P9-CRH-916

ANTHROPOLOGICAL THEORY

An Introductory History

ANTHROPOLOGICAL THEORY

An Introductory History

FIFTH EDITION

R. Jon McGee

Richard L. Warms

ANTHROPOLOGICAL THEORY: AN INTRODUCTORY HISTORY, FIFTH EDITION

Published by McGraw-Hill, a business unit of The McGraw-Hill Companies, Inc., 1221 Avenue of the Americas, New York, NY 10020. Copyright © 2012 by The McGraw-Hill Companies, Inc. All rights reserved. Previous editions © 2008 and 2004. No part of this publication may be reproduced or distributed in any form or by any means, or stored in a database or retrieval system, without the prior written consent of The McGraw-Hill Companies, Inc., including, but not limited to, in any network or other electronic storage or transmission, or broadcast for distance learning.

Some ancillaries, including electronic and print components, may not be available to customers outside the United States.

This book is printed on acid-free paper.

2 3 4 5 6 7 8 9 0 DOC/DOC 1 0 9 8 7 6 5 4 3

ISBN 978-0-07-803488-6
MHID 0-07-803488-4

Vice President & Editor-in-Chief: *Michael Ryan*
Vice President & Director Specialized Publishing: *Janice M. Roerig-Blong*
Editorial Director: *William Glass*
Executive Editor: *Gina Boedeker*
Senior Sponsoring Editor: *Debra B. Hash*
Project Manager: *Melissa M. Leick*
Director Sales & Marketing: *Jennifer J. Lewis*
Design Coordinator: *Margarite Reynolds*
Cover Designer: *Studio Montage, St. Louis, Missouri*
Cover Image: *TRBfoto/Getty Images*
Buyer: *Nicole Baumgartner*
Media Project Manager: *Sridevi Palani*
Compositor: *Aptara®, Inc.*
Typeface: *10/11.5 Fairfield Medium*
Printer: *R.R. Donnelley*

All credits appearing on page or at the end of the book are considered to be an extension of the copyright page.

Library of Congress Cataloging-in-Publication Data

McGee, R. Jon, 1955–
Anthropological theory: an introductory history / R. Jon McGee, Richard L. Warms.—5th ed.
    p. cm.
  Includes bibliographical references and index.
  ISBN-13: 978-0-07-803488-6
  ISBN-10: 0-07-803488-4
  1. Anthropology—Philosophy. 2. Anthropology—Methodology. I. Warms, Richard L. II. Title.
GN33.M33 2011
301.01—dc22

2011008998

www.mhhe.com

CONTENTS

v

Anthropology and Gender 396

Symbolic and Interpretive Anthropology 438

Background to Postmodernism 488

Postmodernism and Its Critics 520

Globalization, Power, and Agency 565

PREFACE

Theory is the core of anthropology. Theories determine the types of questions anthropologists ask and the sorts of information they collect. Without a solid understanding of the history of theory, anthropological data is nothing more than a collection of exotic ethnographic vignettes. With a knowledge of theory, these vignettes become attempts to answer critical philosophical and practical problems. Thus it is crucial for anthropologists to understand theory and its historical context. Students face two choices, then, if they wish to understand the theoretical perspectives that ultimately drive ethnographic fieldwork: They can read theoretical articles or they can read someone's interpretations of those articles. For readers who are not well versed in anthropological theory, neither choice is ideal. We created this volume to provide a more accessible means of introducing students to the past century and a half of theory in anthropology.

We believe that it is essential for students to read original essays by the field's important thinkers. Reading original works promotes depth of understanding and opens possibilities of analysis that even the best books describing the history of theory can never provide. What better introduction to Herbert Spencer, Karl Marx, or Lévi-Strauss than actually reading them? Yet many students find reading original essays extremely demanding. The language is sometimes difficult, and the intellectual disputes, references to other thinkers, and historical contexts are often obscure. We have attempted to make the task less onerous by providing detailed commentary, in close proximity to difficult passages in the original essays, to illuminate obscure references, arcane language, and unfamiliar contexts.

As we have repeatedly revised *Anthropological Theory*, our goals for the book have grown. *Anthropological Theory* is primarily a textbook designed for students in advanced undergraduate and beginning graduate classes. However, we have increasingly tried to write a reference work that both students and professors will want to keep within easy reach. We have done this by writing extensive footnotes on an enormous variety of individuals and topics and providing an extensive two-level index with well over 1,000 entries. You will find basic information on everyone from Leo Frobenius to Daisy Bates, from Ibn Khaldun to Solly Zuckerman. Of course, no book can possibly include information on everyone and everything, but we believe that there is no other single book in anthropology that has as much basic information about as many different theories and people as the current volume.

APPROACH

We have assembled a diverse collection of essays by authors we believe are important thinkers in anthropology. We also deliberately favor essays that are ethnographic examples of theoretical positions over those that are simply declarations of theory. Wherever possible, we have atempted to select essays that are well written, concise, and accessible. The collection begins in the mid-nineteenth century and ends in 2006. It is divided into sections encompassing well-known theoretical positions that are represented by authors generally considered to be the outstanding spokespersons for their points of view, or essays that are especially vivid illustrations of a perspective.

PEDAGOGY

We have provided extensive support material to help students understand the forty-one essays that make up this volume. Each of the fifteen sections begins with an introduction to acquaint readers with some of the most important proponents of a school of thought, the problems they set out to solve, the methods they used, and the dilemmas they faced. Extensive editorial footnotes that provide additional information to help the reader understand and interpret the reading accompany each essay. In addition to providing definitions, translations of foreign phrases, and historical information, the notes help students trace the intellectual connections among thinkers both inside and outside of anthropology. The notes are meant to inform, raise interesting questions, and foster further creative and original thinking. They make essential but sometimes difficult information accessible to students and provide some interesting little-known background details. Anthropological theory, even that of a century ago, is alive and vital. We hope our commentary helps readers see it that way.

No book of theory and commentary can ever be entirely without bias, but we have tried to come as close to this ideal as we can. In our introductions and commentary, we point to both the strengths and weaknesses of each theoretical position. Although astute readers can probably figure out which perspectives we like and which we dislike, we do not intend to promote one theory at the expense of another. In fact, we come from quite different theoretical perspectives, and our ideas have evolved through the years as we teach our theory classes and prepare new editions of this text. Every introductory section and note in this volume was written and rewritten by both of us, and we have been willing to accept substantial criticism and revision of ideas we hold dear.

For us, editing this volume continues to be an exciting process of discovery and interpretation. Research, careful reading, discussion, and argumentation, as well as the comments of numerous reviewers and readers of earlier editions, have greatly deepened our understanding of the works of the great thinkers in anthropology. Writing this book has forced us to rethink what we believed we knew, and in the process we have become better scholars of theory. Selecting these essays and writing the introductions and commentary for them has been profoundly rewarding for us. We hope that reading the essays and our comments will be as productive for students and colleagues.

NEW TO THIS EDITION

This fifth edition contains a great deal of new material. Preparing it has given us a chance to reconsider our selection of essays, the notes we wrote as commentary, and our introductions. We have made substantial improvements in all of these, incorporating new information and bringing an expanded selection of authors and opinions to the volume. Most notably, this edition includes a new section called "Background to Postmodernism," which features essays by two of the seminal authors of the postmodern movement—Pierre Bordieu and Michel Foucault—and contains discussions of Jacque Derrida, Louis Athusser, and other important postmodern thinkers.

In addition to the new final section we have improved existing sections with several new essays. In the section on Culture and Personality we have included Mead's introduction to Coming of Age in Samoa. In the section on Anthropology and Gender we include a dynamic essay by David Valentine: "I Went to Bed with My Own Kind Once: The Erasure of Desire in the Name of Identity." In Part Four we have added the new section Background to Postmodernism with two new essays by Bordieu and Foucault and a new essay by Hanson—"The Making of the Maori: Cultural Invention and its Logic"—in the Postmodern section. We have also added a new essay by Bestor, "*Kaiten-Zushi* and *Konbini*: Japanese Food Culture in the Age of Mechanical Reproduction" in our final section Globalization, Power, and Agency.

In addition to the new essays, each of the section introductions has been updated. Because it is not possible to have selections from all the great thinkers who have made significant contributions to anthropological thought, we have tried to include as many as possible in the section introductions and the notes. Thus you will find discussions of figures such as Jeremy Bentham, A. C. Haddon, James Frazer, Antonio Gramsci, Monica Wilson, Andrew Vayda, Michelle Rosaldo, and scores of others whose work has played a major role in anthropological theory. Needless to say, the correction and revision of footnotes has been an ongoing process; we have also revised the index, increasing the level of detail and making the book a more useful research tool.

We have been particularly gratified by the reactions of readers of the first four editions. We have received many letters and e-mails from the United States, Canada, and Europe. Both professors and students have asked questions, sent thoughtful commentary, and offered recommendations. We have been able to incorporate some of these into this edition. We deeply regret that editorial constraints and issues of timing and space have prevented us from including more of these suggestions, but we appreciate your feedback and hope you will continue to advise us. As always, you can contact us at rm08@txstate.edu for McGee and r.warms@txstate.edu for Warms.

ACKNOWLEDGMENTS

Writing this book has involved the labor and forbearance of many people. First and foremost, we would like to thank our families—Stacie, Jacob, and Hannah McGee and Karen, Benjamin, and Nathan Warms. Without their support, this project would have been impossible.

One unintended consequence of writing this kind of book is that we have had the privilege of having contact with several of the scholars whose work appears in this volume. We are indebted to the many people who made suggestions, reviewed, and commented on the text in various stages of preparation. Our work has benefited greatly from their comments, and our ideas were altered by their insights. We deeply appreciate their advice even though we were not always able to follow it. Since the publication of the first edition of this book, we have benefited from the insights and advice of numerous individuals. These include Roy Rappaport, Marvin Harris, Robert Launay, Roy D'Andrade, Joe Heyman, George Marcus, Naomi Quinn, Claudia Strauss, and Ann Stoler. This edition would not have been possible without the careful analysis and useful suggestions from our reviewers, and we thank them for the time and energy they put into analyzing our work:

Karin Enstam Jaffe,
Sonoma State University

Mary Jo Schneider,
University of Arkansas

Marjorie Snipes,
University of West Georgia

John Chance,
Arizona State University

Laura Ogden,
Florida International University

Richard Senghas,
Sonoma State University

Kathleen Brelsford,
University of South Florida

Gareth Barkin,
University of Puget Sound

David Kideckel,
Central Connecticut State University

Deborah Tooker,
Le Moyne College

Introduction

Anthropology is concerned with understanding the "other." Typically anthropologists study the behavior, beliefs, and lifestyles of people in other cultures. Some examine current cultures; others study the remains of past societies to re-create the lives of people who disappeared long ago; still others study primates to see what our closest relatives can tell us about being human. What unites this diverse work is a common ground in some fundamental theoretical ideas concerning biological evolution and social behavior.

We teach both undergraduate and graduate courses in anthropological theory at Texas State University. Each year as the semester begins, we face the same issues: Some students want to know why if they are studying X (fill in the blank) the theory course is required, and others worry about reading original works by authors and delving into a subject that seems esoteric. Because both matters are important, we begin this book by telling you why we think theory is essential in anthropology and why it is valuable to read original works rather than predigested theoretical summaries.

WHY STUDY THEORY?

Theory is critical because, although anthropologists collect data through fieldwork, data in and of themselves are meaningless. Whether plainly stated or assumed, theories are the tools anthropologists use to decide what data to collect and how to give meaning to their data. Anthropologists in the field are confronted with an almost infinite amount of data that could be collected. No one can record everything that happens to them or everything they witness. Anthropologists record those things they think are important . . . but what one thinks is important is determined, explicitly or implicitly, by one's theoretical perspective. A structuralist interested in the unconscious meaning of mythology probably will not spend too much time studying subsistence patterns. An economic anthropologist might ignore ritual and religion. Without theory, no data collection is possible.

One's theoretical perspective also influences how data is interpreted. How are we to understand designs carved into a rock ten thousand years ago, a cache of silver coins buried with a victim of the plague in fourteenth-century London, or the meaning of a wink? Theories guide our understandings. They are the tools we use to sort what we believe is significant from what we believe is meaningless.

Although this is a book about theory in sociocultural anthropology, the different branches of anthropology have always freely borrowed ideas from one another and from other fields of study. In the nineteenth century, Herbert Spencer's theories were deeply influenced by ideas drawn from biology. Franz Boas was deeply influenced by his doctoral mentor, the physicist Gustav Karsten and later by the biologist Rudolf Virchow. His student, A. L. Kroeber, had a Master's degree in English for which he had written a thesis on the English heroic play. Kroeber's student Julian Steward had undergraduate majors in zoology and geology. Sociobiologists study human behavior in terms of evolutionary biology and cultural adaptations. Symbolic anthropologists and postmodernists rely on tools developed in the study of literature. In the course of their research, anthropologists today delve into biology, geology, psychology, history, literature, physics, chemistry, medicine, and other subjects.

Modern anthropology is built on the work of earlier generations of theorists. Indeed, anthropologists today ask many of the same questions that occupied scholars in the nineteenth and early twentieth centuries. Nineteenth-century theories continue to resonate in popular culture. Have you ever heard the phrase "survival of the fittest," for example? It was coined by Herbert Spencer in the middle part of the nineteenth century. Do you think that technology is a measure of a society's development? Then you will be comfortable reading Lewis Henry Morgan's *Ancient Society*, first published in 1877. To fully comprehend anthropological writing, you must appreciate the history of the ideas that inform it. These are, ultimately, the principles on which current work is based.

Anthropological theory is also important because it helps us think about who and what we are as human beings. It does this by asking us to consider the ways in which we view and understand each other. At its most basic level, anthropology asks how we are to understand other people in the world, those who look different from us and have different languages and customs (what anthropologists have come to call different cultures). Are such people inferior to us, superior to us, or just different? Are their cultures unchanging, following their own paths of evolution, or bound to ours in a grand evolutionary scheme? How should we behave toward such people?

At a second level, anthropology forces us to consider the otherness of nature itself. It forces us to ask if we, as human beings, are fundamentally part of the natural world. If so, perhaps we can be studied by the scientific methods and principles used by biologists, physicists, and other scholars in the traditional physical sciences. Alternatively, are human beings sufficiently different from the rest of the world that

studying them with these methods will produce only trivial and confusing results? If that is true, the skills needed might be creative insight, imaginative interpretation, and empathy—analytic tools traditionally associated with the arts and humanities.

A final level of discourse deals with the otherness of culture itself. By directing us to the comparison of cultures, anthropology ultimately points toward the study of universal human nature. If we could strip away the cultural clothing of all peoples, would we be left with some set of basic principles or underlying essence? Would this be equivalent to finding human nature before us in the buff? If so, how are we to understand human culture? Is it that which permits the full and satisfying expression of human nature, or that which prevents human nature from destroying human society?

At some level, all theory in anthropology, whether written in the eighteenth, nineteenth, twentieth, or twenty-first centuries, addresses these essential questions. Sometimes, individual theorists take extreme postures and for a time quiet the voices of those who hold alternative positions. However, no definitive conclusion has ever been reached on any of these issues. Perhaps these questions are ultimately unanswerable by their very nature. But the fact that no authoritative conclusion has been reached does not lessen the importance of the debate, for how we answer these questions has practical applications in our world. The answers determine our understanding of ourselves and our behavior toward other individuals and groups. In a world of instantaneous communication and virtually unlimited capacity for violence, in a world of ethnic strife and national warfare, surely these are among the most important questions that face us.

WHY READ ORIGINAL WORKS?

We believe it is important to read original works for several reasons. First, commentary on a theory cannot replace the original work because commentators unavoidably (and frequently intentionally) place their own interpretations on the material. For instance, Robert Lowie's 1937 *History of Ethnological Theory* and Marvin Harris' 1968 *The Rise of Anthropological Theory* are both comprehensive summaries of anthropological theory, but they provide strikingly different perspectives on the field.

Second, part of the importance of classic works in theory is their subtlety and complexity. The creation of theory is part of an ongoing dialogue with earlier thinkers, and these essays (and many others) are a portion of that dialogue. As our understanding changes, we return to these older works. Sometimes we find insights that advance our thinking or react to errors we perceive in original works. Through this process, new theory is generated. When works are summarized or when we read only analyses, the theoretical dialogue is flattened, simplified, and ultimately impoverished. In this volume, we provide what we believe is useful commentary on the essays we present, but reading such analysis cannot replace careful reading of the original text. As new insights are made, many of our notes may become outdated. The essays themselves have a much longer shelf life.

Finally, a firsthand reading of the original sources helps one avoid inaccuracies. In preparing this text, we have run across numerous cases in which the popularly accepted information passed to us by our professors or found in textbooks was incorrect. Some of the folk wisdom of anthropology consists of half-truths or is frankly inaccurate. We bring this up not to point fingers or assign blame but to suggest that reading original sources can serve as a partial corrective for this problem.

USING THIS TEXTBOOK

This book is designed to help you understand where some of the great minds in anthropology have been before you and to help you formulate your theoretical position in the field today. It is a historical overview of some of the principal developments in culture theory since the 1850s. The book is different from others because it contains our introductions and paragraph-by-paragraph

comments to inform your reading and raise interesting points or questions.

Theory texts are problematic because their contents tend to become accepted doctrine. Readers and critics suppose that the authors of such a text have chosen to present those pieces universally considered the most important works in the field. When the editors of such a volume have the audacity to write detailed comments on the essays they have chosen, they seem to elevate these texts to scripture and their work to Talmudic authority. Should you entertain these notions, let us disabuse you of them. No group of professional anthropologists, however small, will agree on a single set of critical essays. We have selected what we feel are representative articles by individuals traditionally associated with particular theories works that seem to us to be good examples of theories in practice. We will gladly agree with anyone who claims that better works can be found, but we insist that this will always be the case. An enormous corpus of work in anthropology now exists. We believe that the best way to study anthropological theory is to read as widely as possible. No collection of essays, however artfully chosen, will be able to substitute for years of reading in the field, and that is what is ultimately required for a solid background in theory.

You will find that our commentary on the texts varies from extremely straightforward definitions and explanations to fairly elaborate speculation on the motives of authors and influences on them. Although it is almost impossible to entirely eliminate mistakes, we have checked our work carefully; when we point to a fact, you may be reasonably certain that it is correct. However, please remember that our interpretations are just that. They are meant to guide your reading, stimulate discussion, call your attention to certain ideas, and get you to think about different issues. You are invited to disagree with them and propose alternatives. If you read through this book and find nothing with which to disagree, you are not reading carefully enough or critically enough.

Although our likes and dislikes may become apparent to the careful reader, we do not intend to promote any particular viewpoint. In fact, we were trained in very different theoretical perspectives (McGee in interpretive-symbolic and Warms in positivist-materialist). We have tried to present the key strengths and weaknesses of each position, but we frequently differ in our interpretations of theory and amuse our students by arguing about them. In short, although we hope that readers will agree with most of what we have written, we have tried to write at least something bound to rile your theoretical sensibilities, no matter who you are. You are invited to disagree with the text and debate us about it if you wish, or at the very least contact us if you have a question. We can be contacted by e-mail at r.warms@ txstate.edu for Warms or rm08@txstate.edu for McGee or by traditional mail at the Department of Anthropology, Texas State University, San Marcos, TX 78666.

THE ARRANGEMENT OF ESSAYS AND THE NOTATIONAL SYSTEM

The arrangement of essays presents a surprising number of problems. Should they be arranged strictly chronologically or by intellectual association or descent? If the text is to be divided into sections, what about those authors who do not quite fit? We have taught our theory course both chronologically and thematically and concluded that a chronological presentation works best. Thus we have chosen to arrange the theories in a rough chronological order to show readers the progression of ideas in cultural anthropology and to demonstrate the relationship between concepts. We have divided our chronology into named sections. Each begins with an introduction describing the theorists represented in the section and the principal ideas presented in their work. However, our scheme is not entirely consistent. Different schools of thought often overlap both intellectually and chronologically. Exploiting these inconsistencies and thinking about other possible arrangements of the text may prove an intellectually useful experience. New arrangements may provide new insights.

Space limitations and, occasionally, copyright regulations have forced us to make difficult decisions about the essays we have reprinted. Essays included in earlier drafts of the book have been removed from the final, and we have added or subtracted essays as our own knowledge base grows. More important, we have occasionally eliminated fairly large passages of some essays or chosen to remove particularly lengthy sets of original footnotes or endnotes. These are not decisions we took lightly, nor do they indicate that we believe the notes and passages removed were of no significance. It was simply a question of choosing between removing notes and passages or losing several entire essays. Although there are good intellectual reasons for selecting either of these options, we believe that most readers are better served by the first. In doing this editing, we have tried to preserve a sense of the original by including notes telling the reader exactly how much text was removed and briefly summarizing the content of the lost passage. We also note how many footnotes appeared in those passages, which allows readers to see the subjects about which the authors wrote notes and those they did not and gives a feel for the frequency and pacing of notes.

Each essay in the volume is accompanied by our notes, which appear as footnotes and are numbered with Arabic numerals. Footnotes or endnotes created by the original authors are indicated by lowercase letters and appear as endnotes to the essays. Where authors have provided references in their work, they appear at the end of the essay. Our own references along with an index appear at the end of the volume.

Part One

HISTORICAL FOUNDATIONS
OF ANTHROPOLOGICAL THEORY

Nineteenth-Century Evolutionism

In the English-speaking world, the word *anthropologist* first appeared in print in 1805 (Kuklick 1991:6). It was another seventy-nine years before the first university position in anthropology was created. The discipline of anthropology, however, did not just appear but rather combined three long-existing streams of thought. The first was the study of what we have come to call cultural differences among societies. The second dealt with the struggle to explain the antiquity of humans and the artifacts left from these ancient lives. The final line of thought, closely related to the second, was the investigation of the biological origins of humans and other species. All of these areas have been the subject of investigation and speculation for much of the past millennium. Though it is far beyond the scope of this text to analyze all the antecedents of anthropology, we will briefly review some of the principal developments that led to its origin before exploring evolutionary and anthropological thinking in the nineteenth century.

It is probably fair to say that wherever literate civilizations came into contact with members of different societies, something like ethnographic writing occurred. For example, ancient authors such as Herodotus, a Greek historian of the fifth century B.C.E., offered readers fanciful descriptions of other societies. In the fourteenth century, Ibn Khaldun, a Tunisian politician and historian, wrote the *Muqaddimah,* or *Introduction to History,* in which he proposed that the study of human civilization and social organization was an independent science (quoted in Lacoste 1984:169).

In Europe there was a long tradition of interest in the exotic. Writings such as *The Wonders of the East* and *The Travels of Marco Polo* had fascinated Europeans. Until the fifteenth century, however, Europe remained relatively isolated and provincial. Then, developments in sailing technology and advances in weaponry allowed Europeans to expand their influence across the globe. For the first time, they were in frequent contact with people from societies radically different from their own. This exposure raised a host of philosophical problems. Were these other people human in the same way that Europeans were? Did their societies function according to brute natural law, or were they moral beings possessed of a free will? How were social differences to be explained?

From the Renaissance until the eighteenth century, the concept of degenerationism provided Europeans with a biblically based explanation of cultural diversity. In this view, prior to the destruction of the Tower of Babel, all people belonged to a single civilization. When God destroyed the Tower, creating differences in language and dispersing the people, some degenerated, losing their civilization and eventually becoming savages. Much of the European experience seemed to confirm degenerationism. For example, the recovery of texts and artifacts from ancient Greek and Roman civilizations seemed to show that these were far more advanced than those of later date.

Progressivism was an alternative view of social life. Progressivists believed that, rather than deteriorating from a previously civilized condition, societies had started out primitive but were progressing toward a more advanced state. One proponent of this approach was the British philosopher John Locke (1632–1704). In *Essay Concerning Government,* published in 1690, Locke proposed that the human mind was a blank slate and that knowledge and reason were derived from experience. Thus different sorts of experiences would provide different sorts of ideas. Individuals growing up in different societies would have varied experiences. These would produce varied ideas and thus explain the differences among human societies.

The idea that people had progressed rather than degenerated became popular as scientific investigation and empirical observation increasingly yielded both academic and commercial results. By the late 1700s, few Europeans doubted that humankind was making progress, and that they were the most advanced of all people.

With the general idea of progress firmly entrenched, philosophers devised various schemes to explain the nature and course of this social evolution. Their goal was to construct a universal history of humankind that moved from a primitive past to the development of European nations. One of the most influential of these works was Edward Gibbon's (1737–1794) *The History of the Decline and Fall of the Roman Empire* (1776–1788), but there were others as well. Italian philosopher Giambattista Vico (1668–1744) in his 1744 work *The New Science,* attempted to write a universal history of humanity. Vico believed that human nature was shaped by history and hence changed over time. Thus, he thought that history was a better guide to understanding humanity than the natural sciences. French statesman Anne Robert Jacques Turgot (1727–1781) published *Plan for Two Discourses on Universal History* in 1750. He argued that, after the biblical flood, humans had passed through stages of savagery and barbarism to agriculture and urban-based civilization. One last example of this perspective is *Sketch for a Historical Picture of the Progress of the Human Mind,* written by Marie Jean Antoine Nicolas Caritat, the Marquis de Condorcet (1743–1794). Condorcet proposed a ten-stage scheme describing human progress from early tribal society through the founding of the French Republic and beyond, to a future in which human society was perfected.

Condorcet was a *philosophe,* a friend of Turgot and of Voltaire, Franklin, and Paine as well. He was a widely respected mathematician who became the secretary of the Legislative Assembly after the French Revolution. Condorcet supported liberal and rationalist causes but fell out of favor as the radical Montagnards rose in power. His opposition to the execution of the king and the constitution proposed by the Montagnards led the increasingly powerful radicals to consider him a traitor and call for his arrest. In 1793 Condorcet went into hiding at a friend's home in Paris. *Sketch for a Historical Picture of the Progress of the Human Mind* was written in the months that followed. In 1794, fearing his hiding place was no longer safe, he attempted to flee Paris but was arrested and imprisoned. He was found dead in his cell two days later. Controversy remains over whether he committed suicide or was murdered.

The rise of the violent and radical Montagnards and the death of Condorcet signal an important moment in British, American, and French social thought. The late eighteenth century had been characterized by optimism, progressivism, rationalism, and secularism. The violent overthrow of the social order in France, the increasing disorder and poverty of urban life in England, and the destruction of factories by Luddites in Nottinghamshire and Lancashire led to a retreat from these values. The result was a revival of religion and deep questioning of the notion of progress. There had been clear advances in technology, and for many the standard of living had improved. However, the French Revolution and turbulence among the British lower classes suggested that optimism for humanity's future might not be justified. Clearly, if progress was being made, its course was not smooth. How were intellectuals to reconcile ideas of progress and rationalism with an increasingly disordered society?

The European expansion that began in the fifteenth century had a profound effect on the natural sciences as well as philosophy. Explorers' accounts of the flora and fauna of new lands challenged the biblical view of life, based on Genesis, particularly on the stories of creation and the flood. Long before Darwin, naturalists were confronted with distributions and variations in plants and animals that could not be explained in biblical terms. Scholars also struggled to explain evidence of human antiquity that did not correspond to biblical chronologies. This evidence became more widely available in the early nineteenth century as large-scale, nationwide engineering projects, such as the construction of canal and railroad systems, exposed geological strata, fossils, and human artifacts to the study of naturalists and geologists. Scientists were confronted with questions such as why objects of human manufacture were found in association with extinct mammals.

The foundation of biological-evolutionary speculation was laid down in the descriptive writings of seventeenth-century naturalists such as Gilbert White (1720–1793) and John Ray (1627–1705), who attempted to classify and describe the diversity of life-forms they observed (Eiseley 1961). Ray influenced Carol Linné (Latinized as Carolus Linnaeus) (1707–1778), best known for his taxonomic categorization of life-forms presented in *Systema Naturae* in 1735. Previously, no single naming system for plants and animals existed and identical species were called by different names in different places. Linnaeus' taxonomic system provided the systematic, organized, and for Europeans, universal framework for the classification of life-forms that was necessary for the scientific investigation of biological evolution to take place.

Immutability of species was one aspect of thinking in the natural philosophy of Linnaeus' era. Almost all scholars believed that life-forms were created separately by God in their present form and could not change. The task of biology was to name and classify them. However, challenges to this position were developed by a number of scholars. For example, in *Telliamed: or Discourses Between an Indian Philosopher and a French Missionary on the Diminution of the Sea, the Formation of the Earth, the Origin of Men and Animals, etc.*, a book widely read in the mid-eighteenth century, Benoit de Maillet (1656–1738) outlined a scheme for biological evolution. He speculated that the age of the earth was much greater than popularly believed, recog-

nized that fossils were the remains of life-forms, and suggested that some of these fossils represented extinct species. Not daring to speak of his theories in his own voice, de Maillet chose instead to frame his work as a conversation between Telliamed, a fictitious Indian philosopher, and a Christian missionary placing the radical observations in the mouth of the Indian. Alert readers will realize that "Telliamed" is "de Maillet" spelled backwards.

Another naturalist, second in importance only to Linnaeus, was Georges Louis Leclerc, Comte de Buffon (1707–1788). The forty-four volumes of Buffon's Natural History (1752–1799) outlined an evolutionary theory that he called "degeneration" but which contained many of the elements that Darwin used in his theory of natural selection more than 100 years later. Some of Buffon's key observations were that physical variation occurred within species; that different animals had underlying structural similarities; that life multiplied faster than its food supply, promoting a struggle for existence; and that some life-forms had become extinct.

Jean Lamarck (1744–1829) and Charles Darwin's grandfather, Erasmus Darwin (1731–1802), were two great evolutionists of the late eighteenth century whose work exerted a profound influence on the development of later evolutionary theory. Although they held similar views, Lamarck's theories were more systematically presented, and his work is better known today. Lamarck believed that changes in geographic and climatic areas placed pressures on plant and animal life. In his view, changes in environmental conditions led to changes in animal species. Species had not gone extinct but rather changed their forms as their environments had changed. Lamarck argued that changed conditions would place stresses on particular body parts, requiring them to be used more often or in new ways. Body parts thus used would grow in size and strength. Changes acquired through use and disuse of body parts during the life of individuals would be passed on to their offspring. Lamarck's most famous example was the giraffe. Lamarck argued that as the climate changed, the acacia leaves on which giraffes fed grew higher and higher. As a result, giraffes were forced to stretch to reach them. Thus, giraffes lengthened their necks and forelimbs during their lifetimes. These changes were then passed down to their offspring. The result of this process was that the height of the entire species increased over time. This aspect of Lamarck's work is referred to as the inheritance of acquired characteristics. Although the idea of the inheritance of acquired characteristics was deeply influential in the biology of the nineteenth and early twentieth centuries (for example, agricultural policies of the Soviet Union through much of the twentieth century was based upon it), it is a fallacy. Heritable biological changes must be based on changes in DNA and these cannot be acquired through use and disuse. However, the same is not true of cultural changes: individuals can be taught new cultural characteristics and pass these acquired traits to their offspring.

By the end of the eighteenth century, the philosophical and biological frameworks for anthropology were in place. Nineteenth-century thinkers, driven by an abundance of new data, from fossil finds in England to explorers' accounts of Africa, built on this framework. They produced new theories of biological and social evolution that were key to the development of anthropology. The insights of Charles Darwin (1809–1882) and Herbert Spencer (1820–1903) were particularly important.

Between 1831 and 1836 Darwin traveled on the H.M.S. Beagle. When he returned, he published a journal of his voyages (1839) as well as a major multivolume work on coral reefs (1846) and several works on barnacles (1851–1854). In 1837 he also began to write secret notebooks in which he organized his thoughts about evolution. He studied the materials he had collected and gave considerable attention to commercial plant and animal breeders in whose work he saw a practical application of his concepts. He collected data, organized his notes, and in 1844 composed a draft of his ideas that he showed to his close friend, the eminent botanist Joseph Dalton Hooker (1817–1911). However, aware of the controversy his ideas would arouse, he refrained from publishing his work.

Darwin had been refining his ideas for twenty years when he received a letter in June of 1858 from a young naturalist with whom he had been corresponding, Alfred Russell Wallace (1823–1913). From his own observations in Malaysia, Wallace had independently formulated the theory that Darwin had been working so diligently to substantiate. Darwin was greatly disheartened by Wallace's letter, but his colleagues Charles Lyell (1797–1875) and Joseph Hooker arranged the joint presentation of the two men's ideas in July 1858, and Darwin was granted the opportunity to publish first. He published *On the Origin of Species by Means of Natural Selection* in November 1859.

Darwin held that change within species must follow natural laws like those found in the physical sciences. In *On the Origin of Species,* he outlined a theory he called *natural selection* and proposed that it was the fundamental principle of biological change. Darwin began with the idea that more organisms were born than survived to adulthood, a widely accepted concept derived in part from *An Essay on the Principle of Population,* published in 1798 by Thomas Malthus (1766–1834), then speculated about the factors that determined which individuals survived and which did not. Darwin observed that no two individuals of any species were precisely alike; small variations occur in the appearance or behavioral characteristics of members of any population. Darwin hypothesized that some variations were better than others in that they led those who possessed them to more successfully compete for food, shelter, and mates. These individuals would subsequently produce more offspring who themselves survived and reproduced. Darwin called the characteristics that led to increased numbers of surviving and reproducing offspring "adaptive." Though he did not have any understanding of the mechanisms of heredity, he observed that parents were capable of passing traits to their offspring and that those possessing the adaptive traits were "naturally selected" over those who lacked them. Consequently, over a long period, and through the slow, incremental accumulation of adaptive traits, the appearance of a species could be altered or a new species could develop.

Darwin's theory was extraordinarily important for several reasons. First, it was a scientifically convincing explanation of the ways in which life-forms could change over time and new species emerge. As such, it is the basis of much of modern biology. In addition, Darwin's theory was a powerful social metaphor. Darwin's theory was capable of explaining how it was possible to have both progress and social disruption. It showed how progress, rather than being a smooth upward climb, was achieved through struggle and conflict.

Darwin's work was controversial in religious circles and met with ridicule from the popular press. It was disparaged by French intellectuals (who presented it in seriously flawed mistranslation when it first appeared) and generally rejected in Germany until the turn of the twentieth century. However, in Britain and America, scholars had been moving toward a theory of evolution for half a century. Darwin had become extremely well respected in scientific circles for his publications on his voyages, on the geology of coral reefs, and on barnacles. His support made the ideas of evolution and transmutation of species much more popular in both scientific and popular circles. However, many scientists of Darwin's era rejected natural selection. Some, such as William Thompson, Lord Kelvin, argued that even though the earth was ancient, it was not ancient enough to provide the time necessary for natural selection to occur. Others, such as Fleeming Jenkin believed that any favorable mutations that did occur would be swamped by the size of existing populations. George Douglas Campbell, Duke of Argyle, proposed that natural selection could not account for the beauty of the world. Darwin answered the Duke of Argyle's objections with the theory of sexual selection, but the problems raised by Lord Kelvin and Fleeming Jenkin were not solved until the late nineteenth and early twentieth century when radioactivity and genetics were better understood.

Herbert Spencer was one of those whose work gained increased credibility because of Darwin. Spencer had been working on a theory of human social evolution years before Darwin published *Origin of Species* and Darwin had even applied some of Spencer's concepts in his work.

Though Herbert Spencer was the son of a schoolmaster, he was largely self-educated. He worked as a civil engineer for the Birmingham and London Railway and then as a subeditor for *The Economist,* a news magazine that promoted free market capitalism. In 1853, having received a small inheritance, Spencer was able to leave *The Economist* to devote himself full time to writing.

Spencer was interested in evolution as a general phenomenon, and he applied his evolutionary approach to many fields of study. Garbarino (1977:21) calls him a "philosopher of universal evolution" because Spencer considered evolution to be one of the fundamental natural processes in the universe. His ideas had enormous impact in Britain and the United States, not only on anthropology and sociology but on literature, politics, and popular culture as well (Carneiro 1967:xi). Spencer believed that evolution was progressive and that it moved from small to large, simple to complex, and independent to interdependent. He believed that evolution was a pervasive force in the universe. It was not only people and societies that were evolving, but all things. Among people, however, Spencer believed that evolution was driven by a struggle for survival in which only those with superior skills and traits succeeded. It was Spencer who coined the term "survival of the fittest."

Spencer is also famous for his organic analogy. As illustrated in the selection in this book, "The Social Organism," Spencer compared human societies with biological organisms. He used this analogy to link biological and social evolution, implying both followed the same processes and direction. This suggested that societies could be studied in the same fashion as biological organisms. In making the analogy between societies and biological organisms, Spencer was also proposing that there was an analogy between the organs within an organism and the various parts of society. This implied a research agenda: these social organs should be accurately identified and their role and function in maintaining society described. This idea, in various forms, set the agenda for much of anthropology in the century following the publication of "The Social Organism."

Darwin adopted Spencer's phrase "survival of the fittest" in later editions of *On the Origin of Species* and this has tended to obscure the very important differences between the two. Spencer and Darwin understood the mechanisms of evolution in very different ways. For Spencer, "survival of the fittest" meant that evolution favored the physically strong, intellectually clever, and, among humans, financially most prosperous. For Darwin, fitness was a matter of reproduction. The most fit were those most successful in producing fertile off-spring. Although Spencer viewed Darwin's work as supporting his own, there is little evidence Spencer understood what Darwin meant by natural selection. All humans are ethnocentric to one degree or another, and nineteenth-century Europeans and Americans were no exception. Looking with pride at their industrial advances and burgeoning economic and military power, members of Western societies believed they were at the pinnacle of social evolution. One consequence of Spencer's work was the popularization of a point of view called social darwinism. Social darwinists interpreted theories of evolution to mean that progress could only be achieved through the strong dominating the weak. They equated strength with military and financial power. Thus, they believed that it was not only the right, it was the obligation of the rich to dominate the poor and Western powers to dominate those who were less technologically advanced. It was only in this manner that humanity as a whole could progress. This was a convenient philosophy for the rapidly expanding European powers and was used to justify their imperialism, colonialism, and racism. In the United States, social darwinism was invoked as a justification for free enterprise capitalism.

It should be remembered, however, that while most of the evolutionary thinkers represented here thought Western society more highly evolved than any other, they were also highly critical of it. They believed that evolution moved continually toward perfection. Western society might be more advanced than any other, but it was very far from perfect. It is true that Spencer argued, on one hand, that state welfare, education, and public health programs were contrary to the laws of nature and should be avoided because they slowed the evolutionary process that was weeding out the unfit members of society. On the other hand, he also argued against the military, the Church of England, and the perquisites of the landowning class. Despite the use of theories like

his to justify colonial conquest, Spencer himself was an adamant opponent of British imperialism. In his autobiography, he wrote that as early as 1879 he had:

> Spoken to friends concerning the possibility of doing something towards checking the aggressive tendencies displayed by us [the British] all over the world—sending as pioneers, missionaries of "the religion of love," and then picking quarrels with the native races and taking possession of their lands (1904:443).

Two other nineteenth-century anthropologists interested in the evolution of culture as a general human phenomenon were the American Lewis Henry Morgan (1818–1881) and the Englishman Sir Edward Burnett Tylor (1832–1917). Both men believed there were universal evolutionary stages of cultural development that characterized the transition from primitive to complex societies. Because of this belief, Morgan and Tylor are known as unilineal evolutionists. Although Morgan and Tylor shared a similar evolutionary framework, their studies examined different aspects of culture. Morgan focused on the evolution of elements such as the family and subsistence patterns, whereas Tylor's work concentrated on the idea that one could trace the evolution of a society by studying "survivals," a form of cultural remnant. He is best known for his theory of the evolution of religion.

Morgan's early interest in Native American cultures, in particular, patterns of marriage and descent, led to his 1871 book, *Systems of Consanguinity and Affinity*, the first comparative study of kinship, but his most famous work was *Ancient Society*, published in 1877. There he attempted to trace the evolution of human society from primeval times to the Victorian era (which he considered the high point of human civilization). Following Turgot and other eighteenth-century writers, he divided human cultural development into three grand stages—savagery, barbarism, and civilization—with the first two stages further subdivided into lower, middle, and upper phases. Morgan accepted Spencer's idea that evolution proceeded from simple to complex and, in *Ancient Society*, outlined this progress by correlating

states of social evolution with specific developments in family structure, subsistence, and technology. For example, in Morgan's scheme, middle
savagery begins with the acquisition of fish subsistence, whereas upper savagery is marked by the invention of the bow and arrow. Unlike Spencer,
Morgan believed that evolutionary progress was not
achieved through competition but was propelled by
the "flowering" of "germs of thought." The increasingly complex technologies produced after such
events were markers of evolutionary progress.

E. B. Tylor was a contemporary of Morgan
and probably the leading English anthropologist
of the nineteenth century. In his principal work,
Primitive Culture (1871), Tylor outlined two
ideas for which he is remembered today. First, he
argued that one could reconstruct earlier stages
of cultural evolution by studying "survivals." Tylor
believed that virtually everything in contemporary society that did not have a function he understood was a survival from a previous stage of
cultural evolution. Therefore, one could learn
something about past stages of a society's development through the study of these cultural left-
overs. His second idea concerned the evolution of
religion, Tylor's special interest and the subject
of the second volume of *Primitive Culture*. He
postulated that the most basic concept underlying the invention of religion was animism, the
belief that all objects and aspects of the world are
imbued with spirit. He outlined a developmental
sequence for religion that began with this idea,
evolved into polytheism, and finally progressed
into what he viewed as the highest form of religious belief, enlightened monotheism.

Both Morgan and Tylor believed in the fundamental similarity of human thought around the
world, a concept called the *psychic unity of humankind*. This belief was the foundation for their
unilineal evolutionary views and supported their
contention that societies progressed through parallel (but independent) evolutionary stages.

The unilineal evolutionary perspective of the
late nineteenth century revolved around several
related themes. First, it was generally supposed
that all societies evolved through the same stages
and were progressing toward civilization. Victorian society represented civilization in its highest

currently extant form but would be surpassed by
future societies. Second, the whole perspective
was rooted in the comparative method. In the
nineteenth century the term *comparative method*
referred to the belief that contemporary "primitive" cultures were like "living fossils," similar to
early stages of current advanced cultures. As
such, they were clues to cultural evolutionary development. One could study the evolutionary history of Western society by examining contemporary
primitive societies. The validity of the comparative method rested on an acceptance of the concept of psychic unity. Simple and complex societies
were comparable because human minds were believed to develop along the same lines. If the human mind worked the same way in all cultures,
then it was assumed that unrelated societies would
develop in a parallel fashion. Beliefs in the comparative method, psychic unity, parallel evolution,
and progress were woven together to support the
unilineal view of social evolution.

Karl Marx (1818–1883) and his frequent co-
author Friedrich Engels (1820–1895) are far
better known for their contributions to other disciplines—in particular, economic and political
theory—than for their studies in anthropology.
Despite this, their ideas are critical to anthropology and have been the subject of much debate
among anthropologists.

Marx derived his theory of social evolution
from the theory of dialectical change advanced
by the philosopher Georg Wilhelm Friedrich
Hegel (1770–1831), from the materialism of
British philosophers such as Adam Smith, and the
romantic utopianism of French thinkers such as
Pierre-Joseph Proudhon (1809–1865) and Henri
de San Simon (1760–1825). Whereas scholars
such as Locke and Tylor believed that cultural
institutions were the product of rational thought,
Marx believed that all thought was a product of
cultural institutions rather than their cause. Marx,
a materialist philosopher, gave primacy to the analysis of the conditions of production within society.

Much of the work of Marx and Engels examined the conflict generated by the increasing
wealth of the capitalists (bourgeoisie) at the expense of the working class (proletariat), who only
sunk deeper into poverty. Marx and Engels viewed

social change as an evolutionary process marked by revolution in which new levels of social, political, and economic development were achieved through class struggle. They viewed history as a sequence of evolutionary stages, each marked by a unique mode of production. Just as unilineal evolutionary theorists traced the social evolution of humans from savagery to civilization, Marx and Engels saw the history of Europe in terms of the transition from feudalism, to capitalism, and on to communism—which they believed was the next inevitable step in this process.

In their later work, Marx and Engels were deeply influenced by the work of Lewis Henry Morgan. In *Ancient Society,* Morgan correlated evolutionary stages of human culture with material achievements and technology. Marx and Engels viewed Morgan as a materialist and believed that his work validated their evolutionary theory. Although Marx despised Spencer (whom he viewed as an apologist for capitalism), both focused on the notion of conflict as the mechanism for social evolution.

Marx's work drew little attention in early twentieth-century anthropology. Although some scholars such as Durkheim were political socialists, until the late 1920s Marx had relatively little effect on ethnographic analysis outside of the Soviet Union. However, since that time, anthropologists have come to depend increasingly on his ideas. Many theories in both cultural anthropology and archaeology have come to rely on Marxist insights. This is particularly true of cultural ecologists, neomaterialist, feminist, and postmodern thinkers discussed in Parts Three and Four of this book. Today, a background in Marxist thought is basic to reading culture theory.

---

1. *The Social Organism*

HERBERT SPENCER (1820–1903)

SIR JAMES MACINTOSH got great credit for the saying that "constitutions are not made, but grow." In our day the most significant thing about this saying is, that it was ever thought so significant. As from the surprise displayed by a man at some familiar fact you may judge of his general culture: so from the admiration which an age accords a new thought, its average degree of enlightenment may be safely inferred. That this apothegm of Macintosh should have been quoted and requoted as it has, shows how profound has been the ignorance of social science—how a small ray of truth has seemed brilliant, as a distant rushlight looks like a star in the surrounding darkness.[1] Such a conception could not indeed fail to be startling when let fall in the midst of a system

From *The Westminster Review* (1860)

---

[1] Spencer begins with a quote from the Scottish philosopher and politician, James Macintosh (1765–1832). Although Spencer seems to dismiss the importance of Macintosh's insight, it is critical. The French Revolution set the stage for many of the nineteenth-century debates in social science. Edmond Burke (1729–1797), a conservative critic of the revolution wrote *Reflections on the Revolution in France* (1790). Macintosh, an early supporter of the revolutionaries wrote *Vindiciae Gallicae* (1791) attacking Burke's position. Although Macintosh penned the line about growth, it became identified with Burke who argued that government must be grounded in the mysticism and traditions of the past. Attempts to create new social forms were doomed to failure. Thus, government must grow from its roots rather than being manufactured by human reason. For Spencer, society is neither grounded in organic, mystical traditions nor a result of rational human design. Rather, society reflects natural laws. It is the ever-changing result of conflict and struggle. Spencer sees society as growing from the past, but for him, this growth is a challenge to tradition, not its defense.

of thought to which it was utterly alien. Universally in Macintosh's day, as by an immense majority in our own day, all things were explained on the hypothesis of manufacture, rather than that of growth. It was held that the planets were severally projected round the sun from the Creator's hand, with exactly the velocity required to balance the sun's attraction. The formation of the earth, the separation of the sea from land, the production of animals, were mechanical works from which God rested as a laborer rests. Man was supposed to be molded after a manner somewhat akin to that in which a modeler makes a clay figure. And of course, in harmony with such ideas, societies were tacitly assumed to be arranged thus or thus by direct interposition of Providence; or by the regulations of law-makers; or by both.[2]

Yet that societies are not artificially put together, is a truth so manifest, that it seems wonderful men should have ever overlooked it. Perhaps nothing more clearly shows the small value of historical studies as they have been commonly pursued. You need but to look at the changes going on around, or observe social organization in its leading peculiarities, to see that these are neither supernatural, nor are determined by the wills of individual men, as by implication historians commonly teach; but are consequent on general natural causes. The one case of the division of labor suffices to show this. It has not been by the command of any ruler that some men have become manufacturers, while

others have remained cultivators of the soil. In Lancashire millions have devoted themselves to the making of cotton fabrics; in Yorkshire, perhaps another million live by producing woollens; and the pottery of Staffordshire, the cutlery of Sheffield, the hardware of Birmingham, severally occupy their hundreds of thousands. These are large facts in the structure of English society; but we can ascribe them neither to miracle, nor to legislation. It is not by "the hero as king," any more than by "collective wisdom," that men have been segregated into producers, wholesale distributors, and retail distributors. The whole of our industrial organization, from its most conspicuous features down to its minutest details, has become what it is, not only without legislative guidance, but, to a considerable extent, in spite of legislative hindrances. It has arisen under the pressure of human wants and activities.[3] While each citizen has been pursuing his individual welfare, and none taking thought about division of labor, or indeed conscious of the need for it, division of labor has yet been ever becoming more complete. It has been doing this slowly and silently; scarcely any having observed it until quite modern times. By steps so small, that year after year the industrial arrangements have seemed to men just what they were before—by changes as insensible as those through which a seed passes into a tree; society has become the complex body of mutually dependent workers which we now see. And this economic organization, mark, is the

---

[2] Note that in this paragraph Spencer seems to misunderstand the importance of Macintosh's words. Spencer was an important thinker but many in his own day questioned his wisdom. For example, in a letter written to Darwin a few years after this essay, J.D. Hooker reports that Spencer is "very ingenious and very voluble" but often "out of his depth" (Hooker to Darwin, 24 Jan. 1864, letter 4396) http://www.darwinproject.ac.uk

[3] Here Spencer claims that societies were not supernaturally manufactured but evolved through a natural process of growth, which he illustrates with examples from the social changes in English society caused by industrialization. Spencer's thinking reflected both evolutionism and the work of economist Adam Smith (1723–1790). Smith held that through pursuit of self-interest, individuals would

be guided, as though by an invisible hand, to activities leading to the betterment of society. Spencer presents a similar idea here. There is also an evolutionary undercurrent. Like Darwin, Spencer conceived of evolution as operating through the accumulation of minute changes over long periods of time. Spencer contrasts this idea with the notion that society is the work of individuals. His use of the phrase "the hero as king" is a reference to Thomas Carlyle (1795–1881). In *Lectures on Heroes, Hero-Worship, and the Heroic in History* (1841), Carlyle argued that history was driven by great men. "The hero as king" is the title of one of the chapters of Carlyle's book. Carlyle was a frequent target of American anthropologists in the first half of the twentieth century. Both Kroeber and White argued against the importance of the individual in society.

all-essential organization. Through the combination thus spontaneously evolved it is, that every citizen is supplied with daily necessaries, at the same time that he yields some product or aid to others. That we are severally alive today, we owe to the regular working of this combination during the past week; and could it be suddenly abolished, a great proportion of us would be dead before another week was ended. If these most conspicuous and vital arrangements of our social structure have arisen without the devising of any one, but through the individual efforts of citizens severally to satisfy their own wants, we may be tolerably certain that all the other less important social arrangements have similarly arisen.[4]

"But surely," it will be said, "the social changes directly produced by law cannot be classed as spontaneous growths. When parliaments or kings dictate this or that thing to be done, and appoint officials to do it, the process is clearly artificial; and society to this extent becomes a manufacture rather than a growth." No, not even these changes are exceptions, if they be real and permanent changes. The true sources of such changes lie deeper than the acts of legislators. To take first the simplest instance:—we all know that the enactments of representative governments ultimately depend on the national will: they may for a time be out of harmony with it, but eventually they have to conform to it. And to say that the national will is that which finally determines them, is to say that they result from the average of individual desires; or in other words—from the average of individual natures. A law so initiated, therefore, really grows out of the popular character.[5] In the case of a Government representing but a limited class, the same thing still holds, though not so manifestly. For the very existence of a supreme class monopolizing all power, is itself due to certain sentiments in the commonalty. But for the feeling of loyalty on the part of retainers, a feudal system could not exist. We see in the protest of the Highlanders against the abolition of heritable jurisdictions,[6] that they preferred that kind of local rule. And if thus to the popular nature must be ascribed the growth of an irresponsible ruling class; then to the popular nature must be ascribed the social arrangements which that class creates in the pursuit of its own ends. Even where the Government is despotic, the doctrine still holds. It is not simply that the existence of such a form of government is consequent on the character of the people, and that, as we have abundant proof, other forms suddenly created will not act, but rapidly retrograde to the old form; but it is that such regulations as a despot makes,

---

[4] For Spencer, social evolution was driven by competition among people, through which the best suited to survive were selected. Following this line of thought, he coined the phrase "survival of the fittest." Though this process may have meant misery for some, Spencer believed that it would lead to the perfection of society. His ideas, popularized largely by others as social darwinism, were often used to justify the American and English class systems and colonial political system. However, it is important to note that Spencer himself was deeply critical of both imperialism and the landed aristocracy (for example, see *Facts and Comments* (1902) in which Spencer argues that imperialism makes all men slaves of the state). In America, however, Spencer's work was seen as supporting both the wealthy and imperial expansion. William Graham Sumner (1840–1910) was one of Spencer's most prominent followers and among the best known promoters of social darwinism. In an essay defending the concentration of wealth, he wrote: "No man can acquire a million without helping a million men to increase their little fortunes. . . . The millionaires are a product of natural selection. . . . They may fairly be regarded as the naturally selected agents of society for certain work" (1963 [1914]:156–157).

[5] Spencer here suggests that there is some palpable force in a society that conditions its members to act in certain ways. Even actions that appear to be extremely personal are ultimately the result of this social force. This suggestion provides a portion of the foundation for Émile Durkheim's idea of collective consciousness (see essay 5) and A. L. Kroeber's of the superorganic (see essay 9). Notice that he says that actions by rulers or other individuals may disturb evolution's workings, but that the general process is natural and beyond human control.

[6] Spencer refers to the Heritable Jurisdiction act of 1746 which abolished the traditional rights of Scottish clan chiefs. Spencer is disingenuous in that in objecting to this act, the Scots were protesting rule by London, and not necessarily supporting their own aristocrats.

if really operative, are so because of their fitness to the social state. Not only are his acts very much swayed by general opinion—by precedent, by the feeling of his nobles, his priesthood, his army—and are so in part results of the national character; but when they are out of harmony with the national character, they are soon practically abrogated. The utter failure of Cromwell permanently to establish a new social condition, and the rapid revival of suppressed institutions and practices after his death, show how powerless is a monarch to change the type of the society he governs. He may disturb, he may retard, or he may aid the natural process of organization; but the general course of this process is beyond his control.[7]

Thus that which is so obviously true of the industrial structure of society, is true of its whole structure. The fact that constitutions are not made, but grow, is simply a fragment of the much larger fact, that under all its aspects and through all its ramifications, society is a growth and not a manufacture.

A dim perception that there exists some analogy between the body politic and a living individual body, was early reached, and from time to time re-appeared in literature. But this perception was necessarily vague and more or less fanciful. In the absence of physiological science, and especially of those comprehensive generalizations which it has but recently reached, it was impossible to discern the real parallelisms.

[*It is a law of nature, in Spencer's view, that societies change from simple to complex. The purposes of his article are to outline this process of change and to demonstrate the similarities to the corresponding process in biological organisms. In an 850-word passage eliminated from this edition, Spencer discusses analogies similar to his own made by Plato and Thomas Hobbes. Plato, in* The Republic, *compares society with the human psyche. Hobbes, in* Leviathan, *compares it with the human body. Spencer finds that both of these analogies result in inconsistencies. He also faults Plato and Hobbes for suggesting that society was created by man and hence mechanical rather than grown as a human body or mind and hence organic.*]

Notwithstanding errors, however, these speculations have considerable significance. That such analogies, however crudely conceived, should have arrested the attention, not only of Plato and Hobbes, but of many others, is a reason for suspecting that *some* analogy exists. The untenableness of the particular comparisons above instanced is no ground for denying an essential parallelism; for early ideas are usually but vague adumbrations[8] of the truth. Lacking the great generalizations of biology, it was, as we have said, impossible to trace out the real relations of social organizations to organizations of another order. We propose here to show what are the analogies which modern science discloses to us.

Let us set out by succinctly stating the points of similarity and the points of difference. Societies agree with individual organisms in three conspicuous peculiarities:—

1. That commencing as small aggregations they insensibly augment in mass; some of them

---

[7] Spencer offers the example of Oliver Cromwell's rule of England. Cromwell (1599–1658) rose to power during the English Civil Wars of the mid-seventeenth century. He ruled as Lord Protector of England from 1653–1658. King Charles I was executed in 1649, his death warrant signed by Cromwell himself. However, in 1660, two years after Cromwell's death, Charles' son, Charles II (1630–1685), returned to England and was crowned king. Spencer seems to suggest that the Civil War and Cromwell's rule changed nothing in Britain. This, however, is peculiar. The Interregnum (the period between 1649 and 1660) permanently changed Britain, ending the absolutist monarchy and establishing the dominance of Protestantism. Al-though Spencer wrote about the English Civil War, he may have had the more recent French revolutions of the 1780s and 1840s in mind. These revolutions and the violence that accompanied them shocked and frightened the English upper classes, who interpreted the mass riots as evidence of the bestiality of the working class. The restoration of the monarchy in France was a comforting reassurance that the upper class was indeed superior and that the social evolutionary scheme of things had balanced out. As Spencer writes, "other forms suddenly created will not act, but rapidly retrograde to the old form."

[8] *Adumbrations:* faint shadows or sketches.

reaching eventually perhaps a hundred thousand times what they originally were.

2. That while at first so simple in structure as to be almost considered structureless, they assume, in the course of their growth, a continually increasing complexity of structure.

3. That though in their early undeveloped state there exists in them scarcely any mutual dependence of parts, these parts gradually acquire a mutual dependence, which becomes at last so great, that the activity and life of each part is made possible only by the activity and life of the rest.[9]

These three parallelisms will appear the more significant the more we contemplate them. Observe that, while they are points in which societies agree with individual organisms, they are points in which all individual organisms agree with each other, and disagree with everything else. In the course of its existence, every plant and animal increases in mass, which, with the exception of crystals, can be said of no inorganic objects. The orderly progress from simplicity to complexity displayed by societies in common with every living body whatever, is a characteristic which substantially distinguishes living bodies from the inanimate bodies amid which they move. And that functional dependence of parts, which is scarcely more manifest in animals or plants than in societies, has no counterpart elsewhere. Moreover, it should be remarked, not only that societies and organisms are alike in these peculiarities, in which they are unlike all other

things; but, further, that the highest societies, like the highest organisms, exhibit them in the greatest degree. Looking at the facts in their ensemble, we may observe that the lowest types of animals do not increase to anything like the size of the higher ones; and similarly we see that aboriginal societies are comparatively limited in their growth. In complexity, our large civilized nations as much exceed the primitive savage ones, as a vertebrate animal does a zoophyte. And while in simple communities, as in simple creatures, the mutual dependence of parts is so slight, that subdivision or mutilation causes but little inconvenience; in complex communities as in complex creatures, you cannot remove or injure any considerable organ without producing great disturbance or death of the rest.[10]

On the other hand, the leading differences between societies and individual organisms are these:

1. That they have no specific external forms. This, however, is a point of contrast which loses much of its importance, when we remember that throughout the entire vegetal kingdom, as well as in some lower divisions of the animal kingdom, the forms are very indefinite, and are manifestly in part determined by surrounding physical circumstances, as the forms of societies are. If, too, it should eventually be shown, as we believe it will, that the form of every species of organism has resulted from the average play of the external forces to which it has been subject during its evolution as a species; then, that the external forms of

---

[9] This paragraph contains the fundamental ideas on which Spencer builds his evolutionary theory. He writes that societies are like organisms in three ways: (1) they grow from small groups to large aggregations; (2) they grow from simple to complex structures; and (3) they grow from a collection of independent units to an organism composed of interdependent parts. The second and third points are particularly important to his theory and were incorporated into most of the evolutionary theories of the nineteenth and twentieth centuries. Durkheim, for example, used the idea of directional movement from simplicity to complexity and relational movement from independence to interdependence in his formulation of the

differences between mechanical and organic solidarity (see essay 5).

[10] Note that Spencer's analogy proceeds on two levels. He argues that individual bodies grow in size, complexity, and interdependence and that species also evolve in these same directions. He will similarly argue that both individual groups within society and society itself evolve in this fashion. Evolution is progressive and societies that are large, complex, and integrated are more evolved than those that are not. Industrialized Europe was, in Spencer's view, the best society that evolution had thus far created.

societies should depend, as they do, on surrounding conditions, will be a further point of community.[11]

2. That whereas the living tissue whereof an individual organism consists, forms one continuous mass, the living elements which make up a society, do not form a continuous mass, but are more or less widely dispersed over some portion of the earth's surface. This, which at first sight appears to be a fundamental distinction, is one which yet to a great extent disappears when we contemplate all the facts.

[*In a 400-word passage, Spencer argues that human society is in this respect similar to several primitive life-forms. He further suggests, though not in these terms, that the environment in which people live must be considered part of the social organism and that, if this is taken into account, societies do form a continuous mass.*]

3. That while the ultimate living elements of an individual organism are mostly fixed in their relative positions, those of the social organism are capable of moving from place to place, seems a marked point of disagreement. But here, too, the disagreement is much less than would be supposed. For while citizens are locomotive in their private capacities, they are fixed in their public capacities. As farmers, manufacturers, or traders, men carry on their businesses at the same spots, often throughout their whole lives; and if they go away for a time, they leave behind others to discharge their functions in their absence. Not only does each great center of pro-

duction, each manufacturing town or district, continue always in the same place; but many of the firms in such town or district are for generations carried on either by the descendants or successors of those who founded them. Just as in a living body, the individual cells that make up some important organ, severally perform their functions for a time and then disappear, leaving others to supply their vacant places; so in each part of a society, while the organ remains, the persons who compose it change. Thus, in social life, as in the life of an animal, the units as well as the larger agencies composed of them, are in the main stationary as respects the places where they discharge their duties and obtain their sustenance. So that the power of individual locomotion does not practically affect the analogy.[12]

4. That while in the body of an animal only a special tissue is endowed with feeling, in a society all the members are endowed with feeling, is the last and perhaps the most important distinction. Even this distinction, however, is by no means a complete one. For in some lower divisions of the animal kingdom, characterized by the absence of a nervous system, such sensitiveness as exists is possessed by all parts. It is only in the more organized forms that feeling is monopolized by one particular class of vital elements. Moreover, we must not forget that societies, too, are not without a certain differentiation of this kind. Though the units of a community are all sensitive, yet they are so in unequal degrees. The classes engaged in agriculture and laborious occupations in general, are

---

[11] Spencer glosses over a critical difference between species and societies: species have consistent physical shapes in ways that societies do not. However, he suggests that in time it will be shown that such physical forms are the result of environment and in this finds a commonality. The notion that the environment in which a society exists affects its form became an important element in the environmental determinism of scholars such as Friedrich Ratzel (1844–1904), and influenced Julian Steward and the American cultural ecologists almost a century later.

[12] Spencer writes that communities and businesses exist independently of the individuals who compose them. He says, "so in each part of a society, while the organ remains, the persons who compose it change." The idea that institutions exist independently of the people who compose them is an important insight for both anthropology and sociology in the twentieth century, variously echoed in Durkheim's notion of the collective conscious, Weber's work on bureaucracy, Kroeber's on the superorganic, and Radcliffe-Brown's work on social structure.

far less susceptible, intellectually and emotionally, than the rest; and especially less so than the classes of highest mental culture. Still we have here a tolerably decided contrast between bodies politic and individual bodies. And it is one which we should keep constantly in view. For it reminds us that while in individual bodies the welfare of all other parts is rightly subservient to the welfare of the nervous system, whose pleasurable or painful activities make up the good or evil of life; in bodies politic the same thing does not hold good, or holds good to but a very slight extent. It is well that the lives of all parts of an animal should be merged in the life of the whole, because the whole has a corporate consciousness capable of happiness or misery. But it is not so with a society; since its living units do not and cannot lose individual consciousness; and since the community as a whole has no general or corporate consciousness distinct from those of its components. And this is an everlasting reason why the welfare of its citizens cannot rightly be sacrificed to some supposed benefit of the State; but why, on the other hand, the State must be regarded as existing solely for the benefit of citizens. The corporate life must here be subservient to the life of the parts, instead of the life of the parts being subservient to the corporate life.[13]

Such, then, are the points of analogy and the points of difference. May we not say that the points of difference serve but to bring into clearer light the points of analogy? While comparison makes definite the obvious contrast between organisms commonly so called, and the social organism, it shows that even these contrasts are not nearly so decided as was to be expected. The indefiniteness of form, the discontinuity of the parts, the mobility of the parts, and the universal sensitiveness, are not only peculiarities of the social organism which have to be stated with considerable qualifications; but they are peculiarities to which the inferior classes of animals present approximations. Thus we find but little to conflict with the all important analogies. That societies slowly augment in mass; that they progress in complexity of structure; that at the same time their parts become more mutually dependent; and further, that the extent to which they display these peculiarities is proportionate to their vital activity; are traits that societies have in common with all organic bodies. And these traits in which they agree with all organic bodies and disagree with all other things—these traits which in truth constitute the very essence of organization, entirely subordinate the minor distinctions: such distinctions being scarcely greater than those which separate one half of the organic kingdom from the other. The *principles* of organization are the same; and the differences are simply differences of application.

Thus a general survey of the facts seems quite to justify the comparison of a society to a living body. We shall find that the parallelism becomes the more marked the more closely it is traced. Let us proceed to consider it in detail.

---

[13] In this paragraph Spencer clearly expresses his conviction that some groups of people (particularly those of the "highest mental culture" that is the educated elites) are better than others. In this case, he argues that the intellectual classes are capable of greater feeling than the laboring classes. Statements such as these have led most scholars since the early twentieth century to be highly critical of Spencer, considering him an apologist for ethnocentrism and racism.

The second half of this paragraph is a statement of Spencer's political views. Spencer tells us that the state exists solely for the benefit of its citizens. He understands this as being the promotion of the most complete possible individual freedom of action, a radical form of laissez-faire that rejects almost all forms of collective action. For example, in *TheMan Versus the State* Spencer opposes government expenditures on ". . . free libraries, public museums, washhouses, recreation grounds, etc . . . " as well as many other things. He argues that all of these involve coercion and restrict the freedom since, "the implied address accompanying every additional exaction is – 'Hitherto you have been free to spend this portion of your earnings in any way which pleased you; hereafter you shall not be free so to spend it, but we will spend it for the general benefit.'" (1894:13).

The lowest forms of animal and vegetable life—*Protozoa* and *Protophyta*—are chiefly inhabitants of the water.[14] They are minute bodies, most of which are made individually visible only by the microscope. All of them are extremely simple in structure; and some of them, as the *Amoeba* and *Actinophris,* almost structureless. Multiplying, as they do, by the spontaneous division of their bodies, they produce halves, which may either become quite separate and move away in different directions, or may continue attached. And by the repetition of this process of fission, aggregations of various sizes and kinds are formed. Thus among the *Protophyta* we have some classes, as the *Diatomacea* and the yeast-plant, in which the individuals may be either separate, or attached in groups of two, three, four or more; other classes in which a considerable number of individual cells are united into a thread (*Conferva, Monilia*); others in which they form a network (*Hydrodictyon*); others in which they form plates (*Ulva*); and others in which they form masses (*Laminaria, Agaricus*): all which vegetal forms, having no distinction of root, stem or leaf, are called *Thallogens*. Among the *Protozoa* we find parallel facts. Immense numbers of *Amoeba*-like creatures massed together in a framework of horny fibers, are found in the extensive family of the sponges. In the *Foraminifera* we see smaller groups of such creatures arranged into more definite shapes. Not only do these almost structureless *Protozoa* unite into regular or irregular aggregations of various sizes; but among

some of the more organized ones, as the *Vorticellae*, there are also produced clusters of individuals, proceeding from a common stock. But these little societies of monads, or cells, or whatever else we may call them, are societies in the lowest sense: there is no subordination of parts among them—no organization. Each of the component units lives by and for itself, neither giving nor receiving aid; there is no mutual dependence, save that consequent upon mere mechanical union.[15]

Now do we not here clearly discern analogies to the first stages of human societies? Among the lowest races, as the Bushmen, we find but incipient aggregations: sometimes single families, sometimes two or three families wandering about together. The number of associated units is small and variable, and their union inconstant. No division of labor exists except between the sexes; and the only kind of mutual aid is that of joint attack or defense. We have nothing beyond an undifferentiated group of individuals forming the germ of a society; just as in the groups of similar cells above described, we have only the initial stage of animal and vegetal organization.

[*In a 1,475-word passage removed from this edition, Spencer elaborates on his analogy. Just as more advanced plants and animals show some specialization of function, more advanced societies show evidence of social structure. Beyond sexual division of labor, government is the first structure to emerge. However, as in lower plants, specialization*

---

[14] In this paragraph and below, Spencer makes a highly detailed argument for the analogy between the evolution of biological organisms and that of society. The ideas of simple and complex societies, social structures, and social functions explored here imply a research program. That is, the goal of anthropology (or sociology) should be to identify social "organs" and describe their functioning. Contemporaneously with this essay, Spencer issued a prospectus for a future work, *Principles of Sociology,* in which he proposed to derive empirical generalizations from the comparative study of society (Carneiro 1967). This project was never fully realized, but Spencer's research agenda was central to the development of social anthropology in this century and influenced such thinkers as Emile Durkheim, A. R. Radcliffe-Brown, Julian Steward, and

George Peter Murdock. His ideas continue to be important today.

[15] Notice that Spencer here describes the relationship between these *Protozoa* and *Protophyta* as being "mere mechanical union." Durkheim will later use the term "mechanical solidarity" to describe social relations in small societies. The similarity is probably not accidental. Although Durkheim disagreed with Spencer on many things, he was a close reader of Spencer and developed his own theories both in agreement and in contrast to Spencer's work. Durkheim develops his ideas about mechanical and organic solidarity in *The Division of Labor in Society* (1893). The index to that work cites Spencer almost 50 times (Corning 1982:359).

remains imprecise. Cells can change function and a society's leaders may also do other jobs. The next phase is the spread of similar biological or social units across the landscape. Physical barriers may cause such social units to coalesce into nations. Spencer argues that just as some individuals among a large aggregate of hydra will develop special functions, some communities within a large society will develop specific functions.]

The general doctrine of the progressive division of labor, to which we are here introduced, is more or less familiar to all readers. And further, the analogy between the economical division of labor and the "physiological division of labor" is so striking, as long since to have drawn the attention of scientific naturalists: so striking, indeed, that the expression "physiological division of labor," has been suggested by it. It is not needful, therefore, that we should treat this part of our subject in great detail. We shall content ourselves with noting a few general and significant facts not manifest on a first inspection.

Throughout the whole animal kingdom, from the *Coelenterata* upwards, the first stage of evolution is the same.[16] Equally in the germ of a polype and in the human ovum, the aggregated mass of cells out of which the creature is to arise, gives origin to a peripheral layer of cells, slightly differing from the rest which they include; and this layer subsequently divides into two—the inner one lying in contact with the included yolk being commonly called the mucous layer, and the outer exposed to surrounding agencies being called the serous layer: or in the terms used by Professor Huxley,[17] in describing the development of the *Hydrozoa*—the endoderm and the ectoderm. This primary division marks out the fundamental contrast of parts in the future organism. Out of the mucous layer or endoderm is developed the apparatus of nutrition; while out of the serous layer, or ectoderm, is developed the apparatus of external action. From the one arise the organs by which food is prepared and absorbed, oxygen imbibed, and blood purified; while out of the other arise the nervous, muscular, and osseous[18] systems, by whose combined actions the movements of the body as a whole are effected. Though this is not a rigorously correct distinction, seeing that some organs involve both of these primitive membranes, yet the highest authorities agree in stating it as a broad general one. Well, in the evolution of a society we see a primary differentiation of analogous kind, which similarly underlies the whole future structure.[19] As already pointed out, the only contrast of parts which is visible in primitive

---

[16] The vocabulary Spencer uses when describing biology is quite technical, especially considering that this essay appeared in a general intellectual journal rather than one specifically devoted to biology. The vocabulary he uses when referring to social formations, on the other hand, is quite simple. The effect of combining the technical language of biology with the rather simple vocabulary of society is to make Spencer's comments on society seem much more scientifically compelling than they actually are. Of course, in a modern sense, Spencer's argument is simply an argument by analogy and is not scientific at all. It is neither an attempt to explore and describe the range of human social organization nor a set of conclusions based on controlled experimentation.

[17] Thomas Henry Huxley (1825–1895), sometimes called "Darwin's bulldog," was a prominent biologist famous for his defense of Darwin and the theory of natural selection. Huxley and Spencer knew each other well. Along with Hooker, (mentioned in note 2) they were members of the X Club, a dining club composed of leading scientists, devoted, in the words of one of its members, to: "science, pure and free, untrammelled by religious dogmas" (in Gardner and Wilson 1993:832). Huxley and Spencer later split over Spencer's radical political views; Huxley, writing to Hooker, described Spencer as "long winded vanitous pedant" with "as much tact as a hippopotamus" (in Desmond 2001:3).

[18] *Osseous:* bony; the osseous system refers to the skeleton.

[19] Embryology was one of the leading fields of study of Spencer's day and he was strongly influenced by it, particularly by the work of the pioneering German-Russian embryologist Karl Ernst von Baer (1792–1876). von Baer argued that structures that form early in embryological development are more widely distributed among groups of organisms than structures that arise later in development, an idea now called von Baer's law. Spencer believed von Baer's work demonstrated that movement from homogeneity to heterogeneity was a law of organic progress and proposed that it was a general law of all progress

societies, is that between the government and the governed. In the least organized tribes, the council of chiefs may be a body of men distinguished simply by greater courage or experience. In more organized tribes, the chief-class is definitely separated from the lower class, and often regarded as different in nature—sometimes as god-descended. And later we find these two becoming respectively freemen and slaves, or nobles and serfs. A glance at their respective functions makes it obvious that the great divisions thus early formed, stand to each other in a relation similar to that in which the primary divisions of the embryo stand to each other. For from its first appearance, the class of chiefs is that by which the external actions of the society are controlled: alike in war, in negotiation, and in migration. As we advance, we see that while the upper class grows distinct from the lower, and at the same time becomes more and more exclusively regulative and defensive in its functions, alike as kings and subordinate rulers, as priests, and as military leaders; the inferior class becomes more and more exclusively occupied in providing the necessaries of life for the community at large. From the soil, with which it comes in most direct contact, the mass of the people takes up and prepares for use the food and such rude articles of manufacture as are known; while the overlying mass of superior men, supplied with the necessaries of life by those below them, deals with circumstances external to the community—circumstances with which, by position, it is more immediately concerned. Ceasing by-and-by to have any knowledge of, or power over, the concerns of the society as a whole, the serf class becomes devoted to the processes of alimentation; while the noble class, ceasing to take any part in the process of alimentation, becomes devoted to the co-ordination and movements of the entire body politic.

Equally remarkable is a further analogy of like kind. After there has taken place in the embryo the separation of the mucous and serous layers, there presently arises between the two, a third, known to physiologists as the vascular layer—a layer out of which is developed the system of blood-vessels. The mucous layer absorbs nutriment from the mass of yolk it encloses; this nutriment has to be transferred to the overlying serous layer, out of which the nervo-muscular system is being developed; and between the two arises the system of vessels by which the transfer is effected—a system of vessels which continues ever after to be the transferrer of nutriment from the places where it is absorbed and prepared, to the places where it is needed for growth and repair. Well, may we not clearly trace a parallel step in social progress? Between the governing and the governed there at first exists no intermediate class; and even in some societies that have reached a considerable size, there are scarcely any but the nobles and their kindred on the one hand, and the serfs on the other: the social structure being such, that the transfer of commodities takes place directly from slaves to their masters. But in societies of a higher type, there grows up between these two primitive classes, another—the trading or middle class. Equally at first as now, we may see that, speaking generally, this middle class is the analogue of the middle layer in the embryo. For all traders are essentially distributors. Whether they be wholesale dealers, who collect into large masses the commodities of various producers; or whether they be retailers, who divide out to those who want them the masses of commodities thus collected together; all mercantile men are agents of transfer from the places where things are produced to the places where they are consumed. Thus the distributing apparatus of a

---

(1857:446 [Progress, its law and causes]). Spencer, and others, particularly the German biologist Ernst Heinrich Haeckel (1834–1919) also believed that von Baer's work suggested that the embryological development of an organism illustrated all the stages of its evolution. In 1866 (six years after this essay) Haeckel famously (and incorrectly) proclaimed that "ontogeny recapitulates phylogeny"; that is, the embryological growth of an individual

repeats the evolutionary history of its phylum. When applied to the evolution of society, this meant that the growth of individuals within advanced societies mirrored the stages through which human social evolution had passed. Someone believing this would conclude that adults in primitive societies were very similar to children in advanced societies. Spencer had frequent recourse to "the child/savage equation" (Stocking 1987:22).

society answers to the distributing apparatus in a living body, not only in its functions, but in its intermediate origin and subsequent position, and in the time of its appearance.

Without enumerating the minor differentiations which these three great classes afterwards undergo, we will merely note that throughout, they follow the same general law with the differentiations of an individual organism. In a society, as in a rudimentary animal, we have seen that the most general and broadly contrasted divisions are the first to make their appearance; and of the subdivisions it continues true in both cases, that they arise in the order of their generality.[20]

[*In an 875-word passage, Spencer argues that both societies and organisms develop in the direction of increased specialization of function. He compares the development of states with that of segmented worms. Among these, he says, lower forms are composed of many identical segments, while higher forms have organs that transcend segments. Similarly, early states are composed of many similar independent fiefdoms, but larger states have structures that completely transcend them.*]

If, after contemplating these analogies of structure, we inquire whether there are any such analogies between causes and processes of organic growth, the answer is—yes. The causes which lead to the increase of bulk in any part of the body politic, are strictly analogous to those which lead to increase of bulk in any part of an individual body. In both cases the antecedent is greater functional activity consequent on greater demand. Each limb, viscus, gland, or other member of an animal, is developed by exercise—by actively discharging the duties which the body at large requires of it; and similarly, any class of laborers or artisans, any manufacturing center, or any official agency, begins to enlarge when the community devolves upon it an increase of work.[21] Moreover, in each case growth has its conditions and its limits. That any organ in a living being may grow by exercise, there needs a due supply of blood: all action implies waste; blood brings the materials for repair; and before there can be growth, the quantity of blood supplied must be more than that requisite for repair only. So is it in a society. If to some district which elaborates for the community particular commodities—say the woollens of Yorkshire—there comes an augmented demand; and if in fulfillment of this demand a certain expenditure and wear of the manufacturing organization are incurred; and if in payment for the extra supply of woollens sent away, there comes back only such quantity of commodities as replaces the expenditure and makes good the waste of life and machinery; there can clearly be no growth. That there may be growth, the commodities obtained in return must be somewhat more than is required for these ends; and just in proportion as the excess is great will the growth be rapid. Whence it is manifest that what in commercial affairs we call *profit*, answers to the excess of nutrition over waste in a living body. To which let us add that, in both cases, where the functional activity is great and the nutrition defective, there results not growth but decay. If in an animal any organ is worked so

---

[20] Here and below Spencer reiterates a basic principle of evolution as he understood it: Evolution proceeds from simple to complex, or in his terminology, from the general to the specialized. This understanding was shared by most nineteenth-century thinkers and many more recent scholars. Today it is largely rejected. Evolution may sometimes proceed from simple to complex but probably just as frequently from complex to simple (Mayr 2004).

[21] Note that the description of the evolution of both organisms and society presented here is Lamarckian rather than Darwinian. Spencer says that organs that are used more grow more. Despite the fact that his use of the phrase "survival of the fittest" and his belief in the virtues of competition tie Spencer to Darwin, his version of evolution was formulated independently of Darwin's and was not based on natural selection. Rather, he believed in the inheritance of acquired characteristics. For example, in 1855, he wrote as follows about the personality traits of members of different societies: "there can be no question that these varieties of disposition, which have a more or less evident relation to the habits of life, have been gradually induced and established in successive generations *and have become* organic" (quoted in Stocking 1987:141, emphasis added).

hard that the channels which bring blood cannot furnish enough for repair, the organ dwindles; and if in the body politic some part has been stimulated into great productivity, and cannot afterwards get paid for all its produce, certain of its members become bankrupt and it decreases in size.

One more parallelism to be here noted is, that the different parts of the social organism, like the different parts of an individual organism, compete for nutriment; and obtain more or less of it according as they are discharging more or less duty. If a man's brain be suddenly very much excited, it will abstract blood from his viscera and stop digestion; or, digestion actively going on will so affect the circulation through the brain as to cause drowsiness; or great muscular exertion will determine such a quantity of blood to the limbs as to arrest digestion or cerebral action, as the case may be. And in like manner in a society, it frequently happens that great activity in some one direction causes partial arrests of activity elsewhere, by abstracting capital, that is, commodities: as instance the way in which the sudden development of our railway system hampered commercial operations; or the way in which the raising of a large military force temporarily stops the growth of leading industries.

The last few paragraphs naturally introduce the next division of our subject. Almost unawares we have come upon the analogy which exists between the blood of a living body and the circulating mass of commodities in the body politic. We have now to trace out this analogy from its simplest to its most complex manifestations.

[*In a 2,200-word passage, Spencer compares certain aspects of society with the blood and circulatory system of organisms. Lower animals have no blood or circulatory system; every cell feeds for itself. Similarly, he claims that in primitive tribes there is no system of exchange, and every family fends for itself. Somewhat more complex organisms have extremely simple digestive tracts; likewise, somewhat more complex societies have some trade in agricultural commodities along simple paths. As specialization proceeds in an organism, blood and a circulatory system are required to nourish the now* specialized organs. As societies become more complex, the demands for circulation of products between laboring groups similarly increase. Spencer notes that the circulatory material (either blood for organisms or products for societies) increases not only in quantity but in complexity as well. As animals evolve, they develop what Spencer calls "blood discs" (corpuscles) to facilitate nutrition. In societies money plays a similar role, elaborated in a sequence of analogies. Like blood cells, money itself is not consumed. Blood cells are found in greatest abundance in large organs, and money in greatest abundance in large cities. Blood in lower animals has no corpuscles, and lower societies have no money. Just as lower animals have minimally organized circulatory systems, countries where civilization is beginning have only rudimentary paths for the exchange of goods. More advanced animals have blood vessels, and more advanced societies have fenced and graveled roads. In the highest organisms and societies, there are major blood vessels and capillaries or large main roads and small minor ones. The development of railroads that have a track for each direction is analogous to veins and arteries in a body. The analogy between society and organisms includes not only the circulatory system but also the pattern of motion of nutrients through it. In low creatures, the movement is a slow reciprocating motion. Similarly in lower societies there is movement now toward this fair or market, now toward that. In more advanced societies and animals there are "constant currents in definite directions." Moreover, as organisms evolve, they develop hearts that pump blood through the circulatory system, and societies develop large commercial centers. Blood flows more rapidly the closer it is to the heart, and trains move more rapidly and frequently the closer they are to commercial centers.*]

Thus, then, we find between the distributing system in living bodies and in the body politic, wonderfully close parallelisms. In the lowest forms of both there exists neither prepared nutriment nor a distributing apparatus; and in both, these, arising as necessary accompaniments of the differentiation of parts, approach perfection as this differentiation approaches completeness.

In animals, as in societies, the distributing agencies begin to show themselves at the same relative period, and in the same relative position. In the one, as in the other, the nutritive materials circulated are at first crude and simple, gradually becoming better elaborated and more heterogeneous, and have eventually added to them a new element facilitating the nutritive processes. The channels of communication pass through similar phases of development which bring them to analogous forms. And the direction, rhythm, and rate of the circulation, progress by like steps to final conditions.[22]

We come at length to the nervous system.[23] Having noticed the primary differentiation of societies into the governing and governed classes, and observed its analogy to the differentiation of the two primary tissues which respectively develop into the organs of alimentation and those of external action; having noticed some of the leading analogies between the development of industrial organization and that of the alimentary apparatus; and having above more fully traced the analogies between the distributing systems, social and individual; we have now to compare the appliances by which a society, as a whole, is regulated, with those by which the movements of an organism are regulated. We shall find here parallelisms equally striking with those already detailed.

The class out of which governmental organization originates is, as we have said, analogous, by origin and position, to the ectoderm of the lowest animals and of embryonic forms. And as this primitive membrane, out of which the nervo-muscular system is evolved, must, even in the first stage of its differentiation, be slightly distinguished from the rest by that greater impressibility and contractility[24] characterizing the organ to which it gives rise; so, in that superior class which is eventually transformed into the nervo-muscular system of a society (its legislative and defense appliances), does there exist in the beginning a larger endowment of the capacities required for these higher social functions. Always, in rude assemblages of men, there is a tendency for the strongest, most courageous, and most sagacious to become rulers and leaders; and in a tribe of some standing, this results in the establishment of a ruling class characterized on the average by those mental and bodily qualities which fit them for deliberation and vigorous combined action. Very significant, too, is the fact that those units of a society, who from the beginning discharge the directive and executive functions, are those in whom the directive and executive organs predominate: in other words, that what by analogy we call the nervo-muscular apparatus of a society begins to grow out of those units whose nervo-muscular systems are most developed. For the chiefs who, as individuals, or as a class, first separate themselves from the mass of a tribe, and begin to exercise control over their respective dependents and over the society as a whole, are men who have the greatest bodily vigor, the greatest bravery, or the greatest cunning—more powerful limbs, or more powerful brains, or both; while those to whom the industrious processes are chiefly left—in the smallest tribes the women,

---

[22] Spencer, like most nineteenth-century evolutionists, saw both biological and social evolution leading to more and more perfect societies. In the twentieth century, this view found an echo in the work of Leslie White (see essay 16), but few current evolutionists share it.

[23] By this point you may be tiring of Spencer's examples. To modern readers Spencer's writing style may seem repetitive. However, he was writing for an audience that was largely unfamiliar with the ideas he was presenting. Further, his readers had time to read and an aesthetic taste for copious examples. Gould (1994) has pointed out that, while modern American museums concentrate on the display of one or a few specimens with elaborate explana-tion, Victorian museums attempted to overwhelm the senses through the display of the enormous variety of nature but had relatively little explanation. Here Spencer, a model Victorian, does the same thing with words. We have removed about 40 percent of Spencer's original 14,250-word essay, but we have tried to leave enough of what, by modern standards, is excess verbiage for you to get a feel for this sort of writing.

[24] Spencer uses the words *impressibility* and *contractility* to refer to the ability of the ectoderm, or outer cell layer, in a very simple animal or an embryo to remember (or learn) and to move.

and in larger ones the least masculine men—are of less nervo-muscular power. Thus that greater impressibility and contractility which in the rudest animal forms characterize the units of the ectoderm, characterize also the units of the primitive social ectoderm; since impressibility and contractility are the respective roots of intelligence and strength.[25]

Again, in the unmodified ectoderm, as we see it in the Hydra, the units are all endowed both with impressibility and contractility; but as we ascend to higher types of organization, the ectoderm differentiates into classes of units which divide those two functions between them: some, becoming exclusively impressible, cease to be contractile; while some, becoming exclusively contractile, cease to be impressible. Similarly with societies. In an aboriginal tribe the directive and executive functions are more or less equally diffused throughout the whole governing class. Each minor chief not only commands those under him, but, if need be, himself coerces them into obedience. The council of chiefs itself carries out on the battle-field its own decisions. The head chief not only makes laws, but administers justice with his own hands. But in larger and more settled communities, the directive and executive agencies begin to grow distinct from each other. As fast as his duties accumulate, the head chief, or king, confines himself more and more to directing public affairs, and leaves the execution of his will to others: he deputes others to enforce submission, to inflict punishments, or to carry out minor acts of offence and defence; and only on occasions when perhaps the safety of the society and his own supremacy are at stake, does he be-

gin to act as well as direct. As this differentiation establishes itself, we see that the characteristics of the ruler begin to change. No longer, as in an aboriginal tribe, the strongest and most daring man, the tendency is for him to become the man of greatest cunning, foresight, and skill in the management of others; for in societies that have advanced beyond the first stage, it is chiefly such qualities that insure success in obtaining supreme power, and holding it against internal and external enemies. That is to say, that individual of the governing class who comes to be the chief directing agent, and so plays the same part that a rudimentary nervous center does in an unfolding organism, is usually one endowed with some superiorities of nervous organization.

When, advancing a stage, we contemplate communities somewhat larger and more complex, in which there have arisen, perhaps, a separate military class, a priesthood, and dispersed masses of population requiring local control, there necessarily grow up subordinate governing agents; who, as their duties accumulate, severally become more directive and less executive in their characters. And when, as commonly happens, the king begins to collect round himself a number of advisors who aid him by communicating information, preparing subjects for his judgement, and issuing his orders; we may say that the form of organization is comparable to one very general among inferior types of animals, in which there exists a chief ganglion with a few dispersed minor ganglia under its control.

The analogies between the evolution of governmental structure in a society, and the evolution of governmental structures in living bodies, are, however, more strikingly displayed during

---

[25] In this passage, Spencer focuses on the relationship among fitness, power, and leadership. For him, those who lead society are the most fit, distinguished by physical strength, bravery, and intelligence. Thus, social arrangements are the result of natural law and the power of elites is justified by evolution. Spencer was a member of the rising middle classes and his support of elites was not unconditional. Born to relative poverty, in his early career he opposed the power of the landed aristocracy, writing in *Social Statics* (1865) that "Equity does not permit private property in land . . . [as] . . . exclusive possession of the soil

necessitates infringement of the law of equal freedom" (1865:132). Later in his career he reversed this position, joining the Liberty and Property Defense League and writing in support of the wealthy and powerful regardless of the way in which their wealth was obtained. Similarly, in *Social Statics* Spencer argued for the equality of men and women, writing that "the law of equal freedom applies to both sexes" (1865: 192), but by the time this essay was published, he had reversed this position. He later suggested that the needs of reproduction arrested the mental evolution of females at an early age (Stocking 1987:205).

the formation of nations by the coalescence of small communities—a process already shown to be in several respects parallel to the development of those creatures that primarily consist of many like segments. Among the other points of community between the successive rings which make up the body in the lower *Articulata*, is the possession of similar pairs of ganglia. These pairs of ganglia, though united together by nerves, are very incompletely dependent on any general controlling power. Hence it results, that when the body is cut in two, the hinder part continues to move forward under the propulsion of its numerous legs; and that when the chain of ganglia has been divided without severing the body, the hinder limbs may be seen trying to propel the body in one direction, while the fore limbs are trying to propel it in another. Among the higher *Articulata*, however, a number of the anterior pairs of ganglia, besides growing severally much larger, unite into one mass; and this great cephalic ganglion, becoming the coordinator of all the creature's movements, there no longer exists much local independence. Now may we not in the growth of a consolidated kingdom out of petty sovereignties or baronies, observe analogous changes. Like the chiefs and primitive rulers above described, feudal lords, exercising supreme power over their respective groups of retainers, discharge functions analogous to those rudimentary nervous centers; and we know that at first they, like their prototypes, were distinguished by superiority of directive and executive organization. Among these local governing centers, we see in early feudal times very little subordination. They are in frequent antagonism; they are individually restrained chiefly by the influence of large parties in their own class; and are but imperfectly and irregularly subject to that most powerful member of their order who has gained the position of head suzerain or king. Gradually, however, as the growth and organization of the society progresses, we find these local directive centers falling more and more under the control of a chief directive center. Closer commercial and distributive union between the several segments, is accompanied by closer governmental union; and these minor rulers end in being little more than agents who superintend the execution of the commands of the supreme ruler; just as the local ganglia, above described, eventually become agents which enforce in their respective segments the orders of the cephalic ganglion. Note now a further step in which the parallelism equally holds. We remarked above, when speaking of the rise of aboriginal kings, that in proportion as their territories and duties became greater, they were obliged not only to perform their executive functions by deputy, but also to gather round themselves advisers to aid them in their directive functions; and that thus, in place of a solitary governing unit, there grew up a group of governing units, comparable to a ganglion consisting of many cells. Let us here further remark, that the advisers and chief officers who thus form the rudiment of a ministry, tend from the beginning to exercise a certain control over the ruler. By the information they give and the opinions they express, they sway his judgement and affect his commands. To this extent he therefore becomes a channel through which are communicated the directions originating with them; and in course of time, when the advice of ministers becomes the acknowledged source of a king's actions, we see that he assumes very much the character of an automatic center reflecting the impressions made upon him from without.[26]

Beyond this complication in the governmental structure, many societies do not progress; but in some a much further development takes place. Our own case best illustrates this further development, and its further analogies. To kings and their ministries have been added in course of

---

[26] Here Spencer claims that the best case to illustrate the highest stages of social evolution is his own society and defends the intricacies of the British parliamentary system. Throughout the essay he has compared primitive societies with simple life forms such as yeast and hydra. Here, however, he compares British governmental structures with the brain. It is important to remember the historical context within which Spencer wrote. He was writing in Britain's great period of empire building. His discussion refers to the development of British parliamentary government, and readers applied his ideas to the expansion of the British Empire.

time other great directive centers, exercising a control which, at first small, has been gradually becoming predominant; as with the great governing ganglia that especially distinguish the highest class of living beings. Strange as the assertion will be thought, our Houses of Parliament discharge in the social economy, functions that are in sundry respects comparable to those discharged by the great cerebral masses in a vertebrate animal. As it is in the nature of a single ganglion to be affected only by special stimuli from particular parts of the body; so it is in the nature of a single ruler to be swayed in his acts by exclusive personal or class interests. As it is in the nature of an aggregation of ganglia, closely connected with the primary one, to convey to it a greater variety of influences from more numerous organs, and thus to make its acts conform to more numerous requirements; so it is in the nature of a king surrounded by subsidiary controlling powers to adapt his rule to a greater number of public exigencies. And as it is in the nature of those great and latest developed ganglia which distinguish the highest creatures, to interpret and combine the more numerous and more complex impressions conveyed to them from all parts of the system, and to regulate the actions in such a way as duly to regard them all; so it is in the nature of those great and latest developed legislative bodies which distinguished the most advanced societies, to interpret and combine the wishes and complaints of all classes and localities, and to regulate public affairs as much as possible in harmony with the general wants. It is the function of the cerebrum to coordinate the countless heterogeneous considerations which affect the present and future welfare of the individual as a whole; and it is the function of the House of Commons to coordinate the countless heterogeneous considerations which affect the immediate and remote welfare of the entire community. We may describe the office of the brain as that of *averaging* the interests of life, physical, intellectual, moral, social; and a good brain is one in which the desires answering to these respective interests are so balanced, that the conduct they jointly dictate, sacrifices none of them. Similarly, we may describe the office of a Parliament as that of *averaging* the interests of the various classes in a community; and a good parliament is one in which the parties answering to these respective interests are so balanced, that their united legislation concedes to each class as much as consists with the good of the rest.[27] Besides being comparable in their duties, these great directive centers, social and individual, are also comparable in the processes by which their duties are discharged. It is now a well-understood fact in Psychology, that the cerebrum is not occupied with direct impressions from without, but with the ideas of such impressions: instead of the actual sensations produced in the body, and directly appreciated by the sensory ganglia or primitive nervous centers, the cerebrum receives only the representations of these sensations; and its consciousness is called *representative* consciousness, to distinguish it from the original or *presentative* consciousness. Is it not significant that we have hit upon the same word to distinguish the function of our House of Commons?[28] We call it a representative

---

[27] Throughout this passage Spencer argues that the purpose of government is to regulate and benefit society. Spencer's understanding of the role of government was strongly influenced by John Locke (1632–1704) as well as Jeremy Bentham (1748–1832) and John Stuart Mill (1806–1873). Mill and Spencer were well known to each other. In fact, Mill had offered to cover the entire cost of publication of Spencer's work in the early 1860s (Derry 1902:3). Though not a member, Mill was also associated with the X Club (Barton 1998: 439). Locke, Bentham, and Mill championed the freedom and rights of individuals. Bentham and Mill are associated with the idea that societies should attempt to achieve the greatest good for the greatest number, a key tenet of Utilitarianism. Utilitarianism is deeply embedded in this passage. It is important to note, however, that the liberal, utilitarian understanding of government is not well supported by the history of state level societies. These frequently existed for the benefit of those who ruled them rather than to provide any benefit to the ruled.

[28] Spencer here presents the ideas of representative and presentative consciousness as if they were well established in philosophic discourse. In fact, they are Spencer's own terms and his division of consciousness was widely discussed and critiqued in his own lifetime (see Laveleye 1885, Mercier 1883).

body, because the interests with which it deals—the pains and pleasures about which it consults—are not directly presented to it, but represented to it by its various members; and a debate is a conflict of representations of the evils or benefits likely to follow from a proposed course—a description which applies with equal truth to a debate in the individual consciousness. Further it should be remarked, that in both cases, these great governing masses take no part in the executive functions. As, after a conflict of motives in the cerebrum, those which finally predominate act on the subjacent ganglia, and through their instrumentality determine the bodily actions; so the parties who, after a parliamentary struggle, finally gain the victory, do not themselves carry out their desires, but get them carried out by the executive divisions of the Government. The fulfillment of all legislative decisions continues still to devolve upon the original directive centers—the impulse passing from the Parliament to the Ministers, and from the Ministers to the King, in whose name everything is done; just as those smaller first developed ganglia, which in the lowest vertebrata are the chief controlling agents, are still in a man's brain, the agents through which the dictates of the cerebrum are worked out. And yet once more, observe that in both cases these original centers become more and more automatic. In the individual they have now little function beyond that of executing the determinations of the larger centers. In the State we see that the monarch has long been lapsing into a mere passive agent of Parliament; and that now ministries are rapidly falling into the same position. Nay, between the two cases there is a parallelism, even in respect of the exceptions to this automatic action. For in the individual it happens that under circumstances of sudden alarm, as from a loud sound close at hand, an unexpected object starting up in front, or a slip from insecure footing, the danger is guarded against by some

quick involuntary jump, or adjustment of the limbs, that takes place before there is time to consider the impending evil, and take deliberate measures to avoid it: the rationale of which is, that these violent impressions produced on the senses are reflected from the sensory ganglia to the spinal cord and muscles, without, as in ordinary cases, first passing through the cerebrum. In like manner on national emergencies calling for prompt action, the king and ministry, not having time to lay the matter before the great deliberative bodies, themselves issue commands for the requisite movements or precautions: the primitive, and now almost automatic directive centers resume for a moment their original uncontrolled power. And then, strangest of all, observe that in either case there is an after-process of approval or condemnation. The individual, on recovering from his automatic start, at once contemplates the cause of his fright; and, according to the case, concludes that it was well he moved as he did, or condemns himself for his groundless alarm. In like manner the deliberative powers in the State, discuss, as soon as may be, the unauthorized acts of the executive powers; and, deciding that the reasons were or were not sufficient, grant or withhold a bill of indemnity.[29]

Thus far in comparing the governmental organization of the body politic with that of an individual body, we have considered only the respective coordinating centers. We have yet to consider the channels through which these coordinating centers receive information and convey commands. In the simplest societies, as in the simplest organisms, there is no "internuncial apparatus," as Hunter styled the nervous system. Consequently, impressions can be but slowly propagated from unit to unit throughout the whole mass. The same progress, however, which in animal organization shows itself in the establishment of ganglia or directive centers, shows itself also in the establishment of nerve-threads,

---

[29] The defense of representative government and executive action in the second half of this paragraph must be read in the context of its time. Recall that Karl Marx's *Communist Manifesto* had been published in 1848, a year in which a series of unsuccessful revolutions had swept through Europe. One of the demands of the communists and other revolutionaries was the abolition of both representative government and monarchies. By his argument, Spencer suggested that the superiority of British parliamentary government (and to some extent the governments of other European nations) was established in natural law.

through which the ganglia receive and convey impressions, and so control remote organs. And in societies the like eventually takes place. After a long period during which the directive centers communicate with the various parts of the society through other means, there at length comes into existence an "internuncial apparatus" analogous to that found in individual bodies. The comparison of telegraph wires to nerves is familiar to all. It applies, however, to an extent not commonly supposed. We do not refer to the near alliance between the subtle forces employed in the two cases; though it is now held that the nerve-force, if not literally electric, is still a special form of electric action, related to the ordinary form much as magnetism is. But we refer to the structural arrangements of our telegraph system. Note first the fact that throughout the vertebrate sub-kingdom, we find the great nerve-bundles diverging from the vertebrate axis, side by side with the great arteries; and similarly we see that our groups of telegraph-wires are carried along the sides of our railways. But the most striking parallelism is this—that into each great bundle of nerves as it leaves the axis of the body along with an artery, there enters a branch of the sympathetic nerve, which branch, accompanying the artery through-

out its ramifications, has the function of regulating its diameter and otherwise controlling the flow of blood through it according to the local requirements. In like manner we find that in the group of telegraph wires running alongside each railway, there is one for the purpose of regulating the traffic—for retarding or expediting the flow of passengers and commodities as the local conditions demand. Probably when our now rudimentary telegraph system is fully developed, other analogies will be traceable.[30]

Such, then, is a general outline of the evidence which justifies in detail the comparison of a society to a living organism. The general peculiarities that societies gradually increase in mass, that they become little by little more complex, and that at the same time their parts grow more mutually dependent—these broad peculiarities which societies display in common with all living bodies, and in which they and living bodies differ from everything else; we find to involve minor analogies far closer than might have been expected. To these we would gladly have added others. We had hoped to say something respecting the different types of social organization, and something also on social metamorphoses; but we have reached our assigned limits.

---

[30] For the modern reader one of the most striking things about Spencer is the extraordinary degree of analogical detail he claims. Today, some of his suggestions can sound comic. In *Principles of Sociology* vol. 1 (1916:477, orig.1874) he compares the transition from guild to factory-based production with processes within the human liver. Here he suggests that like the human nervous system, the telegraph, one of the most spectacular technological achievements of his day, appeared as the result of natural law. Spencer had, incidentally, begun his career as a civil engineer working for the London and Birmingham Railway. One wonders what analogies he might have made had he lived in a world of wireless computing and cell phones.

---

2. *The Science of Culture*

Sir Edward Burnett Tylor (1832–1917)

Culture or civilization, taken in its wide ethnographic sense, is that complex whole which includes knowledge, belief, art, morals, law, custom, and any other capabilities and habits acquired by man as a member of society. The condition of culture among the various societies of mankind, in so

---

From *Primitive Culture* (1871)

far as it is capable of being investigated on general principles, is a subject apt for the study of laws of human thought and action.[1] On the one hand, the uniformity which so largely pervades civilization may be ascribed, in great measure, to the uniform action of uniform causes; while on the other hand its various grades may be regarded as stages of development or evolution each the outcome of previous history, and about to do its proper part in shaping the history of the future. To the investigation of these two great principles in several departments of ethnography, with especial consideration of the civilization of the lower tribes as related to the civilization of the higher nations, the present volumes are devoted.

Our modern investigators in the sciences of inorganic nature are foremost to recognize, both within and without their special fields of work, unity of nature, the fixity of its laws, the definite sequence of cause and effect through which every fact depends on what has gone before it, and acts upon what is to come after it. They grasp firmly the Pythagorean doctrine of pervading order in the universal Kosmos. They affirm, with Aristotle, that nature is not full of incoherent episodes, like a bad tragedy. They agree with Leibnitz in what he calls "my axiom, that nature never acts by leaps (La nature n'agit jamais par saut),"[2] as well as in his "great principle, commonly little employed, that nothing happens without its sufficient reason." Nor, again, in studying the structure and habits of plants and animals, or in investigating the lower functions even of man, are these leading ideas unacknowledged. But when we come to talk of the higher processes of human feeling and action, of thought and language, knowledge and

art, a change appears in the prevalent tone of opinion. The world at large is scarcely prepared to accept the general study of human life as a branch of natural science, and to carry out, in a large sense, the poet's injunction to "Account for moral as for natural things." To many educated minds there seems something presumptuous and repulsive in the view that the history of mankind is part and parcel of the history of nature, that our thoughts, wills, and actions accord with laws as definite as those which govern the motion of waves, the combination of acids and bases, and the growth of plants and animals.

The main reasons of this state of the popular judgment are not far to seek. There are many who would willingly accept a science of history if placed before them with substantial definiteness of principle and evidence, but who not unreasonably reject the systems offered to them, as falling too far short of a scientific standard. Through resistance such as this, real knowledge always sooner or later makes its way, while the habit of opposition to novelty does such excellent service against the invasions of speculative dogmatism, that we may sometimes even wish it were stronger than it is. But other obstacles to the investigation of laws of human nature arise from considerations of metaphysics and theology. The popular notion of free human will involves not only freedom to act in accordance with motive, but also a power of breaking loose from continuity and acting without cause,—a combination which may be roughly illustrated by the simile of a balance sometimes acting in the usual way, but also possessed of the faculty of turning by itself without or against its weights. This view of an anomalous action of the

---

[1] Throughout this essay, Tylor reaffirms his faith in the possibility of a science of human society analogous to the physical sciences. In this he is very much like the other thinkers of his era, particularly Herbert Spencer. The opening sentence of this essay is one of the most frequently quoted definitions of culture in anthropology. Despite this, Tylor's understanding of the meaning of culture is clearly very different from that of most modern anthropologists. Whereas most anthropologists today believe that there are a great many different cultures, Tylor believed that "Culture" was, ultimately, a single body of information of which different human groups had greater or lesser amounts. This understanding was based on his belief in the psychic unity of humankind, here referred to as "the uniform action of uniform causes."

[2] *La nature n'agit jamais par saut:* a French phrase meaning "nature never acts by leaps." Darwin also used this phrase in an 1858 essay on variation in species (in Latin rather than French) to express the gradualism of his evolutionary theory. Tylor frequently uses foreign phrases in this essay. They almost always repeat the sentence that precedes them.

will, which it need hardly be said is incompatible with scientific argument, subsists as an opinion patent or latent in men's minds, and strongly affecting their theoretic views of history, though it is not, as a rule, brought prominently forward in systematic reasoning. Indeed the definition of human will, as strictly according with motive, is the only possible scientific basis in such enquiries. Happily, it is not needful to add here yet another to the list of dissertations on supernatural intervention and natural causation, on liberty, predestination, and accountability. We may hasten to escape from the regions of transcendental philosophy and theology, to start on a more hopeful journey over more practicable ground. None will deny that, as each man knows by the evidence of his own consciousness, definite and natural cause does, to a great extent, determine human action. Then, keeping aside from considerations of extranatural interference and causeless spontaneity, let us take this admitted existence of natural cause and effect as our standing ground, and travel on it so far as it will bear us. It is on this same basis that physical science pursues, with ever-increasing success, its quest of laws of nature. Nor need this restriction hamper the scientific study of human life, in which the real difficulties are the practical ones of enormous complexity of evidence, and imperfection of methods of observation.[3]

Now it appears that this view of human will and conduct, as subject to definite law, is indeed recognized and acted upon by the very people who oppose it when stated in the abstract as a general principle, and who then complain that it

annihilates man's free will, destroys his sense of personal responsibility, and degrades him to a soul-less machine. He who will say these things will nevertheless pass much of his own life in studying the motives which lead to human action, seeking to attain his wishes through them, framing in his mind theories of personal character, reckoning what are likely to be the effects of new combinations, and giving to his reasoning the crowning character of true scientific enquiry, by taking it for granted that in so far as his calculation turns out wrong, either his evidence must have been false or incomplete, or his judgment upon it unsound. Such a one will sum up the experience of years spent in complex relations with society, by declaring his persuasion that there is a reason for everything in life, and that where events look unaccountable, the rule is to wait and watch in hope that the key to the problem may some day be found. This man's observation may have been as narrow as his inferences are crude and prejudiced, but nevertheless he has been an inductive philosopher "more than forty years without knowing it." He has practically acknowledged definite laws of human thought and action, and has simply thrown out of account in his own studies of life the whole fabric of motiveless will and uncaused spontaneity.[4] It is assumed here that they should be just so thrown out of account in wider studies, and that the true philosophy of history lies in extending and improving the methods of the plain people who form their judgments upon facts, and check them upon new facts.[5] Whether the doctrine be wholly or but partly

---

[3] In this passage, Tylor rejects both religious explanations of social phenomena and objections to social science based on the supposition of human free will. Tylor was stridently anticlerical. He saw human history as proceeding toward increasing rationality. His own religious background is significant in this context. Tylor was from a Quaker family and was highly influenced by Quaker theology. Quakers (members of the Society of Friends) do not believe in the clergy; instead, they believe that God speaks through each individual. This background had important implications for Tylor's work. Since Quakers believed in the essential unity of humankind, they emphasized a degree of tolerance and humanitarianism frequently absent in this era. The Quaker belief in a single spiritual destiny of

humankind is reflected in Tylor's understanding of human social evolution.

[4] In this passage Tylor continues his attack on those he considers the enemies of the application of scientific method to social science. His key method is really a call for introspection, which has some roots in the Quaker call to introspective prayer.

[5] Notice that Tylor here refers to his work as creating a philosophy of history. Tylor's anthropology required re-creation of the history of humankind's evolution to civilization. Many later anthropologists rejected such historical re-creation as unscientific or impossible.

true, it accepts the very condition under which we search for new knowledge in the lessons of experience, and in a word the whole course of our rational life is based upon it.

"One event is always the son of another, and we must never forget the parentage," was a remark made by a Bechuana chief to Casalis the African missionary. Thus at all times historians, so far as they have aimed at being more than mere chroniclers, have done their best to show not merely succession, but connection, among the events upon their record. Moreover, they have striven to elicit general principles of human action, and by these to explain particular events, stating expressly or taking tacitly for granted the existence of a philosophy of history.[6] Should any one deny the possibility of thus establishing historical laws the answer is ready with which Boswell in such a case turned on Johnson:[7] "Then, sir, you would reduce all history to no better than almanack." That nevertheless the labors of so many eminent thinkers should have as yet brought history only to the threshold of science need cause no wonder to those who consider the bewildering complexity of the problems which come before the general historian. The evidence from which he is to draw his conclusions is at once so multifarious and so doubtful that a full and distinct view of its bearing on a particular question is hardly to be attained, and thus the temptation becomes all but irresistible to garble it in support of some rough and ready theory of the course of events. The philosophy of history at large, explaining the past and predicting the future phenomena of man's life in the world by reference to general laws, is in fact a subject with which, in the present state of knowledge, even genius aided by wide research seems but hardly able to cope. Yet there are departments of it which, though difficult enough, seem compara-

tively accessible. If the field of inquiry be narrowed from History as a whole to that branch of it which is here called Culture, the history, not of tribes or nations, but of the condition of knowledge, religion, art, custom, and the like among them, the task of investigation proves to lie within far more moderate compass. We suffer still from the same kind of difficulties which beset the wider argument, but they are much diminished. The evidence is no longer so wildly heterogeneous, but may be more simply classified and compared, while the power of getting rid of extraneous matter, and treating each issue on its own proper set of facts, makes close reasoning on the whole more available than in general history. This may appear from a brief preliminary examination of the problem, how the phenomena of Culture may be classified and arranged, stage by stage, in a probable order of evolution.

Surveyed in a broad view, the character and habit of mankind at once display that similarity and consistency of phenomena which led the Italian proverb-maker to declare that "all the world is one country" "tutto il mondo e paese." To general likeness in human nature on the one hand, and to general likeness in the circumstances of life on the other, this similarity and consistency may no doubt be traced, and they may be studied with especial fitness in comparing races near the same grade of civilization. Little respect need be had in such comparisons for date in history or for place on the map; the ancient Swiss lake-dweller may be set beside the medieval Aztec, and the Ojibwa of North America beside the Zulu of South Africa. As Dr. Johnson contemptuously said when he had read about Patagonians and South Sea Islanders in Hawkesworth's *Voyages*, "one set of savages is like another." How true a generalization this really is, any Ethnological Museum may show. Examine

---

[6] In this passage Tylor argues that the success of a philosophy of history depends on restricting the subject matter: by focusing on culture, the historian may ignore specific events in favor of general developmental trends. Because Tylor understood culture as a unitary phenomenon that characterized peoples to one degree or another, the project was practical. For Tylor, describing culture as an evolutionary phenomenon implied tracing the history of its

development. Simple societies could be understood as living history or living fossils, a term coined by Darwin (see Morgan, note 13).

[7] Dr. Samuel Johnson (1709–1784), considered by many to be the greatest eighteenth-century English author, is mentioned several times in this essay. James Boswell (1740–1795) was his biographer and frequent companion.

for instance the edged and pointed instruments in such a collection; the inventory includes hatchet, adze, chisel, knife, saw, scraper, awl, needle, spear and arrow-head, and of these most or all belong with only differences of detail to races the most various.[8] So it is with savage occupations; the wood-chopping, fishing with net and line, shooting and spearing game, fire-making, cooking, twisting cord and plaiting baskets, repeat themselves with wonderful uniformity in the museum shelves which illustrate the life of the lower races from Kamchatka to Tierra del Fuego, and from Dahome to Hawaii. Even when it comes to comparing barbarous hordes with civilized nations, the consideration thrusts itself upon our minds, how far item after item of the life of the lower races passes into analogous proceedings of the higher, in forms not too far changed to be recognized, and sometimes hardly changed at all. Look at the modern European peasant using his hatchet and his hoe, see his food boiling or roasting over the log-fire, observe the exact place

which beer holds in his calculation of happiness, hear his tale of the ghost in the nearest haunted house, and of the farmer's niece who was bewitched with knots in her inside till she fell into fits and died. If we choose out in this way things which have altered little in a long course of centuries, we may draw a picture where there shall be scarce a hand's breadth difference between an English ploughman and a negro of Central Africa. These pages will be so crowded with evidence of such correspondence among mankind, that there is no need to dwell upon its details here, but it may be used at once to override a problem which would complicate the argument, namely, the question of race. For the present purpose it appears both possible and desirable to eliminate considerations of hereditary varieties or races of man, and to treat mankind as homogeneous in nature, though placed in different grades of civilization.[9] The details of the enquiry will, I think, prove that stages of culture may be compared without taking into account how far tribes who

---

[8] When Tylor speaks here about "comparing races near the same grade of civilization" and placing ethnographic materials next to each other on display, he is probably thinking about actual museum displays. In 1816, Christian Jürgensen Thomsen (1788–1865) became curator of the Museum of Northern Antiquities in Copenhagen (later the National Museum of Denmark). Because he had no means by which to date artifacts in the museum's collection, he attempted to arrange the museum's collections chronologically based on the material and style of their construction. In so doing, he established the sequence of stone to bronze to iron. Thomsen's "three-age system" became extremely influential in European archaeology and the display of museum collections worldwide. One example was the Crystal Palace exhibition of 1851. The Great Exhibition held in London in the summer of that year, brought together some 14,000 international exhibitors. It not only showed the latest technology, but archaeological and current artifacts from around the world. Both ancient and modern artifacts were displayed together in order of their presumed technical sophistication. More than six million people attended the exhibition and it had a profound influence on both the general public and scholars of the era. Tylor had a personal connection to the exhibition. His friend and mentor the Quaker ethnologist and archaeologist Henry Christi was a juror for it.

The method of display developed by Thomsen and used in the Crystal Palace showed similarities between ancient European artifacts and current-day items from indigenous societies. It seemed to demonstrate that societies could be placed in evolutionary sequence with "Little respect . . . for date in history or place on the map," an idea that became a cornerstone of the comparative method in anthropology.

[9] Tylor here appears to reject racist explanations of cultural differences. Tylor's Quaker theology committed him to the notion of monogenesis—the belief that all human races belonged to the same species and shared the same evolutionary origins. He wrote: "the facts collected seem to favor the view that the wide differences in the civilization and mental state of the various races of mankind are rather differences of development than of origin, rather of degree than kind" (quoted in Stocking 1987:159). This notion was contested by the Americans Samuel G. Morton (1799–1851) and Louis Agassiz (1807–1873), key promoters of polygenesis, a theory that argued human races represented different and unequal species and was used as a "scientific" justification for slavery. Although to modern readers some of Tylor's writing has a decidedly racist cast, he was liberal by the standards of his day.

use the same implement, follow the same custom, or believe the same myth may differ in their bodily configuration and the color of their skin and hair.

A first step in the study of civilization is to dissect it into details, and to classify these in their proper groups. Thus, in examining weapons, they are to be classed under spear, club, sling, bow and arrow, and so forth; among textile arts are to be ranged matting, netting, and several grades of making and weaving threads; myths are divided under such headings as myths of sunrise and sunset, eclipse-myths, earthquake-myths, local myths which account for the names of places by some fanciful tale, eponymic myths which account for the parentage of a tribe by turning its name into the name of an imaginary ancestor; under rites and ceremonies occur such practices as the various kinds of sacrifice to the ghosts of the dead and to other spiritual beings, the turning to the east to worship, the purification of ceremonial or moral uncleanness by means of water or fire. Such are a few miscellaneous examples from a list of hundreds, and the ethnographer's business is to classify such details with a view to making out their distribution in geography and history, and the relations which exist among them. What this task is like may be almost perfectly illustrated by comparing these details of culture with the species of plants and animals as studied by the naturalist. To the ethnographer, the bow and arrow is a species, the habit of flattening children's skulls is a species, the practice of reckoning numbers by tens is a species. The geographical distribution of these things, and their transmission from region to region, have to be studied as the naturalist studies the geography of his botanical and zoological species. Just as certain plants and animals are peculiar to certain districts, so it is with such instruments as the Australian boomerang, the Polynesian stick-and-groove for fire-making, the tiny bow and arrow used as a lancet or phleme by tribes about the Isthmus of Panama, and in like manner with many an art, myth, or custom found isolated in a particular field. Just as the catalogue of all the species of plants and animals of a district represents its Flora and Fauna, so the list of all the items of the general life of a people represents that whole which we call its culture. And just as distant regions so often produce vegetables and animals which are analogous, though by no means identical, so it is with the details of the civilization of their inhabitants.[10] How good a working analogy there really is between the diffusion of plants and animals and the diffusion of civilization comes well into view when we notice how far the same causes have produced both at once. In district after district, the same causes which have introduced the cultivated plants and domesticated animals of civilization, have brought in with them a corresponding art and knowledge. The course of events which carried horses and wheat to America carried with them the use of the gun and the iron hatchet, while in return the old world received not only maize, potatoes, and turkeys, but the habit of smoking and the sailor's hammock.[11]

It is a matter worthy of consideration that the accounts of similar phenomena of culture, recurring in different parts of the world, actually supply incidental proof of their own authenticity.[12] Some years since, a question which brings out

---

[10] Tylor, like Spencer, draws an analogy between cultural and biological evolution. In Tylor's view, the ethnographer's job is to catalog all the practices of humankind and then arrange them into evolutionary and hierarchical order, producing something analogous to the Linnaean classification of plants and animals. The phleme (or fleam) mentioned above is a tool used for bloodletting.

[11] Unlike modern anthropologists, who tend to see field research as inseparable from the practice of anthropology, Tylor did not believe that it was necessary for anthropologists to be involved in data collection. It was their primary job to compile, organize, and classify data. Despite this, Tylor did have some field experience. During a year he spent in North America in 1856, he traveled for four months by horseback in Mexico with his friend Christi. He published an account of this trip (*Anahuac: Or Mexico and the Mexicans, Ancient and Modern*) in 1861.

[12] The argument here is tautological. Above, Tylor maintains that the repeated occurrence of cultural traits in widely disparate locations is evidence of the psychic unity of mankind. Here he contends that he can verify or refute claims about the existence of cultural traits by reference to

this point was put to me by a great historian, "How can a statement as to customs, myths, beliefs, &c., of a savage tribe be treated as evidence where it depends on the testimony of some traveller or missionary, who may be a superficial observer, more or less ignorant of the native language, a careless retailer of unsifted talk, a man prejudiced or even willfully deceitful?" This question is, indeed, one which every ethnographer ought to keep clearly and constantly before his mind. Of course he is bound to use his best judgment as to the trustworthiness of all authors he quotes, and if possible to obtain several accounts to certify each point in each locality. But it is over and above these measures of precaution that the test of recurrence comes in. If two independent visitors to different countries, say a medieval Mohammedan in Tartary and a modern Englishman in Dahome, or a Jesuit missionary in Brazil and a Wesleyan in the Fiji Islands, agree in describing some analogous art or rite or myth among the people they have visited, it becomes difficult or impossible to set down such correspondence to accident or willful fraud. A story by a bushranger in Australia may, perhaps, be objected to as a mistake or an invention, but did a Methodist minister in Guinea conspire with him to cheat the public by telling the same story there? The possibility of intentional or unintentional mystification is often barred by such a state of things as that a similar statement is made in two remote lands, by two witnesses, of whom A lived a century before B, and B appears never to have heard of A. How distant are the countries, how wide apart the dates, how different the creeds and characters of the observers, in the catalogue of facts of civilization, needs no farther showing to any one who will even glance at the foot-notes of the present work. And the more odd the statement, the less likely that several people in several places should have made it wrongly. This being so, it seems reasonable to judge that the statements are in the main truly given, and that their close and regular coincidence is due to the cropping up of similar facts in various districts of culture. Now the most important facts of ethnography are vouched for in this way. Experience leads the student after a while to expect and find that the phenomena of culture, as resulting from widely-acting similar causes, should recur again and again in the world. He even mistrusts isolated statements to which he knows of no parallel elsewhere, and waits for their genuineness to be shown by corresponding accounts from the other side of the earth, or the other end of history. So strong, indeed, is this means of authentication that the ethnographer in his library may sometimes presume to decide, not only whether a particular explorer is a shrewd and honest observer, but also whether what he reports is conformable to the general rules of civilization. "Non quis, sed quid."[13]

To turn from the distribution of culture in different countries, to its diffusion within these countries. The quality of mankind which tends most to make the systematic study of civilization possible is that remarkable tacit consensus or agreement which so far induces whole populations to unite in the use of the same language, to follow the same religion and customary law, to settle down to the same general level of art and knowledge. It is this state of things which makes it so far possible to ignore exceptional facts and to describe nations by a sort of general average. It is this state of things which makes it so far possible to represent immense masses of details by a few typical facts, while, these once settled, new cases recorded by new observers simply fall into their places to prove the soundness of the classification. There is found to be such regularity in the composition of societies of men that we can drop individual differences out of sight, and thus can generalize on the arts and opinions of whole nations, just as, when looking down upon an army from a hill, we forget the individual soldier,

---

the theory of psychic unity. If a traveler asserted that he found traits different from others around the world, then his claims must be false. The use of this sort of reasoning was one factor that led Franz Boas and his followers to attack the work of Tylor and other evolutionists as unscientific.

[13] *Non quis, sed quid:* a Latin phrase meaning "not who, but what." It is not who made the report that is important, but rather what they reported.

whom, in fact, we can scarce distinguish in the mass, while we see each regiment as an organized body, spreading or concentrating, moving in advance or in retreat. In some branches of the study of social laws it is now possible to call in the aid of statistics, and to set apart special actions of large mixed communities of men by means of tax-gatherers' schedules, or the tables of the insurance-office. Among modern arguments on the laws of human action, none have had a deeper effect than generalizations such as those of M. Quetelet,[14] on the regularity, not only of such matters as average stature and the annual rates of birth and death, but the recurrence, year after year, of such obscure and seemingly incalculable products of national life as the numbers of murders and suicides, and the proportion of the very weapons of crime. Other striking cases are the annual regularity of persons killed accidentally in the London streets, and of undirected letters dropped into post-office letterboxes. But in examining the culture of the lower races, far from having at command the measured arithmetical facts of modern statistics, we may have to judge of the condition of tribes from the imperfect accounts supplied by travellers or missionaries, or even to reason upon relics of prehistoric races of whose very names and languages we are hopelessly ignorant. Now these may seem at the first glance sadly indefinite and unpromising materials for a scientific enquiry. But in fact they are neither indefinite nor unpromising, but give evidence that is good and definite, so far as it goes. They are data which, for the distinct way in which they severally denote the condition of the tribe they belong to, will actually bear comparison with the statistician's returns. The fact is that a stone arrow-head, a carved club, an idol, a grave-mound where slaves and property have been buried for the use of the dead, an account of a sorcerer's rites in making rain, a table of numerals, the conjugation of a verb, are things which each express the state of a people as to one particular point of culture, as truly as the tabulated numbers of deaths by poison, and of chests of tea imported, express in a different way other partial results of the general life of a whole community.

That a whole nation should have a special dress, special tools and weapons, special laws of marriage and property, special moral and religious doctrines is a remarkable fact, which we notice so little because we have lived all our lives in the midst of it. It is with such general qualities of organized bodies of men that ethnography has especially to deal. Yet, while generalizing on the culture of a tribe or nation, and setting aside the peculiarities of the individuals composing it as unimportant to the main result, we must be careful not to forget what makes up this main result. There are people so intent on the separate life of individuals that they cannot grasp a notion of the action of a community as a whole—such an observer, incapable of a wide view of society, is aptly described in the saying that he "cannot see the forest for the trees." But, on the other hand, the philosopher may be so intent upon his general laws of society as to neglect the individual actors of whom that society is made up, and of him it may be said that he cannot see the trees for the forest. We know how arts, customs, and ideas are shaped among ourselves by the combined actions of many individuals, of which actions both motive and effect often come quite distinctly within our view. The history of an invention, an opinion, a ceremony, is a history of suggestion and modification, encouragement and opposition, personal gain and party prejudice, and the individuals concerned act each according to his own motives, as determined by his character and circumstances. Thus sometimes we watch individuals acting for

---

[14] Adolphe J. Quetelet (1796–1874) was a mathematician who showed that the behavior of large groups of people could be predicted through the use of statistics. Quetelet called his theory "social physics," implying that he had created a science of society similar to physics. In Tylor's time, statistics was a relatively recent and influential discovery. By providing a way to match numbers with social phenomena, statistics seemed to be a method by which natural laws determining human behavior could be ascertained. Here, Tylor tries to show that ethnographic data are comparable to demographic data and can be considered equally valid. This proposition, if accepted, would provide further evidence that a valid science of culture was possible.

their own ends with little thought of their effect on society at large, and sometimes we have to study movements of national life as a whole, where the individuals co-operating in them are utterly beyond our observation. But seeing that collective social action is the mere resultant of many individual actions, it is clear that these two methods of enquiry, if rightly followed, must be absolutely consistent.

In studying both the recurrence of special habits or ideas in several districts and their prevalence within each district, there come before us ever reiterated proofs of regular causation producing the phenomena of human life, and of laws of maintenance and diffusion according to which these phenomena settle into permanent standard conditions of society, at definite stages of culture.[15] But, while giving full importance to the evidence bearing on these standard conditions of society, let us be careful to avoid a pitfall which may entrap the unwary student. Of course the opinions and habits belonging in common to masses of mankind are to a great extent the results of sound judgment and practical wisdom. But to a great extent it is not so. That many numerous societies of men should have believed in the influence of the evil eye and the existence of a firmament, should have sacrificed slaves and goods to the ghosts of the departed, should have handed down traditions of giants slaying monsters and men turning into beasts—all this is ground for holding that such ideas were indeed produced in men's minds by efficient causes, but it is not ground for holding that the rites in question are profitable, the beliefs sound, and the history authentic. This may seem at the first glance a truism, but, in fact, it is the denial of a fallacy which deeply affects the minds of all but a small

critical minority of mankind. Popularly, what everybody says must be true, what everybody does must be right—"Quod ubique, quod semper, quod ab omnibus creditum est, hoc est vere proprieque Catholicum"—and so forth.[16] There are various topics, especially in history, law, philosophy, and theology, where even the educated people we live among can hardly be brought to see that the cause why men do hold an opinion, or practice a custom, is by no means necessarily a reason why they ought to do so. Now collections of ethnographic evidence, bringing so prominently into view the agreement of immense multitudes of men as to certain traditions, beliefs, and usages, are peculiarly liable to be thus improperly used in direct defence of these institutions themselves, even old barbaric nations being polled to maintain their opinions against what are called modern ideas. As it has more than once happened to myself to find my collections of traditions and beliefs thus set up to prove their own objective truth, without proper examination of the grounds on which they were actually received, I take this occasion of remarking that the same line of argument will serve equally well to demonstrate, by the strong and wide consent of nations, that the earth is flat, and nightmare the visit of a demon.

It being shown that the details of Culture are capable of being classified in a great number of ethnographic groups of arts, beliefs, customs, and the rest, the consideration comes next how far the facts arranged in these groups are produced by evolution from one another.[17] It need hardly be pointed out that the groups in question, though held together each by a common character, are by no means accurately defined. To take up again the natural history illustration, it may be said that they are species which tend to run

---

[15] Tylor's goal in *Primitive Culture* was to scientifically examine the development of religion and expose laws underlying its evolution. He aimed to show that the history of religion is characterized by increasing rationality. The path of his argument led him to explain the rationality of many "primitive" practices. Here he distinguishes between explaining such practices and defending them; it was important to him that his work was perceived as an explanation of religion rather than a defense of particular beliefs.

[16] Tylor quotes St Vincent of Lerins' (d. circa 445) famous definition of orthodoxy. The translation is "That which is believed everywhere, always, and by everyone, this is truly and properly Catholic."

[17] Tylor believed in both evolution and human progress. He refers in the opening of this passage to the debate between biological evolutionists and creationists, still raging in 1871 when this piece was first published. For Tylor, the

widely into varieties. And when it comes to the question what relations some of these groups bear to others, it is plain that the student of the habits of mankind has a great advantage over the student of the species of plants and animals. Among naturalists it is an open question whether a theory of development from species to species is a record of transitions which actually took place or a mere ideal scheme serviceable in the classification of species whose origin was really independent. But among ethnographers there is no such question as to the possibility of species of implements or habits or beliefs being developed one out of another, for development in culture is recognized by our most familiar knowledge. Mechanical invention supplies apt examples of the kind of development which affects civilization at large. In the history of fire-arms, the clumsy wheellock, in which a notched steel wheel was turned by a handle against the flint till a spark caught the priming, led to the invention of the more serviceable flintlock, of which a few still hang in the kitchens of our farm-houses, for the boys to shoot small birds with at Christmas; the flintlock in time passed by an obvious modification into the percussion-lock, which is just now changing its old-fashioned arrangement to be adapted from muzzle-loading to breechloading. The medieval astrolabe passed into the quadrant, now discarded in its turn by the seaman, who uses the more delicate sextant, and so it is through the history of one art and instrument after another. Such examples of progression are known to us as direct history, but so thoroughly is this notion of development at home in our minds,

that by means of it we reconstruct lost history without scruple, trusting to general knowledge of the principles of human thought and action as a guide in putting the facts in their proper order. Whether chronicle speaks or is silent on the point, no one comparing a longbow and a cross-bow would doubt that the cross-bow was a development arising from the simpler instrument. So among the fire-drills for igniting by friction, it seems clear on the face of the matter that the drill worked by a cord or bow is a later improvement on the clumsier primitive instrument twirled between the hands. That instructive class of specimens which antiquaries sometimes discover, bronze celts modelled on the heavy type of the stone hatchet, are scarcely explicable except as first steps in the transition from the Stone Age to the Bronze Age, to be followed soon by the next stage of progress, in which it is discovered that the new material is suited to a handier and less wasteful pattern. And thus, in the other branches of our history, there will come again and again into view series of facts which may be consistently arranged as having followed one another in a particular order of development, but which will hardly bear being turned round and made to follow in reversed order.[18] Such for instance are the facts I have here brought forward in a chapter on the Art of Counting, which tend to prove that as to this point of culture at least, savage tribes reached their position by learning and not unlearning, by elevation from a lower rather than by degradation from a higher state.

Among evidence aiding us to trace the courses which the civilization of the world has actually

---

proposition that societies evolved from the most simple to most complex was self-evident. He wrote, "the educated world of Europe and America practically settles a standard by simply placing its own nations at one end of the social series and savage tribes at the other, arranging the rest of mankind between these limits according as they correspond more closely to savage or cultured life" (quoted in Stocking 1987:162). For Tylor, the force driving this evolution was the natural development of increasingly rational thinking. Although Tylor's thinking is evolutionary, he downplayed the importance of Darwinian evolution. In the preface to the 1873 edition of *Primitive Culture,* he ex-

plained the absence of references to Darwin and Spencer in the work by claiming that his work came "scarcely into contact of detail with the previous works of these eminent philosophers." However, the close connection between the work of Darwin and that of Tylor is shown by Darwin's extensive referencing of Tylor in *The Descent of Man* (1871).

[18] A popular theory in Tylor's time held that some peoples were primitive because they had degenerated from an earlier state. Tylor rejected this idea and discusses it further on in this essay.

followed, is that great class of facts to denote which I have found it convenient to introduce the term "survivals."[19] These are processes, customs, opinions, and so forth, which have been carried on by force of habit into a new state of society different from that in which they had their original home, and they thus remain as proofs and examples of an older condition of culture out of which a newer has been evolved. Thus, I know an old Somersetshire woman whose handloom dates from the time before the introduction of the "flying shuttle," which new-fangled appliance she has never even learnt to use, and I have seen her throw her shuttle from hand to hand in true classic fashion; this old woman is not a century behind her times, but she is a case of survival.[20] Such examples often lead us back to the habits of hundreds and even thousands of years ago. The ordeal of the Key and Bible, still in use, is a survival; the Midsummer bonfire is a survival; the Breton peasants' All Souls' supper for the spirits of the dead is a survival. The simple keeping up of ancient habits is only one part of the transition from old into new and changing times. The serious business of ancient society may be seen to sink into the sport of later generations, and its serious belief to linger on in nursery folk-lore, while superseded habits of old-world life may be modified into new-world forms still powerful for good and evil. Sometimes old thoughts and practices will burst out afresh, to the amazement of a world that thought them long

since dead or dying; here survival passes into revival, as has lately happened in so remarkable a way in the history of modern spiritualism, a subject full of instruction from the ethnographer's point of view.[21] The study of the principles of survival has, indeed, no small practical importance, for most of what we call superstition is included within survival, and in this way lies open to the attack of its deadliest enemy, a reasonable explanation. Insignificant, moreover, as multitudes of the facts of survival are in themselves, their study is so effective for tracing the course of the historical development through which alone it is possible to understand their meaning, that it becomes a vital point of ethnographic research to gain the clearest possible insight into their nature. This importance must justify the detail here devoted to an examination of survival, on the evidence of such games, popular sayings, customs, superstitions, and the like, as may serve well to bring into view the manner of its operation.

Progress, degradation, survival, revival, modification are all modes of the connexion that binds together the complex network of civilization.[22] It needs but a glance into the trivial details of our own daily life to set us thinking how far we are really its originators, and how far but the transmitters and modifiers of the results of long past ages. Looking round the rooms we live in, we may try here how far he who only knows his own time can be capable of rightly comprehending even that. Here is the "honeysuckle" of Assyria, there

---

[19] Although other thinkers such as Henry Sumner Maine (see footnote 27) also used the idea of survivals, it is considered one of Tylor's key contributions to anthropology. To him, almost any practice that seemed illogical or smacked of superstition was an example of the survival of the traits and beliefs of an earlier social form. Studying survivals was crucial, since through them—and with the theory of psychic unity—a researcher could trace the course of cultural evolution.

[20] Notice Tylor's frequent references to the customs of English peasantry in this passage. For Tylor and other evolutionists, European peasantry represented a crucial intermediate step between civilization and savagery.

[21] Tylor wrote in an era when the occult was becoming a popular middle-class pastime. He himself had seen and

written on psychic phenomena. Although he did not believe in psychic phenomena, he did admit to being very impressed by the demonstrations he witnessed and was unable to offer rational explanations of them (Stocking 1987:191).

[22] Here Tylor gives numerous examples of survivals. Tylor's great strength is his ability as a cultural historian; he was a master of the many details of cultural life. This passage also affirms his faith that laws of culture, similar in nature to the cause-and-effect principles of Newtonian physics, could be found. Virtually every paragraph of this essay stresses the ability of rational thinking men to divine cause-and-effect relationships.

the fleur-de-lis of Anjou, a cornice with a Greek border runs round the ceiling, the style of Louis XIV and its parent the Renaissance share the looking-glass between them. Transformed, shifted, or mutilated, such elements of art still carry their history plainly stamped upon them; and if the history yet farther behind is less easy to read, we are not to say that because we cannot clearly discern it there is therefore no history there. It is thus even with the fashion of the clothes men wear. The ridiculous little tails of the German postilion's[23] coat show themselves how they came to dwindle to such absurd rudiments; but the English clergyman's bands no longer so convey their history to the eye, and look unaccountable enough till one has seen the intermediate stages through which they came down from the more serviceable wide collars, such as Milton wears in his portrait, and which gave their name to the "band-box" they used to be kept in. In fact, the books of costume, showing how one garment grew or shrank by gradual stages and passed into another, illustrate with much force and clearness the nature of the change and growth, revival and decay, which go on from year to year in more important matters of life. In books, again, we see each writer not for and by himself, but occupying his proper place in history; we look through each philosopher, mathematician, chemist, poet, into the background of his education—through Leibnitz into Descartes, through Dalton into Priestley, through Milton into Homer. The study of language has, perhaps, done more than any other in removing from our view of human thought and action the ideas of chance and arbitrary invention, and in substituting for them a theory of development by the co-operation of individual men,

through processes ever reasonable and intelligible where the facts are fully known.[24] Rudimentary as the science of culture still is, the symptoms are becoming very strong that even what seem its most spontaneous and motiveless phenomena will, nevertheless, be shown to come within the range of distinct cause and effect as certainly as the facts of mechanics. What would be popularly thought more indefinite and uncontrolled than the products of the imagination in myths and fables? Yet any systematic investigation of mythology, on the basis of a wide collection of evidence, will show plainly enough in such efforts of fancy at once a development from stage to stage, and a production of uniformity of result from uniformity of cause. Here, as elsewhere, causeless spontaneity is seen to recede farther and farther into shelter within the dark precincts of ignorance; like chance, that still holds its place among the vulgar as a real cause of events otherwise unaccountable, while to educated men it has long consciously meant nothing but this ignorance itself. It is only when men fail to see the line of connexion in events that they are prone to fall upon the notions of arbitrary impulses, causeless freaks, chance and nonsense, and indefinite unaccountability. If childish games, purposeless customs, absurd superstitions are set down as spontaneous because no one can say exactly how they came to be, the assertion may remind us of the like effect that the eccentric habits of the wild rice-plant had on the philosophy of a Red Indian tribe, otherwise disposed to see in the harmony of nature the effects of one controlling personal will. The Great Spirit, said these Sioux theologians, made all things except the wild rice; but the wild rice came by chance.

---

[23] *Postilion:* a person who rides the horse on the left of the leading pair when four or more horses are used to draw a carriage, or simply the horse on the left when only one pair is used.

[24] Tylor had an early interest in linguistics and was particularly influenced by Friedrich Max Müller (1823–1900). Linguistic scholarship in Tylor's day was almost primarily historical, and Müller used the study of Sanskrit writings to discover the histories of Indo-European languages. Müller

identified speakers of Indo-European languages as descendants of an ancient Aryan race. He is generally remembered as a humanist and, late in life, clearly opposed those who used the term *Aryan* as a racial category, but Stocking (1987:59) notes that "many of his more rhapsodic passages are . . . resonant of Aryanist racial ideology," and some of his work was later used in Nazi Germany to construct an intellectual pedigree for that regime's racist philosophy.

"Man," said Wilhelm von Humboldt,[25] "ever connects on from what lies at hand (der Mensch Knüpft immer an Vorhandenes an)." The notion of the continuity of civilization contained in this maxim is no barren philosophic principle, but is at once made practical by the consideration that they who wish to understand their own lives ought to know the stages through which their opinions and habits have become what they are. Auguste Comte[26] scarcely overstated the necessity of this study of development, when he declared at the beginning of his "Positive Philosophy" that "no conception can be understood except through its history" and his phrase will bear extension to culture at large. To expect to look modern life in the face and comprehend it by mere inspection is a philosophy whose weakness can easily be tested. Imagine any one explaining the trivial saying, "a little bird told me" without knowing of the old belief in the language of birds and beasts, to which Dr. Dasent, in the introduction to the Norse Tales, so reasonably traces its origin. To ingenious attempts at explaining by the light of reason things which want the light of history to show their meaning, much of the learned nonsense of the world has indeed been due. Sir H. S. Maine,[27] in his "Ancient Law," gives a perfect instance. In all the literature which enshrines the pretended philosophy of law, he remarks, there is nothing more curious than the pages of elaborate sophistry in which Blackstone attempts to explain and justify that extraordinary rule of English law, only recently repealed, which prohibited sons of

the same father by different mothers from succeeding to one another's land. To Sir H. S. Maine, knowing the facts of the case, it was easy to explain its real origin from the "Customs of Normandy" where according to the system of agnation, or kinship on the male side, brothers by the same mother but by different fathers were of course no relations at all to one another. But when this rule "was transplanted to England, the English judges, who had no clue to its principle, interpreted it as a general prohibition against the succession of the half-blood, and extended it to consanguineous brothers, that is to sons of the same father by different wives." Then, ages after, Blackstone sought in this blunder the perfection of reason, and found it in the argument that kinship through both parents ought to prevail over even a nearer degree of kinship through but one parent.[a] Such are the risks that philosophers run in detaching any phenomenon of civilization from its hold on past events, and treating it as an isolated fact, to be simply disposed of by a guess at some plausible explanation.

In carrying on the great task of rational ethnography, the investigation of the causes which have produced the phenomena of culture, and the laws to which they are subordinate, it is desirable to work out as systematically as possible a scheme of evolution of this culture along its many lines.[28] In the following chapter [of *Primitive Culture*], on the Development of Culture, an attempt is made to sketch a theoretical course of civilization among mankind, such as appears on

---

[25] Wilhelm von Humboldt (1767–1835) was a German diplomat, a humanist, and the founder of the University of Berlin. Humboldt's enduring legacy was his work in language. His appreciation of linguistic differences foreshadowed the work of Edward Sapir (1884–1939) and Benjamin L. Whorf (1897–1941) in the twentieth century. In 1820 he wrote: "The differences between languages are not those of sounds and signs but those of differing world view" (1963:246).

[26] Auguste Comte (1798–1857) was one of the architects of the philosophical school of positivism. Comte and other positivists denied the possibility of metaphysical knowledge, asserting that social phenomena were subject to general laws that could be discovered using the scientific

method. He proposed a science of society and is often considered a founder of sociology. Comte had a profound influence on the social scientists of Tylor's generation and was a particularly powerful influence on Émile Durkheim and his followers in the early years of the twentieth century.

[27] Sir Henry Sumner Maine (1822–1888) was a legal historian and cultural evolutionist whose *Ancient Law* (1863) informed many of the anthropological discussions of Tylor's day. This passage shows an example of Maine's use of survivals.

[28] These passages contain numerous examples of the use of the comparative method, which is held together, of course, by the belief in the psychic unity of humankind. If

the whole most accordant with the evidence. By comparing the various stages of civilization among races known to history, with the aid of archaeological inference from the remains of prehistoric tribes, it seems possible to judge in a rough way of an early general condition of man, which from our point of view is to be regarded as a primitive condition, whatever yet earlier state may in reality have lain behind it. This hypothetical primitive condition corresponds in a considerable degree to that of modern savage tribes, who, in spite of their difference and distance, have in common certain elements of civilization, which seem remains of an early state of the human race at large. If this hypothesis be true, then, notwithstanding the continual interference of degeneration, the main tendency of culture from primeval up to modern times has been from savagery towards civilization.[29] On the problem of this relation of savage to civilized life, almost every one of the thousands of facts discussed in the succeeding chapters has its direct bearing. Survival in Culture, placing all along the course of advancing civilization way-marks full of meaning to those who can decipher their signs, even now sets up in our midst primeval monuments of barbaric thought and life. Its investigation tells strongly in favor of the view that the European may find among the Greenlanders or Maoris many a trait for reconstructing the picture of his own primitive ancestors. Next comes the problem of the Origin of Language. Obscure as many parts of this problem still remain, its clearer positions lie open to the investigation whether speech took its origin among mankind in the savage state, and

the result of the enquiry is that, consistently with all known evidence, this may have been the case. From examination of the Art of Counting a far more definite consequence is shown. It may be confidently asserted that not only is this important art found in a rudimentary state among savage tribes, but that satisfactory evidence proves numeration to have been developed by a rational invention from this low stage up to that in which we ourselves possess it. The examination of Mythology contained in the first volume is for the most part made from a special point of view, on evidence collected for a special purpose, that of tracing the relation between the myths of savage tribes and their analogues among more civilized nations. The issue of such enquiry goes far to prove that the earliest myth-maker arose and flourished among savage hordes, setting on foot an art which his more cultured successors would carry on, till its results came to be fossilized in superstition, mistaken for history, shaped and draped in poetry, or cast aside as lying folly.

Nowhere, perhaps, are broad views of historical development more needed than in the study of religion.[30] Notwithstanding all that has been written to make the world acquainted with the lower theologies, the popular ideas of their place in history and their relation to the faiths of higher nations are still of the mediæval type. It is wonderful to contrast some missionary journals with Max Müller Essays, and to set the unappreciating hatred and ridicule that is lavished by narrow hostile zeal on Brahmanism, Buddhism, Zoroastrism, beside the catholic sympathy with which deep and wide knowledge can survey those ancient

---

the presumption of psychic unity was incorrect, there would be no reason that societies must inevitably follow the same stages of cultural evolution.

[29] Degenerationism was a popular idea of the eighteenth and early nineteenth centuries that is explained in the introduction to this section. Tylor felt that degeneration of particular societies was possible, but he held that the general path of human society was progress, not degeneration.

[30] This and the following paragraphs introduce much of the rest of *Primitive Culture,* which is devoted to an analysis of religion. Many of Tylor's contemporaries suggested

that since primitive religion was illogical and irrational, it did not lend itself to scientific study. These included Lewis Henry Morgan, who, though he did write on Iroquois beliefs, considered all primitive religion "to some extent unintelligible" (see essay 3). Tylor, on the other hand, asserted that, properly understood, primitive religious beliefs had rational bases. He further insisted that the development of religion, like most everything else, followed progressive, evolutionary laws. In much of the book that follows, Tylor traced what he believed was the evolution of religion from animism (a term he coined) to "enlightened Christianity."

and noble phases of man's religious consciousness; nor, because the religions of savage tribes may be rude and primitive compared with the great Asiatic systems, do they lie too low for interest and even for respect. The question really lies between understanding and misunderstanding them. Few who will give their minds to master the general principles of savage religion will ever again think it ridiculous, or the knowledge of it superfluous to the rest of mankind. Far from its beliefs and practices being a rubbish-heap of miscellaneous folly, they are consistent and logical in so high a degree as to begin, as soon as even roughly classified, to display the principles of their formation and development; and these principles prove to be essentially rational, though working in a mental condition of intense and inveterate ignorance. It is with a sense of attempting an investigation which bears very closely on the current theology of our own day, that I have set myself to examine systematically, among the lower races, the development of Animism; that is to say, the doctrine of souls and other spiritual beings in general. More than half of the present work is occupied with a mass of evidence from all regions of the world, displaying the nature and meaning of this great element of the Philosophy of Religion, and tracing its transmission, expansion, restriction, modification, along the course of history into the midst of our own modern thought. Nor are the questions of small practical moment which have to be raised in a similar attempt to trace the development of certain prominent Rites and Ceremonies—customs so full of instruction as to the inmost powers of religion, whose outward expression and practical result they are.

In these investigations, however, made rather from an ethnographic than a theological point of view, there has seemed little need of entering into direct controversial argument, which indeed I have taken pains to avoid as far as possible.[31] The connexion which runs through religion, from its rudest forms up to the status of an enlightened Christianity, may be conveniently treated of with little recourse to dogmatic theology. The rites of sacrifice and purification may be studied in their stages of development without entering into questions of their authority and value, nor does an examination of the successive phases of the world's belief in a future life demand a discussion of the arguments adduced for or against the doctrine itself. The ethnographic results may then be left as materials for professed theologians, and it will not perhaps be long before evidence so fraught with meaning shall take its legitimate place. To fall back once again on the analogy of natural history, the time may soon come when it will be thought as unreasonable for a scientific student of theology not to have a competent acquaintance with the principles of the religions of the lower races, as for a physiologist to look with the contempt of fifty years ago on evidence derived from the lower forms of life, deeming the structure of mere invertebrate creatures matter unworthy of his philosophic study.

Not merely as a matter of curious research, but as an important practical guide to the understanding of the present and the shaping of the future, the investigation into the origin and early development of civilization must be pushed on zealously. Every possible avenue of knowledge must be explored, every door tried to see if it is open. No kind of evidence need be left untouched on the score of remoteness or complexity, of minuteness or triviality. The tendency of modern enquiry is more and more toward the conclusion that if law is anywhere, it is everywhere. To despair of what a conscientious collection and study of facts may lead to, and to declare any problem insoluble because difficult and far off, is distinctly to be on the wrong side in science; and he who will choose a hopeless task may set himself to discover the limits of discovery. One remembers Comte starting in his account of astronomy

---

[31] Tylor is careful to distinguish his ethnographic work from a theological defense of or attack on particular beliefs. However, notice the passage here about his evidence taking its legitimate place. Tylor believed that rational, scientific knowledge was displacing religious belief. Although Tylor was certainly no atheist, he implies that many of the religious practices of his own day are survivals of early humans' misunderstanding of the world. Note the anticlerical undercurrents in these passages. Tylor obliquely implies that Christianity itself was a survival and would not survive rational examination.

with a remark on the necessary limitation of our knowledge of the stars: we conceive, he tells us, the possibility of determining their form, distance, size, and movement, whilst we should never by any method be able to study their chemical composition, their mineralogical structure, &c. Had the philosopher lived to see the application of spectrum analysis to this very problem his proclamation of the dispiriting doctrine of necessary ignorance would perhaps have been recanted in favor of a more hopeful view. And it seems to be with the philosophy of remote human life somewhat as with the study of the nature of the celestial bodies. The processes to be made out in the early stages of our mental evolution lie distant from us in time as the stars lie distant from us in space, but the laws of the universe are not limited with the direct observation of our senses. There is vast material to be used in our enquiry; many workers are now busied in bringing this material into shape, though little may have yet been done in proportion to what remains to do; and already it seems not too much to say that the vague outlines of a philosophy of primaeval history are beginning to come within our view.[32]

NOTE

[a]Blackstone, "Commentaries," "As every man's own blood is compounded of the bloods of his respective ancestors, he only is properly of the whole or entire blood with another, who hath (so far as the distance of degrees will permit), all the same ingredients in the composition of his blood that the other hath," etc.

---

[32] Tylor had an important influence on both his generation and future generations of anthropologists, but his attempt to establish anthropology as a university discipline was largely frustrated. Backed by wealthy and influential friends, he held university positions at Oxford from 1884 until his death and received a knighthood in 1912, but a permanent position in anthropology was not established at Oxford during his lifetime. Many American anthropologists, particularly Boas and his students, rejected Tylor's work. However, some, including Leslie White and his students, looked to Tylor for inspiration. Notice the similarity between this paragraph and the last paragraph of White's "Energy and the Evolution of Culture" (essay 16), written more than seventy years later.

---

3. *Ethnical Periods*

Lewis Henry Morgan (1818–1881)

The latest investigations respecting the early condition of the human race are tending to the conclusion that mankind commenced their career at the bottom of the scale and worked their way up from savagery to civilization through the slow accumulations of experimental knowledge.[1]

From *Ancient Society* (1877)

---

[1] In this first paragraph, Morgan shows that he, like other nineteenth-century anthropologists, viewed cultural evolution as progressive. His statement that humans worked their way up "to civilization through the slow accumulations of experimental knowledge" sounds Darwinian, but the relationship between Morgan and Darwin's work is difficult to judge. Morgan had corresponded with Darwin and visited him at Down House in 1871. However, Morgan's ideas are closer to Lamarck's than to Darwin's. Further, his understanding of the progressive nature of human evolution was rooted in the Presbyterian theology of his close friend Joshua McIlvaine (1815–1897). McIlvaine was a philologist who lectured at Princeton and University of Pennsylvania. He opposed degenerationism and supported the idea that humanity had risen from low origins to a high estate. However, McIlvaine (and probably Morgan as well) rejected any possibility of a biological connection between humans and nonhuman animals. McIlvaine wrote: "Man has come up from a low state and there is a splendid future before him. But he never came from the beast" (quoted in Service 1981:28).

As it is undeniable that portions of the human family have existed in a state of savagery, other portions in a state of barbarism, and still other portions in a state of civilization, it seems equally so that these three distinct conditions are connected with each other in a natural as well as necessary sequence of progress. Moreover, that this sequence has been historically true of the entire human family, up to the status attained by each branch respectively, is rendered probable by the conditions under which all progress occurs, and by the known advancement of several branches of the family through two or more of these conditions.

An attempt will be made in the following pages to bring forward additional evidence of the rudeness of the early condition of mankind, of the gradual evolution of their mental and moral powers through experience, and of their protracted struggle with opposing obstacles while winning their way to civilization. It will be drawn, in part, from the great sequence of inventions and discoveries which stretches along the entire pathway of human progress; but chiefly from domestic institutions, which express the growth of certain ideas and passions.[2]

As we re-ascend along the several lines of progress toward the primitive ages of mankind, and eliminate one after the other, in the order in which they appeared, inventions and discoveries on the one hand, and institutions on the other, we are enabled to perceive that the former stand to each other in progressive, and the latter in unfolding relations. While the former class have had a connection, more or less direct, the latter have been developed from a few primary germs of thought. Modern institutions plant their roots in the period of barbarism, into which their germs were transmitted from the previous period of savagery. They have had a lineal descent through the ages, with the streams of the blood, as well as a logical development.[3]

Two independent lines of investigations thus invite our attention. The one leads through inventions and discoveries, and the other through primary institutions. With the knowledge gained therefrom, we may hope to indicate the principal stages of human development. The proofs to be adduced will be drawn chiefly from domestic institutions; the references to achievements more strictly intellectual being general as well as subordinate.[4]

The facts indicate the gradual formation and subsequent development of certain ideas, passions, and aspirations. Those which hold the most prominent positions may be generalized as growths of the particular ideas with which they severally stand connected. Apart from inventions and discoveries they are the following:

I.	*Subsistence,*	V.	*Religion,*
II.	*Government,*	VI.	*House Life and*
III.	*Language,*		*Architecture,*
IV.	*The Family,*	VII.	*Property.*

First. Subsistence has been increased and perfected by a series of successive arts, introduced at

---

[2] Like many others of his day, Morgan held that progress was a moral force. Humanity had not only developed increasingly complex and sophisticated institutions and technologies, modern people were also morally superior to "savages" who he described as "held down by [their] low animal appetites and passions" (1910:41). Notice that Morgan speaks of "winning" civilization. The influence of the concept of evolution as a battle for survival is evident in Morgan's characterization of cultural evolution as a "protracted struggle."

[3] Several aspects of Morgan's thought are evident in this paragraph. Note that Morgan discusses two different types of evolution: first, the growth of intelligence, illustrated by inventions and discoveries and second, evolution of institutions. Part one of *Ancient Society* deals with the first of

these. The remaining three parts deal with the growth of institutions that Morgan deemed central: government, the family, and property.

[4] Morgan was interested in the evolution of culture as a pan-human event but divides the evidence used in his analysis. He proposed to trace the development of "inventions and discoveries" but considered them subordinate to the development of the primary institutions of government, family, and property. Morgan believed that inventions and discoveries were correlated with stages of cultural evolution but developed by different processes. Inventions evolve by logically building from one to the next. Primary institutions have "unfolding relations." They were seeded as germs of thought in the period of Savagery, germinated in the period of Barbarism, and flowered in Civilization.

long intervals of time, and connected more or less directly with inventions and discoveries.[5]

Second. The germ of government must be sought in the organization into gentes[6] in the Status of savagery; and followed down, through the advancing forms of this institution, to the establishment of political society.

Third. Human speech seems to have been developed from the rudest and simplest forms of expression. Gesture or sign language, as intimated by Lucretius,[a] must have preceded articulate language, as thought preceded speech. The monosyllabical preceded the syllabical, as the latter did that of concrete words. Human intelligence, unconscious of design, evolved articulate language by utilizing the vocal sounds. This great subject, a department of knowledge by itself, does not fall within the scope of the present investigation.[7]

Fourth. With respect to the family, the stages of its growth are embodied in systems of consanguinity and affinity, and in usages relating to marriage, by means of which, collectively, the family can be definitely traced through several successive forms.[8]

Fifth. The growth of religious ideas is environed with such intrinsic difficulties that it may never receive a perfectly satisfactory exposition. Religion deals so largely with the imaginative and emotional nature, and consequently with such uncertain elements of knowledge, that all primitive religions are grotesque and to some extent

---

[5] The importance Morgan places on the role of subsistence has given rise to a long debate on the role of materialism in his work. Marx and Engels believed that Morgan's work was materialist and supported their own. In 1884, Engels wrote: "Within the limits set by his subject, Morgan discovered independently the Marxian materialistic view of history" (in Schott 1976:732). Marxist anthropologists such as Eleanor Leacock have also seen Morgan as a materialist. However, there are also very clear differences between Morgan and Marx. To be truly materialist, Morgan must believe that social evolution is driven by the physical conditions of society. However, in many places it is clear that he believes that social evolution has biological roots and is associated with the "gradual enlargement of the brain itself, particularly of the cerebral portion (1910: 36). For example, in *Ancient Society,* Morgan writes: "We have the same brain . . . which worked in the skulls of barbarians . . . It is the same brain grown older and larger with the experience of the ages . . . Out of a few germs of thought have been evolved all the principal institutions of mankind . . . The evolution of these germs of thought as been guided by a natural logic which formed an essential attribute of the brain itself" (1910: 59–60). In another section of *Ancient Society,* Morgan speaks of the inferior brain size of Native Americans and the "preeminent endowment" of the Aryan and Semitic families. Morgan's understanding of the brain sizes of different groups was based on the work of Samuel G. Morton (1799–1851). Trautmann and Kabelac's 1994 study of Morgan's library shows he had taken notes on Morton's work. In his most famous works *Crania Americana* (1839) and *Crania Aegyptica* (1844) Morton claimed that whites had bigger brains than any other group and concluded that they were intellectually and morally superior to those

other groups. Morton's data (although not his conclusions) stood unquestioned until 1981 when Harvard biologist Stephen Jay Gould published an analysis showing Morton had committed gross errors in sampling and had incorrectly analyzed his own data. Gould corrected these errors and reanalyzed the skulls in Morton's collection. He found no significant differences between the skull volumes of different ethnic groups in Morton's collection.

[6] *Gentes:* Latin for a "patrilineal clan."

[7] Morgan here refers to the Roman philosopher and poet Lucretius (96?–55 B.C.E.), author of *De rerum natura,* a lengthy poem that explicates his understanding of Epicurean philosophy. Morgan gives the Latin original in note a. The translation (by Ellery 1916) is "And urged for children and the womankind/ Mercy, of fathers, whilst with cries and gestures/ They stammered hints how meet it was that all/ Should have compassion on the weak." Book five of *De rerum* was an important text for many nineteenth century scholars. In it, Lucretius describes the origin and evolution of animals and plants, the origins of humanity and its rise from savagery to civilization. Although Lucretius' version of evolution is fanciful, it clearly shows movement from the simple to the complex.

[8] The evolution of the family had long been a major focus of Morgan's work. He had published *Systems of Kinship and Affinity of the Human Family,* one of the founding documents of kinship studies, in 1871. In *Systems* Morgan divides all kinship systems into descriptive and classificatory systems and identifies the kinships now known as Omaha, Crow, Iroquois, and Malayan. Morgan understood the family as evolving from primitive promiscuity to civilized monogamy.

unintelligible. This subject also falls without the plan of this work excepting as it may prompt incidental suggestions.[9]

Sixth. House architecture, which connects itself with the form of the family and the plan of domestic life, affords a tolerably complete illustration of progress from savagery to civilization. Its growth can be traced from the hut of the savage, through the communal houses of the barbarians, to the house of the single family of civilized nations, with all the successive links by which one extreme is connected with the other. This subject will be noticed incidentally.

Lastly. The idea of property was slowly formed in the human mind, remaining nascent and feeble through immense periods of time. Springing into life in savagery, it required all the experience of this period of barbarism to develop the germ, and to prepare the human brain for the acceptance of its controlling influence. Its dominance as a passion over all other passions marks the commencement of civilization. It not only led mankind to overcome the obstacles which delayed civilization, but to establish political society on the basis of territory and of property. A critical knowledge of the evolution of the idea of property would embody, in some respects, the most remarkable portion of the mental history of mankind.[10]

It will be my object to present some evidence of human progress along these several lines, and through successive ethnical periods, as it is revealed by inventions and discoveries, and by the growth of the ideas of government, of the family, and of property.

It may be here premised that all forms of government are reducible to two general plans, using the word plan in its scientific sense. In their bases the two are fundamentally distinct. The first, in the order of time, is founded upon persons, and upon relations purely personal, and may be distinguished as a society (*societas*). The gens is the unit of this organization; giving as the successive stages of integration, in the archaic period, the gens, the phratry, the tribe, and the confederacy of tribes, which constituted a people or nation (*populus*).[11] At a later period a coalescence of tribes in the same area into a nation took the place of a confederacy of tribes occupying independent areas. Such, through prolonged ages, after the gens appeared, was the substantially universal organization of ancient society; and it remained among the Greeks and Romans after civilization supervened. The second is founded upon territory and upon property, and may be distinguished as a state (*civitas*). The township or ward, circumscribed by metes and bounds[12] with

---

[9] The idea that religion was not fit for scientific study because it was "imaginative and emotional" was common among nineteenth-century anthropologists. However, it was specifically rejected by E. B. Tylor, who attempted to trace the evolutionary history of religion in *Primitive Culture* (see essay 2).

[10] Morgan's assertion that the concept of property led to the beginning of civilization as well as the establishment of political organizations may have had its origin in the work of John Locke, but it dovetails nicely with Marxist concerns. One can see why Karl Marx and Friedrich Engels were so interested in Morgan's work. Marx read and extensively annotated *Ancient Society* but died before he was able to publish anything about it. Thus, it was Engels who had the task of integrating Morgan into Marxist theory. Engels claimed that Morgan's comparisons of different societies had led him to the same conclusions as Marx (Resek 1960:161). In 1884, Engels, working from Marx's annotations, published *The Origin of the Family, Private*

Property and the State, which he subtitled *In the Light of the Researches of Lewis Henry Morgan.* There, he claimed Morgan had proven Marx's theory by demonstrating that private property and the state were only passing phases in the continuing evolution of human society. Although Engels believed *Ancient Society* confirmed the truth of Marxist analysis, Morgan was not a Marxist. His ideas of psychic unity and unilineal evolution are very different from Marx's notions that human nature is contingent and created through labor (see pages 57–58).

[11] Gens and gentes are synonymous terms for patrilineal clans. A phratry is a unilineal descent group composed of related clans. Morgan postulated that there were two basic forms of government: those based on kinship and those based on property. He believed that the modern state was founded on notions of territory and property rather than kinship.

[12] Metes and bounds is a method of describing real estate common in the United States. A "mete" is a straight run.

the property it contains, is the basis or unit of the latter, and political society is the result. Political society is organized upon territorial areas, and deals with property as well as with persons through territorial relations. The successive stages of integration are the township or ward, which is the unit of organization; the county or province, which is an aggregation of townships or wards; and the national domain or territory, which is an aggregation of counties or provinces; the people of each of which are organized into a body politic. It taxed the Greeks and Romans to the extent of their capacities, after they had gained civilization, to invent the deme or township and the city ward; and thus inaugurate the second great plan of government, which remains among civilized nations to the present hour. In ancient society this territorial plan was unknown. When it came in it fixed the boundary line between ancient and modern society, as the distinction will be recognized in these pages.

It may be further observed that the domestic institutions of the barbarous, and even of the savage ancestors of mankind, are still exemplified in portions of the human family with such completeness that, with the exception of the strictly primitive period, the several stages of this prog-

ress are tolerably well preserved. They are seen in the organization of society upon the basis of sex, then upon the basis of kin, and finally upon the basis of territory; through the successive forms of marriage and of the family, with the systems of consanguinity thereby created; through house life and architecture; and through progress in usages with respect to the ownership and inheritance of property.[13]

The theory of human degradation to explain the existence of savages and of barbarians is no longer tenable. It came in as a corollary from the Mosaic cosmogony, and was acquiesced in from a supposed necessity which no longer exists. As a theory, it is not only incapable of explaining the existence of savages, but it is without support in the facts of human experience.[14]

The remote ancestors of the Aryan nations presumptively passed through an experience similar to that of existing barbarous and savage tribes. Though the experience of these nations embodies all the information necessary to illustrate the periods of civilization, both ancient and modern, together with a part of that in the Later period of barbarism, their anterior experience must be deduced, in the main, from the traceable connection between the elements of their existing institutions and inventions, and similar

---

[13] This passage clearly illustrates Morgan's ideas of unilineal evolution and "living fossils." If all human societies are evolving along a single path, and if Europeans have the most advanced society, then it follows that non-European societies are earlier stages of European society. We can understand the development of European civilization by studying these primitive societies. The term "living fossils" was coined by Darwin in *Origin of Species,* where he uses it to describe Ganoid fishes (fish with thick boney scales and a shiny covering). Darwin said: "And it is in freshwater basins that we find seven genera of Ganoid fishes, remnants of a once preponderant order . . . which, like fossils, connect . . . orders at present widely sundered in the natural scale. These anomalous forms may be called living fossils; they have endured to the present day, from having inhabited a confined area, and from having been exposed to less varied, and therefore less severe, competition" (1864: 100). Notice that Darwin's understanding includes competition, an element generally lacking in Morgan's work.

[14] The "theory of degradation," or degenerationism, based on Genesis (Morgan's "Mosaic cosmology")and is briefly explained on page 6. A leading degenerationist, W. Cooke Taylor outlined this view in *Natural History of Society* (1840). He "insisted upon a literal sequence of fall, flood, Babel, and diaspora. Some groups thereafter degenerated in savagery, but others, aided by God, progressed towards new heights of civilization" (Harris 1968:58). The "supposed necessity" Morgan mentions here refers to the view that there had been a relatively brief period of time since creation. If humans had only been in existence for 5,000 years, then there was time for them to degenerate from a perfect state but, scholars of the nineteenth century believed, insufficient time for them to advance from a primitive state. Morgan thought that advances in geology, particularly the work of Charles Lyell, had shown that the earth had great antiquity. He begins the preface of *Ancient Society* by declaring that "The great antiquity of mankind upon the earth has been conclusively established" (1910, v). Thus, there was adequate time for societies to evolve.

elements still preserved in those of savage and barbarous tribes.[15]

It may be remarked finally that the experience of mankind has run in nearly uniform channels; that human necessities in similar conditions have been substantially the same; and that the operations of the mental principle have been uniform in virtue of the specific identity of the brain of all the races of mankind. This, however, is but a part of the explanation of uniformity in results. The germs of the principal institutions and arts of life were developed while man was still a savage. To a very great extent the experience of the subsequent periods of barbarism and of civilization have been expended in the further development of these original conceptions. Wherever a connection can be traced on different continents between a present institution and a common germ, the derivation of the people themselves from a common original stock is implied.[16]

The discussion of these several classes of facts will be facilitated by the establishment of a certain number of Ethnical Periods; each representing a distinct condition of society, and distinguishable by a mode of life peculiar to itself. The terms "Age of Stone," "of Bronze," and "of Iron," introduced by Danish archaeologists, have been extremely useful for certain purposes, and will remain so for the classification of objects of ancient art; but the progress of knowledge has rendered other and different subdivisions necessary. Stone implements were not entirely laid aside with the introduction of tools of iron, nor of those of bronze. The invention of the process of smelting iron ore created an ethnical epoch, yet we could scarcely date another from the production of bronze. Moreover, since the period of stone implements overlaps those of bronze and of iron, and since that of bronze also overlaps that of iron, they are not capable of a circumscription that would leave each independent and distinct.[17]

It is probable that the successive arts of subsistence which arose at long intervals will ultimately, from the great influence they must have exercised

---

[15] Morgan, like Tylor (see note 24 page 41) follows the German linguist Max Müller in his use of the term Aryan. Morgan had purchased a book of Muller's lectures in 1862 and was much impressed with his use of linguistic techniques to discover the relationships among people (Tooker 1992: 365). He was particularly attracted by Muller's argument that the root of the word "Aryan" was derived from a word that meant "those who plow" (Tooker 1992:365). Morgan adopted the word Aryan and argued that Aryans represented the highest degree of civilization.

Although he does not make it explicit, Morgan is referring in this paragraph to E. B. Tylor's concept of survivals. For more on survivals, see notes 19 and 22, page 40.

[16] This paragraph contains a brief powerful expression of several of Morgan's key ideas. He argues that all human societies have followed (and will follow) similar paths because all humans have similar brains and similar mental processes (this is the result of the common origin of all humanity). However, this message of uniformity is modified by the second half of the paragraph. There he argues that although the origins of the principal institutions of human society date to the period of savagery, these institutions have developed through later periods. In the last sentence, he implies that this development is, at root, bio-logical. The presence of similar, more advanced institutions in different places implies a common biological origin of the people whose society exhibits these institutions.

Morgan believed that his work showed that all humans were descendent from a single creation and all societies had the potential to evolve. Thus, he believed that all humans had the potential to be equal. However, do not mistake this for belief actual current day equality. Morgan, like most scientists of his day, believed people of Northern European descent were superior to all others. You will note that he consistently identifies the Greek, Roman, and Aryan peoples as evolving first and fastest, consigning Asian, African, and Mesoamerican civilizations to earlier stages in his evolutionary scheme.

[17] The terms Stone Age, Bronze Age, and Iron Age were introduced by the first curator of the Danish National Museum, Christian J. Thomsen (1788–1865), in order to chronologically rank European artifacts in an 1807 exhibit. This "three-age system," as it came to be known, was soon widely used throughout Europe (Fagan 1989:34). Morgan critiques Thomsen's system as unable to create historically consistent nonoverlapping classes of society. Ironically, this was a criticism later leveled against Morgan's work.

upon the condition of mankind, afford the most satisfactory bases for these divisions. But investigation has not been carried far enough in this direction to yield the necessary information. With our present knowledge the main result can be attained by selecting such other inventions or discoveries as will afford sufficient tests of progress to characterize the commencement of successive ethnical periods. Even though accepted as provisional, these periods will be found convenient and useful. Each of those about to be proposed will be found to cover a distinct culture, and to represent a particular mode of life.[18]

The period of savagery, of the early part of which very little is known, may be divided, provisionally, into three subperiods. These may be named respectively the Older, the Middle, and the Later period of savagery; and the condition of society in each, respectively, may be distinguished as the Lower, the Middle, and the Upper Status of savagery.[19]

In like manner, the period of barbarism divides naturally into three sub-periods, which will be called, respectively, the Older, the Middle, and the Later period of barbarism; and the condition of society in each, respectively, will be distinguished as the Lower, the Middle, and the Upper Status of barbarism.

It is difficult, if not impossible, to find such tests of progress to mark the commencement of these several periods as will be found absolute in their application, and without exceptions upon all the continents. Neither is it necessary, for the purpose in hand, that exceptions should not exist. It will be sufficient if the principal tribes of mankind can be classified, according to the degree of their relative progress, into conditions which can be recognized as distinct.

I. LOWER STATUS OF SAVAGERY[20]

This period commenced with the infancy of the human race, and may be said to have ended with the acquisition of a fish subsistence and of a knowledge of the use of fire. Mankind were then living in their original restricted habitat, and subsisting upon fruits and nuts. The commencement of articulate speech belongs to this period. No exemplification of tribes of mankind in this condition remained to the historical period.

II. MIDDLE STATUS OF SAVAGERY

It commenced with the acquisition of a fish subsistence and a knowledge of the use of fire, and ended with the invention of the bow and arrow. Mankind, while in this condition, spread from their original habitat over the greater portion of the earth's surface. Among tribes still existing it will leave in the Middle Status of savagery, for example, the Australians and the greater part of the Polynesians when discovered. It will be sufficient to give one or more exemplifications of each status.

---

[18] Morgan's goal was to outline the stages of cultural evolution. He proposed that the transition between stages could be marked by the acquisition of certain kin patterns and modes of subsistence and the development of certain technological innovations. He gives special priority to changes in modes of subsistence. However, it is not clear if changes in subsistence create cultural evolution or simply mark the different stages. Half a century later, the links Morgan made between subsistence, technology, and cultural evolution would be essential in the work of the neo-evolutionists Leslie White and Julian Steward (essays 16 and 17). White in particular would see Morgan's work as an inspiration for his own. In the next several paragraphs, Morgan outlines his design for separating one stage of cultural evolution from another.

[19] Note that Morgan tells us that the oldest periods of savagery are very little known. This is because he believed that all societies had already passed through these periods, and thus, no current day ethnographic example of them could be found to study. They remained conjectural.

[20] Here Morgan begins to outline the factors by which he distinguishes the stages of cultural evolution. Much of the criticism of his theory was based on the fact that Morgan's system created illogical groupings, lumping together societies that we now consider to have vastly different levels of social organization. This critique was first pointed out by Franz Boas in the early part of the twentieth century.

III. UPPER STATUS OF SAVAGERY

It commenced with the invention of the bow and arrow, and ended with the invention of the art of pottery. It leaves in the Upper Status of Savagery the Athapascan tribes of the Hudson's Bay Territory, the tribes of the valley of the Columbia, and certain coast tribes of North and South America; but with relation to the time of their discovery. This closes the period of Savagery.

IV. LOWER STATUS OF BARBARISM

The invention or practice of the art of pottery, all things considered, is probably the most effective and conclusive test that can be selected to fix a boundary line, necessarily arbitrary, between savagery and barbarism. The distinctness of the two conditions has long been recognized, but no criterion of progress out of the former into the latter has hitherto been brought forward. All such tribes, then, as never attained to the art of pottery will be classed as savages, and those possessing this art but who never attained a phonetic alphabet and the use of writing will be classed as barbarians.

The first sub-period of barbarism commenced with the manufacture of pottery, whether by original invention or adoption. In finding its termination, and the commencement of the Middle Status, a difficulty is encountered in the unequal endowments of the two hemispheres, which began to be influential upon human affairs after the period of savagery had passed. It may be met, however, by the adoption of equivalents. In the Eastern hemisphere, the domestication of animals, and the Western, the cultivation of maize and plants by irrigation, together with the use of adobe brick and stone in house building have been selected as sufficient evidence of progress to work a transition out of the Lower and into the Middle Status of barbarism. It leaves, for example, in the Lower Status, the Indian tribes of the United States east of the Missouri River, and such tribes of Europe and Asia as practiced the art of pottery, but were without domestic animals.

V. MIDDLE STATUS OF BARBARISM

It commenced with the domestication of animals in the Eastern hemisphere, and in the Western with cultivation by irrigation and with the use of adobe brick and stone in architecture, as shown. Its termination may be fixed with the invention of the process of smelting iron ore. This places in the Middle Status, for example, the Village Indians of New Mexico, Mexico, Central America and Peru, and such tribes in the Eastern hemisphere as possessed domestic animals but were without a knowledge of iron. The ancient Britons, although familiar with the use of iron, fairly belong in this connection. The vicinity of more advanced continental tribes had advanced the arts of life among them far beyond the state of development of their domestic institutions.[21]

VI. UPPER STATUS OF BARBARISM

It commenced with the manufacture of iron, and ended with the invention of a phonetic alphabet, and the use of writing in literary composition. Here civilization begins. This leaves in the Upper Status, for example, the Grecian tribes of the Homeric age, the Italian tribes shortly before the founding of Rome, and the Germanic tribes of the time of Caesar.

VII. STATUS OF CIVILIZATION

It commenced, as stated, with the use of a phonetic alphabet and the production of literary records, and divides into Ancient and Modern. As an equivalent, hieroglyphical writing upon stone may be admitted.

---

[21] A society's evolutionary stage was gauged by its technology, subsistence pattern, and kin and family structure together. Consequently, although groups such as the ancient Britons had acquired technological achievements of more advanced societies, such as the use of iron (diagnostic of Upper Barbarism), Morgan believes that the development of their domestic institutions places them squarely in the stage of Middle Barbarism.

RECAPITULATION

Periods	*Conditions*
I. *Older Period of Savagery,*	I. *Lower Status of Savagery,*
II. *Middle Period of Savagery,*	II. *Middle Status of Savagery,*
III. *Later Period of Savagery,*	III. *Upper Status of Savagery,*
IV. *Older Period of Barbarism,*	IV. *Lower Status of Barbarism,*
V. *Middle Period of Barbarism,*	V. *Middle Status of Barbarism,*
VI. *Later Period of Barbarism,*	VI. *Upper Status of Barbarism,*

VII. *Status of Civilization*

I. *Lower Status of Savagery,*	*From the Infancy of the Human Race to the Commencement of the next Period.*
II. *Middle Status of Savagery,*	*From the acquisition of a fish subsistence and a knowledge of the use of fire, to etc.*
III. *Upper Status of Savagery,*	*From the Invention of the Bow and Arrow, to etc.*
IV. *Lower Status of Barbarism,*	*From the Invention of the Art of Pottery, to etc.*
V. *Middle Status of Barbarism,*	*From the Domestication of animals on the Eastern hemisphere, and in the Western from the cultivation of maize and plants by Irrigation, with the use of adobe brick and stone, to etc.*
VI. *Upper Status of Barbarism,*	*From the Invention of the process of Smelting Iron Ore, with the use of iron tools, to etc.*
VII. *Status of Civilization,*	*From the Invention of a Phonetic Alphabet, with the use of writing to the present time.*

Each of these periods has a distinct culture and exhibits a mode of life more or less special and peculiar to itself. This specialization of ethnical periods renders it possible to treat a particular society according to its condition of relative advancement, and to make it a subject of independent study and discussion. It does not affect the main result that different tribes and nations on the same continent, and even of the same linguistic family, are in different conditions at the same time, since for our purpose the condition of each is the material fact, the time being immaterial.

Since the use of pottery is less significant than that of domestic animals, of iron, or of a phonetic alphabet, employed to mark the commencement of subsequent ethnical periods, the reasons for its adoption should be stated. The manufacture of pottery presupposes village life, and considerable progress in the simple arts.[b] Flint and stone implements are older than pottery, remains of the former having been found in ancient repositories in numerous instances unaccompanied by the latter. A succession of inventions of greater need and adapted to a lower condition must have occurred before the want of pottery would be felt. The commencement of village life, with some degree of control over subsistence, wooden vessels and utensils, finger weaving with filaments of bark, basket making, and the bow and arrow make their appearance before the art of pottery. The Village Indians who were in the Middle Status of barbarism, such as the Zuñians, the Aztecs and the Cholulans, manufactured pottery in large quantities and in many forms of considerable excellence; the partially Village Indians of the United States, who were in the Lower Status of barbarism, such as the Iroquois, the Choctas, and the Cherokees, made it in smaller quantities and in a limited number of forms; but the non-horticultural Indians, who were in the Status of savagery, such as the Athapascans, the tribes of California and of the valley of the Columbia, were ignorant of its use.[c] In Lubbock's *Pre-Historic Times,* in Tylor's *Early History of Mankind,* and in Peschel's *Races of Man,* the particulars respecting this art, and the extent of its distribution, have been collected with remarkable breadth of research. It was unknown in Polynesia (with the exception of the

Islands of the Tongans and Fijians), in Australia, in California, and in the Hudson's Bay Territory. Mr. Tylor remarks that "the art of weaving was unknown in most of the Islands away from Asia," and that "in most of the South Sea Islands there was no knowledge of pottery."[d] The Rev. Lorimer Fison, an English missionary residing in Australia, informed the author in answer to inquiries, that "the Australians had no woven fabrics, no pottery, and were ignorant of the bow and arrow." This last fact was also true in general of the Polynesians. The introduction of the ceramic art produced a new epoch in human progress in the direction of an improved living and increased domestic conveniences. While flint and stone implements—which came in earlier and required long periods of time to develop all their uses—gave the canoe, wooden vessels and utensils, and ultimately timber and plank in house architecture,[e] pottery gave a durable vessel for boiling food, which before that had been

rudely accomplished in baskets coated with clay, and in ground cavities lined with skin, the boiling being effected with heated stones.[f22]

Whether the pottery of the aborigines was hardened by fire or cured by the simple process of drying, has been made a question. Prof E. T. Cox.[23] of Indianapolis, has shown by comparing the analyses of ancient pottery and hydraulic cements, "that so far as chemical constituents are concerned it (the pottery) agrees very well with the composition of hydraulic stones." He remarks further, that "all the pottery belonging to the mound-builders' age, which I have seen, is composed of alluvial clay and sand, or a mixture of the former with pulverized freshwater shells. A paste made of such a mixture possesses in a high degree the properties of hydraulic Puzzuolani and Portland cement, so that vessels formed of it hardened without being burned, as is customary with modern pottery. The fragments of shells served the purpose of gravel or fragments of

---

[22] In this paragraph Morgan defends his choice of pottery as a marker of evolutionary stages. However, the passage is noted chiefly for the ways in which Morgan cites some of the key scholars of his age. Morgan begins by citing Tylor, Lubbock, and Fison whose works were important influences on his own.

John Lubbock (1834–1913), also known as Lord Avebury, was an amateur ethnologist and natural historian. A prosperous banker and liberal member of Parliament, Lubbock served as president of the Royal Anthropological Institute and Ethnological Society of London. His boyhood home was near that of Darwin, with whom he became a close friend. Later Lubbock staunchly defended *Origin of Species*. Lubbock developed an evolutionary theory of human society based on his study of European and North American archaeology. He proposed a natural progression of social evolution from the primitive to the civilized, and he coined the terms paleolithic and neolithic. He published his ideas in *Prehistoric Times* (1865) and *The Origin of Civilization* (1870). Morgan had met Lubbock on his European tour in 1870 and purchased his books on his return to the United States (Tooker 1992:369).

Lorimer Fison (1832–1907) was a missionary, journalist, and anthropologist. Morgan's studies of kinship were based on extensive questionnaires sent to European travelers and missionaries. While in Fiji in 1869, Fison received one of these. It drew his interest to anthropology and he

became an ardent follower of Morgan, with whom he corresponded extensively. Fison's research into Australian aboriginal kinship systems, based on interviews with European settlers, provided important data for E. B. Tylor, J. G. Frazer, and Émile Durkheim as well as Morgan.

Morgan also cites the German Geographer Oscar Peschel (1826–1875 whose most famous work *Races . . .* (1876) purported to be about geography but focused on customs. In an 1876 review, Alfred Russel Wallace wrote that the book "impresses one painfully with the still chaotic state of the infant science of anthropology." Wallace complained that Peschel focused on easily obtainable facts rather than on information that could only be obtained by systematic, long-term observation. Thus Wallace anticipated some of the later critique of nineteenth century evolutionary anthropology.

Also note that in this paragraph Morgan places Polynesians in Middle Savagery together with Australian Aborigines. Morgan's later critics saw this as an example of an illogical grouping created by his theory. Aboriginal society was organized by family-based foraging bands. Polynesian society, though without pottery or the technological innovations Morgan mentions here, was composed of highly stratified chiefdoms and was far more complex.

[23] Edward Travers Cox (1821–1907) was the state geologist for Indiana.

stone as at present used in connection with hydraulic lime for the manufacture of artificial stone."[g] The composition of Indian pottery in analogy with that of hydraulic cement suggests the difficulties in the way of inventing the art, and tends also to explain the lateness of its introduction in the course of human experience. Notwithstanding the ingenious suggestion of Prof. Cox, it is probable that pottery was hardened by artificial heat. In some cases the fact is directly attested. Thus Adair, speaking of the Gulf Tribes, remarks that "they make earthen pots of very different sizes, so as to contain from two to ten gallons, large pitchers to carry water, bowls, dishes, platters, basins, and a prodigious number of other vessels of such antiquated forms as would be tedious to describe, and impossible to name. Their method of glazing them is, they place them over a large fire of smoky pitch-pine, which makes them smooth, black and firm."[h]

Another advantage of fixing definite ethnical periods is the direction of special investigation to those tribes and nations which afford the best exemplification of each status, with the view of making each both standard and illustrative. Some tribes and families have been left in geographical isolation to work out the problems of progress by original mental effort; and have, consequently, retained their arts and institutions pure and homogeneous; while those of other tribes and nations have been adulterated through external influence.

Thus, while Africa was and is an ethnical chaos of savagery and barbarism, Australia and Polynesia were in savagery, pure and simple, with the arts and institutions belonging to that condition. In like manner, the Indian family of America, unlike any other existing family, exemplified the condition of mankind in three successive ethnical periods. In the undisturbed possession of a great continent, of common descent, and with homogeneous institutions, they illustrated, when discovered, each of these conditions, and especially those of the Lower and of the Middle Status of barbarism, more elaborately and completely than any other portion of mankind. The far northern Indians and some of the coast tribes of North and South America were in the Upper Status of savagery, the partially Village Indians east of the Mississippi were in the Lower Status of barbarism, and the Village Indians of North and South America were in the Middle Status. Such an opportunity to recover full and minute information of the course of human experience and progress in developing their arts and institutions through these successive conditions has not been offered within the historical period. It must be added that it has been indifferently improved. Our greatest deficiencies relate to the last period named.[24]

Differences in the culture of the same period in the Eastern and Western hemispheres undoubtedly existed in consequence of the unequal endowments of the continents; but the condition

---

[24] For Morgan, all humans shared a single origin but different groups represented different branches on a human evolutionary tree. Africans, described as being in "ethnical chaos" in this passage were particularly problematic. In *Systems of Consanguinity* (1997:462 orig. 1870) Morgan wrote: "The people of pure negro stock are known to be limited in numbers on the African continent . . . A portion of the west coast, between the Senegal and the Congo, and some other small and isolated portions of the interior are in the possession of this family, leaving the remainder of the continent in the occupation of nations of more or less immediate Asiatic affiliations. Unimportant in numbers, feeble in intellect, and inferior in rank to every other portion of the human family, they yet center in themselves, in their unknown past and mysterious present, one of the greatest problems in the science of the families of mankind." Of

Morgan's understanding of the African presence in the United States, Ben-Zvi (2007:209) writes: "By leaping from an imagined Native American past to the post–Civil War United States, Morgan imagines that slavery never existed, and portrays the colonization of Native American lands as a natural event. The existence of Africans is perceived as an aberration in national, scientific, and human terms." Hume (2008:146) notes that Morgan argued in favor of interbreeding of Europeans and Native Americans and believed that it would benefit both groups. The same was not true of interbreeding with Africans. Morgan hoped the biological and cultural mixing of Europeans and Native Americans "establish a new national and scientific order that would absorb red into white and make black disappear" (Ben-Zvi 2007:209).

of society in the corresponding status must have been, in the main, substantially similar.

The ancestors of the Grecian, Roman, and German tribes passed through the stages we have indicated, in the midst of the last of which the light of history fell upon them. Their differentiation from the undistinguishable mass of barbarians did not occur, probably, earlier than the commencement of the Middle Period of barbarism. The experience of these tribes has been lost, with the exception of so much as is represented by the institutions, inventions and discoveries which they had brought with them, and possessed when they first came under historical observation. The Grecian and Latin tribes of the Homeric and Romulian periods afford the highest exemplification of the Upper Status of barbarism.[25] Their institutions were likewise pure and homogeneous, and their experience stands directly connected with the final achievement of civilization.

Commencing, then, with the Australians and Polynesians, following with the American Indian tribes, and concluding with the Roman and Grecian who afford the highest exemplifications respectively of the six great stages of human progress, the sum of their united experiences may be supposed fairly to represent that of the human family from the Middle Status of savagery to the end of ancient civilization. Consequently, the Aryan nations will find the type of the condition of their remote ancestors, when in savagery, in that of the Australians and Polynesians; when in the Lower Status of barbarism in that of the partially Village Indians of America; and when in the Middle Status in that of the Village Indians, with which their own experience in the Upper Status directly connects. So essentially identical are the arts, institutions and mode of life in the same status upon all the continents, that the archaic form of the principal domestic institutions of the Greeks and Romans must even now be sought in the corresponding institution of the American aborigines, as will be shown in the course of this volume. This fact forms a part of the accumulating evidence tending to show that the principal institutions of mankind have been developed from a few primary germs of thought; and that the course and manner of their development was predetermined, as well as restricted within narrow limits of divergence, by the natural logic of the human mind and the necessary limitations of its powers. Progress has been found to be substantially the same in kind in tribes and nations inhabiting different and even disconnected continents, while in the same status, with deviations from uniformity in particular instances produced by special causes. The argument when extended tends to establish the unity of origin of mankind.

In studying the condition of tribes and nations in these several ethnical periods we are dealing, substantially, with the ancient history and condition of our own remote ancestors.[26]

NOTES

[a] Et pueros commendarunt mulierbreque saeclum
Vocibus, et gestu, cum balbe significarent,
Imbecillorum esse aequm miserier omnium.
      —*De Rerum Natura*, lib. v, 1020.

[b] Mr. Edwin B. Tylor observes that Goquet "first propounded, in the last century, the notion that the way in which pottery came to be made, was that people daubed such combustible vessels as these with clay to

---

[25] The Homeric and Romulian periods refers to the times of Homer, the Greek poet of the eighth century B.C.E., and Romulus, mythological founder of Rome in 753 B.C.E.

[26] In these concluding paragraphs Morgan outlines key aspects of his theory. Societies evolve through specific stages from savagery to civilization. Because all human minds operate by the same "natural logic" (an idea often called Psychic Unity), the course of this evolution is virtually identical everywhere. Thus, currently existing non-European societies may be compared with earlier states of today's most advanced societies (an idea often called the comparative method). The doctrine of psychic unity justified the use of the comparative method, which formed the basis for the belief in unilineal theories of cultural evolution. However, the circular logic used in this argument: why are there universals of cultural evolution? Because of the psychic unity of humankind. How do we know psychic unity is a valid concept? Because we see common patterns of cultural development.

protect them from fire, till they found that clay alone would answer the purpose, and thus the art of pottery came into the world."—*Early History of Minkind,* p. 237. Goquet relates of Capt. Gonneville who visited the southeast coast of South America in 1503, that he found "their household utensils of wood, even their boiling pots, but plastered with a kind of clay, a good finger thick, which prevented the fire from burning them."—Ib. 273.[27]

[c] Pottery has been found in aboriginal mounds in Oregon within a few years past.—Foster's *Pre-Historic Races of the United States,* I, 152. The first vessels of pottery among the Aborigines of the United States seem to have been made in baskets of rushes or willows used as moulds which were burned off after the vessel hardened.—Jones'*Antiquities of Southern Indians,* p. 461. Prof. Rau's article on Pottery, *Smithsonian Report,* 1866, p. 352.

[d] *Early History of Mankind,* p. 181; *Pre-Historic Times,* pp. 437, 441, 462, 477, 533, 542.

[e] Lewis and Clarke (1805) found plank in use in houses among the tribes of the Columbia River.—*Travels,*

Longman's Ed., 1814, p. 503. Mr. John Keast Lord found "cedar plank chipped from the solid tree with chisels and hatchets made of stone," in Indian houses on Vancouver's Island.—*Naturalist in British Columbia,* I, 169.

[f] Tylor's *Early History of Mankind,* p. 265, et seq.

[g] *Geological Survey of Indiana,* 1873, p. 119. He gives the following analysis:

Ancient Pottery, "Bone Bank," Posey Co., Indiana.

Moisture at 212°F.,	1.00	Alumina,	5.00
Silica,	36.00	Peroxide of Iron,	5.50
		Sulphuric Acid.	.20
Carbonate of Lime.	25.50	Organic Matter (alkalies and loss),	23.60
Carbonate of Magnesia	3.02		100.00

[h] *History of the American Indians,* Lond. ed., 1775, p. 424. The Iroquois affirm that in ancient times their forefathers cured their pottery before a fire.

---

[27] It's interesting to note the typographical errors in Morgan's footnote. Morgan substitutes Edwin for Edward and Minkind for Mankind. These errors date to the original 1877 edition of the work (in the British edition the Minkind/Mankind error is corrected but the Edwin/Edward error is not) and are reproduced in many subsequent editions.

---

4. *Feuerbach: Opposition of the Materialist and Idealist Outlook*

KARL MARX (1818–1883) AND FRIEDRICH ENGELS (1820–1895)

THE ILLUSIONS OF GERMAN IDEOLOGY

As we hear from German ideologists, Germany has in the last few years gone through an unparalleled revolution.[1] The decomposition of the

Hegelian philosophy, which began with Strauss, has developed into a universal ferment into which all the "powers of the past" are swept. In the general chaos mighty empires have arisen only to meet with immediate doom, heroes have emerged momentarily only to be hurled back into obscurity

---

From *The German Ideology* (1845–1846)

---

[1] Marx and Engels, living in exile in Belgium, collaborated on *The German Ideology* in 1845 and 1846. They sent the manuscript to Germany for publication, but political crises prevented it from appearing. Marx later remarked that it had been abandoned to "the gnawing criticism of the mice" (2005:181 orig 1859). At the time *The German Ideology* was written, Marx and Engels were developing a thoroughly materialist worldview, which separated them

by bolder and stronger rivals. It was a revolution beside which the French Revolution was child's play, a world struggle beside which the struggles of the Diadochi [successors of Alexander the Great] appear insignificant. Principles ousted one another, heroes of the mind overthrew each other with unheard-of rapidity, and in the three years 1842–45 more of the past was swept away in Germany than at other times in three centuries.

All this is supposed to have taken place in the realm of pure thought.

Certainly it is an interesting event we are dealing with: the putrescence of the absolute spirit. When the last spark of its life had failed, the various components of this *caput mortuum*[2] began to decompose, entered into new combinations and formed new substances. The industrialists of philosophy, who till then had lived on the exploitation of the absolute spirit, now seized upon the new combinations.[3] Each with all possible zeal set about retailing his apportioned share. This naturally gave rise to competition,

which, to start with, was carried on in moderately staid bourgeois fashion. Later when the German market was glutted, and the commodity in spite of all efforts found no response in the world market, the business was spoiled in the usual German manner by fabricated and fictitious production, deterioration in quality, adulteration of the raw materials, falsification of labels, fictitious purchases, bill-jobbing and a credit system devoid of any real basis. The competition turned into a bitter struggle, which is now being extolled and interpreted to us as a revolution of world significance, the begetter of the most prodigious results and achievements.

If we wish to rate at its true value this philosophic charlatanry, which awakens even in the breast of the honest German citizen a glow of national pride, if we wish to bring out clearly the pettiness, the parochial narrowness of this whole Young Hegelian movement and in particular the tragicomic contrast between the illusions of these heroes about their achievements and the actual achievements themselves, we must look at the

---

from other German philosophers. This work is the first relatively complete statement of this worldview, although the materialist position it presents is foreshadowed in works like "On the Jewish Question" (1963, orig. 1844) and "The Holy Family" (1975, orig. 1845). The complete version of *The German Ideology* was not available until the 1930s. Thus, while European and American theorists of the early twentieth century were profoundly affected by Marx, they did not have this particular work. Ludwig Andreas Feuerbach (pronounced to rhyme with "lawyer-lock") (1804–1872) was a radical Hegelian philosopher whose critical work *The Essence of Christianity* had appeared in 1841. Feuerbach argues that religion in general and Christianity in particular are projections of human nature. Attributes such as love and charity are not divine because God possesses them but rather God possesses them because humans think they are divine. Thus, he proposed that religion had a material basis in human thought (and no "real" God existed). Marx was deeply impressed by Feuerbach's work. Shortly before writing *The German Ideology* he penned his *Theses on Feuerbach* which consists of 11 brief responses to Feuerbach's work. The *Theses on Feuerbach* was originally published as an appendix to Engels' 1888 work *Ludwig Feuerbach and the End of Classical German Philosophy*.

[2] *Caput mortuum*: Latin for "death's head," also referred in chemistry and alchemy to the worthless residue of a chemical operation.

[3] Marx, like all German philosophers of the nineteenth century, was profoundly influenced by the work of Georg Wilhelm Friedrich Hegel (1770–1831). Hegel's philosophy described history as the complex relationship between human beings and absolute spirit or God. Hegel related the history of this relationship to human freedom under different political conditions. Hegel was both deeply religious and conservative. In this and subsequent paragraphs, Marx and Engels satirically describe history of philosophy in Germany after Hegel's death. After Hegel's death, his followers split into two camps: the Right Hegelians and the Young Hegelians. The Right Hegelians stayed very close to Hegel's teaching, concerning themselves with a spiritual and essentially conservative understanding of philosophy. The Young Hegelians, with whom Marx associated as a young man, held on to Hegel's ideas of historical progress toward freedom but rejected the notion that freedom was possible under existing forms of the state. They supported political programs varying from liberal democracy to anarchism.

whole spectacle from a standpoint beyond the frontiers of Germany.[4]

German criticism has, right up to its latest efforts, never quitted the realm of philosophy. Far from examining its general philosophic premises, the whole body of its inquiries has actually sprung from the soil of a definite philosophical system, that of Hegel. Not only in their answers but in their very questions there was a mystification. This dependence on Hegel is the reason why not one of these modern critics has even attempted a comprehensive criticism of the Hegelian system, however much each professes to have advanced beyond Hegel. Their polemics against Hegel and against one another are confined to this—each extracts one side of the Hegelian system and turns this against the whole system as well as against the sides extracted by the others. To begin with they extracted pure unfalsified Hegelian categories such as "substance" and "self-consciousness," later they desecrated these categories with more secular names such as "species," "the Unique," "Man," etc.

The entire body of German philosophical criticism from Strauss to Stirner is confined to criticism of *religious* conceptions. The critics started from real religion and actual theology. What religious consciousness and a religious conception really meant was determined variously as they went along. Their advance consisted in subsuming the allegedly dominant metaphysical, political, juridical, moral and other conceptions under the class of religious or theological conceptions; and similarly in pronouncing political, juridical, moral consciousness as religious or theological, and the political, juridical, moral man—"*man*" in the last resort—as religious. The dominance of religion was taken for granted. Gradually every dominant relationship was pronounced a religious relationship and transformed into a cult, a cult of law, a cult of the State, etc. On all sides it was only a question of dogmas and belief in dogmas. The world sanctified to an ever-increasing extent till at last our venerable Saint Max was able to canonize it *en bloc* and thus dispose of it once for all.[5]

The Old Hegelians had *comprehended* everything as soon as it was reduced to an Hegelian category. The Young Hegelians *criticized* everything by attributing to it religious conceptions or by pronouncing it a theological matter. The Young Hegelians are in agreement with the Old Hegelians in their belief in the rule of religion, of concepts, of a universal principle in the existing world.

---

[4] Note that Marx takes the Young Hegelians, the group with whom he had formerly been associated as his target, rather than the Right Hegelians, the conservatives he had opposed and will continue to oppose. Notice as well that Marx writes from a position outside of Germany. In 1842, Marx had become editor of a liberal newspaper called *Rheinische Zeitung*. In this position, he published increasingly radical critiques of the Prussian government and calls for democratization. This resulted in government censorship. In March 1843, the Prussian government closed the paper and Marx fled to Paris. He lived in Paris from 1843 to 1845 when the French government, acting on a request from the Prussian government expelled him. He moved on to Brussels, where he remained until 1848. *The German Ideology* was begun during Marx's stay in Paris but completed in Belgium.

[5] Much of *The German Ideology* is a critique of the Young Hegelians, a group of which Strauss and Stirner were prominent members. Strauss and Stirner were both radical and influential. In *Life of Jesus* (1835) David Friedrich Strauss (1808–1874) argued that the gospels were not literally true and that Jesus was not divine but simply a historic human figure. The gospels were poetic evidence of man's desire to transcend history in a reach for the absolute spirit described by Hegel. The anarchist Max Stirner (1806–1856, born Kaspar Schmidt), ridiculed here as Saint Max, bears the brunt of Marx and Engels' attack. Stirner's influential book, *The Ego and Its Own* had been published in 1844. Stirner attacked Feuerbach, pointing out inconsistencies in his analysis of Christianity and calling for a radical atheism. For Stirner, oppression and alienation are created through ideas that people accept as holy or sacred (hence Marx and Engels' epithets "holy" and "Saint"); freedom, on the other hand, originates through the ego's creation of its own ideas. The implication of this was individualist anarchy: people should be concerned only with their own welfare and accept no constraints on their actions. Identification with groups such as social classes was a form of oppression. For Marx and Engels, who saw individuals as existing primarily within social groups such as classes, this notion was radically wrong.

Only, the one party attacks this dominion as usurpation, while the other extols it as legitimate.[6]

Since the Young Hegelians consider conceptions, thoughts, ideas, in fact all the products of consciousness, to which they attribute an independent existence, as the real chains of men (just as the Old Hegelians declared them the true bonds of human society) it is evident that the Young Hegelians have to fight only against these illusions of consciousness. Since, according to their fantasy, the relationships of men, all their doings, their chains and their limitations are products of their consciousness, the Young Hegelians logically put to men the moral postulate of exchanging their present consciousness for human, critical or egoistic consciousness, and thus of removing their limitations. This demand to change consciousness amounts to a demand to interpret reality in another way, i.e. to recognize it by means of another interpretation. The Young Hegelian ideologists, in spite of their allegedly "world-shattering" statements, are the staunchest conservatives. The most recent of them have found the correct expression for their activity when they declare they are only fighting against *"phrases."* They forget, however, that to these phrases they themselves are only opposing other phrases, and that they are in no way combating the real existing world when they are merely combating the phrases of this world. The only results

which this philosophic criticism could achieve were a few (and at that thoroughly one-sided) elucidations of Christianity from the point of view of religious history;—all the rest of their assertions are only further embellishments of their claim to have furnished, in these unimportant elucidations, discoveries of universal importance.

It has not occurred to any one of these philosophers to inquire into the connection of German philosophy with German reality, the relation of their criticism to their own material surroundings.[7]

FIRST PREMISES OF MATERIALIST METHOD

The premises from which we begin are not arbitrary ones, not dogmas, but real premises from which abstraction can only be made in the imagination. They are the real individuals, their activity and the material conditions under which they live, both those which they find already existing and those produced by their activity. These premises can thus be verified in a purely empirical way.[8]

The first premise of all human history is, of course, the existence of living human individuals. Thus the first fact to be established is the physical organization of these individuals and their consequent relation to the rest of nature. Of course, we cannot here go either into the actual

---

[6] Both the Right Hegelians (here the Old Hegelians) and the Young Hegelians were much concerned with the issues of religion. However, religion was largely a surrogate for discussing politics and the state, taboo subjects for debate within Germany. Hegel had been quite conservative. He saw the relationship of individuals to the state as a historical and spiritual process fueled by dialectical contradiction and culminating in absolute freedom. He believed this freedom was possible under the Prussian monarchy (which, incidentally, employed him). In supporting the truths of religion, the Right Hegelians were closely following Hegel and supporting the Prussian state. In arguing that religion could not be understood as truth, the Young Hegelians were arguing against the state.

[7] Marx and Engels accuse the Hegelians of believing that criticism of religion, understandings of society that argue that institutions such as law are simply human devices given spiritual dimensions, and changes in the way peo-

ple think in general can lead to changes in the world. For example Selsem and Martel write that for Stirner "All one had to do to get rid of the state, of religion, of poverty, etc., was to recognize that they were merely spooks, and to assert in the loudest possible tones that the only thing that counts is one's own ego" (1987:280). In the 11th Thesis on Feuerbach, Marx wrote: "The philosophers have only interpreted the world, in various ways; the point is to change it."

[8] For Hegel and his followers, the world was conditioned by ideas, and history was about the progress of the human spirit. For Marx, human society was based in particular material conditions, and history was driven by conflicts at the core of society. This is the root of Marx and Engels' disagreements with Hegelians. Here and in following paragraphs they lay out a materialist understanding of the world, beginning with real people and the conditions under which they live.

physical nature of man, or into the natural conditions in which man finds himself—geological, oreohydrographical,[9] climatic and so on. The writing of history must always set out from these natural bases and their modification in the course of history through the action of men.

Men can be distinguished from animals by consciousness, by religion or anything else you like. They themselves begin to distinguish themselves from animals as soon as they begin to *produce* their means of subsistence, a step which is conditioned by their physical organization. By producing their means of subsistence men are indirectly producing their actual material life.[10]

The way in which men produce their means of subsistence depends first of all on the nature of the actual means of subsistence they find in existence and have to reproduce. This mode of production must not be considered simply as being the production of the physical existence of the individuals. Rather it is a definite form of activity of these individuals, a definite form of expressing their life, a definite *mode of life* on their part. As individuals express their life, so they are. What they are, therefore, coincides with their production, both with *what* they produce and with *how* they produce. The nature of individuals thus depends on the material conditions determining their production.[11]

This production only makes its appearance with the *increase of population*. In its turn this presupposes the *intercourse* of individuals with one another. The form of this intercourse is again determined by production.

The relations of different nations among themselves depend upon the extent to which each has developed its productive forces, the division of labour and internal intercourse. This statement is generally recognized. But not only the relation of one nation to others, but also the whole internal structure of the nation itself depends on the stage of development reached by its production and its internal and external intercourse. How far the productive forces of a nation are developed is shown most manifestly by the degree to which the division of labour has been carried. Each new productive force, insofar as it is not merely a quantitative extension of productive forces already known (for instance the bringing into cultivation of fresh land), causes a further development of the division of labour.[12]

The division of labour inside a nation leads at first to the separation of industrial and commercial from agricultural labour, and hence to the separation of *town* and *country* and to the conflict of their interests. Its further development leads to the separation of commercial from industrial labour. At the same time through the division of labour inside these various branches there develop various divisions among the individuals co-operating in definite kinds of labour. The relative position of these individual groups is determined by the methods employed in agriculture, industry and commerce (patriarchalism, slavery, estates, classes). These same conditions are to be seen (given a more developed

---

[9] Oreohydrography: the study of drainage phenomena in mountains.

[10] This paragraph contains a critical Marxist insight. For Hegel, humans are separated from animals by self-consciousness but this self consciousness entails alienation from God. For Marx and Engels, humans are distinguished from all other creatures by awareness and conscious control of the processes of production. Animals simply eat. Humans, on the other hand, must produce their food. Thus, humans are conscious of labor. Other characteristics unique to humans derive from this fact.

[11] Here Marx and Engels pursue the importance of labor further: production is more than simply feeding oneself; through labor people create their society. Since human na-

ture is determined by the social conditions under which people live, humans, through labor, create their own nature.

[12] Note that Marx believes that history is characterized by evolutionary progress through a series of stages. Like the Hegelians, Marx and Engels believed that history had a beginning and an end. For Marx, its beginning was awareness of production and its end the emergence of a communist society. Between these two, society passed through a series of scientifically knowable stages, each characterized by a particular mode of production and its associated forms of property. Changes in human consciousness are part of this historical progression. There can be no experience of transcendental human nature before the end of history and the emergence of a communist society.

intercourse) in the relations of different nations to one another.[13]

The various stages of development in the division of labour are just so many different forms of ownership, i.e. the existing stage in the division of labour determines also the relations of individuals to one another with reference to the material, instrument, and product of labour.[14]

The first form of ownership is tribal ownership. It corresponds to the undeveloped stage of production, at which a people lives by hunting and fishing, by the rearing of beasts or, in the highest stage, agriculture. In the latter case it presupposes a great mass of uncultivated stretches of land. The division of labour is at this stage still very elementary and is confined to a further extension of the natural division of labour existing in the family. The social structure is, therefore, limited to an extension of the family; patriarchal family chieftains, below them the members of the tribe, finally slaves. The slavery latent in the family only develops gradually with the increase of population, the growth of wants, and with the extension of external relations, both of war and of barter.[15]

The second form is the ancient communal and State ownership which proceeds especially from the union of several tribes into a *city* by agreement or by conquest, and which is still accompanied by slavery. Beside communal ownership we already find movable, and later also immovable, private property developing, but as an abnormal form subordinate to communal ownership. The citizens hold power over their labouring slaves only in their community, and on this account alone, therefore, they are bound to the form of communal ownership. It is the communal private property which compels the active citizens to remain in this spontaneously derived form of association over against their slaves. For this reason the whole structure of society based on this communal ownership, and with it the power of the people, decays in the same measure as, in particular, immovable private property evolves. The division of labour is already more developed. We already find the antagonism of town and country; later the antagonism between those states which represent town interests and those which represent country interests, and inside the towns themselves the antagonism between industry and maritime commerce. The class relation between citizens and slaves is now completely developed.[16]

---

[13] This is a critical passage. The developments Marx and Engels outline here seem reminiscent of Adam Smith's (1723–1790) work on the division of labor. Marx had read Smith's *The Wealth of Nations* in 1843 (Levine 1987: 435) and was deeply influenced by his work. However, while Smith saw the division of labor as leading to the achievement of the greatest good for the greatest number, Marx and Engels focused the conflicts and oppression it generates. For them, these conflicts were critical to social development.

[14] The interplay between technology and the social relationships through which technology is put to work is central to Marx and Engels' theory. The idea of ownership is key to this. In these paragraphs, the authors describe the history of Rome and Europe as a progression of different forms of ownership (tribal, state, then feudal) and, hence, different modes of production.

[15] Marx and Engels have stated that humans produce their own nature through labor. However, in this passage they ground their analysis in a claim about the "natural division of labour existing in the family." These assertions seem to contradict each other. Note that Marx and Engels envision the "natural" family as consisting of a patriarch who con-

trols the members of his tribe. Although a powerful male head of the household was a feature of European society of their time, it is hardly a universal aspect of primitive societies. In addition, Marx and Engels cite no evidence to support their understanding of the family. They were aware of this problem, but almost thirty years would pass before the publication of Morgan's *Ancient Society* in 1877, which they believed resolved this issue. Also note that Marx and Engels understanding of primitive society bears little resemblance to current day ideas. In this paragraph, they lump hunters and gatherers and agricultural societies into the same general category.

[16] Marx and Engels' description of the evolution of society is fanciful but note that the emphasis in this paragraph is on groups of individuals who stand in particular relationships to each other (town and country, citizen and slave, industry and commerce). Marx and Engels see the actions of individuals as largely subordinate to the key social classes of which they are members. Note as well that the relationships among these groups are characterized by conflict. Marx and Engels believed that progress was driven by conflict between groups.

With the development of private property, we find here for the first time the same conditions which we shall find again, only on a more extensive scale, with modern private property. On the one hand, the concentration of private property, which began very early in Rome (as the Licinian agrarian law[17] proves) and proceeded very rapidly from the time of the civil wars and especially under the Emperors; on the other hand, coupled with this, the transformation of the plebeian small peasantry into a proletariat, which, however, owing to its intermediate position between propertied citizens and slaves, never achieved an independent development.[18]

The third form of ownership is feudal or estate property. If antiquity started out from the *town* and its little territory, the Middle Ages started out from the *country*. This different starting-point was determined by the sparseness of the population at that time, which was scattered over a large area and which received no large increase from the conquerors. In contrast to Greece and Rome, feudal development at the outset, therefore, extends over a much wider territory, prepared by the Roman conquests and the spread of agriculture at first associated with it. The last centuries of the declining Roman Empire and its conquest by the barbarians destroyed a number of productive forces; agriculture had declined, industry had decayed for want of a market, trade had died out or been violently suspended,

the rural and urban population had decreased. From these conditions and the mode of organization of the conquest determined by them, feudal property developed under the influence of the Germanic military constitution. Like tribal and communal ownership, it is based again on a community; but the directly producing class standing over against it is not, as in the case of the ancient community, the slaves, but the enserfed small peasantry. As soon as feudalism is fully developed, there also arises antagonism to the towns. The hierarchical structure of landownership, and the armed bodies of retainers associated with it, gave the nobility power over the serfs. This feudal organization was, just as much as the ancient communal ownership, an association against a subjected producing class; but the form of association and the relation to the direct producers were different because of the different conditions of production.[19]

This feudal system of landownership had its counterpart in the *towns* in the shape of corporative property, the feudal organization of trades. Here property consisted chiefly in the labour of each individual person. The necessity for association against the organized robber nobility, the need for communal covered markets in an age when the industrialist was at the same time a merchant, the growing competition of the escaped serfs swarming into the rising towns, the feudal structure of the whole country: these

---

[17] The Licinian law (367 B.C.E.) limited the amount of common land a Roman citizen could hold to about 300 acres. Classical Greece and Rome provided key texts for authors of the nineteenth century. Most scholars of this era had an intimate knowledge of Greek and Roman history and philosophy (Marx himself had written his doctoral thesis on an issue in classical Greek philosophy). In addition, because human life on earth was generally assumed to have a fairly brief history, scholars assumed that the practices of early Greeks and Romans were fairly close to those of the most primitive people.

[18] Notice here that Marx identifies three social classes in the late Roman Republic and early empire (so starting around 90 BCE): the land owners, the proletariat (those who sold their labor to the land owners for wages) and slaves.

[19] In Marx and Engels' view, feudal ownership derived from the material conditions of the end of the Roman Empire, in particular the collapse of the Roman economy. Both feudalism and the ancient society that preceded it involved the oppression of those who produced. The differences between these societies resulted from their use of different types of production technology. Once again social form is vitally influenced by production. Marx's understanding of the conditions of Roman land ownership and European feudalism as well as the importance these played in understanding society was deeply influenced by the members of the German historical school, particularly Georg Niebuhr (1776–1831). Niebuhr had argued that there were five forms of property ownership: oriental, tribal, classical, feudal, and modern (Levine 1987: 446). Marx built on this idea in this and other works.

combined to bring about the *guilds*. The gradually accumulated small capital of individual craftsmen and their stable numbers, as against the growing population, evolved the relation of journeyman and apprentice, which brought into being in the towns a hierarchy similar to that in the country.[20]

Thus the chief form of property during the feudal epoch consisted on the one hand of landed property with serf labour chained to it, and on the other of the labour of the individual with small capital commanding the labour of journeymen. The organization of both was determined by the restricted conditions of production—the small-scale and primitive cultivation of the land, and the craft type of industry.[21] There was little division of labour in the heyday of feudalism. Each country bore in itself the antithesis of town and country; the division into estates was certainly strongly marked; but apart from the differentiation of princes, nobility, clergy and peasants in the country, and masters, journeymen, apprentices and soon also the rabble of casual labourers in the towns, no division of importance took place. In agriculture it was rendered difficult by the strip-system,[22] beside which the cottage industry of the peasants themselves emerged. In industry there was no division of labour at all in the individual trades themselves, and very little between them. The separation of industry and commerce was found already in existence in older towns; in the newer it only developed later, when the towns entered into mutual relations.

The grouping of larger territories into feudal kingdoms was a necessity for the landed nobility as for the towns. The organization of the ruling class, the nobility, had, therefore, everywhere a monarch at its head.

The fact is, therefore, that definite individuals who are productively active in a definite way enter into these definite social and political relations. Empirical observation must in each separate instance bring out empirically, and without any mystification and speculation, the connection of the social and political structure with production. The social structure and the State are continually evolving out of the life-process of definite individuals, but of individuals, not as they may appear in their own or other people's imagination, but as they *really* are; i.e. as they operate, produce materially, and hence as they work under definite material limits, presuppositions and conditions independent of their will.[23]

The production of ideas, of conceptions, of consciousness, is at first directly interwoven with the material activity and the material intercourse of men, the language of real life. Conceiving, thinking, the mental intercourse of men, appear at this stage as the direct efflux[24] of their material behaviour. The same applies to mental production as expressed in the language of politics, laws, morality, religion, metaphysics, etc. of a people. Men are the producers of their conceptions, ideas, etc.—real, active men, as they are conditioned by a definite development of their productive forces and of the intercourse corresponding

---

[20] Guilds are created as a result of purely material processes. The urban organization masters (or small capitalist), journeyman, apprentice, recapitulates the rural social organization of lord, military retainers, ensurfed peasant. Notice that Marx and Engels understood property as including both material goods and labor. The idea of labor as a commodity that can be bought and sold is crucial to their later analysis of capitalism.

[21] Marx and Engels give priority to the conditions of production in determining society. It is, however, important to distinguish this stance from ecological determinism. The processes that Marx and Engels list as restricting production are all created by human agency rather than ecological necessity. Production is a human activity.

[22] Strip system: in Medieval farming, peasant families had the right to a small strip of land (or several strips) within a large open field. Since only one crop was planted in a field, the strip system meant that many farming decisions had to be made by the community rather than the individual farmer.

[23] Here Marx and Engels repeatedly stress that the processes they are talking about concern particular physical individuals and their specific physical actions. They mean to distinguish their materialist approach from the idealism of many Hegelians. It is particular individuals and what they do, not the idea of the individual or individualism that is important. This idea is repeated numerous times in the next several paragraphs.

[24] efflux: flowing outward.

to these, up to its furthest forms. Consciousness can never be anything else than conscious existence, and the existence of men is their actual life-process. If in all ideology men and their circumstances appear upside-down as in a *camera obscura,* this phenomenon arises just as much from their historical life-process as the inversion of objects on the retina does from their physical life-process.[25]

In direct contrast to German philosophy which descends from heaven to earth, here we ascend from earth to heaven. That is to say, we do not set out from what men say, imagine, conceive, nor from men as narrated, thought of, imagined, conceived, in order to arrive at men in the flesh. We set out from real, active men, and on the basis of their real life-process we demonstrate the development of the ideological reflexes and echoes of this life-process. The phantoms formed in the human brain are also, necessarily, sublimates of their material life-process, which is empirically verifiable and bound to material premises. Morality, religion, metaphysics, all the rest of ideology and their corresponding forms of consciousness, thus no longer retain the semblance of independence. They have no history, no development; but men, developing their material production and their material intercourse, alter,

along with this their real existence, their thinking and the products of their thinking. Life is not determined by consciousness, but consciousness by life. In the first method of approach the starting-point is consciousness taken as the living individual; in the second method, which conforms to real life, it is the real living individuals themselves, and consciousness is considered solely as *their* consciousness.[26]

This method of approach is not devoid of premises. It starts out from the real premises and does not abandon them for a moment. Its premises are men, not in any fantastic isolation and rigidity, but in their actual, empirically perceptible process of development under definite conditions. As soon as this active life-process is described, history ceases to be a collection of dead facts as it is with the empiricists (themselves still abstract), or an imagined activity of imagined subjects, as with the idealists.[27]

Where speculation ends—in real life—there real, positive science begins: the representation of the practical activity, of the practical process of development of men. Empty talk about consciousness ceases, and real knowledge has to take its place. When reality is depicted, philosophy as an independent branch of knowledge loses its medium of existence. At the best its place can only be

---

[25] Camera obscura: what we might call a pinhole camera. Marx is arguing that society is created by the lives and actions of people as they exist in particular historical contexts. In 1852, in *The Eighteenth Brumaire of Louis Bonaparte,* Marx famously wrote: "Men make their own history, but they do not make it just as they please; they do not make it under circumstances chosen by themselves, but under circumstances directly encountered, given and transmitted from the past." Marx further argues that if history appears to be made by changes in ideas alone, this inversion is a product of men's lives and actions. Ideas appear to be the driving force of society in much the same way that an image appears upside down in a pinhole camera . . . nothing more than an inversion of the physical world created by natural law. But notice that Marx and Engels have created an argument impossible to refute. If you disagree with Marx and Engels, claiming that ideas drive social forms, they reply that your very perception that such might be the case is created by the natural world in which material processes create social forms.

[26] In this famous passage, Marx and Engels declare that consciousness does not create the material conditions of life but rather arises from them. Engels later said that with Hegel, the dialectic "is standing on its head. It must be turned right side up again, if you would discover the rational kernel within the mystical shell" (Engels 1878). Jonathan Friedman (1974) stresses the importance of understanding this passage. He points out that Marx and Engels are not promoting simple materialist determinism (which, following Marx, he calls vulgar materialism) but dialectical materialism, a process of change driven by opposition and contradiction.

[27] In philosophy a premise is a statement presumed to be true as the basis of a logical argument. Such premises are frequently unverifiable statements about the world such as Hegel's presumption that absolute spirit exists. Marx, on the other hand, claims that his presumption is the existence of physical, empirical men living in verifiable historical conditions (see Newman and Holzman 1993:12).

taken by a summing-up of the most general results, abstractions which arise from the observation of the historical development of men. Viewed apart from real history, these abstractions have in themselves no value whatsoever. They can only serve to facilitate the arrangement of historical material, to indicate the sequence of its separate strata. But they by no means afford a recipe or schema, as does philosophy, for neatly trimming the epochs of history. On the contrary, our difficulties begin only when we set about the observation and the arrangement—the real depiction—of our historical material, whether of a past epoch or of the present. The removal of these difficulties is governed by premises which it is quite impossible to state here, but which only the study of the actual life-process and the activity of the individuals of each epoch will make evident. We shall select here some of these abstractions, which we use in contradistinction to the ideologists, and shall illustrate them by historical example.[28]

HISTORY: FUNDAMENTAL CONDITIONS

Since we are dealing with the Germans, who are devoid of premises, we must begin by stating the first premise of all human existence and, therefore, of all history, the premise, namely, that men must be in a position to live in order to be able to "make history." But life involves before every-thing else eating and drinking, a habitation, clothing and many other things. The first historical act is thus the production of the means to satisfy these needs, the production of material life itself. And indeed this is an historical act, a fundamental condition of all history, which today, as thousands of years ago, must daily and hourly be fulfilled merely in order to sustain human life. Even when the sensuous world is reduced to a minimum, to a stick as with Saint Bruno, it presupposes the action of producing the stick. Therefore in any interpretation of history one has first of all to observe this fundamental fact in all its significance and all its implications and to accord it its due importance. It is well known that the Germans have never done this, and they have never, therefore, had an *earthly* basis for history and consequently never an historian. The French and the English, even if they have conceived the relation of this fact with so-called history only in an extremely one-sided fashion, particularly as long as they remained in the toils of political ideology, have nevertheless made the first attempts to give the writing of history a materialistic basis by being the first to write histories of civil society, of commerce and industry.[29]

The second point is that the satisfaction of the first need (the action of satisfying, and the instrument of satisfaction which has been acquired) leads to new needs; and this production of new needs is the first historical act. Here we recognize immediately the spiritual ancestry of

---

[28] Notice the emphasis throughout this portion of the text on empiricism and science. Marx and Engels considered their theory to be scientific in the same sense as the physical sciences. In this passage, Marx and Engels argue that human societies (and human beings themselves) can only be understood in historical perspective and that there are fundamental laws that drive the process of history. They propose to sketch a brief outline of these laws in the following section.

[29] Marx and Engels open this section with yet another satirical attack on the Young Hegelians, particularly Bruno Bauer (their "Saint Bruno"). They also focus their attention on their first premise: the physical, material conditions of life, and the necessity of production to have any life at all. Bruno Bauer was author of *Critique of the Evangelical Gospels* (1841–1842), which traced the Greco-Roman roots of Christianity. Originally a conservative, Bauer had moved steadily to the left and by 1840 was associated with the Young Hegelians. Marx and Engels assertion that Germans have never had historians may strike the reader as odd, given Marx's reliance on German historians in the preceding paragraphs. However, by this, Marx and Engels intend to suggest that the German historical school is flawed since it is based primarily in ideas rather than actual practices. The French and English referred to here are most likely the British economists Adam Smith and Davie Ricardo (1772–1823) and the French anarchist thinker Pierre-Joseph Proudhon (1809–1865). Although Marx and Engels disagreed with these thinkers, they were profoundly influenced by them.

the great historical wisdom of the Germans who, when they run out of positive material and when they can serve up neither theological nor political nor literary rubbish, assert that this is not history at all, but the "prehistoric era." They do not, however, enlighten us as to how we proceed from this nonsensical "prehistory" to history proper; although, on the other hand, in their historical speculation they seize upon this "prehistory" with especial eagerness because they imagine themselves safe there from interference on the part of "crude facts," and, at the same time, because there they can give full rein to their speculative impulse and set up and knock down hypotheses by the thousand.[30]

The third circumstance which, from the very outset, enters into historical development, is that men, who daily remake their own life, begin to make other men, to propagate their kind: the relation between man and woman, parents and children, the *family*. The family, which to begin with is the only social relationship, becomes later, when increased needs create new social relations and the increased population new needs, a subordinate one (excepting Germany), and must then be treated and analyzed according to the existing empirical data, not according to "the concept of the family," as is the custom in Germany.[a] These three aspects of social activity are not of course to be taken as three different stages, but just as three aspects or, to make it clear to the Germans, three "moments," which have existed simultaneously since the dawn of history and the first men, and which still assert themselves in history today.[31]

The production of life, both of one's own in labour and of fresh life in procreation, now appears as a double relationship: on the one hand as a natural, on the other as a social relationship. By social we understand the co-operation of several individuals, no matter under what conditions, in what manner and to what end. It follows from this that a certain mode of production, or industrial stage, is always combined with a certain mode of co-operation, or social stage, and this mode of co-operation is itself a "productive force." Further, that the multitude of productive forces accessible to men determines the nature of society, hence, that the "history of humanity" must always be studied and treated in relation to the history of industry and exchange. But it is also clear how in Germany it is impossible to write this sort of history, because the Germans lack not only the necessary power of comprehension and the material but also the "evidence of their senses," for across the Rhine you cannot have any experience of these things since history has stopped happening. Thus it is quite obvious from the start that there exists a materialistic connection of men with one another, which is determined by their needs and their mode of production, and which is as old as men themselves. This connection is ever taking on new forms, and thus presents a "history" independently of the existence of any political or religious nonsense which in addition may hold men together.[32]

---

[30] Marx and Engels' style is important. Their mixture of name-calling, satirical intellectual humor, polemic, and hyperbole set the tone for much of later writing by Marxists. Their indulgence in these tactics marginalized Marxists within academic discourse. This hyperbole may have been useful for political propaganda, but it made their work easy for others to dismiss.

[31] Here Marx and Engels turn from production to the reproduction of society. They understood reproduction as including both the biological process of human reproduction and the reproduction of social forms through time. Just as people must produce to live, societies must reproduce themselves to survive. Marx and Engels satirically describe the three points they have just described (people

must produce to live, such production creates new needs, people must reproduce) as three "moments." Hegel and his followers described three moments: the subjective, the objective, and the absolute.

[32] In this paragraph, Marx and Engels have described one of their most fundamental concepts, the "mode of production." A mode of production involves the combination of a specific technologies and resources with a particular type of social relationship. Marx and Engels view history as a series of such relationships and say that the study of history must be focused on issues of resources, technology, and associated social relationships. They continue their satirical attack on German philosophers, claiming that in Germany, history has ended. The Right Hegelians

Only now, after having considered four moments, four aspects of the primary historical relationships, do we find that man also possesses "consciousness," but, even so, not inherent, not "pure" consciousness. From the start the "spirit" is afflicted with the curse of being "burdened" with matter, which here makes its appearance in the form of agitated layers of air, sounds, in short, of language. Language is as old as consciousness, language *is* practical consciousness that exists also for other men, and for that reason alone it really exists for me personally as well; language, like consciousness, only arises from the need, the necessity, of intercourse with other men. Where there exists a relationship, it exists for me: the animal does not enter into *"relations"* with anything, it does not enter into any relation at all. For the animal, its relation to others does not exist as a relation. Consciousness is, therefore, from the very beginning a social product, and remains so as long as men exist at all. Consciousness is at first, of course, merely consciousness concerning the *immediate* sensuous environment and consciousness of the limited connection with other persons and things outside the individual who is growing self-conscious. At the same time it is consciousness of nature, which first appears to men as a completely alien, all-powerful and unassailable force, with which men's relations are purely animal and by which they are overawed like beasts; it is thus a purely animal consciousness of nature (natural religion) just because nature is as yet hardly modified historically. (We see here immediately: this natural religion or this particular relation of men to nature is determined by the form of society and vice versa. Here, as everywhere, the identity of nature and man appears in such a way that the restricted relation of men to nature determines their restricted relation to one another, and their restricted relation to one another determines men's restricted relation to nature.) On the other hand, man's consciousness of the necessity of associating with the individuals around him is the beginning of the consciousness that he is living in society at all. This beginning is as animal as social life itself at this stage. It is mere herd-consciousness, and at this point man is only distinguished from sheep by the fact that with him consciousness takes the place of instinct or that his instinct is a conscious one. This sheep-like or tribal consciousness receives its further development and extension through increased productivity, the increase of needs, and, what is fundamental to both of these, the increase of population. With these there develops the division of labour, which was originally nothing but the division of labour in the sexual act, then that division of labour which develops spontaneously or "naturally" by virtue of natural predisposition (e.g. physical strength), needs, accidents, etc. etc. Division of labour only becomes truly such from the moment when a division of material and mental labour appears. (The first form of ideologists, *priests*, is concurrent.) From this moment onwards consciousness *can* really flatter itself that it is something other than consciousness of existing practice, that it *really* represents something without representing something real; from now on consciousness is in a position to emancipate itself from the world and to proceed to the formation of "pure" theory, theology, philosophy, ethics, etc. But even if this theory, theology, philosophy, ethics, etc. comes into contradiction with the existing relations, this can only occur because existing social relations have come into contradiction with existing forces of production; this, moreover, can also occur in a particular national sphere of relations through the appearance of the contradiction, not within the national orbit, but between this national consciousness and the practice of other nations, i.e. between the national and the

---

asserted that Germans had attained freedom under the Prussian monarchy. Marx and Engels (as well as the Young Hegelians in Germany) thought this assertion absurd. Note also that Marx and Engels assert that real history is the history of people's needs and modes of production.

Matters of religion and daily politics are simply the surface manifestation of these underlying forces. Thus, the real forces that drive society are hidden from view, comprehensible only through Marxist analysis.

general consciousness of a nation (as we see it now in Germany).[33]

Moreover, it is quite immaterial what consciousness starts to do on its own: out of all such muck we get only the one inference that these three moments, the forces of production, the state of society, and consciousness, can and must come into contradiction with one another, because the *division of labour* implies the possibility, nay the fact that intellectual and material activity—enjoyment and labour, production and consumption—devolve on different individuals, and that the only possibility of their not coming into contradiction lies in the negation in its turn of the division of labour. It is self-evident, moreover, that "specters," "bonds," "the higher being," "concept," "scruple," are merely the idealistic, spiritual expression, the conception apparently of the isolated individual, the image of very empirical fetters and limitations, within which the mode of production of life and the form of intercourse coupled with it move.[34]

PRIVATE PROPERTY AND COMMUNISM

With the division of labour, in which all these contradictions are implicit, and which in its turn is based on the natural division of labour in the family and the separation of society into individual families opposed to one another, is given simultaneously the *distribution,* and indeed the *unequal* distribution, both quantitative and qualitative, of labour and its products, hence property: the nucleus, the first form, of which lies in the family, where wife and children are the slaves of the husband. This latent slavery in the family, though still very crude, is the first property, but even at this early stage it corresponds perfectly to the definition of modern economists who call it the power of disposing of the labour-power of others. Division of labour and private property are, moreover, identical expressions: in the one the same thing is affirmed with reference to activity as is affirmed in the other with reference to the product of the activity.[35]

Further, the division of labour implies the contradiction between the interest of the separate individual or the individual family and the communal interest of all individuals who have intercourse with one another. And indeed, this communal interest does not exist merely in the imagination, as the "general interest," but first of all in reality, as the mutual interdependence of the individuals among whom the labour is divided. And finally, the division of labour offers us the first example of how, as long as man remains in natural society, that is, as long as a cleavage exists between the particular and the common

---

[33] In this long paragraph, Marx and Engels make one of their key assertions: it is production and social life that creates consciousness, not consciousness that creates social life. They describe human language being linked to consciousness and resulting from problems posed by the processes of production and material life (Holborrow 2006). They further argue that particular forms of consciousness arise from specific modes of production. The earliest of these is simply the consciousness of being part of a society and different than the natural world. Under such conditions, consciousness is very limited. Marx and Engels describe it as "herd-consciousness." The development of consciousness that is distinctly human is dependent on increased population and division of labor. As the division of labor becomes more complex, consciousness appears to seem independent of the world, but this is illusion.

[34] Marx and Engels conclude this section by focusing on conflict. They argue that the division of labor leads to different sorts of consciousnesses and gives different people different interests and positions within society. This necessarily leads to conflict and such conflict drives history. Like all Hegelians, Marx and Engels believed that history was propelled by dialectical conflict. Each state of society (and for Marx and Engels, this meant each mode of production) could be considered a thesis. Each was characterized by internal contradictions which, in time, manifested as an antithesis. This led to a revolutionary clash between thesis and antithesis which resulted in a synthesis that, at the same time, was a new thesis.

[35] Marx and Engels argue that the division of labor entails both inequality and the origin of private property. The division of labor implies control over both a portion of the

interest, as long, therefore, as activity is not voluntarily, but naturally, divided, man's own deed becomes an alien power opposed to him, which enslaves him instead of being controlled by him. For as soon as the distribution of labour comes into being, each man has a particular, exclusive sphere of activity, which is forced upon him and from which he cannot escape. He is a hunter, a fisherman, a shepherd, or a critical critic, and must remain so if he does not want to lose his means of livelihood; while in communist society, where nobody has one exclusive sphere of activity but each can become accomplished in any branch he wishes, society regulates the general production and thus makes it possible for me to do one thing today and another tomorrow, to hunt in the morning, fish in the afternoon, rear cattle in the evening, criticize after dinner, just as I have a mind, without ever becoming hunter, fisherman, shepherd or critic. This fixation of social activity, this consolidation of what we ourselves produce into an objective power above us, growing out of our control, thwarting our expectations, bringing to naught our calculations, is one of the chief factors in historical development up till now.[36]

(And out of this very contradiction between the interest of the individual and that of the community the latter takes an independent form as the *State*, divorced from the real interests of individual and community, and at the same time as an illusory communal life, always based, however, on the real ties existing in every family and tribal conglomeration—such as flesh and blood, language, division of labour on a larger scale, and other interests—and especially, as we shall enlarge upon later, on the classes, already determined by the division of labour, which in every such mass of men separate out, and of which one dominates all the others. It follows from this that all struggles within the State, the struggle between democracy, aristocracy, and monarchy, the struggle for the franchise, etc. etc. are merely the illusory forms in which the real struggles of the different classes are fought out among one another. Of this the German theoreticians have not the faintest inkling, although they have received a sufficient introduction to the subject in the *Deutsch-Französische Jahrbücher* and *Die Heilige Familie*.[37] Further, it follows that every class which is struggling for mastery, even when its domination, as is the case with the proletariat, postulates the abolition of the old form of society in its entirety and of domination itself, must first conquer for itself political power in order to represent its interest in turn as the general interest, which immediately it is forced to do. Just because individuals seek *only* their particular interest, which for them does not coincide with their communal interest, the latter will be imposed on them as an interest "alien" to them, and "independent" of them, as in its turn a

---

labor process and the products of that process. Notice the concern with gender and the subjugation of women and children present in this paragraph. Because it was a good tool for analyzing relations of inequality, Marxism proved appealing to many feminist scholars. See Eleanor Leacock's essay 29 in this volume for an example of Marxist-feminist scholarship.

[36] Division of labor makes society possible, but it also destroys freedom and creates alienation. Alienation or estrangement, a key Marxist concept, refers to the separation of the individual from either the preconditions or the products of labor, or, in this case, from life's necessities. Alienation was understood by Marx and Engels as antithetical to freedom. Here, they argue that specializing in one activity necessarily creates alienation in all others. Marx and Engels believed that history would eventually produce communist society. They envisioned such a society as being completely without contradictions. Since they also believed that contradictions created the historical process, the arrival of communism would end the historical process. Time, of course, would continue; but history would end. Almost all of Marx and Engels' work is devoted to describing and analyzing history and the rise of capitalism. They devote relatively little space to describing how a communist society might actually be structured. Here they suggest that people in such a society might occupy any job they feel like at any time they feel like it. But can one be an engineer one day and a doctor the next?

[37] *Deutsch-Französische Jahrbücher* (The German-French Annals, 1844) was a radical periodical edited in France by Marx and Arnold Ruge (1802–1880). Only one issue appeared. *Die Heilige Familie* (The Holy Family, 1845) was Marx and Engels' first collaboration. It was a mocking attack on Bruno Bauer and other Young Hegelians.

particular, peculiar "general" interest; or they themselves must remain within this discord, as in democracy. On the other hand, too, the *practical* struggle of these particular interests, which constantly *really* run counter to the communal and illusory communal interests, makes *practical* intervention and control necessary through the illusory "general" interest in the form of the State.)[38]

The social power, i.e. the multiplied productive force, which arises through the co-operation of different individuals as it is determined by the division of labour, appears to these individuals, since their cooperation is not voluntary but has come about naturally, not as their own united power, but as an alien force existing outside them, of the origin and goal of which they are ignorant, which they thus cannot control, which on the contrary passes through a peculiar series of phases and stages independent of the will and the action of man, nay even being the prime governor of these.[39]

How otherwise could for instance property have had a history at all, have taken on different forms, and landed property, for example, according to the different premises given, have proceeded in France from parcellation to centralization in the hands of a few, in England from centralization in the hands of a few to parcellation, as is actually the case today? Or how does it happen that trade, which after all is nothing more than the exchange of products of vari-

ous individuals and countries, rules the whole world through the relation of supply and demand—a relation which, as an English economist says, hovers over the earth like the fate of the ancients, and with invisible hand allots fortune and misfortune to men, sets up empires and overthrows empires, causes nations to rise and to disappear—while with the abolition of the basis of private property, with the communistic regulation of production (and, implicit in this, the destruction of the alien relation between men and what they themselves produce), the power of the relation of supply and demand is dissolved into nothing, and men get exchange, production, the mode of their mutual relation, under their own control again?[40]

In history up to the present it is certainly an empirical fact that separate individuals have, with the broadening of their activity into world-historical activity, become more and more enslaved under a power alien to them (a pressure which they have conceived of as a dirty trick on the part of the so-called universal spirit, etc.), a power which has become more and more enormous and, in the last instance, turns out to be the *world market*. But it is just as empirically established that, by the overthrow of the existing state of society by the communist revolution (of which more below) and the abolition of private property which is identical with it, this power, which so baffles the German theoreticians, will be dissolved;

---

[38] This entire paragraph appeared as a marginal note to the paragraph above it in the original manuscript. Several important Marxist principles are laid out in it. First, as Marx and Engels were to write in the Communist Manifesto of 1848, "The history of all hitherto existing society is the history of class struggles." Second, this class struggle is the hidden, underlying dynamic driving political and economic history. Third, the state is an instrument of control and oppression, and seizing control of the state is a necessary step in changing society.

[39] In this and the next paragraph, Marx and Engels argue that although people actually create society, it seems to be something external to them with a life of its own. Similarly Hegel had argued that that the spirit is part of humanity but appears to be separated from humanity. Hegel viewed history as the process of dissolving the alienation between

humanity and spirit. Marx and Engels view history as the process of dissolving the alienation between human beings and society.

[40] Marx refers here to Adam Smith's idea of the invisible hand. In discussing domestic and foreign investment, Smith had written that individuals, intending their own gain are frequently "led by an invisible hand" to promote the interests of society. He continues with the caution that those who claim to make their economic decisions to promote the public good rarely do much good. Thus, Smith sees the invisible hand as a generally positive force. Marx and Engels, however, see it as a force of alienation, causing nations to rise and fall in arbitrary ways. They suggest that the laws of supply and demand are the products of society, an alien force that exists outside of people. Marx and Engels propose that in a communist society, such laws would cease to exist.

and that then the liberation of each single individual will be accomplished in the measure in which history becomes transformed into world history. From the above it is clear that the real intellectual wealth of the individual depends entirely on the wealth of his real connections. Only then will the separate individuals be liberated from the various national and local barriers, be brought into practical connection with the material and intellectual production of the whole world and be put in a position to acquire the capacity to enjoy this all-sided production of the whole earth (the creations of man). *All-round* dependence, this natural form of the *world-historical* co-operation of individuals, will be transformed by this communist revolution into the control and conscious mastery of these powers, which, born of the action of men on one another, have till now overawed and governed men as powers completely alien to them. Now this view can be expressed again in speculative-idealistic, i.e. fantastic, terms as "self-generation of the species" ("society as the subject"), and thereby the consecutive series of interrelated individuals connected with each other can be conceived as a single individual, which accomplishes the mystery of generating itself. It is clear here that individuals certainly make *one another,* physically and mentally, but do not make themselves.[41]

This "alienation" (to use a term which will be comprehensible to the philosophers) can, of course, only be abolished given two *practical* premises. For it to become an "intolerable" power, i.e. a power against which men make a revolution, it must necessarily have rendered the great mass of humanity "propertyless," and produced, at the same time, the contradiction of an existing world of wealth and culture, both of which conditions presuppose a great increase in productive power, a high degree of its development. And, on the other hand, this development of productive

forces (which itself implies the actual empirical existence of men in their *world-historical,* instead of local, being) is an absolutely necessary practical premise because without it *want* is merely made general, and with *destitution* the struggle for necessities and all the old filthy business would necessarily be reproduced; and furthermore, because only with this universal development of productive forces is a *universal* intercourse between men established, which produces in all nations simultaneously the phenomenon of the "propertyless" mass (universal competition), makes each nation dependent on the revolutions of the others, and finally has put *world-historical,* empirically universal individuals in place of local ones. Without this, (1) communism could only exist as a local event; (2) the *forces* of intercourse themselves could not have developed as *universal,* hence intolerable powers: they would have remained home-bred conditions surrounded by superstition; and (3) each extension of intercourse would abolish local communism. Empirically, communism is only possible as the act of the dominant peoples "all at once" and simultaneously, which presupposes the universal development of productive forces and the world intercourse bound up with communism. Moreover, the mass of *propertyless* workers—the utterly precarious position of labour-power on a mass scale cut off from capital or from even a limited satisfaction and, therefore, no longer merely temporarily deprived of work itself as a secure source of life—presupposes the *world market* through competition. The proletariat can thus only exist *world-historically,* just as communism, its activity, can only have a "world-historical" existence. World historical existence of individuals means, existence of individuals which is directly linked up with world history.

Communism is for us not a *state of affairs* which is to be established, an *ideal* to which reality

---

[41] In this and the next paragraph, Marx emphasizes that the movement toward communism must be a world-historical movement. Communist revolution in one place will lead to communist revolution in all places. Such a revolution would enable individuals to transcend the alienation be-

tween humans and society. Marx followed Hegel in believing that humans created themselves ("self-generation of the species"). However, whereas for Hegel this was an intellectual movement of the spirit, for Marx and Engels, it was a social movement of labor (Thompson 1982:84).

[will] have to adjust itself. We call communism the *real* movement which abolishes the present state of things. The conditions of this movement result from the premises now in existence.[42]

NOTE

[a]The building of houses. With savages each family has as a matter of course its own cave or hut like the separate family tent of the nomads. This separate domestic economy is made only the more necessary by the further development of private property. With the agricultural peoples a communal domestic economy is just as impossible as a communal cultivation of the soil. A great advance was the building of towns. In all previous periods, however, the abolition of individual economy, which is inseparable from the abolition of private property, was impossible for the simple reason that the material conditions governing it were not present. The setting-up of a communal domestic economy presupposes the development of machinery, of the use of natural forces and of many other productive forces—e.g., of water-supplies, of gas-lighting, steam-heating, etc., the removal [of the antagonism] of town and country. Without these conditions a communal economy would not in itself form a new productive force; lacking any material basis and resting on a purely theoretical foundation, it would be a mere freak and would end in nothing more than a monastic economy—What was possible can be seen in the towns brought about by condensation and the erection of communal buildings for various definite purposes (prisons, barracks, etc.). That the abolition of individual economy is inseparable from the abolition of the family is self-evident.

---

[42] Marx and Engels understand history as having created ever more oppressive conditions and people as ever more enslaved. At the same time, they saw that the prosperity of certain sectors of society was increasing. They argue here that the contradiction between the poverty and property-less condition of the masses and the wealth produced by industrialization would lead to revolution. This revolution would logically begin where both industrial wealth and poverty were most developed. From there it would quickly spread to become a general world revolution. In 1845, as they wrote *The German Ideology* Marx and Engels believed that the conditions for such a revolution were rapidly being met. In 1848, when revolution did break out in Germany, they believed it to be the beginnings of world communist revolution. Marx and Engels hurriedly returned to Germany where Marx began to publish another radical newspaper, the *Neue Rheinische Zeitung* (recall that the paper he has originally edited was called the *Rheinische Zeitung*). However, the 1848 revolutions were quickly and violently suppressed. In the spring of 1849 the government closed the newspaper and Marx was forced to flee to England, where he spent the remainder of his life.

The communist revolution as predicted by Marx did not happen. The movements remained, in Marx's phrase, "local events." But as you read the last three paragraphs of this essay in which Marx describes the conditions that would generate the universal communist movement he proposed, think about the economic events of the last few years. Today we live in a world of vast wealth and equally vast poverty, where the investment speculations of global corporations caused the near economic collapse of the largest nations in the world. Today we may be closer to the world forecast by Marx than he could have dreamed in 1848.

The Foundations of Sociological Thought

Like anthropology, sociology is based on the work of philosophers and scientists of the nineteenth century, and the two disciplines share many ideas in common. Indeed, at the end of the nineteenth century, there was no clear distinction between anthropology and sociology. The theories of the early sociological thinkers are worth exploring because they exerted a profound effect on anthropology that continues to be felt today. In fact, all of the theoreticians discussed here adopted a cross-cultural approach in their work.

One individual central in the creation of modern sociology is Émile Durkheim (1858–1917). Durkheim is responsible for formulating some of the basic concepts of the discipline and training the first generation of French sociologists at the beginning of the twentieth century. Durkheim had studied the works of the positivist philosopher Auguste Comte (1798–1857) as well as those of Herbert Spencer. In agreement with both of these scholars, Durkheim believed that human society followed laws, just like the natural laws of physics or biology, that could be discovered by empirical observation and testing. In 1885 to 1886, Durkheim took a leave of absence from high school teaching to do research in Germany, in the psychological laboratories of Wilhelm Wundt (1832–1920). His experiences with Wundt convinced him that a scientific study of society was possible.

Durkheim wished to substantiate his belief that society was much more than simply a collection of individuals and to discover the laws and principles by which society operated. He began by questioning the nature of social cohesion (the term he used was social solidarity): What was it exactly that held societies together? He concluded that social solidarity was primarily the result of a force arising from participation in a shared system of beliefs and values, which molded and controlled individual behavior. Durkheim called this force "l'âme collective," a phrase usually translated into English as "the collective conscience." However, the French word "âme" can also be translated as "soul," "spirit," "sentiment," or "sensibility," and Durkheim intended all of these meanings. In this book we will preserve the French "l'âme collective" but frequently use it with the English article "the."

Durkheim believed that the collective conscience originated in the communal interactions and experiences of members of a society. Because people were born and raised within this shared context of the collective conscience, it determined their values, beliefs, and behaviors. Ultimately, it made life possible and meaningful. For the most part, social cohesion was maintained because everyone in a society participated in the l'âme collective. As you can see, Durkheim's collective conscience foreshadowed the modern concept of culture, although he was not familiar with the term and did not use it in his work.

Durkheim argued that the collective conscience was a psychological entity that, although carried by members of a society, superseded individual existence and could not be explained in terms of individual behavior. Once called into existence (through a process Durkheim called social condensation), it had a life of its own and operated by its own rules. In other words, the collective conscience was not contained within any individual organism; it was superorganic. Given that it was not a material thing, how could the collective conscience be scientifically studied? Durkheim proposed that the appropriate units of analysis were social facts. These were the social and behavioral rules and principles that exist in a society before an individual is born and which that person learns and observes as a member of their society. Social facts can be recognized by their pervasiveness within a society (they are not individualistic) and because they are coercive. People feel obligated to observe their constraints. Durkheim believed that such social facts could be observed in people's actions and studied independently through the use of statistics. His 1897 book, *Suicide,* is a classic example of this form of analysis.

Like the other theorists of his day, Durkheim supposed technologically primitive peoples to be examples of earlier stages of cultural evolution. Though he did no fieldwork himself, he studied reports of primitive societies, in particular the Australian Aborigines, attempting to determine the form and nature of the collective conscience in these societies. In his analysis, he applied the concepts of mechanical and organic solidarity he had developed in his earlier work, The Division of Labor in Society, published in 1893. Primitive societies are held together by what Durkheim called mechanical solidarity. He believed that in such societies, there are no individuals in the modern sense. Rather, "collective conscience completely envelopes [individual] conscience and coincides with it at every point" (1933[1893]:43). Such societies lack internal differentiation; their parts are interchangeable. Therefore, segments can break away without disrupting the functioning of the entire society. In these societies, kinship forms the primary bond between people.

Industrialized societies, on the other hand, are held together by organic solidarity. In such societies collective conscience is at least partially differentiated from individual conscience. One result is occupational specialization—people

need each other to function. In this type of society, the primary ties between individuals come from economic and occupational interdependence and cooperation rather than from kinship. Durkheim believed that individual freedom and ultimately happiness were maximized under organic solidarity.

The influence of nineteenth-century evolutionary thought can be clearly seen in Durkheim's study of primitive societies. He believed that societies evolved from mechanical to organic solidarity, that is, from simple undifferentiated groups into more advanced differentiated societies. In this respect, his work developed some of the implications of Herbert Spencer's organic analogy (see essay 1). Unlike Spencer, Darwin, and Marx, who wrote in terms of the human struggle for survival, Durkheim focused on the solidarity within a society. Spencer, Darwin, and Marx saw competition and conflict as the motors driving evolution. Durkheim, on the other hand, believed that social evolution toward increased complexity was driven by the need to achieve social solidarity at higher and higher population levels. Although he certainly did not view complex societies as free from conflict (some of his best known work is on suicide), Durkheim believed that social differentiation and specialization led to increased social cohesion and broadened the possibilities for individuals to achieve their full potential as human beings. Strife in modern society resulted from the incomplete elaboration of organic solidarity. Ultimately, it would greatly diminish. Durkheim and many of his followers had a profound faith in the ability of science and rationality to help people create a better, more peaceful society in the future. This faith was sorely tested as Europe descended into World War I.

Durkheim postulated that all people understood the world through socially created systems of classification. He argued that such systems were not derived from simple observation of nature. Rather, they were social facts. Thus, systems of classification did not reflect the natural world but rather imposed the structure of society upon the natural world. In other words, classification systems were specific to individual societies and reflected the social organization of those societies. Durkheim developed this idea in *Primitive Classification* (Durkheim and Mauss 1963, orig. 1903) and *The Elementary Forms of the Religious Life* (1965, orig. 1912). In these works, Durkheim argued that human societies project their social organization on the material world. In the realm of religion, this classification system becomes sacred. Thus, when societies engage in religious worship, what they are actually praising is their own social order. This act of praise invests society itself with a sacred character and is a critical element in creating and maintaining social solidarity.

Durkheim made many additional points in these works, but two that are of enduring importance are, first, that the processes he analyzed in Aboriginal society are essentially the same processes that occur in all societies. Thus, primitive societies are not simply living fossils but rather simplified versions of more complex societies in which universal social processes can be seen more clearly. Second, Durkheim proposed that some social facts are universal. For example, he claimed that all human thought was dualistic. In all human societies, people have a tendency to classify by dividing everything into things and their opposites (good/bad, day/night, right/left, and so on). Further, he proposed that the most fundamental of these divisions was into the categories of sacred and profane. Durkheim's emphasis on systems of classification and binary opposition would have enormous effect on later theories, in particular, French structuralism, ethnoscience, and cognitive anthropology.

Durkheim adopted what anthropologists in later decades termed a "functionalist" approach to the analysis of society. His analysis of social institutions and beliefs was often couched in terms of their contribution to promoting and maintaining social solidarity. This aspect of his work is central to the work of many of Durkheim's students and forms the basis of the British functionalist and structural-functionalist schools of anthropological thought exemplified by Bronislaw Malinowski and A. R. Radcliffe-Brown (see essays 11 and 12).

Around 1900, Durkheim's work attracted a very influential group of scholars, some of whom

were his relatives. Together, between 1898 and 1912, they published a journal called *L'Année Sociologique*. As a result, they are collectively known as the *L'Année Sociologique* school. Unhappily, World War I exacted a profound toll on Durkheim and his students. Fearing German nationalism and anti-Semitism, Durkheim had supported the war. He was on numerous war-related committees and wrote several propaganda pamphlets against German expansionism particularly criticizing the work of Heinrich von Treitschke (1834–1896), a profoundly nationalist and anti-Semitic German politician and author. However, a great many of Durkheim's students were killed in the war. These included Maxime David, Antoine Bianconi, Robert Hertz, Jean Reynier, and R. Gelly, all of whom were in their very early thirties. Even more important, Durkheim's only son, André, a promising young linguist, died in 1915 during the retreat from Serbia. André was initially listed as missing, so Durkheim did not definitively know about his death for most of a year. Bereft of his son, Durkheim withdrew into silence. LaCapra writes: "Iron self-discipline remained the dominant force in Durkheim's life, and it finally broke him. In 1917 he died of what has been called a 'broken heart'" (1972:78).

Durkheim's nephew Marcel Mauss (1872–1950), one of the few members of L'Année Sociologique to survive the war, was considered one of the school's leading thinkers. In the wake of the disaster that had befallen his friends and colleagues, however, he neglected his own work to concentrate on publishing the work of his mentor, Durkheim, and his deceased colleagues. In 1925, in the first issue of *L'Année Sociologique* to appear after the war, Mauss wrote: "Let us then carry on the work for a few more years. Let us try to do the kind of work which will bring honor to their memory, and which will not be too unworthy of the work begun by our Master" (in Leacock 1954:59). In that same year, he published "Essai sur le don" ("The Gift"), a portion of which is reprinted here. In this essay, Mauss shows that gift-giving in primitive societies is often a part of political and social obligations, reflecting or expressing the society's underlying social structure. He also proposes a special class of social facts called total social phenomena and illustrates this concept in his discussion of the potlatch.

The last contributor to this section is the German sociologist Max Weber (1864–1920). Although best known for his work in sociology, Weber was trained in law and history and held academic posts in economics. Unlike Durkheim, Weber was concerned with the action of individuals as well as social groups. According to Weber, the ultimate base of social action is individual behavior a person undertakes in relation to others; that behavior is best judged by whether the action is rational or not. Weber was relatively poorly versed in the ethnography of "primitive" societies, but he was extremely interested in Asia and wrote extensively on religion in China and India.

Much of Weber's work was influenced by Marx, and he attempted to develop Marx's thoughts on social class. Like Marx, he believed that social class was related to property ownership and control of the means of production. Unlike Marx, he believed that classes, in and of themselves, could not act and that status (or honor) and party could also cut across class lines. In his essay "Class, Status, Party," Weber develops this theory of class stratification and parties (groups that exist to pursue power) and their relationship to the role of the individual in society.

Another critical feature that differentiates Weber's work from Marx's is the prominent place he gave to individual action and ideology. Both Marx and Weber saw these as ultimately grounded in systems of production, but in Weber's work individuals and ideologies take on the capacity for action and culture change that is much less evident in Marx.

The Protestant Ethic and the Spirit of Capitalism, originally published in 1930, is perhaps Weber's best known explanation of the role of ideology. Like Marx, Weber analyzed the rise of capitalism and, like Marx, he saw the roots of capitalism in fundamental changes in relations of production, such as the displacement of peasants. However, unlike Marx, he found these material causes insufficient to explain the emergence and success of capitalism. Instead, he proposed that it was material factors, coupled with a new Calvinist ethic emphasizing moral accountability and self-discipline that explained capitalism's rise. It is critical to Weber's point that Calvinism did not emerge from capitalism. It was aimed at ensuring personal salvation, not profits. However, coinciding with changes in relations of production, it greatly favored the emergence of a powerful capitalist bourgeoisie.

Weber believed that individuals could profoundly affect their societies. Prophets could emerge who could change the way people thought. He called the ability of an individual to influence others charisma, which he defined in *The Sociology of Religion* (1993, orig. 1920) as an "extraordinary power," a sort of spiritual force possessed by an individual. Weber did not explain the source of charisma, asserting that it simply exists naturally in some people; in others, it is a germ that must be awakened. The power of charisma enables certain individuals to lead their societies and change the thinking of those around them. The notion of charisma gives the individual a place in Weber's work that is lacking in Marx's theory.

Weber's influence on later anthropological work is subtle but significant. His emphasis on individual, rational, social action was incorporated by Bronislaw Malinowski into his theory of psychological functionalism. His work on forms of authority influenced many anthropological thinkers (see Morton Fried, essay 18), as did his analysis of the Protestant ethic and capitalism (see Julian Steward, essay 17, and Clifford Geertz, essay 33). Weber's work on religion influenced Roy Rappaport (Rappaport 1994:167) as well as Anthony F. C. Wallace, Peter Worsley, and Jean and John Comaroff (Erickson 1998:112). Especially important to contemporary anthropologists is his notion of "verstehen," usually translated as "understanding." Weber used the term to mean the empathetic identification with those you are observing in order to better understand their motives and the meaning of their behavior. This is one of the fundamental concepts of the school of symbolic anthropology. In particular, Clifford Geertz and Renato Rosaldo (essays 33 and 36) illustrate how this principle has been used by anthropologists.

5. *What Is a Social Fact?*

ÉMILE DURKHEIM (1858–1917)

BEFORE INQUIRING INTO the method suited to the study of social facts, it is important to know which facts are commonly called "social." This information is all the more necessary since the designation "social" is used with little precision. It is currently employed for practically all phenomena generally diffused within society, however small their social interest. But on that basis, there are, as it were, no human events that may not be called social. Each individual drinks, sleeps, eats, reasons; and it is to society's interest that these functions be exercised in an orderly manner. If, then, all these facts are counted as "social" facts, sociology would have no subject matter exclusively its own, and its domain would be confused with that of biology and psychology.[1]

But in reality there is in every society a certain group of phenomena which may be differentiated from those studied by the other natural sciences. When I fulfill my obligations as brother, husband, or citizen, when I execute my contracts, I perform duties which are defined, externally to myself and my acts, in law and in custom. Even if they conform to my own sentiments and I feel their reality subjectively, such reality is still objective, for I did not create them; I merely inherited them through my education. How many times it happens, moreover, that we are ignorant of the details of the obligations incumbent upon us, and that in order to acquaint ourselves with them we must consult the law and its authorized interpreters! Similarly, the church-member finds the beliefs and practices of his religious life ready-made at birth; their existence prior to his own implies their existence outside of himself. The system of signs I use to express my thought, the system of currency I employ to pay my debts, the instruments of credit I utilize in my commercial relations, the practices followed in my profession, etc., function independently of my own use of them. And these statements can be repeated for each member of society. Here, then, are ways of acting, thinking, and feeling that present the noteworthy property of existing outside the individual consciousness.

These types of conduct or thought are not only external to the individual but are, moreover, endowed with coercive power, by virtue of which they impose themselves upon him, independent of his individual will. Of course, when I fully consent and conform to them, this constraint is felt only slightly, if at all, and is therefore unnecessary. But it is, nonetheless, an intrinsic characteristic of these facts, the proof thereof being that it asserts itself as soon as I attempt to resist it. If I attempt to violate the law, it reacts against me so as to prevent my act before its accomplishment, or to nullify my violation by restoring the damage, if it is accomplished and reparable, or to make me expiate it if it cannot be compensated for otherwise.[2]

From *Rules of the Sociological Method* (1895)

---

[1] Durkheim's goal in writing this essay was to show that sociology could be a field of study distinct from other sciences. He wrote at a time when the divisions between anthropology, sociology, and psychology, as we know them today, did not exist. Durkheim was concerned to establish what he considered a new and independent science, which required having something in particular to study, a subject matter that could distinguish it from other sciences. That subject matter, Durkheim proposed, was social facts. As a follower of the French positivist Auguste Comte (1798–1857), Durkheim was vitally concerned with establishing the reality of social facts. Comte insisted that philosophy (and social science) be based on precise, observable facts subject to general laws. If the existence of such facts could not be demonstrated, sociology had no place in science.

[2] Durkheim argues that social facts are real because their effects can be felt. People are compelled to live according to the rules of their society and violate them at their peril.

In the case of purely moral maxims; the public conscience exercises a check on every act which offends it by means of the surveillance it exercises over the conduct of citizens, and the appropriate penalties at its disposal. In many cases the constraint is less violent, but nevertheless it always exists. If I do not submit to the conventions of society, if in my dress I do not conform to the customs observed in my country and in my class, the ridicule I provoke, the social isolation in which I am kept, produce, although in an attenuated form, the same effects as a punishment in the strict sense of the word. The constraint is nonetheless efficacious for being indirect. I am not obliged to speak French with my fellow-countrymen nor to use the legal currency, but I cannot possibly do otherwise. If I tried to escape this necessity, my attempt would fail miserably. As an industrialist, I am free to apply the technical methods of former centuries; but by doing so, I should invite certain ruin. Even when I free myself from these rules and violate them successfully, I am always compelled to struggle with them. When finally overcome, they make their constraining power sufficiently felt by the resistance they offer. The enterprises of all innovators, including successful ones, come up against resistance of this kind.[3]

Here, then, is a category of facts with very distinctive characteristics: it consists of ways of acting, thinking, and feeling, external to the individual, and endowed with a power of coercion, by reason of which they control him. These ways of thinking could not be confused with biological phenomena, since they consist of representations and of actions; nor with psychological phenomena, which exist only in the individual consciousness and through it. They constitute, thus, a new variety of phenomena; and it is to them exclusively that the term "social" ought to be applied. And this term fits them quite well, for it is clear that, since their source is not in the individual, their substratum can be no other than society, either the political society as a whole or some one of the partial groups it includes, such as religious denominations, political, literary, and occupational associations, etc. On the other hand, this term "social" applies to them exclusively, for it has a distinct meaning only if it designates exclusively the phenomena which are not included in any of the categories of facts that have already been established and classified. These ways of thinking and acting therefore constitute the proper domain of sociology. It is true that, when we define them with this word "constraint," we risk shocking the zealous partisans of absolute individualism. For those who profess the complete autonomy of the individual, man's dignity is diminished whenever he is made to feel that he is not completely self-determinant. It is generally accepted today, however, that most of our ideas and our tendencies are not developed by ourselves but come to us from without. How can they become a part of us except by imposing themselves upon us? This is the whole meaning of our definition. And it is generally accepted, moreover, that social constraint is not necessarily incompatible with the individual personality.[a]

Since the examples that we have just cited (legal and moral regulations, religious faiths, financial systems, etc.) all consist of established beliefs and practices, one might be led to believe

---

Fertile ground for discovering examples of social facts can be found in a society's general rules of behavior, such as the informal rules about what is appropriate to eat and how to eat. Most readers of this book probably have an aversion to eating insects—not because there is a law against eating them but because of informal rules that shape behavior. Even thinking about eating insects probably disgusts most Americans, which is how the effects of the social fact can be observed.

[3] Although Durkheim refers to social facts as "laws" and speaks of "executing contracts," he is not just thinking of laws in the legal sense. He was referring to the general rules of behavior that people unconsciously follow; rules we internalize through growing up in a society—what he calls "moral maxims." He argues that public opinion also controls people's conduct, in particular, through mechanisms such as shaming, ridicule, and ostracism. For instance, it is not illegal to pick your nose in public, but it does violate an informal rule of behavior. Taking this action provokes reactions of disgust from onlookers, and the offender would feel embarrassed or ashamed and probably not repeat the action.

that social facts exist only where there is some social organization. But there are other facts without such crystallized form which have the same objectivity and the same ascendancy over the individual. These are called "social currents." Thus the great movements of enthusiasm, indignation, and pity in a crowd do not originate in any one of the particular individual consciousnesses. They come to each one of us from without and can carry us away in spite of ourselves. Of course, it may happen that, in abandoning myself to them unreservedly, I do not feel the pressure they exert upon me. But it is revealed as soon as I try to resist them. Let an individual attempt to oppose one of these collective manifestations and the emotions that he denies will turn against him. Now, if this power of external coercion asserts itself so clearly in cases of resistance, it must exist also in the first-mentioned cases, although we are unconscious of it. We are then victims of the illusion of having ourselves created that which actually forced itself from without. If the complacency with which we permit ourselves to be carried along conceals the pressure undergone, nevertheless it does not abolish it. Thus, air is no less heavy because we do not detect its weight. So, even if we ourselves have spontaneously contributed to the production of the common emotion, the impression we have received differs markedly from that which we would have experienced if we had been alone. Also, once the crowd has dispersed, that is, once these social influences have ceased to act upon us and we are alone again, the emotions which have passed through the mind appear strange to us, and we no longer recognize them as ours. We realize that these feelings have been impressed upon us

to a much greater extent than they were created by us. It may even happen that they horrify us, so much were they contrary to our nature. Thus, a group of individuals, most of whom are perfectly inoffensive, may, when gathered in a crowd, be drawn into acts of atrocity. And what we say of these transitory outbursts applies similarly to those more permanent currents of opinion on religious, political, literary, or artistic matters which are constantly being formed around us, whether in society as a whole or in more limited circles.[4]

To confirm this definition of the social fact by a characteristic illustration from common experience, one need only observe the manner in which children are brought up. Considering the facts as they are and as they have always been, it becomes immediately evident that all education is a continuous effort to impose on the child ways of seeing, feeling, and acting which he could not have arrived at spontaneously. From the very first hours of his life, we compel him to eat, drink, and sleep at regular hours; we constrain him to cleanliness, calmness, and obedience; later we exert pressure upon him in order that he may learn proper consideration for others, respect for customs and conventions, the need for work, etc. If, in time, this constraint ceases to be felt, it is because it gradually gives rise to habits and to internal tendencies that render constraint unnecessary; but nevertheless it is not abolished, for it is still the source from which these habits were derived. It is true that, according to Spencer, a rational education ought to reject such methods, allowing the child to act in complete liberty; but as this pedagogic theory has never been applied by any known people, it must be accepted only as an expression of personal opinion, not as a fact

---

[4] Durkheim differentiates social facts, which are enduring, from transitory social currents. Social currents, such as the momentary emotions sweeping a crowd, give a taste of the power of social facts. As members of a crowd, we are clearly capable of emotions (and actions) beyond our own individual capabilities or desires.

Issues of crowd behavior were very much on the minds of writers of this era. The unsuccessful European revolutions of 1848 and the Paris Commune of 1871 had included striking displays of mob and government vio-

lence. In 1894, a year before the publication of this essay, Alfred Dreyfus (1859–1935), the only Jewish officer in the French army's General Staff, was wrongly convicted of spying for the Germans. The affair inflamed mob passions against Jews, socialists, and other minorities. The proto-fascist politician and author Maurice Barrès (1862–1923) called for a leader who would be an embodiment of the collective will of the masses. Durkheim, as a secular, Jewish socialist, must have been deeply impressed and concerned.

which can contradict the aforementioned observations. What makes these facts particularly instructive is that the aim of education is, precisely, the socialization of the human being; the process of education, therefore, gives us in a nutshell the historical fashion in which the social being is constituted. This unremitting pressure to which the child is subjected is the very pressure of the social milieu which tends to fashion him in its own image, and of which parents and teachers are merely the representatives and intermediaries.[5]

It follows that sociological phenomena cannot be defined by their universality. A thought which we find in every individual consciousness, a movement repeated by all individual manifestations, is not thereby a social fact. If sociologists have been satisfied with defining them by this characteristic, it is because they confused them with what one might call their reincarnation in the individual. It is, however, the collective aspects of the beliefs, tendencies, and practices of a group that characterize truly social phenomena. As for the forms that the collective states assume when refracted in the individual, these are things of another sort. This duality is clearly demonstrated by the fact that these two orders of phenomena are frequently found dissociated from one another. Indeed, certain of these social manners of acting and thinking acquire, by reason of their repetition, a certain rigidity which on its own account crystallizes them, so to speak, and isolates them from the particular events which reflect them. They thus acquire a body, a tangible form, and constitute a reality in their own right, quite distinct from the individual facts which produce it. Collective habits are inherent not only in the successive acts which they determine but, by a privilege of which we find no example in the biological realm, they are given permanent expression in a formula which is repeated from mouth to mouth, transmitted by education, and fixed even in writing. Such is the origin and nature of legal and moral rules, popular aphorisms and proverbs, articles of faith wherein religious or political groups condense their beliefs, standards of taste established by literary schools, etc. None of these can be found entirely reproduced in the applications made of them by individuals, since they can exist even without being actually applied.[6]

No doubt, this dissociation does not always manifest itself with equal distinctness, but its obvious existence in the important and numerous cases just cited is sufficient to prove that the social fact is a thing distinct from its individual manifestations. Moreover, even when this dissociation is not immediately apparent, it may often be disclosed by certain devices of method. Such dissociation is indispensable if one wishes to separate social facts from their alloys in order to observe them in a state of purity. Currents of opinion, with an intensity varying according to the time and place, impel certain groups either to more marriages, for example, or to more suicides, or to a higher or lower birthrate, etc. These currents are plainly social facts. At first sight they seem inseparable from the forms they take in individual cases. But statistics furnish us with

---

[5] Today, anthropologists call this process "enculturation" and believe that it is largely unconscious. In other words, we think and act the way we do largely because of the unconscious internalization of cultural constraints imposed on us during childhood, not because of conscious, rational choice. Durkheim's citation of Herbert Spencer here is strange because the name that would come to the mind of any French intellectual reading this passage is Jean-Jacques Rousseau (1712–1778), whose 1762 book Émile proposed a similar theory of "natural" education. So why does Durkheim, writing in French, cite Spencer, an Englishman, and not Rousseau, who was French? Probably because he considered Spencer a scientist and Rousseau a philosopher and wished to emphasize the scientific nature of his work.

[6] Since they are beyond the individual, social facts must have an existence apart from their individual manifestations. Indeed, individual behavior can only approximate the rules of behavior. Durkheim was familiar with Platonic philosophy and his argument parallels that perspective. Plato, in his *Republic,* proposed that objects on earth are imperfect representations of ideal forms existing beyond human consciousness; Durkheim suggests that actual behavior is the imperfect representation of crystallized social facts existing beyond individual awareness. A problem with this view is that a social fact must somehow be teased out of a myriad of individual manifestations, none of which accurately reflects it. Will all observers find the same social facts?

the means of isolating them. They are, in fact, represented with considerable exactness by the rates of births, marriages, and suicides, that is, by the number obtained by dividing the average annual total of marriages, births, suicides, by the number of persons whose ages lie within the range in which marriages, births, and suicides occur.[b] Since each of these figures contains all the individual cases indiscriminately, the individual circumstances which may have had a share in the production of the phenomenon are neutralized and, consequently, do not contribute to its determination. The average, then, expresses a certain state of the group mind (l'âme collective).[7]

Such are social phenomena, when disentangled from all foreign matter. As for their individual manifestations, these are indeed, to a certain extent, social, since they partly reproduce a social model. Each of them also depends, and to a large extent, on the organopsychological constitution of the individual and on the particular circumstances in which he is placed. Thus they are not sociological phenomena in the strict sense of the word. They belong to two realms at once; one could call them sociopsychological. They interest the sociologist without constituting the immediate subject matter of sociology. There exist in the interior of organisms similar phenomena, compound in their nature, which form in their turn the subject matter of the "hybrid sciences," such as physiological chemistry, for example.

The objection may be raised that a phenomenon is collective only if it is common to all members of society, or at least to most of them—in other words, if it is truly general. This may be true; but it is general because it is collective (that is, more or less obligatory), and certainly not collective because general. It is a group condition repeated in the individual because imposed on him. It is to be found in each part because it exists in the whole, rather than in the whole because it exists in the parts.[8] This becomes conspicuously evident in those beliefs and practices which are transmitted to us ready-made by previous generations; we receive and adopt them because, being both collective and ancient, they are invested with a particular authority that education has taught us to recognize and respect. It is, of course, true that a vast portion of our social culture is transmitted to us in this way; but even when the social fact is due in part to our direct collaboration, its nature is not different. A collective emotion which bursts forth suddenly and violently in a crowd does not express merely what all the individual sentiments had in common; it is something entirely different, as we have shown. It results from their being together, a product of the actions and reactions which take place between individual consciousnesses; and if each individual consciousness echoes the collective sentiment, it is by virtue of the special energy resident in its collective origin. If all hearts beat in unison, this is not the result of a spontaneous and pre-established harmony but rather because an identical force propels them in the same direction. Each is carried along by all.[9]

We thus arrive at the point where we can formulate and delimit in a precise way the domain of sociology.[10] It comprises only a limited group of phenomena. A social fact is to be recognized by the power of external coercion which it exercises

---

[7] The use of statistics to predict behavior was of relatively recent origin when Durkheim wrote this article. The astronomer-turned-statistician Adolphe J. Quetelet published two volumes, *A Treatise on Man and the Development of His Faculties* (1835) and *Of the Social System and the Laws Which Rule It* (1848), in which probability theory was first applied to population characteristics (Tylor also refers to Quetelet in essay 2). Because the behavioral characteristics of a population are predictable through statistical analysis, Durkheim saw statistics as a scientific method for identifying social facts. In this paragraph he mentions their use in analyzing suicide rates. One of Durkheim's

most influential works was *Suicide: A Study in Sociology* (1897), which appeared two years after this essay and makes extensive use of statistics.

[8] Although the wording may be confusing, Durkheim makes an important point at the outset of this paragraph. He thought that a belief or behavior held in common by members of a society was prevalent because it was a collective phenomenon. Everyone shares social facts because they are collective; they are not collective simply because everyone shares them. Social facts precede individuals and are imposed on them.

or is capable of exercising over individuals, and the presence of this power may be recognized in its turn either by the existence of some specific sanction or by the resistance offered against every individual effort that tends to violate it. One can, however, define it also by its diffusion within the group, provided that, in conformity with our previous remarks, one takes care to add as a second and essential characteristic that its own existence is independent of the individual forms it assumes in its diffusion. This last criterion is perhaps, in certain cases, easier to apply than the preceding one. In fact, the constraint is easy to ascertain when it expresses itself externally by some direct reaction of society, as is the case in law, morals, beliefs, customs, and even fashions.[11] But when it is only indirect, like the constraint which an economic organization exercises, it cannot always be so easily detected. Generality combined with externality may, then, be easier to establish. Moreover, this second definition is but another form of the first; for if a mode of behavior whose existence is external to individual consciousnesses becomes general, this can only be brought about by its being imposed upon them.[c]

But these several phenomena present the same characteristic by which we defined the others. These "ways of existing" are imposed on the individual precisely in the same fashion as the "ways of acting" of which we have spoken. Indeed, when we wish to know how a society is divided politically, of what these divisions themselves are composed, and how complete is the fusion existing between them, we shall not achieve our purpose by physical inspection and by geographical observations; for these phenomena are social, even when they have some basis in physical nature. It is only by a study of public law that a comprehension of this organization is possible, for it is this law that determines the organization, as it equally determines our domestic and civil relations. This political organization is, then, no less obligatory than the social facts mentioned above. If the population crowds into our cities instead of scattering into the country, this is due to a trend of public opinion, a collective drive that imposes this concentration upon the individuals. We can no more choose the style of our houses than of our clothing—at least, both are equally obligatory. The channels of communication prescribe the direction of internal migrations and commerce, etc., and even their extent.[12] Consequently, at the very most, it should be necessary to add to the list of phenomena which we have enumerated as presenting the distinctive criterion of a social fact only one additional category, "ways of existing"; and as this enumeration was not meant to be rigorously exhaustive, the addition would not be absolutely necessary.

Such an addition is perhaps not necessary, for these "ways of existing" are only crystallized "ways of acting." The political structure of a

---

[9] In this paragraph, Durkheim returns once again to the problem of the crowd. He suggests that by virtue of coming together, people create a "special energy," which in *The Elementary Forms of the Religious Life* (1965 [1912]), he called "l'âme collective." The use of the term "energy" is important. Durkheim wished to show that sociology was a science and borrowed some of the vocabulary of physics to make his point. Just as the physicists of his day were concerned with the discovery of laws of energy, Durkheim wanted to uncover the laws underlying the behavior of this "social energy."

[10] In this paragraph, Durkheim summarizes the characteristics of social facts: They are external to individuals and coercive. Sometimes social facts are enshrined in law or can be recognized by the negative reaction of others when a principle is violated. Frequently they can be determined by the statistical analysis of a population's behavior.

[11] Durkheim says that the constraint exercised by social facts is easily recognized when expressed "externally by some direct reaction of society, as is the case in law, morals, beliefs, customs and even fashions." Compare this statement with Tylor's famous definition of culture, which opens *Primitive Culture* (1871; see essay 2): "Culture or civilization, taken in its wide ethnographic sense, is that complex whole which includes knowledge, belief, art, morals, law, custom, and any other capabilities and habits acquired by man as a member of society." Although not cited, it appears Durkheim's formulation was influenced by Tylor's definition. He may well have conceived of society as a collection of social facts.

[12] Durkheim contends in this paragraph that social movements, such as the change from rural to predominantly urban lifestyles, are driven by collective opinion, revealing himself as a strict idealist. Unlike Marxists, cultural

society is merely the way in which its component segments have become accustomed to live with one another. If their relations are traditionally intimate, the segments tend to fuse with one another, or, in the contrary case, to retain their identity. The type of habitation imposed upon us is merely the way in which our contemporaries and our ancestors have been accustomed to construct their houses. The methods of communication are merely the channels which the regular currents of commerce and migrations have dug, by flowing in the same direction. To be sure, if the phenomena of a structural character alone presented this permanence, one might believe that they constituted a distinct species. A legal regulation is an arrangement no less permanent than a type of architecture, and yet the regulation is a "physiological" fact. A simple moral maxim is assuredly somewhat more malleable, but it is much more rigid than a simple professional custom or a fashion. There is thus a whole series of degrees without a break in continuity between the facts of the most articulated structure and those free currents of social life which are not yet definitely molded. The differences between them are, therefore, only differences in the degree of consolidation they present. Both are simply life, more or less crystallized.[13] No doubt, it may be of some advantage to reserve the term "morphological" for those social facts which concern the social substratum, but only on condition of not overlooking the fact that they are of the same nature as the others. Our definition will then include the whole relevant range of facts if we say: A social fact is every way of acting, fixed or not, capable of exercising on the individual an external constraint; or again, every way of acting which is general throughout a given society, while

at the same time existing in its own right independent of its individual manifestations.[d]

ACKNOWLEDGEMENT

Émile Durkheim, "What Is a Social Fact?" Reprinted with the permission of The Free Press, a division of Simon & Schuster, Inc., from *The Rules of Sociological Method* by Émile Durkheim, translated by Sarah A. Solovay and John H. Mueller. Edited by George E. G. Catlin. Copyright © 1938 by George E. G. Catlin. Copyright © renewed 1966 by Sarah A. Solovay, John H. Mueller, George E. G. Catlin. All rights reserved.

NOTES

[a] We do not intend to imply, however, that all constraint is normal. We shall return to this point later.

[b] Suicides do not occur at every age, and they take place with varying intensity at the different ages in which they occur.

[c] It will be seen how this definition of the social fact diverges from that which forms the basis of the ingenious system of M. Tarde. First of all, we wish to state that our researches have nowhere led us to observe that preponderant influence in the genesis of collective facts which M. Tarde attributes to imitation. Moreover, from the preceding definition, which is not a theory but simply a résumé of the immediate data of observation, it seems indeed to follow, not only that imitation does not always express the essential and characteristic features of the social fact, but even that it never expresses them. No doubt, every social fact is imitated; it has, as we have just shown, a tendency to become general, but that is because it is social, i.e., obligatory. Its power of expansion is not the cause but the consequence of its sociological character. If, further, only social facts produced this consequence, imitation could perhaps serve, if not to explain them, at least to define them. But an individual condition which produces a whole series of effects remains individual nevertheless. Moreover, one may ask whether the word "imitation" is indeed fitted to designate an effect due to a coercive influence. Thus, by this single expression,

---

ecologists, and cultural materialists, Durkheim attributes social changes to changes in ideas and opinions rather than changes in material structures such as the development of industrial capitalism.

[13] It is easy to see the coercive element in illegal or immoral acts, whereby violation of a rule results (at least theoretically) in punishment. However, Durkheim points out that coercion is also present in ways of behaving that are outside of the individual and general

throughout society, such as participation in the capitalist economic system or living in a certain type of house. Durkheim calls these phenomena "ways of existing." He further suggests that ways of existing and acting are variable in degree of flexibility. A moral maxim he says, is more rigid than a fashion, custom less rigid than law, but both exist on a continuum and are included in Durkheim's famous definition of social facts presented at the end of the paragraph.

very different phenomena, which ought to be distinguished, are confused.

[d] This close connection between life and structure, organ and function, may be easily proved in sociology because between these two extreme terms there exists a whole series of immediately observable intermediate stages which show the bond between them. Biology is not in the same favorable position. But we may well believe that the inductions on this subject made by sociology are applicable to biology and that, in organisms as well as in societies, only differences in degree exist between these two orders of facts.

---

6. *Excerpts from the Gift*

Marcel Mauss (1872–1950)

[*Our reprint of Mauss' work opens with section three of Chapter 2. In sections one and two of that chapter, comprising about 5,000 words, Mauss describes the rules of generosity on the Andaman Islands and the Kula trade in Melanesia, as well as other associated exchange practices. These exchanges, he believes, are the material expressions of what Durkheim called social facts. They are used to forge and maintain alliances, and they replicate the divisions between the people involved in them. The interdependence of the exchange network increases social solidarity. He continues here with a discussion of potlatch among Native Americans.*]

3. HONOUR AND CREDIT (NORTH-WEST AMERICA)

From these observations on Melanesian and Polynesian peoples our picture of gift economy is already beginning to take shape.[1] Material and moral life, as exemplified in gift exchange, functions there in a manner at once interested and obligatory. Furthermore, the obligation is expressed in myth and imagery, symbolically and collectively; it takes the form of interest in the objects exchanged; the objects are never completely separated from the men who exchange them; the communion and alliance they establish are well-nigh indissoluble. The lasting influence of the objects exchanged is a direct expression of the manner in which sub-groups within segmentary societies of an archaic type are constantly embroiled with and feel themselves in debt to each other.

Indian societies of the American North-West have the same institutions, but in a more radical and accentuated form.[2] Barter is unknown there. Even now after long contact with Europeans it does not appear that any of the considerable and continual transfers of wealth take place otherwise than through the formality of the potlatch.* We now describe this institution as we see it.

First, however, we give a short account of these societies.[3] The tribes in question inhabit the North-West American coast—the Tlingit and Haida of Alaska,* and the Tsimshian and Kwakiutl of British Columbia.* They live on the sea or on the rivers and depend more on fishing

From *The Gift* (1925)

---

[1] The parts of Mauss' essay reproduced here contain more than 100 notes. Space limitations prevent us from reproducing them here, but asterisks have been included to give the reader an idea of the volume of notes Mauss wrote. The intrepid reader can look them up in a complete version of *The Gift*.

[2] Mauss implies here that the purpose of these practices cannot be explained simply by economics. If their root purposes were economic, they would have disappeared with European contact.

[3] The next several paragraphs provide a broad ethnographic description of the potlatch customs of several Northwest Native American groups, much of which is drawn from Franz Boas' work. Mauss' description is a catalog of material culture, but his real interests lie in examining patterns of social interaction.

than on hunting for their livelihood; but in contrast to the Melanesians and Polynesians they do not practice agriculture. Yet they are very wealthy, and even at the present day their fishing, hunting and trapping activities yield surpluses which are considerable even when reckoned on the European scale. They have the most substantial houses of all the American tribes, and a highly evolved cedar industry. Their canoes are good; and although they seldom venture out on to the open sea they are skillful in navigating around their islands and in coastal waters. They have a high standard of material culture. In particular, even back in the eighteenth century, they collected, smelted, molded and beat local copper from Tsimshian and Tlingit country. Some of the copper in the form of decorated shields they used as a kind of currency. Almost certainly another form of currency was the beautifully embellished Chilkat blanket-work still used ornamentally, some of it being of considerable value.* The peoples are excellent carvers and craftsmen. Their pipes, clubs and sticks are the pride of our ethnological collections. Within broad limits this civilization is remarkably uniform. It is clear that the societies have been in contact with each other from very early days, although their languages suggest that they belong to at least three families of peoples.*

Their winter life, even with the southern tribes, is very different from their summer life. The tribes have a two-fold structure: at the end of spring they disperse and go hunting, collect berries from the hillsides and fish the rivers for salmon; while in winter they concentrate in what are known as towns. During this period of concentration they are in a perpetual state of effervescence.[4] The social life becomes intense in the extreme, even more so than in the concentrations of tribes that manage to form in the summer. This life consists of continual movement. There are constant visits of whole tribes to others, of clans to clans and families to families. There is feast upon feast, some of long duration. On the occasion of a marriage, on various ritual occasions, and on social advancement, there is reckless consumption of everything which has been amassed with great industry from some of the richest coasts of the world during the course of summer and autumn. Even private life passes in this manner; clansmen are invited when a seal is killed or a box of roots or berries opened; you invite everyone when a whale runs aground.

Social organization, too, is fairly constant throughout the area though it ranges from the matrilineal phratry (Tlingit and Haida) to the modified matrilineal clan of the Kwakiutl; but the general characters of the social organization and particularly of totemism are repeated in all the tribes. They have associations like those of the Banks Islanders of Melanesia, wrongly called "secret societies," which are often inter-tribal; and men's and women's societies among the Kwakiutl cut across tribal organization. A part of the gifts and counterprestations[5] which we shall discuss goes, as in Melanesia,* to pay one's way into the successive steps* of the associations. Clan and association ritual follows the marriage of chiefs, the sale of coppers, initiations, shamanistic séances and funeral ceremonies, the latter being more particularly pronounced among the Tlingit and Haida. These are all accomplished in the course of an indefinitely prolonged series of potlatches. Potlatches are given in all directions, corresponding to other potlatches to which they

---

[4] For Durkheim and his followers, members of the *L'Année Sociologique* school, the idea of periods of "effervescence" was critical in the binary separation of sacred and profane. For example, discussing the Australian Aborigines in *The Elementary Forms of the Religious Life,* Durkheim wrote that sacred times, when people assemble, were marked by "a sort of electricity . . . which transports them to exaltation. Every sentiment expressed finds a place without resistance in all the minds . . . each re-echoes the others, and is re-echoed by the others. . . . How could such experiences

as these . . . fail to leave [an individual convinced] that there really exist two heterogeneous and mutually incomparable worlds?" (1965:245–50).

[5] Mauss' work deals with a class of phenomena he calls "prestations," which are a type of gift exchange between groups. They appear "disinterested and spontaneous" but are, in reality, neither. Rather, they are obligatory and enacted under a highly specific system of reciprocity.

are the response. As in Melanesia the process is one of constant give-and-take.

The potlatch, so unique as a phenomenon, yet so typical of these tribes, is really nothing other than gift-exchange.[6] The only differences are in the violence, rivalry and antagonism aroused, in a lack of jural[7] concepts, and in a simpler structure. It is less refined than in Melanesia, especially as regards the northern tribes, the Tlingit and the Haida,* but the collective nature of the contract is more pronounced than in Melanesia and Polynesia.* Despite appearances, the institutions here are nearer to what we call simple total prestations. Thus the legal and economic concepts attached to them have less clarity and conscious precision. Nevertheless, in action the principles emerge formally and clearly.

There are two traits more in evidence here than in the Melanesian potlatch or in the more evolved and discrete institutions of Polynesia: the themes of credit and honour.*

As we have seen, when gifts circulate in Melanesia and Polynesia the return is assured by the virtue of the things passed on, which are their own guarantees. In any society it is in the nature of the gift in the end to being its own reward. By definition, a common meal, a distribution of *kava*,[8] or a charm worn, cannot be repaid at once. Time has to pass before a counterprestation can be made. Thus the notion of time is logically implied when one pays a visit, contracts a marriage or an alliance, makes a treaty, goes to organized games, fights or feasts of others, renders ritual and honorific service and "shows respect," to use the Tlingit term.* All these are

things exchanged side by side with other material objects, and they are the more numerous as the society is wealthier.

On this point, legal and economic theory is greatly at fault.[9] Imbued with modern ideas, current theory tends towards *a priori* notions of evolution,* and claims to follow a so-called necessary logic; in fact, however, it remains based on old traditions. Nothing could be more dangerous than what Simiand[10] called this "unconscious sociology." For instance, Cuq could still say in 1910: "In primitive societies barter alone is found; in those more advanced, direct sale is practiced. Sale on credit characterizes a higher stage of civilization; it appears first in an indirect manner, a combination of sale and loan."* In fact the origin of credit is different. It is to be found in a range of customs neglected by lawyers and economists as uninteresting: namely the gift, which is a complex phenomenon especially in its ancient form of total prestation which we are studying here. Now a gift necessarily implies the notion of credit. Economic evolution has not gone from barter to sale and from cash to credit. Barter arose from the system of gifts given and received on credit, simplified by drawing together the moments of time which had previously been distinct. Likewise purchase and sale—both direct sale and credit sale—and the loan, derive from the same source. There is nothing to suggest that any economic system which has passed through the phase we are describing was ignorant of the idea of credit, of which all archaic societies around us are aware. This is a simple and realistic manner of dealing with the problem, which

---

[6] Mauss follows Durkheim's idea of social evolution from mechanical to organic solidarity. Simple societies, such as those he is describing, are characterized by mechanical solidarity, which means that their social institutions are not separated, as in complex society. Instead, a few phenomena—called total social phenomena—simultaneously express a great many institutions. Potlatch exchange, as Mauss details below, is such a phenomenon.

[7] Jural: legal.

[8] Kava: a Polynesian ritual beverage consumed to produce a euphoric state. Made from the roots of the kava plant, *Piper methysticum*.

[9] Here Mauss takes aim at simple linear evolutionary schemes. Durkheim and Mauss were hostile to Darwinian models of social evolution, which stressed conflict and competition. In Durkheim's model, social evolution is driven by the need to achieve social solidarity at greater levels of population density and complexity.

[10] François Simiand (1873–1935) was a French economic historian. A student of Durkheim and a socialist, he was critical of scholars of his day and suggested that history could not be studied apart from social and economic structures.

Davy[11] has already studied, of the "two moments of time" which the contract unites.*

No less important is the role which honour plays in the transactions of the Indians. Nowhere else is the prestige of an individual as closely bound up with expenditure, and with the duty of returning with interest gifts received in such a way that the creditor becomes the debtor. Consumption and destruction are virtually unlimited. In some potlatch systems one is constrained to expend everything one possesses and to keep nothing.* The rich man who shows his wealth by spending recklessly is the man who wins prestige.[12] The principles of rivalry and antagonism are basic. Political and individual status in associations and clans, and rank of every kind, are determined by the war of property, as well as by armed hostilities, by chance, inheritance, alliance or marriage.* But everything is conceived as if it were a war of wealth.* Marriage of one's children and one's position at gatherings are determined solely in the course of the potlatch given and returned. Position is also lost as in war, gambling,* hunting and wrestling.* Sometimes there is no question of receiving return; one destroys simply in order to give the appearance that one has no desire to receive anything back.* Whole cases of candlefish or whale oil,* houses, and blankets by the thousand are burnt; the most valuable coppers are broken and thrown into the sea to level and crush a rival. Progress up the social ladder is made in this way not only for one-self but also for one's family. Thus in a system of this kind much wealth is continually being consumed and transferred. Such transfers may if desired be called exchange or even commerce or sale;* but it is an aristocratic type of commerce characterized by etiquette and generosity; moreover, when it is carried out in a different spirit, for immediate gain, it is viewed with the greatest disdain.*

We see, then, that the notion of honour, strong in Polynesia, and present in Melanesia, is exceptionally marked here. On this point the classical writings made a poor estimate of the motives which animate men and of all that we owe to societies that preceded our own. Even as informed a scholar as Huvelin[13] felt obliged to deduce the notion of honour—which is reputedly *without* efficacy—from the notion of magical efficacy.* The truth is more complex. The notion of honor is no more foreign to these civilizations than the notion of magic.* Polynesian *mana* itself symbolizes not only the magical power of the person but also his honour, and one of the best translations of the word is "authority" or "wealth."* The Tlingit or Haida potlatch consists in considering mutual services as honours.* Even in really primitive societies like the Australian, the "point of honor" is as ticklish as it is in ours; and it may be satisfied by prestations, offerings of food, by precedence or ritual, as well as by gifts.* Men could pledge their honor long before they could sign their names.[14]

---

[11] Georges Davy (1883–1955) was a member of the *L'Année Sociologique* school and a specialist in the sociology of law. He made extensive use of Mauss' analysis of the potlatch in describing the transition from statute to contractual law.

[12] For Mauss, neither psychology nor economics could explain the vast destruction of property caused by the potlatch or the seemingly illogical behavior of its participants. Instead, he believed that potlatch was about the status of groups, their maintenance of internal cohesion, and their relations with one another.

[13] Paul Huvelin (1873–1924) was a specialist in Roman Law and a member of the law faculty at the University of Lyon. He was a friend of Mauss and an important member of the *L'Année Sociologique* group. Huvelin theorized that the origins of law were magical.

[14] Here, and in other passages, Mauss attacks simplistic understandings of primitive people as morally inferior to Europeans. Although optimistic about the future of civilization, he was highly critical of his own society and, to some degree, romanticized the primitive. In the conclusion to *The Gift*, he wrote, "Hence, we should return to the old and elemental. Once again we shall discover . . . the joy of giving in public, the delight in generous artistic expenditure, the pleasure of hospitality in the public or private feast. . . . We can visualize a society in which these principles obtain. . . . For honour, disinterestedness and corporate solidarity are not vain words, nor do they deny the necessity for work" (1967:67).

The North-West American potlatch has been studied enough as to the form of the contract. But we must find a place for the researches of Davy and Adam in the wider framework of our subject. For the potlatch is more than a legal phenomenon; it is one of those phenomena we propose to call "total." It is religious, mythological and shamanistic because the chiefs taking part are incarnations of gods and ancestors, whose names they bear, whose dances they dance and whose spirits possess them.* It is economic; and one has to assess the value, importance, causes and effects of transactions which are enormous even when reckoned by European standards. The potlatch is also a phenomenon of social morphology; the reunion of tribes, clans, families and nations produces great excitement. People fraternize but at the same time remain strangers; community of interest and opposition are revealed constantly in a great whirl of business.* Finally, from the jural point of view, we have already noted the contractual forms and what we might call the human element of the contract, and the legal status of the contracting parties—as clans or families or with reference to rank or marital condition; and to this we now add that the material objects of the contracts have a virtue of their own which causes them to be given and compels the making of counter-gifts.

It would have been useful, if space had been available, to distinguish four forms of American potlatch: first, potlatch where the phratries and chiefs' families alone take part (Tlingit); second, potlatches in which phratries, clans, families and chiefs take more or less similar roles (Haida); third, potlatch with chiefs and their clans confronting each other (Tsimshian); and fourth, potlatch of chiefs and fraternities (Kwakiutl). But this would prolong our argument, and in any case three of the four forms (with the exception of the Tsimshian) have already been comparatively described by Davy.* But as far as our study is concerned all the forms are more or less identical as regards the elements of the gift, the obligation to receive and the obligation to make a return.

4. THE THREE OBLIGATIONS: GIVING, RECEIVING, REPAYING[15]

THE OBLIGATION TO GIVE

This is the essence of potlatch. A chief must give a potlatch for himself, his son, his son-in-law or daughter* and for the dead.* He can keep his authority in his tribe, village and family, and maintain his position with the chiefs inside and outside his nation,* only if he can prove that he is favorably regarded by the spirits, that he possesses fortune* and that he is possessed by it.* The only way to demonstrate his fortune is by expending it to the humiliation of others, by putting them "in the shadow of his name."* Kwakiutl and Haida noblemen have the same notion of "face" as the Chinese mandarin or officer.* It is said of one of the great mythical chiefs who gave no feast that he had a "rotten face."* The expression is more apt than it is even in China; for to lose one's face is to lose one's spirit, which is truly the "face," the dancing mask, the right to incarnate a spirit and wear an emblem or totem. It is the veritable *persona* which is at stake, and it can be lost in the potlatch* just as it can be lost in the game of gift-giving,* in war,* or through some error in ritual.* In all these societies one is anxious to give; there is no occasion of importance (even outside the solemn winter gatherings) when one is not obliged to invite friends to share the produce of the chase or the forest which the gods or totems have sent;* to redistribute everything received at a potlatch; or to recognize services* from chiefs, vassals or relatives* by means of gifts. Failing these obligations—at least for the nobles—etiquette is violated and rank is lost.*

---

[15] In this section, Mauss describes what he believes is a fundamental pattern underlying prestations. Since prestations are total social phenomena, this same pattern must also underlie other aspects of society. This insight was of crucial importance in the development of Lévi-Strauss' French structural anthropology (see essays 22 and 23). Lévi-Strauss said, on reading *The Gift,* that his mind was "overcome by the certainty as yet undefinable of assisting in a decisive event in the evolution of science" (quoted in Harris 1968:484).

The obligation to invite is particularly evident between clans or between tribes. It makes sense only if the invitation is given to people other than members of the family, clan or phratry.* Everyone who can, will or does attend the potlatch must be invited.* Neglect has fateful results.* An important Tsimshian myth* shows the state of mind in which the central theme of much European folklore originated: the myth of the bad fairy neglected at a baptism or marriage.[16] Here the institutional fabric in which it is sewn appears clearly, and we realize the kind of civilization in which it functioned. A princess of one of the Tsimshian villages conceives in the "Country of the Otters" and gives birth miraculously to "Little Otter." She returns with her child to the village of her father, the chief. Little Otter catches halibut with which her father feeds all the tribal chiefs. He introduces Little Otter to everyone and requests them not to kill him if they find him fishing in his animal form: "Here is my grandson who has brought for you this food with which I serve you, my guests." Thus the grandfather grows rich with all manner of wealth brought to him by the chiefs when they come in the winter hunger to eat whale and seal and the fresh fish caught by Little Otter. But one chief is not invited. And one day when the crew of a canoe of the neglected tribe meets Little Otter at sea the bowman kills him and takes the seal. The grandfather and all the tribes search high and low for Little Otter until they hear about the neglected tribe. The latter offers its excuses; it has never heard of Little Otter. The princess dies of grief; the involuntarily guilty chief brings the grandfather all sorts of gifts in expiation. The myth ends: "That is why the people have great feasts when a chief's son is born and gets a name; for none may be ignorant of him."* The potlatch—the distribution of goods—is the fundamental act of public recognition in all spheres, military, legal, economic and religious. The chief or his son is recognized and acknowledged by the people.

Sometimes the ritual in the feasts of the Kwakiutl and other tribes in the same group expresses this obligation to invite.* Part of the ceremonial opens with the "ceremony of the dogs." These are represented by masked men who come out of one house and force their way into another. They commemorate the occasion on which the people of the three other tribes of Kwakiutl proper neglected to invite the clan which ranked highest among them, the Guetela who, having no desire to remain outsiders, entered the dancing house and destroyed everything.*

THE OBLIGATION TO RECEIVE

This is no less constraining.[17] One does not have the right to refuse a gift or a potlatch.* To do so would show fear of having to reply, and of being abased in default. One would "lose the weight" of one's name by admitting defeat in advance.* In certain circumstances, however, a refusal can be an assertion of victory and invincibility.* It appears at least with the Kwakiutl that a recognized position in the hierarchy, or a victory through previous potlatches, allows one to refuse an invitation or even a gift without war ensuing. If this is so, then a potlatch must be carried out by the man who refuses to accept the invitation. More particularly, he has to contribute to the "fat festival" in which a ritual of refusal may be observed.* The chief who considers himself superior refuses the spoonful of fat offered him: he fetches his copper and returns with it to "extinguish the fire" (of the fat). A series of formalities follow which mark the challenge and oblige the chief who has refused to give another potlatch or fat festival.* In principle, however, gifts are always accepted and praised.* You must speak your appreciation of food prepared for you.* But you

---

[16] The comparison of the Tsimshian myth with European folklore here presupposes an evolutionary framework. Mauss, like many other social thinkers of the time, saw primitive cultures as living fossils. Given this premise, it followed that current Tsimshian myths were equivalent to ancient European folktales.

[17] Notice that, while Mauss has said that prestations do sometimes serve an economic role, his discussion of potlatch is not economic. Instead, the potlatch is seen as symbolic of social relations between groups, which is why he can say that the obligation to receive is "no less constraining" than the obligation to give.

accept a challenge at the same time.* You receive a gift "on the back." You accept the food and you do so because you mean to take up the challenge and prove that you are not unworthy.* When chiefs confront each other in this manner they may find themselves in odd situations and probably they experience them as such. In like manner in ancient Gaul and Germany, as well as nowadays in gatherings of French farmers and students, one is pledged to swallow quantities of liquid to "do honor" in grotesque fashion to the host. The obligation stands even although one is only heir to the man who bears the challenge.* Failure to give or receive,* like failure to make return gifts, means a loss of dignity.*

THE OBLIGATION TO REPAY

Outside pure destruction the obligation to repay is the essence of potlatch.* Destruction is very often sacrificial, directed towards the spirits, and apparently does not require a return unconditionally, especially when it is the work of a superior clan chief or of the chief of a clan already recognized as superior.* But normally the potlatch must be returned with interest like all other gifts. The interest is generally between 30 and 100 per cent a year. If a subject receives a blanket from his chief for a service rendered he will return two on the occasion of a marriage in the chief's family or on the initiation of the chief's son. But then the chief in his turn redistributes to him whatever he gets from the next potlatch at which rival clans repay the chief's generosity.

The obligation of worthy return is imperative.* Face is lost for ever if it is not made or if equivalent value is not destroyed.*

The sanction for the obligation to repay is enslavement for debt. This is so at least for the Kwakiutl, Haida and Tsimshian. It is an institution comparable in nature and function to the Roman *nexum*.[18] The person who cannot return a loan or potlatch loses his rank and even his status of a free man. If among the Kwakiutl a man of poor credit has to borrow he is said to

"sell a slave." We need not stress the similarity of this expression with the Roman one.* The Haida say, as if they had invented the Latin phrase independently, that a girl's mother who gives a betrothal payment to the mother of a young chief "puts a thread on him."

Just as the Trobriand *kula* is an extreme case of gift exchange, so the potlatch in North-West America is the monster child of the gift system. In societies of phratries, amongst the Tlingit and Haida, we find important traces of a former total prestation (which is characteristic of the Athabascans, a related group). Presents are exchanged on any pretext for any service, and everything is returned sooner or later for redistribution.* The Tsimshian have almost the same rules.* Among the Kwakiutl these rules, in many cases, function outside the potlatch.* We shall not press this obvious point; old authors described the potlatch in such a way as to make it doubtful whether it was or was not a distinct institution.* We may recall that with the Chinook, one of the least known tribes but one which would repay study, the word "potlatch" means "gift."*

5. THE POWER IN OBJECTS OF EXCHANGE

Our analysis can be carried farther to show that in the things exchanged at a potlatch there is a certain power which forces them to circulate, to be given away and repaid.

To begin with, the Kwakiutl and Tsimshian, and perhaps others, make the same distinction between the various types of property as do the Romans, Trobrianders and Samoans. They have the ordinary articles of consumption and distribution and perhaps also of sale (I have found no trace of barter). They have also the valuable family property—talismans, decorated coppers, skin blankets and embroidered fabrics.* This class of articles is transmitted with that solemnity with which women are given in marriage, privileges are endowed on sons-in-law, and names and status

---

[18] The *nexum* was a system of contracting a loan in ancient Rome in which the loan was made in the presence of five witnesses. Debtors could be held in bondage for failure to repay.

are given to children and daughters' husbands.* It is wrong to speak here of alienation, for these things are loaned rather than sold and ceded.[19] Basically they are *sacra*[20] which the family parts with, if at all, only with reluctance.

Closer observation reveals similar distinctions among the Haida. This tribe has in fact sacralized, in the manner of Antiquity, the notions of property and wealth.[21] By a religious and mythological effort of a type rare enough in the Americas they have managed to reify an abstraction: the "Property Woman," of whom we possess myths and a description.* She is nothing less than the mother, the founding goddess of the dominant phratry, the Eagles. But oddly enough—a fact which recalls the Asiatic world and Antiquity—she appears identical with the "queen," the principal piece in the game of tip-cat, the piece that wins everything and whose name the Property Woman bears. This goddess is found in Tlingit* country and her myth, if not her cult, among the Tsimshian* and Kwakiutl.*

Together these precious family articles constitute what one might call the magical legacy of the people; they are conceived as such by their owner, by the initiate he gives them to, by the ancestor who endowed the clan with them, and by the founding hero of the clan to whom the spirits gave them.* In any case in all these clans they are spiritual in origin and nature.* Further, they are kept in a large ornate box which itself is endowed with a powerful personality, which speaks, is in communion with the owner, contains his soul, and so on.*

Each of these precious objects and tokens of wealth has, as amongst the Trobrianders, its name,* quality and power.* The large *abalone* shells,* the shields covered with them, the decorated blankets with faces, eyes, and animal and human figures embroidered and woven into them, are all personalities.* The houses and decorated beams are themselves beings.* Everything speaks—roof, fire, carvings and paintings; for the magical house is built not only by the chief and his people and those of the opposing phratry but also by the gods and ancestors; spirits and young initiates are welcomed and cast out by the house in person.*

Each of these precious things has, moreover, a productive capacity within it.* Each, as well as being a sign and surety of life, is also a sign and surety of wealth, a magico-religious guarantee of rank and prosperity.* Ceremonial dishes and spoons decorated and carved with the clan totem or sign of rank, are animate things.* They are replicas of the never ending supply of tools, the creators of food, which the spirits gave to the ancestors. They are supposedly miraculous. Objects are confounded with the spirits who made them, and eating utensils with food. Thus Kwakiutl dishes and Haida spoons are essential goods with a strict circulation and are carefully shared out between the families and clans of the chiefs.

6. MONEY OF RENOWN (RENOMMIERGELD)*

Decorated coppers* are the most important articles in the potlatch, and beliefs and a cult are attached to them. With all these tribes copper, a living being, is the object of cult and myth.* Copper, with the Haida and Kwakiutl at least, is identified with salmon, itself an object of cult.* But in addition to this mythical element each copper is by itself an object of individual belief.* Each principal copper of the families of clan chiefs has its name and individuality;* it has also its own value,* in the full magical and economic sense of the word which is regulated by the vicissitudes of

---

[19] Mauss' comment on alienation illustrates his insistence that the transactions he describes are not economic—that is, they are not driven by the desire to maximize material profit or minimize loss. Therefore, he believed that the term *alienation* (frequently used by Marxist economists) was not appropriate.

[20] *Sacra*: Latin for objects of devotion.

[21] Durkheim and his followers divided the cultural world into the sacred and profane. Here, Mauss demonstrates the sacred nature of gift-giving. Twenty years later, Lévi-Strauss and his followers emphasized the binary division of sacred and profane employed by *L'Année Sociologique* thinkers, along with the use of binary opposition by structural linguists (see essays 22 and 23).

the potlatches through which it passes and even by its partial or complete destruction.*

Coppers have also a virtue which attracts other coppers to them, as wealth attracts wealth and as dignity attracts honours, spirit-possession and good alliances.* In this way they live their own lives and attract other coppers.* One of the Kwakiutl coppers is called "Bringer of Coppers" and the formula describes how the coppers gather around it, while the name of its owner is "Copper-Flowing-Towards-Me."* With the Haida and Tlingit, coppers are a "fortress" for the princess who owns them; elsewhere a chief who owns them is rendered invincible.* They are the "flat divine objects" of the house.* Often the myth identifies together the spirits who gave the coppers, the owners and the coppers themselves.* It is impossible to discern what makes the power of the one out of the spirit and the wealth of the other; a copper talks and grunts, demanding to be given away or destroyed;* it is covered with blankets to keep it warm just as a chief is smothered in the blankets he is to distribute.*

From another angle we see the transmission of wealth and good fortune.* The spirits and minor spirits of an initiate allow him to own coppers and talismans which then enable him to acquire other coppers, greater wealth, higher rank and more spirits (all of these being equivalents). If we consider the coppers with other forms of wealth which are the object of hoarding and potlatch—masks, talismans and so on—we find they are all confounded in their uses and effects.* Through them rank is obtained; because a man obtains wealth he obtains a spirit which in turn possesses him, enabling him to overcome obstacles heroically. Then later the hero is paid for his shamanistic services, ritual dances and trances. Everything is tied together; things have personality, and personalities are in some manner the permanent possession of the clan. Titles, talismans, coppers and spirits of chiefs are homonyms and synonyms, having the same nature and function.* The circulation of goods follows that of men, women and children, of festival ritual, ceremonies and dances, jokes and injuries. Basically they are the same. If things are given and returned it is precisely because one gives and returns "respects" and "courtesies." But in addition, in giving them, a man gives himself, and he does so because he owes himself—himself and his possessions—to others.[22]

7. PRIMARY CONCLUSION

From our study of four important groups of people we find the following: first, in two or three of the groups, we find the potlatch, its leading motive and its typical form. In all groups we see the archaic form of exchange—the gift and the return gift. Moreover, in these societies we note the circulation of objects side by side with the circulation of persons and rights. We might stop at this point. The amount, distribution and importance of our data authorize us to conceive of a regime embracing a large part of humanity over a long transitional phase, and persisting to this day among peoples other than those described. We may then consider that the spirit of gift exchange is characteristic of societies which have passed the phase of "total prestation" (between clan and clan, family and family) but have not yet reached the stage of pure individual contract, the money market, sale proper, fixed price, and weighed and coined money.[23]

[The Gift, *in its entirety, is a reasonably short essay (only about 80 pages plus extensive notes in the Norton Library edition). The passage you have just*

---

[22] In this paragraph, Mauss claims that the goods given in potlatch are, in essence, indistinguishable from the people giving them. The goods have personalities and are members of households. Giving them is then spiritually the same as the movement of people from household to household. Twenty five years later, in his first major work, *Les Structures Élémentaires de la Parenté* (1949)

(The Elementary Structures of Kinship), Lévi-Strauss expanded this line of argument by analyzing the exchange of women between groups as a fundamental social phenomenon.

[23] This conclusion points once again to the evolutionary nature of Mauss' thinking.

read is the conclusion of Chapter 2. Chapter 3, titled "Survivals in Early Literature," discusses written evidence for Mauss' theory of gift-giving from ancient Roman law, ancient Hindu legal documents, early Germanic society, and, very briefly, Chinese law. Chapter 4 is titled "Conclusions." The first two sections, which we have excluded here, are moral conclusions and political and economic conclusions. They consist of about 4,750 words and 23 footnotes. We rejoin the text with the sociological and ethical conclusions with which Mauss ends his essay.]

3. SOCIOLOGICAL AND ETHICAL CONCLUSIONS

We may be permitted another note about the method we have used. We do not set this work up as a model; it simply proffers one or two suggestions. It is incomplete: the analysis could be pushed farther.* We are really posing questions for historians and anthropologists and offering possible lines of research for them rather than resolving a problem and laying down definite answers. It is enough for us to be sure for the moment that we have given sufficient data for such an end.

This being the case, we would point out that there is a heuristic element in our manner of treatment.[24] The facts we have studied are all "total" social phenomena. The word "general" may be preferred although we like it less. Some of the facts presented concern the whole of society and its institutions (as with potlatch, opposing clans, tribes on visit, etc.); others, in which exchanges and contracts are the concern of individuals embrace a large number of institutions.

These phenomena are at once legal, economic, religious, aesthetic, morphological and so on. They are legal in that they concern individual and collective rights, organized and diffuse morality;

they may be entirely obligatory, or subject simply to praise or disapproval. They are at once political and domestic, being of interest both to classes and to clans and families. They are religious; they concern true religion, animism, magic and diffuse religious mentality. They are economic, for the notions of value, utility, interest, luxury, wealth, acquisition, accumulation, consumption and liberal and sumptuous expenditure are all present, although not perhaps in their modern senses. Moreover, these institutions have an important aesthetic side which we have left unstudied; but the dances performed, the songs and shows, the dramatic representations given between camps or partners, the objects made, used, decorated, polished, amassed and transmitted with affection, received with joy, given away in triumph, the feasts in which everyone participates—all these, the food, objects and services, are the source of aesthetic emotions as well as emotions aroused by interest.* This is true not only of Melanesia but also, and particularly, of the potlatch of North-West America and still more true of the market-festival of the Indo-European world. Lastly, our phenomena are clearly morphological. Everything that happens in the course of gatherings, fairs and markets or in the feasts that replace them, presupposes groups whose duration exceeds the season of social concentration, like the winter potlatch of the Kwakiutl or the few weeks of the Melanesian maritime expeditions. Moreover, in order that these meetings may be carried out in peace, there must be roads or water for transport and tribal, inter-tribal or international alliances—*commercium and connubium.*[25]

We are dealing then with something more than a set of themes, more than institutional elements, more than institutions, more even than systems of institutions divisible into legal, economic, religious and other parts. We are concerned with "wholes," with systems in their entirety. We have not described them as if they were fixed, in a static

---

[24] In this paragraph and below, Mauss provides a comprehensive definition of total social phenomena, suggesting that the investigation of such phenomena provides an outstanding pathway for developing an understanding of society in general. Mauss claims that total social phenomena

are morphological. That is, they reveal the underlying structure of the groups practicing them.

[25]*Commercium and connubium:* Latin for "commerce and intermarriage."

or skeletal condition, and still less have we dissected them into the rules and myths and values and so on of which they are composed. It is only by considering them as wholes that we have been able to see their essence, their operation and their living aspect, and to catch the fleeting moment when the society and its members take emotional stock of themselves and their situation as regards others. Only by making such concrete observation of social life is it possible to come upon facts such as those which our study is beginning to reveal. Nothing in our opinion is more urgent or promising than research into "total" social phenomena.[26]

The advantage is twofold. Firstly there is an advantage in generality, for facts of widespread occurrence are more likely to be universal than local institutions or themes, which are invariably tinged with local color. But particularly the advantage is in realism. We see social facts in the round, as they really are. In society there are not merely ideas and rules, but also men and groups and their behaviours. We see them in motion as an engineer sees masses and systems, or as we observe octopuses and anemones in the sea. We see groups of men, and active forces, submerged in their environments and sentiments.[27]

Historians believe and justly resent the fact that sociologists make too many abstractions and separate unduly the various elements of society.[28] We should follow their precepts and observe what is given. The tangible fact is Rome or Athens or the average Frenchman or the Melanesian of some island, and not prayer or law as such. Whereas formerly sociologists were obliged to

analyze and abstract rather too much, they should now force themselves to reconstitute the whole. This is the way to reach incontestable facts. They will also find a way of satisfying psychologists who have a pronounced viewpoint, and particularly psycho-pathologists, since there is no doubt that the object of their study is concrete. They all observe, or at least ought to, minds as wholes and not minds divided into faculties. We should follow suit. The study of the concrete, which is the study of the whole, is made more readily, is more interesting and furnishes more explanations in the sphere of sociology than the study of the abstract. For we observe complete and complex beings. We too describe them in their organisms and *psychai* as well as in their behavior as groups, with the attendant psychoses: sentiments, ideas and desires of the crowd, of organized societies and their sub-groups. We see bodies and their reactions, and their ideas and sentiments as interpretations or as motive forces. The aim and principle of sociology is to observe and understand the whole group in its total behavior.

It is not possible here—it would have meant extending a restricted study unduly—to seek the morphological implications of our facts. It may be worth while, however, to indicate the method one might follow in such a piece of research.

All the societies we have described above with the exception of our European societies are segmentary. Even the Indo-Europeans, the Romans before the Twelve Tables, the Germanic societies up to the *Edda*,[29] and Irish society to the time of its chief literature, were still societies based on

---

[26] Here Mauss seems to emphasize the holism that was part of American anthropology of his era, particularly the work of Boas. Mauss cites Boas' work many times in the present article. However, the application of holism to total social phenomena is distinctly his own. Boas and his followers did not believe that total social phenomena existed; they tended to believe that the different aspects of culture were of equal importance.

[27] Mauss relies on Durkheim's idea of a social fact. For Durkheim, sociology was the analysis of social facts. He defines these as "every way of acting, fixed or not, capable of exercising on the individual an external constraint; or again, every way of acting which is general throughout a

given society, while at the same time existing in its own right independent of its individual manifestations" (see essay 5).

[28] At the turn of the century, academic disciplines were not divided the same way they are today. One of Durkheim's concerns, here echoed by Mauss, was to show that sociology was a discipline with its own area of study and was distinct from history or psychology. The concern of modern anthropologists is frequently the reverse. Recent theorists such as Renato Rosaldo have explored how history and psychology provide fundamental insights into anthropology (see essay 36).

[29] The *Edda* refers to a poetry and prose collection of Norse mythology written in Iceland in the thirteenth century.

the clan or on great families more or less undivided internally and isolated from each other externally. All these were far removed from the degree of unification with which historians have credited them or which is ours today. Within these groups the individuals, even the most influential, were less serious, avaricious and selfish than we are; externally at least they were and are generous and more ready to give. In tribal feasts, in ceremonies of rival clans, allied families or those that assist at each other's initiation, groups visit each other; and with the development of the law of hospitality in more advanced societies, the rules of friendship and the contract are present—along with the gods—to ensure the peace of markets and villages; at these times men meet in a curious frame of mind with exaggerated fear and an equally exaggerated generosity which appear stupid in no one's eyes but our own. In these primitive and archaic societies there is no middle path. There is either complete trust or mistrust. One lays down one's arms, renounces magic and gives everything away, from casual hospitality to one's daughter or one's property. It is in such conditions that men, despite themselves, learnt to renounce what was theirs and made contracts to give and repay.

But then they had no choice in the matter. When two groups of men meet they may move away or in case of mistrust or defiance they may resort to arms; or else they can come to terms. Business has always been done with foreigners, although these might have been allies. The people of Kiriwina said to Malinowski:[30] "The Dobu man is not good as we are. He is fierce, he is a man-eater. When we come to Dobu, we fear him, he might kill us! But see! I spit the charmed ginger root and their mind turns. They lay down their spears, they receive us well."* Nothing better expresses how close together lie festival and warfare.

Thurnwald describes with reference to another Melanesian tribe, with genealogical material, an actual event which shows just as clearly how these people pass in a group quite suddenly from a feast to a battle.* Buleau, a chief, had invited Bobal, another chief, and his people to a feast which was probably to be the first of a long series. Dances were performed all night long. By morning everyone was excited by the sleepless night of song and dance. On a remark made by Buleau one of Bobal's men killed him; and the troop of men massacred and pillaged and ran off with the women of the village. "Buleau and Bobal were more friends than rivals," they said to Thurnwald. We all have experience of events like this.

It is by opposing reason to emotion and setting up the will for peace against rash follies of this kind that peoples succeed in substituting alliance, gift and commerce for war, isolation and stagnation.

The research proposed would have some conclusion of this kind.[31] Societies have progressed in the measure in which they, their sub-groups and their members, have been able to stabilize their contracts and to give, receive and repay. In order to trade, man must first lay down his spear. When that is done he can succeed in exchanging goods and persons not only between clan and clan but

---

[30] Mauss refers to anthropologist Bronislaw Malinowski, best known for his work in the Trobriand Islands. We present an extract from Malinowski's *Argonauts of the Western Pacific (1922)* in essay 11. Richard Thurnwald (1869–1954), mentioned in the next paragraph, led research expeditions to the South Pacific in the early twentieth century. He was the founder of the journal *Sociologus* and a key voice in midcentury German anthropology.

[31] According to Durkheim's ideas about evolution, primitive mechanical solidarity gives way to modern organic solidarity. In this scheme, there is constant progress toward interdependence, and society reaches ever higher levels of integration. Rather than segments of society being opposed to each other in class warfare, as Marxist analysts claim, or engaged in a Malthusian struggle for survival, as Spencerians believed, every part of society should be seen as working for the peace and benefit of the whole.

Although Mauss and Durkheim believed that social evolution would be characterized by a progression of ever better social forms, Mauss' life was tragic. His mentor Durkheim died in 1917. Few of the members of *L'Année Sociologique,* many of whom were his close friends, survived World War I. When *The Gift* was published, in 1925, conditions in Europe were far from stable. These concluding paragraphs to *The Gift* must be read in this context. They are, at the same time, an affirmation of Durkheim's belief in progress and a plea for peace and harmony in the aftermath of war.

between tribe and tribe and nation and nation, and above all between individuals. It is only then that people can create, can satisfy their interests mutually and define them without recourse to arms. It is in this way that the clan, the tribe and nation have learnt—just as in the future the classes and nations and individuals will learn—how to oppose one another without slaughter and to give without sacrificing themselves to others. That is one of the secrets of their wisdom and solidarity.

There is no other course feasible. The *Chronicles of Arthur** relate how King Arthur, with the help of a Cornish carpenter, invented the marvel of his court, the miraculous Round Table at which his knights would never come to blows. Formerly because of jealousy, skirmishes, duels and murders had set blood flowing in the most sumptuous of feasts. The carpenter says to Arthur: "I will make thee a fine table, where sixteen hundred may sit at once, and from which none need be excluded . . . And no knight will be able to raise combat, for there the highly placed will be on the same level as the lowly." There was no "head of the table" and hence no more quarrels. Wherever

Arthur took his table, contented and invincible remained his noble company. And this today is the way of the nations that are strong, rich, good and happy. Peoples, classes, families and individuals may become rich, but they will not achieve happiness until they can sit down like the knights around their common riches. There is no need to seek far for goodness and happiness. It is to be found in the imposed peace, in the rhythm of communal and private labor, in wealth amassed and redistributed, in the mutual respect and reciprocal generosity that education can impart.

Thus we see how it is possible under certain circumstances to study total human behavior; and how that concrete study leads not only to a science of manners, a partial social science, but even to ethical conclusions—"civility," or "civics" as we say today. Through studies of this sort we can find, measure and assess the various determinants, aesthetic, moral, religious and economic, and the material and demographic factors, whose sum is the basis of society and constitutes the common life, and whose conscious direction is the supreme art—politics in the Socratic sense of the word.

---

7. *Class, Status, Party*

MAX WEBER (1864–1920)

I: ECONOMICALLY DETERMINED POWER AND THE SOCIAL ORDER[a]

Law exists when there is a probability that an order will be upheld by a specific staff of men who will use physical or psychical compulsion with the intention of obtaining conformity with the order, or of inflicting sanctions for infringement

of it. The structure of every legal order directly influences the distribution of power, economic or otherwise, within its respective community. This is true of all legal orders and not only that of the state. In general, we understand by "power" the chance of a man or of a number of men to realize their own will in a communal action even against the resistance of others who are participating in the action.[1]

From *Economy and Society* (1922)

---

[1] This essay was part of Weber's massive posthumous work, *Wirtschaft und Gesellschaft (Economy and Society)*. Probably written between 1915 and 1920, it was first published in 1922. *Wirtschaft und Gesellschaft* was one volume of an extensive series of studies in the social sciences that Weber organized for the German publishing house Siebeck. Much of Weber's work was written in response to Karl Marx (see essay 4), and the relationship between the

"Economically conditioned" power is not, of course, identical with "power" as such. On the contrary, the emergence of economic power may be the consequence of power existing on other grounds. Man does not strive for power only in order to enrich himself economically. Power, including economic power, may be valued "for its own sake." Very frequently the striving for power is also conditioned by the social "honor" it entails. Not all power, however, entails social honor: The typical American Boss, as well as the typical big speculator, deliberately relinquishes social honor. Quite generally, "mere economic" power, and especially "naked" money power, is by no means a recognized basis of social honor. Nor is power the only basis of social honor. Indeed, social honor, or prestige, may even be the basis of political or economic power, and very frequently has been. Power, as well as honor, may be guaranteed by the legal order, but, at least normally, it is not their primary source. The legal order is rather an additional factor that enhances the chance to hold power or honor; but it cannot always secure them.[2]

The way in which social honor is distributed in a community between typical groups participating in this distribution we may call the "social order." The social order and the economic order are, of course, similarly related to the "legal order."

However, the social and the economic order are not identical. The economic order is for us merely the way in which economic goods and services are distributed and used. The social order is of course conditioned by the economic order to a high degree, and in turn it reacts upon it.[3]

Now: "classes," "status groups," and "parties" are phenomena of the distribution of power within a community.

2: DETERMINATION OF CLASS-SITUATION BY MARKET-SITUATION

In our terminology, "classes" are not communities; they merely represent possible, and frequent, bases for communal action. We may speak of a "class" when (1) a number of people have in common a specific causal component of their life chances, in so far as (2) this component is represented exclusively by economic interests in the possession of goods and opportunities for income, and (3) is represented under the conditions of the commodity or labor markets.[4] [These points refer to "class situation," which we may express more briefly as the typical chance for a supply of goods, external living conditions, and personal life experiences, in so far as this chance

---

two is complex. The first section of the essay sets Weber's argument. In contrast to Marx, Weber insists that individual identity is not subsumed by class identity. Status and party may, and frequently do, cut across class membership. In this essay, he presents and discusses each of these forms of identity.

[2] Social thinkers and political activists (and Weber was both) in the Germany of Weber's time were extreme conservatives (generally members of the landowning upper class) or radicals who often espoused Marxist ideals (generally those identified with industrial workers). Weber—from a family whose wealth was based in textile manufacturing—identified with neither the conservative landowners nor the radical workers, but was a political liberal trying to sit midway between the two.

[3] Weber felt that Marx's methods of analysis produced valuable insights. However, he believed that they leaned

too heavily on economics and dialectical conflict between forces of production and relations of production as the motor driving social evolution. Weber incorporated much Marxist thought into his theories, yet he was not a Marxist and did not believe in a communist utopia. In the days of the cold war, this might have been a factor in his appeal to American sociologists and anthropologists.

[4] Weber's definition of class overlapped Marx's, yet differed from it. For Marx, class signified a specific relationship to the means of production. In a class society, one class has ownership or control of the means of production, and another is employed producing surplus for that owner class. Further, classes are born in the struggle for control of the means of production. For Marx, understanding the role of class was key to the analysis of society; all other identifications were secondary. Although focused on ownership of property as the constitutive element of class, Weber downplayed other elements of Marx's analysis. In

is determined by the amount and kind of power, or lack of such, to dispose of goods or skills for the sake of income in a given economic order. The term "class" refers to any group of people that is found in the same class situation.]

It is the most elemental economic fact that the way in which the disposition over material property is distributed among a plurality of people, meeting competitively in the market for the purpose of exchange, in itself creates specific life chances. According to the law of marginal utility this mode of distribution excludes the non-owners from competing for highly valued goods; it favors the owners and, in fact, gives to them a monopoly to acquire such goods. Other things being equal, this mode of distribution monopolizes the opportunities for profitable deals for all those who, provided with goods, do not necessarily have to exchange them. It increases, at least generally, their power in price wars with those who, being propertyless, have nothing to offer but their services in native form or goods in a form constituted through their own labor, and who above all are compelled to get rid of these products in order barely to subsist. This mode of distribution gives to the propertied a monopoly on the possibility of transferring property from the sphere of use as a "fortune," to the sphere of "capital goods"; that is, it gives them the entrepreneurial function and all chances to share directly or indirectly in returns on capital. All this holds true within the area in which pure market conditions prevail. "Property" and "lack of property" are, therefore, the basic categories of all class situations. It does not matter whether these two categories become effective in price wars or in competitive struggles.

Within these categories, however, class situations are further differentiated: on the one hand, according to the kind of property that is usable for returns; and, on the other hand, according to the kind of services that can be offered in the market. Ownership of domestic buildings; productive establishments; warehouses; stores; agriculturally usable land, large and small holdings—quantitative differences with possibly qualitative consequences—; ownership of mines; cattle; men (slaves); disposition over mobile instruments of production, or capital goods of all sorts, especially money or objects that can be exchanged for money easily and at any time; disposition over products of one's own labor or of others' labor differing according to their various distances from consumability; disposition over transferable monopolies of any kind—all these distinctions differentiate the class situations of the propertied just as does the "meaning" which they can and do give to the utilization of property, especially to property which has money equivalence. Accordingly, the propertied, for instance, may belong to the class of rentiers or to the class of entrepreneurs.

Those who have no property but who offer services are differentiated just as much according to their kinds of services as according to the way in which they make use of these services, in a continuous or discontinuous relation to a recipient. But always this is the generic connotation of the concept of class: that the kind of chance in the *market* is the decisive moment which presents a common condition for the individual's fate. "Class situation" is, in this sense, ultimately "market situation." The effect of naked possession *per se* which among cattle breeders gives the non-owning slave or serf into the power of the cattle owner, is only a forerunner of real "class" formation. However, in the cattle loan and in the naked severity of the law of debts in such communities, for the first time mere "possession" as such emerges as decisive for the fate of the individual.

---

particular, Weber suggested that class does not necessarily have analytic primacy—other elements of identity may be of equal or greater importance. Moreover, Weber gave conflict less of a role in generating and maintaining class relationships than Marx did. For Marx, this conflict was critical since it drove history (recall *The Communist Manifesto* [1972 {1848}:241]): "The history of all hitherto existing society is the history of class struggles"). For Weber, other forces are of much greater importance in social change. For example, Weber saw social evolution as a generalized process toward increased rationalization and bureaucratization that necessarily entailed the destruction of individual liberties. He believed that charisma acted in opposition to this force. Through strength of personality, the charismatic individual was able to break the bonds of routine and radically redirect society.

This is very much in contrast to the agricultural communities based on labor. The creditor-debtor relation becomes the basis of "class situations" only in those cities where a "credit market," however primitive, with rates of interest increasing according to the extent of dearth and a factual monopolization of credits, is developed by a plutocracy. Therewith "class struggles" begin.

Those men whose fate is not determined by the chance of using goods or services for themselves on the market, e.g., slaves, are not, however, a "class" in the technical sense of the term. They are, rather, a "status group."

3: COMMUNAL ACTION FLOWING FROM CLASS INTEREST

According to our terminology, the factor that creates "class" is unambiguously economic interest, and indeed, only those interests involved in the existence of the "market." Nevertheless, the concept of "class-interest" is an ambiguous one: even as an empirical concept it is ambiguous as soon as one understands by it something other than the factual direction of interests following with a certain probability from the class situation for a certain "average" of those people subjected to the class situation. The class situation and other circumstances remaining the same, the direction in which the individual worker, for instance, is likely to pursue his interests may vary widely, according to whether he is constitutionally qualified for the task at hand to a high, to an average, or to a low degree. In the same way, the direction of interests may vary according to whether or not a *communal* action of a larger or smaller portion of those commonly affected by the "class situation," or even an association among them, e.g., a "trade union," has

grown out of the class situation from which the individual may or may not expect promising results. [Communal action refers to that action which is oriented to the feeling of the actors that they belong together. Societal action, on the other hand, is oriented to a rationally motivated adjustment of interests.] The rise of societal or even of communal action from a common class situation is by no means a universal phenomenon.[5]

The class situation may be restricted in its effects to the generation of essentially *similar* reactions, that is to say, within our terminology, of "mass actions." However, it may not have even this result. Furthermore, often merely an amorphous communal action emerges. For example, the "murmuring" of the workers known in ancient oriental ethics: the moral disapproval of the work-master's conduct, which in its practical significance was probably equivalent to an increasingly typical phenomenon of precisely the latest industrial development, namely, the "slow down" (the deliberate limiting of work effort) of laborers by virtue of tacit agreement. The degree in which "communal action" and possibly "societal action," emerges from the "mass actions" of the members of a class is linked to general cultural conditions, especially to those of an intellectual sort. It is also linked to the extent of the contrasts that have already evolved, and is especially linked to the *transparency* of the connections between the causes and the consequences of the "class situation." For however different life chances may be, this fact in itself, according to all experience, by no means gives birth to "class action" (communal action by the members of a class). The fact of being conditioned and the results of the class situation must be distinctly recognizable.[6] For only then the contrast of life chances can be felt not as an absolutely given fact to be

---

[5] Underlying Weber's analysis is a concern for the issues of action and abstraction. For Weber, a class was an abstraction and therefore, in and of itself, could perform no action; thus the actions that flow from class interest were problematic. In order to act, any group must be organized. In this passage, Weber shows that the actions of classes must be mediated by individuals. However, individual variation within a class may be so great that it prevents the

emergence of any generalized class consciousness or class struggle. Parties and status groups, discussed below, play key roles in organizing classes.

[6] Like the Marxists, Weber saw ideology as frequently masking the true nature of relations among people. Society could be understood by debunking the myths and ideological assertions that often cover economically or

accepted, but as a resultant from either (1) the given distribution of property, or (2) the structure of the concrete economic order. It is only then that people may react against the class structure not only through acts of an intermittent and irrational protest, but in the form of rational association. There have been "class situations" of the first category (1), of a specifically naked and transparent sort, in the urban centers of Antiquity and during the Middle Ages; especially then, when great fortunes were accumulated by factually monopolized trading in industrial products of these localities or in foodstuffs.[7] Furthermore, under certain circumstances, in the rural economy of the most diverse periods, when agriculture was increasingly exploited in a profit-making manner. The most important historical example of the second category (2) is the class situation of the modern "proletariat."

4: TYPES OF CLASS STRUGGLE

Thus every class may be the carrier of any one of the possibly innumerable forms of "class action," but this is not necessarily so. In any case, a class does not in itself constitute a community. To treat "class" conceptually as having the same value as "community" leads to distortion. That men in the same class situation regularly react in mass actions to such tangible situations as economic ones in the direction of those interests that are most adequate to their average number is an important and after all simple fact for the understanding of historical events. Above all, this fact must not lead to that kind of pseudo-scientific operation with the concepts of "class" and "class interests" so frequently found these days and which has found its most classic expression in the statement of a talented author, that the individual may be in error concerning his interests but that the "class" is "infallible" about its interests.[8] Yet, if classes as such are not communities, nevertheless class situations emerge only on the basis of communalization. The communal action that brings forth class situations, however, is not basically action between members of the identical class; it is an action between members of different classes. Communal actions that directly determine the class situation of the worker and the entrepreneur are: the labor market, the commodities market, and the capitalistic enterprise. But, in its turn, the existence of a capitalistic enterprise presupposes that a very specific communal action exists and that it is specifically structured to protect the possession of goods *per se* and especially the power of individuals to dispose, in principle freely, over the means of production. The existence of a capitalistic enterprise is preconditioned by a specific kind of "legal order." Each kind of class situation, and above all when it rests upon the power of property *per se*, will become most clearly efficacious when all other determinants of reciprocal relations are, as far as possible,

---

politically motivated action. Here he suggests that in order for class action to take place, class consciousness must already exist. However, various ideological structures may prevent classes from becoming aware of the true nature of their oppression and hence prevent the formation of class consciousness.

[7] Although Weber wrote on India and China, by far his primary interest was European history and society, and most of his analysis was driven by his understanding of these. His original scholarly interest was in history, and he wrote his doctoral thesis on trading companies during the Middle Ages. He later wrote essays on the social structure of ancient society. He refers frequently to both the European Middle Ages and to ancient Greece and Rome throughout his writing.

[8] The talented author Weber refers to in this passage is, of course, Marx. The point here is to highlight his disagreement with the Marxists. Marxism is a theory of class and group action in which the individual plays little role. For Weber, on the other hand, individuals and their relationships to social groups were of great importance. For Marxists, conflict between social groups was the key force that drives history. Weber suggests that such conflict can only exist when classes and groups are organized under quite specific conditions. A class, in the example here, cannot be infallible about its interests because a class is an abstraction and cannot have interests outside of a very particular context. In this passage he illustrates some of the conditions under which class interests and struggle are likely to exist or historically did exist.

eliminated in their significance. It is in this way that the utilization of the power of property in the market obtains its most sovereign importance.

Now "status groups" hinder the strict carrying through of the sheer market principle. In the present context they are of interest to us only from this one point of view. Before we briefly consider them, note that not much of a general nature can be said about the more specific kinds of antagonism between "classes" (in our meaning of the term). The great shift, which has been going on continuously in the past, and up to our times, may be summarized, although at the cost of some precision: the struggle in which class situations are effective has progressively shifted from consumption credit toward, first, competitive struggles in the commodity market and, then, toward price wars on the labor market. The "class struggles" of antiquity—to the extent that they were genuine class struggles and not struggles between status groups—were initially carried on by indebted peasants, and perhaps also by artisans threatened by debt bondage and struggling against urban creditors. For debt bondage is the normal result of the differentiation of wealth in commercial cities, especially in seaport cities. A similar situation has existed among cattle breeders. Debt relationships as such produced class action up to the time of Cataline.[9] Along with this, and with an increase in provision of grain for the city by transporting it from the outside, the struggle over the means of sustenance emerged. It centered in the first place around the provision of bread and the determination of the price of bread. It lasted throughout antiquity and the entire Middle Ages. The propertyless as such flocked together against those who actually and supposedly were interested in the dearth of bread. This fight spread until it involved all those commodities essential to the way of life and to handicraft production. There were only incipient discussions of wage disputes in antiquity and in the Middle Ages. But they have been slowly increasing up into modern times. In the earlier periods they were completely secondary to slave rebellions as well as to fights in the commodity market.[10]

The propertyless of antiquity and of the Middle Ages protested against monopolies, preemption, forestalling, and the withholding of goods from the market in order to raise prices. Today the central issue is the determination of the price of labor.

This transition is represented by the fight for access to the market and for the determination of the price of products. Such fights went on between merchants and workers in the putting-out system of domestic handicraft during the transition to modern times. Since it is quite a general phenomenon we must mention here that the class antagonisms that are conditioned through the market situation are usually most bitter between those who actually and directly participate as opponents in price wars. It is not the rentier, the share-holder, and the banker who suffer the ill will of the worker, but almost exclusively the manufacturer and the business executives who are the direct opponents of workers in price wars. This is so in spite of the fact that it is precisely the cash boxes of the rentier, the share-holder, and the banker into which the more or less "unearned" gains flow, rather than into the pockets of the manufacturers or of the business executives.[11] This simple state of affairs has very frequently been decisive for the role the class situation has played in the formation of political parties. For example, it has made possible

---

[9] Cataline: Lucius Sergius Catilina (108–62 B.C.E.) was a soldier and politician in the Roman Republic.

[10] In this passage Weber presents a very rough outline of the history of European class struggles. Weber viewed sociology as the background information necessary to do history. The goal of his sociology was to propose general principles, but he believed that the actual unfolding of history was predicated on individual action and thus beyond any law. He wrote that "The reduction of empirical reality . . . to 'laws' is meaningless" and that "A systematic science of culture . . . would be senseless in itself" (quoted in Ritzer 1992:114). Franz Boas was probably quite familiar with Weber's work and had a similar understanding of the role of the individual. He, too, was suspicious of any attempt to make anthropology a science of culture based on the discovery of natural laws.

[11] Here Weber points out that class struggles are often misdirected, a significant critique of the Marxist view. If class struggles were truly between classes, owners such as rentiers, shareholders, and bankers should suffer the wrath of

the varieties of patriarchal socialism and the frequent attempts—formerly, at least—of threatened status groups to form alliances with the proletariat against the "bourgeoisie."

5: STATUS HONOR

In contrast to classes, *status groups* are normally communities.[12] They are, however, often of an amorphous kind. In contrast to the purely economically determined "class situation" we wish to designate as "status situation" every typical component of the life fate of men that is determined by a specific, positive or negative, social estimation of *honor*. This honor may be connected with any quality shared by a plurality, and, of course, it can be knit to a class situation: class distinctions are linked in the most varied ways with status distinctions. Property as such is not always recognized as a status qualification, but in the long run it is, and with extraordinary regularity. In the subsistence economy of the organized neighborhood, very often the richest man is simply the chieftain. However, this often means only an honorific preference. For example, in the so-called pure modern "democracy," that is, one devoid of any expressly ordered status privileges for individuals, it may be that only the families coming under approximately the same tax class dance with one another. This example is reported of certain smaller Swiss cities. But status honor need not necessarily be linked with a "class situation." On the contrary, it normally stands in sharp opposition to the pretensions of sheer property.

Both propertied and propertyless people can belong to the same status group, and frequently they do with very tangible consequences. This "equality" of social esteem may, however, in the long run become quite precarious. The "equality" of status among the American "gentlemen," for instance, is expressed by the fact that outside the subordination determined by the different functions of "business," it would be considered strictly repugnant—wherever the old tradition still prevails—if even the richest "chief," while playing billiards or cards in his club in the evening, would not treat his "clerk" as in every sense fully his equal in birthright. It would be repugnant if the American "chief" would bestow upon his "clerk" the condescending "benevolence" marking a distinction of "position," which the German chief can never dissever from his attitude. This is one of the most important reasons why in America the German "clubby-ness" has never been able to attain the attraction that the American clubs have.[13]

6: GUARANTEES OF STATUS STRATIFICATION

In content, status honor is normally expressed by the fact that above all else a specific *style of life* can be expected from all those who wish to belong to the circle. Linked with this expectation are restrictions on "social" intercourse (that is, intercourse which is not subservient to economic or any other of business's "functional" purposes). These restrictions may confine normal marriages

---

the working class as much as manufacturers and business executives. Weber claims, however, that they do not because they are less likely to be in direct contact with the workers.

[12] Above, Weber has described the operation of class within society. Here and below, he adds what he considers two other forces that cut across class identification and compete with it for prominence in social action: status and party. For Weber, class, status, and party are overlapping identifications. None of them has universal analytic priority, but rather identification with one or the other is dependent on circumstances. This idea of overlapping

identities anticipates much of current interpretive and postmodern anthropology.

[13] Weber's 1904 visit to America made a profound and lasting impression on him. Though greatly disturbed by the position of African Americans and immigrants, in many respects he viewed America as, for better and worse, the model of a new society. He felt that in America, rationalization and bureaucratization had proceeded to the greatest extent. The example of boss and worker treating each other as equals may appear fanciful to the modern reader, but for Weber, it illustrated the compartmentalization and bureaucratization of American life.

to within the status circle and may lead to complete endogamous closure. As soon as there is not a mere individual and socially irrelevant imitation of another style of life, but an agreed-upon communal action of this closing character, the "status" development is under way.

In its characteristic form, stratification by "status groups" on the basis of conventional styles of life evolves at the present time in the United States out of the traditional democracy.[14] For example, only the resident of a certain street ("the street") is considered as belonging to "society," is qualified for social intercourse, and is visited and invited. Above all, this differentiation evolves in such a way as to make for strict submission to the fashion that is dominant at a given time in society. This submission to fashion also exists among men in America to a degree unknown in Germany. Such submission is considered to be an indication of the fact that a given man *pretends* to qualify as a gentleman. This submission decides, at least *prima facie*,[15] that he will be treated as such. And this recognition becomes just as important for his employment chances in "swank" establishments, and above all, for social intercourse and marriage with "esteemed" families, as the qualification for dueling among Germans in the Kaiser's day. As for the rest: certain families resident for a long time, and, of course, correspondingly wealthy, e.g., "F.F.V., i.e., First Families of Virginia," or the actual or alleged descendants of the "Indian Princess" Pocahontas, of the Pilgrim fathers, or of the

Knickerbockers,[16] the members of almost inaccessible sects and all sorts of circles setting themselves apart by means of any other characteristics and badges . . . all these elements usurp "status" honor. The development of status is essentially a question of stratification resting upon usurpation. Such usurpation is the normal origin of almost all status honor. But the road from this purely conventional situation to legal privilege, positive or negative, is easily traveled as soon as a certain stratification of the social order has in fact been "lived in" and has achieved stability by virtue of a stable distribution of economic power.

7: "ETHNIC" SEGREGATION AND "CASTE"

Where the consequences have been realized to their full extent, the status group evolves into a closed "caste."[17] Status distinctions are then guaranteed not merely by conventions and laws, but also by *rituals*. This occurs in such a way that every physical contact with a member of any caste that is considered to be "lower" by the members of a "higher" caste is considered as making for a ritualistic impurity and to be a stigma which must be expiated by a religious act. Individual castes develop quite distinct cults and gods.

In general, however, the status structure reaches such extreme consequences only where there are underlying differences which are held to be "ethnic." The "caste" is, indeed, the normal

---

[14] Although Weber recognized a link between economic position and status, he also believed that there were many other ways to acquire status. The examples he uses here are drawn from American society but reflect the extremely status-conscious German society. Weber himself came from a family of factory owners. He had trained in law at Heidelberg and been a member of his father's prestigious dueling fraternity. He had scars from the dueling he refers to in this passage. After his studies and a year of military training, he was commissioned as an officer in the German army.

[15] *Prima facie:* Latin for "at first sight."

[16] *Knickerbockers* refers to descendants of the Dutch settlers of New York.

[17] Weber developed his notions of caste more fully in his work on the Indian caste system, but he clearly believed the term *caste* applied to a wide variety of social systems. He spends a good deal of time discussing caste here because he sees it as an extreme manifestation of status differences. One of Weber's contributions to sociology is the idea of the ideal type, a "one-sided accentuation of one or more points of view" (1999 [orig 1904]: 248). Weber uses *ideal* in the sense of the most extreme logical possibility rather than in the sense of best. He looked for, or logically constructed, extreme examples to gain insight into more typical social forms. Although the use of ideal types provides clear examples amenable to analysis, it may also obscure the complexity of social life.

form in which ethnic communities usually live side by side in a "societalized" manner. These ethnic communities believe in blood relationship and exclude exogamous marriage and social intercourse. Such a caste situation is part of the phenomenon of "pariah" peoples and is found all over the world. These people form communities, acquire specific occupational traditions of handicrafts or of other arts, and cultivate a belief in their ethnic community. They live in a "diaspora" strictly segregated from all personal intercourse, except that of an unavoidable sort, and their situation is legally precarious. Yet, by virtue of their economic indispensability, they are tolerated, indeed, frequently privileged, and they live in interspersed political communities. The Jews are the most impressive historical example.

A "status" segregation grown into a "caste" differs in its structure from a mere "ethnic" segregation: the caste structure transforms the horizontal and unconnected coexistences of ethnically segregated groups into a vertical social system of super- and subordination. Correctly formulated: a comprehensive societalization integrates the ethnically divided communities into specific political and communal action.[18] In their consequences they differ precisely in this way: ethnic coexistences condition a mutual repulsion and disdain but allow each ethnic community to consider its own honor as the highest one; the caste structure brings about a social subordination and an acknowledgment of "more honor" in favor of the privileged caste and status groups. This is due to the fact that in the caste structure ethnic distinctions as such have become "functional" distinctions within the political societalization (warriors, priests, artisans that are politically im-

portant for war and for building, and so on). But even pariah people who are most despised are usually apt to continue cultivating in some manner that which is equally peculiar to ethnic and to status communities: the belief in their own specific "honor." This is the case with the Jews.

Only with the negatively privileged status groups does the "sense of dignity" take a specific deviation. A sense of dignity is the precipitation in individuals of social honor and of conventional demands which a positively privileged status group raises for the deportment of its members. The sense of dignity that characterizes positively privileged status groups is naturally related to their "being" which does not transcend itself, that is, it is to their "beauty and excellence" ($\kappa\alpha\lambda o\kappa\dot\alpha\gamma\alpha\vartheta\iota\alpha$). Their kingdom is "of this world." They live for the present and by exploiting their great past. The sense of dignity of the negatively privileged strata naturally refers to a future lying beyond the present, whether it is of this life or of another. In other words, it must be nurtured by the belief in a providential "mission" and by a belief in a specific honor before God. The "chosen people's" dignity is nurtured by a belief either that in the beyond "the last will be the first," or that in this life a Messiah will appear to bring forth into the light of the world which has cast them out the hidden honor of the pariah people. This simple state of affairs, and not the "resentment" which is so strongly emphasized in Nietzsche's much admired construction in the *Genealogy of Morals*, is the source of the religiosity cultivated by pariah status groups. In passing, we may note that resentment may be accurately applied only to a limited extent; for one of Nietzsche's main examples, Buddhism, it is not at all applicable.[19]

---

[18] Notice Weber's use of the words *society* and *societalization*. He theorized that there were three basic types of social structure: the community, the association, and the society (Gerth and Mills 1946:57). To some degree, he understood history as a progression from community to society, with society marked by increased rationalization and bureaucratization. In Weber's usage, society is what modern anthropologists might refer to as state-level society. For Weber, when a group became societalized, it also became bureaucratized.

[19] The work of Friedrich Wilhelm Nietzsche (1844–1900) was extremely influential for German social thinkers of the late nineteenth century. He was concerned, among other things, with the benefit that people gained from holding certain types of ideas. Simply put, his resentment theory (from *On the Genealogy of Morals* [1967 {1887}]) states that, because they cannot bear the psychological burden of low position, oppressed people turn the characteristics of their subjugation into sources of honor. Thus, Nietzsche believed that ascetic Christian morality

Incidentally, the development of status groups from ethnic segregations is by no means the normal phenomenon. On the contrary, since objective "racial differences" are by no means basic to every subjective sentiment of an ethnic community, the ultimately racial foundation of status structure is rightly and absolutely a question of the concrete individual case.[20] Very frequently a status group is instrumental in the production of a thoroughbred anthropological type. Certainly a status group is to a high degree effective in producing extreme types, for they select personally qualified individuals (e.g., the Knighthood selects those who are fit for warfare, physically and psychically). But selection is far from being the only, or the predominant, way in which status groups are formed: Political membership or class situation has at all times been at least as frequently decisive. And today the class situation is by far the predominant factor, for of course the possibility of a style of life expected for members of a status group is usually conditioned economically.

8: STATUS PRIVILEGES

For all practical purposes, stratification by status goes hand in hand with a monopolization of ideal and material goods or opportunities, in a manner we have come to know as typical.[21] Besides the specific status honor, which always rests upon distance and exclusiveness, we find all sorts of material monopolies. Such honorific preferences may consist of the privilege of wearing special costumes, of eating special dishes taboo to others, of carrying arms—which is most obvious in its consequences—the right to pursue certain non-professional dilettante artistic practices, e.g., to play certain musical instruments. Of course, material monopolies provide the most effective motives for the exclusiveness of a status group; although, in themselves, they are rarely sufficient, almost always they come into play to some extent. Within a status circle there is the question of intermarriage: the interest of the families in the monopolization of potential bridegrooms is at least of equal importance and is parallel to the interest in the monopolization of daughters. The daughters of the circle must be provided for. With an increased enclosure of the status group, the conventional preferential opportunities for special employment grow into a legal monopoly of special offices for the members. Certain goods become objects for monopolization by status groups. In the typical fashion these include "entailed estates" and frequently also the possessions of serfs or bondsmen and, finally, special trades. This monopolization occurs positively when the status group is exclusively entitled to own and to manage them; and negatively when, in order to maintain its specific way of life, the status group must *not* own and manage them.

The decisive role of a "style of life" in status "honor" means that status groups are the specific bearers of all "conventions."[22] In whatever way it may be manifest, all "stylization" of life either

---

reflected the resentment of early Christians who were often slaves (Gerth and Mills 1946:62). Although Weber is concerned with individual psychology, he understands the attribution of elevated moral status to oppressed peoples as a group function—one that maintains the status differentials of the caste system—rather than as an individual psychological coping mechanism. Weber probably considered resentment theory inapplicable to Buddhism because that religion's founder, the Indian prince Siddhartha Gautama (563?–483? B.C.E.), was a man of high status.

[20] Note that Weber argues that caste groups may be separated by perceived racial distinctions but are not *created* by these. Rather, differential status may, in time, create distinctions that are then *perceived* as racial. This is a fairly radical point.

[21] Weber suggests that while economic privileges are frequently one important aspect of status, they are rarely sufficient to explain stratification. Other, less material privileges may well be more important.

[22] In his emphasis on consumption as a marker of status, Weber may have been strongly influenced by the economic and social theorist Thorstein Veblen (1857–1929). Veblen's *The Theory of the Leisure Class* (1912 [1899]) suggested that there was a conflict between making goods and making money: Moneyed classes increasingly freed themselves from any involvement in labor. Weber expands on this topic in the section below.

originates in status groups or is at least conserved by them. Even if the principles of status conventions differ greatly, they reveal certain typical traits, especially among those strata which are most privileged. Quite generally, among privileged status groups there is a status disqualification that operates against the performance of common physical labor. This disqualification is now "setting in" in America against the old tradition of esteem for labor. Very frequently every rational economic pursuit, and especially "entrepreneurial activity," is looked upon as a disqualification of status. Artistic and literary activity is also considered as degrading work as soon as it is exploited for income, or at least when it is connected with hard physical exertion. An example is the sculptor working like a mason in his dusty smock as over against the painter in his salon-like "studio" and those forms of musical practice that are acceptable to the status group.

9: ECONOMIC CONDITIONS AND EFFECTS OF STATUS STRATIFICATION

The frequent disqualification of the gainfully employed as such is a direct result of the principle of status stratification peculiar to the social order, and of course, of this principle's opposition to a distribution of power which is regulated exclusively through the market. These two factors operate along with various individual ones, which will be touched upon below.

We have seen above that the market and its processes "knows no personal distinctions": "functional" interests dominate it. It knows nothing of "honor." The status order means precisely the reverse, viz.: stratification in terms of "honor" and of styles of life peculiar to status groups as such. If mere economic acquisition and naked economic power still bearing the stigma of its extra-status origin could bestow upon anyone who has won it the same honor as those who are interested in status by virtue of style of life claim for themselves, the status order would be threatened at its very root. This is the more so as, given equality of status honor, property *per se* represents an addition even if it is not overtly acknowledged to be such. Yet if such economic acquisition and power gave the agent any honor at all, his wealth would result in his attaining more honor than those who successfully claim honor by virtue of style of life. Therefore all groups having interests in the status order react with special sharpness precisely against the pretensions of purely economic acquisition. In most cases they react the more vigorously the more they feel themselves threatened.[23] Calderon's respectful treatment of the peasant, for instance, as opposed to Shakespeare's simultaneous and ostensible disdain of the *canaille* illustrates the different way in which a firmly structured status order reacts as compared with a status order that has become economically precarious.[24] This is an example of a state of affairs that recurs everywhere. Precisely because of the rigorous reactions against the claims of property *per se* the "parvenu"[25] is never accepted, personally and without reservation, by the privileged status groups, no matter how completely his style of life has been adjusted to theirs. They will only accept his descendants who have been educated in the conventions of their status group and who have never besmirched its honor by their own economic labor.

As to the general *effect* of the status order, only one consequence can be stated, but it is a very important one: the hindrance of the free development of the market occurs first for those

---

[23] To a modern American reader, this passage may sound terribly anachronistic. For most of us, enormous wealth is likely to confer status almost instantly. In Weber's nineteenth-century world, quick wealth was often considered tainted, and the old rich had little respect for those who acquired their money more recently. To Weber—member of a dueling society, officer, and nationalist—

honor and the acquisition of status played a role that is, for most of us today, quite alien.

[24] *Calderon* refers to Spanish playwright Pedro Calderon de la Barca (1600–1681). A *canaille* is a mob.

[25] *Parvenu:* people with manners that ill-fit their newfound wealth.

goods which status groups directly withheld from free exchange by monopolization.[26] This monopolization may be effected either legally or conventionally. For example, in many Hellenic cities during the epoch of status groups, and also originally in Rome, the inherited estate (as is shown by the old formula for indiction against spendthrifts) was monopolized just as were the estates of knights, peasants, priests, and especially the clientele of the craft and merchant guilds. The market is restricted, and the power of naked property *per se* which gives its stamp to "class formation," is pushed into the background. The results of this process can be most varied. Of course, they do not necessarily weaken the contrasts in the economic situation. Frequently they strengthen these contrasts, and in any case, where stratification by status permeates a community as strongly as was the case in all political communities of antiquity and of the Middle Ages, one can never speak of a genuinely free market competition as we understand it today. There are wider effects than this direct exclusion of special goods from the market. From the contrariety between the status order and the purely economic order mentioned above, it follows that in most instances the notion of honor peculiar to status absolutely abhors that which is essential to the market: higgling. Honor abhors higgling among peers and occasionally it taboos higgling for the members of a status group in general. Therefore, everywhere some status groups, and usually the most influential, consider almost any kind of overt participation in economic acquisition as absolutely stigmatizing.

With some over-simplification, one might thus say that "classes" are stratified according to their relations to the production and acquisition of goods; whereas "status groups" are stratified according to the principles of their *consumption* of goods as represented by special "styles of life."

An "occupational group" is also a status group. For normally, it successfully claims social honor only by virtue of the special style of life which may be determined by it. The differences between classes and status groups frequently overlap. It is precisely those status communities most strictly segregated in terms of honor (viz. the Indian castes) who today show, although within very rigid limits, a relatively high degree of indifference to pecuniary income. However, the Brahmins seek such income in many different ways.

As to the general economic conditions making for the predominance of stratification by "status," only very little can be said.[27] When the bases of the acquisition and distribution of goods are relatively stable, stratification by status is favored. Every technological repercussion and economic transformation threatens stratification by status and pushes the class situation into the foreground. Epochs and countries in which the naked class situation is of predominant significance are regularly the periods of technical and economic transformations. And every slowing down of the shifting of economic stratifications leads, in due course, to the growth of status structures and makes for a resuscitation of the important role of social honor.

10: PARTIES

Whereas the genuine place of "classes" is within the economic order, the place of "status groups" is within the social order, that is, within the sphere of the distribution of "honor." From within these spheres, classes and status groups influence one another and they influence the legal order and are in turn influenced by it. But "parties" live in a house of "power."

Their action is oriented toward the acquisition of social "power," that is to say, toward influencing a communal action no matter what its content may be. In principle, parties may exist in a social "club" as well as in a "state." As over

---

[26] In this paragraph, Weber provides a concise summary of his understanding of class and status.

[27] Compare the conception of change here with Marx's understanding of change caused by conflict between classes. In both cases, conflict between ideological superstructure and technological base plays a crucial role.

against the actions of classes and status groups, for which this is not necessarily the case, the communal actions of "parties" always mean a societalization. For party actions are always directed toward a goal which is striven for in planned manner. This goal may be a "cause" (the party may aim at realizing a program for ideal or material purposes), or the goal may be "personal" (sinecures, power, and from these, honor for the leader and the followers of the party). Usually the party action aims at all these simultaneously. Parties are, therefore, only possible within communities that are societalized, that is, which have some rational order and a staff of persons available who are ready to enforce it. For parties aim precisely at influencing this staff, and if possible, to recruit it from party followers.[28]

In any individual case, parties may represent interests determined through "class situation" or "status situation," and they may recruit their following respectively from one or the other. But they need be neither purely "class" nor purely "status" parties. In most cases they are partly class parties and partly status parties, but sometimes they are neither.[29] They may represent ephemeral or enduring structures. Their means of attaining power may be quite varied, ranging from naked violence of any sort to canvassing for votes with coarse or subtle means: money, social influence, the force of speech, suggestion, clumsy hoax, and so on to the rougher or more artful tactics of obstruction in parliamentary bodies.

The sociological structure of parties differs in a basic way according to the kind of communal action which they struggle to influence. Parties also differ according to whether or not the community is stratified by status or by classes. Above all else, they vary according to the structure of domination within the community. For their leaders normally deal with the conquest of a community. They are, in the general concept which is maintained here, not only products of specially modern forms of domination. We shall also designate as parties the ancient and medieval "parties," despite the fact that their structure differs basically from the structure of modern parties. By virtue of these structural differences of domination it is impossible to say anything about the structure of parties without discussing the structural forms of social domination *per se*. Parties, which are always structures struggling for domination, are very frequently organized in a very strict "authoritarian" fashion.

Concerning "classes," "status groups," and "parties," it must be said in general that they necessarily presuppose a comprehensive societalization, and especially a political framework of communal action, within which they operate. This does not mean that parties would be confined by the frontiers of any individual political community. On the contrary, at all times it has been the order of the day that the societalization (even when it aims at the use of military force in common) reaches beyond the frontier of politics.[30] This has been the case in the solidarity of interests among the oligarchs and among the democrats in Hellas, among the Guelfs and among Ghibellines in the Middle Ages, and within the Calvinist party during the period of religious struggles.[31] It has been the case up to the solidarity of the landlords

---

[28] Weber understood parties very broadly as any group committed to using power to achieve a certain goal. Thus, his understanding of party was not limited to official state political parties. For Weber, two things separated parties from classes and status groups: They existed to pursue power, and they strove to achieve a specific goal or cause. These gave them much more definite shape than Weber perceives in either class or status groups.

[29] Just as class and status sometimes coincide, party may as well. However, such overlapping cannot be assumed. Class, status, and party are often different and contradictory institutions.

[30] Weber's description of parties reaching across political communities must be considered in the context of the debate between Weber and the Marxists. Communist parties of Weber's era were aimed precisely at political action across international boundaries. Unlike the Marxists, Weber does not view these parties as historically unique and is equivocal about their chances for success.

[31] Hellas refers to classical Greece. The Guelfs and the Ghibellines were the major political factions of twelfth- and thirteenth-century Italy. The Guelfs defeated the Ghibellines in 1268.

(international congress of agrarian landlords) and has continued among princes (holy alliance, Karlsbad decrees), socialist workers, conservatives (the longing of Prussian conservatives for Russian intervention in 1850). But their aim is not necessarily the establishment of new international political, i.e., *territorial,* dominion. In the main they aim to influence the existing dominion.

[The posthumously published text breaks off here. We omit an incomplete sketch of types of "warrior estates."]

NOTE

[a] *Wirtschaft und Gesellschaft,* part III, chap. 4, pp. 631–40. The first sentence in paragraph one and the several definitions in this chapter that are in brackets do not appear in the original text. They have been taken from other contexts of *Wirtschaft und Gesellschaftbb.*

Part Two

CULTURE THEORY IN THE EARLY
TWENTIETH CENTURY

Historical Particularism

A great deal of ethnographic writing took place in late nineteenth-century America. We have already discussed the anthropological theorist Lewis Henry Morgan, who published his major works between 1851 and 1881 (see essay 3). In addition to Morgan, early ethnologists such as Alice Fletcher (1838–1923) were actively pursuing ethnographic investigations. The Bureau of American Ethnology (BAE) together with the Smithsonian Institution also sponsored the work of many scholars, including Otis Mason (1838–1908), James Mooney (1861–1921), and Frank Cushing (1857–1900). The BAE was a division of the Smithsonian created in 1879 to organize anthropological research in America. Its first director was John Wesley Powell (1834–1902), better known as the explorer of the Grand Canyon. Despite this variety of anthropological activity, it was not until the turn of the twentieth century that anthropology coalesced as an academic discipline in America. When it did, the ideas of a single individual, Franz Boas (1858–1942), had enormous impact. The method of research Boas pioneered, later labeled *historical particularism,* is widely considered the first American-born school of anthropological thought, and he is considered one of the founders of American anthropology.

Boas was born to a secular and intellectual German Jewish family. His father was a merchant of liberal political views and his mother a radical freethinker, the founder of a kindergarten devoted to the "consciousness of mutual interdependence" in children (Frank 1997:733). Boas described his home as a place in which "the ideals

of the revolution of 1848 were a living force (1974 [1938]:41)." His upbringing emphasized the freedom, dignity, and fundamental equality of all peoples, and Boas remained deeply devoted to these ideas throughout his life.

Boas' education emphasized the physical sciences of his day. After graduating from gymnasium in 1877, he went first to the University of Heidelberg, then to Bonn, and finally to Kiel, where he received his Ph.D. His examination subjects were geography, physics, and philosophy, and his dissertation was titled *Contribution to the Understanding of the Color of Water.* Although his training emphasized quantitative data, he later wrote that these studies caused him to realize that "there are domains of our experience in which the concepts of quantity . . . are not applicable" (1974 [1938]:42). Although Boas believed in a science of anthropology, he recognized a distinction between the social and natural sciences.

As a Jewish liberal, Boas had few opportunities for academic employment in late nineteenth-century Germany and, by 1882, he had begun contemplating immigration to the United States. In 1883, he seized an opportunity to do research on migration patterns and seawater among the Eskimo on Baffin Island. Boas spent fifteen months in "the sublime loneliness of the arctic" (quoted in Stocking 1974:22), and the experience changed him from a geographer to an ethnographer. Living among the Eskimo convinced him that the liberal and humanistic values of his childhood could be applied to the study of human society.

Not long before Boas left for Baffin Island, he had become engaged to Marie Krackoweiser. During his fieldwork, he kept a diary in the form of a single long letter to her. In an oft-quoted passage written on December 23, 1883, he wrote:

> I believe, if this trip has for me (as a thinking person) a valuable influence, it lies in the strengthening of the viewpoint of the relativity of all cultivation and that the evil as well as the value of a person lies in the cultivation of the heart, which I find or do not find here just as much as amongst us, and that all service, therefore, which a man can perform for humanity must serve to promote truth. (quoted in Cole 1983)

A month later, on January 22, 1884, he wrote:

> I do not want a German professorship because I know I would be restricted to my science and to teaching, for which I have little inclination. I should much prefer to live in America in order to be able to further those ideas for which I live. . . . What I want to live and die for, is equal rights for all, equal possibilities to learn and work for poor and rich alike! Don't you believe that to have done even the smallest bit for this, is more than all science taken together? (quoted in Cole 1983)

After spending the winter of 1884–1885 in New York, Boas returned to Germany in 1885 to take positions at the Berlin Ethnological Museum (the *Musuum fur Volkenkunde*) and the University of Berlin. However, he soon left Germany once more, this time to visit the Kwakiutl and other tribes on Northern Vancouver Island in Canada, groups he was to study for the rest of his life. In 1886, after a brief return to Germany, he decided to immigrate to the United States.

His first position in America was at Clark University, where he taught from 1888 to 1892. Boas left Clark during a faculty strike in 1892 and accepted a job with the Columbian Exposition of 1893, a fair held in Chicago to celebrate the four-hundredth anniversary of Columbus' arrival in America. The Field Museum of Anthropology grew out of this exhibition. Boas briefly served as the curator of anthropology there but left after quarreling with the museum's administration. In 1896 he moved to Columbia University as a lec-turer in physical anthropology and in 1899 became a professor of anthropology. Boas spent the rest of his career at Columbia. He retired in 1936 but remained extremely active in anthropology until his death six years later.

Boas began his career at a time when anthropology was not recognized as a science or even as a field of university study. With his training in the physical sciences, he brought a rigorous approach to ethnographic fieldwork. Boas' emphasis on the careful collection of ethnographic data and his rejection of nineteenth-century evolutionary theories in favor of ethnographic field experience were, in part, a reaction to the uncritical use of the comparative method by the unilineal evolutionists of his day.

Though Boas recognized that humans and other primates shared common ancestry, he was also deeply influenced by Rudolph Virchow, one of his mentors, who was skeptical of Darwinian evolution. Boas seems never to have fully understood or accepted the Darwinian process of natural selection (Caspari 2003:68). Boas strongly repudiated the social Darwinism and evolutionary speculation of his day. These beliefs may have influenced his views of natural selection. In fact, his famous study of changing head size among immigrants and their children (1912) was more Lamarckian than Darwinian. According to Boas, children, because they had better nutrition, had larger head sizes than their immigrant parents. Thus they had acquired a trait that might be passed to future generations.

Boas maintained that the sweeping generalizations of the unilineal social evolutionists were not scientifically valid. He based much of his attack on the distinction between convergent and parallel evolution. Evolutionists assumed that similar cultural traits were the result of parallel development driven by universal evolutionary law. Boas showed that it was possible for the same characteristics to come about through different processes. In "The Limitations of the Comparative Method in Anthropology" (1896), he demonstrated that cultures may have similar traits for a variety of reasons, including diffusion and trade. Corresponding environments or historical accident may produce similar cultural traits independent of any universal evolutionary process. Thus, the existence of such traits could not be used as evidence for universal stages of cultural evolution.

Boas believed that to explain cultural customs, one must examine them from three fundamental perspectives: the environmental conditions under which they developed, psychological factors, and historical connections. Of these, the third was the most important. He felt that societies were created by their own historical circumstances. Thus the best explanations of cultural phenomena were to be acquired by studying the historical development of the societies in which they were found. Because Boas focused on the specific histories of individual societies, his approach to anthropology is called historical particularism, although he never used this label. It was coined by Marvin Harris in the 1960s.

Boas advocated a four-field perspective that included studying prehistory, linguistics, and physical anthropology in addition to the observation of culture. This idea shaped the anthropology department Boas created at Columbia and the departments his students founded at other universities. The hallmark of Boasian-style anthropology became the intensive study of specific cultures through long periods of fieldwork. Boas argued that it was only through living with a people and learning their language that one could develop an accurate understanding of a culture.

Boas and his students were driven by the belief that "primitive" societies were rapidly disappearing. In particular, the situation of Native Americans, forced onto reservations and their populations decimated, gave Boas and his students a sense of urgency. They believed that if these cultures were not recorded immediately, knowledge of them would be lost entirely. The sense that anthropology was an urgent salvage operation conditioned much of the theory and method in American anthropology and caused it to develop in a very different direction than anthropology in Britain and France.

Boas also pioneered the concept that has become known as *cultural relativism*. He himself never used the term, which was coined in the 1950s, but, like historical particularism, it accurately describes his position. As we have noted

above, cultural evolutionists had argued that all societies were following the same path of development from savagery to civilization. If this was so, then it was perfectly reasonable to say that some societies were more or less advanced, more or less savage than others. Boas rejected parallel evolution and argued that societies were the result of their own unique histories. If this was the case, then there could be no universal yardstick by which to judge them. Their traits were the result of their historical and environmental circumstance and could only be understood within that context. Consequently, terms such as *primitive, inferior,* and *superior* could not apply.

Because Boas discredited the unilineal evolutionary schemes popular in his day and insisted that societies were the result of their particular histories and could not be compared, he is often perceived as antitheoretical. Some of Boas' students argued that this was not the case; he recognized the need for new theoretical perspectives but believed that more general theories of human behavior would become obvious once enough data had been collected (for example, see Lesser 1981). However, it is clear that Boas was uninterested in theory building, and the central tenet of historical particularism, that cultures are primarily the result of their unique histories, is inimical to any general theory of culture.

Though he did not leave a coherent theory, Boas had a profound effect on the development of anthropology. He almost single-handedly trained the first generation of American anthropologists and directed their initial field studies. Individuals such as Alfred Louis Kroeber (1876–1960), Robert Lowie (1883–1957), Edward Sapir (1884–1939), Margaret Mead (1901–1978), Melville Herskovits (1895–1963), Paul Radin (1883–1959), Ruth Fulton Benedict (1887–1948), Clark Wissler (1870–1947), Ashley Montagu (1905–1999), and many others, were his students. Several of these researchers have works that appear or are mentioned later in this text.

In addition to training students, Boas lived his life as a citizen scientist, true to the ideals he had expressed in his Baffin Island letter-diary. He was an indefatigable campaigner for justice, equality, and the rights of individuals. He spoke out against World War I and the xenophobia and jingoism the war had triggered in America. A staunch champion of the rights of immigrants and African Americans, he fought against the poll tax, racial discrimination, the intimidation of teachers in colleges and high schools, and the rise of Nazism in Europe.

In particular, Boas was deeply involved in the early years of the NAACP. He contributed the lead article for the second issue of that organization's journal, *The Crisis*, and spoke out on the subject of race and racism repeatedly throughout his life. Boas died in 1942 at a luncheon in honor of Paul Rivet, a founder of French anthropology, whose escape from Nazi-occupied France Boas had championed. Rivet reported that Boas' last words were, "One must never tire of repeating that racism is a monstrous error or an impudent lie" (in Lewis 2001:456).

Boas and his students dominated American anthropology from about 1911 until after World War II (Stocking 1992:117), but he was not unopposed. In the late nineteenth century, anthropology in America was controlled by scholars from Harvard (sometimes called the Maya Group, after their interest in Mayan Studies) and the Smithsonian (called the Washington Group). Academics from these institutions, drawn largely from old WASP families, subscribed to programs of evolutionary anthropology. Many were devoted to race-science attempts to prove the superiority of Northern Europeans. Anthropologists in the Maya and Washington Groups objected to Boas and his students, most of whom were either immigrants themselves or the sons and daughters of immigrants, and many of whom were Jewish. They opposed Boas' notions of cultural relativism and racial equality. Boas' most virulent enemies were members of the anthropology division of the National Research Council (an organization founded to promote American aims in World War I) and the Galton Society, which promoted racial science and eugenics. Key members of both organizations included Charles B. Davenport (1866–1944), Madison Grant (1865–1937), and Ales Hrdlicka (1869–1943) (Stocking 1968:289).

Boas was also deeply disturbed by the race-based anthropology practiced by physical anthro-

pologists in the late nineteenth and early twentieth centuries. Virchow taught Boas anthropometrics, or techniques of human measurement, which he later put to use in his studies, debunking the notion that race was a factor in cultural development (Caspari 2003:68).

Boas' conflicts with other anthropologists over cultural relativism, racism, eugenics, and opposition to immigrants were intensified by his pacifism and opposition to World War I. In 1919, Boas wrote a letter to *The Nation* castigating unnamed anthropologists for working as spies for the American government. He wrote that such actions undermined belief in the "truthfulness of science" and "raised a new barrier" against international scientific cooperation (quoted in Stocking 1968:274). In addition, he called President Woodrow Wilson a hypocrite. The letter brought a series of old grievances and resentments against Boas to the surface at the American Anthropological Association (AAA) meeting ten days after its publication. The Harvard and Smithsonian anthropologists moved successfully to have Boas censured by the AAA and stripped of membership in its governing council; he was also pressured to resign from the National Research Council (Stocking 1968:273). Despite these setbacks, Boas and his students already controlled key positions in anthropology departments around the country and were the most important group of scholars shaping the direction of American anthropology. Although the place of Boas and his students in American anthropology was assured by the 1920s, the AAA censure of Boas stood for ninety-six years. In 2005, by a vote of 1245 to 73, the organization finally rescinded and repudiated its 1919 motion of censure.

Next to Boas, the most influential figure in American anthropology during the first half of the last century was A. L. Kroeber. Kroeber was the first of Boas' students at Columbia to receive a doctorate in anthropology, which he earned in 1901. In that same year, Kroeber was hired by the University of California at Berkeley. At the age of twenty-five, he became the first instructor in the newly created anthropology program and the curator for the university's museum of anthropology. Kroeber stayed at Berkeley for the rest of his career, retiring in 1946. He stayed active in research and writing until his death in 1960.

Throughout his life Kroeber maintained a Boasian perspective. Both Kroeber and Boas were antievolutionists, believed in integrating the four subfields of anthropology, and taught that a historical perspective was necessary to understand other cultures. However, Kroeber split from Boas over two critical issues. Their first disagreement concerned Kroeber's rejection of Boas' idea that anthropology was ultimately a discipline devoted to the study of humankind's origins. Their second disagreement is more significant to contemporary anthropology. Boas believed that individuals played a significant role in a culture's development and change. Kroeber argued that this was not the case, adopting a view of culture very close to that expressed by the French sociologist Émile Durkheim (see essays 5 and 6). The Kroeber essay we have chosen for this volume consists of a series of statements or "professions" about the nature of anthropology. Kroeber argues that although culture came from and is carried by human beings, it cannot be reduced to individual psychology. He maintains that culture is a pattern that transcends and controls individuals and plays a powerful determining role in individual human behavior. This idea is very similar to Durkheim's "collective conscience." In Kroeber's view, individual accomplishment results from historical trends within society rather than anything important about the individual. These ideas are further developed in Kroeber's 1917 essay, "The Superorganic."

Kroeber also pursued the Boasian notion of studying cultures in relation to their environmental surroundings. Much of his research consisted of surveys of culture traits among Native Americans in California and on the Great Plains. Unlike Boas, who advocated the intensive study of individual societies, Kroeber was more interested in mapping the distribution of cultural traits into larger geographic patterns (Jacknis 2002:525). As early as 1903, he had already conceived of the ethnological survey that would become his 1925 volume, the *Handbook of the Indians of California*. In his study *Cultural and Natural Areas of Native North America* (1939), he mapped geographic, climatological, and vegetation distribution in rela-

tion to Native American cultures. This work was influential among his students, particularly Julian Steward, who went on to develop the cultural ecological approach to the analysis of culture.

Whereas Kroeber believed that the individual was unimportant in cultural analysis, other students of Boas saw individuals as of paramount importance to anthropology. Among them Paul Radin, in particular, typified this approach. For example, Radin's 1926 book *Crashing Thunder: The Autobiography of an American Indian*—was an ethnography in the form of a single individual's life history. Like Boas, Radin believed that it was only through long-term intensive study, including the mastery of language, that an anthropologist could fully comprehend another culture. Following this principle, Radin studied Winnebago society for fifty years, producing a comprehensive record of the culture. Curiously, Radin's focus on the individual distanced him from Boas' own conviction that anthropology was a natural science. His emphasis on life histories moved anthropology in the direction of biography and literature.

The final essay in this section is the work of one of the best-known linguists of the Boasian era, Benjamin Lee Whorf (1897–1941). Whorf earned a degree in chemical engineering at the Massachusetts Institute of Technology in 1918, then worked for the Hartford Fire Insurance Company in Connecticut. He pursued his interests in language primarily as a hobby. Although Whorf received several offers of professorships, he refused them, claiming that his work with the insurance company provided him with greater freedom and more money than an academic position could (Lavery 2001). In 1931, Whorf began to study linguistics at Yale University with Edward Sapir (1884–1939), one of the leading linguists of the period.

Whorf's main area of interest was the languages of Mesoamerica. However, he is most remembered for his work on the Hopi language and the *Sapir-Whorf hypothesis*, which he developed with his mentor, Sapir. The Sapir-Whorf hypothesis contains two basic elements: linguistic determinism and linguistic relativity. The first deals with the manner in which the structure of a language affects cognition. Sapir and Whorf proposed that the grammatical and lexical categories of the language a person speaks organize the way they think and shape their behavior. Linguistic relativity is the idea that the grammatical and lexical categories of a language are unique to that language and thus speakers of different languages inhabit separate conceptual worlds. Sapir was a student of Boas and you can see how the notion of linguistic relativity reflects the Boasian view of culture.

The work of Sapir and Whorf inspired research on the relationship between language and culture for almost two decades. Through the 1950s and 1960s, linguists and psychologists sought to test the notion of linguistic determinism. The concept of linguistic relativity was instrumental in the development of the ethnoscience and cognitive anthropology schools. In particular, the influence of the Sapir-Whorf hypothesis is evident in the studies of subjects such as ethnobotany and ethnomedicine in the 1960s and in work such as Conklin's (see essay 24).

The essay chosen for this volume is Whorf's "The Relation of Habitual Thought and Behavior

to Language." It is one of Whorf's best known statements of linguistic determinism, containing many examples derived from his investigative work for the Hartford Insurance Company and his study of the Hopi language.

In most European universities, archaeology and linguistics are separate departments from social anthropology, and biological anthropology is typically a part of biology. The four-field focus of anthropology departments in American universities today is a reflection of Boas and his students' view of anthropology.

Though anthropologists today rarely identify themselves as historical particularists, it is almost impossible to overestimate the influence of Boas and historical particularism on mainstream American anthropology. The effects of Boas' critical insights are seen most clearly in the work of his students in the first half of this century, but clear echoes of Boasian thought are present in ethnoscience and cognitive anthropology, as well as in the symbolic and postmodern approaches to the study of culture.

8. *The Methods of Ethnology*

Franz Boas (1858–1942)

During the last ten years the methods of inquiry into the historical development of civilization have undergone remarkable changes. During the second half of the last century evolutionary thought held almost complete sway and investigators like Spencer, Morgan, Tylor, Lubbock, to mention only a few, were under the spell of the idea of a general, uniform evolution of culture in which all parts of mankind participated. The newer development goes back in part to the influence of Ratzel, whose geographical training

impressed him with the importance of diffusion and migration. The problem of diffusion was taken up in detail particularly in America, but was applied in a much wider sense by Foy and Graebner, and finally seized upon in a still wider application by Elliot Smith and Rivers, so that at the present time, at least among certain groups of investigators in England and also in Germany, ethnological research is based on the concept of migration and dissemination rather than upon that of evolution.[1]

From *American Anthropologist* (1920)

[1] In this essay, Boas attacks evolutionary theorists such as those represented in this volume. He also attacks diffusionists, whom we have discussed in notes only He mentions some particularly eminent diffusionists here. Fritz Graebner (1877–1934) and Friedrich Ratzel (1844–1904) were founders of the German Kulturkreis ("culture circle")

A critical study of these two directions of inquiry shows that each is founded on the application of one fundamental hypothesis.[2] The evolutionary point of view presupposes that the course of historical changes in the cultural life of mankind follows definite laws which are applicable everywhere, and which bring it about that cultural development is, in its main lines, the same among all races and all peoples. This idea is clearly expressed by Tylor in the introductory pages of his classic work "Primitive Culture." As soon as we admit that the hypothesis of a uniform evolution has to be proved before it can be accepted, the whole structure loses its foundation. It is true that there are indications of parallelism of development in different parts of the world, and that similar customs are found in the most diverse and widely separated parts of the globe. The occurrence of these similarities, which are distributed so irregularly that they cannot readily be explained on the basis of diffusion, is one of the foundations of the evolutionary hypothesis, as it was the foundation of Bastian's[3] psychologizing treatment of cultural phenomena. On the other hand, it may be recognized that the hypothesis implies the thought that our modern Western European civilization represents the highest cultural development towards which all other more primitive cultural types tend, and that, therefore, retrospectively, we construct an orthogenetic[4] development towards our own modern civilization. It is clear that if we admit that there may be different ultimate and co-existing types of civilization, the hypothesis of one single general line of development cannot be maintained.

Opposed to these assumptions is the modern tendency to deny the existence of a general evolutionary scheme which would represent the history of the cultural development the world over.[5] The hypothesis that there are inner causes which bring about similarities of development in remote parts of the globe is rejected and in its place it is assumed that identity of development in two different parts of the globe must always be due to migration and diffusion. On this basis historical contact is demanded for enormously large areas. The theory demands a high degree of stability of cultural traits such as is apparently observed in many primitive tribes, and it is furthermore based on the supposed correlation between a number of diverse and mutually independent cultural traits which reappear in the same combinations in distant parts of the world. In this sense, modern investigation takes up anew Gerland's theory of the persistence of a number of cultural traits which were developed in one center and carried by man in his migrations from continent to continent.[6]

It seems to me that if the hypothetical foundations of these two extreme forms of ethnological research are broadly stated as I have tried to

---

school of diffusionism. Kulturkreis members were tightly linked to the Catholic Church, and in much of their work they attempted to make newly available ethnographic data correspond with prevailing biblical interpretation (Harris 1968:379). In Cologne, Graebner worked as assistant to museum director Willy Foy (1873–1929). Graebner and Foy collaborated on Graebner's book *Die Methode der Ethnologie* (1911), which Boas brutally critiqued in an essay in *Science* that same year. Grafton Elliot Smith (1871–1937) and William Halse Rivers Rivers (that's right, Rivers Rivers) (1864–1922) were radical English diffusionists who believed that all civilization had diffused from Egypt.

[2] Boas' attack on the evolutionists rested on what he considered a logical flaw in their argument. According to him, their argument assumes what it is trying to prove: that historical changes in human culture follow general laws.

Boas supported the Darwinian model of biological evolution but was hostile to its application to social evolution.

[3] Adolf Bastian (1826–1905) was a German theorist of psychic unity who believed that a few fundamental ideas, common to humankind, were the building blocks of culture. Bastian was acquainted with Boas in Berlin in the early 1880s.

[4] Orthogenetic: evolution along definite, predetermined lines.

[5] Above, Boas has focused his assault on cultural evolutionists. Here he turns his attack to the diffusionists.

[6] Georg Gerland (1833–1919) was a German geographer and a student of the anthropologist Theodor Waitz (1821–1864). Waitz also had a strong influence on Boas. Gerland argued against the idea of geographical influences on human societies.

do here, it is at once clear that the correctness of the assumptions has not been demonstrated, but that arbitrarily the one or the other has been selected for the purpose of obtaining a consistent picture of cultural development.[7] These methods are essentially forms of classification of the static phenomena of culture according to two distinct principles, and interpretations of these classifications as of historical significance, without, however, any attempt to prove that this interpretation is justifiable. To give an example: It is observed that in most parts of the world there are resemblances between decorative forms that are representative and others that are more or less geometrical. According to the evolutionary point of view, their development is explained in the following manner: the decorative forms are arranged in such order that the most representative forms are placed at the beginning. The other forms are so placed that they show a gradual transition from representative forms to purely conventional geometric forms. This order is then interpreted as meaning that geometric designs originated from representative designs which gradually degenerated. This method has been pursued, for instance, by Putnam, Stolpe, Balfour, and Haddon, and by Verworn and, in his earlier writings, by von den Steinen. While I do not mean to deny that this development may have occurred, it would be rash to generalize and to claim that in every case the classification which has been made according to a definite principle represents an historical development. The order might as well be reversed and we might begin with a simple geometric element which, by the addition of new traits, might be developed into a

representative design, and we might claim that this order represents an historical sequence. Both of these possibilities were considered by Holmes[8] as early as 1885. Neither the one nor the other theory can be established without actual historical proof.

The opposite attitude, namely, origin through diffusion, is exhibited in Heinrich Schurtz's attempt to connect the decorative art of Northwest America with that of Melanesia. The simple fact that in these areas elements occur that may be interpreted as eyes, induced him to assume that both have a common origin, without allowing for the possibility that the pattern in the two areas—each of which shows highly distinctive characteristics—may have developed from independent sources. In this attempt Schurtz followed Ratzel, who had already tried to establish connections between Melanesia and Northwest America on the basis of other cultural features.

While ethnographical research based on these two fundamental hypotheses seems to characterize the general tendency of European thought, a different method is at present pursued by the majority of American anthropologists. The difference between the two directions of study may perhaps best be summarized by the statement that American scholars are primarily interested in the dynamic phenomena of cultural change, and try to elucidate cultural history by the application of the results of their studies; and that they relegate the solution of the ultimate question of the relative importance of parallelism of cultural development in distant areas, as against worldwide diffusion, and stability of cultural traits over long periods to a future time

---

[7] This paragraph is typical of Boas' method of attack: He does not attack particular examples but looks for flaws in methodology. Trained in physics, mathematics, and geography, Boas strived for a meticulous scientific methodology in anthropological research. Essentially, he faults his opponents for sloppy thinking. Writing in this way, he seems to imply that a rigorously scientific presentation of the data might allow the construction of an evolutionary model of human society. In fact Boas staunchly opposed evolutionary explanations. He believed profoundly in human equality and viewed social evolutionary theories as

undermining this position. Thus, while Boas couches his arguments against social evolution in methodological terms, his ultimate reasons for making such arguments are deeply held moral convictions.

[8] Notice Boas' passing reference to William Henry Holmes (1846–1933), who was John Wesley Powell's successor at the Bureau of American Ethnology. In 1919, the year before this essay was published, Holmes led the American Anthropological Association's successful effort to censure Boas.

when the actual conditions of cultural change are better known.[9] The American ethnological methods are analogous to those of European, particularly of Scandinavian, archaeology, and of the researches into the prehistoric period of the eastern Mediterranean area.

It may seem to the distant observer that American students are engaged in a mass of detailed investigations without much bearing upon the solution of the ultimate problems of a philosophic history of human civilization. I think this interpretation of the American attitude would be unjust because the ultimate questions are as near to our hearts as they are to those of other scholars, only we do not hope to be able to solve an intricate historical problem by a formula.[10]

First of all, the whole problem of cultural history appears to us as an historical problem. In order to understand history it is necessary to know not only how things are, but how they have come to be. In the domain of ethnology, where, for most parts of the world, no historical facts are available except those that may be revealed by archaeological study, all evidence of change can be inferred only by indirect methods. Their character is represented in the researches of students of comparative philology.[11] The method is based on the comparison of static phenomena combined with the study of their distribution. What can be done by this method is well illustrated by Dr. Lowie's[12] investigations of the military societies of the Plains Indians, or by the modern investigation of American mythology. It is, of course, true that we can never hope to obtain incontrovertible data relating to the chronological sequence of

events, but certain general broad outlines can be ascertained with a high degree of probability, even of certainty.

As soon as these methods are applied, primitive society loses the appearance of absolute stability which is conveyed to the student who sees a certain people only at a certain given time. All cultural forms rather appear in a constant state of flux and subject to fundamental modifications.

It is intelligible why in our studies the problem of dissemination should take a prominent position. It is much easier to prove dissemination than to follow up developments due to inner forces, and the data for such a study are obtained with much greater difficulty. They may, however, be observed in every phenomenon of acculturation in which foreign elements are remodeled according to the patterns prevalent in their new environment, and they may be found in the peculiar local developments of widely spread ideas and activities. The reason why the study of inner development has not been taken up energetically is not due to the fact that from a theoretical point of view it is unimportant, it is rather due to the inherent methodological difficulties. It may perhaps be recognized that in recent years attention is being drawn to this problem as is manifested by the investigations on the processes of acculturation and of the interdependence of cultural activities which are attracting the attention of many investigators.

The further pursuit of these inquiries emphasizes the importance of a feature which is common to all historic phenomena. While in natural sciences we are accustomed to consider a given

---

[9] When Boas speaks here of American anthropologists, he is really referring to himself and the many students he trained. The particular issue of cultural change with which they were concerned was the acculturation and disappearance of Native American groups. Despite Boas' claim that American anthropologists analyze culture change, he and his followers were often faulted for producing an essentially static anthropology unable to deal effectively with change.

[10] Boas was concerned with methodology rather than theory. European anthropologists often accused Boas and his

students of producing an atheoretical anthropology concerned only with the collection of data. In the following paragraphs, he attempts to answer this charge.

[11] Philology: the study of written records, their authenticity and original form, and the determination of their meaning.

[12] Robert Lowie (1883–1957), a student of Boas and, later, professor of anthropology at Berkeley, was an influential voice in American anthropology in the 1930s and 1940s. Boas' reference here is to Lowie's 1913 article, "Military Societies of the Crow Indians."

number of causes and to study their effects, in historical happenings we are compelled to consider every phenomenon not only as effect but also as cause.[13] This is true even in the particular application of the laws of physical nature, as, for instance, in the study of astronomy in which the position of certain heavenly bodies at a given moment may be considered as the effect of gravitation, while, at the same time, their particular arrangement in space determines future changes. This relation appears much more clearly in the history of human civilization. To give an example: a surplus of food supply is liable to bring about an increase of population and an increase of leisure, which gives opportunity for occupations that are not absolutely necessary for the needs of everyday life. In turn the increase of population and of leisure, which may be applied to new inventions, gives rise to a greater food supply and to a further increase in the amount of leisure, so that a cumulative effect results.

Similar considerations may be made in regard to the important problem of the relation of the individual to society, a problem that has to be considered whenever we study the dynamic conditions of change.[14] The activities of the individual are determined to a great extent by his social environment, but in turn his own activities influence the society in which he lives, and may bring about modifications in its form. Obviously, this problem is one of the most important ones to be taken up in a study of cultural changes. It is also beginning to attract the attention of students who are no longer satisfied with the systematic enumeration of standardized beliefs and customs of a tribe, but who begin to be interested in the question of the way in which the individual reacts to his whole social environment, and to the differences of opinion and of mode of action that occur in primitive society and which are the causes of far-reaching changes.

In short then, the method which we try to develop is based on a study of the dynamic changes in society that may be observed at the present time. We refrain from the attempt to solve the fundamental problem of the general development of civilization until we have been able to unravel the processes that are going on under our eyes.[15]

Certain general conclusions may be drawn from this study even now. First of all, the history of human civilization does not appear to us as determined entirely by psychological necessity that leads to a uniform evolution the world over. We rather see that each cultural group has its own unique history, dependent partly upon the peculiar inner development of the social group, and partly upon the foreign influences to which it has been subjected. There have been processes of gradual differentiation as well as processes of leveling down differences between neighboring cultural centers, but it would be quite impossible to understand, on the basis of a single evolutionary scheme, what happened to any particular people. An example of the contrast between the two points of view is clearly indicated by a comparison of the treatment of Zuñi civilization by Frank

---

[13] Boas here defines the position that came to be called "historical particularism": Rather than operating under the constraints of some universal law, cultures are sui generis (that is, they create themselves). Thus, cultures can only be understood with reference to their particular historical development.

[14] Notice Boas' focus on the effects of an individual on society. During his life, Boas moved from a position that gave individuals little importance to one that gave them much more. The issue split Boas' followers. Kroeber argued that individuals had little importance (see essay 9); others such as Paul Radin contended that anthropology should concentrate on individual life histories.

[15] In other words, Boas' approach was to be purely inductive. Theoretical claims, he believed, could not be supported without the collection of large amounts of data. He is generally understood to have believed that the attempt to formulate a general theory was not wrong, just extremely premature. However, Boas insisted that cultures could only be understood with respect to their unique historical development. Building theory, on the other hand, necessarily involves comparison and generalization. Thus, it seems unlikely that Boasian-style anthropology could ever generate broad theoretical propositions. Harris has noted that Boas "could never . . . feel at ease in the presence of a generalization" (1968:260).

Hamilton Cushing[16] on the one hand, on the other by modern students, particularly by Elsie Clews Parsons, A. L. Kroeber and Leslie Spier.[17] Cushing believed that it was possible to explain Zuñi culture entirely on the basis of the reaction of the Zuñi mind to its geographical environment, and that the whole of Zuñi culture could be explained as the development which followed necessarily from the position in which the people were placed. Cushing's keen insight into the Indian mind and his thorough knowledge of the most intimate life of the people gave great plausibility to his interpretations. On the other hand, Dr. Parsons' studies prove conclusively the deep influence which Spanish ideas have had on Zuñi culture, and, together with Professor Kroeber's investigations, give us one of the best examples of acculturation that have come to our notice. The psychological explanation is entirely misleading, notwithstanding its plausibility; and the historical study shows us an entirely different picture, in which the unique combination of ancient traits (which in themselves are undoubtedly complex) and of European influences has brought about the present condition.

Studies of the dynamics of primitive life also show that an assumption of long continued stability such as is demanded by Elliot Smith[18] is without any foundation in fact. Wherever primitive conditions have been studied in detail, they can be proved to be in a state of flux, and it would seem that there is a close parallelism between the history of language and the history of general cultural development. Periods of stability are followed by periods of rapid change. It is exceedingly improbable that any customs of primitive people should be preserved unchanged for thousands of years. Furthermore, the phenomena of acculturation prove that a transfer of customs from one

region into another without concomitant changes due to acculturation is very rare. It is, therefore, very unlikely that ancient Mediterranean customs could be found at the present time practically unchanged in different parts of the globe, as Elliot Smith's theory demands.

While on the whole the unique historical character of cultural growth in each area stands out as a salient element in the history of cultural development, we may recognize at the same time that certain typical parallelisms do occur. We are, however, not so much inclined to look for these similarities in detailed customs but rather in certain dynamic conditions which are due to social or psychological causes that are liable to lead to similar results. The example of the relation between food supply and population to which I referred before may serve as an example. Another type of example is presented in those cases in which a certain problem confronting man may be solved by a limited number of methods only. When we find, for instance, marriage as a universal institution, it may be recognized that marriage is possible only between a number of men and a number of women; a number of men and one woman; a number of women and one man; or one man and one woman. As a matter of fact, all these forms are found the world over and it is, therefore, not surprising that analogous forms should have been adopted quite independently in different parts of the world, and, considering both the general economic conditions of mankind and the character of sexual instinct in the higher animals, it also does not seem surprising that group marriage and polyandrous marriages should be comparatively speaking rare. Similar considerations may also be made in regard to the philosophical views held by mankind. In short, if we look for laws, the laws relate to the effects of

---

[16] Frank Hamilton Cushing (1857–1900) spent five years with the Zuñi people (1879–1884) and was initiated into their Bow Priest Society. He wrote extensively on Zuñi religion and technology. Here, Boas critiques Cushing's work as ahistorical.

[17] Kroeber and Leslie Spier (1893–1961) were trained by Boas. Elsie Clews Parsons (1875–1941) worked extensively with him (one of his monographs is dedicated to her).

[18] As mentioned above, the diffusionist Grafton Elliot Smith had theorized that all complex cultural traits diffused from Egypt. The radical diffusionists believed that humans were not inherently inventive, and as a result, societies remained static for long periods. Boas disagreed with this contention.

physiological, psychological, and social conditions, not to sequences of cultural achievement.[19]

In some cases a regular sequence of these may accompany the development of the psychological or social status. This is illustrated by the sequence of industrial inventions in the Old World and in America, which I consider as independent. A period of food gathering and of the use of stone was followed by the invention of agriculture, of pottery and finally of the use of metals. Obviously, this order is based on the increased amount of time given by mankind to the use of natural products, of tools and utensils, and to the variations that developed with it. Although in this case parallelism seems to exist on the two continents, it would be futile to try to follow out the order in detail. As a matter of fact, it does not apply to other inventions. The domestication of animals, which, in the Old World must have been an early achievement, was very late in the New World, where domesticated animals, except the dog, hardly existed at all at the time of discovery. A slight beginning had been made in Peru with the domestication of the llama, and birds were kept in various parts of the continent.[20]

A similar consideration may be made in regard to the development of rationalism. It seems to be one of the fundamental characteristics of the development of mankind that activities which have developed unconsciously are gradually made the subject of reasoning.[21] We may observe this process everywhere. It appears, perhaps, most clearly in the history of science which has gradually extended the scope of its inquiry over an ever-widening field and which has raised into consciousness human activities that are automatically performed in the life of the individual and of society.

I have not heretofore referred to another aspect of modern ethnology which is connected with the growth of psycho-analysis. Sigmund Freud has attempted to show that primitive thought is in many respects analogous to those forms of individual psychic activity which he has explored by his psycho-analytical methods. In many respects his attempts are similar to the interpretation of mythology by symbolists like Stucken. Rivers has taken hold of Freud's suggestion as well as of the interpretations of Graebner and Elliot Smith, and we find, therefore, in his new writings a peculiar disconnected application of a psychologizing attitude and the application of the theory of ancient transmission.[22]

While I believe some of the ideas underlying Freud's psycho-analytic studies may be fruitfully applied to ethnological problems, it does not seem to me that the one-sided exploitation of this method will advance our understanding of the development of human society. It is certainly true that the influence of impressions received during the first few years of life has been entirely underestimated and that the social behavior of man depends to a great extent upon the earliest habits which are established before the time when connected memory begins, and that many so-called

---

[19] Equifinality is a key aspect of Boas' theoretical position. He argues that the presence of similar traits in many societies is not necessarily evidence either for psychic unity or large-scale diffusion. They may be the result of convergent evolution and independent invention. Note also a key point in this passage: Boas says that one reason for the development of similar institutions is that logically, certain things can only be done in a limited number of ways. Thus, in his example here, one reason for similarities in marriage patterns is the low number of ways it is possible to construct an institution such as marriage.

[20] This paragraph is an attack on Morgan (see essay 3), who used the presence of specific technologies or items of material culture to mark eras in his scheme of cultural evolution.

[21] It is curious that, having attacked the principle of psychic unity, Boas here relies on a statement about the universal nature of humankind.

[22] Freud's psychoanalytic theory was extremely popular in the 1920s. Although Boas and his students were profoundly affected by portions of Freud's work, they entirely rejected his treatment of the origins and development of society. However, for many of Boas' students, some of Freud's other insights were critical. Margaret Mead and Ruth Benedict developed their views on culture and personality partially in reaction to Freud's ideas. Others, such as Cora Du Bois (1903–1991) and Abram Kardiner (1891–1981), attempted to apply Freudian psychology to anthropology (see the section "Culture and Personality" in this volume).

racial or hereditary traits are to be considered rather as a result of early exposure to a certain form of social conditions. Most of these habits do not rise into consciousness and are, therefore, broken with difficulty only. Much of the difference in the behavior of adult male and female may go back to this cause. If, however, we try to apply the whole theory of the influence of suppressed desires to the activities of man living under different social forms, I think we extend beyond their legitimate limits the inferences that may be drawn from the observation of normal and abnormal individual psychology. Many other factors are of greater importance. To give an example: The phenomena of language show clearly that conditions quite different from those to which psycho-analysts direct their attention determine the mental behavior of man.[23] The general concepts underlying language are entirely unknown to most people. They do not rise into consciousness until the scientific study of grammar begins. Nevertheless, the categories of language compel us to see the world arranged in certain definite conceptual groups which, on account of our lack of knowledge of linguistic processes, are taken as objective categories and which, therefore, impose themselves upon the form of our thoughts. It is not known what the origin of these categories may be, but it seems quite certain that they have nothing to do with the phenomena which are the subject of psycho-analytic study.

The applicability of the psycho-analytic theory of symbolism is also open to the greatest doubt. We should remember that symbolic interpretation has occupied a prominent position in the philosophy of all times. It is present not only in primitive life, but the history of philosophy and of theology abounds in examples of a high development of symbolism, the type of which depends upon the general mental attitude of the philosopher who develops it. The theologians who interpreted the Bible on the basis of religious symbolism were no less certain of the correctness of their views, than the psycho-analysts are of their interpretations of thought and conduct based on sexual symbolism. The results of a symbolic interpretation depend primarily upon the subjective attitude of the investigator who arranges phenomena according to his leading concept. In order to prove the applicability of the symbolism of psycho-analysis, it would be necessary to show that a symbolic interpretation from other entirely different points of view would not be equally plausible, and that explanations that leave out symbolic significance or reduce it to a minimum would not be adequate.[24]

While, therefore, we may welcome the application of every advance in the method of psychological investigation, we cannot accept as an advance in ethnological method the crude transfer of a novel, one-sided method of psychological investigation of the individual to social phenomena the origin of which can be shown to be historically determined and to be subject to influences that are not at all comparable to those that control the psychology of the individual.[25]

---

[23] Linguistics was a particular interest of Boas and his students. In this paragraph, Boas refers to the idea that language determines the categories we use to think. This line of reasoning was pursued by Boas' student Edward Sapir (1884–1939) and Sapir's student and colleague, Benjamin Lee Whorf (1897–1941). Today, it is known as the Sapir-Whorf hypothesis.

[24] Boas' assault on psychoanalysis is similar to his attack on evolutionists and diffusionists: He faults it on methodological grounds. All of Boas' criticisms are intended to reinforce his call for an inductive methodology in anthropology. He insisted that it was only through the meticulous collection of empirical data that anthropologists could hope to understand cultures.

[25] The particular attacks Boas makes in this essay are repeated frequently in anthropology. For example, Boas' criticism of psychology as dependent on "[the] subjective attitude of the investigator who arranges phenomena according to his leading concept" is repeated almost word for word by ethnoscientists and cognitive anthropologists in the 1950s and 1960s in their critique of other forms of anthropology (see essays 24 and 25) and in slightly different form by postmodernists as well (see essays 36, 37, and 38).

9. *Eighteen Professions*[1]

A. L. KROEBER (1876–1960)

ANTHROPOLOGY TODAY INCLUDES two studies which fundamental differences of aim and method render irreconcilable. One of these branches is biological and psychological; the other, social or historical.[2]

There is a third field, the special province of anthropology, concerned with the relation of biological and social factors. This is no-man's-land, and therefore used as a picnic-ground by whosoever prefers pleasure excursions to the work of cultivating a patch of understanding. Some day this tract will also be surveyed, fenced, and improved. Biological science already claims it; but the title remains to be established. For the present, the labor in hand is the delimitation of the scope of history from that of science.[3]

In what follows, historical anthropology, history, and sociology are referred to as history. Physical anthropology and psychology are included in biology.[4]

1. *The aim of history is to know the relations of social facts to the whole of civilization.*

Civilization means civilization itself, not its impulses. Relation is actual connection, not cause.[5]

_____

From *American Anthropologist* (1915)

---

[1] Readers expecting an excursion into the uses of anthropology in the early twentieth century are bound to be disappointed by this essay. Kroeber uses the word *professions* to mean items of belief rather than jobs that an anthropologist might do. Most Boasian anthropologists prided themselves on replacing what they considered the empty theorizing of nineteenth-century scholars such as Morgan and Tylor with the scientific reasoning of Franz Boas. They often reminded students that Boas was trained in the physical sciences. By using the word *professions,* Kroeber is emphasizing the notion that he considers these points to be the bedrock of anthropology.

Kroeber's early training was in English, and he held both a B.A. and an M.A. in that subject. Even though he earned a Ph.D. in anthropology (his doctoral dissertation was a twenty-eight-page paper on Arapaho art that attacked nineteenth-century evolutionary assumptions about the meaning and form of symbols), he retained a deep interest in history and the humanities throughout his life. He believed that anthropology should be objective, but he differed with Boas on its subject matter. Boas believed that anthropologists should focus on the intensive study of a single society. Kroeber was more interested in regional surveys of general traits (Jacknis 2002:525).

[2] Anthropologists today often bemoan the collapse of the four-field approach, the notion that they should be trained in physical, archaeological, linguistic, and cultural anthropology. We tend to look at the early American anthropologists as masters of all of these fields. However, tension among the fields dates from the early twentieth century, and even Boas and his students argued about whether all of these areas could be covered in a single field of study. Kroeber devoted his life to the study of cultural anthropology, archaeology, and linguistics but did little with physical anthropology.

[3] At the time this essay was published in *American Anthropologist* (1915) very little was known of human evolution and the biology of human variation. In this paragraph, Kroeber is making fun of the physical anthropology of his era. Much anthropology of this time was devoted to showing that people other than Europeans were biologically, intellectually, and socially inferior. Here he pokes fun at this work but his comments indicate that he considers biology's claim to physical anthropology to be an open issue.

[4] Like Boas, Kroeber understands anthropology as a type of cultural history. Cultures are created by their own histories, and therefore understanding them is a form of historical research.

[5] Kroeber uses the term *social facts* in his first profession. In doing so, he is referencing Durkheim (see essay 5). Kroeber looked to both Durkheim and Spencer as critical nineteenth-century thinkers in anthropology and sociology. To some extent, this essay and Durkheim's are designed to serve similar ends. In both, the authors try to

2. *The material studied by history is not man, but his works.*

It is not men, but the results of their deeds, the manifestations of their activities, that are the subject of historical inquiry.[6]

3. *Civilization, though carried by men and existing through them, is an entity in itself, and of another order from life.*

History is not concerned with the agencies producing civilization, but with civilization as such. The causes are the business of the psychologist. The entity civilization has intrinsically nothing to do with individual men nor with the aggregates of men on whom it rests. It springs from the organic, but is independent of it. The mental processes of groups of men are, after all, only the collected processes of individuals reacting under certain special stimuli. Collective psychology is therefore ultimately resolvable into individual human psychology, just as this in turn is resolvable into organic psychology and physiology. But history deals with material which is essentially non-individual and integrally social. History is not concerned with the relations of civilization to men or organisms, but with the interrelations of civilization. The psychic organization of man in the abstract does not exist for it, save as something given directly and more or less completely to the student's consciousness. The uncivilized man does not exist; if he did, he would mean nothing to the historian. Even civilized man is none of history's business; its sphere is the civilization of which man is the necessary basis but which is inevitable once this basis exists.[7]

4. *A certain mental constitution of man must be assumed by the historian, but may not be used by him as a resolution of social phenomena.*

The historian can and should obtain for himself the needed interpretation of man's mind from familiarity with social facts and the direct application to them of his own psychic activities. This interpretation is likely to be of service in proportion as it emanates immediately from himself and not from the formulated laws of the biological psychologist. Whether an understanding of civilization will or will not help the psychologist is for the latter to determine.[8]

---

delineate anthropology or sociology as particular fields of study separate from other fields. However, there are several critical differences. First, Kroeber uses the term *social fact* without defining it. This makes its meaning much broader than that given to it by Durkheim. Second, Durkheim set out to model sociology on the natural sciences, but Kroeber was opposed to such modeling.

[6] In this profession Kroeber is emphasizing the Boasian focus on fieldwork and patterns of diffusion between areas. Further, although we do not remember Kroeber as a museum curator today, a major part of his early work at Berkeley was setting up the anthropology museum there, collecting material for exhibits, and curating those collections. The focus on material works in the second profession reflects Kroeber's background in museum work and emphasis on the diffusion of cultural traits in his research.

[7] In professions 3 and 4, Kroeber proclaims that civilization is totally separate from the individuals who compose it. Like Durkheim, he rejects the notion that culture or society can be reduced to the actions of human minds, working either separately or as a group. One of the key tenants of Kroeber's anthropology (and one that he will develop further in this essay) is that individuals count for little or nothing in culture. Following Spencer and Durkheim, Kroeber claims that culture is superorganic; that is, that it has an existence separate from the human beings who compose it, and follows a pattern of its own.

Kroeber also argues here that the focus of anthropological research should be on wide cultural patterns that could be demonstrated by studying the diffusion of cultural traits. Despite Boas' urgings for him to settle down and study one group, Kroeber was more interested in conducting comparative surveys of data over large geographic areas (Jacknis 2002:525–526). These interests are the background for his statements about "civilization," by which he means culture, as an entity in itself.

[8] There are two very important aspects of this statement. First, note the primacy that Kroeber gives to social facts and culture. He notes that psychology, "man's mind," cannot explain culture, but rather culture, social facts, can be used to help explain human psychology. Second, note that Kroeber advises historians to examine their own minds. In so doing, he reflects his own experience and the dictates of Freudian psychoanalysis. This essay was written in 1915, in the years that Kroeber called his "Hegira," a word

5. *True instincts lie at the bottom and origin of social phenomena, but cannot be considered or dealt with by history.*

History begins where instincts commence to be expressed in social facts.

6. *The personal or individual has no historical value save as illustration.*

Ethnological genealogies are valuable material. So are the actions of conspicuous historical personages. But their dramatic, anecdotic, or biographic recital is biographic or fictional art, or possibly psychology, not history.[9]

7. *Geography, or physical environment, is material made use of by civilization, not a factor shaping or explaining civilization.*

Civilization reacts to civilization, not to geography. For the historian, geography does not act on civilization, but civilization incorporates geographical circumstances. Agriculture presupposes a climate able to sustain agriculture, and modifies itself according to climatic conditions. It is not caused by climate. The understanding of agricultural activity is to be sought in the other phenomena of civilization affecting it.[10]

8. *The absolute equality and identity of all human races and strains as carriers of civilization must be assumed by the historian.*

The identity has not been proved nor has it been disproved. It remains to be established, or to be limited, by observations directed to this end, perhaps only by experiments. The historical and

---

generally used to refer to the prophet Mohammad's years of exile from Mecca. It was a tragic era in Kroeber's life that began with the death of his first wife, Henriette Rothschild, in 1913. There were numerous calamities in the years that followed, including the death of Ishi, a Yana Indian who had lived and worked with Kroeber. Throughout it all, Kroeber had an ear infection that was misdiagnosed as "neurasthenia," a nineteenth- and early twentieth-century term for a neurotic mental disorder. This, combined with an apparent midlife crisis, led Kroeber to psychoanalysis in 1917. After undergoing analysis by a student of Freud, he returned to California and practiced for several years as a Freudian psychoanalyst, taking partial leave from his university position to do so.

[9] Here again, Kroeber stresses the importance of the social and cultural above the individual. Kroeber and many other American anthropologists arrayed themselves against the Great Man theory of history. Much of history was then (and still is) taught as biography. Historians and students tend to understand policies and practices as the result of the ideas and will of single individuals. Thus, books about the American presidents are extraordinarily popular and people debate whether or not World War II would have happened without Hitler. Kroeber and others such as Leslie White (1949) argued that such individuals made no difference at all; they were merely placeholders, representing trends and tendencies in their social and cultural systems.

Kroeber's radical de-emphasis of the individual led him away from Boas and others such as Sapir and Radin, who believed that culture was the result of the interplay of individuals and their society. Kroeber's condemnation of the use of the individual to explain history raises another issue: Kroeber himself developed a close personal and research relationship with a single individual, Ishi, and relied primarily on information from Ishi in his work on the Yana. If culture was really superorganic and "ethnological genealogies" are not history, i.e., anthropology, then why did Kroeber go to such great lengths to cultivate and maintain his relationship with Ishi?

[10] In profession 7, Kroeber rejects any role of environment in shaping culture. In this he follows his mentor Boas. The idea that environment determined culture was popular in the late nineteenth and early twentieth centuries. Europeans and white Americans often explained cultural differences by reference to climate and geography. One typical example was the notion that northern Europeans were hardworking and hardy because they had to deal with harsh winters, whereas Africans, Mexicans, and so on, were uncivilized because tropical climates made them lazy. The Boasians rejected formulations such as this. In the 1880s, Boas was interested in the relationship between environment, geography, and society, but this interest clearly waned after his experiences on Baffin Island. According to his student Gladys A. Reichard (1893–1955), Boas came to believe that the Eskimo "did things in spite of rather than because of the environment" (quoted in Herskovitz 1957:115). Most Boasians followed this line of reasoning and saw very little connection between culture and environment.

Kroeber's student Julian Steward (see essay 17), was an important exception. Steward formulated a theory in which the relationship between environment and culture was the cornerstone of anthropological study.

social influences affecting every race and every large group of persons are closely intertwined with the alleged biological and hereditary ones, and have never yet been sufficiently separated to allow demonstration of the actual efficiency of either. All opinions on this point are only convictions falsely fortified by subjectively interpreted evidence. The biologist dealing with man must assume at least some hereditary differences, and often does assume biological factors as the only ones existent. The historian, until such differences are established and exactly defined, must assume their non-existence. If he does not base his studies on this assumption, his work becomes a vitiated mixture of history and biology.[11]

9. *Heredity cannot be allowed to have acted any part in history.*

Individual hereditary differences undoubtedly exist, but are not historical material because they are individual. Hereditary differences between human groups may ultimately be established, but like geography must in that event be converted into material acted upon by the force of civilization, not treated as causes of civilization.

10. *Heredity by acquirement is equally a biological and historical monstrosity.*

This naive explanation may be eliminated on the findings of biology; but should biology ever determine that such heredity operates through a mechanism as yet undiscovered, this heredity must nevertheless be disregarded by history together with congenital heredity. In the present stage of understanding, heredity by acquirement is only too often the cherished inclination of those who confuse their biological thinking by the introduction of social aspects, and of those who confound history by deceiving themselves that they are turning it into biology.[12]

11. *Selection and other factors of organic evolution cannot be admitted as affecting civilization.*

It is actually unproved that the processes of organic evolution are materially influencing civilization or that they have influenced it. Civilization obviously introduces an important factor which is practically or entirely lacking in the existence of animals and plants, and which must at least largely neutralize the operation of any kind of selection. Prehistoric archaeology shows with certainty that civilization has changed profoundly without accompanying material alterations in the human organism. Even so far as biological evolution may ultimately be proved in greater or less degree for man, a correspondence between organic types and civilizational forms will have to be definitely established before history can concern itself with these organic types or their changes.[13]

---

[11] The complete rejection of biologically based racism was one of the most critical achievements of Boas and his students. Boas fought long and hard against the idea of race and the practice of racism. He attracted students sympathetic to his notions about race and imbued them with a passion for the idea that all human differences are the result of culture rather than biology. In this profession and the several following, Kroeber summarizes and reiterates this Boasian belief.

Kroeber's discussion of profession 8 closely resembles the argument that Boas made when attacking theories of unilineal evolution (essay 8). Like Boas, Kroeber says that the evidence is inadequate to conclude whether or not the human races and their cultures are equal or not, and until better data can be gathered, one must assume their equality.

[12] This profession was more controversial in 1915 than it sounds today. Kroeber is not typically remembered for his political or social activism, but this statement was a major

stand on his part. In Kroeber's day, Lamarckian evolution (the inheritance of acquired characteristics, or "heredity by acquirement") was a common belief. Mendel's laws of genetics had been rediscovered only recently and were not very widely known. It was popularly believed that undesirable behaviors such as crime, prostitution, and alcoholism were hereditary and that certain classes and ethnic groups were predisposed to these behaviors. This belief in part fed the American eugenics movement of the first decades of the twentieth century during which there was a call for the involuntary sterilization of "undesirables." It is this sort of public policy that Kroeber is calling "monstrous."

[13] Like those above it, this profession continues Kroeber's direct attack on scientific racism and the notion that there were superior or inferior cultures. Much of anthropology (particularly physical anthropology) between the Civil War and the 1920s was aimed at proving the hereditary

12. *The so-called savage is no transition be-tween the animal and the scientifically educated man.*

All men are totally civilized. All animals are totally uncivilized because they are almost totally uncivilizable. The connecting condition which it is universally believed must have existed, is entirely unknown. If ever it becomes known, it can furnish to the historian only an introduction to history. There is no higher and lower in civilization for the historian. The ranging of the portions of civilization in any sequence, save the actual one of time, place, and connection, is normally misleading and always valueless. The estimation of the adult savage as similar to the modern European child is superficial and prevents his proper appreciation either biologically or historically.[14]

13. *There are no social species or standard cultural types or stages.*

A social species in history rests on false analogy with organic species. A stage in civilization is merely a preconception made plausible by arbitrarily selected facts.[15]

14. *There is no ethnic mind, but only civilization.*

There are only individual minds. When these react on each other cumulatively, the process is merely physiological. The single ethnic or social existence is civilization, which biologically is resolvable purely into a product of physiological forces, and historically is the only and untranscendable entity.[16]

15. *There are no laws in history similar to the laws of physico-chemical science.*

All asserted civilizational laws are at most tendencies, which, however determinable, are not permanent quantitative expressions. Nor are such

---

and biological superiority of northern Europeans. Social Darwinists of Kroeber's day argued that the technological superiority of the industrialized nations was proof that they were evolutionarily superior. Kroeber, like Boas, rejects all notions of biological superiority or inferiority.

[14] This profession is a resounding statement of Boasian cultural relativism and an attack on the social evolutionary theories of the nineteenth and early twentieth centuries. Throughout this essay, Kroeber has used the term *civilization* as synonymous with culture. He does so to shock the reader and make a point. In Kroeber's day, readers would have been surprised by the usage because scholars equated civilization with either ancient state-level society or the fine arts. The notion that technologically simple societies were civilized would strike them as incongruous. Today, the usage is equally surprising but for a different reason. Now, anthropologists generally equate civilization with state-level societies and use the term *culture* to speak of all societies. However, by insisting that all human societies are civilizations and all humans are equally civilized, Kroeber proposes radical equality, not only of societies but, by implication, of individual human beings as well. This was a touchstone of Boasian anthropology.

Note too that in profession 12, Kroeber explicitly rejects the unilineal evolutionary theories popular in the late nineteenth century and the "ontogeny recapitulates phylogeny" argument that was common in the fields of biology, psychology, and medicine in the nineteenth and early

twentieth centuries. This is discussed in greater detail in the note 19 on pages 21 and 22.

The notion that an adult savage was equivalent to a European child was widely popularized by Freud's 1913 book, *Totem and Taboo*. In that work, Freud proposed a psychoanalytic theory for the origin of culture that depended on the notion that primitive people were similar to European children and neurotics. Given his deep involvement in psychoanalysis, it is curious that Kroeber so willingly attacked one of Freud's cherished ideas.

[15] In this profession, Kroeber provides a one-sentence summary of Boas' argument against evolutionism. Boas charged that evolutionist thinking was unscientific because evolutionists chose facts without regard to their historical and ethnographic context in order to fit their theories (see essay 8).

[16] In other words, culture is superorganic. It generates itself and cannot be reduced to the group thinking of the individuals who compose it. However, it is interesting that while many of Kroeber's statements closely track Durkheim's notions of social facts and *l'âme collective*, here he makes a decisive break. Durkheim proposed that the origin of culture was a process of "social condensation" created by a critical mass of individuals coming together. Here Kroeber says that when minds react cumulatively the result is purely physiological. He is unwilling to speculate on the origin of culture.

tendencies the substitute which history has for the laws of science. History need not deny them and may have to recognize them, but their formulation is not its end.[17]

16. *History deals with conditions sine qua non, not with causes.*

The relations between civilizational phenomena are relations of sequence, not of effect. The principles of mechanical causality, emanating from the underlying biological sciences, are applicable to individual and collective psychology. Applied to history, they convert it into psychology. An insistence that all treatment of civilizational data should be by the methods of mechanical causality is equivalent to a denial of the valid existence of history as a subject of study. The only antecedents of historical phenomena are historical phenomena.[18]

17. *The causality of history is teleological.*

Psychological causes are mechanical. For history, psychology is assumable, not demonstrable. To make the object of historical study the proving of the fundamental identity of the human mind by endless examples is as tedious as barren. If the process of civilization seems the worthwhile end of knowledge of civilization, it must be sought as a process distinct from that of mechanical causality, or the result will be a reintegration that is not history. Teleology of course does not suggest theology to those free from the influence of theology. The teleology of history involves the absolute conditioning of historical events by other historical events. This causality of history is as completely unknown and unused as chemical causality was a thousand and physical causality three thousand years ago.[19]

18. *In fine, the determinations and methods of biological, psychological, or natural science do not exist for history, just as the results and the manner of operation of history are disregarded by consistent biological practice.*

---

[17] In many of the earlier professions, Kroeber's ideas seem similar to Durkheim's: Kroeber mentions social facts and he talks about the existence of something that sounds very much like Durkheim's notion of *l'âme collective* (in 1917, two years after this paper, Kroeber published a famous essay, called "The Superorganic" in which he described his notion of culture in greater detail). However, in profession 15 he breaks from Durkheim and from the British social anthropologists who followed Durkheim. For Durkheim, the point of describing social facts and *l'âme collective* was to search for the laws by which societies happen. Durkheim believed that a science of society similar to the natural sciences could be developed. Kroeber rejects these notions entirely. In professions 15 and 16, he claims that though laws might exist, anthropologists should not be interested in finding them. Like Boas, Kroeber believes that cultures are understandable only in the context of their own historical and environmental circumstances.

[18] Here Kroeber says that the cause-and-effect relationships seen in the biological sciences do not apply to cultural phenomena. It is interesting that Kroeber rejects the notion that anthropology can be scientific but supports the idea that psychology is scientific. On the one hand, in the nineteenth century, Wilhelm Wundt and others developed a psychology that was based on laboratory experiments. Clearly, using such a technique was not possible for anthropologists. On the other hand, the form of psychology to which Kroeber was personally drawn was Freudian psychoanalysis, one of the least scientific theories of psychology imaginable.

[19] In this profession, Kroeber uses the word *teleology* in an interesting fashion. Teleology is the study of ultimate causes and is often linked to some religious conception of the world; the search for ultimate causes usually implies a series of beliefs about human destiny. Thus, Herbert Spencer's theory that evolution was a universal force driving everything to a destiny of perfection was teleological. Echoing Boas, Kroeber says that the cause of history is history, or in other words, culture is *sui generis*. In the last sentence of the profession, Kroeber declares himself to be at the dawn of a new era of study. History has been dominated by studies of great men and the acts of literate nation-states. Now that we understand that history is anthropology and that it is not the biography of the great or the property of technologically advanced nations, Kroeber says, we can begin to document and understand it. For Kroeber, the goal of anthropology was to be knowledge itself—understanding for understanding's sake. In 1959, only a year before his death, Kroeber wrote: "The pursuit of anthropology must often have seemed strange and useless to many people, but no one has ever called it an arid or a toneless or a dismal science" (1959:404).

Most biologists have implicitly followed their aspect of this doctrine, but their consequent success has tempted many historians, especially sociologists, anthropologists, and theorists, to imitate them instead of pursuing their proper complementary method.[20]

[20] Kroeber and most other Boasians maintained a strong stance against an anthropology based on the hypothesis testing model of the natural sciences throughout their lives. In the same essay quoted above, Kroeber writes:

> Now, maturity has stolen upon us. The times and utilitarianism have caught up with us, and we find ourselves classified and assigned to the social sciences. . . . As our daily bread, we invent hypotheses in order to test them, as we are told is the constant practice of the high tribe of physicists. If at times some of you, like myself, feel somewhat ill at ease in the house of social science, do not wonder; we are changelings therein; our true paternity lies elsewhere. (1959:404)

10. *The Relation of Habitual Thought and Behavior to Language*

BENJAMIN L. WHORF (1897–1941)

Human beings do not live in the objective world alone, nor alone in the world of social activity as ordinarily understood, but are very much at the mercy of the particular language which has become the medium of expression for their society. It is quite an illusion to imagine that one adjusts to reality essentially without the use of language and that language is merely an incidental means of solving specific problems of communication or reflection. The fact of the matter is that the "real world" is to a large extent unconsciously built up on the language habits of the group. . . . We see and hear and otherwise experience very largely as we do because the language habits of our community predispose certain choices of interpretation.

—*Edward Sapir*[1]

THERE WILL PROBABLY be general assent to the proposition that an accepted pattern of using words is often prior to certain lines of thinking and forms of behavior, but he who assents often sees in such a statement nothing more than a platitudinous recognition of the hypnotic power of philosophical and learned terminology on the one hand or of catchwords, slogans, and rallying cries on the other. To see only thus far is to miss the point of one of the important interconnections

From *Language, Culture, and Personality: Essays in Memory of Edward Sapir* (1941)

[1] Whorf opens this essay with a quote from his friend and mentor, Edward Sapir, that is a strong statement of linguistic relativity and determinism, the principles underlying the Sapir-Whorf hypothesis. This essay, written in 1939, was first published in Language, Culture, and Personality (Spier, Hallowell, and Newman, eds.), a 1941 memorial volume dedicated to Sapir, who died in 1939. The fundamental point of the essay is to demonstrate some ways in which grammatical categories in language unconsciously influence the ways in which people interpret the world around them and thus direct their behavior (linguistic determinism). Whorf argues that speakers of different languages think and act differently because their languages create different conceptual worlds (linguistic relativity).

which Sapir saw between language, culture, and psychology, and succinctly expressed in the introductory quotation. It is not so much in these special uses of language as in its constant ways of arranging data and its most ordinary everyday analysis of phenomena that we need to recognize the influence it has on other activities, cultural and personal.[2]

THE NAME OF THE SITUATION AS AFFECTING BEHAVIOR

I came in touch with an aspect of this problem before I had studied under Dr. Sapir, and in a field usually considered remote from linguistics. It was in the course of my professional work for a fire insurance company, in which I undertook the task of analyzing many hundreds of reports of circumstances surrounding the start of fires, and in some cases, of explosions. My analysis was directed toward purely physical conditions, such as defective wiring, presence or lack of air spaces between metal flues and woodwork, etc., and the results were presented in these terms. Indeed it was undertaken with no thought that any other significances would or could be revealed. But in due course it became evident that not only a

physical situation *qua* physics, but the meaning of that situation to people, was sometimes a factor, through the behavior of the people, in the start of the fire. And this factor of meaning was clearest when it was a *linguistic meaning,* residing in the name or the linguistic description commonly applied to the situation. Thus, around a storage of what are called "gasoline drums," behavior will tend to a certain type, that is, great care will be exercised; while around a storage of what are called "empty gasoline drums," it will tend to be different—careless, with little repression of smoking or of tossing cigarette stubs about. Yet the "empty" drums are perhaps the more dangerous, since they contain explosive vapor. Physically the situation is hazardous, but the linguistic analysis according to regular analogy must employ the word "empty," which inevitably suggests lack of hazard. The word "empty" is used in two linguistic patterns: (1) as a virtual synonym for "null and void, negative, inert," (2) applied in analysis of physical situations without regard to, e.g., vapor, liquid vestiges, or stray rubbish, in the container. The situation is named in one pattern (2) and the name is then "acted out" or "lived up to" in another (1), this being a general formula for the linguistic conditioning of behavior into hazardous forms.[3]

---

[2] Whorf begins by noting that there "will probably be general assent" to the notion that language precedes thought. This is, in fact, a very controversial proposition (see Pinker 1994). To some degree, by claiming "general assent," Whorf assumes what he is trying to prove, that language asserts a controlling influence on thought and action.

[3] Whorf is an unusual figure in the history of anthropology in that he is a widely known theorist who never held a regular academic position. Although he was an honorary research fellow at Yale in the mid-1930s, He was educated as a chemical engineer and he spent his career working for the Hartford Fire Insurance Company. Whorf began his studies with Sapir in 1931 during the Great Depression, at a time when academic jobs were difficult to find and did not pay well. Apparently Whorf considered himself lucky to have had a lucrative job that allowed him time to pursue his intellectual interests. Whorf became aware of the effect of language on thought, as he says at the start of this section, while investigating the

causes of fires. In this section Whorf provides a series of examples from his work as an insurance inspector. He claims that in these cases, fires started because the language people used did not adequately describe physical reality. He proposes that the "empty" gasoline drums were not really empty and the "spun limestone" was not stone. The implication is that the language we use for things can affect our actions because it influences the way we think about things. However, Whorf's examples are somewhat troubling. We really don't know how much of the workers' behavior was actually driven by the data and how much of it was Whorf's interpretation. For example, was the "spun limestone" allowed to catch fire because workers thought of it as stone, or did they and the owners who bought the metal stills simply assume that the manufacturer provided safe equipment? Did the workers know the name of the insulation at all? Since Whorf does not provide us with his interview data, we don't know the answer to these questions.

In a wood distillation plant the metal stills were insulated with a composition prepared from limestone and called at the plant "spun limestone." No attempt was made to protect this covering from excessive heat or the contact of flame. After a period of use, the fire below one of the stills spread to the "limestone," which to everyone's great surprise burned vigorously. Exposure to acetic acid fumes from the stills had converted part of the limestone (calcium carbonate) to calcium acetate. This when heated in a fire decomposes, forming inflammable acetone. Behavior that tolerated fire close to the covering was induced by use of the name "limestone," which because it ends in "stone" implies noncombustibility.

A huge iron kettle of boiling varnish was observed to be overheated, nearing the temperature at which it would ignite. The operator moved it off the fire and ran it on its wheels to a distance, but did not cover it. In a minute or so the varnish ignited. Here the linguistic influence is more complex; it is due to the metaphorical objectifying (of which more later) of "cause" as contact or the spatial juxtaposition of "things"—to analyzing the situation as "on" versus "off" the fire. In reality, the stage when the external fire was the main factor had passed; the overheating was now an internal process of convection in the varnish from the intensely heated kettle, and still continued when "off" the fire.

An electric glow heater on the wall was little used, and for one workman had the meaning of a convenient coat hanger. At night a watchman entered and snapped a switch, which action he verbalized as "turning on the light." No light appeared, and this result he verbalized as "light is burned out." He could not see the glow of the heater because of the old coat hung on it. Soon the heater ignited the coat, which set fire to the building.

A tannery discharged waste water containing animal matter into an outdoor settling basin partly roofed with wood and partly open. This situation is one that ordinarily would be verbalized as "pool of water." A workman had occasion to light a blowtorch near by, and threw his match into the water. But the decomposing waste matter was evolving gas under the wood cover, so that the setup was the reverse of "watery." An instant flare of flame ignited the woodwork, and the fire quickly spread into the adjoining building.

A drying room for hides was arranged with a blower at one end to make a current of air along the room and thence outdoors through a vent at the other end. Fire started at a hot bearing on the blower, which blew the flames directly into the hides and fanned them along the room, destroying the entire stock. This hazardous setup followed naturally from the term "blower" with its linguistic equivalence to "that which blows," implying that its function necessarily is to "blow." Also its function is verbalized as "blowing air for drying," overlooking that it can blow other things, e.g., flames and sparks. In reality, a blower simply makes a current of air and can exhaust as well as blow. It should have been installed at the vent end to *draw* the air over the hides, then through the hazard (its own casing and bearings), and thence outdoors. Beside a coal-fired melting pot for lead reclaiming was dumped a pile of "scrap lead"—a misleading verbalization, for it consisted of the lead sheets of old radio condensers, which still had paraffin paper between them. Soon the paraffin blazed up and fired the roof, half of which was burned off.

Such examples, which could be greatly multiplied, will suffice to show how the cue to a certain line of behavior is often given by the analogies of the linguistic formula in which the situation is spoken of, and by which to some degree it is analyzed, classified, and allotted its place in that world which is "to a large extent unconsciously built up on the language habits of the group." And we always assume that the linguistic analysis made by our group reflects reality better than it does.

GRAMMATICAL PATTERNS AS INTERPRETATIONS OF EXPERIENCE

The linguistic material in the above examples is limited to single words, phrases, and patterns of limited range. One cannot study the behavioral compulsiveness of such material without suspecting a much more far-reaching compulsion from large-scale patterning of grammatical categories, such as plurality, gender and similar classifications (animate, inanimate, etc.), tenses, voices, and other verb forms, classifications of the type of "parts of speech," and the matter of whether a given experience is denoted by a unit morpheme, an inflected word, or a syntactical combination. A category such as number (singular vs. plural) is an attempted interpretation of a whole large order of experience, virtually of the world or of nature; it attempts to say how experience is to be segmented, what experience is to be called "one" and what "several." But the difficulty of appraising such a far-reaching influence is great because of its background character, because of the difficulty of standing aside from our own language, which is a habit and a cultural *non estdisputandum,* and scrutinizing it objectively.[4] And if we take a very dissimilar language, this language becomes a part of nature, and we even do to it what we have already done to nature. We tend to think in our own language in order to examine the exotic language. Or we find the task of unraveling the purely morphological intricacies so gigantic that it seems to absorb all else. Yet the problem, though difficult, is feasible; and the best approach is through an exotic language, for in its study we are at long last pushed willy-nilly out of our ruts. Then we find that the exotic language is a mirror held up to our own.

In my study of the Hopi language, what I now see as an opportunity to work on this problem was first thrust upon me before I was clearly aware of the problem. The seemingly endless task of describing the morphology did finally end. Yet it was evident, especially in the light of Sapir's lectures on Navaho, that the description of the

language was far from complete. I knew for example the morphological formation of plurals, but not how to use plurals. It was evident that the category of plural in Hopi was not the same thing as in English, French, or German. Certain things that were plural in these languages were singular in Hopi. The phase of investigation which now began consumed nearly two more years. The work began to assume the character of a comparison between Hopi and western European languages. It also became evident that even the grammar of Hopi bore a relation to Hopi culture, and the grammar of European tongues to our own "Western" or "European" culture. And it appeared that the interrelation brought in those large subsummations of experience by language, such as our own terms "time," "space," "substance," and "matter." Since, with respect to the traits compared, there is little difference between English, French, German, or other European languages with the *possible* (but doubtful) exception of Balto-Slavic and non-Indo-European, I have lumped these languages into one group called SAE, or "Standard Average European."[5]

That portion of the whole investigation here to be reported may be summed up in two questions: (1) Are our own concepts of "time," "space," and "matter" given in substantially the same form by experience to all men, or are they in part conditioned by the structure of particular languages? (2) Are there traceable affinities between (a) cultural and behavioral norms and (b) large-scale linguistic patterns? (I should be the last to pretend that there is anything so definite as "a correlation" between culture and language, and especially

---

[4] *Non est disputandum* is Latin for indisputable. Whorf is suggesting that it is very difficult to understand the effects of language on culture because we perceive all cultures through our own language, which is filled with fundamental assumptions about the nature of the world. In other words, it is difficult to study the linguistic categories of another language because we must ultimately perceive these through the linguistic categories of our own language. Whorf suggests that the way around this problem is to examine an exotic language, since becoming familiar with such a language can give us a new point of view from which to examine our own.

[5] European scholars have been speculating about the nature of language and cognition and the differences between languages since the late seventeenth century. Echoing the Boasian rejection of unilineal evolutionary thinking and the related ranking of races that was common at the time, Sapir and Whorf rejected the ranking of cultures or languages. Here Whorf begins to use his concept of linguistic relativity, the notion that different languages reflect different cultural conceptions of reality. He aims to demonstrate that European concepts of time, space, and matter are not universal, but take different conceptual forms in different cultures and that these differences are the result of differences in language.

between ethnological rubrics such as "agricultural, hunting," etc., and linguistic ones like "inflected," "synthetic," or "isolating."[a] When I began the study, the problem was by no means so clearly formulated, and I had little notion that the answers would turn out as they did.

PLURALITY AND NUMERATION IN SAE AND HOPI

In our language, that is SAE, plurality and cardinal numbers are applied in two ways: to real plurals and imaginary plurals. Or more exactly if less tersely: perceptible spatial aggregates and metaphorical aggregates. We say "ten men" and also "ten days." Ten men either are or could be objectively perceived as ten, ten in one group perception[b]— ten men on a street corner, for instance. But "ten days" cannot be objectively experienced. We experience only one day, today; the other nine (or even all ten) are something conjured up from memory or imagination. If "ten days" be regarded as a group it must be as an "imaginary," mentally constructed group. Whence comes this mental pattern? Just as in the case of the fire-causing errors, from the fact that our language confuses the two different situations, has but one pattern for both. When we speak of "ten steps forward, ten strokes on a bell," or any similarly described cyclic sequence, "times" of any sort, we are doing the same thing as with "days." *Cyclicity* brings the response of imaginary plurals. But a likeness of cyclicity to aggregates is not unmistakably given by experience prior to language, or it would be found in all languages, and it is not.[6]

Our *awareness* of time and cyclicity does contain something immediate and subjective—the basic sense of "becoming later and later." But, in the habitual thought of us SAE people, this is covered under something quite different, which though mental should not be called subjective. I call it *objectified,* or imaginary, because it is patterned on the *outer* world. It is this that reflects our linguistic usage. Our tongue makes no distinction between numbers counted on discrete entities and numbers that are simply "counting itself." Habitual thought then assumes that in the latter the numbers are just as much counted on "something" as in the former. This is objectification. Concepts of time lose contact with the subjective experience of "becoming later" and are objectified as counted *quantities,* especially as lengths, made up of units as a length can be visibly marked off into inches. A "length of time" is envisioned as a row of similar units, like a row of bottles.[7]

In Hopi there is a different linguistic situation. Plurals and cardinals are used only for entities that form or can form an objective group. There are no imaginary plurals, but instead ordinals used with singulars. Such an expression as "ten days" is not used. The equivalent statement is an operational one that reaches one day by a suitable count. "They stayed ten days" becomes "they stayed until the eleventh day" or "they left after the tenth day." "Ten days is greater than nine days" becomes "the tenth day is later than the ninth." Our "length of time" is not regarded as a length but as a relation between two events in lateness. Instead of our linguistically promoted objectification of that datum of consciousness we call "time," the Hopi language has not laid down any pattern that would cloak the subjective "becoming later" that is the essence of time.[8]

---

[6] In this section Whorf argues that SAE speakers use the same grammatical construction for physical things that we can experience at a single time such as "ten men" and things that we can only experience as a sequence such as ten days. He refers to the first of these as "real" plurals and the second as "imaginary" plurals.

[7] Whorf claims that because SAE speakers treat the abstract concept of numbers, particularly numbers of days, as if they were physical objects, SAE speakers have con-

structed a linear concept of time as a line of units that stretches out before us into the future and behind us in the past. He makes this point because he is preparing readers for a discussion of the cyclical nature of time in Hopi thought.

[8] In other words, while speakers of SAE think of time as an imaginary plural "ten days" speakers of Hopi think of it as a series of concrete events, day following day, getting later. This makes sense to McGee, because a similar situation

NOUNS OF PHYSICAL QUANTITY IN SAE AND HOPI

We have two kinds of nouns denoting physical things: individual nouns, and mass nouns, e.g., water, milk, wood, granite, sand, flour, meat. Individual nouns denote bodies with definite outlines: a tree, a stick, a man, a hill. Mass nouns denote homogeneous continua without implied boundaries. The distinction is marked by linguistic form; e.g., mass nouns lack plurals,[c] in English drop articles, and in French take the partitive article *du, de la, des*. The distinction is more widespread in language than in the observable appearance of things. Rather few natural occurrences present themselves as unbounded extents; air of course, and often water, rain, snow, sand, rock, dirt, grass. We do not encounter butter, meat, cloth, iron, glass, or most "materials" in such kind of manifestation, but in bodies small or large with definite outlines. The distinction is somewhat forced upon our description of events by an unavoidable pattern in language. It is so inconvenient in a great many cases that we need some way of individualizing the mass noun by further linguistic devices. This is partly done by names of body-types: stick of wood, piece of cloth, pane of glass, cake of soap; also, and even more, by introducing names of containers though their contents be the real issue: glass of water, cup of coffee, dish of food, bag of flour, bottle of beer. These very common container formulas, in which "of" has an obvious, visually perceptible meaning ("contents"), influence our feeling about the less obvious type-body formulas: stick of wood, lump of dough, etc. The formulas are very similar: individual noun plus a similar relator (English "of").

In the obvious case this relator denotes contents. In the inobvious one it "suggests" contents. Hence the lumps, chunks, blocks, pieces, etc., seem to contain something, a "stuff," "substance," or "matter" that answers to the water, coffee, or flour in the container formulas. So with SAE people the philosophic "substance" and "matter" are also the naïve idea; they are instantly acceptable, "common sense." It is so through linguistic habit. Our language patterns often require us to name a physical thing by a binomial that splits the reference into a formless item plus a form.

Hopi is again different. It has a formally distinguished class of nouns. But this class contains no formal subclass of mass nouns. All nouns have an individual sense and both singular and plural forms. Nouns translating most nearly our mass nouns still refer to vague bodies or vaguely bounded extents. They imply indefiniteness, but not lack, of outline and size. In specific statements, "water" means one certain mass or quantity of water, not what we call "the substance water." Generality of statement is conveyed through the verb or predicator, not the noun. Since nouns are individual already, they are not individualized by either type-bodies or names of containers, if there is no special need to emphasize shape or container. The noun itself implies a suitable type-body or container. One says, not "a glass of water" but *kə·yi* "a water," not "a pool of water" but *pa·hə,*[d] not "a dish of cornflour" but n*ə*mni "a (quantity of) cornflour," not "a piece of meat" but *sikʷi* "a meat." The language has neither need for nor analogies on which to build the concept of existence as a duality of formless item and form. It deals with formlessness through other symbols than nouns.[9]

---

exists in Lacandon, Maya. When speaking in Maya, many Lacandon talk of time in terms of phases of the moon. For example, if McGee is staying in a community for two weeks, he describes this as "half a moon." Two weeks is an imaginary plural, fourteen days lined up in front of us that we will experience one day at a time. But the phases of the moon are something that can be concretely experienced. One can see when the moon is halfway through its cycle.

[9] In this section Whorf says that SAE has mass nouns such as "glass" and "water" that require us to individualize them by adding a qualifier such as "pane of glass" or a container such as "glass of water." However, he claims that Hopi has no mass nouns; rather, Hopi nouns for indefinite objects such as water imply outline size or quantity. It is curious that Whorf chooses the example of water to illustrate this point, because water is a case in English in which one can construct nouns in the same manner as Hopi. The nouns *puddle, pond,* and *lake* all imply a certain size and quantity of water. *Twig, stick,* and *board* are other examples in the case of wood. Maybe the differences between SAE and Hopi noun construction are not as absolute as Whorf claims.

PHASES OF CYCLES IN SAE AND HOPI

Such terms as summer, winter, September, morning, noon, sunset are with us nouns, and have little formal linguistic difference from other nouns. They can be subjects or objects, and we say "at" sunset or "in" winter just as we say at a corner or in an orchard.[e] They are pluralized and numerated like nouns of physical objects, as we have seen. Our thought about the referents of such words hence becomes objectified. Without objectification, it would be a subjective experience of real time, i.e. of the consciousness of "becoming later and later"—simply a cyclic phase similar to an earlier phase in that ever-later-becoming duration. Only by imagination can such a cyclic phase be set beside another and another in the manner of a spatial (i.e., visually perceived) configuration. But such is the power of linguistic analogy that we do so objectify cyclic phasing. We do it even by saying "a phase" and "phases" instead of, e.g., "phasing." And the pattern of individual and mass nouns, with the resulting binomial formula of formless item plus form, is so general that it is implicit for all nouns, and hence our very generalized formless items like "substance," "matter," by which we can fill out the binomial for an enormously wide range of nouns. But even these are not quite generalized enough to take in our phase nouns. So for the phase nouns we have made a formless item, "time." We have made it by using "a time," i.e. an occasion or a phase, in the pattern of a mass noun, just as from "a summer" we make "summer" in the pattern of a mass noun. Thus with our binomial formula we can say and think "a moment of time," "a second of time," "a year of time." Let me again point out that the pattern is simply that of "a bottle of milk" or "a piece of cheese." Thus we are assisted to imagine that "a summer" actually contains or consists of such-and-such a quantity of "time."

In Hopi however all phase terms, like summer, morning, etc., are not nouns but a kind of adverb, to use the nearest SAE analogy. They are a formal part of speech by themselves, distinct from nouns, verbs, and even other Hopi "adverbs." Such a word is not a case form or a locative pattern, like "des Abends" or "in the morning." It contains no morpheme like one of "in the house" or "at the tree."[f] It means "when it is morning" or "while morning-phase is occurring." These "temporals" are not used as subjects or objects, or at all like nouns. One does not say "it's a hot summer" or "summer is hot"; summer is not hot, summer is only *when* conditions are hot, *when* heat occurs. One does not say "*this* summer," but "summer now" or "summer recently." There is no objectification, as a region, an extent, a quantity, of the subjective duration-feeling. Nothing is suggested about time except the perpetual "getting later" of it. And so there is no basis here for a formless item answering to our "time."[10]

TEMPORAL FORMS OF VERBS IN SAE AND HOPI

The three-tense system of SAE verbs colors all our thinking about time. This system is amalgamated with that larger scheme of objectification of the subjective experience of duration already noted in other patterns—in the binomial formula applicable to nouns in general, in temporal nouns, in plurality and numeration. This objectification enables us in imagination to "stand time units in a row." Imagination of time as like a row harmonizes with a system of *three* tenses; whereas a system of *two*, an earlier and a later, would seem

---

[10] Building on his discussions of plurality and mass nouns, Whorf proposes here that SAE terminology for phases of time such as summer or morning quantify these imaginary nouns as if they were a quantity of concrete, observable items. In fact, in the Western calendar the seasons are specific series of days that disregard local environmental conditions. This is another example of the Western objectification of time. In contrast, he says the Hopi use phase terms in the manner of adverbs. For example, summer is not hot (because summer is not a concrete thing that contains heat). Summer for the Hopi is when conditions are hot. From Whorf's description we can see that, in general, Hopi is a concrete language that reflects people's physical experience. This is a point that is dealt with in greater detail in the next section in the discussion of verb forms.

to correspond better to the feeling of duration as it is experienced. For if we inspect consciousness we find no past, present, future, but a unity embracing complexity. *Everything* is in consciousness, and everything in consciousness *is,* and is together. There is in it a sensuous and a nonsensuous. We may call the sensuous—what we are seeing, hearing, touching—the "present" while in the nonsensuous the vast image-world of memory is being labeled "the past" and another realm of belief, intuition, and uncertainty "the future"; yet sensation, memory, foresight, all are in consciousness together-one is not "yet to be" nor another "once but no more." Where real time comes in is that all this in consciousness is "getting later," changing certain relations in an irreversible manner. In this "latering" or "durating" there seems to me to be a paramount contrast between the newest, latest instant at the focus of attention and the rest—the earlier. Languages by the score get along well with two tense-like forms answering to this paramount relation of later to earlier. We can of course *construct and contemplate in thought* a system of past, present, future, in the objectified configuration of points on a line. This is what our general objectification tendency leads us to do and our tense system confirms.

In English the present tense seems the one least in harmony with the paramount temporal relation. It is as if pressed into various and not wholly congruous duties. One duty is to stand as objectified middle term between objectified past and objectified future, in narration, discussion, argument, logic, philosophy. Another is to denote inclusion in the sensuous field: "I *see* him." Another is for nomic, i.e. customarily or generally valid, statements: "We *see* with our eyes." These varied uses introduce confusions of thought, of which for the most part we are unaware.[11]

Hopi, as we might expect, is different here too. Verbs have no "tenses" like ours, but have validity-forms ("assertions"), aspects, and clause-linkage forms (modes), that yield even greater precision of speech. The validity-forms denote that the speaker (not the subject) reports the situation (answering to our past and present) or that he expects it (answering to our future)[g] or that he makes a nomic statement (answering to our nomic present). The aspects denote different degrees of duration and different kinds of tendency "during duration." As yet we have noted nothing to indicate whether an event is sooner or later than another when both are *reported.* But need for this does not arise until we have two verbs: i.e., two clauses. In that case the "modes" denote relations between the clauses, including relations of later to earlier and of simultaneity. Then there are many detached words that express similar relations, supplementing the modes and aspects. The duties of our three-tense system and its tripartite linear objectified "time" are distributed among various verb categories, all different from our tenses; and there is no more basis for an objectified time in Hopi verbs than in other Hopi patterns; although this does not in the least hinder the verb forms and other patterns from being

---

[11] Whorf points out that SAE requires one to think and speak in a three-tense system. However, there is no past, present, or future in our consciousness. We live in a continual present and experience our memories (past), sensations (present), and anticipation of things (future) all together in "real time." This is another example of the way that SAE steers its speakers toward the Western objectification of time. Hopi, however, is different, as Whorf explains later. Besides outlining how he thinks Hopi speakers understand the world, Whorf's claim has much larger implications. Whorf is saying that the physical phenomenon of consciousness can be divided into two categories: the sensuous, that is, what we are experiencing at this instant, and the nonsensuous, everything else (memories, anticipations, anxieties, and so on). Because of the structure of our language, we carve three tenses out of this phenomenon: past, present, and future. In fact, as a physical phenomenon, the only thing that actually exists is the process of getting later. In this, Whorf understands consciousness in a fashion that is consistent with Boasian thinking. Consciousness is essentially undifferentiated . . . a blank slate, or tabula rasa. Understandings are created by culture and environment rather than by any preexisting tendency of the brain to work in particular ways. Here, Whorf focuses on an important, and very Boasian, debate: Are notions such as past, present, and future related to aspects of human physiology or is human behavior virtually completely flexible? Are they learned, cultural phenomena?

closely adjusted to the pertinent realities of actual situations.[12]

[*Because of space constraints we have skipped a 590-word section of Whorf's essay called "Duration, Intensity, and Tendency in SAE and Hopi." In this section Whorf discusses how duration, intensity, and tendency are expressed metaphorically in SAE. For example, an event that concludes quickly is "short." Someone with an injury may suffer a "sharp" pain, and as the oil market reacts to shifting supplies of crude oil caused by political and environmental events the price of gasoline "rises" and "falls." Whorf concludes that this is part of the whole process in SAE of objectifying or spatializing qualities and events that are not concrete or spatial. He says that we can hardly refer to the simplest nonspatial situation without using physical metaphors. For example, do you "grasp" this point, or is it "over your head"? Whorf concludes this section by saying that the Hopi language does not use these physical metaphors because Hopi has "tensors," a class of words that denotes intensity, tendency and duration.*]

HABITUAL THOUGHT IN SAE AND HOPI

The comparison now to be made between the habitual thought worlds of SAE and Hopi speakers is of course incomplete. It is possible only to touch upon certain dominant contrasts that appear to stem from the linguistic differences already noted. By "habitual thought" and "thought world" I mean more than simply language, i.e., than the linguistic patterns themselves. I include all the analogical and suggestive value of the patterns (e.g., our "imaginary space" and its distant implications), and all the give-and-take between language and the culture as a whole, wherein is a vast amount that is not linguistic but yet shows the shaping influence of language. In brief, this "thought world" is the microcosm that each man carries about within himself, by which he measures and understands what he can of the macrocosm.[13]

The SAE microcosm has analyzed reality largely in terms of what it calls "things" (bodies and quasibodies) plus modes of extensional but formless existence that it calls "substances" or "matter." It tends to see existence through a binomial formula that expresses any existent as a spatial form plus a spatial formless continuum related to the form, as contents is related to the outlines of its container. Nonspatial existents are imaginatively spatialized and charged with similar implications of form and continuum.

The Hopi microcosm seems to have analyzed reality largely in terms of *events* (or better "eventing"), referred to in two ways, objective and subjective. Objectively, and only if perceptible physical experience, events are expressed mainly as outlines, colors, movements, and other perceptive reports. Subjectively, for both the physical and nonphysical, events are considered the

---

[12] As Whorf indicates, many languages like Hopi have two tense forms (past and present) and numerous aspect forms that indicate duration or whether an action is about to happen, is ongoing, or has been completed.

[13] Up to this point Whorf has spent his time (whoops, another metaphor objectifying time as a quantity) discussing how SAE and Hopi grammatical categories are different. In this section he now turns his attention to the relationship between language, thought, and behavior. Whorf argues that cultural differences are not simply reflected in language. Rather, the cultural differences "stem from" linguistic differences. He proposes that each person carries within themselves a "thought world," shaped by language, through which they understand the world around them. In the discussion that follows, Whorf is proposing that language and culture are homogeneous phenomena. An individual is born into both and they are largely responsible for shaping that person's worldview. In fact, this notion of the thought world is similar to Ruth Benedict's concept of a cultural configuration (see essay 14). Although he does not cite Benedict in his essay, both Whorf and Benedict were close friends of Edward Sapir and shared his interests in the relationship between psychology and culture. Romanucci-Ross reports that Sapir was "intimately friendly with Ruth [Benedict] and even more involved with Margaret [Mead]" (2001:1176). Benedict's *Patterns of Culture* was published in 1934, just at the time Whorf was first formulating his thoughts on the role of language in anthropology. It is clear here that Whorf was familiar with Benedict's work.

expression of invisible intensity factors, on which depend their stability and persistence, or their fugitiveness and proclivities.[14] It implies that existents do not "become later and later" all in the same way; but some do so by growing like plants, some by diffusing and vanishing, some by a procession of metamorphoses, some by enduring in one shape till affected by violent forces. In the nature of each existent able to manifest as a definite whole is the power of its own mode of duration: its growth, decline, stability, cyclicity, or creativeness. Everything is thus already "prepared" for the way it now manifests by earlier phases, and what it will be later, partly has been, and partly is in act of being so "prepared." An emphasis and importance rests on this preparing or being prepared aspect of the world that may to the Hopi correspond to that "quality of reality" that "matter" or "stuff" has for us.[15]

HABITUAL BEHAVIOR FEATURES OF HOPI CULTURE

Our behavior, and that of Hopi, can be seen to be coordinated in many ways to the linguistically conditioned microcosm. As in my fire casebook, people act about situations in ways which are like the ways they talk about them. A characteristic of Hopi behavior is the emphasis on preparation. This includes announcing and getting ready for events well beforehand, elaborate precautions to insure persistence of desired conditions, and

stress on good will as the preparer of right results. Consider the analogies of the day-counting pattern alone. Time is mainly reckoned "by day" (*taLk, tala*) or "by night" (*tok*), which words are not nouns but tensors, the first formed on a root "light, day," the second on a root "sleep." The count is by *ordinals*. This is not the pattern of counting a number of different men or things, even though they appear successively, for, even then, they *could* gather into an assemblage. It is the pattern of counting successive reappearances of the *same* man or thing, incapable of forming an assemblage. The analogy is not to behave about day-cyclicity as to several men ("several days"), which is what *we* tend to do, but to behave as to the successive visits of the *same man*. One does not alter several men by working upon just one, but one can prepare and so alter the later visits of the same man by working to affect the visit he is making now. This is the way the Hopi deal with the future—by working within a present situation which is expected to carry impresses, both obvious and occult, forward into the future event of interest. One might say that Hopi society understands our proverb "Well begun is half done," but not our "Tomorrow is another day." This may explain much in Hopi character.[16]

This Hopi preparing behavior may be roughly divided into announcing, outer preparing, inner preparing, covert participation, and persistence. Announcing, or preparative publicity, is an important function in the hands of a special official, the Crier Chief. Outer preparing is preparation

---

[14] Fugitiveness and proclivities: in this context, instabilities and tendencies.

[15] In other words, whereas SAE is characterized by "being," Hopi is characterized by "becoming." This is an interesting point, because Whorf's concerns here dovetail key interests of philosophers of his era, particularly the phenomenologists. Edmund Husserl and his student Martin Heidegger had both published works on the nature of time in the 1920s. Heidegger published *Being and Time* in 1927 and Husserl *Lectures on the Phenomenology of Internal Time Consciousness* in 1928. In these works they explore various objective and subjective experiences of time.

[16] In this section Whorf seeks to make the connection between Hopi language and behavior. He says that as with

the insurance cases he has investigated, the Hopi act in ways that are similar to the way they talk and he provides several examples that contrast the Hopi point of view with that of SAE speakers. The examples speak for themselves and do not need our explanation. It is worth pointing out that Whorf is firmly Boasian in using Hopi language as a way of explaining the Hopi worldview. This was a position Boas first formulated in 1911 in the introduction to his *Handbook of American Indian Languages*. However, unlike Boas and following Sapir, Whorf believed that psychology (rather than history) provided the explanatory tools that anthropology needed to analyze the relationship between humans and culture, and he saw linguistics as the bridge between anthropology and psychology.

involving much visible activity, not all necessarily directly useful within our understanding. It includes ordinary practicing, rehearsing, getting ready, introductory formalities, preparing of special food, etc. (all of these to a degree that may seem overelaborate to us), intensive sustained muscular activity like running, racing, dancing, which is thought to increase the intensity of development of events (such as growth of crops), mimetic and other magic, preparations based on esoteric theory involving perhaps occult instruments like prayer sticks, prayer feathers, and prayer meal, and finally the great cyclic ceremonies and dances, which have the significance of preparing rain and crops. From one of the verbs meaning "prepare" is derived the noun for "harvest" or "crop": *na'twani*, "the prepared" or the "in preparation."[h]

Inner preparing is use of prayer and meditation, and at lesser intensity good wishes and good will, to further desired results. Hopi attitudes stress the power of desire and thought. With their "microcosm" it is utterly natural that they should. Desire and thought are the earliest, and therefore the most important, most critical and crucial, stage of preparing. Moreover, to the Hopi, one's desires and thoughts influence not only his own actions, but all nature as well. This too is wholly natural. Consciousness itself is aware of work, of the feel of effort and energy, in desire and thinking. Experience more basic than language tells us that, if energy is expended, effects are produced. *We* tend to believe that our bodies can stop up this energy, prevent it from affecting other things until we will our *bodies* to overt action. But this may be so only because we have our own linguistic basis for a theory that formless items like "matter" are things in themselves, malleable only by similar things, by more matter, and hence insulated from the powers of life and thought. It is no more unnatural to think that thought contacts everything and pervades the universe than to think, as we all do, that light kindled outdoors does this. And it is not unnatural to suppose that thought, like any other force, leaves everywhere traces of effect. Now, when *we* think of a certain actual rosebush, we do not suppose that our thought goes to that actual bush, and engages with it, like a searchlight turned upon it. What then do we suppose our consciousness is dealing with when we are thinking of that rosebush? Probably we think it is dealing with a "mental image" which is not the rosebush but a mental surrogate of it. But why should it be *natural* to think that our thought deals with a surrogate and not with the real rosebush? Quite possibly because we are dimly aware that we carry about with us a whole imaginary space, full of mental surrogates. To us, mental surrogates are old familiar fare. Along with the images of imaginary space, which we perhaps secretly know to be imaginary only, we tuck the thought-of actually existing rosebush, which may be quite another story, perhaps just because we have that very convenient "place" for it. The Hopi thought-world has no imaginary space. The corollary to this is that it may not locate thought dealing with real space anywhere but in real space, nor insulate real space from the effects of thought. A Hopi would naturally suppose that his thought (or he himself) traffics with the actual rosebush—or more likely, corn plant—that he is thinking about. The thought then should leave some trace of itself with the plant in the field. If it is a good thought, one about health and growth, it is good for the plant; if a bad thought, the reverse.[17]

The Hopi emphasize the intensity-factor of thought. Thought to be most effective should be vivid in consciousness, definite, steady, sustained, charged with strongly felt good intentions. They render the idea in English as "concentrating," "holding it in your heart," "putting your mind on

---

[17] This section is a brilliant example of culturally relativistic writing, and we want to draw your attention to the skill with which Whorf explains how a Hopi views his place in the world. Boas believed that one of the goals of anthropology was to understand the "native" worldview. Here Whorf not only explains the Hopi view of things, he does it in such a way that highlights the contrasts between Hopi and SAE and makes Hopi seem reasonable. It is good to point out here that the clarity of Whorf's presentation does not mean he was correct. Linguists and psychologists have been experimenting with different aspects of Whorf's ideas for half a century without reaching any definitive conclusions.

it," "earnestly hoping." Thought power is the force behind ceremonies, prayer sticks, ritual smoking, etc. The prayer pipe is regarded as an aid to "concentrating" (so said my informant). Its name, *na'twanpi,* means "instrument of preparing."

Covert participation is mental collaboration from people who do not take part in the actual affair, be it a job of work, hunt, race, or ceremony, but direct their thought and good will toward the affair's success. Announcements often seek to enlist the support of such mental helpers as well as of overt participants, and contain exhortations to the people to aid with their active good will.[i] A similarity to our concepts of a sympathetic audience or the cheering section at a football game should not obscure the fact that it is primarily the power of directed thought, and not merely sympathy or encouragement, that is expected of covert participants. In fact these latter get in their deadliest work before, not during, the game! A corollary to the power of thought is the power of wrong thought for evil; hence one purpose of covert participation is to obtain the mass force of many good wishers to offset the harmful thought of ill wishers. Such attitudes greatly favor cooperation and community spirit. Not that the Hopi community is not full of rivalries and colliding interests. Against the tendency to social disintegration in such a small, isolated group, the theory of "preparing" by the power of thought, logically leading to the great power of the combined, intensified, and harmonized thought of the whole community, must help vastly toward the rather remarkable degree of cooperation that, in spite of much private bickering, the Hopi village displays in all the important cultural activities.

Hopi "preparing" activities again show a result of their linguistic thought background in an emphasis on persistence and constant insistent repetition. A sense of the cumulative value of innumerable small momenta is dulled by an objectified, spatialized view of time like ours, enhanced by a way of thinking close to the subjective awareness of duration, of the ceaseless "latering" of events. To us, for whom time is a motion on a space, unvarying repetition seems to scatter its force along a row of units of that space, and be wasted. To the Hopi, for whom time is not a motion but a "getting later" of everything that has ever been done, unvarying repetition is not wasted but accumulated. It is storing up an invisible change that holds over into later events.[j] As we have seen, it is as if the return of the day were felt as the return of the same person, a little older but with all the impresses of yesterday, not as "another day," i.e. like an entirely different person. This principle joined with that of thought-power and with traits of general Pueblo culture is expressed in the theory of the Hopi ceremonial dance for furthering rain and crops, as well as in its short, piston-like tread, repeated thousands of times, hour after hour.[18]

SOME IMPRESSES OF LINGUISTIC HABIT IN WESTERN CIVILIZATION

It is harder to do justice in few words to the linguistically conditioned features of our own culture than in the case of the Hopi, because of both vast scope and difficulty of objectivity—because of our deeply ingrained familiarity with the attitudes to be analyzed. I wish merely to sketch certain characteristics adjusted to our linguistic

---

[18] Here Whorf uses his discussion of the Hopi conception of time and their views on the physical power of thought to make sense of Hopi ritual activity. He says that because their language treats time fundamentally differently than SAE, repetition, for the Hopi, is an essential part of their ceremonies. However, Whorf claims that SAE speakers as a result of their language cannot conceive of time in this "becoming later" fashion and therefore do not see the same value to repetition as do the Hopi. We are not in a position to quibble with Whorf over his observations of

the Hopi, but we feel that Whorf overlooked the history of traditional Christian religious ceremony all over Europe. Much Christian ritual activity involves repetition. It would be hard to look at the life of people in Catholic monastic orders, for example, and not see that the lives of monks and nuns are structured around a repetitive prayer and ritual cycle. Catholic penance may involve repeated sayings of specific prayers. The last line in this paragraph could apply equally well to Christian pilgrims, whose every footstep may be considered a prayer in exactly the same way.

binomialism of form plus formless item or "substance," to our metaphoricalness, our imaginary space, and our objectified time. These, as we have seen, are linguistic.

From the form-plus-substance dichotomy the philosophical views most traditionally characteristic of the "Western world" have derived huge support. Here belong materialism, psychophysical parallelism, physics at least in its traditional Newtonian form—and dualistic views of the universe in general. Indeed here belongs almost everything that is "hard, practical common sense." Monistic,[19] holistic, and relativistic views of reality appeal to philosophers and some scientists, but they are badly handicapped in appealing to the "common sense" of the Western average man—not because nature herself refutes them (if she did, philosophers could have discovered this much), but because they must be talked about in what amounts to a new language. "Common sense," as its name shows, and "practicality" as its name does not show, are largely matters of talking so that one is readily understood. It is sometimes stated that Newtonian space, time, and matter are sensed by everyone intuitively, whereupon relativity is cited as showing how mathematical analysis can prove intuition wrong. This, besides being unfair to intuition, is an attempt to answer offhand question (1) put at the outset of this paper, to answer which this research was undertaken. Presentation of the findings now nears its end, and I think the answer is clear. The offhand answer, laying the blame upon intuition for our slowness in discovering mysteries of the Cosmos, such as relativity, is the wrong one. The right answer is: Newtonian space, time, and matter are no intuitions. They are recepts [*sic*] from culture and language. That is where Newton got them.[20]

Our objectified view of time is, however, favorable to historicity and to everything connected with the keeping of records, while the Hopi view is unfavorable thereto. The latter is too subtle, complex, and ever-developing, supplying no ready-made answer to the question of when "one" event ends and "another" begins. When it is implicit that everything that ever happened still is, but is in a necessarily different form from what memory or record reports, there is less incentive to study the past. As for the present, the incentive would be not to record it but to treat it as "preparing." But *our* objectified time puts before imagination something like a ribbon or scroll marked off into equal blank spaces, suggesting that each be filled with an entry. Writing has no doubt helped toward our linguistic treatment of

---

[19] Monism is the philosophical principle that mind and matter are essentially the same.

[20] Because he studied engineering Whorf had a better background in the physical sciences than most of his colleagues, and he continued to follow developments in the sciences throughout his career. He was familiar with Einstein's work on relativity and saw a link between relativity in physics and cultural relativity in the study of human societies, namely, that "reality" depends on the positioning of the observer. Here this leads him to an extremely radical claim: that we experience Newtonian physics (things such as the effects of gravity, the consistency of time, or mass) not because these things are "real" but because our language and culture cause us to perceive and believe them. By implication, if we had a different language and culture (like the Hopi) we might perceive what SAE speakers call time, gravity, and mass differently. It's an intriguing notion, and one needs to be careful not to misunderstand his point. Whorf is not arguing here that the physical laws that govern the universe are different in different cultures because people speak differently, but that the cultural reality or how events are defined may be different.

Whorf is arguing a linguistic version of cultural relativity. However, his work is closer than most Boasians to *hermeneutics*, the study of the interpretation of meaning. Hermeneutics was developed in Europe in the early twentieth century by philosophers such as Martin Heidegger and Hans-Georg Gadamer. Hermeneuticists argued that one could not have objective knowledge about the world because people necessarily understood the world through their cultural, linguistic, and intellectual models.

In American anthropology Boas and his students used the notion of cultural relativity to argue against racism and discrimination and to support the notion of cultural equality. Unfortunately, in post–World War I Germany political leaders used ideas from hermeneutics to argue for German cultural superiority that lead to a rise in nationalism, anti-Semitism, and the ascendance of Hitler and the National Socialist Party.

time, even as the linguistic treatment has guided the uses of writing. Through this give-and-take between language and the whole culture we get, for instance:

1. Records, diaries, bookkeeping, accounting, mathematics stimulated by accounting.
2. Interest in exact sequence, dating, calendars, chronology, clocks, time wages, time graphs, time as used in physics.
3. Annals, histories, the historical attitude, interest in the past, archaeology, attitudes of introjection toward past periods, e.g., classicism, romanticism.[21]

Just as we conceive our objectified time as extending in the future in the same way that it extends in the past, so we set down our estimates of the future in the same shape as our records of the past, producing programs, schedules, budgets. The formal equality of the spacelike units by which we measure and conceive time leads us to consider the "formless item" or "substance" of time to be homogeneous and in ratio to the number of units. Hence our prorata[22] allocation of value to time, lending itself to the building up of a commercial structure based on time-prorata

values: time wages (time work constantly supersedes piece work), rent, credit, interest, depreciation charges, and insurance premiums. No doubt this vast system, once built, would continue to run under any sort of linguistic treatment of time; but that it should have been built at all, reaching the magnitude and particular form it has in the Western world, is a fact decidedly in consonance with the patterns of the SAE languages. Whether such a civilization as ours would be possible with widely different linguistic handling of time is a large question—in our civilization, our linguistic patterns and the fitting of our behavior to the temporal order are what they are, and they are in accord. We are of course stimulated to use calendars, clocks, and watches, and to try to measure time ever more precisely; this aids science, and science in turn, following these well-worn cultural grooves, gives back to culture an ever-growing store of applications, habits, and values, with which culture again directs science. But what lies outside this spiral? Science is beginning to find that there is something in the Cosmos that is not in accord with the concepts we have formed in mounting the spiral. It is trying to frame a NEW LANGUAGE by which to adjust itself to a wider universe.[23]

---

[21] Whorf here mentions the influence of writing on our objectified concept of time. Some more recent authors argue that writing has a profound influence on the way people think and communicate. For example, in *Orality and Literacy* (1982) Ong argues that literacy transforms thought in ways possible only after the technology of writing has been adopted. Whereas Whorf believed the differences he found between SAE and Hopi speakers were due to the grammar of the languages, a generation later scholars such as Ong and Goody argued that these differences were due to literacy and writing. Goody in particular chides Whorf for failing to see that the features of SAE are shared in common in part because they are written languages (1977:161).

Beyond this, note that Whorf's notion of society is thoroughly idealist. It is entirely determined by thinking. Most modern theorists would probably link the development of record keeping to commerce, taxation, and the emergence of state-level society. For Whorf, it is a function of language. Whereas Hopi language seems to virtually prohibit record keeping, SAE compels it.

[22] *Prorata:* on a proportional basis.

[23] Here Whorf suggests that language directs our scientific thinking and that scientific thinking in turn reinforces our "well-worn cultural grooves." Although Whorf here is talking about SAE-speaking society and not the Hopi, following this reasoning implies that the Hopi could never have come up with ideas such as payment for hourly labor or either Einsteinian or Newtonian physics. Their language would have prevented them from seeing the world in the way necessary for these concepts. At the time Whorf wrote, relativity was a fairly new concept (Whorf published this piece in 1941, Einstein published the theory of specific relativity in 1905). Whorf argues that language had not yet adapted to Einstein's discoveries.

Relativity creates an interesting problem for Whorf. If language controls thought to the degree that Whorf suggests, then how could Einstein discover concepts for which there were no words (that required a "NEW LANGUAGE")? Whorf attempts to solve this problem by proposing a feedback loop. Language creates science, which, in turn creates new vocabularies.

It is clear how the emphasis on "saving time" which goes with all the above and is very obvious objectification of time, leads to a high valuation of "speed," which shows itself a great deal in our behavior.

Still another behavioral effect is that the character of monotony and regularity possessed by our image of time as an evenly scaled limitless tape measure persuades us to behave as if that monotony were more true of events than it really is. That is, it helps to routinize us. We tend to select and favor whatever bears out this view, to "play up to" the routine aspects of existence. One phase of this is behavior evincing a false sense of security or an assumption that all will always go smoothly, and a lack in foreseeing and protecting ourselves against hazards. Our technique of harnessing energy does well in routine performance, and it is along routine lines that we chiefly strive to improve it—we are, for example, relatively uninterested in stopping the energy from causing accidents, fires, and explosions, which it is doing constantly and on a wide scale. Such indifference to the unexpectedness of life would be disastrous to a society as small, isolated, and precariously poised as the Hopi society is, or rather once was.

Thus our linguistically determined thought world not only collaborates with our cultural idols and ideals, but engages even our unconscious personal reactions in its patterns and gives them certain typical characters. One such character, as we have seen, is *carelessness,* as in reckless driving or throwing cigarette stubs into waste paper. Another of different sort is *gesturing* when we talk. Very many of the gestures made by English-speaking people at least, and probably by all SAE speakers, serve to illustrate, by a movement in space, not a real spatial reference but one of the nonspatial references that our language handles by metaphors of imaginary space. That is, we are more apt to make a grasping gesture when we speak of grasping an elusive idea than when we speak of grasping a doorknob. The gesture seeks to make a metaphorical and hence somewhat unclear reference more clear. But, if a language refers to nonspatials without implying a spatial analogy, the reference is not made any clearer by gesture.

The Hopi gesture very little, perhaps not at all in the sense we understand as gesture.

It would seem as if kinesthesia, or the sensing of muscular movement, though arising before language, should be made more highly conscious by linguistic use of imaginary space and metaphorical images of motion. Kinesthesia is marked in two facets of European culture: art and sport. European sculpture, an art in which Europe excels, is strongly kinesthetic, conveying great sense of the body's motions; European painting likewise. The dance in our culture expresses delight in motion rather than symbolism or ceremonial, and our music is greatly influenced by our dance forms. Our sports are strongly imbued with this element of the "poetry of motion." Hopi races and games seem to emphasize rather the virtues of endurance and sustained intensity. Hopi dancing is highly symbolic and is performed with great intensity and earnestness, but has not much movement or swing.

Synesthesia, or suggestion by certain sense receptions of characters belonging to another sense, as of light and color by sounds and *vice versa,* should be made more conscious by a linguistic metaphorical system that refers to nonspatial experiences by terms for spatial ones, though undoubtedly it arises from a deeper source. Probably in the first instance metaphor arises from synesthesia and not the reverse; yet metaphor need not become firmly rooted in linguistic pattern, as Hopi shows. Nonspatial experience has one well-organized sense, *hearing*—for smell and taste are but little organized. Nonspatial consciousness is a realm chiefly of thought, feeling, and *sound.* Spatial consciousness is a realm of light, color, sight, and touch, and presents shapes and dimensions. Our metaphorical system, by naming nonspatial experiences after spatial ones, imputes to sounds, smells, tastes, emotions, and thoughts qualities like the colors, luminosities, shapes, angles, textures, and motions of spatial experience. And to some extent the reverse transference occurs; for, after much talking about tones as high, low, sharp, dull, heavy, brilliant, slow, the talker finds it easy to think of some factors in spatial experience as like factors of tone. Thus we speak of "tones" of color, a gray "monotone," a "loud" necktie, a "taste" in dress: all spatial metaphor in reverse. Now European art is distinctive in the way it seeks deliberately to play with synesthesia. Music tries to suggest scenes, color, movement, geometric design; painting and sculpture are often consciously guided by the analogies of music's rhythm; colors are conjoined with feeling for the analogy to concords and discords. The European theater and opera seek a synthesis of many arts. It may be that in this way our metaphorical language that is in some sense a confusion of thought is producing, through art, a result of far-reaching value—a deeper esthetic sense leading toward a more direct apprehension of underlying unity behind the phenomena so variously reported by our sense channels.[24]

HISTORICAL IMPLICATIONS

How does such a network of language, culture, and behavior come about historically? Which was first: the language patterns or the cultural norms? In main they have grown up together, constantly influencing each other. But in this partnership the nature of the language is the factor that limits free plasticity and rigidifies channels of development in the more autocratic way. This is so because a language is a system, not just an assemblage of norms. Large systematic outlines can change to something really new only very slowly, while many other cultural innovations are made with comparative quickness. Language thus represents the mass mind; it is affected by inventions and innovations, but affected little and slowly, whereas to inventors and innovators it legislates with the decree immediate.[25]

The growth of the SAE language-culture complex dates from ancient times. Much of its metaphorical reference to the nonspatial by the spatial was already fixed in the ancient tongues, and more especially in Latin. It is indeed a marked trait of Latin. If we compare, say Hebrew, we find that, while Hebrew has some allusion to not-space as space, Latin has more. Latin terms for nonspatials, like *educo, religio, principia, comprehendo,* are usually metaphorized physical references: lead out, tying back, etc. This is not true of all languages—it is quite untrue of Hopi. The fact that in Latin the direction of development happened to be from spatial to nonspatial (partly because of secondary stimulation to abstract thinking when the intellectually crude Romans encountered Greek culture) and that later tongues were strongly stimulated to mimic Latin, seems a likely reason for a belief, which still lingers on among linguists, that this is the natural direction of semantic change in all languages, and for the persistent notion in Western learned circles (in strong contrast to Eastern ones) that objective experience is prior to subjective. Philosophies make out a weighty case for the reverse, and certainly the direction of development is sometimes the reverse. Thus the Hopi word for "heart" can be shown to be a late formation within Hopi from a root meaning think or remember. Or consider what has happened to the word "radio" in such a sentence as "he bought a new radio," as compared to its prior meaning "science of wireless telephony." In the Middle

---

[24] Earlier in the essay, Whorf pointed out that SAE speakers typically use physical metaphors to talk about nonphysical things. For example, the phrase "I take your point." Here Whorf makes the interesting suggestion that this phenomenon developed from synesthesia. Yet if we accept Whorf's idea, this raises an interesting (and presumably unsolvable) problem. Whorf says that linguistic metaphor perhaps arose from the experience of synesthesia, which, presumably, all humans are capable of having. An interesting question, then, is why certain metaphors become "rooted" in one language but not others.

[25] Here Whorf outlines a view of language that parallels his Boasian colleagues' view of culture. He refuses to speculate on whether language or culture came first, saying only that they form a network of factors that developed together and influenced each other. One can also see Whorf's linguistic determinism in the conclusion of this paragraph where he says that while language is little affected by inventions and changes slowly, it has an immediate power over the inventors.

Ages the patterns already formed in Latin began to interweave with the increased mechanical invention, industry, trade, and scholastic and scientific thought. The need for measurement in industry and trade, the stores and bulks of "stuffs" in various containers, the type-bodies in which various goods were handled, standardizing of measure and weight units, invention of clocks and measurement of "time," keeping of records, accounts, chronicles, histories, growth of mathematics and the partnership of mathematics and science, all cooperated to bring our thought and language world into its present form.

In Hopi history, could we read it, we should find a different type of language and a different set of cultural and environmental influences working together. A peaceful agricultural society isolated by geographic features and nomad enemies in a land of scanty rainfall; arid agriculture that could be made successful only by the utmost perseverance (hence the value of persistence and repetition), necessity for collaboration (hence emphasis on the psychology of teamwork and on mental factors in general), corn and rain as primary criteria of value, need of extensive *preparations* and precautions to assure crops in the poor soil and precarious climate, keen realization of dependence upon nature favoring prayer and a religious attitude toward the forces of nature, especially prayer and religion directed toward the ever-needed blessing, rain—these things interacted with Hopi linguistic patterns to mold them, to be molded again by them, and so little by little to shape the Hopi world outlook.[26]

To sum up the matter, our first question asked in the beginning (p. 134) is answered thus: Concepts of "time" and "matter" are not given in substantially the same form by experience to all men but depend upon the nature of the language or languages through the use of which they have been developed. They do not depend so much

upon *any one system* (e.g., tense, or nouns) within the grammar as upon the ways of analyzing and reporting experience which have become fixed in the language as integrated "fashions of speaking" and which cut across the typical grammatical classifications, so that such a "fashion" may include lexical, morphological, syntactic, and otherwise systemically diverse means coordinated in a certain frame of consistency. Our own "time" differs markedly from Hopi "duration." It is conceived as like a space of strictly limited dimensions, or sometimes as like a motion upon such a space, and employed as an intellectual tool accordingly. Hopi "duration" seems to be inconceivable in terms of space or motion, being the mode in which life differs from form, and consciousness *in toto* from the spatial elements of consciousness. Certain ideas born of our own time-concept, such as that of absolute simultaneity, would be either very difficult to express or impossible and devoid of meaning under the Hopi conception, and would be replaced by operational concepts. Our "matter" is the physical subtype of "substance" or "stuff," which is conceived as the formless extensional item that must be joined with form before there can be real existence. In Hopi there seems to be nothing corresponding to it; there are no formless extensional items; existence may or may not have form, but what it also has, with or without form, is intensity and duration, these being nonextensional and at bottom the same.

But what about our concept of "space," which was also included in our first question? There is no such striking difference between Hopi and SAE about space as about time, and probably the apprehension of space is given in substantially the same form by experience irrespective of language. The experiments of the Gestalt psychologists with visual perception appear to establish this as a fact. But the *concept* of *space* will vary

---

[26] Here Whorf summarizes how language and culture developed together and influenced each other to produce Western society as we know it, and how a different language and different set of cultural and environmental influences produced a very different type of culture among the Hopi. This is classic statement of the historical-particularistic view of culture.

somewhat with language, because, as an intellectual tool,[k] it is so closely linked with the concomitant employment of other intellectual tools, of the order of "time" and "matter," which are linguistically conditioned. We see things with our eyes in the same space forms as the Hopi, but our idea of space has also the property of acting as a surrogate of nonspatial relationships like time, intensity, tendency, and as a void to be filled with imagined formless items, one of which may even be called "space." Space as sensed by the Hopi would not be connected mentally with such surrogates, but would be comparatively "pure," unmixed with extraneous notions.

As for our second question (p. 134): There are connections but not correlations or diagnostic correspondences between cultural norms and linguistic patterns. Although it would be impossible to infer the existence of Crier Chiefs from the lack of tenses in Hopi, or vice versa, there is a relation between a language and the rest of the culture of the society which uses it. There are cases where the "fashions of speaking" are closely integrated with the whole general culture, whether or not this be universally true, and there are connections within this integration, between the kind of linguistic analyses employed and various behavioral reactions and also the shapes taken by variouscultural developments. Thus the importance of Crier Chiefs does have a connection, not with tenselessness itself, but with a system of thought in which categories different from our tenses are natural. These connections are to

be found not so much by focusing attention on the typical rubrics of linguistic, ethnographic, or sociological description as by examining the culture and the language (always and only when the two have been together historically for a considerable time) as a whole in which concatenations that run across these departmental lines may be expected to exist, and, if they do exist, eventually to be discoverable by study.[27]

NOTES

[a] We have plenty of evidence that this is not the case. Consider only the Hopi and the Ute, with languages that on the overt morphological and lexical level are as similar as, say, English and German. The idea of "correlation" between language and culture, in the generally accepted sense of correlation, is certainly a mistaken one.

[b] As we say, "ten at the *same time*," showing that in our language and thought we restate the fact of group perception in terms of a concept "time," the large linguistic component of which will appear in the course of this paper.

[c] It is no exception to this rule of lacking a plural that a mass noun may sometimes coincide in lexeme with an individual noun that of course has a plural; e.g., "stone" (no pl.) with "a stone" (pl. "stones"). The plural form denoting varieties, e.g., "wines" is of course a different sort of thing from the true plural; it is a curious outgrowth from the SAE mass nouns, leading to still another sort of imaginary aggregates, which will have to be omitted from this paper.

[d] Hopi has two words for water quantities; kə·yi and pa·hə. The difference is something like that between "stone" and "rock" in English, pa·hə implying greater

---

[27] In this essay, Whorf supplies a series of linguistic examples that seem to be compelling evidence in support of linguistic determinism. He concludes however, that what he has demonstrated are "connections but not correlations or diagnostic correspondences between cultural norms and linguistic patterns." Whorf the scientist recognized that his work was not proof of his ideas in a scientific sense. Reviewing almost fifty years of work on different aspects of the Sapir-Whorf hypothesis, Lucy argues that there has been no sustained program of empirical research that supports it (1997:291–292). He points out that work such as Whorf's typically highlights features of a language that the researcher assumes to be relevant to a behavior. However, even though the feature of the language may stand out to

the observer, it may not be structurally or functionally important in the language. One doesn't know unless there is a formal analysis of the language (Lucy 1997:302). More particularly, Whorf's knowledge and understanding of Hopi have been questioned. In 1983, Ekkehart Malotki argued that Whorf simply got it wrong and that claims that Hopi do not use expressions such as "ten days" are incorrect. Malotki argued that the Hopi conception of time was not radically different from our own (1983: 529–530). Still, Whorf and Sapir's notion that there is a relationship between language, thought, and behavior seems intuitively obvious and retains a strong presence in some branches of anthropological thinking.

size and "wildness"; flowing water, whether or not out-doors or in nature; is pa·hə; so is "moisture." But, un-like "stone" and "rock," the difference is essential, not pertaining to a connotative margin, and the two can hardly ever be interchanged.

[e] To be sure, there are a few minor differences from other nouns, in English for instance in the use of the articles.

[f] "Year" and certain combinations of "year" with name of season, rarely season names alone, can occur with a locative morpheme "at," but this is exceptional. It appears like historical detritus of an earlier different patterning, or the effect of English analogy, or both.

[g] The expective and reportive assertions contrast according to the "paramount relation." The expective expresses anticipation existing *earlier* than objective fact, and coinciding with objective fact *later* than the status quo of the speaker, this status quo, including all the subsummation of the past therein, being expressed by the reportive. Our notion "future" seems to represent at once the earlier (anticipation) and the later (after-wards, what will be), as Hopi shows. This paradox may hint of how elusive the mystery of real time is, and how artificially it is expressed by a linear relation of past-present-future.

[h] The Hopi verbs of preparing naturally do not corre-spond neatly to our "prepare"; so that *na'twani* could also be rendered "the practiced-upon," "the tried-for," and otherwise.

[i] See, e.g., Ernest Beaglehole, *Notes on Hopi economic life* (Yale University Publications in Anthropology, no. 15, 1937), especially the reference to the an-nouncement of a rabbit hunt, and on p. 30, description of the activities in connection with the cleaning of To-reva Spring—announcing, various preparing activities, and finally, preparing the continuity of the good results already obtained and the continued flow of the spring.

[j] This notion of storing up power, which seems implied by much Hopi behavior, has an analog in physics: ac-celeration. It might be said that the linguistic back-ground of Hopi thought equips it to recognize naturally that force manifests not as motion or velocity, but as cumulation or acceleration. Our linguistic background tends to hinder in us this same recognition, for having legitimately conceived force to be that which produces change, we then think of change by our linguistic *met-aphorical* analog, motion, instead of by a pure motion-less changingness concept, i.e. accumulation or acceleration. Hence it comes to our naïve feeling as a shock to find from physical experiments that it is not possible to define force by motion, that motion and speed, as also "being at rest," are wholly relative, and that force can be measured only by acceleration.

[k] Here belong "Newtonian" and "Euclidean" space, etc.

Functionalism

In the first thirty years of the twentieth century, Franz Boas and his students were clearly the dominant anthropological thinkers in America, and the evolutionary model was temporarily abandoned. In Britain, on the other hand, the reaction to cultural evolution did not occur with the same force. With no single figure comparable to Boas, British anthropologists were divided into two camps: the diffusionists and the functionalists. It is the latter group that concerns us here.

In the 1880s and 1890s, a new group of anthropological thinkers, led by Alfred Cort Haddon (1855–1940) emerged in Britain. Haddon was trained in anatomy and zoology but was deeply influenced by Tylor, Frazer, and Spencer. In the 1880s, he held a position at the Royal College of Science in Dublin. In 1888, dissatisfied with life in Dublin, Haddon journeyed to the Torres Straits, between New Guinea and Australia, in the hopes that an important expedition might get him a better job (Stocking 1992:21). Haddon went primarily to study coral reefs, but he brought several works of anthropology along, including *Notes and Queries on Anthropology for the Use of Travelers and Residents in Uncivilized Lands*. This was a book-length questionnaire designed to help untrained observers collect information of use to anthropologists. *Notes and Queries* was a collaborative work by many anthropologists, but Tylor was the primary author of the nineteenth-century editions. Using *Notes and Queries* Haddon collected information from the islanders and, by the time he returned he was committed to anthropology.

Back in England, Haddon moved to Cambridge University, where he became the first lecturer in physical anthropology. He published some of the data he had collected in the Torres Straits but soon became convinced that another expedition was essential. He hoped to make a comprehensive study of native body types, psychology, language, and material culture. To this end, he enlisted an interdisciplinary team of scholars, including the physician Charles Seligman (1873–1940), the experimental psychologist W. H. R. (William Halse Rivers) Rivers (1864–1922), and his students, William McDougall (1871–1938) and C. S. Myers (1873–1946). Other team members included linguist S. H. Ray and A. Wilkin, who served as photographer and studied land tenure issues. The team arrived in the Torres Straits in April 1898. Group members stayed for varying lengths of time, but all left within six months.

Despite its relative brevity, the Torres Straits expedition was a defining moment in the development of both anthropology and psychology in Britain. Most expedition members went on to hold important professorships in England and the United States. Haddon and Rivers were at Cambridge, Seligman at the London School of Economics. Myers worked first as an assistant to Rivers at Cambridge but then moved to London, founding the Institute of Industrial Psychology in 1921. McDougall taught at Oxford, then at Harvard and Duke.

Haddon and his colleagues made fieldwork a critical component of British anthropology. While on the expedition they worked largely by summoning people to speak with them through translators, but they encouraged their students to learn local languages and live in far closer proximity to those they studied. After their return to England, they published extensive accounts of their research. Perhaps more important, Haddon, Rivers, and Seligman were critical in the training of the key thinkers of British functionalist anthropology.

Although Haddon and his colleagues were profoundly affected by Tylor and the evolutionism of the nineteenth century, the focus of their research was different. They were strongly influenced by Spencer and Durkheim and attempted to carry out the research agenda implied by Spencer's organic analogy and Durkheim's *Rules of Sociological Method*. If, as Spencer claimed, society was like an organism, anthropologists should be able to describe the different social "organs" that composed a society. If, as Durkheim claimed, a positivist science of society was possible, then anthropologists should be able to find social facts and discover the laws that determine how they operate. The functionalists set out to accomplish just these things.

Functionalism in anthropology is generally divided into two schools of thought, each associated with a key personality. Psychological functionalism is linked to Bronislaw Malinowski (1884–1942). For the psychological functionalists, cultural institutions function to meet the basic physical and psychological needs of people in a society. Like Boas, Malinowski's method was based on extensive in-depth fieldwork during which he gathered evidence to support his theoretical position. The second school, structural functionalism, is associated with A. R. Radcliffe-Brown (1881–1955). Structural functionalists, who drew heavily on Durkheim's work, sought to understand how cultural institutions maintained the equilibrium and cohesion of a society.

Though Bronislaw Malinowski was interested in religion and folklore and had read Frazer's *The Golden Bough* as a young man, he was trained in the physical sciences and received a Ph.D. in physics and mathematics in 1908. The following year, he did advanced studies in Leipzig, where he, like Durkheim, was deeply influenced by Wilhelm Wundt and took classes with Karl Bücher (1847–1930), an economist who specialized in gift-and-exchange economies. His time with Wundt and Bücher led him to an interest in folk psychology, and from there, to anthropology (Gross 1986). In 1910 Malinowski traveled to England and enrolled in the London School of Economics (LSE), where he studied anthropology under Charles Seligman. At the outbreak of World War I, Malinowski was traveling in the British-controlled South Pacific. He had intended that the trip, undertaken for ethnographic research, be relatively brief. However, Malinowski was from Krakow, in a part of Polish Galicia that had been controlled by Austria since 1849. Thus he was considered an enemy national, and the British forbade his return to Europe. They did permit him to stay in the Trobriand Islands from 1915 to 1918, and he conducted ethnographic research there for almost two years. Malinowski's intensive day-to-day contact with his informants and his familiarity with the local language set a high standard for modern ethnographic fieldwork. After the war, Malinowski returned to England and accepted a teaching position at the LSE, where he spent most of his career, training many of the finest English anthropologists of his era. These included E. E. Evans-Pritchard (1902–1973), Isaac Schapera (1905–2003), Audrey Richards (1899–1984), Raymond Firth (1901–2002), Meyer Fortes (1906–1983), Lucy Mair (1901–1986), and S. F. Nadel (1903–1956).

At the time functionalism emerged, anthropology did not have a particularly good reputation. Traveling to distant locations to study natives was exciting and exotic, but also uncouth. It probably didn't help that Seligman, as well as many of his students (and those of Haddon and Rivers) were Jewish. As a result, in the early years of the century, anthropology languished at Oxford and Cambridge, the most prestigious universities. Cambridge anthropologists Haddon and Rivers (1864–1922) were considered ungentlemanly by other members of the faculty (Leach 1984:5). However, anthropology prospered at the LSE, an institution founded by members of the socialist Fabian Society. While Malinowski built the anthropology program at the LSE, at Cambridge his books *Sex and Repression in Savage Society,* first published in 1927, and *The Sexual Life of Savages in Northwestern Melanesia* (1929b) were kept in a special section of the library and could only be read with the permission of a senior college official (Leach 1984:8).

Malinowski was concerned with how individuals pursued their own ends within the constraints of their culture. He believed that culture existed to satisfy seven basic human needs: nutrition, reproduction, bodily comforts, safety, relaxation, movement, and growth (1939). He wished to demonstrate how various cultural beliefs and practices contributed to the smooth functioning of society while providing individual biological or psychological benefits. For example, in his 1925 essay, "Magic, Science, and Religion," Malinowski discussed the nature of thought in primitive societies and demonstrated the psychological functions served by supernatural beliefs such as magic. By basing his theory on physiological and biopsychological needs, Malinowski gave his theory of culture a universal character. Because these needs were satisfied through cultural institutions, he was able to identify particular cultural and societal formations set up to fulfill them (Applebaum 1987:1–12). Malinowski was famous for his ethnographic reporting, and he was skilled at weaving theoretical ideas into his ethnographic discussions. His concept of psychological functionalism is represented by "The Essentials of the Kula," chapter 3 of his groundbreaking ethnography, *Argonauts of the Western Pacific* (1922). In this chapter, Malinowski offers a description of the trade in kula valuables that has become a classic of anthropology. The chapter showcases Malinowski's skill as an ethnographer but also illustrates many of his fundamental ideas.

Radcliffe-Brown, who studied anthropology at Cambridge under Haddon and Rivers. Although he did fieldwork in the Andaman Islands and Australia, Radcliffe-Brown was more interested in deriving social laws governing behavior from the comparative study of different cultures than in cultural description based on intensive fieldwork in one culture. Durkheim's influence is evident in Radcliffe-Brown's attempts to illustrate how cultural systems function to maintain a society's equilibrium.

Although he used the term *culture* in his early work, Radcliffe-Brown rejected the concept later in his career. He believed that culture was an abstract concept and that, because the values and norms of a society could not be observed, a science of culture was impossible (Garbarino 1977:58). Radcliffe-Brown preferred to limit his research to social structures—to the principles that organize persons in a society (such as kinship) and to the actual roles and relationships that can be observed firsthand. To illustrate this perspective, Radcliffe-Brown used Spencer's organic analogy In 1935, he wrote:

> An animal organism is an agglomeration of cells and interstitial fluids arranged in relation to one another not as an aggregate but as an integrated living whole. The system of relations by which these units are related is the organic structure. As the terms are here used the organism is not itself the structure; it is a collection of units (cells or molecules) arranged in a structure, i.e., in a set of relations; the organism has a structure. The structure is thus to be defined as a set of relations between entities. Over a period its constituent cells do not remain the same. But the structural arrangement of the constituent units does remain similar. (Radcliffe-Brown 1965b [1935]:178–179)

Applying this analogy to anthropological data, Radcliffe-Brown argued that it is more useful to study kinship systems than to study the individuals in a society because, although people die, the kin structure remains the same from generation to generation. In Radcliffe-Brown's view, Malinowski's focus on individuals led nowhere. To use a cliché, Radcliffe-Brown thought that Malinowski did not see the forest for the trees.

We have chosen two articles to represent structural functionalism. In the first, "On Joking Relationships (1940)," Radcliffe-Brown argues that structural relations between people in certain positions in kinship systems lead to conflicts of interest. Such conflict could threaten the stability of society. However, this problem is solved through ritualized joking or avoidance between people in such positions. Thus, when conflict threatens stability, society develops social institutions to mediate oppositions and preserve social solidarity.

The second structural-functionalist essay, "The Licence in Ritual," is by Max Gluckman. Gluckman (1911–1975) was born in South Africa and trained there. He studied at the University of Witwatersrand under Winnifred Hoernle (1885–1960) and Isaac Schapera, both of whom had studied with Radcliffe-Brown at Oxford. In addition, Hoernle studied psychology with Wundt and sociology with Durkheim (Stocking 1995). From South Africa, Gluckman went to Oxford, where he studied with Robert Marett (1866–1943). Marett was a student of Tylor but turned against his evolutionary ideas and became one of the first British intellectuals to use Durkheim's work in social analysis (Stocking 1995:169). Besides doing extensive fieldwork among South African groups, including the Zulu (1936–1938) and the Barotse (1939–1941), Gluckman held a series of important academic positions. He was head of the Rhodes-Livingstone Institute from 1941 to 1947 and then served for two years as a lecturer at Oxford. In 1949 he moved to Manchester, where he founded the Department of Social Anthropology at the University of Manchester. Gluckman brought a group of outstanding scholars to Manchester, including Elizabeth Colson, Victor Turner, Frederick Bailey, Edmund Leach, and Fredrik Barth. Together they forged a distinctive anthropological style focusing on process, change, and the maintenance of social order. The department became known as the Manchester School, and although the ideas and scholars associated with Manchester have changed over the past few decades, it continues to exert a powerful influence.

In many ways Gluckman's work represents the culmination of British functionalist thought. A specialist in political anthropology, he is especially known for his analysis of political systems among different groups in Africa, especially the functions of feuds and conflicts. Two of Gluckman's most famous books on this theme are *Rituals of Rebellion in South-East Africa* (1954) and *Custom and Conflict in Africa* (1956). His essay in this volume is an example of this type of work. In "The Licence in Ritual" Gluckman shows how ritualized reversals of social roles, seemingly acts of rebellion, act instead to support a society's social order and political systems.

We stated in the first section of this book that scientific theories are a product of the social and cultural context in which they are conceived. Functionalism was conceived and practiced largely by European anthropologists in territories that were European colonial possessions such as the Trobriand Islands, Australia, India, and East Africa. Given this context, it is surely no accident that these thinkers studied the function of cultural institutions in relation to the maintenance of social order and the smooth working of society. This focus was precisely the aspect of non-Western societies in which colonial governments were most interested.

The nature of the relationship between anthropology and colonialism is highly equivocal. It is certain that British anthropologists often thought about their usefulness to colonial administrations. From the turn of the twentieth century until World War II, most anthropologists wanted to provide their expertise to governments. A. C. Haddon, for example, campaigned persistently (but unsuccessfully) for an "imperial bureau of ethnology," designed to help the state deal with "conflicts derived from racial and cultural variation that arose both in the colonies and at home" (Kuklick 1991:44). Radcliffe-Brown held positions in Cape Town and Sydney, in which he was responsible for training officials to govern indigenous peoples (Max Gluckman was one notable exception to this trend. A political activist, he campaigned openly against colonialism and apartheid policies of his native South Africa). Both Radcliffe-Brown and Malinowski often pointed out ways in which anthropology could be useful to the colonial enterprise. Governments, however, were not particularly interested in either funding or listening to anthropologists. Most of the money that supported the functionalists came from the Rockefeller Foundation and other charitable organizations. The British government provided almost nothing (Goody 1995). In addition, governments were deeply suspicious of anthropologists. Colonial officials were most often political conservatives, whereas anthropologists tended to be liberals. Officials generally believed that anthropologists were too close to the natives and were more likely to see their efforts as undermining than supporting colonialism.

One other observation about functionalism is warranted: The functionalists typically were only marginally interested in history. Whereas American anthropology at this time was based largely on reconstructing cultures from interviews with informants, British anthropologists were directly observing native societies in action (or thought they were). Under these circumstances, they believed that issues of the functioning of the current system were of primary importance. They asserted that historical reconstruction did little to clarify the current functioning of social institutions— indeed, they were deeply skeptical of historical reconstructions. Many functionalists held that since most of the societies they studied lacked writing, such reconstructions could be little more than fictions. As a result, they examined societies as if they were timeless and thus were unable to account for social change.

Functionalism lost its place of theoretical prominence after World War II. Because of the massive social, cultural, and political transformations that resulted from the war, interest in how societies maintained social stability declined, to be replaced by concern with cultural change. Despite this, the work of Malinowski, Radcliffe-Brown, and their students Fortes, Gluckman, Schapera, Richards, and others continues to be widely read and to provide inspiration for modern anthropologists. Although few people would refer to themselves as structural-functionalist anthropologists today, and virtually no explicitly functionalist theoretical papers are being published, key functionalist concepts are still implicit in a great deal of anthropology. Functionalism continues to be a powerful idea, and many anthropologists are probably more functionalist than they generally acknowledge.

11. *The Essentials of the Kula*

Bronislaw Malinowski (1884–1942)

I

Having thus described the scene, and the actors, let us now proceed to the performance.[1] The Kula is a form of exchange, of extensive, intertribal character; it is carried on by communities inhabiting a wide ring of islands, which form a closed circuit. This circuit can be seen on Map V, where it is represented by the lines joining a number of islands to the North and East of the East end of New Guinea. Along this route, articles of two kinds, and these two kinds only, are constantly travelling in opposite directions. In

the direction of the hands of a clock, moves constantly one of these kinds—long necklaces of red shell, called *soulava* . . . In the opposite direction moves the other kind—bracelets of white shell called *mwali*. Each of these articles, as it travels in its own direction on the closed circuit, meets on its way articles of the other class, and is constantly being exchanged for them. Every movement of the Kula articles, every detail of the transactions is fixed and regulated by a set of traditional rules and conventions, and some acts of the Kula are accompanied by an elaborate magical ritual and public ceremonies.

From *Argonauts of the Western Pacific* (1922)

---

[1] "The Essentials of the Kula" is the third chapter of Malinowski's 1922 monograph *Argonauts of the Western Pacific*. In the introduction and first two chapters of the work, Malinowski discusses his research methods, the ge-ography of the region, and the different "races" of people who inhabit it, as well as their notions of magic, sorcery, and power. Here he begins his discussion of the Kula, perhaps the thing for which this book is best remembered.

MAP V   The Kula ring

On every island and in every village, a more or less limited number of men take part in the Kula—that is to say, receive the goods, hold them for a short time, and then pass them on. Therefore every man who is in the Kula, periodically though not regularly, receives one or several *mwali* (arm-shells), or a *soulava* (necklace of red shell discs), and then has to hand it on to one of his partners, from whom he receives the opposite commodity in exchange. Thus no man ever keeps any of the articles for any length of time in his possession. One transaction action does not finish the Kula relationship, the rule being "once in the Kula, always in the Kula," and a partnership between two men is a permanent and lifelong affair. Again, any given *mwali* or *soulava* may always be found travelling and changing hands, and there is no question of its ever settling down, so that the principle "once in a Kula, always in a Kula" applies also to the valuables themselves.

The ceremonial exchange of the two articles is the main, the fundamental aspect of the Kula. But associated with it, and done under its cover, we find a great number of secondary activities and features.[2] Thus, side by side with the ritual exchange of arm-shells and necklaces, the natives carry on ordinary trade, bartering from one island to another a great number of utilities, often

---

[2] Malinowski's theoretical position is known as psychological functionalism. In a 1939 essay "The Group and The Individual in Functionalist Analysis," Malinowski argued that there were seven universal biological and psychological needs. These individual needs were converted to cultural behavior through the use of symbols, which also served to mold individual behavior to group standards. The task of the psychological functionalist was to describe these symbols and demonstrate how social institutions operated to fill psychological needs. However, it is not clear to what extent Malinowski had worked out these ideas when he wrote Argonauts and his other book-length

unprocurable in the district to which they are imported, and indispensable there. Further, there are other activities, preliminary to the Kula, or associated with it, such as the building of sea-going canoes for the expeditions, certain big forms of mortuary ceremonies, and preparatory taboos.

The Kula is thus an extremely big and complex institution, both in its geographical extent, and in the manifoldness of its component pursuits. It welds together a considerable number of tribes, and it embraces a vast complex of activities, interconnected, and playing into one another, so as to form one organic whole.[3]

Yet it must be remembered that what appears to us an extensive, complicated, and yet well ordered institution is the outcome of ever so many doings and pursuits, carried on by savages, who have no laws or aims or characters definitely laid down.[4] They have no knowledge of the *total outline* of any of their social structure. They know their own motives, know the purpose of individual actions and the rules which apply to them, but how, out of these, the whole collective insti-

tution shapes, this is beyond their mental range. Not even the most intelligent native has any clear idea of the Kula as a big, organized social construction, still less of its sociological function and implications. If you were to ask him what the Kula is, he would answer by giving a few details, most likely by giving his personal experiences and subjective views on the Kula, but nothing approaching the definition just given here. Not even a partial coherent account could be obtained. For the integral picture does not exist in his mind; he is in it, and cannot see the whole from the outside.

The integration of all the details observed, the achievement of a sociological synthesis of all the various, relevant symptoms, is the task of the Ethnographer. First of all, he has to find out that certain activities, which at first sight might appear incoherent and not correlated, have a meaning. He then has to find out what is constant and relevant in these activities and what accidental and inessential, that is, to find out the laws and rules of all the transactions. Again, the Ethnographer

---

accounts of the Trobriand Islands, most of which were published in the 1920s. In these he seems far more interested in portraying the experiences of the Trobrianders in ways that make them comprehensible to audiences in Europe and America than in examining the ways in which institutions such as the Kula fill specific psychological needs. The degree to which psychological functionalism is actually represented in Argonauts is unclear. On the one hand, it is true that the Kula does serve at least some of the seven psychological functions Malinowski enumerated in 1939: It increases their safety by setting up networks of trading partners and allies and may allow for movement and growth. On the other hand, Malinowski does not address these issues anywhere in Argonauts, and there is little evidence he had them in mind as he was writing this book.

[3] Malinowski takes pains throughout this chapter to emphasize the size and complexity of the Kula. His understanding of it was conditioned by Spencer's notion of the social organism as a complex system of interrelated parts. The influence of Durkheim is also evident. Mauss did not describe total social phenomena until *The Gift* in 1925. However, it is clear that the Kula is a total social phenomenon and in *The Gift* Mauss frequently refers to Malinowski's work on the Kula.

[4] Notice Malinowski's characterization of the Trobriand Islanders in this and the next paragraph as aware of their individual actions and motives but unable to see their entire system. It takes an outsider, the ethnographer according to Malinowski, to conduct an objective analysis of a society and its institutions (a point echoed by the interpretive anthropologist Victor Turner in essay 32.) Malinowski is not denigrating the intelligence of the Trobriand Islanders here, for he believed the same principle to be true for people in Western societies. The point that a person cannot objectively analyze the system in which he or she participates is a central tenet of psychoanalytic thought. A selection of Freud's work was made available to Malinowski in the field by his professor Charles G. Seligman (1873–1940), and Malinowski's opinion on the issue may have been influenced by Freud's writings. Seligman, a medical doctor, was a member of the Torres Straits expedition and wrote the groundbreaking *The Melanesians of British New Guinea* (1910), which set the stage for Malinowski's research. Seligman found Freud useful in his work with victims of shell shock during World War I. Malinowski, on the other hand, became a key critic of Freud and used data from the Trobriands to attack Freud's Oedipal theory in *Sex and Repression in Savage Society* (1955 [1927]). Note also the analogy Malinowski makes between ethnography and the physical sciences.

has to *construct* the picture of the big institution, very much as the physicist constructs his theory from the experimental data, which always have been within reach of everybody but which needed a consistent interpretation. I have touched on this point of method in the Introduction (Divisions V and VI), but I have repeated it here, as it is necessary to grasp it clearly in order not to lose the right perspective of conditions as they really exist among the natives.

II

In giving the above abstract and concise definition, I had to reverse the order of research, as this is done in ethnographic fieldwork, where the most generalised inferences are obtained as the result of long inquiries and laborious inductions. The general definition of the Kula will serve as a sort of plan or diagram in our further concrete and detailed descriptions. And this is the more necessary as the Kula is concerned with the exchange of wealth and utilities, and therefore it is an economic institution, and there is no other aspect of primitive life where our knowledge is more scanty and our understanding more superficial than in Economics. Hence misconception is rampant, and it is necessary to clear the ground when approaching any economic subject.

Thus in the Introduction we called the Kula a "form of trade," and we ranged it alongside other systems of barter. This is quite correct, if we give the word "trade" a sufficiently wide interpretation, and mean by it any exchange of goods. But the word "trade" is used in current Ethnography and economic literature with so many different implications that a whole lot of misleading, preconceived ideas have to be brushed aside in order to grasp the facts correctly. Thus the *a priori* current notion of primitive trade would be that of an exchange of indispensable or useful articles, done without much ceremony or regulation, under stress of dearth or need, in spasmodic, irregular intervals—and this done either by direct barter, everyone looking out sharply not to be done out of his due, or, if the savages were too timid and distrustful to face one another, by some customary arrangement, securing by means of heavy penalties compliance in the obligations incurred or imposed.[a5] Waiving for the present the question how far this conception is valid or not in general—in my opinion it is quite misleading—we have to realise clearly that the Kula contradicts in almost every point the above definition of "savage trade." It shows us primitive exchange in an entirely different light.

The Kula is not a surreptitious and precarious form of exchange. It is, quite on the contrary, rooted in myth, backed by traditional law, and surrounded with magical rites. All its main transactions are public and ceremonial, and carried out according to definite rules. It is not done on the spur of the moment, but happens periodically, at dates settled in advance, and it is carried on along definite trade routes, which must lead to fixed trysting places. Sociologically, though transacted between tribes differing in language, culture, and probably even in race, it is based on a fixed and permanent status, on a partnership

[5] In his first footnote, Malinowski references the German economist Carl Bücher (1847–1930). Bücher's *Industrial Evolution,* first published in Germany in 1893, was enormously influential in Europe, and by 1901 had been translated into English, French, and Russian. Bücher developed a three-stage view of economic evolution, proposing that households led to towns, which led to national economies. The factor that differentiated these stages was the role of exchange. He believed that contemporary primitive societies represented a preeconomic stage of society (Firth 1964:210). Bücher writes that "primitive man lives only for the present . . . shuns all regular work . . . has not the conception of duty, not of a vocation as a moral function in life" (1968 [1901]:82). These views influenced the work of scholars such as Max Weber (see essay 7) and Marcel Mauss (see essay 6). Malinowski—though sympathetic to Bücher's attempts to understand primitive economy—wrote *Argonauts of the Western Pacific* as a reaction to this view of primitive humans, using the Kula as a counterexample. Later in *Argonauts* he wrote, "Now I hope that whatever the meaning of the Kula might be for Ethnology, for the general science of culture, the meaning of the Kula will consist in being instrumental to dispel such crude, rationalistic conceptions of primitive mankind, and to induce both the speculator and the observer to deepen the analysis of economic facts" (1922:516).

which binds into couples some thousands of individuals. This partnership is a lifelong relationship, it implies various mutual duties and privileges, and constitutes a type of inter-tribal relationship on an enormous scale. As to the economic mechanism of the transactions, this is based on a specific form of credit, which implies a high degree of mutual trust and commercial honour—and this refers also to the subsidiary, minor trade, which accompanies the Kula proper. Finally, the Kula is not done under stress of any need, since its main aim is to exchange articles which are of no practical use.

From the concise definition of Kula given at the beginning of this chapter, we see that in its final essence, divested of all trappings and accessories, it is a very simple affair, which at first sight might even appear tame and unromantic. After all it only consists of an exchange, interminably repeated, of two articles intended for ornamentation, but not even used for that to any extent. Yet this simple action—this passing from hand to hand of two meaningless and quite useless objects—has somehow succeeded in becoming the foundation of a big inter-tribal institution, in being associated with ever so many other activities. Myth, magic and tradition have built up around it definite ritual and ceremonial forms, have given it a halo of romance and value in the minds of the natives, have indeed created a passion in their hearts for this simple exchange.[6]

The definition of the Kula must now be amplified, and we must describe one after the other its fundamental characteristics and main rules, so that it may be clearly grasped by what mechanism the mere exchange of two articles results in an institution so vast, complex, and deeply rooted.

III

First of all, a few words must be said about the two principal objects of exchange, the arm-shells (*mwali*) and the necklaces (*soulava*). The arm-shells are obtained by breaking off the top and the narrow end of a big, cone-shaped shell (*Conus millepunctatus*) and then polishing up the remaining ring. These bracelets are highly coveted by all the Papuo-Melanesians of New Guinea, and they spread even into the pure Papuan district of the Gulf.[b] The manner of wearing the arm-shells is illustrated by Plate XVII, where the men have put them on on purpose to be photographed.[7]

---

[6] Malinowski believed that technologically primitive peoples were fully rational and just as intelligent as "civilized" people, but the point of the economic discussion in *Argonauts* is to critique the concept of "economic man." This is the notion that human beings rationally deploy limited resources to competing ends in such a way as to increase their personal benefit. This idea lies behind Adam Smith's *Wealth of Nations* (1976 [1776]) and most of Western economics. Malinowski's attack at its most vitriolic is found on page 60 of *Argonauts,* where he writes,

> Another notion which must be exploded, once and forever, is that of the Primitive Economic Man of some current economic textbooks. This fanciful, dummy creature, who has been very tenacious of existence in popular and semi-popular economic literature and whose shadow haunts even the minds of competent anthropologists, blighting their outlook with a preconceived idea, is an imaginary, primitive man, or savage, prompted in all his actions by a rationalistic concept of self-interest, and achieving his aims directly with the minimum of effort.

Malinowski wanted "rational man" but not "economic man," and he needed to show that it was possible to have one without the other. In large part, this is the goal of the Kula discussion. To Malinowski, the Kula is a highly elaborate and rational system of exchange that has an economically irrational end: the distribution of goods that have no utilitarian value. Much of later substantivist economics treated Malinowski's attack as virtually a founding document of their form of analysis. On the other hand, Firth says Malinowski's attack was essentially against a straw man (1964:217).

[7] Unusually for the period in which this was written, Malinowski tells the reader about the conditions under which the photograph was taken. This is a level of ethnographic reporting that did not become common until the 1970s and 1980s. You will find references to additional photographic plates in this essay, however, no photos are included in this volume.

The use of the small discs of red spondylus shell out of which the *soulava* are made, is also of very wide diffusion. There is a manufacturing centre of them in one of the villages in Port Moresby, and also in several places in Eastern New Guinea, notably in Rossell Island, and in the Trobriands. I have said "use" on purpose here, because these small beads, each of them a flat, round disc with a hole in the centre, coloured anything from muddy brown to carmine red, are employed in various ways for ornamentation. They are most generally used as part of earrings, made of rings of turtle shell, which are attached to the ear lobe, and from which hang a cluster of the shell discs. These earrings are very much worn, and, especially among the Massim, you see them on the ears of every second man or woman, while others are satisfied with turtle shell alone, unornamented with the shell discs. Another everyday ornament, frequently met with and worn, especially by young girls and boys, consists of a short necklace, just encircling the neck, made of the red spondylus discs, with one or more cowrie shell pendants. These shell discs can be, and often are, used in the make-up of the various classes of the more elaborate ornaments, worn on festive occasions only. Here however, we are more especially concerned with the very long necklaces, measuring from two to five metres, made of spondylus discs, of which there are two main varieties, one, much the finer, with a big shell pendant, the other made of bigger discs, and with a few cowrie shells or black banana seeds in the centre (see Plate XVIII)

The arm-shells on the one hand, and the long spondylus shell strings on the other, the two main Kula articles, are primarily ornaments. As such, they are used with the most elaborate dancing dress only, and on very festive occasions such as big ceremonial dances, great feasts, and big gatherings, where several villages are represented, as can be seen in Plate VI. Never could they be used as everyday ornaments, nor on occasions of minor importance such as a small dance in the village, a harvest gathering, a love-making expedition, when facial painting, floral decoration and smaller though not quite everyday ornaments are worn (see Plates XII and XIII). But even though usable and sometimes used, this is not the main function of these articles. Thus, a chief may have several shell strings in his possession, and a few arm-shells. Supposing that a big dance is held in his or in a neighbouring village, he will not put on his ornaments himself if he goes to assist at it, unless he intends to dance and decorate himself, but any of his relatives, his children or his friends and even vassals, can have the use of them for the asking. If you go to a feast or a dance where there are a number of men wearing such ornaments, and ask anyone of them at random to whom it belongs, the chances are that more than half of them will answer that they themselves are not the owners, but that they had the articles lent to them. These objects are not owned in order to be used; the privilege of decorating oneself with them is not the real aim of possession.

Indeed—and this is more significant—by far the greater number of the arm-shells, easily ninety percent, are of too small a size to be worn even by young boys and girls. A few are so big and valuable that they would not be worn at all, except once in a decade by a very important man on a very festive day. Though all the shell-strings can be worn, some of them are again considered too valuable, and are cumbersome for frequent use, and would be worn on very exceptional occasions only.

This negative description leaves us with the questions: why, then, are these objects valued, what purpose do they serve? The full answer to this question will emerge out of the whole story contained in the following chapters, but an approximate idea must be given at once. As it is always better to approach the unknown through the known, let us consider for a moment whether among ourselves we have not some type of objects which play a similar role and which are used and possessed in the same manner. When, after a six years' absence in the South Seas and Australia, I returned to Europe and did my first bit of sight-seeing in Edinburgh Castle, I was shown the Crown Jewels. The keeper told many stories of how they were worn by this or that king or queen on such and such occasion, of how some of them had been taken over to London, to the great and just indignation of the whole Scottish nation, how they were restored, and how now everyone can be pleased, since they are safe under lock and key, and no one can touch them. As I was looking at them and thinking how ugly, useless, ungainly, even tawdry they were, I had the feeling that something similar had been told to me of late, and that I had seen many other objects of this sort, which made a similar impression on me.[8]

And then arose before me the vision of a native village on coral soil, and a small, rickety platform temporarily erected under a pandanus thatch, surrounded by a number of brown, naked men, and one of them showing me long, thin red strings, and big, white, worn-out objects, clumsy to sight and greasy to touch. With reverence he also would name them, and tell their history, and by whom and when they were worn, and how they changed hands, and how their temporary possession was a great sign of the importance and glory of the village. The analogy between the European and the Trobriand *vaygu'a* (valuables) must be delimited with more precision. The Crown Jewels, in fact, any heirlooms too valuable and too cumbersome to be worn, represent the same type as *vaygu'a* in that they are merely possessed for the sake of possession itself, and the ownership of them with the ensuing renown is the main source of their value. Also both heirlooms and *vaygu'a* are cherished because of the historical sentiment which surrounds them. However, ugly, useless, and—according to current standards—valueless an object may be, if it has figured in historical scenes and passed through the hands of historic persons, and is therefore an unfailing vehicle of important sentimental associations, it cannot but

be precious to us. This historic sentimentalism, which indeed has a large share in our general interest in studies of past events, exists also in the South Seas. Every really good Kula article has its individual name, round each there is a sort of history and romance in the traditions of the natives. Crown Jewels or heirlooms are insignia of rank and symbols of wealth respectively, and in olden days with us, and in New Guinea up till a few years ago, both rank and wealth went together. The main point of difference is that the Kula goods are only in possession for a time, whereas the European treasure must be permanently owned in order to have full value.[9]

Taking a broader, ethnological view of the question, we may class the Kula valuables among the many "ceremonial" objects of wealth; enormous, carved and decorated weapons, stone implements, articles of domestic and industrial nature, too well decorated and too clumsy for use. Such things are usually called "ceremonial," but this word seems to cover a great number of meanings and much that has no meaning at all. In fact, very often, especially on museum labels, an article is called "ceremonial" simply because nothing is known about its uses and general nature. Speaking only about museum exhibits from New Guinea, I can say that many so-called ceremonial objects are nothing but simply overgrown objects of use, which preciousness of material and amount of labour expended have transformed into reservoirs of condensed economic value. Again, others are used on festive occasions, but play no part whatever in rites and ceremonies, and serve

---

[8] Malinowski is considered one of the great ethnographers in anthropological history in part because of his gift for ethnographic reportage. He believed it was important to understand how natives perceived their world and passed this understanding on to his readers by comparisons such as that presented here between *vaygu'a* and the crown jewels of Scotland. Like the jewels, *vaygu'a* do not have a practical utility; rather their value is symbolic, derived from their age and history. In making this comparison, Malinowski uses a nontechnical example easily accessible to a popular audience. *Argonauts,* like many of Malinowski's other works, was designed to be read by educated laypersons as well as professional anthropologists.

[9] In the passage above, Malinowski tries to give us a native's perspective when he explains what the Kula items mean to their recipients. Malinowski's writing style gave him a reputation as a man with great personal empathy for the people he studied. Admirers of Malinowski were greatly disillusioned when his diaries were published in 1967 *(A Diary in the Strict Sense of the Term)*. The diaries showed that Malinowski was intensely unhappy and lonely much of the time, was constantly preoccupied with his health, and often spoke of the Trobriand Islanders in racist terms. In other words, he reacted like most people of his era (and perhaps our own) when forced into unfamiliar circumstances for a long period of time.

for decoration only, and these might be called *objects of parade* (compare Chap. VI, Div. I). Finally, a number of these articles function actually as instruments of a magical or religious rite, and belong to the intrinsic apparatus of a ceremony. Such and such only could be correctly called *ceremonial*. During the *So'i* feasts among the Southern Massim, women carrying polished axe blades in fine carved handles, accompany with a rhythmic step to the beat of drums, the entry of the pigs and mango saplings into the village (see Plates V and VI). As this is part of the ceremony and the axes are an indispensable accessory, their use in this case can be legitimately called "ceremonial." Again, in certain magical ceremonies in the Trobriands, the *towosi* (garden magician) has to carry a mounted axe blade on his shoulders, and with it he delivers a ritual blow at a *kamkokola* structure (see Plate LIX; compare Chapter II Division IV).

The *vaygu'a*—the Kula valuables—in one of their aspects are overgrown objects of use. They are also, however, *ceremonial* objects in the narrow and correct sense of the word. This will become clear after perusal of the following pages, and to this point we shall return in the last chapter.

It must be kept in mind that here we are trying to obtain a clear and vivid idea of what the Kula valuables are to the natives, and not to give a detailed and circumstantial description of them, nor to define them with precision. The comparison with the European heirlooms or Crown Jewels was given in order to show that this type of ownership is not entirely a fantastic South Sea custom, untranslatable into our ideas. For—and this is a point I want to stress—the comparison I have made is not based on purely external, superficial similarity. The psychological and sociological forces at work are the same, it is really the same mental attitude which makes us value our heirlooms, and makes the natives in New Guinea value their *vaygu'a*.

IV

The exchange of these two classes of *vaygu'a*, of the arm-shells and the necklaces, constitutes the main act of the Kula. This exchange is not done freely, right and left, as opportunity offers, and where the whim leads. It is subject indeed to strict limitations and regulations. One of these refers to the sociology of the exchange, and entails that Kula transactions can be done only between partners. A man who is in the Kula—for not everyone within its district is entitled to carry it on—has only a limited number of people with whom he deals. This partnership is entered upon in a definite manner, under fulfillment of certain formalities, and it constitutes a life-long relationship. The number of partners a man has varies with his rank and importance. A commoner in the Trobriands would have a few partners only, whereas a chief would number hundreds of them. There is no special social mechanism to limit the partnership of some people and extend that of the others, but a man would naturally know to what number of partners he was entitled by his rank and position. And there would be always the example of his immediate ancestors to guide him. In other tribes, where the distinction of rank is not so pronounced, an old man of standing, or a headman of a hamlet or village would also have hundreds of Kula associates, whereas a man of minor importance would have but few.

Two Kula partners have to *kula* with one another, and exchange other gifts incidentally; they behave as friends, and have a number of mutual duties and obligations, which vary with the distance between their villages and with their reciprocal status. An average man has a few partners near by, as a rule his relations-in-law or his friends, and with these partners, he is generally on very friendly terms. The Kula partnership is one of the special bonds which unite two men into one of the standing relations of mutual exchange of gifts and services so characteristic of these natives. Again, the average man will have one or two chiefs in his or in the neighbouring districts with whom he *kulas*. In such a case, he would be bound to assist and serve them in various ways, and to offer them the pick of his *vaygu'a* when he gets a fresh supply. On the other hand he would expect them to be specially liberal to him.

The overseas partner is, on the other hand, a host, patron and ally in a land of danger and insecurity. Nowadays, though the feeling of danger still persists, and natives never feel safe and comfortable in a strange district, this danger is rather felt as a magical one, and it is more the fear of foreign sorcery that besets them. In olden days, more tangible dangers were apprehended, and the partner was the main guarantee of safety. He also provides with food, gives presents, and his house, though never used to sleep in, is the place in which to foregather while in the village. Thus the Kula partnership provides every man within its ring with a few friends near at hand, and with some friendly allies in the far-away, dangerous, foreign districts. These are the only people with whom he can *kula,* but, of course, amongst all his partners, he is free to choose to which one he will offer which object.[10]

Let us now try to cast a broad glance at the cumulative effects of the rules of partnership. We see that all around the ring of Kula there is a network of relationships, and that naturally the whole forms one interwoven fabric. Men living at hundreds of miles' sailing distance from one another are bound together by direct or intermediate partnership, exchange with each other, know of each other, and on certain occasions meet in a large inter-tribal gathering (Plate XX). Objects given by one, in time reach some very distant indirect partner or other, and not only Kula objects, but various articles of domestic use and minor gifts. It is easy to see that in the long run, not only objects of material culture, but also customs, songs, art motives and general cultural influences travel along the Kula route. It is a vast, inter-tribal net of relationships, a big institution, consisting of thousands of men,—all bound together by one common passion for Kula exchange, and secondarily, by many minor ties and interests.[11]

Returning again to the personal aspect of the Kula, let us take a concrete example, that of *an average man* who lives, let us assume, in the village of Sinaketa, an important Kula centre in the

Southern Trobriands. He has a few partners, near and far, but they again fall into categories, those who give him arm-shells, and those who give him necklaces. For it is naturally an invariable rule of the Kula that arm-shells and necklaces are never received from the same man, since they must travel in different directions. If one partner gives the arm-shells, and I return to him a necklace, all future operations have to be of the same type. More than that, the nature of the operation between me, the man of Sinaketa, and my partner, is determined by our relative positions with regard to the points of the compass. Thus I, in Sinaketa, would receive from the North and East only arm-shells; from the South and West, necklaces are given to me. If I have a near partner next door to me, if his abode is North or East of mine, he will always be giving me arm-shells and receiving necklaces from me. If, at a later time, he were to shift his residence within the village, the old relationship would obtain, but if he became a member of another village community on the other side of me the relationship would be reversed. The partners in villages to the North of Sinaketa, in the district of Luba, Kulumata, or Kiriwina all supply me with arm-shells. These I hand over to my partners in the South, and receive from them necklaces. The South in this case means the southern districts of Boyowa, as well as the Amphletts and Dobu.

Thus every man has to obey definite rules as to the geographical direction of his transactions. At any point in the Kula ring, if we imagine him turned towards the centre of the circle, he receives the arm-shells with his left hand, and the necklaces with his right, and then hands them both on. In other words, he constantly passes the arm-shells from left to right, and the necklaces from right to left.

Applying this rule of personal conduct to the whole Kula ring, we can see at once what the aggregate result is. The sum total of exchanges will

---

[10] Here Malinowski provides a clear example of the role of *kula* trade in filling the biopsychological need for safety.

[11] Following Spencer's organic analogy, functionalists tended to see societies as collections of interrelated parts that worked together to promote the society's smooth

functioning and equilibrium. Malinowski's emphasis on the Kula as a mechanism for establishing ties between people on different islands is apparent in the previous few paragraphs. He characterizes the Kula as a "vast, inter-tribal net of relationships."

not result in an aimless shifting of the two classes of article, in a fortuitous come and go of the arm-shells and necklaces. Two continuous streams will constantly flow on, the one of necklaces following the hands of a clock, and the other, composed of the arm-shells, in the opposite direction. We see thus that it is quite correct to speak of the *circular* exchange of the Kula, of a ring or circuit of moving articles (comp. Map V). On this ring, all the villages are placed in a definitely fixed position with regard to one another, so that one is always on either the arm-shell or on the necklace side of the other.

Now we pass to another rule of the Kula, of the greatest importance. As just explained "the arm-shells and shellstrings always travel in their own respective directions on the ring, and they are never, under any circumstances, traded back in the wrong direction. Also, they never stop. It seems almost incredible at first, but it is the fact, nevertheless, that no one ever keeps any of the Kula valuables for any length of time. Indeed, in the whole of the Trobriands there are perhaps only one or two specially fine armshells and shell necklaces permanently owned as heirlooms, and these are set apart as a special class, and are once and for all out of the Kula. 'Ownership,' therefore, in Kula, is quite a special economic relation. A man who is in the Kula never keeps any article for longer than, say, a year or two. Even this exposes him to the reproach of being niggardly, and certain districts have the bad reputation of being 'slow' and 'hard' in the Kula. On the other hand, each man has an enormous number of articles passing through his hands during his life time, of which he enjoys a temporary possession, and which he keeps in trust for a time. This possession hardly ever makes him use the articles, and he remains under the obligation soon again to hand them on to one of his partners. But the temporary ownership allows him to draw a great deal of renown, to exhibit his article, to tell how he obtained it, and to plan to whom he is going to give it. And all this forms one of the favourite subjects of tribal conversation and gossip, in which the feats and the glory in Kula of chiefs or commoners are constantly discussed and re-discussed."c Thus every article moves in one direction only, never comes back, never permanently stops, and takes as a rule some two to ten years to make the round.[12]

This feature of the Kula is perhaps its most remarkable one, since it creates a new type of ownership, and places the two Kula articles in a class of their own. Here we can return to the comparison drawn between the *vaygu'a* (Kiriwinian valuables) and the European heirlooms. This comparison broke down on one point: in the European objects of this class, permanent ownership, lasting association with the hereditary dignity or rank or with a family, is one of its main features.

In this the Kula articles differ from heirlooms, but resemble another type of valued object, that is, trophies, gauges of superiority, sporting cups, objects which are kept for a time only by the winning party, whether a group or an individual. Though held only in trust, only for a period, though never used in any utilitarian way, yet the holders get from them a special type of pleasure by the mere fact of owning them, of being entitled to them. Here again, it is not only a superficial, external resemblance, but very much the same mental attitude, favoured by similar social arrangements. The resemblance goes so far that in the Kula there exists also the element of pride in merit, an element which forms the main ingredient in the pleasure felt by a man or group holding a trophy. Success in Kula is ascribed to special, personal power, due mainly to magic, and men are very proud of it. Again, the whole community glories in a specially fine Kula trophy, obtained by one of its members.

---

[12] Malinowski was concerned with differentiating his brand of functionalism from that of A. R. Radcliffe-Brown (see essay 12). Malinowski's theory was derived from his personal experiences in the field and was concerned with behavior within a cultural context, whereas Radcliffe-Brown studied social structure as an abstract representation that he believed existed independent of human beings. One of the most important differences between the two theorists was that Malinowski believed in the importance of individuals within a culture. Here he speaks of the Kula as many individual transactions taking place simultaneously. Radcliffe-Brown, on the other hand, believed that the study of culture as individual human behavior was impossible.

All the rules so far enumerated—looking at them from the individual point of view—limit the social range and the direction of the transactions as well as the duration of ownership of the articles. Looking at them from the point of view of their integral effect, they shape the general outline of the Kula, give it the character of the double-closed circuit. Now a few words must be said about the nature of each individual transaction, in so far as its *commercial technicalities* are concerned. Here very definite rules also obtain.

V

The main principle underlying the regulations of actual exchange is that the Kula consists in the bestowing of a ceremonial gift, which has to be repaid by an equivalent counter-gift, after a lapse of time, be it a few hours or even minutes, though sometimes as much as a year or more may elapse between payments.[d] But it can never be exchanged from hand to hand with the equivalence between the two objects discussed, bargained about and computed. The decorum of the Kula transaction is strictly kept, and highly valued. The natives sharply distinguish it from barter, which they practise extensively, of which they have a clear idea, and for which they have a settled term—in Kiriwinian: *gimwali*. Often, when criticising an incorrect, too hasty, or indecorous procedure of Kula, they will say: "He conducts his Kula as if it were *gimwali*."

The second very important principle is that the equivalence of the counter-gift is left to the giver, and cannot be enforced by any kind of coercion. A partner who has received a Kula gift is expected to give back fair and full value, that is, to give as good an arm-shell as the necklace he receives, or vice versa. Again, a very fine article must be replaced by one of equivalent value, and not by several minor ones, though intermediate gifts may be given to mark time before the real repayment takes place.[13]

If the article given as counter-gift is not equivalent, the recipient will be disappointed and angry, but he has no direct means of redress, no means of coercing his partner, or of putting an end to the whole transaction. What then are the forces at work which keep the partners to the terms of the bargain? Here we come up against a very important feature of the native's mental attitude towards wealth and value. The great misconception of attributing to the savage a pure economic nature, might lead us to reason incorrectly thus: "The passion of acquiring, the loathing to lose or give away, is the fundamental and most primitive element in man's attitude to wealth. In primitive man, this primitive characteristic will appear in its simplest and purest form. *Grab and never let go* will be the guiding principle of his life."[e] The fundamental error in this reasoning is that it assumes that "primitive man," as represented by the present-day savage, lives, at least in economic matters, untrammeled by conventions and social restrictions. Quite the reverse is the case. Although, like every human being, the Kula native loves to possess and therefore desires to acquire and dreads to lose, the social code of rules, with regard to give and take by far overrides his natural acquisitive tendency.[14]

---

[13] Malinowski's Kula description is considered one of the seminal works in the development of economic anthropology and had a major impact on scholars of his day. Mauss, as we have seen, made extensive use of *Argonauts of the Western Pacific* in *The Gift*. For example, the first two principles of the Kula outlined at the start of this section are fundamental elements of prestation adopted and discussed by Mauss in his work (see essay 6).

[14] Structural functionalists such as Radcliffe-Brown trace their intellectual descent directly from Durkheim. Malinowski was a bitter rival of Radcliffe-Brown, but he too was influenced by the French sociologist. In one article

Malinowski called social structure a "vast conditioning apparatus" (Malinowski 1939), and here he says it overrides a person's natural acquisitiveness. In some respects these comments seem to echo Durkheim's definition of a social fact (essay 5), but there are critical differences. Durkheim emphasized the independent nature of the collective conscience, which he believed had an existence apart from any individual and operated by its own laws. Malinowski, on the other hand, believed that culture existed to serve human needs and that, ultimately, these needs were individual physiological and psychological requirements.

This social code, such as we find it among the natives of the Kula is, however, far from weakening the natural desirability of possession; on the contrary, it lays down that to possess is to be great, and that wealth is the indispensable appanage of social rank and attribute of personal virtue. But the important point is that with them to possess is to give—and here the natives differ from us notably. A man who owns a thing is naturally expected to share it, to distribute it, to be its trustee and dispenser. And the higher the rank the greater the obligation. A chief will naturally be expected to give food to any stranger, visitor, even loiterer from another end of the village. He will be expected to share any of the betel-nut or tobacco he has about him. So that a man of rank will have to hide away any surplus of these articles which he wants to preserve for his further use. In the Eastern end of New Guinea a type of large basket, with three layers, manufactured in the Trobriands, was specially popular among people of consequence, because one could hide away one's small treasures in the lower compartments. Thus the main symptom of being powerful is to be wealthy, and of wealth is to be generous. Meanness, indeed, is the most despised vice, and the only thing about which the natives have strong moral views, while generosity is the essence of goodness.

This moral injunction and ensuing habit of generosity, superficially observed and misinterpreted, is responsible for another wide-spread misconception, that of the *primitive communism of savages*. This, quite as much as the diametrically opposed figment of the acquisitive and ruthlessly tenacious native, is definitely erroneous, and this will be seen with sufficient clearness in the following chapters.[15]

Thus the fundamental principle of the natives' moral code in this matter makes a man do his fair share in Kula transaction and the more important he is, the more will he desire to shine by his generosity. *Noblesse oblige*[16] is in reality the social norm regulating their conduct. This does not mean that people are always satisfied, and that there are no squabbles about the transactions, no resentments and even feuds. It is obvious that, however much a man may want to give a good equivalent for the object received, he may not be able to do so. And then, as there is always a keen competition to be the most generous giver, a man who has received less than he gave will not keep his grievance to himself, but will brag about his own generosity and compare it to his partner's meanness; the other resents it, and the quarrel is ready to break out. But it is very important to realise that there is no actual haggling, no tendency to do a man out of his share. The giver is quite as keen as the receiver that the gift should be generous, though for different reasons. Then, of course, there is the important consideration that a man who is fair and generous in the Kula will attract a larger stream to himself than a mean one.[17]

The two main principles, namely, first that the Kula is a gift repaid after an interval of time by a counter-gift, and not a bartering; and second, that the equivalent rests with the giver, and cannot be enforced, nor can there be any haggling or going back on the exchange—these underlie all the transactions. A concrete outline of how they are carried on, will give a sufficient preliminary idea.

"Let us suppose that I, a Sinaketa man, am in possession of a pair of big arm-shells. An overseas expedition from Dobu in the d'Entrecasteaux

---

[15] Malinowski was writing just a few years after the Russian Revolution, when communist rhetoric was fashionable in Europe and the United States. This comment on primitive communism is a critique of the Marxist five-stage theory of history—Marx had suggested that European society had evolved through stages of primitive communism, ancient slave societies, feudalism, and capitalism. He believed that this evolution would end with the stage of socialism-communism. Many Marxists believed these stages could be found in all societies.

[16] *Noblesse oblige:* benevolent and honorable behavior, originally thought to be an obligation of persons of high rank.

[17] Notice how Malinowski acknowledges the presence of conflict but minimizes its effect. For him, conflict exists but does not drive the system; rather, it is an aberration in what is generally a smoothly functioning organism.

Archipelago, arrives at my village. Blowing a conch shell, I take my arm-shell pair and I offer it to my overseas partner, with some words as 'This is a *vaga* (opening gift)—in due time, thou returnest to me a big *soulava* (necklace) for it!' Next year, when I visit my partner's village, he either is in possession of an equivalent necklace, and this he gives to me as *yotile* (return gift), or he has not a necklace good enough to repay my last gift. In this case he will give me a small necklace—avowedly not equivalent to my gift— and he will give it to me as *basi* (intermediary gift). This means that the main gift has to be re-paid on a future occasion, and the *basi* is given in token of good faith—but it, in turn, must be re-paid by me in the meantime by a gift of small arm-shells. The final gift, which will be given to me to clinch the whole transaction, would then be called *kudu* (clinching gift) in contrast to *basi*" (loc. cit., p. 99).

Although haggling and bargaining are com-pletely ruled out of the Kula, there are customary and regulated ways of bidding for a piece of *vaygu'a* known to be in the possession of one's partner. This is done by the offer of what we shall call solicitary gifts, of which there are several types. "If I, an inhabitant of Sinaketa, happen to be in possession of a pair of arm-shells more than usually good, the fame of it spreads, for it must be remembered that each one of the first-class arm-shells and necklaces has a personal name and a history of its own, and as they circulate around the big ring of the Kula, they are all well known, and their appearance in a given district always creates a sensation. Now, all my partners—whether from overseas or from within the district—compete for the favour of receiving this particular article of mine, and those who are specially keen try to ob-tain it by giving me *pokala* (offerings) and *kaributu* (solicitary gifts). The former (*pokala*) consist as a rule of pigs, especially fine bananas, and yams or taro; the latter (*kaributu*) are of greater value: the valuable, large axe blades (called *beku*), or lime spoons of whale bone are given" (loc. cit., p. 100). The further complication in the repayment of these solicitary gifts and a few more technicalities and technical expressions connected herewith will be given later on in Chapter IV.

VI

I have enumerated the main rules of the Kula in a manner sufficient for a preliminary definition, and now a few words must be said about the as-sociated activities and secondary aspects of the Kula. If we realise that at times the exchange has to take place between districts divided by danger-ous seas, over which a great number of people have to travel by sail, and do so keeping to ap-pointed dates, it becomes clear at once that con-siderable preparations are necessary to carry out the expedition. Many preliminary activities are intimately associated with the Kula. Such are, particularly, the building of canoes, preparation of the outfit, the provisioning of the expedition, the fixing of dates and social organisation of the enterprise. All these are subsidiary to the Kula, and as they are carried on in pursuit of it, and form one connected series, a description of the Kula must embrace an account of these prelimi-nary activities. The detailed account of canoe-building, of the ceremonial attached to it, of the incidental magical rites, of the launching and trial run, of the associated customs which aim at preparing the outfit—all this will be described in detail in the next few chapters.

Another important pursuit inextricably bound up with the Kula, is that of the *secondary trade*. Voyaging to far-off countries, endowed with natu-ral resources unknown in their own homes, the Kula sailors return each time richly laden with these, the spoils of their enterprise. Again, in or-der to be able to offer presents to his partner, every outward bound canoe carries a cargo of such things as are known to be most desirable in the overseas district. Some of this is given away in presents to the partners, but a good deal is carried in order to pay for the objects desired at home. In certain cases, the visiting natives exploit on their own account during the journey some of the natu-ral resources overseas. For example, the Sinaketans dive for the spondylus in Sanaroa Lagoon, and the Dobuans fish in the Trobriands on a beach on the southern end of the island. The second trade is complicated still more by the fact that such big Kula centres as, for instance, Sinaketa, are not efficient in any of the industries of special value to the Dobuans. Thus, Sinaketans have to procure the necessary store of goods from the inland villages of Kuboma, and this they do on minor trading expeditions preliminary to the Kula. Like the canoe-building, the secondary trading will be described in detail later on, and has only to be mentioned here.[18]

Here, however, these subsidiary and associated activities must be put in proper relation with regard to one another and to the main transaction. Both the canoe-building and the ordinary trade have been spoken of as secondary or subsidiary to the Kula proper. This requires a comment. I do not, by thus subordinating the two things in importance to the Kula mean to express a philosophical reflection or a personal opinion as to the relative value of these pursuits from the point of view of some social teleology. Indeed, it is clear that if we look at the acts from the outside, as comparative sociologists and gauge their real utility, trade and canoe-building will appear to us as the really important achievements, whereas we shall regard the Kula only as an indirect stimulus, impelling the natives to sail and to trade. Here, however, I am not dealing in sociological, but in pure ethnographical description and any sociological analysis I have given is only what has been absolutely indispensable to clear away misconceptions and to define terms.[f,19]

By ranging the Kula as the primary and chief activity, and the rest as secondary ones, I mean that this precedence is implied in the institutions themselves. By studying the behaviour of the natives and all the customs in question, we see that the Kula is in all respects the main aim: the dates are fixed, the preliminaries settled, the expeditions arranged, the social organisation determined, not with regard to trade, but with regard to Kula. On an expedition, the big ceremonial feast, held at the start, refers to the Kula; the final ceremony of reckoning and counting the spoil refers to Kula, not to the objects of trade obtained. Finally, the magic, which is one of the main factors of all the procedure, refers only to the Kula, and this applies even to a part of the magic carried out over the canoe. Some rites in the whole cycle are done for the sake of the canoe itself, and others for the sake of Kula. The construction of the canoes is always carried on directly in connection with a Kula expedition. All this, of course, will become really clear and convincing only after the detailed account is given. But it was necessary at this point to set the right perspective in the relation between the main Kula and the trade.

Of course not only many of the surrounding tribes who know nothing of the Kula do build canoes and sail far and daringly on trading expeditions, but even within the Kula ring, in the Trobriands for instance, there are several villages who do not *kula*, yet have canoes and carry on energetic overseas trade. But where the Kula is practiced, it governs all the other allied activities, and canoe-building and trade are made subsidiary to it. And this is expressed both by the nature of

---

[18] Later theorists were critical of Malinowski's comments on the nature of primitive economies. Malinowski insisted that the Kula was a rational system directed toward nonrational ends, that is, the exchange of items with only symbolic value. Because of this, he gives little weight to the fact that the offerings given to induce a partner to part with good *vaygu'a* are utilitarian items such as pigs, bananas, yams, and axe blades. Although this secondary trade is repeatedly mentioned, Malinowski does not analyze it to see if participants gain an economic benefit. Critics suggest that in insisting that his perspective on the Kula is the right one, Malinowski ignores the data that disprove his theory.

[19] Malinowski's footnote is important because it is directed at the diffusionists and the Boasians, whose ideas were popular at this time. Participant observation and the integration of culture were central aspects of the work of Franz Boas (see essay 8), and Malinowski's work consistently incorporates these ideas. However, Boas and Malinowski disagreed on the importance of history. Boas believed that the current state of a culture could only be understood through the study of its history. Malinowski vehemently disagreed. In this note, Malinowski says that reconstructing history is an "unpardonable sin" and that he is unconcerned with searching for origins of institutions, preferring to spend his time working out the interrelations of elements within a society. Similarly, Malinowski dismissed popular diffusionists such as W. H. R. Rivers and Grafton Elliot Smith (1871–1937), who were trying to prove that all culture began in ancient Egypt and diffused from there.

the institutions and the working of all the arrangements on the one hand, and by the behaviour and explicit statements of the natives on the other.

The Kula—it becomes, I hope, more and more clear—is a big, complicated institution, insignificant though its nucleus might appear. To the natives, it represents one of the most vital interests in life, and as such it has a ceremonial character and is surrounded by magic. We can well imagine that articles of wealth might pass from hand to hand without ceremony or ritual, but in the Kula they never do. Even when at times only small parties in one or two canoes sail overseas and bring back *vaygu'a*, certain taboos are observed, and a customary course is taken in departing, in sailing, and in arriving; even the smallest expedition in one canoe is a tribal event of some importance, known and spoken of over the whole district. But the characteristic expedition is one in which a considerable number of canoes take part, organised in a certain manner, and forming one body. Feasts, distributions of food and other public ceremonies are held, there is one leader and master of the expedition, and various rules are adhered to, in addition to the ordinary Kula taboos and observances.

The ceremonial nature of the Kula is strictly bound up with another of its aspects—magic. "The belief in the efficiency of magic dominates the Kula, as it does ever so many other tribal activities of the natives. Magical rites must be performed over the sea-going canoe when it is built, in order to make it swift, steady and safe; also magic is done over a canoe to make it lucky in the Kula. Another system of magical rites is done in order to avert the dangers of sailing. The third system of magic connected with overseas expeditions is the *mwasila* or the Kula magic proper. This sys-

tem consists in numerous rites and spells, all of which act directly on the mind (*nanola*) of one's partner, and make him soft, unsteady in mind, and eager to give Kula gifts" (loc. cit., p. 100).[20]

It is clear that an institution so closely associated with magical and ceremonial elements, as is the Kula, not only rests on a firm, traditional foundation, but also has its large store of legend. "There is a rich mythology of the Kula in which stories are told about far-off times when mythical ancestors sailed on distant and daring expeditions. Owing to their magical knowledge they were able to escape dangers to conquer their enemies, to surmount obstacles, and by their feats they established many a precedent which is now closely followed by tribal custom. But their importance for their descendants lies mainly in the fact that they handed on their magic, and this made the Kula possible for the following generations" (loc. cit., p. 100).

The Kula is also associated in certain districts, to which the Trobriands do not belong, with the mortuary feasts called *so'i*. The association is interesting and important and in Chapter 20 [of Malinowski's book] an account of it will be given.

The big Kula expeditions are carried on by a great number of natives, a whole district together. But the geographical limits, from which the members of an expedition are recruited, are well defined. Glancing at Map V, "we see a number of circles, each of which represents a certain sociological unit which we shall call a Kula community. A Kula community consists of a village or a number of villages, who go out together on big overseas expeditions, and who act as a body in the Kula transactions, perform their magic in common, have common leaders, and have the same outer and inner social sphere, within which

---

[20] Magic plays an important role in Trobriand Island society, and Malinowski discusses the subject in other chapters of *Argonauts* and in his later works *Magic, Science, and Religion* (1954 [1925]) and *Coral Gardens and Their Magic* (1935). Malinowski was reacting against the theory of one of his mentors, Sir James Frazer. Frazer, a popular theorist of anthropology and religion, argued that people in primitive societies had magical beliefs and other superstitions because they had some form of primitive mentality and were incapable of scientific thought. Concerned with presenting people in simple societies as rational, Malinowski was careful to distinguish the contexts in which magic was used. He argued that the Trobrianders were just as intelligent as anyone else and used magic in circumstances that were beyond rational control. Thus, magic had a psychological function: to reassure individuals in unpredictable situations.

they exchange their valuables. The Kula consists, therefore, first of the small, internal transactions within a Kula community or contiguous communities, and secondly, of the big overseas expeditions in which the exchange of articles takes place between two communities divided by the sea. In the first, there is a chronic, permanent trickling of articles from one village to another, and even within the village. In the second, a whole lot of valuables, amounting to over a thousand articles at a time, are exchanged in one enormous transaction, or, more correctly, in ever so many transactions taking place simultaneously" (loc. cit., p. 101).[21] "The Kula trade consists of a series of such periodical overseas expeditions, which link together the various island groups, and annually bring over big quantities of *vaygu'a* and of subsidiary trade from one district to another. The trade is used and used up, but the *vaygu'a*—the arm-shells and necklets—go round and round the ring" (loc. cit., p. 105).

In this chapter, a short, summary definition of the Kula has been given. I enumerated one after the other its most salient features, the most remarkable rules as they are laid down in native custom, belief and behaviour. This was necessary in order to give a general idea of the institution before describing its working in detail. But no abridged definition can give to the reader the full understanding of a human social institution. It is necessary for this, to explain its working concretely, to bring the reader into contact with the people, show how they proceed at each successive stage, and to describe all the actual manifestations of the general rules laid down in abstract.

As has been said above, the Kula exchange is carried on by enterprises of two sorts; first there are the big overseas expeditions, in which a more or less considerable amount of valuables are carried at one time. Then there is the inland trade in which the articles are passed from hand to hand, often changing several owners before they move a few miles.

The big overseas expeditions are by far the more spectacular part of the Kula. They also contain much more public ceremonial, magical ritual, and customary usage. They require also, of course, more of preparation and preliminary activity. I shall therefore have a good deal more to say about the overseas Kula expeditions than about the internal exchange.

As the Kula customs and beliefs have been mainly studied in Boyowa, that is, the Trobriand Islands, and from the Boyowan point of view, I shall describe, in the first place, the typical course of an overseas expedition, as it is prepared, organized, and carried out from the Trobriands. Beginning with the construction of the canoes, proceeding to the ceremonial launching and the visits of formal presentation of canoes, we shall choose then the community of Sinaketa, and follow the natives on one of their overseas trips, describing it in all details. This will serve us as a type of a Kula expedition to distant lands. It will then be indicated in what particulars such expeditions may differ in other branches of the Kula, and for this purpose I shall describe an expedition from Dobu, and one between Kiriwina and Kitava. An account of inland Kula in the Trobriands, of some associated forms of trading and of Kula in the remaining branches will complete the account.

In the next chapter I pass, therefore, to the preliminary stages of the Kula, in the Trobriands, beginning with a description of the canoes.

NOTES

[a] By "current view," I mean such as is to be found in textbooks and in passing remarks, scattered through economic and ethnological literature. As a matter of fact, Economics is a subject very seldom touched upon either in theoretical works or Ethnology, or in accounts of field-work. I have enlarged on this deficiency in the article on "Primitive Economics," published in the *Economic Journal*, March, 1921.

The best analysis of the problem of savage economy is to be found, in spite of its many shortcomings, in K. Bücher's "Industrial Evolution," English translation,

---

[21] The above paragraphs demonstrate Malinowski's belief that culture was a system of interrelated parts. One cannot study the Kula alone, because it is interconnected with other aspects of Trobriand life such as canoe-building, magic, and family structure. Spencer's organic analogy can be seen behind Malinowski's model of the Kula. The Kula is a system in a physical sense; it can be diagrammed like the circulatory system of the body.

1901. On primitive trade, however, his views are inadequate. In accordance with his general view that savages have no national economy, he maintains that any spread of goods among natives is achieved by non-economic means, such as robbery, tributes and gifts. The information contained in the present volume is incompatible with Bücher's views, nor could he have maintained them had he been acquainted with Barton's description of the Hiri (contained in Seligman's "Melanesians").

A summary of the research done on Primitive Economics, showing, incidentally, how little real, sound work has been accomplished, will be found in Pater W. Kopper's "Die Ethnologische Wirtschaftsforschung" in *Anthropos,* X–XI, 1915–16, pp. 611–651, and 971–1079. The article is very useful, where the author summarises the views of others.

[b] Professor C. G. Seligman, op. cit., p. 93, states that arm-shells, *toea,* as they are called by the Motu, are traded from the Port Moresby district westward to the Gulf of Papua. Among the Motu and Koita, near Port Moresby, they are highly valued, and nowadays attain very high prices, up to £30, much more than is paid for the same article among the Massim.

[c] This and the following quotations are from the Author's preliminary article on the Kula in *Man,* July, 1920. Article number 51, p. 100.

[d] In order not to be guilty of inconsistency in using loosely the word "ceremonial" I shall define it briefly. I shall call an action ceremonial, if it is (1) public; (2) carried on under observance of definite formalities; (3) if it has sociological, religious, or magical import, and it carries with it obligations.

[e] This is not a fanciful construction of what an erroneous opinion might be, for I could give actual examples proving that such opinions have been set forth, but as I am not giving here a criticism of existing theories of Primitive Economics, I do not want to overload this chapter with quotations.

[f] It is hardly necessary perhaps to make it quite clear that all questions of origins of development or history of the institutions have been rigorously ruled out of this work. The mixing up of speculative or hypothetical views with an account of facts is, in my opinion an unpardonable sin against ethnographic method.

---

12. *On Joking Relationships*[a]

A. R. RADCLIFFE-BROWN (1881–1955)

THE PUBLICATION OF Mr. F. J. Pedler's note[b] on what are called "joking relationships," following on two other papers on the same subject by Professor Henri Labouret[c] and Mademoiselle Denise Paulme,[d] suggests that some general theoretical discussion of the nature of these relationships may be of interest to readers of Africa[e,1]

What is meant by the term "joking relationship" is a relation between two persons in which one is by custom permitted, and in some instances

From *Africa* (1940)

---

[1] Radcliffe-Brown begins his essay, which first appeared in the journal *Africa,* by mentioning several other anthropologists of his era. F. J. Pedler (1908–1991), later Sir Frederick Pedler, was a colonial administrator and diplomat who became the director of the United Africa Company and wrote several books on Africa. In the note referenced here, Pedler reports on a legal case involving a joking relationship called *utani.* We will return to that case below. Henri Labouret (1878–1959) was a soldier, colonial administrator, linguist, and ethnographer who played a critical role in West African ethnography in the early twentieth century. Denise Paulme (1909–1998) was a student of Marcel Mauss who became one of the leading French Africanist scholars. Her book *Femmes d'Afrique Noire* (1960), a volume of essays about African women written entirely by female anthropologists, is an early classic of feminist anthropology. All of the work cited by Radcliffe-Brown, as well as this essay itself, appeared in the journal *Africa: Journal of the International Africa Institute.* National traditions in anthropology tended to be located in specific places. Much American anthropology was done among Native American groups in the United States or among people living on American controlled territories, particularly in the Pacific Islands. British and French anthropology tended to focus on Africa or Southeast Asia, where these nations had colonial possessions.

required, to tease or make fun of the other, who in turn is required to take no offence. It is important to distinguish two main varieties. In one the relation is symmetrical; each of the two persons teases or makes fun of the other. In the other variety the relation is asymmetrical; A jokes at the expense of B and B accepts the teasing good humouredly but without retaliating; or A teases B as much as he pleases and B in return teases A only a little. There are many varieties in the form of this relationship in different societies. In some instances the joking or teasing is only verbal, in others it includes horse-play; in some the joking includes elements of obscenity, in others not.

Standardized social relationships of this kind are extremely widespread, not only in Africa but also in Asia, Oceania and North America. To arrive at a scientific understanding of the phenomenon it is necessary to make a wide comparative study. Some material for this now exists in anthropological literature, though by no means all that could be desired, since it is unfortunately still only rarely that such relationships are observed and described as exactly as they might be.[2]

The joking relationship is a peculiar combination of friendliness and antagonism. The behavior is such that in any other social context it would express and arouse hostility; but it is not meant seriously and must not be taken seriously. There is a pretence of hostility and a real friendliness. To put it in another way, the relationship is one of permitted disrespect. Thus any complete theory of it must be part of, or consistent with, a theory of the place of respect in social relations and in social life generally. But this is a very wide and very important sociological problem; for it is evident that the whole maintenance of a social order depends upon the appropriate kind and degree of respect being shown towards certain persons, things and ideas or symbols.[3]

Examples of joking relationships between relatives by marriage are very commonly found in Africa and in other parts of the world. Thus Mademoiselle Paulme[f] records that among the Dogon a man stands in a joking relationship to his wife's sisters and their daughters. Frequently the relationship holds between a man and both the brothers and sisters of his wife. But in some instances there is a distinction whereby a man is on joking terms with his wife's younger brothers and sisters but not with those who are older than she is. This joking with the wife's brothers and sisters is usually associated with a custom requiring extreme respect, often partial or complete avoidance, between a son-in-law and his wife's parents.[g]

The kind of structural situation in which the associated customs of joking and avoidance are found may be described as follows. A marriage involves a readjustment of the social structure whereby the woman's relations with her family are greatly modified and she enters into a new and very close relation with her husband. The latter is at the same time brought into a special relation with his wife's family, to which, however, he is an outsider. For the sake of brevity, though at the risk of over-simplification, we will consider only the husband's relation to his wife's family. The relation can be described as involving both attachment and separation, both social conjunction and social disjunction, if I may use the terms. The man has his own definite position in the social structure, determined for him by his birth into a certain family, lineage or clan. The great body of his rights and duties and the interests and activities that he shares with others are the result of his position. Before the marriage his wife's family are outsiders for him as he is an outsider for them. This constitutes a social disjunction which is not destroyed by the marriage. The social conjunction results from the continuance, though in altered

---

[2] Note that Radcliffe-Brown says his goal is to provide a scientific understanding of joking relationships. He hoped to make anthropology a science and believed that it was possible to discover universal laws and principles underlying the structure of human society. These laws were to be discovered through the comparative analysis of social structure.

[3] Following Durkheim, and using the concept of the organic analogy developed by Spencer, Radcliffe-Brown's key concern was the maintenance of social order. He understood society as composed of a series of institutions, each of which could be understood in terms of its function (hence functionalism). An institution's function was the role it played in maintaining social order.

form, of the wife's relation to her family, their continued interest in her and in her children. If the wife were really bought and paid for, as ignorant persons say that she is in Africa, there would be no place for any permanent close relation of a man with his wife's family. But though slaves can be bought, wives cannot.[4]

Social disjunction implies divergence of interests and therefore the possibility of conflict and hostility, while conjunction requires the avoidance of strife. How can a relation which combines the two be given a stable, ordered form? There are two ways of doing this. One is to maintain between two persons so related an extreme mutual respect and a limitation of direct personal contact. This is exhibited in the very formal relations that are, in so many societies, characteristic of the behavior of a son-in-law on the one side and his wife's father and mother on the other. In its most extreme form there is complete avoidance of any social contact between a man and his mother-in-law.

This avoidance must not be mistaken for a sign of hostility. One does, of course, if one is wise, avoid having too much to do with one's enemies, but that is quite a different matter. I once asked an Australian native why he had to avoid his mother-in-law, and his reply was, "Because she is my best friend in the world; she has given me my wife." The mutual respect between son-in-law and parents-in-law is a mode of friendship. It prevents conflict that might arise through divergence of interest.

The alternative to this relation of extreme mutual respect and restraint is the joking relationship, one, that is, of mutual disrespect and licence. Any serious hostility is prevented by the playful antagonism of teasing, and this in its regular repetition is a constant expression or reminder of that social disjunction which is one of the essential components of the relation, while the so-

cial conjunction is maintained by the friendliness that takes no offence at insult.[5]

The discrimination within the wife's family between those who have to be treated with extreme respect and those with whom it is a duty to be disrespectful is made on the basis of generation and sometimes of seniority within the generation. The usual respected relatives are those of the first ascending generation, the wife's mother and her sisters, the wife's father and his brothers, sometimes the wife's mother's brother. The joking relatives are those of a person's own generation; but very frequently a distinction of seniority within the generation is made; a wife's older sister or brother may be respected while those younger will be teased.

In certain societies a man may be said to have relatives by marriage long before he marries and indeed as soon as he is born into the world. This is provided by the institution of the required or preferential marriage. We will, for the sake of brevity, consider only one kind of such organisations. In many societies it is regarded as preferable that a man should marry the daughter of his mother's brother; this is a form of the custom known as cross-cousin marriage. Thus his female cousins of this kind, or all those women whom by the classificatory system he classifies as such, are potential wives for him, and their brothers are his potential brothers-in-law. Among the Ojibwa Indians of North America, the Chiga of Uganda, and in Fiji and New Caledonia, as well as elsewhere, this form of marriage is found and is accompanied by a joking relationship between a man and the sons and daughters of his mother's brother. To quote one instance of these, the following is recorded for the Ojibwa. "When cross-cousins meet they must try to embarrass one another. They 'joke' one another, making the most vulgar allegations, by their standards as well

---

[4] Radcliffe-Brown sees a critical contradiction at the core of marriage. A husband does not become part of his wife's family but neither is he entirely separate from them. A wife does not become part of her husband's family, and her family of origin continues to have interest in her and her children. This contradiction creates the preconditions for conflict between the two families. For society to function smoothly there must be an institution to resolve this conflict.

[5] Thus, society functions smoothly because the contradiction between husband and wife's family is resolved either by avoidance or joking. Radcliffe-Brown shows that these are two related phenomena.

as ours. But being 'kind' relations, no one can take offence. Cross-cousins who do not joke in this way are considered boorish, as not playing the social game."[h]

The joking relationship here is of fundamentally the same kind as that already discussed. It is established before marriage and is continued, after marriage, with the brothers- and sisters-in-law.

In some parts of Africa there are joking relationships that have nothing to do with marriage. Mr. Pedler's note, mentioned above, refers to a joking relationship between two distinct tribes, the Sukuma and the Zaramu, and in the evidence it was stated that there was a similar relation between the Sukuma and the Zigua and between the Ngoni and the Bemba. The woman's evidence suggests that this custom of rough teasing exists in the Sukuma tribe between persons related by marriage, as it does in so many other African tribes.[i,6]

While a joking relationship between two tribes is apparently rare, and certainly deserves, as Mr. Pedler suggests, to be carefully investigated, a similar relationship between clans has been observed in other parts of Africa. It is described by Professor Labouret and Mademoiselle Paulme in the articles previously mentioned, and amongst the Tallensi it has been studied by Dr. Fortes, who will deal with it in a forthcoming publication.[j,7]

The two clans are not, in these instances, specially connected by intermarriage. The relation between them is an alliance involving real friendliness and mutual aid combined with an appearance of hostility.

The general structural situation in these instances seems to be as follows. The individual is a member of a certain defined group, a clan, for example, within which his relations to others are defined by a complex set of rights and duties, referring to all the major aspects of social life, and supported by definite sanctions. There may be another group outside his own which is so linked with his as to be the field of extension of jural and moral relations of the same general kind. Thus, in East Africa, as we learn from Mr. Pedler's note, the Zigua and the Zaramu do not joke with one another because a yet closer bond exists between them since they are ndugu (brothers). But beyond the field within which social relations are thus defined there lie other groups with which, since they are outsiders to the individual's own group, the relation involves possible or actual hostility. In any fixed relations between the members of two such groups the separateness of the groups must be recognised. It is precisely this separateness which is not merely recognised but emphasised when a joking relationship is established. The show of hostility, the perpetual disrespect, is a continual expression of that social disjunction which is an essential part of the whole structural situation, but over which, without destroying or

---

[6] Be sure to read Radcliffe-Brown's original footnote here. Pedler had reported a court case involving a joking relationship. Radcliffe-Brown uses this as a springboard to argue that anthropology should be involved in colonial administration. He had been a colonial administrator himself (director of education in Tonga from 1916 to 1920) and like other functionalists, saw service to the colonial administrations as one aim of their work. Malinowski argued, in an article entitled "Practical Anthropology" (1929a), that such service should be a key goal. Then (as today) access to funding was an important reason for stressing the applied aspects of anthropological research: Much of the money that funded research projects came from the Colonial Social Science Research Council. In general, functionalists did not question the basic fact of colonization or the subservient position of the colonized. Both paternalism and social evolutionism were implied in their writings. They believed that benevolent colonialism

offered native societies the chance for progress. On the other hand, they considered themselves friends of those they studied and argued on their behalf before colonial administrations. Colonial administrations, for their part, were deeply suspicious of anthropologists, considering them too liberal and too close to the natives (Goody 1995). The same Malinowski who authored "Practical Anthropology" also authored the preface to Jomo Kenyatta's *Facing Mount Kenya: The Traditional Life of the Gikuyu* (1979 [1938]). Kenyatta, a student of Malinowski, is better remembered as a leader of Kenya's fight for independence and that nation's first president.

[7] Fortes (1906–1983) was a member of the group of students who gathered around Malinowski and Radcliffe-Brown in the years between World War I and II. He is discussed more fully in the next essay see note 21, p. 191 in this volume.

even weakening it, there is provided the social conjunction of friendliness and mutual aid.

The theory that is here put forward, therefore, is that both the joking relationship which constitutes an alliance between clans or tribes, and that between relatives by marriage, are modes of organising a definite and stable system of social behaviour in which conjunctive and disjunctive components, as I have called them, are maintained and combined.[8]

To provide the full evidence for this theory by following out its implications and examining in detail its application to different instances would take a book rather than a short article. But some confirmation can perhaps be offered by a consideration of the way in which respect and disrespect appear in various kinship relations, even though nothing more can be attempted than a very brief indication of a few significant points.[9]

In studying a kinship system it is possible to distinguish the different relatives by reference to the kind and degree of respect that is paid to them.[k] Although kinship systems vary very much in their details there are certain principles which are found to be very widespread. One of them is that by which a person is required to show a marked respect to relatives belonging to the generation immediately preceding his own. In a majority of societies the father is a relative to whom marked respect must be shown. This is so even in many so-called matrilineal societies, i.e. those which are organised into matrilineal clans or lineages. One can very frequently observe a tendency

to extend this attitude of respect to all relatives of the first ascending generation and, further, to persons who are not relatives. Thus in those tribes of East Africa that are organised into age-sets a man is required to show special respect to all men of his father's age-set and to their wives.[10]

The social function of this is obvious. The social tradition is handed down from one generation to the next. For the tradition to be maintained it must have authority behind it. The authority is therefore normally recognised as possessed by members of the preceding generation and it is they who exercise discipline. As a result of this the relation between persons of the two generations usually contains an element of inequality, the parents and those of their generation being in a position of superiority over the children who are subordinate to them. The unequal relation between a father and his son is maintained by requiring the latter to show respect to the former. The relation is asymmetrical.

When we turn to the relation of an individual to his grandparents and their brothers and sisters we find that in the majority of human societies relatives of the second ascending generation are treated with very much less respect than those of the first ascending generation, and instead of a marked inequality there is a tendency to approximate to a friendly equality.

Considerations of space forbid any full discussion of this feature of social structure, which is one of very great importance. There are many instances in which the grandparents and their

---

[8] Thus, that which is true within a group, is also true between groups. Just as the potential conflicts between husband's and wife's families are resolved by avoidance and joking, so too potential conflicts between related tribes may be resolved by avoidance or joking.

[9] Passages such as this are very typical of Radcliffe-Brown's work. He frequently claims that the idea he wishes to demonstrate or the theory he wishes to prove would require a substantial body of work, but he never provides that work. Radcliffe-Brown constructs his arguments based almost exclusively on his reading of the ethnographic reports of others. His own fieldwork is rarely mentioned. He had done fieldwork among the Andaman Islanders and among the Kariera in Australia but he was not known for his ethno-

graphic talents and had little interest in writing ethnography. Almost the whole of his work consists of relatively brief essays such as this one, and addresses. He published one full-length ethnography *The Andaman Islanders,* his account of his 1906–1908 fieldwork, but even this was not published until 1922, well over a decade after his return from the field.

[10] Much of Radcliffe-Brown's work focused on kinship. He was guided in this in part by his mentor, W. H. R. Rivers. Rivers, a medical doctor who had joined the 1898 Torres Straits expedition, devised what he called the "genealogical method." He suggested that a truly scientific anthropology could be achieved through the study of kinship (Rivers 1910).

grandchildren are grouped together in the social structure in opposition to their children and parents. An important clue to the understanding of the subject is the fact that in the flow of social life through time, in which men are born, become mature and die, the grandchildren replace their grandparents.

In many societies there is an actual joking relationship, usually of a relatively mild kind, between relatives of alternate generations. Grandchildren make fun of their grandparents and of those who are called grandfather and grandmother by the classificatory system of terminology, and these reply in kind.

Grandparents and grandchildren are united by kinship; they are separated by age and by the social difference that results from the fact that as the grandchildren are in process of entering into full participation in the social life of the community the grandparents are gradually retiring from it. Important duties towards his relatives in his own and even more in his parents' generation impose upon an individual many restraints; but with those of the second ascending generation, his grandparents and collateral relatives, there can be, and usually is, established a relationship of simple friendliness relatively free from restraint. In this instance also, it is suggested, the joking relationship is a method of ordering a relation which combines social conjunction and disjunction.

This thesis could, I believe, be strongly supported if not demonstrated by considering the details of these relationships. There is space for only one illustrative point. A very common form of joke in this connection is for the grandchild to pretend that he wishes to marry the grandfather's wife, or that he intends to do so when his grandfather dies, or to treat her as already being his wife. Alternatively the grandfather may pretend that the wife of his grandchild is, or might be, his

wife.[l] The point of the joke is the pretence at ignoring the difference of age between the grandparent and the grandchild.[11]

In various parts of the world there are societies in which a sister's son teases and otherwise behaves disrespectfully towards his mother's brother. In these instances the joking relationship seems generally to be asymmetrical. For example the nephew may take his uncle's property but not vice versa; or, as amongst the Nama Hottentots, the nephew may take a fine beast from his uncle's herd and the uncle in return takes a wretched beast from that of the nephew.[m]

The kind of social structure in which this custom of privileged disrespect to the mother's brother occurs in its most marked forms, for example the Thonga of South-East Africa, Fiji and Tonga in the Pacific, and the Central Siouan tribes of North America, is characterised by emphasis on patrilineal lineage and a marked distinction between relatives through the father and relatives through the mother.

In a former publication[n] I offered an interpretation of this custom of privileged familiarity towards the mother's brother. Briefly it is as follows. For the continuance of a social system children require to be cared for and to be trained. Their care demands affectionate and unselfish devotion; their training requires that they shall be subjected to discipline. In the societies with which we are concerned there is something of a division of function between the parents and other relatives on the two sides. The control and discipline are exercised chiefly by the father and his brothers and generally also by his sisters; these are relatives who must be respected and obeyed. It is the mother who is primarily responsible for the affectionate care; the mother and her brothers and sisters are therefore relatives who can be looked to for assistance and indulgence. The mother's

---

[11] Once again, Radcliffe-Brown alludes to evidence but fails to present anything more than anecdote. At this point, his thesis seems to be that joking is found in relationships where there is conjuncture and disjuncture. As with in-laws and in his examples of other groups, grandchildren are conjoined to their grandparents by being members of the same family but disjoined because they are separated by the generation of parents. This may be true but raises a problem: Because we are all individuals, no two human beings have exactly the same interests. Therefore, couldn't any two individuals be said to have both conjoined and disjoined interests? The question highlights the difficulties in trying to explain the behavior of groups of individuals through abstract and generalized theoretical constructs.

brother is called "male mother" in Tonga and in some South African tribes.[12]

I believe that this interpretation of the special position of the mother's brother in these societies has been confirmed by further field work since I wrote the article referred to. But I was quite aware at the time it was written that the discussion and interpretation needed to be supplemented so as to bring them into line with a general theory of the social functions of respect and disrespect.

The joking relationship with the mother's brother seems to fit well with the general theory of such relationships here outlined. A person's most important duties and rights attach him to his paternal relatives, living and dead. It is to his patrilineal lineage or clan that he belongs. For the members of his mother's lineage he is an outsider, though one in whom they have a very special and tender interest. Thus here again there is a relation in which there is both attachment, or conjunction, and separation, or disjunction, between the two persons concerned.

But let us remember that in this instance the relation is asymmetrical.[o] The nephew is disrespectful and the uncle accepts the disrespect. There is inequality and the nephew is the superior. This is recognised by the natives themselves. Thus in Tonga it is said that the sister's son is a "chief" (eiki) to his mother's brother, and Junod[p] quotes a Thonga native as saying "The uterine nephew is a chief! He takes any liberty he likes with his maternal uncle." Thus the joking relationship with the uncle does not merely annul the usual relation between the two generations, it reverses it. But while the superiority of the father and the father's sister is exhibited in the respect that is shown to them the nephew's superiority to

his mother's brother takes the opposite form of permitted disrespect.

It has been mentioned that there is a widespread tendency to feel that a man should show respect towards, and treat as social superiors, his relatives in the generation preceding his own, and the custom of joking with, and at the expense of, the maternal uncle clearly conflicts with this tendency. This conflict between principles of behaviour helps us to understand what seems at first sight a very extraordinary feature of the kinship terminology of the Thonga tribe and the VaNdau tribe in South-East Africa. Amongst the Thonga, although there is a term malume (5 male mother) for the mother's brother, this relative is also, and perhaps more frequently, referred to as a grandfather (kokwana) and he refers to his sister's son as his grandchild (ntukulu). In the VaNdau tribe the mother's brother and also the mother's brother's son are called "grandfather" (tetekulu, literally "great father") and their wives are called "grandmother" (mbiya), while the sister's son and the father's sister's son are called "grandchild" (muzukulu).

This apparently fantastic way of classifying relatives can be interpreted as a sort of legal fiction whereby the male relatives of the mother's lineage are grouped together as all standing towards an individual in the same general relation. Since this relation is one of privileged familiarity on the one side, and solicitude and indulgence on the other, it is conceived as being basically the one appropriate for a grandchild and a grandfather. This is indeed in the majority of human societies the relationship in which this pattern of behaviour most frequently occurs. By this legal fiction the mother's brother ceases to belong to the first ascending generation, of which it is felt that the members ought to be respected.[13]

---

[12] The former publication is "Mother's Brother in South Africa," found in the earlier editions of this book. In that essay, in addition to making the point he just described, Radcliffe-Brown argues that matrilineal kinship systems are not survivals of earlier stages of human evolution (as Morgan, Junod, and Bachofen had argued) but a fully functioning part of current-day societies. In the present essay he attempts to place "Mother's Brother" in a more general theory of kin relations.

[13] Keep in mind that in kinship studies (particularly those by functionalist authors) kin names such as "grandfather" or "male mother" refer primarily to behavioral expectations rather than biological linkages. So, if a Thonga youth calls his mother's brother "grandfather," he behaves to him as he behaves to his father's father (whom he also calls "grandfather").

It may be worth while to justify this interpretation by considering another of the legal fictions of the VaNdau terminology. In all these southeastern Bantu tribes both the father's sister and the sister, particularly the elder sister, are persons who must be treated with great respect. They are also both of them members of a man's own patrilineal lineage. Amongst the VaNdau the father's sister is called "female father" (tetadji) and so also is the sister.[9] Thus by the fiction of terminological classification the sister is placed in the father's generation, the one that appropriately includes persons to whom one must exhibit marked respect.

In the south-eastern Bantu tribes there is assimilation of two kinds of joking relatives, the grandfather and the mother's brother. It may help our understanding of this to consider an example in which the grandfather and the brother-in-law are similarly grouped together. The Cherokee Indians of North America probably numbering at one time about 20,000, were divided into seven matrilineal clans.[r] A man could not marry a woman of his own clan or of his father's clan. Common membership of the same clan connects him with his brothers and his mother's brothers. Towards his father and all his relatives in his father's clan of his own or his father's generation he is required by custom to show a marked respect. He applies the kinship term for "father" not only to his father's brothers but also to the sons of his father's sisters. Here is another example of the same kind of fiction as described above; the relatives of his own generation whom he is required to respect and who belong to his father's matrilineal lineage are spoken of as though they belonged to the generation of his parents. The body of his immediate kindred is included in these two clans, that of his mother and his father. To the other clans of the tribe he is in a sense an outsider. But with two of them he is connected, namely with the clans of his two grandfathers, his father's father and his mother's father. He speaks of all the members of these two clans, of whatever age, as "grandfathers" and "grandmothers". He stands in a joking relationship with all of them. When a man marries he must respect his wife's parents but jokes with her brothers and sisters.

The interesting and critical feature is that it is regarded as particularly appropriate that a man should marry a woman whom he calls "grandmother," i.e., a member of his father's father's clan or his mother's father's clan. If this happens his wife's brothers and sisters, whom he continues to tease, are amongst those whom he previously teased as his "grandfathers" and "grandmothers." This is analogous to the widely spread organisation in which a man has a joking relationship with the children of his mother's brother and is expected to marry one of the daughters.[14]

It ought perhaps to be mentioned that the Cherokee also have a one-sided joking relationship in which a man teases his father's sister's husband. The same custom is found in Mota of the Bank Islands. In both instances we have a society organised on a matrilineal basis in which the mother's brother is respected, the father's sister's son is called "father" (so that the father's sister's husband is the father of a "father"), and there is a special term for the father's sister's husband. Further observation of the societies in which this custom occurs is required before we can be sure of its interpretation. I do not remember that it has been reported from any part of Africa.

What has been attempted in this paper is to define in the most general and abstract terms the kind of structural situation in which we may expect to find well-marked joking relationships. We have been dealing with societies in which the basic social structure is provided by kinship. By reason of his birth or adoption into a certain position in the social structure an individual is connected with a large number of other persons. With some of them he finds himself in a definite and specific jural relation, i.e., one which can be denned in terms of rights and duties. Who these persons will be and what will be the rights and duties depend on the form taken by the social structure.

---

[14] In other words, in this example, a man jokes with his potential marriage partners and their families. He continues to joke with their families after his marriage.

As an example of such a specific jural relation we may take that which normally exists between a father and son, or an elder brother and a younger brother. Relations of the same general type may be extended over a considerable range to all the members of a lineage or a clan or an age-set. Besides these specific jural relations which are defined not only negatively but also positively, i.e. in terms of things that must be done as well as things that must not there are general jural relations which are expressed almost entirely in terms of prohibitions and which extend throughout the whole political society. It is forbidden to kill or wound other persons or to take or destroy their property. Besides these two classes of social relations there is another, including many very diverse varieties, which can perhaps be called relations of alliance or consociation. For example, there is a form of alliance of very great importance in many societies, in which two persons or two groups are connected by an exchange of gifts or services.[s] Another example is provided by the institution of blood-brotherhood which is so widespread in Africa.

The argument of this paper has been intended to show that the joking relationship is one special form of alliance in this sense. An alliance by exchange of goods and services may be associated with a joking relationship, as in the instance recorded by Professor Labouret.[t] Or it may be combined with the custom of avoidance. Thus in the Andaman Islands the parents of a man and the parents of his wife avoid all contact with each other and do not speak; at the same time it is the custom that they should frequently exchange presents through the medium of the younger married couple.[15]

But the exchange of gifts may also exist without either joking or avoidance, as in Samoa, in the exchange of gifts between the family of a man and the family of the woman he marries or the very similar exchange between a chief and his "talking chief."

So also in an alliance by blood-brotherhood there may be a joking relationship as amongst the Zande;[u] and in the somewhat similar alliance formed by exchange of names there may also be mutual teasing. But in alliances of this kind there may be a relation of extreme respect and even of avoidance. Thus in the Yaralde and neighbouring tribes of South Australia two boys belonging to communities distant from one another, and therefore more or less hostile, are brought into an alliance by the exchange of their respective umbilical cords. The relationship thus established is a sacred one; the two boys may never speak to one another. But when they grow up they enter upon a regular exchange of gifts, which provides the machinery for a sort of commerce between the two groups to which they belong.

Thus the four modes of alliance or consociation, (1) through intermarriage, (2) by exchange of goods or services, (3) by blood-brotherhood or exchanges of names or sacra, and (4) by the joking relationship, may exist separately or combined in several different ways. The comparative study of these combinations presents a number of interesting but complex problems. The facts recorded from West Africa by Professor Labouret and Mademoiselle Paulme afford us valuable material. But a good deal more intensive field research is needed before these problems of social structure can be satisfactorily dealt with.

---

[15] Radcliffe-Brown was very deeply influenced by his reading of Durkheim and Durkheim's followers. This is evident in many ways in this essay. First, Radcliffe-Brown makes very heavy use of the ideas of Marcel Mauss and Mauss' student, Paulme. Beyond this, his overriding concern is the same as Durkheim's. Durkheim was particularly concerned with the ways in which social solidarity is developed and maintained. In other words, he focused on the mechanisms that held societies together. He found these in notions of the collective conscience, social facts, and collective representations. Radcliffe-Brown has simi-lar concerns. For him, kinship is the critical institution holding societies together (and this is consistent with his mentor Rivers' ideas as well as a general concern within Anglo-American anthropology). Within kinship, the relations of law and alliance that he discusses here function to hold society together and maintain it. Notice that the system is very neat: Where there are possibilities of disjuncture and rupture, society creates institutions such as joking and avoidance relationships to smooth the disjunctures over and avoid conflict.

What I have called relations by alliance need to be compared with true contractual relations. The latter are specific jural relations entered into by two persons or two groups, in which either party has definite positive obligations towards the other, and failure to carry out the obligations is subject to a legal sanction. In an alliance by blood-brotherhood there are general obligations of mutual aid, and the sanction for the carrying out of these, as shown by Dr. Evans-Pritchard, is of a kind that can be called magical or ritual. In the alliance by exchange of gifts failure to fulfil the obligation to make an equivalent return for a gift received breaks the alliance and substitutes a state of hostility and may also cause a loss of prestige for the defaulting party. Professor Mauss[v] has argued that in this kind of alliance also there is a magical sanction, but it is very doubtful if such is always present, and even when it is it may often be of secondary importance.

The joking relationship is in some ways the exact opposite of a contractual relation. Instead of specific duties to be fulfilled there is privileged disrespect and freedom or even licence, and the only obligation is not to take offence at the disrespect so long as it is kept within certain bounds defined by custom, and not to go beyond those bounds. Any default in the relationship is like a breach of the rules of etiquette; the person concerned is regarded as not knowing how to behave himself.

In a true contractual relationship the two parties are conjoined by a definite common interest in reference to which each of them accepts specific obligations. It makes no difference that in other matters their interests may be divergent. In the joking relationship and in some avoidance relationships, such as that between a man and his wife's mother, one basic determinant is that the social structure separates them in such a way as to make many of their interests divergent, so that conflict or hostility might result. The alliance by extreme respect, by partial or complete avoidance, prevents such conflict but keeps the parties conjoined. The alliance by joking does the same thing in a different way.

All that has been, or could be, attempted in this paper is to show the place of the joking relationship in a general comparative study of social structure. What I have called, provisionally, relations of consociation or alliance are distinguished from the relations set up by common membership of a political society which are defined in terms of general obligations, of etiquette, or morals, or of law. They are distinguished also from true contractual relations, defined by some specific obligation for each contracting party, into which the individual enters of his own volition. They are further to be distinguished from the relations set up by common membership of a domestic group, a lineage or a clan, each of which has to be defined in terms of a whole set of socially recognised rights and duties. Relations of consociation can only exist between individuals or groups which are in some way socially separated.[16]

This paper deals only with formalised or standardised joking relations. Teasing or making fun of other persons is of course a common mode of behaviour in any human society. It tends to occur in certain kinds of social situations. Thus I have observed in certain classes in English-speaking countries the occurrence of horse-play between

---

[16] Radcliffe-Brown's goal was to create a science of society. He proposes that this essay is a step toward a science of social structure. Functionalist anthropology in general (and Radcliffe-Brown in particular) were scathingly critiqued by American anthropologists for their failure (so the Americans believed) to effectively do this. In 1951 George Peter Murdock wrote an essay cataloging the sins of functionalism. Of Radcliffe-Brown's attempts at scientific theorizing, he says:

> Radcliffe-Brown is responsible for two serious distortions of scientific method from which his followers

have never freed themselves, namely (1) the notion that universal "laws" are discoverable from the intensive study of a very few societies without reference to their representativeness and (2) the misconception that such laws can be adequately expressed by verbal statements which do not specify the concomitant behavior of variables (1951:469).

Later in the same essay, he accuses functionalist anthropologists of having a "predilection" for "'sociologistic' verbalisms as a substitute for scientific laws" (1951:472).

young men and women as a preliminary to court-ship, very similar to the way in which a Cherokee Indian jokes with his "grandmothers." Certainly these unformalised modes of behaviour need to be studied by the sociologist. For the purpose of this paper it is sufficient to note that teasing is always a compound of friendliness and antagonism.

The scientific explanation of the institution in the particular form in which it occurs in a given society can only be reached by an intensive study which enables us to see it as a particular example of a widespread phenomenon of a definite class. This means that the whole social structure has to be thoroughly examined in order that the particu-lar form and incidence of joking relationships can be understood as part of a consistent system. If it be asked why that society has the structure that it does have, the only possible answer would lie in its history. When the history is unrecorded, as it is for the native societies of Africa, we can only indulge in conjecture, and conjecture gives us neither scientific nor historical knowledge.[w,17]

NOTES

[a] Reprinted from *Africa,* Vol. XIII, No. 3, 1940, pp. 195–210.

[b] "Joking Relationships in East Africa," *Africa,* Vol. XIII, p. 170.

[c] "La Parenté à Plaisanteries en Afrique Occidentale," *Africa,* Vol. II, p. 244.

[d] "Parenté à Plaisanteries et Alliance par le Sang en Afrique Occidentale," *Africa,* Vol. XII, p. 433.

[e] Professor Marcel Mauss has published a brief theo-retical discussion of the subject in the *Annuaire de l'École Pratique des Hautes Etudes, Section des Sci-ences religieuses,* 1927–8. It is also dealt with by Dr. F. Eggan in *Social Anthropology of North American Tribes,* 1937, pp. 75–81.

[f] *Africa,* Vol. XII, p. 438.

[g] Those who are not familiar with these widespread customs will find descriptions in Junod, *Life of a South African Tribe,* Neuchatel, Vol. I, pp. 220–37, and in *Social Anthropology of North American Tribes,* edited by F. Eggan, Chicago, 1937. pp. 55–7.

[h] Ruth Landes in Mead, *Co-operation and Competition among Primitive Peoples,* 1937, p. 103.

[i] Incidentally it may be said that it was hardly satisfac-tory for the magistrate to establish a precedent whereby the man, who was observing what was a permitted and may even have been an obligatory custom, was de-clared guilty of common assault, even with extenuating circumstances. It seems quite possible that the man may have committed a breach of etiquette in teasing the woman in the presence of her mother's brother, for in many parts of the world it is regarded as improper for two persons in a joking relationship to tease one an-other (particularly if any obscenity is involved) in the presence of certain relatives of either of them. But the breach of etiquette would still not make it an assault. A little knowledge of anthropology would have enabled the magistrate, by putting the appropriate questions to the witnesses, to have obtained a fuller understanding of the case and all that was involved in it.

[j] Fortes, M., *The Dynamics of Clanship among the Tallensi.* Oxford University Press, 1945.

[k] See, for example, the kinship systems described in *Social Anthropology of North American Tribes,* edited by Fred Eggan, University of Chicago Press, 1937; and Margaret Mead, "Kinship in the Admiralty Islands," *Anthropological Papers of the American Museum of Natural History,* Vol. XXXIV, pp. 243–56.

[l] For examples see Labouret, *Les Tribus du Rameau Lobi,* 1931, p. 248 and Sarat Chandra Roy, *The Oraons of Chota Nagpur,* Ranchi, 1915, pp. 352–4.

[m] A. Winifred Hoernle, "Social Organisation of the Nama Hottentot," *American Anthropologist,* N.s., Vol. XXVII, 1925, pp. 1–24.

[n] "The Mother's Brother in South Africa," *South Afri-can Journal of Science,* Vol. XXI, 1924. See Chapter I.

[o] There are some societies in which the relation be-tween a mother's brother and a sister's son is approxi-

---

[17] In this last paragraph, Radcliffe-Brown attacks Boasian anthropologists. The Boasians insisted that societies were the *sui generis* results of their own historical development. They had a strong distaste for general theories of society. Radcliffe-Brown argues that the histories of nonliterate so-cieties are unknowable (and therefore, Boasian anthropol-ogy essentially groundless). Earlier, he had written that those who hold that laws of human society do not exist (i.e., Boas and his followers) must hold that "in the field of

social phenomena, in contradistinction to physical and biological phenomena, any attempt at the systematic test-ing of existing generalizations or toward the discovery and verification of new ones is, for some unexplained reason, futile, or as Dr. Radin puts it, 'crying for the moon'" (1965b [1935]:187). He viewed this as a clearly irrational belief and suggested that arguing against such lack of logic was a waste of time.

mately symmetrical, and therefore one of equality. This seems to be so in the Western Islands of Torres Straits, but we have no information as to any teasing or joking, though it is said that each of the two relatives may take the property of the other.

p *Life of a South African Tribe*, Vol. I, p. 255.

q For the kinship terminology of the VaNdau see Boas, "Das Verwandtschafts system der Vandau," in *Zeitschrift für Ethnologie*. 1922, pp. 41–51.

r For an account of the Cherokee see Gilbert, in *Social Anthropology of North American Tribes*, pp. 285–338.

s See Mauss, "Essai sur le Don," *Année Sociologique*, Nouvelle Série, tome I, pp. 30–186.

t *Africa*. Vol. II, p. 245.

u Evans-Pritchard, "Zande Blood-brotherhood," *Africa*, Vol. VI, 1933, pp. 369–401.

v "Essai sur le Don."

w The general theory outlined in this paper is one that I have presented in lectures at various universities since 1909 as part of the general study of the forms of social structure. In arriving at the present formulation of it I have been helped by discussions with Dr. Meyer Fortes.

---

13. *The Licence in Ritual*

Max Gluckman (1911–1975)

In certain armed services at Christmas, and at Christmas only, the officers wait at table on the men. This kind of reversal of role is well-known in ceremonial and ritual. It was one of the problems which lay at the heart of Sir James Frazer's monumental study, *The Golden Bough*. In his attempt to interpret the situation of the Roman priest-king who had to defend his life against his would-be successor, Frazer went on to consider ceremonies in which people of lower social categories are made temporary kings, in which women act as men and men act as women, and so forth.[1] These rites of reversal obviously include a protest against the established order. Yet they are intended to preserve and even to strengthen the established order; and in many rituals their performance is believed to achieve success and prosperity for the group which practices them. Therefore they fall squarely within the general problem which I am discussing in this series of lectures—the problem of how custom in Africa emphasizes conflicts in certain ranges of social relationship and yet establishes cohesion in the wider society or over a longer period of time. It is with this problem in mind that I am going to try to interpret ceremonies in which women don men's clothing and do things normally prohibited to them, such as herding cattle, and also to interpret

---

From *Custom and Conflict in Africa* (1956)

---

[1] Gluckman begins this essay with a brief example of a custom from the British military to prepare his readers for his discussion of comparable rituals in the African societies that are the subject of his essay. This was a common technique of many functionalists who looked for universal cultural patterns or laws that were true for any society. Another technique of these anthropologists was to make customs that appear strange more familiar by comparing them with customs of British society (for example, in essay 11 Malinowski compares kula items with the crown jewels of Scotland).

This opening paragraph mentions Sir James George Frazer (1854–1941), a towering figure in British anthro-pology in the late nineteenth and early twentieth centuries. Frazer was a key influence on British anthropologists of Gluckman's generation. He is best known for his comparative study of religion and folklore, *The Golden Bough* (1890). The purpose of this book was to trace the evolutionary development of thought from magical to religious thinking to the rational/scientific thought of civilized societies. Frazer's evolutionary thinking was soon replaced by diffusionist and functionalist theories, but his work synthesized a huge volume of cross-cultural material that influenced the work of later generations of anthropologists. For example, Gluckman here refers to Frazer's work on the rituals of divine kingships in African societies.

great political feasts in which kings are pitied and insulted and threatened.[2]

Before I go on with this description and its interpretation, I must stress that African ritual and religion form a vast field of study. Many psychological and sociological—indeed physiological—combinations are required for a full analysis. I am not attempting this impossible task. I am discussing only one aspect of ritual—how its protest against the established order is licensed and even encouraged. This encouragement must be explained by some theory which demonstrates that the ritual is socially valuable. And I am going to deal mainly with rituals which contain this element of protest—which are organized to exhibit rebellion. There are many rituals which are not organized thus.[3]

I start from the empirical fact that African rituals are frequently organized to exhibit rebellion and protest, and to emphasize the conflicts which exist between those who participate in the rituals. Thus there are descriptions of Zulu agricultural rites—no longer performed—in which women and girls committed public obscenities and acted as if they were men. More strikingly, the ceremonies were said to be performed in order to propitiate a certain goddess named Nomkubulwana. She is described 'as being robed with light as a garment and having come down from heaven to teach people to make beer, to plant, to harvest, and all the useful arts. . . . She is a maiden and she makes her visit to the earth in the Spring of the year. She is also described as presenting the appearance of a beautiful landscape with verdant forests on some parts of her body, grass-covered slopes on others, and cultivated slopes on others.

She is said to be the maker of the rain.' The ceremonies to supplicate a good harvest from the goddess were comparatively simple. I describe only their core. The young unmarried girls donned men's garments and carried shields and assagais.[4] They drove the cattle out to pasture and milked them, though cattle were normally taboo to females. Meanwhile their mothers planned a garden for the goddess far out in the veld, and poured a libation of beer to her. Thereafter this garden was neglected. At various stages of the ceremonies women and girls went naked, and sang lewd songs. Men and boys hid inside the huts, and might not go near the women. If they did, the women and girls could attack them.

This goddess and her ceremonies are interesting for many reasons. The Zulu and other South African tribes have very little mythology and have not elaborated descriptions of any other of their spirits—of their High-God who, after making the world, withdrew from direct interest in it, or of the power of the Sky, or of ancestral spirits. Why should there be this clearer idea of an unusual naturalistic anthropomorphic goddess, connected with rites in which women behaved both lewdly and as if they were men? A search for the information on the surrounding tribes produced no similar goddess, but I found in them items of these lewd and other protests by women against established rules. To the south, the Tembu women behaved thus when they were celebrating a girl's puberty; to the north, Tsonga women went naked and sang lewd songs and maltreated any man they might meet, when they were trying to get rid of a crop-pest. These obscene and domineering acts by the women were encouraged, for

---

[2] Gluckman mentions a "series of lectures." This essay is a written version of one of six lectures that were presented on BBC radio in Britain in 1955. This was the fifth such lecture. The titles of the others are: (1) "The Peace in the Feud," (2) "The Frailty in Authority," (3) "Estrangement in the Family," (4) "The Logic in Witchcraft," and (6) "The Bonds in the Color-Bar." The lectures were published in book form under the title *Custom and Conflict in Africa* (1956). This volume became one of Gluckman's best known works. In the preface, he writes that he has published the lectures as he delivered them.

[3] Note here another central tenet of structural functionalism: Society is composed of institutions such as religion. These institutions exist because they serve functions for society, thus, they are socially valuable. In this series of essays, Gluckman takes as his task to show that rituals that appear to be disruptive of society actually serve to support it.

[4] An *assagai* is a light spear or javelin.

they were believed to achieve a blessing for the community—good crops, the fertility and good health of a nubile girl, the riddance of crop-pest. I am recounting here the personal experience which first brought me up against the problem of how the customary exaggeration of conflict achieves a social blessing; and beyond that, the problem of how conflicts are built into a system of social order.[5]

I set out to trace the roles of women in all other social situations. I found that there were a whole series of beliefs and customs which emphasized that women as such were ritually ambivalent for the Zulu—that is, they had in them power for evil, and power for good. The power for evil existed in them independently of their conscious volition. Whenever they menstruated they threatened danger to warriors, crops, and cattle, by what we call supernatural means. They became witches harming others, by attracting to themselves sexual familiars. As ancestral-spirits, they were capriciously evil, while male spirits sent merited misfortune. These beliefs were extended into the wider world, for dangerous forked lightning was female, and sheet lightning was male. And so forth. On the other hand, their menstrual blood was important for it helped to make children, and their pregnant condition was magically fertilizing. The striking fact was that these capacities for good and for evil were inherent in being a female. Men had no such conflicting capacities, in their very nature as men. Men had deliberately to seek to do magical evil, by performing actions of sorcery. They could learn to be good magicians. But for women to become good magicians they had to undergo a painful illness as-

cribed to possession by a spirit. This was the ritual difference between men and women.[6]

After surveying Zulu culture, I worked out that a woman was in law—in law, not always in practice—subject to the control of some man—either her father or brother, or after marriage her husband. The prime effect of this subordination was to give these men control over the woman's capacities as wife and as child-bearer. In exchange for transferring to the husband a woman's capacity as a wife, including her work in the gardens, and her capacity as a bearer of children, the husband handed over to her male relatives cattle which were taboo to her—she could not touch them or go into their corral. Here there seemed to me to be a fundamental conflict involved in the social position of a woman in Zulu society, a conflict which I've described in earlier lectures, but which I sharpen now in order to focus the problems of ritual. Zulu kinship groups are built on the principle of descent from men going on through men; succession to office and inheritance of property pass in this line, and the line of descent through women is completely excluded. That is, the line of descent through women as sisters and as daughters transmitted neither power nor property. But in practice the line of a man descends to his sons through his wife or wives. The Romans had a similar system, and they have a paradoxical legal maxim which sums up admirably this conflict which centres on the woman: *mulier et origo et finis familiae est*—a woman is the beginning and the end of a family. In Roman and Zulu society a woman as wife perpetuates her husband's line, as a daughter she is the end of her father's line. And her transference to the position of wife from that of daughter is

---

[5] The way that Gluckman poses his problem is very different from the way that a Boasian anthropologist might. Whereas Boasians insisted that anthropology was fundamentally about cultural description, British social anthropologists looked for general principles underlying human society. Thus, Gluckman is drawn to these rituals because similar events seem to appear in different societies. Most of Boas' students probably would have argued that such superficial similarities may mask profound differences, thus events in each society must be understood in their

context. Gluckman assumes that, in southern Africa at least, if there are similar customs in different groups, they are likely to have similar causes and meanings.

[6] Gluckman seems to be saying that the ability of women to perform rituals of reversal is related to their ambivalent position in society. Men are viewed as having a single nature, whereas women are conflicted. By their nature they bring both good and ill.

achieved by the wedding-ceremony, in which she carries a man's shield and assagai, and by the handing-over of cattle.[7]

Other evidence showed strongly that the approach of marriage was a period of great distress for Zulu girls: they were subject to frequent attacks of hysteria which were ascribed to the love-magic of their suitors. Marriage itself was a difficult relation, requiring adjustment to a strange family where the girl was hedged with many taboos. She had to avoid important parts of her husband's home village and even parts of her own hut. She had to alter her language so as not to use any word containing the root of her husband's name or the names of her senior male relatives-in-law. Her stressed function was to be a dutiful, hard-working, faithful, and decorous wife, bearing children for her husband, and caring for those children. Only when they grew up, could she become independent, as the mother of grown sons. And after her death it was believed that her spirit would send them capricious misfortune, not deserved by evil deeds; nor would she withdraw it after sacrifice, as a male spirit did. But in fulfilling her duty as a wife, she weakened her husband's group as well as strengthening it. On the one hand she gave her husband's group more members, fresh recruits; and on the other hand she produced competitors for power and for property in the group. Here is a second conflict in the position of a woman in these groups. These conflicts centering on the position of woman as wife and as child-bearer both hinge on the cattle which regulate Zulu marriage—

Zulu say, therefore, 'cattle beget children.' Hence it seemed to me that cattle, and the herding of cattle, might well symbolize the whole legal subordination of women. Allowing them to herd the cattle would be a reward and a release, especially while they were also allowed to go naked and sing lewd songs and attack wandering men. This statement, that performing these normally tabooed actions is a reward and release, seems to be justified by the descriptions we have. But part of its interpretation involves psychological analysis for which there is no evidence.[8]

Socially, the lifting of the normal taboos and restraints obviously serves to emphasize them. It is this aspect of the ceremony which most interests me. Zulu custom emphasizes the difference between men and women, beyond their biological differences. Women cannot approach cattle; women must be decorous in public; women do not take part in national life or national ceremonies; women, when they menstruate, are full of mystical danger. This is part of woman's social position, and the customs and beliefs emphasize her distinction and her separateness from men. For men herd cattle, they can be forward in national life and in national ceremonies, they do not menstruate and are not full of this mystical danger. But on one occasion in the year—the time of planting when they begin their arduous agricultural labours—women are allowed to act as if they were men. They are not only licensed to do so, but they are encouraged and even enjoined to do so in the interests of the community. When I was working in Zululand in 1937 these ceremonies were no

---

[7] British social anthropology frequently focused on systems of kinship (see Radcliffe-Brown, essay 12), and it is there that Gluckman identifies a central issue in Zulu society. The kinship system fictionally excludes women, passing property and power from father to son. However, women, of course, are necessary to procreation. Thus, the ritual in Zulu society must somehow reconcile the conflict between women excluded from kinship but central to its composition. Gluckman's job is now to show what the handing over of cattle and the wearing of men's clothing have to do with this conflict.

[8] There are, of course, two classic forms of functionalism: psychological and structural, the former promoted by

Malinowski, the latter by Radcliffe-Brown. Gluckman was influenced far more by Radcliffe-Brown and Evans-Pritchard than by Malinowski. In fact, Gluckman attacked Malinowski for psychologizing culture and abstracting it from its historical and political context (Gluckman 1947, 1949). In this paragraph, he suggests that allowing women to herd cattle might serve a psychological function: the release of tension caused by the conflict between women and their marriage families. However, he ends the paragraph by dismissing psychological analysis in general, suggesting there is no evidence for it. It is not clear what sort of evidence Gluckman has in mind.

longer performed: old men told me that therefore crops were poor. Hence the lifting of the taboos not only rewarded the women but it also brought benefits to the men who allowed this lifting and subjected themselves to the temporarily dominant women. I suggest that this was possible, and effective in ways we do not yet fully understand, because the women as well as the men accepted the general nature of Zulu society—as good and valuable. That is, this particular ritual, by allowing people to behave in normally prohibited ways, gave expression, in a reversed form, to the normal rightness of a particular kind of social order. And the ritual would continue to be effective in this sense, and yet be rewarding to the women, so long as the women accepted Zulu arrangements as good. They were not suffragettes and feminists seeking to alter Zulu society in order to strengthen their own position. Had they been in revolt against Zulu rules, the ritual could not be effective in stating moral principles by reversal, with the belief that this reversal would bring the social blessing of rich harvests.[9]

My analysis of the deeper social alignments affecting the position of women in this ritual is supported when we examine other rites among these peoples. Take this description of the Tsonga ritual which organizes the moving of a village. A Tsonga village is inhabited by a headman, with his wives and children, and the wives and children of his married sons. When they are ready to move, the headman goes first to examine some spots where he would like to build. He breaks small twigs from various trees and these are tested by the divining bones to see which spot will be prosperous. Building material is then collected at the chosen spot, and the headman and

his principal wife leave the old village finally. They have ritual sexual relations on the new site and in the morning tie a knot in grass over which all the villagers should step. This ties the village to the headman and his principal wife. Now begins a month of taboo, especially on sexual relations by the villagers. Breach of this taboo may make the headman ill; it does not make the offender ill. The huts of the old village are carried to the new site by the men, who sing obscene songs insulting the women. Later when the women smear the floors of the huts with mud they retaliate with obscene songs at the men's expense. A Tsonga said of these songs: 'The village is broken to pieces, so are the ordinary laws. The insults which are taboo are now allowed.' The village is fenced with magical substances to obstruct the entry of witches. Finally the new home is ready. All couples have ritual sexual relations in order of precedence, and then the final rite of establishing the headman has to be performed. The headman's principal wife takes his assagai and shield and closes the gate of the village. She makes an offering to the ancestral spirits and prays for the people: 'Be not tied by the village! Bring forth children; live and be happy and get everything. You gods, see! I have no bitterness in my heart. It is pure. I was angry because my husband abandoned me, he said I was not his wife; he loved his younger wives. Now, this is finished in my heart. We shall have friendly relations together.' They then feast together.[10]

This ceremony again requires that in the ritual there should be an emphatic statement of those conflicts within the village which are likely to lead to its break-up. In the end, indeed, over time these conflicts do lead to the splitting of the

---

[9] This paragraph contains the center of Gluckman's argument, and it displays some of the weaknesses and strengths of structural-functionalist thinking. He begins by stating that it is obvious that the lifting of taboos serves to emphasize them. Is this in fact obvious? Gluckman then observes that the reversals of taboos can serve to strengthen society. Thus, he proposes to explain that rituals that seemingly disrupt society in fact support it and lead to its continuation. British structural anthropologists were often masterful in showing that apparent contradictions were surface manifestations of underlying agreements. Things were not necessarily what they seemed.

[10] Note in this description of ritual that individuals who break taboos do not themselves suffer; it is the headman who suffers. Thus, the villagers are declaring their support of their headman and affirming the structure of the village despite the ceremonies in which they publically revile each other.

village. The conflicts centre on the marital relations of the different men in the village; for through these marital relations each man gets children who may eventually enable him to set up his own village. Sexual relations are therefore banned during the period when the old village is deserted but the new village is not yet built—the period when dissident villagers may decide to leave. Normal restraints are lifted and obscenity is allowed. And a breach of the taboo on marital relations does not lead to mystical punishment of the wrongdoer, but to mystical threats to the headman. For it is his authority which is threatened by the marriages which lead to the independence of each man from the group. Finally, the principal wife takes the place of her husband, carrying his weapons, to symbolize the unity of the group of males and their wives, despite the fact that it is through the wives, who bear children, that the group will ultimately split. Women and men are shown to be identified in the interests of village unity. In her prayer the principal wife states the conflicts which exist between herself and other wives of the headman. She says they are jealous for his attentions; but it is also because they are jealous for the rights of their own children. The general opposition of the group of male kin to the stranger women whom they marry, and who bring dissension into the village, is stated in the obscene songs. This ritual again emphasizes conflicts which threaten the unity of the village. And it is carried out even if in practice everyone lives together harmoniously. But by this statement of the conflicts, the ritual emphasizes that the conflicts exist, and indeed it may exaggerate them. Yet the Tsonga believe that the effect of the ceremony is to bless the village with fertility and prosperity. This belief can be held so long as the members of the village accept the unity of the village as a good thing. These same conflicts appear in many other rituals of these tribes. The desire of each group of male kin

for wives, and yet their rejection of the wives as trouble-makers between them, is clearly stated in Zulu wedding ceremonies. The two intermarrying groups insult one another and threaten one another with weapons, they dance competitively against one another, the bride attempts to run away and has to be captured by her husband. Most clearly, this symbolism appears in the bride's carrying a small shield and a knife or assagai, as if she were a man, an enemy threatening her husband's group. And for long periods of the ceremony she has to sit with downcast head while her husband's kin insult her as a lazy good-for-nothing, of bad family, who is going to introduce quarrels into their happy home. Again, the ritual of marriage states in advance the conflicts that will hinge on her position, and this statement is believed to bless the marriage. Open expression of conflict within the group is believed to bring success, and to achieve the unity and prosperity of the wider group.[11]

These rituals contain the belief that if people perform certain actions they will influence the course of events so that their group be made richer, more prosperous, more successful, and so forth. Some of us therefore call these actions 'ritual,' and say that they contain 'mystical notions'—notions that their performance will in some mysterious way affect the course of events. 'Ritual' in this definition is contrasted with 'ceremonial' which consists of similar actions but has no such mystical notions associated with it.

Rituals of this kind, in which people perform actions in terms of their social roles, are very widespread in the so-called primitive societies. They occur in the round of agriculture, in hunting and herding and manufacturing, and in military operations. They also occur when villages are moved or established and persons of authority are installed, and at different stages during the growing-up of individuals—at birth, puberty, marriage. Finally, they are important in funerals.

---

[11] In several ways, this passage expresses the critical points made above. The rebellious acts expressed in rituals are real in that they are about points of conflict in society: Women really do hold conflicted positions that are necessary to the survival of the lineage, but as outsiders they are also dangerous to it; villages do eventually split up over conflicts between different families. But allowing the expression of these real conflicts in ritual somehow controls them and promotes the stability of the village rather than its destruction.

We find that different societies ritualize these events to very different degrees, and different societies seize on different occasions to perform ritual. But overall a high ritualization of these social occasions is characteristic of the simpler societies, when compared with developed industrial civilizations. This rule is general, not absolute: for many simple societies, including those which belong to Islam, are not thus full of ritual.

The characteristic feature of this type of ritualization is that it makes use of the details of particular social relationships—of relationships between parents and children, maternal uncle and sister's son, men and women, king and princes and subjects. Indeed, the performance of specific ritual acts by persons in a particular kind of relationship with one another, is an essential element of that relationship. In many patriarchal societies, for example, it is the mother's brother who offers support to a lad at certain crises, by assisting him through initiation and other rituals. And provision of this ritual support, or the performance of any rite in a ceremony involving some related person, is strongly enforced. Failure to conform is believed to lead to severe mystical penalties. Thus these ritual obligations are a very significant part of each relationship, and mark it off from other relationships. The varying ritual role of any person marks out his or her particular relationship with the person concerned; and the mystical penalties ensure that attention shall be paid to this role.[12]

This being so, the ritual of each African tribe is built about the framework of its own forms of organization. Generally each tribe has distinctive sets of rituals for particular occasions, and in these rituals persons appear according to their relationships with one another in secular life. What

happens is, that the various persons involved act out their roles, either directly or by reversal of normal behaviour or by special symbolic rites. The Zulu bride carries shield and assagai, but she also carries a child of her husband's village on her back. She aggressively hurls an assagai into her husband's cattle-kraal; but she also meekly and ceremoniously collects firewood, cooks, and sweeps. In one set of rites she reverses her role, in the other set of rites she performs her future duties. The rites thus exhibit the ambivalence of her total role. In national ceremonies the king is insulted; but he is also lauded as all-powerful.[13]

To say that African rituals have this high degree of particularism is not to deny that they deal with some of the general problems of social and human existence which have faced men everywhere. Some problems are universal. What is man? Whence does he come and whither does he go? Why should there be good and evil, prosperity and misfortune? How is human society set in the world of nature? What of the relations of men and women, parents and children, magistrates and people? What of the dealings of different groups with one another? These problems may be summed up, perhaps, in the general question: What is man's place, as a member of society, in the world? The answer is given partly in myth and legend, partly in dogma, and largely in rituals, like the Zulu ritual of women propitiating the goddess Nomkubulwana.

Africans have not worked out elaborate dogmas to explain the nature of the universe, though there are important exceptions to this generalization. Partly, they lack professional theologians. Hence, too, they do not strive to make their dogmas consistent. Their different rituals often embody inconsistent, and even contradictory,

---

[12] Here Gluckman is outlining a function of ritual that is lifted straight from Durkheim via Radcliffe-Brown. He says that certain ritual roles are prescribed for individuals with specific relationships to each other and are sanctioned by mystical penalties. Thus the rituals emphasize certain kin ties and reinforce the social order.

[13] Note the emphasis in this passage on the roles that individuals fill. People do not act out their personal rebellions in these ceremonies, but rather they play parts that are dictated by their social roles. Structural functionalists tended to think of society as a series of social roles standing in particular relationships to each other. Personalities of individuals were not relevant to their analysis. This was not a denial that people in primitive societies had emotions and were able to rebel; rather, the structural functionalists understood these as psychological factors and not part of anthropological understandings.

principles and values. For they reflect the existence in social life of different principles of social organization, which work out against each other, as we have seen. A wife is a blessing and a danger. These different principles compensate for one another, so that after a period of time or in a wider range of social relations conflicts in particular relationships are redressed, and the social pattern is re-established or duplicated. The village remains united, or two similar villages are built. This repetitive process in African social life allows the use of ritual statement of conflict. For social processes are working through quarrels and disputes to produce the same kind of social relationships, and not different new relationships. After their orgy of cattle-herding, Zulu women return to their daily tasks: they do not seek for a different set of feminist laws. The rituals are statements of rebellion, and never of revolution.[14]

This tendency appears very markedly in the great national ceremonies of the tribes who dwell in Southeast Africa. At sowing, first fruits and harvest, and before war, the Zulu nation performed, and the Swazi still perform, great military rituals. These rituals are believed to strengthen the nation, and to ensure national prosperity and victory. Yet they consist largely of statements of rebellion against the king, by his brother-princes and by his subjects, and of affirmations that he is unworthy of his high office. Dr. Hilda Kuper[15] has brought this out in a brilliant description and analysis of the Swazi ceremonies. She also brings out the smallness of the universe within which Swazi cosmology is established, and the particularistic nature of their answer to the problem,

what is man? The world is seen as a setting for the Swazi, in competition with neighbouring nations, and not for humanity in general. The king has to race the sun by beginning the first fruits ceremony before the sun reaches the Tropic of Capricorn; but he has also to begin the ceremony at the last wane of the moon when man's powers go into decline, in order that a fortnight later the ritual climax may occur at the full moon when man's powers are at their height.

The ceremony itself is strikingly an acting out of the whole of Swazi political relations, so that Dr. Kuper calls it 'a drama of kingship.' The king and queen-mother and queens, princes and councillors, men in their regiments, commoner chiefs, women, all have specific roles in the ritual which are related to their roles in everyday life. But the rites affirm not only the unity of the nation about the kingship, but also all the conflicts around the person of the reigning king: the resentment of his subjects against authority, the jealousy of his brother-princes who covet the throne, and so forth. Indeed, the ritual exaggerates the conflicts. Whether or not princes covet the throne they are made to act as if they do so covet it. At critical points when loyalty to the king is being affirmed, they have to leave the arena. And even their unborn children are also involved in the conflict—for the pregnant wife of a prince must also withdraw. At particular points in the ceremony a black bull is required: these bulls are stolen from commoner subjects who are thus made "angry and proud," say the Swazi—an apt description of the ambivalent attitudes involved in being a member of an authoritative nation.[16] There are,

---

[14] This passage does two critical things. First, it reminds us that although the rituals Gluckman has been discussing are intended to strike the Western audience for whom the lecture was planned as exotic, the people performing them are dealing with fundamental issues that are faced by people everywhere; hence we should be able to think about similar rituals in our society. Second, Gluckman once again emphasizes that while the rituals have the appearance of rebellion, they are really nothing of the kind. In fact, they support the societies in which they are found and reproduce the same social forms they critique.

[15] Hilda Kuper (1911–1992), like Gluckman, was an African-born anthropologist. She was from Bulawayo in

Rhodesia (now Zimbabwe). Like Gluckman, she studied anthropology at the University of Witwatersrand under A. Winnifred Hoernle and Isaac Schapera. Kuper did extensive fieldwork among the Swazi and in the slums of South Africa. Like Gluckman, she was concerned with racism and the problems of apartheid.

[16] It would have been hard to read this last sentence in the 1950s without thinking of both Nazi Germany and the Soviet Union, authoritarian nations with angry and proud citizens. Gluckman is trying to make his anthropology germane to the daily concerns of his audience.

of course, also rites which affirm the support of the king both by princes and by subjects, but the general tone is as much one of rejection of the king as of triumph in his might. Here are typical songs:

> You hate the child king,
> You hate the child king;

and

> You hate him,
> Mother, the enemies are the people.
> You hate him,
> The people are wizards.
> Admit the treason of Mabedla—
> You hate him,
> You have wronged,
> Bend great neck,
> Those and those they hate him,
> They hate the king;

and

> King, alas for thy fate,
> King, they reject thee,
> King, they hate thee.

Those who hate the king are those who reject him: enemies within the tribe, not external enemies, his brothers and his discontented subjects. His fate is sad because he carries the burden of office, and the hatred that is the lot of office.

This theme of rejection and hatred of the king is so built into this great national ceremony that we have to ask, again, how the affirmation of rebellion can be so strong in a ritual which the people believe unifies and blesses their nation. And the king not only allows them to reject, and also to insult him; by doing so they are believed to support him in his arduous office.

Obviously there may be high psychological catharsis and relief in the princes and subjects who are required thus publicly to express hidden resentments. This problem lies outside my province. But again, as a sociologist, I am interested in the fact that this affirmation of rebellion goes on within an accepted order. The kingship is sacred, and its sacred strength is necessary for the nation—not only for its political strength, but also for the fertility of its women, fields, and cattle. The acceptance of the established order as right and good, and even sacred, seems to allow unbridled licence, very rituals of rebellion, for the order itself keeps this rebellion within bounds. Hence to act the conflicts, whether directly or by inversion or in other symbolical forms, emphasizes the social cohesion within which the conflicts exist. As the social order always contains a division of rights and duties, and of privileges and powers as against responsibilities, the ritual enactment of the order states its rightness. The ritual states that in virtue of their social position princes and people hate the king, but nevertheless they support him. They support him despite the conflicts between them. Or, at least, if they don't support the particular king, they support the kingship. For in the conditions of Swazi polity, as I've explained in an earlier lecture, malcontents did not attempt to subvert the social order, but to install a new king in the old kingship. Swazi were rebels, never revolutionaries. Should a particular king be a tyrant, his people's redress was not to seek to establish a republic, but to find some good prince in the king's family; for only a member of that family could hold the sacred kingship.[17]

I myself believe that in the undeveloped Swazi economy, with its poor communications, different territorial sections of the nation developed strong autonomous tendencies, and tendencies to break out of the national hegemony. But these tendencies to fragment were canalized into a struggle to put particular princes on to the throne: the sections fought for the sacred kingship, and not for independence from it. Hence I have argued that in these African states periodic rebellions strengthened, and did not weaken, the

---

[17] Note two ideas drawn directly from Durkheim in this passage: First, ritual is about social cohesion. Much of Durkheim's work focused on the problem of social cohesion: How exactly were societies held together? Both Durkheim and Gluckman agree that the process has a great deal to do with the rituals that the society conducts.

Second: Consider that what Gluckman is really saying in this passage is that when society conducts these religious rituals, it is really, in fact, worshiping itself, or more specifically its social order, a central point of Durkheim's *The Elementary Forms of Religious Life* (1965 [1912]).

political system. If this argument is acceptable, it is possible to see that the Swazi may be right when they say their great ceremony, so openly affirming conflicts, is a source of unity and strength—of cohesion. For the 'drama of kingship' states a process that is present in actual political life. It affirms the acceptance of kingship as such, as the source of law and moral order for the Swazi, against internal traitors and external foes. It does so by stating that those who are hostile to the ruling king, nevertheless support him because they support the kingship. And the possibility that the king may be personally inadequate, and may desecrate the values of the kingship, is admitted in the insults he suffers. This does not invalidate the kingship itself.[18]

The general theme I have been putting forward emerges with great force from an account by Delegorgue, an early French traveller, of the Zulu ceremony.[19] His account is the more telling because he did not understand what he was looking at. He described the Zulu government as despotic, and commented on the ceremony: 'It is at the time of the general assembly of warriors (towards December 8th) when the maize ripens, that lively discussion takes place. There are free interrogations which the king must immediately answer, and in a manner which will satisfy the people. I have seen at that time ordinary warriors come leaping out of their ranks, transformed into orators full of spirit, extremely excited, not only returning the fiery glance of the king, but even denouncing him before everyone, blaming his actions, stigmatizing them as base and cowardly,

obliging him to explain, destroying the reasoning in his answers, dissecting them and unmasking their falsehood; then proudly threatening him and ending with a gesture of contempt. I have also seen, after such discussions,' Delegorgue goes on, 'I have also seen the king's party and that of the opposition on the point of hurling themselves upon one another. I have seen that the voice of the despot was no longer heeded, and that a revolution could have exploded then and there had a single ambitious man come forward to profit by the indignation of the party opposed to the king. But what surprised me no less, was the order which succeeded the end of this kind of popular tribunal.' It is the surprise of M. Delegorgue that I am trying to explain away. Clearly no revolutionary leader could come forward at that point. The attack on the king was demanded by tradition and it naturally culminated in the warriors exhorting the king to lead them to war. For the attack must have been on the king, as shown by Delegorgue's words, for failing to live up to the standards of kingship—it exhibited the conflict between the kingship and the human frailty of the king, between subjects and king. But it affirmed the value of kingship.[20]

I could demonstrate the extent to which conflict is thus used in ritual in many other political ceremonies, both in states and in societies without governmental institutions. A remarkable example among a people without government occurs among the Tallensi of the Gold Coast. Professor Fortes has shown there that different groups are involved in a series of rites, so that

---

[18] Note again that what is ritually supported and reinforced is not the individuals who hold social roles (as Gluckman points out, these may be either good or bad) but the roles themselves.

[19] Adulphe Delegorgue (1814–1850) was a French explorer and naturalist who visited South Africa between 1838 and 1844. His two-volume *Travels in Southern Africa,* originally published in 1847, is a classic of exploration literature.

[20] Delegorgue misunderstands the actions he witnesses because he puts them in European social context: He thinks he is witnessing a potential revolution. He explains them in a way that was probably both ethnocentric and

racist: The Zulu lack the incentive and ambition to change their system. Gluckman provides an alternative explanation that he believes is neither ethnocentric nor racist: Delegorgue wasn't witnessing a rebellion at all; what he saw was a ceremony confirming and reinforcing the values of the Zulu kingship.

Also note that Delegorgue believes that the rebellion he witnessed failed because there was no individual who had the personal ambition and talent to seize control. However, functionalists such as Gluckman minimize the role of personal characteristics as forces driving society. They find explanatory power in social and structural positions. Individual initiative has little to do with social action.

each group must perform its part of a cycle of rituals if all are to be prosperous.[21] One lot of groups is responsible for rain, another for fertility of the crops. And what is important for my purpose is that when each lot performs its rites the other must remain shut up in its homes, under pain of mystical punishment. Unity and interdependence are again stressed by mutual exclusion, to achieve prosperity for all. For this unity and this interdependence are made up by the separateness of the component groups. It is significant, too, that marriages are banned in this period, for marriages establish special links between the independent groups and conflicts within each group which I've already discussed. Herein, I venture to suggest, lies the origin of the ban on Christian marriages in Lent, and of Jewish marriages at the same period. This, in the Mediterranean, is the period between first fruits and harvest, and the period of great national rites in the ancient civilizations. Marriages, as the source of unity across division, were taboo.

These rebellious rituals thus occur in national ceremonies and in domestic ceremonies. At the installation of a village headman in many Central African tribes he is insulted and told he is unworthy of office: the Yao strike him on the head to knock him out, ritually to kill him. Here successors to headmanship are also tested for witchcraft, because it is believed they may have killed their predecessor and their rivals. In these small political groups the struggle for power cuts deep into personal relations, and this is used in the ritual to cleanse the headman and to install him so that he may rule wisely and to the benefit of the villagers. But the statement of conflict in ritual is not carried into the smallest grouping of society, and that a very important one—the elementary family. No ceremony that I know allows the open statement of hostility by children to parents, by parents to children, or by brothers and sisters to one another. Psychologists will probably say that may be because the conflicts here cut too near the bone: the relationship could not be reestablished if the conflicts repressed in these most intimate sentiments were exhibited. As a social anthropologist I seek for an explanation of a different kind. The rites I have been considering all go on in groups which endure despite the life and death of members, or their geographical movements. They are on the whole enduring groups—nations, interlinked political groups, villages, local districts of women in the Zulu goddess's ritual. The family is not such an enduring group: it breaks up with the death of the parents and with the marriages of the children. It has not the same sort of cohesion as the other groups. And the basis of my argument is that the licensed ritual of protest and of rebellion is effective so long as there is no querying of the order within which the ritual of protest is set, and the group itself will endure.[22]

But family relationships are altered when children grow up and when they marry. Here the ritual

---

[21] Meyer Fortes (1906–1983) was another of the African-born anthropologists around Gluckman. He was trained at the University of Capetown and later under Malinowski, who wrote that "for sheer brilliancy and real capacity and intelligence [he is] the best pupil I have ever had" (quoted in Goody 1995:28). However, like Gluckman, Fortes was ultimately more drawn to the structural side of functionalism than the psychological.

Also note that Gluckman points out that the Tallensi are a people without governmental institutions. The maintenance of order in societies without government was a central problem for the British structural-functionalist anthropologists (and not unrelated to British colonization).

[22] In this passage, Gluckman's thinking is very close to Durkheim's. The enduring groups and practices he discusses are essentially the same as Durkheim's ideas of collective conscience and social fact. Both Durkheim and Gluckman focus specifically on superorganic entities that exist independent of the individuals who are members of the social group or participate in the rituals.

Note also the tendency throughout this essay to view society as unchanging. The functionalists were strongly criticized, particularly by American anthropologists, for painting a static portrait of society. If, as Gluckman argues in this essay, personal psychological factors are irrelevant to social analysis and acts of rebellion within the social system can be interpreted as supporting that system, it is hard to see what dynamic might drive change in society.

which involves their separation from their parents does not state that the parents resent the adulthood of their children or their marriages. Commonly, the parents may abstain from being present. When a Tsonga girl reaches puberty, her mother does not attend the rites: she is looked after by a substitute mother. This in itself signifies a breaking away from her mother's apron-strings. Barotse parents do not attend their children's marriages. Absence in this way may be ritually effective in symbolizing a change of relationships; in the Tallensi political ceremonies I've quoted (where political groups which are interlinked hide when their peers are performing their ceremonies) absence is effective in allowing the ceremony to achieve the blessing of prosperity for all. Prescribed absence from a ritual is thus a form of participation in it: though it is not a protest, it states that there is a conflict present in the social process.

I myself was fortunate to observe this process vividly in certain boys' circumcision ceremonies in North-western Rhodesia.[23] There are many similar rituals throughout South-central Africa. Earlier descriptions of these rituals all just stressed that they were taboo to women, who had to remain away. I found that the absence of the women was part of their contribution to the ritual which aimed to help their sons grow up. By not being present they assisted their sons to break away from them, and become men, associated with their fathers. But through the ritual as a whole, the women had to abstain for periods, and then join actively in certain rites. The rites involved a symbolic marriage of men and women to give rebirth to the boys as complete men. This symbolic marriage was based on the idea that the mating of sexes for procreation involves the union of two opposed but complementary persons—man and woman. Male and female symbols were linked throughout the camp where the boys were isolated. And men and women successively fought one another, separated, united in joy at the growing-up of their sons. The ceremony was compared for me with marital

relations—a "fighting with joy," a union fraught with conflict, but a union which would be successful if the proper rites were observed, as ordained by the ancestors. Again, the open statement, the exaggeration of conflict, was believed to achieve a generally desired end—the maturity and fruitfulness of the boys. It did so because women agreed in wanting their sons to become men, like their husbands. There was no division over the ultimate rightness of the social order.

I have been arguing that the emphatic dramatizing of conflict within a particular type of social order may be believed to bless that order, so long as it is unquestioned. People are required to express their hostilities to one another so as to secure a blessing: they assert acceptance of common goals despite these hostilities. I have also suggested reasons why rituals of licence do not occur inside the elementary family. But I have still to deal with other rituals where the element of conflict is not expressed, and the aim of the ritual is secured by straightforward affirmations of unity and identity of purpose. This is a complex problem, but I believe the clue to the answer was given by Delegorgue's description of the Zulu national ceremonies. In all the ceremonies I've been describing this evening, despite the conflicts, there is no division about the desired end, and no doubt about which is the dominant moral rule or social relationship. The Zulu and Swazi states were strong and unquestioned. In domestic life, the Zulu had a very strong patriarchy, under the dominance of the eldest son of a man's chief wife. It was difficult for men to leave their paternal kin, or for women to leave their husbands. The strength of this system may allow the women's licence in ritual; as the strength of the army structure allows the Christmas reversal of roles when officers wait on men. Similarly, in the Polish ghettoes, where the rabbis were powerful, once a year a sermon attacking them was preached in the synagogue by a wastrel; this was not found where the rabbinate was weak.[24] In

---

[23] Northwestern Rhodesia is now Zambia.

[24] Gluckman was Jewish, like many of his colleagues in British social anthropology, including Charles Seligman (a

member of the Torres Straits expedition), Isaac Schapera, Meyer Fortes, S. F. Nadel, Hortense Powdermaker, and Ashley Montague. Many of Gluckman's essays contain references to Jewish history and Jewish law.

Swaziland, if the king was still a boy, the rites of rebellion were not practised. I don't know the full answer to this, but I am suggesting that where the relationships involved are weak, there cannot be licence in ritual.[25]

The weakness of a relationship may lie in its own structure. But it may also be weak because it involves conflicts of social principles which are immediately obvious and which cannot be reconciled. Then, I think, the ritual will affirm the principles separately, and it will not stress the conflict between them. Finally, another profitable line of inquiry seems to lie in the contrast of ritual handling of conflict with the secular handling of conflict. For example, the political conflicts which I described for the Zulu and Swazi, are also present in Barotse life. Yet the Barotse do not have rituals of rebellion. But their political system is so organized—as the systems of Zulu and Swazi are not—that all these conflicts are built into an elaborate series of councils. The conflicts are exhibited and expressed in differentiated secular relationships. And here, I believe, lies an important clue to understanding why rituals are so few in our own society. There must be many reasons for this, but I put only the lessons of rites of protest.

I have been advancing two lines of argument in my attempt to understand these rites. First, in Africa, on the whole, a man does everything with the same set of fellows—he works with them, plays with them, acts politically with them, worships with them. An intricate set of relationships

is woven in which every interest for the people depends on right relationship with the same lot of their fellows. A quarrel with your brother or your wife upsets your subsistence activities, for example. Wider ties in the society are developed by extending the ties inside the family: and the result is an intricate mesh of relationships in which the same people depend on one another for many things. Custom marks out the individuality of different relationships within the whole. And the customs of ritual are used to indicate any change in the relationships, or change in the activities within them. So that the birth of a child, or a boy's attainment of maturity or marriage, a man's going hunting or the taking in of harvest, and so forth—all these change the whole pattern of social life. The intricate set of relationships is disturbed, and thus the moral order of the society. This has to be righted. And it is righted by reaffirming the general moral order, through stating both the cohesion and the conflicts which exist within that cohesion. The conflicts can be stated openly wherever the social order is unquestioned and indubitable—where there are rebels, and not revolutionaries. In such a system, the licensed statement of conflict can bless the social order.[26]

This hypothesis of how rituals of protest can occur in certain societies, also implies why they cannot exist in other types of society, such as our own. First, we have revolutionaries as well as rebels, suffragettes as well as good wives and mothers—indeed, good wives and mothers are

---

[25] Once again, Gluckman is proposing but not elaborating on a general law of social behavior: There is an inverse relationship between the strength of a social relationship and the existence of rebellious ritual. Where social relationships are strong, such rituals are likely; where they are weak, such rituals are unlikely. Now, near the end of his essay, Gluckman returns to a Durkheimian theme. In this passage, Gluckman is arguing that the societies he has been describing are held together by mechanical solidarity. In these societies, "a man does everything with the same set of fellows" and the social order is unquestioned and unquestionable. Gluckman argues that a ritual of rebellion is most effective under these circumstances. Since the social order is ultimately unquestionable, such rituals bless it rather than threaten it.

[26] Continuing the Durkheimian theme, Gluckman proposes that modern society is held together by organic solidarity: It is composed of many groups with different interests that both collaborate and compete. Because, in such a situation, revolution is a distinct possibility, rituals that emphasize conflicts pose a danger to the entire system. They are also, to a great extent, unnecessary. Rather than experience conflict, an individual can, in many cases, move to a different social group. Durkheim believed that systems of organic solidarity were preferable to systems of mechanical solidarity because the former allowed for a greater development of human individuality and the human spirit. Gluckman seems to share this belief.

often suffragettes. Once there is questioning of the social order, the ritual of protest is inappropriate, since the purpose of the ritual is to unite people who do not or cannot query their social roles. And beyond this, our society is composed of highly fragmented and divided relationships—our interests lead us into association with a whole variety of different persons, in the family, schools, pubs, workplaces, churches, political organizations, recreational clubs, and so on. The dissatisfied person can change his membership of groups, vote for a new government, join a new club, seek work in a new factory, move away from his family when he marries. In African society, a man could not do this so easily; and my impression is that rites of protest are less developed in those societies where some movement is possible. Hence, I suggest—the problem is too complex for a strong affirmation—hence, I suggest, we do not have the many rituals of Africa. They are inappropriate in the family, our single many-interest group. They are inappropriate in the state, because we have revolutionaries as well as rebels. All our other groups have voluntary and not compelled membership. And many differentiated secular institutions, with great freedom of movement, allow for the temporary solution of personal and sectional conflicts.

We don't have rituals in the sense that we believe that the acting of social roles will in some supernatural manner affect our prosperity and unity in this way. But, of course, we have many ceremonials expressing unity. And a few of these are recognized to state conflicts. Yet I am also sometimes tempted to regard as 'ceremonies' other squabbling actions in our social life, which are usually assumed to be realistic. Parliamentary debates and election campaigns are full of dispute: I wonder how realistic much of this is, and what relation it bears to the actual taking of political decisions. Periodic scandals, say about the actions of the Civil Service, may lead to the affirmation of general principles about how the country should be run, as if there were not posed impossible reconciliations of different interests. These inquiries may not alter what actually happens, but they affirm an ideal condition of unity and justice. Even some strikes appear to be ceremonials of rebellion in the national industrial system. For some of them end, and apparently for a time happily, without changing conditions; and others lead to a change which might have been achieved without the demonstration. Yet the demonstration appears to be a preliminary necessity. African society was not changing in its structure, and rituals of rebellion worked because ultimate values, some contradictory, were put on a mystical plane where they could not be questioned. Ours is a rapidly changing society. Nevertheless, I am not sure that these processes which are like those we find in Africa, may not act to persuade us that there is great persistence notwithstanding the change.[27]

---

[27] In closing the essay, Gluckman revises what he has said above, arguing that perhaps some actions in modern society are like rituals of rebellion. He is trying to make his essay relevant to his audience, but given his background as a social activist it is a rather cynical point of view. It seems unlikely that union members on strike or candidates fighting elections believe that their actions are designed to preserve the status quo. However, it is a profoundly functionalist point of view: The purpose of elections is not to choose among candidates (for that ultimately makes little difference) but to celebrate, and thus perpetuate, the political system of our society.

Culture and Personality

The fact that British functionalists relied on Spencer's organic analogy and Durkheim's notion of the collective conscience necessarily gave their work a holistic quality. In America, Franz Boas insisted that anthropology was holistic but lacked any compelling unifying theory that either required or demonstrated this feature. Although Boas used the rhetoric of holism, many of the historical particularists tended to treat culture as a chance association of disparate features. In 1920, Boas' student Robert Lowie (1883–1957) concluded *Primitive Society* with an attack on the notion of historical laws of cultural evolution. Quoting Gilbert and Sullivan's operetta *The Mikado,* he wrote: "To that planless hodge-podge, that thing of shreds and patches called civilization, its historian can no longer yield superstitious reverence." Lowie later wrote that he was critiquing American civilization in the post–World War I years, not proposing that all cultures were things of shreds and patches (Lowie 1946:119). However, many took his words as a general statement on the impossibility of finding coherent regularities in culture. Whatever Lowie's intentions, Boas and his followers were certainly open to this critique.

One way that several of Boas' students sought to circumvent this problem without challenging the bases of historical particularism was through ideas borrowed from Gestalt psychology and psychoanalysis. Gestalt psychologists examined personality as an interrelated psychological pattern rather than a collection of separate elements. This insight particularly influenced the work of Ruth Fulton Benedict (1887–1948), who focused on the psychological concept of personality as her unifying theme. However, many of the other great culture and personality theorists took their lead from the work of Sigmund Freud. Margaret Mead (1901–1978), for example, was keenly interested in the effect of early childhood influences on adult personality and behavior.

Sigmund Freud (1856–1939) was an Austrian physician and neurologist who founded the field of psychoanalysis. Psychoanalytic theory, with its emphasis on unconscious psychological processes and psychological defense mechanisms such as repression, projection, and sublimation, captured the popular imagination of his day and became an important part of anthropological thought in the first decades of the twentieth century. Freud proposed that a person's mind contained three "mental organs" called the id, ego, and superego, and that these struggled for control over behavior. He postulated that certain psychological processes and responses were innate and universal, believing, for example, that all humans evolved through a universal series of psychosexual phases he named the oral, anal, genital, latency, and genital primacy stages of development.

Freud is best known for his study and treatment of neurosis through psychoanalysis and his work on dreams. The latter is summarized in his first book, *On Dreams* (1963, orig. 1900). Here, Freud challenged the popular European view that dreams were insignificant, calling them the "royal road to the unconscious" and outlining his method for examining their symbolic and unconscious meanings.

Freud, was also fascinated by history and anthropology and was familiar with anthropological theory of the nineteenth century. Starting about 1910 on a quest that would occupy him for the rest of his life, Freud wrote a series of books and articles attempting to demonstrate how psychoanalysis could explain the origins of cultural institutions. Two of the most famous are *Totem and Taboo* (1950, orig. 1913) and *Civilization and Its Discontents* (1961, orig. 1930). Freud believed that he could analyze cultural institutions in a way that was analogous to his method of analyzing the neurotic symptoms of his patients. In fact, the subtitle of *Totem and Taboo* is *Some Points of Agreement between the Mental Lives of Savages and Neurotics.*

Few people today would describe themselves as Freudian anthropologists. However, Freud's influence on the discipline was profound. His evolutionary ideas, in particular the notion that adults in primitive tribes were similar to children in civilized society, were widely popularized. The antievolutionary ideas of Boasian anthropology of the early twentieth century served, in part, to counter Freud's theories.

Although anthropologists rejected Freud's evolutionism, they were interested in the relationship between culture and the individual and were drawn to his ideas about the importance of early childhood and the significance of sexual symbolism. They believed that psychoanalysis was a powerful tool for probing the human psyche. Kroeber, though not a culture and personality theorist, actually practiced psychoanalysis in San Francisco from 1921 to 1923. Following Freud, many American anthropologists from the 1920s through the 1950s focused attention on the importance of weaning and toilet training in the development of adult personalities and cultural institutions. More recently, symbolic and interpretive anthropologists of the 1960s, 1970s, and 1980s were attracted to the Freudian notion that many cultural ideas and symbols reflected unconscious impulses or deep-seated sexual tensions (see, for example, Obeyesekere 1981).

Ruth Benedict, Margaret Mead, Edward Sapir, Abram Kardiner (1891–1981), and Cora Du Bois (1903–1991) examined different aspects of the problem of how humans acquired culture and culture's relationship to individual personality. Because they focused on the interaction between individual personality and culture, they became known as founding members of the culture and personality school. There are two broad themes within this perspective: the relationship between culture and individual personality (represented here by Benedict's essay "Psychological Types in the Cultures of the Southwest") and the relationship between culture and human nature (represented here by Mead's introduction to her 1928 book, *Coming of Age in Samoa*).

The major figures associated with the founding of the culture and personality school all had close ties to Boas and to each other. For example, Edward Sapir was one of Boas' most gifted students. Although primarily known for his work in linguistics (see pages 116–117), Sapir was well versed in psychoanalytic literature and was good friends with Benedict, who taught at Columbia University with Boas. Their correspondence played an important role in shaping Benedict's theories. Mead was one of Benedict's first students and also studied under Boas.

Benedict came to anthropology from literature. She had taught secondary-school English and published numerous poems of her own before starting her career in anthropology. Her interest in the interplay between culture and personality was encouraged by her friend Sapir and her mentor, Boas. Benedict was an ardent cultural relativist. For example, in "Anthropology and the Abnormal" (1934), she argued that normal and abnormal were culturally determined and that what was abnormal in one culture might be perfectly acceptable in another. The most comprehensive expression of Benedict's ideas was her book *Patterns of Culture* (1934). Here, Benedict proposed that each culture had a unique pattern, called a *cultural configuration,* which determined the fundamental personality characteristics of its members. To illustrate this concept, Benedict selected three societies: Zuni, Dobu, and Kwakiutl. Relying on her own and Elsie Clews Parsons' (1875–1941) observations among the Zuni, Reo Fortune's (1903–1979) work with the people of Dobu, and Boas' writings on the Kwakiutl, she described the configuration for each society based on the dominant personality characteristics observed in those cultures. Famously, she argued that culture was "personality writ large." Although this idea was a guiding principle in her work, Benedict offered little explanation of why a culture or its members should have a particular personality or how it was passed from generation to generation.

Margaret Mead and later culture and personality theorists largely accepted Benedict's notion of cultural configuration and focused on discovering its sources. Their investigations centered on the interplay of biological and cultural factors, most significantly on Freud's notion that childrearing practices had profound effects on adult personality. Margaret Mead's work clearly illustrates this theme. In a series of studies, starting with *Coming of Age in Samoa* (1928) and continuing with *Growing up in New Guinea* (1930) and one of her more controversial books, *Sex and Temperament in Three Primitive Societies* (1935), Mead attempted to separate the biological and cultural factors that control human behavior and personality development. Together with Benedict's *Patterns of Culture* (1934b), Mead's trilogy established the cultural configuration and national character approaches in American anthropology.

Mead was also one of the most colorful figures in American anthropology. She was born in Philadelphia, the daughter of a professor at the Wharton School of the University of Pennsylvania. Like her mentor, Ruth Benedict, she had an early interest in literature. During her undergraduate career at Barnard College in New York City, she was a member of a literary group called the Ash Can Cats (Lutkehaus 1995:189).

In 1923, Mead began her graduate career at Columbia University, working with both Ruth Benedict and Franz Boas. Her relationship with her mentor Benedict was particularly intense. Mead and Benedict became lovers after the completion of her dissertation, a relationship that continued until Benedict's death in 1948 (Bateson 1984:117).

In 1925 Mead did her first fieldwork in Samoa. Her Samoan experience was the only fieldwork she was to undertake alone, and it became the basis of her first book, *Coming of Age in Samoa*. This book was an immediate hit and launched Mead on a long career as one of anthropology's most prolific authors. She published thirty-nine books (fifteen of them collaborations) and almost fourteen hundred other pieces of various kinds. Many of these were brief essays designed for popular consumption. She wrote regularly for *The Nation* and *The New York Times*. For seventeen years, with her collaborator, Rhoda Metraux (1914–2003), she wrote a monthly column for the women's magazine *Redbook*. In addition to this she made films and appeared frequently on radio and television. By the late 1950s her regular appearances on television talk shows made her one of the best known academics in American life, and certainly the best known anthropologist. Publication in the popular press placed Mead squarely in the tradition of Franz Boas, who frequently wrote for a general, rather than professional, audience.

Mead's personal life was particularly tumultuous. In addition to her long affair with Benedict, she was married three times. Her first marriage to her childhood sweetheart, Luther Cressman, began in 1923. Cressman was ordained an Episcopal priest that same year but also studied sociology and anthropology at Columbia, receiving a Ph.D. in sociology in 1928. In 1925, Cressman left New York to continue his studies in theology in Europe, and Mead began her fieldwork in Samoa. On the way back from Samoa, she met and fell in love with the Australian anthropologist and psychologist Reo Fortune. She divorced Cressman and married Fortune in 1928. Cressman went on to found the anthropology department at the University of Oregon and conducted some of the first research in the history and prehistory of the Northwest.

In the late 1920s and early 1930s Fortune and Mead continued to do fieldwork together in New Guinea. In 1932, while working on the Sepik River in New Guinea, they met British anthropologist and psychologist Gregory Bateson. From 1932 to 1935, Mead, Fortune, and Bateson worked together and occasionally lived together. During this time, Mead fell in love with Bateson.

When the three returned from the field in 1935, Mead divorced Fortune and in 1936 married Bateson. Soon after, they left to conduct research together in Bali. Mead's only child, Mary Catherine Bateson, was born to the couple in 1939. Catherine Bateson is today a linguist and anthropologist specializing in Middle Eastern culture. Mead and Gregory Bateson divorced in 1950.

In 1942 Mead began a professional collaboration with her research assistant, Rhoda Metraux. In 1955, after Metraux's divorce, Mead and Metraux began to share the same residence. This relationship continued for twenty-three years until Mead's death in 1978. In addition to their columns for *Redbook,* Mead and Metraux collaborated on several books.

We are often asked why we choose to present Mead's personal life in these pages. After all, we don't tell you about Radcliffe-Brown's or Boas' family, so why should we talk about Mead and Benedict? There are several reasons. First, all serious students of anthropology will surely hear something of Mead's private life and, because of this, it is important that the outline of her life and context of her many relationships be presented clearly. Second, there is a complex relationship between Mead's sexual and family life and her work, which focused extensively on family and sexual roles in different societies. Clearly, readers of Mead should ask to what extent her personal life colored her research and vice versa. For example, the research Mead did for *Sex and Temperament in Three Primitive Societies,* was done while she, Fortune, and Bateson lived together in New Guinea. Mead's daughter later wrote:

> It is not accidental that when Margaret was on the Sepik, struggling with the question of diversity in herself and in her ways of loving, she was formulating the contrasts between three New Guinea peoples who dealt very differently with maleness and femaleness, with assertion and creativity. (Bateson 1984:160)

The introduction to *Coming of Age in Samoa* clearly shows Mead's interest in culture as a primary factor determining the experience of adolescence and the social and behavioral characteristics of adolescents. The book, written for a popular rather than a professional audience, aimed to promote the Boasian notion of cultural relativity and increase the readers' appreciation for cultural diversity.

Mead was always a controversial scholar, both within anthropology and outside of it. Books such as *Coming of Age in Samoa* were intended as a critique of American culture and read as such. Mead was involved in politics for much of her life and consistently stood for liberal causes. Wilton Dillon wrote that "perhaps no citizen in modern times has testified on so many different topics before more different professional committees as Mead" (1980:327). Although Mead posthumously received the Presidential Medal of Freedom in 1979, she also made many enemies in the course of her life, particularly among conservative thinkers. *Coming of Age in Samoa* figures prominently on several lists put together by conservative organizations. In fact, the archconservative Intercollegiate Studies Institute named it the number one worst book of the century (www.isi.org/journals/ir/50best_worst/50worst.html). Within academia, Mead's work, as well as Benedict's, also faced criticism. Benedict was critiqued for ignoring aspects of culture that did not fit her cultural configuration model, such as the drunkenness affecting Pueblo Indians and the calculating self-control practiced by the Kwakiutl. In 1983, five years after Mead's death, Australian anthropologist Derek Freeman (1916–2001) ignited a controversy with the publication of *Margaret Mead and Samoa: The Making and Unmaking of an Anthropological Myth,* in which he claimed that Mead's *Coming of Age in Samoa* was factually incorrect. Freeman charged that Mead's informants, embarrassed by her questions about intimate matters, deceived her with wild tales of sexual abandon. Debate over Freeman's assertions was a major issue in anthropology in the 1980s and early 1990s and still remains unresolved.

Essentially, culture and personality theorists of the 1930s were interested in learning more about the specific ways in which a culture determined the personality of its members. Psychoanalyst Abram Kardiner, in collaboration with anthropologists Du Bois, Sapir, and Ralph Linton (1893–1953), among others, developed a neo-Freudian approach to the study of this issue. According to Langness (1987), Kardiner was influenced by reading *The Future of an Illusion,* first published in 1928, in which Freud proposed that children's early life experiences determine their later religious beliefs. For example, children raised in a household with a strict authoritarian father conceptualized their deities as demanding, always observant, and strict disciplinarians. In accord with this line of thought, Kardiner advanced a theory that explained the mechanism by which culture determined personality.

Kardiner proposed what he called the *basic personality structure,* a collection of fundamental personality traits shared by the normal members of a society. Following Freud, he hypothesized that the foundations of personality development were set in early childhood. He argued that since childrearing procedures such as disciplining, weaning, and toilet training (what Kardiner termed *primary institutions*) are generally standardized within a society, all members of that society are subjected to the same basic influences on their personality development. Consequently, a society's primary institutions lead to the formation of its basic personality structure. Personality, in turn, influences culture through the creation of secondary institutions. These are cultural institutions, such as religion, created to satisfy the needs of personality through the psychological mechanism of projection.

Organizing a series of seminars in 1936 and 1937, Kardiner tested his theory with data supplied by his anthropologist colleagues. It soon became apparent to Kardiner that no data had been collected specifically for the sort of analysis he proposed. To resolve this issue, anthropologist Cora Du Bois traveled to the island of Alor in the Dutch East Indies to gather the appropriate types of information. Du Bois collected a variety of ethnographic and psychological data (such as Rorschach tests, life histories, and reports of dreams) from Alorese informants. After her return in 1939, Du Bois, Kardiner, and other independent analysts reviewed the data; they all reached the same fundamental conclusions concerning the basic characteristics of Alorese personality.

A weakness in Kardiner's theory was that the basic personality structure could not account for the variation in personality present in even the smallest society. To finesse this problem, Du Bois proposed the *modal personality,* the personality type that was statistically most common in a society. Like Kardiner, Du Bois hypothesized that primary institutions would lead to the formation of a basic set of personality characteristics (as illustrated by her research on the Alorese) but that there would also exist individual variation in how personalities developed and were expressed. Thus the concept of modal personality provided a theoretical tool for examining the interplay of personality and culture while allowing for the psychological variation that invariably exists among the members of a given society.

The outbreak of World War II provided anthropologists with opportunities to push culture and personality research still further. In the 1940s and during the cold war, the United States became vitally interested in studying the psychology of the citizens of the nations with which it was in conflict. The culture and personality theorists responded with *national character studies.* These studies differed from the modal personality work in scale and methodology. First, the national character studies dealt with industrial nation-states rather than simple societies. Second, culture and personality theorists typically worked with small numbers of people and relied on information gathered through participant observation. However, national character studies involved nations with millions of people and because the nations being studied were sometimes hostile, participant observation was inappropriate and often impractical. To find their way around these problems, anthropologists interviewed immigrants, analyzed literature and films, and searched government records. The results were mixed.

Two of the most famous national character studies are Benedict's *The Chrysanthemum and the Sword* (1946), a study of the Japanese, and Geoffrey Gorer (1905–1985) and John Rickman's (1891–1951) *The People of Great Russia: A Psychological Study* (1949). Both followed a neo-Freudian approach, attempting to relate childrearing practices to adult personality types. Benedict, for example, examined Japanese toilet-training practices in relation to the alleged Japanese preoccupation with obedience and order. Gorer and Rickman hypothesized that the Russian national character (supposedly a manic-depressive personality type) resulted from the practice of swaddling infants. It is easy to see how this study fit into the politics of the cold war.

The Chrysanthemum and the Sword, though it undoubtedly contains many inaccuracies and was strongly critiqued by both American and Japanese scholars (for example Bennett and Nagai 1953, Lummis 1982), proved highly influential. The book played an important role in determining the nature of the American occupation of Japan (1945–1952) and has been much discussed and debated since, particularly in Japan. In 1999 Fukui reported that over 2.3 million copies of the book had been sold in Japan and its pocket-size Japanese edition, first published in 1967, has gone through more than 100 printings (Ryang 2004). Gorer and Rickman's work has not fared nearly so well. As with most national character studies, subsequent research has shown it to be inaccurate. The practice of swaddling, for example, was not widespread in Russia; thus it could not explain the Russian personality type—if such a thing existed. Such errors cast doubts on whether or not anthropological techniques could ever be appropriate to the analysis of large-scale societies, and played a large part in the declining popularity of culture and personality studies. By the 1960s, most anthropologists had moved away from the examination of enculturation and its relationship to personality development. Though Benedict's work continued to be read and Mead became increasingly popular with the public, within anthropology, their work was sidelined.

Despite their lack of scholarly acceptance, culture and personality studies, and national character studies in particular, remain keen areas of popular interest. Introductory textbooks in cultural anthropology still reference Mead's and Benedict's work. Numerous books, such as Harrison and Huntington's *Culture Matters: How Values Shape Human Progress* (2001), continue to be published detailing aspects of the cultural personality of this or that group. As in the case of Copeland's *Going International: How to Make Friends and Deal Effectively in the Global Marketplace* (1985) or Thomas and Inkson's *Cultural Intelligence: People Skills for Global Business* (2004), these works are usually marketed as guides for businesspeople.

---

14. *Psychological Types in the Cultures of the Southwest*

Ruth Fulton Benedict (1887–1948)

THE CULTURE OF the Pueblo Indians is strongly differentiated from that of surrounding peoples.[1] Most obviously, all aspects of their life are highly ritualized, highly formalized. No one has lived among them who has not been struck by the im- portance of the formal detail in rite and dance, the intricate interrelations of the ceremonial organization, the lack of concern with personal religious experience or with personal prestige or exploit. The emphasis in their all-absorbing ceremonial

From Proceedings of the Twenty-third International Congress of Americanists, September 1928 (New York, 1930), 572–81

---

[1] Benedict did fieldwork among the Zuñi, Cochiti, and Pima throughout the mid-1920s. This paper, presented in 1928, was her first major analysis of her experiences there. In it, she develops themes later elaborated in *Patterns of Culture,* published in 1934. Perhaps because it was designed for a popular audience and written in an engaging style, *Patterns of Culture* became an enduring classic of anthropology—one still frequently read by students in introductory courses. Despite frequent criticism, Benedict's descriptions of Native American cultures and her theoretical position have had an important effect on American anthropology.

routine is placed where it was in the medieval Roman church of certain periods, on the formal observance, the ritualistic detail for its own sake.

This is so conspicuously true for the Southwest peoples that in descriptions of their culture we have been content to let the matter rest with this characterization. Yet in a civilization such as that of the North American Indians high ritualistic development sets no group off in any definitive fashion from the vast majority of peoples. The ritual of the sun dance, the peace pipe ceremonies, the cult groups, and age-societies of the Plains, or the winter ceremonial of the Northwest Coast bulk perhaps slightly less prominently in the total life of these people than the calendric dances and retreats of the Southwest, but it is not by any such matter of gradation that the Southwest is set off from other American Indian cultures. There is in their cultural attitudes and choices a difference in psychological type fundamentally to be distinguished from that of surrounding regions. It goes deeper than the presence or the absence of ritualism; ritualism itself is of a fundamentally different character within this area, and without the understanding of this fundamental psychological set among the Pueblo peoples we must be baffled in our attempts to understand the cultural history of this region.[a]

It is Nietzsche who has named and described, in the course of his studies in Greek tragedy, the two psychological types which have established themselves in the region of the Southwest in the cultures of the Pueblo.[2] He has called them the Dionysian and the Apollonian. He means by his classification essentially confidence in two diametrically different ways of arriving at the values of existence.[b] The Dionysian pursues them through "the annihilation of the ordinary bounds and limits of existence"; he seeks to attain in his most valued moments escape from the boundaries imposed upon him by his five senses, to break through into another order of experience. The desire of the Dionysian, in personal experience or in ritual, is to press beyond, to reach a certain psychological state, to achieve excess. The closest analogy to the emotions he seeks is drunkenness, and he values the illuminations of frenzy. With Blake,[3] he believes "the path of excess leads to the palace of wisdom." The Apollonian distrusts all this, if by chance he has any inkling of the occurrence of such experiences; he finds means to outlaw them from his conscious life. He "knows but one law, measure in the Hellenic sense." He keeps the middle of the road, stays within the known map, maintains his control over all disruptive psychological states. In Nietzsche's fine phrase, even in the exaltation of the dance, "he remains what he is, and retains his civic name."[c]

The Southwest Pueblos are, of course, Apollonian, and in the consistency with which they pursue the proper valuations of the Apollonian they contrast with very nearly the whole of aboriginal America. They possess in a small area, islanded in the midst of predominantly Dionysian cultures, an *ethos* distinguished by sobriety, by its distrust of excess, that minimizes to the last possible vanishing point any challenging or dangerous experiences. They have a religion of fertility without orgy, and absorption in the dance without using it to arrive at ecstasy. They have abjured torture. They indulge in no wholesale destruction of property at death. They have never made or bought intoxicating liquors in the fashion of

---

[2] Benedict derives her categories of Apollonian and Dionysian from *The Birth of Tragedy* (published in 1872), a study of the origins of Greek drama by German philosopher Friedrich Nietzsche (1844–1900). Some biographers have suggested that Benedict's intellectual preference for this classification scheme was related to her experience as a very young child, when, at her father's open-casket funeral, she experienced the contrast between her mother's open grief and her father's calm, tragic corpse (Modell 1983:1).

[3] The reference is to William Blake (1757–1827), an English poet, painter, and visionary. Benedict, who had studied English literature at Vassar College, was a more artful writer than most anthropologists. In addition to her anthropological works, Benedict wrote poetry under the pen name of Anne Singleton, a name that may be revealing of her personality. Her poems appeared in literary magazines, but she was unable to get a collection of them published. Thankfully for anthropology, her inability to find a publisher for her book dissuaded her from a career in poetry.

other tribes about them, and they have never given themselves up to the use of drugs. They have even stripped sex of its mystic danger. They allow to the individual no disruptive role in their social order. Certainly in all of these traits they stand so strikingly over against their neighbors that it is necessary to seek some explanation for the cultural resistances of the Pueblos.[4]

The most conspicuous contrast, in the Pueblos, is their outlawry of the divine frenzy and the vision. Now in North America at large the value of ecstatic experience in religion is a cornerstone of the whole religious structure. It may be induced by intoxicants and drugs; it may be self-induced— which may include such means as fasting and torture—or it may be achieved in the dance.

We may consider first the ecstasy induced by intoxicants and drugs.[5] For the neighboring Pima, who share the culture of the primitive tribes of northern Mexico, intoxication is the visible mirroring of religion, it is the symbol of its exaltation, the pattern of its mingling of clouded vision and of insight. Theory and practice are explicitly Dionysian.

> "And I was made drunk and given the sacred songs;"
> "He breathed the red liquor into me,"

are in their songs common forms of reference to the shamanistic experience. Their great ceremony is the drinking of the "tizwin," the fermented juice of the fruit of the giant cactus. The ceremony begins with all religious formality and the recitation of ritual, but its virtue lies in the intoxication itself; the desired state is that of roused excitement, and they accept even extreme violence more readily than a state of lethargy. Their ideal is to stave off the final insensibility indefinitely while achieving the full excitation of the intoxicant. This is of course a form of fertility and health magic and is in complete accord with the Dionysian slant of their culture.

It is much commoner, north of Mexico, to use drugs rather than intoxicants for religious ends. The peyote or mescal bean of northern Mexico has been traded up the Mississippi Valley as far as the Canadian border, and has been the occasion of serious religious movements among many tribes. It gives supernormal experiences with particularly strong affect, no erotic excitation, very often brilliant color images. The cult is best described for the Winnebago[d] where the peyote is identified with the supernatural. "It is the only holy thing I have been aware of in all my life"; "this medicine alone is holy and has rid me of all evil."[e] It was eaten everywhere with the object of attaining the trance or supernormal sensations which the drug can give. The Arapaho ate it in an all-night ceremony after which the effects of the drug prolonged themselves throughout the following day.[f] The Winnebago speak of eating it for four days and nights without sleep.

---

[4] Many of the claims that Benedict makes in this passage are flatly contradicted by evidence from the Pueblos. For example, here we read that the Puebloans never drink but many others report that they do. For example, according to Smith and Roberts (1954:58) the most common "crimes" at Zuñi are drunkenness and drunken driving. However as Barnouw (1957:535) points out, although Benedict's errors of fact and interpretation should be pointed out, there is much of value in her observations.

Benedict speaks here of seeking explanation for Pueblo Apollonian behavior, but offers none. Benedict saw culture as personality writ large. She believed that societies were able to choose their cultures out of the full range of human variability, but she was not concerned with understanding why a society would choose one type of culture rather than another. Although Benedict's work offered many examples of Pueblo Apollonian behavior, it provided no historical context—she made no attempt to explain the origins of the cultural personalities she documented. The lack of history is surprising, since Franz Boas, her teacher, placed such an emphasis on historical reconstruction. Despite their Boasian backgrounds, culture and personality writers were generally ahistorical.

[5] Benedict's anthropology is psychological, but it is not Freudian. Like other Boasians, she rejected Freud's notions of cultural evolution as nonscientific and ethnocentric. She traced her intellectual descent from the German psychologist Wilhelm Dilthey (1883–1911), who believed that the goal of psychology was to understand the inner life of the mind. He also proposed the existence of different *weltanshauungen,* or worldviews, which were categories much like Benedict's Apollonian and Dionysian cultures.

The *datura* is a more drastic poison. I have been told by the Serrano[6] and Cahuilla of boys who have died as a result of the drink, and the Luiseño tell also the same story.[g] It was used by the tribes of Southern California, and north including the Yokuts, for the initiation of boys at puberty. Among the Serrano the boys were overcome by the drug during the night and lay in a comatose condition through the next day and night, during which time they were granted visions. On the following day they ran a race.[h] Among the Luiseño it seems to have been the same, four nights of trance being spoken of as excessive.[i] The Diegueño reckon only one night of complete stupefaction.[j] The Mohave drank *datura* in order to gain luck in gambling; they were said to be unconscious for four days,[k] during which time they received their power in a dream.

None of these alcohol- and drug-induced excitations have gained currency among the Pueblos.[7] The Pima are the nearest settled neighbors of the Zuñi to the southwest and easily accessible; tribes of the Plains with which the eastern Pueblos came in contact are the very ones in which peyote practices are important; and to the west the tribes of Southern California share certain characteristic traits of this very Pueblo culture. The absence of these traits in the Pueblos is therefore not due to the cultural isolation of impassable barriers. We know too that the period of time during which the Pueblos and their neighbors have been settled relatively near to one another is of considerable antiquity. But the Pueblos have defended themselves against the use of drugs and intoxicants to produce trance or excitement even in cases where the drugs themselves are known among them. Any Dionysian effect from them is, we may infer, repulsive to the Pueblos, and if they receive cultural recognition at all it is in a guise suited to Apollonian sobriety. They did not themselves brew any native intoxicant in the old days, nor do they now. Alone among the Indian reservations, the whiskey of the whites has never been a problem in the Southwest. When, in 1912, drinking seemed to be making some headway among the younger generation in Zuñi, it was the Pueblo elders themselves who took the matter in hand. It is not that it is a religious taboo; it is deeper than that, it is uncongenial. The peyote has been introduced only in Taos, which is in many ways marginal to Pueblo culture.

Datura is used in Zuñi as it was in ancient Mexico[l] in order to discover a thief, and Mrs. Stevenson[8] gives an account of the manner of its use.[m] Read in connection with her quotations on *datura* poisoning and the two to four day trances of the Mohave and Mission Indians, it is a classic example of the Apollonian recasting of a Dionysian technique. In Zuñi the man who is to take the drug has a small quantity put in his mouth by the officiating priest, who then retires to the next room and listens for the incriminating name from the lips of the man who has taken the *datura*. He is not supposed to be comatose at any time; he alternately sleeps and walks about the room. In the morning he is said to have no memory of the insight he has received. The chief care is to remove every trace of the drug and two common desacratizing techniques are employed: first, he

---

[6] Although Benedict here mentions her own 1922 study of the Serrano, she did little fieldwork, preferring instead to draw on studies from many sources.

[7] Benedict started her career in ethnology as a student of Elsie Clew Parsons (1875–1941) at the New School for Social Research but soon went to study under Franz Boas at Columbia. After the completion of her dissertation, she remained with Boas until his retirement in 1936; she herself continued at Columbia until her death in 1948. The particularly close relationship between Boas and Benedict gave her exceptional access to the work and friendship of his other students, particularly Sapir, Mead (essay 15), and Kroeber (see essay 9). Both their work and her conversations and correspondence with them had a profound influence on Benedict's anthropology. Note the strong reliance on work by Boas, his students, and friends in Benedict's notes to this essay.

[8] Matilda Stevenson (1849–1915) was a pioneering American ethnographer who did extensive fieldwork among the Zuñi between 1879 and 1915 and published several monographs on them. Stevenson, founder and first president of the Women's Anthropological Society, was one of the first ethnographers to do work that centered on women and children.

is given an emetic, four times, till every vestige of the drug is supposed to be ejected; then his hair is washed in yucca suds.[9] The other Zuñi use of *datura* is even further from any connection with a Dionysian technique; members of the priestly orders go out at night to plant prayer sticks on certain occasions "to ask the birds to sing for rain," and at such times a minute quantity of the powdered root is put into the eyes, ears, and mouth of each priest. Here any connections with the physical properties of the drug are lost sight of.

Much more fundamental in North America than any use of drugs or alcohol to induce ecstasy was the cult of the self-induced vision. This was a near-universality from ocean to ocean, and everywhere it was regarded as the source of religious power. The Southwest is by no means beyond the southern limits of its distribution, but it is the one outstanding area of North America where the characteristic development of the vision is not found. This experience has several quite definite characteristics for North America: it is achieved characteristically in isolation, and it gives to the successful individual a personal manitou or guardian spirit who stands to him in a definite life-long relationship. Though west of the Rockies it is often regarded as an involuntary blessing available only for those of a particular psychological make-up, throughout the great extent of the continent it is sought by isolation and fasting, and in the central part of the continent often by self-torture. This "vision," from which supernatural power was supposed to flow, did not by any means

signify only supernormal or Dionysian experiences, but it provided always a pattern within which such an experience had peculiar and institutionalized value; and in the great majority of cases it was these more extreme experiences that were believed to give the greater blessing.

The absence of this vision complex in the Southwest is one of the most striking cases of cultural resistance or of cultural reinterpretation that we know in North America. The formal elements are found there: the seeking of dangerous places, the friendship with a bird or animal, fasting, the belief in special blessings from supernatural encounters. But they are no longer instinct with the will to achieve ecstasy. There is complete reinterpretation. In the pueblos they go out at night to feared or sacred places and listen for a voice, not that they may break through to communication with the supernatural, but that they may take the omens of good luck and bad. It is regarded as a minor ordeal during which you are badly frightened, and the great taboo connected with it is that you must not look behind you on the way home no matter what seems to be following you. The objective performance is much the same as in the vision quest; in each case, they go out during the preparation for a difficult undertaking—in the Southwest often a race—and make capital of the darkness, the solitariness, the appearance of animals. But the significance is utterly different.[10]

Fasting, the technique most often used in connection with the self-induced vision, has received

---

[9] Two aspects of Boasian thought exerted particularly strong influences on Benedict. The first was cultural relativism. Notice that her language describing the use of hallucinogens, an exotic and possibly offensive cultural practice, is matter-of-fact and nonjudgmental. Although Apollonian culture traits might seem more desirable to upper-middle-class intellectual Americans (her primary audience), her writing here and in *Patterns of Culture* describes Apollonian and Dionysian cultures as equally attractive.

The second Boasian influence was an emphasis on holism. Boas suggested that cultures were integrated; Benedict pushed this idea further. She saw culture as having internal logical consistency and being characterized by a single dominant trend or pattern. This essay is largely

an exercise in the demonstration of the holism that she saw in culture in general and among the Pueblo peoples in particular. Throughout the essay, she tries to show that all Pueblo practices, even the use of hallucinogenic drugs, fit the restrained, Apollonian worldview.

[10] Benedict's focus here is not on the actions performed, but on how the actors interpret their actions. Boas wanted to build anthropology on a scientific, empirical model; Benedict came to see anthropology as an interpretive art, as much a part of the humanities as a social science. At the end of her life, she wrote that anthropology stood at the boundary between science and the humanities (1948:585). This view has made her an important figure for many interpretive and postmodern anthropologists.

the same sort of reinterpretation in the South-west. It is no longer utilized to dredge up experiences that normally lie below the level of consciousness; it is here a requirement for ceremonial cleanness. Nothing could be more unexpected to a Pueblo Indian than any theory of a connection between fasting and any sort of exaltation. Fasting is required during all retreats, before participation in a dance, in a race, etc., etc., but it is never followed by power-giving experience; it is never Dionysian. Fasting, also, like drugs and visions, has been revamped to the requirements of the Apollonian.

Torture, on the contrary, has been much more nearly excluded.[11] It is important only in the initiations and dances of certain curing societies[n] and in these cases there is no suggestion of any states of self-oblivion. It is interesting that the Pueblos have been exposed to self-torture practices, both in the aboriginal culture of the Plains, and in European-derived practices of the Mexican Penitentes.[12] The eastern Pueblos are in the very heart of the Santa Fe Penitentes country and these Mexicans attend their dances and ceremonies regularly and without hindrance. Much in their practice they have in common with the Indians: the retreats in the ceremonial house, the organization of the brotherhood (priesthood, for the Indian), the planting of crosses. But the self-lashing with cactus whips, the crucifixion on Good Friday, are alien; torture has not penetrated Pueblo life either from these practices or from those of the Plains or of California. Among the Pueblos, every man's hand has its five fingers,[13] and unless he has been tortured as a witch, he is unscarred.

No more than the Pueblos have allowed ecstasy as induced by alcohol or drugs, or under the guise of the vision, have they admitted it as induced by the dance. Perhaps no people in North America spend more time in dance than the Southwest Pueblos. But its use as the most direct technique at our command for the inducement of supernormal experience is alien to them. With the frenzy of a Nootka bear dance, of a Kwakiutl cannibal dance, of a ghost dance, of a Mexican whirling dance, their dancing has nothing in common. It is rather a technique of monotonous appeal, of unvarying statement; always, in the phrase of Nietzsche's I used before, "they remain as they are and retain their civic names." Their theory seems to be that by the reiteration of the dance they can exercise compulsion upon the forces they wish to influence.

There are several striking instances of the loss, for the Pueblos, of the Dionysian significance of specific dance behavior, the objective aspects of which they still share with their neighbors. The best is probably the dance upon the altar. For the Cora of northern Mexico the climax of the whirling dance is reached in the dancer's ecstatic, and otherwise sacrilegious, dancing upon the ground altar itself. In his madness it is destroyed, trampled into the sand again.[o] But this is also a Pueblo pattern. Especially the Hopi at the climax of their dances in the kivas dance upon the altar destroying the ground painting. Here there is no ecstasy; it is raw material used to build up one of the common Pueblo dance patterns where two "sides" which have previously come out alternately from opposite sides, now come out together for the dance climax. In the snake dance, for instance,[p] in the first set Antelope (dancer of Antelope society) dances, squatting, the circuit of the altar, retires; Snake (dancer of Snake society) repeats. In the second set Antelope receives a vine in his mouth and dances before the initiates trailing it over their knees; retires; Snake repeats with a live rattlesnake held in the same fashion. In the final set Antelope and Snake come out together, dancing together upon the altar, still in the squatting position, and destroy the ground painting. It is a formal sequence, like a Morris dance.[14]

---

[11] Notice that Benedict offers no reason why the Pueblo have rejected torture. It is simply an aspect of their culture, and culture is an independent force creating itself.

[12] *Penitentes* are individuals who, at Easter, imitate the suffering of Jesus by whipping themselves and imitating his crucifixion.

[13] *Five fingers* refers to a common Plains Indian practice of chopping off a finger joint in mourning or for spiritual purposes.

[14] Critics have frequently accused Benedict of being so guided by her vision of the logical constancy of culture that she distorted her data. They point out that, Benedict's

It is evident that ecstatic experience is not recognized in the Southwest and that the techniques associated with it in other areas are reinterpreted or refused admittance. The consequence of this is enormous: it rules out shamanism. For the shaman, the religious practitioner whose power comes from experiences of this type, is everywhere else in North America of first rate importance. Wherever the authority of religion is derived from his solitary mental aberrations and stress experiences and his instructions derived therefrom are put into practice by the tribe as a sacred privilege, that people is provided with a technique of cultural change which is limited only by the unimaginativeness of the human mind.[15] This is a sufficient limitation; so much so that it has never been shown that cultures which operate on this basic theory are more given to innovation than those which disallow such disruptive influences. This should not blind us to the fact, however, that the setting in these two cultures for the exercise of individuality is quite different; individual initiative which would be fully allowed in the one case[q] would in the other be suspect, and these consequences are fully carried out in the Southwest. They have hardly left space for an impromptu individual act in their closely knit religious program; if they come across such an act they label the perpetrator a witch. One of the Zuñi tales I have recorded tells of the chief priest of Zuñi who made prayer sticks and went out to deposit them. It was not the time of the moon when prayer sticks must be planted by members of the curing societies, and the people said, "Why does the chief priest plant prayer sticks? He must be conjuring." As a matter of fact he was calling an earthquake for a private revenge. If this is so in the most personal of Zuñi religious acts, that of planting prayer sticks, it is doubly so of more formal activities like retreats, dances, etc. Even individual prayers of the most personal sort—those where cornmeal is scattered—must be said at sunrise, or over a dead animal, or at a particular point in a program, etc.; the times and seasons are always stipulated. No one must ever wonder why an individual was moved to pray.

Instead therefore of shamans with their disruptive influence upon communal practices and settled traditions, the Southwest has religious practitioners who become priests by rote memorizing and by membership in societies and cult groups. This membership is determined by heredity and by payment[r] for though in their own theory serious illness or an accident like snake bite or being struck by lightning are the accepted reasons for membership in certain societies, there are always alternative ways of joining even the curing societies so that no man with interest and sufficient means remains outside. In Zuñi heredity is the chief factor in membership in the priestly groups, payment in the curing societies; in neither is individual supernatural power ever claimed by any member as a result of personal illumination. Those who practice curing in Zuñi are merely those who by payment and by knowledge of ritual have reached the highest orders of the curing societies and received the personal corn fetish, the *mili*.

If the ecstasy of the Dionysian has been rejected in the Southwest with all its implications,

----

claims to the contrary, alcoholism was common on the Pueblo reservations during her fieldwork (and is so today). In this passage, Benedict suggests that a dance done with a live rattlesnake in the mouth is not an ecstatic ritual, but rather like a Morris dance, a rather staid and orderly form of British folk dancing. Perhaps so, but this assertion raises important questions of interpretation. Most observers would consider dancing with live rattlesnakes an ecstatic rite. However, few members of any religion would use such words to describe their actions. So, is it or is it not ecstatic? If we accept that dancing with live rattlesnakes is

not an ecstatic ritual, does the phrase have any meaning; can any ritual be described as ecstatic? Such issues of interpretation became the subject of intense anthropological debate in the 1950s and 1960s and to some extent remain so today.

[15] Benedict comments in passing on the "unimaginativeness of the human mind." Like Boas, Benedict believed that within a culture, most traits originated by diffusion rather than independent invention. However, neither agreed at all with the radical European diffusionist thinkers.

so too has the orgy.[16] There is no doubt that the idea of fertility bulks large in the religious practices of the Southwest,[s] and with fertility rites we almost automatically couple orgy, so universally have they been associated in the world. But the Southwest has a religion of fertility founded on other associations. Haeberlin's study gives a useful summary of the type of ritual that is here considered to have this efficacy.[t] The cylinders the men carry and the amulets carried by the women in ceremonies are sex symbols and are thrown by them into springs or onto ground paintings; or in the women's dance two are dressed as male dancers and shoot arrows into a bundle of cornhusks; or a line of women with yucca rings run in competition with a line of men with kicking sticks. In Peru in a race of exactly similar import, men racing women, the men ran naked and violated every woman they overtook.[u] The pattern is self-evident and common throughout the world, but not in the Southwest. In Zuñi there are three occasions on which laxness is countenanced. One of these is in the retreat of the Tlewekwe society, which has power over cold weather. The priestesses of the medicine bundle of this society (*te etone*) and the associated bundle (*mu etone*) during one night receive lovers, and they collect a thumb's length of turquoise from their partners to add to the decorations of their bundles. It is an isolated case in Zuñi and the society can no longer be very satisfactorily studied. The other two cases are rather a relaxation of the customary strict chaperonage of the young people, and occur at the ceremonial rabbit hunt[v] and on the nights of the scalp dance; children conceived on these nights are said to be exceptionally vigorous. Doctor Bunzel[17] writes, "These occasions on which boys and girls dance together or are out together at night provide an opportunity for sweethearts. There is no promiscuity, and they are never, never orgiastic in character. There is amiable tolerance of sexual laxity; a 'boys will be boys' attitude." It is all very far indeed from the common Dionysian sex practices for the sake of fertility.

It is not only in connection with fertility and sex that orgy is common among the peoples of America. In the region immediately surrounding the Southwest, there is on the one hand the orgy of sun dance torturing to the east and the orgy of wholesale destruction in the mourning ceremonies to the west. As I have said, torture plays a very slight role in the Southwest, orgiastic or otherwise. Mourning is made oppressive by fear of the dead, but there is no trace of abandon. Mourning here is made into the semblance of an anxiety complex; it is a completely different thing from the wild scenes of burning the dead in a bonfire of offered property and of clothes stripped from the mourner's backs that the Mohave practice[w] and that is found in such Dionysian fullness commonly in California, where among the Maidu mourners have to be forcibly restrained from throwing themselves into the flames,[x] and among the Pomo they snatch pieces of the corpse and devour them.[y]

One Dionysian ceremony of wide American distribution has established itself in the Southwest—the scalp dance.[18] This is the victory dance of the Plains, or the women's dance, and the position of

---

[16] Throughout this essay, but particularly here and below, the examples given are quite sensational, even risqué. This is typical of much of the anthropology of Benedict's time and, in her case, there were at least two reasons for it. First, she often wrote for a popular audience, and like Freud, Mead, and Malinowski, used the lure of the discussion of forbidden topics such as sex to attract and hold her audience. Second, she was a firm believer in cultural relativism. Showing exotic cultural practices that were unacceptable to her audience in a calm and rational light helped build the case for the acceptance of all cultures as equally valid. In this connection, it should be noted that Benedict practiced what she preached. She was a bitter opponent of racism and a forceful advocate for tolerance within her own society.

[17] Like many of those that Benedict mentions, Ruth Bunzel (1898–1990) was a student of Boas and a member of Benedict's own circle. She is particularly remembered for her studies of Zuñi pottery making.

[18] In this passage, Benedict seems to allow that an Apollonian society can include some Dionysian practices. However, this apparent contradiction is resolved by the fact that those who perform the Dionysian act dread participating in it.

honor given to women in it, the four-circle coil danced around the encampment, the close-fitting war bonnet, certain treatments of the scalp, are the same in the Southwest as on the Plains. The wilder abandons of the Plains dance are, as we should expect, omitted, but there occurs in this dance, at least in Zuñi, one of the few ritual Dionysian acts of the Southwest—the washing and biting of the scalp. For the repulsion against contact with bones or a corpse is intense among these people, so that it makes an occasion for horror out of placing a scalp between the teeth, whereas placing a snake between the teeth in the snake dance is no such matter. The woman who carries the scalp in the dance—the position of honor—must rise to this pitch and every girl is said to dread being called out for the role.

Ecstasy and orgy, therefore, which are characteristic of America at large are alien in the Southwest. Let me illustrate this fundamental Apollonian bent in the Southwest by certain specific examples of the way in which it has worked itself out in their culture.

There is considerable emphasis in North America upon the ritualistic eating of filth and it is in this category that the very slightly developed cannibalistic behavior of the Northwest Coast belongs.[19] That is, the emphasis there is never, as so often in cannibalism, upon the feast, nor on doing honor to or reviling the dead. The cannibal dance of the Kwakiutl is a typically Dionysian ritual.[z] It is not only that it is conceived as a dramatization of a condition of ecstasy which the main participant must dance to its climax before he can be restored to normal life; every ritualistic arrangement is designed—I do not mean consciously—to heighten the sense of the anti-natural act. A long period of fasting and isolation precedes the rite, the dance itself is a crouching, ecstatic pursuit of the prepared body held outstretched toward him by a woman attendant. With the required ritualistic bites the anti-natural climax is conceived to be attained, and prolonged vomiting and fasting and isolation follows.

In the filth eating of the Southwest, which is the psychological equivalent to this initiation of the Kwakiutl cannibal, the picture is entirely different. The rite is not used to attain horror, nor to dramatize a psychological climax of tension and release. Captain Bourke has recorded the Newekwe feast he attended with Cushing, at which gallon jars of urine were consumed by the members of the society. The picture is as far from that of the Kwakiutl rite as any buffoonery of our circus clowns. The atmosphere was one of coarse joviality, each man trying to outdo the others. "The dancers swallowed huge decanters, smacked their lips, and amid the roaring merriment of the spectators, remarked that it was very, very good. The clowns were now upon their mettle, each trying to surpass his neighbors in feats of nastiness." [aa,20]

The same comment is true not only of filth eating but of clowning in the Southwest in general.[21]

---

[19] Here, as in *Patterns of Culture,* Benedict uses the Kwakiutl as her chief example of a Dionysian culture. In so doing, she relied almost entirely on the work of Boas. She had access not only to Boas' published work, but also to his notebooks and journals. More important, she worked closely with Boas for almost twenty years.

[20] Captain John G. Bourke (1843–1896) and Frank Hamilton Cushing (1857–1900) were key figures in nineteenth century American ethnography. Bourke was a civil war veteran and West Point graduate who served in the American West from the late 1860s to the mid 1880s. He wrote extensively about Native American practices that he witnessed and was a particular expert on the use of human excrement in religious ritual. Cushing was, at a very young age, curator of the ethnological department at the National Museum in Washington D.C. He was a protégé of John Wesley Powell. Cushing lived at Zuñi Pueblo for several years in the 1880s and became a Zuñi priest. He was eventually forced to leave Zuñi after he attempted to protect Zuñi lands against Army encroachment. Cushing wrote extensively about his experiences in Zuñi, both for professional and popular audiences. Part showman, part scholar, Cushing has long been a controversial figure in anthropology (see Parezo 2007, McGee et al 1900).

[21] Notice Benedict's use of the first person in this paragraph and below. Her reporting of Pueblo clowning is not couched in neutral, scientific language; rather she focuses on how things seemed to her. This articulates well with her view of anthropology as an interpretive art.

I take it that the true Dionysian use of clowning is as comic relief in sacred ceremonial where the release from tension is as full of meaning as the preceding tension, and serves to accentuate it. This use of clowning seems to have been developed, for instance, in the ancient Aztec rites. Now I have never seen any clowning in the Pueblos that seemed to me remotely even to partake of this character, and I do not know of any description which would indicate its presence. Clowning can be buffoonery with no Dionysian implications, as we know well enough from the examples in our own civilization. It is this same use that is most prominent in the Southwest, but clowning is used there also for social satire, as in the take-offs of agents, churches, Indian representatives, etc., and it is common too as a substitute for the joking relationship, which is absent here, and its license for very personal public comment.

Another striking example of the Southwest Apollonian bent is their interpretation of witch power. The Southwest has taken the European witch complex with all its broomsticks and witches' animal suits and eyes laid on a shelf, but they have fitted it into their own *Weltanschauung*. The most articulate statement that I know of a widespread attitude is still in manuscript in Doctor Parson's monograph on Isleta.[22] The difference, for Isleta, between witch power and good power is simply that good supernatural power is always removed from you as soon as you have put it to the use you intended; witch power is nonremovable, it rides you for life. Their practice perfectly agrees with this; after every sacred investiture every participant in any rite is desacratized, the unwanted mysterious power is laid aside. Nothing could conceptualize more forcibly their discomfort in the face of mystery. Even the best supernatural power is uncanny.

Their lack of comprehension of suicide is, I think, another specific Apollonian trait. The Pima tell many stories of men who have killed themselves for women, and the Plains made suicide a ceremonial pattern; fundamentally their vows to assume the slit sash were suicide pledges in order to raise their rank. But the Pueblos tell the most inept stories[bb] which are obvious misunderstandings of the concept. Again and again I have tried to convey the general idea of suicide to different Pueblo Indians, either by story or by exposition. They always miss the point. Yet in their stories they have the equivalent. There are a number of Zuñi stories[cc] which tell of a man or woman whose spouse has been unfaithful—or of priests whose people have been unruly; they send messengers, often birds, to the Apache and summon them against their pueblo. When the fourth day has come—nothing ever happens in the Southwest till the fourth day—they wash themselves ceremonially and put on their finest costumes and go out to meet the enemy that they may be the first to be killed. When I have asked them about suicide no one has ever mentioned these stories, though they had perhaps been told that very day, and indeed they do not see them in that light at all. They are ritual revenge and the Dionysian gesture of throwing away one's life is not in question.

The cultural situation in the Southwest is in many ways hard to explain.[23] With no natural barriers to isolate it from surrounding peoples, it presents probably the most abrupt cultural break

---

[22] Benedict draws much of her information on the Pueblos from the work of Parsons, her first teacher, who worked extensively among the Pueblos and published many books on them. Boas and Parsons were very close friends and did some of their research together. Parsons, daughter of a wealthy banking family and wife of a U.S. Congressman did pioneering work on many subjects including feminism, race, and Native Americans. In the early years of the twentieth century, she argued for "trial marriage, divorce by mutual consent, access to reliable contraception, independence and elasticity within rela-tionships" (Deacon xii). She did extensive fieldwork in the American Southwest, Mexico, and the Carribean. She became the first female president of the American Anthropological Association in 1941.

[23] In conclusion, Benedict again declares the fundamental inexplicability of culture. In *Patterns of Culture,* she used a Digger Indian myth to explain cultural origins and differences: "God gave to every people . . . a cup of clay, and from this cup they drank their life. . . . They all dipped in the water but their cups were different" (1934b:33).

that we know in America. All our efforts to trace out the influences from other areas are impressive for the fragmentariness of the detail; we find bits of the weft or woof of the culture, we do not find any very significant clues to its pattern. From the point of view of the present paper this clue is to be found in a fundamental psychological set which has undoubtedly been established for centuries in the culture of this region, and which has bent to its own uses any details it imitated from surrounding peoples and has created an intricate cultural pattern to express its own preferences. It is not only that the understanding of this psychological set is necessary for a descriptive statement of this culture; without it the cultural dynamics of this region are unintelligible. For the typical choices of the Apollonian have been creative in the formation of this culture, they have excluded what was displeasing, revamped what they took, and brought into being endless demonstrations of the Apollonian delight in formality, in the intricacies and elaborations of organization.

NOTES

[a] For the theoretical justification of this position in the study of culture see Benedict, Ruth, "Cultures and Psychological Types," *American Anthropologist*, N. S., in press.

[b] I have not followed Nietzsche's definitions in their entirety; I have used that aspect which is pertinent to the problems of the Southwest.

[c] *Birth of Tragedy*, p. 68.

[d] Radin, Paul, "The Winnebago Tribe," *Thirty-seventh Annual Report, Bureau of American Ethnology*, Washington, 1923, 388–426.

[e] Ibid., pp. 408; 392.

[f] Kroeber, A. L., "The Arapaho," *Bulletin, American Museum of Natural History*, vol. 18, New York, 1907, p. 398.

[g] Kroeber, A. L., "Handbook of the Indians of California," *Bulletin 78, Bureau of American Ethnology*, Washington, 1925, p. 669.

[h] Benedict, Ruth, "A Brief Sketch of Serrano Culture," *American Anthropologist*, N. S., vol. 26, pp. 366–392, 1924, p. 383.

[i] Kroeber, A. L., "Handbook," p. 669.

[j] Ibid.

[k] Ibid., p. 779.

[l] Safford, William E., "Narcotic Daturas of the Old and New World; an Account of Their Remarkable Properties and Their Uses as Intoxicants and in Divination," *Annual Report, Smithsonian Institution for 1920*, pp. 537–567, Washington, 1922, p. 551.

[m] Stevenson, Matilda C., "The Zuñi Indians, Their Mythology, Esoteric Fraternities and Ceremonies," *Twenty-third Annual Report, Bureau of American Ethnology*, Washington, 1904, p. 89.

[n] Cushing, F. H., "My Experience in Zuñi," *Century Magazine*, N. S., 4, p. 31; Stevenson, M. A., *The Zuñi Indians*, p. 503. "All are filled with the spirit of good nature."

[o] Preuss, K. T., *Die Nayarit-Expedition*. Leipzïg, 1912, p. 55.

[p] Voth, H. R., "Oraibi Summer Snake Ceremony," *Field Columbian Museum, Publication 83*. Chicago, 1903, p. 299.

[q] See Radin, Paul, *Primitive Man as Philosopher*. New York and London, 1927, pp. 257–275, for discussion of the wide limits of individualism among the Winnebago.

[r] Except for the war chiefs' societies where it was necessary to have taken a scalp.

[s] Haeberlin, H. K., "The Idea of Fertilization in the Culture of the Pueblo Indians," *Memoirs, American Anthropological Association*, vol. 3, no. 1, 1916.

[t] Ibid., especially p. 39 ff.

[u] Arriaga, P. J., *Extirpacion de la Idolotria del Peru*. Lima, 1621, p. 36 sq.

[v] Information from Dr. Ruth Bunzel.

[w] Kroeber, "Handbook," p. 750.

[x] Ibid., p. 431.

[y] Ibid., p. 253.

[z] Boas, Franz, "The Social Organization and Secret Societies of the Kwakiutl," *Report, United States National Museum for 1895*, Washington, 1897, p. 537 sq.

[aa] Bourke, John G., *Compilation of Notes and Memoranda Bearing on the Use of Human Ordure and Human Urine in Rites of a Religious or Semi-religious Character among Various Nations*. Washington, 1888, p. 9.

[bb] Parsons, Elsie Clews, "A Zuñi Detective," *Man*, vol. 16, pp. 168–170, London, 1916, p. 169.

[cc] Benedict, R., Mss.

15. *Introduction to Coming of Age in Samoa*

MARGARET MEAD (1901–1978)

DURING THE LAST hundred years parents and teachers have ceased to take childhood and adolescence for granted. They have attempted to fit education to the needs of the child, rather than to press the child into an inflexible educational mould. To this new task they have been spurred by two forces, the growth of the science of psychology, and the difficulties and maladjustments of youth. Psychology suggested that much might be gained by a knowledge of the way in which children developed, of the stages through which they passed, of what the adult world might reasonably expect of the baby of two months or the child of two years. And the fulminations of the pulpit, the loudly voiced laments of the conservative social philosopher, the records of juvenile courts and social agencies all suggested that something must be done with the period which science had named adolescence. The spectacle of a younger generation diverging ever more widely from the standards and ideals of the past, cut adrift without the anchorage of respected home standards or group religious values, terrified the cautious reactionary, tempted the radical propagandist to missionary crusades among the defenceless youth, and worried the least thoughtful among us.[1]

In American civilisation, with its many immigrant strains, its dozens of conflicting standards of conduct, its hundreds of religious sects, its shifting economic conditions, this unsettled, disturbed status of youth was more apparent than in the older, more settled civilisation of Europe. American conditions challenged the psychologist, the educator, the social philosopher, to offer acceptable explanations of the growing children's plight. As today in post-war Germany, where the younger generation has even more difficult adjustments to make than have our own children,[2] a great mass of theorising about adolescence is flooding the book shops; so the psychologist in America tried to account for the restlessness of youth. The result was works like that of Stanley Hall on "Adolescence," which ascribed to the period through which the children were passing, the causes of their conflict and distress. Adolescence was characterised as the period in which idealism flowered and rebellion against authority

From *Coming of Age in Samoa* (1928)

[1] *Coming of Age in Samoa* was published in 1928. However, the adolescent issues with which Mead starts this essay—education, child psychology, juvenile crime, rebellion against home and parents, etc., sound timely to a modern reader. It is easy to see how Mead, always unconventional, would be drawn to the topic of sexuality and adolescence. Although elders have complained about the decadence of the young from at least the time of Ancient Greece, the 1920s truly were an era of radical cultural change: movies, radio, jazz, flappers, modern art, etc. It was an era far more similar to the 1960s than to the 2010s.

The passage also reflects Mead's interest in psychology. She mentions Hall below and she was interested in Freud. However, Levine (2007) argues that the culture and personality anthropologists were far more affected by the Neo-Freudian psychologists, particularly Harry Stack Sullivan, Karen Horney, and Eric Fromm. These theorists deemphasized the role of sexuality and universal psychosexual stages in childhood. Instead they focused on the quality of the children's early experiences with parents and siblings. Because these clearly varied from culture to culture, ethnography was critical to the Neo-Freudian viewpoint.

[2] Mead's reference to the difficult adjustments facing post-war children in Germany refers to the terrible economic and social conditions faced by Germans during the collapse of German society after World War I.

waxed strong, a period during which difficulties and conflicts were absolutely inevitable.[3]

The careful child psychologist who relied upon experiment for his conclusions did not subscribe to these theories. He said, "We have no data. We know only a little about the first few months of a child's life. We are only just learning when a baby's eyes will first follow a light. How can we give definite answers to questions of how a developed personality, about which we know nothing, will respond to religion?" But the negative cautions of science are never popular. If the experimentalist would not commit himself, the social philosopher, the preacher and the pedagogue tried the harder to give a short-cut answer. They observed the behaviour of adolescents in our society, noted down the omnipresent and obvious symptoms of unrest, and announced these as characteristics of the period. Mothers were warned that "daughters in their teens" present special problems. This, said the theorists, is a difficult period. The physical changes which are going on in the bodies of your boys and girls have their definite psychological accompaniments. You can no more evade one than you can the other; as your daughter's body changes from the body of a child to the body of a woman, so inevitably will her spirit change, and that stormily. The theorists looked about them again at the adolescents in our civilisation and repeated with great conviction, "Yes, stormily."[4]

Such a view, though unsanctioned by the cautious experimentalist, gained wide currency, influenced our educational policy, paralysed our parental efforts. Just as the mother must brace herself against the baby's crying when it cuts its first tooth, so she must fortify herself and bear with what equanimity she might the unlovely, turbulent manifestations of the "awkward age." If there was nothing to blame the child for, neither was there any programme except endurance which might be urged upon the teacher. The theorist continued to observe the behaviour of American adolescents and each year lent new justification to his hypothesis, as the difficulties of youth were illustrated and documented in the records of schools and juvenile courts.

But meanwhile another way of studying human development had been gaining ground, the approach of the anthropologist, the student of man in all of his most diverse social settings. The anthropologist, as he pondered his growing body of material upon the customs of primitive people, grew to realise the tremendous role played in an

---

[3] Granville Stanley Hall (1844–1924) was the founder of the American Journal of Psychology and first president of the American Psychological Association. In the late nineteenth and early twentieth centuries, he was one of the leading psychologists in the United States, and a pioneer of educational psychology. Hall earned his doctorate in 1878 under the supervision of the pioneering American psychologist, William James, brother of the novelist Henry James. He then visited Germany to study experimental psychology with Wilhelm Wundt, and while there was introduced to German biologist Ernst Haeckel's recapitulation theory (see Spencer, note 19). Following Haeckel, Hall proposed that children developed through psychological stages that reflected the evolutionary history of humankind and that educational curricula for children should be developed to track with these stages.

Hall's most famous work was *Adolescence,* published in 1904. In this work he popularized the notion that adolescence was a time of stress characterized by conflict with one's parents, mood swings, and risk taking. Hall was a social Darwinist who believed in forced sterilization and was against helping those who were socially or physically defective because this would slow the improvement of humanity. He proposed that the purpose of high schools should be to indoctrinate students with the ideals of military discipline, patriotism, and love of authority.

By the time Mead wrote *Coming of Age in Samoa,* Hall's influence in Psychology was in decline. In fact, Mead's work helped show that the experience of adolescence was not universally stressful or conflict-ridden. However, Hall's view of adolescence is still popular today.

[4] After the publication of *Coming of Age in Samoa,* Mead became one of the better-known social scientists of her day. Reading these first paragraphs it is easy to see why. She discussed socially controversial topics in a reasonable and often light-hearted tone. Here she makes fun of "the social philosopher, the preacher and the pedagogue." You can just see old guys with beards and monocles saying "yes, stormily."

individual's life by the social environment in which each is born and reared. One by one, aspects of behaviour which we had been accustomed to consider invariable complements of our humanity were found to be merely a result of civilisation, present in the inhabitants of one country, absent in another country, and this without a change of race. He learned that neither race nor common humanity can be held responsible for many of the forms which even such basic human emotions as love and fear and anger take under different social conditions.

So the anthropologist, arguing from his observations of the behaviour of adult human beings in other civilisations, reaches many of the same conclusions which the behaviourist reaches in his work upon human babies who have as yet no civilisation to shape their malleable' humanity.

With such an attitude towards human nature the anthropologist listened to the current comment upon adolescence. He heard attitudes which seemed to him dependent upon social environment—such as rebellion against authority, philosophical perplexities, the flowering of idealism, conflict and struggle—ascribed to a period of physical development. And on the basis of his knowledge of the determinism of culture, of the plasticity of human beings, he doubted. Were these difficulties due to being adolescent or to being adolescent in America?[5]

For the biologist who doubts an old hypothesis or wishes to test out a new one, there is the biological laboratory. There, under conditions over which he can exercise the most rigid control, he can vary the light, the air, the food, which his plants or his animals receive, from the moment of birth throughout their lifetime. Keeping all the conditions but one constant, he can make accurate measurement of the effect of the one. This is the ideal method of science, the method of the controlled experiment, through which all hypotheses may be submitted to a strict objective test.

Even the student of infant psychology can only partially reproduce these ideal laboratory conditions. He cannot control the pre-natal environment of the child whom he will later subject to objective measurement. He can, however, control the early environment of the child, the first few days of its existence, and decide what sounds and sights and smells and tastes are to impinge upon it. But for the student of the adolescent there is no such simplicity of working conditions. What we wish to test is no less than the effect of civilisation upon a developing human being at the age of puberty. To test it most rigorously we would have to construct various sorts of different civilisations and subject large numbers of adolescent children to these different environments. We would list the influences the effects of which we wished to study. If we wished to study the influence of the size of the family, we would construct a series of civilisations alike in every respect except in family organisation. Then if we found differences in the behaviour of our adolescents we could say with assurance that size of family had caused the difference, that, for instance, the only child had a more troubled adolescence than the child who was a member of a large family. And so we might proceed through a dozen possible situations—early or late sex knowledge, early or late sex-experience, pressure towards precocious development, discouragement of precocious development, segregation of the sexes or coeducation from infancy, division of labour between the sexes or common tasks for both, pressure to make religious choices young or the lack of such pressure. We would vary one factor, while the others remained quite constant,

---

[5] In the previous paragraphs Mead has been questioning Hall and the popular wisdom concerning the turmoil of adolescence. As a devoted disciple of Boas, she looked to cultural explanations for human behavior. Like Boas, she argued that race and culture are not connected with each other. Like Boas she rejected the idea that "common humanity" ("psychic unity") can explain the diversity of forms that culture takes. Here she proposes the experience of adolescence is a cultural phenomenon. Based on her work in Samoa she argued that the stress psychologists associated with adolescence is not so much due to the inevitable biological and social pressures all humans face at that age as it is to the culturally specific effects of adolescence in America.

and analyse which, if any, of the aspects of our civilisation were responsible for the difficulties of our children at adolescence.

Unfortunately, such ideal methods of experiment are denied to us when our materials are humanity and the whole fabric of a social order. The test colony of Herodotus, in which babies were to be isolated and the results recorded, is not a possible approach. Neither is the method of selecting from our own civilisation groups of children who meet one requirement or another. Such a method would be to select five hundred adolescents from small families and five hundred from large families, and try to discover which had experienced the greatest difficulties of adjustment at adolescence. But we could not know what were the other influences brought to bear upon these children, what effect their knowledge of sex or their neighbourhood environment may have had upon their adolescent development.[6]

What method then is open to us who wish to conduct a human experiment but who lack the power either to construct the experimental conditions or to find controlled examples of those conditions here and there throughout our own civilisation? The only method is that of the anthropologist, to go to a different civilisation and make a study of human beings under different cultural conditions in some other part of the world. For such studies the anthropologist chooses quite simple peoples, primitive peoples, whose society has never attained the complexity of our own. In this choice of primitive peoples like the Eskimo, the Australian, the South Sea islander, or the Pueblo Indian, the anthropologist is guided by the knowl-edge that the analysis of a simpler civilisation is more possible of attainment.

In complicated civilisations like those of Europe, or the higher civilisations of the East, years of study are necessary before the student can begin to understand the forces at work within them. A study of the French family alone would involve a preliminary study of French history, of French law, of the Catholic and Protestant attitudes towards sex and personal relations. A primitive people without a written language present a much less elaborate problem and a trained student can master the fundamental structure of a primitive society in a few months.

Furthermore, we do not choose a simple peasant community in Europe or an isolated group of mountain whites in the American South, for these people's ways of life, though simple, belong essentially to the historical tradition to which the complex parts of European or American civilisation belong. Instead, we choose primitive groups who have had thousands of years of historical development along completely different lines from our own, whose language does not possess our Indo-European categories, whose religious ideas are of a different nature, whose social organisation is not only simpler but very different from our own. From these contrasts, which are vivid enough to startle and enlighten those accustomed to our own way of life and simple enough to be grasped quickly, it is possible to learn many things about the effect of a civilisation upon the individuals within it.[7]

So, in order to investigate the particular problem, I chose to go not to Germany or to Russia,

---

[6] Here Mead confronts one of the most fundamental shortcomings of trying to conduct experimental science in the social sciences. Because social scientists cannot control the variables in the lives of humans as one can do for laboratory animals, it is not possible to set up the same kind of experimental situations or test hypothesis with the same scientific rigor as that found in the physical sciences. For Mead and the other students of Boas the answer to this issue was conducting fieldwork in other societies. Her comment about the "Test colony of Herodotus" refers to the Ancient Greek historian Herodotus's (c484–c425 BCE) account of an experiment supposedly performed by the Pharaoh Psammetichus. In an effort to discover the oldest language, Psammetichus ordered two infants raised for two years in acoustic isolation. Psammetichus believed that the language that infants raised under these conditions first spoke would necessarily be the language of the earliest humans. According to Herodotus, Psammetichus believed his experiment proved that the Phrygians (from West Central Turkey) were the most ancient people.

[7] The Boasian perspective that each society is the result of its own unique historical circumstances is today called historical particularism. Because this viewpoint emphasized cultural relativism and the incommensurability of different cultures, it was a potent counterpoint to the evolutionary

but to Samoa, a South Sea island about thirteen degrees from the Equator, inhabited by a brown Polynesian people. Because I was a woman and could hope for greater intimacy in working with girls rather than with boys, and because owing to a paucity of women ethnologists our knowledge of primitive girls is far slighter than our knowledge of boys, I chose to concentrate upon the adolescent girl in Samoa.[8]

But in concentrating, I did something very different from what I would do if I concentrated upon a study of the adolescent girl in Kokomo, Indiana. In such a study, I would go right to the crux of the problem; I would not have to linger long over the Indiana language, the table manners or sleeping habits of my subjects, or make an exhaustive study of how they learned to dress themselves, to use the telephone, or what the concept of conscience meant in Kokomo. All these things are the general fabric of American life, known to me as investigator, known to you as readers.

But with this new experiment on the primitive adolescent girl the matter was quite otherwise. She spoke a language the very sounds of which were strange, a language in which nouns became verbs and verbs nouns in the most sleight-of-hand fashion. All of her habits of life were different.

She sat cross-legged on the ground, and to sit upon a chair made her stiff and miserable. She ate with her fingers from a woven plate; she slept upon the floor. Her house was a mere circle of pillars, roofed by a cone of thatch, carpeted with water-worn coral fragments. Her whole material environment was different. Cocoanut palm, breadfruit, and mango trees swayed above her village. She had never seen a horse, knew no animals except the pig, dog and rat. Her food was taro, breadfruit and bananas, fish and wild pigeon and half-roasted pork, and land crabs. And just as it was necessary to understand this physical environment, this routine of life which was so different from ours, so her social environment in its attitudes towards children, towards sex, towards personality, presented as strong a contrast to the social environment of the American girl.[9]

I concentrated upon the girls of the community. I spent the greater part of my time with them. I studied most closely the households in which adolescent girls lived. I spent more time in the games of children than in the councils of their elders. Speaking their language, eating their food, sitting barefoot and cross-legged upon the pebbly floor, I did my best to minimise the differences between us and to learn to know and understand

---

and diffusionist theories of the late nineteenth century. Here Mead expresses the view that Samoan culture is an anthropological laboratory because it developed on its own uninfluenced by the Western world. However, today the notion that a society could exist in a "pure" form is considered naive. Archaeological evidence indicates that Samoa was settled around 1500 B.C.E. and had a relationship with the polities of Fiji and Tonga. Europeans first arrived in the Samoan islands in the early 1700s, missionaries a hundred years later. In other words, despite Mead's observations about the importance of working in non-western societies she was living among people influenced by European colonialism for almost two hundred years. In Mead's defense, this notion that Western societies are "complicated" and that indigenous societies are somehow unspoiled remains a powerful theme in modern popular thought.

[8] Although Mead's statement about working with young women because she was a woman and little research had been done with indigenous women seems obvious today, the anthropology of her day was male dominated and largely oblivious to the importance of gender in anthropo-

logical field work. In 1928, the highlighting of gender in her work was innovative.

[9] Read the last two paragraphs again and think about Mead's comments concerning the "culture" of teenage girls in Kokomo, Indiana, and her description of the life of a teenage girl in Samoa. The simplicity of Mead's concept of culture is striking. For Mead, culture is the language, food, customs, and material goods of a people. This understanding is little different than the definition of culture first published by E.B. Tylor in Primitive Culture in 1871 (see essay 2). However, work by scholars in the 1970s and 1980s challenged this static view of culture. A good example of this is the Hanson essay (number 38 in this book) which looks at the processes by which cultural traditions are invented and interpreted by different groups in the same society. Further, it is always easy to think of the past as a simpler time. The cultural homogeneity assumed in Mead's description may not really have existed in the Samoan villages she visited or in Kokomo, Indiana in 1928. It may be an artifact of the way anthropologists of her era understood culture.

all the girls of three little villages on the coast of the little island of Tau, in the Manu'a Archipelago.

Through the nine months which I spent in Samoa, I gathered many detailed facts about these girls, the size of their families, the position and wealth of their parents, the number of their brothers and sisters, the amount of sex experience which they had had. All of these routine facts are summarised in a table in the appendix. They are only the barest skeleton, hardly the raw materials for a study of family situations and sex relations, standards of friendship, of loyalty, of personal responsibility, all those impalpable storm centres of disturbances in the lives of our adolescent girls. And because these less measurable parts of their lives were so similar, because one girl's life was so much like another's, in an uncomplex, uniform culture like Samoa, I feel justified in generalising although I studied only fifty girls in three small neighbouring villages.

In the following chapters I have described the lives of these girls, the lives of their younger sisters who will soon be adolescent, of their brothers with whom; a strict taboo forbids them to speak, of their older sisters who have left puberty behind them, of their elders, the mothers and fathers whose attitudes towards life determine the attitudes of their children. And through this description I have tried to answer the question which sent me to Samoa: Are the disturbances which vex our adolescents due to the nature of adolescence itself or to the civilisation? Under different conditions does adolescence present a different picture?

Also, by the nature of the problem, because of the unfamiliarity of this simple life on a small Pacific island, I have had to give a picture of the whole social life of Samoa, the details being selected always with a view to illuminating the problem of adolescence. Matters of political or-ganisation which neither interest nor influence the young girl are not included. Minutiae of relationship systems or ancestor cults, genealogies and mythology, which are of interest only to the specialist, will be published in another place. But I have tried to present to the reader the Samoan girl in her social setting, to describe the course of her life from birth until death, the problems she will have to solve, the values which will guide her in her solutions, the pains and pleasures of her human lot cast on a South Sea island.[10]

Such a description seeks to do more than illuminate this particular problem. It should also give the reader some conception of a different and contrasting civilisation, another way of life, which other members of the human race have found satisfactory and gracious. We know that our subtlest perceptions, our highest values, are all based upon contrast; that light without darkness or beauty without ugliness would lose the qualities which they now appear to us to have. And similarly, if we would appreciate our own civilisation, this elaborate pattern of life which we have made for ourselves as a people and which we are at such pains to pass on to our children, we must set our civilisation over against other very different ones. The traveller in Europe returns to America, sensitive to nuances in his own manners and philosophies which have hitherto gone unremarked, yet Europe and America are parts of one civilisation. It is with variations within one great pattern that the student of Europe today or the student of our own history sharpens his sense of appreciations. But if we step outside the stream of Indo-European culture, the appreciation which we can accord our civilisation is even more enhanced. Here in remote parts of the world, under historical conditions very different from those which made Greece and Rome flourish and fall, groups of human beings have worked

---

[10] In this paragraph Mead makes clear she is writing for a popular American audience and takes a gentle poke at the anthropology prominent in her day. She says descriptions of political organization, relationship systems, ancestor cults, genealogies, and mythology, "which are of interest only to the specialist" are not dealt with in this book be-cause they are not of interest to the girls she studied. Political organization, kinship, and religion are precisely the topics that were the focus of much of the anthropology of previous decades. Her study is among the first to focus on women and their lives.

out patterns of life so different from our own that we cannot venture any guess that they would ever have arrived at our solutions. Each primitive people has selected one set of human gifts, one set of human values, and fashioned for themselves an art, a social organisation, a religion, which is their unique contribution to the history of the human spirit.[11]

Samoa is only one of these diverse and gracious patterns, but as the traveller who has been once from home is wiser than he who has never left his own door step, so a knowledge of one other culture should sharpen our ability to scrutinise more steadily, to appreciate more lovingly, our own.

And, because of the particular problem which we set out to answer, this tale of another way of life is mainly concerned with education, with the process by which the baby, arrived cultureless upon the human scene, becomes a full-fledged adult member of his or her society. The strongest light will fall upon the ways in which Samoan education, in its broadest sense, differs from our own. And from this contrast we may be able to turn, made newly and vividly self-conscious and self-critical, to judge anew and perhaps fashion differently the education we give our children.[12]

---

[11] In this paragraph Mead attacks the notion that one can predict the future of a society based on its current state. In so doing, she is echoing Boas' attack on the unilineal evolutionists.

[12] Mead's cultural relativism and appreciation for other cultures shines through in these final paragraphs. One reason she was such a popular figure was her ability to make her readers appreciate the lifestyles of other peoples. Note too her argument that in learning about other cultures we are better able to understand and appreciate our own. Mead was raised in an unconventional household. Her father, Edward Sherwood Mead (1874–1956) was a professor of finance at the University of Pennsylvania. Her mother, Emily Fogg Mead (1871–1950) had been a teacher and during Margaret's childhood studied Italian immigrants in Hammonton, New Jersey, while working on a never-to-be-completed Master's degree in sociology. Growing up, Margaret was encouraged to explore her interests and have a career at a time before women were even allowed to vote. In these last paragraphs she invites us all to open our minds, broaden our horizons, and value the diversity of cultures in the world as she had learned to do.

Part Three

THEORY AT MIDCENTURY

The Reemergence of Evolutionary Thought

A major theoretical shift occurred in American anthropology in the late 1940s and the 1950s. For the first half of the century, the principal work in American anthropology was based on the Boasian tradition or the neo-Freudian approach of the culture and personality school. Beginning in the 1930s, the antievolutionary perspective of the Boasian tradition had once again to compete with new and more sophisticated evolutionary approaches proposed by Julian Steward (1902–1972), Leslie White (1900–1975), and George Peter Murdock (1897–1985).

Steward and White developed a techno-environmental approach to cultural change and both were influenced by Marxist thought. Steward's ecological approach focused on the adaptation of individual cultures to specific environmental circumstances. White is best known for his formulation of a general evolutionary theory of culture, an approach that had been abandoned after Boas thrashed unilineal evolutionary theory at the turn of the century. George Peter Murdock was influential in resurrecting the sort of large-scale cross-cultural comparisons that had been the basis of the work of nineteenth-century anthropologists such as Lewis Henry Morgan and E. B. Tylor. He is best known for his creation of the Human Relations Area Files, or HRAF. Harris (1968:606) credits Murdock, Steward, and White's revival of cross-cultural comparison with the "mid-century collapse of historical particularism." Although Harris' eulogy for historical particularism was premature, these three men set the foundation for the formulation of ecological

anthropology and cultural materialism, two of the most influential forms of anthropological analysis since the 1960s.

Julian Steward grew up in Washington, D.C., but at age sixteen went to the newly founded Deep Springs Preparatory School (today Deep Springs College). Deep Springs almost surely had a profound effect on Steward. It was then, as today, an extremely small school (about twenty students) where intense study and debate was combined with strenuous physical labor. Deep Springs is also in an extraordinarily spectacular physical setting in the deserts and mountains of Eastern California. At Deep Springs, Steward became interested in the local Paiute and Shoshoni communities and may well have been impressed with the way in which these groups had survived in this beautiful but harsh environment. After completing his undergraduate education at the University of California–Berkeley and Cornell University, Steward studied anthropology at Berkeley, as a student of A. L. Kroeber. Since Steward was interested in discovering the causes of cultural traits and Kroeber insisted that such causes were not "a proper concern of anthropology" (Manners 1973:889) their relationship was contentious. Steward devoted most of his energy to the study of the environmental adaptation of specific societies. His first research was in archaeology, but he then moved to ethnography and worked with the Shoshoni, the Pueblo, and later the Carrier Indians in British Columbia. Steward also devoted a great deal of energy to the investigation of parallel developmental sequences in the evolution of civilizations in the New and Old Worlds.

Steward proposed that cultures in similar environments would tend to follow the same developmental sequences and formulate similar responses to their environmental challenges. He termed those cultural features most closely associated with subsistence practices the *cultural core* (1955). Cultures that shared similar core features belonged to the same *culture type*. Having identified these culture types, he compared and sorted them into a hierarchy arranged by complexity. Steward's original ranking was family, multifamily, and state-level societies. His followers later refined these categories into the now familiar classifications of band, tribe, chiefdom, and state.

Steward did not believe that cultures followed a single universal sequence of development. He proposed instead that cultures could evolve in any number of distinct patterns depending on their environmental circumstances. He called his theory *multilinear evolution* to distinguish it from nineteenth-century unilineal evolutionary theories. The methodology Steward outlined for multilinear evolution involved a field of study he called *cultural ecology*—that is, the examination of the cultural adaptations formulated by human beings to meet the challenges posed by their environments. The selection of Steward's work we have chosen, "The Patrilineal Band," clearly shows how he viewed culture as an evolutionary adaptation to the environment.

Leslie White studied at the University of Chicago under Edward Sapir, a student of Boas. White was thus trained in Boasian historical particularism but found this approach intellectually unsatisfying. At his first teaching post at the University of Buffalo, he read the work of nineteenth-century evolutionists such as Herbert Spencer and particularly Lewis Henry Morgan. Morgan had been vilified by Boas and was the target of attacks by many of Boas' students. White, however, argued that much of what Morgan wrote was correct. Specifically, White agreed that cross-cultural comparison showed that cultural evolution did exist and that this evolution was in the direction of increasing complexity. The problem with the evolutionary thinkers of the nineteenth

century, White argued, was that they failed to develop a non-ethnocentric, scientific method of accurately assessing cultural complexity. Therefore, although their general idea was correct, many of their specific examples were in error. White proposed to remedy this by developing a quantifiable, universal standard of measurement. In his 1943 essay, "Energy and the Evolution of Culture," White proposed that the control of energy was a key factor in cultural evolution and could serve as the standard by which to measure evolutionary progress. He traced the history of human culture, arguing that changes in technology marked evolutionary stages. White understood culture as the means by which humans adapted to nature. As members of societies learned to capture energy, they were able to make their lives increasingly secure and so culture advanced. White proposed a grand, universal law of cultural evolution: Culture advances as the amount of energy harnessed per capita per year increases, or as the efficiency with which energy is used increases.

Inspired by his reading of Marx, White separated culture into three analytical levels: technological, sociological, and ideological. Like Marx, he believed that all the institutions of society contributed to the evolution of culture; however, technology played the primary role in social evolution and changes in technology affected a society's institutions and value systems.

George Peter Murdock was another important anthropologist deeply influenced by the work of Spencer and Morgan. He received his undergraduate and graduate degrees at Yale University and taught there for thirty-two years. He also rejected the Boasian approach to anthropology. Murdock was interested in the statistical testing of cross-cultural hypotheses, in direct opposition to Boas' avoidance of cross-cultural generalizations. Toward this end he established the Cross-Cultural Survey in 1937, which a decade later formed the basis of the Human Relations Area Files (HRAF), a huge bank of ethnographic data on more than one thousand societies indexed according to standardized categories. Using this information, one can conduct cross-cultural quantitative analyses and test cultural hypotheses in a wide variety of societies.

In addition to creating the HRAF, Murdock is remembered for his 1949 book *Social Structure*. He believed that a universal set of principles governed the relationship between family structure, kinship, and marriage practices. In *Social Structure* Murdock attempted to determine these principles through quantitative analysis and, using comparative data from 250 societies, he was able to demonstrate the utility of the HRAF.

Murdock generally saw his work as deriving from the positivist approach of Spencer, but he recognized that Morgan's (1871) study of kinship was instrumental in shaping the quantitative-comparative approach he developed in *Social Structure*. On the opening page of his chapter on kinship, Murdock wrote, "The scientific significance of kinship systems was first appreciated by Morgan in what is perhaps the most original and brilliant single achievement in the history of anthropology" (1960:61). In addition, Morgan is one of the anthropologists to whom *Social Structure* is dedicated.

Although White, Steward, and Murdock were evolutionists, they had very different ideas of what cultural evolution meant and how it happened. Steward did not focus on any general, overall pattern of cultural evolution. His vision of evolution was specific and relativistic; he viewed a society's core features as cultural adaptations to their specific environment. On the other hand, White, like L. H. Morgan, looked at evolution as a general overall pattern of technological development. White argued that cultural progress can be measured by specific, absolute standards and can be ranked on a universal scale. He proposed that the key factor driving evolutionary change was revolutionary changes in technology. In the 1960s, Marshall Sahlins (b. 1930) and Elman Service (1915–1996) attempted to reconcile these two approaches. Based on yet another analogy with biological evolution, they suggested that evolution follows two paths. The first is general evolution, a grand movement from simple to complex. The second is specific evolution, the change of individual cultures in response to their particular environmental circumstances (Sahlins and Service 1960).

Murdock's cross-cultural comparisons of cultural traits in many ways paralleled Steward's theory of multilinear evolution, and his attempts to statistically demonstrate universal principles of kin relations resembled White's effort to formulate a universal theory of cultural evolution. However, Murdock focused his efforts on the evolution of aspects of social structure such as kin terminology, family structure, and marriage patterns.

No theoretical viewpoint is immune to the political context in which it develops, and cultural ecology is a particularly good example of this point. The cultural ecologists relied heavily on the insights of Marxist analysis, but given the virulently anticommunist political climate of the United States at the time, they generally did not cite Marx openly. Steward made no reference at all to the influence of Marx in his work and was thus able to avoid controversy. White, to the contrary, often courted controversy.

Like many American scholars of the 1920s, White was drawn to Soviet communism. He visited the Soviet Union for eight weeks in the summer of 1929 and by the time he returned, he was convinced that "the Russian Revolution was the most significant event in modern history" (Peace 1998:85). When the American Association for the Advancement of Science met in 1930, White gave an address, called "An Anthropological Appraisal of the Russian Revolution," praising the Soviet Union and predicting disaster for capitalist nations. The address received front-page attention in *The New York Times* and *Pravda* (the official state newspaper of the Soviet Union), and created a firestorm. Burnt by this experience, White became much more cautious in expressing his political views. He concealed his political activities and avoided public statements of his attachment to either authors or individuals associated with the left. In the 1930s, as the nature of Stalin's dictatorship became apparent, White became a fierce opponent and critic of Soviet communism but he remained a committed socialist. He wrote articles and letters for *The Weekly People,* the newspaper of the Socialist Labor Party of America, under the pseudonym of John Steele (Shankman and Dino 2001).

We should note that many anthropologists have paid a heavy price for their political activism. Boas, as you will recall, was censured for criticizing the government. Other anthropologists were followed and harassed by the FBI. These include

Melville Jacobs, Paul Radin, Elman Service, Oscar Lewis, Margaret Mead, and Cora Du Bois. The Boasian Ashley Montagu was fired from Rutgers University after giving a speech condemning Senator Joseph McCarthy (Price 2004 [1960]). Boas' student Gene Weltfish (1902–1980) was a specialist on the Pawnee and author, with Ruth Benedict, of an extremely influential antiracist pamphlet *The Races of Mankind* distributed to troops during World War II (but recalled because it suggested that northern blacks were intellectually superior to southern whites). Weltfish was called to testify before McCarthy and the House Committee on Un-American Activities. *The Races of Mankind* was declared subversive material, and Weltfish's teaching position at Columbia not renewed (Shipp 1980, Pathe 1988).

White was pleased by the attention his views generated, but he was also worried for his position at the University of Michigan. His ideas were repeatedly attacked, and attempts to have him fired were a recurring theme of his career. The university denied him promotion and pay raises for thirteen years. Nevertheless, White remained there and at the end of his career felt that he owed a great debt to the university. He wrote that the university's "devotion to its own ideals made it possible for a nonconformist to stay there and keep being a nonconformist" (in Peace 1998:89; see also Peace and Price 2001).

Eventually, White's work was widely acclaimed. In the late '50s and '60s, he received numerous awards, two honorary degrees, and was elected president of the American Anthropological Association. His prominence allowed him to be politically active once more. In 1957, just after the Russians launched the satellite Sputnik, White said, "A cultural system that can launch earth satellites can dispense with gods entirely." This statement was quoted by the *New York Times,* and clergy in Michigan responded by calling for White's dismissal from the university. White later responded to the situation by asking whether God "need[ed] a protective clergyman to defend Him" (in Carneiro 1981).

Although a materialist, Murdock was at the opposite end of the political spectrum from White and thus avoided the kinds of public political controversies in which White became embroiled. However, in recent years Murdock has come under scrutiny for his political activities during the 1940s and 1950s. Based on files recovered under the Freedom of Information Act, David Price discovered that Murdock, as an informant for the FBI, reported on the activities of many of his professional colleagues. For example, in 1949 he corresponded directly with J. Edgar Hoover, naming a dozen anthropologists who he was convinced were communists (Price 2004).

Murdock's research has also not escaped the critical appraisal of other anthropologists. One of the most telling criticisms of Murdock's work is the same as that which Boas leveled at the nineteenth-century evolutionists in his 1896 article, "The Limitations of the Comparative Method in Anthropology." That is, the data on which Murdock's analyses were based were taken out of their appropriate cultural contexts, thus invalidating the reliability of the analysis. Murdock's popularity was largely limited to American anthropologists. Many British social anthropologists considered Murdock's work to be nothing more than classification of data.

---

16. *Energy and the Evolution of Culture*

LESLIE WHITE (1900–1975)

EVERYTHING IN THE universe may be described in terms of energy.[a] Galaxies, stars, molecules and atoms may be regarded as organizations of energy.

Living organisms may be looked upon as engines which operate by means of energy derived directly or indirectly from the sun. The civilizations, or

---

From *American Anthropologist* (1943)

cultures of mankind, also, may be regarded as a form of organization of energy. Culture is an organization of phenomena—material objects, bodily acts, ideas, and sentiments—which consists of or is dependent upon the use of symbols. Man, being the only animal capable of symbol-behavior, is the only creature to possess culture.[b] Culture is a kind of behavior. And behavior, whether of man, mule, plant, comet or molecule, may be treated as a manifestation of energy. Thus we see, on all levels of reality,[c] that phenomena lend themselves to description and interpretation in terms of energy. Cultural anthropology is that branch of natural science[d] which deals with matter-and-motion, i.e., energy, phenomena in cultural form, as biology deals with them in cellular, and physics in atomic, form.[1]

The purpose of culture is to serve the needs of man. These needs are of two kinds: (1) those which can be served or satisfied by drawing upon resources within the human organism alone. Singing, dancing, myth-making, forming clubs or associations for the sake of companionship, etc., illustrate this kind of needs and ways of satisfying them. (2) The second class of needs can be satisfied only by drawing upon the resources of the external world, outside the human organism. Man must get his food from the external world. The tools, weapons, and other materials with which man provides himself with food, shelter from the elements, protection from his enemies, must likewise come from the external world. The satisfaction of spiritual and aesthetic needs through singing, dancing, myth-making, etc., is possible,

however, only if man's bodily needs for food, shelter, and defense are met. Thus the whole cultural structure depends upon the material, mechanical means with which man articulates himself with the earth. Furthermore, the satisfaction of human needs from "inner resources" may be regarded as a constant,[e] the satisfaction of needs from the outer resources a variable. Therefore, in our discussion of cultural development we may omit consideration of the constant factor and deal only with the variable—the material, mechanical means with which man exploits the resources of nature.

The articulation-of-man-with-the-earth process may be analyzed and resolved into the following five factors: (1) the human organism, (2) the habitat, (3) the amount of energy controlled and expended by man, (4) the ways and means in which energy is expended, and (5) the human-need-serving product which accrues from the expenditure of energy. This is but another way of saying that human beings, like all other living creatures, exploit the resources of their habitat, in one way or another in order to sustain life and to perpetuate their kind.

Of the above factors, we may regard the organic factor as a constant. Although peoples obviously differ from each other physically, we are not able to attribute differences in culture to differences in physique (or "mentality"). In our study of culture, therefore, we may regard human race as of uniform quality, i.e., as a constant, and, hence, we eliminate it from our study.[2]

No two habitats are alike; every habitat varies in time. Yet, in a study of culture as a whole,[f] we

---

[1] This arresting opening passage reveals several aspects of White's thinking at this stage of his career. Because he saw anthropology as a branch of natural science, he believed that the research methods used in the sciences, when applied to anthropology, would reveal the laws of culture. Later in this essay, White provides a materialist and functionalist basis for the analysis of culture. His "functions and needs" approach is reminiscent of Bronislaw Malinowski, whom he admired (see essay 11), and Herbert Spencer (see essay 1). However, his emphasis on "material, mechanical means" reflects his grounding in Marxist thought (see essay 4).

White was trained in the Boasian tradition. He studied at the New School for Social Research under Alexander

Goldenweiser (1880–1940), a student of Franz Boas and the mentor of Ruth Benedict. At Chicago, where he received his Ph.D., he worked with Edward Sapir, another of Boas' students. However, his theoretical work diverged sharply from that of the Boasians.

[2] As a teenager, White was interested in astronomy and intended to become a physicist. His style of writing and of argument reflect this background. White argues in a scientific idiom—defining and eliminating or analyzing variables and describing laws. Like other Boasians, he discounts the effects of race.

may regard the factor of habitat as a constant: we simply reduce the need-serving, welfare-promoting resources of particular habitats to an average. (In a consideration of particular manifestations of culture we would of course have to deal with their respective particular habitats.) Since we may regard habitat as a constant, we exclude it, along with the human organism, from our study of the development of culture.[3]

This leaves us, then, three factors to be considered in any cultural situation: (1) the amount of energy per capita per unit of time harnessed and put to work within the culture, (2) the technological means with which this energy is expended, and (3) the human-need-serving product that accrues from the expenditure of energy.[4] We may express the relationship between these factors in the following simple formula: $E \times T = P$ in which E represents the amount of energy expended per capita per unit of time, T the technological means of its expenditure, and P the magnitude of the product per unit of time. This may be illustrated concretely with the following simple example: A man cuts wood with an axe. Assuming the quality of the wood and the skill of the workman to be constant, the amount of wood cut in a given period of time, say an hour, depends, on the one hand upon the amount of energy the man expends during this time: the more energy expended, the more wood cut. On the other hand, the amount of wood cut in an hour depends upon the kind of axe used. Other things being equal, the amount of wood cut varies with the quality of the axe: the better the axe the more wood cut. Our workman can cut more wood with an iron, or steel, axe than with a stone axe.

The efficiency with which human energy is expended mechanically depends upon the bodily skills of the persons involved, and upon the nature of the tools employed. In the following discussion we shall deal with skill in terms of averages.[5] It is obvious, of course, that, other things being equal, the product of the expenditure of human energy varies directly as the skill employed in the expenditure of this energy. But we may reduce all particular skills, in any given situation, to an average which, being constant, may be eliminated from our consideration of culture growth. Hereafter, then, when we concern ourselves with the efficiency with which human energy is expended mechanically, we shall be dealing with the efficiency of tools only.

With reference to tools, man can increase the efficiency of the expenditure of his bodily energy in two ways: by improving a tool, or by substituting a better tool for an inferior one. But with regard to any given kind of tool, it must be noted that there is a point beyond which it cannot be improved. The efficiency of various tools of a certain kind varies; some bows are better than others. A bow, or any other implement, may vary in efficiency between 0 per cent and 100 per cent. But there is a maximum, theoretically as well as actually, which cannot be exceeded. Thus, the efficiency of a canoe paddle can be raised or lowered by altering its length, breadth, thickness, shape, etc. Certain proportions or dimensions would render it useless, in which case its efficiency would be 0 per cent. But, in the direction of improvement, a point is reached, ideally as well as practically, when no further progress can be made—any further change would be a detriment.

---

[3] Although White was concerned with the relationship between humans and nature, he did not share Steward's interest in the effects of specific environments on culture (see essay 17).

[4] The concerns on which White focuses in this essay, especially technology, reflect the influence of Marx on his works. White visited the Soviet Union in 1929 and, while there, was inspired by his reading of Marx and Engels. He later corresponded briefly with Leon Trotsky (Beardsley 1976:619). He told one of his students that he had profitably read the last chapter of Marx's work *Capital* sixteen times (Carneiro 1981).

[5] Here and later, White refers to numbers and writes equations, suggesting that he is measuring attributes that can be quantified, perhaps with relative ease. However, White and his followers had great trouble actually providing agreed-on, concrete, quantitative measures of the variables they discussed. As a result, critics considered their work pseudoscientific.

Its efficiency is now at its maximum (100 per cent). So it is with a canoe, arrow, axe, dynamo, locomotive, or any other tool or machine.

We are now ready for some generalizations about cultural development.[6] Let us return to our formula, but this time let us write it E × F = P, in which E and P have the same values as before—E, the amount of energy expended; P the product produced—while F stands for the efficiency of the mechanical means with which the energy is expended. Since culture is a mechanism for serving human needs, cultural development may be measured by the extent to which, and the efficiency with which, need-serving goods or services are provided. P, in our formula, may thus stand for the total amount of goods or services produced in any given cultural situation. Hence P represents the status of culture, or, more accurately, the degree of cultural development. If, then, F, the efficiency with which human energy is expended, remains constant, then P, the degree of cultural development, will vary as E, the amount of energy expended per capita per year[8] varies:

$$\frac{E_1 \times F}{E_2 \times F} = \frac{P_1}{P_2}$$

Thus we obtain the first important law of cultural development: *Other things being equal, the degree of cultural development varies directly as the amount of energy per capita per year harnessed and put to work.*[7]

Secondly, if the amount of energy expended per capita unit of time remains constant, then P varies as F:

$$\frac{E \times F_1}{E \times F_2} = \frac{P_1}{P_2}$$

and we get the second law of cultural development: *Other things being equal, the degree of cultural development varies directly as the efficiency of the technological means with which the harnessed energy is put to work.*

It is obvious, of course, that E and F may vary simultaneously, and in the same or in opposite directions. If E and F increase simultaneously P will increase faster, naturally, than if only one increased while the other remained unchanged. If E and F decrease simultaneously P will decrease more rapidly than if only one decreased while the other remained constant. If E increases while F decreases, or vice versa, then P will vary or remain unchanged, depending upon the magnitude of the changes of these two factors and upon the proportion of one magnitude to the other. If an increase in E is balanced by a decrease in F, or vice versa, then P will remain unchanged. But should E increase faster than F decreases or vice versa, then P would increase; if E decreases faster than F increases, or vice versa, then P would decrease.

We have, in the above generalizations *the law of cultural evolution: culture develops when the amount of energy harnessed by man per capita per year is increased; or as the efficiency of the technological means of putting this energy to work is increased; or, as both factors are simultaneously increased.*

All living beings struggle to live, to perpetuate their respective kinds.[8] In the human species the struggle for survival assumes the cultural form. The human struggle for existence expresses itself in a never-ending attempt to make of culture a more effective instrument with which to provide security of life and survival of the species. And one of the ways of making culture a more powerful

---

[6] In this passage, White writes of degrees of cultural development. This places him in direct opposition to most Boasians, who held that comparing cultures in this manner was impossible and came dangerously close to ethnocentrism.

[7] Here and later, White offers several laws of culture. These occasioned a dispute between White and Steward. Steward argued that White's laws were so general as to be virtually self-evident and told nothing about the specifics of change within a culture. White responded that this, while true, was the fundamental nature of universal laws. Sup-

porting White's defense of his laws, Harris (1968:649) asks, "Does the law of gravitation tell us nothing about particulars? When one predicts a particular eclipse on a particular planet . . . has this no relation to the general law?"

[8] White's emphasis on struggle reflects his reading of both Darwin and Marx. Compare his statement here with Marx's famous dictum that all history is the history of class struggle. In Marx, social classes struggle for control of the means of production. For White, the struggle is for increased control of energy and increased efficiency of energy usage.

instrument is to harness and to put to work within it more energy per capita per year. Thus, wind, and water and fire are harnessed; animals are domesticated, plants cultivated; steam engines are built. The other way of improving culture as an instrument of adjustment and control is to invent new and better tools and improve old ones. Thus energy for culture-living and culture-building is augmented in quantity, is expended more efficiently, and culture advances.

Thus we know, not only *how* culture evolves, but *why*, as well. The urge, inherent in all living species, to live, to make life more secure, more rich, more full, to insure the perpetuation of the species, seizes upon, when it does not produce, better[h] (i.e., more effective) means of living and surviving. In the case of man, the biological urge to live, the power to invent and to discover, the ability to select and use the better of two tools or ways of doing something—these are the factors of cultural evolution.[9] Darwin could tell us the consequences of variations, but he could not tell us how these variations were produced. We know the motive force as well as the means of cultural evolution. The culturologist[10] knows more about cultural evolution than the biologist, even today, knows about biological evolution.[i]

A word about man's motives with regard to cultural development. We do not say that man deliberately set about to improve his culture. It may well have been, as Morgan[j] suggested, decades before Lowie[k] emphasized the same point, that animals were first domesticated through whim or caprice rather than for practical, utilitarian reasons. Perhaps agriculture came about through accident. Hero's steam engine was a plaything. Gunpowder was first used to make pretty fireworks. The compass began as a toy. More than this, we know that peoples often resolutely oppose technological advances with a passionate devotion to the past and to the gods of their fathers. But all of this does not alter the fact that domesticated animals and cultivated plants have been used to make life more secure. Whatever may have been the intentions and motives (if any) of the inventors or discoverers of the bow and arrow, the wheel, the furnace and forge, the steam engine, the microscope, etc., the fact remains that these things have been seized upon by mankind and employed to make life more secure, comfortable, pleasant, and permanent. So we may disregard the psychological circumstances under which new cultural devices were brought into being. What is significant to the cultural evolutionist is that inventions and discoveries have been made, new tools invented, better ways of doing things found, and that these improved tools and techniques are kept and used until they are in turn replaced.

So much for the laws, or generalizations, derived from our basic formula. Let us turn now to concrete facts and see how the history of culture is illuminated and made intelligible by these laws.

In the beginning of culture history, man had only the energy of his own body under his control and at his disposal for culture-living and culture-building. And for a very long period of time this was

---

[9] Much of American anthropology has denied the existence of any but the most rudimentary human instincts. White goes against this trend. Here he relies on the existence of a biologically based drive to use culture to make life "more rich, more full."

[10] As this essay shows, White was much given to inventing new words and phrases. White called his work *culturology* rather than anthropology. He proposed that culturology was a science and that it treated cultural phenomena as obeying their own laws, distinct from human biology or individual psychology. In this, he was clearly influenced by Kroeber's idea of the superorganic (see essay 9) and Durkheim's notion of the collective conscience (see essay 5). White once wrote that great men were no more personally effective in shaping the general course of culture than a "sack of sawdust" (1949:279).

White's insistence that culture follows its own path independent of individual humans, however, seems to contradict his notion that culture exists to make life more secure for humans. At the end of his life, he confronted this problem. White's emphasis on the notion of culture as a system and evidence that culture was often maladaptive led him to reject the idea that culture exists to serve people's needs. In his last work he wrote, "We no longer think of culture as designed to serve the needs of man; culture goes its own way in accordance with laws of its own. Man lives within the embrace of cultural systems, and enjoys or suffers whatever they mete out to him" (1975:159).

almost the only source of energy available to him. Wind, water, and fire were but rarely used as forms of energy. Thus we see that, in the first stage of cultural development, the only source of energy under man's control and at his disposal for culture-building was, except for the insignificant and limited use of wind, water and fire, his own body.

The amount of energy that could be derived from this source was very small. The amount of energy at the disposal of a community of 50, 100, 300 persons would be 50, 100, or 300 times the energy of the average member of the community, which, when infants, the sick, the old and feeble are considered, would be considerably less than one "man-power" per capita. Since one "manpower" is about one-tenth of one horsepower, we see that the amount of energy per capita in the earliest stage of cultural development was very small indeed—perhaps 1/20th horsepower per person.

Since the amount of energy available for culture-building in this stage was finite and limited, the extent to which culture could develop was limited. As we have seen, when the energy factor is a constant, cultural progress is made possible only by improvements in the means with which the energy is expended, namely, the technology. Thus, in the human-energy stage of cultural development progress is achieved only by inventing new tools—the bow and arrow, harpoon, needle, etc., by improving old ones—new techniques of chipping flint implements, for example. But when man has achieved maximum efficiency in the expenditure of energy, and when he has reached the limits of his finite bodily energy resources, then his culture can develop no further. Unless he can harness additional quantities of energy—by tapping new sources—cultural development will come to an end. Man would have remained on the level of savagery[1] indefinitely if he had not learned to augment the amount of energy under his control and at his disposal for culture-building by harnessing new sources of energy. This was first accomplished by the domestication of animals and by the cultivation of plants.[11]

Man added greatly to the amount of energy under his control and at his disposal for culture-building when he domesticated animals and brought plants under cultivation.[12] To be sure, man nourished himself with meat and grain and clothed himself with hides and fibers long before animal husbandry and agriculture came into being. But there is a vast difference between merely exploiting the resources of nature and harnessing the forces of nature. In a wild food economy, a person, under given environmental conditions, expends a certain amount of energy (we will assume it is an average person so that the question of skill may be ignored) and in return he will secure, on the average, so much meat, fish, or plant food. But the food which he secures is itself a form and a magnitude of energy. Thus the hunter or wild plant-food gatherer changes one magnitude of energy for another: m units of labor for n calories of food. The ratio between the magnitude of energy obtained in the form of food and

---

[11] White's description of the relationship between technology and culture was heavily influenced by Marx's idea of a mode of production. Marxists understand different societies as being determined by particular combinations of relations of production and forces of production (see essays 4, 29, and 40). White's analysis is similar but perhaps less complex. He sees different types of society as fundamentally conditioned by the different types of technology they use.

[12] The evolutionary perspective of the nineteenth century was largely abandoned by American cultural anthropologists, but after World War I it was rehabilitated by archaeologists and European anthropologists. Although they explicitly rejected the ethnocentric and racist formulations of nineteenth-century evolutionary theory, they retained and elaborated its basic elements. White saw little resemblance between his work and that of V. Gordon Childe (1892–1957), but this passage, and much of White's analysis later, shows that influence (Service 1976:613). Childe was an Australian-born archaeologist and culture theorist who lived and worked largely in Great Britain. Openly Marxist, he is remembered for, among other things, coining the term *Neolithic Revolution*. He and others conducted studies of cultural evolution based on archaeological data for a number of years before White published this essay. White, along with Steward, returned the evolutionary element to American cultural anthropology. The evolutionary materialism of these thinkers is reflected in much of American archaeology in the second half of the twentieth century.

the magnitude expended in hunting and gathering may vary. The amount obtained may be greater than, less than (in which case the hunter-gatherer would eventually perish), or equal to, the amount expended. But although the ratio may vary from one situation to another, it is in any particular instance fixed: that is, the magnitude of energy-value of the game taken or plant-food gathered remains constant between the time that it is obtained and the time of its consumption. (At least it does not increase, it may in some instances decrease through natural deterioration.)

In a wild food economy, an animal or a plant is of value to man only after it has ceased to be an animal or a plant, i.e., a living organism. The hunter kills his game, the gatherer digs his roots and bulbs, plucks the fruit and seeds. It is different with the herdsman and the farmer. These persons make plants and animals work for them.[13]

Living plants and animals are biochemical mechanisms which, of themselves, accumulate and store up energy derived originally from the sun. Under agriculture and animal husbandry these accumulations can be appropriated and utilized by man periodically in the form of milk, wool, eggs, fruits, nuts, seeds, sap, and so on. In the case of animals, energy generated by them may be utilized by man in the form of work, more or less continuously throughout their lifetime. Thus, when man domesticated animals and brought plants under cultivation, he harnessed powerful forces of nature, brought them under his control, and made them work for him just as he has harnessed rivers and made them run mills and dynamos, just as he has harnessed the tremendous reservoirs of solar energy that are coal and oil. Thus the difference between a wild plant and animal economy and a domestic economy is that in the former the return for an expenditure of human energy, no matter how large, is fixed, limited, whereas in agriculture and animal husbandry the initial return for the expenditure of human labor, augments itself indefinitely. And so it has come about that with the development and perfection of the arts of animal husbandry and agriculture—selective breeding, protection from their competitors in the Darwinian struggle for survival, feeding, fertilizer, irrigation, drainage, etc.—a given quantity of human labor produces much more than it could before these forces were harnessed. It is true, of course, that a given amount of human labor will produce more food in a wild economy under exceptionally favorable circumstances, such, e.g., as in the Northwest Coast of America where salmon could be taken in vast numbers with little labor, or in the Great Plains of North America where, after the introduction of the horse and in favorable circumstances, a large quantity of bison meat could be procured with but little labor,—than could be produced by a feeble development of agriculture in unfavorable circumstances. But history and archaeology prove that, by and large, the ability of man to procure the first necessity of life, food, was tremendously increased by the domestication of animals and by the cultivation of plants. Cultural progress was extremely rapid after the origin of agriculture.[m] The great civilizations of China, India, Mesopotamia, Egypt, Mexico, and Peru sprang up quickly after the agricultural arts had attained to some degree of development and maturity. This was due, as we have already observed, to the fact that, by means of agriculture man was able to harness, control, and put to work for himself powerful forces of nature. With greatly augmented energy resources man was able to expand and develop his way of life, i.e., his culture.[14]

In the development of culture, agriculture is a much more important and powerful factor than animal husbandry.[n] This is because man's control

---

[13] In these passages White, following Childe (1942)—who followed Morgan (see essay 3)—provides criteria for distinguishing savagery, barbarism, and civilization. Compare White's criteria with Childe's comment that "upper Paleolithic societies must be designated savage inasmuch as they relied for a livelihood on hunting, fishing, and collecting" (1942:37), or his statement that the development of agriculture was the first step in the Neolithic Revolution and distinguishes barbarism from savagery (1942:48).

[14] As these passages illustrate, for White, human cultural evolution was best understood as a process of increasing human control over the natural environment. This is a teleological vision of evolution, much like that of the

over the forces of nature is more immediate and more complete in agriculture than in animal husbandry. In a pastoral economy man exerts control over the animals only, he merely harnesses solar energy in animal form. But the animals themselves are dependent upon wild plants. Thus pastoral man is still dependent to a great extent upon the forces and caprices of nature. But in agriculture, his control is more intimate, direct, and, above all, greater. Plants receive and store up energy directly from the sun. Man's control over plants is direct and immediate. Further independence of nature is achieved by means of irrigation, drainage, and fertilizer. To be sure, man is always dependent upon nature to a greater or less extent; his control is never complete. But his dependence is less, his control greater, in agriculture than in animal husbandry. The extent to which man may harness natural forces in animal husbandry is limited. No matter how much animals are improved by selective breeding, no matter how carefully they are tended—defended from beasts of prey, protected from the elements—so long as they are dependent upon wild plant food, there is a limit, imposed by nature, to the extent to which man can receive profitable returns from his efforts expended on his herds. When this limit has been reached no further progress can be made. It is not until man controls also the growth of the plants upon which his animals feed that progress in animal husbandry can advance to higher levels. In agriculture, on the other hand, while there may be a limit to the increase of yield per unit of human labor, this limit has not yet been reached, and, indeed it is not yet even in sight. Thus there appears to be a limit to the return from the expenditure of a given amount of human labor in animal husbandry. But in agriculture this techno-

logical limit, if one be assumed to exist, lies so far ahead of us that we cannot see it or imagine where it might lie.

Added to all of the above, is the familiar fact that a nomadic life, which is customary in a pastoral economy, is not conducive to the development of advanced cultures. The sedentary life that goes with agriculture is much more conducive to the development of the arts and crafts, to the accumulation of wealth and surpluses, to urban life.

Agriculture increased tremendously the amount of energy per capita available for culture-building, and, as a consequence of the maturation of the agricultural arts, a tremendous growth of culture was experienced. Cultural progress was very slow during Eolithic and Paleolithic times. But after a relatively brief period in the Neolithic age, during which the agricultural arts were being developed, there was a tremendous acceleration of culture growth and the great cultures of China, India, Mesopotamia, Egypt, Mexico, and Peru, came rapidly into being.

The sequence of events was somewhat as follows: agriculture transformed a roaming population into a sedentary one. It greatly increased the food supply, which in turn increased the population. As human labor became more productive in agriculture, an increasing portion of society became divorced from the task of food-getting, and was devoted to other occupations. Thus society becomes organized into occupational groups: masons, metal workers, jade carvers, weavers, scribes, priests. This has the effect of accelerating progress in the arts, crafts, and sciences (astronomy, mathematics, etc.), since they are now in the hands of specialists, rather than jacks-of-all-trades. With an increase in manufacturing, added to division

---

nineteenth-century evolutionists. For White, cultural evolution has a single goal: virtually complete human control of the environment. This vision accords very well with the times in which White wrote. In the 1940s and (particularly) the 1950s, people foresaw a not-too-distant future of domed, climate-controlled cities. Childe, for example, wrote in 1942 that the development of agriculture turned humans into "active partners with nature instead of parasites on nature" (1942:48). Today, our understanding of

human ability to exert control over nature, as well as its desirability, is considerably different. Would a modern textbook, for example, refer to hunters and gatherers as parasites on nature? The theories we produce today tend to emphasize the limits of human abilities and the impossibility of determining the direction of biological or cultural evolution. Perhaps our vision of the world is conditioned by the economics and politics of our own day just as White's was by events of his era.

of society into occupational groups, comes production for exchange and sale (instead of primarily for use as in tribal society), mediums of exchange, money, merchants, banks, mortgages, debtors, slaves. An accumulation of wealth and competition for favored regions provoke wars of conquest, and produce professional military and ruling classes, slavery and serfdom. Thus agriculture wrought a profound change in the life-and-culture of man as it had existed in the human-energy stage of development.[15]

But the advance of culture was not continuous and without limit. Civilization had, in the main, reached the limit of its development on the basis of a merely agricultural and animal husbandry technology long before the next great cultural advance was initiated by the industrial revolution. As a matter of fact, marked cultural recessions took place in Mesopotamia, Egypt, Greece, Rome, perhaps in India, possibly in China. This is not to say that no cultural progress whatsoever was made; we are well aware of many steps forward from time to time in various places. But so far as general type of culture is concerned, there is no fundamental difference between the culture of Greece during the time of Archimedes and that of Western Europe at the beginning of the eighteenth century.

After the agricultural arts had become relatively mature, some six, eight or ten thousand years before the beginning of the Christian era, there was little cultural advance until the nineteenth century A.D. Agricultural methods in Europe and the United States in 1850 differed very little from those of Egypt of 2000 B.C. The Egyptians did not have an iron plow, but otherwise there was little difference in mode of production. Even today in many places in the United States and in Europe we can find agricultural practices which, the use of iron excepted, are essentially like those of dynastic Egypt. Production in other fields was essentially the same in western Europe at the beginning of the eighteenth (we might almost say nineteenth) century as in ancient Rome, Greece, or Egypt. Man, as freeman, serf, or slave, and beasts of burden and draft animals supplemented to a meager extent by wind and water power, were the sources of energy. The Europeans had gunpowder whereas the ancients did not. But gunpowder cannot be said to be a culture-builder.[o] There was no essential difference in type of social–political and economic–institutions. Banks, merchants, the political state, great land-owners, guilds of workmen, and so on were found in ancient Mesopotamia, Greece, and Rome.

Thus we may conclude that culture had developed about as far as [it] could upon the basis of an agricultural-animal husbandry economy, and that there were recessions from peaks attained in Mesopotamia, Egypt, Greece and Rome long before the beginning of the eighteenth century A.D. We may conclude further, that civilization would never have advanced substantially beyond the levels already reached in the great

---

[15] In this passage, White presents an evolutionary model that derives from Childe (1942: chapters 3 and 4) but is ultimately based on Spencer. He saw cultural evolution as a process of increasing differentiation and specialization. White's evolutionism, like that of other twentieth-century thinkers, lacks the explicit ethnocentrism and racism of nineteenth-century evolutionists. A key difference is probably the experience of World Wars I and II. It was, perhaps, easy for an English intellectual at the end of the nineteenth century to maintain that the Victorian Age represented the pinnacle of currently achieved evolution. To continue to hold this position after the carnage of battles like the Somme, where the British took 60,000 casualties on the first day of fighting and where there were a total of more than 1.2 million casualties, however, required considerable mental gymnastics. White enlisted to fight in World War I and served in the Navy in 1918 and 1919. He saw no action but his Navy experiences and the war clearly changed his life. He became opposed to all war. Of his experiences in World War I, he wrote: "I was awed and appalled by the war; I could not understand it. And I had the sickening feeling that our verbal explanations and professions did not really account for our behavior. I wanted to know *why* millions of men should murder and mangle each other, and why women and priests should urge them to do it . . ." Of World War II he wrote: "This war sickens me. The lying, cheating bragging; the nauseating hypocrisy, the parading of vicious hate, envy greed, as holy and noble striving and idealism. Using the war and patriotism to shackle and enslave-to humiliate and discredit—the working class—while at the same time proclaiming that this is a war of the common man—is sickening" (in Peace 2004: 9).

cultures of antiquity if a way had not been found to harness a greater magnitude of energy per capita per unit of time, by tapping a new source of energy: fuel.[16]

The invention of the steam engine, and of all subsequent engines which derive power from fuels, inaugurated a new era in culture history. When man learned to harness energy in the form of fuel he opened the door of a vast treasure house of energy. Fuels and engines tremendously increased the amount of energy under man's control and at his disposal for culture-building. The extent to which energy has been thus harnessed in the modern world is indicated by the eminent physicist, Robert A. Millikan[17] (1939:211) as follows:[p]

> In this country [the U.S.A.] there is now expended about 13.5 horsepower hours per day per capita—the equivalent of 100 human slaves for each of us; in England the figure is 6.7, in Germany 6.0, in France 4.5, in Japan 1.8, in Russia 0.9, China, 0.5.

Let us return now, for a moment, to our basic principle—culture develops as (1) the amount of energy harnessed and put to work per capita per unit of time increases, and (2) as the efficiency of the means with which this energy is expended increases—and consider the evolution of culture from a slightly different angle. In the course of human history various sources of energy are tapped and harnessed by man and put to work at culture-living and culture-building. The original source of energy was, as we have seen, the hu-

man organism. Subsequently, energy has been harnessed in other forms—agriculture, animal husbandry, fire,[q] wind, water, fuel. Energy is energy, and from the point of view of technology it makes no difference whether the energy with which a bushel of wheat is ground comes from a free man, a slave,[r] an ox, the flowing stream or a pile of coal. But it makes a big difference to human beings where the energy comes from,[s] and an important index of cultural development is derived from this fact.

To refer once more to our basic equation: On the one hand we have energy expended; on the other, human-need-serving goods and services are produced. Culture advances as these two factors increase, hand in hand. But the energy component is resolvable into two factors: the human energy, and the non-human energy, factors. Of these, the human energy factor is a constant; the non-human energy factor, a variable. The increase in quantity of need-serving goods goes hand in hand with an increase in the amount of non-human energy expended. But, since the human energy factor remains constant, an increase in amount of goods and services produced means more goods and services per unit of human labor. Hence, we obtain the law: *Other things being equal, culture evolves as the productivity of human labor increases.*[18]

In Savagery (wild food economy) the productivity of human labor is low; only a small amount of human-need-serving goods and services are produced per unit of human energy. In Barbarism

---

[16] White's evolutionism was modified by his reading of Marx. Most nineteenth-century evolutionists saw evolution as a process of gradual incremental change without major breaks, but Marx saw cultural evolution as proceeding by revolution: long periods of relative stasis broken by cataclysmic upheaval. White's vision in these passages is close to this view: He saw long epochs without change broken by quantum changes in energy production and consumption.

[17] White had an interest in physics and would certainly have been aware of quantum mechanics. Although there is no direct link between White's theories here and quantum theory, which developed in the late 1920s and the 1930s, the parallel is suggestive. Quantum mechanics de-

scribed abrupt changes in the levels of energy of subatomic particles; White describes abrupt changes in the levels of energy available to cultures.

He quotes Robert Millikan twice in this article. Millikan (1868–1953) won the Nobel Prize in 1923, primarily for his famous oil drop experiment. Using a simple but ingenious apparatus, Millikan determined the electrical charge of an electron and discovered that it was constant. The experiment is a classic of scientific literature, and its results were fundamental building blocks of quantum mechanics.

[18] In *Capital* (1930 [1867]), Marx argues that it is human labor that gives value to goods and services. White may have considered that as he wrote this passage.

(agriculture, animal husbandry), this productivity is greatly increased. And in Civilization (fuels, engines) it is still further increased.

We must now consider another factor in the process of cultural development, and an important one it is, viz., *the social system within which energy is harnessed and put to work.*

We may distinguish two kinds of determinants in social organization, two kinds of social groupings.[19] On the one hand we have social groupings which serve those needs of man which can be fed by drawing upon resources within man's own organism: clubs for companionship, classes or castes in so far as they feed the desire for distinction, will serve as examples. On the other hand, social organization is concerned with man's adjustment to the external world; social organization is the way in which human beings organize themselves for the three great processes of adjustment and survival—food-getting, defense from enemies, protection from the elements. Thus, we may distinguish two factors in any social system, those elements which are *ends in themselves*, which we may call E; and elements which are *means to ends* (food, defense, etc.) which we may term M.

In any social system M is more important than E, because E is dependent upon M. There can be no men's clubs or classes of distinction unless food is provided and enemies guarded against. In the development of culture, moreover, we may regard E as a constant: a men's club is a men's club whether among savage or civilized peoples. Being a constant, we may ignore factor E in our consideration of cultural evolution and deal only with the factor M.

M is a variable factor in the process of cultural evolution.[20] It is, moreover, a dependent variable, dependent upon the technological way which energy is harnessed and put to work. It is obvious, of course, that it is the technological activities of hunting people that determine, in general, their form of social organization (in so far as that social organization is correlated with hunting rather than with defense against enemies). We of the United States have a certain type of social system (in part) because we have factories, railroads, automobiles, etc.; we do not possess these things as a consequence of a certain kind of social system. Technological systems engender social systems rather than the reverse. Disregarding the factor E, social organization is to be regarded as the way in which human beings organize themselves to wield their respective technologies. Thus we obtain another important law of culture: *The social organization (E excluded) of a people is dependent upon and determined by the mechanical means with which food is secured, shelter provided, and defense maintained.* In the process of cultural development, *social evolution is* [a] *consequence of technological evolution.*

But this is not the whole story. While it is true that social systems are engendered by, and dependent upon, their respective underlying technologies, it is also true that social systems condition the operation of the technological systems upon which they rest; the relationship is one of mutual, though not necessarily equal, interaction and influence. A social system may foster the effective operation of its underlying technology or it may tend to restrain and thwart it. In short, in any given situation the social system may play a progressive role or it may play a reactionary role.

We have noted that after the agricultural arts had attained a certain degree of development, the

---

[19] White distinguished three components in the analysis of culture: technological, sociological, and ideational-attitudinal. He gave priority to the technological. He saw social organization and beliefs as arising primarily from the constraints and possibilities of technology (1959:18–28). These ideas are variations on Marx's analytical divisions: forces of production, relations of production, base, and superstructure.

[20] Here, without crediting Marx, White lays out some principles of materialist thinking. Marx had written that the mode of economic production determines the general character of the social, political, and spiritual processes of life. White uses American society in an example of precisely this sort of thinking. Marx believed that the ultimate result of the thwarting of technology by society was revolution and the emergence of new social structures. In the passages below, White echoes this belief.

great civilizations of China, India, Egypt, the Near East, Central America and Peru came rapidly into being as a consequence of the greatly augmented energy resources of the people of these regions. But these great civilizations did not continue to advance indefinitely. On the contrary they even receded from maximum levels in a number of instances. Why did they not continue progressively to advance? According to our law culture will advance, other things being equal, as long as the amount of energy harnessed and put to work per capita per unit of time increases. The answer to our question, Why did not these great cultures continue to advance? is, therefore, that the amount of energy per capita per unit of time, *ceased to increase,* and furthermore, the efficiency of the means with which this energy was expended *was not advanced beyond a certain limit.* In short, there was no fundamental improvement in the agricultural arts from say 2000 B.C. to 1800 A.D.

The next question is, Why did not the agricultural arts advance and improve during this time? We know that the agricultural arts are still capable of tremendous improvement, and the urge of man for plenty, security and efficiency was as great then as now. Why, then, did agriculture fail to progress beyond a certain point in the great civilizations of antiquity? The answer is, the social system, within which these arts functioned, curbed further expansion, thwarted progress.

All great civilizations resting upon intensive agriculture are divided into classes: a ruling class and the masses who are ruled.[21] The masses produced the means of life. But the distribution of these goods is in accordance with rules which are administered by the ruling class. By one method of control or another—by levies, taxes, rents, or some other means—the ruling class takes a portion of the wealth produced by the masses from them, and consumes it according to their liking or as the exigencies of the time dictate.

In this sort of situation cultural advancement may cease at a certain point for lack of incentive. No incentive to progress came from the ruling class in the ancient civilizations of which we are speaking. What they appropriated from their subjects they consumed or wasted. To obtain more wealth the ruling class merely increased taxes, rents, or other levies upon the producers of wealth. This was easier, quicker, and surer than increasing the efficiency of production and thereby augmenting the total product. On the other hand, there was no incentive to progress among the masses—if they produced more by increasing efficiency it would only mean more for the tax-gatherers of the ruling class. The culture history of China during the past few centuries, or indeed, since the Han dynasty, well illustrates situations of this sort.

We come then to the following conclusion: *A social system may so condition the operation of a technological system as to impose a limit upon the extent to which it can expand and develop. When this occurs, cultural evolution ceases.* Neither evolution nor progress in culture is inevitable (neither Morgan nor Tylor ever said, or even intimated, that they are). When cultural advance has thus been arrested, it can be renewed only by tapping some new source of energy and by harnessing it in sufficient magnitude to burst asunder the social system which binds it. Thus freed the new technology will form a new social system, one congenial to growth, and culture will again advance until, perhaps, the social system once more checks it.[22]

It seems quite clear that mankind would never have advanced materially beyond the maximum levels attained by culture between 2000 B.C. and 1700 A.D. had it not tapped a new source of energy (fuel) and harnessed it in substantial magnitudes. The speed with which man could travel, the range of his projectiles, and many other things, could not have advanced beyond a certain point had he

---

[21] Notice, here and below, the direct use of class analysis. White does not quote Marx directly, but the Marxist view of history as class struggle is very much evident in these passages.

[22] Here White diverges critically from Marx. Marx believed that social evolution toward communism was inevitable, though its rate might be affected by human action. White claims that "neither evolution nor progress in culture is inevitable."

not learned to harness more energy in new forms. And so it was with culture as a whole.

The steam engine ushered in a new era. With it, and various kinds of internal combustion engines, the energy resources of vast deposits of coal and oil were tapped and harnessed in progressively increasing magnitudes. Hydroelectric plants contributed a substantial amount from rivers. Populations grew, production expanded, wealth increased. The limits of growth of the new technology have not yet been reached; indeed, it is probably not an exaggeration to say that they have not even been foreseen, so vast are the possibilities and so close are we still to the beginning of this new era. But already the new technology has come into conflict with the old social system.[23] The new technology is being curbed and thwarted. The progressive tendencies of the new technology are being held back by a social system that was adapted to pre-fuel technology. This fact has become commonplace today.

In our present society, goods are produced for sale at a profit. To sell one must have a market. Our market is a world market, but it is, nevertheless, finite in magnitude. When the limit of the market has been reached production ceases to expand: no market, no sale; no sale, no profit; no profit, no production. Drastic curtailment of production, wholesale destruction of surpluses follow. Factories, mills, and mines close; millions of men are divorced from industrial production and thrown upon relief. Population growth recedes. National incomes cease to expand. Stagnation sets in.

When, in the course of cultural development, the expanding technology comes into conflict with the social system, one of two things will happen: either the social system will give way, or technological advance will be arrested. If the latter occurs, cultural evolution will, of course, cease. The outcome of situations such as this is not preordained. The triumph of technology and the continued evolution and progress of culture are not assured merely because we wish it or because it would be better thus.[24] In culture as in mechanics, the greater force prevails. A force is applied to a boulder. If the force be great enough, the rock is moved. If the rock be large enough to withstand the force, it will remain stationary. So in the case of technology-institutions conflicts: if the force of the growing technology be great enough, the restraining institutions will give way; if this force is not strong enough to overcome institutional opposition, it must submit to it.

There was undoubtedly much institutional resistance to the expanding agricultural technology in late Neolithic times. Such staunch institutions as the tribe and clan which had served man well for thousands of years did not give way to the political state without a fight; the "liberty, equality and fraternity" of primitive society were not surrendered for the class-divided, serf and lord, slave and master, society of feudalism without a struggle.[25] But the ancient and time-honored institutions of tribal society could not accommodate the greatly augmented forces of the agricultural technology. Neither could they successfully oppose these new forces. Consequently, tribal institutions gave way and a new social system came into being.

Similarly in our day, our institutions have shown themselves incapable of accommodating the vast technological forces of the Power Age. What the outcome of the present conflict between modern fuel technology and the social system of an earlier era will be, time alone will tell. It seems likely, however, that the old social system is now in the process of destruction. The tremendous forces of the Power Age are not to be denied. The

---

[23] White's distaste for capitalism is evident in passages such as this. When White wrote this essay in 1943, World War II was raging, and the memory of the Depression was still very fresh in people's minds. White believed that capitalism inevitably entailed a cycle of depression and destructive warfare. Although he was appalled by Stalin's policies in Russia and considered the members of the American Communist Party "a bunch of stooges for Stalin" (quoted in Peace 1998), he was a committed socialist.

[24] White's absolute faith in the desirability of technological progress is characteristic of the era in which he wrote. Modern anthropologists have lost much of this faith.

[25] White again echoes Marx's dictum that change comes about through revolutionary struggle rather than gradual evolutionary progress.

great wars of the twentieth century derive their chief significance from this fact: they are the means by which an old social order is to be scrapped, and a new one to be brought into being. The first World War wiped out the old ruling families of the Hapsburgs, Romanoffs, and Hohenzollerns, hulking relics of Feudalism, and brought Communist and Fascist systems into being. We do not venture to predict the social changes which the present war will bring about. But we may confidently expect them to be as profound and as far-reaching as those effected by World War I.[26]

Thus, in the history of cultural evolution, we have witnessed one complete cultural revolution, and the first stage of a second. The technological transition from a wild food economy to a relatively mature agricultural and animal husbandry economy was followed by an equally profound institutional change: from tribal society to civil society. Thus the first fundamental and all-inclusive cultural change, or revolution, took place. At the present time we are entering upon the second stage of the second great cultural revolution of human history. The Industrial Revolution was but the first stage, the technological stage, of this great cultural revolution. The Industrial Revolution has run its course, and we are now entering upon the second stage, one of profound institutional change, of social revolution. Barring collapse and chaos, which is of course possible, a new social order will emerge. It appears likely that the human race will occupy the earth for some million years to come. It seems probable, also, that man, after having won his way up through Savagery and Barbarism, is not likely to stop, when at last he finds himself upon the very threshold of Civilization.[27]

The key to the future, in any event, lies in the energy situation. If we can continue to harness as much energy per capita per year in the future as we are doing now, there is little doubt but that our old social system will give way to a new one, a new era of civilization. Should, however, the amount of energy that we are able to harness diminish materially, then culture would cease to advance or even recede. A return to a cultural level comparable to that of China during the Ming dynasty is neither inconceivable nor impossible. It all depends upon how man harnesses the forces of nature and the extent to which this is done.

At the present time "the petroleum in sight is only a twelve year supply, . . . and new discoveries [of oil] are not keeping pace with use."[t] Coal is more abundant. Even so, many of the best deposits in the United States—which has over half of the world's known coal reserves—will some day be depleted.[28] "Eventually, no matter how much we conserve, this sponging off past ages for fossil energy must cease . . . What then?"[u] The answer is, of course, that culture will decline unless man is able to maintain the amount of energy harnessed per capita per year by tapping new sources.

Wind, water, waves, tides, solar boilers, photochemical reactions, atomic energy, etc., are sources which might be tapped or further exploited. One of the most intriguing possibilities is that of harnessing atomic energy. When the nucleus of an atom of uranium (U235) is split it "releases 200,000,000 electron volts, the largest conversion of mass into energy that has yet been produced by terrestrial means."[v] Weight for weight, uranium (as a source of energy produced by nuclear fission) is 5,000,000 times as effective as coal.[w] If harnessing sub-atomic energy could be made a practical success, our energy resources would be multiplied a thousand fold. As Dr. R. M. Langer,[x]

---

[26] This essay was first published in 1943. It was most likely penned in late 1942 and early 1943, during the middle of World War II and before it was clear what the outcome of that war would be. White had predicted war between capitalist nations since at least the late 1920s. In 1931 he had written "Anyone who has any vision and grasp of cultural processes must realize war is not only likely but even imminent. Indeed, one might say that capitalism needs a war now…" (in Peace 2007:11). White believed that warfare would lead to the destruction of the capitalist system.

[27] Notice a strong utopian thread in White's writing here and later. Provided enough energy can be found, the destiny of humanity is civilization and a new social order. It follows from White's logic that the new social order, since it is better matched to technology, will be superior to the old. Progress is our most important product.

[28] Fears about limits of the world's energy supplies are nothing new. The estimates White cites here are similar to some of those given during the energy crisis thirty years later.

research associate in physics at California Institute of Technology, has put it:

> The face of the earth will be changed. . . . Privilege and class distinctions will become relics because things that make up the good life will be so abundant and inexpensive. War will become obsolete because of the disappearance of those economic stresses that immemorially have caused it. . . . The kind of civilization we might expect . . . is so different in kind from anything we know that even guesses about it are futile.

To be able to harness sub-atomic energy would, without doubt, create a civilization surpassing sober imagination of today. But not everyone is as confident as Dr. Langer that this advance is imminent. Some experts have their doubts, some think it a possibility. Time alone will tell.[29]

But there is always the sun, from which man has derived all of his energy, directly or indirectly, in the past. And it may be that it will become, directly, our chief source of power in the future. Energy in enormous amounts reaches the earth daily from the sun. "The average intensity of solar energy in this latitude amounts to about 0.1 of a horse power per square foot" (Furnas 1941:426). "Enough energy falls on about 200 square miles of an arid region like the Mojave Desert to supply the [present needs of the] United States" (Furnas 1941:427). But the problem is, of course, to harness it effectively and efficiently.[y] The difficulties do not seem insuperable. It will doubtless be done, and probably before a serious diminution of power from dwindling resources of oil and coal overtakes us. From a power standpoint the outlook for the future is not too dark for optimism.

We turn now to an interesting and important fact, one highly significant to the history of anthropology: The thesis set forth in the preceding pages is substantially the same as that advanced by Lewis H. Morgan and E. B. Tylor many decades ago.[30] We have expounded it in somewhat different form and words; our presentation is, perhaps, more systematic and explicit. At one point we have made a significant change in their theoretical scheme: we begin the third great stage of cultural evolution with engines rather than with writing. But essentially our thesis is that of the Evolutionist school as typified by Morgan and Tylor.

According to Morgan, culture developed as man extended and improved his control over his environment, especially with regard to the food supply.[31] The "procurement of subsistence" is man's "primary need" (p. 525).[z]

> The important fact that mankind commenced at the bottom of the scale and worked up, is revealed in an expressive manner by their

---

[29] White wrote this before the invention of the atomic bomb and the nuclear power plant. In the 1950s, his writing seemed almost prescient. Many people then believed that nuclear energy would result in electric power so inexpensive it would not be worth metering. White, and others, pointed out that such a development would have profound effects on social structure. Langer (quoted here) is perhaps disingenuous when he writes that guesses are futile; the type of society he describes is precisely that predicted by Marx.

[30] There are many references to Morgan's and Tylor's scheme of cultural evolution in the preceding passages. Here, White makes their contribution to his work explicit. White's detailed acknowledgment of Morgan and Tylor must be seen as an attack on most of American anthropology of his time—much of Boasian anthropology was a reaction against the evolutionism of nineteenth-century writers such as Morgan and Tylor. Boas and his students dismissed their work as logically flawed, insufficiently scientific, and implicitly racist. White's rehabilitation of

Morgan and Tylor in the pages of *American Anthropologist* (where this essay first appeared) must have seemed audacious to his contemporaries. His repeated quotation of them in these passages was a goad to established anthropological opinion. White later wrote, "I was ridiculed and scoffed at. Everyone knew that evolutionism was dead." He quotes Ralph Linton (1893–1953), an eminent anthropologist of the time, as saying that he, White, "ought to be given the courtesy extended to suspected horse thieves and shady gamblers in the days of the Wild West, namely, to allow them to get out of town before sundown" (quoted in Carneiro 1981:229).

[31] White's first teaching post was at Buffalo, Morgan's hometown. While there, he read Morgan's work and was profoundly affected by it. He later edited Morgan's letters and journals and produced a definitive edition of Morgan's *Ancient Society*. He was certainly the greatest scholar of Morgan's work of his era. Harris has written, "In every respect, White's *The Evolution of Culture* is the modern equivalent of Morgan's *Ancient Society*" (1968:643).

successive arts of subsistence. Upon their skill in this direction, the whole question of human supremacy on the earth depended. Mankind are the only beings who may be said to have gained an absolute control over the production of food; which at the outset they did not possess above other animals. Without enlarging the basis of subsistence, mankind could not have propagated themselves into other areas not possessing the same kinds of food, and ultimately over the whole surface of the earth; and, lastly, without obtaining an absolute control over both its variety and amount, they could not have multiplied into populous nations. It is accordingly probable that the great epochs of human progress have been identified, more or less directly, with the enlargement of the sources of subsistence (p. 19). When the great discovery was made that the wild horse, cow, sheep, ass, sow and goat might be tamed, and, when produced in flocks and herds, become a source of permanent subsistence, it must have given a powerful impulse to human progress (p. 534).

And

the acquisition of farinaceous food by cultivation must be regarded as one of the greatest events in human experience (p. 42).

Morgan is much concerned with the significance of technology and its development:

"The domestic animals supplementing human muscle with animal power, contributed a new factor of the highest value" (p. 26). The bow and arrow, "the first deadly weapon for the hunt, . . . must have given a powerful upward influence to ancient society," since it made man more effective in the food quest (pp. 21–22). "The plow drawn by animal power may be regarded as inaugurating a new art" (p. 26). The "production of iron gave the plow with an iron point and a better spade and axe" (p. 26). Many other inventions, such as pottery, adobe brick, metallurgy—when man "had invented the furnace, and produced iron from ore, nine tenths of the battle for civilization was won" (p. 43)—are emphasized as motive forces of cultural development. "The most advanced portion of the human race were halted, so to express it, at certain stages of progress, until some great invention or discovery, such as the domestication of

animals or the smelting of iron ore, gave a new and powerful impulse forward" (pp. 39–40).

Morgan shows how technological advance brings about social change: technological evolution produces social evolution. In many places, but particularly in Part IV of *Ancient Society,* he shows how property, which accumulates through "an enlargement of the means of subsistence" and through a development of the individual arts, affects and changes the constitution of society. "Property and office were the foundations upon which aristocracy planted itself" (p. 551). Also,

From . . . the increased abundance of subsistence through field agriculture, nations began to develop, numbering many thousands under one government. . . . The localization of tribes in fixed areas and in fortified cities, with the increase of the numbers of the people, intensified the struggle for the possession of the most desirable territories. It tended to advance the art of war, and to increase the rewards of individual prowess. These changes of condition and of the plan of life indicate the approach of civilization which was to overthrow gentile and establish political society (p. 540).

We find essentially the same ideas in Tylor. Like Morgan, Tylor declares that man's "first need is to get his daily food" (p. 206).[aa] Culture develops as man's control over his environment, especially over the food supply, increases. Mankind advanced from savagery to barbarism when they took to agriculture: "With the certain supply of food which can be stored until next harvest, settled village and town life is established, with immense results in the improvement of arts, knowledge, manners and government" (p. 24). "Those edible grasses," says Tylor, "which have been raised by cultivation into the cereals, such as wheat, barley, rye, and by their regular and plentiful supply have become the mainstay of human life and the *great moving power of civilization*" (p. 215; emphasis ours).

A pastoral economy, according to Tylor, is superior to that of a hunting and gathering (wild food) economy, but inferior to an agricultural economy. A combination of agriculture and animal husbandry is superior to either way of life by itself (pp. 24, 220).

Social evolution comes as a consequence of technological development: To this "change of habit [i.e., from a wild food economy to agriculture] may be plainly in great part traced the expansion of industrial arts and the creation of higher social and political institutions" (p. 118; article "Anthropology," in *Encyclopaedia Britannica*, 11th ed.).

With the development of agriculture and the industrial arts comes a struggle for the most desirable territories (as Morgan puts it) and warfare "for gain" rather than "for quarrel or vengeance" (Tylor, p. 225). The consequences of this warfare for gain are tremendous: ". . . captives, instead of being slain, are brought back for slaves, and especially set to till the ground. By this agriculture is much increased, and also a new division of society takes place . . . Thus we see how in old times the original equality of men broke up, a nation dividing into an aristocracy of warlike freemen, and an inferior laboring caste" (p. 225). "It was through slave labor that agriculture and industry increased, that wealth accumulated, and leisure was given to priests, scribes, poets, philosophers, to raise the level of men's minds" (p. 435). Furthermore, according to Tylor, warfare, among culturally advanced peoples, produces "two of the greatest facts in history— the organized army . . . and the confederation of tribes . . ." (pp. 432–433); tribes become states, primitive society gives way to civil society.

Tylor is much interested in the ways in which man harnesses the forces of nature and the extent to which energy is harnessed. "It was a great movement in civilization," he says, when man harnessed water power (p. 204). He speaks of the "civilized world . . . drawing an immense supply of power from a new source, the coal burnt in the furnace of the steam-engine, which is already used so wastefully that economists are uneasily calculating how long this stored-up fossil force will last, and what must be turned to next—tide force or sun's heat—to labor for us" (pp. 204–205).

Tylor clearly recognizes the problem we have dealt with in this essay when he speculates: "It is an interesting problem in political economy to reckon the means of subsistence in our country during the agricultural and pastoral period, and to compare them with the resources we now gain from coal, in doing home-work and manufacturing goods to exchange for foreign produce. Perhaps the best means of realizing what coal is to us, will be to consider, that of three Englishmen now [1881], one at least may be reckoned to live by coal, inasmuch as without it the population would have been so much less" (p. 272). The energy significance of modern civilization lies in the fact that "in modern times, man seeks more and more to change the laborer's part he played in early ages, for the higher duty of director or controller of the world's forces" (p. 205).

Thus, we see that our essay is substantially a systematic exposition of the ideas of Morgan and Tylor.[32] Man is an animal. His first and greatest need is food. Control over habitat in general and food supply in particular is effected by means of tools (of all kinds, weapons included). Through invention and discovery the technological means of control are extended and improved. Social evolution follows upon technological evolution.

At one point we have made an innovation. Both Morgan (p. 12) and Tylor (p. 24) use the origin of writing to mark the beginning of the third great era of cultural development, "Civilization." In our scheme, "civilization" begins with the invention of the steam engine as a practical means of harnessing energy.[33]

---

[32] White's portrayal of Morgan and Tylor conceals a very important difference between their thinking and his own. Morgan and Tylor, like many other nineteenth-century evolutionists, generally saw social change as driven by psychic unity. Although the material aspects of a society may indicate the level of evolution it had attained, progress was ultimately dependent on the organic unfolding of germs of thought. White, on the other hand, proposed that humans' biologically based need to make life secure was the force driving cultural evolution.

[33] White's appreciation of Morgan was enhanced by the importance given him by Marx and Engels, who saw Morgan's *Ancient Society* as providing independent confirmation of their model of social and historical development. For this reason, Soviet communists in the first half of this century often had an unusually detailed understanding of Morgan. White would have been exposed to this on his trip to the Soviet Union in 1929.

Although Morgan and Tylor both deal directly with the energy factor in cultural development, they lose sight of it when they consider writing. Writing is not a motive force. What change would writing have effected in the culture of the Arunta, or the Eskimo, or the Iroquois? It would not have altered their way of life in any essential respect. The culture of the ancient Peruvians, which lacked writing, was quite as advanced as that of the Aztecs who had writing. And in our own culture, writing has served to preserve and perpetuate—when it has not sanctified—the ignorance and superstitions of our barbaric ancestors quite as much as it has promoted progress and enlightenment.

But, if writing is not to be considered a motive force in cultural development, the human organism, domesticated animals, cultivated plants, water wheels, windmills, steam engines, etc., are motive forces (or the means of harnessing energy). What we have done is to reduce all specific, concrete motive forces in cultural development to a single, abstract, common term: energy. To classify cultures as "wild food, domestic food, and literate," as Morgan and Tylor did, is illogical; it is like classifying vehicles as "three-wheeled, four-wheeled, and pretty." We classify cultures according to the way, or ways, in which they harness energy and the manner in which it is put to work to serve human needs.

In the foregoing we have, we believe, a sound and illuminating theory of cultural evolution. We have hold of principles, fundamental principles, which are operative in all cultures at all times and places. The motive force of cultural evolution is laid bare, the mechanisms of development made clear. The nature of the relationship between social institutions on the one hand and technological instruments on the other is indicated. Understanding that the function of culture is to serve the needs of man, we find that we have an objective criterion for evaluating culture in terms of the extent to which, and the efficiency with which, human needs are satisfied by cultural means. We can measure the amounts of energy expended; we can calculate the efficiency of the expenditure of energy in terms of measurable quantities of goods and services produced. And, finally, as we see, these measurements can be expressed in mathematical terms.[34]

The theory set forth in the preceding pages was, as we have made clear, held by the foremost thinkers of the Evolutionist school of the nineteenth century, both in England and in America. Today they seem to us as sound as they did to Tylor and Morgan, and, if anything, more obvious. It seems almost incredible that anthropologists of the twentieth century could have turned their backs upon and repudiated such a simple, sound, and illuminating generalization, one that makes the vast range of tens of thousands of years of culture history intelligible. But they have done just this.[bb] The anti-evolutionists, led in America by Franz Boas, have rejected the theory of evolution in cultural anthropology and have given us instead a philosophy of "planless hodge-podge-ism."[35]

It is not surprising, therefore, to find at the present time the most impressive recognition of the significance of technological progress in cultural evolution in the writings of a distinguished physicist, the Nobel prize winner, Robert A. Millikan:[cc]

The changes that have occurred within the past hundred years not only in the external conditions under which the average man, at least in this

---

[34] Boas and most of his students believed that universal laws of the evolution of human culture could not be formulated and that thinkers such as Morgan and Tylor were ethnocentric. However, Boas' specific criticism of the evolutionists was based on flaws in their method—he claimed that they were insufficiently scientific. Here, White answers this criticism by showing what he believes are objective, empirical criteria for the comparison of cultures.

[35] The "planless hodge-podge-ism" refers to a frequently quoted passage in the work of Robert Lowie (1883–1957),

a student of Boas. In the final paragraph of his widely read *Primitive Society,* Lowie wrote, "To that planless hodge-podge, that thing of shreds and patches called civilization, its historian can no longer yield superstitious reverence" (1920:441). Although it stands at variance with much of Lowie's other work, this statement has often been used to caricature historical particularism.

western world, passes life on earth, but in his superstitions . . . his fundamental beliefs, in his philosophy, in his conception of religion, in his whole world outlook, are probably greater than those that occurred during the preceding four thousand years all put together. Life seems to remain static for thousands of years and then shoot forward with amazing speed. The last century has been one of those periods of extraordinary change, the most amazing in human history. If, then, you ask me to put into one sentence the cause of that recent rapid and enormous change I should reply: "It is found in the discovery and utilization of the means by which heat energy can be made to do man's work for him."

Tucked away in the pages of Volume II of a manual on European archaeology, too, we find a similar expression from a distinguished American scholar, George G. MacCurdy:[dd,36]

The *degree of civilization* of any epoch, people, or group of peoples *is measured by ability to utilize energy for human advancement or needs.* Energy is of two kinds, internal and external or free. Internal energy is that of the human body or machine, and its basis is food. External energy is that outside the human body and its basis is fuel. Man has been able to tap the great storehouse of external energy. Through his internal energy and that acquired from external sources, he has been able to overcome the opposing energy of his natural environment. *The difference between these two opposing forces is the gauge of civilization* (emphasis ours).

Thus, this view is not wholly absent in anthropological theory in America today although extremely rare and lightly regarded. The time will come, we may confidently expect, when the theory of evolution will again prevail in the science of culture as it has in the biological and the physical sciences. It is a significant fact that in cultural anthropology alone among the sciences is a philosophy of anti-evolutionism respectable—a fact we would do well to ponder.[37]

NOTES

[a] By "energy" we mean "the capacity for performing work."

[b] Cf. Leslie A. White, *The Symbol: The Origin and Basis of Human Behavior* (Philosophy of Science, Vol. 7, October, 1940), pp. 451–463.

[c] See Leslie A. White, *Science Is Sciencing* (Philosophy of Science, Vol. 5, October, 1938), pp. 369–389, for a discussion of this general point of view.

[d] "Natural science" is a redundancy. All science is natural; if it is not natural it is not science.

[e] Actually, of course, it is not wholly constant; there may be progress in music, myth-making, etc., regardless of technology. A men's club, however, is still a men's club, whether the underlying technology be simple and crude or highly developed. But, since the overwhelming portion of cultural development is due to technological progress, we may legitimately ignore that small portion which is not so dependent by regarding it a constant.

[f] "There is only one cultural reality that is not artificial, to wit: the culture of all humanity at all periods and in all places," R. H. Lowie, *Cultural Anthropology: A Science* (American Journal of Sociology, Vol. 42, 1936), p. 305.

[g] We say "per year" although "per unit of time" would serve as well, because in concrete cultural situations a year would embrace the full round of the seasons and the occupations and actions appropriate thereto.

---

[36] George G. MacCurdy (1863–1947) was a founding member of the American Anthropological Association and its president in 1931. An expert on European Prehistory, he was curator of Yale's Peabody Museum and, in 1921, the first director of the American School for Prehistoric Research, an important archaeological research organization between World Wars I and II.

[37] Despite his rejection by the Boasians, White had a profound effect on many younger scholars. He spent almost his entire forty-year academic career at the University of Michigan and was known as a brilliant and challenging teacher. Through his students, he had a powerful impact not only on cultural anthropology but on archaeology and physical anthropology as well. His students include cultural anthropologists Robert Carneiro, David Kaplan, and Napoleon Chagnon; archaeologists Louis Binford and Jeffrey Parsons; and physical anthropologists Frank Livingston, George Armelagos, and Jack Kelso, as well as many others in each of these fields.

^h The cultural evolutionists have been criticized for identifying progress with evolution by pointing out that these two words are not synonymous. It is as true as it is obvious that they are not synonymous—in the dictionary. But by and large, in the history of human culture, progress and evolution *have gone hand in hand*.

ⁱ See Tylor, *Primitive Culture,* Vol. I, p. 14 (London, 1929 printing) for another respect in which, in the theory of evolution, "the student of the habits of mankind has a great advantage over the student of the species of plants and animals."

^j "Commencing probably with the dog . . . followed . . . by the capture of the young of other animals and rearing them, not unlikely, *from the merest freak of fancy,* it required time and experience to discover the utility of each . . ." (emphasis ours). Morgan, *Ancient Society,* p. 42 (Holt ed.).

^k *Introduction to Cultural Anthropology* (New York, 1940 ed.), pp. 51–52. In this argument Lowie leans heavily upon Eduard Hahn, whose work, incidentally, appeared many years after *Ancient Society* ("Subsistence," p. 303, in *General Anthropology,* F. Boas, ed., New York, 1938; *History of Ethnological Theory,* p. 112 ff., New York, 1937).

^l Following Morgan and Tylor, we use "savagery" to designate cultures resting upon a wild-food basis, "barbarism" for cultures with a domestic food basis. Our use of "civilization," however, differs from that of Tylor and Morgan (see p. 355).

^m "Finds in the Near East seem to indicate that the domestication of plants and animals in that region was followed by an extraordinary flowering of culture," Ralph Linton, *The Present Status of Anthropology* (Science, Vol. 87, 1938), p. 245.

ⁿ But this does not mean that agriculture *must be preceded* by a pastoral economy in the course of cultural development. Contrary to a notion current nowadays, none of the major evolutionists ever maintained that farming must be preceded by herding.

^o It is true, of course, that powder is used in blasting in quarries, etc., and is to this extent a motive force in culture-building. But energy employed in this way is relatively insignificant quantitatively. The bow and arrow inaugurated cultural advance because in its economic context it provided man with food in greater quantity or with less effort. The gun, in its hunting context, has had the opposite effect, that of reducing the food supply by killing off the game. In their military contexts, neither the bow and arrow or the gun has been a culture-builder. The mere conquest or extermination of one tribe or nation by another, the mere change from one dynasty or set of office holders to another, is not culture-building.

^p *Science and the World Tomorrow* (Scientific Monthly, Sept. 1939) p. 211. These figures do not, however, tell the whole story for they ignore the vast amount of energy harnessed in the form of cultivated plants and domesticated animals.

^q We may be permitted thus to distinguish two different ways of harnessing energy although each involves fire and fuel. By "fire" we indicate such energy uses of fire which preceded the steam engine—clearing forests, burning logs to make dugout canoes, etc. By "fuel" we designate energy harnessed by steam, gasoline, etc., engines.

^r Technologically a freeman and a slave are equal, both being energy in homo sapiens form. Sociologically, there is, of course, a vast difference between them. Sociologically, a slave is not a human being; he is merely a beast of burden who can talk.

^s According to E. H. Hull, of the General Electric Research Laboratory, the power equivalent of "a groaning and sweating slave" is "75 watts of electricity, which most of us can buy at the rate of two-fifths of a cent an hour." *Engineering: Ancient and Modern* (Scientific Monthly, November, 1939), p. 463.

^t C. C. Furnas, *Future Sources of Power* (Science, Nov. 7, 1941), p. 425.

^u Ibid., p. 426.

^v Herbert L. Anderson, *Progress in Harnessing Power from Uranium* (Scientific Monthly, June 1940).

^w Robert D. Potter, *Is Atomic Power at Hand?* (Scientific Monthly, June, 1940), p. 573.

^x *Fast New World* (Collier's, July 6, 1940).

^y See C. C. Abbot, *Utilizing Heat from the Sun* (Smithsonian Miscellaneous Collections, Vol. 98, No. 5, March 30, 1939).

^z The page references are to Morgan's *Ancient Society,* Henry Holt edition.

^{aa} Page references are to Tylor's *Anthropology* (New York, Appleton & Co. edition of 1916).

^{bb} One distinguished anthropologist has gone so far as to declare that "the theory of cultural evolution [is] to my mind the most inane, sterile, and pernicious theory ever conceived in the history of science . . ." B. Laufer, in a review of Lowie's *Culture and Ethnology* (American Anthropologist, Vol. 20, 1918), p. 90.

^{cc} Op. cit., p. 211.

^{dd} *Human Origins* (New York, 1933), Vol. II, pp.134–135.

17. *The Patrilineal Band*[a]

JULIAN STEWARD (1902–1972)

LOOSE AGGREGATES OF comparatively independent families such as those of the Shoshoni occur only rarely because in most parts of the world subsistence patterns required sufficient regularity of cooperation and leadership to give definite form and stability to multifamily social groups. There are many kinds of such multifamily groups of which the patrilineal band is but one.

The patrilineal band illustrates several concepts. First, it is a cultural type whose essential features- -patrilineality, patrilocality, exogamy, land ownership, and lineage composition—constituted a cultural core which recurred cross-culturally with great regularity, whereas many details of technology, religion, and other aspects of culture represent independent variables, the nature of which was determined by diffusion or by unique local circumstances. Second, its cultural core resulted from ecological adaptations which, under the recurrent conditions of environment and subsistence technology, could vary only within minor limits. Third, it represents a level of sociocultural integration slightly higher than that of the Shoshoni family; for its multifamily aggregates found cohesion not only in kinship relations but in cooperative hunting, in common landownership, and to some extent in joint ceremonies.[1]

I shall analyze the cultures of these bands as they occurred among the Bushmen of South Africa, some of the Congo Negritos of Central Africa, some Philippine Negritos, the Australians, the Tasmanians, some southern California Shoshonean-speaking groups, and the Ona of Tierra del Fuego. Other tribes besides those covered in the present survey no doubt had the same pattern.

The essential features of these bands are most readily explained as the independent product of similar patterns of adaptation of technology and certain social forms to the environment. There are only two other possible explanations of the patrilineal band. First, that the pattern was borrowed from neighboring tribes. This explanation is untenable since their neighbors did not have the pattern. Second, that the pattern is the heritage of some archaic culture which developed at an early period of human history and has been preserved ever since. Perhaps some social patterns do have great persistence, but they must meet some need. It would be stretching credulity much too far to suppose that a pattern which is closely adapted to a special kind of subsistence had persisted for thousands of years among tribes who had wandered through dozens of unlike environments to the remotest corners of the earth, especially when other hunting and gathering tribes had lost these patterns and acquired types of society appropriate to their mode of life. Moreover, like most cultural historical theories, neither the hypothesis of diffusion nor of archaic heritage provides an explanation of how and why the patrilineal band developed in the first place.

From *Theory of Culture Change, the Methodology of Multilinear Evolution* (1955)

---

[1] Steward's preoccupation with the causes of culture is immediately evident in this first passage. Unlike the historical particularists, Steward was interested in discovering general laws of culture.

Steward divided culture into core and secondary features. He probably got the division from his professor A. L. Kroeber, who divided culture into value and utility components—Steward's *culture core* was similar to Kroeber's *utility culture*. It consisted of those cultural traits that Steward felt were closest to subsistence activities and economic arrangements. A key difference between the two men is that Kroeber thought the value culture more interesting and important than the utility culture, whereas Steward focused his studies on the utility features. Collections of elements of the culture core that regularly occur cross-culturally, such as the patrilineal band described here, he termed *culture types*.

The cultural ecological hypothesis on the other hand is not only explanatory but it is by far the simplest and most consistent with the facts.[2]

The cultural ecological explanation of the patrilineal band hinges on an identity of exploitative patterns rather than of technology or environment. Technology and environment were similar in crucial respects, but they were not identical in their totality. Cultures do not exploit their entire environments, and it is, therefore, necessary to consider only those features which bear upon the productive patterns.[3] The environments of the patrilineal bands were similar in that, first, they had limited and scattered food resources, which not only restricted population to a low density but which prevented it from assembling in large, permanent aggregates. Second, the principal food resource was game, which unlike wild seeds, may be profitably taken collectively. Third, the game occurred in small, nonmigratory bands rather than in large, migratory herds. This kind of game can support only small aggregates of people, who remain within a restricted territory. Large herds, on the other hand, support much larger aggregates who can remain together as they follow the herds. These latter aggregates were bilateral or composite bands.

Dispersed and small game herds are, therefore, a condition of patrilineal bands, but this does not mean identity of environment, for deserts, jungles, and mountains tend to limit the number of game and the distance it could wander.[4] Of the tribes examined here, the Bushmen, Australians, and southern California Shoshoneans lived in areas which had sparse game because of extreme aridity. Moreover, all were affected by the limited sources of water. In Tierra del Fuego, the habitat is one of wet plains but guanaco[5] and small rodents, the principal foods, were scattered and nonmigratory. The Congo Negritos[6] and the Philippine Negritos lived in the tropical rain forests, the former in lowlands and the latter in mountains.

Exploitative technology of these societies varied considerably in detail, but in all cases it included weapons of about equal efficiency and

---

[2] In this passage, Steward differentiates his own cultural ecological approach from that of the historical particularists. He believed historical particularism had little explanatory power. He further distinguished himself from the nineteenth-century evolutionists such as Morgan and Tylor, who saw the existence of such bands as survivals of some preexisting social form, precisely the second possibility that Steward mentions and discounts here. Unlike other Boasians, Steward's research emphasized cross-cultural comparison, but his rejection of the idea of psychic unity separates his work from the comparative method of the nineteenth-century evolutionists.

[3] Steward's cultural ecology is often misunderstood as a sort of ecological determinism, but his emphasis was on the process of human labor within the environment. Steward was concerned with the technological process by which people exploited their environment, and his analysis focused on how different subsistence strategies required different social structures. This emphasis derives from Steward's reading of Marx.

[4] Here and below, Steward focuses on the interplay between environment and technology. The idea that environment determined culture—a position known as geographical determinism—was not new. One prominent advocate was

the British historian Henry Thomas Buckle (1821–1862), who believed history to be governed by laws of nature. The development of nations could be explained by the general effect of nature on the human mind as well as the specific effects of climate, food, soil, and so on. American anthropologist Clark Wissler (1870–1947), a student of Boas, was also interested in environment and culture. His research convinced him that there was a relationship between the two. In a series of works, including *The Relation of Nature to Man in Aboriginal America* (1926), Wissler attempted to map American cultural areas based on the principal modes of food production. Steward was not a geographic determinist such as Buckle, and his formulation was more sophisticated than that of Wissler. He believed that certain types of society are extremely likely to occur under particular conditions of technology and environment.

[5] *Guanaco:* a South American ruminant, of which the llama and alpaca are domesticated varieties.

[6] *Negrito:* In Steward's day, the parlance of racial classification included the term *Negrito,* used for short, dark-skinned peoples. These included people in Africa, India, the Philippines, and the Malay Peninsula. The term is rarely used today.

hunting patterns which entailed as much co-operation as circumstances permitted. The Bushmen used bows, poisoned arrows, clubs, pitfalls, poisoned springs, grass fires, dogs, and surrounds. The Congo Negritos employed bows, poisoned and nonpoisoned arrows, spears, knives, and long game nets. The Shoshoneans had bows, thrown clubs, traps, nets, surrounds, and drives. The Ona used bows, spears, clubs, slings, and spring pole nooses. Australian technology may have been less efficient in that it lacked the bow, but it included clubs, spears, and the spear-thrower. The sociological effect of hunting scattered game individually or collectively was the same everywhere.

The interaction between a bow-spear-club technology and a small, nonmigratory herd food resource tended to produce the patrilineal band. This type of band was the normal result of the adaptive processes of cultural ecology, and though various factors constantly operated to destroy the ideal pattern, as will be shown, interaction of technology and environment was such as to restore it. Only a basic change in environment or technology could have eliminated the patrilineal band. The inevitability of such bands under the given conditions is shown by its persistence along with clans, moieties, and other special patterns in the different groups, and, in the case of the Congo, an interdependence of the hunting Negritos and farming Bantu tribes who inhabited the same area.

With a given population density, the size of the territory and of the band which owns it are direct variables. If the group is enlarged the territory must also be increased in order to support it. Among the ethnic groups in question, however, the population is sparse, ranging from a maximum which seldom exceeds one person per 5 square miles to one person per 50 or more square miles. This prevents indefinite enlargement of the band because there would be no means of transporting the food to the people or the people to the food. The area which the band can conveniently forage averages some 100 square miles and seldom exceeds 500 square miles, a tract roughly 20 miles to a side. Consequently, the band averages 50 individuals and seldom exceeds 100.[b] Only in regions of unusual resources—for example, where there are herds of migratory game—does the group size surpass these figures.

We now have to consider why these bands are patrilineal. First, it is characteristic of hunters in regions of sparse population for postmarital residence to be patrilocal. This has several causes. If human beings could be conceived stripped of culture, it is not unreasonable to suppose that innate male dominance would give men a commanding position.[c] If, in addition to native dominance, however, the position of the male is strengthened by his greater economic importance, as in a hunting culture,[d] or even if women are given greater economic importance than men, it is extremely probable that postmarital residence will be patrilocal.[7]

But in these small bands patrilocal residence will produce the fact or fiction that all members of the band are patrilineally related[e] and hence matrimonially taboo. Band exogamy—that is local exogamy—is therefore required. Probably at one time or another such bands have actually consisted of relatives with traceable connection. Genealogical data on the tribes of southern California, for example, show that more often than not the band comprises a true patrilineal lineage. Because life is so precarious that increase of the total population is impossible and budding collateral lineages often become extinct, the possibility is small that several independent families which have no traceable connection will develop in any band. Such families will occur only if the band is extraordinarily large. And even in this case, the fiction of relationship may be perpetuated after the connection is forgotten if

---

[7] Rather than arguing that material conditions (hunting) give rise to social forms (patrilineality), Steward here relies on the supposition of biological differences between males and females to explain the origins of patrilineality. It is an uncharacteristically weak explanation, especially given the last line of this paragraph, when he asserts the adoption of patrilocality regardless of whether males or females are relatively more influential in a society.

group unity is reinforced by patronymy, myths, and other factors.[f,8]

For these reasons, the bands of hunters who live in sparsely populated areas must ordinarily be patrilineal. But special factors may make them temporarily composite. Thus, if unrelated and hence intermarriageable families exist within a band, local exogamy and patrilocal residence with respect to the band are unnecessary. This will occur when parallel-cousin marriage is permitted or where bands have, for various reasons, become unusually large and lack any factor that would create or perpetuate a fiction of relationship between its members. Occasionally, matrilocal residence will introduce families which are not related patrilineally into a band. This will prevent strictly patrilineal inheritance of band territory and tend to weaken the fiction of relationship between band members. For these reasons, patrilineal bands at certain times or places deviate from the ideal pattern and consist of unrelated families. In this respect, they resemble composite bands, but whereas the latter normally must remain composite, patrilineal bands tend to return to their typical pattern. The factors which produce composite bands will be analyzed subsequently.

Political unity in all bands is very similar. Centralized control exists only for hunting, for rituals, and for the few other affairs that are communal. Consequently, the leader has temporary and slight authority. In patrilineal bands, he is usually the head of the lineage, which, being a status based on kinship, is usually not formally institutionalized. The shaman, however, controls many collective activities, and he is feared and respected for his supernatural power, which often gives him more influence than the other leaders. Bands which are ordinarily autonomous may temporarily unite for special occasions such as Australian and Fuegian initiation ceremonies. Although the reason for this larger unity is religious and social, food supply strictly limits the duration of multiband gatherings.

The occurrence of clans among Australians, Ojibway, and others, of moieties in Australia and in southern California, and of other social forms in no way affects the cause-and-effect relationships involved in the formation of the patrilineal band.[9] Such institutions are variables with respect to the pattern we have analyzed. Their presence or absence is to be explained by diffusion or by some special local factors and not by adaptations of technology to environment.[10]

TRIBES WITH THE PATRILINEAL BAND

In the following pages some patrilineal bands will be discussed in detail, showing reasons in each case for departures from the ideal pattern.[11]

---

[8] Notice that Steward's explanation is generally materialist. Cultural fictions (the name of the patrilineage for example) are necessitated by ecological conditions.

This materialist basis was influenced by Marx (see essay 4). The intellectual climate of his day prevented Steward from referencing Marx, but he had read Marx's work. Despite this, Steward cannot be considered a Marxist, nor was he as heavily influenced by Marx as was Leslie White, the other major American materialist of this era (see essay 16). Unlike Steward, White's work was concerned with establishing an overall evolutionary scheme for society and with the roles of conflict and class within society; these are typically Marxist issues. Steward's work lacks the characteristically Marxist emphasis on conflict as a motor of evolution. He was far more interested in showing the specific interrelations among technology, environment, and society. Further, as Harris (1968) notes, although Steward's division of culture into core and secondary features sounds superficially like Marx's division of society into base and superstructure, it is quite different. Marx saw superstructure as arising from base; Steward generally saw secondary features as virtually unrelated to the core.

[9] When the members of a tribe are divided into two groups, these divisions are called *moieties*.

[10] Critics of Steward's work point out that he explained away those things that did not fit the patterns he outlined by suggesting, as he does here, that they were secondary features resulting from diffusion or the specific history of the group under study.

[11] In this section of the essay, Steward cites evidence from a wide variety of societies to support his contention that certain environmental and technological constraints lead to the formation of patrilineal bands.

The Bushmen[g]

A hunting and gathering culture imposed upon an arid and unproductive native environment produced a sparse population among the Bushmen. Population aggregates were necessarily small[h] and the group that co-operated in various undertakings was a politically autonomous patrilineal lineage. Although the band or lineage split seasonally into smaller units, probably family groups, it owned and communally utilized a definite territory. Some hunting required joint effort of all band members, and game was often shared by all.

The bands of the Northwestern Bushmen, including the Heikum, were ordinarily patrilineal owing to patrilocal residence and local or band exogamy. The Naron bands, however, were sometimes composite because matrilocal residence, which was practiced occasionally in order that the wife's mother might help the wife with her children, introduced families which were not related patrilineally into the same band. This weakened patrilineal inheritance of the estate and tended to obviate the necessity of band exogamy, which, however, was preferred (Schapera 1930: 81–85). The Cape, Namib, and !Okung bands also tended to be composite because, although band exogamy was preferred, matrilocal residence, for a reason which has not been revealed, was sometimes practiced. Band endogamy, moreover, was facilitated by cousin marriage, parallel or cross, which was barred among the Northwestern groups (Schapera 1930:82–83;102–07).[12]

Schebesta (1931) reports what appears to be an identical pattern. The Bambuti, Efe, Bac'wa,

and Batwa of the Belgian Congo had exogamous, patrilocal, and generally autonomous sibs ("sippe") or families of male relatives numbering sixty to sixty-five persons each. Apparently, the "totemic clans" of these people were the same as lineages, that is, they were localized clans or sibs.[13]

Central African Negritos

Several scattered groups of Negritos or pygmies living in the dense tropical rain forests of the Congo in equatorial Africa also belonged to the patrilineal band type. The bands were predominantly hunters, and the exploitative patterns produced the features typical of the patrilineal band despite the fact that the pygmies lived in a close dependency relationship with the Bantu Negroes.[14]

In the Ituri Forest (Putnam 1948:322–42), a Negro village and a pygmy band jointly owned about 100 square miles of country. The Negroes were largely farmers, and the pygmies were entirely hunters, the latter supplying the former with meat in exchange for vegetable foods. The dependence of the pygmy upon the Negro might account for the cohesion of the pygmy band and for the pattern of land-tenure, but it would not account for the patrilineality and exogamy, which must be explained by the low population density, the small band size, and the predominance of hunting.

The bands ranged in size from 100 to 200 persons, 150 being the average. All families were normally related through the male line, and the band, therefore, constituted a locally exogamous and patrilocal group. The cohesion of the lineage or band was reinforced by the belief that a totemic

---

[12] Harris (1968:667) claims that Steward's listing of factors responsible for patrilineal, complex, or matrilineal band formation are "fortuitous and quixotic." Note the reliance in this passage and later in this essay on "a reason which has not been revealed" and other such devices.

[13] Steward makes extensive use of the works of Paul Schebesta (1887–1967) a German Catholic Priest and missionary who did extensive work in anthropology. Schebesta worked in Japan, Zambia, Malaysia, the Philippines, and the Congo and wrote more than 150 books and articles. Although he was trained in the diffusionist anthropology of another German priest, Father Wilhelm Schmidt

(1868–1954, also mentioned in this essay and see note 5 in essay 38), his theoretical perspective was closer to functionalism (Dupré 1969).

[14] The fact that hunting bands of pygmies lived in close proximity to agricultural Bantus was critical for Steward. Traditional evolutionary schemes had placed agriculture far above hunting and gathering. If diffusion alone could account for cultural traits and agriculture was superior to hunting and gathering, why had the pygmies not adopted it? Steward felt he could solve this problem using a cultural-ecological approach.

animal was the ancestor of the band and by myths. The band contained unrelated families only when exceptional circumstances introduced a man from some other band, for example, when a man could not get along in his own band or when he had trouble with his Negro group. The patrilineal features resulted from the hunting pattern. The men spent all their time hunting for game which was normally scattered. They used nets in collective drives or else bows, spears, and knives in individual stalking. The game was varied and included turtles, rats, antelope, buffalo, and elephants. Hunting was restricted to the band's territory, the size of which must be interpreted as the optimum which can be exploited. Had the territory been substantially larger, the band would have surpassed a kin group in size and therefore ceased to be exogamous and patrilocal. However, the sparse population, the limitations upon the area which could be hunted, and the patrilocality after marriage produced localized lineages.

These bands sometimes tended to be composite for two reasons. First, it was customary at marriage for the husband's band to furnish a woman who married a member of his wife's band. When no woman was available, the man lived with his wife's people. Second, band endogamy, that [is], marriage between related members of the band, though felt to be a breach of incest laws, was often practiced when other bands were remote and inaccessible (Schmidt 1910:173).

The Negritos of Gabon in French Equatorial Africa were grouped in some 100 or 150 villages, each of which usually comprised one family "rangée sous l'autorité d'un seul chef, le père du clan, généralement de 30 à 35 individus mâles."[15] These seemed to be independent, patrilocal, and exogamous, and therefore true patrilineal bands.

But they belonged to some kind of larger patrilineal totemic clans, which were preferably, but not always, exogamous (Trilles 1932:20–23, 143–51, 409–18).[16]

Semang

The more or less inadequate information now available indicates that many of the Negritos of the Malay peninsula possessed the patrilineal band. Largely hunters and gatherers and more or less isolated in the sparsely settled mountain forests, the Semang groups were small, ranging, according to fragments of evidence recorded by Schebesta (1929), from individual families which were probably temporary subdivisions to groups of 50 or more persons. These seem to have been politically autonomous, landowning bands. Skeat and Blagden (1900:495–97) say that the Kedah Semang band often amounted to an enlarged family and, somewhat obscurely, that the chief was practically "the head of a family, which in this case is represented by a larger family, the tribe." It may be, however, that band territory was sometimes further subdivided among bilateral families so that each owned an area for its durian trees. Schebesta says (1929:83, 234, 279) that "the individual groups wander within the tribal boundaries but always return to their family territory, especially at the time of the durian crop" and that the trees are owned by men as family heads. These family tracts were, perhaps, comparable to the Algonkian and Althabaskan beaver-trapping territories.

That these bands were truly patrilineal is indicated by Schebesta's statement (1929) that the unit of society was the "sib" like that of the Congo Negritos, but he does not particularize its

---

[15] *"rangée . . . mâles"*: The French comment means "placed under the authority of a single leader, usually the eldest of the clan, and consisting of thirty to thirty-five men."

[16] In assembling his cases, Steward relied on historical accounts as well as then-current ethnography. The use of these sources was important for him since his intellectual achievement was to explain the presence of the band in very different and widely distributed locales. Use of his-

torical accounts was problematic, however, since it led him to use sources that were not very reliable and to discuss groups, such as the Tasmanians, which had disappeared by his era. Further, much of the information he presents here, for example, his description of the Central African Negritos, has since been shown to be invalid, or, at best, only partially correct. Does this invalidate his argument?

characteristics. Elsewhere he observes that there was considerable band exogamy and patrilocal residence, although he recorded one band that was composite. One reason for the occurrence of the latter among the Kenta Semang was that durian trees were sometimes inherited matrilineally. This would, of course, favor matrilocal residence and tend to set up a composite band.

Philippine Negritos

The predominantly hunting and gathering Philippine Negritos lived in comparative isolation from the Malaysians. They were clustered in bands which Vanoverbergh (1925:430–33), says comprise "a certain group of families." These remained in the same portion of the forest and seasonally exploited different parts of an area which had a radius of not over twenty miles. Trespass on the land of neighboring bands was not forbidden but was avoided. The land was hunted communally by its owners, but cultivated trees and honey nests were privately owned. It is not recorded, however, how trees were inherited. Bands seem to have been politically autonomous, but the lack of an institutionalized band chief is implied by the somewhat vague statement that authority rested in the father of the family.

There is some indication that Philippine Negrito bands have recently changed from patrilineal to composite.[17] Schmidt (1910:72–73), quoting Blumentritt on the Zambales-Bataam, says that the bands are now endogamous but at the end of the eighteenth century were exogamous. Present-day endogamy is further shown by the presence of unrelated families in the same band.[i] Nevertheless, patrilocal residence is re-

corded, although it is not clear whether residence is patrilocal with respect to the band or the family.

There is, therefore, some doubt as to the frequency of the two types of bands and the customs concerning residence and other matters which would produce them. It appears, however, that some factor has tended to produce a change from patrilineal to composite bands during the past century. At least one important cause of composite bands today is the practice of marrying cousins. Although marriage was preferably between cross-cousins, parallel-cousins were eligible for matrimony (Vanoverbergh 1925:425–28).[18]

Australians[j]

The relatively low productivity of Australia permitted but a sparse population which averaged only 1 person per 12 square miles for the entire continent.[k] The population was grouped into relatively small, autonomous bands which Radcliffe-Brown calls hordes. Each band comprised 20 to 50 individuals and owned 100 to 150 square miles of land. The male members of the band inherited and communally hunted their tract, which was definitely bounded and protected from trespass.[l]

These bands were truly patrilineal, and they approximated male lineages. They were almost universally exogamous and patrilocal. The idea of relationship between band members was further reinforced by kinship terminology. Even those ethnic groups which had moieties, sections (formerly called "marriage classes"), and matrilineal clans and totems had not, except in a portion of western Australia, lost the patrilineal band (Radcliffe-Brown 1931:438).

---

[17] Tracing out the ways in which culture changed was to become one of Steward's key concerns. He is known as the creator of multilinear evolutionism, which he contrasted with nineteenth-century unilineal evolution and his contemporary Leslie White's universal evolution. He argued that unlike White and his nineteenth-century predecessors, he was not interested in formulating a general, universal plan of evolution but rather with showing how particular cultures changed and developed (1955:11–19).

[18] Steward's is an uneasy evolutionism. It is perhaps best seen as a compromise between his historical-particularist training and his goal of creating an anthropology based in the discovery of causal principles. He placed societies in an essentially unilineal evolutionary scheme from family to multifamily to state civilization. He then focused on the multiple pathways that societies may take between evolutionary stages.

Tasmanians

Information on the Tasmanians, though incomplete, indicates the aboriginal presence of the patrilineal band. The scant population[m] was divided into autonomous bands of 30 to 40 persons each. Each band owned a tract of land on which it wandered seasonally in search of food. It protected its hunting rights against trespass, which was a common cause of war (Roth 1899:58–59, 104–07).

The Tasmanian band must have been patrilineal, for evidence assembled by Roth indicates, although it does not prove beyond question, that the band was exogamous and marriage patrilocal.

The Ona of Tierra del Fuego

The Ona of Tierra del Fuego fall strictly into the patrilineal band pattern. The low subsistence level, based largely upon guanaco hunting, produced a population of only one individual to 4.5 or 5 square miles. This was grouped in politically independent bands of 40 to 120 persons, each owning an average of 410 square miles. Gusinde (1931) believes that the manner of life would not have supported larger aggregates. Each territory was named, band rights to it were sanctioned by myths, and hunting privileges were protected against trespass. Although each band was politically autonomous, there was no institution of chief.

The band was patrilineal because it was exogamous and patrilocal. Local exogamy was required even among the large bands in which relationship between members was not traceable, for native theory held that each band was a male lineage.

Tehuelche of Patagonia

The Tehuelche of Patagonia, although very incompletely known, are instructive when compared with the Ona. Also dependent largely upon herds of guanaco, their economic life appears formerly to have resembled that of the Fuegians. There is evidence that they were divided into bands, each having some degree of localization[n] and led in its travels, etc., by a patrilineal chief (Outes and Bruch, 1910:126; Beerbohm 1881:93) who was called "father" (Musters 1873:194). The band chief, however, acknowledged a general cacique, who, according to Musters, had very little authority. The institution of general or tribal cacique[19] may easily have developed subsequent to the arrival of the European.

The introduction of the horse about a century and a half ago completely altered ecological conditions in Patagonia. It enabled people to move widely in pursuit of guanaco herds and to transport foods considerable distances. This would, of course, have tended to eliminate band ownership of small parcels of territory, even had it existed. It also permitted enlargement of population aggregates far beyond the size of the usual lineage. Further motivation for amalgamation of formerly separate bands was provided by internecine strife, which was stimulated by competition for foods and war against the white man. The political unit consequently increased in size and had a single, although not absolute, chief. Thus, in 1871, bands numbered as many as 400 or 500 persons, although they occasionally split into smaller groups (Musters 1873:64, 70, 96–97, 117, 188). As there is no mention of exogamy of any form, it must be assumed that these bands were composite. This is common elsewhere in bands of such size.[20]

---

[19] *Cacique* refers to a leader in Mesoamerican Indian communities.

[20] Here Steward gives an example of the effect of technological change on social structure: The introduction of the horse led to an increase in band size. Examples linking technology and social structure were essential because they were the sort of things that would leave traces in the archaeological record, which meant that archaeological data could be used to bolster Steward's theoretical position. This connection between theory in cultural anthropology and archaeology was one of the factors leading to the emergence of the new archaeology in the 1960s. Steward had, in fact, begun his career as an archaeologist working in the Columbia River valley.

Southern Californians

The Shoshonean-speaking Serrano, Cahuilla, and Luiseño, and some of the Yuman-speaking Diegueño of southern California were divided into patrilineal bands.[21] This region is exceptional in that abundance of acorns and other wild seeds permitted the unusually dense native population of one person per square mile. But this great density was accompanied by small territory size rather than large band size, probably because the very few and small sources of water prevented greater concentration of people. Therefore, bands averaged only fifty individuals and the territory only fifty square miles.

The other factors producing the patrilineal bands were those which operated elsewhere. Because of patrilocal residence coupled with the small size of the bands, most of them were actual patrilineal lineages so local exogamy was required. In addition, a band chief, "priest," ceremonies, ceremonial house and bundle, and myths contributed to group cohesion (Strong, 1927, 1929; Gifford, 1918, 1926, 1931; Kroeber, 1925, 1934). This strongly fortified patrilineal pattern may also have served to maintain the band at lineage size.

The culturally similar neighboring Cupeño provide an illuminating contrast to these groups. Because the local abundance of food and water permitted greater concentration, they were able to live in two permanent towns, each numbering some 250 persons. Each village contained several lineages and had a chief. Bands were, therefore, of the composite type (Gifford, 1926:394–96; Strong 1929:188–90, 233).

CAUSAL FORMULATION FOR PATRILINEAL BANDS

In any society there are certain cultural factors which potentially give cohesion to aggregates of several families: marriage, extension of kinship ties and corollary extensions of incest taboos, group ceremonies, myths, games, and other features. These features may be derived from cultural heritage of the group or they may be borrowed from neighboring tribes. In each group they are integrated in a total sociocultural system, but the nature of this system is not explained merely by tracing the diversified history of the features or by describing the functional interdependency of the parts. These features must be adjusted to the subsistence patterns that are established through the exploitation of a particular habitat by means of a particular technology; and the subsistence patterns are only partly explainable in terms of culture history. The use of bows and arrows, traps, hunting nets, game drives, or grass firing can generally be traced to diffusion, but the hunting patterns and the social effect of these patterns are quite unlike in areas of sparse and scattered game and in areas of large herds of migratory game. Among societies which devote a very great portion of their time and energy to food-getting, these differences in hunting patterns will greatly affect the size, permanency, composition, and general behavior patterns of the group. The extent and degree to which subsistence patterns affect the total structure of the society and the functional integration of its various parts are questions to be answered by empirical procedure.[22]

---

[21] Steward's most protracted fieldwork was among the Shoshoni in Utah, and here, as he describes Southern California peoples, he is closest to his own fieldwork interests. His fieldwork experiences were important for two reasons. First, working among the traditional Shoshoni, he was struck by the small group size and the extremely demanding environment they inhabited. In the deserts of the Great Basin, the powerful influences of environment and technology might have been more evident than they were in many other places. Second, Steward was known for his fieldwork technique. He was highly critical of ethnographic studies that used material collected from people no longer engaged in aboriginal lifestyles. He encouraged an ethnography based on recording actual behavior rather than one based on what people said about past behavior. It is ironic that in developing multilinear evolution, he, of necessity, had to rely on secondhand data collected under conditions that were not well known, precisely the type of information he distrusted.

[22] This passage contains a critique of historical particularism and functionalism and outlines Steward's theoretical position. Staking out this position brought him into direct conflict with many other Boasians. For example, in this

The patrilineal band represents a social type the principal features of which are determined within exceedingly narrow limits by the cultural ecology—by the interaction of technology and environment. Other features, such as clans, moieties, age-grades, men's tribal societies, group ceremonialism, totemism, and mythology may or may not also be present. If they do form part of the cultural inventory of the band, they are integrated to the patrilineal pattern. A causal formulation of the factors producing the patrilineal band may therefore omit these various historically-derived features, for the latter are of interest only when attention is shifted to the uniqueness of each culture and they do not help explain the patrilineal features which are the subject of inquiry.

The factors which produce the patrilineal band are:[23]

1. A population density of one person or less—usually much less—per square mile, which is caused by a hunting and gathering technology in areas of scarce wild foods;
2. An environment in which the principal food is game that is nonmigratory and scattered, which makes it advantageous for men to remain in the general territory of their birth;
3. Transportation restricted to human carriers;
4. The cultural-psychological fact, which cannot be explained by local adaptation, that groups of kin who associate together intimately tend to extend incest taboos from the biological family to the extended family thus requiring group exogamy.

These four factors interact as follows: The scattered distribution of the game, the poor transportation, and the general scarcity of the population make it impossible for groups that average over 50 or 60 persons and that have a maximum of about 100 to 150 persons to associate with one another frequently enough and to carry out sufficient joint activities to maintain social cohesion. The band consists of persons who habitually exploit a certain territory over which its members can conveniently range. Customary use leads to the concept of ownership. Were individual families to wander at will, hunting the game in neighboring areas, competition would lead to conflict. Conflict would call for alliance with other families, allies being found in related families. As the men tend to remain more or less in the territory in which they have been reared and with which they are familiar, patrilineally related families would tend to band together to protect their game resources. The territory would therefore become divided among these patrilineal bands.

It is worth noting that the nature of Great Basin Shoshonean land-use precluded the banding together of patrilineal families and landownership. For two reasons, the pine nut, which was the principal food, had a very different sociological effect than game hunting. First, good crops were so abundant that there was never competition for it. Second, abundant crops occurred

---

passage, Steward discards unique historically derived features as having no explanatory value. However, it was precisely these unique features that Kroeber and many other historical particularists were interested in documenting. They believed these showed the creative genius of humankind. Unsurprisingly, the relationship between Kroeber and Steward was not close. Kroeber considered Steward a promising but not particularly interesting student. Steward respected Kroeber but was fundamentally at odds with most of what he stood for (Wolf 1981:63).

[23] Although Steward rejected much of what his professors believed, his work was not unprecedented in American anthropology. Earlier, members of the culture area school attempted to map North and South America into a series of areas of similar cultures, which, they noted, tended to overlap with ecological zones. Otis Mason (1838–1908) formulated one such version in the 1890s, but Boas and his students Kroeber and Wissler created a more definitive mapping in the teens and early twenties (see Mason 1895, Holmes 1914, Wissler 1917). The culture area theorists tended to see environment as a passive factor placing broad restrictive limits on cultural possibilities. Steward saw the combination of technology and environment as playing a far more causal role in determining social systems.

each year in very different localities and they brought different groups together each time.[24]

Among the patrilineal bands, the component biological families associated together sufficiently often to permit an extension of incest taboos to all members. Prohibition of marriage within the immediate biological family is universal among mankind. There are generally extensions of marriage restrictions to collateral relatives of the second or third degree, though cross-cousins may marry in certain cultures. The patrilineal bands were so small that they usually consisted of known relatives who commonly fall within the prohibited degrees of relationship, and cross-cousins—the father's sister's daughter or the mother's brother's daughter—would normally be in another band. Band exogamy is therefore required.

The several features of the patrilineal band reinforce one another. Patrilocal residence after marriage because the male wishes to remain in country he knows causes an area to be habitually occupied, utilized, and defended by patrilineally-related families. Local exogamy prevents the introduction into the band of unrelated families, so that the band becomes in fact, a patrilineal lineage.[25]

The requirement that the band be exogamous may persist after traceable kinship relations in the group are forgotten if the patrilineal complex is reinforced by other features, such as names, kinship terminology, myths, ceremonies, totems, and the like. Thus, the bands of Australia, southern California, and Tierra del Fuego conform more rigidly to the pattern because they possess such supports. Among the Bushmen and Negritos patrilineal bands may often temporarily become composite bands when special conditions exist.

A theory of the patrilineal band which sought its origin in purely cultural-historical terms would be confronted by insuperable difficulties.[26] Such a theory would have to assume either that the band inherited the basic patrilineal pattern from some archaic world-wide culture or that it borrowed it from some neighboring tribes. As we have seen, primitive nonagricultural peoples in areas of seed resources, of fish, or of large game herds do not have the patrilineal band because these areas are not conducive to the exploitation of a certain restricted territory by small groups of men in the manner found among the patrilineal band peoples. It is inconceivable that this pattern could have survived the migrations of mankind over dozens of unlike environments during thousands of years. The theory of borrowing from neighbors will not stand up because the neighbors of these tribes simply do not have patrilineal bands.

A holistic or functional explanation minimizes the importance of cultural ecology by insisting that all features of the culture are equally cause and effect.[27] This simply evades the issue of causality. As we have seen, the clans, moieties, men's tribal societies, and other special features occur with only some of the patrilineal patterns and they also occur among quite different kinds

---

[24] Steward was also influenced by his work with Carl Sauer (1889–1975), a geographer interested in anthropology and archaeology who stressed an approach to geography based on the interaction of humans and environment. Sauer, who was at Berkeley during Steward's time there, had an important impact on Kroeber and his students. Sauer, incidentally, is also infamous for his belief that Irish monks visited North America before the Vikings.

[25] Steward's approach is oriented toward technology and environment, but he frequently refers to psychology as an important factor (as here, where he discusses the male's wishes). Steward's work is contemporaneous with the culture and personality school (see essays 14 and 15), which relied heavily on psychological explanations.

[26] In this passage and later, Steward attacks the other prominent theoretical positions of his time. This paragraph dismisses historical particularism; later he takes on functionalism and diffusionism.

[27] When Steward presented the first version of this paper in 1936, British functionalism was growing increasingly important in this country. A. R. Radcliffe-Brown, then at the University of Chicago, was a loud and eloquent critic of the Boasians. This passage is aimed directly at his thinking. Radcliffe-Brown identified an ecological-adaptive aspect of social structure but assigned it no particular importance. Steward argues that because of this, Radcliffe-Brown's system describes but does not explain culture.

of societies. There is a functional interrelationship between hunting in a restricted area, the male's continued residence in that area, patrilocality, and local exogamy. Exogamy within a localized patrilineal group causes the men to hunt scattered game in certain ways. The groups hunt what is available with devices at their command; men best remain in the territory where they were raised; their wives come to their territory after marriage; and the bands are so small that people are related and, given concepts of incest, local exogamy is practiced. It is not claimed that the cultural ecological factors explain everything about the patrilineal band. They explain why these bands differ from other bands which have a similar technology and similar potentialities for extending incest taboos outward from the biological family.

A common explanation of the patrilineal band is that it is merely a localized clan, and diffusionists seek to trace its source to clans elsewhere. Societies which have clans may influence patrilineal bands in two ways; first, borrowed clans may crosscut the bands but fail to change their basic patterns; second, clan myths, ceremonies, and other features may be borrowed by the band and reinforce its local unity. But diffused unilateral structure and exogamy cannot explain the adjustment of male lineages to exploitative activities. In fact, the concept of the patrilineal band has greater value in explaining the clan than vice versa. If, for reasons stated here, a localized patrilineal group develops, it is in effect a localized clan. Whether it should properly be called a clan, however, would depend upon whether it is

exogamous regardless of locality. Those groups which have reinforcing features, such as the southern California Shoshoneans, the Australians, and others, would be clans if exogamy continued after they were dislocated from their territories and the different bands mixed up. Evidently this has happened often in human history and clans have developed in many places. We shall subsequently show how the data of archaeology and ethnography support such an interpretation of the origin of clans among the Pueblo Indians of the Southwest.[28]

CULTURAL VARIABLES AND THE PATRILINEAL BAND

The features of the patrilineal band which must be explained by ecological factors are patrilineality, patrilocality, exogamy, landownership, and informal and limited leadership.[29] Many other features, however, were fairly variable in form despite this basic pattern. A substantial range of possible alternatives made diffusion a more direct explanation of their presence.

Some of the technological traits secondary to the main hunting patterns were extremely variable. Containers used in transporting, preparing, and storing food, for example, could not be elaborate, heavy, or numerous because of the nomadic life, but the materials of which they were made, their specific forms, and their decorations were quite variable. The Congo Negritos, Semang, Shoshoneans, and Ona used basketry of various weaves, shapes, and ornamentation; the Bushmen

---

[28] Kroeber had done important work in tracing the diffusion of cultural traits throughout the Southwest. In addition, radical diffusionist theories were popular in Britain and Germany when Steward wrote (see essay 8, note 1). Steward's point is that while diffusion of traits can be shown to exist, the traits are always modified to fit the ecological conditions of the society accepting them.

[29] In this section, Steward explores cultural variables that he considers secondary features, those aspects of culture not closely tied to the cultural core and determined by purely cultural-historical factors such as random innovation and diffusion. This section of the essay is fairly long

(more than 1,300 words), but much of it is a simple cataloging of cultural traits with little or no analysis of them. This presentation reflects two factors: first, Steward's training in historical particularism (the collection and cataloging of cultural traits was precisely the sort of anthropology Kroeber urged on his followers) and, second, the likelihood that Steward placed little importance on the information he presents here. From the lack of analysis and the fact that this section is only weakly articulated with the rest of the essay, it appears that Steward considered this material a collection of virtually random facts of no particular interest.

and Congo Negritos employed some pottery; the other areas utilized skins, shells, bark, or other convenient materials. Fire was made with the wooden drill by the Bushmen and Shoshoneans, with the fire saw by the Semang, and with pyrite and stone by the Ona. The Congo Negritos had no means of making fire and were forced to borrow it if their own went out. Shelters were limited by the requirement that they be quickly and easily put together of materials available. These bands used natural shelters, such as caves, when possible. Otherwise, they built mere windbreaks, brush- or skin-covered conical lodges, or dome-shaped brush houses. Similar huts are found scattered throughout the world among primitive peoples, and it would be rather profitless to speculate as to whether they diffused or not, for they are so elementary that it would require no great ingenuity to invent them. Clothing was scant and made with simple skills, but styles varied locally: string skirts or aprons, wrap-around skin skirts, breechclouts, robes, and the like, or perhaps nothing but a few smudges of paint.

Musical instruments and games were generally simple, for extensive paraphernalia was out of the question. The former were generally learned from neighboring tribes. For example, the Semang used flutes, jew's-harps, guitars, and drums borrowed from their Malay neighbors; and the Bushmen had musical bows, flutes, cocoon rattles, and drums, all probably acquired from the Bantu; while the southern California Shoshoneans used only flutes and rattles; the Australians swung bull-roarers and pounded sticks on rolled-up hides; the Ona struck sticks together; and the African Negritos thumped hollow logs.

A certain distinctiveness is evident in many features of social organization. While the formal aspects of these are attributable to diffusion, their functional significance was very similar because of their role in the total culture. Several of the bands had men's tribal societies—religious organizations into which young men were initiated during rites from which women and children were barred. The neophytes were scarified,

given hunting tests, and made to observe food taboos while religion was explained to them. The Australian societies used bull-roarers in their ceremonies, whereas the Ona used masks and special huts and had rites based on the concept of death and resurrection of the initiate. Southern California Shoshoneans lacked such societies, but their group fetish bundle, ritual, and ceremonial leader had a similar function in reinforcing group cohesion. These and other social features, however, were not necessary to existence of the patrilineal band pattern, and they can hardly constitute the primary basis of cultural typology. The Semang have no men's society.

The presence in any society of the patrilineal band and the tribal society must be "explained" in different terms. The secret society is scattered throughout the world in many kinds of cultures and there is little doubt that it represents a very ancient pattern which has fitted certain psychological-cultural needs as well as a variety of cultural functions so well that it has persisted in spite of tremendous cultural change and that it has even diffused from one type of culture to another. The secret society can in no way be considered a cause of the patrilineal pattern or of the type of land use that underlies this pattern.[30]

There were other social features which, from the point of view of the patrilineal pattern, were secondary or variable and which were found also among tribes lacking the patrilineal band. Some of the northern Australians had matrilineal moieties, which were probably diffused from Melanesia. The combination of these with localized patrilineal, exogamous groups created a very complex organization. The uniqueness of this organization—the fact that it consisted of functionally interrelated parts—does not mean that the origin of its parts cannot be treated separately and in causal terms. The southern California Shoshoneans had moieties which cut across localized patrilineal bands, but these functioned primarily at death ceremonies.

The religious patterns of these tribes were affected by the ecological adjustments principally

---

[30] Here and later, Steward attempts to demonstrate that the cultural features he believes are secondary have little causal significance for the cultural core: subsistence, technology, and social structure.

in a negative sense: they lacked complicated and institutionalized worship of the kinds found among more developed cultures, there being little ceremonialism dedicated to group purposes. Rites were concerned primarily with birth, puberty, sickness, death, and other crisis situations of individuals. The patterns of these crisis rites and of shamanism show certain general similarity to one another and very probably they represent in large part an ancient heritage which survived throughout the world in cultures of many kinds. That is, these rites show a great deal of stability, their basic patterns persisting in many cultural contexts which are quite dissimilar. This fact makes it obviously quite absurd to conceive that religion could be the starting point, the primary factor, in an investigation of the origin of social forms and economic patterns. Religion was a functional part of each culture, but from the point of view of the basic social types and cultural ecological determinants its form was a relatively independent variable.[31]

The local forms and functions of the puberty rites are an illustration of the considerable range of variations that could be woven into the basic pattern of the patrilineal band.[32] We have already seen how puberty rites stressed the maturing of young men among the Northwest Bushmen, the Australians, and the Ona to the extent that the adult males constituted a secret organization. The Congo Negritos may also have had such societies; at least, it is clear that in the Ituri Forest young Pygmy men together with the sons of their Negro overlords were circumcised in groups every few years, each group becoming an age-grade society. The other tribes wholly lacked any such

formal grouping of their males. Among the Semang, children of both sexes were merely inducted into the status of puberty by a simple rite at which they were painted, tattooed, scarified, and had their teeth filed. The Shoshoneans of southern California, like their nonpatrilineal neighbors, had observances for both sexes. Pubescent girls were "roasted" in a pit and required to race each day, to scratch themselves only with a stick, and to refrain from drinking cold water. Boys were drugged, lectured on tribal lore and morality, subjected to biting ants, and required to dance. Among the Semang both sexes were painted, scarified, and tattooed at adolescence.

In all these tribes, as in hundreds of others throughout the world, the shaman's chief function was to cure disease by supernatural means, generally through singing and sucking out the supposed cause of disease. He had certain other functions, however, which varied with the special local patterning of religion. Among the Bushmen, for example, he officiated at puberty ceremonies, and among the Semang he mediated between mankind and the thunder god.

Death observances were matters of private ritual among most of these bands, but the Shoshoneans of southern California developed them into a ceremony which greatly strengthened group cohesion. An annual mourning ceremony was held under the direction of a special ceremonial leader, while images of the deceased were burned and myths were recited to commemorate the dying god. This ceremony seems to have contributed greatly to the cohesion of Shoshonean bands, and it may partly explain why the bands continued to regard themselves as kin

---

[31] Here Steward reaffirms his basic materialism: Material conditions influence ideas, not vice versa. This passage seems to be a direct attack on Tylor, who saw the progressive rationalization of religion as one of the fundamental processes driving cultural change (see essay 2). But why would Steward attack Tylor more than a half century after the publication of *Primitive Culture* and two decades after the latter's death? It is more likely that he was thinking of Max Weber. The English translation of Weber's highly influential *The Protestant Ethic and the Spirit of Capitalism*

had been published in 1930, not many years before the first appearance of Steward's essay. In this book Weber argued that Protestant theology was critical to the advent of capitalism in Europe.

[32] Steward turns the historical particularists' practice of cataloging cultural traits against them. Here, his style of writing is significant. By presenting a seemingly random listing of traits, he draws the reader to the conclusion that such a presentation, and hence the historical-particularist research program, can have little explanatory value.

groups and to practice exogamy after they became dislocated from their territories, scattered, and lost genealogical knowledge of their relationship to one another.[33]

NOTES

[a] This is an adaptation and expansion of the article, "The Economic and Social Basis of Primitive Bands," in *Essays in Honor of A. L. Kroeber* (University of California Press, 1936), pp. 331–50.

[b] Wilhelm Koppers observes that 15 to 20 individuals is common and about 100 the probable limit. See Wilhelm Koppers, *Die Anfänge des menschlichen Gemeinschaftslebens* (Vienna, 1921), p. 72.

[c] Bingham observed gorillas in a state of nature in groups of eight to twenty-two individuals, each group under a dominant male; chimpanzees are said to be similar; and it is probable that the males among the baboons observed in nature by Zuckerman had a comparable dominance. See Harold C. Bingham, *Gorillas in a Native Habitat*. Report Joint Expedition of 1929–1932 by Yale University and Carnegie Institution of Washington for Psychobiological Study of Mountain Gorillas (*Gorilla berengei*) in Parc National Albert, Belgian Congo Africa (1932). Also see S. Zuckerman, *The Social Life of Monkeys and Apes* (New York: Harcourt, Brace and Company, 1932).

[d] E.g., the extraordinarily low status of women in the arduous hunting area of northern Canada. Radcliffe-Brown has observed that Australian hunters would be much less successful in territory which was not known to them from childhood.

[e] Relationship is seldom traced beyond three generations among these people.

[f] I make no effort to solve the very difficult problem of why there are incest laws at all. Marriage with relatives to the third generation, i.e., cousins, is taboo in most of these cases, although cross-cousin and even parallel-cousin marriage is permitted among several.

[g] This section is based on I. Schapera, "A Preliminary Consideration of the Relationship between the Hottentots and the Bushmen," *South African Journal of Science*, XXIII (1926), 833–66; I. Schapera, *The Khoisan Peoples of South Africa* (London, 1930); S. S. Dornan, *Pygmies and Bushmen of the Kalahari* (London, 1925);

E. J. Dunn, *The Bushman* (London, 1931); George W. Stow, *The Native Races of South Africa* (New York, 1905); S. Passarge, *Die Buschmanner der Kalahari* (Berlin, 1907).

[h] Schapera, *The Khoisan Peoples of South Africa*, pp. 67–81, has gleaned a few figures on band size from various sources: Cape Bushmen, who were seriously affected by foreign contacts, 100 to 150, according to one estimate, and 3 to 4 families each, according to a more recent figure; Heichware, 20; Kalahari, 30; !Okung, not exceeding 30; Northwestern Bushmen, ranging from 20 to 150 and probably averaging 50 to 60 each.

[i] Morice Vanoverbergh, "Negritos of Northern Luzon," *Anthropos*, XXV (1930), 538–39, found that some bands contained related males and also that related males occurred in different bands.

[j] This material is largely from A. R. Radcliffe-Brown, "Former Numbers and Distribution of the Australian Aborigines," *Official Yearbook of the Commonwealth of Australia*, No. 23 (1930), pp. 671–96, and Radcliffe-Brown, "The Social Organization of Australian Tribes, I–III," *Oceania* I (1930, 1931) 34–63, 204–46, 426–56 (especially pp. 436–39, 455).

[k] Radcliffe-Brown, *Official Yearbook of the Commonwealth of Australia*, No. 23 (1930), p. 696. The population range was 1 person per 2 square miles in the most fertile section to 1 per 38 square miles in the more arid regions.

[l] D. Sutherland Davidson, "The Family Hunting Territory in Australia," *American Anthropologist*, n.s., XXX (1928), 614–32. Davidson has collected evidence that in some localities the landowning group was the bilateral family. It is the opinion of Radcliffe-Brown, *Oceania*, I (1931), 438, however, that "the particularism of the family whereby it might tend to become an isolated unit is neutralized by the horde [i.e., band] solidarity."

[m] Radcliffe-Brown, *Official Yearbook of the Commonwealth of Australia*, No. 23 (1930), p. 695, gives the aboriginal total as probably 2,000 or 3,000, which is one person to 8 or 13 square miles.

[n] Antonio Serrano, *Los Primitivos Habitantes del Territorio Argentina* (Buenos Aires, 1930), p. 157. Nuñoz, quoted by Serrano, says that among the Northern Tehuelche the head chief owned the land and that the lesser chiefs could not change their land without giving notice to him.

---

[33] Steward's work had a profound effect on the anthropologists of his day. Although his career, unlike that of Boas or White, was characterized by many short stays at different universities, he was a charismatic professor and attracted an important following. Among the students of Steward who later became prominent anthropologists were Stanley Diamond (1922–1991), Morton H. Fried (1923–1986) (see essay 18), Sidney Mintz (b. 1922), Elman Service (1915–1996), Elliott Skinner (b. 1924), and Eric Wolf (1923–1999) (see essay 21).

REFERENCES

Beerbohn, Julius. 1881. *Wanderings in Patagonia or Life Among the Ostrich-Hunters*. London.

Dornan, S. S. 1925. *Pygmies and Bushmen of the Kahlahari*. London.

Dunn, E. J. 1931. *The Bushman*. London.

Gifford, E. W. 1918. "Clans and Moieties in Southern California," *University of California Publications in American Archaeology and Ethnology*, XIV, 155–219.

———. 1926. "Miwok Lineages and the Political Unit in Aboriginal California," *American Anthropologist*, n.s., XXVIII, 389–401.

———. 1931. "The Kamia of the Imperial Valley," *Bureau of American Ethnology Bulletin* 97.

Gusinde, Martin. 1931. "Die Feuerland Indianer. Bande I. Die Selk'nam. Verlag der Internationalen Zeitschrift," *Anthropos*, pp. 302–06.

Kroeber, A. L. 1925. "Handbook of the Indians of California," *Bureau of American Ethnology Bulletin* 78.

———. 1934. "Native American Population," *American Anthropologist*, n.s., XXXVI, No. 1, pp. 1–25.

Musters, George C. 1873. *At Home with the Patagonians. A Year's Wandering over Untrodden Ground from the Straits of Magellan to the Rio Negro*. London.

Outes, Felix, F., and Carlos Bruch. 1910. *Los Aborigines de la Republica Argentina*. Buenos Aires.

Putnam, Patrick. 1948. "The Pygmies of the Ituri Forest," in Carleton S. Coon, *A General Reader in Anthropology*. New York: H. Holt and Company, pp. 322–342.

Radcliffe-Brown, A. R. 1930. "Former Numbers and Distribution of the Australian Aborigines," *Official Yearbook of the Commonwealth of Australia* No. 23, pp. 671–96.

———. 1931. "The Social Organization of Australian Tribes, III," *Oceania*, I, 426–56.

Roth, H. Ling. 1899. *The Aborigines of Tasmania*. Halifax (England): F. King and Sons.

Schapera, I. 1926. "A Preliminary Consideration of the Relationship between the Hottentots and the Bushmen." *South African Journal of Science*, XXIII, 833–66.

———. 1930. *The Khosian Peoples of South Africa*. London.

Schebesta, Paul. 1929. *Among the Forest Dwarfs of Malaya*. London.

———. 1931. "Erste Mitteilungen uber die Ergebnisse meiner Forschungsreise bei den Pygmaen in Belgische-Kongo," *Anthropos*, XXVI, 1–17.

Schmidt, P. W. 1910. "Die Stellung der Pygmaenvolker in der Entwicklungsgeschichte des Menshen," *Studien u. Forschungen zur Menschen-u.Volkerkunde*. Stuttgart.

Skeat, W. W., and C. O. Blagden. 1900. *Pagan Races of the Malay Peninsula*. London and New York: The Macmillan Company.

Strong, W. D. 1927. "An Analysis of Southwestern Society," *American Anthropologist*, n.s., XXIX, 1–61.

———. 1929. "Aboriginal Society in Southern California," *University of California Publications in American Archaeology and Ethnology*, XXVI, 1–358.

Trilles, R. P. 1932. "Les Pygmées de la Forêt Equatorial," *Anthropos*, III, 1–530.

Neomaterialism: Evolutionary, Functionalist, Ecological, and Marxist

Julian Steward and Leslie White set the stage for ecological anthropology and materialist cultural analysis, but it was the next generation of anthropologists who really developed these fields of inquiry. By midcentury, two types of materialism were becoming popular in anthropology: ecological-materialist approaches and neo-Marxist approaches.

The ecological-materialist approach to anthropology was heavily influenced by the field of cybernetics, general systems theory, and the growing science of ecology. They commonly assumed that societies were homeostatic, that is, that cultural institutions functioned as feedback mechanisms (like thermostats) to maintain a balance between energy production and expenditure and the productive capacity of the environment. Typically, ecological materialists examined culture using an equilibrium model that traced energy flow within an ecosystem. For example, a society might be analyzed in terms of its food production and the caloric expenditure of human energy required to maintain the society in equilibrium.

In addition, ecological-materialist studies differed from those of Steward and White in that the former tended to take local populations rather than cultures as their units of analysis. Ecological materialists examined the interactions between populations and environments rather than treating the environment as a passive background that shapes culture but is not influenced by it.

Ecological materialism can be subdivided into two different approaches: neoevolutionism and neofunctionalism (Orlove 1980). Like Lewis Henry Morgan (see essay 3), neoevolutionists were primarily interested in the origins of cultural phenomena and in particular, the rise of civilization. Examples of this work include Morton H. Fried's (1923–1986) *The Evolution of Political Society* (1967), Elman Service's (1915–1996) *Primitive Social Organization: An Evolutionary Perspective* (1962), and Kent Flannery's (b. 1934) "The Cultural Evolution of Civilizations" (1972). (Archaeological research has been a major part of this field as well but is beyond the scope of this book.)

The neoevolutionists were often concerned with the identification of stages through which cultural phenomena developed. For instance, the famous bands-tribes-chiefdoms-states sequence of cultural development was proposed by Service (1962), a student of both White and Steward. The essay we chose to represent this school of thought is by Morton Fried. Fried was first a graduate student and then a professor at Columbia University. He was deeply affected by classes he took from Julian Steward as well as by his fellow students, including Elman Service, Stanley Diamond (1922–1991), Eric Wolf (1923–1999), and Robert Manners (1913–1996). He also credited Leslie White and V. Gordon Childe with making major contributions to his understanding of social evolution (Service 1988). Fried's principal area of field research was China; he made numerous trips to the mainland as well as to Chinese communities in other parts of the world.

In the essay presented here, Fried examines the evolution of social stratification in relation to the control and distribution of resources. Fried developed this perspective more fully in *The Evolution of Political Society,* where he examined the development of social inequality, proposing the evolutionary stages of egalitarian, ranked, stratified, and state societies.

Like the psychological and structural functionalists of the first half of the twentieth century, neofunctionalists were interested in the function and purpose of institutions and beliefs. However, whereas the functionalists described institutions in terms of their contribution to individual needs or social stability, neofunctionalists were interested in adaptation. They focused on the ways in which particular cultural beliefs, practices, and institutions allowed populations to maintain and reproduce themselves successfully within specific physical, political, and economic environments. The dominant perspective within neofunctionalism is called cultural materialism, and Marvin Harris (1927–2001) was its leading proponent.

Harris did both his undergraduate and graduate training at Columbia University, where he also served as a professor from 1953 to 1980. His mentor was Charles Wagley (1913–1991), a student of Boas. Harris took courses from Steward and was attracted by White's critique of the Boasians, but during his career as a student, these experiences did not have a very profound effect on him. He moved decisively toward materialism after his fieldwork in Mozambique. His experiences of Portuguese colonialism there convinced him that systems of production were fundamental to any understanding of culture (Harris: 1994:75–76).

Harris' work followed the Marxist perspective resurrected by Leslie White. Marx was a dialectical materialist, and believed that production played the primary role in social evolution (see essay 4). While rejecting Marxist dialectics, cultural materialists firmly insist on the primacy of modes of production and reproduction—what Harris (1979) called "infrastructure"—in determining behaviors and beliefs within a society. Much of Harris' work was an attack on what he considered to be the obscurant, spiritualized explanations of symbolic and interpretive anthropology, as well as religion and various "consciousness"

movements. Harris wrote that Americans have "been taught to value elaborate 'spiritualized' explanations of cultural phenomena. . . ." He, on the other hand, intended to show

> that even the most bizarre-seeming beliefs and practices turn out on closer inspection to be based on ordinary, banal, one might say "vulgar" conditions, needs, and activities. What I mean by a banal or vulgar solution is that it rests on the ground and that it is built up out of guts, sex, energy, wind, rain, and other palpable and ordinary phenomena. (1974:2–3)

Cultural materialism has been one of the most powerful and enduring theoretical positions within modern American anthropology, partly because Harris himself was an extremely successful and indefatigable promoter of it. Generations of graduate students have read Harris' classic *The Rise of Anthropological Theory* (1968). You may have noticed that we frequently refer to it in this volume. Harris' book is a comprehensive analysis of the history of anthropology, but it is also a polemic promoting cultural materialism.

In addition to copious work designed for professional consumption, Harris also wrote many books for popular audiences, including *Cows, Pigs, Wars and Witches: The Riddles of Culture* (1974), *Cannibals and Kings: The Origins of Culture* (1977), *Good to Eat: Riddles of Food and Culture* (1985), and many others. These books, which give cultural-materialist explanations of cultural phenomena, are written in an extremely accessible and engaging style and had enormous popular success.

Cultural-materialist analysis was extremely popular in the 1970s and 1980s and continues to command a large following today. However, it is also frequently attacked as naive positivism, "rooted in a mechanical, naturalistic mode that fails to reckon with the fact that the mind is more than a tabula rasa" (Murphy 1994:58). Harris vehemently resisted such charges, while insisting that an objective, positivist science of society is not only possible but necessary. His position is perhaps best summed up in the title of one of his essays, "Cultural Materialism Is Alive and Well and Won't Go Away Until Something Better Comes Along" (1994).

Our example of cultural materialism is Harris' 1966 article, "The Cultural Ecology of India's Sacred Cattle." Writing for a technical audience, Harris argues that the Hindu prohibition on killing cattle should be understood in relation to the role that cattle play in the production of food crops, fuel, and fertilizer. He convincingly demonstrates the material and ecological importance of cattle to Indian society and argues that this, rather than Hindu religious doctrine, is the ultimate basis of the ban on killing and eating cattle. In fact, in line with Marxist thinking, Harris argues the sacredness of cattle is a result of their productive importance.

A second orientation in neofunctionalist materialism comes from the work of Roy Rappaport (1926–1997). Whereas Fried and Harris drew their inspiration from Marx, Rappaport was more deeply affected by the work of ecological biologists. Like Fried and Harris, Rappaport was a student at Columbia. However, although influenced by White's notions concerning cultural evolution, Rappaport was more deeply affected by classes he took with Harold Conklin (b. 1926) and Conrad Arensburg (1912–1997), and fieldwork seminars with Margaret Mead (Rappaport 1994:166). His deep reading in biological ecology led to his dissertation under Andrew P. Vayda, an anthropologist vitally interested in ecology. Rappaport and Vayda believed that general laws of biological ecology could be used to study human populations, a belief they sought to substantiate in their fieldwork.

Rappaport and other neofunctionalist anthropologists adopted the concept of feedback from cybernetics to explain cultural stability. In the essay reproduced here, "Ritual Regulation of Environmental Relations Among a New Guinea People," Rappaport proposes that the sacrifice of pigs in the *kaiko* ritual of the Tsembaga of New Guinea is a feedback mechanism that regulates the ecological relationship between men, pigs, local food supplies, and warfare. He outlined this point of view in greater detail in his 1967 work, *Pigs for the Ancestors*.

The neo-Marxist approach was developed in Europe at about the same time that neoevolutionism and neofunctionalism were becoming popular in the United States. Neofunctionalism and neoevolutionism were primarily American theoretical developments that, despite their reliance on insights from Marxist scholarship, rejected key elements of Marxist doctrine, particularly the dialectic. Neo-Marxism was centered in Europe, where political conditions made strictly Marxist anthropology more feasible. There, a tradition of rigorously Marxist research already existed. Much of this was inspired by Soviet ethnographers, who generally reflected Stalinist and Leninist interpretations of Marx. However, in the 1960s, particularly in France, a group of Marxist thinkers emerged that challenged Soviet ethnographic hegemony. This group, including Claude Meillassoux (1925–2005) and Maurice Godelier (b. 1934) suggested that Marx's work provided the basic insights for the analysis of traditional society but that, because his writings had focused primarily on the development of capitalism in Europe, they could not be applied directly to ethnographic analysis. The neo-Marxists modified Marx's work to adapt it for this purpose. In particular, they described new modes of production and proposed new evolutionary sequences. Unlike almost all other anthropologists of their era, they had a keen critical eye for the effects of colonialism and international economic exchanges.

Whereas American materialists tended to focus on feedback mechanisms and stable adaptations, the neo-Marxists directed their attention to dialectical contradiction. They viewed society in terms of the struggle of different social groups (which they frequently insisted were classes) for control and power. They were often brutally critical of American materialist approaches that minimized the role of conflict or ignored the dialectic. A particularly good example of this criticism is the essay "Marxism, Structuralism, and Vulgar Materialism" (1974), in which Jonathan Friedman provides an extensive critique of Harris' ideas on Indian cattle worship and Rappaport's understanding of the ecological importance of pigs and ritual. Friedman argues that, by ignoring the dialectic, American anthropologists transform subtle and sophisticated Marxist analysis to mechanistic "vulgar materialism." As a result, they misunderstand the insights Marxist analysis can provide.

Neo-Marxist analysis is represented in this section by an essay from Eric Wolf (1923–1999). Wolf was one of the most influential neo-Marxist thinkers in the United States. Born in Vienna, he emigrated first to England, then, in 1940, to New York. After service in World War II during which he was decorated for bravery, he went on to earn his Ph.D. at Columbia, where he studied with Ruth Benedict, Stanley Diamond, Sidney Mintz, Morton Fried, and Julian Steward.

Because of his contact with Fried, Steward, and others, Wolf's work was informed by Marx's notion of society as a historical and material process. His first book, *Sons of the Shaking Earth* (1959), explored the rise of Mesoamerican cultures in relation to the geography, ecology, and ethnic diversity of the area and examined effects of the Spanish conquest.

Wolf began to conduct cultural analysis in openly Marxist terms in *Peasants* (1966), the first chapter of which is presented here. In *Peasants* Wolf examines the structure of peasant societies and their relation to industrialized states. *Peasants* was followed in 1969 by *Peasant Wars of the Twentieth Century,* a book that applied Marxist thinking to a series of conflicts in Mexico, Russia, China, Algeria, and Cuba. Wolf was a strong critic of the war in Vietnam. Along with Marshal Sahlins, he helped start the "teach-in" movement at the University of Michigan (Wolf and Jorgensen 1970). Teach-ins were part of the 1960s and early 1970s protest against the Vietnam War and soon spread to many universities. Students and faculty would meet to debate, question, challenge assumptions and learn about the Vietnam War. Wolf intended *Peasant Wars* to be a text used at such meetings. As a result of their activism, Wolf and Sahlins both came under FBI scrutiny in the late 1960s, as did Morton Fried (Price 2004).

Wolf's most influential book was *Europe and the People Without History* (1982). Wolf was deeply influenced by the economist Andre Gunder Frank (1929–2005) and the sociologist Immanuel Wallerstein (b. 1930), who were leading thinkers of dependency theory and World System theory. In the 1960s, economists such as W. W. Rostow proposed that poor nations could become wealthy by repeating the historical experience of wealthy nations—the premise of what came to be called modernization theory. Frank and others argued that modernization in undeveloped nations could not succeed because their wealth and labor had been systematically siphoned from them by Europe and the United States. Poor nations had not simply failed to modernize and develop. They had been systematically underdeveloped by wealthy nations.

In *Europe and the People Without History* Wolf takes the expansion of European capitalism as his central subject. He shows how the mercantile and capitalist expansion of Europe affected and undermined indigenous cultural systems throughout the Third World and how this process produced great wealth and great suffering. The book is critical because it moved American neo-Marxists and neofunctionalists away from the study of small-scale isolated systems to large-scale social analysis. However, Wolf's analysis had effects well beyond neo-Marxist circles. His revisionist approach to world history championed the voices of the poor and oppressed. He cast doubt on the coherence of ethnic groupings and identities, pointing out that these were often created by the forces of capital. He reminded readers that the dominant narrative of history was generally told only from the point of view of the wealthy and powerful, which was a very biased perspective. Wolf attempted to give voice to the poor and oppressed in his telling of history.

Wolf's work was particularly influential because it combined the concern for the downtrodden that was an important element of Boasian thinking with a powerful neo-Marxist analysis. At a time when postmodernism was emerging as an important force within anthropology, Wolf drew attention to the issue of voice, of who has the authority to tell history and how that authority is constituted, and to the historical and contingent nature of identity.

18. *On the Evolution of Social Stratification and the State*

Morton H. Fried (1923–1986)

The evolutionists never discussed in detail—still less observed—what actually happened when a society in Stage A changed into a society at Stage B; it was merely argued that all Stage B societies must somehow have evolved out of the Stage A societies.

—E. R. Leach, 1954, p. 283

To some extent E. R. Leach's charge, which relates to the evolution of political organization, is unfair. The climate in which pristine systems of state organization took shape no longer exists. The presence of numerous modern states and the efficiency of communications have converted all movements toward state level organization into acculturation phenomena of some degree. In fact, it seems likely that the only truly pristine states—those whose origin was *sui generis*,[1] out of local conditions and not in response to pressures emanating from an already highly organized but separate political entity—are those which arose in the great river valleys of Asia and Africa and the one or two comparable developments in the Western Hemisphere. Elsewhere the development of the state seems to have been "secondary" and to have depended upon pressures, direct or indirect, from existing states. Where such pressures exist, the process of development is accelerated, condensed, and often warped, so that a study of contemporary state formation is a murky

mirror in which to discern the stages in the development of the pristine states.

Further, the conditions of emergence of rank and stratification as pristine phenomena are similarly obscured when the impetus to change is the introduction of aspects of a market economy, money as a medium of exchange, rationalization of production, and the transformation of labor into a commodity. It would be extremely gratifying to actually observe societies in transition from a "Stage A" (egalitarian organization) to a "Stage B" (rank society) and from there to a "Stage C" (stratification society) and finally from that stage to a "Stage D" (state society).[2] Indeed, some of these observations have been made, though no one has yet been able to follow a single society or even selected exemplars from a group of genetically related societies through all these stages. Instead a variety of unrelated societies are selected, each representing one or another of the several possible transitions. Mr. Leach himself has contributed one of the most valuable of the

From *Culture in History: Essays in Honor of Paul Radin* (1960)

---

[1] *Sui generis:* Latin for "of its own kind," here meaning "unique" or "individual."

[2] In this article, Fried proposes an evolutionary model of society. Ever since Morgan, cultural-evolutionary studies have tended to be synchronic—comparing contemporary societies at different levels of development to try to reconstruct the process by which simple societies evolved into more complex forms. (On the other hand, archaeological studies of cultural evolution tend to be diachronic—studying the de-

velopment of one society in a specific area through time.) Fried posits that state-level societies are the final product of an evolutionary sequence that begins with egalitarian bands and progresses first to ranked and then to stratified societies. The mechanisms that propel societies through this evolutionary sequence are material factors such as economy, population, and environment. Fried also points out that the evolutionary sequence he is proposing has never actually been observed. Pristine traditional systems no longer exist.

accounts dealing with this matter in his analysis of the movement from *gumlao* to *gumsa* organization among the Kachin of northern Burma.[3]

Following leads supplied in the data of such accounts as that of Leach, just mentioned, of Douglas Oliver (1955), and others, it is our intention to discuss in detail the things which it seems to us must have occurred in order to make the previous transitions possible. Since the data are largely contemporary, the statements are to be viewed as hypotheses in their application to pristine situations beyond even archaeological recall.

Here then is what we seek to accomplish: (1) to suggest some specific institutional developments, the occurrences of which are normal and predictable in viable societies under certain conditions, and in the course of which the whole society perforce moves into a new level of socio-cultural organization; (2) to suggest some of the conditions under which these institutional developments occurred and came to florescence; (3) to indicate as a by-product, that the movement occurs without conscious human intervention, the alterations tak-

ing place slowly enough and with such inevitability that the society is revolutionized before the carriers of the culture are aware of major changes.[4]

In approaching this task, it seems wise, if only to head off needless argument, to deny any intention of supplying a single master key to a lock that has defied the efforts of great talents from the time of the Classical civilizations to the present. It seems obvious that other sequences of events than those sketched here could, under proper circumstances, have had similar results. Indeed, the writer is eager to entertain other possibilities and hopes hereby to stimulate others to offer counter suggestions. It will also be obvious to the reader that substantial trains of thought herein stated are merely borrowed and not created by the writer. The recent strides in economic anthropology, and I refer primarily to the work of Polanyi, Arensberg, and Pearson (1957), the clarification of some basic concepts in the study of social organization, and the incentives provided by a seminal paper by Paul Kirchhoff (1935) have all been combined in the present effort.[5]

---

[3] Fried cites Edmund Leach's (1911–1989) classic 1954 study, *Political Systems of Highland Burma,* which describes the evolution of a political system. A weakness of the functionalists was their tendency to view cultures as static. *Political Systems of Highland Burma* was a structural-functionalist study, but Leach saw Kachin political structure as dynamic, alternating between egalitarian and stratified forms. His book emphasized the evolution of political systems in relation to ecology, subsistence, and historical political forces outside of the control of culture members. This work, coming just six years before Fried's, had a major impact on Fried's own analysis of social stratification. Fried in fact used Leach's data in formulating his own theory. Note that the quotation at the opening of this article is from Leach's book.

[4] Note the third goal listed in this paragraph. Fried's comments are reminiscent of the nineteenth-century Spencerian view of social evolution. Recall that Spencer described evolution as superorganic, occurring without the conscious awareness or intervention of the members of society. The evolutionary process was inevitable and resulted from the slow accumulation of social changes. The course of evolution was from simple undifferentiated societies to increasingly complex and specialized societies. Similarly, in Fried's evolutionary model, egalitarian bands evolve

into increasingly complex societies with internal social differentiation.

[5] The 1957 work by Polanyi, Arensberg, and Pearson, *Trade and Market in the Early Empires,* was a seminal document in economic anthropology. Karl Polanyi (1886–1964), a historian, suggested that economies could be organized by ideas other than the market and that the rules of economic analysis developed for use in capitalist societies did not apply to other societies. This perspective came to be known as substantivism and was important to economic anthropologists of the 1960s. According to Polanyi, societies could be organized either by reciprocity, redistribution, or some form of market. Fried makes great use of this theory later in this article. You should also remember the principles of prestation Marcel Mauss outlined in *The Gift* (see essay 6) when reading Fried's discussion of Polanyi.

Paul Kirchhoff (1900–1972) was a German-Mexican ethnologist who studied theology, comparative religion, and psychology as well as anthropology. Kirchhoff spent the majority of his career working in Mexico. His primary work was on the Indians of North and South America, and he coined the term *Mesoamerica.* Kirchohoff was alsoa cofounder of the Escuela Nacional de Anthropología e Historia. The work Fried refers to is a manuscript called "The Principles of Clanship in Human Society."

THE NON-RANK, NON-STRATIFIED SOCIETY

Every human society differentiates among its members and assigns greater or less prestige to individuals according to certain of their attributes. The simplest and most universal criteria of differential status are those two potent axes of the basic division of labor, age and sex. Beyond are a host of others which are used singly or in combination to distinguish among the members of a category otherwise undifferentiated as to sex or age group. Most important of the characteristics used in this regard are those which have a visible relation to the maintenance of subsistence, such as strength, endurance, agility, and other factors which make one a good provider in a hunting and gathering setting. These characteristics are ephemeral; moreover, the systems of enculturation prevalent at this level, with their emphasis upon the development of subsistence skills, make it certain that such skills are well distributed among the members of society of the proper sex and age groups.

The major deviation from this system of subsistence-oriented statuses is associated with age. However, it makes no difference to the argument of this paper whether the status of the old is high or low since the basis of its ascription is universal. Anyone who is of the proper sex and manages to live long enough automatically enters into its benefits or disabilities.

Given the variation in individual endowment which makes a chimera[6] of absolute equality, the primitive societies which we are considering are sufficiently undifferentiated in this respect to permit us to refer to them as "egalitarian societies." An egalitarian society can be defined more precisely: it is one in which there are as many positions of prestige in any given age-sex grade as there are persons capable of filling them. If within a certain kin group or territory there are four big men, strong, alert, keen hunters, then there will be four "strong men"; if there are six, or three, or one, so it is. Eskimo society fits this general picture. So do many others. Almost all of these societies are founded upon hunting and gathering and lack significant harvest periods when large reserves of food are stored.

There is one further point I wish to emphasize about egalitarian society. It accords quite remarkably with what Karl Polanyi has called a reciprocal economy.[a]

Production in egalitarian society is characteristically a household matter. There is no specialization; each family group repeats essentially similar tasks. There may be individuals who make certain things better than do others, and these individuals are often given recognition for their skills, but no favored economic role is established, no regular division of labor emerges at this point, and no political power can reside in the status (Leacock, 1958). Exchange in such a society takes place between individuals who belong to different small-scale kin groups; it tends to be casual and is not bound by systems of monetary value based upon scarcity. Such exchanges predominate between individuals who recognize each other as relatives or friends, and may be cemented by such procedures as the provision of hospitality and the granting of sexual access to wives.

Within the local group or band the economy is also reciprocal, but less obviously so. Unlike the exchanges between members of different local groups which, over the period of several years, tend to balance, the exchanges within a group may be quite asymmetrical over time. The skilled and lucky hunter may be continually supplying others with meat; while his family also receives shares from the catch of others, income never catches up with the amounts dispensed. However, the difference between the two quantities is made up in the form of prestige, though, as previously mentioned, it conveys no privileged economic or political role. There frequently is a feeling of transience as it is understood that the greatest hunter can lose his luck or his life, thereby making his family dependent on the largesse of others.

In all egalitarian economies, however, there is also a germ of redistribution. It receives its

---

[6] *Chimera:* something unreal or imaginary.

simplest expression in the family but can grow no more complex than the pooling and redisbursing of stored food for an extended family. In such an embryonic redistributive system the key role is frequently played by the oldest female in the active generation, since it is she who commonly coordinates the household and runs the kitchen.

THE RANK SOCIETY

Since a truly egalitarian human society does not exist, it is evident that we are using the word "rank" in a somewhat special sense. The crux of the matter, as far as we are concerned, is the structural way in which differential prestige is handled in the rank society as contrasted with the way in which egalitarian societies handle similar materials. If the latter have as many positions of valued status as they have individuals capable of handling them, the rank society places additional limitations on access to valued status. The limitations which are added have nothing to do with sex, age group, or personal attributes. Thus, the rank society is characterized by having fewer positions of valued status than individuals capable of handling them. Furthermore, most rank societies have a fixed number of such positions, neither expanding them nor diminishing them with fluctuations in the populations, save as totally new segmented units originate with fission or disappear as the result of catastrophe or sterility.

The simplest technique of limiting status, beyond those already discussed, is to make succession to status dependent upon birth order. This principle, which is found in kinship-organized societies, persists in many more complexly organized societies. At its simplest, it takes the form of primogeniture or ultimogeniture on the level of the family, extended family, or lineage.[7] In more complex forms it may be projected through time so that only the first son of a first son of a first son enjoys the rights of succession, all others having been excluded by virtue of ultimate descent from a positionless ancestor. There are still other variants based on the theme: the accession to high status may be by election, but the candidates may come only from certain lineages which already represent selection by birth order.

The effects of rules of selection based on birth can be set aside by conscious action. Incompetence can be the basis for a decision to by-pass the customary heir, though it would seem more usual for the nominal office to remain vested in the proper heir while a more energetic person performed the functions of the status. A strategic murder could also accomplish the temporary voiding of the rule, but such a solution is much too dangerous and extreme to be practical on the level which we are considering. It is only in rather advanced cultures that the rewards associated with such statuses are sufficient to motivate patricide and fratricide.

Whether accomplished by a rule of succession or some other narrowing device, the rank society as a framework of statuses resembles a triangle, the point of which represents the leading status hierarchically exalted above the others. The hierarchy thus represented has very definite economic significance, going hand in hand with the emergence of a superfamilial redistributive network. The key status is that of the central collector of allotments who also tends to the redistribution of these supplies either in the form of feasts or as emergency seed and provender in time of need. Depending on the extent and maturity of the redistributive system, there will be greater or lesser development of the hierarchy. Obviously, small-scale networks in which the members have a face-to-face relationship with the person in the central status will have less need of a bureaucracy.[8]

In the typical ranked society there is neither exploitative economic power nor genuine political power. As a matter of fact, the central status

---

[7] *Primogeniture* is inheritance by the firstborn son; *ultimogeniture* is inheritance by the lastborn.

[8] In Fried's theory one can see Marx's idea that modes of production determine the ideological features of society. Fried believes that the force that drives political evolution is the control over production and distribution of resources. Egalitarian societies are marked by universal access to prestige and reciprocity of resources. A key feature of rank societies is that their members have unequal access to prestige that results from the power of high-prestige individuals to control the distribution of resources.

closely resembles its counterpart in the embryonic redistributive network that may be found even in the simplest societies. This is not surprising, for the system in typical rank societies is actually based upon a physical expansion of the kin group and the continuation of previously known kinship rights and obligations. The kingpin of a redistributive network in an advanced hunting and gathering society or a simple agricultural one is as much the victim of his role as its manipulator. His special function is to collect, not to expropriate; to distribute, not to consume. In a conflict between personal accumulation and the demands of distribution it is the former which suffers. Anything else leads to accusations of hoarding and selfishness and undercuts the prestige of the central status; the whole network then stands in jeopardy, a situation which cannot be tolerated. This, by the way, helps to explain that "anomaly" that has so frequently puzzled students of societies of this grade: why are their "chiefs" so often poor, perhaps poorer than any of their neighbors? The preceding analysis makes such a question rhetorical.[9]

It is a further characteristic of the persons filling these high status positions in typical rank societies that they must carry out their functions in the absence of political authority. Two kinds of authority they have: familial, in the extended sense, and sacred, as the redistributive feasts commonly are associated with the ritual life of the community. They do not, however, have access to the privileged use of force, and they can use only diffuse and supernatural sanctions to achieve their ends. Indeed, the two major methods by which they operate are by setting personal examples, as of industriousness, and by utilizing the principles of reciprocity to bolster the emergent redistributive economy.[b]

Despite strong egalitarian features in its economic and political sectors, the developing rank society has strong status differentials which are marked by sumptuary specialization and ceremonial function.[10] While it is a fact that the literature abounds in references to "chiefs" who can issue no positive commands and "ruling classes" whose members are among the paupers of the realm, it must be stated in fairness that the central redistributive statuses *are* associated with fuss, feathers, and other trappings of office. These people sit on stools, have big houses, and are consulted by their neighbors. Their redistributive roles place them automatically to the fore in the religious life of the community, but they are also in that position because of their central kinship status as lineage, clan,[c] or kindred heads.[11]

FROM EGALITARIAN TO RANK SOCIETY

The move from egalitarian to rank society is essentially the shift from an economy dominated by reciprocity to one having redistribution as a major device. That being the case, one must look for the causes of ranking (the limitation of statuses such that they are fewer than the persons capable of handling them) in the conditions which enable the redistributive economy to emerge from its position of latency in the universal household economy, to dominate a network of kin groups which extend beyond the boundaries of anything known on the reciprocal level.

Though we shall make a few suggestions relating to this problem, it should be noted that the focus of this paper does not necessitate immediate disposition of this highly complicated question. In view of the history of our topic, certain negative conclusions are quite significant. Most important of all is the deduction that the roots of

---

[9] Fried, although strongly influenced by Marx, does not believe in revolutionary dialectical change. Instead, he says that the transition from egalitarian to rank societies is characterized by the continuation of previously known rights and obligations. Like Darwin and Spencer, Fried believed that evolutionary change occurred in slow incremental stages. Further, in his discussion of "mature" and "embryonic" redistributive networks, Fried's terminology harkens back to the organic analogy of the nineteenth century.

[10] *Sumptuary specialization:* specialized clothing marking one's status.

[11] Max Weber conducted some of the early work on the distinction between types of authority and power. Fried's distinction between political versus familial and sacred authority is clearly part of the same tradition.

ranking do not lie in features of human personality. The structural approach obviates, in this case, psychological explanations. To be precise, we need assume no universal human drive for power[d] in comprehending the evolution of ranking.[12]

It is unthinkable that we should lead a reader this far without indicating certain avenues whereby the pursuit of the problem may be continued. We ask, therefore, what are the circumstances under which fissioning kin or local groups retain active economic interdigitation,[13] the method of interaction being participation in the redistributive network?

In a broad sense, the problem may be seen as an ecological one. Given the tendency of a population to breed up to the limit of its resources and given the probably universal budding of kin and local groups which have reached cultural maxima of unit size, we look into different techno-geographical situations for clues as to whether more recently formed units will continue to interact significantly with their parent units, thereby extending the physical and institutional range of the economy. Such a situation clearly arises when the newer group moves into a somewhat different environment while remaining close enough to the parent group to permit relatively frequent interaction among the members of the two groups. Given such a condition, the maintenance of a redistributive network would have the effect of diversifying subsistence in both

units and also providing insurance against food failures in one or the other. This is clearly something of a special case; one of its attractions is the amount of work that has been done upon it by another student of the problem (Sahlins, 1957, 1958).[14]

It is possible to bring to bear upon this problem an argument similar to that employed by Tylor in the question of the incest taboo (Tylor, 1888, p. 267; White, 1948), to wit: the redistributive network might appear as a kind of random social mutation arising out of nonspecific factors difficult to generalize, such as a great personal dependence of the members of the offspring unit upon those they have left behind. Whatever the immediate reason for its appearance, it would quickly show a superiority over simple reciprocal systems in (a) productivity, (b) timeliness of distribution, (c) diversity of diet, and (d) coordination of mundane and ceremonial calendars (in a loose cyclical sense). It is not suggested that the success of the institution depends upon the rational cognition of these virtues by the culture carriers; rather the advantages of these institutions would have positive survival value over a long period of time.[15]

We should not overlook one other possibility that seems less special than the first one given above. Wittfogel has drawn our attention on numerous occasions to the social effects of irrigation (see Wittfogel, 1957, for a summation of his latest thinking). The emergence of the superfamilial

---

[12] Here Fried rejects all psychological explanations for the evolutionary shift from egalitarian to rank societies, pointing instead to the change from one form of economic distribution to another. By linking the evolution from egalitarian to rank society to the shift from a reciprocal economy to one dominated by redistribution, Fried echoes the Marxist-materialist perspective as interpreted in Polanyi's work.

[13] *Interdigitation:* interlocking, like the fingers of both hands.

[14] Fried attempts here to expand the scientific basis for his argument (which is essentially a hypothetical reconstruction) by incorporating the field of cultural ecology, which was relatively new at this time. Notice that the reader is taken from a discussion of kin groups, economies, and prestige to breeding populations and ecology. In particular, he cites Marshall Sahlins (b. 1930), a fellow evolutionist and a leading proponent of cultural ecology. See, for example, Sahlins' article "Culture and Environment: The Study of Cultural Ecology" (1964).

[15] Fried cannot definitively outline the rationale behind the transition from egalitarian to rank society, so he offers three possibilities. The first is the fissioning of related kin groups in expanded redistributive networks. The second is an argument borrowed from evolutionary biology: The development of ranking may be a random "social mutation" that conveyed a selective advantage or "positive survival value" on those who adopted the trait. The third is Wittfogel's hydro-agriculture hypothesis, which is discussed in the next paragraph. Karl A. Wittfogel (1896–1988) was an archaeologist who proposed that irrigation was a primary factor in the development of stratified societies. Wittfogel felt that the origins of social stratification and the state lay in the formation of a body of ruler-managers who oversaw the construction and maintenance of large-scale irrigation systems necessary for intensive agriculture. As a universal explanation, this theory was refuted by Adams (1966) and Carneiro (1970).

redistributive network and the rank society seem to go well with the developments he has discussed under the rubric "hydro-agriculture," in which some supervision is needed in order to control simple irrigation and drainage projects yet these projects are not large enough to call into existence a truly professional bureaucracy.

It may be wondered that one of the prime explanations for the emergence of ranking, one much favored by notable sociologists of the past, has not appeared in this argument. Reference is to the effects of war upon a society. I would like in this article to take a deliberately extreme stand and assert that military considerations serve to institutionalize rank differences only when these are already implicit or manifest in the economy. I do not believe that pristine developments in the formalization of rank can be attributed to even grave military necessity.[16]

THE STRATIFIED SOCIETY

The differences between rank society and stratified society are very great, yet it is rare that the two are distinguished in descriptive accounts or even in the theoretical literature. Briefly put, the essential difference is this: the rank society operates on the principle of differential status for members with similar abilities, but these statuses are devoid of privileged economic or political power, the former point being the essential one for the present analysis. Meanwhile, the stratified society is distinguished by the differential relationships between the members of the society and its subsistence means—some of the members of the society have unimpeded access to its strategic resources[e] while others have various impediments in their access to the same fundamental resources.[17]

With the passage to stratified society man enters a completely new area of social life. Whereas the related systems of redistribution and ranking rest upon embryonic institutions that are as universal as family organization (*any* family, elementary or extended, conjugal or consanguineal, will do equally well), the principles of stratification have no real foreshadowing on the lower level.

Furthermore, the movement to stratification precipitated many things which were destined to change society even further, and at an increasingly accelerated pace. Former systems of social control which rested heavily on enculturation, internalized sanctions, and ridicule now required formal statement of their legal principles, a machinery of adjudication, and a formally constituted police authority. The emergence of these and other control institutions were associated with the final shift of prime authority from kinship means to territorial means and describes the evolution of complex forms of government associated with the state. It was the passage to stratified society which laid the basis for the complex division of labor which underlies modern society. It also gave rise to various arrangements of socio-economic classes and led directly to both classical and modern forms of colonialism and imperialism.[18]

---

[16] The most notable of the sociologists referred to by Fried was Spencer, whose views on stratification and war he quotes several times in *The Evolution of Political Society*. The role of warfare in the evolution of society has long been a contentious issue among anthropologists. Here and in *The Evolution of Political Society* Fried argues emphatically that warfare was not a primary catalyst in the formation of stratified societies, an opinion based on his belief that primitive societies are not typically warlike. He cites several ethnographic examples supporting this view in his book. In contrast, Robert Carneiro (b. 1927) is one of the strongest advocates for the role of warfare in the origin of state-level societies (Carneiro 1970).

[17] The description Fried gives in this paragraph stands today as the standard definition of social stratification. It can be found virtually verbatim in most introductory cultural anthropology texts.

[18] For Fried, the development of stratification was a revolutionary step that defined the transition to state-level societies. The influence of nineteenth-century evolutionary thought is evident in this paragraph. Like the Spencerians, Fried focuses on increasing complexity, specialization, and the shift from autonomous individuals to interdependency of occupations and classes. The shift from kin-based to property-based authority is derived from Marx and Morgan. In Morgan's view, the modern state was founded on the notions of territory and property (see essay 3).

THE TRANSITION TO STRATIFIED SOCIETY

The decisive significance of stratification is not that it sees differential amounts of wealth in different hands but that it sees two kinds of access to strategic resources. One of these is privileged and unimpeded; the other is impaired, depending on complexes of permission which frequently require the payment of dues, rents, or taxes in labor or in kind. The existence of such a distinction enables the growth of exploitation, whether of a relatively simple kind based upon drudge slavery or of a more complex type associated with involved divisions of labor and intricate class systems. The development of stratification also encourages the emergence of communities composed of kin parts and non-kin parts which, as wholes, operate on the basis of non-kin mechanisms.[19]

So enormous is the significance of the shift to stratification that previous commentators have found it essential that the movement be associated with the most powerful people in the society. Landtman, for example, says:

"It is in conjunction with the dissimilarity of individual endowments that inequality of wealth has conduced to the rise of social differentiation. As a matter of course the difference as regards property in many cases goes hand in hand with difference in personal qualities. A skillful hunter or fisher, or a victorious warrior, has naturally a better prospect of acquiring a fortune than one who is inferior to him in these respects" (Landtman, 1938, p. 68).

If our analysis is correct, however, such is definitely not the case. The statuses mentioned by Landtman are not those which stand to make great accumulations but rather stand to make great give-aways. Furthermore, the leap from distribution to power is unwarranted by the ethnographic evidence.[20]

There are unquestionably a number of ways in which secondary conditions of stratification can emerge. That is, once the development of stratification proceeds from contact with and tutelage by cultures which are at the least already stratified and which may be the possessors of mature state organization, there are many specific ways in which simpler cultures can be transformed into stratified societies. The ways which come quickest to mind include the extension of the complex society's legal definitions of property to the simpler society, the introduction of all-purpose money and wage labor, and the creation of an administrative system for the operation of the simpler society on a basis which is acceptable to the superordinate state. Often the external provenance of these elements is obvious in their misfit appearance. A sharper look may reveal, indeed, that the stratified system is a mere facade operated for and often by persons who have no genuine local identities, while the local system continues to maintain informally, and sometimes in secrecy, the older organization of the society. Put more concretely, this means that "government" appointed chiefs are respected only in certain limited situations and that the main weight of social control continues to rest upon traditional authorities and institutions which may not even be recognized by the ruling power.[21]

---

[19] Although Fried, like most materialists at this time, did not cite Marx, the Marxist view of stratification and class exploitation is clearly expressed in this paragraph. This is particularly evident in his use of the term *exploitation,* the meaning of which is different for Marxists and non-Marxists. For non-Marxists, exploitation refers to receiving unfair returns for labor. To Marxists, exploitation is the appropriation of the surplus value of labor, which is inherently unfair. Fried is using the term in the Marxist sense.

[20] Fried explicitly rejects the claim that social stratification is founded on the differences between people's personal qualities and skills, an idea reminiscent of nineteenth-century social darwinism. He provides ethnographic evidence in his discussion of redistribution in rank societies to refute this doctrine.

[21] Remember that Fried is writing at the end of the period of European colonialism in the Pacific, Africa, and Asia and the beginning of the "development" of the Third World. His comments about local systems operating in secrecy and government-appointed chiefs refer to this situation. These remarks are an early example of the anthropological critique of colonialism; earlier theorists had often discussed how their work was useful to colonial administrators. Fried says that colonialism does not work.

An excellent climate for the development of stratification in a simple society can be supplied in a relatively indirect way by a society of advanced organization. Let us take the situation in which a culture has no concept of nuclear family rights to land. The economy is based upon hunting, trapping, and fishing, with the streams and forests being associated in a general way with weakly organized bands which have a decided tendency to fragment and reconstitute, each time with potentially different membership. Subvert this setup with an external market for furs and a substantial basis for stratification has been laid. This system, like the direct intervention of a superordinate state, also seems to have certain limitations for there is ample evidence that the development of private property in such a system as that just mentioned is confined to trapping lines and does not extend to general subsistence hunting and fishing in the area (see Leacock, 1958).

Another situation that bears study is one in which important trade routes linking two or more advanced societies traverse marginal areas in which simple societies are located. Certain geographical conditions make it possible for the relatively primitive folk to enhance their economies with fruits derived from the plunder of this trade or, in a more mature system, by extorting tribute from the merchants who must pass by. The remoteness of these areas, the difficulty of the terrain and the extreme difficulties and costs of sending a punitive force to pacify the area often enables the simpler people to harass populations whose cultural means for organized violence far exceeds their own. Be this as it may, the combination of the examples of organization presented by the outposts of complexly organized societies and the availability of commodities which could not be produced in the simple culture may combine to lay the basis for an emergence of stratification. Precisely such conditions seem partially responsible for the political developments described for the Kachin (Leach, 1954, esp. pp. 235, 247 ff.).

None of this seems to apply to the pristine emergence of stratification. As a matter of fact, it is not even particularly suggestive. There is, however, one particular ecological condition that appears in highland Burma which also has been noted elsewhere, each time in association with rather basic shifts in social organization paralleling those already sketched in the previous section of this paper. We refer to the shift from rainfall to irrigation farming, particularly to the construction of terraced fields. This is admittedly a restricted ethnographic phenomenon and as such it cannot bear the weight of any general theory. It is the suggestive character of these developments and the possibility of extrapolating from them to hypothetical pristine conditions that makes them so interesting.[22]

In brief, the shift to irrigation and terracing is from swiddens or impermanent fields to plots which will remain in permanent cultivation for decades and generations. Whereas we have previously stressed the possible role of hydro-agriculture in the transition from egalitarian to rank society, we now note its possible role in the transition to stratification. This it could accomplish by creating conditions under which access to strategic resources, in this case land and water, would be made the specific prerogative of small-scale kin groups such as minimal lineages or even stem families. Through the emergence of hydro-agriculture a community which previously acknowledged no *permanent* association between particular component units and particular stretches of land now begins to recognize such permanent and exclusive rights. Incidentally, the evidence seems to indicate that the rank-forming tendencies of hydro-agriculture need not occur prior to the tendencies toward stratification: both can occur concomitantly. This in turn suggests that we must be cautious in constructing our theory not to make stratification emerge from ranking, though under particular circumstances this is certainly possible.[23]

A point of considerable interest about hydro-agriculture is that it seems to present the possibility

---

[22] The passage refers back to Wittfogel's hydraulic hypothesis, discussed above. Fried wrote this article at a time when Wittfogel's hypothesis was popular, before major criticisms of the theory had been published.

[23] An important point is being made here. Although Fried has proposed a materialist analysis of the relationship between stratification (differential access to prestige and wealth) and ranking, he allows for the possibility that

of an emergence of stratification in the absence of a problem of overpopulation or resource limitation. We need a great deal of further thought on the matter. Studies of the last two decades, in which a considerably higher degree of agricultural expertise on the part of the fieldworkers has been manifested than was formerly the case, have increasingly tended to show that hydro-agriculture does not invariably out-produce slash and burn and that, other things being equal, a population does not automatically prefer hydro-agriculture as a more rationalized approach to agricultural subsistence. Here we can introduce a factor previously excluded. The hydro-agricultural system invariably has a higher degree of settlement concentration than swiddens. Accordingly, it would seem to have considerable value in the maintenance of systems of defense, given the presence of extensive warfare. Here then, is a point at which military considerations would seem to play an important if essentially reinforcing role in the broad evolutionary developments which we are considering.

The writer is intrigued with another possibility for the emergence of stratification. Once again, the conditions involved seem a little too specific to serve the purpose of a single unified theory. It requires the postulation of a society with a fixed rule of residence, preferably one of the simpler ones such as patrilocality/virilocality or matrilocality/uxorilocality[f] and a fixed rule of descent, preferably one parallel to the residence rule.[24] It further postulates a condition of population expansion such that, given slash and burn agriculture, the society is very near the limits of the carrying capacity of the system. Such conditions are very likely to develop at varying speeds within an area of several hundred miles due to obvious imbalances in reproductive rates and to

micro-ecological variation. Now, as long as there is no notable pressure of people on the land, deviation in residence and even in descent will be expectable though quite unusual and lacking in motivation. As the situation grows grave in one area but remains relatively open in another, there may be a tendency for a slight readjustment in residence rules to occur. For example, in a normally virilocal society, the woman who brings her husband back to her natal group transgresses a few customary rules in doing so but presents her agnates with no basic problems in resource allocation since she, as a member of the agnatic group, has her own rights of access which may be shared by the spouse during her lifetime. The complication arises at her death when her husband and all of her children discover themselves to be in an anomalous position since they are not members of the kin community. Where local land problems are not severe and where such breaches of the residence pattern are yet uncommon, it is not unlikely that the aliens will be accepted as *de facto* members of the community with the expectation that future generations will revert to custom, the unorthodox switch of residence fading in memory with the passage of time. Here we have a crude and informal *ambil-anak*.[25] But as the local community enters worsening ecological circumstances and as the exceptional residence becomes more frequent, the residence and descent rules, particularly the latter, assume greater and greater importance. As the situation continues, the community is slowly altered, though the members of the community may be unable to state exactly what the changes are. The result, however, is clear. There are now two kinds of people in the village where formerly there was only one. Now there are kernel villagers, those who have unimpaired access to

---

ranking precedes stratification. In other words, he hedges on a strictly Marxist interpretation. Do you see how nicely this statement ties into Julian Steward's views on multilinear evolution? In fact, Steward's *Theory of Culture Change: The Methodology of Multilinear Evolution* had been published in 1955, just five years before this article.

[24] *Virilocality:* customary residence with the husband's father's kin after marriage; *uxorilocality:* customary residence with the wife's kin after marriage.

[25] *Ambil-anak:* a form of marriage occurring among the otherwise patrilocal Batak people of Indonesia. There, under certain conditions, rather than paying bridewealth, a man may move in with his wife's family. The children of such a marriage will be members of the wife's father's lineage.

land, and those whose tenure rests upon other conditions, such as loyalty to a patron, or tribute, or even a precarious squatter's right.[26]

THE STATE SOCIETY

The word should be abandoned entirely . . . after this chapter the word will be avoided scrupulously and no severe hardship in expression will result. In fact, clarity of expression demands this abstinence (Easton, 1953, p. 108).

The word was "state" and the writer, a political scientist, was reacting to some of the problems in his own field in making this judgment, but it does look as if he was pushed to drastic action by the work of some anthropologists in whose hands the concept of state lost all character and utility, finally ending as a cultural universal. E. Adamson Hoebel, one of the few United States anthropologists to make a serious specialization in the field of law and the state, formerly introduced students to this question by remarking that

where there is political organization there is a state. If political organization is universal, so then is the state. One is the group, the other an institutionalized complex of behavior (Hoebel, 1949, p. 376).[27]

In a revision of the same book after a few years, Hoebel's treatment of the subject seems to indicate that he is in the process of rethinking the matter. His summary words, however, repeat the same conclusion:

Political organization is characteristic of every society. . . . That part of culture that is recognized as political organization is what constitutes the state (Hoebel, 1958, p. 506).

This is a far cry from the approach of evolutionists to the state as exemplified in Sumner and Keller (1927, I, p. 700):

The term state is properly reserved for a somewhat highly developed regulative organization. . . . It is an organization with authority and discipline essential to large-scale achievements, as compared with the family, for example, which is an organization on the same lines but simpler and less potent.

Without making a special issue of the definition of the state (which would easily consume the entire space of this article, if not the volume) let me note one used by the jurist Léon Duguit which conveys the sense most useful to the point of view of this paper:

En prenant le mot dans son sens le plus général, on peut dire qu'il y a unEtattoutes les foi squ'ilexistedansunesociétédonnéeunedifférenci ationpolitique, quelquerudimentaireouquelquecompliquée et developéequ'ellesoit. Le mot Etatdesignesoit les gouvernantsoù le pouvoir-politique, soit la sociétéellemême, oùexistecet-tedifférenciation entre gouvernantsetgouvernés et oùexiste par làmêmeune puissance politique (Duguit, 1921, p. 395).[28]

---

[26] In this paragraph Fried is trying to describe an ecological scenario in which population pressure in an area of limited resources leads to the formation of stratification within a formerly egalitarian society. He proposes that stratification may evolve in a society of swidden horticulturalists when an expanding population taxes the carrying capacity of the local environment. The change is propelled by the potential conflict between the patrilineal inheritance of land and the demand for land by people who are related matrilineally to those in the village. Understanding a change in the structure of society as a result of a conflict is a very Marxist view.

[27] E. Adamson Hoebel (1907–1993) was an American anthropologist who specialized in the study of politics and law in primitive societies. He was a student of Franz Boas,

author of a famous ethnography of the Cheyenne, and president of the American Anthropology Association. Hoebel represents the Boasian relativism to which Fried is reacting. The source of the first quotation is the first edition of Hoebel's book, *Man in the Primitive World* (1949); the quotation that follows is from a revised edition.

[28] Leon Duguit (1859–1928) was a French political scientist whose work focused on the government and the state. The translation of this quotation is:

Taking the word in its most general sense, one could say that there is a state every time a political disparity, however simple or however complex and well developed, exists within a given society. The word state can refer either to governments or political

The difference between Hoebel and Duguit seems to be in the clear statement of power. Reviewing our own paper in the light of this difference we note our previous emphasis on the absence of coercive economic or political power in the egalitarian and rank societies. It is only in the stratified society that such power emerges from embryonic and universal foreshadowings in familial organization.[29]

The maturation of social stratification has manifold implications depending on the precise circumstances in which the developments take place. All subsequent courses, however, have a certain area of overlap; the new social order, with its differential allocation of access to strategic resources, must be maintained and strengthened. In a simple stratified society in which class differentials are more implicit than explicit the network of kin relations covers a sufficient portion of the total fabric of social relations so that areas not specifically governed by genuine kinship relations can be covered by their sociological extensions. The dynamic of stratification is such that this situation cannot endure. The stratified kin group emphasizes its exclusiveness: it erodes the corporative economic functions formerly associated with stipulated kinship and at every turn it amputates extensions of the demonstrated kin unit. The result of this pruning is that the network of kin relations fails more and more to coincide with the network of personal relations. Sooner or later the discrepancy is of such magnitude that, were non-kin sanctions and non-kin agencies absent or structured along customary lines only, the society would dissolve in uncomposable conflict.

The emergent state, then, is the organization of the power of the society on a supra-kin basis. Among its earliest tasks is the maintenance of general order but scarcely discernible from this is its need to support the order of stratification. The defense of a complete system of individual statuses is impossible so the early state concentrates on a few key statuses (helping to explain the tendency to convert any crime into either sacrilege or *lèse majesté*) and on the basic principles of organization, e.g., the idea of hierarchy, property, and the power of the law.

The implementation of these primary functions of the state gives rise to a number of specific and characteristic secondary functions, each of which is associated with one or more particular institutions of its own. These secondary functions include population control in the most general sense (the fixing of boundaries and the definition of the unit; establishment of categories of membership; census). Also a secondary function is the disposal of trouble cases (civil and criminal laws moving toward the status of codes; regular legal procedure; regular officers of adjudication). The protection of sovereignty is also included (maintenance of military forces; police forces and power; eminent domain). Finally, all of the preceding require fiscal support, and this is achieved in the main through taxation and conscription.[30]

In treating of this bare but essential list of state functions and institutions the idea of the state as a universal aspect of culture dissolves as a fantasy. The institutions just itemized may be made to appear in ones or twos in certain primitive societies by exaggeration and by the neglect of known history. In no egalitarian society and in no rank society do a majority of the functions enumerated appear regardless of their guise. Furthermore there is no indication of their appearance as a unified functional response to basic socio-cultural needs except in those stratified societies which are verging upon statehood.

---

power or to the society itself, where there is a difference between governors and governed and where, accordingly, political power exists.

[29] Fried says that social stratification is foreshadowed in "familial organization"; that is, it lies in differential access to resources between small-scale kin groups.

[30] At the time Fried wrote this article there was a controversy over how to define a state. Archaeologists argued that features such as monumental architecture, urban populations, and large-scale public works were indicative of state-level societies. Here Fried is defining a state by complexity of social organization and stratification.

THE TRANSITION TO STATE

Just as stratified society grew out of antecedent forms of society without the conscious awareness of the culture carriers, so it would seem that the state emerged from the stratified society in a similar, inexorable way.[31] If this hypothesis is correct, then such an explanation as the so-called "conquest theory" can be accepted only as a special case of "secondary-state" formation. The conquests discussed by such a theorist as Franz Oppenheimer (1914) established not stratification but super-stratification, either the conqueror or the conquered, or perhaps even both, already being internally stratified.[32]

The problem of the transition to state is so huge and requires such painstaking application to the available archaeological and historical evidence that it would be foolish to pursue it seriously here. Let us conclude, therefore, by harking back to statements made at the outset of this paper, and noting again the distinction between pristine and secondary states. By the former term is meant a state that has developed *sui generis* out of purely local conditions. No previous state, with its acculturative pressures, can be discerned in the background of a pristine state. The secondary state, on the other hand, is pushed by one means or another toward a higher form of organization by an external power which has already been raised to statehood.

The number of pristine states is strictly limited; several centuries, possibly two millennia, have elapsed since the last one emerged in Meso-America, and there seems to be no possibility that any further states of the pristine type will evolve, though further research may bring to light some of the distant past of which we yet have no positive information. In all, there seems to have been some six centers at which pristine states emerged, four in the Old World and two in the New: the Tigris-Euphrates area, the region of the lower Nile, the country drained by the Indus and the middle course of the Huang Ho where it is joined by the Han, Wei, and Fen. The separate areas of Peru-Bolivia and Meso-America complete the roster.

If there is utility in the concept of the pristine state and if history has been read correctly in limiting the designation to the six areas just enumerated, then we discover a remarkable correlation between areas demanding irrigation or flood control and the pristine state. Certainly this is no discovery of the author. It is one of the central ideas of Wittfogel's theory and has received extensive treatment from Julian Steward and others (see Steward, 1955, pp. 178–209; Steward *et al.*, 1955). The implication of the "hydraulic theory" for this paper, however, is that the development of the state as an internal phenomenon is associated with major tasks of drainage and irrigation. The emergence of a control system to ensure the operation of the economy is closely tied to the appearance of a distinctive class system and certain constellations of power in the hands of a managerial bureaucracy which frequently operates below a ruler who commands theoretically unlimited power.

It is an interesting commentary on nineteenth-century political philosophy that the starting point of so many theories was, of necessity, the Classical world of Greece and Rome. According to the present hypothesis, however, both of these great political developments of antiquity were not pristine but secondary formations which built on cultural foundations laid two thousand

---

[31] When Fried talks about the inexorability of the emergence of the state, can there be any doubt about the influence of nineteenth-century evolutionism on his thinking?

[32] Franz Oppenheimer (1864–1943) was a German sociologist best known for his book *The State: Its History and Development Viewed Sociologically* (1914). Most previous scholars viewed the state as the result of a social contract in which individuals surrendered some rights in return for protection from foes outside the state and chaos within it. Oppenheimer argued that the state, in every case, was the result of war and the subjugation of one people by another. He wrote that the state "is a social institution, forced by a victorious group of men on a defeated group, with the sole purpose of regulating the dominion of the victorious group over the vanquished, and securing itself against revolt from within and attacks from abroad (Oppenheimer 1914:15).

years and more before the rise of Greece. Furthermore, it would seem that the active commercial and military influences of the truly ancient pristine states, mediated through the earliest of the secondary states to appear in Asia Minor and the eastern Mediterranean littoral, were catalysts in the events of the northern and western Mediterranean.

CONCLUSION

The close of a paper like this, which moves like a gadfly from time to time, place to place, and subject matter to subject matter, and which never pauses long enough to make a truly detailed inquiry or supply the needed documentation, the close of such a paper requires an apology perhaps more than a conclusion.

I have been led to write this paper by my ignorance of any modern attempt to link up the contributions which have been made in many sub-disciplines into a single unified theory of the emergence of social stratification and the state. That the theory offered here is crude, often too special, and by no means documented seems less important than that it may be used as a sitting duck to attract the fire and better aim of others.[33]

NOTES

[a] The reader may object to crediting Polanyi with the concept of a reciprocal economy. While it is true that Thurnwald and Malinowski earlier expressed similar concepts, and Durkheim, with his distinction between segmental and organic societies, also foreshadows this development, it awaited Polanyi's analysis to place reciprocal economies into systematic harmony with other, more complex types of economy, such as the redistributive type discussed later on, and the market kind as well. For Polanyi's definitions of each of these types see Polanyi, Arensberg and Pearson, 1957, pp. 250–56.

[b] For an ethnographic illustration of this point see Oliver, 1955, pp. 422 ff.

[c] These, of course, would be ranked lineages or ranked clans. Cf. Fried, 1957, pp. 23–26.

[d] As does Leach, 1954, p. 10.

[e] Strategic resources are those things which, given the technological base and environmental setting of the culture, maintain subsistence. See Fried, 1957, p. 4.

[f] Our residence terms follow usage suggested by J. L. Fischer, 1958.

REFERENCES

Dugui, Léon. 1921. Traité de droit constitutionnel. 2d ed. Vol. 1 Paris.

Easton, David. 1953. The Political System. New York.

Fischer, J. L. 1958. "The Classification of Residence in Censuses," *American Anthropologist*, 60:508–17.

Fried, Morton H. 1957. "The Classification of Corporate Unilineal Descent Groups," *Journal of the Royal Anthropological Institute*, 87:1–29.

Hoebel, E. Adamson. 1949. Man in the Primitive World. 1st ed. New York.

——1958. Man in the Primitive World. 2nd ed. New York.

Kirchhoff, Paul. 1935. "The Principles of Clanship in Human Society." (Ms; cf. *Davidson Journal of Anthropology* 1 [1955]).

Landtman, Gunnar. 1938. The Origin of the Inequality of the Social Classes. London.

Leach, E.R. 1954. Political Systems of Highland Burma. Cambridge, Mass.

Leacock, Eleanor. 1958. "Status among the Montagnais-Naskapi of Labrador," *Ethnohistory*, 5:Part 3:200–209.

Oliver, Douglas. 1955. A Solomon Island Society. Cambridge, Mass.

Oppenheimer, Franz. 1914. The State; Its History and Development Viewed Sociologically. New York.

Polanyi, Karl, Conrad M. Arensberg, and Harry W. Pearson, eds. 1957. Trade and Market in the Early Empires. Glencoe, Ill.

Sahlins, Marshall. 1958. Social Stratification in Polynesia. Seattle.

——1957. "Differentiation by Adaptation in Polynesian Societies," *Journal of the Polynesian Society*, 66:291–300.

Steward, Julian H. 1955. Theory of Culture Change. Urban, Ill.

Steward, Julian H., *et al.* 1955. Irrigation Civilizations: A Comparative Study. Social Science Monographs #1, Washington, D.C.

[33] When Fried speaks of linking the contributions of many subdisciplines into a single unified theory, he refers, in particular, to the exchange between archaeology and cultural ecology and materialism. The transfer of ideas between these areas resulted in the publication of numerous works on cultural evolution for almost two decades.

Summer, W.G., and A.G. Keller. 1927. The Science of Society. New Haven, Conn.

Tylor, Edward B. 1888. "On a Method of Investigating the Development of Institutions; Applied to Laws of Marriage and Descent," *Journal of the Royal Anthropological Institute*, 18:245–69.

White, Leslie. 1948. "The Definition and Prohibition of Incest," *American Anthropologist*, 50:416–35.

Wittfogel, Karl A. 1957. Oriental Despotism. New Haven, Conn.

19. *The Cultural Ecology of India's Sacred Cattle*

MARVIN HARRIS (1927–2001)

I<small>N THIS PAPER</small> I attempt to indicate certain puzzling inconsistencies in prevailing interpretations of the ecological role of bovine cattle in India. My argument is based upon intensive reading—I have never seen a sacred cow, nor been to India. As a non-specialist, no doubt I have committed blunders an Indianist would have avoided. I hope these errors will not deprive me of that expert advice and informed criticism which alone can justify so rude an invasion of unfamiliar territory.[1]

I have written this paper because I believe the irrational, non-economic, and exotic aspects of the Indian cattle complex are greatly overemphasized at the expense of rational, economic, and mundane interpretations.

My intent is not to substitute one dogma for another, but to urge that explanation of taboos, customs, and rituals associated with management of Indian cattle be sought in "positive-functioned" and probably "adaptive" processes of the ecological system of which they are a part,[a] rather than in the influence of Hindu theology.[2]

Mismanagement of India's agricultural resources as a result of the Hindu doctrine of *ahimsa*,[b] especially as it applies to beef cattle, is frequently noted by Indianists and others concerned with the relation between values and behavior. Although different antirational, dysfunctional, and inutile aspects of the cattle complex are stressed by different authors, many agree that *ahimsa* is a prime example of how men will diminish their material welfare to obtain spiritual satisfaction in obedience to nonrational or frankly irrational beliefs.

A sample opinion on this subject is here summarized: According to Simoons (1961:3), "irrational ideologies" frequently compel men "to overlook foods that are abundant locally and are of high nutritive value, and to utilize other scarcer foods of less value." The Hindu beef-eating taboo is one of Simoons' most important cases. Venkatraman (1938:706) claims, "India is unique in possessing an enormous amount of cattle without making profit from its slaughter." The Ford Foundation (1959:64) reports "widespread recognition

From *Current Anthropology* (1960)

---

[1] In the 1960s ethnographic experience was the cornerstone of authority in American anthropology (and to some extent still is today). Harris' upfront admission that he had never been to India was a challenge to this prevailing anthropological opinion and is related to his views on the emic-etic debate that was raging within the profession at this time. (For more on emics and etics, see footnote 5.)

[2] Harris makes his materialist and neofunctionalist position clear in the opening paragraphs of this essay. As a material-

ist, Harris presumes that Indian beliefs about the sacredness of cattle have a rational economic explanation that takes precedence over references to Hindu theology. In addition, Harris' statement that the explanation for Indian cattle management can be found in the "adaptive processes of the ecological system of which they are a part" clearly demonstrates the influence of the cultural ecology of Julian Steward (see essay 17). His claim that he does not wish to substitute one dogma for another is disingenuous—Harris is brilliant, but he is one of the more polemic writers in anthropology.

not only among animal husbandry officials, but among citizens generally, that India's cattle population is far in excess of the available supplies of fodder and feed . . . At least ⅓, and possibly as many as ½, of the Indian cattle population may be regarded as surplus in relation to feed supply." Matson (1933:227) writes it is a commonplace of the "cattle question that vast numbers of Indian cattle are so helplessly inefficient as to have no commercial value beyond that of their hides." Srinivas (1952:222) believes "Orthodox Hindu opinion regards the killing of cattle with abhorrence, even though the refusal to kill the vast number of useless cattle which exist in India today is detrimental to the nation."

According to the Indian Ministry of Information (1957:243), "The large animal population is more a liability than an asset in view of our land resources." Chatterjee (1960) calculates that Indian production of cow and buffalo milk involves a "heavy recurring loss of Rs 774 crores. This is equivalent to 6.7 times the amount we are annually spending on importing food grains." Knight (1954:141) observes that because the Hindu religion teaches great reverence for the cow, "there existed a large number of cattle whose utility to the community did not justify economically the fodder which they consumed." Das and Chatterji (1962:120) concur: "A large number of cattle in India are old and decrepit and constitute a great burden on an already impoverished land. This is due to the prejudice among the Hindus against cow killing." Mishra (1962) approvingly quotes Lewis (1955:106): "It is not true that if economic and religious doctrines conflict the economic interest will always win. The Hindu cow has remained sacred for centuries, although this is plainly contrary to economic interest." Darling (1934:158) asserts, "By its attitude to slaughter Hinduism makes any planned improvement of cattle breeding almost impossible." According to Desai (1959:36), "The cattle population is far in excess of the available fodder and feeds."[3]

[*In a 400-word passage eliminated from this edition, Harris continues his catalog of experts and government agencies that have declared Indian cattle practices uneconomic.*]

In spite of the sometimes final and unqualified fashion in which "surplus," "useless," "uneconomic," and "superfluous" are applied to part or all of India's cattle, contrary conclusions seem admissible when the cattle complex is viewed as part of an *eco-system* rather than as a sector of a national price market. Ecologically, it is doubtful that any component of the cattle complex is "useless," i.e., the number, type, and condition of Indian bovines do not *per se* impair the ability of the human population to survive and reproduce. Much more likely the relationship between bovines and humans is symbiotic[c] instead of competitive. It probably represents the outcome of intense Darwinian pressures acting upon human and bovine population, cultigens, wild flora and fauna, and social structure and ideology. Moreover presumably the degree of observance of taboos against bovine slaughter and beef-eating reflect the power of these ecological pressures rather than *ahimsa*; in other words, *ahimsa* itself derives power and sustenance from the material rewards it confers upon both men and animals.[4] To support these

---

[3] Harris' materialist point of view has been so successful in the last few decades that it should be noted that Westerners really used to think that Indian cattle usage was irrational. In fact, the view that non-Western people's traditional practices were irrational formed one of the cornerstones of colonial ethnocentrism. From the Western point of view, the irrationality of Indian culture was demonstrated by the failure of Indians to conform to European notions of animal husbandry, a failure that confirmed the British in their self-perceived civilizing mission. So, while Harris is doing a cultural-materialist analysis, he is also working in a form of analysis that would have made Franz Boas proud.

[4] Harris' debt to the cultural ecology of Steward is clear in this paragraph. His statement that the features of the cattle complex are the consequence of Darwinian pressures within an ecological system sounds very much like Steward's concept of the cultural core. Harris doesn't spell out exactly how these pressures operate, but the invocation of Darwin increases the scientific feel of the article by associating it with a well-established scientific position.

hypotheses, the major aspects of the Indian cattle complex will be reviewed under the following headings: (1) Milk Production, (2) Traction, (3) Dung, (4) Beef and Hides, (5) Pasture, (6) Useful and Useless Animals, (7) Slaughter, (8) Anti-Slaughter Legislation, (9) Old-Age Homes, and (10) Natural Selection.

MILK PRODUCTION

In India the average yield of whole milk per Zebu cow is 413 pounds, compared with the 5,000-pound average in Europe and the U.S.[d] (Kartha 1936:607; Spate 1954:231). In Madhya Pradesh yield is as low as 65 pounds, while in no state does it rise higher than the barely respectable 1,445 pounds of the Punjab (Chatterjee 1960:1347). According to the 9th Quinquennial Livestock Census (1961) among the 47,200,000 cows over 3 years old, 27,200,000 were dry and/or not calved (Chaudri and Giri 1963:598).

These figures, however, should not be used to prove that the cows are useless or uneconomic, since milk production is a minor aspect of the sacred cow's contribution to the *eco-system*. Indeed, most Indianists agree that it is the buffalo, not the Zebu, whose economic worth must be judged primarily by milk production. Thus, Kartha (1959:225) writes, "the buffalo, and not the Zebu, is the dairy cow." This distinction is elaborated by Mamoria (1953:255):

> Cows in the rural areas are maintained for producing bullocks rather than for milk. She-buffaloes, on the other hand, are considered to be better dairy animals than cows. The male buffaloes are neglected and many of them die or are sold for slaughter before they attain maturity.

Mohan (1962:47) makes the same point:

> For agricultural purposes bullocks are generally preferred, and, therefore, cows in rural areas are primarily maintained for the production of male progeny and incidentally only for milk.

It is not relevant to my thesis to establish whether milk production is a primary or secondary objective or purpose of the Indian farmer. Failure to separate emics from etics (Harris 1964) contributes greatly to confusion surrounding the Indian cattle question.[5] The significance of the preceding quotations lies in the agreement that cows contribute to human material welfare in more important ways than milk production. In this new context, the fact that U.S. cows produce 20 times more milk than Indian cows loses much of its significance. Instead, it is more relevant to note that, despite the marginal status of milking in the symbiotic syndrome, 46.7% of India's dairy products come from cow's milk (Chatterjee 1960:1347). How far this production is balanced by expenditures detrimental to human welfare will be discussed later.

TRACTION

The principal positive ecological effect of India's bovine cattle is in their contribution to production of grain crops, from which about 80% of the human calorie ration comes. Some form of animal traction is required to initiate the agricultural cycle, dependent upon plowing in both rainfall and irrigation areas. Additional traction for hauling, transport, and irrigation is provided by animals, but by far their most critical kinetic contribution is plowing.

---

[5] The terms *emic* and *etic* were coined in 1954 by the missionary-linguist Kenneth Pike (1912–2000). Emic statements refer to meaning as it is perceived by the natives of a culture, and emic anthropologists tried to outline the models by which natives understood their society. By definition, emic understanding is culture-bound. In contrast, etic meanings are those arrived at by empirical investigation. Etic anthropologists aim at producing generalizations that are cross-culturally valid using methods of investigation that can be verified and replicated by anyone using a similar investigative process. Etic analyses are typically perceived to be more scientific, and Harris' analysis of cattle in India is an etic study. Harris believes that many studies mix etic and emic data together, thus confounding the analysis. Here he says the same problem "contributes greatly to confusion surrounding the Indian cattle question." Harris claims that when the situation is examined from an etic perspective (energy contribution of cows versus energy expenditures of cows within an overall ecosystem), it is clear that the treatment of cattle in India is adaptive.

Although many authorities believe there is an overall surplus of cattle in India, others point to a serious shortage of draught animals. According to Kothavala (1934:122), "Even with . . . overstocking, the draught power available for land operations at the busiest season of the year is inadequate. ..." For West Bengal, the National Council of Applied Economic Research (1962:56) reports:

> However, despite the large number of draught animals, agriculture in the State suffers from a shortage of draught power. There are large numbers of small landholders entirely dependent on hired animal labour.

Spate (1954:36) makes the same point, "there are too many cattle in the gross, but most individual farmers have too few to carry on with." Gupta (1959:42) and Lewis and Barnouw (1958:102) say a pair of bullocks is the minimum technical unit for cultivation, but in a survey by Diskalkar (1960:87), 18% of the cultivators had only 1 bullock or none. Nationally, if we accept a low estimate of 60,000,000 rural households (Mitra 1963:298) and a high estimate of 80,000,000 working cattle and buffaloes (Government of India 1962:76), we see at once that the allegedly excess number of cattle in India is insufficient to permit a large portion, perhaps as many as ⅓, of India's farmers to begin the agricultural cycle under conditions appropriate to their techno-environmental system.

Much has been made of India's having 115 head of cattle per square mile, compared with 28 per square mile for the U.S. and 3 per square mile for Canada. But what actually may be most characteristic of the size of India's herd is the low ratio of cattle to people. Thus, India has 44 cattle per 100 persons, while in the U.S. the ratio is 58 per 100 and in Canada, 90 (Mamoria 1953:256). Yet, in India cattle are employed as a basic instrument of agricultural production.

Sharing of draught animals on a cooperative basis might reduce the need for additional animals. Chaudhri and Giri point out that the "big farmer manages to cultivate with a pair of bullock a much larger area than the small cultivators"

(1963:596). But, the failure to develop cooperative forms of plowing can scarcely be traced to *ahimsa*. If anything, emphasis upon independent, family-sized farm units follows intensification of individual land tenure patterns and other property innovations deliberately encouraged by the British (Bhatia 1963:18 on). Under existing property arrangements, there is a perfectly good economic explanation of why bullocks are not shared among adjacent households. Plowing cannot take place at any time of the year, but must be accomplished within a few daylight hours in conformity with seasonal conditions. These are set largely by summer monsoons, responsible for about 90% of the total rainfall (Bhatia 1963:4). Writing about Orissa, Bailey (1957:74) notes:

> As a temporary measure, an ox might be borrowed from a relative, or a yoke of cattle and a ploughman might be hired . . . but during the planting season, when the need is the greatest, most people are too busy to hire out or lend cattle.

According to Desai (1948:86):

> . . . over vast areas, sowing and harvesting operations, by the very nature of things, begin simultaneously with the outbreak of the first showers and the maturing of crops respectively, and especially the former has got to be put through quickly during the first phase of the monsoon. Under these circumstances, reliance by a farmer on another for bullocks is highly risky and he has got, therefore, to maintain his own pair.

Dube (1955:84) is equally specific:

> The cultivators who depend on hired cattle or who practice cooperative lending and borrowing of cattle cannot take the best advantage of the first rains, and this enforced wait results in untimely sowing and poor crops.

Wiser and Wiser (1963:62) describe the plight of the bullock-short farmer as follows, "When he needs the help of bullocks most, his neighbors are all using theirs." And Shastri (1960:1592) points out, "Uncertainty of Indian farming due to dependence on rains is the main factor creating obstacles in the way of improvements in bullock labor."

It would seem, therefore, that this aspect of the cattle complex is not an expression of spirit and ritual, but of rain and energy.[6]

DUNG

In India cattle dung is the main source of domestic cooking fuel. Since grain crops cannot be digested unless boiled or baked, cooking is indispensable. Considerable disagreement exists about the total amount of cattle excrement and its uses, but even the lowest estimates are impressive. An early estimate by Lupton (1922:60) gave the BTU equivalent of dung consumed in domestic cooking as 35,000,000 tons of coal or 68,000,000 tons of wood. Most detailed appraisal is by National Council of Applied Economic Research (1959:3), which rejects H. J. Bhabha's estimate of 131,000,000 tons of coal and the Ministry of Food and Agriculture's 112,000,000 tons. The figure preferred by the NCAER is 35,000,000 tons anthracite or 40,000,000 tons bituminous, but with a possible range of between 35–45,000,000 of anthracite dung-coal equivalent. This calculation depends upon indications that only 36% of the total wet dung is utilized as fuel (p. 14), a lower estimate than any reviewed by Saha (1956:923). These vary from 40% (Imperial Council on Agricultural Research) to 50% (Ministry of Food and Agriculture) to 66.6% (Department of Education, Health and Lands). The

NCAER estimate of a dung-coal equivalent of 35,000,000 tons is therefore quite conservative; it is nonetheless an impressive amount of BTU's to be plugged into an energy system.

Kapp (1963:144 on), who discusses at length the importance of substituting tractors for bullocks, does not give adequate attention to finding cooking fuel after the bullocks are replaced. The NCAER (1959:20) conclusion that dung is cheaper than coke seems an understatement. Although it is claimed that wood resources are potentially adequate to replace dung the measures advocated do not involve *ahimsa* but are again an indictment of a land tenure system not inspired by Hindu tradition (NCAER 1959:20 on; Bansil 1958:97 on). Finally, it should be noted that many observers stress the slow burning qualities of dung and its special appropriateness for preparation of *ghi* and deployment of woman-power in the household (Lewis and Barnouw 1958:40; Mosher 1946:153).[7]

As manure, dung enters the energy system in another vital fashion. According to Mujumdar (1960:743), 300,000,000 tons are used as fuel, 340,000,000 tons as manure, and 160,000,000 tons "wasted on hillsides and roads." Spate (1954:238) believes that 40% of dung production is spread on fields, 40% burned, and 20% "lost." Possibly estimates of the amount of dung lost are grossly inflated in view of the importance of "roads and hillsides" in the grazing pattern (see Pasture). Similarly artificial and culture- or even class-bound judgments refer to utilization of India's night soil. It is usually assumed that Chinese

---

[6] Harris was taking a fairly radical position at this time, therefore he presents quotation after quotation supporting his views when one or two would suffice. Note that he relies almost exclusively on statistical rather than ethnographic data. True to his etic perspective, Harris provides the reader with a statistical portrait of Indian society. It is also instructive to examine Harris' writing style. Although not as polemical an author as Marx, who called one of his opponents "Saint Max" (see essay 4), Harris undercuts his opponents through rhetorical style as well as scientific argument. Throughout this section—as he does here—Harris concludes points by saying, in effect, you do not

need religion to explain this. The cumulative effect is to make the position he is opposing look silly.

[7] Harris' statement about "a land tenure system not inspired by Hindu tradition" is an allusion to British colonialism. As Friedman points out in his 1974 critique of Harris' analysis, Harris never really deals with the cultural context in which the traditions he analyzes take place—that is, centuries of British colonial rule.

Ghi, or *ghee,* is clarified butter made from the butterfat of milk.

and Indian treatment of this resource are radically different, and that vast quantities of nitrogen go unused in agriculture because of Hindu-inspired definitions of modesty and cleanliness. However, most human excrement from Indian villages is deposited in surrounding fields; the absence of latrines helps explain why such fields raise 2 and 3 successive crops each year (Mosher 1946:154, 33; Bansil 1958:104). More than usual caution, therefore, is needed before concluding that a significant amount of cattle dung is wasted. Given the conscious premium set on dung for fuel and fertilizer, thoughtful control maintained over grazing patterns (see Pasture), and occurrence of specialized sweeper and gleaner castes, much more detailed evidence of wastage is needed than is now available. Since cattle graze on "hillsides and roads," dung dropped there would scarcely be totally lost to the *eco-system*, even with allowance for loss of nitrogen by exposure to air and sunlight. Also, if any animal dung is wasted on roads and hillsides it is not because of *ahimsa* but of inadequate pasturage suitable for collecting and processing animal droppings. The sedentary, intensive rainfall agriculture of most of the subcontinent is heavily dependent upon manuring. So vital is this that Spate (1954:239) says substitutes for manure consumed as fuel "must be supplied, and lavishly, even at a financial loss to government." If this is the case, then old, decrepit, and dry animals might have a use after all, especially when, as we shall see, the dung they manufacture employs raw materials lost to the culture-energy system unless processed by cattle, and especially when many apparently moribund animals revive at the next monsoon and provide their owners with a male calf.[8]

BEEF AND HIDES[9]

Positive contributions of India's sacred cattle do not cease with milk-grazing, bullock-producing, traction, and dung-dropping. There remains the direct protein contribution of 25,000,000 cattle and buffalo which die each year (Mohan 1962:54). This feature of the eco-system is reminiscent of the East African cattle area where, despite the normal taboo on slaughter, natural deaths and ceremonial occasions are probably frequent enough to maintain beef consumption near the ecological limit with dairying as the primary function (Schneider 1957:278 on). Although most Hindus probably do not consume beef, the *eco-system* under consideration is not confined to Hindus. The human population includes some 55,000,000 "scheduled" exterior or untouchable groups (Hutton 1961:vii), many of whom will consume beef if given the opportunity (Dube 1955:68–69), plus several million more Moslems and Christians. Much of the flesh on the 25,000,000 dead cattle and buffalo probably gets consumed by human beings whether or not the cattle die naturally. Indeed, could it be that without the orthodox Hindu beef-eating taboo, many marginal and depressed castes would be deprived of an occasional, but nutritionally critical, source of animal protein?

It remains to note that the slaughter taboo does not prevent depressed castes from utilizing skin, horns and hoofs of dead beasts. In 1956 16,000,000 cattle hides were produced (Randhawa 1962:322). The quality of India's huge leather industry—the world's largest—leaves much to be desired, but the problem is primarily outmoded tanning techniques and lack of capital, not *ahimsa*.

---

[8] Since the publication of Leslie White's "Energy and the Evolution of Culture" in 1943, energy has had a significant role in American anthropology. Harris' discussion of dung as an energy source is an early example of the type of analysis that became a mainstay of the ecological and evolutionary approaches in cultural anthropology.

[9] This section may be the weakest in Harris' argument. Notice the absence of statistical support in his discussion of beef eating and the leather industry. He writes, "The quality of India's huge leather industry—the world's largest—leaves much to be desired, but the problem is primarily outmoded tanning techniques and lack of capital, not *ahimsa*." But one could easily argue that it is precisely *ahimsa* that keeps the industry outmoded since, because of *ahimsa*, no one with prestige or capital will invest in tanning. Treating hides is the domain of the lowest castes. This point does not really damage his argument, but it is typical of Harris' dogmatism: He will allow no explanatory power to *ahimsa* at all.

PASTURE

The principal positive-functioned or useful contributions of India's sacred cattle to human survival and well-being have been described. Final evaluation of their utility must involve assessment of energy costs in terms of resources and human labor input which might be more efficiently expended in other activities.

Direct and indirect evidence suggests that in India men and bovine cattle do not compete for existence. According to Mohan (1962:43 on):

> . . . the bulk of the food on which the animals subsist . . . is not the food that is required for human consumption, i.e., fibrous fodders produced as incidental to crop production, and a large part of the crop residues or byproducts of seeds and waste grazing.

On the contrary, "the bulk of foods (straws and crop residues) that are ploughed into the soil in other countries are converted into milk" (p. 45).

The majority of the Indian cattle obtain their requirements from whatever grazing is available from straw and stalk and other residues from human foodstuffs, and are starved seasonally in the dry months when grasses wither.

In Bengal the banks and slopes of the embankments of public roads are the only grazing grounds and the cattle subsist mainly on paddy straw, paddy husks and . . . coarse grass. . . . (Mamoria 1953:263–64).

According to Dube (1955:84), ". . . the cattle roam about the shrubs and rocks and eat whatever fodder is available there." This is confirmed by Moomaw (1949:96): "Cows subsist on the pasture and any coarse fodder they can find. Grain is fed for only a day or two following parturition." The character of the environmental niche reserved for cattle nourishment is described by Gourou (1963:123), based on data furnished by Dupuis (1960) for Madras:

> Iffautvoirclairementque le faiblerendement du bétailindienn'est pas un gaspillage:
> cebétailn'entre pas en concurrence avec la consommation de produitsagricoles . . . ils ne leursacrifient pas des surfaces agricoles, ouayant un potential agricole.[10]

NCAER (1961:57) confines this pattern for Tripura: "There is a general practice of feeding livestock on agricultural by-products such as straw, grain wastes and husks"; for West Bengal (NCAER 1962:59): "The state has practically no pasture or grazing fields, and the farmers are not in the habit of growing green fodders . . . livestock feeds are mostly agricultural by-products"; and for Andhra Pradesh (NCAER 1962:52): "Cattle are stall-fed, but the bulk of the feed consists of paddy straw. . . . "

The only exceptions to the rural pattern of feeding cattle on waste products and grazing them on marginal or unproductive lands involve working bullocks and nursing cows:

> The working bullocks, on whose efficiency cultivation entirely depends, are usually fed with chopped bananas at the time of fodder scarcity. But the milch cows have to live in a semi-starved condition, getting what nutrition they can from grazing on the fields after their rice harvest (Gangulee 1935:17). At present cattle are fed largely according to the season. During the rainy period they feed upon the grass which springs up on the *uncultivated* hillsides. . . . But in the dry season there is hardly any grass, and cattle wander on the *cropless* lands in an often halfstarved condition. True there is some fodder at these times in the shape of rice-straw and dried copra, but it is not generally sufficient, and is furthermore given mainly to the animals actually *working* at the time (Mayer 1952:70, italics added).

There is much evidence that Hindu farmers calculate carefully which animals deserve more food and attention. In Madras, Randhawa, et al. (1961:117) report: "The cultivators pay more attention to the male stock used for ploughing and for draft. There is a general neglect of the cow and the

---

[10] The translation of this passage is: "One needs to see clearly that the small return of Indian cattle is not waste: These beasts do not compete for the consumption of agricultural produce . . . neither fields nor areas that could be used for agriculture are sacrificed to them."

female calf even from birth . . ." Similar discrimination is described by Mamoria (1953:263 on):

> Many plough bullocks are sold off in winter or their rations are ruthlessly decreased whenever they are not worked in full, while milch cattle are kept on after lactation on poor and inadequate grazing. . . . The cultivator feeds his bullocks better than his cow because it pays him. He feeds his bullocks better during the busy season, when they work, than during the slack season, when they remain idle. Further, he feeds his more valuable bullocks better than those less valuable. . . . Although the draught animals and buffaloes are properly fed, the cow gets next to nothing of stall feeding. She is expected to pick up her living on the bare fields after harvest and on the village wasteland. . . .

The previously cited NCAER report on Andhra Pradesh notes that "Bullocks and milking cows during the working season get more concentrates. . . ." (1962:52). Wiser and Wiser (1963:71) sum up the situation in a fashion supporting Srinivas' (1958:4) observation that the Indian peasant is "nothing if he is not practical":

> Farmers have become skillful in reckoning the minimum of food necessary for maintaining animal service. Cows are fed just enough to assure their calving and giving a little milk. They are grazed during the day on lands which yield very little vegetation, and are given a very sparse meal at night.

Many devout Hindus believe the bovine cattle of India are exploited without mercy by greedy Hindu owners. *Ahimsa* obviously has little to do with economizing which produces the famous *phooka* and *doom dev* techniques for dealing with dry cows.[11] Not to Protestants but to Hindus did Gandhi (1954:7) address lamentations concerning the cow:

> How we bleed her to take the last drop of milk from her, how we starve her to emaciation, how we ill-treat the calves, how we deprive them of their portion of milk, how cruelly we treat the oxen, how we castrate them, how we beat them, how we overload them. . . . I do not know that the condition of the cattle in any other part of the world is as bad as in unhappy India.

USEFUL AND USELESS ANIMALS

How then, if careful rationing is characteristic of livestock management, do peasants tolerate the widely reported herds of useless animals? Perhaps "useless" means one thing to the peasant and quite another to the price-market-oriented agronomist. It is impossible at a distance to judge which point of view is ecologically more valid, but the peasants could be right more than the agronomists are willing to admit.

Since non-working and non-lactating animals are thermal and chemical factories which depend on waste lands and products for raw materials, judgment that a particular animal is useless cannot be supported without careful examination of its owner's household budget. Estimates from the cattle census which equate useless with dry or non-working animals are not convincing. But even if a given animal in a particular household is of less-than-marginal utility, there is an additional factor whose evaluation would involve long-range bovine biographies. The utility of a particular animal to its owner cannot be established simply by its performance during season or an animal cycle. Perhaps the whole system of Indian bovine management is alien to costing procedures of the West. There may be a kind of low-risk sweepstakes which drags on for 10 or 12 years before the losers and winners are separated.

As previously observed, the principal function of bovine cows is not their milk-producing but their bullock-producing abilities. Also established is the fact that many farmers are short of bullocks. Cows have the function primarily to produce male offspring, but when? In Europe and America, cows become pregnant under well-controlled, hence predictable, circumstances and a farmer with

---

[11] The "*famous*" *phooka* and *doom dev* techniques Harris refers to are procedures Indians use to stimulate a cow's flow of milk. As described by Harris in his 1974 book *Cows, Pigs, Wars, and Witches*, *phooka* is blowing air into the cow's uterus through a hollow pipe; *doom dev* refers to stuffing the cow's tail into its vagina.

many animals can count on male offspring in half the births. In India, cows become pregnant under quite different circumstances. Since cows suffer from malnutrition through restriction to marginal pasture, they conceive and deliver in unpredictable fashion. The chronic starvation of the inter-monsoon period makes the cow, in the words of Mamoria (1953:263), "an irregular breeder." Moreover, with few animals, the farmer may suffer many disappointments before a male is born. To the agriculture specialist with knowledge of what healthy dairy stock look like, the hot weather herds of walking skeletons "roaming over the bare fields and dried up wastes" (Leake 1923:267) must indeed seem without economic potential. Many of them, in fact, will not make it through to the next monsoon. However, among the survivors are an unknown number still physically capable of having progeny. Evidently neither the farmer nor the specialist knows which will conceive, nor when. To judge from Bombay city, even when relatively good care is bestowed on a dry cow, no one knows the outcome: "If an attempt is made to salvage them, they have to be kept and fed for a long time. Even then, it is not known whether they will conceive or not" (Nandra, *et al.* 1955:9).

In rural areas, to judge a given animal useless may be to ignore the recuperative power of these breeds under conditions of erratic rainfall and unpredictable grazing opportunities. The difference of viewpoint between the farmer and the expert is apparent in Moomaw's (1949) incomplete attempt to describe the life history of an informant's cattle. The farmer in question had 3 oxen, 2 female buffaloes, 4 head of young cattle and 3 "worthless" cows (p. 23). In Moomaw's opinion, "the three cows . . . are a liability to him, providing no income, yet consuming feed which might be placed to better use." Yet we learn, "The larger one had a calf about once in three years"; moreover 2 of the 3 oxen were "raised" by the farmer himself. (Does this mean that they were the progeny of the farmer's cows?) The farmer tells Moomaw, "The young stock get some fodder, but for the most part they pasture with the village herd. The cows give nothing and I cannot afford to feed them." Whereupon Moomaw's *non sequitur:* "We spoke no more of his cows, for like many a farmer he just keeps them, without inquiring whether it is profitable or not" (p. 25).

The difficulties in identifying animals that are definitely uneconomic for a given farmer are reflected in the varying estimates of the total of such animals. The Expert Committee on the Prevention of Slaughter of Cattle estimated 20,000,000 uneconomic cattle in India (Nandra, *et al.* 1953:62). Roy (1955:14) settles for 5,500,000, or about 3.5%. Mamoria (1953:257), who gives the still lower estimate of 2,900,000, or 2.1%, claims most of these are males. A similarly low percentage—2.5%—is suggested for West Bengal (NCAER 1962:56). None of these estimates appears based on bovine life histories in relation to household budgets; none appears to involve estimates of economic significance of dung contributions of older animals.[12]

Before a peasant is judged a victim of Oriental mysticism, might it not be well to indicate the devastating material consequences which befall a poor farmer unable to replace a bullock lost through disease, old age, or accident? Bailey (1957:73) makes it clear that in the economic life of the marginal peasantry, "Much the most devastating single event is the loss of an ox (or a plough buffalo)." If the farmer is unable to replace the animal with one from his own herd, he must borrow money at usurious rates. Defaults on such loans are the principal causes of transfer of land titles from peasants to landlords. Could this explain why the peasant is not overly perturbed that some of his animals might turn out to be only dung-providers? After all, the real threat to his existence does not arise from animals but from people ready to swoop down on him as soon as one of his beasts

---

[12] Harris' concern is for the economics of cattle at the level of the Indian peasant household, but the statistics he cites are national or state-level figures. Millions of starving cattle wandering around might present state-level problems not experienced by an individual farmer—the level at which a problem is examined affects one's analysis. Both Harris and the government figures he cites may be correct, but in different ways. The only macro-level view Harris takes is farther down, when he discusses the political significance of cattle slaughter bans.

falters. Chapekar's (1960:27) claim that the peasant's "stock serve as a great security for him to fall back on whenever he is in need" would seem to be appropriate only in reference to the unusually well-established minority. In a land where life expectancy at birth has only recently risen to 30 years (Black 1959:2), it is not altogether appropriate to speak of security. The poorest farmers own insufficient stock. Farm management studies show that holdings below $2/3$ of average area account for $2/5$ of all farms, but maintain only $1/4$ of the total cattle on farms. "This is so, chiefly because of their limited resources to maintain cattle" (Chaudhri and Giri 1963:598).

SLAUGHTER

Few, if any, Hindu farmers kill their cattle by beating them over the head, severing their jugular veins or shooting them. But to assert that they do not kill their animals when it is economically important for them to do so may be equally false. This interpretation escapes the notice of so many observers because the slaughtering process receives recognition only in euphemisms. People will admit that they "neglect" their animals, but will not openly accept responsibility for the *etic* effects, i.e., the more or less rapid death which ensues. The strange result of this euphemistic pattern is evidenced in the following statement by Moomaw (1949:96): "All calves born, however inferior, are allowed to live until they die of neglect." In the light of many similar but, by Hindu standards, more vulgar observations, it is clear that this kind of statement should read, "Most calves born are not allowed to live, but are starved to death."

This is roughly the testimony of Gourou (1963:125), "Le paysan conserve seulement les veaux qui deviendrontboeufs de labourouvacheslaitières; les autressontécartés . . . etmeur-

ent d'epuisement."[13] Wiser and Wiser (1963:70) are even more direct:

> Cows and buffaloes too old to furnish milk are not treated cruelly, but simply allowed to starve. The same happens to young male buffaloes. . . . The males are unwanted and little effort is made to keep them alive.

Obviously, when an animal, undernourished to begin with, receives neither food nor care, it will not enjoy a long life (compare Gourou 1963: 124). Despite claims that an aged and decrepit cow "must be supported like an unproductive relative, until it dies a natural death" (Mosher 1946:124), ample evidence justifies belief that "few cattle die of old age"[e] (Bailey 1957:75). Dandekar (1964:352) makes the same point: "In other words, because the cows cannot be fed nor can they be killed, they are neglected, starved and left to die a 'natural' death."

The farmer culls his stock by starving unwanted animals and also, under duress, sells them directly or indirectly to butchers. With economic pressure, many Indians who will not kill or eat cows themselves:

> are likely to compromise their principles and sell to butchers who slaughter cows, thereby tacitly supporting the practice for other people. Selling aged cows to butchers has over the centuries become an accepted practice along side the *mos* that a Hindu must not kill cattle (Roy 1955:15)

Determining the number of cattle slaughtered by butchers is almost as difficult as determining the number killed by starvation. According to Dandekar (1964:351), "Generally it is the useless animals that find their way to the slaughter house." Lahiry (n.d.:140) says only 126,900 or.9% of the total cattle population is slaughtered per year. Darling (1934:158) claims:

> All Hindus object to the slaughter and even to the sale of unfit cows and keep them

---

[13] The translation of this quotation is "The peasant only saves those cows that will become traction animals or milk cows. The others are taken away and die of starvation."

indefinitely. . . . rather than sell them to a cattle dealer, who would buy only for the slaughter house, they send them to a *gowshala* or let them loose to die. Some no doubt sell secretly, but this has its risks in an area where public opinion can find strong expression through the *panchayat*.[14]

Such views would seem to be contradicted by Sinha (1961:95): "A large number of animals are slaughtered privately and it is very difficult to ascertain their numbers." The difficulty of obtaining accurate estimates is also implied by the comment of the Committee on the Prevention of Slaughter that "90% of animals not approved for slaughter are slaughtered stealthily outside of municipal limits" (Nandra, *et al.* 1955:11).[15]

An indication of the propensity to slaughter cattle under duress is found in connection with the food crisis of World War II. With rice imports cut off by Japanese occupation of Burma (Thirumalai 1954:38; Bhatia 1963:309 on), increased consumption of beef by the armed forces, higher prices for meat and foodstuffs generally, and famine conditions in Bengal, the doctrine of *ahimsa* proved to be alarmingly ineffectual. Direct military intervention was required to avoid destruction of animals needed for plowing, milking, and bullock-production:

> During the war there was an urgent need to reduce or to avoid the slaughter for food of animals useful for breeding or for agricultural work. For the summer of 1944 the slaughter was prohibited of: 1) Cattle below three years of age; 2) Male cattle between two and ten years of age which were being used or were likely to be used as working cattle; 3) All cows between three and ten years of age, other than

cows which were unsuitable for bearing offspring; 4) All cows which were pregnant or in milk (Knight 1954:141).

Gourou (1963:124–25), aware that starvation and neglect are systematically employed to cull Indian herds, nonetheless insists that destruction of animals through starvation amounts to an important loss of capital. This loss is attributed to the low price of beef caused by the beef-eating taboo, making it economically infeasible to send animals to slaughter. Gourou's appraisal, however, neglects deleterious consequences to the rural tanning and carrion-eating castes if increased numbers of animals went to the butchers. Since the least efficient way to convert solar energy into comestibles is to impose an animal converter between plant and man (Cottrell 1955), it should be obvious that without major technical and environmental innovations or drastic population cuts, India could not tolerate a large beef-producing industry. This suggests that insofar as the beef-eating taboo helps discourage growth of beef-producing industries, it is part of an ecological adjustment which maximizes rather than minimizes the calorie and protein output of the productive process.

ANTI-SLAUGHTER LEGISLATION AND GOWSHALAS[16]

It is evident from the history of anti-slaughter agitation and legislation in India that more than *ahimsa* has been required to protect Indian cattle from premature demise. Unfortunately, this legislation is misinterpreted and frequently cited as

---

[14] *Gowshala:* an "old age home" for cattle; *panchayat:* a village council.

[15] One thing to keep in mind while reading all these statements is that cattle slaughter is a sensitive political topic in India; those making the statements may be politically motivated to take one or another position. It is possible that such statements are more revealing of Indian politics than the conditions of Indian cattle. Currently, in most Indian states cattle slaughter is illegal.

[16] Having discussed the utility of *ahimsa* to Indian peasant farmers, Harris turns to a discussion of the social and

political ramifications of the practice. Here he injects an element of class conflict into his argument. Discussing the disparity between wealthy landowners and the landless he writes, "To have one's cow eat other people's crops may be a very fine solution to the subsistence problem of those with no crops of their own." However, while Harris sees conflict, he doesn't make it the engine of cultural change. The system he describes is essentially static. A true Marxist would bring this conflict to the center of the analysis.

evidence of the anti-economic effect of Hinduism. I am unable to unravel all the tangled economic and political interests served by the recent anti-slaughter laws of the Indian states. Regardless of the ultimate ecological consequences of these laws, however, several points deserve emphasis. First it should be recalled that cow protection was a major political weapon in Gandhi's campaign against both British and Moslems. The sacred cow was the ideological focus of a successful struggle against English colonialism; hence the enactment of total anti-slaughter legislation obviously had a relational base, at least among politicians who seized and retained power on anti-English and anti-Moslem platforms. It is possible that the legislation will now backfire and upset the delicate ecological balance which now exists. The Committee on the Prevention of Slaughter claimed that it

actually saw in Pepsu (where slaughter is banned completely) what a menace wild cattle can be. Conditions have become so desperate there, that the State Government have got to spend a considerable sum for catching and re-domesticating wild animals to save the crops (Nandra, *et al.* 1955:11).

According to Mayadas (1954:29):

The situation has become so serious that it is impossible in some parts of the country to protect growing crops from grazing by wandering cattle. Years ago it was one or two stray animals which could either be driven off or sent to the nearest cattle pound. Today it is a question of constantly being harassed day and night by herds which must either feed on one's green crops, or starve. How long can this state of affairs be allowed to continue?

Before the deleterious effects of slaughter laws can be properly evaluated, certain additional evolutionary and functional possibilities must be examined. For example, given the increasing growth rate of India's human population, the critical importance of cattle in the *eco-system,* and the absence of fundamental technical and environmental changes, a substantial increase in cattle seems necessary and predictable, regardless of slaughter legislation. Furthermore, there is some indication, admittedly incomplete but certainly

worthy of careful inquiry, that many who protest most against destructiveness of marauding herds of useless beasts may perceive the situation from very special vantage points in the social hierarchy. The implications of the following newspaper editorial are clear:

The alarming increase of stray and wild cattle over wide areas of Northern India is fast becoming a major disincentive to crop cultivation. . . . Popular sentiment against cow slaughter no doubt lies at the back of the problem. People prefer to let their aged, diseased, and otherwise useless cattle live at the expense of *other people's crops* (Indian Express, New Delhi, 7 February 1959, italics added).

Evidently we need to know something about whose crops are threatened by these marauders. Despite post-independence attempts at land reform, 10% of the Indian agricultural population still owns more than ½ the total cultivated area and 15,000,000, or 22%, of rural households own no land at all (Mitra 1963:298). Thorner and Thorner (1962:3) call the land reform program a failure, and point out how "the grip of the larger holder serves to prevent the lesser folk from developing the land. . . . " Quite possibly, in other words, the anti-slaughter laws, insofar as they are effective, should be viewed as devices which, contrary to original political intent, bring pressure to bear upon those whose lands are devoted to cash crops of benefit only to narrow commercial, urban, and landed sectors of the population. To have one's cows eat other people's crops may be a very fine solution to the subsistence problem of those with no crops of their own. Apparently, in the days when animals could be driven off or sent to the pound with impunity, this could not happen, even though *ahimsa* reigned supreme then as now.

Some form of anti-slaughter legislation was required and actually argued for, on unambiguously rational, economic, and material grounds. About 4% of India's cattle are in the cities (Mohan 1962:48). These have always represented the best dairy stock, since the high cost of feeding animals in a city could be offset only by good milking qualities. A noxious consequence of this dairy pattern was the slaughter of the cow at the end of its first urban lactation period because it was too expensive to maintain while awaiting another pregnancy. Similarly, and by methods previously discussed, the author calf was killed after it had stimulated the cow to "let down." With the growth of urban milk consumption, the best of India's dairy cattle were thus systematically prevented from breeding, while animals with progressively poorer milking qualities were preserved in the countryside (Mohan 1962:48; Mayadas 1954:29; Gandhi 1954:13 on). The Committee on the Prevention of Slaughter of Cattle (Nandra, *et al.* 1955:2) claimed at least 50,000 high-yielding cows and she-buffaloes from Madras, Bombay, and Calcutta were "annually sent to premature slaughter" and were "lost to the country." Given such evidence of waste and the political potential of Moslems being identified as cow-butchers and Englishmen as cow-eaters (Gandhi 1954:16), the political importance of *ahimsa* becomes more intelligible. Indeed, it could be that the strength of Gandhi's *charisma* lay in his superior understanding of the ecological significance of the cow, especially in relation to the underprivileged masses, marginal low caste and out caste farmers. Gandhi (p. 3) may have been closer to the truth than many a foreign expert when he said:

> Why the cow was selected for apotheosis is obvious to me. The cow was in India the best companion. She was the giver of plenty. Not only did she give milk but she also made agriculture possible.

OLD-AGE HOMES

Among the more obscure aspects of the cattle complex are bovine old-age homes, variously identified as *gowshalas, pinjrapoles,* and, under the Five-Year Plans, as *gosadans*. Undoubtedly some of these are "homes for cows, which are supported by public charity, which maintain the old and derelict animals till natural death occurs" (Kothavala 1934:123). According to Gourou (1963:125), however, owners of cows sent to these religious institutions pay rent with the understanding that if the cows begin to lactate they will be returned. The economics of at least some

of these "charitable" institutions is, therefore, perhaps not as quaint as usually implied. It is also significant that, although the 1st Five-Year Plan called for establishment of 160 *gosadans* to serve 320,000 cattle, only 22 *gosadans* servicing 8,000 cattle were reported by 1955 (Government of India Planning Commission 1956:283).

NATURAL SELECTION

Expert appraisers of India's cattle usually show little enthusiasm for the typical undersized breeds. Much has been made of the fact that 1 large animal is a more efficient dung, milk, and traction machine than 2 small ones. "Weight for weight, a small animal consumes a much larger quantity of food than a bigger animal" (Mamoria 1953:268). "More dung is produced when a given quantity of food is consumed by one animal than when it is shared by two animals" (Ford Foundation 1959:64). Thus it would seem that India's smaller breeds should be replaced by larger, more powerful, and better milking breeds. But once again, there is another way of looking at the evidence. It might very well be that if all of India's scrub cattle were suddenly replaced by an equivalent number of large, high-quality European or American dairy and traction animals, famines of noteworthy magnitude would immediately ensue. Is it not possible that India's cattle are undersized precisely because other breeds never could survive the atrocious conditions they experience most of the year? I find it difficult to believe that breeds better adapted to the present Indian *eco-system* exist elsewhere.

> By nature and religious training, the villager is unwilling to inflict pain or to take animal life. But the immemorial grind for existence has hardened him to an acceptance of survival of the fittest (Wiser and Wiser 1963).

Not only are scrub animals well adapted to the regular seasonal crises of water and forage and general year-round neglect, but long-range selective pressures may be even more significant. The high frequency of drought-induced famines in India (Bhatia 1963) places a premium upon drought-resistance plus a more subtle factor: A herd of smaller animals, dangerously thinned by famine or pestilence, reproduces faster than an equivalent group of larger animals, despite the fact that the larger animal consumes less per pound than 2 smaller animals. This is because there are 2 cows in the smaller herd per equivalent large cow. Mohan (1962:45) is one of the few authorities to have grasped this principle, including it in defense of the small breeds:

> Calculations of the comparative food conversion efficiency of various species of Indian domestic livestock by the writer has revealed, that much greater attention should be paid to small livestock than at present, not only because of their better conversion efficiency for protein but also because of the possibilities of bringing about a rapid increase in their numbers.

CONCLUSION[17]

The probability that India's cattle complex is a positive-functioned part of a naturally selected *eco-system* is at least as good as that it is a negative-functioned expression of an irrational ideology. This should not be interpreted to mean that no "improvements" can be made in the system, nor that different systems may not eventually evolve. The issue is not whether oxen are more efficient than tractors. I suggest simply that many features of the cattle complex have been erroneously reported or interpreted. That Indian cattle are weak and inefficient is not denied, but there is doubt that this situation arises from and is mainly perpetuated by Hindu ideology. Given the techno-environmental base, Indian property relationships, and political organization, one need not involve the doctrine of *ahimsa* to understand fundamental features of the cattle complex. Although the cattle population of India has risen by 38,000,000 head since 1940, during the same period, the human population has risen by 120,000,000. Despite the anti-slaughter legislation, the ratio of cattle to humans actually declined from 44:100 in 1941 to 40:100 in 1961 (Government of India 1962:74; 1963:6). In the absence of major changes in environment, technology or property relations, it seems unlikely that the cattle population will cease to accompany the rise in the human population. If *ahimsa* is negative-functioned, then we must be prepared to admit the possibility that all other factors contributing to the rapid growth of the Indian human and cattle populations, including the germ theory of disease, are also negative-functioned.[18]

ACKNOWLEDGEMENT

Marvin Harris, excerpts from "The Cultural Ecology of India's Sacred Cattle," *Current Anthropology*, vol. 7, no. 1 (1966), 51–59. Copyright © 1966 by the Wenner-Gren Foundation for Anthropological Research, Inc. Reprinted by permission of the University of Chicago Press.

---

[17] At the time Harris wrote this essay, an approach called ethnoscience, or the new ethnography, was very popular. With a focus on the emic perspective, an underlying assumption of ethnoscience was that culture was a mental model that people acted out. One goal of ethnoscience was to re-create these models so that anthropologists could understand the world in the same way as their informants. Harris, however, disagrees strongly with this view of culture, arguing against it in *The Rise of Anthropological Theory* (1968). According to Harris, culture should be defined as behavior that is determined by techno-environmental factors. Harris' article is both an example of a materialist perspective and a challenge to ethnoscience.

[18] Harris is certainly one of the most colorful and polemical figures in contemporary anthropology. For the last thirty years, while other perspectives have come and gone, Harris has stood firm as one of the leading proponents of cultural materialism and the etic approach. Starting as an intellectual approach to cultural analysis, his advocacy of cultural materialism has taken on a moral-ideological dimension. For example, in the introduction to his book *America Now*, Harris wrote:

> The task of this book is to reassert the primacy of rational endeavor and objective knowledge in the struggle to save and renew the American dream. . . . Anthropologists regard it as their solemn duty to represent the hopes and fears, values and goals, beliefs and rituals of different groups and communities seen from within, the way people who belong to these groups and communities perceive them to be, and the way they want them to be seen by others. But that can be only half the job. The other half is to describe and explain what people are actually saying and doing from the standpoint of the objective study of culture and history (Harris 1981:15).

NOTES

[a]The author (1960) suggested that the term "adaptive" be restricted to traits, biological or cultural, established and diffused in conformity with the principle of natural selection. Clearly, not all "positive-functioned," i.e., useful, cultural traits are so established.

[b]*Ahimsa* is the Hindu principle of unity of life, of which sacredness of cattle is principal sub-case and symbol.

[c]According to Zeuner (1954:328), "Symbiosis includes all conditions of the living together of two different species, provided both derive advantages therefrom. Cases in which both partners benefit equally are rare." In the symbiosis under consideration, men benefit more than cattle.

[d]The U.S. Census of Agriculture (1954) showed milk production averaging from a low of 3,929 pounds per cow in the Nashville Basin sub-region to 11,112 pounds per cow in the Southern California sub-region.

[e]Srinivas (1962:126) declared himself properly skeptical in this matter: "It is commonly believed that the peasant's religious attitude to cattle comes in the way of the disposal of useless cattle. Here again, my experience of Rampura makes me skeptical of the general belief. I am not denying that cattle are regarded as in some sense sacred, but I doubt whether the belief is as powerful as it is claimed to be. I have already mentioned that bull-buffaloes are sacrificed to village goddesses. And in the case of the cow, while the peasant does not want to kill the cow or bull himself he does not seem to mind very much if someone else does the dirty job out of his sight."

REFERENCES

Bailey, F. G. 1957. *Caste and the economic frontier.* Manchester: University of Manchester Press.

Bansil, P. C. 1958. *India's food resources and population,* p. 104. Bombay: Vora. p. 97 (if 1959).

Bhatia, B. M. 1963. *Famines in India.* New York: Asia Publishing House.

Black, John D. 1959. Supplementary to the Ford Foundation team's report: India's food crisis and steps to meet it. *The Indian Journal of Agricultural Economics* 14:1–6.

Chapekar, L. N. 1960. *Thakurs of the Sahyadri.* Oxford: Oxford University Press.

Chatterjee, I. 1960. Milk production in India. *Economic Weekly* 12:1347–48.

Chaudhri, S. C., and R. Giri. 1963. Role of cattle in India's economy. *Agricultural situation in India* 18:591–99.

Cottrell, Fred. 1955. *Energy and society.* New York: McGraw-Hill.

Dandekar, U. M. 1964. Problem of numbers in cattle development. *Economic Weekly* 16:351–355.

Darling, M. L. 1934. *Wisdom and waste in a Punjab village.* London: Oxford University Press.

Das, A. B., and M. N. Chatterji. 1962. *The Indian economy.* Calcutta: Bookland Private.

Desai, M. B. 1948. *The rural economy of Gujarat.* Bombay: Oxford University Press.

——. 1959. India's food crisis. *The Indian Journal of Agricultural Economics* 14: 27–37.

Diskalkar, P. D. 1960. *Resurvey of a Deccan village Pimple Sandagar.* Bombay: The Indian Society of Agricultural Economics.

Dube, S. C. 1955. *Indian village.* Ithaca: Cornell University Press.

Dupuis, J. 1960. *Madras et le nord du Coromandel; étude des conditions de la vie indienne dans un cadre géografique.* Paris: Maisonneuve.

Ford Foundation. 1959. *Report on India's food crisis and steps to meet it.* New Delhi: Government of India, Ministry of Food and Agriculture and Ministry of Community Development and Cooperation.

Gandhi, M. K. 1954. *How to serve the cow.* Edited by Bharaton Kumarappa. Ahmedabad: Navajivan Publishing House.

Gangulee, N. 1935. *The Indian peasant and his environment.* London: Oxford University Press.

Gourou, Pierre. 1963. Civilisation et economie pastorale. *L'Homme* 123–29.

Government of India. 1956. *Second five-year plan.* Planning Commission. New Delhi.

——. 1962. *Statistical Abstract of the Indian Union* 11. Cabinet Secretariat. New Delhi.

Gupta, S. C. 1959. *An economic survey of Shamaspur village.* New York: Asia Publishing House.

Harris, Marvin. 1964. *The nature of cultural things.* New York: Random House.

Hutton, J. H. 1961. *Caste in India,* p. VII. London: Oxford University Press.

Kapp, K. W. 1963. *Hindu culture, economic development and economic planning in India.* New York: Asia Publishing House.

Kartha, K. P. R. 1936. A note on the comparative economic efficiency of the Indian cow, the half breed cow, and the buffalo as producers of milk and butter fat. *Agriculture and Livestock in India* 4: 605–23.

——. 1959. "Buffalo," in *An introduction to animal husbandry in the Tropics.* Edited by G. Williamson and W. J. A. Payne. London: Longmans, Green.

Knight, Henry. 1954. *Food administration in India 1939–47.* Stanford: Stanford University Press.

Kothavala, Zal R. 1934. Milk production in India. *Agriculture and Livestock in India* 2:122–29.

Lahiry, N. L. n.d. "Conservation and utilization of animal food resources," in Proceedings of symposium on food needs and resources. *Bulletin of the National Institute of Sciences of India* 20:140–44.

Leake, H. Martin. 1923. *The foundations of Indian agriculture.* Cambridge: W. Heffer.

Lewis, Oscar, and Victor Barnouw. 1958. *Village life in northern India.* Urbana: University of Illinois Press.

Lewis, W. A. 1955. *The theory of economic growth.* Homewood, Ill.: R. D. Irwin.

Lupton, Arnold. 1922. *Happy India.* London: G. Allen & Unwin.

Mamoria, C. B. 1953. *Agricultural problems of India.* Allahabad: Kitab Mahal.

Matson, J. 1933. Inefficiency of cattle in India through disease. *Agriculture and Livestock in India* 1:227–28.

Mayadas, C. 1954. *Between us and hunger.* London: Oxford University Press.

Mayer, Adrian. 1952. *Land and society in Malabar.* Bombay: Oxford University Press.

Mishra, Vikas. 1962. *Hinduism and economic growth.* London: Oxford University Press.

Mitra, Ashok. 1963. "Tax burden for Indian agriculture," in *Traditions, values, and socio-economic development.* Edited by R. Braibanti and J. J. Spengler, pp. 281–303. Durham: Duke University Press.

Mohan, S. N. 1962. Animal husbandry in the Third Plan. *Bulletin of the National Institute of Sciences of India* 20: 41–54.

Moomaw, I. W. 1949. *The farmer speaks.* London: Oxford University Press.

Mosher, Arthur T. 1946. *The economic effect of Hindu religion and social traditions on agricultural production by Christians in North India.* Unpublished Ph.D. dissertation, University of Chicago. (Also microfilms T 566.)

Mujumdar, N. A. 1960. Cow dung as manure. *Economic Weekly* 12:743–44.

Nandra, P. N., *et al.* 1955. Report of the expert committee on the prevention of *slaughter of cattle in India.* New Delhi: Government of India Press.

National Council of Applied Economic Research. 1959. *Domestic fuels in India.* New York: Asia Publishing House.

——. 1960. *Techno-economic survey of Madhya Pradesh.* New Delhi.

——. 1961. *Techno-economic survey of Tripura.* New Delhi.

——. 1962a. *Techno-economic survey of Andhra Pradesh.* New Delhi.

——. 1962b. *Techno-economic survey of Punjab.* New Delhi.

——. 1962c. *Techno-economic survey of West Bengal.* New Delhi.

——. 1963. *Techno-economic survey of Rajasthan.* New Delhi.

Randhawa, M. S. 1962. *Agriculture and animal husbandry in India.* New Delhi. Indian Council of Agricultural Research.

Randhawa, M. S., *et al.* 1961. *Farmers of India.* 2 vols. New Delhi: Indian Council of Agricultural Research.

Roy, Prodipto. 1955. The sacred cow in India. *Rural sociology* 20:8–15.

Saha, M. N. 1956. Fuel in India. *Nature* 177:923–24.

Schneider, Harold. 1957. The subsistence role of cattle among the Pakot and in East Africa. *American Anthropologist* 59:278–300.

Shastri, C. P. 1960. Bullock labour utilization in agriculture. *Economic Weekly* 12:1585–92.

Simoons, F. J. 1961. *Eat not this flesh.* Madison: University of Wisconsin Press.

Sinha, R. P. 1961. *Food in India.* London: Oxford University Press.

Spate, Oskar Hermann. 1954. *India and Pakistan: A general and regional geography.* London: Methuen.

Srinivas, M. N. 1952. *Religion and society among the Coorgs of South India.* Oxford: Oxford University Press.

——. 1958. India's cultural values and economic development. *Economic Development and cultural change* 7:3–6.

——. 1962. *Caste in modern India.* New York: Asia Publishing House.

Statistical atlas for the Madras Presidency. 1895. Madras Government Press. [JM]

Thirumalai, Shri. 1954. *Post-war agricultural problems and policies in India,* p. 38. New York: Institute of Pacific Relations.

Thorner, Daniel, and Alice Thorner. 1962. *Land and labour in India.* New York: Asia Publishing House.

U.S. Census of Agriculture. 1954. "Dairy producers and dairy production." in *Farmers and farm production in the United States* 3, part 9, chap. V.

Venkatraman, R. B. 1938. The Indian village, its past, present, future. *Agriculture and Livestock in India* 7:702–10.

Wiser, William H., and C. V. Wiser. 1963. *Behind mud walls: 1930–1960.* Berkeley: University of California Press.

Zeuner, F. E. 1954. "Domestication of animals," in *A history of technology.* Edited by C. Singer, *et al.,* pp. 327–52. New York: Oxford University Press.

20. *Ritual Regulation of Environmental Relations among a New Guinea People*[a]

Roy A. Rappaport (1926–1997)

Most functional studies of religious behavior in anthropology have as an analytic goal the elucidation of events, processes, or relationships occurring within a social unit of some sort.[1] The social unit is not always well defined, but in some cases it appears to be a church, that is, a group of people who entertain similar beliefs about the universe, or a congregation, a group of people who participate together in the performance of religious rituals. There have been exceptions. Thus Vayda,[2] Leeds, and Smith (1961) and O. K. Moore (1957) have clearly perceived that the functions of religious ritual are not necessarily confined within the boundaries of a congregation or even a church. By and large, however, I believe that the following statement by Homans (1941:172) represents fairly the dominant line of anthropological thought concerning the functions of religious ritual:

> Ritual actions do not produce a practical result on the external world—that is one of the reasons why we call them ritual. But to make this statement is not to say that ritual has no function. Its function is not related to the world external to the society but to the internal constitution of the society. It gives the members of

the society confidence, it dispels their anxieties, it disciplines their social organization.

No argument will be raised here against the sociological and psychological functions imputed by Homans, and many others before him, to ritual. They seem to me to be plausible. Nevertheless, in some cases at least, ritual does produce, in Homans' terms, "a practical result on the world" external not only to the social unit composed of those who participate together in ritual performances but also to the larger unit composed of those who entertain similar beliefs concerning the universe. The material presented here will show that the ritual cycles of the Tsembaga, and of other local territorial groups of Maring speakers living in the New Guinea interior, play an important part in regulating the relationships of these groups with both the nonhuman components of their immediate environments and the human components of their less immediate environments, that is, with other similar territorial groups.[3] To be more specific, this regulation helps to maintain the biotic communities existing within their territories, redistributes land among people and people over land, and limits the frequency of

From *Ethnology* (1967)

---

[1] In the opening passage of this essay, Rappaport critiques functionalism in much the same way Julian Steward did almost thirty years previously. That is, holistic functional explanations do not generally show causes, only interrelations among parts within a system. Functionalists suppose that social systems are only weakly connected with their environments. Rappaport, following the cultural-ecology model, wishes to show that religion, at least among those he studies, is articulated with, and has a profound effect on, the natural world.

[2] Andrew P. Vayda (b. 1931) was Rappaport's dissertation advisor at Columbia and was in New Guinea with Rappaport when the fieldwork that formed the basis for this essay was done.

[3] One of the principal influences on Rappaport and many other social scientists of the 1960s was general systems theory. This approach, developed primarily by Austrian biologist Ludwig von Bertalanffy (1901–1972), was a way of providing a mathematical description of a physical system. It encouraged anthropologists to examine cultures as systems composed of both human and nonhuman elements. It presumed that the normal state of a system was equilibrium and described the various methods by which systems deviated from states of balance and were returned to them. In this essay, Rappaport describes Tsembaga culture as just such a system, highlighting the role of religious practices as mechanisms that return the system to equilibrium.

fighting. In the absence of authoritative political statuses or offices, the ritual cycle likewise provides a means for mobilizing allies when warfare may be undertaken. It also provides a mechanism for redistributing local pig surpluses in the form of pork throughout a large regional population while helping to assure the local population of a supply of pork when its members are most in need of high quality protein.

Religious ritual may be defined, for the purposes of this paper, as the prescribed performance of conventionalized acts manifestly directed toward the involvement of nonempirical or supernatural agencies in the affairs of the actors. While this definition relies upon the formal characteristics of the performances and upon the motives for undertaking them, attention will be focused upon the empirical effects of ritual performances and sequences of ritual performances. The religious rituals to be discussed are regarded as neither more nor less than part of the behavioral repertoire employed by an aggregate of organisms in adjusting to its environment.[4]

The data upon which this paper is based were collected during fourteen months of field work among the Tsembaga, one of about twenty local groups of Maring speakers living in the Simbai and Jimi Valleys of the Bismarck Range in the Territory of New Guinea. The size of Maring local groups varies from a little over 100 to 900. The Tsembaga, who in 1963 numbered 204 persons, are located on the south wall of the Simbai Valley. The country in which they live differs from the true highlands in being lower, generally more

rugged, and more heavily forested. Tsembaga territory rises, within a total surface area of 3.2 square miles, from an elevation of 2,200 feet at the Simbai river to 7,200 feet at the ridge crest. Gardens are cut in the secondary forests up to between 5,000 and 5,400 feet, above which the area remains in primary forest. Rainfall reaches 150 inches per year.

The Tsembaga have come into contact with the outside world only recently; the first government patrol to penetrate their territory arrived in 1954.[5] They were considered uncontrolled by the Australian government until 1962, and they remain unmissionized to this day.

The 204 Tsembaga are distributed among five putatively patrilineal clans, which are, in turn, organized into more inclusive groupings on two hierarchical levels below that of the total local group.[b] Internal political structure is highly egalitarian. There are no hereditary or elected chiefs nor are there even "big men" who can regularly coerce or command the support of their clansmen or coresidents in economic or forceful enterprises.

It is convenient to regard the Tsembaga as a population in the ecological sense, that is, as one of the components of a system of trophic[6] exchanges taking place within a bounded area. Tsembaga territory and the biotic community existing upon it may be conveniently viewed as an ecosystem. While it would be permissible arbitrarily to designate the Tsembaga as a population and their territory with its biota as an ecosystem, there are also nonarbitrary reasons for doing so.[7] An ecosystem is a system of material exchanges,

---

[4] Notice Rappaport's style—he writes in a scientific trope, frequently referring to those he studies as "biological organisms" rather than people or individuals. His goal is to analyze human behavior in a fashion analogous to that used by biologists examining animal behavior. Ethology, the study of animal behavior, was becoming an increasingly important field within biology at this time. Austrian ethologist Konrad Lorenz (1901–1989) published his popular account of animal behavior, *King Solomon's Ring,* in 1952. This had an important impact on many scholars in this era.

[5] A criticism sometimes made of this essay (and this style of analysis) is that it makes very little reference to history. This brief paragraph is virtually the only reference to the

history of the Tsembaga or their relations with outside (European) powers.

[6] *Trophic:* relating to nutrition.

[7] Notice that Rappaport again treats humans simply as organisms within an ecosystem. Given this, how would Rappaport define culture? In the epilogue to the second edition of Rappaport's book-length treatment of this material, *Pigs for the Ancestors* (1984:371–403), Rappaport writes: "cultures . . . constitute the major and most distinctive means by which human populations maintain common sets of material relations with other components of the ecosystems in which they participate" (1984:384). However, a paragraph later he tells us that "If the concept

and the Tsembaga maintain against other human groups exclusive access to the resources within their territorial borders. Conversely, it is from this territory alone that the Tsembaga ordinarily derive all of their foodstuffs and most of the other materials they require for survival. Less anthropocentrically, it may be justified to regard Tsembaga territory with its biota as an ecosystem in view of the rather localized nature of cyclical material exchanges in tropical rainforests.

As they are involved with the nonhuman biotic community within their territory in a set of trophic exchanges, so do they participate in other material relationships with other human groups external to their territory. Genetic materials are exchanged with other groups, and certain crucial items, such as stone axes, were in the past obtained from the outside. Furthermore, in the area occupied by the Maring speakers, more than one local group is usually involved in any process, either peaceful or warlike, through which people are redistributed over land and land redistributed among people.

The concept of the ecosystem, though it provides a convenient frame for the analysis of interspecific trophic exchanges taking place within limited geographical areas, does not comfortably accommodate intraspecific exchanges taking place over wider geographic areas. Some sort of geographic population model would be more useful for the analysis of the relationship of the local ecological population to the larger regional population of which it is a part, but we lack even a set of appropriate terms for such a model. Suffice it here to note that the relations of the Tsembaga to the total of other local human populations in their vicinity are similar to the relations of local aggregates of other animals to the totality of their species occupying broader and more or less continuous regions. This larger, more inclusive aggregate may resemble what geneticists mean by the term population, that is, an aggregate of interbreeding organisms persisting through an indefinite number of generations and either living or capable of living in isolation from similar aggregates of the same species. This is the unit which survives through long periods of time while its local ecological (*sensu stricto*)[8] subunits, the units more or less independently involved in interspecific trophic exchanges such as the Tsembaga, are ephemeral.

Since it has been asserted that the ritual cycles of the Tsembaga regulate relationships within what may be regarded as a complex system, it is necessary, before proceeding to the ritual cycle itself, to describe briefly, and where possible in quantitative terms, some aspects of the place of the Tsembaga in this system.[9]

All gardens are mixed, many of them containing all of the major root crops and many greens. Two named garden types are, however, distinguished by the crops which predominate in them. "Taro-yam gardens" were found to produce, on the basis of daily harvest records kept on entire gardens for close to one year, about 5,300,000 calories[c] per acre during their harvesting lives of 18 to 24 months; 85 percent of their yield is harvested between 24 and 76 weeks after planting. "Sugar-sweet potato gardens" produce about 4,600,000 calories per acre during their harvesting lives, 91 percent being taken between 24 and 76 weeks after planting. I estimated that approximately 310,000 calories per acre is expended on cutting, fencing, planting, maintaining, harvesting, and walking to and from taro-yam gardens. Sugar-sweet potato gardens required an expenditure of

---

of culture as adaptation is the truth, it is not the whole truth . . ." Once cultures are established, "It becomes no longer clear whether culture is a symbolic means to organic ends or organisms living means to cultural ends . . ." (1984:385).

[8] *Sensu stricto:* Latin for "strictly speaking."

[9] Rappaport's description focuses on those aspects of Tsembaga life that are of direct concern to his theoretical approach, particularly gardening. Within this framework, he discusses the Tsembaga as calorie producers and consumers. Note also Rappaport's quantification of data, which reflects his desire to make his work scientifically rigorous. Subsistence activities form the basis of his analysis. Other cultural features arise as a secondary result of subsistence or are historically particular and of less analytic importance. Rappaport's treatment is similar to Steward's idea of the culture core.

approximately 290,000 calories per acre.[d] These energy ratios, approximately 17:1 on taro-yam gardens and 16:1 on sugar-sweet potato gardens, compare favorably with figures reported for swidden cultivation in other regions.[e]

Intake is high in comparison with the reported dietaries of other New Guinea populations. On the basis of daily consumption records kept for ten months on four households numbering in total sixteen persons, I estimated the average daily intake of adult males to be approximately 2,600 calories, and that of adult females to be around 2,200 calories.[10] It may be mentioned here that the Tsembaga are small and short-statured.[11] Adult males average 101 pounds in weight and approximately 58.5 inches in height; the corresponding averages for adult females are 85 pounds and 54.5 inches.[f]

Although 99 percent by weight of the food consumed is vegetable, the protein intake is high by New Guinea standards. The daily protein consumption of adult males from vegetable sources was estimated to be between 43 and 55 grams, of adult females 36 to 48 grams. Even with an adjustment for vegetable sources, these values are slightly in excess of the recently published WHO/FAO daily requirements (Food and Agriculture Organization of the United Nations 1964). The same is true of the younger age categories, although soft and discolored hair, a symptom of protein deficiency, was noted in a few children. The

WHO/FAO protein requirements do not include a large "margin for safety" or allowance for stress; and, although no clinical assessments were undertaken, it may be suggested that the Tsembaga achieve nitrogen balance at a low level. In other words, their protein intake is probably marginal.[12]

Measurements of all gardens made during 1962 and of some gardens made during 1963 indicate that, to support the human population, between .15 and .19 acres are put into cultivation per capita per year. Fallows range from 8 to 45 years. The area in secondary forest comprises approximately 1,000 acres, only 30 to 50 of which are in cultivation at any time. Assuming calories to be the limiting factor, and assuming an unchanging population structure, the territory could support—with no reduction in lengths of fallow and without cutting into the virgin forest from which the Tsembaga extract many important items—between 290 and 397 people if the pig population remained minimal. The size of the pig herd, however, fluctuates widely. Taking Maring pig husbandry procedures into consideration, I have estimated the human carrying capacity[13] of the Tsembaga territory at between 270 and 320 people.

Because the timing of the ritual cycle is bound up with the demography of the pig herd, the place of the pig in Tsembaga adaptation must be examined.[14]

First, being omnivorous, pigs keep residential areas free of garbage and human feces. Second,

---

[10] Rappaport is giving many figures here, but they are based on observation of a small number of people: 16 in four families. In most studies in biology or ecology, this would be a very small sample. What sort of questions does this raise about his conclusions? Despite the small numbers, it should be noted that, at the time this essay was published, it was probably the most detailed and comprehensive body of data ever collected on swidden agriculturalists. In keeping with the biological model on which he based this work, all of the data is available for inspection in the appendices to *Pigs for the Ancestors* (1967).

[11] In *Pigs for the Ancestors* (1967), a picture shows the five-foot, ten-inch Rappaport towering over a group of Tsembaga men.

[12] Rappaport's analysis, clearly materialist, is functionalist rather than Marxist; there is no reference to the evolution

of culture in this essay. Further, for Marxists, conflict drives progressive change, but for Rappaport, conflict is a feature that returns the cultural system to a state of equilibrium.

[13] Rappaport again uses a concept borrowed from biology—carrying capacity, which is the number of individuals of a species that a given ecosystem can support without suffering degradation. Notice that for humans, the technology of food production must be taken into account, a point also discussed by Steward.

[14] When Rappaport did his graduate training at Columbia, thinking there was dominated by the ideas of White and Steward. Rappaport thus went into the field with a background in cultural ecology. Once there, his experiences compelled him to take a position in some ways more extreme than these classic cultural ecologists. Steward had supposed that, though environment had a profound

limited numbers of pigs rooting in secondary growth may help to hasten the development of that growth. The Tsembaga usually permit pigs to enter their gardens one and a half to two years after planting, by which time second-growth trees are well established there. The Tsembaga practice selective weeding; from the time the garden is planted, herbaceous species are removed, but tree species are allowed to remain. By the time cropping is discontinued and the pigs are let in, some of the trees in the garden are already ten to fifteen feet tall. These well-established trees are relatively impervious to damage by the pigs, which, in rooting for seeds and remaining tubers, eliminate many seeds and seedlings that, if allowed to develop, would provide some competition for the established trees. Moreover, in some Maring-speaking areas swiddens are planted twice, although this is not the case with the Tsembaga. After the first crop is almost exhausted, pigs are penned in the garden, where their rooting eliminates weeds and softens the ground, making the task of planting for a second time easier. The pigs, in other words, are used as cultivating machines.

Small numbers of pigs are easy to keep. They run free during the day and return home at night to receive their ration of garbage and substandard tubers, particularly sweet potatoes. Supplying the latter requires little extra work, for the substandard tubers are taken from the ground in the course of harvesting the daily ration for humans. Daily consumption records kept over a period of some months show that the ration of tubers received by the pigs approximates in weight that consumed by adult humans, i.e., a little less than three pounds per day per pig.

If the pig herd grows large, however, the substandard tubers incidentally obtained in the course of harvesting for human needs become insufficient, and it becomes necessary to harvest especially for the pigs. In other words, people must work for the pigs and perhaps even supply them with food fit for human consumption. Thus, as Vayda, Leeds, and Smith (1961:71) have pointed out, there can be too many pigs for a given community.

This also holds true of the sanitary and cultivating services rendered by pigs. A small number of pigs is sufficient to keep residential areas clean, to suppress superfluous seedlings in abandoned gardens, and to soften the soil in gardens scheduled for second plantings. A larger herd, on the other hand, may be troublesome; the larger the number of pigs, the greater the possibility of their invasion of producing gardens, with concomitant damage not only to crops and young secondary growth but also to the relations between the pig owners and garden owners.

All male pigs are castrated at approximately three months of age, for boars, people say, are dangerous and do not grow as large as barrows. Pregnancies, therefore, are always the result of unions of domestic sows with feral males. Fecundity is thus only a fraction of its potential. During one twelve-month period only fourteen litters resulted out of a potential 99 or more pregnancies. Farrowing generally takes place in the forest and mortality of the young is high. Only 32 of the offspring of the above mentioned fourteen pregnancies were alive six months after birth. This number is barely sufficient to replace the number of adult animals which would have died or been killed during most years without pig festivals.

The Tsembaga almost never kill domestic pigs outside of ritual contexts. In ordinary times, when there is no pig festival in progress, the rituals are almost always associated with misfortunes or emergencies, notably warfare, illness, injury, or death. Rules state not only the contexts in which pigs are to be ritually slaughtered, but also who may partake of the flesh of the sacrificial animals. During warfare it is only the men participating in the fighting who eat the pork. In

---

impact on human society, humans were, in fundamental ways, so different from other creatures that natural laws that applied to populations of other animals could not be applied to them. (This view was consistent with his training in historical particularism.) Rappaport, on the other hand, came to believe that while the human possession of culture does separate us from other animals, as biological organisms we are subject to the same fundamental laws. In this essay he repeatedly compares humans with other species.

cases of illness or injury, it is only the victim and certain near relatives, particularly his co-resident agnates and spouses, who do so.

It is reasonable to assume that misfortune and emergency are likely to induce in the organisms experiencing them a complex of physiological changes known collectively as "stress." Physiological stress reactions occur not only in organisms which are infected with disease or traumatized, but also in those experiencing rage or fear (Houssay et al. 1955:1096), or even prolonged anxiety (National Research Council 1963:53). One important aspect of stress is the increased catabolization of protein (Houssay et al. 1955:451; National Research Council 1963:49), with a net loss of nitrogen from the tissues (Houssay et al. 1955:450).[15] This is a serious matter for organisms with a marginal protein intake. Antibody production is low (Berg 1948:311), healing is slow (Large and Johnston 1948:352), and a variety of symptoms of a serious nature are likely to develop (Lund and Levenson 1948:349; Zintel 1964:1043). The status of a protein-depleted animal, however, may be significantly improved in a relatively short period of time by the intake of high quality protein, and high protein diets are therefore routinely prescribed for surgical patients and those suffering from infectious diseases (Burton 1959:231; Lund and Levenson 1948:350; Elman 1951:85ff.; Zintel 1964:1043ff.).

It is precisely when they are undergoing physiological stress that the Tsembaga kill and consume their pigs, and it should be noted that they limit the consumption to those likely to be experiencing stress most profoundly.[8] The Tsembaga, of course, know nothing of physiological stress. Native theories of the etiology and treatment of disease and injury implicate various categories of spirits to whom sacrifices must be made. Nevertheless, the behavior which is appropriate in terms of native understandings is also appropriate to the actual situation confronting the actors.

We may now outline in the barest of terms the Tsembaga ritual cycle. Space does not permit a description of its ideological correlates. It must suffice to note that the Tsembaga do not necessarily perceive all of the empirical effects which the anthropologist sees to flow from their ritual behavior. Such empirical consequences as they may perceive, moreover, are not central to their rationalizations of the performances. The Tsembaga say that they perform the rituals in order to rearrange their relationships with the supernatural world. We may only reiterate here that behavior undertaken in reference to their "cognized environment"—an environment which includes as very important elements the spirits of ancestors—seems appropriate in their "operational environment," the material environment specified by the anthropologist through operations of observation, including measurement.[16]

Since the rituals are arranged in a cycle, description may commence at any point.[17] The operation of the cycle becomes clearest if we begin

---

[15] One element of Rappaport's argument is that pig consumption is driven by exceptional demand for protein. This is based on the idea that humans in crisis situations or about to do strenuous work experience a physiological need for protein. Even when this article was written, in 1967, this was a controversial position, and there was evidence in the scientific literature pointing against it (see Keys 1943, 1946; Mayer and Bullen 1960). Today, most nutritionists would probably agree that what people in these conditions need is not protein but carbohydrates. Rappaport reconsidered the protein issue in the appendix of the 1984 edition of *Pigs for the Ancestors* and suggested that he was probably mistaken about protein intake, but for a different reason—further fieldwork revealed that the stressed person generally does not get to eat much of the pig sacrificed for him.

[16] The focus of much of Rappaport's work is the relationship between the cognized and operational environments. This distinction is similar to the one Marvin Harris and others have made between etic and emic analysis (see essay 19, footnote 5). Although this essay focuses on describing the Tsembaga in ecosystem terms, *Pigs for the Ancestors* contains an extensive treatment of the Tsembaga's understanding of their environment.

[17] The idea of a cycle is quite important and again relates to developments in biology in the 1960s. Biologists viewed ecosystems in terms of nutrient cycles. Rappaport applies the same sort of logic to the system he describes here. Note, however, that Rappaport was in the field for only fourteen months, from October 1962 to December 1963. He was thus unable to observe a single complete cycle, which takes place over a period of a decade or more.

with the rituals performed during warfare. Opponents in all cases occupy adjacent territories, in almost all cases on the same valley wall. After hostilities have broken out, each side performs certain rituals which place the opposing side in the formal category of "enemy." A number of taboos prevail while hostilities continue. These include prohibitions on sexual intercourse and on the ingestion of certain things—food prepared by women, food grown on the lower portion of the territory, marsupials, eels, and while actually on the fighting ground, any liquid whatsoever.

One ritual practice associated with fighting which may have some physiological consequences deserves mention. Immediately before proceeding to the fighting ground, the warriors eat heavily salted pig fat. The ingestion of salt, coupled with the taboo on drinking, has the effect of shortening the fighting day, particularly since the Maring prefer to fight only on bright sunny days. When everyone gets unbearably thirsty, according to informants, fighting is broken off.

There may formerly have been other effects if the native salt contained sodium (the production of salt was discontinued some years previous to the field work, and no samples were obtained). The Maring diet seems to be deficient in sodium. The ingestion of large amounts of sodium just prior to fighting would have permitted the warriors to sweat normally without a lowering of blood volume and consequent weakness during the course of the fighting. The pork belly ingested with the salt would have provided them with a new burst of energy two hours or so after the commencement of the engagement. After fighting was finished for the day, lean pork was consumed, offsetting, at least to some extent, the nitrogen loss associated with the stressful fighting (personal communications from F. Dunn, W. McFarlane, and J. Sabine, 1965).

Fighting could continue sporadically for weeks. Occasionally it terminated in the rout of one of the antagonistic groups, whose survivors would take refuge with kinsmen elsewhere. In such instances, the victors would lay waste to their opponents' groves and gardens, slaughter their pigs, and burn their houses. They would not, however, immediately annex the territory of the vanquished. The Maring say that they never take over the territory of an enemy for, even if it has been abandoned, spirits of their ancestors remain to guard it against interlopers. Most fights, however, terminated in truces between the antagonists.

With the termination of hostilities a group which has not been driven off its territory performs a ritual called "planting the *rumbim*." Every man puts his hand on the ritual plant, rumbim (*Cordyline fruticosa* (L.), A. Chev; *C. terminalis*, Kunth), as it is planted in the ground. The ancestors are addressed, in effect, as follows:[18]

> We thank you for helping us in the fight and permitting us to remain on our territory. We place our souls in this *rumbim* as we plant it on our ground. We ask you to care for this *rumbim*. We will kill pigs for you now, but they are few. In the future, when we have many pigs, we shall again give you pork and uproot the *rumbim* and stage a *kaiko* (pig festival). But until there are sufficient pigs to repay you the *rumbim* will remain in remain the ground. This ritual is accompanied by the wholesale slaughter of pigs. Only juveniles remain alive.

All adult and adolescent animals are killed, cooked, and dedicated to the ancestors. Some are consumed by the local group, but most are distributed to allies who assisted in the fight.

Some of the taboos which the group suffered during the time of fighting are abrogated by this ritual. Sexual intercourse is now permitted, liquids may be taken at any time, and food from any part of the territory may be eaten. But the group is still in debt to its allies and ancestors. People say it is still the time of the *bamp ku*, or "fighting

---

[18] Notice that Rappaport does not report what people *said* on a particular occasion, but rather the kind of thing they are *likely to say*. He cannot report verbatim because he was not present at a *rumbim* planting. Anthropologists who view culture in primarily mentalistic terms, such as structuralists and ethnoscientists, would have trouble with such a reconstruction. They would most likely be concerned with the specifics of *rumbim* symbolism and would see such a reconstruction as doing violence to the data. Because Rappaport's view of culture is primarily materialistic, the reconstruction adds a bit of ethnographic interest and is largely irrelevant to the data.

stones," which are actual objects used in the rituals associated with warfare. Although the fighting ceases when *rumbim* is planted, the concomitant obligations, debts to allies and ancestors, remain outstanding; and the fighting stones may not be put away until these obligations are fulfilled. The time of the fighting stones is a time of debt and danger which lasts until the *rumbim* is uprooted and a pig festival (*kaiko*) is staged.

Certain taboos persist during the time of the fighting stones. Marsupials, regarded as the pigs of the ancestors of the high ground, may not be trapped until the debt to their masters has been repaid. Eels, the "pigs of the ancestors of the low ground," may neither be caught nor consumed. Prohibitions on all intercourse with the enemy come into force. One may not touch, talk to, or even look at a member of the enemy group, nor set foot on enemy ground. Even more important, a group may not attack another group while its ritual plant remains in the ground, for it has not yet fully rewarded its ancestors and allies for their assistance in the last fight. Until the debts to them have been paid, further assistance from them will not be forthcoming. A kind of "truce of god" thus prevails until the *rumbim* is uprooted and a *kaiko* completed.[19]

To uproot the *rumbim* requires sufficient pigs. How many pigs are sufficient, and how long does it take to acquire them? The Tsembaga say that, if a place is "good," this can take as little as five years; but if a place is "bad," it may require ten years or longer. A bad place is one in which misfortunes are frequent and where, therefore,

ritual demands for the killing of pigs arise frequently. A good place is one where such demands are infrequent. In a good place, the increase of the pig herd exceeds the ongoing ritual demands, and the herd grows rapidly. Sooner or later the substandard tubers incidentally obtained while harvesting become insufficient to feed the herd, and additional acreage must be put into production specifically for the pigs.

The work involved in caring for a large pig herd can be extremely burdensome. The Tsembaga herd just prior to the pig festival of 1962–63, when it numbered 169 animals, was receiving 54 percent of all the sweet potatoes and 82 percent of all the manioc harvested. These comprised 35.9 percent by weight of all root crops harvested. This figure is consistent with the difference between the amount of land under cultivation just previous to the pig festival, when the herd was at maximum size, and that immediately afterwards, when the pig herd was at minimum size. The former was 36.1 percent in excess of the latter.[20]

I have estimated, on the basis of acreage yield and energy expenditure figures, that about 45,000 calories per year are expended in caring for one pig 120–150 pounds in size. It is upon women that most of the burden of pig keeping falls. If, from a woman's daily intake of about 2,200 calories, 950 calories are allowed for basal metabolism, a woman has only 1,250 calories a day available for all her activities, which include gardening for her family, child care, and cooking, as well as tending pigs. It is clear that no woman can feed many pigs; only a few had as many as

---

[19] Rappaport's description of the relationship between ritual and environment is heavily influenced by cybernetics, which was considered an important new field at the time the essay was written. Cybernetics had begun in the 1940s and was concerned with environmental feedback to automatic devices, particularly antiaircraft guns. By the time Rappaport was writing, the principles of cybernetics were being applied to computers and the human nervous system as well. Here, the ritual planting of the *rumbim* is understood as a switch that turns hostilities off.

[20] Rappaport goes to lengths to prove that the Tsembaga hold festivals when the burden of caring for pigs becomes excessive. Critics ask why the Tsembaga don't control

herd size simply by killing and eating pigs when they are too numerous. Rappaport does not address these issues here, preferring to concentrate on the functioning of the *kaiko* rather than its origin, but he did respond to such questions at length in the epilogue to the 1984 edition of *Pigs for the Ancestors*. Functionalism did, of course, have an important effect on Steward and other key thinkers in cultural ecology. They criticized functionalism because it did not give enough attention to the relation between people and their environment and because it did not produce empirically testable hypotheses. Rappaport's work is, in part, a functional analysis that attempts to respond to these problems.

four in their care at the commencement of the festival; and it is not surprising that agitation to uproot the *rumbim* and stage the *kaiko* starts with the wives of the owners of large numbers of pigs.

A large herd is not only burdensome as far as energy expenditure is concerned; it becomes increasingly a nuisance as it expands. The more numerous pigs become, the more frequently are gardens invaded by them. Such events result in serious disturbances of local tranquility. The garden owner often shoots, or attempts to shoot, the offending pig; and the pig owner commonly retorts by shooting, or attempting to shoot, either the garden owner, his wife, or one of his pigs. As more and more such events occur, the settlement, nucleated when the herd was small, disperses as people try to put as much distance as possible between their pigs and other people's gardens and between their gardens and other people's pigs. Occasionally this reaches its logical conclusion, and people begin to leave the territory, taking up residence with kinsmen in other local populations.

The number of pigs sufficient to become intolerable to the Tsembaga was below the capacity of the territory to carry pigs. I have estimated that, if the size and structure of the human population remained constant at the 1962–1963 level, a pig population of 140 to 240 animals averaging 100 to 150 pounds in size could be maintained perpetually by the Tsembaga without necessarily inducing environmental degradation. Since the size of the herd fluctuates, even higher cyclical maxima could be achieved. The level of toleration, however, is likely always to be below the carrying capacity, since the destructive capacity of the pigs is dependent upon the population density of both people and pigs, rather than upon population size. The denser the human population, the fewer pigs will be required to disrupt social life. If the carrying capacity is exceeded, it is likely to be exceeded by people and not by pigs.

The *kaiko* or pig festival, which commences with the planting of stakes at the boundary and the uprooting of the *rumbim*, is thus triggered by either the additional work attendant upon feeding pigs or the destructive capacity of the pigs themselves. It may be said, then, that there are sufficient pigs to stage the *kaiko* when the relationship of pigs to people changes from one of mutualism to one of parasitism or competition.[21]

A short time prior to the uprooting of the *rumbim*, stakes are planted at the boundary. If the enemy has continued to occupy its territory, the stakes are planted at the boundary which existed before the fight. If, on the other hand, the enemy has abandoned its territory, the victors may plant their stakes at a new boundary which encompasses areas previously occupied by the enemy. The Maring say, to be sure, that they never take land belonging to an enemy, but this land is regarded as vacant, since no *rumbim* was planted on it after the last fight. We may state here a rule of land redistribution in terms of the ritual cycle: *If one of a pair of antagonistic groups is able to uproot its rumbim before its opponents can plant their rumbim, it may occupy the latter's territory.*[22]

Not only have the vanquished abandoned their territory; it is assumed that it has also been abandoned by their ancestors as well. The surviving members of the erstwhile enemy group have by this time resided with other groups for a number of years, and most if not all of them have already had occasion to sacrifice pigs to their ancestors at their new residences. In so doing they have invited these spirits to settle at the new locations of the living, where they will in the future receive sacrifices. Ancestors of vanquished

---

[21] Here Rappaport again relies on the vocabulary of biology. *Mutualism* is a relationship between any two species in which both species benefit. *Parasitism* is such a relationship in which only one benefits.

[22] In this paragraph and below, Rappaport builds a formal model (or part of one) by stating a series of rules. This is similar to White's style of writing (see essay 16). Unlike White, whose rules are evolutionary and intended to apply to all cultures, however, Rappaport's rules are specific to Tsembaga culture and say nothing about the long-term direction of cultural change.

groups thus relinquish their guardianship over the territory, making it available to victorious groups. Meanwhile, the *de facto* membership of the living in the groups with which they have taken refuge is converted eventually into *de jure* membership.[23] Sooner or later the groups with which they have taken up residence will have occasion to plant *rumbim*, and the refugees, as co-residents, will participate, thus ritually validating their connection to the new territory and the new group. *A rule of population redistribution may thus be stated in terms of ritual cycles: A man becomes a member of a territorial group by participating with it in the planting of rumbim.*[24]

The uprooting of the *rumbim* follows shortly after the planting of stakes at the boundary. On this particular occasion the Tsembaga killed 32 pigs out of their herd of 169. Much of the pork was distributed to allies and affines outside of the local group.

The taboo on trapping marsupials was also terminated at this time.[25] Information is lacking concerning the population dynamics of the local marsupials, but it may well be that the taboo which had prevailed since the last fight—that against taking them in traps—had conserved a fauna which might otherwise have become extinct.

The *kaiko* continues for about a year, during which period friendly groups are entertained from time to time. The guests receive presents of vegetable foods, and the hosts and male guests dance together throughout the night.

These events may be regarded as analogous to aspects of the social behavior of many non-human animals. First of all, they include massed epigamic,[26] or courtship, displays (Wynne-Edwards 1962:17). Young women are presented with samples of the eligible males of local groups with which they may not otherwise have had the opportunity to become familiar. The context, moreover, permits the young women to discriminate amongst this sample in terms of both endurance (signaled by how vigorously and how long a man dances) and wealth (signaled by the richness of a man's shell and feather finery).

More importantly, the massed dancing at these events may be regarded as epideictic display,[27] communicating to the participants information concerning the size or density of the group (Wynne-Edwards 1962:16). In many species such displays take place as a prelude to actions which adjust group size or density, and such is the case among the Maring. The massed dancing of the visitors at a *kaiko* entertainment communicates to the hosts, while the *rumbim* truce is still in force, information concerning the amount of support they may expect from the visitors in the bellicose enterprises that they are likely to embark upon soon after the termination of the pig festival.

Among the Maring there are no chiefs or other political authorities capable of commanding the support of a body of followers, and the decision to assist another group in warfare rests with each individual male. Allies are not recruited by appealing for help to other local groups as such. Rather, each member of the groups primarily involved in the hostilities appeals to his cognatic and affinal kinsmen in other local groups. These men, in turn, urge other of their co-residents and kinsmen to "help them fight." The channels through which invitations to dance are extended are precisely those through which appeals for military support are issued. The invitations go not from group to group, but from kinsman to kinsman, the recipients of invitations urging their co-residents to "help them dance."

---

[23] *De facto* means "in actuality," *de jure* means "in law."

[24] In a personal communication Rappaport noted that participating in the planting of a *rumbim* is how the Tsembaga themselves understand becoming a member of a territorial group. What is important for Rappaport's approach, however, is that participation in this ceremony provides a clear operational and behavioral way of determining group membership, whether perceived that way by the Tsembaga or not.

[25] Notice that Rappaport suggests that other aspects of the system he has identified also serve ecological functions.

[26] *Epigamic:* related to the mating of animals and particularly the use of color to attract the opposite sex.

[27] *Epideictic:* In ornithology, this refers to collective displays and other conventional behaviors, which are believed to have evolved from the need to control population.

Invitations to dance do more than exercise the channels through which allies are recruited; they provide a means for judging their effectiveness. Dancing and fighting are regarded as in some sense equivalent. This equivalence is expressed in the similarity of some pre-fight and pre-dance rituals, and the Maring say that those who come to dance come to fight. The size of a visiting dancing contingent is consequently taken as a measure of the size of the contingent of warriors whose assistance may be expected in the next round of warfare.[28]

In the morning the dancing ground turns into a trading ground. The items most frequently exchanged include axes, bird plumes, shell ornaments, an occasional baby pig, and, in former times, native salt. The *kaiko* thus facilitates trade by providing a market-like setting in which large numbers of traders can assemble. It likewise facilitates the movement of two critical items, salt and axes, by creating a demand for the bird plumes which may be exchanged for them.

The *kaiko* concludes with major pig sacrifices. On this particular occasion the Tsembaga butchered 105 adult and adolescent pigs, leaving only 60 juveniles and neonates alive. The survival of an additional fifteen adolescents and adults was only temporary, for they were scheduled as imminent victims. The pork yielded by the Tsembaga slaughter was estimated to weigh between 7,000 and 8,500 pounds, of which between 4,500 and 6,000 pounds were distributed to members of other local groups in 163 separate presentations. An estimated 2,000 to 3,000 people in seventeen local groups were the beneficiaries of the redistribution. The presentations, it should be mentioned, were not confined to pork. Sixteen Tsembaga men presented bridewealth or child-wealth, consisting largely of axes and shells, to their affines at this time.[29]

The *kaiko* terminates on the day of the pig slaughter with the public presentation of salted pig belly to allies of the last fight. Presentations are made through the window in a high ceremonial fence built specially for the occasion at one end of the dance ground. The name of each honored man is announced to the assembled multitude as he charges to the window to receive his hero's portion. The fence is then ritually torn down, and the fighting stones are put away. The pig festival and the ritual cycle have been completed, demonstrating, it may be suggested, the ecological and economic competence of the local population. The local population would now be free, if it were not for the presence of the government, to attack its enemy again, secure in the knowledge that the assistance of allies and ancestors would be forthcoming because they have received pork and the obligations to them have been fulfilled.[30]

Usually fighting did break out again very soon after the completion of the ritual cycle. If peace still prevailed when the ceremonial fence had rotted completely—a process said to take about three years, a little longer than the length of time required to raise a pig to maximum size—*rumbim* was planted as if there had been a fight, and all adult and adolescent pigs were killed. When the

---

[28] Notice that the flow of information is important in Rappaport's description. Information theory, developed in the 1950s, provided a way of expressing the transmission of certain types of information in energy terms. It was useful because, in principle, when combined with nutritional analysis, it provided a way of measuring the flow of both food and information through a cultural system in terms of energy. In practice, it proved extremely difficult to apply.

[29] Rappaport, here and above, briefly mentions the economic functions of the *kaiko* but does not elaborate on them, and below he mentions some specifics about how pork is distributed. Rappaport frequently supplies ethnographic details, like Steward, but they play a different role for each researcher. For Steward, details of ceremonies are generally secondary cultural features determined by the specific history of the group and therefore not meaningful for analysis. For Rappaport, they are part of the critical interface between culture and environment.

[30] The Tsembaga were under the administration of the Australian government when Rappaport worked with them, and the government had suppressed fighting among the different groups. Rappaport describes a *kaiko* festival he witnessed. However, he was unable to witness the cycle of warfare that led to it, which took place before his arrival. This element of his description is thus reconstructed from the memories of informants he interviewed.

pig herd was large enough so that the *rumbim* could be uprooted, peace could be made with former enemies if they were also able to dig out their *rumbim*. To put this in formal terms: *If a pair of antagonistic groups proceeds through two ritual cycles without resumption of hostilities their enmity may be terminated.*[h]

The relations of the Tsembaga with their environment have been analyzed as a complex system composed of two subsystems. What may be called the "local subsystem" has been derived from the relations of the Tsembaga with the nonhuman components of their immediate or territorial environment. It corresponds to the ecosystem in which the Tsembaga participate. A second subsystem, one which corresponds to the larger regional population of which the Tsembaga are one of the constituent units and which may be designated as the "regional subsystem," has been derived from the relations of the Tsembaga with neighboring local populations similar to themselves.[31]

It has been argued that rituals, arranged in repetitive sequences, regulate relations both within each of the subsystems and within the larger complex system as a whole. The timing of the ritual cycle is largely dependent upon changes in the states of the components of the local subsystem. But the *kaiko*, which is the culmination of the ritual cycle, does more than reverse changes which have taken place within the local subsystem. Its occurrence also affects relations among the components of the regional subsystem. During its performance, obligations to other local populations are fulfilled, support for future military enterprises is rallied, and land from

which enemies have earlier been driven is occupied. Its completion, furthermore, permits the local population to initiate warfare again. Conversely, warfare is terminated by rituals which preclude the reinitiation of warfare until the state of the local subsystem is again such that a *kaiko* may be staged and completed. Ritual among the Tsembaga and other Maring, in short, operates as both transducer, "translating" changes in the state of one subsystem into information which can effect changes in a second subsystem, and homeostat, maintaining a number of variables which in sum comprise the total system within ranges of viability. To repeat an earlier assertion, the operation of ritual among the Tsembaga and other Maring helps to maintain an undegraded environment, limits fighting to frequencies which do not endanger the existence of the regional population, adjusts man-land ratios, facilitates trade, distributes local surpluses of pig throughout the regional population in the form of pork, and assures people of high quality protein when they are most in need of it.[32]

Religious rituals and the supernatural orders toward which they are directed cannot be assumed *a priori* to be mere epiphenomena.[33] Ritual may, and doubtless frequently does, do nothing more than validate and intensify the relationships which integrate the social unit, or symbolize the relationships which bind the social unit to its environment. But the interpretation of such presumably *sapiens*-specific phenomena as religious ritual within a framework which will also accommodate the behavior of other species shows, I think, that religious ritual may do much more

---

[31] In this paper, because of space limitations imposed by the original publication format, Rappaport tells us little about data collection. In his book-length treatment of this material, however, he includes a good deal of information on data collection and extensive appendices with raw data. Rappaport was unusual for his time. Most ethnographic work of this era did not include this sort of information and was strongly criticized on that basis by anthropologists in the 1970s and 1980s.

[32] When Rappaport's work on the Tsembaga was published in the late 1960s, it fell on fertile ground. It seemed

to many to demonstrate the ecological soundness and wisdom of traditional society. This idea was appealing in the late 1960s and the 1970s, when many in academia were concerned with ecology and the value of traditional communities and folks were busy developing communes. Criticism of his work grew as these ideas fell out of popularity and political conservatism became increasingly dominant.

[33] *Epiphenomena:* secondary events.

than symbolize, validate, and intensify relationships. Indeed, it would not be improper to refer to the Tsembaga and the other entities with which they share their territory as a "ritually regulated ecosystem," and to the Tsembaga and their human neighbors as a "ritually regulated population."[34]

NOTES

[a] The field work upon which this paper is based was supported by a grant from the National Science Foundation, under which Professor A. P. Vayda was principal investigator. Personal support was received by the author from the National Institutes of Health. Earlier versions of this paper were presented at the 1964 annual meeting of the American Anthropological Association in Detroit, and before a Columbia University seminar on Ecological Systems and Cultural Evolution. I have received valuable suggestions from Alexander Alland, Jacques Barrau, William Clarke, Paul Collins, C. Glen King, Marvin Harris, Margaret Mead, M. J. Meggitt, Ann Rappaport, John Street, Marjorie Whiting, Cherry Vayda, A. P. Vayda and many others, but I take full responsibility for the analysis presented herewith.

[b] The social organization of the Tsembaga will be described in detail elsewhere.

[c] Because the length of time in the field precluded the possibility of maintaining harvest records on single gardens from planting through abandonment, figures were based, in the case of both "taro-yam" and "sugar-sweet potato" gardens, on three separate gardens planted in successive years. Conversions from the gross weight to the caloric value of the yield were made by reference to the literature. The sources used are listed in Rappaport (1966: Appendix VIII).

[d] Rough time and motion studies of each of the tasks involved in making, maintaining, harvesting, and walking to and from gardens were undertaken. Conversion to energy expenditure values was accomplished by reference to energy expenditure tables prepared by Hipsley and Kirk (1965:43) on the basis of gas exchange measurements made during the performance of garden tasks by the Chimbu people of the New Guinea highlands.

[e] Marvin Harris, in an unpublished paper, estimates the ratio of energy return to energy input on Dyak

(Borneo) rice swiddens at 10:1. His estimates of energy ratios on Tepoltzlan (Meso-America) swiddens range from 13:1 on poor land to 29:1 on the best land.

[f] Heights may be inaccurate. Many men wear their hair in large coiffures hardened with pandanus grease, and it was necessary in some instances to estimate the location of the top of the skull.

[g] The possible significance of pork consumption by protein-short people during periods of physiological stress was unknown to me while I was in the field. I did not, therefore, investigate this matter in full detail. Georgeda Bick and Cherry Vayda, who visited the Maring area in 1966, have investigated the circumstances surrounding pork consumption further, and will publish their more detailed materials elsewhere.

[h] After this article had gone to press in *Ethnology*, where it was originally published, I learned from A. P. Vayda, who spent the summer of 1966 in the Maring area, that he received somewhat different accounts of peace-making mechanisms, both from informants in other Maring local groups and from the Tsembaga man who had supplied me with the only full account which I was able to obtain (details of his account were, however, corroborated by information obtained from other Tsembaga men). According to Vayda's account, when the ceremonial fence had rotted away completely, some, but not all, adult and adolescent pigs were slain and offered to certain ancestral spirits to insure the health and fecundity of the remaining pigs, and no *rumbim* was planted. When the herds of the erstwhile antagonists again reached maximum size peace could be made.

It is important to note here that the other rituals treated in this paper were either observed by me or described by a number of informants who had participated in them, but none of either Vayda's informants or mine had ever participated in peace-making procedures, for none had taken place during the adult life of any of them. They were only reporting what they remembered from their childhood or what they had heard from their fathers or grandfathers. It is likely, therefore, that none of the informants are particularly well-versed in the details of the procedure. However, it is also important to note that all of the informants are in basic agreement upon what is in the present context the most important aspects of peace-making: that the rituals were not performed until pig herds of the erstwhile antagonists had reached maximum size. The rule

---

[34] The functions Rappaport identifies for religion here fit well with those Bronislaw Malinowski noted in his work among the people of the Trobriand Islands. Although Rappaport's work is limited to the Maring, it suggests that ecological, homeostatic functions be looked for in other religions as well.

which I have proposed would seem to stand if it is understood that the second ritual cycle of the sequence may differ from the first in that *rumbim* might not be planted, and if it is understood that the truce may not be sanctified during the second cycle of the sequence.

REFERENCES

Berg, C. 1948. Protein deficiency and its relation to nutritional anemia, hypoproteinemia, nutritional edema, and resistance to infection. In *Protein and amino acids in nutrition*, ed. M. Sahyun, pp. 290–317. New York: Reinhold.

Burton, B. T., ed. 1959. The Heinz handbook of nutrition. New York: McGraw-Hill.

Elman, R. 1951. Surgical Care. New York: Appleton-Century-Crofts.

Food and Agriculture Organization of the United Nations. 1964. Protein: At the heart of the world food problem. World Food Problems 5. Rome: FAO.

Hipsley, E., and N. Kirk. 1965. Studies of the dietary intake and energy expenditure of New Guineans. South Pacific Commission, Technical Paper 147. Noumea: South Pacific Commission.

Homans, G. C. 1941. Anxiety and ritual: The theories of Malinowski and Radcliffe-Brown. American Anthropologist 43:164–172.

Houssay, B. A., et al. 1955. Human physiology, 2nd ed. New York: McGraw-Hill.

Large, A., and C. G. Johnston. 1948. Proteins as related to burns. *In* Proteins and amino acids in nutrition, ed. M. Sahyun, pp. 386–396. New York: Reinhold.

Lund, C. G., and S. M. Levenson. 1948. Protein nutrition in surgical patients. *In* Proteins and amino acids in nutrition, ed. M. Sahyun, pp. 349–363. New York: Reinhold.

Moore, O. K. 1957. Divination—a new perspective. American Anthropologist 59:69–74.

National Research Council. 1963. Evaluation of protein quality. National Academy of Sciences—National Research Council Publication 1100. Washington: NAS/NRC.

Rappaport, R. A. 1966. Ritual in the ecology of a New Guinea people. Unpublished doctoral dissertation. Columbia University.

Vayda, A. P., A. Leeds, and D. B. Smith. 1961. The place of pigs in Melanesian subsistence. In proceedings of the 1961 Annual Spring Meeting of the American Ethnological Society, ed. V. E. Garfield, pp. 69–77. Seattle: University of Washington Press.

Wynne-Edwards V. C. 1962. Animal dispersion in relation to social behavior. Edinburgh and London: Oliver & Boyd.

Zintel, Harold A. 1964. Nutrition in the care of the surgical patient. *In* Modern nutrition in health and disease. ed. M. G. Wohl and R. S. Goodhart, pp. 1043–1064, 3rd ed. Philadelphia: Lea and Febiger.

21. *Peasantry and Its Problems*

Eric Wolf (1923–1999)

THIS BOOK IS about peasants; its approach is anthropological. Although anthropology had its beginnings in the investigation of the so-called primitive peoples of the world, in recent years anthropologists have become increasingly interested in rural populations that form part of larger, more complex societies. Where an anthropologist previously examined the life-ways of a roaming band of desert hunters or of migratory cultivators occupying a hamlet in some tropical forest, now he often sets himself the task of investigating a village in Ireland, in India, or in China, in areas of the world that have long supported a variegated and rich cultural tradition carried on by many different kinds of people. Among these, rural cultivators constitute only one—though an important—segment. Thus, the people now under anthropological scrutiny are in continuous interaction and communication with other social groups. What goes on in Gopalpur, India or Alcala de la Sierra in Spain cannot be explained in terms of that village alone; the explanation must include

From *Peasants* (1966)

consideration both of the outside forces impinging on these villages and of the reactions of villagers to these forces.[1]

PEASANTS AND PRIMITIVES

Our first question, then, is to ask what distinguishes peasants from the primitives more often
studied by anthropologists. We have spoken of
peasants as rural cultivators; that is, they raise
crops and livestock in the countryside, not in
greenhouses in the midst of cities or in aspidistra
boxes on the windowsill.[2] At the same time they
are not *farmers*, or agricultural entrepreneurs as
we know them in the United States. The American farm is primarily a business enterprise, combining factors of production purchased in a
market to obtain a profit by selling advanta-
geously in a products market. The peasant, however, does not operate an enterprise in the
economic sense; he runs a household, not a business concern. But there are also primitive peoples who live in the countryside and raise crops
and livestock. What then is the distinguishing
mark of the peasant, as opposed to the primitive
cultivator?

One way of approaching this question has
been to say that peasants form part of a larger,
compound society, whereas a primitive band or

tribe does not. But this answer hardly does justice to the question. For primitives seldom live
in isolation. There are exceptions, like the Polar
Eskimos who were cut off from all outside contact until rediscovered for the larger world by
Admiral Peary in his attempt to reach the North
Pole. But much more frequently, primitive tribes
also entertain relations with their neighbors.
Even the simple hunters and gatherers of the
Australian deserts maintain ties which bring together groups of people, often widely dispersed,
into systematic economic and ritual exchanges.
The tribes of the Amazon basin, apparently isolated in separate pockets of the tropical forest,
trade with one another, or marry one another, or
fight one another—for warfare is indeed also a
kind of relationship. We owe to anthropologists
like Bronislaw Malinowski, the author of *Argonauts of the Western Pacific* (1922) descriptions
and analyses of the trade uniting the east end of
New Guinea and the adjacent archipelagoes into
a network of ceremonial and commercial transactions. Similarly, the Plains Indians of the
United States, we now see, were part and parcel
of American history, influenced by the advancing
frontier and influencing its advance in turn.

The distinction between primitives and peasants thus does not lie in the greater or lesser outside involvement of one or the other, but in the
character of that involvement. Marshall D. Sahlins

---

[1] This essay is the opening chapter of a brief book called *Peasants* (1966). It appeared as part of a series called *The Foundations of Modern Anthropology*, which also in-cluded books on hunters, tribesmen, the formation of the state, and numerous other subjects. The series was pub-lished for the college market in the mid-1960s and de-signed to introduce undergraduate students to then cur-rent thinking in anthropology. By current-day standards, the opening paragraph seems unexceptional, even com-monsensical in its insistence that anthropologists be con-cerned with outside forces impinging on village life. In its era, however, this statement was considerably more radi-cal. Anthropology in the first half of the twentieth century did have precisely this problem. Anthropologists tended to study communities as if they were self-contained. Al-though in beginning chapters or forewords ethnographers often referred to the broader setting of the society they

were studying, they then tended to focus entirely on the social dynamics within that community. A good example of this is Robert Redfield's work on Chan Kom, a Maya village in the Yucatan. Wolf's work, and other neo-Marxist work from the 1960s to the current day, focuses on the connections and exchanges that bind the local commu-nity to the economic aspects of the wider world. Wolf's book is ostensibly aimed at introductory students, but his references show that he clearly has a professional audi-ence in mind as well—the examples in this paragraph are anything but random. Golpalpur refers to Alan R. Beals' 1962 book *Gopalpur: A South Indian Village* (1962), and Alcala de la Sierra refers to Julian Pitt-Rivers' *The People of the Sierra* (1961); both are important and, at that time, recently published ethnographies.

[2] *Aspidistra* is a popular indoor plant.

has characterized the economic and social world of primitives as follows:

> In primitive economies, most production is geared to use of the producers or to discharge of kinship obligations, rather than to exchange and gain. A corollary is that de facto control of the means of production is decentralized, local, and familial in primitive society. The following propositions are then implied: (1) economic relations of coercion and exploitation and the corresponding social relations of dependence and mastery are not created in the system of production; (2) in the absence of the incentive given by exchange of the product against a great quantity of goods on a market, there is a tendency to limit production to goods that can be directly utilized by the producers.[a]

Thus, in primitive society, producers control the means of production, including their own labor, and exchange their own labor and its products for the culturally defined equivalent goods and services of others. In the course of cultural evolution, however, such simple systems have been superseded by others in which control of the means of production, including the disposition of human labor, passes from the hands of the primary producers into the hands of groups that do not carry on the productive process themselves, but assume instead special executive and administrative functions, backed by the use of force. The constitution of society in such a case is no longer based on the equivalent and direct

exchanges of goods and services between one group and another; rather, goods and services are first furnished to a center and only later redirected. In primitive society, surpluses are exchanged directly among groups or members of groups; peasants, however, are rural cultivators whose surpluses are transferred to a dominant group of rulers that uses the surpluses both to underwrite its own standard of living and to distribute the remainder to groups in society that do not farm but must be fed for their specific goods and services in turn.[3]

CIVILIZATION

The development of a complex social order based on a division between rulers and food-producing cultivators is commonly referred to as the development of civilization. Civilization has a long and involved history; the archaeological record indicates a great diversity in the processes which allowed men in different parts of the world to make the transition from primitives to peasants. Nevertheless, gross features of the process stand out. In the Old World, for example, cultivation and animal domestication seem to have been under way in Southwestern Asia as early as 9000 B.C., and it is probable that sedentary farming villages were established in the same area by 6000 B.C. Similarly, finds in Northeastern Mexico suggest that experiments with food production were begun

---

[3] Wolf does not refer directly to Marx in this passage. Nevertheless, it would be difficult to find a more solidly Marxist approach to anthropology in America in this era. In this passage, Wolf clearly defines the peasantry as a specific mode of production. You will recall that the notion of a mode of production is central to Marxist thinking. A mode of production is briefly defined as the set of material factors and social relations that any society uses to produce its sustenance. In this passage Wolf identifies three modes of production: (1) The American farmer whose goal is to use resources to create a profit represents the capitalist mode of production. (2) The primitive who uses resources to supply the family and satisfy kinship demands represents what Marshal Sahlins will call the familial or domestic mode of production (1968). (3) The peasant is defined by a mode of production in which surpluses are siphoned

away to rulers with higher standards of living and, largely through them, to nonfarming specialists.

Wolf relies here on the work of Marshal Sahlins (b. 1930). A student of Leslie White, Sahlins was also deeply influenced by Julian Steward. He was one of the co-authors of the critical volume *Evolution and Culture* (1960), which attempted to synthesize the work of Steward and White. Like Wolf, he was deeply affected by Marxist ideas as well as the work of the economist Karl Polanyi (1886–1964; see footnote 6). Sahlins wrote the volume *Tribesman* for the "Foundations of Modern Anthropology Series," though this did not appear until 1968, two years after Wolf's volume. He is probably best known for his 1972 book *Stone Age Economics,* in which he presents a materialist analysis of band and tribal societies based on the notion of the domestic mode of production.

around 7000 B.C., with full-fledged cultivation firmly established around 1500 B.C. From these or similar original centers, cultivation spread out with variable speed in different directions, being adapted to the demands of new climates and new social exigencies. But not all areas of the world were caught up equally in this process. The people in some areas never accepted cultivation or accepted it only reluctantly, while others forged ahead to attain the new levels of productivity and social organization which permitted the unfolding of the functional division of labor between cultivators and rulers which we have defined as the hallmark of civilization.[4]

CALORIC MINIMA AND SURPLUSES

It is sometimes said that the capacity to sustain a functional division of labor between cultivators and rulers is a simple consequence of the capacity of a society to produce a surplus above and beyond the minimum required to sustain life. This minimum can be defined quite rigorously in physiological terms as the daily intake of food calories required to balance the expenditures of energy a man incurs in his daily output of labor. This amount has been put at roughly between 2000 and 3000 calories per person per day. It is probably not amiss to point out that this daily minimum is still not met in most parts of the world. About half the population of the world has an average daily per capita ration of less than 2250 calories. This category includes Indonesia (with 1750 calories), China (with 1800 calories) and India (with 1800 calories). Two-tenths of the world's population fall into the category receiving

an average daily per capita ration between 2250 and 2750 calories. This group includes Mediterranean Europe and the Balkan countries. Only three-tenths of the world's population—the United States, the British dominions, Western Europe, and the Soviet Union—attain figures higher than 2750.[b] Even this last achievement must be seen in historical perspective. In the seventeenth century for example, France—now among the fortunate three-tenths—attained the amount of 3000 daily calories per person (represented by half a loaf of bread per day) in only one out of every five years. In the eighteenth century, this accomplishment became possible in one out of four years. In the off years, the average daily ration clearly fell below minimum requirements.[c]

Cultivators must not only furnish themselves with minimal caloric rations; they must also raise enough food beyond this caloric minimum to provide sufficient seed for next year's crop, or to provide adequate feed for their livestock. Thus, for example, a 40-acre farm in Mecklenburg northeastern Germany, during the fourteenth and fifteenth centuries produced 10,200 pounds of grain crops, of which 3400 pounds had to be set aside for seed and 2800 pounds to feed four horses. More than half of the total yield was thus committed in advance to seed and feed.[d] This amount is therefore not absolute surplus, but an amount destined for the upkeep of the instruments of production. The cultivator had to set aside time and effort to repair his tools, to sharpen his knives, to caulk his storage bin, to fence his yard, to shoe his work animals, perhaps to make and set up a scarecrow to keep the eager birds out of his fields. Moreover, he had to replace such things as a leaky roof, a broken pot, or

---

[4] Wolf's use of the concept of civilization is striking here and differentiates him clearly from Boasian anthropologists and culture and personality theorists. For Wolf, civilization is a distinct mode of production involving plant and animal domestication and a division of society into social levels. Boasians and culture and personality theorists tended to use *civilization* as synonymous with *culture.* They spoke frequently of "primitive civilization" (for example, Boas 1901:8; Goldenweiser 1917:449; Sapir 1924:416). For them the separation of societies into the

primitive and civilized was dangerously ethnocentric. Even current-day anthropologists often prefer the term *state-level-society* to *civilization,* perhaps for this reason. Wolf clearly has no qualms about describing certain types of societies as civilizations. However, for Wolf, as for other neo-Marxists, *civilization* refers to a society with specific social and political characteristics. A principal characteristic of civilization is not that it is superior to other forms of society but that it is more oppressive, as you will see in Wolf's examples below.

his clothing when it became too tattered and torn. The amount needed to replace his minimum equipment for both production and consumption was his *replacement fund*.[5]

It is important that we think of this replacement fund not merely in purely technical terms, but in cultural terms as well. The instruments and techniques of a particular technology are the product of a prolonged process of cultural accumulation in the past. There are technologies without pottery or storage bins or work animals. Once a technology has come to include these items, however, they become part and parcel of everyday existence, and hence culturally necessary. Like the Greek philosopher Diogenes, a man can rid himself of his last cup, since he need not suffer thirst as long as he can make a cup of his hands. But once pottery cups are a part of a man's cultural expectations, they become more than that—they become something he must commit himself to obtain. Hence, a drought or an invasion of locusts or any other misfortune which endangers the replacement fund threatens not only a man's minimal biological existence but also his capacity to meet his cultural necessities.

It is conceivable that a cultivator might cease his productive efforts on the land once his caloric minimum and his replacement fund are assured. Thus, for example, the Kuikuru Indians of the Amazon are able to reach their caloric minimum and replacement requirements by working only three-and-a-half hours each day, and do not work beyond this time. There are neither technical nor social reasons why they should add additional hours to their daily labor budget.[e] Production beyond the level of the caloric minimum and the replacement level obeys social incentives and dictates. At stake is a major issue in economic anthropology. There are some who argue that the appearance of surpluses generates further development; others hold that potential surpluses are universal and what counts is the institutional means for mobilizing them.[6]

SOCIAL SURPLUSES

Ceremonial Fund

There are two such sets of social imperatives. The first of these occurs in any society. Even where men are largely self-sufficient in food and goods, they must entertain social relations with their fellows. They must, for example, marry outside the household into which they were born, and this requirement means that they must have social contacts with people who are their potential or actual in-laws. They must also join with their fellow men in keeping order, in ensuring the rudimentary acceptances of certain rules of conduct so as to render life predictable and livable. They may be required to help each other in some phase of the food quest. But social relations of any kind are never completely utilitarian and instrumental.

---

[5] Note Wolf's interest in the caloric production of societies. In "Energy and the Evolution of Culture" (1943), White had argued that culture evolves as the amount of energy it produces increases. For White's students and others, one way of accessing this was through counting how many calories a society could produce. A second of Wolf's concerns is evident in this passage. He is deeply concerned with world history. In particular, he is concerned with correcting the misapprehension that European societies have always been wealthy and technologically advanced in comparison with the rest of the world. This theme is explored in much greater depth in *Europe and the People Without History* (1982).

[6] Thus, Wolf argues, biological reproduction is different from cultural reproduction. Reproducing a society is not just providing enough calories for people to live, but enough calories for people to recreate the social and material conditions of their own society. This concern with social reproduction is central to Marxist thought.

In the final two sentences, Wolf refers to a major issue in economic anthropology. This probably refers to the then-current debate between "formalist" and "substantivist" economic anthropologists. Formalists (such as Harold Schneider and Scott Cook) held that the principles of new-classical Western economics could be used to understand all economic systems ("the appearance of surpluses generates further development"). Substantivists (such as Paul Bohannan and George Dalton) held that economic principles were conditioned by social institutions. Substantivist thinkers were deeply influenced by the socialist economic historian Karl Polanyi, whose book *The Great Transformation* (1944) argued that the development of capitalism and free market economics were linked to the historic rise of the nation-state.

Each is always surrounded with symbolic constructions which serve to explain, to justify, and to regulate it. Thus, a marriage does not involve merely the passage of a spouse from one house to another. It also involves gaining the goodwill of the spouse-to-be and of her kinfolk; it involves a public performance in which the participants act out, for all to see, both the coming of age of the marriage partners and the social realignments which the marriage involves; and it involves also the public exhibition of an ideal model of what marriages—all marriages—ought to do for people and how people should behave once they have been married. All social relations are surrounded by such ceremonial, and ceremonial must be paid for in labor, in goods, or in money. If men are to participate in social relations, therefore, they must also work to establish a fund against which these expenditures may be charged. We shall call this the *ceremonial fund*.

The ceremonial fund of a society—and hence the ceremonial fund of its members—may be large or small. Size is once again a relative matter. The ceremonial funds of Indian villages in Mexico and Peru, for example, are very large when compared to their caloric budgets and their replacement funds, for there a man must expend a great deal of effort and goods in the sponsorship of ceremonials that serve to underline and exemplify the solidarity of the community to which he belongs.[f] Ceremonial expenditures are a matter of cultural tradition, and will vary from culture to culture. Yet everywhere the need to establish and maintain such a ceremonial fund will result in the production of surpluses beyond the replacement fund discussed above.

It is important at this point, however, to remember that the efforts of a peasantry are not governed wholly by the exigencies internal to its own way of life. A peasantry always exists within a larger system. Hence the size of the effort which it must put forward to replace its means of production or to cover its ceremonial costs is also a function of the ways in which labor is divided within the society to which the peasant belongs, and of the regulations governing that division of labor. Thus, in some societies, the amount of effort required to meet these needs may be quite small. This is true, for example, in a society where a man grows his own food and makes his own basic equipment. For him the amount of surplus required to obtain articles from the outside is reduced; indeed, it is identical with his replacement fund. This is also true in societies where different households manufacture different objects or provide different services that are exchanged in equivalent reciprocal relations. If I grow grain, but do not make my own blankets, I may exchange a given amount of grain for a given number of blankets; the blanket-maker thus gets food in return for his labor. In such situations men obtain goods through exchanges, but—and this is an important but—the amount of food they must grow to get needed blankets or pots is still chargeable to their replacement fund, even though the manner by which they replace goods they do not make themselves is indirect. But it is possible, and increasingly so as societies have grown more complex, that the exchange ratios between units of food produced by the cultivator and units of goods produced are not exchanged in equivalencies determined by the face-to-face negotiation of producer and consumer, but according to asymmetrical ratios of exchange determined by external conditions. Where the networks of exchange are restricted and localized, the participants must adjust the prices of their goods to the purchasing power of their potential customers. But where exchange networks are far-flung and obey pressures which take no account of the purchasing power of a local population, a cultivator may have to step up his production greatly to obtain even the items that are required for replacement. Under such conditions, a considerable share of the peasant's replacement fund may become somebody else's fund of profit.[7]

---

[7] Here, Wolf once again reminds us of the ways that communities articulate with the outside world. A farmer can exchange food with a blanket maker in a simple system at rates that are equitable for both and which both parties agree too. What happens, however, if, because of global connections, the blanket maker has an opportunity to sell his wares to wealthy collectors? The price of blankets rises and the farmer is placed in competition with the wealthy collector. The blanket maker has opportunities that are not available (or not equally available) to the farmer, and the producers of blankets will find that their livelihoods will be affected by external forces outside of their control.

Funds of Rent

There is yet a second set of social imperatives which may produce surpluses beyond the caloric minimum and replacement level. The relation of the cultivator to other craft specialists may be symmetrical, as we have seen above. They may exchange different products, but at traditional and long-established ratios. However, there exist in more complex societies social relations which are not symmetrical, but are based, in some form, upon the exercise of power. In the case of the Mecklenburg farm mentioned above, for example, the 4000 pounds of grain left over after the cultivator had subtracted his committed replacement fund for seed and feed were not consumed by the cultivator's household alone. Twenty-seven hundred pounds, or more than half of the effective yield, went in payment of dues to a lord who maintained jurisdiction, or domain, over the land. Only 1300 pounds remained to feed the cultivator and his family, yielding a per capita daily ration of 1600 calories.[8] To sustain minimal caloric levels, therefore, the cultivator was forced to seek additional sources of calories, such as he could derive from his garden or from livestock of his own. This peasant, then, was subject to asymmetrical power relations which made a permanent charge on his production. Such a charge, paid out as the result of some superior claim to his labor on the land, we call rent, regardless of whether that rent is paid in labor, in produce, or in money. Where someone exercises an effective superior power, or domain, over a cultivator, the cultivator must produce a fund of rent.

It is this production of a fund of rent which critically distinguishes the peasant from the primitive cultivator. This production in turn is spurred by the existence of a social order in which some men can through power demand payments from others, resulting in the transfer of wealth from one section of the population to another. The peasant's loss is the power-holder's gain, for the fund of rent provided by the peasant is part of the fund of power on which the controllers may draw.

It is important to note, though, that there are many different ways in which this fund of rent is produced, and many different ways in which it is siphoned from the peasant stratum into the hands of the controlling group. Since the distinctions in the exercise of this power have important structural effects on the way the peasantry is organized, there are consequently many kinds of peasantry, not just one. So far, then, the term "peasant" denotes no more than an asymmetrical structural relationship between producers of surplus and controllers; to render it meaningful, we must still ask questions about the different sets of conditions which will maintain this structural relationship.

THE ROLE OF THE CITY

The development of civilization has commonly been identified with the development of cities, hence the peasant has commonly been defined as a cultivator who has an enduring relationship with the city. It is certainly true that, in the course of cultural evolution, the rulers have commonly settled in special centers which have often become cities. Yet, in some societies, the rulers merely "camped" among the peasantry, as the Watusi rulers did until very recently among the Bahutu peasantry of Ruanda Urundi. Or the rulers may have lived at religious centers such as tombs or shrines to which produce was brought by the peasantry. In ancient Egypt, the Pharaoh set up his temporary capital near the pyramid being built in his honor; the role of cities remained insignificant. Among the Peten Maya, political integration appears to have been achieved without the emergence of densely settled urban zones.[h] The city is therefore a likely, but not an inevitable, product of the increasing complexity of society. I should like to think of it as a settlement in which a combination of functions are exercised, and which becomes useful because in time greater efficiency is obtained by having these functions concentrated in one site.[8]

---

[8] In twentieth-century anthropology, there was often much debate over what exactly was necessary for a society to be considered a civilization or state-level society. Cities being widely considered a central feature of civilizations, their presence was one classic diagnostic tool. In fact, the word *civilization* has its roots in the Latin word for city (*civis*).

Yet there remain very different kinds of cities. In India, until recently, some large settlements contained the castle and power apparatus of military rulers, and served as administrative centers. Others, the sites of famous shrines, functioned primarily as religious centers, attracting devotees in periodic pilgrimages to its temples. Still others were settlements of literati, specialists in elaborating some aspect of the intellectual tradition of the country.[i] It is only where one or another of these functions comes to overshadow all the others and exerts a powerful attraction on others that these come to be concentrated under one roof or in one site. But there are areas where no such dominant centers arise, where political, religious, or intellectual functions remain dispersed in the countryside. Wales, for instance, and Norway are areas in which many functions remain dispersed over the countryside, and the development of cities is weak. The presence or absence of cities will certainly affect the pattern of a society but the particular seat for the apparatus of power and influence is only one phase in the establishment of power and influence, not its totality. A piano is an instrument for making polyphonic music; but it is possible to make polyphonic music without pianos. Similarly, the city is but one—though common—form in the orchestration of power and influence, but not its exclusive or even decisive form.

Thus, it is the crystallization of executive power which serves to distinguish the primitive from the civilized, rather than whether or not such power controls are located in one kind of place or another. Not the city, but the state is the decisive criterion of civilization and it is the appearance of the state which marks the threshold of transition between food cultivators in general and peasants. Thus, it is only when a cultivator is integrated into a society with a state—that is, when the cultivator becomes subject to the demands and sanctions of power-holders outside his social stratum—that we can appropriately speak of peasantry.

It is, of course, difficult to place this threshold of civilization in terms of time and space. Nevertheless, on the basis of such data as we now possess, we may mark the beginnings of the state and hence of a peasantry at around 3500 B.C. in the Near East and around 1000 B.C. in Middle America. We must emphasize that the processes of state-building are multiple and complex. Different areas were integrated into states in markedly different ways and at different times. In some areas of the world these processes have not yet run their course, and in a few places we can still witness the encounter between primitive cultivators and state societies which impinge on the primitive and try to bring them within control.

THE PLACE OF PEASANTRY IN SOCIETY

Not only does our world contain both primitives on the verge of peasantry and full-fledged peasants, but it also contains both societies in which the peasant is the chief producer of the store of social wealth and those in which he has been relegated to a secondary position. There are still large areas of the world in which peasants who cultivate the land with their traditional tools not only form the vast majority of the population, but also furnish the funds of rent and profit which underwrite the entire social structure. In such societies, all other social groups depend upon peasants both for their food and for any income that may accrue to them. There are other societies, however, in which the Industrial Revolution has created vast complexes of machines that produce goods quite independently of peasants. If there are any peasants left in such societies, they occupy a secondary position in the creation of wealth. Moreover, the vast and growing numbers

---

Wolf's neo-Marxist position is reflected in his insistence here that the presence or absence of cities is incidental to civilization; rather, civilization is defined by social relations of production. Critical to those are the relations of exploitation that link the peasant to the landowner and to the state (in Wolf's words, "to power holders outside his social stratum").

of industrial workers who man the wealth-creating machines must also be fed. More often than not the provision of food for these workers is no longer in the hands of peasants who work small units of land with traditional techniques, but in the hands of new "factories in the field," which apply the technology of the Industrial Revolution to the growing of food on large, heavily capitalized, scientifically operated farms.[j] Such farms are staffed not by peasants, but by agricultural workers who are paid wages for their work much as an industrial worker is paid for running a blast furnace or a spinning machine. Both kinds of society contain threats to the peasant, whether these threats emanate from demands for surplus, or from competition which may render the peasant economically useless.[9]

THE PEASANT DILEMMA

The outsider may look down upon the peasant as upon a sheep to be shorn periodically of its wool: "three bags full—one for my master, one for my dame, and one for the little boy who lives down the lane." But to the peasant, his caloric minimum and his replacement fund will be primary, together with such ceremonial payments as he must make to maintain the social order of his narrow peasant world. These needs, as we have indicated above, are culturally relative; they will differ in China from what they are in Puerto Rico. Yet they are both functionally and logically prior to the demands of the outsider, whether lord or merchant. This attitude is neatly implied

in the old song, sung during the peasant uprisings of the late European Middle Ages:

> When Adam delved and Eve span,
> Who was then the gentleman?

Peasant needs—the requirement to maintain a caloric minimum, a replacement fund, and a ceremonial fund—will often conflict with the requirements imposed by the outsider.

Yet if it is correct to define the peasantry primarily in terms of its sub-ordinate relationships to a group of controlling outsiders, it is also correct to assert as a corollary of this definition that a peasantry will be forced to maintain a balance between its own demands and the demands of the outsiders and will be subject to the tensions produced by this struggle to keep the balance. The outsider sees the peasant primarily as a source of labor and goods with which to increase his fund of power. But the peasant is at once an economic agent and the head of a household. His holding is both an economic unit and a home.[10]

The peasant unit is thus not merely a productive organization constituted of so many "hands" ready to labor in the fields; it is also a unit of consumption, containing as many mouths as there are workers. Moreover, it does not merely feed its members; it also supplies them with many other services. In such a unit children are raised and socialized to the demands of the adult world. Old people may be cared for until their death, and their burial paid for from the unit's stock of wealth. Marriage provides sexual satisfaction, and relationships within the unit generate affection which ties the members to each

---

[9] This passage mirrors the one above it. In the previous passage, Wolf reminded us that cities were not essential to a state. Here he reminds us that people are not peasants just because they cultivate the land. It is the social relations of production that are critical to understanding the mode of production. People who are paid wages to cultivate the land are capitalist workers—members of the proletariat. People who work the land and pay rents to absentee landowners and the state are more likely to be peasants.

[10] A critical feature that differentiates Marxist analysis in all of its forms is an emphasis on conflict. Up until now, Wolf has described the fundamental relations of produc-

tion for the peasantry. Here and below, he delves into sources of conflict. If the peasant considers his replacement fund and ceremonial fund to have priority over payments to landowners and states, these later will rarely share that opinion—and are generally armed as well. Thus, a fundamental conflict of interests shapes the livelihoods of peasants. Most other forms of anthropology (particularly functionalism) consider conflict to be mediated by ritual. According to Wolf, it is more likely to be mediated by armed uprising. Wolf explored this theme in substantial detail in his subsequent book, *Peasant Wars of the Twentieth Century* (1969).

other. Using its ceremonial fund, such a unit pays "the costs of representation" incurred by its members within the larger community. Hence, labor is contributed as needed in a great number of different contexts; its expenditure is not prompted directly by the existence of an economic system governed by prices and profits.

We are, of course, familiar with this kind of economic behavior in our own society. A mother will also sit up all night with a sick child or cook a meal for the family, without reckoning the cost of her labor. A father may do minor repairs around the house; a teen-age son may mow the lawn. Purchased in the open market, such services would cost a good deal. It has been estimated, for example, that in our society a man can save annually $6000–$8000 in payments for economic services if he gets married, rather than paying for their performance by specialists at prices current in the open market. Within the family, such labors of love are performed readily, without the need for cost accounting.

Peasant households function similarly. Certainly peasants are aware of the price of labor and goods in the market—their economic and social survival depends on it. The shrewdness of peasants is proverbial. Certainly many anthropologists would second Sol Tax, who concluded in a study of Indian peasants in Guatemala that "the purchasers of goods make a choice of markets according to what they want to buy and how much time they are willing to spend to get it more cheaply and closer to its source."[k] However, to the extent that a peasant holding serves to provision a group of people, every decision made in terms of the external market also has its internal, domestic aspect.[11]

This fact has caused the Russian economist A. V. Chaianov to speak of a special kind of peasant economics. He explains this concept in the following terms:

> The first fundamental characteristic of the farm economy of the peasant is that it is a family economy. Its whole organization is determined by the size and composition of the peasant family and by the coordination of its consumptive demands with the number of its working hands. This explains why the conception of profit in peasant economy differs from that in capitalist economy and why the capitalistic conception of profit cannot be applied to peasant economy. The capitalistic profit is a net profit computed by subtracting all the expenses of production from the total income. The computation of profit in this manner is inapplicable in a peasant economy because in the latter the elements entering into expenses of production are expressed in units incomparable to those in a capitalist economy.
>
> In peasant economy, as in capitalist economy, gross income and material expenditures can be expressed in rubles; but labor expended can neither be expressed in, nor measured by, rubles of paid wages, but only in the labor effort of the peasant family itself. These efforts cannot be subtracted from, or added to, money units; they can merely be confronted with rubles. The comparison of the value of a certain effort of the family with the value of a ruble would be very subjective; it would vary with the degree to which the demands of the family were satisfied and with the hardships involved in the working effort itself, as well a with other conditions.
>
> So long as the requirements of the peasant family are unsatisfied, since the subjective significance of its satisfaction is valued more highly than the burden of labor necessary for such satisfaction, the peasant family will work for a small remuneration that would be definitely unprofitable in a capitalistic economy.

---

[11] Sol Tax (1907–1995) was an influential American anthropologist of the mid-twentieth century. He studied at the University of Chicago under the Boasian Ralph Linton. One of the founders of the journal *Current Anthropology*, he was also known for promoting "action anthropology," (1960) which was based on the notion that anthropologists should discover and promote the interests of the communities in which they work. Tax believed that anthropology should increase scientific knowledge but also improve community welfare (Rylko-Bauer, Singer, and Van Willigen 2006). Rather than providing reports to government authorities, anthropologists should provide indigenous communities with alternative courses of action and help them pursue those they choose. A great many anthropologists today would subscribe to this position, but it was radical in the 1950s when Tax promoted it.

Since the principal object of peasant economy is the satisfaction of the yearly consumption budget of the family, the fact of most interest is not the remuneration of the labor unit (the working day), but the remuneration of the whole labor year. Of course, if there is an abundance of land any working unit expended by the family will tend to receive the maximum wage for that unit, whether it be a peasant or capitalistic economy. Under such conditions, peasant economy often results in more extensive cultivation than the economy of privately (entrepreneurially) owned land. There will be a smaller income from a unit of land but higher wages for a unit of work. But when the amount of available land is limited and is under a normal degree of intensity of cultivation, the peasant family cannot use all its labor forces on its own land if it practices extensive cultivation. Having a surplus of these forces and being unable to secure all its necessities with the income derived from the annual wage of its members, the peasant family can utilize the surplus of labor in a more intensive cultivation of its land. In this way it can increase the yearly income of its working members, though the remuneration for each unit of their work will be lower. . . . For the same reason the peasant family often rents land at an exceedingly high price, unprofitable from a purely capitalistic standpoint, and buys land for a price considerably exceeding the capitalized rent. This is done in order to find a use for the surplus labor of the family, which (otherwise) could not be utilized under conditions of land scarcity.[1,12]

The perennial problem of the peasantry thus consists in balancing the demands of the external world against the peasants' need to provision their households. Yet in meeting this root problem peasants may follow two diametrically opposed strategies. The first of these is to increase production; the second, to curtail consumption.

If a peasant follows the first strategy, he must step up the output of labor upon his own holding, in order to raise its productivity and to increase the amount of produce with which to enter the market. His ability to do so depends largely on how easy it is for him to mobilize the needed factors of production—land, labor, capital (whether in the form of savings, ready cash, or credit)—and, of course, on the general condition of the market. Let us remember that among peasants factors of production are usually heavily encumbered with prior commitments, especially in the form of committed surpluses for ceremonial expenditure and for the payment of rent. It is very rare, if not impossible, for a man to raise himself singlehandedly by his economic bootstraps to a level of productivity above and beyond that demanded by the mandatory payments. It is also difficult for most peasants to see their possessions in an economic context divorced from the provisioning of the household. A piece of land, a house, are not merely factors of production; they are also loaded with symbolic values. Family jewelry is not merely a form of cold cash; it is often an heirloom, encumbered with sentiments. Yet

---

[12] Wolf uses this long Chayanov quote to support his contention that the primary interest of peasant households is their own support and sustenance. Alexander Chayanov (also, less commonly, spelled Chaianov [1888–1937]) was an influential Soviet economist, essayist, and author. As seen in this passage, he argued that peasant economic behavior was fundamentally different from capitalist behavior. Peasants were vitally concerned with supplying their own needs, which are, in part, a function of the family cycle. Children are unproductive but must be fed. Therefore peasants will work very hard, often buying resources at unattractive prices and toiling at extremely low effective rates of pay. In other words, they end up exploiting themselves. Contrary to Lenin and other Soviet thinkers, Chayanov argued that these activities did not represent protocapitalism. Surplus could not be easily extracted

from the peasantry. Any surplus generated would ultimately not be reinvested in productive resources. Rather, as children grew up and married, resources would be split up and the cycle would begin again. Chayanov's theories drew him into conflict with the Stalinist state in the 1930s. Stalin persecuted wealthier peasants (*kuluks*) as emerging capitalists and therefore enemies of the state. Chayanov's theory of cyclical accumulation went against this interpretation. He was repeatedly arrested in the Stalinist purges of the 1930s and probably executed in either 1937 or 1939. Though Wolf cites a Chayanov essay that had been published in 1931, Chayanov's *Theory of Peasant Economy*, originally published in Russian in 1926, was first available in English translation in 1966, the year of Wolf's essay. Chayanov was increasingly influential in the economic anthropology of the late 1960s and 1970s.

our analysis can tell us also when we may expect increasing numbers of peasants to follow the strategy of increasing production.

First, this becomes possible when traditional liens on the peasants' funds of rent have weakened—a condition likely to occur when the power structure through which funds have been siphoned off to traditional overlords has become ineffective. Second, we may expect to find this phenomenon where it has become possible for the peasant to escape the demands placed on him to underwrite with ceremonial expenditures the traditional social ties with his fellows. If he can refuse to commit his surplus to ceremonial outlays, he can use the funds so released to support his economic ascent. The two changes frequently go together. As the overarching power structure weakens, many traditional social ties also lose their particular sanctions. The peasant community, under such circumstances, may see the rise of wealthy peasants who shoulder aside their less fortunate fellows and move into the power vacuum left by the retreating superior holders of power. In the course of their rise, they frequently violate traditional expectations of how social relations are to be conducted and symbolized—frequently they utilize their newly won power to enrich themselves at the cost of their neighbors. Such men were the rising *yeomen* of sixteenth century England, the rich peasants of China, the *kulaki* or "fists" of pre-revolutionary Russia. In other cases, large numbers of peasants may end their ceremonial commitments, as happened among many Middle American Indian groups who have abandoned their traditional Catholic folk rituals—with their great costs paid out in the support of religious organizations and events—and have turned to a sober Protestantism for which such expenditures are not required.[m,13]

The alternative strategy is to solve the basic peasant dilemma by curtailing consumption. The peasant may reduce his caloric intake to the most basic items of food; he may cut his purchases in the outside market to a few essential items only. Instead, he may rely as much as possible on the labor of his own domestic group to produce both food and needed objects, within the confines of his own homestead. Such efforts to balance accounts by underconsumption go a long way towards explaining why peasants tend to cleave to their traditional way of life, why they fear the new as they would fear temptation: Any novelty may undermine their precarious balance. At the same time, such peasants will also support the maintenance of traditional social relations and the expenditure of ceremonial funds required to sustain them. As long as these can be upheld, a peasant community can ward off the further penetration of outside demands and pressures, while at the same time forcing its more fortunate members to share some of their labor and goods with their less fortunate neighbors.

In many parts of the world, therefore—even in those where the peasantry has been relegated to a secondary role in the total social order—we shall encounter the phenomenon of peasants striving to stay alive without undue commitments to the larger system. At the same time, it must be remembered that in many situations—especially during wartime and depressions—peasant holdings represent sanctuaries from the ravages which afflict people in cities and industrial centers. A man with 40 acres and a mule has a hard row to hoe; at the same time he has at least some measure of probable caloric output when others may have to seek their sustenance in the garbage cans of crumbling towns. The peasant retains—in his control of land and his capacity to raise

---

[13] The subtext here is probably economic development. In the 1950s and 1960s, many anthropologists were concerned with cultural change and the "modernization" of "traditional" society. Here, Wolf explains how in the peasant context such modernization may occur. Note in addition the contrast with Max Weber's notions. In *The Protestant Ethic and the Spirit of Capitalism*, (1958 [1930])

Weber argued that the move from Catholicism to Protestantism encouraged the development of a work ethic that led to capitalism. Here, Wolf the materialist argues that economic interests may influence a peasant's move from Catholicism to Protestantism because the latter places fewer economic demands on him.

crops on it—both his autonomy and his capacity to survive when others, more delicately dependent upon the larger society, find such survival difficult.

While the two strategies of peasant operations point in entirely different directions, we must not, however, think of them as mutually exclusive. We have seen that their relative dominance is largely a function of the larger social order within which the peasant must make his living. To the extent, then, that a social order grows in strength or weakens, the peasants will favor one or the other, sometimes playing both at the same time in different contexts. Periods in which the first strategy is strongly favored may be followed by others when the peasant retrenches and renews his social fabric within a narrower orbit. Similarly, at any given time, there will be some individuals who will risk the social ostracism involved in testing the limits of traditional social ties, while others prefer the security involved in following the norm that has been tried, and is therefore thought to be true. Literary clichés about the immovable peasantry to the contrary, a peasantry is always in a dynamic state, moving continuously between two poles in the search for a solution of its basic dilemma.[14]

The existence of a peasantry thus involves not merely a relation between peasant and nonpeasant, but a type of adaptation, a combination of attitudes and activities designed to sustain the cultivator in his effort to maintain himself and his kind within a social order which threatens that maintenance. In this study, we shall attempt to outline both the kinds of relations peasants entertain with outsiders and the strategies they follow in modifying or neutralizing the effects of these relations.

ACKNOWLEDGEMENT

Eric R. Wolf, "Peasantry and Its Problems" from *Peasants,* 1st Edition, © 1966, pp. 1–17. Reprinted by permission of Pearson Education, Inc., Upper Saddle River, NJ.

NOTES

[a] Marshall D. Sahlins, "Political Power and the Economy in Primitive Society," in *Essays in the Science of Culture: In Honor of Leslie A. White,* eds. Gertrude E. Dole and Robert L. Carneiro (New York: Thomas Y. Crowell Company, 1960), p. 408.

[b] Jean Fourastié, *The Causes of Wealth* (Glencoe: The Free Press, 1960), pp. 102–103.

[c] *Ibid.,* p. 41.

[d] Wilhelm Abel, *Geschichte der deutschen Landwirtschaft vom frühen Mittelalter bis zum 19. Jahrhundert,* Deutsche Agrargeschichte II (Stuttgart: Eugen Ulmer, 1962), p. 95.

[e] Robert L. Carneiro, "Slash-and-Burn Cultivation among the Kuikuru and its Implications for Cultural Development in the Amazon Basin," in *The Evolution of Horticultural Systems in Native South America: Causes and Consequences,* ed. Johannes Wilbert, *Antropologica,* Supplement, No. 2 (1961), p. 49.

[f] Evidence from Middle America indicates that a man may have to expend at least the equivalent of one year's local wages to act as a sponsor in a community ceremonial. Expenditures of two to twenty times this amount are noted for particular communities. For examples, see Ralph Beals, *Cherán, a Sierra Tarascan Village,* Smithsonian Institution Institute of Social Anthropology, Publication No. 2 (Washington D.C.: United States Government Printing Office, 1946), p. 85; Calixta Guiteras-Holmes, *Perils of the Soul: The World View of a Tzotzil Indian* (New York: The Free Press, 1961), p. 58; Sol Tax, *Penny Capitalism: A Guatemalan Indian Economy,* Smithsonian Institution, Institute of Social Anthropology, Publication No. 16 (Washington, D.C.: United States Government Printing Office, 1953), pp. 177–178. For the Andes, see William W. Stein,

---

[14] In these final paragraphs, Wolf portrays the peasant world as a dialectical system, characterized by a set of embedded contradictions: The contradiction between the production of surplus (at the expense of community) and the necessity to curtail consumption, is set within the contradiction between the interests of peasants (to retain as much of their surplus as possible) and those of the landlords (to strip the peasantry of as much surplus as possible). Wolf portrays this as a dynamic but continuous state of affairs. In other words, peasants negotiate and renegotiate their livelihoods within a more or less stable framework of peasant-landlord relations. However, it is also a potentially revolutionary state of affairs. The peasantry as a class may rise against the landlords as a class in an attempt at revolutionary change. Elsewhere, Wolf argues that such revolt was particularly likely to occur as the spread of capitalism from North America and Europe weakened the power of preexisting elites, opened new possibilities for peasants, and made the structures that protected them from risk less dependable.

Hualcan: Life in the Highlands of Peru (Ithaca: Cornell University Press, 1961), p. 52, 236, 255.

[g] Abel, *Geschichte der deutschen Landwirtschaft*, p. 95.

[h] On Watusi and Bahutu settlement pattern, see Pierre B. Gravel, *The Play for Power: Description of a Community in Eastern Ruanda* (Ann Arbor: Department of Anthropology, University of Michigan, Ph.D. Thesis, 1962). On Egypt, see Henri Frankfort, *The Birth of Civilization in the Near East* (Garden City, N.Y.: Doubleday and Company, 1956), pp. 97–98, and John A. Wilson, *The Culture of Ancient Egypt* (Chicago: University of Chicago Press, 1951), p. 37, pp. 97–98. On the Maya, see Gordon R. Willey, "Mesoamerica," in *Courses Toward Urban Life*, eds. Robert J. Braidwood and Gordon R. Willey (Chicago: Aldine Publishing Company, 1962), p. 101, and Michael Coe, "Social Typology and the Tropical Forest Civilizations," *Comparative Studies in Society and History*, IV, No. 1 (1961), p. 66.

[i] McKim Mariott and Bernard C. Cohn, "Networks and Centers in the Integration of Indian Civilization," *Journal of Social Research* (Ranchi, Bihar, India), I, No. 1 (1958).

[j] For a discussion of the plantation see Eric R. Wolf and Sidney W. Mintz, "Haciendas and Plantations in Middle America and the Antilles," *Social and Economic Studies*, VI, No. 3 (1957), and *Plantation Systems of the New World*. Papers and discussion summaries of the Seminar held in San Juan, Puerto Rico, Social Science Monographs, VII, Pan American Union, Washington, D.C., 1959. For a good case study of the replacement of peasants by plantations see Ramiro Guerra y Sánchez, *Sugar and Society in the Caribbean* (New Haven: Yale University Press, 1964).

[k] Sol Tax, *Penny Capitalism*, p. 14.

[l] A. V. Chaianov, "The Socio-economic Nature of Peasant Farm Economy," in *A Systematic Source Book in Rural Sociology*, eds. Pitirim A. Sorokin, Carle C. Zimmerman, and Charles J. Galpin (Minneapolis: The University of Minnesota Press, 1931) II, pp. 144–145.

[m] See, for instance, June Nash, "Protestantism in an Indian Village in the Western Highlands of Guatemala," *The Alpha Kappa Deltan*, XXX, No. 1 (1960), p. 50.

Structuralism

Claude Lévi-Strauss (1908–2009) almost single-handedly founded the field of structuralism. He began with the assumption that culture was, first and foremost, a product of the mind. Since all human brains are biologically similar, he reasoned, there must be deep-seated similarities among cultures. The goal he set for anthropology was to discover the fundamental structure of human cognition, the underlying patterns of human thought that produce the great variety of current and historical cultures. Pursuing this quest, he spent his career conducting cross-cultural studies of kinship, myths, and religion.

Lévi-Strauss believed that the underlying processes tying cultures together were found in bits of information that provide messages about the structuring of society. However, each culture is also the product of its own history and its technological adaptation to the world. These processes have combined, altered, transfigured, and modified the original bits of information. Transmitting culture is rather like playing "telephone" or "whispering down the alley" in a crowded bus station. Messages are apt to get jumbled. This jumble is the result of the particular history and technological adaptation of each culture. Lévi-Strauss hoped that by breaking down cultures into their elemental parts he could get beyond this "noise" and return to the original message.

Lévi-Strauss' structuralism was heavily influenced by the great French scholars of the previous generation, particularly Émile Durkheim and Marcel Mauss. In fact, the title of his first major work, *The Elementary Structures of Kinship* (1949), echoes the title of Durkheim's great work on religion, *The Elementary Forms of the Religious Life* (1965, orig. 1912). The Prague School of structural linguistics, organized in 1926, also played a major role in the conception of his theory. This group of scholars, led by the linguists Roman Jakobson (1896–1982) and Nikolai Troubetzkoy (1890–1938), emphasized the synchronic (descriptive) rather than diachronic (historical) study of language and promoted the theory that linguistic meaning was built on contrasts between sounds, or phonemes. Members of the Prague School defined and characterized the phonemic study of languages. This work, and his study of Durkheim, provided Lévi-Strauss with the concept of binary contrasts that was fundamental to his formulation of structuralism.

Perhaps the simplest way to explain the theoretical basis of structuralism is to compare it with linguistics. All languages are composed of arbitrary groups of sounds called *phonemes*. Phonemes by themselves are meaningless. It is only when they are combined into larger units (morphemes, words, phrases, and so on) according to certain patterns (the rules of syntax and grammar) that phonemes form meaningful units (speech). Most speakers of a language cannot articulate the underlying rules that structure their use of phonemes in creating meaningful communication, yet all are able to use language to communicate successfully with one another. Therefore, at a subconscious level we must all "know" the rules that structure our use of language. The job of a linguist is to analyze the outward use of language in such a way as to discover these unconscious principles. In the same fashion, Lévi-Strauss tried to design a technique for studying the unconscious principles that structure human culture.

To Lévi-Strauss, culture, like language, was essentially a collection of arbitrary symbols. He was not interested in the specific meaning of the symbols any more than a linguist is interested in the phonemes of a language. Rather, he was concerned with the patterning of elements, the way cultural elements relate to one another to form the overall system (Lévi-Strauss 1963c:208).

A key insight of the Prague School was that words were built on contrasts (binary oppositions) between phonemes rather than simply being groups of sounds. Following this linguistic model, Lévi-Strauss proposed that the fundamental pattern of human thought also uses binary contrasts such as black-white, night-day, and hot-cold. This insight dovetailed nicely with Durkheim's and Hertz's proposition that distinctions such as sacred-profane and right-left were fundamental manifestations of the collective conscious.

Lévi-Strauss used the notion of the binary structure of human thought to analyze kinship. He followed the work of Marcel Mauss, who in *The Gift* (1967, orig. 1925) had tried to demonstrate that exchange in primitive societies was driven not by economic motives but by rules of reciprocity on which the solidarity of society depended. In *Elementary Structures of Kinship* (1969, orig. 1949) Lévi-Strauss took Mauss' concept of reciprocity and applied it to marriage in primitive societies, arguing that in those societies women were a commodity that could be exchanged. Lévi-Strauss contended that one of the first and most important distinctions a human makes is between self and others. This "natural" binary distinction then leads to the formation of the incest taboo, which necessitates choosing spouses from outside of one's family. In this fashion, the binary distinction between kin and non-kin is resolved in primitive societies by the reciprocal exchange of women and the formation of kin networks.

Lévi-Strauss is best known today for his analysis of myth. He proposed that studying the mythologies of primitive peoples allowed him to examine the unconscious universal patterning of human thought in its least contaminated form. In Lévi-Strauss' view, the mythology of primitive peoples was closer to these universal principles than are Western beliefs because the training we receive in Western society buries the logical structure he seeks under layers of "cultural interference" created by our social environment.

In his work on myths, folktales, and religion, Lévi-Strauss elaborated on the notion that binary oppositions were the basis of human cognition. He proposed that a fundamental characteristic of human thought was the desire to find a midpoint between such oppositions, a category that transcends and somehow resolves them. In Lévi-Strauss' view, the elements of myth, like the phonemes of a language, acquired meaning only as a consequence of certain structural relations. Therefore, to uncover the unconscious meaning of myth, the structuralist must break myth into its constituent elements and examine the rules that govern their relationships. This hidden structural core will reveal the essential patterns and processes of human thought.

The articles we have chosen for this section are examples of the application of structural analysis to different areas of study over several decades. In the essay "Four Winnebago Myths: A Structural Sketch," published in 1960, Lévi-Strauss outlines the fundamental aspects of his methodology by comparing four Native American myths collected by Paul Radin. In his analysis Lévi-Strauss attempts to show how the four stories contain the same logical pattern of oppositions and are thus different themes with the same logical structure.

The second selection in this section is a structural analysis of gender stratification by the American anthropologist Sherry Ortner (b. 1941). Although her first work was in symbolic anthropology, in the last few decades Ortner has become known for her contributions to the field of feminist anthropology. In particular, her volume *Sexual Meanings: The Cultural Construction of Gender and Sexuality,* (edited with Harriet Whitehead and originally published in 1974), is considered a classic in the field. Ortner's essay, drawn from this volume, examines the issue of gender inequality. Echoing Lévi-Strauss, Ortner suggests that gender stratification is based on the fundamental opposition between nature and culture. Women, she proposes, because of pregnancy and childbirth, are universally associated with nature. Men, because they are unable to bear children, create in the realm of culture and are thus accorded higher status.

Structuralism had a profound effect on American anthropology. In particular, it influenced symbolic anthropology, which was popular in the 1970s, cognitive anthropology, and postmodernism, which achieved notoriety in the 1980s.

22. *Four Winnebago Myths: A Structural Sketch*

CLAUDE LÉVI-STRAUSS (1908–2009)

AMONG THE MANY talents which make him one of the great anthropologists of our time, Paul Radin has one which gives a singular flavor to his work. He has the authentic esthetic touch, rather uncommon in our profession. This is what we call in French *flair:* the gift of singling out those facts, observations, and documents which possess an especially rich meaning, sometimes undisclosed at first, but likely to become evident as one ponders the implications woven into the material. A crop harvested by Paul Radin, even if he does not choose to mill it himself, is always capable of providing lasting nourishment for many generations of students.[1]

This is the reason why I intend to pay my tribute to the work of Paul Radin by giving some thought to four myths which he has published under the title *The Culture of the Winnebago: As Described by Themselves.*[a] Although Radin himself pointed out in the Preface: "In publishing these texts I have only one object in view, to put at the disposal of students, authentic material for the study of Winnebago culture," and although

the four myths were each obtained from different informants, it seems that, on a structural level, there was good reason for making them the subject of a single publication. A deep unity underlies all four, notwithstanding the fact that one myth, as Radin has shown in his introduction and notes, appears to differ widely in content, style, and structure from the other three. My purpose will be to analyze the structural relationships between the four myths and to suggest that they can be grouped together not only because they are part of a collection of ethnographic and linguistic data referring to one tribe, which Radin too modestly claimed as his sole purpose, but because they are of the same genre, i.e., their meanings logically complement each other.[2]

The title of the first myth is "The Two Friends Who Became Reincarnated: The Origin of the Four Nights' Wake." This is the story of two friends, one of them a chief's son, who decide to sacrifice their lives for the welfare of the community. After undergoing a series of ordeals in the underworld, they reach the lodge of Earthmaker,

From *Culture in History: Essays in Honor of Paul Radin* (1960)

[1] This article first appeared in a volume called *Culture in History: Essays in Honor of Paul Radin* (1960), edited by Stanley Diamond and published soon after Radin's death.

[2] "Four Winnebago Myths" is a short example of Lévi-Strauss' structural analysis of myth. His goal is to understand the unconscious structure of the human mind and thought processes. In his opinion, myths of aboriginal so-

cieties are the perfect vehicles for that endeavor because such mythology has less "cultural interference" to filter out than stories in Western industrial societies. The outward story line of the myth is irrelevant, but by analyzing the logical relationships between elements of the myth Lévi-Strauss believes he can arrive at the unconscious message the myth conveys.

who permits them to become reincarnated and to resume their previous lives among their relatives and friends.

As explained by Radin in his commentary,[b] there is a native theory underlying the myth: every individual is entitled to a specific quota of years of life and experience. If a person dies before his time, his relatives can ask the spirits to distribute among them what he has failed to utilize. But there is more in this theory than meets the eye. The unspent life-span given up by the hero, when he lets himself be killed by the enemies, will be added to the capital of life, set up in trust for the group. Nevertheless, his act of dedication is not entirely without personal profit: by becoming a hero an individual makes a choice, he exchanges a full life-span for a shortened one, but while the full life-span is unique, granted once and for all, the shortened one appears as a kind of lease taken on eternity. That is, by giving up one full life, an indefinite succession of half-lives is gained. But since all the unlived halves will increase the life expectancy of the ordinary people, everybody gains in the process: the ordinary people whose average life expectancy will slowly but substantially increase generation after generation, and the warriors with shortened but indefinitely renewable lives, provided their minds remain set on self-dedication.

It is not clear, however, that Radin pays full justice to the narrator when he treats as a "secondary interpretation" the fact that the expedition is undertaken by the heroes to show their appreciation of the favors of their fellow villagers.[c] My contention is that this motive of the heroes deserves primary emphasis, and it is supported by the fact that there are two war parties. The first one is undertaken by the warriors while the heroes are still in their adolescent years, so they are neither included in, nor even informed of it; they hear about the party only as a rumor[d] and they decide to join it uninvited. We must conclude

DIAGRAM 1

then that the heroes have no responsibility for the very venture wherein they distinguish themselves, since it has been instigated and led by others. Moreover, they are not responsible for the second war party, during which they are killed, since this latter foray has been initiated by the enemy in revenge for the first.[3]

The basic idea is clear: the two friends have developed into successful social beings;[e] accordingly, they feel obliged to repay their fellow tribesmen who have treated them so well.[f] As the story goes, they set out to expose themselves in the wilderness; later they die in an ambush prepared by the enemy in revenge for the former defeat. The obvious conclusion is that the heroes have willingly died for the sake of their people. And because they died without responsibility of their own, but instead that of others, those will inherit the unspent parts of their lives, while the heroes themselves will be permitted to return to earth and the same process will be repeated all over again. This interpretation is in agreement with information given elsewhere by Radin: i.e., in order to pass the test of the Old Woman who rids the soul of all the recollections belonging to its earthly life, each soul must be solicitous not of its own welfare but of the welfare of the living members of the group.

Now at the root of this myth we find—as the phonologist would say—a double opposition. First there is the opposition between *ordinary life* and *heroic life*, the former realizing a full life-span, not renewable, the latter gambling with life for the benefit of the group. The second opposition

---

[3] Like the Freudian analyst, Lévi-Strauss is searching for unconscious meaning, freeing him to interpret the motives of the myth's characters and place emphasis on the elements of the story he feels are significant regardless of the storyline. According to Lévi-Strauss, the structural analyst is not interested in individual story elements but combinations of those elements. Examining the relationship between combinations of elements provides the analyst with the unconscious meaning the myth.

is between two kinds of death, one "straight" and final, although it provides a type of unearthly immortality in the villages of the dead; the other "undulating," and swinging between life and death. Indeed one is tempted to see the reflection of this double fate in the Winnebago symbol of the ladder of the afterworld as it appears in the Medicine Rite. One side is "like a frog's leg, twisted and dappled with light-and-life. The other [is] like a red cedar, blackened from frequent usage and very smooth and shiny."[g,4]

To sum up the meaning of the myth so far: if one wants a full life one gets a full death; if one renounces life and seeks death, then one increases the full life of his fellow-tribesmen, and, moreover, secures for oneself a state composed of an indefinite series of half-lives and half-deaths. Thus we have a triangular system.

The second myth, entitled "The Man Who Brought His Wife Back from Spiritland," is a variation on the same theme, although there is a significant difference involved. Here too, we find a hero—the husband—ready to sacrifice his unspent life-span; not, as in the first myth, for the benefit of the group, but rather for the benefit of only one individual, his beloved wife. Indeed, the hero is not aware at first that by seeking death he will secure a new lease on life for both his dead wife and himself. Had he been so aware, and this holds equally for the protagonists in the first myth, the essential element of sacrifice would have been missing. In both cases the result is

similar: an altruistic loss of life means life regained, not only for the self-appointed victim, but also for the one or more persons to whom the sacrifice was consecrated.

The third myth, "The Journey of the Ghost to Spiritland, as Told in the Medicine Rite," belongs, as the title suggests, to a religious society. It explains how the members of the Medicine Rite, after death, undergo (as do the protagonists of the other myths) several tests in Spiritland, which they overcome, thus gaining the right to become reincarnated.[5]

At first sight this situation seems to differ from the others, since nobody sacrificed his life. However, the members of the Medicine Rite actually spend their lives in symbolic sacrifice. As Radin has shown, in *The Road of Life and Death* and elsewhere, the Medicine Rite follows the familiar pattern of letting oneself be "killed" and then "revived." Thus the only departure consists in the fact that whereas in the first and second myths the heroes are willing to die once and, so they anticipate, permanently, the heroes of the third myth (the members of the Rite) repeatedly, though symbolically, have trained themselves to self-sacrifice. They have, so to speak, mithridatized[6] themselves against a full death by renouncing a full ordinary life which is replaced, in ritual practice, by a lifelong succession of half-lives and half-deaths. Therefore we are entitled to assume that, in this case too, the myth is made up of the same elements, although Ego—and not another

---

[4] Lévi-Strauss follows the Hegelian idea that the structure of human perception is dialectical. In his structural analyses of myth he looks for binary oppositions within the elements of the story and the factors that mediate them. For example, in the Winnebago myth described here, the opposition between life and death is mediated by reincarnation. The myth's message is derived from the logical relationships between patterns of such oppositions.

[5] Notice that Lévi-Strauss writes in the tradition of the French sociological school that preceded him: His method is comparative. He chooses those pieces of traditions or beliefs from different societies that fit his view regardless of the cultural context in which these elements are found. Lévi-Strauss interprets these myths for his readers without giving them the full text of the stories or providing any

background information about Winnebago society. This is a typical French structuralist approach: Because the unconscious structure of human thought is universal, the cultural context of the myths is superficial and irrelevant to the myths' underlying message. For this kind of analysis, he says, the meaning of the myths is not found in the history or culture of the Winnebago. The only context Lévi-Strauss requires is the myths themselves. American anthropologists, as inheritors of the Boasian tradition, are inclined to place more emphasis on the specific cultural contexts in which events occur.

[6] *Mithridatized:* to develop a tolerance or immunity to something by taking small doses of it, from the Greek myth of King Mithridates, who in this way developed an immunity to poison.

person, nor the group as a whole—is conceived as the primary beneficiary.

Let us now consider the fourth myth, "How an Orphan Restored the Chief's Daughter to Life," a tale which has given Radin some concern. This myth, he says, is not only different from the other three, its plot appears unusual relative to the rest of Winnebago mythology. After recalling that in his book *Method and Theory of Ethnology*[h] he suggested that this myth was a version, altered almost beyond recognition, of a type which he then called village-origin myths, he proceeds to explain in *The Culture of the Winnebago*[i] why he can no longer support his earlier interpretation.

It is worthwhile to follow closely Radin's new line of reasoning. He begins by recapitulating the plot—such a simple plot, he says, that there is practically no need for doing so: "The daughter of a tribal chief falls in love with an orphan, dies of a broken heart and is then restored to life by the orphan who must submit to and overcome certain tests, not in spiritland but here, on earth, in the very lodge in which the young woman died."[j]

If this plot is "simplicity itself," where do the moot points lie? Radin lists three which he says every modern Winnebago would question: (1) the plot seems to refer to a highly stratified society; (2) in order to understand the plot one should assume that in that society women occupied a high position and that, possibly, descent was reckoned in the matrilineal line; (3) the tests which in Winnebago mythology take place, as a rule, in the land of ghosts occur, in this instance, on earth.

After dismissing two possible explanations—that we are dealing here with a borrowed European tale or that the myth was invented by some Winnebago radical—Radin concludes that the myth must belong to "a very old stratum of Winnebago history." He also suggests that two distinct types of literary tradition, divine tales on the one hand and human tales on the other, have merged while certain primitive elements have been reinterpreted to make them fit together.[k]

I am certainly not going to challenge this very elegant reconstruction backed by an incomparable knowledge of Winnebago culture, language, and history. The kind of analysis I intended to offer is no alternative to Radin's own analysis. It lies on a different level, logical rather than historical. It takes as its context the three myths already discussed, not Winnebago culture, old or recent. My purpose is to explicate the structural relationship—if any—which prevails between this myth and the other three.

First, there is a theoretical problem which should be noted briefly. Since the publication of Boas' *Tsimshian Mythology*, anthropologists have often simply assumed that a full correlation exists between the myths of a given society and its culture. This, I feel, is going further than Boas intended. In the work just referred to, he did not suppose that myths automatically reflect the culture, as some of his followers seem always to anticipate. Rather, he tried to find out how much of the culture actually did pass into the myths, if any, and he convincingly showed that *some* of it does. It does not follow that whenever a social pattern is alluded to in a myth this pattern must correspond to something real which should be attributed to the past if, under direct scrutiny, the present fails to offer an equivalent.[7]

There must be, and there is, a correspondence between the unconscious meaning of a myth—the problem it tries to solve—and the conscious content it makes use of to reach that end, i.e., the plot. However, this correspondence should not always be conceived as a kind of mirror-image, it can also appear as a *transformation*.[8] If the problem is presented in "straight" terms, that is, in the way the social life of the

---

[7] Franz Boas was a vehement cultural relativist. Here Lévi-Strauss tries to reconcile French structuralism with Boasian particularism.

[8] In his first great book, *The Elementary Structures of Kinship* (1949), Lévi-Strauss postulated that there was a universal psychological need to give and receive gifts. He believed that this was based on a fundamental dialectic of the human mind—the distinction between self and others. He devoted an entire chapter to child psychology in an attempt to justify this claim (Harris 1968:491). Here Lévi-Strauss once again resorts to psychological theory, in this case psychoanalysis, to justify his point of view. He states that there must be some agreement between a

group expresses and tries to solve it, the overt content of the myth, the plot, can borrow its elements from social life itself. But should the problem be formulated, and its solution sought for, "upside down," that is *ab absurdo,* then the overt content will become modified accordingly to form an inverted image of the social pattern actually present to the consciousness of the natives.

If this hypothesis is true, it follows that Radin's assumption that the pattern of social life referred to in the fourth myth must belong to a past stage of Winnebago history, is not inescapable.

We may be confronted with the pattern of a nonexistent society, contrary to the Winnebago traditional pattern, only because the structure of that particular myth is itself inverted, in relation to those myths which use as overt content the traditional pattern. To put it simply, if a certain correspondence is assumed between A and B, then if A is replaced by 2A, B must be replaced by 2B, without implying that, since B corresponds to an external object, there should exist another external object 2B, which must exist somewhere: either in another society (borrowed element) or in a past stage of the same society (survival).

Obviously the problem remains: why do we have three myths of the A type and one of the 2A type? This could be the case because 2A is older than A, but it can also be because 2A is one of the transformations of A which is already known to us under three different guises: A_1A_2, A_3, since we have seen that the three myths of the assumed A type are not identical.

We have already established that the group of myths under consideration is based upon a fundamental opposition: on the one hand, the lives of ordinary people unfolding towards a natural death, followed by immortality in one of the spirit villages—; and, on the other hand, heroic life, self-abridged, the gain being a supplementary life quota for the others as well as for oneself. The former alternative is not envisaged in this group of myths which, as we have seen, is mostly con-

cerned with the latter. There is, however, a secondary difference which permits us to classify the first three myths according to the particular end assigned to the self-sacrifice in each. In the first myth the group is intended to be the immediate beneficiary, in the second it is another individual (the wife), and in the third it is oneself.

When we turn to the fourth myth, we may agree with Radin that it exhibits "unusual" features in relation to the other three. However, the difference seems to be of a logical more than of a sociological or historical nature. It consists in a new opposition introduced within the first pair of opposites (between "ordinary" life and "extraordinary" life). Now there are two ways in which an "extraordinary" phenomenon may be construed as such; it may consist either in a *surplus* or in a *lack.* While the heroes of the first three myths are all overgifted, through social success, emotions or wisdom, the heroes of the fourth myth are, if one may say so, "below standard," at least in one respect.

The chief's daughter occupies a high social position; so high, in fact, that she is cut off from the rest of the group and is therefore paralyzed when it comes to expressing her feelings. Her exalted position makes her a defective human being, lacking an essential attribute of life. The boy is also defective, but socially, that is, he is an orphan and very poor. May we say, then, that the myth reflects a stratified society? This would compel us to overlook the remarkable symmetry which prevails between our two heroes, for it would be wrong to say simply that one is high and the other low: as a matter of fact, each of them is high in one respect and low in the other, and this pair of symmetrical structures, wherein the two terms are inverted relative to each other, belongs to the realm of ideological constructs rather than of sociological systems. We have just seen that the girl is "socially" above and "naturally" below. The boy is undoubtedly very low in the social scale; however, he is a miraculous hunter, i.e. he

---

myth's underlying meaning and its plot. However, the correspondence between meaning and plot may appear as a "transformation," or an "upside down" version of the apparent meaning. There is no question that this is an impor-

tant insight for both psychology and myth analysis, but it offers dangers as well. If used carelessly, this concept can be used to justify any flight of imagination that may occur to the interpreter.

entertains privileged relations with the natural world, the world of animals. This is emphasized over and over again in the myth.[1]

Therefore may we not claim that the myth actually confronts us with a polar system consisting in two individuals, one male, the other female, and both exceptional insofar as each of them is overgifted in one way (1) and undergifted in the other (2).[9]

The plot consists in carrying this disequilibrium to its logical extreme; the girl dies a *natural* death, the boy stays alone, i.e. he also dies, but in a *social* way. Whereas during their ordinary lives the girl was overtly above, the boy overtly below, now that they have become segregated (either from the living or from society) their positions are inverted: the girl is below (in her grave), the boy above (in his lodge). This, I think, is clearly implied in a detail stated by the narrator which seems to have puzzled Radin: "On top of the grave they then piled loose dirt, placing everything in such a way that nothing could seep through."[m] Radin comments: "I do not understand why piling the dirt loosely would prevent seepage. There must be something else involved that has not been mentioned."[n] May I suggest that this detail be correlated with a similar detail about the building of the young man's lodge: ". . . the bottom was piled high with dirt so that, in this fashion, they could keep the lodge warm."[o] There is implied here, I think, not a reference to recent or past custom but rather a clumsy attempt to emphasize that, relative to the earth's surface, i.e. dirt, the boy is now above and the girl below.

This new equilibrium, however, will be no more lasting than the first. *She who was unable to live cannot die;* her ghost lingers "on earth." Finally she induces the young man to fight the ghosts and take her back among the living. With a wonderful symmetry, the boy will meet, a few years later, with a similar, although inverted, fate; "Although I am not yet old, he says to the girl

DIAGRAM 2

(now his wife), I have been here (lasted) on earth as long as I can. . . ."[p] *He who overcame death, proves unable to live.* This recurring antithesis could develop indefinitely, and such a possibility is noted in the text (with an only son surviving his father, he too an orphan, he too a sharpshooter) but a different solution is finally reached. The heroes, equally unable to die or to live, will assume an intermediate identity, that of twilight creatures living under the earth but also able to come up on it; they will be neither men nor gods, but wolves, that is, ambivalent spirits combining good and evil features. So ends the myth.

If the above analysis is correct, two consequences follow: first, our myth makes up a consistent whole wherein the details balance and fit each other nicely; secondly, the three problems raised by Radin can be analyzed in terms of the myth itself; and no hypothetical past stage of Winnebago society need be invoked.

Let us, then, try to solve these three problems, following the pattern of our analysis.

1. The society of the myth appears stratified, only because the two heroes are conceived as a pair of opposites, but they are such both from the point of view of nature *and* of culture. Thus, the so-called stratified society should be interpreted not as a sociological vestige but as a projection of a logical structure wherein everything is given both in opposition and correlation.

2. The same answer can be given to the question of the assumed exalted position of the women. If I am right, our myths state three propositions,

---

[9] The opposition of nature and culture illustrated in the figure and explained later is one of the fundamental principles in French structuralist thought and finds expression in a variety of forms. See for example, Lévi-Strauss' book *The Raw and the Cooked* (1969).

the first by implication, the second expressly stated in myths 1, 2 and 3, the third expressly stated in myth 4.

These propositions are as follow:

a. Ordinary people live (their full lives) and die (their full deaths).
b. Positive extraordinary people die (earlier) and live (more).
c. Negative extraordinary people are able neither to live nor to die.

Obviously proposition c offers an inverted demonstration of the truth of a and b. Hence, it must use a plot starting with protagonists (here, man and woman) in inverted positions. This leads us to state that a plot and its component parts should neither be interpreted by themselves nor relative to something outside the realm of the myth proper, but as *substitutions* given in, and understandable only with reference to *the group made up of all the myths of the same series.*

3. We may now revert to the third problem raised by Radin about myth 4, that is, the contest with the ghosts takes place on earth instead of, as was usually the case, in spiritland. To this query I shall suggest an answer along the same lines as the others.

It is precisely because our two heroes suffer from a state of *under-life* (in respect either to culture or nature) that, in the narrative, the ghosts become a kind of *super-dead.* It will be recalled that the whole myth develops and is re-solved on an intermediary level, where humans become underground animals and ghosts linger on earth. It tells about people who are, from the start, half-alive and half-dead while, in the preceding myths, the opposition between life and death is strongly emphasized at the beginning, and overcome only at the end. Thus, the integral meaning of the four myths is that, in order to be overcome, the opposition between life and death should be first acknowledged, or else the ambiguous state will persist indefinitely.[10]

I hope to have shown that the four myths under consideration all belong to the same *group* (understood as in *group theory*) and that Radin was even more right than he supposed in publishing them together. In the first place, the four myths deal with extraordinary, in opposition to ordinary, fate. The fact that ordinary fate is not illustrated here and thus is reckoned as an "empty" category, does not imply, of course, that it is not illustrated elsewhere. In the second place, we find an opposition between two types of extraordinary fate, positive and negative. This new dichotomy which permits us to segregate myth 4 from myths 1, 2 and 3 corresponds, on a logical level, to the discrimination that Radin makes on psychological, sociological, and historical grounds. Finally, myths 1, 2 and 3 have been classified according to the purpose of the sacrifice which is the theme of each.[11]

Thus the four myths can be organized in a dichotomous structure of correlations and oppositions. But we can go even further and try to order them on a common scale. This is suggested

---

[10] Lévi-Strauss presents his analysis with unquestioned skill, but is erudition the same as accuracy? One of the principal criticisms of Lévi-Strauss' structuralism is that he presents masterful analyses that seem to be based in his own fantastic imagination and forceful writing style. Attempts to replicate his analyses usually fail or arrive at different conclusions.

[11] Lévi-Strauss has done anthropology a tremendous service by outlining a methodology for the sorting of anthropological data. As a method of analysis, structuralism can lead to valuable interpretive insights where other theoretical perspectives may fail. But as a means for proving the binary structure of the mind, structuralism has failed. Lévi-Strauss is no closer to proving his hypothesis about the unconscious structure of human thought than Sigmund Freud who proposed a theory of the unconscious more than a century ago. In spite of the dialectical nature of Lévi-Strauss' theory and his self-professed allegiance to Marxist thought, materialists have provided some of the most telling critiques of structuralism. Those who view anthropology as a science generally discount Lévi-Strauss' structuralism because the reality he claims to present is an unconscious one and thus unverifiable (Malefijt 1974:330). Marvin Harris, for example, says that a "paralysis of reality" spreads over his entire work (1968:497).

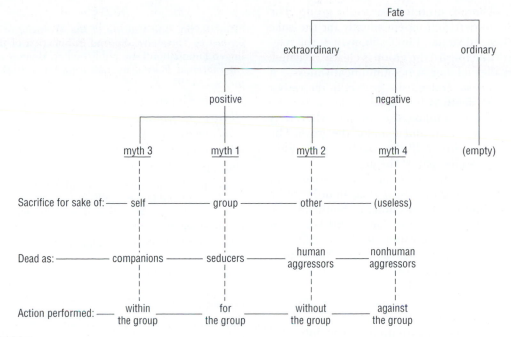

DIAGRAM 3

by the curious variations which can be observed in each myth with respect to the kind of test the hero is put to by the ghosts. In myth 3 there is no test at all, so far as the ghosts are concerned. The tests consist in overcoming material obstacles while the ghosts themselves figure as indifferent fellow travelers. In myth 1 they cease to be indifferent without yet becoming hostile. On the contrary, the tests result from their overfriendliness, as inviting women and infectious merry-makers. Thus, from *companions* in myth 3 they change to seducers in myth 1. In myth 2 they still behave as human beings, but they now act as *aggressors*, and permit themselves all kinds of rough play. This is even more evident in myth 4, but here the human element vanishes; it is only at the end that we know that ghosts, not crawling insects,

are responsible for the trials of the hero. We have thus a twofold progression, from a *peaceful* attitude to an *aggressive* one, and from *human* to *nonhuman* behavior.

This progression can be correlated with the kind of relationship which the hero (or heroes) of each myth entertain with the social group. The hero of myth 3 belongs to a ritual brotherhood: he definitely assumes his (privileged) fate as a member of a group, he acts with and in his group.

The two heroes of myth 1 have resolved to part from the group, but the text states repeatedly that this is in order to find an opportunity to achieve something beneficial for their fellow tribesmen. They act, therefore, for the group. But in myth 2 the hero is only inspired by his love for

Even one of Lévi-Strauss' greatest admirers, Edmund Leach, says:

> I am ready to concede that the structures which he displays are products of an unconscious mental process, but I can see no reason to believe that they are

human universals. Bereft of Lévi-Strauss' resourceful special pleading they appear to be local, functionally determined attributes of particular individuals or of particular cultural groups. (Leach 1976:126) his wife. There is no reference to the group. The action is undertaken independently for the sake of another individual. Finally, in myth 4, the negative attitude toward the group is clearly revealed; the girl dies of her "uncommunicativeness," if one may say so. Indeed she prefers to die rather than speak; death is her "final" exile. As for the boy, he refuses to follow the villagers when they decide to move away and abandon the grave. The segregation is thus willfully sought on all sides; the action unrolls against the group.

The accompanying chart summarizes our discussion. I am quite aware that, in order to be fully convincing, the argument should not be limited to the four myths considered here, but include more of the invaluable Winnebago mythology which Radin has given us. But I hope that by integrating more material the basic structure outlined has become richer and more complex, without being impaired. By singling out one book which its author would perhaps consider a minor contribution, I have intended to emphasize, in an indirect way, the fecundity of the method followed by Radin, and the lasting value of the problems he poses for the anthropologist.[12]

NOTES

[a] Paul Radin, *The Culture of the Winnebago: As Described by Themselves* Special Publication of the Bollingen Foundation (also published as Memoir 2 of the *International Journal of American Linguistics*, 1949, pp. iv, 1–119).

[b] *Ibid.,* p. 41, para. 32.

[c] *Ibid.,* p. 37, para. 2.

[d] *Ibid.,* paras. 11–14.

[e] *Ibid.,* paras. 66–70.

[f] *Ibid.,* para. 72.

[g] *Ibid.,* p. 71, paras. 91–93; see also Paul Radin, *The Road of Life and Death,* Bollingen Series, Vol. V (New York, 1945), especially the author's illuminating comments on pp. 63–65.

[h] Paul Radin, *Method and Theory of Ethnology* (New York, 1933), pp. 238–45.

[i] Radin, *The Culture of the Winnebago,* pp. 74 ff.

[j] *Ibid.,* p. 74.

[k] *Ibid.,* pp. 74–77.

[l] *Ibid.,* see paras. 10–14, 17–18, 59–60, 77–90.

[m] *Ibid.,* p. 87, para. 52.

[n] *Ibid.,* p. 100, n. 40.

[o] *Ibid.,* p. 87, para. 74.

[p] *Ibid.,* p. 4, para. 341.

---

[12] It is ironic that in the last paragraph of this essay Lévi-Strauss states he intended to emphasize the "fecundity of the method followed by Radin." Radin was the quintessential historical particularist who spent much of his career studying the Winnebago in extensive detail. With its emphasis on universal structures of the mind and large-scale cross-cultural comparisons, nothing could be further from Radin's approach than Lévi-Strauss' structuralism. Lévi-Strauss was perhaps aware of this irony.

---

23. *Is Female to Male as Nature Is to Culture?*

SHERRY B. ORTNER (b. 1941)

MUCH OF THE CREATIVITY of anthropology derives from the tension between two sets of demands: that we explain human universals, and that we explain cultural particulars. By this canon, woman provides us with one of the more challenging problems to be dealt with. The secondary status of woman in society is one of the true universals, a pan-cultural fact. Yet within that universal fact, the specific cultural conceptions and symbolizations of woman are extraordinarily diverse and even mutually contradictory. Further, the actual treatment of women and their relative power and contribution vary enormously from culture to culture, and over different periods in

---

From *Women Culture and Society* (1974)

the history of particular cultural traditions. Both of these points—the universal fact and the cultural variation—constitute problems to be explained.[1]

My interest in the problem is of course more than academic: I wish to see genuine change come about, the emergence of a social and cultural order in which as much of the range of human potential is open to women as is open to men. The universality of female subordination, the fact that it exists within every type of social and economic arrangement and in societies of every degree of complexity, indicates to me that we are up against something very profound, very stubborn, something we cannot rout out simply by rearranging a few tasks and roles in the social system, or even by reordering the whole economic structure. In this paper I try to expose the underlying logic of cultural thinking that assumes the inferiority of women; I try to show the highly persuasive nature of the logic, for if it were not so persuasive, people would not keep subscribing to it. But I also try to show the social and cultural sources of that logic, to indicate wherein lies the potential for change.[2]

It is important to sort out the levels of the problem. The confusion can be staggering. For example, depending on which aspect of Chinese culture we look at, we might extrapolate any of several entirely different guesses concerning the status of women in China. In the ideology of Taoism, *yin*, the female principle, and *yang*, the male principle, are given equal weight; "the opposition, alternation, and interaction of these two forces give rise to all phenomena in the universe" (Siu, 1968:2). Hence we might guess that maleness and femaleness are equally valued in the general ideology of Chinese culture.[a] Looking at the social structure, however, we see the strongly emphasized patrilineal descent principle, the importance of sons, and the absolute authority of the father in the family. Thus we might conclude that China is the archetypal patriarchal society. Next, looking at the actual roles played, power and influence wielded, and material contributions made by women in Chinese society—all of which are, upon observation, quite substantial—we would have to say that women are allotted a great deal of (unspoken) status in the system. Or

---

[1] Early feminist critiques assumed the universal subordination of women; for instance, in her opening paragraph, Ortner states that the secondary status of women is a "pancultural fact." The purpose of the article is to formulate a theory that explains this universal gender asymmetry.

Feminist scholars dealt with the question of gender asymmetry in a variety of ways. Leacock (essay 29 in this volume), for example, approached the issue from a Marxist perspective, claiming that gender subordination was a product of external factors—namely, the introduction of capitalism and men's control of the forces of production in society. Ortner's answer to this issue turns inward. Rather than finding the answer to her questions in the material factors of society, she looks for the answer in the structure of human thought. Structuralists believe that cultural phenomena are the product of universal logical processes that organize human thought. And a fundamental characteristic of human thought, according to structuralists, is to sort data into binary oppositions. Therefore, one should be able to identify cross-cultural patterns of oppositions associated with men and women. This is exactly what Ortner sets out to do in this essay.

A decade later, theorists abandoned the view that women were everywhere and always subordinate to men in favor of a more sophisticated view that exam-

ined the cultural construction of relationships between men and women. But in the 1970s, within the political context of the women's movement, the domination of women by men was accepted doctrine for feminist anthropologists.

[2] Most anthropological theory, though influenced by prevailing political events or philosophies, is not written with an openly political objective. With rare exceptions, such as Gorer and Rickman's *The People of Great Russia* (1962 [1949]), it was not until the 1970s, when college campuses were extremely politicized, that anthropologists such as Ortner started writing politically charged work.

Ortner talks about exposing the "underlying logic of cultural thinking." The notion that a hidden logic underlies human thought is basic to structuralism. The fundamental dichotomy she has constructed for analysis is male-power versus female-subordination. Ortner's argument is based directly on the work of Lévi-Strauss, whose books *The Elementary Structures of Kinship* (1969 [1949]) and *The Raw and the Cooked* (1969) are cited in her paper. In fact, the title of one section of her essay ("Nature and Culture") is a direct reference to Lévi-Strauss' proposition that a fundamental opposition through which humans conceptualize the world is between nature and culture.

again, we might focus on the fact that a goddess, Kuan Yin, is the central (most worshiped, most depicted) deity in Chinese Buddhism, and we might be tempted to say, as many have tried to say about goddess-worshiping cultures in prehistoric and early historical societies, that China is actually a sort of matriarchy. In short, we must be absolutely clear about *what* we are trying to explain before explaining it.

We may differentiate three levels of the problem:

1. The universal fact of culturally attributed second-class status of women in every society. Two questions are important here. First, what do we mean by this; what is our evidence that this is a universal fact? And second, how are we to explain this fact, once having established it?

2. Specific ideologies, symbolizations, and socio-structural arrangements pertaining to women that vary widely from culture to culture. The problem at this level is to account for any particular cultural complex in terms of factors specific to that group—the standard level of anthropological analysis.

3. Observable on-the-ground details of women's activities, contributions, powers, influence, etc., often at variance with cultural ideology (although always constrained within the assumption that women may never be officially preeminent in the total system). This is the level of direct observation, often adopted now by feminist-oriented anthropologists.

This paper is primarily concerned with the first of these levels, the problem of the universal devaluation of women. The analysis thus depends not upon specific cultural data but rather upon an analysis of "culture" taken generically as a special sort of process in the world. A discussion of the second level, the problem of cross-cultural variation in conceptions and relative valuations of women, will entail a great deal of cross-cultural research and must be postponed to another time. As for the third level, it will be obvious from my approach that I would consider it a misguided endeavor to focus only upon women's actual though culturally unrecognized and unvalued powers in any given society, without first understanding the overarching ideology and deeper assumptions of the culture that render such powers trivial.[3]

THE UNIVERSALITY OF FEMALE SUBORDINATION

What do I mean when I say that everywhere, in every known culture, women are considered in some degree inferior to men? First of all, I must stress that I am talking about *cultural* evaluations; I am saying that each culture, in its own way and on its own terms, makes this evaluation. But what would constitute evidence that a particular culture considers women inferior?

Three types of data would suffice: (1) elements of cultural ideology and informants' statements that *explicitly* devalue women, according them, their roles, their tasks, their products, and their social milieux less prestige than are accorded men and the male correlates; (2) symbolic devices, such as the attribution of defilement, which may be interpreted as *implicitly* making a statement of inferior valuation; and (3) social structural arrangements that exclude women from participation in or contact with some realm in which the highest powers of the society are felt

---

[3] The issue that Ortner seeks to address here is universal female subordination. She proposes that there are three levels of this problem to examine, but she is most interested in the first.

Ortner's focus on the first level follows from her structuralist theoretical position. A basic principle of structuralism is that a single universal cultural patterning underlies all individual cultures. Therefore, structuralism should be a good method for explaining universal cultural characteristics. It would be less effective at explaining the specifics of cultural symbols (Ortner's second level). In fact, structuralists do not generally consider the meanings of individual symbols important. It is their pattern that is critical. The third level is of even less interest for structuralists. Since they believe that culture is a mental model, structuralists are much more concerned with what people think and say than what they do.

to reside.[b] These three types of data may all of course be interrelated in any particular system, though they need not necessarily be. Further, any one of them will usually be sufficient to make the point of female inferiority in a given culture. Certainly, female exclusion from the most sacred rite or the highest political council is sufficient evidence. Certainly, explicit cultural ideology devaluing women (and their tasks, roles, products, etc.) is sufficient evidence. Symbolic indicators such as defilement are usually sufficient, although in a few cases in which, say, men and women are equally polluting to one another, a further indicator is required—and is, as far as my investigations have ascertained, always available.

On any or all of these counts, then, I would flatly assert that we find women subordinated to men in every known society.[4] The search for a genuinely egalitarian, let alone matriarchal, culture has proved fruitless. An example from one society that has traditionally been on the credit side of this ledger will suffice. Among the matrilineal Crow, as Lowie[5] (1956) points out, "Women had highly honorific offices in the Sun Dance; they could become directors of the Tobacco Ceremony and played, if anything, a more conspicuous part in it than the men; they sometimes played the hostess in the Cooked Meat Festival; they were not debarred from sweating or doctoring or from seeking a vision" (p. 61). Nonetheless, "Women [during menstruation] formerly rode inferior horses and evidently this loomed as a source of contamination, for they were not allowed to approach either a wounded man or men starting on a war party. A taboo still lingers against their coming near sacred

objects at these times" (p. 44). Further, just before enumerating women's rights of participation in the various rituals noted above, Lowie mentions one particular Sun Dance Doll bundle that was not supposed to be unwrapped by a woman (p. 60). Pursuing this trail we find: "According to all Lodge Grass informants and most others, the doll owned by Wrinkled-face took precedence not only of other dolls but of all other Crow medicines whatsoever. This particular doll was not supposed to be handled by a woman" (p. 229).[c]

In sum, the Crow are probably a fairly typical case. Yes, women have certain powers and rights, in this case some that place them in fairly high positions. Yet ultimately the line is drawn: menstruation is a threat to warfare, one of the most valued institutions of the tribe, one that is central to their self-definition; and the most sacred object of the tribe is taboo to the direct sight and touch of women.

Similar examples could be multiplied ad infinitum, but I think the onus is no longer upon us to demonstrate that female subordination is a cultural universal; it is up to those who would argue against the point to bring forth counter examples. I shall take the universal secondary status of women as a given, and proceed from there.[6]

NATURE AND CULTURE[d]

How are we to explain the universal devaluation of women? We could of course rest the case on biological determinism. There is something genetically inherent in the male of the species, so

---

[4] In this paragraph, Ortner sets out the basic criteria that she believes prove a culture considers women inferior. Below, she provides examples of these different classes of evidence from different societies. However, she doesn't give the reader all three types of evidence for any single society. Ortner says that although the three types of data may all be found in one system, any single one of them is sufficient to prove female inferiority in a given culture.

If one accepts the structuralist premise that cultural patterns originate in the way the brain processes information, this is an acceptable methodological technique. However, her methods seem little different from those of the nineteenth-century evolutionists who validated their

cross-cultural comparative analyses using the concept of psychic unity.

[5] Austrian-born anthropologist Robert Lowie (1883–1957) was a student of Franz Boas. Lowie wrote extensively on the Crow as well as other Plains Indians. Be sure to read Ortner's footnote "c" about Lowie and his doll.

[6] Ortner says that even in societies in which women may hold high status and powerful positions, one can still find evidence indicating that they are inferior to men. She declares her case to be proven and places the burden of disproof on those who disagree. Are you convinced? Does the Crow example she provides bear this out?

the biological determinists would argue, that makes them the naturally dominant sex; that "something" is lacking in females, and as a result women are not only naturally subordinate but in general quite satisfied with their position, since it affords them protection and the opportunity to maximize maternal pleasures, which to them are the most satisfying experiences of life. Without going into a detailed refutation of this position, I think it fair to say that it has failed to be established to the satisfaction of almost anyone in academic anthropology. This is to say, not that biological facts are irrelevant, or that men and women are not different, but that these facts and differences only take on significance of superior/inferior within the framework of culturally defined value systems.[7]

If we are unwilling to rest the case on genetic determinism, it seems to me that we have only one way to proceed. We must attempt to interpret female subordination in light of other universals, factors built into the structure of the most generalized situation in which all human beings, in whatever culture, find themselves. For example, every human being has a physical body and a sense of nonphysical mind, is part of a society of other individuals and an inheritor of a cultural tradition, and must engage in some relationship, however mediated, with "nature," or the non-human realm in order to survive. Every human being is born (to a mother) and ultimately dies, all are assumed to have an interest in personal survival, and society/culture has its own interest in (or at least momentum toward) continuity and survival, which transcends the lives and deaths of particular individuals. And so forth. It is in the realm of such universals of the human condition that we must

seek an explanation for the universal fact of female devaluation.

I translate the problem, in other words, into the following simple question. What could there be in the generalized structure and conditions of existence, common to every culture, that would lead every culture to place a lower value upon women? Specifically, my thesis is that woman is being identified with—or, if you will, seems to be a symbol of—something that every culture devalues, something that every culture defines as being of a lower order of existence than itself. Now it seems that there is only one thing that would fit that description, and that is "nature" in the most generalized sense. Every culture, or, generically, "culture," is engaged in the process of generating and sustaining systems of meaningful forms (symbols, artifacts, etc.) by means of which humanity transcends the givens of natural existence, bends them to its purposes, controls them in its interest. We may thus broadly equate culture with the notion of human consciousness, or with the products of human consciousness (i.e., systems of thought and technology), by means of which humanity attempts to assert control over nature.[8]

Now the categories of "nature" and "culture" are of course conceptual categories—one can find no boundary out in the actual world between the two states or realms of being. And there is no question that some cultures articulate a much stronger opposition between the two categories than others—it has even been argued that primitive peoples (some or all) do not see or intuit any distinction between the human cultural state and the state of nature at all. Yet I would maintain that the universality of ritual betokens an assertion in

---

[7] The reference to biological determinism in this paragraph is an allusion to theories popular at the time this essay was written. In addition, books such as Ardrey's 1961 *African Genesis,* which emphasized the aggressive nature of men, had captured the popular imagination.

[8] The idea that all humans make a fundamental distinction between culture and nature, and that in every society, culture is believed to be superior to nature, is basic to the work of Lévi-Strauss. In the two paragraphs you have just read, Ortner paraphrases him. In *The Elementary Structures of Kinship* Lévi-Strauss wrote:

. . . it is easy to recognize universality as the criterion of nature, for what is constant in man falls necessarily beyond the scope of customs, techniques, and institutions. . . . Let us suppose that everything universal in man relates to the natural order . . . and that everything subject to a norm is cultural and is both relative and particular. (quoted in Boyne 1966:200)

Ortner's comments here directly reflect Lévi-Strauss' statement. She reasons from this passage that if everything universal relates to nature, and if female subordination is universal, then female subordination must relate to nature.

all human cultures of the specifically human ability to act upon and regulate, rather than passively move with and be moved by, the givens of natural existence. In ritual, the purposive manipulation of given forms toward regulating and sustaining order, every culture asserts that proper relations between human existence and natural forces depend upon culture's employing its special powers to regulate the overall processes of the world and life.[9]

One realm of cultural thought in which these points are often articulated is that of concepts of purity and pollution. Virtually every culture has some such beliefs, which seem in large part (though not, of course, entirely) to be concerned with the relationship between culture and nature (see Ortner, 1973, n.d.). A well-known aspect of purity/pollution beliefs cross-culturally is that of the natural "contagion" of pollution; left to its own devices, pollution (for these purposes grossly equated with the unregulated operation of natural energies) spreads and overpowers all that it comes in contact with. Thus a puzzle—if pollution is so strong, how can anything be purified? Why is the purifying agent not itself polluted? The answer, in keeping with the present line of argument, is that

purification is effected in a ritual context; purification ritual, as a purposive activity that pits self-conscious (symbolic) action against natural energies, is more powerful than those energies.[10]

In any case, my point is simply that every culture implicitly recognizes and asserts a distinction between the operation of nature and the operation of culture (human consciousness and its products); and further, that the distinctiveness of culture rests precisely on the fact that it can under most circumstances transcend natural conditions and turn them to its purposes. Thus culture (i.e., every culture) at some level of awareness asserts itself to be not only distinct from but superior to nature, and that sense of distinctiveness and superiority rest precisely on the ability to transform—to "socialize" and "culturalize"—nature.[11]

Returning now to the issue of women, their pan-cultural second-class status could be accounted for, quite simply, by postulating that women are being identified or symbolically associated with nature, as opposed to men, who are identified with culture. Since it is always culture's project to subsume and transcend nature, if women were considered part of nature, then culture would find it "natural" to subordinate,

---

[9] A critical element of structuralist thought is expressed in this passage. Ortner notes that there is no boundary in the physical world between nature and culture. The boundary is a product of human thinking. Structuralists believe that the human mind imposes order by *parsing,* or breaking down, the world into culturally meaningful bits. Structuralists try to discover the fundamental principles by which humans accomplish this parsing.

[10] Having rejected biological foundations for the universal subordination of women, Ortner must formulate a cultural explanation. Following Lévi-Strauss, she chooses ritual as the focus of her analysis, as the place where cultures attempt to regulate and sustain order. Lévi-Strauss authored two studies of mythology—*The Raw and the Cooked* (1969) and *From Honey to Ashes* (1973)—based on what he claimed to be a fundamental opposition between nature and culture. Following Lévi-Strauss, Ortner states that humans transcend and control nature through the use of symbols. In particular, we distinguish ourselves from the natural world and regulate it through the use of ritual. It is through ritual that the natural, dangerous, and unacceptable are transformed into the cultural, acceptable, and safe.

The focus on ritual symbols and their power is not new for Ortner. In 1973, the year before the publication of this essay, Ortner published an article in *American Anthropologist* called "On Key Symbols," in which she discusses how symbols operate in ritual thought and action. Then in 1975 she published another analysis titled "Gods' Bodies, Gods' Food: A Symbolic Analysis of Sherpa Ritual," which was inspired by the work of Clifford Geertz (see essay 33).

[11] Lévi-Strauss' ideas, like those of other theorists, were not uniformly accepted. Anthropologist Carol MacCormack (1934–1997), for example, criticized Lévi-Strauss' nature-culture formulation. Whereas he saw the nature-culture contrast as timeless and value-free, MacCormack concluded that such ideas were culturally specific. MacCormack wrote:

There is no way to absolutely verify that the nature-culture opposition exists as an essential feature of universal unconscious structure, and there is ethnographic evidence to suggest that in the form in which Europeans now conceive it, the contrast is not a universal feature of consciously-held folk models. (1980:10) not to say oppress, them. Yet although this argument can be shown to have considerable force, it seems to oversimplify the case. The formulation I would like to defend and elaborate on in the following section, then, is that women are seen "merely" as being *closer* to nature than men. That is, culture (still equated relatively unambiguously with men) recognizes that women are active participants in its special processes, but at the same time sees them as being more rooted in, or having more direct affinity with, nature.

The revision may seem minor or even trivial, but I think it is a more accurate rendering of cultural assumptions. Further, the argument cast in these terms has several analytic advantages over the simpler formulation; I shall discuss these later. It might simply be stressed here that the revised argument would still account for the pan-cultural devaluation of women, for even if women are not equated with nature, they are nonetheless seen as representing a lower order of being, as being less transcendental of nature than men are. The next task of the paper, then, is to consider why they might be viewed in that way.[12]

WHY IS WOMAN SEEN AS CLOSER TO NATURE?

It all begins of course with the body and the natural procreative functions specific to women alone. We can sort out for discussion three levels at which this absolute physiological fact has significance: (1) woman's *body and its functions,* more involved more of the time with "species life,"

seem to place her closer to nature, in contrast to man's physiology, which frees him more completely to take up the projects of culture; (2) woman's body and its functions place her in *social roles* that in turn are considered to be at a lower order of the cultural process than man's; and (3) woman's traditional social roles, imposed because of her body and its functions, in turn give her a different *psychic structure,* which, like her physiological nature and her social roles, is seen as being closer to nature. I shall discuss each of these points in turn, showing first how in each instance certain factors strongly tend to align woman with nature, then indicating other factors that demonstrate her full alignment with culture, the combined factors thus placing her in a problematic intermediate position. It will become clear in the course of the discussion why men seem by contrast less intermediate, more purely "cultural" than women. And I reiterate that I am dealing only at the level of cultural and human universals. These arguments are intended to apply to generalized humanity; they grow out of the human condition, as humanity has experienced and confronted it up to the present day.

1. *Woman's physiology seen as closer to nature.* This part of my argument has been anticipated, with subtlety, cogency, and a great deal of hard data, by De Beauvoir (1953).[13] De Beauvoir reviews the physiological structure, development, and functions of the human female and concludes that "the female, to a greater extent than the male, is the prey of the species" (p. 60). She points out that many major areas and processes of the woman's body serve no apparent

---

[12] Ortner's distinction between women as identified with nature and women as "merely" closer to nature is subtle and performs two tasks in this essay. First, it makes her case more compelling but less amenable to testing. If Ortner said that women were identified wholly with nature, one or two counterexamples could easily disprove her point. However, she suggests that women are merely closer to nature than men. This means that in every case where anthropologists find women associated with culture rather than nature, they must ask, "Well, are men even more associated with culture?" This is a difficult proposition to test. Second, it opens the possibility that women mediate be-

tween culture and nature. This issue is discussed further below (see esp. notes 17, 18, and 20).

[13] Simone de Beauvoir (1908–1986) was a French existentialist author of plays and novels and the companion of the philosopher Jean-Paul Sartre (1905–1980). The reference is to her book *The Second Sex* (1952), which analyzes women's inferior positions in society. In *The Second Sex,* de Beauvoir used existential argument and ethnographic data to compare women with oppressed minorities and proposed that women's status was the result of social conditions rather than biological factors. Today, *The Second Sex* is considered a fundamental document of modern feminism.

function for the health and stability of the individual; on the contrary, as they perform their specific organic functions, they are often sources of discomfort, pain, and danger. The breasts are irrelevant to personal health; they may be excised at any time of a woman's life. "Many of the ovarian secretions function for the benefit of the egg, promoting its maturation and adapting the uterus to its requirements; in respect to the organism as a whole, they make for disequilibrium rather than for regulation—the woman is adapted to the needs of the egg rather than to her own requirements" (p. 24). Menstruation is often uncomfortable, sometimes painful; it frequently has negative emotional correlates and in any case involves bothersome tasks of cleansing and waste disposal; and—a point that De Beauvoir does not mention—in many cultures it interrupts a woman's routine, putting her in a stigmatized state involving various restrictions on her activities and social contacts. In pregnancy many of the woman's vitamin and mineral resources are channeled into nourishing the fetus, depleting her own strength and energies. And finally, childbirth itself is painful and dangerous (pp. 24–27 *passim*). In sum, De Beauvoir concludes that the female "is more enslaved to the species than the male, her animality is more manifest" (p. 239).

While De Beauvoir's book is ideological, her survey of woman's physiological situation seems fair and accurate. It is simply a fact that proportionately more of woman's body space, for a greater percentage of her lifetime, and at some—sometimes great—cost to her personal health, strength, and general stability, is taken up with the natural processes surrounding the reproduction of the species.

De Beauvoir goes on to discuss the negative implications of woman's "enslavement to the species" in relation to the projects in which humans engage, projects through which culture is generated and defined. She arrives thus at the crux of her argument (pp. 58–59):

Here we have the key to the whole mystery. On the biological level a species is maintained only by creating itself anew; but this creation results

only in repeating the same Life in more individuals. But man assures the repetition of Life while transcending Life through Existence [i.e., goal-oriented, meaningful action]; by this transcendence he creates values that deprive pure repetition of all value. In the animal, the freedom and variety of male activities are vain because no project is involved. Except for his services to the species, what he does is immaterial. Whereas in serving the species, the human male also remodels the face of the earth, he creates new instruments, he invents, he shapes the future.

In other words, woman's body seems to doom her to mere reproduction of life; the male, in contrast, lacking natural creative functions, must (or has the opportunity to) assert his creativity externally, "artificially," through the medium of technology and symbols. In so doing, he creates relatively lasting, eternal, transcendent objects, while the woman creates only perishables—human beings.

This formulation opens up a number of important insights. It speaks, for example, to the great puzzle of why male activities involving the destruction of life (hunting and warfare) are often given more prestige than the female's ability to give birth, to create life. Within De Beauvoir's framework, we realize it is not the killing that is the relevant and valued aspect of hunting and warfare; rather, it is the transcendental (social, cultural) nature of these activities, as opposed to the naturalness of the process of birth: "For it is not in giving life but in risking life that man is raised above the animal; that is why superiority has been accorded in humanity not to the sex that brings forth but to that which kills" (*ibid.*).

Thus if male is, as I am suggesting, everywhere (unconsciously) associated with culture and female seems closer to nature, the rationale for these associations is not very difficult to grasp, merely from considering the implications of the physiological contrast between male and female. At the same time, however, woman cannot be consigned fully to the category of nature, for it is perfectly obvious that she is a full-fledged human being endowed with human consciousness just as a man is; she is half of the human race, without whose cooperation the whole enterprise would collapse. She may seem more in the possession of nature than man, but having consciousness, she thinks and speaks; she generates, communicates, and manipulates symbols, categories, and values. She participates in human dialogues not only with other women but also with men. As Lévi-Strauss says, "Woman could never become just a sign and nothing more, since even in a man's world she is still a person, and since insofar as she is defined as a sign she must [still] be recognized as a generator of signs" (1969a:496).[14]

Indeed, the fact of woman's full human consciousness, her full involvement in and commitment to culture's project of transcendence over nature, may ironically explain another of the great puzzles of "the woman problem"—woman's nearly universal unquestioning acceptance of her own devaluation. For it would seem that, as a conscious human and member of culture, she has followed out the logic of culture's arguments and has reached culture's conclusions along with the men. As De Beauvoir puts it (p. 59):

> For she, too, is an existent, she feels the urge to surpass, and her project is not mere repetition but transcendence towards a different future—in her heart of hearts she finds confirmation of the masculine pretensions. She joins the men in the festivals that celebrate the successes and victories of the males. Her misfortune is to have been biologically destined for the repetition of Life, when even in her own view Life does not carry within itself its reasons for being, reasons that are more important than life itself.

In other words, woman's consciousness—her membership, as it were, in culture—is evidenced in part by the very fact that she accepts her own devaluation and takes culture's point of view.

I have tried here to show one part of the logic of that view, the part that grows directly from the physiological differences between men and women. Because of woman's greater bodily involvement with the natural functions surrounding reproduction, she is seen as more a part of nature than man is. Yet in part because of her consciousness and participation in human social dialogue, she is recognized as a participant in culture. Thus she appears as something intermediate between culture and nature, lower on the scale of transcendence than man.[15]

2. *Woman's social role seen as closer to nature.* Woman's physiological functions, I have argued, may tend in themselves to motivate[e] a view of woman as closer to nature, a view she herself, as an observer of herself and the world, would tend to agree with. Woman creates naturally from within her own being, whereas man is free to, or forced to, create artificially, that is, through cultural means, and in such a way as to sustain culture. In addition, I now wish to show how woman's physiological functions have tended universally to limit her social movement, and to confine her universally to certain social contexts which *in turn* are seen as closer to nature. That is, not only her bodily processes but the social situation in which her bodily processes locate her may carry this significance. And insofar as

---

[14] Lévi-Strauss' comments on women and signs are from his 1949 book *The Elementary Structures of Kinship*. There, he uses the notion of sign taken from the turn-of-the-century Swiss structural linguist Ferdinand de Saussure (1857–1913). Contrary to the popular views of his time, Saussure argued that the meanings of the majority of words in a language are derived from the arbitrary association of sound and meaning. Each idea in language is arbitrarily associated with a sound. The sound, Saussure called the "signifier"; the idea, the "signified." Together they form, in Saussure's terminology, a linguistic "sign." So, Ortner is saying that although devalued, women are still "generators of signs."

[15] Although Lévi-Strauss proposed that human thinking always parsed the world into binary oppositions, he also believed that the mind was dissatisfied with such oppositions and always searched for a mediator for them. A mediating category was a category that was not subsumed by either part of the binary but somehow transcended them. He argued that this mediator was always problematic. It was privileged, special, or ambiguous. In positioning women as "merely" closer to nature than men, and in insisting that women, while identified with nature, are in truth part of society's cultural project, Ortner is beginning to build a case that women are the mediating element in the culture-nature binary.

she is permanently associated (in the eyes of culture) with these social milieux, they add weight (perhaps the decisive part of the burden) to the view of woman as closer to nature. I refer here of course to woman's confinement to the domestic family context, a confinement motivated, no doubt, by her lactation processes.

Woman's body, like that of all female mammals, generates milk during and after pregnancy for the feeding of the newborn baby. The baby cannot survive without breast milk or some similar formula at this stage of life. Since the mother's body goes through its lactation processes in direct relation to a pregnancy with a particular child, the relationship of nursing between mother and child is seen as a natural bond, other feeding arrangements being seen in most cases as unnatural and makeshift. Mothers and their children, according to cultural reasoning, belong together. Further, children beyond infancy are not strong enough to engage in major work, yet are mobile and unruly and not capable of understanding various dangers; they thus require supervision and constant care. Mother is the obvious person for this task, as an extension of her natural nursing bond with the children, or because she has a new infant and is already involved with child-oriented activities. Her own activities are thus circumscribed by the limitations and low levels of her children's strengths and skills:[f] she is confined to the domestic family group; "woman's place is in the home."[16]

Woman's association with the domestic circle would contribute to the view of her as closer to nature in several ways. In the first place, the sheer fact of constant association with children plays a role in the issue; one can easily see how infants and children might themselves be considered part of nature. Infants are barely human and utterly unsocialized; like animals they are unable to walk upright, they excrete without control, they do not speak. Even slightly older children are clearly not yet fully under the sway of culture. They do not yet understand social duties, responsibilities, and morals; their vocabulary and their range of learned skills are small. One finds implicit recognition of an association between children and nature in many cultural practices. For example, most cultures have initiation rites for adolescents (primarily for boys; I shall return to this point below), the point of which is to move the child ritually from a less than fully human state into full participation in society and culture; many cultures do not hold funeral rites for children who die at early ages, explicitly because they are not yet fully social beings. Thus children are likely to be categorized with nature, and woman's close association with children may compound her potential for being seen as closer to nature herself. It is ironic that the rationale for boys' initiation rites in many cultures is that the boys must be purged of the defilement accrued from being around mother and other women so much of the time, when in fact much of the woman's defilement may derive from her being around children so much of the time.[17]

The second major problematic implication of women's close association with the domestic context derives from certain structural conflicts

---

[16] Ortner, like all authors, writes within a historical and political context. Her remarks on mother-child bonds and mother's nursing are an interesting reflection of this. American middle-class women "rediscovered" breastfeeding in the 1970s. Nursing became part of a political movement that included campaigns against corporations such as Nestlé, which sold infant formula, especially in poor nations. There was also much popular writing on the importance of mother-infant bonding. Ortner may have had these things in mind as she wrote these passages.

[17] Ortner has constructed an elegant argument, but like Lévi-Strauss before her, has based her logic on a set of ar-

bitrary assumptions. Why, for example, is the link between women and nature assumed as fact? As she herself states, women socialize children into cultural beings and turn raw substances into edible meals. So why are women not closer to culture? She answers by saying that socialization activities are taken over by men in adolescence. But why should this time period be inherently more important than earlier childhood in determining the relation of men and women to culture? Further, Ortner does not deal with activities that seem to place men close to nature. Shouldn't adult men, who are presumably out in nature hunting and killing, be closer to nature than women?

between the family and society at large in any social system. The implications of the "domestic/public opposition" in relation to the position of women have been cogently developed by Rosaldo (1974), and I simply wish to show its relevance to the present argument. The notion that the domestic unit—the biological family charged with reproducing and socializing new members of the society—is opposed to the public entity—the superimposed network of alliances and relationships that is the society—is also the basis of Lévi-Strauss's argument in the *Elementary Structures of Kinship* (1969a). Lévi-Strauss argues not only that this opposition is present in every social system, but further that it has the significance of the opposition between nature and culture. The universal incest prohibition[g] and its ally, the rule of exogamy (marriage outside the group), ensure that "the risk of seeing a biological family become established as a closed system is definitely eliminated; the biological group can no longer stand apart, and the bond of alliance with another family ensures the dominance of the social over the biological, and of the cultural over the natural" (p. 479). And although not every culture articulates a radical opposition between the domestic and the public as such, it is hardly contestable that the domestic is always subsumed by the public; domestic units are allied with one another through the enactment of rules that are logically at a higher level than the units themselves; this creates an emergent unit—society—that is logically at a higher level than the domestic units of which it is composed.[18]

Now, since women are associated with, and indeed are more or less confined to, the domestic context, they are identified with this lower order of social/cultural organization. What are the implications of this for the way they are viewed? First, if the specifically biological (reproductive) function of the family is stressed, as in Lévi-Strauss's formulation, then the family (and hence woman) is identified with nature pure and simple, as opposed to culture. But this is obviously too simple; the point seems more adequately formulated as follows: the family (and hence woman) represents lower-level, socially fragmenting, particularistic sort of concerns, as opposed to interfamilial relations representing higher-level, integrative, universalistic sorts of concerns. Since men lack a "natural" basis (nursing, generalized to child care) for a familial orientation, their sphere of activity is defined at the level of interfamilial relations. And hence, so the cultural reasoning seems to go, men are the "natural" proprietors of religion, ritual, politics, and other realms of cultural thought and action in which universalistic statements of spiritual and social synthesis are made. Thus men are identified not only with culture, in the sense of all human creativity, as opposed to nature; they are identified in particular with culture in the old-fashioned sense of the finer and higher aspects of human thought—art, religion, law, etc.[19]

Here again, the logic of cultural reasoning aligning woman with a lower order of culture than man is clear and, on the surface, quite compelling. At the same time, woman cannot be fully consigned to nature, for there are aspects of her situation, even within the domestic context, that undeniably demonstrate her participation in the cultural process. It goes without saying, of course,

---

[18] Ortner is referring here to Lévi-Strauss' contention that one of the most basic of binary oppositions is between us and them, kin and nonkin. This relates to the nature-culture opposition because of the universal rules of incest.

In addition, Ortner mentions Michelle Rosaldo's (1944–1981) article on gender inequality. There, Rosaldo presented a structuralist argument, but one that relied on a sociocultural rather than a biological explanation. She focused on the domestic-public opposition between men and women. She argued that men are typically associated with higher prestige public activities, while women, be-

cause they raise children, are limited to less prestigious domestic tasks.

Michelle Rosaldo, the wife of Renato Rosaldo, was killed in an accident during field research in October 1981 Renato Rosaldo's attempt to deal with his wife's death forms the core of his article "Grief and a Headhunter's Rage" (essay 36).

[19] When Ortner talks of culture in the old-fashioned sense, she is referring to Tylor's nineteenth-century definition of culture (arts, laws, morals, etc.; see essay 2) as opposed to a Boasian notion of culture.

that except for nursing newborn infants (and artificial nursing devices can cut even this biological tie), there is no reason why it has to be mother—as opposed to father, or anyone else—who remains identified with child care. But even assuming that other practical and emotional reasons conspire to keep woman in this sphere, it is possible to show that her activities in the domestic context could as logically put her squarely in the category of culture.

In the first place, one must point out that woman not only feeds and cleans up after children in a simple caretaker operation; she in fact is the primary agent of their early socialization. It is she who transforms newborn infants from mere organisms into cultured humans, teaching them manners and the proper ways to behave in order to become full-fledged members of the culture. On the basis of her socializing functions alone, she could not be more a representative of culture. Yet in virtually every society there is a point at which the socialization of boys is transferred to the hands of men. The boys are considered, in one set of terms or another, not yet "really" socialized; their entree into the realm of fully human (social, cultural) status can be accomplished only by men. We still see this in our own schools, where there is a gradual inversion in the proportion of female to male teachers up through the grades: most kindergarten teachers are female; most university professors are male.[h]

Or again, take cooking. In the overwhelming majority of societies cooking is the woman's work. No doubt this stems from practical considerations—since the woman has to stay home with the baby, it is convenient for her to perform the chores centered in the home. But if it is true, as Lévi-Strauss has argued (1969b), that transforming the raw into the cooked may represent, in many systems of thought, the transition from nature to culture, then here we have woman aligned with this important culturalizing process, which could easily place her in the category of culture, triumphing over nature. Yet it is also interesting to note that when a culture (e.g., France or China) develops a tradition of *haute cuisine*—"real" cooking, as opposed to trivial ordinary domestic cooking—the high chefs are almost always men. Thus the pattern replicates that in the area of socialization—women perform lower-level conversions from nature to culture, but when the culture distinguishes a higher level of the same functions, the higher level is restricted to men.

In short, we see once again some sources of woman's appearing more intermediate than man with respect to the nature/culture dichotomy. Her "natural" association with the domestic context (motivated by her natural lactation functions) tends to compound her potential for being viewed as closer to nature, because of the animal-like nature of children, and because of the infra-social connotation of the domestic group as against the rest of society. Yet at the same time her socializing and cooking functions within the domestic context show her to be a powerful agent of the cultural process, constantly transforming raw natural resources into cultural products. Belonging to culture, yet appearing to have stronger and more direct connections with nature, she is once again seen as situated between the two realms.

[*We have omitted most of the last two sections of Ortner's article, about 3,000 words, called "Woman's Psyche Seen as Closer to Nature" and "The Implications of Intermediacy." In the first section she argues that women not only have a different body and a different social importance than men but also a different psychic structure. In support of this view she relies mainly on an argument developed by Chodorow (1974), who claimed that men are more objective than women and communicate in terms of relatively abstract categories whereas women are subjective and relate in terms of relatively concrete phenomena. She argued that these differences are not innate but are due to the fact that "women, universally, are largely responsible for early care and for (at least) later female socialization" (1974:43).*

The last section, "The Implications of Intermediacy," summarizes the essay's main points and discusses the implications of women's mediation between nature and culture. Ortner says that women are universally seen as occupying a middle status on a hierarchy of being from culture to nature. As a result they are lower than men and less capable of achieving transcendence of nature. Ortner believes that this position assigns them greater symbolic ambiguity. She says,

> *Thus we can account easily for both the subversive feminine symbols (witches, evil eye, menstrual pollution, castrating mothers) and the feminine symbols of transcendence (mother goddesses, merciful dispensers of salvation, female symbols of justice, and the strong presence of feminine symbolism in the realms of art, religion, ritual, and law). Feminine symbolism, far more often than masculine symbolism, manifests this propensity toward polarized ambiguity—sometimes utterly exalted, sometimes utterly debased, rarely within the normal range of human possibilities.*

Ortner concludes this section as follows:]

In short, the postulate that woman is viewed as closer to nature than man has several implications for further analysis, and can be interpreted in several different ways. If it is viewed simply as a *middle* position on a scale from culture down to nature, then it is still seen as lower than culture and thus accounts for the pan-cultural assumption that woman is lower than man in the order of things. If it is read as a *mediating* element in the culture-nature relationship, then it may account in part for the cultural tendency not merely to devalue woman but to circumscribe and restrict her functions, since culture must maintain control over its (pragmatic and symbolic) mechanisms for the conversion of nature into culture. And if it is read as an *ambiguous* status between culture and nature, it may help account for the fact that, in specific cultural ideologies and symbolizations, woman can occasionally be aligned with culture, and in any event is often assigned polarized and contradictory meanings within a single symbolic system. Middle status, mediating functions, ambiguous meaning—all are different readings, for different contextual purposes, of woman's being seen as intermediate between nature and culture.

CONCLUSIONS

Ultimately, it must be stressed again that the whole scheme is a construct of culture rather than a fact of nature. Woman is not "in reality" any closer to (or further from) nature than man—both have consciousness, both are mortal. But there are certainly reasons why she appears that way, which is what I have tried to show in this paper. The result is a (sadly) efficient feedback system: various aspects of woman's situation (physical, social, psychological) contribute to her being seen as closer to nature, while the view of her as closer to nature is in turn embodied in institutional forms that reproduce her situation. The implications for social change are similarly circular: a different cultural view can only grow out of a different social actuality; a different social actuality can only grow out of a different cultural view.

It is clear, then, that the situation must be attacked from both sides. Efforts directed solely at changing the social institutions—through setting quotas on hiring, for example, or through passing equal-pay-for-equal-work laws—cannot have far-reaching effects if cultural language and imagery continue to purvey a relatively devalued view of women. But at the same time efforts directed solely at changing cultural assumptions—through male and female consciousness-raising groups, for example, or through revision of educational materials and mass-media imagery—cannot be successful unless the institutional base of the society is changed to support and reinforce the changed cultural view. Ultimately, both men and women can and must be equally involved in projects of creativity and transcendence. Only then will women be seen as aligned with culture, in culture's ongoing dialectic with nature.[20]

---

[20] In the final paragraph Ortner seems to be caught on the horns of a dilemma. She advocates political action to end what she considers the universal subordination of women but cannot accommodate this notion within structuralism.

Structuralism is designed to find consistencies within different cultures in order to reconstruct fundamental patterns of human thought. Because of this, culture change is irrelevant to structuralist analysis. In addition, Ortner has

NOTES

The first version of this paper was presented in October 1972 as a lecture in the course "Women: Myth and Reality" at Sarah Lawrence College. I received helpful comments from the students and from my co-teachers in the course: Joan Kelly Gadol, Eva Kollisch, and Gerda Lerner. A short account was delivered at the American Anthropological Association meetings in Toronto, November 1972. Meanwhile, I received excellent critical comments from Karen Blu, Robert Paul, Michelle Rosaldo, David Schneider, and Terence Turner, and the present version of the paper, in which the thrust of the argument has been rather significantly changed, was written in response to those comments. I, of course, retain responsibility for its final form. The paper is dedicated to Simone De Beauvoir, whose book *The Second Sex* (1953), first published in French in 1949, remains in my opinion the best single comprehensive understanding of "the woman problem."

[a] It is true of course that *yin*, the female principle, has a negative valence. Nonetheless, there is an absolute complementarity of *yin* and *yang* in Taoism, a recognition that the world requires the equal operation and interaction of both principles for its survival.

[b] Some anthropologists might consider this type of evidence (social-structural arrangements that exclude women, explicitly or de facto, from certain groups, roles, or statuses) to be a subtype of the second type of evidence (symbolic formulations of inferiority). I would not disagree with this view, although most social anthropologists would probably separate the two types.

[c] While we are on the subject of injustices of various kinds, we might note that Lowie secretly bought this doll, the most sacred object in the tribal repertoire, from its custodian, the widow of Wrinkled-face. She asked $400 for it, but this price was "far beyond [Lowie's] means," and he finally got it for $80 (p. 300).

[d] With all due respect to Lévi-Strauss (1969a, b, and *passim*).

[e] Semantic theory uses the concept of motivation of meaning, which encompasses various ways in which a meaning may be assigned to a symbol because of certain objective properties of that symbol, rather than by arbitrary association. In a sense, this entire paper is an inquiry into the motivation of the meaning of woman as a symbol, asking why woman may be unconsciously assigned the significance of being closer to nature. For a concise statement on the various types of motivation of meaning, see Ullman (1963).

[f] A situation that often serves to make her more child-like herself.

[g] David M. Schneider (personal communication) is prepared to argue that the incest taboo is not universal, on the basis of material from Oceania. Let us say at this point, then, that it is virtually universal.

[h] I remember having my first male teacher in the fifth grade, and I remember being excited about that—it was somehow more grown up.

REFERENCES

Carlson, Rae. 1971. "Sex Differences in Ego Functioning: Exploratory Studies of Agency and Communion," *Journal of Consulting and Clinical Psychology*, 37:267–77.

De Beauvoir, Simone. 1953. *The Second Sex*. New York.

Lévi-Strauss, Claude. 1969a. *The Elementary Structures of Kinship*. Trans. J. H. Bell and J. R. von Sturmer; ed. R. Needham. Boston.

———. 1969b. *The Raw and the Cooked*. Trans. J. and D. Weightman. New York.

Lowie, Robert. 1956. *The Crow Indians*. New York. Originally published in 1935.

Ortner, Sherry B. 1973. "Sherpa Purity," *American Anthropologist*, 75:49–63.

———. n.d. "Purification Beliefs and Practices," *Encyclopedia Britannica*, forthcoming.

Pitt-Rivers, Julian. 1961. People of the Sierra. Chicago.

Rosaldo, Michelle. 1974. "Women, Culture, and Society: A Theoretical Overview," Michelle Rosaldo and Louise Lamphere, eds., *Women, Culture, and Society*, pp. 14–42. Palo Alto, Calif.: Stanford University Press.

Siu, R. G. H. 1968. *The Man of Many Qualities*. Cambridge, Mass.

Ullman, Stephen. 1963. "Semantic Universals," in Joseph H. Greenberg, ed., *Universals of Language*. Cambridge, Mass.(1952)

---

located the source of female oppression in the fact that members of societies universally parse their worlds into nature and culture and universally assign women to a mediating category between them. One can easily imagine political action designed to improve the conditions of women in a society, but how can one ever change a culturally universal pattern of thought?

Ethnoscience and Cognitive Anthropology

It has long been evident that a major weakness in anthropology is the underdeveloped condition of ethnographic method. Typologies and generalizations abound, but their descriptive foundations are insecure. Anthropology is in the natural history stage of development rather than the "stage of deductively formulated theory" (Northrup 1947).

What is needed is the improvement of ethnographic method, to make cultural descriptions replicable and accurate, so that we know what we are comparing. Ethnoscience shows promise as the New Ethnography required to advance the whole of cultural anthropology (Sturtevant 1987:131–132).

Beginning in the mid-1950s, ethnographers constructed a new methodological program for conducting fieldwork: ethnoscience, or the new ethnography. Ethnoscience was based on a critique of traditional fieldwork. Ethnoscientists claimed that for several reasons, ethnography had been unscientific. They complained that there was no single way of doing ethnography. Each anthropologist studied and wrote in his or her own, idiosyncratic way. As a result, ethnographies contained different sorts of information and were not analytically comparable with one another. Further, ethnographers tried to describe native society and native understandings, but they did so using the conceptual categories of Western society. Critics claimed that this distorted the results. To make anthropology more scientific and ethnographic descriptions more accurate, ethnoscientists argued, anthropologists should attempt to reproduce cultural reality as it was perceived and lived by members of society. To this end, they urged that descriptions of culture be couched in terms of native thought. Understanding native conceptual categories was key to this task. The ideal ethnoscientific ethnography would include all the rules, principles, and categories that natives must know in order to understand and act appropriately in social situations within their cultures.

The underlying theoretical assumption of ethnoscience was that a culture was a set of mental models. It was the job of ethnographers to duplicate the features of those cognitive models so that they could "think like a native." An ethnographer's model was presumed correct if it allowed him or her to replicate the way a native categorized phenomena.

Because no one has direct access to another person's mind, the cognitive models drawn by ethnographers were based on what informants told them. Thus, the new ethnography drew heavily on the techniques of linguistic analysis. In particular, they adopted the methodology developed in the 1920s by members of the Prague School of linguistics. Members of the Prague School such as Jakobson and Troubetzkoy were interested in the structure of languages, in particular, phonology. They studied the phonetic structure of languages by contrasting sounds in order to analyze the features that made sounds distinct. Ethnoscientists incorporated this idea into their research by creating diagrams in which contrasts of meaning could be outlined and the features of native conceptual categories distinguished.

Another set of linguistic principles on which ethnoscience is based can be traced to the 1930s and the work of Edward Sapir and Benjamin L. Whorf. As we have seen (essay 10), Sapir and Whorf were interested in the relationship between language and thought. Together they formulated the Sapir-Whorf hypothesis, proposing that language was not just a means of communication but also shaped people's perceptions of the world. Whorf wrote:

> We dissect nature along lines laid down by our native languages. . . . We cut nature up, organize it into concepts, and ascribe significances as we do, largely because we are parties to an agreement to organize it in this way—an agreement that holds throughout our speech community and is codified in the patterns of our language. (1956:213)

Sapir and Whorf's emphasis on the linguistic determinism of perception was one element that led the ethnoscientists to see a close connection between culture and language. They reasoned that replicating the classification system of any language would give them the ability to view the world in the same way as native speakers of that language.

William Sturtevant outlined the fundamental principles of this new approach in his 1964 article, "Studies in Ethnoscience," published in *American Anthropologist*. However, other ethnoscientists were already outlining the new research methodologies. Individuals such as Ward Goodenough and Charles Frake described specific ways to conduct fieldwork and analyze data (Goodenough 1956, Frake 1962). The key instrument to be used in fieldwork was the highly structured interview, aimed specifically at eliciting native conceptual categories, which ethnoscientists called *domains*. They then used a technique called *componential analysis* to determine the definitive characteristics by which the objects and ideas in each domain were sorted. Ethnoscientists believed that the members of domains (and domains themselves) were organized following

one of several logical possibilities, including the paradigm, the taxonomy, the congerie, and the type-token. In theory, data collection in this manner was more systematic and replicable and thus, followers claimed, more scientific. Once the appropriate model was selected, the ethnographer could classify information according to native conceptual categories. Some ethnoscientists claimed that this allowed them to think like a native member of that culture.

Early attempts at this form of classification, such as Lounsbury's (1956), concentrated on kin terminologies, but the methodology was easily applicable to other areas and soon applied in a variety of research situations. Notable examples of this are Conklin's study of Hanunóo color categories reprinted in this section, Metzger and Williams' study of Tzeltal Maya categories of firewood (1966), Berlin, Breedlove, and Raven's 1974 analysis of Tzeltal Maya plant terminology, and a more contemporary example, Holland and Skinner's 1987 study of the cultural models behind American gender types.

The ethnoscientists' focus on the native point of view was not new. In the introduction to *Argonauts of the Western Pacific*, Bronislaw Malinowski had written that the final goal of ethnography was "to grasp the native's point of view, his relation to life, to realise *his* vision of his world" (1922:25, emphasis in original). The search for the native viewpoint also had strong resonances with Boasian historical particularism. Franz Boas and his students insisted on the uniqueness of each culture. They collected masses of physical data on the material and behavioral existence of the people they studied, and made the doctrine of cultural relativism an item of faith among American anthropologists. Ethnoscientists continued the Boasian insistence on culture being *sui generis* and extended the search for data from the material to the mental, something Boas had first suggested half a century previously.

Ethnoscience, like Boasian anthropology, implied an extreme cultural relativism—an approach that presented problems. Critics maintained that this approach made cross-cultural comparison impossible. If each culture had a unique way of conceptualizing the world and could only be described in its own terms, how could cultures be compared? Lévi-Strauss' structuralism was seen by some as the answer to this dilemma, but skeptics argued that it was impossible for either ethnoscientists or structuralists to get inside another's head and see how they think or what they believe. A further problem concerned individual variation within society. When ethnoscientists said they were trying to re-create cultural reality from a native's point of view, an obvious question to ask was, "Which native?" (Kaplan and Manners 1972:185). Despite these criticisms, ethnoscience was an important factor in the development of at least two other theoretical approaches—cognitive anthropology and symbolic anthropology—that both achieved major prominence in the following decades.

In the late 1960s and early 1970s the focus of ethnoscientific work shifted. Instead of simply outlining native categories of thought, anthropologists proposed that by analyzing these, one could learn how the human mind functioned. They called this approach *cognitive anthropology*. Like structuralists and most linguists, cognitive anthropologists of the 1970s believed that there were universal cognitive processes that reflect an innate structure of the human brain. Taking their cue from the ethnoscientists, they proposed that linguistic analysis was the best way to understand these structures and gain insight into human thought and culture. Cognitive anthropologists attempted to understand the abstract thinking patterns of people in various cultures, studying not only the content of cognition but also the mental processes by which ideas and symbols were related (Applebaum 1987:407).

Anthropologists have long debated the nature of their field. Some argue that anthropology should be an empirical science similar to biology or physics. Others think that anthropology is an interpretive art. Cognitive anthropologists such as Stephen A. Tyler (b. 1932) conceptualized culture as a mental model and focused on the rules by which things were categorized. They believed that anthropology should be more like philosophy or mathematics, with anthropologists searching for formal logical models.

Although cognitive anthropology never achieved the prominence hoped for by its practitioners, the anthropological study of cognition remains an active field of research that has moved far from its ethnoscientific beginnings. By the mid-1970s, advances in anthropology, psychology, and the field of artificial intelligence had made it apparent that human cognition was much more complex than the models of native classification derived from componential analysis. The earlier focus on domains and taxonomies has given way to work in schema theory and connectionism.

A fundamental part of ethnoscience and early cognitive anthropology was the idea that people classified objects in their world by checking off a mental list of essential features (apple = red, round, stem). Cognitive anthropologists today argue that people conceptualize by reference to general mental prototypes called *schemas*, or *schemata*. Cognitive psychologist George Mandler describes schema in the following manner:

> The schema that is developed as a result of prior experiences with a particular kind of event is not a carbon copy of that event; schemas are abstract representations of environmental regularities. We comprehend events in terms of the schemas they activate.
>
> Schemas are also processing mechanisms; they are active in selecting evidence, in parsing the data provided by our environment, and in providing appropriate general or specific hypotheses. Most, if not all, of the activation processes occur automatically and without awareness on the part of the perceiver-comprehender. (Mandler in D'Andrade 1995a:122)

Thus, according to schema theory, a child will recognize an object that is green, round, and has no stem as an apple because it activates an "appleness" schema, rather than because it matches an exact list of traits.

Contrary to the view assumed by Tyler in essay 25 in this volume, it is now understood that much knowledge is nonlinguistic and is not governed by the linear logic of language. Thinking, in the view of Tyler (1969) and his contemporaries, involved a process whereby one element followed another in a linear sequence much like a computer program.

However, this model does not account for the speed and efficiency with which we process information and perform tasks. To explain non-sequential thought processes in areas where thinking is non-linguistic, contemporary cognitive anthropologists and psychologists have turned to the notion of *connectionism*. Connectionism suggests that knowledge is linked, networked, and widely distributed by "processing units" that work like neurons (Strauss and Quinn 1994:286) and that we access and analyze information through these processing units. Because these units are connected and work simultaneously, we can process information much faster than any computer.

Looking at thinking and knowledge using the connectionist model has two advantages over the old ethnoscientific view. First, it acknowledges that information and knowledge do not have to be language-based, and second, it is compatible with our ability to perform commonplace but complex actions rapidly and without conscious thought.

The experience of learning to drive a car illustrates the difference between language-based rule learning and nonverbal connectionist learning based on the networking of schemas (D'Andrade 1995). Driving involves both connectionist networks and verbally based knowledge. One can be told that the brake pedal is on the left, gas pedal on the right, and that in the United States one drives on the right side of the road. This type of learning is rapid and easy to change. However, verbal instruction is very different from the physical process of driving. It may require hundreds of driving experiences to make basic driving actions such as shifting gears smooth and automatic. The automatic driving reactions that come from practice and experience are based on schema networks that are set down and interconnected through observation and trial and error, not verbal instruction. If you learned to drive as McGee did, in a car with a manual transmission, you remember the practice it took to shift smoothly, something that no amount of verbal instruction could help. It is connectionist networks based on experience that allow you to drive without conscious thought, reacting quickly and automatically to situations around you. For example, if a child runs out into the street in front of your car, you do not go through a thought process that ends with the conclusion that it would be logical in this situation to slow your vehicle. You simply and automatically apply the brakes.

A major consequence of the development of schema and connectionist theories of cognition was a shift in how cognitive anthropologists looked at the concept of culture. For the ethnoscientists of the 1950s and 1960s, culture was a mental model in the heads of native informants that could be diagrammed and replicated using the proper interviewing techniques. However, schema theorists have argued that a great deal of what goes on in the minds of human beings is certainly cultural, but not verbal, not conscious, and not able to be elicited through questioning. Thus the old definition of culture is inadequate. A solution to this problem proposed by Hutchins (1994) is to define culture as a process. In this view, culture is not simply mental content; rather, it involves the process of thinking and interacting in and with the physical world. These interactions build the schemas and create the mental connections in the brain that make cognition possible. Today, with their emphasis on brain structure and cognitive processes, cognitive anthropologists have moved away from traditional notions of cultural anthropology and edged closer to the field of evolutionary psychology.

The articles chosen for this section reflect the development of ethnoscientific and cognitive anthropological thought through the last half century. The first article, Harold C. Conklin's 1955 study, is a classic piece of ethnoscientific work in which he outlines the features by which the Hanunóo categorize colors. The second essay is the introduction from Stephen A. Tyler's 1969 edited volume *Cognitive Anthropology*. There, he describes some of the conceptual models that he proposes underlie human thought. Though he has since changed his mind, at the time he wrote this introduction, he believed he was examining the fundamental processes by which people classify information.

24. *Hanunóo Color Categories*[a]

HAROLD C. CONKLIN (b. 1926)

In the following brief analysis of a specific Philippine color system I shall attempt to show how various ethnographic field techniques may be combined profitably in the study of lexical sets relating to perceptual categorization.[1]

Recently, I completed more than a year's field research on Hanunóo folkbotany.[b] In this type of work one soon becomes acutely aware of problems connected with understanding the local system of color categorization because plant determinations so often depend on chromatic differences in the appearance of flowers or vegetative structures—both in taxonomic botany and in popular systems of classification. It is no accident that one of the most detailed accounts of native color terminology in the Malayo-Polynesian area was written by a botanist.[c] I was, therefore, greatly concerned with Hanunóo color categories during the entire period of my ethnobotanical research. Before summarizing the specific results of my analysis of the Hanunóo material, however, I should like to draw attention to several general considerations.[2]

1. Color, in a western technical sense, is not a universal concept and in many languages such as Hanunóo there is no unitary terminological equivalent. In our technical literature definitions state that color is the evaluation of the visual sense of that quality of light (reflected or transmitted by some substance) which is basically determined by its spectral composition.

The spectrum is the range of visible color in light measured in wave lengths (400 [deep red] to 700 [blue-violet] millimicrons).[d] The total color sphere—holding any set of external and surface conditions constant—includes two other dimensions, in addition to that of spectral position or hue. One is saturation or intensity (chroma), the other brightness or brilliance (value). These three perceptual dimensions are usually combined into a coordinate system as a cylindrical continuum known as the color solid. Saturation diminishes toward the central axis which forms the achromatic core of neutral grays from the white at the end of greatest brightness to black at the opposite extremity. Hue varies with circumferential position. Although technically speaking *black* is the absence of any "color," *white*, the presence of all visible color wave lengths, and neutral *grays* lack spectral distinction, these achromatic positions within the color solid are often included with spectrally-defined positions in the categories distinguished in popular color systems.

2. Under laboratory conditions, color *discrimination* is probably the same for all human populations, irrespective of language; but the manner in which different languages classify the millions[e] of "colors" which every normal individual can discriminate *differ*. Many stimuli are classified as equivalent, as extensive, cognitive—or

From *Southwestern Journal of Anthropology* (1955)

---

[1] The focus of ethnoscientific studies were usually *domains*, which are patterns of classification of objects in a society. For example, sofas, chairs, and desks fall within the domain of furniture. Most of the early ethnoscientific studies concentrated on outlining the domains of limited phenomena such as native conceptions of disease or ethnobotany. Conklin's essay is a classic example of such a study.

[2] In the two numbered paragraphs, Conklin is setting up the framework on which he is going to build his presentation of Hanunóo color categories. He first provides a scientific

definition of color, states that all humans are equally able to discriminate between colors, and postulates that color vocabulary influences the perception of color. Note here that Conklin is not saying that color vocabularies determine color perception, an implication of the Sapir-Whorf hypothesis described in the introduction to this section. Rather, he sets out to prove that color vocabularies influence color classification and thus the criteria by which people define colors. He wants to show the culturally specific criteria by which the Hanunóo classify color.

perceptual—screening takes place.[f] Requirements of specification may differ considerably from one culturally-defined situation to another. The largest collection[g] of English color names runs to over 3,000 entries, yet only eight of these occur very commonly.[h] Recent testing by Lenneberg and others[i] demonstrates a high correlation in English and in Zuñi between ready color vocabulary and *ease in recognition of colors*. Although this is only a beginning it does show how the structure of a lexical set may affect color perception. It may also be possible to determine certain nonlinguistic correlates for color terminology. Color terms are a part of the vocabulary of particular languages and only the intracultural analysis of such lexical sets and their correlates can provide the key to their understanding and range of applicability. The study of isolated and assumed translations in other languages can lead only to confusion.[j]

In the field I began to investigate Hanunóo color classification in a number of ways, including the eliciting of linguistic responses from a large number of informants to painted cards, dyed fabrics, other previously prepared materials,[k] and the recording of visual-quality attributes taken from descriptions of specific items of the natural and artificial surroundings. This resulted in the collection of a profusion of attributive words of the nonformal—and therefore in a sense "color"—type. There were at first many inconsistencies and a high degree of overlap for which the controls used did not seem to account. However, as the work with plant specimens and minute floristic differentiation progressed, I noted that in *contrastive* situations this initial confusion and incongruity of informants' responses did not usually occur. In such situations, where the "nonformal (i.e., not spatially organized) visible quality"[l] of one substance (plant part, dyed thread, or color card) was to be related to and contrasted with that of another, both of which were either at hand or well known, terminological agreement was reached with relative ease. Such a defined situation seemed to provide the frame necessary for establishing a known level of specification. Where needed, a greater degree of specification (often employing different root morphemes) could be and was made. Otherwise, such finer distinctions were ignored. This hint of terminologically significant levels led to a reexamination of all color data and the following analysis emerged.[3]

Color distinctions in Hanunóo are made at two levels of contrast. The first, higher, more general level consists of an all-inclusive, coordinate, four-way classification which lies at the core of the color system. The four categories are mutually exclusive in contrastive contexts, but may overlap slightly in absolute (i.e., spectrally, or in other measurable) terms. The second level, including several sublevels, consists of hundreds of specific color categories, many of which overlap and interdigitate. Terminologically, there is "unanimous agreement"[m] on the designations for the four Level I categories, but considerable lack of unanimity—with a few explainable exceptions—in the use of terms at Level II.[4]

---

[3] Ethnoscience is primarily based on linguistic analysis of information elicited from informants in highly structured interviews. The data is then subjected to componential analysis. In componential analysis one identifies the defining attributes of a cultural category (in Conklin's case, colors) by discovering and describing contrasts within the category (Spradley 1980:133). In the following pages, Conklin describes the criteria used by the Hanunóo to classify different colors.

[4] Conklin says that the Hanunóo classify colors at two levels. The more general level of classification, upon which there is a high level of agreement, is a set of four terms—darkness, lightness, redness, and greenness—that are mutu-

ally exclusive contrasts. At the second level, hundreds of specific color names can overlap, and there is a lack of exact agreement. We have found an analogous situation during tests in our large classes. We color-code exams, asking students to identify the color of their exam on their answer sheets. Students easily distinguish between red, green, yellow, and blue (Conklin's Level I categorization) because these terms are mutually exclusive contrasts—if something is red, it cannot be blue. But there is a great deal of disagreement about softer pastel colors. For example, students typically do not differentiate well between gold and orange. Although all agree they are different colors, where does gold end and orange begin? This situation is analogous to Conklin's Level II Hanunóo color distinctions.

The four Level I terms are:

1. (ma) biru[n] "relative darkness (of shade of color); blackness" (black)
2. (ma) lagti[?] "relative lightness (or tint of color); whiteness" (white)
3. (ma) rara[?] "relative presence of red; redness" (red)
4. (ma) latuy "relative presence of light greenness; greenness" (green).

The three-dimensional color solid is divided by this Level I categorization into four unequal parts; the largest is *mabiru,* the smallest *malatuy.* While boundaries separating these categories cannot be set in absolute terms, the focal points (differing slightly in size, themselves) within the four sections, can be limited more or less to black, white, orange-red, and leaf-green respectively. In general terms, *mabiru* includes the range usually covered in English by black, violet, indigo, blue, dark green, dark gray, and deep shades of other colors and mixtures; *malagti[?],* white and very light tints of other colors and mixtures; *marara[?],* maroon, red, orange, yellow, and mixtures in which these qualities are seen to predominate; *malatuy,* light green, and mixtures of green, yellow, and light brown. All color terms can be reduced to one of these four but none of the four is reducible. This does not mean that other color terms are synonyms, but that they designate color categories of greater specification within four recognized color realms.

The basis of this Level I classification appears to have certain correlates beyond what is usually considered the range of chromatic differentiation, and which are associated with nonlinguistic phenomena in the external environment. First, there is the opposition between light and dark, obvious in the contrasted ranges of meaning of *lagti[?]* and *biru.* Second, there is an opposition between dryness or desiccation and wetness or freshness (succulence) in visible components of the natural environment which are reflected in the terms *rara[?]* and *latuy* respectively. This distinction is of particular significance in terms of plant life. Almost all living plant types possess some fresh, succulent, and often "greenish" parts. To eat any kind of raw, uncooked food, particularly fresh fruits or vegetables, is known as *pag-laty-un* (<*latuy*). A shiny, wet, *brown*-colored section of newly-cut bamboo is *malatuy* (not *marara[?]*). Dried-out or matured plant material such as certain kinds of yellowed bamboo or hardened kernels of mature or parched corn are *marara[?].* To become desiccated, to lose all moisture, is known as *mamara[?]* (<*para•* "desiccation"; and parenthetically, I might add that there are morphological and historical reasons—aside from Hanunóo folk etymologizing—to believe that at least the final syllables of these two forms are derived from a common root). A third opposition, dividing the two already suggested, is that of deep, unfading, indelible, and hence often more desired material as against pale, weak, faded, bleached, or "colorless" substance, a distinction contrasting *mabiru* and *marara[?]* with *malagti[?]* and *malatuy.* This opposition holds for manufactured items and trade goods as well as for some natural products (e.g., red and white trade beads, red being more valuable by Hanunóo standards; indigo-dyed cotton sarongs, the most prized being those dyed most often and hence of the deepest indigo color—sometimes obscuring completely the designs formed originally by *white* warp yarns; etc.). Within each of these Level I categories, increased esthetic value attaches as the focal points mentioned above are approached. There is only one exception: the color which is most tangibly visible in their jungle surroundings, the green (even the focal point near light- or yellow-green) of the natural vegetation, is *not* valued decoratively. Green beads, for example, are "unattractive," worthless. Clothing and ornament are valued in proportion to the sharpness of contrast between, and the intensity (lack of mixture, deep quality) of "black," "red," and "white."[5]

---

[5] Ethnoscientists asserted that their method of analysis helped anthropologists see how people in different cultures conceptualize their world. Hanunóo color categories incorporate distinctions that are not made in the American definition of color. For example, a factor that influences Hanunóo color identification is the perceived moisture content of the object. Conklin says the Hanunóo also pay attention to the texture and shine of the object's surface.

Level II terminology is normally employed only when greater specification than is possible at Level I is required, or when the name of an object referred to happens also to be a "color" term (e.g., *bulawon* "gold; golden [color]"). Level II terms are of two kinds: relatively specific color words like *(ma)dapug* "gray" (, *dapug* "hearth; ashes"), *(ma)ʔarum* "violet," *(ma)dilaw* "yellow" (, *dilaw* "tumeric"); and constructions, based on such specific terms—or on Level I names—but involving further derivations, such as *mabirubiru* "somewhat *mabiru*" (more specific than *mabiru* alone only in that a color which is *not* a solid, deep, black is implied, i.e., a color classed within the *mabiru* category at Level I, but not at or near the focal point), *mabiru (gid)* "very *mabiru*" (here something close to the focal center of jet black is designated), and *madilawdilaw* "weak yellow." Much attention is paid to the texture of the surface referred to, the resulting degree and type of reflection (iridescent, sparkling, dull), and to admixture of other nonformal qualities. Frequently these noncolorimetric aspects are considered of primary importance, the more spectrally-definable qualities serving only as secondary attributes. In either case polymorphemic descriptions are common.

At Level II there is a noticeable difference in the ready color vocabulary of men as compared to women. The former excel (in the degree of specification to which they carry such classification terminologically) in the ranges of "reds" and "grays" (animals, hair, feather, etc.); the latter, in "blues" (shades of indigo-dyed fabrics). No discernible similar difference holds for the "greens" or "whites."

In short, we have seen that the apparent complexity of the Hanunóo color system can be reduced at the most generalized level to four basic terms which are associated with lightness, darkness, wetness, and dryness. This intracultural analysis demonstrates that what appears to be color "confusion" at first may result from an inadequate knowledge of the internal structure of a color system and from a failure to distinguish sharply between sensory reception on the one hand and perceptual categorization on the other.[6]

NOTES

[a] Fieldwork among the Hanunóo on Mindoro Island (1952–1954) was supported by grants from the Social Science Research Council, the Ford Foundation, and the Guggenheim Foundation.

[b] Conklin, 1954a, 1954b.

[c] Bartlett, 1929.

[d] Osgood, 1953, p. 137.

[e] Estimates range from 7,500,000 to more than 10,000,000 (Optical Society of America, 1953; Evans, 1948, p. 230).

[f] Lounsbury, 1953.

[g] Maerz and Paul, 1930.

[h] Thorndike and Lorge, 1944.

[i] Lenneberg, 1953, pp. 468–471; Lenneberg and Roberts, 1954; Brown and Lenneberg, 1954.

[j] Lenneberg, 1953, pp. 464–466; Hjelmslev, 1953, p. 33.

[k] Cf. Ray, 1952, 1953.

[l] The lack of a term similar in semantic range to our word "color" makes abstract interrogation in Hanunóo about such matters somewhat complicated. Except for leading questions (naming some visual-quality attribute as a possibility), only circumlocutions such as *kabitay tida nu pagbantayun?* "How is it to look at?" are possible. If this results in a description of spatial organization or form, the inquiry may be narrowed by the specification *bukun kay? anyu?* "not its shape (or form)."

[m] Lenneberg, 1953, p. 469.

[n] These forms occur as attributes with the prefix *ma* "exhibiting, having" as indicated above in parentheses, or as free words (abstracts).

REFERENCES

Bartlett, Harley Harris. 1929. *Color Nomenclature in Batak and Malay.* (Papers, Michigan Academy of Science, Arts, and Letters, vol. 10, pp. 1–52, Ann Arbor).

---

[6] Conklin's conclusion is a classic ethnoscientific statement: What researchers had considered "color confusion" by the Hanunóo is actually a lack of understanding of the criteria by which the Hanunóo distinguish colors. Although ethnoscientists soon realized that complete descriptions of all the domains of a society would be impossible to achieve, studies such as Conklin's, though limited in scale, provided valuable information about the beliefs of people in other societies. Ethnoscientists believed they had developed a method for the analysis of society that provided scientific results that could be replicated. One can see how much promise the first ethnoscientists saw in their method and why they called it the new ethnography.

Brown, Roger W., and Eric H. Lenneberg. 1954. A Study in Language and Cognition. (*Journal of Abnormal and Social Psychology,* vol. 49, pp. 454–462).

Conklin, Harold C. 1954a. *The Relation of Hanunóo Culture to the Plant World* (Doctoral dissertation, Yale University, New Haven).

_____.1954b. *An Ethnoecological Approach to Shifting Agriculture* (Transactions, New York Academy of Sciences, ser. II, vol. 17, pp. 133–142, New York).

Evans, Ralph M. 1948. *An Introduction to Color* (New York: Wiley).

Hjelmslev, Louis. 1953. *Prolegomena to a Theory of Language* (Indiana University Publications in Anthropology and Linguistics, Memoir 7 of the International Journal of American Linguistics [translated by Francis J. Whitfield], Bloomington).

Lenneberg, Eric H. 1953. *Cognition in Ethnolinguistics* (Language, vol. 29, pp. 463–471, Baltimore).

Lenneberg, Eric H., and John M. Roberts. 1954. *The Language of Experience, a Case Study* (Communications Program, Center of International Studies, Massachusetts Institute of Technology, Cambridge: hectographed, 45 pp. and 9 figs.).

Lounsbury, Floyd G. 1953. "Introduction" [section on Linguistics and Psychology] (in *Results of the Conference of Anthropologists and Linguists,* pp. 47–49, Memoir 8, International Journal of American Linguistics, Baltimore).

Maerz, A., and M. R. Paul. 1930. *A Dictionary of Color* (New York: McGraw-Hill).

Optical Society of America, Committee on Colorimetry. 1953. *The Science of Color* (New York: Crowell).

Osgood, Charles E. 1953. *Method and Theory in Experimental Psychology* (New York: Oxford University Press).

Ray, Verne F. 1952. *Techniques and Problems in the Study of Human Color Perception* (Southwestern Journal of Anthropology, vol. 8, pp. 251–259).

_____. 1953. *Human Color Perception and Behavioral Response* (Transactions, New York Academy of Sciences, ser. II, vol. 16, pp. 98–104, New York).

Thorndike, E. L., and I. Lorge. 1944. *The Teacher's Word Book of 30,000 Words* (Teacher's College, Columbia University, New York).

25. *Introduction to Cognitive Anthropology*

Stephen A. Tyler (b.1932)

THE OLD AND THE NEW[a]

The history of all scientific disciplines is marked by periods of intense theoretical innovation followed by relatively quiescent periods of consolidation and refinement. When the descriptive facts of science no longer fit the older explanatory models, it becomes necessary to discover new theories which will more adequately explain the accumulated data. Anthropology is currently in one of these periods of innovation.

On every hand, the various subdisciplines of anthropology are astir with new formulations challenging and supplementing established concepts and methods. The very lexicon of anthropology reflects this ferment. The journals are full of articles on *formal analysis, componential analysis, taxonomy, ethnoscience, ethnosemantics,* and *sociolinguistics,* to list but a few. Nearly all of these topics have appeared in the brief span of approximately ten years, with increasing frequency in the last three or four years.[1]

From *Cognitive Anthropology* (1969)

---

[1] The model of science that Tyler outlines here resembles that in Thomas Kuhn's *The Structure of Scientific Revolutions.* This book, which first appeared in 1962, had a substantial impact on American science and social science. Kuhn proposed that paradigms—models used to describe the natural world—shifted when scientific explanation no longer accounted accurately for data. Tyler suggests that such a paradigm shift was happening in anthropology. The "scientific" approach he takes throughout this essay evokes Kuhn's ideas.

Assessment of such new departures is always difficult. What are their historical antecedents and what do they augur for the future of anthropology? Are these genuinely viable reformulations or are they simply short-lived fads and blind alleys, detrimental in the long run to significant research?

Enough has been presented in symposia and journals for us to feel that we are witnessing a quiet revolution in anthropology—quiet because the new departures are firmly rooted in the past. Formal analysis derives in part from the work of such anthropological titans as Radcliffe-Brown, Lévi-Strauss, and Nadel. Folk taxonomies are foreshadowed in the writings of Mauss, Boas, and Evans-Pritchard.[2] That great ethnographer Malinowski would have been no stranger to recent developments in sociolinguistics. The concern for psychological validity is congruent with much of Sapir's work and, to a lesser extent, with some of Kroeber's. And, perhaps, most relevant of all is the work of Bateson.[3]

Yet, these developments constitute more than a disconnected reworking of disparate themes from out of the past. These new formulations contrast sharply with many of the aims, assumptions, goals, and methods of an earlier anthropology. Previous theoretical orientations in anthropology can in a very general way be classed into two types—those concerned primarily with change and development and those concerned with static descriptions. Thus, the evolutionists and the diffusionists concentrated on patterns of change, while the functionalists eschewed this work as mere "speculative history," and focused on the internal organization and comparison of systems, hoping thereby to discover general laws of society. Some culture and personality studies attempted to characterize whole cultures with such concepts as "national character" and "modal personality type," while other culture and personality studies utilized a comparative approach in an attempt to correlate psychological and cultural features.

These formulations were attempts to construct universal organizational types which were linked either by similar processes of change or by similarities of internal structure. In order to achieve this goal, only certain kinds of information were accepted as relevant, and concrete ethnographic data had to be elevated to more abstract forms such as index variables and typological constructs. Consequently, abstract definitions of these features were necessary, and much of the discussion in books and journals concerned the adequacy of these definitions.[4] Once a corporate lineage, for example, had been defined in a particular way, it

---

[2] Later in the essay, Tyler elaborates on formal analysis. A formal analysis is a set of logical principles. A good example would be a set of postulates and their implications applied to a proof in geometry.

[3] Tyler positions his work as a logical extension of many strands of theory in anthropology, but most of the theorists he mentions here, some of whom have essays in this volume, probably would not have supported his ideas. Tyler gives particular credit to Gregory Bateson, calling his ideas "most relevant of all." Bateson studied anthropology at Cambridge under Alfred Cort Haddon and did fieldwork in New Guinea. *Naven* (1958 [1936]), an important anthropological study of the religion and culture of the Iatmul of New Guinea, came from this field work *Naven* is crucial to Tyler because Bateson proposed a definition of culture very close to the one Tyler uses in this essay. Bateson defined culture as "a collective term for the coherent 'logical' system which may be constructed by the scientist, fitting together the various premises of the cul-

ture" (1958:218). He further specified that "we must expect to find different systems of logic, different modes of building together of premises, in different cultures" (1958:219).

[4] Ethnoscientists and cognitive anthropologists were concerned with problems of classification. Their critique of earlier anthropology was really much like Boas' attack on unilineal evolution half a century earlier. Boas had criticized evolutionists for theorizing in advance of data; the ethnoscientists criticized the methods by which anthropological data was obtained. The cornerstone of their critique was that the ethnographic method was fundamentally subjective because anthropologists applied their own classification systems to the societies they studied. Therefore, data from one ethnographic study could not be compared easily with data from another. The proliferation of categories Tyler mentions here is an artifact of that problem—evidence, to him, that anthropological theories no longer fit the data being collected.

was only a matter of time before some fieldworker returned to his desk and elatedly reported that his tribe did not conform to the received definition. One way around this problem was to construct more types and subtypes, and broader, more abstract definitions. It was generally accepted that neither the types nor the definitions actually corresponded to anything in the "real world." They were merely convenient methods of ordering the data at hand. Proliferation of types, however, was dangerous, for as the types proliferated, so did the processes linking the types and their constituents. Contrary to expectations, anthropology became more and more particularistic rather than more general and universal.

This concern with typology and definition is an index to another feature characteristic of this period in anthropology. Anthropologists were really much more concerned with discovering what anthropology was than, for example, what an Eskimo was.[5] In a sense anthropologists were studying only one small culture—the culture of anthropology.

Aside from the diffusionists, these earlier theories can be characterized as attempts to construct monolithic, unitary systems which purported to either explain cultures or their development. Such concepts as cultural core, cultural norm, structure, modal structure, pattern, and others were used to describe these systems. These ideas are symptomatic of a quest for the typical, the normal, the usual, for those definitely bounded phenomena which would systematically differentiate one culture from another. In fact the very concept of culture is but another of these labels for some arbitrarily bounded unit within which certain types of behavior, norms, artifacts, and emotions are typical (cf. Sapir 1932:515; 1934:593–595). The atypical, especially as expressed in patterns

of variation, were either simply dismissed or artificially worked into the scheme as indices of change, diffusion, survival, innovation, dysfunction, abnormality, cultural disintegration, opportunities for the exercise of social control and the like. The only important variations were variations between cultures.

In contrast to these approaches, cognitive anthropology constitutes a new theoretical orientation. It focuses on *discovering* how different people organize and use their cultures. This is not so much a search for some generalized unit of behavioral analysis as it is an attempt to understand the *organizing principles underlying* behavior. It is assumed that each people has a unique system for perceiving and organizing material phenomena—things, events, behavior, and emotions (Goodenough 1957). The object of study is not these material phenomena themselves, but the way they are organized in the minds of men. Cultures then are not material phenomena; they are cognitive organizations of material phenomena.[b] Consequently cultures are neither described by mere arbitrary lists of anatomical traits and institutions such as house type, family type, kinship type, economic type and personality type, nor are they necessarily equated with some over-all integrative pattern of these phenomena. Such descriptions may tell us something about the way an anthropologist thinks about a culture, but there is little, if any, reason to believe that they tell us anything of how the people of some culture think about their culture.[6]

In essence, cognitive anthropology seeks to answer two questions: What material phenomena are significant for the people of some culture; and, how do they organize these phenomena? Not only do cultures differ among one another in their organization of material phenomena, they

---

[5] The idea that traditional ethnology is really anthropology studying itself rather than making objective statements about others is a crucial insight of postmodern theorists. Many of them see themselves as direct descendants of the ethnoscientists. In his critique Tyler explains that in traditional ethnography, culture is a creation of the anthropologists rather than the people they are studying. By defining some aspects of behavior as *culture core* (a term from Julian Steward and the cultural ecologists) or *modal culture*

(a term from the culture and personality theorists), anthropologists inappropriately classify behavior according to their own idiosyncratic standards.

[6] Although Tyler does not use the term, ethnoscientists and cognitive anthropologists proposed an *emic* approach to anthropology. The critical distinction between emics and etics was first made by the linguist Kenneth Pike in 1954 based on the use of the words *phonetics* and *phonemics* in

differ as well in the kinds of material phenomena they organize. The people of different cultures may not recognize the same kinds of material phenomena as relevant, even though from an outsider's point of view the same material phenomena may be present in every case. For example, we distinguish between dew, fog, ice, and snow, but the Koyas of South India do not. They call all of these *mancu*. Even though they can perceive the differences among these if asked to do so, these differences are not significant to them. On the other hand, they recognize and name at least seven different kinds of bamboo, six more than I am accustomed to distinguish. Similarly, even though I know that my cousin George is the son of my mother's sister, while my cousin Paul is the son of my mother's brother, this objective difference is irrelevant to my system of classification. They are both "cousins." If I were a Koya, however, this difference would be highly important. I would call my mother's brother's son *baaTo* and my mother's sister's son *annaal*. Even though the same material phenomena are objectively present, they are subjectively perceived and organized differently by Koyas than they are by Americans.[c] Furthermore, there is no apparent over-all integrative pattern which relates the classification of bamboo to the classification of relatives. These are separate classes of phenomena with distinctive and unrelated principles of organization.

Not only may the same phenomena be organized differently from culture to culture, they may also be organized in more than one way in the same culture. There is, then, *intracultural* variation as well as *intercultural* variation. Some intracultural variations may be idiosyncratic, but more important from the anthropologist's point of view are those variations which are used by different classes of people and/or occur in different situations and contexts (cf. Goodenough 1963:257–264). For example, if we are interested in describing the way people classify colors we may discover that there are variant patterns dependent upon the sex or age of our informant as well as his general experience with colors. Thus, females in our culture can generally discriminate and name more colors than males. Or, to take another example, the classification of relatives may be partially dependent on the social statuses of the people talking about relatives, the relationship between them, and the social context in which they are conversing. A Telugu refers to his younger sister as *celli* when talking to another member of his family, but when speaking to a person outside his family group, he uses the term *cellelu*, which may mean younger sister, or mother's sister's daughter, or father's brother's daughter.[7]

---

linguistics. Phonetics is the study of the production and transmission of language sounds in general. Phonemics is the study of the ways in which sounds are organized within a language—that is, it analyzes units of sound that are psychologically distinct for speakers of a particular language. In anthropology, those studying emics strive to reproduce the meanings and understandings of the members of a culture. Those studying etics strive to analyze culture in terms meaningful to the scientific community though not necessarily to the members of the culture under observation. Cognitive anthropologists and ethnoscientists thus viewed culture as a mental construct or template. The principal tool they used to examine culture was linguistic analysis. They based their use of language on the work of Edward Sapir, a student of Boas best known for his work on Native American languages and cognition. Sapir argued that language determined those things people habitually noticed and, by extension, the manner in which they organized their worlds. An analysis of language could then be used to examine how people understood their worlds. In the later passages, Tyler points out several examples of distinctions between linguistic classification and empirical reality.

[7] Tyler's discussion of variation within cultures reflects the concern of ethnoscientists and their intellectual descendants with describing the precise nature of a culture. That culture is not a unitary phenomenon is a critical insight that distinguishes cognitive anthropology from many traditional approaches. However, it also leads to several logical problems. If culture is a mental template and can be approached through linguistic classification, then in what sense can individuals who have different systems of classification be said to be members of the same culture? In addition, can one draw valid conclusions about a culture based on data from only a few informants?

These sorts of problems could lead to two distasteful possibilities. On the one hand, since no two people have

A consequence of this interest in variation is the idea that cultures are not unitary phenomena, that is, they cannot be described by only one set of organizing principles. For each class of relevant phenomena there may be several alternative organizations. The realization or choice of one alternative to the exclusion of some other is dependent upon a variety of factors. For example, some people have more or less knowledge of some phenomena, or certain alternatives may be acceptable only in particular contexts (cf. Hymes 1964b:41). If these variants are used only in certain identified situations, or if there is a hierarchy of choice so that variants are ordered on the basis of their relative desirability, we can say that they are in complementary distribution and do not conflict with one another. In such a situation it is possible for a large number of variants to coexist. But, if the variants conflict in their organization and the situations in which they occur, there must be some means of harmonizing the contrast. This can be achieved by some change in the principles of organization or in the situation in which they occur. For example, among the Koyas, the pig is classed as an edible animal, but among neighboring Muslims the pig is classed as inedible and defiling. Suppose a Koya woman were married to a Muslim man.[8] While in her husband's home she could not act on her classification of pig as an edible by eating pork; while visiting her parents in the absence of her husband she could. So long as the two systems of classification can be realized in these isolated contexts there is no necessary conflict between

them, and both may persist. If these contexts were not in complementary distribution, some rearrangement of the two contrasting systems of classification would have to take place if the marriage were to persist.[d]

In fact, this is an argument for a different kind of unitary description which sees unity as emerging from the ordered relations between variants and contexts. Variants are not mere deviations from some assumed basic organization; with their rules of occurrence *they are the organization*. (Wallace 1961:29–41; Hymes 1964a:386–387). It must be emphasized, however, that such a unitary description can be achieved only by the anthropologist. It is highly unlikely that the members of a culture ever see their culture as *this kind of* unitary phenomenon. Each individual member may have a unique unitary model of his culture, but is not necessarily cognizant of all unique, unitary models held by other members of his culture. He will be aware of and use some, but it is only the anthropologist who completely transcends these particular models and constructs a single, unitary model.[9] This cognitive organization exists solely in the mind of the anthropologist (cf. Bateson 1958:294). Yet, to the extent that it will generate concept models used by the people of a particular culture, it is a model of their cognitive systems.[e]

The "theory" here is not so much a THEORY OF CULTURE as it is *theories of cultures*, or a theory of descriptions. The aim of such a theory is to provide answers to the questions: How would the people of some other culture expect me to behave

---

exactly the same system of classification, each person may be a culture unto himself. On the other hand, if we look for the "average" system of classification, that shared by most people, we are back once again with a modal culture, precisely what Tyler says cognitive anthropology avoids.

[8] Another problem Tyler faces is that a single person, such as the Koya woman mentioned here, might hold more than one system of classification. This presents a problem because ethnoscience, as a logical system, should have no inconsistencies. Tyler deals with this by suggesting that an individual may hold differing systems of classification as long as these are used in different situations, but a person may not hold two conflicting classification systems in the

same situation. However, it is worth asking if people *do* simultaneously hold conflicting ideas.

[9] Tyler is extremely equivocal about the ability of cognitive anthropologists to think like natives. In this passage he first states that models generated by cognitive anthropologists exist only in their own minds. This would seem to suggest that an anthropologist might learn to speak and behave as a native but not actually think like one. However, Tyler then asserts that to the extent that such a model generates conceptual models used by the people of a culture, it is a model of *their* (emphasis added) cognitive systems. This claim comes perilously close to claiming to think like the natives.

if I were a member of their culture; and what are the rules of appropriate behavior in their culture? Answers to these questions are provided by an adequate description of the rules used by people in that culture. Consequently, this description itself constitutes "theory" for that culture, for it represents the conceptual model of organization used by its members. Such a theory is validated by our ability to predict how these people would expect us to behave if we were members of the culture.

ORDER OUT OF CHAOS

In a sense, cognitive anthropology is not a new departure. Many anthropologists have expressed an interest in how the natives see their world. Yet, there is a difference of focus between the old and the new. Where earlier anthropologists sought categories of description in their native language, cognitive anthropologists seek categories of description in the language of their natives.[f] Ultimately, this is the old problem of what do we describe and how do we describe it? Obviously, we are interested in the mental codes of other peoples, but how do we infer these mental processes? Thus far, it has been assumed that the easiest entry to such processes is through language, and most of the recent studies have sought to discover codes that are mapped in language.[10] Nearly all of this work has been concerned with how other peoples "name" the "things" in their environment and how these names are organized into larger groupings. These names are thus both an index to what is significant in the environment of some other people, and a means of discovering how these people organize their perceptions of the environment. Naming is seen as one of the chief methods for imposing order on perception.[g]

In a very real sense, the anthropologist's problem is to discover how other people create order out of what appears to him to be utter chaos. Imagine, for a moment, a being from another planet equipped with all our sensory apparatus who perceives for the first time the infinite variety of sight and sound in which we live. Suppose further that he is attempting to describe this world in a scientific report for his colleagues at home. At first, everything would be chaotic. Each sound and object would seem to be unlike any other. His experience would be similar to what we feel the first time we hear a language we have never heard before. But, with infinite time and patience, let us assume that he is able to describe everything he perceives—that is, the total environment of earth. Probably he would eventually be able to organize his report around concepts acceptable to his world or devise new ones as he saw fit. Yet, would anyone of us accept his report as an accurate account of the world as we see and live in it? If he in fact describes everything, we would not. Nor would we accept his organization of the things he perceived, for they would almost certainly not fit our own system of organization. Unlike this mythical creature, we do not live in a world in which we discriminate among all the possible sensory stimuli in our environment, nor do we react to each stimulus as if it were totally new and foreign. In effect, we choose to ignore many of those perceptual differences which make each object unique. In large part, we do this by naming. By naming we classify and put objects which to us are similar into the same category, even though we can perceive differences among them (cf. Boas 1938:208–214). For example, the chair in which I sit has a nick in the left leg, yet I class it as a "straight chair" no different from others like it in the room.[11]

---

[10] At the core of ethnoscience and cognitive anthropology is an analogy between culture and language. One key source of this insight was Sapir, who has already been mentioned. Another was the work of Lévi-Strauss and, through him, that of the Prague School linguistic theorists, described in the Introduction to Structuralism, pages 320–21. Many social scientists working in the 1950s and 1960s considered linguistics to be the most advanced of all the social sciences and believed that it could provide a model for other social sciences.

[11] A key insight of cognitive anthropology, derived from Sapir and Lévi-Strauss (who in his turn was inspired by Durkheim and Mauss), was that humans order their world through classification. The world presents us with chaos. We make sense of it by noticing some phenomena and

FIGURE 1   Taxonomy of furniture

We classify because life in a world where nothing was the same would be intolerable. It is through naming and classification that the whole rich world of infinite variability shrinks to manipulable size and becomes bearable. Our methods of classification are entirely arbitrary and subjective. There is nothing in the external world which demands that certain things go together and others do not. It is our perception of similarities and differences together with a set of hierarchical cues that determine which things go together. We not only react to certain discriminable stimuli as if they were the same, we name them and organize them into groupings. Thus, for example, there are objects with a seat, a back and four legs which we label *chairs*, even though no two of these objects are exactly alike. The word *chair* then stands as a sign for a whole class of objects with a seat, a back, and four legs. This sign, too, is arbitrary—we might as well call these objects *argoboos*. Just as there is no inherent quality in an object that forces us to perceive it in

exactly one way, neither is there an intrinsic characteristic associating an object with its name. Consequently, with the passage of time, a class of objects may be renamed, but the class of objects denoted by this name does not change, or, conversely, the class of objects denoted by a name may change, but the name does not.

Thus, we subjectively group the phenomena of our perceptual world into named classes. These classes are not disparate and singular. They are organized into larger groupings.[12] To the extent that these groupings are hierarchically arranged by a process of inclusion, they form a taxonomy. To continue the example of chairs, there are other objects in our homes which are not chairs. There are sofas, tables, desks, cabinets, and the like. Each of these constitutes a separate class, some with many subclasses. For example there are end tables, dining tables, and coffee tables, but each of these is also a member of some more inclusive class—the class of things called "furniture." A portion of this taxonomy is shown in Fig. 1.

ignoring others or by grouping some things together and excluding others. Both French and American thinkers arrived at this conclusion, but it implied different things to each of them. Working in the tradition of Durkheim and the evolutionists, Lévi-Strauss and his followers understood classification as reflecting underlying universal principles of organization, perhaps rooted in human biology.

Working in the tradition of Boasian cultural relativism, ethnoscientists and cognitive anthropologists attempted no such search for universal laws or generalizations. Instead, they viewed the classification system of each culture as more or less unique, reflecting that culture's specific history. Thus, as Tyler noted earlier, cognitive anthropology produces not a theory of culture, but essentially incommensurate theories of culture. Cognitive anthropologists proposed that ultimately, universal laws of culture might be derived from their work, but like Boas, they believed that this goal required massive data collection and could only be attained in the distant future. Moreover, they presented

no logical framework in which to move from such theories of culture to one overarching theory.

[12] As noted in footnote 1, essay 24, ethnoscientific work has generally consisted of describing *domains*—categories of cultural meaning that include other, smaller categories. Tyler, as he notes later, conceives of culture as consisting of a collection of domains. One has described a culture completely when one has outlined all of its domains.

A domain must be organized by some logical principle. Here and in later passages, Tyler provides three different examples of this: taxonomy, paradigm, and tree. These are the most common principles of data organization used by ethnoscientists, but elsewhere Tyler lists more including key, partonomy, congeries, type-token, and several others (Tyler 1978:255).

Note that when Tyler uses these terms (particularly *taxonomy* and *paradigm*), he is assigning new meanings to them that are specific to cognitive anthropology.

FIGURE 2   Branching diagram

Figure 1 illustrates two processes characteristic of taxonomies: (1) items at the same level contrast with one another; (2) items at different levels are related by inclusion. At the bottom level are the more highly discriminated classes, at the top is the most inclusive class. Thus, end tables are kinds of tables as tables are kinds of furniture; end tables are not the same as dining tables just as tables are not the same as chairs. These relationships could also be represented in a branching diagram as in Fig. 2.

This particular taxonomy constitutes one *semantic domain* in our culture. A semantic domain consists of a class of objects all of which share at least one feature in common which differentiates them from other semantic domains. Chairs, sofas, desks, end tables, and dining tables have in common the designation *furniture*.

Note that Fig. 2 tells us nothing of the things which distinguish a chair from a table. It tells us only that they are different. Suppose you had to tell someone how you know that one object is a chair and the other is a table. In the process of doing this, you might describe certain underlying features, some of which both chairs and tables share and some of which they do not. For example, you might say a chair has four legs, a seat, and a back, but a table has four legs and a top. Chairs would thus differ from tables by the presence of two features—a seat and a back, and the absence of one feature—a top. These underlying features are *components* or *features* of meaning.

They are some of the dimensions of meaning underlying the general domain of *furniture*. That these are not the only dimensions is apparent in the contrasts between desk and table. Both pieces of furniture have four legs and a top. Using only the two features you have isolated, it is not possible to say how a table differs from a desk. Should you wish to show how each of these items differs from the other you would have to discover other features of meaning.[13]

Semantic features, like labels, are also organized. A part of the taxonomy of "animals" in American English consists of the following lexemes: cow, bull, heifer, calf, steer, mare, stallion, filly, foal, colt, gelding, sow, boar, gilt, barrow, shoat, piglet, ewe, ram, wether, lamb, livestock, cattle, swine, horse, sheep. This taxonomy is arranged in Table 1.

On even casual examination the items occurring in the lowest level of Table 1 seem to be related in some way. Closer inspection reveals that similar distinctions are made under each major category of livestock. The contrast between cow and bull, for example, is the same as the contrast between boar and sow; ram and ewe; stallion and mare. We can readily identify this contrast as one of sex or gender, male versus female. Similarly, there is an identical contrast between bull and steer; ram and wether; stallion and gelding; boar and barrow. Again, we would identify this as a contrast between male animals versus neutered animals. In addition to this sex contrast there is a

---

[13] Once a domain has been identified, ethnoscientists and cognitive anthropologists attempted to perform componential analyses, which James P. Spradley (1933–1982) defined as "the systematic search for the attributes (components of meaning) associated with cultural categories" (1980:130). To do componential analysis, ethnoscientists search for how items in a domain systematically differ from one another. They construct a series of categories on which elements of the domain contrast. Tyler uses the example of horse and swine below. The contrasting categories are related to the sex of the animal. He calls the diagrams showing these contrasts *paradigms*.

TABLE 1   Taxonomy of "Livestock"

	ANIMAL		
	LIVESTOCK		
cattle	horse	sheep	swine
cow	mare	ewe	sow
bull	stallion	ram	boar
steer	gelding	wether	barrow
heifer	filly	lamb	gilt
calf	colt		shoat
	foal		piglet

further contrast between mature and immature animals. A calf is an immature cow or bull and a heifer is an "adolescent" cow. All the lexemes in the lowest level of Table 1 reflect the two semantic features of sex and maturity. Each of these has three values: sex (male, female, neuter); maturity (adult, adolescent, child). Note, however, that horse and pig have an additional feature of maturity denoting "newborn" or "baby" (piglet and foal).

Using symbols: ♂—male; ♀—female; ∅—neuter; M^{-1} adult; M^{-2} adolescent; M^{-3} child; M^{-4} baby; H—horse; P—swine; C—cattle; S—sheep; the distribution of features for each label can be stated in formulae as follows:

stallion	$H \, ♂ \, M^{-1}$	boar	$P \, ♂ \, M^{-1}$
mare	$H \, ♀ \, M^{-1}$	sow	$P \, ♀ \, M^{-1}$
gelding	$H \, ∅ \, M^{-1}M^{-2}$	barrow	$P \, ∅ \, M^{-1}M^{-2}$
filly	$H \, ♀ \, M^{-2}$	gilt	$P \, ♀ \, M^{-2}$
colt	$H \, ♂♀ \, M^{-3}$	shoat	$P \, ♂♀ \, M^{-3}$
foal	$H \, ♂♀ \, M^{-4}$	piglet	$P \, ♂♀ \, M^{-4}$

The first formula reads: a stallion is a horse, male, adult, or more appropriately, a stallion is an adult male horse. Such formulae are simply expressions of the distribution of features for each separate label. A box figure shows how these features distribute across the whole set of labels.

Reading from the diagram, a stallion is an adult male horse and a mare is an adult female horse. The features "adult" and "male" *intersect* at the space containing the label "stallion," while the features "adult" and "female" intersect at the space containing the label "mare." Since this diagram has two major features (maturity and sex) which cut across (intersect) one another, it is a *paradigm*. Features are paradigmatically arranged when they are: (1) multiple; (2) intersect.[h]

Paradigms and taxonomies are different kinds of semantic arrangements. In contrast to a paradigm, a taxonomy orders its labels by contrast and inclusion. A taxonomy typically asserts that items in lower levels are *kinds* of items in higher levels. A horse, for example, is a *kind* of livestock. A paradigm makes no such assertion. In Fig. 3 for example, a shoat is not necessarily a kind of boar.[14]

In addition to taxonomies and paradigms semantic features may be arranged on a branching diagram called a *tree*.[15] Features in a tree are ordered by sequential contrast of only one feature at a time. Trees are thus based on successive choices between only two alternatives. Such a semantic arrangement is most frequently encountered in zoological or botanical texts. Figure 4 is a simplified example of a tree.

A reading of Fig. 4 would be: Are the flowers spurred? If yes, are the flowers regular? If they are regular, then this is a delphinium. Unlike a paradigm, the features of a tree do not intersect, and unlike a taxonomy items at lower levels are not included in higher levels. Consequently, paradigms, taxonomies and trees are fundamentally different kinds of semantic arrangements. Each semantic domain of a culture may be ordered by one or more of these arrangements.

A culture consists of many semantic domains organized around numerous features of meaning, and no two cultures share the same set of semantic domains or features of meaning, nor do they

---

[14] Although paradigms and taxonomies are different, they are not mutually exclusive. The same lexical elements may be arranged into both paradigms and taxonomies.

[15] Binary distinctions underlie many forms of organization but are most evident in trees. This emphasis on dual-

ity and opposition reflects the influence of Prague School linguistics, perhaps largely as filtered by Lévi-Strauss (see essay 22), a powerful influence on ethnoscientists.

		Sex		
		male ♂	female ♀	neuter ∅
Maturity	adult M⁻¹	stallion boar	mare sow	gelding barrow
	adolescent M⁻²		filly gilt	
	child M⁻³	colt shoat		
	baby M⁻⁴	foal piglet		

FIGURE 3 Paradigm of features for "horse" and "swine." For cattle and sheep the contrast between baby and child would be omitted. Sheep also omits the adolescent distinction. There is however an archaic form for newborn sheep viz. "Yearling."

share the same methods of organizing these features. The problem for the anthropologist is to discover these semantic domains and their features, for an anthropologist in the field is much like our interplanetary visitor. There is no familiar order to the way these strange people organize their world. But, unlike our visitor, the anthropologist must avoid imposing his own semantic categories on what he perceives. He must attempt to discover the semantic world in which these people live. There are, then, two ways of bringing order out of apparent chaos—*impose* a preexisting order on it, or *discover* the order underlying it.[i] Nearly all of earlier anthropology was characterized by the first method. By contrast, cognitive anthropology seeks to develop methods which can be used for discovering and describing these principles of organization.[16]

Since such semantic systems are implicit in our use of language, they constitute one of the most significant features of human communication. Yet, what can be communicated and how it is communicated is not solely determined by this kind of semantic feature. Other semantic features deriving from the context of communication are equally important. Context includes the manner of communication (for example, verbal and written), the social setting, and the linguistic repertories of speaker and hearer. Contextual semantic features and their mutual interdependence are as much a part of the cognitive system as taxonomies and semantic domains.

There still remains the question of how we discover features in cultures other than our own. If you will attempt to complete the statement of semantic features for the taxonomy of furniture,

[16] The ethnoscientists' key critique of earlier anthropology was that it artificially imposed order on the data. Interestingly, at the same time that ethnoscience was emerging, George Peter Murdock was developing the Human Relations Area Files (HRAF). Begun in 1937, the HRAF project was (and continues to be) a massive effort to provide a universal index to anthropological literature. Using the HRAF, a researcher may look up a single topic, say friendship, and find information indexed as friendship in ethnographies on many different societies. Murdock's statistical comparative approach was favored by materialists such as Marvin Harris and modern evolutionists such as Morton Fried.

Ethnoscientists and cognitive anthropologists were very critical of Murdock's approach on two levels: First, it was not clear that a classification such as friendship has the same meaning from culture to culture. Second, it was not clear that the various people who indexed the work had the same ideas about the meaning of friendship. Thus, critics claimed that the index compared apples with oranges, which meant that reliable generalizations could not be drawn.

FIGURE 4   A tree arrangement. Plus (+) indicates presence of the feature, minus (−) its absence. Thus, if a flower is not spurred, has no petals, and no involucre, it is a clematis.

you will see that the discovery of these features is difficult enough in your native language. It is even more difficult in a strange language. As a consequence, new fieldwork techniques and methods have had to be devised. Most important among these are techniques of *controlled eliciting* and methods of *formal analysis.*[17]

Controlled eliciting utilizes sentence frames derived from the language of the people being studied. The aim of such eliciting is to enable the ethnographer to behave linguistically in ways appropriate to the culture he is studying. This involves the use of linguistically correct questions which relate concepts meaningful in that cul-

ture. Suppose you are a foreigner attempting to learn something about American culture. On seeing an object for which you do not know an English term, one possible sequence of related questions and responses might be:

Q: What is this?

A: This is a sow.

Q: Is that a sow, too?

A: No, that's a boar.

Q. Is a boar a kind of sow?

A: No, a boar is a kind of livestock.

Q: Is a sow a kind of livestock?

A: Yes.

Q: How many kinds of livestock are there?

A: There are pigs, horses, mules, sheep, goats, and others.

This sequence indicates that sows and boars are conceptually linked and that there are numerous other things grouped with them in the taxonomy of livestock. Note that decisions concerning the inclusion of items within this taxonomy are made by the informant, not by the investigator. Contrast this procedure with a familiar questionnaire technique derived from handbooks on social science methodology. Is the cow very like; somewhat like; only a little like; not at all like a god (check one). Aside from the spurious scaling, this question would be meaningful only in societies of English speakers in which there were: (a) cows, (b) gods, (c) some evidence that gods and cows were conceptually linked, or

---

[17] Ethnoscientists and cognitive anthropologists criticized early anthropology in general and Murdock in particular for their lack of systematic methods of data collection.

It is certainly true that, until recently, graduate-level texts or courses that dealt with field methods were few and far between. Michael Agar (1980) tells the story of a student of Kroeber who went to ask the grand old man for advice on the ways to do fieldwork. "After several passes by the open door, she entered and nervously cleared her throat. Kroeber was typing (naturally) and did not look up for a minute or so. When he did, the student . . . asked for advice. 'Well,' said Kroeber, returning to his typing, 'I suggest that you buy a notebook and a pencil.'"

The key point made by cognitive anthropologists and ethnoscientists was that since ethnographers did not use consistent data collection techniques, and since they used categories from their own cultures that they defined imprecisely, they could neither accurately reflect native understandings of the world nor make useful generalizations across cultures. They claimed that Murdock's HRAF was meaningless because it implied the existence of "natural" domains, that is, domains that have the same boundaries in every culture. Ethnoscientists and cognitive anthropologists believed that such things were theoretically possible but not likely to exist. Their position mirrors Boas' ideas on natural laws pertaining to cultures.

(d) sociologists. In this technique, the investigator has already made all the decisions about conceptual relevance. The informant's responses can only be replications in one way or another of the investigator's judgments about conceptual relevance. In a sense, such a method merely tells you what you already know. Controlled eliciting, on the other hand, is designed to provide the ethnographer with not only the answers, but also to assist him in discovering the relevant questions. It clearly derives from the fact that the questioning process is itself the dominant factor in scientific investigation (Collingwood 1929:29–43). Where the procedures and results of controlled eliciting are contained in the report, two things are achieved: (1) there is an explicit record of how the data were gathered; (2) a public record of the results is available.

Formal analysis is simply one method of stating the results of such controlled eliciting. It differs from other methods in its emphasis on internal consistency, completeness, and form. A particular set of data relating to some semantic domain must be explained by the relationship between units comprising that domain—not by determinants outside it.[18] The problem of external determinants is delayed until internal determinants are analyzed. For example, the question of whether I call my mother's sister's son "cousin" determined until I know the system of relations between cousin, brother, and all the other kin terms in the English system. A formal analysis is complete when the relations among all the units comprising a semantic domain are described.

THE NEW ORDER

The aims and methods of cognitive anthropology have important implications for cultural anthropology. They entail a rethinking of the culture concept, the comparative method, and of ethnography.

In this discussion culture has been identified with cognition. This must strike some cultural anthropologists as a truncated version of the culture concept, for it neglects many of their traditional interests. They might well ask, What about process? What about behavior? What about motivation? Implicit in these questions is an assumption that in addition to cognitive systems a theory of culture must explain cultures as systems emerging from patterned frequencies of observed behavior and processes of development and change (cf. Goodenough 1964). *As a general statement of anthropological goals, these are relevant considerations, but they are not relevant to a theory of culture.* There is no necessity to assume that the cognitive order is either systematically a derivative of or a predictor of substantive actions.[19] Just as the grammar of a language provides no information on what all individual speakers will say on any given occasion, so too a cognitive description of a culture does not pretend to predict the actual behavior of any individual. The formal analysis of culture, like a grammar, is concerned only with what is expected and appropriate. And just as an adequate grammar is neither contingent upon prior assumptions concerning developmental processes nor necessarily explains them, a grammar of culture

---

[18] In many ways, cognitive anthropology and ethnoscience represent an extreme logical end of Boasian thinking. In this paragraph, for example, notice the restatement of Boasian cultural relativism in ethnoscientific terms: Semantic domains may only be explained with reference to themselves. Like Boasian culture, they are *sui generis*.

[19] The theoretical battles of the 1950s and 1960s crystallized a profound division in American anthropology—that between materialist and idealist thinkers. This division had

been present in anthropology from the beginning but is probably best seen in this era. Tyler and the cognitive and ethnoscientific anthropologists, who represent one extreme, conceive of culture in purely mentalistic terms. It is created *sui generis* and has no predictable effect on the "real world." The other pole is represented by Harris and the functional materialists and ecologists, who view culture as adaptive. They were concerned with observable behavior and generally less interested in the underlying thoughts of the actors.

need make no assumptions about nor attempt to explain these processes. So construed, neither prediction of actual events nor specification of developmental process is a necessary component of a theory of culture.[j] To paraphrase Collingwood (1956:217), cultural anthropology is not a description of events or an account of change. The cultural anthropologist is only concerned with those events which are expressions of underlying thoughts. His aim is to penetrate beyond mere material representation to the logical nexus of underlying concepts.

Culture, conceived as the totality of human behavior, ideas, history, institutions and artifacts has never been particularly useful as a meaningful method of explaining ethnographic facts.[20] Such a conception merely asserts that culture is equivalent to the whole of human knowledge. As a device which purports to explain all of man's learned behavior, motivations, prehistoric record, ecological adaptations, biological limitations, and evolution it attempts too much. What we need is a more limited notion of culture which stresses *theories of culture.* Rather than attempt to develop a general THEORY OF CULTURE, the best we can hope for at present is particular theories of cultures. These theories will constitute complete, accurate descriptions of particular cognitive systems. Only when such particular descriptions are expressed in a single metalanguage with known logical properties will we have arrived at a general theory of culture. Such a general theory will be equivalent to the language in which we describe cultures (Kay 1965:112). In effect we already have a pseudometalanguage. It is for this reason that nearly all ethnographies have similar chapter headings. The problem with this metalanguage is

that is assumes universality without prior demonstration.[21] Its universality inheres in the language of description and not necessarily in the object being described.[k]

At issue here are two contrasting views of cultural anthropology. The central issue is, is cultural anthropology a *natural* or *formal* science? Traditional cultural anthropology is based on the assumption that its data are discrete material phenomena which can be analyzed like the material phenomena of any other natural science. Cognitive anthropology is based on the assumption that its data are mental phenomena which can be analyzed by formal methods similar to those of mathematics and logic.[l] Each particular culture consists of a set of logical principles which order relevant material phenomena. To the cognitive anthropologist these logical principles rather than the material phenomena are the object of investigation. For the cognitive anthropologist cultural anthropology is a formal science. It seems likely that the logical operations underlying principles of ordering are finite and universal, but capable of generating an infinite number of possible specific orderings (cf. Lévi-Strauss 1966:268). In this limited sense, cognitive anthropology constitutes a return to Bastian's search for the "psychic unity of mankind."[22]

The implications for the comparative method follow directly from the above. The central issue in comparative analysis is, What is the unit of comparison? There have been many attempts to specifically delimit the unit of comparison. Yet most so-called cross-cultural comparisons have really been nothing more than cross-tribal or cross-community comparisons. Obviously, if a culture is the unit of comparison, then we must

---

[20] Tyler here takes aim at E. B. Tylor's classic definition of culture (see essay 2). What he proposes is, in fact, similar to what Boas proposed; that is, detailed descriptions of individual cultures rather than any single overarching analysis of culture. The difference is that Boas did not propose a specific methodology, and Tyler does. In theory, this means that Tyler's theories of culture will be expressed in a consistent manner that might allow a general theory to emerge.

[21] The metalanguage Tyler refers to here is the language that would describe the structure of the domains outlined

by cognitive anthropology and ethnoscience. He claims that current metalinguistic categories, such as kinship, religion, political system, and so on, are inadequate because it has not been shown that they describe cross-culturally consistent domains. He calls these *pseudometalanguage.*

[22] Tyler here describes anthropology as a formal science, not only like math and logic but also like structural linguistics. He opens the possibility that some of the logical principles that will be discovered by cognitive anthropology are universals.

compare whole systems which are bounded in space and time or demonstrate that the parts of systems we are comparing are justifiably isolable (cf. Boas 1940:275). Since most ethnographies are not sufficiently complete for either of these possibilities, the whole comparative approach based on substantive variables must be abandoned if our aim is indeed cultural comparison.[23] Those who insist that no fact has meaning except by comparison are right, but the implication that comparison can occur only between similar facts from different systems does not follow. It is much more pertinent to compare similar, but not identical facts within the same system. This is not so much a total abandonment of the comparative method; it is a matter of priorities. Comparisons between systems can only be useful if the facts compared are truly comparable, and we cannot know what facts are comparable until the facts themselves are adequately described. When this is achieved, the units of comparison will be formal features rather than substantive variables.

PROBLEMS AND PROSPECTS

[*Tyler concludes his essay with a 2,000-word discussion of the problems and prospects of his approach. He discusses research problems in the following areas: arrangements, perception and conception, discourse analysis, propositional analysis, metamessages, historical linguistics, and semantic ontogenesis. Tyler views the problems he has identified as indicative of the vitality of cognitive anthropology rather than as fatal flaws in its theory. He closes with the following passage.*]

These comments are intended as speculations on the possible areas of future development in cognitive anthropology. They do not pretend to be exhaustive nor even representative. Nonetheless, they do indicate that cognitive anthropology has moved into a secondary stage of development. We have a few tentative answers, some new questions, and a host of old questions still unanswered. Fresh ground has been broken and new areas occupied, but still more remote territories have opened up for further research.

Explicit here is a view of culture derived from a kind of ethnography in which the methods of description are public and replicable, and the results predictive of expectations of appropriate behavior.[24] Implicit is the cognitive reorganization of our categories of description and analysis. Cognitive anthropology entails an ethnographic technique which describes cultures from the inside out rather than from the outside in. Categories of description are initially derived from relevant features in a culture rather than from the lexicon of anthropology.

Cognitive reorganization is a familiar process in the history of anthropology—in fact of any scientific discipline. The history of science is but the record of constant reexamination of assumptions, methods, and data. Such new developments in science do not take place in a vacuum. Innovations in one branch of science are complemented by convergent developments in other branches.[25]

---

[23] In this passage, Tyler returns to his critique of traditional ethnography. He touches on a topic that became crucial to anthropologists in the late 1980s—defining the boundaries of cultural groups or subgroups. Tyler suggests that traditional ethnography has not done this in a consistent way that would make comparison possible. Some anthropologists in the 1980s suggested that such definition was by nature an impossible task.

[24] Tyler emphasizes that, in his view, anthropology is a scientific and not an interpretive discipline (though a formal and not a natural science). Its goal is to produce logical, consistent, and public descriptions of culture that will withstand what Tyler considers rigorous testing.

[25] In closing, Tyler returns once again to Kuhn's idea of paradigm shift. He views cognitive anthropology and ethnoscience as new paradigms that will revolutionize anthropology. This assessment of the place of cognitive anthropology was overoptimistic, however. It certainly did not have a revolutionary effect that rendered competing paradigms obsolete. In fact, Tyler later abandoned this approach in favor of postmodernism. Nevertheless, ethnoscience and cognitive anthropology did have powerful impacts on anthropology in the 1960s and 1970s and were crucial to the development of postmodernist thinking in the 1980s.

The psychologist's renewed interest in cognition, the linguist's rediscovery of semantics, the biologist's recent emphasis on taxonomy and species specific behavior, and the sociologist's concern with the presentation of the self all reflect a set of recent developments complementary to one another and to those in anthropology. To be sure, among these disciplines there are differences in emphasis and method, yet each shares with the other a common orientation—the discovery of the organizing principles used by individuals, cultures, and species in manipulating and adapting to their particular life-space.

ACKNOWLEDGEMENT

Stephen A. Tyler, from "Introduction" from *Cognitive Anthropology*, 1st ed., pp. 1–15, 19–23. © 1969 Wadsworth, a part of Cengage Learning, Inc. Reproduced by permission. www.cengage.com/permissions

NOTES

[a] I wish to thank the following people who commented on previous versions of this paper: Brent Berlin, Mary Black, Charles Frake, John Gumperz, Dell Hymes, Paul Kay, Floyd Lounsbury, Ronald Rohner, George and Louise Spindler. I hope it is evident that the views in this chapter are those of the editor and do not necessarily represent a consensus of opinion among the above nor among those whose papers comprise subsequent chapters.

[b] In this, and in much of what follows, there is a pronounced neo-Kantian flavor.

[c] For an instance of a similar distinction between "objective environment" and "perceived life-space," see von Uexküll (1957).

[d] The processes involved in this example are related to theories of cognitive dissonance (cf. Festinger 1957).

[e] The line of argument here derives mainly from Russell (1929:92–98), but see also Bateson (1958:294) and Sapir (1932:515–519).

[f] The most notable exception to this statement is Boas.

[g] It is probably not true that all named things are significant, just as it is not the case that all significant things are named. Yet, as a point of departure, named categories are of primary importance.

[h] Note the two empty spaces in Fig. 3. These indicate that this is not a perfect paradigm. The empty spaces are the result of incomplete combination of semantic components. The combinations ? M^{22}; B M^{23}; B M^{24} do not occur. In a perfect paradigm all possible combinations would be realized. Perfect paradigms occur less frequently than imperfect paradigms. It should also be noted that in some contexts the lexemes "boar" and "stallion" denote not only ? M^{21} but ? M^{21} M^{22}. For "horse" the lexeme "yearling" may sometimes denote ? M^{22}; / M^{22}; B M^{22}. Historically it is interesting to note that all the lexemes denoting "newborn" (?/M^{24}) except piglet are derived from verbs denoting "to give birth to." A cow "calves," a mare "foals," a ewe "lambs," or "yeans," but a sow "farrows." As might be expected the archaic term for a newborn pig is "farrow." The lexeme piglet is recent. Also relevant is the fact that the "wild animal" category denoted by the lexeme "deer" has, except for the neuter category, the same semantic features as the category denoted by cattle. Formerly deer denoted "animal." Finally the features male, female, neuter correspond to the generalized Indo-European classification of nouns as masculine, feminine, neuter. [This note is missing a variety of symbols, JM]

[i] This distinction between a priori and a posteriori models is difficult to maintain, for it impinges directly on the philosophical problem of "other minds." If the mind imposes its own order on the disorderly happenings of the universe, then the investigator of necessity imposes his own logical constructs on the world he believes he is exploring. From this point of view there is no evidence for a belief in the existence of other minds except by analogy. Yet, granted the existence of other minds it is possible to assume that since the logical constructs of an informant and of an investigator are both products of a mind, these constructs are knowable insofar as they are communicable. Hence, the cognitive anthropologist's emphasis on language as both a method of discovery and an object of investigation (cf. Russell 1929:99–103).

[j] This is not to imply that such a theory is incompatible with the study of change and development. The point is that a theory of description constitutes a different order of theory than that required for processes of change (for a discussion of this point, see Bateson 1958:296–300). A theory of change emphasizing cognitive organization would probably demonstrate that most anthropological data on change relate not to cultural change, but merely to epiphenomenal fluctuations.

[k] This is misleading. Scientific laws are of necessity statements of universals in the language of description. All talk of "objects" and an hypothesized relation between "objects" and the language of description is symptomatic of a pernicious kind of dualism. The point is that our current language of description is inadequate either for the description of particular cultures or the development of universals simply because its assumptions are implicit and its operations (when specified) are contradictory. The continuing argument

in descent "theory" is a classic example of the inadequacy of our current "metalanguage." The misleading statement reflects my own vacillation between an "intuitionist" (conceptualist) and "logicist" (realist) point of view (cf. Quine 1952). In general, this chapter is intuitionist with occasional logicist lapses. The lapses create problems like the one referred to above. My assertion that the description of a culture is really a description of the anthropologist's cognitive ordering is pure intuitionism which does not square directly with the Lévi-Straussian quest for a universal pan-human logic expressed in other sections. In a sense, the psychological reality problem is a confrontation between intuitionism and realism or perhaps formalism (nominalism). My belief in the relevance of relevance as an aspect of cognitive anthropology is probably creeping realism.

[1] Leach (1961:6–21) makes a similar point, but with different emphasis. For two discussions of the distinction between formal and factual or natural sciences, see Carnap (1953) and Quine (1960:270–276). The distinction may be somewhat overdrawn, but this should not obscure the fact that cultural anthropology has traditionally emulated a model of scientific method derived from a rather naive nineteenth century scientific materialism. Harris's (1962) quest for elementary units of cultural "matter" is a recent example of this attitude.

REFERENCES

Bateson, Gregory. 1958. *Naven,* 2d ed. Stanford: Stanford University Press.

Boas, Franz. 1938. *The Mind of Primitive Man.* London: Macmillan.

____. 1940. *Race, Language and Culture.* New York: Macmillan.

Carnap, Rudolf. 1953. Formal and factual science. In H. Feigl and M. Brodbeck, eds., *Readings in the philosophy of science.* New York: Appleton.

Collingwood, R. G. 1929. *An Autobiography.* New York: Oxford University Press.

____. 1956. *The Idea of History.* New York: Oxford University Press.

Festinger, Leon. 1957. *A Theory of Cognitive Dissonance.* New York: Harper and Row.

Goodenough, Ward H. 1957. Cultural anthropology and linguistics. In Paul Garvin, ed., Report of the seventh annual round table meeting on linguistics and language study. Georgetown University Monograph Series on Language and Linguistics No. 9.

____. 1963. *Cooperation in Change.* New York: Russell Sage.

____. 1964. Introduction. In W. H. Goodenough, ed., *Explorations in Cultural Anthropology.* New York: McGraw-Hill.

Harris, Marvin. 1964. *The Nature of Cultural Things.* New York: Random House.

Harris, Zellig. 1952. Discourse analysis. *Language* 28:1–30.

Hymes, Dell, ed. 1964a. *Language in Culture and Society.* New York: Harper and Row.

____. 1964b. Directions in (ethno-) linguistic theory. *American Anthropologist* 66 Pt. 2, No. 3:656.

Kay, Paul. 1965. Does anthropology need a metalanguage? Paper presented at the Southwestern Anthropological Association Annual Meeting, 1965.

Leach, E. R. 1961. *Rethinking Anthropology.* London School of Economics Monographs on Social Anthropology No. 22. London: University of London Press.

Lévi-Strauss, Claude. 1966. *The Savage Mind.* Chicago: University of Chicago Press.

Quine, Willard Van Orman. 1960. *Word and Object.* New York: Wiley.

____. 1952. On what there is. In L. Linsky, ed., *Semantics and the Philosophy of Language.* Urbana: University of Illinois Press.

Russell, Bertrand. 1929. *Our Knowledge of the External World.* New York: Norton.

Sapir, Edward. 1932. Cultural anthropology and psychiatry. In D. G. Mandelbaum, ed., *Selected Writings of Edward Sapir.* Berkeley: University of California Press.

____. 1934. The emergence of the concept of personality in a study of cultures. In D. G. Mandelbaum, ed., *Selected Writings of Edward Sapir.* Berkeley: University of California Press.

Uexküll, Jakob von. 1957. A stroll through the world of animals and men: A picture book of invisible worlds. In C. H. Schiller and K. S. Lashley, eds., *Instinctive Behavior: The Development of a Modern Concept.* New York: International Universities.

Wallace, A. F. C. 1961. *Culture and Personality.* New York: Random House.

Woodger, J. H. 1952. *Biology and Language: An Introduction to the Methodology of the Biological Sciences Including Medicine.* Cambridge: University Press.

Part Four

THE LATE TWENTIETH CENTURY AND BEYOND

Sociobiology, Evolutionary Psychology, and Behavioral Ecology

Unlike most other twentieth-century anthropological perspectives, sociobiology, evolutionary psychology, and behavioral ecology seek to explain human behavior in terms of Darwinian evolutionary theory. (In the remainder of this introductory essay, we will use the term *sociobiology* to stand for all three of these fields, except as needed to differentiate viewpoints.) Just as Charles Darwin proposed the theory of natural selection to account for the biological evolution of physical characteristics, sociobiologists propose that differential reproductive success shapes the evolution of social behavior of all organisms, including humans. The basis of Darwinian evolution is that individuals with those variations best adapted to their environment reproduce more than those lacking such variations. As a result, each subsequent generation will include a higher percentage of such individuals. Sociobiologists argue that because humans are biological organisms, they are subject to the same evolutionary laws as other life forms. Given that there is a genetic component to behavior, they say, those behavior patterns that improve an organism's adaptation to its environment will be selected for and reproduced in future generations.

Cultural analogies to evolution are not new in anthropology. As outlined in the first section of this text, many nineteenth-century thinkers believed that the goal of anthropology was to describe and illustrate how culture evolved from primitive to civilized and simple to complex. New work in sociobiology differs from this in fundamental ways. Most important, nineteenth-century thinkers viewed evolution as a metaphor or analogy. Spencer, for example, focused on what he termed the *organic analogy*. For these scholars, the history of society was *like* the evolution of biological organisms. Theirs was an argument by comparison, a literary argument. Further, to the extent that they focused at all on the mechanisms of evolution, they understood these in Lamarckian terms; that is, they believed that cultural innovations were developed in one generation and passed on to the next.

Nineteenth-century evolutionists believed that societies evolved in the direction of increased size, complexity, and interdependence. This process was driven by competition that led to increases in technology and power that could be passed culturally to the next generation. Their vision of evolution had little to do with Darwin's notion of natural selection through reproductive success. In fact, they feared the reproductive success of some segments of society (the poor, the infirm, various minority groups), viewing it as a force that could undermine the evolutionary progress of society. Modern-day sociobiologists, to the contrary, are very specifically concerned with Darwinian fitness. They understand human behavior to be evolving under the pressure of reproductive success: Natural selection favors those behaviors that lead to greater numbers of offspring. This belief points to another important distinction between contemporary sociobiologists and nineteenth-century evolutionists. The work of nineteenth-century scholars was strongly teleological. They believed that the process of evolution created increasingly perfect societies, whereas sociobiologists see no such teleology. The fact that a behavior leads to reproductive success does not, in itself, make that behavior morally superior or inferior to other behaviors. Further, most sociobiologists argue that the evolution of human behavioral characteristics must have happened when humans lived in foraging societies. Social organization above the band level has only existed for a few thousand years, and this is probably not enough time for biological evolution to occur. Consequently, many social problems we experience happen because we live in the twenty-first century with behaviors adapted to ancient foraging lifestyles. Whether this speculation is true or not remains an open question.

Sociobiology grew out of the work of evolutionary biologists, geneticists, ethologists, and anthropologists studying primate behavior. The animal behavior specialists Konrad Lorenz, Karl Von Frisch (1906–1982), and Nikolas Tinbergen (1907–1988) were particularly influential. These three published widely in the 1950s and 1960s and shared a Nobel Prize in 1973. Although some anthropologists and biologists, including Lionel Tiger and Robin Fox, had been publishing on sociobiological themes since the 1960s, the publications that brought sociobiology to the critical attention of anthropologists and the general public were two books published in 1975 and 1976—Harvard biologist E. O. Wilson's (b. 1929) *Sociobiology: The New Synthesis* and *The Selfish Gene* by Richard Dawkins (b. 1941). These authors adopted an approach that saw social behavior as controlled, in principle, by particular genes. In Wilson and Dawkin's view, evolutionary selection for behavior occurred at this level because reproductive success amounted to increasing the frequency of certain genes in future generations. In effect, they proposed that humans were little more than the vehicles genes use to reproduce themselves.

The notion that human cultural behavior could be reduced to genetics violated the fundamental tenets of Boasian anthropology and produced enormous hostility among cultural anthropologists. Of the many criticisms most focused on three points: First, sociobiological studies looked at behavior in terms of reproductive success and population genetics but ignored the effects of culture and learning, which most anthropologists claim are extremely powerful influences on human society. Second, virtually all sociobiological research was conducted on animals and insects rather than humans. Wilson's own work, for example, was concerned with ants. Anthropologists doubted that research findings based on insect behavior were applicable to human behavior. Finally, sociobiology was critically dependent on the notion that specific human behaviors could be linked to specific biological genes. Selection for the behaviors was, in fact, selection for the genes that produced them. These genes and thus the behavior they produced would be inherited by future generations. However, no conclusive link between a specific gene and a specific behavior has ever been demonstrated in "normal" human beings (clearly people with genetic abnormalities such as Down's syndrome do show such gene-specific behaviors). In fact, most anthropologists argued that although genetically based predispositions to behavior may exist, the very diversity of human behavior makes a direct connection between a specific behavior and a particular gene very unlikely (Sahlins 1976, Montagu 1980).

Even though many of the flaws of the early work in sociobiology have been corrected, it remains one of the most contentious areas within anthropology—so contentious that each time this book is reviewed for a new edition, several reviewers encourage us to remove this section. You are reading this over their objections. Part of the hostility is a continuing reaction to the extreme claims sociobiologists made in the 1970s and early 1980s, when they frequently asserted that sociobiology would render all forms of social science obsolete. Today, it would be hard to find a sociobiologist who would support this radical notion. Beyond this, sociobiology is inimical to some of the most dearly held principles of American cultural anthropology. The insistence of sociobiologists on grounding at least some behavior in universal human genetic predispositions runs contrary to cultural anthropologists' emphasis on the primacy of culture itself as the determinant of human social life.

Because of the high level of hostility, the word *sociobiology* has been almost entirely dropped from anthropological discourse, and much of the study of the relationship between biology and human behavior has moved into other academic disciplines, notably psychology. Sociobiology also remains a strong field of study in biology.

Several distinct approaches can be distinguished in current-day sociobiology. Among them are evolutionary psychology, human behavioral ecology, and the study of human universals. Evolutionary psychology is concerned primarily with the analysis of the mind as a device formed by natural selection. Evolutionary psychologists hypothesize that the mind is composed of a large number of functionally specialized neural circuits. These circuits were designed by natural selection to solve adaptive problems faced by our foraging ancestors. Evolutionary psychologists attempt to describe brain circuits, show how they work, what information they are designed to process, and what they were designed to accomplish in a foraging context (Cosmides and Tooby 1997).

A second focus, human behavioral ecology, looks to integrate earlier forms of cultural ecology with more recent understandings of biological ecology. It emphasizes populations rather than cultures (Kormondy and Brown 1998). Rather than focusing on the mind, human behavioral ecologists focus on testing the hypothesis that culturally patterned traits actually enhance fitness.

A third current approach involves the search for human universals (Brown 1991, Fessler 1995, Shapiro 2004, Wierzbica 2005). Followers of this approach concentrate on discovering the characteristics found in all human societies. They presume that ultimately such traits must be primarily based in human evolutionary biology and adaptation but do not focus their studies there.

The articles chosen for this section show some of the evolution of the sociobiological approach. The first selection, the introduction from E. O. Wilson's classic *Sociobiology: The New Synthesis* (1975), is an example of early sociobiology. Wilson's approach is extremely reductionist. His essay here is a polemical statement in support of the idea that all human cultural behavior ultimately will come to be understood as a reflection of underlying genetic forces. The second essay, "The Hunting Handicap" by Rebecca Bliege Bird, Eric Alden Smith, and Douglas W. Bird, takes an approach based in behavioral ecology. It tries to explain how evolution might select for a behavior that is wasteful, in this case the hunting of fish and turtles by means that are more difficult and inefficient than necessary.

Although sociobiology in all of its forms continues to be rejected by most cultural anthropologists, it has increased in popularity, both among anthropologists and the general public, in the last several years. At least two factors help to explain this increasing acceptance. First, recent medical successes and high-profile research such as the Human Genome Project have generally focused attention on the role of genetic inheritance in human life. As evidence emerges that things as diverse as cancers and religious sentiments may have genetic and biochemical bases, people are more willing to examine the connection between biology and behavior (see Sloan 2006). Second, many anthropologists have reacted vehemently against postmodernism and the notion that no objective description of culture (or anything else) is possible. They turn to sociobiology as the branch of anthropology that most resembles the natural sciences. A good example of this is James Lett, whose book *Science, Reason, and Anthropology* is largely an attack on postmodernism. Lett takes postmodern anthropologists to task for their polemic approach to debate and goes on to define anthropology as "the scientific study of human evolution" (1997:121).

26. *The Morality of the Gene*

Edward O. Wilson (b. 1929)

CAMUS SAID THAT the only serious philosophical question is suicide. That is wrong even in the strict sense intended. The biologist, who is concerned with questions of physiology and evolutionary history, realizes that self-knowledge is constrained and shaped by the emotional control centers in the hypothalamus and limbic system of the brain. These centers flood our consciousness with all the emotions—hate, love, guilt, fear, and others—that are consulted by ethical philosophers who wish to intuit the standards of good and evil. What, we are then compelled to ask, made the hypothalamus and limbic system? They evolved by natural selection. That simple biological statement must be pursued to explain ethics and ethical philosophers, if not epistemology and epistemologists, at all depths. Self-existence, or the suicide that terminates it, is not the central question of philosophy. The hypothalamic-limbic complex automatically denies such logical reduction by countering it with feelings of guilt and altruism. In this one way the philosopher's own emotional control centers are wiser than his solipsist consciousness, "knowing" that in evolutionary time the individual organism counts for almost nothing. In a Darwinist sense the organism does not live for itself. Its primary function is not even to reproduce other organisms; it reproduces genes, and it serves as their temporary carrier. Each organism generated by sexual reproduction is a unique, accidental subset of all the genes constituting the species. Natural selection is the process whereby certain genes gain representation in the following generations superior to that of other genes located at the same chromosome positions. When new sex cells are manufactured in each generation, the winning genes are pulled apart and reassembled to manufacture new organisms that, on the average, contain a higher proportion of the same genes. But the individual organism is only their vehicle, part of an elaborate device to preserve and spread them with the least possible biochemical perturbation. Samuel Butler's famous aphorism, that the chicken is only an egg's way of making another egg, has been modernized: the organism is only DNA's way of making more DNA. More to the point, the hypothalamus and limbic system are engineered to perpetuate DNA.[1]

In the process of natural selection, then, any device that can insert a higher proportion of certain genes into subsequent generations will come to characterize the species. One class of such devices promotes prolonged individual survival. Another promotes superior mating performance and care of the resulting offspring. As more complex social behavior by the organism is added to the genes' techniques for replicating themselves, altruism becomes increasingly prevalent and eventually appears in exaggerated forms. This brings us to the central theoretical problem of sociobiology: how can altruism, which by definition reduces personal

From *Sociobiology: The New Synthesis* (1975)

---

[1] This electrifying paragraph, which opens the first chapter of Wilson's book, makes immediately clear why it was so controversial. Wilson begins by quoting Albert Camus (1913–1960), the French existential philosopher and novelist, and then immediately reduces the philosopher's statement to a biological issue. In *Sociobiology*, Wilson proposes a theory in which all human social activity is reduced to evolutionary genetics. Wilson's attempt to tackle what Camus believed was the ultimate problem of human existence is a powerful rhetorical device. It is intended to grab the reader's attention by radically reducing philosophy to a subfield of evolutionary biology. However, the book does not fulfill the promise of this first chapter. Most of it is devoted to animal and insect behavior. Wilson does not return to human sociobiology again until the final chapter, 27. There he explores issues such as culture, religion, ethics, and esthetics, but these together account for five pages of a book of almost 700 pages.

fitness, possibly evolve by natural selection? The answer is kinship: if the genes causing the altruism are shared by two organisms because of common descent, and if the altruistic act by one organism increases the joint contribution of these genes to the next generation, the propensity to altruism will spread through the gene pool. This occurs even though the altruist makes less of a solitary contribution to the gene pool as the price of its altruistic act.[2]

To his own question, "Does the Absurd dictate death?" Camus replied that the struggle toward the heights is itself enough to fill a man's heart. This arid judgment is probably correct, but it makes little sense except when closely examined in the light of evolutionary theory. The hypothalamic-limbic complex of a highly social species, such as man, "knows," or more precisely it has been programmed to perform as if it knows, that its underlying genes will be proliferated maximally only if it orchestrates behavioral responses that bring into play an efficient mixture of personal survival, reproduction, and altruism. Consequently, the centers of the complex tax the conscious mind with ambivalences whenever the organisms encounter stressful situations. Love joins hate; aggression, fear; expansiveness, withdrawal; and so on; in blends designed not to promote the happiness and survival of the individual, but to favor the maximum of the controlling genes.

The ambivalences stem from counteracting pressures of natural selection. Their genetic consequences will be explored formally later in this book. For the moment suffice it to note what is good for the individual can be destructive to the family; what preserves the family can be harsh on both the individual and the tribe to which its family belongs; what promotes the tribe can weaken the family and

destroy the individual; and so on upward through the permutations of levels of organization. Counteracting selection on these different units will result in certain genes being multiplied and fixed, others lost, and combinations of still others held in static proportions. According to the present theory, some of the genes will produce emotional states that reflect the balance of counteracting selection forces at the different levels.

I have raised a problem in ethical philosophy in order to characterize the essence of sociobiology. Sociobiology is defined as the systematic study of the biological basis of all social behavior. For the present it focuses on animal societies, their population structure, castes, and communication, together with all of the physiology underlying the social adaptations. But the discipline is also concerned with the social behavior of early man and the adaptive features of organization in the more primitive contemporary human societies. Sociology *sensu stricto,*[3] the study of human societies at all levels of complexity, still stands apart from sociobiology because of its largely structuralist and nongenetic approach. It attempts to explain human behavior primarily by empirical description of the outermost phenotypes and by unaided intuition, without reference to evolutionary explanations in the true genetic sense. It is most successful, in the way descriptive taxonomy and ecology have been most successful, when it provides a detailed description of particular phenomena and demonstrates first-order correlations with features of the environment. Taxonomy and ecology, however, have been reshaped entirely during the past forty years by integration into neo-Darwinist evolutionary theory—the "Modern Synthesis," as it is often called—in which each phenomenon is

---

[2] Altruism was a problem for sociobiology. If behavior is dictated by natural selection, how can altruistic acts (which may cost the organism food, reproductive potential, living space, and even its life) exist? The answer is called *kin selection theory,* which Wilson explains in this paragraph. The question of altruism came into focus for Wilson through his study of ant colonies. Only queen ants reproduce, and the vast majority of individuals are workers who give up their reproductive potential to support the

queen and the colony. Why should these workers forgo reproduction to facilitate that of the queen? Wilson discovered that a worker ant actually passes on a greater percentage of its genetic material to future generations by supporting the queen, with whom it shares genetic material, rather than by reproducing itself.

[3] *Sensu stricto:* Latin for "in a strict sense."

weighed for its adaptive significance and then related to the basic principles of population genetics. It may not be too much to say that sociology and the other social sciences, as well as the humanities, are the last branches of biology waiting to be included in the Modern Synthesis. One of the functions of sociobiology, then, is to reformulate the foundations of the social sciences in a way that draws these subjects into the Modern Synthesis. Whether the social sciences can be truly biologized in this fashion remains to be seen.[4]

This book makes an attempt to codify sociobiology into a branch of evolutionary biology and particularly of modern population biology. I believe that the subject has an adequate richness of detail and aggregate of self-sufficient concepts to be ranked as coordinate with such disciplines as molecular biology and developmental biology. In the past its development has been slowed by too close an identification with ethology and behavioral physiology. In the view presented here, the new sociobiology should be compounded of roughly equal parts of invertebrate zoology, vertebrate zoology, and population biology. Figure 1 shows the schema with which I closed *The Insect Societies*, suggesting how the amalgam can be achieved.[5] Biologists have always been intrigued by comparisons between societies of invertebrates, especially insect societies, and those of vertebrates. They have dreamed of identifying the common properties of such disparate units in a way that would provide insight into all aspects of social evolution, including that of man. The goal can be expressed in modern terms as follows: when the same parameters and quantitative theory are used to analyze both termite colonies and troops of rhesus macaques, we will have a unified science of sociobiology. This may seem an impossibly difficult task. But as my own studies have advanced, I have been increasingly impressed with the functional similarities between invertebrate and vertebrate societies and less so with the structural differences that seem, at first glance, to constitute such an immense gulf between them. Consider for a moment termites and monkeys. Both are formed into cooperative groups that occupy territories. The group members communicate hunger, alarm, hostility, caste status or rank, and reproductive status among themselves by means of something on the order of 10 to 100 nonsyntactical signals.[6] Individuals are intensely aware of the distinction between groupmates and nonmembers. Kinship plays an important role in group structure and probably served as a chief generative force of sociality in the first place. In both kinds of society there is a well-marked division of labor, although in the insect society there is a much stronger reproductive component. The details of organization have been evolved by an evolutionary optimization process of unknown precision, during which some measure of added fitness was given to individuals with cooperative tendencies—at least toward relatives. The fruits of cooperativeness depend upon the particular conditions of the environment and are available to only a minority of animal species during the course of their evolution.[7]

---

[4] To emphasize his biological perspective, Wilson characterizes sociology as describing "phenotypes"—in other words, behavior is no more than the visible expression of genetic information. Just as Freud tried to unite the social sciences under his theory of psychoanalysis, Wilson states that the social sciences and humanities can be incorporated into the field of biology.

[5] *The Insect Societies*, published in 1971, was Wilson's exhaustive study of the behavior of ants. It was from his study of insects that he derived many of the insights he brought to his work in sociobiological theory.

[6] *Nonsyntactical signals:* nonlinguistic signals, or communications that are not language. Primate call systems, for example, are aural signals but not language.

[7] Wilson's focus on similarities between different species is typical of sociobiological studies. One could, no doubt, find more differences than similarities between termites and monkeys if one chose to look. It is probably no exaggeration to say that most anthropologists would find this list of similarities trivial and the differences one could think of profound. In fact, most cultural anthropologists probably believe that the sorts of behavior that sociobiologists study are relatively trivial and that any genetic universals underlying human behavior are limited and far less interesting than human cultural diversity.

Evolutionary and Ecological Parameters

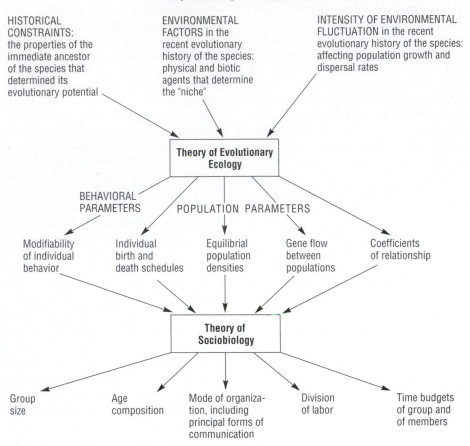

FIGURE 1   The connections that can be made between phylogenetic studies, ecology, and sociobiology. Reprinted by permission of the publisher from "The Morality of the Gene" in *Sociobiology: The New Synthesis* by Edward O. Wilson, p. 5, Cambridge, Mass.: The Belknap Press of Harvard University Press. Copyright © 1975, 2000 by the President and Fellows of Harvard College.

This comparison may seem facile, but it is out of such deliberate oversimplification that the beginnings of a general theory are made. The formulation of a theory of sociobiology constitutes, in my opinion, one of the great manageable problems of biology for the next twenty or thirty years. The prolegomenon of Figure 1 guesses part of its future outline and some of the directions in which it is most likely to lead animal behavior research. Its central precept is that the evolution of social behavior can be fully comprehended only through an understanding, first, of demogra-phy, which yields the vital information concerning population growth and age structure, and, second, of the genetic structure of the populations, which tells us what we need to know about effective population size in the genetic sense, the coefficients of relationship within the societies, and the amounts of gene flow between them. The principal goal of a general theory of sociobiology should be an ability to predict features of social organization from a knowledge of these population parameters combined with information on the behavioral constraints imposed by the genetic constitution of the species. It will be a chief task of evolutionary ecology, in turn, to derive the population parameters from a knowledge of the evolutionary history of the species and of the environment in which the most recent segment of that history unfolded. The most important feature of the prolegomenon, then, is the sequential relation between evolutionary studies, ecology, population biology, and sociobiology.[8]

In stressing the tightness of this sequence, however, I do not wish to underrate the filial relationship that sociobiology has had in the past with the remainder of behavioral biology. Although behavioral biology is traditionally spoken of as if it were a unified subject, it is now emerging as two distinct disciplines centered on neurophysiology and on sociobiology, respectively. The conventional wisdom also speaks of ethology, which is the naturalistic study of whole patterns of animal behavior, and its companion enterprise, comparative psychology, as the central, unifying fields of behavioral biology. They are not; both are destined to be cannibalized by neurophysiology and sensory physiology from one end and sociobiology and behavioral ecology from the other (see Figure 2).[9]

I hope not too many scholars in ethology and psychology will be offended by this vision of the future of behavioral biology. It seems to be indicated both by the extrapolation of current events and by consideration of the logical relationship behavioral biology holds with the remainder of science. The future, it seems clear, cannot be with the ad hoc terminology, crude models, and curve fitting that characterize most of contemporary ethology and comparative psychology. Whole patterns of animal behavior will inevitably be explained within the framework, first, of integrative neurophysiology, which classifies neurons and reconstructs their circuitry, and, second, of sensory physiology, which seeks to characterize the cellular transducers at the molecular level. Endocrinology will continue to play a peripheral role, since it is concerned with the cruder tuning devices of nervous activity. To pass from this level and reach the next really distinct discipline, we must travel all the way up to the society and the population. Not only are the phenomena best described by families of models different from those of cellular and molecular biology, but the explanations become largely evolutionary. There should be nothing surprising in this distinction. It is only a reflection of the larger division that separates the two greater domains of evolutionary biology and functional biology. As Lewontin[10] (1972a) has truly said: "Natural selection of the character states themselves is the essence of Darwinism. All else is molecular biology."[11]

---

[8] Since sociobiology focuses on natural selection and reproductive success as the mechanisms for determining behavior, such factors as population growth, gene flow, and demography are important to it. Behaviors must be analyzed in terms of these factors. Notice that Wilson sees the key issues as entirely within the traditional hard sciences. Anthropology, sociology, economics—not to mention the humanities—are not on the list. This is because sociobiologists, at the time this essay was written, perceived the subject materials of these disciplines as epiphenomenal: They were secondary manifestations of biologically based phenomena and therefore of no interest.

[9] Wilson was profoundly reductionist. He was in search of a few unifying principles that would explain all behavior. According to Wilson, even the fields that gave rise to sociobiology, such as psychology, were due to be subsumed by it or neurophysiology.

[10] Richard Lewontin (b. 1929) is a geneticist and evolutionary biologist.

[11] Wilson's worldview is evident in this passage. He invokes parsimony as one of his guiding principles—explanations must be neat, concise, and leave no loose ends. The vision behind this hearkens back to the science of the nineteenth century and the belief that the world is a rational and orderly place. This view is rejected by most current anthropologists and by many in the hard sciences as well, who see complexity at all levels.

Thirty years have passed since the publication of this essay, and the progress that Wilson predicted for "the next twenty or thirty years" has not taken place. Sociobiology may be a useful theoretical perspective for understanding some aspects of culture, but even its most fervent supporters probably no longer believe that it has the potential to replace the social sciences. By the mid-1980s, Wilson himself adopted a more moderate and sophisticated line on the distinction between evolutionary biology and culture. See, for example, his book *Biophilia* (1984).

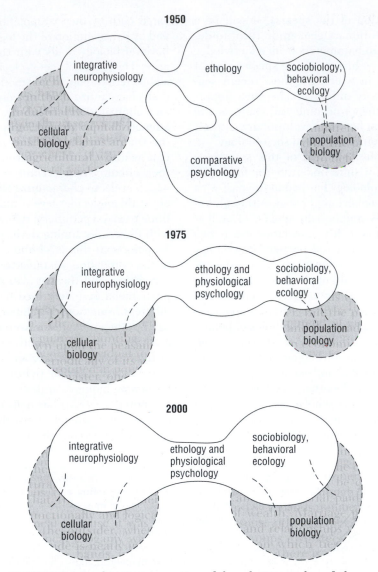

FIGURE 2   A subjective conception of the relative number of ideas in various disciplines in and adjacent to behavioral biology to the present time and as it might be in the future. Reprinted by permission of the publisher from "The Morality of the Gene" in *Sociobiology: The New Synthesis* by Edward O. Wilson, p. 5, Cambridge, Mass.: The Belknap Press of Harvard University Press. Copyright © 1975, 2000 by the President and Fellows of Harvard College.

ACKNOWLEDGEMENT

Reprinted by permission of the publisher from "The Morality of the Gene" in *Sociobiology: The New Synthesis* by Edward O. Wilson, pp. 3–6, Cambridge, Mass.: The Belknap Press of Harvard University Press. Copyright © 1975, 2000 by the President and Fellows of Harvard College.

REFERENCES

Lewontin, R. C. 1972a. Testing the theory of natural selection. (Review of R. Creed, ed., *Ecological genetics and Evolution.* Blackwell Scientific Publications, Oxford, 1971.) *Nature,* London, 236 (5343): 181–182.

27. *The Hunting Handicap: Costly Signaling in Human Foraging Strategies*

Rebecca Bliege Bird, Eric Alden Smith, and Douglas W. Bird

INTRODUCTION

Human foragers often make decisions that lead them to bypass alternative activities with higher energy gain rates, provide widely shared goods without repayment, or incur an increased risk of injury. These decisions have often been explained by the benefits of a sexual division of labor in parental investment (e.g., Hurtado et al. 1992), the optimization of macronutrients (e.g., Hill 1988), or reduction of consumption variance (e.g., Smith 1988). In particular, the practice common to many hunter-gatherer societies of widespread or group-wide sharing of large prey captured by any subset of the group is conventionally explained as a form of risk reduction where all ultimately benefit from a reciprocal sharing of unpredictable harvests (reviews in Hawkes 1992; Winterhalder 1997).[1]

While some types of food seem to be distributed in ways that conform to delayed reciprocity (Gurven et al. 2000), recent studies (Hawkes 1993; Bliege Bird and Bird 1997) have challenged

From *Behavioral Ecology and Sociobiology* (2001)

its ability to explain the wide variety of sharing patterns to which it has been claimed to apply. The cases that seem least congruent with strategies of delayed reciprocity are those associated with public distributions of food in which the acquirer does not control access to the harvest or its distribution, and may not even reserve a portion for him or herself (Wiessner 1996). Under these conditions, acquirers seem unlikely to be able to direct shares to reciprocators and withhold them from free riders, as is required to solve the collective action problem (e.g., prisoner's dilemma) associated with enforcing delayed reciprocity. Similar challenges to the primacy of reciprocal altruism (RA) on both theoretical and empirical fronts are also found in recent literature on non-human behavior (reviews in Dugatkin 1997; Pusey and Packer 1997). Many theorists have suggested the paradigm may require extensive revisions (Clements and Stephens 1995; Connor 1996; Dugatkin 1997; Roberts 1998).[2]

An alternative explanation for such "economically irrational" decisions is that under

---

[1] In ecological and biological approaches to anthropology, it is a fundamental tenet that cultural practices are best explained by underlying ecological reasons and that these are ultimately related to natural selection: Individuals who follow these practices are more likely to be reproductively successful than those who do not. Anthropologists are particularly interested in foraging peoples, reasoning that for most of human existence, people have survived by foraging. Gardening and agriculture appear relatively recently in the archaeological record. Thus, if people are adapted by natural selection to any form of food acquisition, it must be foraging. Given this perspective, the food choices of foraging peoples pose interesting problems. Ecological and biological anthropologists believe that such food choices must reflect the operation of underlying principles rather than historical accident or taste preference. One powerful way of explaining such choices was optimal foraging theory (OFT). This was the idea that human foragers, like other animals, will choose

foods that offer the maximal energy return for the minimal energy investment (Smith 1983; Hill, Kaplan, Hawkes, and Hurtado 1987; Nonacs and Dill 1993). Among some groups, OFT seems to model foraging behavior reasonably well, yet there are a great many deviations from it. This essay (as well as the ones mentioned in this paragraph) is an attempt to use ideas rooted in biology to explain those instances in which OFT fails.

[2] In other words, it's well known that in foraging groups hunters generally share their kill with all members of their group. If all hunters were equally good, then such sharing makes economic sense: Each should ultimately receive as much as he gives. However, all hunters are not equally good, hence those who provide large kills regularly sacrifice without receiving adequate compensation. The prisoner's dilemma is a classic problem in game theory. Here is a brief description: Imagine that two people are held in solitary confinement. They cannot see or talk to each other. The

some circumstances they could serve as an honest signal of one or more dimensions of fitness-related quality (Neiman 1998; Boone 1998; Sosis 2000; Smith and Bliege Bird 2000). Costly signaling theory (CST) provides a powerful framework for explaining two paradoxical observations: the persistence of wasteful phenotypes when natural selection is assumed to create greater efficiency, and the evolution of honest communication despite the pervasive conflicts of interest underlying evolutionary processes (Zahavi 1975, 1977; Grafen 1990; Johnstone 1995, 1997; Getty 1998). CST proposes that communication between individuals with conflicting interests can be evolutionarily stable if the signal honestly advertises an underlying quality of interest to observers. Advertising is kept honest and thus mutually beneficial to both signaler and observer as long as the cost or benefit of advertisement is so closely tied to the quality of the signaler that faking it costs more than the signal is worth. If this holds, the correlation between the quality of a signaler and the quality or intensity of the signal will be maintained by differences in marginal cost or benefit, allowing recipients to reliably discriminate among competing signalers. When these conditions are met, honest signals and reliable communication will be evolutionarily stable, even when signaler and recipient are antagonists or competitors.[3]

The hypothesis that hunting might serve as a form of status competition among men interested

in "showing off" to a public audience is not new (Hawkes 1990, 1991). Here, we recast the "show-off" model using a payoff structure compatible with CST (Smith and Bliege Bird 2000). We propose that individuals of high phenotypic quality might reap higher benefits or pay lower costs to acquire skill based resources or to unconditionally share their harvest. These benefits (material, political, and reproductive) flow from observers who find it in their interest to behave in ways that improve the relative advantage, status, or social dominance of signalers, ultimately enhancing signaler fitness. Analyzed according to CST, this is not delayed reciprocity involving an exchange of substance (to the observer) for social status (to the signaler), but rather a form of by-product mutualism. The payoff to the observer comes from the usefulness of the information inferred from the signal: he or she should be able to evaluate the signaler's suitability as a competitor, mate, or ally by attending to the signal rather than through more costly or unreliable means of assessing the signaler's abilities or hidden qualities. The high cost or low benefit of faking the signal guarantees that signalers will not engage in false advertising, and that observers will pay attention. Costly signaling can thus spread (by natural selection or imitation) because of its mutual benefits to both signalers and observers.[4]

Here, we test the costly signaling hypothesis among the Meriam (a Melanesian people of

---

guards decide to play a little game with them: "If you choose to cooperate with the other prisoner, each of you will receive three candy bars. If one of you chooses to compete and the other to cooperate, the one who competes will receive five candy bars and the one who cooperates, none. If both of you choose to compete, each gets one candy bar. What will your choice be?" There is no real solution to the problem because maximizing one's return depends on guessing what one's fellow prisoner will do. A great deal has been written about the application of the prisoner's dilemma to evolution and economics. A good reference is Robert Axelrod's, *The Evolution of Cooperation* (1984).

[3] So, what the authors propose to demonstrate is that, in some cases, hunters choose to pursue prey neither for their taste nor their nutritional value but rather because so doing demonstrates their ability to undertake difficult tasks successfully, and this tells others, especially potential

mates, that they are particularly desirable. Note the authors' use of the term *phenotype* here and throughout this essay. An individual's behavior could conceivably be related to his or her personal psychology, history, culture, or any of a myriad of factors. A phenotype is the outward observable expression of a genetically based trait. By using *phenotype* to describe behaviors, the authors are proposing that these behaviors are ultimately rooted in some as yet undiscovered genotype. Thus, at root, they are biologically rather than culturally based.

[4] Several key concepts are found in this passage. Note first that the authors describe the behavior they observe as by-product mutualism. Mutualism in this sense refers to cooperation. There is mutualism when two individuals gain a benefit through cooperation. By-product mutualism is a special case. In by-product mutualism, one individual (A) benefits from the actions of another individual (B). But B

Torres Strait, Australia). We evaluate two candidate foraging activities (spearfishing on the reef at low tide, and hunting turtle for public feasts), to determine whether these hunt types meet key criteria for costly signaling in being (1) differentially costly or beneficial in ways that are (2) honestly linked to signaler quality, and (3) designed to effectively broadcast the signal to the intended audience. We propose that accomplished spearfishers signal such qualities as hand-eye coordination, stealth, and patience, while successful turtle hunters signal strength, risk-taking, and (in the case of hunt leaders) a variety of cognitive and leadership abilities to potential allies, mates, and competitors.

METHODS[5]

Mer (a.k.a. Murray Island) is a small (1.6 × 2.2 km) island on the northern end of the Great Barrier Reef, 140 km from New Guinea in Australia's Torres Strait. The island's current population is 430 individuals of Torres Strait Islander descent, scattered in approximately 85 households. The Torres Strait as a whole is administered by the State of Queensland and the Commonwealth of Australia.

Prior to about 1975, when Australian welfare payments were first made available to all indigenous Australians, the Meriam were nearly full-time subsistence horticulturalists and marine foragers planting tropical yams, bananas, sugar cane, and introduced new world crops such as manioc, sweet potatoes, and corn, and harvesting marine fish, shellfish, and sea turtles. Today, fishing and shellfish collecting remain a critical component of Meriam subsistence economy: mean per capita after-sharing consumption rates average 630 kcal of meat and 40 g of protein. More than 80% of these calories are supplied by turtle when in season. For additional ethnographic description and previous work among the Meriam, see Haddon (1906), Beckett (1988), Sharp (1993), Bliege Bird et al. (1995), Bird and Bliege Bird (1997, 2000), Bliege Bird and Bird (1997), and Smith and Bliege Bird (2000).[6]

Observations of Meriam foraging choices, time allocation, and food-sharing strategies reported here were conducted over several periods totaling 27 months between January 1993 and July 1999. Much of this field research was specifically designed to test hypotheses related to the origin and maintenance of the human sexual division of labor, and to determine the nature of the tradeoffs affecting men's and women's foraging decisions.

Time allocation to intertidal activities (spearfishing, shellfish collecting) was measured through focal individual follows occurring during

---

would have done the action and gained the benefits regardless of A (Brown 1983). In the example presented here, benefits are conferred on both the hunter who is signaling and the audience intended to receive the signal, but the hunter would signal even if there were no audience. In this essay, selection is assumed to be primarily at the level of the individual rather than the group. The emphasis throughout is on benefits received by individuals. Second, note that the authors suggest that traits are passed along through either natural selection, implying again a genetic basis for behavior, or through imitation or Lamarckian evolution, thus implying that some of what they observe is culturally rather than biologically based.

[5] In this section, the authors describe the site of their research and some of the basic techniques of hunting that they observed. Note that the description owes much more to ethology, the study of animal behavior, than it does to anthropology. The focus is on the physical characteristics of the setting and on the actions that the people being studied actually performed. In this description we learn very little about Meriam culture or society. The methodology is entirely consistent with the theoretical position of the anthropologists. One of the fundamentals of behavioral ecology is to observe and analyze human behavior to the greatest extent possible as you would observe and analyze the behavior of any other animal. Pay close attention to the descriptions of the turtle hunts in the second half of this section; they are critical for understanding the rest of the essay.

[6] Of historical interest, note that the first reference on the Meriam that the authors cite is from Haddon. Mer was one of the sites investigated in the famous Torres Straits expeditions of the late nineteenth century (see the Introduction to Functionalism for more information on the Torres Straits expedition).

randomly selected days during the spring ebbing tide. Locations along the foreshore were observed from the midpoint of the ebbing tide, before the reef was fully exposed, for at least 2 h or until the last forager had left the reef. During the intertidal sampling period, we recorded the moment-by-moment behavior of at least one individual to arrive during the sample, and if the individual remained after the interval ended, we remained to completely record the episode. We observed the reef flat habitat for a total of 118.5 h over 41 spring ebb tide days, recording 338.1 forager hours of subsistence activity in 210 partial and full foraging follows of 94 men, women, and children entering the reef flat. We then analyzed the percentage of total foraging time each forager devoted to all potential intertidal activities during the follow.

We analyzed the reef as a bounded habitat within which there are "hunt types" sensu (Smith 1991). All hunt types are simultaneously available options within the ecological habitat "reef flat at low tide": reef flat collecting, rocky shore harvesting, and spearfishing (Bird and Bliege Bird 1997, 2000). Reef flat collecting involves mobile search of shellfish, with in situ processing to increase the utility of the load (Bird and Bliege Bird 1997). Spearfishing involves search and travel across the reef looking for encounters with mobile prey (small fish and squid 250 g1) to the exclusion of all other prey; when prey are detected, the hunter stalks the prey and launches his spear from a distance. Both hunt types occur in the same patch during the same period of time, while the reef is exposed at low tide. The hunt types vary in how spatially exclusive they are within the habitat: spearfishing and shellfish collecting are the only two major hunt types in which the forager engaged in exclusive search for prey frequently encounters and ignores prey in the other hunt type. These are not the complete complement of hunt types simultaneously available, but they are the three in which adults spend more than 90% of their foraging time while on the reef at low tide. Other minor hunt types are hand line fishing from the reef edge and in deeper lagoons, netting sardines, hunting octopus, and diving from the reef edge to take underwater prey

by hand. Gross foraging return rates for each hunt type (not including energetic expenditure assumed to be roughly equal for all reef hunt types) were calculated from the moment an individual stepped onto the exposed reef and began to engage in targeted search for particular prey types. The macronutrient content of finfish and shellfish was obtained through published sources and through individual analysis of samples collected on Mer (Hirth 1971; Sidwell 1981; Brand Miller et al. 1993).

For a detailed description of methods used to collect turtle hunting and sharing data see Bliege Bird and Bird (1997); the results presented here on turtle hunting and sharing are a reanalysis of those data. The acquisition of over 120 turtles was noted through daily sampling of the entire village during the nesting season (October–April) in 1994–1995, and ad lib sampling of the village during the 1994 and 1998 hunting seasons (May-September). Nearly every successful hunt or collection of turtle was recorded, with information obtained on acquirer(s), place acquired, method of acquisition, and subsequent distribution through informant interview.

There are two primary types of marine turtle acquisition on Mer: turtle hunting (*nam deraimer*) and turtle collection (*nam terpei*). Turtle hunting occurs throughout the year, but is the only way to acquire turtles between May and September (*Kob Kerker*), when green turtles (*Chelonia mydas*) feed and mate on shallow reefs about 16–20 km from Mer. Field observations indicate that turtles captured on hunts range from 100 to 150 kg live weight, with an average edible yield of 50.1 kg (Bliege Bird and Bird 1997). Hunters head out to the hunting grounds in open boats powered with outboard motors, often in cooperation with at least one other hunting boat. Among Meriam turtle hunters, there are three distinct roles: hunt leader (*ariemer-le*), jumper (*arpeir-le*), and driver, or tiller-man (*korizer-le*). Hunt leaders organize and direct the hunt; there is always only one leader per hunt, regardless of crew size. Hunt leaders bear the cost of organizing the hunt and ensuring boats and fuel to spare. They direct the crew to particular locations, decide whether prey encountered is worth pursuing, orchestrate the chase, and direct jumpers when to jump from the boat to secure the turtle. Hunt leaders are invested with public recognition and receive full credit for the kill regardless of whether or not they directly participate in capture.

The hunt proceeds as follows. While one man drives, the rest of the crew stands toward the bow scanning the reef for signs of turtle. The hunt leader directs the driver and coordinates with crews in other boats if present. When a turtle is spotted, the hunt leader makes a decision whether to pursue it based on its size (large turtles have more meat) and sex (female turtles have more fat). The boat(s) then give chase, keeping the turtle away from the reef edge. When the turtle tires, the hunt leader usually directs his jumper to launch himself from the bow of the boat with a rope attached to his upper arm. The jumper then attempts to secure the turtle by locking his arms around the flippers and, if successful, the crew then pulls him and the turtle on board.

Turtle hunting occurs primarily in the context of public feasting events: hunters choose to hunt in response to a request from feast organizers to provide turtles for consumption at a previously announced feast. The biggest and most elaborate Meriam feasts occur in the context of coming-of-age celebrations and funeral ceremonies (see Smith and Bliege Bird 2000 for further details). In contrast to turtle hunting, turtles are also collected (*n* = 88 events), primarily in the context of household provisioning, but also for feasts, by men of all ages, women, and children. This occurs only when they can be harvested on beaches during the nesting season (*Nam Kerker*: October–April), although during these months some turtles are also hunted on nearby reefs. In the nesting season, turtles are collected at night or during the early morning hours as they crawl onto sandy beaches above the mean high water mark to lay their eggs. Turtles are acquired by flipping them onto their backs, trussing their flippers with ropes, and hauling them by boat back to the acquirer's household where they are kept alive until butchered. When butchered for "private" consumption, turtle shares are distributed in large, uncooked portions (10–11 kg) of meat, fat, organs, and eggs among nearby households, with the size of portions kept by the butchering household determined primarily by the number of demanders (hereafter termed "household consumption," sensu Bliege Bird and Bird (1997)). While hunting a turtle is a costly activity in which the benefit is acquired through the social value of the hunt, collecting a turtle is an activity which has little signaling potential and in which the benefit is primarily nutritional. However, there may be some signal value of displays of generosity among neighbors as turtle portions are shared according to the Meriam ethic of *debe tonar* ("the good way," which involves sharing without expectation of return).

All statistical analyses were performed using Statview (SAS). Large-sample means tests were performed after testing for normality and equality of variance using either one- or two-tailed *t*-tests depending upon the prediction tested, while tests on small samples and those violating the assumptions of parametric tests used two-tailed Mann-Whitney *U*-tests. All means are reported with associated SEs.[7]

---

[7] The authors of this essay take a scientific approach to anthropology. Some hallmarks of modern science are quantification, measurement, and hypothesis testing. The authors use statistical techniques, particularly *t*-tests and *U*-tests, to accomplish these tasks. *U*-tests and *t*-tests are basic statistical tests of the reliability of differences between two groups. Imagine that you can measure some attribute of two different groups, assigning an average to each. Of course, it is very unlikely that the averages of the groups will be identical, but what you would like to know is if the average is just the result of chance, or if it means there is a real difference between the groups. *U*-tests and *t*-tests help you figure this out by allowing you to calculate a probability that the difference between the averages is due to chance. If that probability is less than 5%, the results are deemed "significant." That is, it is considered unlikely that the differences are due to chance. The difference between a *t*-test and a *U*-test has to do with your expectations about the distribution of results. When the distribution of results for each group are "normal," that is, look like a bell curve, *t*-tests are used. If the results are a different shape, a *U*-test is used.

RESULTS

Spearfishing as Costly Signal

There are significant sex differences in time allocation to hunt types in the intertidal: on average, men spend 63% of their reef foraging time spearing, while for women this value is only 9% ($t = 6.00$, $df = 66$, $p = 0.001$), and women spend 76% and men 31% of their time shellfish collecting ($t = 4.50$, $df = 66$, $p = 0.001$).[8] The majority of men never collect shellfish at all, nor do they combine spearing with shellfish collecting in a single visit to the reef at low tide: 78.6% of 21 men in the time allocation sample spent *all* of their foraging time spearfishing.

Is spearfishing a signal? The decision men make to spear fish nearly exclusively (rather than collect shellfish) violates simple energy-maximizing prey choice models, because (1) on average, continuing to search for fish to spear (292 ± 135 kcal/h, $n = 26$) offers lower overall energy returns than shell fishing ($1,492 \pm 173$ kcal/h, $n = 47$) while in the reef flat at low tide ($t = 4.672$, $df = 71$, $p = 0.0001$) and (2) on-encounter returns for the most skilled spearfisher ($2,505 \pm 2778$ kcal/h) are equivalent to the on-encounter returns for the lowest-ranked shellfish prey still in the optimal diet breadth ($2,214 \pm 414$ kcal/h) (see Table 1).[9] [*Space limitations prevent the inclusion of this and other tables and figures with this essay. Table 1 shows the mean calories obtained per encounter, the nutritional content, and the time allotted by men and women for reef collecting, reef spearing, and rocky shore harvesting. It shows that reef spearing has poor returns compared with reef collecting and rocky shore harvesting.*]

One explanation for this pattern might be that spearfishers are not maximizing calories, but other macronutrients. But this appears not to be the case: protein return rates from shellfish collecting at 284 ± 31 g/h are higher than from spearfishing at 6.6 ± 2.9 g/b ($t = 6.78$, $df = 68$, $p = .0001$). Fat return rates are also higher for shellfish collecting at 22 ± 3 g/h than for spearfishing at 1.6 ± 0.7 g/h ($t = 4.808$, $df = 68$, $p = 0.0001$).

Another possibility is that spearfishers prefer other benefits supplied by reef fish: they may be more valuable as trade goods than shellfish prey. But this seems unlikely: shellfish collecting produces larger harvests ($1,962 \pm 247$ g, $n = 44$) than spearing (356 ± 100 g, $n = 26$) ($t = 24.857$, $df = 68$, $p = 0.0001$). Shellfish prey are also more likely to be shared: following a harvest of shellfish, on average 22% of the take is shared to another household, while only 7.5% of a spearing harvest is shared.

Finally, could choosing to spear fish instead of collecting shellfish as women do provide greater consumption benefits in the long-term? The short-term costs are inescapable: while women maximize their patch returns and the size of their meat harvests by stopping to take shellfish when encountered on the reef, male spearfishers take a large cut in protein, fat, and energy income by ignoring shellfish and continuing to

---

[8] Results from *t*- and *U*-tests are generally given in the form (*t* or *U* =, *df* =, *p* =). In this expression, *t* or *U* refers to the *t* or *U* score (in general, the greater the number here, the more certain you are of a real difference between the two groups) and *df* stands for degrees of freedom, a complex concept related to the number of results that are free to vary and the number of variables in the experiment. In *t*- and *U*-tests generally, the larger your sample size, the larger the degrees of freedom and the smaller the *t* or *U* score needed to show differences between groups. Finally, *p* refers to the probability that the two groups are the same. In this case in the essay, *p* = 0.001, so there is only one chance in a thousand that the hunting and shellfish collecting behaviors of men and women are really the same.

[9] As this paragraph shows, spearfishing violates optimal foraging theory. If it has low caloric returns for the calories invested, then an economic fisher would not choose to do it. This makes the fact that most men spearfish an optimal test case for explanations other than OFT. In the next paragraphs, the authors discuss several possible explanations other than costly signaling, dismissing or minimizing the possibilities of each. These include the idea that spearfishers are maximizing fat and protein rather than calories, the idea that there are other economic benefits to spearfishing that are not gained through fish collecting, and that the practice of men spearfishing while women collect maximizes the long-term yield of the collection area.

search for fish to spear. There could be long-term benefits of such specialization if by dividing labor and pooling harvests, male spearfishers and female shellfish collectors maintain long-term shellfishing productivity on the reef. This could happen if the cooperative pooling unit (the household) defended a reef territory, excluding other pooling units from foraging so that the future benefits of conservation could be realized. But they do not: while reef territories are owned, the group sharing use-rights to sections of reef is not equivalent to the pooling unit. Sections of reef are considered extensions of residential plots: use-rights to residential plots are shared by all members of a patriline. Only bounded clam gardens within reef territories are excludable and defendable by single households, and these gardens are approximately 2–4 m in diameter, not large enough to permit spearfishing. Any gains in long-term shellfish productivity would have to be shared by the entire patriline, and all men within the patriline would have to forgo shellfish collecting, which is unlikely since men do vary in the extent to which they collect shellfish. We cannot definitively exclude this possibility, only note that it seems unlikely.

Spearfishers interested in maximizing return rates should not ignore shellfish while foraging on the reef, but most of them do. The costs of choosing to spear fish do not appear to be balanced by benefits received through cooperative gender specialization in macronutrient harvesting, nor through reciprocal sharing. We propose that the benefits of spearfishing are gained through the honest signal value of acquiring the prey rather than through consumption, and that honesty is maintained through differential benefits: men of higher phenotypic quality benefit more than lower quality individuals because

they can signal more intensely each time they signal.

Prediction 1: *men who signal more frequently obtain greater benefits*[10]

If spearfishing is a competitive display, signalers should reap social benefits associated with more frequent spearfishing, such as the benefits from gaining status through building a reputation as a skilled spearfisher. In interviews with 33 Meriam men and women, none would nominate a slate of "the best shellfish collectors," claiming that "being better than others" (i.e., getting larger harvests) depends solely on working long hours, not on qualities intrinsic to the forager, and most nominated the most frequently observed woman on the reef as "hardest-working shellfish collector." Across individuals, shellfish-collecting harvest sizes are strongly contingent upon foraging time, whereas spearfishing harvest sizes are not. . . . [*Figure 1, not included in this edition, shows two graphs. The first compares harvest size with foraging time for spearfishing. The second makes the same comparison for reef shellfish collecting. Together they show that harvest increases with time for reef shellfish collecting, but not with spearfishing.*] All interviewees were willing to nominate a slate of "the best spearfishers." Because there was little variance in signal frequency among the majority of men observed on the reef, we divided the signalers into the most frequent (1 man with 10 observed bouts) and the least frequent (14 men with 19 bouts total). The most frequent signaler obtained 23 out of 61 (37.7%) total nominations by the 32 respondents (who nominated as many as three individuals). More than 75% of respondents named the most frequent signaler as the best spearfisherman. None of the less frequent signalers in our sample obtained any nominations at all. The remainder of

---

[10] In this essay, perhaps more than any other in this book, the authors state general rules for the society they are studying. The essays that come close, those by Radcliffe-Brown, Gluckman, and White, state possible rules in very general terms. The literary technique of stating these principles as predictions is consistent with the scientific trope of the essay. However, the use of the term *prediction* is interesting. Normally, one would expect to make a prediction before collecting data. These predictions, however, seem to have been made after data collection and analysis. Thus, in this case, it is very difficult to tell if the reasoning is truly deductive (if the data were collected in order to test the predictions) or inductive (the predictions derived from data collected).

the nominations went to deceased individuals or those currently not active as spearfishers.[11]

Prediction 2: *signal intensity is linked to phenotypic quality*

For the qualities signaled by spearfishing to be honestly advertised, high quality spearfishers should signal more intensely, because they gain greater marginal benefits or endure lower marginal costs per unit signal. In addition to signal frequency (see above), good measures of signaling intensity are harvest size and success rate. The mean harvest size per bout (in kcal) of the most frequent spearfisher (680 ± 197, $n = 9$) was larger than that obtained by other spearfishers (209 ± 101, $n = 15$; $U = 32$, $p = 0.05$). His hunt type return rates were also higher at 616 ± 356 kg/h versus 137 ± 75 kg/h ($U = 32$, $p = 0.49$), although his bouts were of equal mean length as those of the less frequent signalers (106 ± 17.2 versus 102 ± 15.6 min). The most frequent signaler's return rates were still lower than he could achieve shellfish collecting ($U = 72$, $p = 0.002$). The "frequent signaler" also had a much lower bout failure rate than other men (failure rate per bout = 22.2% versus 66.7%; chi-squared 4.444, $p = 0.03$).[12]

Prediction 3: *the signal is designed to be perceived by the intended audience*

Since spearfishing is a solitary hunting activity that produces no large, widely consumed common good, the signal elements contained in spearfishing are subtle and difficult to observe. Yet reputations are still built in the absence of any overt boasting or tale-telling on the part of the forager himself, who when successful, displays the typical behavior of a male solitary hunter: he returns home carrying his catch quietly, albeit very visibly. The signal elements incorporated in spearfishing are conveyed to observers in three distinct ways. (1) Reef activities are highly visible to a large section of the village surrounding one's residence, which contributes to the ease of observer perception of bout frequency. (2) Spearfishermen make perception of harvest size easier by carrying their harvests openly in hand, rather than carrying them in a bucket, as line fishers and shellfish collectors do. (3) Although bout frequency is the signal element most easily observed, harvest size is usually made known to a large number of individuals through verbal communication. Hunts with large harvests are recounted many times over, and stories about such success become part of local legend.

Turtle Hunting as Costly Signal[13]

Turtle hunting could serve as a competitive display if foragers can distinguish themselves from others based on their skill. The signal(s) thus produced by turtle hunting would depend upon the kinds of costs incurred. If turtle hunting is associated with lower foraging returns than other options, signals of skill sent through hunting could honestly indicate the ability of the forager to expend time and energy in a wasteful pursuit. If hunting has a high return but is associated with wide, unconditional, and costly distributions of food, signals of skill could honestly indicate one's quality (prosocial tendencies, or ability to gain resource reserves through skill in other activities) by expending time and energy in providing goods for public consumption.

---

[11] Note the leap of faith demanded by the authors here. The authors show that there is a fairly high degree of agreement about who the best spearfishermen are (although there also seems to be quite a bit of variability about the rank of most of the men who fish). They suggest that being recognized as the best spearfisherman must, naturally, carry benefits. This is not an unreasonable thing to suggest, but the authors are weak about specifying exactly what those benefits are. Perhaps most Meriam women dislike the best spearfisherman because he is self-centered and always smells like fish.

[12] In other words, the best fisherman was able to get larger harvests with less time expended than other fishermen. Thus it "cost" him less to send a strong signal than it cost other spearfishermen who would have had to expend much more time and energy to bring home the same catch.

[13] In the section above the authors have discussed spearfishing as a costly signal. Now they perform the same task for turtle hunting, a separate and more complex case.

Hunting turtles is indeed a competitive pursuit, with a very different complement of participants than collecting. As the Meriam put it *anyone* can collect turtle in the nesting season, but only certain men have the ability to succeed at turtle hunting. Older and younger men, children, and women of all ages participate in turtle *collecting* during the nesting season: 21% of turtle collections involve adult females. In contrast, for turtle *hunting*, the only participants are males between the ages of 16 and 47 (mean age = 31.6, n = 38). Though a substantial proportion of Meriam men participate in turtle hunting at some point in their lives, relatively few do so with regularity. In our sample of 37 turtle hunts extending over two periods (1994–1995 and 1998), there were a total of 102 man-days expended, or 2.76 hunters per hunt (all hunts last 1 day or less). For the 87 man-days where hunters are individually identified, there were a total of 40 unique individuals, or 2.18 hunts per hunter. But the 3 most active men participated a total of 16 times, or 18.4% of the hunter-days of known individuals. Thus, 44.4% of the 90 Meriam males aged 16–47 hunted at least once in the study period, but the 3 most active participants (3.3% of males) were over five times more likely to engage in a turtle hunt than the average Meriam male in this age range.[14]

Turtle hunting entails a variety of costs that could ultimately be linked to signaler quality in a way that ensures signals sent by hunting will remain honest (Smith and Bliege Bird 2000). Hunting may involve (1) high opportunity costs in the form of passing over opportunities to acquire other resources with a higher rate of return, (2) low consumption return rates (Bliege Bird and Bird 1997) as hunters distribute meat to nonhunters following the hunt, or (3) high energetic, monetary, or time investment costs of preparing for and conducting the hunt that reduce energetic return rates below that of other more easily acquired resources. There may be other costs or risks of a social nature that provide a link between turtle hunting and hunter quality, particularly the loss of social status should a hunter fail to deliver turtles to a feast (see below).[15]

Hunting Season Hunts

During the hunting season, between April and October, the goal of all hunts is to capture turtle for a previously arranged feast. During major feasts, all those who come must be fed by the feast-giving family and their allies, and the family can never predict precisely how many people will come to the feast itself. Theoretically, the entire population of the island (over 400 men, women, and children) plus many off-island visitors could attend, though attendance by 200 or fewer from both on and off the island is typical (mean = 174.9, range = 49–343, n = 54). Failure to provide turtle is a substantial cost to the hunter's status since all feast-goers will note the absence of turtle meat at the feast. Since hunts are only undertaken a day or two prior to a feast, there are only as many hunts as there are feasts during this

---

[14] Interesting points sometimes lie hidden in the numbers. In the methods section above, the authors tell us that there are three different roles in the hunt: the leader, the jumper, and the tillerman. Further, their writing seems to imply that sometimes crews are quite large (for example, they talk about the leader directing jumpers rather than a single jumper). However, notice that the average crew size is only 2.76. That implies that on many hunts not all the roles were filled. In fact, the numbers suggest a few hunts with large crews and many hunts with very small crews. Did the most successful hunters frequently go out with a crew of one?

[15] One issue that the authors do not discuss but that readers might want to keep in mind is the inelastic nature of food demand. That is, the amount of food consumed by well-fed humans is relatively stable. A hunter who captures 100,000 calories can only eat around 2,000 in a day. As long as a hunter is assured of having enough to eat, whether he captures 1,000 or 100,000 might make little difference. Thus passing over rich resources or consuming a low percentage of a catch (points one and two in this paragraph) may not really be irrelevant. In a relatively lush environment like the one the Meriam live in, adequate food supply might be easy to get. This exposes a dilemma in ethological technique. The technique is designed to study nonhuman animals that engage in far less cooperation and planning than do humans. Can such a technique be appropriate to the study of human society?

season: in 1994 there were ten hunts for public feasts. During the hunting season, the turtle patch is more distant, encounters with turtle are less common, and turtles are more difficult to detect and follow under water that is often murky and broken by swells and whitecaps created by the nearly constant 20-knot southeast trade winds during this season. After a successful hunt, hunters could expect to obtain a per capita net return of 4,653 kcal/h if they divided the turtle among themselves; however, all hunts during this season provision feasts, and hunters keep no share of the turtle they provide. Hunters deliver the turtle whole to the feasting location. Hunters thus obtain negative per capita consumption returns of −1,086 kcal/h, including the costs of traveling to the patch (see Bliege Bird and Bird 1997 for details of the method of calculating net returns from turtle hunting).

Nesting Season Hunts

During the remainder of the year, hunts are undertaken for two reasons: to provision previously arranged feasts ($n = 13$), and to provision households ($n = 9$). In this season, hunting is much easier and hunters take on fewer costs: turtles are found on nearby reefs waiting to crawl onto the beaches to lay eggs at night, the trade winds have largely ceased, and in between monsoon storms, the water is clear, calm, and visibility is excellent, allowing hunters to dog turtles more closely, to lose fewer, and to more finely discern size and sex. Considering only successful hunts, hunters in the nesting season could potentially obtain per capita returns of 8,061 kcal/h hunting for household consumption if they did not share the meet with others. But hunters share more widely than collectors during the same season, leaving their personal return rate from hunting for a feast at −1,633, and those from hunting for household consumption at 814 (Table 2). [*Table 2, not included in this edition, shows the mean returns for turtle hunting. It shows that many more turtles were acquired during nesting season than during hunting season. And for turtle hunters, the caloric returns were negative during both hunting and nesting seasons.*] Hunts during the nesting season

should not happen at all if hunters were interested solely in maximizing energetic return rates: during the nesting season, collected turtle offers higher after-sharing energetic returns than hunted turtle. In addition, other available resources are also more energetically productive: sardine netting provides $11,008 \pm 1,705$ ($n = 28$) kcal/h before sharing—sardine harvests are shared only 5% of the time, leaving on average 10,864 kcal/h. If hunting turtle were solely about ensuring feast-goers can eat plenty of meat and fat, men should net 50 kg of sardines with no chance of failure rather than spending the entire day chasing turtle to risk coming back to the feast empty-handed.

Turtle hunting in both seasons thus satisfies two of our criteria for consideration as an honest and costly signal. Unlike turtle collecting, observers can distinguish skilled from unskilled individuals and participation is restricted to a subset of the community; second, hunting has the potential to generate high return rates among simultaneously available foraging alternatives (second only to sardine netting), but does not result in much consumption benefit to the hunters since they share widely and take no portion for themselves. As with spearfishing, we hypothesize that the benefits of hunting are gained through the honest-signal value of acquiring the prey, rather than through consumption, and that honesty is maintained through differential costs and benefits: men of higher phenotypic quality benefit more or pay less than lower-quality individuals per unit signal.

Prediction 1: *turtle hunting is differentially costly or beneficial*

The relative costs and benefits of hunting turtle vary with the season: hunts are less costly in the nesting season because the prey are found closer to home, but they are more ambiguous as a signal, since turtles may also be collected at this time. Since there is the potential for dishonest signaling (acquiring a turtle through collecting and passing it off as a hunted turtle), we predict that the benefits of hunting during the nesting season are lower as well. We would thus expect that more skilled hunters would be over-represented among hunting season hunts, which have the highest cost and the lowest signal ambiguity, while the least skilled hunters would be over-represented among nesting season hunts, when hunts are less costly as well as harder to discriminate from collecting. Among turtle hunt participants, age is usually a good proxy for skill, since hunt participants move up in the hierarchy of roles as they gain in skill over time, and since the skills necessary to be a good hunt leader are not dependent upon size and strength. We thus expect jumpers to make the move to become hunt leaders only during the nesting season. Hunt leaders during the hunting season ($n = 8$) are in fact an average of 7.9 years older than hunt leaders ($n = 22$) during the nesting season, a difference that is statistically significant ($U = 41.5$, $p = 0.05$). In contrast, there is no difference in age of jumper according to season ($df = 37$, $t = 0.253$, $p = 0.80$). Of the 17 known current hunt leaders, the 4 youngest (aged 18–22) were observed as hunt leaders only during the nesting season, and served only as jumpers during the hunting season.[16]

Prediction 2: *signal intensity is linked to phenotypic quality*

Turtle hunting provides evidence of skills that could honestly signal several relevant qualities: environmental and ethological knowledge, risk-taking, strength and agility, leadership and organizational abilities, and prosocial tendencies (e.g., expending time and energy in providing goods for public consumption at feasts). Such information is presumably of interest to potential female mates, their families, potential political alliance partners, or competitors for social status.

As detailed above, the most active hunters are a subset of the adult male population. The best turtle hunt leaders are well known to community members: in a series of 32 interviews we conducted with men and women in which informants were asked to nominate any three individuals of their choice for "best turtle hunters," 3 men (all ones we had observed as the most frequent hunt leaders) garnered 38 (39.6%) of the 96 nominations (a total of 30 men were nominated for "best hunter" out of a pool of 90 or more males aged 16 and older). While several deceased individuals or older men no longer active as hunt leaders were named among the "best hunters," no men currently active solely as jumpers were so named. Jumpers are rarely individually credited by others for acquiring a turtle, and drivers are rarely publicly credited with participation in the hunt. Feast-goers can readily name hunt leaders as providers of the turtle, even several years after the feast, but when pressed for the names of other hunt participants, lump all others together as "the boys." Jumpers may begin in this role as young as 15–17 years old; anecdotal evidence indicates that those who excel in this role and gain increasing knowledge and peer respect eventually become hunt leaders, while others remain jumpers or cease participating in turtle hunting.[17]

Prediction 3: *the signal is designed to be perceived by the intended audience*

Signals do little good if they are not perceived and the information contained is not deciphered. We propose that when signals are designed to

---

[16] Note the very strict adherence to an ethologically based research methodology. The researchers could easily have asked Meriam hunt leaders why they choose to hunt in the hunting or nesting season. They could have asked why they choose turtle hunting over sardine fishing, and the answers might have been enlightening. However, theoretical models built from animal behavior do not admit that type of questioning. They are built almost entirely on the observation of behavior and the assumption that observed behavior is, in some way, fitness enhancing.

[17] In the case of both spearfishing and turtle hunting, sexual selection is being implied. Although the authors do not state this directly, if these behaviors are to have any effect

on natural selection, men must be displaying turtle hunting or spearfishing abilities in much the same way that male peacocks display spectacular tail feathers. Peahens find large tail feather displays sexually attractive and, the authors suggest, human females find turtle hunting and spearfishing displays sexually attractive. If this is so, then over time, one would expect that the Meriam population would be genetically superior at the abilities involved in hunting to other populations not subject to the same pressures. We are not aware that this is indeed the case. However, perhaps all human populations were historically subject to conditions that selected for talents similar to those used in spearfishing and turtle hunting.

acquire general social status or political dominance, broadcast efficiency will be increased by directing them at larger audiences, rather than small subsets of interested parties (as might be predicted if the signal elements of hunting were directed solely at potential mating partners). Thus, we predict that hunted turtles should be shared more widely than collected turtles; in other words, that individuals should choose to hunt for larger audiences, and to collect when audiences (the number of households attracted to the turtle and consuming portions) are predicted to be smaller. Because turtles cannot be collected during the hunting season, we control for the effects of season. We thus predict that audience size should have a significant effect on acquisition method within the nesting season only: when larger audiences are available, men should prefer to hunt rather than collect. During the 1994–1995 nesting season, hunts for which the number of consumers were known ($n = 22$) averaged 26.7 ± 23.7 households, while collections ($n = 80$) averaged 18.7 ± 19.0 households consuming, a significant difference ($t = -1.649$, $df = 100$, $p = 0.05$).[18]

Individuals who acquire turtles for feasts have a large built-in audience; however, turtles acquired for household provisioning will be shared among a smaller number of households. If hunting serves as an honest signal and hunters wish to broadcast the signal widely, turtles acquired for household provisioning should also be shared more widely when hunted than when collected (controlling for season). During the 1994–1995 nesting season, there were 9 hunts and 44 collections to supply turtles for household consumption. . . . As predicted, hunted consumption turtles were shared to more households (7.5 ± 3.0) than collected consumption turtles (4.6 ± 2.5), and the statistical difference is strongly significant ($U = 64$, $p = 0.015$). Because the number of households receiving portions of a hunted turtle is larger than the number receiving portions of a collected turtle, portions shared to each household should be smaller, but they do not seem to be so, because hunters kept less for themselves and their own households than did collectors (mean portion kept [kcal] for hunters $7,780 \pm 2,194$ kcal, $n = 38$; for collectors = $14,387 \pm 2,631$ kcal, $n = 123$) although the difference is not significant (t-test on log-transformed kcal kept, $t = 0.682$, $df = 159$, $p = 0.50$).

DISCUSSION[19]

Although our sample of spearfishers is too small to define a continuum in level of skill, spearfishing does seem to exhibit strong potential for competitive signaling. The most frequent signaler obtains much higher gains per unit patch residence time than other spearfishers. Harvest size (the most easily observed indicator of return rates) is likely to be linked to phenotypic quality in the form of hand-eye coordination, stealth, and patience, and provides an immediate signal of forager quality. Success rate is a signal element contributing to the long-term reputation of the spear-fisher. High success rates in conjunction with large harvest size ensure that large harvests are more likely due to skill (forager-dependent variability) than to luck (forager-independent variability). As a result, the most active spearfisher gains the benefits of an enhanced spearing reputation that more infrequent signalers do not seem to enjoy. Spearing thus has the potential to serve as an honest signal of a spearfisherman's phenotypic quality.

---

[18] Remember that there is a difference between significant and meaningful. The results the authors mention above are significant because there is less than a 5% chance that the average number of people consuming hunted food at an occasion is the same as the number of people consuming gathered food. Notice that despite the statistically significant difference between the two groups, the plus and minus figures tell you that there is a great deal of overlap between them. That doesn't mean that the authors' interpretation is incorrect. The difference between the two groups may be meaningful as well as significant, but it is left to the reader to judge whether the difference in size between the audience for hunting and the audience for collecting is really important.

[19] In this section, the authors recap the critical findings of their research and discuss several problems in it.

Although we have demonstrated the potential for signaling, and the bias in men's foraging toward resources which have high competitive signaling potential, precisely how both signaler and observer ultimately benefit from the signal is not clear. We do know that good spearing men are widely recognized, and that this adds to their social status within the community. Potential competitors might also gain from knowing who is a better man with a spear, although the knowledge certainly would have been more useful in the past when spears were the major means of ambushing competitors. Spearing signals may not be designed to appeal to potential mates interested only in marrying provisioners. A man who demonstrates his intention to provision a household by collecting shellfish may be more attractive to such women than a man who demonstrates his intention to engage in a competitive, status-enhancing pursuit.[20]

Turtle hunters seem to have very different goals than turtle collectors. Compared to collecting, hunting is more costly (in time, energy, and risk), provides meat less efficiently, and is associated with wider distributions of meat and larger audiences to witness the hunters' prowess. Hunters keep no meat for themselves unless (quite rarely) hunting for household consumption, in which case they still keep less and share more than turtle collectors. Hunters take on a variety of costs for which they are not materially compensated: they expend more time and energy in hunting than they do collecting, they spend more money for fuel, they spend time organizing and preparing the hunting team and its equipment prior to the hunt, and they deliver the meat to be consumed by large audiences at feasts. The ability to bear such costs appears to be linked to hunter quality. Because a hunter is an organizer and decision-maker, his abilities peak as he gains

skill and experience: those named as the best hunters are older than other hunt participants, such as jumpers. As we predicted, when hunting was less costly and more difficult to discriminate from collecting (i.e., during the nesting season), hunters were younger, in fact composed almost entirely of ambitious jumpers preparing to be hunt leaders themselves. Furthermore, the signals sent by hunting are efficiently broadcast: hunts were associated with larger numbers of consumers overall than collections during the nesting season and during household consumption events. Most feast-goers (audience members), when quizzed, know the identity of hunters, but not the identity of jumpers.

Since the low take-home returns of hunters providing turtle for household consumption and the negative take-home returns of hunters providing turtle for a feast are due to widespread sharing, the argument could be made that the signal cost is eventually recovered in the form of meat or other goods or services returned as payback for the hunter's gift. In other words, perhaps RA[21] by the recipients of a hunter's largesse erases the cost of his signal (Sosis and Hill 1997). The stable maintenance of RA requires that the provisioning of a turtle be contingent upon the eventual receipt of counterbalancing benefits which compensate the hunter for the marginal cost of giving up turtle that could have been used in other fitness-enhancing ways. Previous tests of predictions based on RA in the form of risk reduction reciprocity for sharing of collected and hunted turtles combined received little support (Bliege Bird and Bird 1997). Further tests of alternative forms of reciprocity are being conducted to evaluate this line of explanation (R. Bliege Bird, G. Kushnik, E. A. Smith, D. Bird, C. Hadley, unpublished data), as will be detailed in future publications.

---

[20] Here the authors face but do not resolve the critical problem we identified earlier in the essay. They clearly show that spearfishing and turtle hunting have characteristics that could qualify them as costly signals. However, the theory can only work if these individuals really do receive benefits, particularly reproductive benefits. It is not unreasonable to suppose that they do, but the authors are unable to show it unambiguously. These passages demonstrate that they are well aware of this problem.

[21] Here the authors once again try to eliminate RA (reciprocal altruism, described in the opening paragraphs of this essay) as the cause of the wide sharing of hunted foods.

While we have measured the cost of hunting using direct material currencies such as time, energy, and money, there are additional social costs that, though difficult to measure, may be of equal or even greater importance. Turtles provided for feasts are needed by community elders (feast hosts) to enhance their own status by ensuring there is plenty of meat for guests. If successful hunting is a reliable signal of the hunter's underlying quality (as defined above), lower-quality individuals would be expected to fail on turtle hunts more often and thus pay a higher marginal cost per turtle delivered to a feast (i.e., per unit signal). Failing to deliver a turtle to a feast also entails significant social costs, since the feast-holders are expected to serve turtle to their guests, and everyone will know when a hunter has failed. High-quality individuals should have a lower probability of failure and thus a high ratio of social benefits (from successful hunts) to costs (from failures). Low-quality individuals may face a large enough risk of failing to produce a net social deficit from their signaling attempts, and hence may avoid signaling at all, making it difficult to test this hypothesis. We do have anecdotal evidence that some men have attempted turtle hunting in the past, and given up when they found they were "no good at it." In addition, the facts (detailed above) that only certain men engage in turtle hunting, that only an older and more experienced subset of these become hunt leaders, and that hunt leader status is widely recognized in the community, all indicate that success in this endeavor is not equally available.[22]

To qualify as costly signaling, hunting must not only be honest, but must also reveal signaler quality. Given the three distinct roles played by hunt participants, we propose (but cannot currently test) that at least four distinct dimensions of underlying quality could be signaled through turtle hunting: (1) physical quality (such as strength, stamina, agility, and risk-taking); (2) cognitive skills (involving the ecological and ethological knowledge needed to successfully locate and capture turtles); (3) leadership skills (charisma and organizational abilities); and (4) generosity (ability and willingness to bear the high immediate cost in time, money, and energy of providing collective goods without direct compensation). We expect the first dimension to apply primarily to the younger men who serve as "jumpers," whereas the other three dimensions refer primarily to hunt leaders.

The results of additional analysis in progress show that the display of such qualities is correlated with higher social status and higher age-specific reproductive success of hunters and their mates than other Meriam (E. A. Smith, R. Bliege Bird, D. Bird, unpublished data). As explained to us by Meriam hunters and their mates, the signals sent by hunters are likely to be part of both political strategies, in which hunters demonstrate to other men their honest intention to work for the public good, and reproductive strategies, in which hunters demonstrate their "willingness to work hard" in order to gain access to the "best girl" (Kaddy, personal communication; Passi, personal communication). Hunters know that spreading one's influence widely via the provisioning of collective goods at feasts increases social status over the long-term among the community as a whole, while less public-minded status enhancing activities (like stealing land or selfishly hoarding resources) provides narrow, short-term status in only a small pool of competitors.[23]

---

[22] Here, again, is one of the most critical elements of the authors' argument: The system works because the signal is costly. That is, although it can be faked (for example, a poor hunter could do enough work to acquire turtles for a feast), the cost of faking is so high in terms of time and energy expended, as well as risk of social embarrassment, that the good achieved (the social benefits of recognition as a good hunter) is not worth the costs incurred. We must

point out, however, that since the authors have not clearly specified the benefits that good hunters achieve, we have no method to judge how much they are worth.

[23] In this paragraph, the authors allow a rare bit of traditional ethnographic data into their essay in the form of interviews with Meriam men.

Implications for the Sexual Division of Labor

One intriguing result of our analysis are the gender differences in participation in those activities with high signaling potential. With spearfishing particularly, the differences were not consistent with the common notion that a sexual division of labor in humans functions to maximize the productivity of a cooperating male-female pair (see Bliege Bird 1999). We propose that the signaling benefits attached to certain foraging strategies may often change the valuation of certain prey items for some individuals. While foraging on the reef, males make choices that fail to maximize their macronutrient return rates. These choices appear to be due to the tradeoffs men face over foraging for highly productive resources which have little signaling value (shellfish) against foraging for less productive resources with high signaling value (speared fish). Likewise, choosing to hunt turtle for feasts provides much lower consumption benefits than collecting turtle for the household, but greater signaling benefits. Adult women only participate in cooperative turtle collection, comprising 21% of all participants, and do not hunt. These data suggest that foraging sex differences may not simply be a result of women preferring plants and men meat, or women preferring small harvests while men prefer large ones, or even women preferring prey which can be more easily harvested while children are present (shellfish are just as difficult as fish to collect with small children). Where there is a choice in foraging method, men seem to prefer to acquire meat through more risky methods that more easily differentiate the skill of individual foragers, while women seem to prefer less risky methods carrying little potential for discrimination of forager quality. We propose that sex-biased foraging preferences may arise due to the differing benefits each sex receives from investing in competition for status through signaling certain genotypic or phenotypic qualities.[24]

Foraging as Communication

As Hawkes (1990, 1991, 1992, 1993) first hypothesized, some kinds of hunting may persist in human populations because some foragers gain benefits from widely disseminating knowledge about their prowess relative to other individuals through the hunting of large and risky prey items. While Hawkes (1993) stressed the benefits that hunters obtain from providing collective goods (as with turtle hunting and unconditional sharing), our results show that benefits may also come in the absence of any material good provided to observers (as with spearfishing) as a result of honestly revealing hidden information to interested parties. Differential costs and benefits for signalers of higher and lower quality serve to keep the information honest and valuable to observers.

Our results suggest that CST has the potential to account for many puzzling aspects of human foraging strategies, and to substantially modify received views about optimal foraging, food sharing, and other phenomena central to studies of human behavioral ecology in small-scale societies (Winterhalder and Smith 2000). CST may illuminate otherwise puzzling behaviors such as preference for prey and patch types which provide fewer energetic benefits than other possible choices and are more costly on other levels, if the costs (or benefits) incurred are linked to signaler quality, so that poorer-quality signalers cannot consistently maintain or reach the same level of signaling as higher-quality signalers. Signaling hypotheses have only just begun to be tested as a cause for variability in human foraging strategies. Sosis (2000) has suggested that the benefits of signaling may explain why Ifaluk men engage in energetically inefficient fishing methods associated with costly ritual preparations. Such benefits may also explain why Ache men prefer to hunt widely shared game even though palm starch collection would offer higher on-encounter energetic returns (Hill et al. 1987; Hawkes 1991).

---

[24] In this passage, the authors level another attack on economic models of forager behavior. Here they insist that the sexual division of labor in these societies occurs not because the group is trying to maximize its caloric return while minimizing its labor, as an economic model might have it. Instead they propose that the division of labor and the particular types of hunting performed by men are explained by competition for status and reproduction rather than calories.

We are not proposing that the signaling benefits provide the *only* motivation for hunters and meat recipients, but simply that they provide an additional factor of evolutionary and motivational significance shaping hunting and sharing decisions. Thus the social and political signaling benefits of at least certain forms of hunting may compensate for any economic "wastefulness," in the same way that Veblen (1899) explained both "conspicuous consumption" of material goods and "conspicuous leisure" as instances of "conspicuous expenditure" designed to gain or maintain social benefits only indirectly related to economic advantage.[25] However, CST has the potential to explain not only "wasteful" foraging activities, but any behavior in which higher-quality individuals obtain higher marginal benefits because they can better absorb the cost of the behavior, and where such behavior is efficiently broadcast to the proper observers (potential mates, allies, or competitors).

ACKNOWLEDGEMENTS

We thank the Meriam community foremost, especially Chairman Ron Day for his foresight and tolerance, our Meriam families, particularly the Passis, and the turtle hunters who volunteered information or invited us on hunts. We also wish to acknowledge the invaluable field assistance of Andrew Passi, Rono "Sonny" Passi, Edna Kabere, Del Passi, and Craig Hadley. For many helpful discussions and comments on the manuscript, we thank Monique Borgerhoff Mulder, Thomas Getty, Craig Hadley, Polly Wiessner, Kristen Hawkes, Kim Hill, Frank Marlowe, Rich Sosis, Steven Siller, and Bruce Winterhalder. Research in 1998–1999 was supported by NSF grant SBR-9616096 to R.B.B. and E.A.S., NSF grant SBR-9616887 to D.W.B. and E.A.S., and research in 1994–1995 was supported by grants to R.B.B. and D.W.B. from AIATSIS, the L.S.B. Leakey Foundation, the Wenner Gren Foundation for Anthropological Research, and an NSF predoctoral fellowship to R.B.B. and an NSF Dissertation Improvement Grant to D.W.B.

REFERENCES

Beckett J. (1988). The Torres Strait Islanders: custom and colonialism. Cambridge University Press, Cambridge, UK.

Bird D. W., Bliege Bird R. (1997). Contemporary shellfish gathering strategies among the Meriam of the Torres Strait Islands, Australia: testing predictions of a central place foraging model. J Archaeol Sci 24:39–63.

Bird D. W., Bliege Bird R. (2000). The ethnoarchaeology of juvenile foragers: shellfishing strategies among Meriam children. J. Anthropol Archaeol 19:461–476.

Bliege Bird R. (1999). Cooperation and conflict: the behavioral ecology of the sexual division of labor. Evol Anthropol 8:65–75.

Bliege Bird R., Bird D. W. (1997). Delayed reciprocity and tolerated theft. Curr Anthropol 38:49–78.

Bliege Bird R., Bird D. W., Beaton J. (1995). Children and traditional subsistence on Mer (Murray Island), Torres Strait. Aust Aboriginal Stud 1:2–17.

Boone J. L. (1998). The evolution of magnanimity: when is it better to give than to receive? Hum Nat 9:1–21.

Brand Miller J., James K., Maggiore P. (1993). Tables of composition of Australian Aboriginal foods. Aboriginal Studies Press, Canberra.

Clements R., Stephens D. C. (1995). Testing models of non-kin cooperation—mutualism and the prisoner's dilemma. Anim Behav 50:527–535.

Connor R. C. (1996). Partner preferences in by-product mutualism and the case of predator inspection in fish. Anim Behav 51:451–454.

Dugatkin L. (1997). Cooperation among animals: an evolutionary perspective. Oxford University Press, New York.

---

[25] Thorstein Veblen (1857–1929) was an economist and social theorist best known for his 1912 work, *The Theory of the Leisure Class.* In that work, he attempted to apply ideas about Darwinian evolution to economic life. In Veblen's analysis, the fundamental conflict and struggle in society is between making goods (the realm of factory workers and engineers) and making money (the realm of bankers and financiers). The goal of economic life in capitalism is "conspicuous consumption," a phrase that Veblen coined. He argued that the wealthy (particularly those who make money rather than goods) consumed conspicuously, buying obviously visible luxuries for the purposes of display rather than for any use value such objects might have. The notion that the most important part of consumption is display fits in well with the key points made in this essay.

Getty T. (1998). Handicap signaling: when fecundity and viability do not add up. Anim Behav 56:127–130.

Grafen A. (1990). Biological signals as handicaps. J Theor Biol 144:517–546.

Gurven M., Hill K., Hurtado A., Lyles R. (2000). Food transfers among Hiwi foragers of Venezuela: tests of reciprocity. Hum Ecol 28:171–218.

Haddon A. C. (1906). Sociology, magic and religion of the Eastern Islanders. Reports of the Cambridge Anthropological Expedition to Torres Straits, vol. 6. Cambridge University Press, Cambridge, UK.

Hawkes K. (1990). Why do men hunt? Some benefits for risky choices. In: Cashdan E. (ed.) Uncertainty in tribal and peasant economies. Westview, Boulder, pp. 145–166.

Hawkes K. (1991). Showing off: tests of another hypothesis about men's foraging goals. Ethol Sociobiol 12:29–54.

Hawkes K. (1992). Sharing and collective action. In: Smith E. A., Winterhalder B. (eds.) Evolutionary ecology and human behavior. de Gruyter, Hawthorne, NY, pp. 269–300.

Hawkes K. (1993). Why hunter-gatherers work. Curr Anthropol 34:341–362.

Hill K. (1988). Macronutrient modifications of optimal foraging theory: an approach using indifference curves applied to some modern foragers. Hum Ecol 16:157–197.

Hill K., Kaplan H., Hawkes K., Hurtado A. M. (1987). Foraging decisions among Ache hunter-gatherers: new data and implications for optimal foraging models. Ethol Sociobiol 8:1–36.

Hirth H. (1971). Synopsis of biological data on the green turtle *Chelonia mydas* (Linnaeus).1758. FAO Fisheries Synopsis No 85. Food and Agriculture Organization of the United Nations, Rome.

Hurtado A. M., Hill K., Kaplan H., Hurtado I. (1992). Trade-offs between female food acquisition and child care among Hiwi and Ache foragers. Hum Nat 3:185–216.

Johnstone R. A. (1995). Sexual selection, honest advertisement and the handicap principle: reviewing the evidence. Biol Rev 70:1–65.

Johnstone R. A. (1997). The evolution of animal signals. In: Krebs J. R., Davies N. B. (eds.) Behavioural ecology: an evolutionary approach. Blackwell, Oxford, pp. 155–178.

Neiman F. D. (1998). Conspicuous consumption as wasteful advertising: a Darwinian perspective on spatial patterns in classic Maya terminal monument dates. In: Barton C. M., Clark G. A. (eds.) Rediscovering Darwin: evolutionary theory and archaeological explanation. Archaeological papers of the American Anthropological Association No 7, pp. 267–290.

Pusey A. E., Packer C. (1997). The ecology of relationships. In Krebs J. R., Davies N. B. (eds.) Behavioural ecology: an evolutionary approach. Blackwell, Oxford, pp. 254–283.

Roberts G. (1998). Competitive altruism: from reciprocity to the handicap principle. Proc R Soc Lond B 265:427–431.

Sharp N. (1993). Stars of Tagai: the Torres Strait Islanders. Aboriginal Studies Press, Canberra.

Sidwell V. (1981). Chemical and nutritional composition of finfishes, whales, crustaceans, mollusks, and their products. NOAA Technical Memorandum. National Marine Fisheries Services, Washington, DC.

Smith E. A. (1988). Risk and uncertainty in the "original affluent society": evolutionary ecology of resource sharing and land tenure. In: Ingold T., Riches D., Woodburn I. (eds.) Hunters and gatherers: history, evolution, and social change. Berg, Oxford, pp. 222–252.

Smith E. A. (1991). Inujjamiut foraging strategies: evolutionary ecology of an Arctic hunting economy. de Gruyter, Hawthorne, NY.

Smith E. A., Bliege Bird R. (2000). Turtle hunting and tombstone opening: public generosity as costly signaling. Evol Hum Behav 21:245–261.

Sosis R. (2000). Costly signaling and torch fishing on Ifaluk Atoll. Evol Hum Behav 21:223–244.

Sosis R., Hill K. (1997). Comment on Bliege Bird and Bird. Curr Anthropol 38:73–74.

Veblen T. (1899). Theory of the leisure class. Macmillan, New York.

Wiessner P. (1996). Leveling the hunter: constraints on the status quest in foraging societies. In: Wiessner P., Schiefenhovel W. (eds.) Food and the status quest. Berghahn, Providence, RI, pp. 171–192.

Winterhalder B. (1997). Gifts given, gifts taken: the behavioral ecology of nonmarket, intragroup exchange. J Archaeol Res 5:121–168.

Winterhalder B., Smith E. A. (2000). Analyzing adaptive strategies: human behavioral ecology at twenty-five. Evol Anthropol 9:51–72.

Zahavi A. (1975). Mate selection—a selection for handicap. J. Theor Biol 53:205–214.

Zahavi A. (1977). Reliability in communication systems and the evolution of altruism. In: Stonehouse B., Perrins C. M. (eds.) Evolutionary ecology. Macmillan, London, pp. 253–259.

Anthropology and Gender

Unlike many disciplines, almost from the discipline's beginning, women in anthropology reached high levels of professional achievement and gained popular recognition for their work. In the twentieth century, women such as Ruth Benedict and Margaret Mead became household names, whereas others such as Mary Douglas (1921–2007), Laura Bohannon (1922–2002), Sherry Ortner (b. 1941), Michelle Rosaldo (1944–1981), Peggy Reeves Sanday (b. 1937), Louise Lamphere (b. 1940), Lila Abu-Lughod (b. 1952), and Marilyn Strathern (b. 1941) and Nancy Scheper-Hughes (b. 1944) are widely known to scholars outside of anthropology.

Despite the achievements of women within anthropology, as Lamphere (2004:127) notes, even such seminal figures as Margaret Mead, Ruth Benedict, and Elsie Clew Parsons were marginalized, pigeonholed, and excluded from important aspects of the discipline. Until the mid-twentieth century, discussions of women in the anthropological literature were usually limited to introductory textbook chapters on marriage, family, and kinship. In the 1960s and 1970s, this situation began to change. The modern feminist movement in anthropology had its beginnings in the social upheavals of the 1960s—the civil rights movement, anti–Vietnam War activism, various consciousness-raising experiments and the wider "second-wave" feminist movement itself. By the early 1970s women anthropologists were incorporating these new perspectives into their research. Feminist anthropologists documented the discipline's neglect of women and gender as significant dimensions of social life and questioned anthropological assumptions they considered male centered. Since that time, interest in the study of gender roles and focus on gender and sexuality in a cross-cultural perspective has increased, and some of the basic assumptions of anthropology have been called into question.

Much of the research by feminist anthropologists in the early 1970s was concerned with documenting women's lives and their roles in societies around the world. Assuming universal sexual asymmetry—that is, the worldwide subordination of women—virtually all of these early studies sought to study this situation through various theoretical perspectives. For example, Friedl (1975) attempted to explain the position of women from a materialist perspective by focusing on women's subsistence roles. Chodorow (1974) examined the issue of subordination from a psychological view, emphasizing the role of childhood socialization in the formation of sex roles. Michelle Rosaldo and Louise Lamphere's 1974 volume, *Women, Culture, and Society*, and Reyna Reiter's 1975 anthology, *Toward an Anthropology of Women*, were two of the defining works in this era of feminist anthropology.

At the same time that feminist cultural anthropologists focused on gender inequality, research on women and gender by feminist archaeologists and physical anthropologists challenged the "man the hunter" version of human evolution. Work on this issue, such as the 1975 essay by physical anthropologist Sally Slocum (b. 1939) in this volume charged that woman's roles in human evolution had been ignored because scholars focused on hunting rather than gathering. For instance, Slocum challenges the popular idea that hunting by men, because it implied tool making, communication, and the development of complex cognitive skills (Washburn and Lancaster 1968), played a pivotal role in our evolutionary past. She stresses that women's gathering and child care also demanded complex communication, cooperation, and tool making. Slocum argues that evidence indicates foraging, not hunting, was the principal economic strategy throughout most of human evolutionary history (Lamphere 1987:16). This "woman the gatherer" approach inspired scholars to revise the standard views on human evolution. One particularly significant study was Tanner and Zihlman's 1976 study of women's activities in economics and technology in relation to the roles that savanna living, foraging, and social organization played in human evolutionary selection.

By the 1980s, anthropological research into issues of gender had broadened substantially. Feminist researchers were increasingly joined by others whose interests not necessarily linked to feminist concerns. Increasingly researchers investigated the complexity and variety of gender roles. Gender identities that did not fit the conventional Western notions of male and female were of particular interest.

Research and analysis in the 1980s moved away from the previous decade's blanket assumptions of gender asymmetry and followed three principal trends. The first of these focused on the social construction of gender. Researchers differentiated sex (a condition of biology) from gender (a social role assigned to an individual) and explored the many permutations of gender and sexuality among the different societies, a field pioneered by Margaret Mead in the 1930s. Good examples of this type of work are Herdt's 1984 examination of ritualized homosexuality among the Sambia of New Guinea and Nanda's examination of the Hijra, a group in India that cannot easily be classified as male or female (1990). In addition, work such as Yanagisako and Collier's *Gender and Kinship* (1987) and Sanday and Goodenough's *Beyond the Second Sex* (1990), fall into this class of study.

Another direction in gender research and analysis took a materialist perspective. Materialist scholars used cross-cultural analysis to explain differences in the roles and power of different gender groups. These researchers were relatively unconcerned with describing the ways in which gender is defined in different societies. They concentrated on research that analyzed gender-related activities using measures of social, economic, and political power (Morgen 1989:4). Many scholars in this area focused on gender as it relates to class, the social relations of power, and changes in modes of production. Essay 29, by Eleanor Leacock (1922–1987), fits this category of study. In this work, which appeared in 1983, Leacock argues that prior to Western contact, gender relations in Native American and Australian aboriginal societies were typically egalitarian because men and women participated equally in the processes of production. She argues that the unequal place of women in these societies today is the result of the subjugation of these societies by Europeans and the imposition of capitalist forms of production.

A third trend of this era concerned the range of variation of experiences of gender, particularly within current industrialized society. As we noted above, feminist anthropology grew from the broader social movements of the 1960s. The feminist movement of that era was dominated by white, middle-class scholars and so largely concerned itself with issues of particular interest to that group. However, by the 1980s, women of different class and ethnic backgrounds were making feminist anthropologists increasingly aware that their interests did not necessarily coincide with those of the white middle-class women who had popularized feminism in anthropology. Micaela di Leonardo writes that feminist scholars were forced to confront "the question of 'difference'— the multiple racial, ethnic, class, sexual, age, regional, and national identities of women—as they noted their own restricted demographic representation and research interests" (1991:18). In the 1990s, "the question of difference" expanded to include gay, lesbian, and transgender issues as studies began to explore the links between sexuality, identity, and social positioning and power.

Scholars following this third trend have emphasized the specificity of gender identities. They have moved away from the earlier theorizing about "man" and "woman" as general concepts to focus on the different ways in which race, class, and gender intersect. Essay #30 by David Valentine (b. 1966) is an example of this type of research. In this essay Valentine points out that those who don't fit the Western homosexual/heterosexual identities are labeled transgender, but their sexual identity and behavior is still classified as either heterosexual or homosexual. By showing how transgendered people talk about sexual desire, Valentine intends to illustrate the inconsistencies in the western concepts of gender identity and sexuality.

The work of anthropologists concerned with gender in the 1980s broadened the focus of anthropology. These anthropologists led the discipline in developing new, experimental forms of ethnographic writing. In particular, current in gender theory follows three trends. First, feminist theorists called the anthropological canon into question. In the introduction to *Women Writing Culture*, for example, Ruth Behar writes:

> Why is it that the legacy of what counts as social theory is traced back only to Lewis Henry Morgan, Karl Marx, Émile Durkheim, Max Weber, Michael Foucault and Pierre Bourdieu? Why is there not a parallel matrilineal genealogy taking off from say, the turn-of-the-century work of Charlotte Perkins Gilman? . . . Why is the culture concept in anthropology only traced through Sir Edward Tylor, Franz Boas, Bronislaw Malinowski, Claude Lévi-Strauss, and Clifford Geertz? Could the writing of culture not be traced, as the essays in this volume suggest, through Elsie Clews Parsons, Ruth Benedict, Margaret Mead, Ella Deloria, Zora Neale Hurston, Ruth Landes, and Barbara Myerhoff to Alice Walker? (1995:11–12)

Second, gender theorists have often led the way in emphasizing multivocality—that is, giving voice to a variety of viewpoints in their ethnographic writing. They question the objectivity of science and argue that anthropologists are not uniquely qualified interpreters of culture. They claim that traditional anthropological writing distanced authors from their subjects. To counter this, gender theorists have encouraged members of marginalized groups to write about their cultures for themselves and challenged anthropologists to take into account "the discriminations of racism, homophobia, sexism, and classism (Behar and Gordon 1995:7)" that they claim are a part of traditional anthropology.

Finally, some gender theorists have emphasized experimentation with nontraditional forms of anthropological writing. Claiming that all ways of knowing are subjective, these authors have offered works of poetry and fiction as new forms of ethnography. Others experiment with the epistemological assumptions of anthropology by introducing their own thoughts and experiences into their research. One form this work has taken is the "autoethnography"—works that combine autobiographical information with anthropological analyses. In "A Tale of Two Pregnancies" (essay 37 in this volume, published in 1995), for example, Lila Abu-Lughod discusses her experience of pregnancy and compares it with the pregnancies of Bedouin women with whom she conducted research.

The past thirty years has seen enormous growth in gender studies. Almost all major universities now have gender studies, or women's studies programs. Men still hold the majority of full professorships in anthropology, but women now make up half of most department faculties. Though these women do not necessarily have a particular interest in issues of gender, it is probably true that the majority are sympathetic to gender-related concerns in university life in general and anthropology in particular.

Despite their success in the academy and after almost five decades of work in the areas of gender and sexuality, anthropologists have not successfully translated their findings to a wider culture beyond an academic context. The cultural clashes over women in the workplace, sexual harassment, marriage of same-sex couples, workplace and legal discrimination against homosexuals, to name a few, continue unabated in the United States more than eighty years after Margaret Mead's groundbreaking studies.

28. Woman the Gatherer: Male Bias in Anthropology

SALLY SLOCUM (b. 1939)

LITTLE SYSTEMATIC ATTENTION has been given in our discipline to an "anthropology of knowledge."[1] While some anthropologists have concerned themselves with knowledge in general, as seen through the varieties of human cultures, few have examined anthropological knowledge itself. An anthropology of knowledge would have several parts. First is what Peter Berger (1967:1–18) has called "philosophical anthropology": a study of the nature of the human species. This has always been a legitimate concern of anthropology, but too often we become so concerned with minute differences that we forget we are studying a single species. Second is how we "know" anything—what is accepted as "proof," what is reality, what are the grounds for rationality (Garfinkel, 1960), what modes are used in gathering knowledge, what are the effects of differences in culture and world view on what we "know." Third is a close examination of the questions asked in anthropology, for questions always determine and limit answers.

It is the third point, the nature of anthropological questions, to which I wish to speak in this paper. We are human beings studying other human beings, and we cannot leave ourselves out of the equation. We choose to ask certain questions, *and not others*. Our choice grows out of the cultural context in which anthropology and anthro-

pologists exist. Anthropology, as an academic discipline, has been developed primarily by white Western males, during a specific period in history. Our questions are shaped by the particulars of our historical situation, and by unconscious cultural assumptions.[2]

Given the cultural and ethnic background of the majority of anthropologists, it is not surprising that the discipline has been biased. There are signs, however, that this selective blindness is beginning to come under scrutiny. For example, in the exchange in the journal *Current Anthropology* (1968), anthropologists like Kathleen Gough and Gerald Berreman point out the unconscious efforts of American political and economic assumptions on our selection of problems and populations to be studied. Restive minority groups in this country are pointing to the bias inherent in anthropological studies of themselves through books such as Vine Deloria's *Custer Died for Your Sins*. We have always encouraged members of American minority groups, and other "foreigners," to take up anthropology because of the perspective on the world that they can supply. The invitation is increasingly being accepted. As we had both hoped and feared, repercussions from this new participation are being felt in theory, method, interpretation, and problem choice, shaking anthropology to the roots.[3]

From *Toward an Anthropology of Women* (1975)

[1] The 1960s and 1970s were an era of radical rethinking within anthropology, with many strands contributing to a broad critique of positivist anthropology. The feminist critique was one of the most powerful, since it attacked what feminists viewed as fundamental biases in a field that prided itself on being relatively bias free. This essay is taken from one of several groundbreaking anthologies of feminist essays in anthropology to appear in the 1970s, *Toward an Anthropology of Women,* edited by Reyna Reiter (1975).

[2] One of the key questions of current anthropology is whether the fact that anthropology is generally done by a

specific group of people fundamentally prejudices its results. Feminists were among the first to pose the question in these terms.

[3] The feminist critique was, of course, part of a broader revision of the social sciences and humanities that has continued in American intellectual culture. This change has been powerfully influenced by popular politics, especially the civil rights and women's movements of the 1960s. Several books aimed at popular rather than scholarly audiences were crucial. *Custer Died* (1969) was one of these. Dee Brown's 1971 *Bury My Heart at Wounded Knee* and Wallenchinsky and Wallace's 1975 *The People's*

The perspective of women is, in many ways, equally foreign to an anthropology that has been developed and pursued primarily by males. There is a strong male bias in the questions asked, and the interpretations given. This bias has hindered the full development of our discipline as "the study of the human animal" (I don't want to call it "the study of man" for reasons that will become evident). I am going to demonstrate the Western male bias by reexamining the matter of evolution of Homo sapiens from our nonhuman primate ancestors. In particular, the concept of "Man the Hunter" as developed by Sherwood Washburn and C. Lancaster (1968) and others is my focus. This critique is offered in hopes of transcending the male bias that limits our knowledge by limiting the questions we ask.[4]

Though male bias could be shown in other areas, hominid evolution is particularly convenient for my purpose because it involves speculations and inferences from a rather small amount of data. In such a case, hidden assumptions and premises that lie behind the speculations and inferences are more easily demonstrated. Male bias exists not only in the ways in which the scanty data are interpreted, but in the very language used. All too often the word "man" is used in such an ambiguous fashion that it is impossible to decide whether it refers to males or to the human species in general, including both males and females. In fact, one frequently is led to suspect that in the minds of many anthropologists, "man," supposedly meaning the human species, is actually exactly synonymous with "males."

This ambiguous use of language is particularly evident in the writing that surrounds the concept of Man the Hunter.[5] Washburn and Lancaster make it clear that it is specifically males who hunt, that hunting is much more than simply an economic activity, and that most of the characteristics which we think of as specifically human can be causally related to hunting. They tell us that hunting is a whole pattern of activity and way of life: "The biology, psychology, and customs that separate us from the apes—all these we owe to the hunters of time past" (1968:303). If this line of reasoning is followed to its logical conclusion, one must agree with Jane Kephart when she says:

> Since only males hunt, and the psychology of the species was set by hunting, we are forced to conclude that females are scarcely human, that is, do not have built-in the basic psychology of the species: to kill and hunt and ultimately to kill others of the same species. The argument implies built-in aggression in human males, as well as the assumed passivity of human females and their exclusion from the mainstream of human development. (1970:5)

To support their argument that hunting is important to human males, Washburn and Lancaster point to the fact that many modern males still hunt, though it is no longer economically necessary. I could point out that many modern males play golf, play the violin, or tend gardens: these, as well as hunting, are things their culture teaches them. Using a "survival" as evidence to demonstrate an important fact of cultural evolution can be accorded

---

Almanac were others. All of these books became best sellers. *Bury My Heart,* first published in January 1971, had gone through thirteen printings by October of that year.

[4] To some it seemed curious that anthropology should be accused of male bias. After all, several key early figures in anthropology had been women, and the best known anthropologist in America in the 1960s was Margaret Mead. However, statistically, anthropology was overwhelmingly dominated by men. Moreover, the institutions anthropologists frequently considered most worthy of study were those controlled by males.

[5] The feminist critique of the specific language used by anthropologists was particularly powerful because it refer-

enced the Sapir-Whorf hypothesis that language shaped worldview, an idea that had been common since the 1930s and one to which most American anthropologists subscribed to one degree or another.

The idea of primitive "man" and "man" the hunter was a particularly apt target. Washburn and Lancaster had theorized that hunting was the most critical activity for early humans and that the most important human adaptations, bipedalism and language, arose as a result of it. This idea found its way into popular culture (where it is still common today). However, research in the 1960s had shown that male hunting played a relatively small role in supplying the nutritional needs of modern hunter-gatherers.

no more validity when proposed by a modern anthropologist than when proposed by Tylor.

Regardless of its status as a survival, hunting, by implication as well as direct statement, is pictured as a male activity to the exclusion of females. This activity, on which we are told depends the psychology, biology, and customs of our species, is strictly male. A theory that leaves out half the human species is unbalanced. The theory of Man the Hunter is not only unbalanced; it leads to the conclusion that the basic human adaptation was the desire of males to hunt and kill.[6] This not only gives too much importance to aggression, which is after all only one factor of human life, but it derives culture from killing. I am going to suggest a less biased reading of the evidence, which gives a more valid and logical picture of human evolution, and at the same time a more hopeful one. First I will note the evidence, discuss the more traditional reading of it, and then offer an alternative reconstruction.

The data we have to work from are a combination of fossil and archaeological materials, knowledge of living nonhuman primates, and knowledge of living humans. Since we assume that the protohominid ancestors of Homo sapiens developed in a continuous fashion from a base of characteristics similar to those of living nonhuman primates, the most important facts seem to be the ways in which humans differ from nonhuman primates, and the ways in which we are similar. The differences are as follows: longer gestation period; more difficult birth; neoteny, in that human infants are less well developed at birth; long period of infant dependency; absence of body hair; year-round sexual receptivity of females, resulting in the possibility of bearing a second infant while the first is still at the breast or still dependent; erect bipedalism; possession of a large and complex brain that makes possible the creation of elaborate symbolic systems, languages, and cultures, and also results in most behavior being under cortical control; food sharing; and finally, living in families. (For the purposes of this paper I define families as follows: a situation where each individual has defined responsibilities and obligations to a specific set of others of both sexes and various ages. I use this definition because, among humans, the family is a *social* unit, regardless of any biological or genetic relationship which may or may not exist among its members.)

In addition to the many well-known close physiological resemblances, we share with nonhuman primates the following characteristics: living in social groups; close mother-infant bonds; affectional relationships; a large capacity for learning and a related paucity of innate behaviors; ability to take part in dominance hierarchies; a rather complex nonsymbolic communication system which can handle with considerable subtlety such information as the mood and emotional state of the individual, and the attitude and status of each individual toward the other members of the social group.[7]

---

[6] In addition to Washburn and Lancaster, popular theory in ethology and evolution in the 1960s gave a very important place to aggression. Ethologist Konrad Lorenz's *On Aggression* (1966) and author Robert Ardrey's *African Genesis* (1961) were popular works that promoted this viewpoint. These works argued for the primacy of hunting and aggression in the evolutionary formation of humanity and more or less ignored the role played by women.

It is interesting to note that most of the primate ethology of the 1960s, particularly that on which Ardrey's popular works were based, was fundamentally flawed. It was derived largely from the work of Sir Solly Zuckerman (1904–1993) and Raymond Dart (1893–1988). Zuckerman drew his conclusions from watching an artificially assembled colony of hamadryas baboons in the London zoo in the 1920s. However, the behavior of these animals in the wild is very different from that of the London zoo colony. Dart, an anatomy professor and fossil hunter, on the basis of minimal evidence, proposed that early hominids had a murderous culture based on bone and wooden weaponry.

[7] Part of Slocum's argument comes from redefining differences between humans and nonhuman primates. In traditional anthropology and popular culture, the key differences between the two were brain size and language. She presents this image below. By 1970 it became clear that anatomical features such as bipedalism preceded language and increases in brain size, and thus were more important in differentiating between hominids and other primates. Notice that the first factors mentioned by Slocum in the previous paragraph all concern women exclusively. She places brain size and language well down the list.

The fossil and archaeological evidence consists of various bones labeled Ramapithecus, Australopithecus, Homo habilis, Homo erectus, etc.; and artifacts such as stone tools representing various cultural traditions, evidence of use of fire, etc. From this evidence we can make reasonable inferences about diet, posture and locomotion, and changes in the brain as shown by increased cranial capacity, ability to make tools, and other evidences of cultural creation. Since we assume that complexity of material culture requires language, we infer the beginnings of language somewhere between Australopithecus and Homo erectus.

Given this data, the speculative reconstruction begins. As I was taught anthropology, the story goes something like this. Obscure selection pressures pushed the protohominid in the direction of erect bipedalism—perhaps the advantages of freeing the hands for food carrying or for tool use. Freeing the hands allowed more manipulation of the environment in the direction of tools for gathering and hunting food. Through a hand-eye-brain feedback process, coordination, efficiency, and skill were increased. The new behavior was adaptive, and selection pressure pushed the protohominid further along the same lines of development. Diet changed as the increase in skill allowed the addition of more animal protein. Larger brains were selected for, making possible transmission of information concerned with tool making, and organizing cooperative hunting. It is assumed that as increased brain size was selected for, so also was neoteny—

immaturity of infants at birth with a corresponding increase in their period of dependency, allowing more time for learning at the same time as this learning became necessary through the further reduction of instinctual behaviors and their replacement by symbolically invented ones.[8]

Here is where one may discover a large logical gap. From the difficult-to-explain beginning trends toward neoteny and increased brain size, the story jumps to Man the Hunter. The statement is made that the females were more burdened with dependent infants and could not follow the rigorous hunt. Therefore they stayed at a "home base," gathering what food they could, while the males developed cooperative hunting techniques, increased their communicative and organizational skills through hunting and brought the meat back to the dependent females and young. Incest prohibitions, marriage, and the family (so the story goes) grew out of the need to eliminate competition between males for females. A pattern developed of a male hunter becoming the main support of "his" dependent females and young (in other words, the development of the nuclear family for no apparent reason). Thus the peculiarly human social and emotional bonds can be traced to the hunter bringing back the food to share. Hunting, according to Washburn and Lancaster, involved "cooperation among males, planning, knowledge of many species and large areas, and technical skill" (1968:296). They even profess to discover the beginnings of art in the weapons of the hunter.

---

[8] Despite the popular interest in the social and behavioral aspects of early humans, physical anthropology was, at the time this article was written, relatively unconcerned with it. Most physical anthropologists interested in evolution focused on recovering and identifying fossils. Although the version of evolution Slocum describes here was taught and generally accepted when she was writing, it was an area that had been relatively unstudied. Research since the 1970s has all but completely discredited this version of human evolution.

Slocum here is intentionally drawing a caricature of Washburn and Lancaster's position, presenting a version that can easily be demolished. Note the polemic tone of her writing. She both describes and ridicules Washburn and Lancaster's theory by using such phrases as "so the story goes" or "poor dependent females." Slocum's use of polemic language was, presumably, intentional. However, some of those she is critiquing, perhaps unintentionally, used language that seems equally polemic, which reinforces her point about bias in the literature. An example of this is an essay by Robin Fox that describes a theory by Chance, another researcher. According to Fox, Chance shows that "the whole process of enlarging the neo-cortex to take-off point was based on a competition between the dominant and sub-dominant males" (1972:373). Fox criticized Chance's view but was wildly condescending. In pointing out problems with the theory, he noted that it "would apply only to the male neo-cortex, and much as we may be mystified at the use made of this organ by the female of the species, she undoubtedly possesses it" (1972:373).

They point out that the symmetrical Acheulian biface tools are the earliest beautiful man-made objects. Though we don't know what these tools were used for, they argue somewhat tautologically that the symmetry indicates they may have been swung, because symmetry only makes a difference when irregularities might lead to deviations in the line of flight. "It may well be that it was the attempt to produce efficient high-speed weapons that first produced beautiful, symmetrical objects" (1968:298).

So, while the males were out hunting, developing all their skills, learning to cooperate, inventing language, inventing art, creating tools and weapons, the poor dependent females were sitting back at the home base having one child after another (many of them dying in the process), and waiting for the males to bring home the bacon. While this reconstruction is certainly ingenious, it gives one the decided impression that only half the species—the male half—did any evolving. In addition to containing a number of logical gaps, the argument becomes somewhat doubtful in the light of modern knowledge of genetics and primate behavior.

The skills usually spoken of as being necessary to, or developed through, hunting are things like coordination, endurance, good vision, and the ability to plan, communicate, and cooperate. I have heard of no evidence to indicate that these skills are either carried on the Y chromosome, or are triggered into existence by the influence of the Y chromosome. In fact, on just about any test we can design (psychological, aptitude, intelligence,

etc.) males and females score just about the same. The variation is on an individual, not a sex, basis.

Every human individual gets half its genes from a male and half from a female; genes sort randomly. It is possible for a female to end up with all her genes from male ancestors, and for a male to end up with all his genes from female ancestors. The logic of the hunting argument would have us believe that all the selection pressure was on the males, leaving the females simply as drags on the species. The rapid increase in brain size and complexity was thus due entirely to half the species; the main function of the female half was to suffer and die in the attempt to give birth to their large-brained male infants. An unbiased reading of the evidence indicates there was selection pressure on both sexes, and that hunting was not in fact the basic adaptation of the species from which flowed all the traits we think of as specifically human. Hunting does not deserve the primary place it has been given in the reconstruction of human evolution, as I will demonstrate by offering the following alternate version.

Picture the primate band: each individual gathers its own food, and the major enduring relationship is the mother-infant bond.[9] It is in similar circumstances that we imagine the evolving protohominids. We don't know what started them in the direction of neoteny and increased brain size, but once begun the trends would prove adaptive. To explain the shift from the primate individual gathering to human food sharing, we cannot simply jump to hunting. Hunting cannot explain its own origin. It is much more logical to

---

[9] The picture of the primate band that Slocum draws here is much closer to that held by current physical anthropologists than the version she presented and ridiculed above. It was, however, only one of several feminist versions of human evolution offered in the early 1970s. The version that was probably most popular with nonprofessionals at that time was the aquatic hypothesis. This view was presented by Elaine Morgan in her 1972 book *The Descent of Woman*. Like Ardrey (who was originally a playwright), Morgan was a writer rather than an anthropologist, and her book was aimed at a popular rather than a professional audience.

Morgan argued that the fundamental human characteristics of bipedalism, language, and tool use resulted from adaptation to living in coastal environments and that the

crucial evolutionary pressures were on females rather than males. Morgan's original work was polemic in tone. She published a more technical version of it called *The Aquatic Ape* in 1982. The aquatic hypothesis enjoyed great popularity among feminists and some cultural anthropologists, but it has been rejected by physical anthropologists as incompatible with the fossil evidence.

Unlike Morgan or Ardrey, Slocum is a physical anthropologist; she did her doctoral work on rhesus monkeys. Thus, her argument comes from within physical anthropology and demonstrates a much greater technical command of the field than Morgan's or Ardrey's work. Despite her background, the essay is aimed at an audience of cultural rather than physical anthropologists.

assume that as the period of infant dependency began to lengthen, *the mothers would begin to increase the scope of their gathering to provide food for their still-dependent infants.* The already strong primate mother-infant bond would begin to extend over a longer time period, increasing the depth and scope of social relationships, and giving rise to the first sharing of food.

It is an example of male bias to picture these females with young as totally or even mainly dependent on males for food. Among modern hunter-gatherers, even in the marginal environments where most live, the females can usually gather enough to support themselves and their families. In these groups gathering provides the major portion of the diet, and there is no reason to assume that this was not also the case in the Pliocene or early Pleistocene. In the modern groups women and children both gather and hunt small animals, though they usually do not go on the longer hunts. So, we can assume a group of evolving protohominids, gathering and perhaps beginning to hunt small animals, with the mothers gathering quite efficiently both for themselves and for their offspring.

It is equally biased, and quite unreasonable, to assume an early or rapid development of a pattern in which one male was responsible for "his" females(s) and young. In most primate groups when a female comes into estrus she initiates coitus or signals her readiness by presenting. The idea that a male would have much voice in "choosing" a female, or maintain any sort of individual, long-term control over her or her offspring, is surely a modern invention which could have had no place in early hominid life. (Sexual control over females through rape or the threat of rape seems to be a modern human invention. Primate females are not raped because they are willing throughout estrus, and primate males appear not to attempt coitus at other times, regardless of physiological ability.) In fact, there seems to me

no reason for suggesting the development of male-female adult pair-bonding until much later. Long-term monogamy is a fairly rare pattern even among modern humans—I think it is a peculiarly Western male bias to suppose its existence in protohuman society. An argument has been made (by Morris, 1967, and others) that traces the development of male-female pair-bonding to the shift of sexual characteristics to the front of the body, the importance of the face in communication, and the development of face-to-face coitus. This argument is insufficient in the first place because of the assumption that face-to-face coitus is the "normal," "natural," or even the most common position among humans (historical evidence casts grave doubt on this assumption). It is much more probable that the coitus position was invented *after* pair-bonding had developed for other reasons.

Rather than adult male-female sexual pairs, a temporary consort-type relationship is much more logical in hominid evolution. It is even a more accurate description of the modern human pattern: the most dominant males (chief, headman, brave warrior, good hunter, etc.), mate with the most dominant females (in estrus, young and beautiful, fertile, rich, etc.), for varying periods of time. Changing sexual partners is frequent and common. We have no way of knowing when females began to be fertile year-round, but this change is not a necessary condition for the development of families. We need not bring in any notion of paternity, or the development of male-female pairs, or any sort of marriage in order to account for either families or food sharing.

The lengthening period of infant dependency would have strengthened and deepened the mother-infant bond; the earliest families would have consisted of *females and their children.* In such groups, over time, the sibling bond would have increased in importance also. The most universal, and presumably oldest, form of incest prohibition is between mother and son.[10] There are

---

[10] Here, in passing, Slocum makes a stab at the origins of the incest taboo, one of the oldest problems in anthropology and one that is still not solved to general satisfaction. In fact, her case here is very weak, since females do not have to be fertile to have sex. However, just as theorists

such as Washburn tried to link the evolution of an enormous number of traits to male hunting, Slocum tries to link a wide range of characteristics to particular aspects of female-led evolution.

indications of such avoidance even among modern monkeys. It could develop logically from the mother-children family: as the period of infant dependency lengthened, and the age of sexual maturity advanced, a mother might no longer be capable of childbearing when her son reached maturity. Another factor which may have operated is the situation found in many primates today where only the most dominant males have access to fertile females. Thus a young son, even after reaching sexual maturity, would still have to spend time working his way up the male hierarchy before gaining access to females. The length of time it would take him increases the possibility that his mother would no longer be fertile.

Food sharing and the family developed from the mother-infant bond. The techniques of hunting large animals were probably much later developments, after the mother-children family pattern was established. When hunting did begin, and the adult males brought back food to share, the most likely recipients would be first their mothers, and second their siblings. In other words, a hunter would share food *not* with a wife or sexual partner, but with those who had shared food with him: his mother and siblings.

It is frequently suggested or implied that the first tools were, in fact, the weapons of the hunters.[11] Modern humans have become so accustomed to the thought of tools and weapons that it is easy for us to imagine the first manlike creature who picked up a stone or club. However, since we don't really know what the early stone tools such as hand-axes were used for, it is equally probable that they were not weapons at all, but rather *aids in gathering*. We know that gathering was important long before much animal protein was added to the diet, and continued to be important. Bones, sticks, and hand-axes could be used for digging up tubers or roots, or to pulverize tough vegetable matter for easier eating. If, however, instead of thinking in terms of tools and weapons, we think in terms of *cultural inventions*, a new aspect is presented. I suggest that two of the *earliest and most important* cultural inventions were containers to hold the products of gathering, and some sort of sling or net to carry babies.[12] The latter in particular must have been extremely important with the loss of body hair and the increasing immaturity of neonates, who could not cling and had less and less to cling to. Plenty of material was available—vines, hides, human hair. If the infant could be securely fastened to the mother's body, she could go about her tasks much more efficiently. Once a technique for carrying babies was developed, it could be extended to the idea of carrying food, and eventually to other sorts of cultural inventions—choppers and grinders for food preparation, and even weapons. Among modern hunter-gatherers, regardless of the poverty of their material culture, food carriers and baby carriers are always important items in their equipment.

A major point in the Man the Hunter argument is that cooperative hunting among males demanded more skill in social organization and communication, and thus provided selection pressure for increased brain size. I suggest that longer periods of infant dependency, more difficult births, and longer gestation periods also demanded more skills in social organization and communication—creating selective pressure for increased brain size without looking to hunting as an explanation. The need to organize for feeding after weaning, learning to handle the more complex social-emotional bonds that were developing, the new skills and cultural inventions surrounding more extensive gathering—all would demand larger brains. Too much attention has been given to the skills required by hunting, and

---

[11] As Slocum attacked male bias in beliefs about evolution, she took on many commonly accepted themes in popular culture. The idea that early tools were offensive weapons came from Dart's work. Compare her analysis here with the story presented in Stanley Kubrick's *2001: A Space Odyssey,* an extremely popular film that appeared in the late 1960s. The opening scenes of the film show the discovery of tools: One ape man picks up a large bone, stares at it, and then uses it to beat a companion over the head.

[12] Here and later Slocum is engaging in pure speculation. Like the sociobiologists, she is arguing by analogy to modern hunting-gathering bands, using them as "living fossils"—a method that hearkens back to the nineteenth century.

too little to the skills required for gathering and the raising of dependent young. The techniques required for efficient gathering include location and identification of plant varieties, seasonal and geographical knowledge, containers for carrying the food, and tools for its preparation. Among modern hunting-gathering groups this knowledge is an extremely complex, well-developed, and important part of their cultural equipment. Caring for a curious, energetic, but still dependent human infant is difficult and demanding. Not only must the infant be watched, it must be taught the customs, dangers, and knowledge of its group. For the early hominids, as their cultural equipment and symbolic communication increased, the job of training the young would demand more skill. Selection pressure for better brains came from many directions.

Much has been made of the argument that cooperation among males demanded by hunting acted as a force to reduce competition for females. I suggest that competition for females has been greatly exaggerated.[13] It could easily have been handled in the usual way for primates— according to male status relationships already worked out—and need not be pictured as particularly violent or extreme. The seeds of male cooperation already exist in primates when they act to protect the band from predators. Such dangers may well have increased with a shift to savannah living, and the longer dependency of infants. If biological roots are sought to explain the greater aggressiveness of males, it would be more fruitful to look toward their function as protectors, rather than any supposedly basic hunting adaptation. The only division of labor that regularly exists in primate groups is the females caring for infants and the males protecting the group from predators. The possibilities for both cooperation and aggression in males lies in this protective function.

The emphasis on hunting as a prime moving factor in hominid evolution distorts the data. It is simply too big a jump to go from the primate individual gathering pattern to a hominid cooperative hunting-sharing pattern without some intervening changes. Cooperative hunting of big game animals could only have developed *after* the trends toward neoteny and increased brain size had begun. Big-game hunting becomes a more logical development when it is viewed as growing out of a complex of changes which included sharing the products of gathering among mothers and children, deepening social bonds over time, increase in brain size, and the beginnings of cultural invention for purposes such as baby carrying, food carrying, and food preparation. Such hunting not only needed the prior development of some skills in social organization and communication, it probably also had to await the development of the "home base." It is difficult to imagine that most or all of the adult primate males in a group would go off on a hunting expedition, leaving the females and young exposed to the danger of predators, without some way of communicating to arrange for their defense, or at least a way of saying, "Don't worry, we'll be back in two days." Until that degree of communicative skill developed, we must assume either that the whole band traveled *and hunted* together, or that the males simply did not go off on large cooperative hunts.

The development of cooperative hunting requires, as a prior condition, an increase in brain size. Once such a trend is established, hunting skills would take part in a feedback process of selection for better brains just as would other cultural inventions and developments such as gathering skills. By itself, hunting fails to explain any part of human evolution and fails to explain itself.

Anthropology has always rested on the assumption that the mark of our species is our ability to *symbol*, to bring into existence forms of behavior and interaction, and material tools with which to adjust and control the environment. To explain human nature as evolving from the desire

---

[13] Early theories about protohuman social organization tended to emphasize violent competition among males for essentially passive females. The popular image is of the caveman dragging the cavewoman off by the hair. More modern theory, however, tends to emphasize the role of females in sexual selection, diminishing the importance of male aggression.

of males to hunt and kill is to negate most of anthropology.[14] Our species survived and adapted through the invention of *culture*, of which hunting is simply a part. It is often stated that hunting *must* be viewed as the "natural" species' adaptation because it lasted as long as it did, nine-tenths of all human history. However:

> Man the Hunter lasted as long as "he" did from no natural propensity toward hunting any more than toward computer programming or violin playing or nuclear warfare, but because that was what the historical circumstances allowed. We ignore the first premise of our science if we fail to admit that "man" is no more natural a hunter than "he" is naturally a golfer, for after symboling became possible our species left forever the ecological niche of the necessity of any one adaptation, and made all adaptations possible for ourselves. (Kephart, 1970:23)

That the concept of Man the Hunter influenced anthropology for as long as it did is a reflection of male bias in the discipline. This bias can be seen in the tendency to equate "man," "human," and "male"; to look at culture almost entirely from a male point of view; to search for examples of the behavior of males and assume that this is sufficient for explanation, ignoring almost totally the female half of the species; and to filter this male bias through the "ideal" modern Western pattern of one male supporting a dependent wife and minor children.[15]

The basis of any discipline is not the answers it gets, but the questions it asks. As an exercise in the anthropology of knowledge, this paper stems from asking a simple question: what were the females doing while the males were out hunting? It was only possible for me to ask this question after I had become politically conscious of myself as a woman. Such is the prestige of males in our society that a woman, in anthropology or any other profession, can only gain respect or be attended to if she deals with questions deemed important by men. Though there have been women anthropologists for years, it is rare to be able to discern any difference between their work and that of male anthropologists. Learning to be an anthropologist has involved learning to think from a male perspective, so it should not be surprising that women have asked the same kinds of questions as men. But political consciousness, whether among women, blacks, American Indians, or any other group, leads to reexamination and reevaluation of taken-for-granted assumptions. It is a difficult process, challenging the conventional wisdom, and this paper is simply a beginning. The male bias in anthropology that I have illustrated here is just as real as the white bias, the middle-class bias, and the academic bias that exist in the discipline. It is our task, as anthropologists, to create a "study of the human species" in spite of, or perhaps because of, or maybe even by means of, our individual biases and unique perspectives.[16]

REFERENCES

Berger, Peter, and T. Luckmann. 1967. *The Social Construction of Reality.* Garden City, N.Y.: Doubleday Anchor.

---

[14] As you read these passages, recall again that this essay first appeared in 1971, close to the height of the movement protesting the Vietnam War. Slocum's suggestion that the hunting hypothesis negates most anthropology seems rash, but the idea that humans did not innately desire to kill was extremely popular in this era and, whether it followed logically or not, increased the emotional appeal of Slocum's argument.

[15] Slocum's suggestion that, even within anthropology, there was a tendency to equate man and human was certainly no exaggeration. Consider C. F. Hockett's 1973 anthropology text called *Man's Place in Nature,* with chapters titled "Man the Tinkerer," "Man the Chatterer," "Man the Worshiper," "Man the Owner," and so on.

[16] Notice the layering of political change, personal change, and theoretical perspective in this final paragraph. Slocum's perception that a change in her political consciousness caused a change in her theoretical position prefigures postmodern anthropology. Compare it with some of Renato Rosaldo's insights in essay 36 in this volume. However, Slocum is certainly no postmodernist, and feminist writers of this era did not make the leap to extreme relativism that characterizes some postmodern writing.

Current Anthropology. 1968. Social Responsibilities Symposium. Reprint from December 1968 issue.

Garfinkel, Harold. 1960. "The Rational Properties of Scientific and Common Sense Activities." *Behavioral Science* 5, no. 1:72–83.

Kephart, Jane. 1970. "Primitive Woman as Nigger, or, The Origin of the Human Family as Viewed Through

the Role of Women." M.A. Dissertation, University of Maryland.

Morris, Desmond. 1967. *The Naked Ape.* New York: McGraw-Hill.

Washburn, Sherwood, and C. Lancaster. 1968. "The Evolution of Hunting." In *Man the Hunter* edited by R. B. Lee and Irven DeVore. Chicago: Aldine.

29. *Interpreting the Origins of Gender Inequality: Conceptual and Historical Problems*

Eleanor Leacock (1922–1987)

For some time I have argued that the analysis of women's oppression and its origins calls for clarification along two lines, historical and conceptual.*[1] The historical dimension requires that the myth of the "ethnographic present" be totally eradicated, and that anthropologists deal fully with the fact that the structure of gender relations among the people they study does not follow from pre-capitalist production relations as such, but from the ways in which these have been affected by particular histories of colonization. The conceptual dimension requires a complete break with the tendency to interpret all cultures in terms of categories derived from capitalist society. Such categories distort the structure of primitive com-munist relations and thereby obscure the sources of hierarchy. Equally critical, as consistently pointed out by feminist scholars, is the need to root out the pervasive assumption that women are not actors on the scene of human history to the same degree as are men. There is still a widespread failure to recognize that correcting the anthropological distortion of women's roles in society has profound implications for the interpretation of social structure generally. In particular, the fact that the French Marxists have not launched a thorough-going criticism of Lévi-Strauss' assumption that the exchange of women by men inaugurated human society has served to weaken their analyses of pre-capitalist production modes.[2]

From *Dialectical Anthropology* (1983)

---

[1] Leacock's original essay contained ninety-six notes. Space limitations prevent us from reproducing them here, but asterisks have been included to show where they were placed.

[2] Leacock's feminist Marxist perspective is immediately apparent in this opening paragraph. Here she touches on a number of issues that were central to feminists and Marxists in the late 1970s and early 1980s. These included a critique of the notion of the ethnographic present (see note 4) as well as a declaration that not only are women of equal importance to men in society but also relationships between men and women are fundamental elements that pattern society.

The notion of primitive communism is very important in this essay. Marx and Engels proposed that early societ-ies were communistic. This idea was given force by Lewis Henry Morgan's description of early societies as having communistic living arrangements and possessing liberty and equality (1871, 1877). These descriptions provided data for Marx and Engels.

In the last sentence of the paragraph, Leacock refers to Lévi-Strauss' work *The Elementary Structures of Kinship*, in which he argues that the fact that women are com-modities exchanged by men is one of the fundamental patterning elements of society. You can find a more thor-ough discussion of Lévi-Strauss' theory in the introduction to the "Structuralism" section in this book. Lévi-Strauss had a critical impact on the development of Marxist thought because many leading French Marxists of the 1960s and 1970s were his students.

ANTHROPOLOGY AND HISTORY

The importance of paying constant attention to history was impressed upon me as a graduate student at Columbia University when I was fortunate enough to take part in Wm. Duncan Strong's seminar on "Time Perspective and the Plains." Strong drew on archaeology and ethnohistory to demonstrate that "typical" Plains culture, as then conceived, was not aboriginal, but had developed in the 18th century when formerly diverse tribes, some agricultural, some hunting-gathering, took advantage of the horse and either moved out onto, or spent more of the year on the prairies. I would add that a greatly expanded market for buffalo hides plus land pressure resulting from European intrusion to the east and south were also important reasons for the move out onto the plains. In a fairly short time, social, ritual, and material traits were borrowed, developed, and/or elaborated upon by different peoples who integrated them into a relatively uniform culture.[3]

Strong's ethnohistorical orientation influenced a number of dissertations, some on Plains peoples,* and some on other areas.* Subsequently, extensive studies of native American social-economic organization and land use were undertaken in connection with the Indian Claims actions initiated in the 1950s.* This work revealed a fact of major significance for understanding the unstratified societies that existed in most of what was to become the United States: bands, villages, and towns were only loosely grouped into what are called tribes; politically, however, they functioned as fully autonomous units. The point was made explicit by Kroeber,* and it has been elaborated upon by Fried in his critique of the concept "tribe."* Kroeber wrote:

The more we review aboriginal America, the less certain does any consistently recurring phenomenon become that matches our usual conventional concept of tribe; and the more largely does this concept appear to be a White man's creation of convenience for talking about Indians, negotiation with them, administering them . . . It was infinitely more convenient and practicable for us to deal with representatives of one large group than with these of ten, twenty, or thirty tiny and shifting ones whose very names and precise habitat often were not known. This was equally so whether treaties were being negotiated for trade, traverse, settlement or resettlement, land cession, peace, subsidy or rationing, administration on a reservation, or abrogating and opening up a reservation. Generally we treated the nationality-"tribes" as if they were sovereign state-tribes, and by sheer pressure of greater strength forced the Indians to submit to our classification of them.*

Kroeber's point that tribes as commonly defined were a product of colonization requires the qualification that tribal organization and leadership were not only imposed from without. They also arose among native Americans as necessary for resisting white invasion. Such warfare as had existed in pre-colonial times usually took the form of petty raiding by young men (and such women as occasionally chose to participate) who tested their mettle in a coup-counting system that deemed it more prestigious to touch enemies than kill them. When warfare for survival became necessary, strong leaders emerged to unite one or more tribes and meet the need.

In any case, Kroeber wrote that the "larger nationalities," i.e., the culturally affiliated groups known as tribes, were "ethnic" but "non-political" in the sense that they held no power over their

---

[3] The archaeologist William Duncan Strong (1899–1962) was a student of A. L. Kroeber and a classmate of Julian Steward. Strong was a major influence on Leacock during her years at Columbia. He conducted extensive research in the western United States, in Labrador, and with his student, Gordon R. Wiley (1913–2002) in Peru. Although not a Marxist, Strong emphasized the role of history in anthropology and critiqued both evolutionism without ad-

equate historical research and functionalist approaches that ignored history, such as those of A. R. Radcliffe-Brown (Solecki and Wagley 1963). After Strong's death, Leacock edited the journals he kept during his fieldwork among the Naskapi Indians. Although she began this project in the early 1960s, the resulting book, *Labrador Winter: The Ethnographic Journals of William Duncan Strong, 1927–1928,* was not published until 1994, seven years after her death.

constituents. It was the "smaller units, whether they be called villages, bands, towns, tribelets, lineages, or something else . . . that were independent, sovereign, and held and used a territory."* However, these smaller units should not be considered miniature tribes in the sense of stable, bonded groups subject to the authority of a chief and/or council. Such a formulation violates the reality of communally organized societies, in which movement among groups was easy and frequent; rights to lands were not viewed as exclusive; decisions about individual activities were made by those who would carry them out; and decisions about group activities, arrived at through consensus, did not bind those who did not agree.* Such a formulation also distorts the working structure of relations among bands and villages and the complex social and ceremonial forms that affirmed cooperation and friendship or ritualized and contained potential animosity.

Kroeber's and Fried's discussions of changing political forms demonstrate how unjustifiable it is to consider the cultures that have been reconstructed from the memories of late 19th and early 20th century elders as "traditional" in the sense of pre-Columbian. To do so is to gloss over the active participation of native Americans in almost 500 years of post-colonial history. It is to present them as cardboard figures, living according to a congeries of "culture traits" within "culture areas," traits that did not change but were "lost" through "acculturation."*[4]

GENDER IN NATIVE NORTH AMERICA

With regard to the position of women, it is equally unjustifiable to make generalizations about one or another Indian culture without consideration of the historical dimension. During the colonial period, male authority was being encouraged by Euro-Americans in their political and military dealings with native Americans at the same time as Indian women were becoming dependent in individual households on wage-earning and trading husbands. For example, after documenting the full social equality of Cherokee women revealed by colonial accounts, Reid, an historian of law, wrote:

> The decline of hunting and the adoption of American ways during the nineteenth century, with the substitution of factory-made for homemade goods . . . freed the Cherokee woman from outdoor labor, placing her in the kitchen and her husband in the fields, but it also deprived her of economic independence, making her politically and legally more like her white sisters.*

A second example of changes in women's position following the colonization of native North America is afforded by the contrast between Lafitau and Morgan on the Iroquois.[5] In his 18th century account, Lafitau stated that Iroquois and/or Huron women were "the souls of the Councils, the arbiters of peace and war," in whom

---

[4] Throughout this section, Leacock shows her concern with the historical background of Native America and attacks the notion of the ethnographic present. Through the first half of the twentieth century, most ethnographies did not pay any particular attention to history. Societies were described either in their current state or as they were remembered by their elder members. For the purposes of their writing, many anthropologists assumed that the societies they studied were relatively isolated from external forces of change, and internally driven change was extremely slow. Thus, notions of history were largely irrelevant to ethnography. In addition, two prominent schools of thought in the 1960s and 1970s were structuralism and ethnoscience (or new ethnography). Members of these schools focused on what they believed to be the fundamental ways in which members of a society understood

their world. They held that the effects of history on such understandings were of little importance. Marxism, on the other hand, is fundamentally concerned with history: Marxists see societies developing as their internal contradictions are worked out. Thus, someone taking a feminist Marxist approach should be vitally concerned with understanding the historical position of women in society.

[5] In this section Leacock begins to build the case that the gender relations reported in most twentieth-century ethnographies are the result of contact with Europeans rather than structural elements of non-European society. Some of the important names Leacock mentions in this section are the Wyandot, Powell, and Lafitau. The Wyandot are better known as the Huron. Powell refers to John Wesley Powell (1834–1902), the founder of the Bureau of American

"all real authority is vested."* In Morgan's 19th century description, despite reference to women's decision-making powers in Iroquois households, he wrote that Iroquois men considered women as "inferior, the dependent, and the servant of men," and that a woman, "from nurture and habit, . . . actually considered herself to be so."* Although the flatness of the latter statement can well be questioned, it was written at the time when Iroquois women had lost their role as major producers and the control over the products of their labor that had insured them personal autonomy and public authority. Their situation was no longer that of 1791, when elder Seneca women informed Colonel Proctor, an envoy from George Washington,

> you ought to hear and listen to what we, women, shall speak, as well as to the sachems; for we are the owners of this land—and it is ours. It is we that plant it for our and their use. Hear us, therefore, for we speak of things that concern us while our men shall say more to you; for we have told them.*

The changing relationship between women's economic role and their decision-making powers among the Iroquois and the Huron is further illuminated by a little known paper on the Wyandot by the early anthropologist Powell. Powell wrote:

> Cultivation is communal; that is, all of the able-bodied women of the gens take part in the cultivation of each household tract in the following manner:

> The head of the household sends her brother or son into the forest or to the stream to bring in game or fish for a feast; then the able-bodied women of the gens are invited to assist in the cultivation of the land, and when this work is done a feast is given.*

Powell stated that women were family heads among the Wyandot, and that four family heads, plus a man of their choosing, made up the clan council. The clan councils together made up the tribal council that was responsible for dividing Wyandot lands among the clans. The women councilors of each clan were in turn responsible for dividing it among the clan households, as well as for matters such as giving personal names and discussing and consenting to marriages. Apparently the entire council, that is, including the male member, handled certain transgressions while others were brought before the tribal council. Warfare was the responsibility of the men; all "able-bodied men" made up what Powell called a "military council" headed by a "military chief." The fact that women were not members of these councils has led to a serious underestimation of their authority in societies organized, as many North American societies were, along lines roughly similar to the Wyandot Huron. First, accounts of military negotiations between the outsiders and "military councils" and "military chiefs" do not recognize the formal structure of women's power which can therefore be interpreted as indirect and "behind the scene."* Second, the imminence of conquest increased the responsibility and power of "military councils." Subsequent economic developments, along with policies such as the Dawes (General Allotment) Act of 1887 (designed to divide all Indian lands into family-owned plots), undercut the collective economic activities traditionally controlled by women. As among the Cherokee and the Iroquois, the egalitarian and reciprocal structure of decision-making among the Huron was destroyed.

CONCEPTUALIZING PRIMITIVE COMMUNISM AND ITS TRANSFORMATION

As the above discussion suggests, the egalitarian relations that obtained in most foraging and many horticultural societies around the world at the time of European expansion rested on the fact that all mature individuals participated directly in

---

Ethnology. Additional information on Powell can be found in the introduction to "Historical Particularism." Joseph-Francois Lafitau (1681–1746), author of *American Savages Compared with Those of Earliest Times* (1724), was a Jesuit missionary who worked among the Iroquois from 1711 to 1717. He wrote on Iroquois kinship systems 100 years before Morgan.

The Late Twentieth Century and Beyond

the full process of production. By "full process" I refer to Marx's concept of production, distribution, exchange, and consumption as "members of one entity, different aspects of one unit,"* as opposed to formulations that limit their emphasis to either work processes or the allocation of produce. The control that all individuals had over the conditions of their labor, over the skills as well as the resources necessary to perform it, and over the disposition and use of its products, distinguishes egalitarian from hierarchically ordered structures.[6]

A Marxist conceptual baseline for analysing egalitarian society, interpreted in these terms, sharpens the fact that the transformation from egalitarian to hierarchical relations was qualitative and not merely quantitative. Such a view contrasts with the common practice of describing egalitarian society in terms of the same features that characterize class society. In formulations of this type, differential access to land and other resources, hereditary authority, and social-economic hierarchies are treated as incipient—as weakly developed tendencies that only needed strengthening to become predominant. Despite caveats to the contrary, history is thereby implied to be unilineal and teleological, with Western society as its ultimate purpose and measure. Alternatives for the future are obscured by the implication that there was no real alternative in the past.[7]

The widely held assumption that female subordination is a universal of human society derives from, and in turn supports, the assumption that primitive communal society was ultimately ordered by the same constraints and compulsions that order class society.* Where institutionalized hostility between the sexes exists, it is interpreted as a variant of a universal battle between the sexes, rather than as evidence of emerging status differentiations among men and among women, as well as between men and women. The critical relationship between the development of ranking and the attempt to subvert women's public and autonomous status (such as in the so-called big men societies of Melanesia) is seldom recognized. In sum, gender hierarchy is all too often taken for granted, and both the structure of primitive communism and the basis for its transformation are thereby mystified.[8]

There is much talk of paradigms these days, and much emphasis on process. Nonetheless, cross-cultural analyses still rely heavily on states or essences as categories, rather than processes or relationships. The mid-century admission that the regularities of social evolution as broadly outlined by Engels and Morgan approximated historical reality, opened the way in anthropology for a dialectical analysis of human history in terms of basic transformations in the ways people interrelated as they reproduced themselves and their social structures. In particular, given the focus on relations between individual and society that characterized the personality and culture school, and its successors in psychological anthropology, the significance of Marx's sixth thesis on Feuerbach could have been explored in

---

[6] In Marxist thought, there is a close link between production and power. Since social relations flow primarily from relations of production, the greater the contribution of an individual to production, the greater that individual's power should be. Leacock is arguing that her reading of the ethnography shows that women and men participated fully in production before their societies were profoundly affected by Europeans. If they did so, then, from a Marxist viewpoint, it would be a logical necessity that both men and women participated fully in political decision making as well.

[7] Although Leacock does not provide any references for what she describes as a common practice—seeing egalitarian societies as incipient states—she is probably think-

ing of Morton Fried's *The Evolution of Political Society* (1967). Fried's book was published several years before this essay, and she cites it repeatedly later in the work.

[8] Many 1970s feminists understood female subordination as a human universal. Ortner, for example, says that female subordination "exists within every type of social and economic arrangement and in societies of every degree of complexity" (see essay 23). When a practice is universal, there is at least the strong suspicion that it is rooted in human nature. However, for a Marxist, there can be no such thing. Human nature is not fixed and universal, but created in the process of production. Therefore, explanations that rely upon human nature cannot be sustained. Leacock makes this point repeatedly in the next several paragraphs.

terms of how individual behavior and societal processes interrelate.[9]

"The essence of man is no abstraction inherent in each separate individual," Marx wrote. "In its reality it is the *ensemble* (aggregate) of social relations."* To Marx and Engels people did not have an intrinsic nature apart from society, but neither were they mere reflections of their society. In a number of oft-quoted passages, Marx and Engels stressed that "men make their own history,"* although the circumstances under which they do so are inherited from the past. Furthermore, the independent unfolding of social forces means that people's actions do not necessarily lead to the intended results. Instead the "simplest determinations," the relations of production, ways people relate to one another as they produce, distribute, exchange, and consume the necessities of life, set processes in motion that lie beyond the wills of the actors.* On the one hand, social structures are created by the behavior of individuals; "the social structure and the State are continually evolving out of the life-processes of definite individuals." On the other hand, however, these life-processes are themselves structured by production relations, as people "are effective, produce materially, and are active under definite material limits, presuppositions and conditions independent of their will."*[10]

Marxist dialectics, then, opened the way for examining the series of interlocking processes—the different levels of integration—that constitute human history. At the individual physiological level, human nature is not a given but a mix of potentials and propensities that are expressed differently under different conditions; at the societal level, social-historical processes are of an altogether different order; in between, mediating the two, at the individual psycho-social or behavioral level, the person operates as a nexus of social-economic relationships; and at the ideological level, people's perceptions of their relations to each other and to nature are patterned by traditional concepts, in part spontaneous and in part manipulated, and with a certain lawfulness of their own that arises from the nature of language as a symbol system.*

Such a line of thinking has been followed through only minimally. Instead, anthropology has been plagued by ever more radically reductionist and anti-historical formulations. In structuralist theory, and more recently in sociobiology, social determinants are defined in terms of behavioral outcomes and ultimately reduced to psycho-biologically fixed entities. Whether these be such grotesque notions as Wilson's "conformer" and other behavior-specific genes, or Lévi-Strauss's more elegant, since undefined, deep structures, or Laughlin and d'Aquili's more scientifically couched, if less euphonious "neuroanatomical-neurophysiological relationships," their inventors all reduce human history and society to mere projections of individual biological propensities, with

---

[9] When Leacock refers to the midcentury admission that Engels and Morgan were approximately correct, she is probably thinking of Leslie White's work on cultural evolution and his editing of Morgan's work (see essay 16). Marx's *Theses on Feuerbach* is a short work written in 1845. It was published as an appendix to Engels' *Ludwig Feuerbach and the End of Classical German Philosophy* (1949 [1888]). It consists of eleven brief points that, in Marx's opinion, separated his own work from Feuerbach's. The sixth thesis, in its entirety, is:

> Feuerbach resolves the religious essence into the human essence. But the human essence is no abstraction inherent in each single individual. In its reality it is the ensemble of the social relations. Feuerbach, who does not enter upon a criticism of this real essence, is consequently compelled: 1) To abstract

from the historical process and to fix the religious sentiment as something by itself and to presuppose an abstract—isolated—human individual. 2) Essence, therefore, can be comprehended only as "genus," as an internal, dumb generality which naturally unites the many individuals.

In the following paragraph, Leacock explains the significance of Marx's point for her own argument.

[10] In this and the following paragraph, Leacock is describing a Marxist dialectic. She is saying that society is not simply a reflection of the structure of production (that is a position that Marxists call "vulgar materialism") but rather emerges from the relations of production and how people think about these relations.

the environment the only independently interacting factor.*[11]

The result of ruling out a level of societal process entirely separate from individual propensities is like attempting to explain the movements of the solar system as flowing from the properties of the atomic particles (or processes) that make it up. To be sure, planetary movements are in a superficial sense the sum total of all movements of subatomic particles, just as social processes are in a trivial sense the sum total of individual behaviors. Scientifically, however, it would be absurd not to recognize that the lawful movements of planetary bodies have their own history of development, and operate at a level of integration independent from the internal processes that characterize their constituent parts. With respect to society, few would argue directly that social processes do not also operate at a level of their own. In effect, however, this is precisely what reductionist formulations imply.

Anthropologists have long been sensitive to biological reductionism with regard to physical variations of a racial order, and somewhat aware that reductionist formulations serve as ideological rationalizations of oppression. Unfortunately, this is not the case with respect to physical variations of a sexual order. Although the fact that physiological sex and social gender are far from isometric is well established and documented in anthropology, cross-cultural discussions of sex roles commonly fall into reductionism in their formulations.[12] Many Marxists, as well as other scholars, translate the gender structure of the hierarchical exploitative society with which they are familiar into innate predispositions and the practice is encouraged by the recent worldwide spread of Western norms, at least on a superficial level. The assumption remains prevalent that physiological differences between the sexes embody hints of female subordination only slightly expressed in egalitarian cultures but that come to full flower in class-based state-organized urban societies. Instead of being treated as an historical development, hierarchy becomes written into human physiology. Despite much citation from Marx and Engels on the part of those who do this, they contradict a fully Marxist view of human nature as informed by the last hundred years of social science research. Their entanglement with male supremacist ideology feeds into and is fed by the failure to deal rigorously with both history and theory in the interpretation of primitive communist society and the source of its transformation.[13]

THE ORIGINS OF HIERARCHY

The two sets of relations defined by Marx and Engels as critical to the emergence of exploitation are: first, the loss of control over the production

---

[11] When this essay was written, French structuralism and sociobiology were extremely popular in the United States. In this paragraph, Leacock takes aim at both, particularly sociobiologist E. O. Wilson's *Sociobiology: The New Synthesis* (1975). (The introduction to Wilson's book is reprinted as essay 26.) Wilson's notion that genes were responsible for much of human nature was anathema to most anthropologists. Behind the notion of the "conformer gene" is the idea that hunting required a high degree of coordination and conformity. Laughlin (mentioned in this paragraph) called hunting the "master behavior pattern of the human species" (cited in Barash 1979:186). Thus, the tendency of humans to conform is genetically based—the result of the fact that, over the millennia, there was strong evolutionary pressure for conformity.

Leacock criticizes French structuralism as reductionist and antihistorical. For Lévi-Strauss, the underlying meaning of myths and other cultural phenomena involves a few universal themes such as resolving humans' relations to nature. The outward form of the stories and the historical circumstances that produced them have no meaning. This perspective is rejected by Leacock.

[12] *Isometric:* of equal measure.

Here, Leacock says that although sex and gender are not equivalent, many scholars still believe that the physiological differences between men and women are the basis for gender inequality. One example of this type of work is Ortner's structural analysis in this volume (essay 23).

[13] In the paragraphs above, Leacock has condemned the sociobiologists and structuralists. Here she takes aim at unnamed Marxists who fail to fully apply Marxist analysis to their subject because they accept the Western ideology of male supremacy. Neo-Marxist authors are well known for attacking one another's positions, and Leacock does not spare those who share her theoretical outlook.

process (i.e., production, exchange, distribution, and consumption) through the division of labor beyond that by sex; and second, the emergence of dyadic relations[14] of dependency within individual families as a public/private dichotomy developed in economic and political life, making families separate economic units rather than parts of encompassing communal groups. The fundamental historical development analysed at length in Marx's opening section of *Capital* and central to Engels' reworking of Morgan's evolutionary hypothesis in *The Origin of the Family, Private Property and the State*, was the transformation from production for use to production for exchange. The emergence of production for exchange meant that value as an attribute of goods began to supersede use as the feature of primary social significance. As a consequence "abstract labor," the labor time represented in an exchangeable object, became separable from concrete work, a development that eventually made it possible for those who controlled exchange to regulate and exploit the productivity of others. Finally, money developed in various forms as a medium of exchange, as a pure commodity. Marx stressed that the money form allowed the fetishistic absurdity whereby relations among people appeared to them as relations among things; thus the structure of exploitation was mystified and the existence of class differences rationalized.[15]

In *The Evolution of Political Society*, Fried raised the question why people accepted control by others over the products of their work and allowed the loss of their independence.[16] Whatever the answer, Fried stated, people did not realize the magnitude of the changes they were bringing about.* To be sure, they did not, since, through exchange and the division of labor, people were simply enriching their lives and cementing interpersonal and intergroup bonds, innocent of the processes thereby set in motion. As Engels put it, "the more a social activity, a series of social processes . . . appears a matter of pure chance, then all the more surely within this chance the laws peculiar to it and inherent in it assert themselves." Commodity production and the division of labor that accompanied it slowly but inexorably led to class stratification; they raised up "incorporeal alien powers . . . too powerful for men's conscious control."*[17]

Simple barter does not separate the producer from control over exchange and distribution. As barter develops in importance, however, it leads to a contradiction between the material benefits to be derived from specialized production for trade and the structure of full egalitarianism. Fried suggested that the elaboration of redistribution was

---

[14] A dyadic relationship is one with two parts. Leacock argues here that the emergence of dyadic relations of dependency within individual families was a second factor explaining the origins of exploitation.

[15] In this paragraph, Leacock is trying to briefly recount Marx's theory of the origins of hierarchy. The first step is a movement from producing things simply to use them (for their "use value") to producing things as commodities that can be sold. Marx argues that this movement allows people in capitalist societies to think of the amount of labor that goes into the production of an object as equivalent to the value of that object. However, capitalist society makes a fetish of the commodity, valuing it over the labor that produced it. Marx's notion is sometimes referred to as the labor theory of value and is one of the most controversial aspects of his philosophy.

The Origin of the Family, Private Property, and the State (1972 [1884]) is a book that Engels wrote based on notes Marx had taken as he read Morgan's *Ancient Society*

(1985 [1877]). Engels' analysis is based on Morgan's notion that families were originally matrilineal. He ties the historic shift from matrilineality to patrilineality to the emergence of private property. Leacock was very familiar with Engels' work. In fact, she wrote an introduction to the 1972 edition.

[16] In this section, Leacock leans heavily on the theory of stratification advanced by Morton Fried in *The Evolution of Political Society* (1967). The essay by Fried in this volume (essay 18), published seven years before his book, is a summary of the principal arguments he advanced there.

[17] In this section, "The Origins of Hierarchy," Leacock points out that social processes are qualitatively different from the actions of individuals. Here, individuals simply pursue their own benefit, but the net result is a social shift to hierarchy that results in their loss of independence. She argues that this same shift also results in the emergence of gender hierarchy.

important to the emergence of ranking, the first form of stratification.* The focus should be sharpened and emphasis placed on the significance of redistribution for the emergence of commodity production with all its consequences. Goods produced for exchange rather than for use create new interest groups. For a long time, egalitarian relationships prevent persons in pivotal positions in networks of exchange and redistribution from exploiting the economic possibilities of their position. Nonetheless, the conflict between egalitarian relations sharpens and, in what are called ranking societies, people begin to accept dependent positions in relation to "big men" and other chiefly people in order to benefit from the hand-outs associated with them. Eventually, unequal appropriation among and within competitively structured lineages is institutionalized, and the conflict between egalitarian distribution and consumption on the one hand, and the potential afforded by exchange and increasing specialization of labor on the other, is partially resolved. New contradictions are already crystallizing, however, between the potentials created by increasingly farflung economic ties and social forms attuned to autonomous kin and village groupings, in turn to be resolved by full stratification and political organization and the familiar conflicts of class society.[18]

To return to the second component of exploitation and stratification, it is in conjunction with the above developments that a public/private dichotomy emerges and dyadic relations of dependence within families as economic units begin to take shape. Lévi-Strauss posits to the contrary, in egalitarian societies, women are not exchanged by men; instead they exchange goods and services with men.* Direct exchange between the sexes, like single barter, does not separate either sex from control over its own production. Instead, alienation develops in tandem with the development of exchange systems, as individuals use lineage and extended family units to compete for ranking positions in relation to control over the production and distribution of valued goods. Gender responsibilities for marketing and exchange vary according to how different environments and histories have patterned the sex division of labor, and women's position in decision-making structures varies correspondingly.* Yet the question remains: when ranking begins to undermine the equal prerogatives of people generally, why is it that the autonomy and authority of women as a sex are threatened rather than those of men? Aside from various formulations of male superiority, it is usually argued that the physical limitations of childbirth and suckling are critical. Yet these do not hinder women in egalitarian societies.* In keeping with my reading of dialectical materialist theory as outlined above, I would say that the significance of women's childbearing ability is transformed by new social relations when they become the producers, not only of people as individuals, but also of what is becoming "abstract"—i.e., exploitable—labor. The origins of gender hierarchy, then, are inextricably meshed with the origins of exploitation and class stratification.*[19]

Engels posed a sharp contrast between the status of women among the egalitarian Iroquois and that in the patriarchal societies of the classical

---

[18] In Marxist thinking, it is the resolution of conflict that creates change between social forms. However, each such resolution contains the germs of a new conflict and, hence, progress to new social forms. In this paragraph, Leacock points first to a conflict between egalitarian social forms and specialization. Since no two specializations are likely to be entirely equal, it is impossible to maintain egalitarian social relations once specialization begins. This problem is resolved in rank societies through a hierarchical ordering of kin groups. Such ranking, however, creates new contradictions because nonkin relations are now available through trade with distant people.

[19] Leacock argues that in egalitarian societies based on barter economics, gender relations are relations of equality. Making a fetish of commodities and making labor a commodity are part of the formation of hierarchical societies, and it is only when egalitarian societies become rank societies that women lose rights and men gain them. This leaves her with a difficult question: Why are women, rather than men, the ones who lose the rights? She rejects explanations rooted in either biology or "human nature" and instead asserts that women are disadvantaged because they are associated with the production of labor power rather than of commodities themselves. Thus, women produce labor, men

Middle East and Mediterranean where control over female sexuality was important for the inheritance of status and property. In his view, the family as an economic unit was of primary importance within the upper class although it had ramifications throughout society. It remained for mid-20th century Marxist-feminist scholarship to add a further dimension to these ramifications. Female subordination within the family as an economic unit also enabled an upper class to squeeze more surplus from workers, serfs and slaves. The fact that domestic work could be separated from a public sphere and assigned to women as the wards of men assured to an upper class the reproduction and maintenance of workers through socially unremunerated—i.e., slave—labor. This is not to say that the arrangement was thought through in advance any more than other major historical developments of the past. However, given the records of women's steady decline in legal and social rights in classical antiquity, it remains to trace some of the steps whereby the household subordination of women was buttressed by ideological and social sanctions as its economic advantages were realized.[*20]

All of this, however, pertains to the final stages of women's subordination. The majority of societies with which anthropology deals involve the most preliminary stages—points at which women's autonomy began to be threatened and a certain hostility between the sexes began to be institutionalized, but that were very far indeed from the legal and political reduction of women to the status of ward that accompanied full-scale stratification. I am suggesting that the structure of gender in such societies needs to be interpreted in relation to: the structure of exchange and the division of labor; the structure of ranking and the degree to which some sections of the society are gaining control over the labor of others; the structure of kinship and the extent to which lineages have become competing sodalities rather than the means for organizing production and distribution in communal villages; the degree to which the well-being of one segment of a society is not merely relative but is actually at the expense of other segments; and, in the light of all this, the structure of marriage in relation to control over children as exploitable labor or as exploiters of labor.[21]

---

produce commodities. Commodities are more valued in hierarchical societies than is labor; therefore men are more highly valued than women. Note that the accuracy of this claim rests wholly on acceptance of Marx's notion of the labor theory of value and the notion of making a fetish of the commodity. Without these ideas, there is no reason why producing labor should be intrinsically more or less valuable than producing commodities.

Interestingly, Leacock's analysis here bears a superficial resemblance to Ortner's notions in "Is Female to Male as Nature Is to Culture?" (essay 23). In that essay, Ortner contends that women are seen as inferior because nature is seen as inferior to culture. Women's production of children ties them to nature, whereas men's production of material ties them to culture. The critical difference between Ortner's structural analysis and Leacock's Marxist analysis is that Ortner sees the relative positions of nature and culture as fundamental features of human consciousness in all societies. Leacock, on the other hand, believes that the position of labor relative to its products is a specific, historical development in capitalist societies.

[20] Leacock is arguing that men were able to reproduce their superior social position by relying on the unpaid domestic work of women. Her argument comes substantially from Engels' *Origin of the Family*. In that work, Engels argues that property was key to marriage among the bourgeoisie, and he likened marriage to prostitution. Women in such marriages traded domestic and sexual service for economic support. Engels argued that after the communist revolution, marriage would be egalitarian since each partner would be equally involved in production.

[21] In this passage, Leacock cites two other prominent feminist anthropologists: Peggy Sanday (b. 1937) and Karen Sacks (b. 1941). When this essay was written, Sanday had recently published *Female Power and Male Dominance: On the Origins of Sexual Inequality* (1981). There, she argued that in "inner oriented" societies—those with abundant food supplies and little threat of outside aggression—people lived in harmony with nature and one another. Gender relations were egalitarian. But in "outer oriented" societies, characterized by food scarcity and warfare, men dominated women. She reported that the number of "outer oriented" societies increased with colonialism. Karen Sacks is also concerned with issues of gender equality and, when this essay was written, had recently published *Sisters and Wives: The Past and Future of Sexual Equality* (1979).

In what are called ranking societies, women's position begins to shift from valued people who cement networks of reciprocal relations and who have access to various publically recognized mechanisms for adjudicating their interests as women, into that of service workers in the households of husbands and their kin groups. Bride wealth begins to take the form of purchasing a woman's children, rather than of gift exchange. Sacks has explored the relation of such developments to the emergence of status difference among women as well as between women and men.* She has demonstrated the usefulness of separating the status of women as wives from that as sisters in order to appreciate the extent to which women exercise publically recognized authority through the manipulation of kin ties in societies where economic stratification and gender hierarchy are emerging. Sanday has stressed the fact that women may protect and maintain their public authority well into the conditions of stratification, a fact attested to by extensive data on West African societies and suggested by the case of ancient Crete.* All told, a focus on the above developments and the particularities of their unfolding in different historical, cultural and environmental contexts, makes clear that changes in women's position are neither secondary phenomena, as some imply, nor prior to economic hierarchy, as argued by others. They are at the core of, and inseparable from, profound transformations that take place in conjunction with the development of exchange and the division of labor.

The social and economic subordination of women was established in some parts of the world millenia ago; it was unfolding in other parts of the world at the time of European exploration and conquest; and it has been developing in yet others in the context of Western colonialism and imperialism.* I am here arguing that in order to interpret this development correctly, it is essential, first: to have a clear concept of primitive communism, divested of stereotypical assumptions that female subordination is a natural rather than historical phenomenon, and second: to place any society under study clearly in the context of its particular history, pre- and post-colonial. I now return to the second point.

THE HISTORICAL CONTEXT OF ANTHROPOLOGICAL ANALYSIS

The actual people contemporary anthropologists study are not autonomous gatherer-hunters or horticulturalists or whatever. In one way or another the relations of capitalism have impinged upon them for a long time. Whatever the specific nature of a people's involvement with capitalism, the *ultimate* direction of change is the same: the individualization and alienation of labor, the individualization of the nuclear family, and the relegation of women both to unrecompensed domestic labor and to public labor as an unstable and underpaid work force. People lose what control over the process and products of their labor they previously had, and their labor itself becomes increasingly transformed into a commodity to be bought, if not outright commandeered. The responsibility for rearing the new generation is progressively transferred from some larger kin or band grouping to individual families. Idealized by missionary teachings as loving care for husband and children, women's labor in the household becomes for all practical purposes a gift to the plantation or mine owner, manufacturer or trader, who draws profits from the work of husbands and sons and then buys women's additional labor at a marginal price.*[22]

Untidy details like plantation labor and commercial transactions have too commonly been ignored when data on so-called traditional societies are codified and punched on IBM cards for

---

[22] Leacock's critical point is that women's domestic labor is essential to the reproduction of the workforce. Without domestic labor, families cannot be maintained and workers cannot be produced. However, the owners of capital (the factory owners or mine owners) pay their workers (usually male) but do not pay the women, whose work enables the production of these workers. Thus, from Leacock's perspective, women's domestic work is a gift to capitalists.

cross-cultural comparison.[23] Not surprisingly, a recent analysis concludes that there are no consistent correlations between women's position in a society and other factors.* Luckily, however, ethnohistorical and archaeological reconstruction of pre-colonial and colonial culture histories is proceeding apace, and it is possible to throw light on puzzling cases where there seems to be little relation between female subordination and economic inequality.[24]

I have already made reference to North America, which, north of Mexico, constitutes the largest world area that was inhabited by egalitarian peoples at the time of European expansion. Ranking was elaborated in coastal areas, especially along the Gulf of Mexico and the northern Pacific, but the vast majority of native North Americans had retained egalitarian socio-economic structures. The Iroquois are the best known example of the gender equality common in North America, and,

contrary to the opinion of Lévi-Strauss,* are not an anomaly. Instead, they afford a well-documented example of the economic and political reciprocity that accompanied the matrilineal-matrilocal organization widespread among North American horticulturalists.* Among hunting-gathering peoples, the Inuit (Eskimo) are commonly cited as an example of masculine brutality toward women in an otherwise egalitarian society, an example seemingly paralleled by accounts of female subordination among the Chipewyan.* However, ethnographic accounts of women's independence and assertiveness among the Inuit indicate that ethno-historical analysis, long overdue, will reveal the latter-day character of male abusiveness as following from the demoralization and drunkenness suffered in many Inuit communities.* As for the Chipewyan case, it is based on an account of middlemen in the fur trade, the "gang" that collected around the unusually dedicated

---

[23] Leacock is attacking George Peter Murdock's Human Relations Area Files project (see the section "The Reemergence of Evolutionary Thought"). Murdock's project was a descendant of the large-scale cross-cultural studies started by Herbert Spencer. Thus it has a history that places it squarely in the anti-Marxist camp. The "Outline of Cultural Materials" Murdock devised to code the HRAF is decidedly non-Marxist, giving little attention to conflict, imperialism, class consciousness, or other interests central to Marxist analysis.

[24] Leacock makes the point in the second half of this essay that European expansion, from the fifteenth century on, had critical effects on people throughout the world. In particular, as capitalist relations of production were imposed on indigenous groups, the social and political position of women suffered. Previously egalitarian societies, in which women enjoyed either full equality with men or very substantial rights, were subverted, and men came to dominate women. Leacock argues that most ethnographic writing simply fails to take the effects of European colonialism into account. Thus ethnographies that showed the oppression of women among indigenous peoples were generally in error. The authors of these monographs, writing in the ethnographic present, fail to realize that the practices they assume to be "traditional" date only from the transformation of these societies by capitalism. If these societies could be seen before the advent of European

expansion, the equality of gender relations in egalitarian and early ranked societies would be apparent. In making this argument Leacock is strongly influenced by World System Theory, a popular neo-Marxist position of the 1960s and 1970s. Although notions of dependency have been around for a long time, World System Theory was promoted by the work of Andre Gunder-Frank (b. 1929) and Immanuel Wallerstein (b.1930). In his most famous essay, "The Development of Underdevelopment" (1966), Gunder-Frank argued that the nations of Latin America were not poor because they failed to industrialize. Rather, the processes of the expansion of capitalism in the wealthy nations, particularly in North America and in northern Europe, had drawn wealth out of Latin America. Thus, the poverty of southern nations was directly linked to the wealth of northern capitalist societies. In 1974 Wallerstein published *The Modern World-System,* in which he traced the development of global capitalism from its origins in the early seventeenth century, emphasizing its deleterious effects on noncapitalist cultures around the world. As did Gunder-Frank, the principal thesis Wallerstein advanced was that the wealth of nations and the poverty of nations are interlinked. Today's wealthy nations became rich by expropriating the wealth of today's poor nations. Although Leacock focuses on gender relations rather than wealth, the fundamental argument is the same. She insists that it was the expansion of capitalist power that undermined the position of women in society after society.

worker for the Hudson's Bay Company, and not on independent Chipewyan hunters. The quality of relations therein described contrasts sharply with the 17th century Jesuit accounts of gender equality among the Montagnais-Naskapi.*

Australia

Aboriginal Australia has furnished ample grounds for arguments that male dominance is a psychosocial or psychobiological universal rather than an historical development. Male control of women's marriage, male inheritance of land, virilocal residence, male brutality towards women, and male exclusion of women from important rituals in a non-stratified society form an imposing package and have been documented again and again. To be sure, data modifying these generalizations are beginning to assert themselves. Older women have a say in marriages along with older men, while young men, like young women, have little say. Just as young women are commonly married the first time to elder men, so are young men often married to elder women. Women have clubs with which they not only defend themselves, but with which they beat men for misbehavior; they are not cowed by men. Furthermore, if wrongfully hit, a woman may simply leave, or may take up residence in the women's section of the camp, taboo to men. Women are important in the conduct of some male rituals, and are indifferent to their exclusion from others; their own, from which men are excluded, hold more interest for them.* Tindale has pointed out that among the Pitjandara of western Australia, women call male rituals to a close if they find themselves walking too far for food and wish to move camp.* Bell worked in a north-central Australian settlement where "the maintenance of law and order . . . is still a cooperative venture between men and women who turn to each other for assistance on some issues and assert their independent rights on others."*

However, while such data qualify the picture of male dominance claimed for Australian gatherer-hunters, the historical setting in which 20th century Aboriginal society has been functioning must be understood if this image is to be contradicted in its entirety. First and foremost, not to evaluate the effects of the brutal genocide native Australians have suffered is as unscientific as it is unethical. Brutality against native Australians has been practiced from the earliest forays by Malays; to the sporadic explorations by Europeans and the 1788 convict settlement at what is now Sydney; through the steady encroachment on Australian lands and the accompanying shooting, poisoning, beating and enslaving, along with disastrous disease; into the brutal policing and racist restrictions of the present. One cannot talk of men hitting women as if apart from a pattern of frontier violence where demoralization is compounded by alcohol.*

Second, it is—or should be—inexcusable to analyse land rights in Australia without considering the impact of forced movements away from coastal areas and the resulting land pressure in interior regions to which many Aborigines fled. Some early meetings between Europeans and Australians were friendly, but the Europeans were over-ready to use their guns, and apparently the Australians sometimes retaliated with the unambiguous act of treating their foes as food. For the most part, therefore, early explorers from Europe were glad to leave the Australians alone, once it was decided that there was no ready gold or other easy wealth on their lands. Then the arrival of the first merino sheep in New South Wales in 1797 was followed in 1813 by the discovery, west of the Blue Mountains, of the immense grasslands that were to make Australia the largest producer of fine wool in the world.* The push was on. The rich southeast, where 400 to 600 people were wont to gather at certain seasons to socialize and live on seafood and crayfish, was soon depopulated of Aborigines. Some were killed, some moved west, and a few married into the white community. The herders too pushed west, enslaving the Aborigines, or pressing them into labor, and brutally suppressing their resistance.* Driven westward and inland, away from expanding centers of white settlement and onto each other's traditional homelands, different peoples turned against each other, fighting and quarrelling. As among native Americans, the recognition of a common identity as Aborigines, with a common history and common struggle, took time to emerge. White Australians of course took advantage of and exacerbated divisiveness among the Aborigines, favoring "pacified" groups and using them to enslave or control others.

The demoralization found among displaced Aboriginal survivors is documented by Daisy Bates, who over a period of some forty years publicized the Aboriginal condition from her isolated camp in South Australia.* Despite the patronization and misinterpretations of her account, many incidents she reports parallel the macabre bitterness of collective suicide described by Turnbull for the Ik.* A particularly bizarre scene ensues when Bates accompanied Radcliffe-Brown to the grim hospital island where sick and fearful Aborigines, separated from their own people, are taken only to die. She describes Radcliffe-Brown asking the old men to sing ritual songs into his phonograph and playing them Tannhauser and Egmont in return.*[25]

By the 20th century, disease and genocide in its various forms had reduced an estimated 300,000 or more people of aboriginal Australia to less than 40,000.* By mid-century, with the "stabilization" of native reserves, and the dispensation of minimal food supplies and medical care by government or mission stations, the Aboriginal population began to rise again. Ritual life, too, began to revive and expand, although serving a new function as a focus for the assertion of identity and self-respect by a people robbed of their independence. Anthropologists also expanded in numbers, typically wishing to study the lives of pristine hunter-gatherers. They usually took care to interview people living a distance from mission stations or cattle ranches, rather than the service workers directly attached to such enterprises. Seldom, however, did they inquire deeply into a people's history, nor even inquire about existing official regulations for Aborigines, such as those that prohibit marriage off of a reserve.*

The point should be clear. To ignore the historical, economic, and political realities of Aboriginal life is to gloss over the effects of conquest and oppression, and therefore to misconstrue the social relations that obtained when Aborigines were autonomous gatherers and hunters in control of their own social world. With respect to relations between the sexes, when one scrapes the surface of ethnohistorical materials, one finds suggestions of women's former importance, such as Howitt's reference to influential elder women in southeastern Australia. Only recently, however, have these begun to be followed up.* As long ago as a hundred years, Spencer and Gillin note a three-day women's section of an initiation ceremony among the Arunta and comment that "there was a time when women played a more important part in regard to such ceremonies than they do at the present time."* Unfortunately, they give no further information except that they personally find the ceremony boring. In his recently republished *Australian Religion*, Mircea Eliade makes ample reference to male high gods, but nowhere mentions the important mythological personage who keeps reappearing in the pages of Spencer and Gillin, the female Sun. Eliade writes that initiation for Australian girls is simpler than for boys, and flatly contradicts ethnographic fact by stating, "as everywhere in the world."*

---

[25] This paragraph contains references to several famous characters. Daisy Bates (1861–1951) was an Irishwoman who lived among the Aborigines for thirty years, beginning in about 1913. Bates wrote several books about her experience. It is impossible to doubt that horrific things happened to the Aborigines, but for their history Daisy Bates might not be the best source. Julia Blackburn, author of *Daisy Bates in the Desert: A Woman's Life Among the Aborigines* (1994), writes that Bates fabricated her life history and that she was unable to separate her experiences from her imagination.

Colin Turnbull (1924–1994) was the author of *The Forest People* (1961) and *The Mountain People* (1972). The first of these describes the idyllic life of the Mbuti of the Ituri Forest and the second, the horrific life of the Ik of Uganda. Both portraits have been heavily critiqued as romantic (or anti-romantic).

A. R. Radcliffe-Brown (see essay 12) lived in Australia from 1926 to 1931. The image Bates and Leacock present here is a compelling one, and it may well have happened. It is clear that Radcliffe-Brown had little interest in history and believed that the social structures he studied had been relatively little affected by colonialism.

Hart and Pilling raise the need for ethno-historical work in their account of the Tiwi.* They describe how missionary influences as well as prostitution encouraged male control over women's sexuality in the early 20th century, and then go on to consider earlier influences on the politics of wife-trading. Archival research is needed, they write, to determine the extent of slave raiding by the Portuguese in the 18th century. Since it was probably the younger men who were taken off to Timor, they suggest the slaving may have encouraged the dominance of old Tiwi men and their monopolization of wives.

[Leacock provides three additional ethnographic examples, but space considerations prevent us from reprinting them here. We summarize them below.

In a 1,100-word section with 12 notes entitled "The Amazon," Leacock first divides Amazonian history into five periods. The first of these is precolonial, but in the others she dwells on the effects of colonization. She then moves to a discussion of the Yanomamo, asserting that their portrayal as "the fierce people" serves to rationalize the destruction of the Amazon forests. Citing geographer William J. Smole (1976), Leacock argues that the Yanomamo studied by Chagnon were made fierce by their contacts with Portuguese and Spanish invaders. Smole also reports that the position of women among the highland Yanomamo he studied was very much better than that reported by Chagnon. Leacock concludes this section by claiming that Chagnon's failure to deal with the Yanomamo history and politics cast doubt on his portrayal of the male aggressiveness and dominance among a virtually pristine egalitarian people.

In an 830-word section with 6 notes entitled "Melanesia," Leacock suggests that the societies of New Guinea are often used as evidence for the subordination of women in egalitarian societies. This portrayal, however, is incorrect since ancient irrigation works and trade connections suggest that stratification had already begun in this area. Further, trade connections with Malays, Chinese, and Europeans may have badly compromised egalitarian relations. The hostility often expressed between men and women is highly suggestive of a society in which rank is being asserted and women are losing

control over their production. The fact that in New Guinea women often respond to their subordination with open anger rather than passive acceptance is strongly suggestive of societies in which the process of stratification is only beginning. These relations may have been further exacerbated by European conquest, which increased conflict between tribes.

A 2,000-word section with 19 notes titled "Africa" includes a substantial critique of the work of French neo-Marxists Claude Meillassoux and Emanuel Terray. Their work was critical in the development of Marxist thought in anthropology during the 1960s and 1970s, and both worked in Africa. The French neo-Marxists broke from Soviet-style Marxist anthropology. Soviet ethnographers insisted on the primacy of the modes of production outlined by Marx and Morgan's scheme for the evolution of society. The French neo-Marxists expanded the notion of mode of production to include new modes germane to the societies anthropologists studied. They were also largely trained by Lévi-Strauss and were deeply influenced by his notions on exchange and the role of women.

Leacock begins by noting that African history is extremely complex but often ignored. Despite some exceptions, the ethnography of African societies portrays women as firmly under male authority. Ethnohistorical work, however, shows that the position of African women deteriorated with the advent of colonial rule. Before colonialism, they often had important public political roles. Although in African hierarchical societies, women's autonomy was undermined, it was not destroyed, except in later Muslim states. Leacock faults the French neo-Marxists for failing to use Engels' notion that the subjugation of women was central to the development of hierarchy in analyzing the emergence of ranked societies in Africa. Because they agree with Lévi-Strauss on the universal subjugation of women, they tend to condense egalitarian and beginning rank societies into a single mode of production. This obscures the critical processes of the emergence of hierarchy. The problem is evident in Terray's work on the Gayman. Terray sees kin relations among the Gayman as exploiting women and youth. These relations were eventually dominated by relations based on slavery. Terray does not, however, look for a reason why women *are exploited in the first place. Leacock, however, finds the answer in Terray's own work. She notes that he says the lineage structure is related to the political structure and did not come before it; further, "youth" was a rank that could include older men. Finally, captive labor was used in the lineage mode of production. Thus, Terray fails to realize that the exploitation of women and youth in the lineage mode of production is integral to the existence of hierarchical society and did not precede it. Terray also fails to consider that the ranked urban portion of society could have affected the more egalitarian rural part of society. His analysis is also weakened by failure to consider changes brought about by exposure to European slaving.]*

CONCLUSION

Across the disciplines, research on the economic and social activities of women has been shaking up some established assumptions about society and history. I have argued that only when gender hierarchy is taken as an historical problematic, rather than a psycho-biological given, can the structure of primitive communist relations be properly understood, and the part played by exchange in the transformation of these relations clearly formulated. The need for an effective theory of exchange in pre-capitalist societies is well recognized by Marxist anthropologists,* but ironically it is associated, especially for those working in the structuralist tradition, with the wholly anti-Marxist concept of woman exchange as basic in primitive communist society.[26] Only when such a formulation is stringently challenged can the first phases of the process whereby women actually became exchanged be understood, for these were inseparable from initial steps in the transformation of use to value, work to abstract labor, and cooperative production to exploitation.

An effective theory of exchange is necessary both for analysing pre-capitalist societies and for interpreting the effects on these societies of colonization and imperialism. Only when the genders in primitive communist societies are understood as economically independent exchangers of goods and services, can the full force of capitalist relations in subverting the labor of women, and therefore transforming the entire structure of relationships in such societies, be appreciated. Until such time, the myth of the ethnographic present will continue to support the assumption, so prevalent in pop-science and the mass media, that the widespread normative ideal of men as household heads who provision dependent women and children reflects some human need or drive. And until such time, the unique and valued culture history and tradition of each Third World people will continue to be distorted, twisted to fit the interests of capitalist exploitation.

---

[26] Here, Leacock is once again attacking the French Marxists she has discussed in her analysis of Africa. We have edited this portion of the essay from the text, but be sure to read our condensation of it.

---

30. *"I Went to Bed with My Own Kind Once": The Erasure of Desire in the Name of Identity*

DAVID VALENTINE (1966-)[a]

INTRODUCTION

What does it mean to talk about erotic desire? By this, I mean two inter-related things: what does it mean to talk about desire in a scholarly context; and what does it mean to talk about one's own desires? In the contemporary USA, popular discussions of erotic desire are drawn inevitably into a discussion of 'sexuality,' one which—again, inevitably—occurs against and invokes the binary

From *Language and Communication* (2003)

of hetero/homo-sexual identity (troubled perhaps by the evidence of bisexuality, though even with bisexuality, desire is seen to lie discretely within the bounds of an identity category, namely 'bisexual'). Within queer, feminist, and anthropological scholarship, Foucault's famous point—that sexual identity has come to stand as the truth of who we are (Foucault, 1990[1980], pp. 51–73)—has been utilized to show how, since the late nineteenth century in the West, the erotic is not expressed as particular desires but, rather, as discrete identities. Foucault and others (e.g. Weeks, 1981; Katz, 1995) have pointed to the power of identity categories to both proliferate discourses about, and simultaneously restrain, talk of erotic desire as an experience which bears the name 'sexuality.' Erotic desires which fall outside the trinary of heterosexuality, homosexuality (either/or) and bisexuality (both/and), or which fail to make sense in terms of their basic logic of binary gender, are rendered unintelligible. Such 'unintelligible' desires present a unique opportunity for scholars to investigate the complexity of erotic desire, its expression in practice (linguistic and otherwise), and its relationship to identity categories.[1]

Yet, despite the influence of Foucault, the troubling nature of desire-beyond-sexual identity has received relatively little attention. Since the early 1990s, many anthropologists have indeed pointed out that Western sexual identities and identity labels cannot make sense of—and indeed, are complicated by—non-Western sexual practices and desires (e.g. Blackwood, 1995;

Donham, 1998; Johnson, 1997; Kulick, 1998). However, there has been little corresponding work which looks explicitly at the erratic connections between erotic desire and identity in US settings outside of immigrant communities (e.g. Manalansan, 1997). Most anthropologists of sexuality in the USA have tended to follow the basic anthropological tenet of using one's informants' categories to describe them. Consequently, gay men and lesbians—the usual subjects of discussions of 'sexuality' in the anthropological literature—are usually discussed in terms of those categories of identity which are meaningful to informants. As a result, the ontological assumptions which underpin these emic categories are left unexamined (e.g. Lewin, 1993; Shokeid, 1995; Weston, 1991). While attention to study subjects' self-categorization is clearly central to the anthropological enterprise, critical analyses of those categorizations is also vital to analysis.[2]

If anthropology (and other social sciences) has neglected the ontological underpinnings of desire, there has been even less work in linguistics and linguistic anthropology which takes up the deeper implications of considering language and desire. As Kulick (2000) points out, much of the work that takes on the relationship between language and erotic desire has coalesced around a discussion of 'sexuality,' usually focusing on gay- and lesbian-identified (and occasionally transgender-identified) subjects. As with the studies I mentioned above, this work similarly depends for its analysis on a close identification

---

[1] Valentine opens his discussion of sexuality and discourse by referencing Foucault (essay 35 in this volume). For Foucault, the control of discourse is an expression of power. Foucault argued that in the West, in the eighteenth and nineteenth centuries, people increasingly became identified with their sexuality. Prior to this era, sex was something that one did or desires one had. After it, a person's expression of sexual desire pigeonholed them as a particular type of person, typically a heterosexual or a homosexual. However, Valentine argues that sexual desire that does not conform to the logic of binary gender challenges our thinking about desire and gender categories. Implicit in this argument is that we tend to think with the categories our culture makes available to us, an idea here drawn largely from French Post Modernism. Experiences that

cannot be easily categorized are "unintelligible." This essay introduces us to individuals whose behavior is unintelligible in this sense.

[2] Here Valentine argues that although anthropologists have long accepted that nonwestern gender categories and sexual behavior may not fit Western models, the underlying assumptions of western gender identity and sexuality have gone largely unexamined. Individuals may classify themselves as gay, straight, or bisexual. Anthropologists assume they know what is meant by those terms. However, Valentine argues that this assumption is unwarranted. Such terms require unpacking and this can be performed through a linguistic analysis of how people talk about desire.

with study participants' self-identity as gay and lesbian. But, as Kulick points out, there is a central flaw in much of this work, drawing as it does on a tautology: people who are lesbian and gay speak in a way that is defined as 'gay language'; and people who talk a 'gay language' are, thus, gay. Kulick argues that such studies continuously capitulate to a sexuality = identity formula. To move beyond this dynamic, Kulick proposes a reorientation of 'language and sexuality' studies from a focus on sexual identity to a focus on desire. He argues that a focus on desire will both complicate understandings of what 'sexuality' is and enable an examination of the relationship between linguistic practices and sexuality that is not constrained by identity categories.[3]

Central to Kulick's argument is a critique of the essentialism implicit in much of the work on language and sexuality. This critique draws on a central tenet of contemporary social theory: that essentialized categories of identity obscure the cross-cutting nature of social experience and identification. Being 'gay' or 'lesbian' for example, is experienced by different people in radically different ways depending on their racial identification, location, age, social class, personal history, and so forth. What is less clear, though, is that such categories of identity achieve a density of meaning through their reiteration, even in scholarly work that attempts to disrupt that meaning. By this I mean that even scholars who take a critical approach to essentialized identities require some baseline understandings about bodies and practices, about the relationship between signifier and signified, in order to mount a critique in the first place.[4]

To take the examples of 'gay' and 'lesbian' once more, while we might accept that very different kinds of people may use these categories in identifying themselves, there are also some basic assumptions that flow from the organization of the categories themselves. Primary among these is that people who identify as 'gay' or 'lesbian' are understood as unambiguously men or women, and that they direct their desire to others who are, respectively, unambiguously men or women. That is, these categories rest implicitly on the logic of binary gender which underpins the homo/hetero identity structure, a structure which requires clearly gendered men and women to desire one another (or each other).

For those people who are not unambiguously gendered, the category 'transgender' has, since the early 1990s, become ubiquitous (by people so identified and in scholarly texts) to encapsulate this experience. 'Transgender' has become both a powerful tool of activism and a convenient label for social scientific research in bringing together a range of social and medicalized identities formerly seen as separate including, but not limited to, transexuals, cross-dressers, drag queens[b], and intersex people. Indeed, the power of the category is that it is actively seen as a collective term to gather in all non-normative expressions of gender, no matter how they are labeled. Another central element of contemporary discourses of 'transgender' is that transgender identities are seen to emanate from the experience of 'gender,' not 'sexuality.' In other words, transgender identities are conceptualized as quite distinct from homosexual identities, which are seen to have their source in 'sexuality.'[5]

---

[3] Don Kulick (1960–) is a Swedish anthropologist whose work has focused around sexuality and language. Considered to be among the foremost Scandinavian Queer Theorists, Kulick has worked in Italy, Brazil, Papua New Guinea, and Sweden.

[4] Kulick's argument, as presented by Valentine, is that in order to communicate about a topic people must share some "baseline" or "essentialized" understandings about that topic. However, these essentialized understandings ignore the individually lived nature of social experience. For example, one can have a conversation about gays or

lesbians but this assumption of identity ignores the individual lives and experiences of gay and lesbian people that are not subsumed by the labels "gay" and "lesbian."

[5] Valentine points out here that while homo- and heterosexuality are labels determined by one's sexual behavior, transgender is different. Transgender is a label that is used to describe all non-normative expressions of gender no matter whether these are based on cultural factors such as dress and surgery, or genital structure. Anyone who blurs the boundaries between the Western homosexual/heterosexual identity structure is labeled transgender. However, in the

At the same time, it is important to note that even in discussions of transgender-identified[c] people, sexual desire is still generally encoded as either heterosexual or homosexual (or, indeed, bisexual). That is, sexual identity is usually claimed by transgender-identified people in accordance with their gender of identity. While most transgender-identified people insist on the differences between homosexuality and transgender identity (a significant point I will return to), many also identify as homosexual, based on their erotic and affective attraction to people who share the same gender category with which they identify. However, to reiterate, in contemporary scholarship and activism these identities are seen to flow from distinct kinds of ontological sources— transgender identity from 'gender,' and homosexual or heterosexual identity from 'sexuality.'[6]

As such, this seems like a very neat system, which accounts both for gender identification and erotic desire within a double binary of homosexual/ heterosexual and masculinity/femininity, with their roots respectively in yet another binary: that of sexuality and gender. But things are not always so clear cut, for frequently, as I will show, erotic desires expressed in speech can conflate, confuse, and contradict this neatness.

LANGUAGE AND DESIRE

As I noted above, 'talking about desire' in this paper refers not only to scholarly discussions of desire, but also points to the place where such an investigation might begin. One of the problems in 'talking about desire' (in a scholarly sense) is defining what 'desire' might mean; indeed there is a great difficulty in defining such an object, particularly for anthropologists, leery of psychological and individualistic explanations for human action (see Kulick, 2000, 2003). Here, however, I propose that one approach may be to simply listen to what people have to say about their desires without trying to account for them only in terms of identity categories. Indeed, my suggestion is to listen to talk-about-desire to see what that talk can tell us about identity categories. In paying attention to expressed erotic desire—whether in the intimacy of a particular encounter, reports of past experiences, or fantasies spoken out loud—the contradictions produced by categories of self-identity can become evident. By so doing, we may expose the complicated politics of the double binary (that is, homosexual/heterosexual and masculinity/femininity), enable a critical approach to the relationship between identity and desire, and a richer analysis of the binary of gender/sexuality that underpins them.[7]

In what follows I will examine: (a) the way erotic desire is expressed in speech, in this case, reports of past experiences; (b) the ways that different kinds of desires are differently adjudicated as valid or invalid; and (c) the historical and cultural conditions that allow such adjudication to take place. Paying attention to what people say about their desire—and the ways such assertions are accepted or rejected—enables us to investigate the power of identity categories to obscure

---

next paragraph Valentine points out that although transgendered people do not neatly fit the Western binary gender identity, their sexual behavior is still classified as either heterosexual or homosexual. Valentine intends to demonstrate the contrary, by showing how transgendered people talk about sexual desire he hopes to illustrate the holes in the western concepts of gender identity and sexuality.

[6] In other words, the true nature of a transgendered person's identity (their ontology) flows from their understanding of their physical appearance (both body and dress). Such people understand themselves as not normatively male or female. This contrasts with homosexual or heterosexual identity which are understood to flow from the sexual desire of one individual for another rather than their body itself.

[7] In many ways Valentine's work echoes the textual deconstruction pioneered by Bourdieu and Derrida (see essay #34, the introductory essay to the Postmodernism section, page 499, and essay 38 note 20). Deconstruction is an attempt to analyze an author's way of thinking by breaking his/ her text apart. Through this process, deconstructionists hope to reveal the unconscious assumptions and biases in the text and hence gain insight into the people who produce and read texts and the societies they represent. Here Valentine intends to deconstruct conversations to make evident the contradictions between categories of self-identity.

particular desires both in people's lives and in scholarly discussion of them. Moreover, this focus also points to a deeper epistemological issue, one which underpins both the question of language and desire but also much contemporary social theory: the relationship between gender and sexuality. In the data I present here, I want to show first that the use of particular kinds of identity categories disable certain kinds of desires from being validated. But second, I want to show that this process rests upon—and reproduces—a central analytic and political proposition in contemporary queer and feminist anthropology, as well as studies of language and sexuality: that those human experiences we call 'gender' and for [sic] 'sexuality' are distinct arenas of social practice, experience, and analysis (see Rubin, 1984). While the separation of gender and sexuality has been a theoretically productive tool, I will argue here that—ironically—this separation implicitly underpins the identity labels that feminist and queer scholars are at pains to deconstruct. Further, this theoretical framework, in which gender and sexuality are seen as separable human experiences, has implications beyond the study of gender and sexuality. My argument is that a progressive political and theoretical move to make a space for 'sexuality' as a field of investigation and activism has unwittingly produced a system whereby those who are already disenfranchised—through poverty and racism—cannot be fully accounted for in contemporary theorizations about gender and sexuality.[8]

A focus on 'desire'—in the form of its expression through speech—enables us to consider the politics of categorizing certain experiences as 'sexual' and others as 'gendered.' To do so, I focus on two aspects of talk: first, the use of identity categories themselves; but second, and equally importantly, what people say about their erotic desires in ways that cannot be accounted for by these categories. The broader question is, therefore: what does the expression—and adjudication—of desire in talk tell us about the politics of sexual and gender identity in the contemporary USA?

THE ALTERNATIVE LIFESTYLES GROUP: 'SOMEONE LIKE ME'

The data I will discuss are drawn from an 'alternative lifestyles' support group at a Lower East Side community project in New York City in the Fall of 1996. I attended this group over the course of that Fall, and on one occasion I was able to tape record the proceedings.[d] The participants were a group of friends and acquaintances who came to the group weekly to talk about their experiences. As a group, they were united primarily by the fact that they all were tenants in low-income housing, for which this organization was a resource and gathering place. However, the core group consisted of mostly young African American or Latina/o people who could be described, or would describe themselves during the meeting as gay, lesbian, bisexual, and transgender

---

[8] This is a critical paragraph. Here Valentine lays out the central elements of his argument which is to examine how:

a. different types of desire are validated or delegitimized and the conditions that allow this to happen.

b. the use of gender identity categories invalidates the expression of certain kinds of desires.

c. the separation of gender and sexuality as distinct areas of study has actually reinforced the gender identity labels that feminist and queer scholars have attempted to critique.

d. the move to make sexuality a separate field of study has further alienated those who because of poverty and racism were already ignored by contemporary gender and sexuality theory.

Valentine has already mentioned Foucault and this paragraph reflects this influence. The key issue is that of licensing certain interpretations and delicensing others. In this case the Gay, Lesbian, and Bisexual community and the academic world license certain kinds of desire and sexuality and delicense others. This marginalizes communities of individuals whose desires and sexualities are not easily subsumed by these categories and interpretations. Note also in the next paragraph Valentine talks about the adjudication of desire, again focusing on what is allowable and not allowable in terms of both discourse and feelings.

(among other categories), even though, as I will show, these identifications were far from stable for all participants. Others came in and out over the weeks I was able to attend this group, and the one I describe here also included a young African American woman whose brother had come out to her as gay (and who was struggling to understand what this meant), as well as Sylvia, a very old white woman in a wheelchair who appeared to attend every group meeting at the center, whatever its topic.

The only outsiders in this group were myself— a white, gay-identified man—and Nora. Nora is Latina, a self-identified heterosexual transsexual woman, a former drug user, and now a peer educator for several NYC social service agencies. In conversation, Nora is explicit about her transsexual history, but refuses to accept that this makes her less of a woman. She has been in recovery from drug addiction since the early 1990s, and part of that recovery and personal growth has been working for social service agencies in New York. Through this experience, Nora has developed an understanding of 'transgender' which has been shaped in contexts of political and social service advocacy since the 1990s: that of a collective category which gathers into it any kind of non-normative gender expression, and which is distinct from homosexuality. This is evident from her explanation of what 'transgender' means to one of the group members early on in the meeting. Transgender, she said, is an

> umbrella term which includes [. . .] transexuals, pre-op, post-op, uh, transvestites, drag queens, female impersonators [. . .] you know, it makes it much easier to define [. . .], a person or group or whatever.

Though Nora and the group participants shared common life experiences—of poverty, racism, drug addiction, and non-normative gender or sexual identity—the way they talked about themselves in this group was quite divergent, a difference underpinned precisely by Nora's experience in social service settings both as a client and as a

counselor where she has learnt this usage of 'transgender.' It is this difference, in particular, the escalation of Nora's attempts to get one of the group members to identify as *either* transgender *or* gay that I will focus on in the analysis below.[9]

At the beginning of this meeting, as we sat gathered around a conference table in an untidy meeting room, Nora introduced herself as follows: 'I'm Nora, I'm transsexual and I'm a woman and transsexual is my alternative lifestyle.' I introduced myself as 'a non-transgender gay man' which got a conversation going about what 'transgender' means (from which I have excerpted Nora's explanation, above). However, not everyone in the room professed such stable identities as Nora and I did. For example, when Ben, another core group member introduced himself, he said: 'I'm Ben, I'm just a male who enjoys . . . male companionship as well as female companionship.' Note that Ben did not refer to himself as 'bisexual' in this statement, though other group members did take on particular identity categories in talking about themselves.

One of them was Miss Angel. We had not been talking long when she entered the room, late as usual. Miss Angel—African American, a former drug user and sex worker—was one of the central participants in the group, the acknowledged linchpin of the core group of friends, who also worked as a chef at the community center. Upon her arrival, everything stopped and we waited as she took her place, made her observations, and came to rest. As she came in, so too did another participant, a woman I had not met before. As such, I introduced myself and explained my presence (and my tape recorder). Ben took this as a sign that I hadn't met Angel before, and he told her to introduce herself to me.

Excerpt A

1. Angel: Introduce ourselves? To whom?
2. Ben: Do you all know each other? [i.e. do Angel and I know each other]

---

[9] Thus, Valentine understands the interactions he observes as a struggle for control of discourse. Nora has learned a social services discourse and seeks to impose this on others in the group. These others have their own meanings and resist this imposition.

3. A: Yes! These homosexuals know each other up in here! They better!

This brief excerpt is significant, particularly for what follows. In noting that we have met before, Angel grouped herself and me (identified to the group in this and earlier meetings as a gay man), as 'homosexuals.' While Ben's earlier cited statement to the group is interesting because he avoided identity categories in talking about himself, Angel's talk is notable because she did not: indeed during the rest of the meeting, she used a plethora of identity categories about herself, 'homosexual' being only the first. When Angel finally sat down and took command of the meeting (as she was wont to do), the following exchange took place:

Excerpt B

1. Angel: My name is Angel, I'm a pre-op transsexual. I dunno what I am, I'm a woman, simply . . . , OK? I'm HIV positive.
2. Nora: A genetic woman?
3. A: I'm a drug addict woman.
4. Interjection: Was!
5. Nora: Was or still are
6. Int: I hope!
7. A: No I was but I'm still, you know, they say you still supposed to say you're a drug addict.
8. Int: Well.
9. A: OK, still a drug addict.
10. N: It's up to you if you want to say that, you know, if you don't want to I mean [you don't have to].
11. A: Well whatever, look I'm telling the story right? Thank you. And I'm 31 years old and I'm a woman.[10]

In this exchange, Angel makes several claims about herself—that she is a pre-operative trans-sexual, a woman, a (former) drug addict, HIV positive and, moreover, that 'I dunno what I am.' In this support group, as indeed in many of this kind, the divulging of personal information such as HIV status or substance abuse history is not uncommon. Nora's question (Excerpt B, line 2), which is meant as a joke, leads Angel to provide another qualifier for 'woman': 'drug addict' (Excerpt B, line 3). This results in a discussion of Angel's history of drug addiction, and a discussion of what you are 'supposed' or 'don't have to' divulge about such details. In the end, Angel asserts her right to say who she is, and says simply: 'I'm 31 years old and I'm a woman.'

Given the distinction made in most contemporary theory and activism between homosexual and transgender/transsexual identity, Angel's claims to be (implicitly) homosexual (Excerpt A, line 3) and a transsexual woman (Excerpt B, line 1) are somewhat confusing; certainly they were confusing to Nora (and to myself), as is evident from an exchange that happened a few minutes later:

Excerpt C

1. Angel: I had to get to know new friends when I turned gay and it's not easy being gay.
2. Nora: How was your experience when you became a woman, a transsexual woman?
3. A: I was 13 years old when I did everything.
4. N: Was it even harder?
5. A: Was it harder? No.
6. N: Did it go from bad to worse?
7. A: No [. . .] Urn, when I was 13. It was hard, I went to school-
8. Ben: With breasts.
9. A: The breasts.

---

[10] Angel is an example of an individual who challenges the boundaries of accepted gender identities. "She" is a "homosexual," a pre-operation transsexual, and a 31-year-old woman. If a person is a biological male, homosexual, a pre-operation transsexual, and a woman all at the same time what does that say about conventional western gender categories? Angel also illustrates Valentine's contention that labeling gender categories with particular sexual desires is problematic. If one is a pre-op transsexual who is sexually attracted to men, is it valid to talk in terms of homo and hetero-sexuality?

This excerpt marks the first point in the conversation in which Nora attempts to disaggregate Angel's different self-identifications: as homosexual and as transgender/transexual. Nora's questions to Angel above (Excerpt C, lines 2, 4, 6) are significant because Nora is implicitly proposing to Angel two different states of coming out: as 'gay' when she was 13, and as a 'transexual woman' at a later date. Angel, however, does not make this distinction: she was 13 when she did 'everything.'

To return to the conceptualization of desire and identity in the contemporary USA, the reason for this misunderstanding is, I would argue, based on different conceptual notions of personhood and identity: Nora, schooled in the language of 'transgender' through her work in social service agencies, sees a necessary division between experiences of being gay (the realm of 'sexuality') and experiences of being transgender (the realm of 'gender': 'how was your experience when you became a woman, a transexual woman?'). Angel does not ('I was 13 years old when I did everything.')[11]

This divergence in understandings became clearer still in a later exchange between them, as they discussed Angel's sexual history. Angel had informed us that she had had sex with straight and gay men, and with women (with one of whom she had had a child). However, all of Nora's questions—her implicit attempts, as in Excerpt C above, to elicit a stable identity from Angel—failed. A crucial point in the conversation occurred when Nora tried to pin Angel down on precisely how she labels herself after Angel made a seemingly oblique statement:

Excerpt D

1. Angel: I went to bed with my own kind. I tried it once.
2. Ben: How was it?

3. A: How was it?
4. B: Uh huh.
5. Nora: Now what is your own kind mean by definition, because you're always telling us
6. A: I'm a woman, well you know.
7. N: You 're a woman, transexual, you're gay, you're homosexual.
8. B: A man.
9. A: Look, me, like me, someone like me. Someone like me. . . .
   Someone like me.
10. N: [who] changes sexuality(e), uh huh
11. B: With breasts.
12. A: With breasts.
13. N: OK.
14. A: I went out with someone like me. Her name was Billie Jean, she lives in Coney Island.

Here Nora finally tried to get Angel to define what her 'own kind' is. She listed the identity categories that Angel had used about herself in this meeting (woman, gay, homosexual, transexual) implying that she cannot be all of these things. To this, Angel insisted: 'look, me, like me, someone like me. Someone like me. . . . Someone like me.' In the end Ben offered: 'with breasts' to which Angel affirmed 'with breasts,' and Nora left it there: 'OK.' However, while Nora's 'OK' indicates she was not willing to draw Angel any further on the topic, the import of her questions in excerpts C and D is that she was attempting to get Angel to channel her expressions (and experiences) of erotic desire—be it her desire for a woman, a man, or for 'someone like her'—through identity categories that cannot, in the end, account for them.[12]

---

[11] Here and below, Valentine examines Nora and Angel's struggle for control of discourse. Nora wishes to use the categories of language as she understands them, to define Angel's identity. Angel constantly redefines and escapes Nora's classification system.

[12] This is the heart of the first part of Valentine's argument. Angel is a male homosexual, a pre-op transsexual, and a woman who has fathered a child and had sex with homosexual and heterosexual men, women, and "someone like me." Typical western categories of gender and sexuality cannot account for a person like Angel. The fluidity of Angel's sexual identity makes it impossible to neatly label her sexuality. However, as Nora tries to force Angel to self-identify into categories that Nora understands, one can

Both in excerpts C and D, Ben offers 'with breasts' by way of explanation of Angel's being, which Angel affirms (in Excerpt D, line 12). This reference to Angel's breasts—the result of hormone therapy—is the final word in both cases. The reference to her body is particularly instructive, for Angel's changing body shifts her—in contemporary progressive understandings—into the category of 'transgender' or more specifically, 'transexual,' a category she indeed uses to describe herself. Yet, as is clear from the preceding conversation, Angel does not always stick to this definition of self. Indeed, Nora's attempts to pin her down on this point relates directly to the double binary I invoked earlier—Angel is conflating gendered and sexual identities, recounting desires which cannot be accounted for in a system which sees gender and sexuality as distinct.

Perhaps in response to this questioning, Angel tried to summarize her theory of sexuality and desire shortly after this exchange. She said:

'When it comes down to sex, I don't think . . . it's two men going to bed with each other, a man and a woman going to bed with it or pre-op or nothing like that. I just think it's just two people having sex, making love to each other, enjoying each other's company, enjoying each other's time, when we're together.

Here Angel is proposing a fluidity to sexual identity that neatly encapsulates a non-identitarian politics of sexual desire. A short while later, Nora made the following comment, which seems to support Angel's theory of desire:

You label yourself what you want to label yourself. Other people don't label you, I mean unless you want to be labeled yourself, you know.

Yet Nora's questioning throughout this meeting points to the ways that such desires and passions are subject, always, to a rigorous system of labeling, whether or not someone wants to be labeled. Those desires that cannot be labeled—or which require different kinds of labels at different times—are produced as incoherent, or, at the very least, the product of confusion.[13]

Later in the group, Nora tells of her days of sex work when non-transgender men who were her clients would ask her what their desire for her meant for their own sexual identity:

Excerpt E

1. Nora: And they're attracted to that [a feminine person with a penis] So they would tell me, 'well what am I?' I said 'well I can't tell you what you are unless you know and I can't not tell you this is what you are and this is what you're gonna be, you know, because it's not my life.' My life, I know what I am.
2. Angel: I'm a woman with a large clit.
3. N: I know what I am.

---

start to see why Valentine (following Foucault) argues that gender identities also reinforce certain avenues of social and political power. Nora and Angel struggle for control of the discourse. However, they are not equals. Nora has the weight of social service and academic establishment on her side. Angel has no such power. The result is that Angel, and those like her, are marginalized because they do not conform to the boundaries of gender and sexuality as these are understood in government, the academy, and broader society.

This passage contains Valentine's opening quote: "I went to bed with my own kind." So, what was Angel's own kind? Was she born with a penis or not? There is no way to find the answer from the information given. There is only interpretation: a deeply postmodern point.

[13] An underlying argument in this essay is that if something can't be classified it will probably be perceived as either incoherent or producing confusion. This is a point of view that has deep resonances in both American anthropology (for example, the work of Sapir and Whorf as well as ethnoscience) as well as much of French postmodern thought. Valentine presents this as a truth but as a philosophical proposition it raises enormous problems. For example, most readers are probably not particularly confused by Angel. We simply accept that, as with many of our experiences, she's not easily classified. Of course, the problem is that, if you get deep enough into the issue of classification, or variation in the way that people classify, there may be nothing but confusion. This is one of the most unmanageable dilemmas of the postmodern thought.

In this excerpt, Nora states 'I know what I am' and her statements of self never vary: she is a heterosexual transexual woman. Nora's claim overlaps yet another assertion by Miss Angel—this time that she is 'a woman with a large clit'—which joins the other categories she has taken on during the meeting: gay, homosexual, and transexual. In contrast to Nora's clear sense of knowing 'what I am' above, Angel claims 'I dunno what I am' (Excerpt B, line 1), an observation that Nora implicitly draws on in asking Angel to adhere to one of them.

I would argue that Nora's attempts to get Angel to pick just one of the definitions of self that she has used during the meeting fail not because Angel cannot account for 'what she is,' but rather because she can account for herself in many different ways. Nora, as I have noted, shares much of Angel's history and experience as a former drug user, sex worker, and person of color. However, Nora differs from Angel in that she has an understanding of gender and sexual identity gained through her contact with the social service agencies she works for, and defined by a distinct split between gay identities on the one hand and transgender identities on the other. Angel has no such model of personhood, and these distinctions do not seem to signify much to her. All she can say when Nora requests a definition of what 'my own kind' might mean is: 'someone like me.'

At the end of the group, Nora said: 'In the long run, as long as you know the truth that's really all that matters.' But what is the truth? And what operations of power—and requirements for asserting identity to make sense of one's desire—make some kinds of desires more true—and more coherent—than others? The ways these different kinds of knowledge are assessed, within this

group and within a broader system of identity, complicates how such assertions of self and expressions of desire—which are expected to be congruent with such identities—are seen as being 'truthful.' Nora's inability to tell her former clients—or to ascertain about Angel—'what' they are points to the place where desires escape identity and become unnameable and, consequently, unrepresentable.[14]

GENDER, SEXUALITY, AND THE NAMING OF DESIRE

The interactions that occurred at the Alternative Lifestyles group and the conceptual mismatches they illustrate only make sense if one considers the history of the last quarter of the twentieth century, in which gay and lesbian (and later, bisexual and transgender) people made their mark in American society. By the end of the 1960s, when the now almost-mythical Stonewall rebellion was about to take place, homosexuality had long been pathologized. But it was also differently conceptualized than it was in the late 1990s when this group meeting took place. Homosexuality was seen in medical and popular understandings as a failure of gendered identity and desire, a phenomenon which produced homosexual men as feminine and homosexual women as masculine. That is, in the pre-Stonewall era, the dominant understanding of homosexuality was that it was caused by—and was manifested in—gender variance. In 1972, Esther Newton, could write that '[d]rag and camp are the most representative and widely used symbols of homosexuality in the English speaking world.' (Newton, 1979[1972], p. 100).[15]

---

[14] It is interesting that Nora pressures Angel to adopt a conventional gender identity because Nora's experience as a sex worker highlights the confusion her transgender status created in her own clients. In this passage, Valentine centers in on one of his key concerns: the relationship between truth and power. This is also a central concern of Postmodernism in general and Michel Foucault in particular. Valentine deconstructs Nora's statement by casting doubt on the idea that the truth is knowable, by associat-

ing the ability to assert truth with the ability to wield power, and by asking what different regimes of power lie behind different assertions of truth.

[15] Valentine refers to the Stonewall rebellion. The Stonewall riots took place in June 1969 when police raided the Stonewall Inn, a well-known gay bar in the Greenwich Village section of New York City. In the 1960s, New York attempted to shut gay bars by revoking liquor licenses and

Thirty years later, it would be harder to make such an argument. It is interesting to note that Nora, in her description of 'transgender' on page 128, includes drag queens in her list of identities that are captured by 'transgender' (as do I in my own list on p. 125; see note 2). While images of drag still figure large in media representations of male homosexuality, nowadays it is far more likely to see both gay men and lesbians in both news and entertainment media as gender normative professionals and citizens: lawyers, teachers, and even parents. These images are the result of decades of gay and lesbian activism in which the link between homosexuality and gender variance have been at least partly replaced by the image of gay men and lesbians who adhere to time-honored white, middle-class American values. This activism has gone hand-in-glove with a call for gay and lesbian civil rights, based on the claim that gay and lesbian Americans are responsible citizens whose sexuality—coded as private in American culture—should not be the purview of public scrutiny or regulation. This schema opposes a still-powerful US American folk model of homosexuality which sees it as a gendered inversion, and, in Urvashi Vaid's words, works to make a claim that 'homosexual sexuality is merely the queer version of heterosexuality' (Vaid, 1995, p. 44). In particular, accommodationist gay and lesbian politics has increasingly worked with a model of 'gay' which implicitly foregrounds the *similarity* of gay and lesbian people to heterosexual people (and, implicitly, an adherence to white middle class American-ness) while, at the same time, highlighting its *difference* from gender variance. This accommodationist

politics took the forefront in many public campaigns for civil rights in the late 1980s and 1990s, and was articulated in high profile debates about homosexuals in the military, adoption, and marriage rights (for the purest examples of this kind of accommodationist politics, see the work of neo-conservative gay scholars and writers such as Andrew Sullivan, 1995, and Bruce Bawer, 1993).[16]

During the same period, from the early 1990s, 'transgender' emerged in contexts of activism and social service provision as a collective category to provide a voice for those who were no longer capable of being accounted for in terms of 'homosexuality.' To be sure, the differences between gender-normative gay men and lesbians and those with variant expressions of gender are not new and the connection between gender variance and homosexual desire has been contested for almost as long as homosexuality has existed as a category (see Chauncey, 1994; Meyerowitz, 2002). However, the advent of gay and lesbian activism in the 1970s resulted in a radical shift in medical and popular understandings of homosexuality, bringing the gender-normative model of homosexuality to the fore. These understandings rest, implicitly, on a theory of gender and sexuality that sees these two experiences as distinct in the sense that one does not have to be—indeed, in the language of much post-Stonewall gay activism, is not—gender variant just because one diverges from the heterosexual norm. This insistence on distinguishing between gender and sexuality allowed for the emergence of a new category, 'transgender', in the 1990s which rests precisely on this assumed distinction.[e17]

---

entrapping clients in solicitation stings. Raids of gay bars were frequent. However, when police raided The Stonewall, the patrons rioted. They were joined by others and the rioting continued the next night as well. The Stonewall Riots are considered the founding event of the Gay Liberation movement.

[16] Urvashi Vaid (1958-) is a prominent Gay, Lesbian, and Transexual Rights activist. A former executive at The National Gay and Lesbian Taskforce, Vaid positions Gay and Lesbian liberation as representing mainstream American values of democracy, pluralism, and freedom (see http://gos.sbc.edu/w/vaid.html).

[17] Note the ways in which Valentine locates systems of classification with respect to history and politics. He argues that for the classification 'transgender' to emerge, homosexuality had first to be differentiated from gender. Thus, it was necessary for homosexual men and lesbian women to be seen as normal males and females with minority sexual preferences rather than as pathological individuals. The normalizing of homosexuals and lesbians was a political process happening largely in the 1970s and 1980s.

So, in the past 30 years in the USA a newly emerging model of gender and sexuality as distinct arenas of social experience and analysis has resulted in the inability of Nora (representative here of larger institutional discourses and practices) to make sense of Miss Angel's expressed desires, because of the requirement that erotic desire be made sense of through sexual identity categories that are distinct from gendered identity categories.

This is not to say that this system is absolute. For one, the folk model of gender and sexuality which see gender and sexuality as intrinsically linked is far from dead. Moreover, activists and scholars have challenged the politics of neo-conservative writers and groups (e.g. Vaid, 1995; Warner, 1999); and feminist and queer scholars continue to query the relationships between 'gender' and 'sexuality' (e.g. Wieringa and Blackwood, 1999; Jolly and Manderson, 1997). Yet at the same time, the explanatory force of this heuristic separation has gained institutional force in the very use of identity category labels—underpinned by that separation—to talk about sexual desire. That is, as 'transgender' becomes a category of personhood but also of activism, politics, and in academic debates, the theoretical distinction between gender and sexuality becomes solidified as fact in every iteration of that category (and the category to which it is opposed: homosexuality). And as such, Miss Angel's voice and her desires are rendered as nonsensical.[18]

Miss Angel's claim to be 'gay,' 'transexual' and 'transvestite' may be seen, by people like Nora and others (e.g. see Plummer, 1992) to hark back to an earlier (and implicitly, outmoded and false) model of homosexuality which conflated sexuality and gender. Yet, Angel's professions of identity and desire are not unique. Among many African American and Latino communities in NYC, such claims are frequently made. In the communities in which I did fieldwork where primarily young, poor, people of color predominated—drag balls, bars, sex work strolls—the category of 'transgender' is rarely used. Rather, categories such as 'fem queen' (another category Angel sometimes used about herself), 'butch queen' (a category that I—as a non-transgender identified gay man—was frequently classed under), and 'butches' (masculine female-bodied people), as well as a range of others, were all seen as united by the overarching category of 'gay.' While the borders between these identity categories were strictly monitored in these communities, as categories generally are, the source of their commonality was never denied, and was seen to flow from a complex nexus between those experiences which, in contemporary social theory, we call 'gender and sexuality.'

In other words, to be 'gay' in these contexts is not necessarily marked by gender normativity. Rather, in those communities, it is the difference *from* hetero-normativity—rather than the difference *between* 'gay' and 'transgender'—which underpins the organization of gender and sexuality. Yet, their unity as 'gay' people, defined by another set of characteristics—the conjunction of their disenfranchisement in terms of both class and racial memberships and their non-normative genders/sexualities—precludes them from membership in the contemporary mainstream understanding of 'gay.'[19]

As such, these desires and senses of self which cannot be made to fit into certain identity

---

[18] Valentine here argues that understanding gender and sexuality as separate phenomena allowed gay men and lesbian women to present themselves as gender normative (despite their choice of sexual partners), and thus more socially acceptable. The problem as Valentine sees it, is that because the theoretical distinction between gender and sexuality has gained institutional force and is widely accepted as fact, people like Miss Angel who do not fit the accepted gender model are marginalized.

[19] The people Valentine has been describing consider themselves gay but commonly used the categories of

"fem queens," "butch queen," "butches," categories of non-normative gender, to talk about themselves. The homosexual and lesbian community has tried to create a definition of gays and lesbians as gender normative but with various sexual desires. However, the community that Valentine describes consists of people who identify themselves as 'gay' but whose gender is very specifically non-normative. Because of race, class, and non-normative gender, although they define themselves as 'gay,' they are excluded from the mainstream understanding of gay.

categories are confusing. Early on in the meeting, Angel had demanded her right to tell her own story ('look I'm telling the story right?' Excerpt A, line 11), but she also recognized the power of institutions to form what one should say about oneself ('they say you still supposed to say you're a drug addict.' Excerpt A, line 7). In the end, Nora cannot push Angel to use a unitary category that makes sense in Nora's conceptualization of gendered and sexual identity, so Angel does get to tell her own story in her own words. But Angel's words, like many of her peers', are also subject to discourses and practices which produce those stories as incoherent. In a conversation with one social worker to whom I related the conversation I discuss here, she argued that Angel was a victim of 'false consciousness' and that she should be educated into a more enlightened understanding of identity. In other words, to paraphrase Miss Angel, 'they say you supposed to say you're transgender.'[20]

For this social worker, and for many other social service providers, activists, and scholars, a model of gender and sexuality as separate experiences underpinning discrete identities is implicitly a truth, and no longer simply an analytic or an activist move. Yet ironically, as I have tried to show here, the practices and politics that have resulted from this shift have, in part, reproduced a set of social relationships whereby those who arguably have the most need for a progressive politics of sexuality and gender are excluded from its explanatory purview by being made to seem confusing and confused.[21]

There are two related theoretical points which can be drawn from this analysis, which map onto the questions I asked at the outset: what does it mean to talk about desire, both in scholarly contexts and in talking about one's own desire? First, I have suggested that the use of identity labels, conceptualized through a binary understanding of 'sexuality' and 'gender,' reproduce a system where desires that span these experiences—and are narrated as such—are difficult to make sense of, or can be dismissed as a kind of 'false consciousness.' Secondly, though, paying attention to such desires, rather than dismissing them, gives us a way of focusing on the practices and desires which underpin the complex lives of human beings, unrestrained as they are experientially by how such desires come to be accounted for. As such, a focus on desire expressed in talk enables a complication of the categories that have gained such force and power in academic, activist, and increasingly, popular understandings of what counts as 'sexuality.'

Looking at what people say about what they desire, who they desire, and how they act upon those desires can highlight for us the political nature of desire and the ways such yearnings are shaped by the identity categories through which they are forced to speak if they wish to get a hearing. Such a focus can enable us to look more closely at the seemingly neutral categories of 'gender' and 'sexuality,' and complicate the relationship between them. And, most usefully, it requires us to not simply assume that desire is self evidently explained by the categories 'gender' and 'sexuality' in using them to talk about the complexity of erotic lives.[22]

---

[20] Note the social worker's use of 'false consciousness,' a term usually associated with Marxist analysis. For Marxists, people have false consciousness when they believe the representations of the dominant classes that serve to obscure the realities of their domination and exploitation. In this case, the social worker, a representative of the middle class, is saying that Angel doesn't understand her own oppression. Valentine's point, of course, is that it is the social worker who doesn't understand.

[21] Valentine says that the system of classification used by the social services makes people like Miss Angel seem confusing and confused. However, it is the social service providers who are confused. Their model of sex and gen-

der does not allow them to comprehend Miss Angel's reality. Valentine's essay is a forceful testament to the power of anthropology to shed light on the human condition in ways that other social sciences cannot.

[22] Valentine concludes that looking at what people say about desire can provide insight into its political nature. His point can be pushed to a much larger scale. Models of gender and sexuality are part of the contemporary political battleground in the United States. To contend that these issues do not carry immense political and social significance is naive. Who hasn't heard of political fights over same-sex marriage, adoption by gay couples, sex education curriculums, and assaults on people thought to

ACKNOWLEDGEMENTS

My thanks to Nora, Miss Angel, Ben, and the other members of the Alternative Lifestyles group for allowing me to tape record and make use of their words in this paper. Thanks also to Don Kulick for his comments and suggestions on this paper. Finally, thanks are due to a core group of readers—Bambi Schieffelin, Henry Gold-schmidt, and Ben Chesluk—whose comments are always supremely helpful. I am also indebted to Dr. Barbara Warren and Rosalyne Blumenstein for facilitating my research. The research upon which this paper is based was assisted by a fellowship from the Sexuality Research Fellowship Program from the Social Science Research Council with funds provided by the Ford Foundation.

NOTES

[a] The inclusion of 'drag queen' in this list is a particular choice on my part, and not one that all transgender-identified people—or drag queens—might agree with. Indeed, I include it here, somewhat reluctantly, only because many of my informants do so in their explanations of what 'transgender' encompasses. As will become apparent later in this paper, 'drag queen' is a central category in thinking about the relationship between identity and desire.

[b] I use the construction 'transgender-identified' to mark the ways in which people both take on the category transgender as something meaningful about themselves; as well as the sense of being identified by others to fall into a category. This is a useful way of dealing with the conceptual mismatches I will be talking about in this paper, but it also speaks to the ways that self identity and identification by others of the self are not separate but complexly related phenomena.

[c] I had, initially, intended my fieldwork to revolve around a linguistic anthropological methodology, and intended to record extensive periods of conversation and talk in a variety of settings to aid my analyses. However, it became clear to me from early in my project that the politics of taping among the people with whom I conducted fieldwork was fraught. Given the nature of social scientific involvements with transgender-identified people's lives (see Valentine, 2003), many people were deeply suspicious of my research goals, and refused to be taped, even when I had gained their trust. Group settings, such as the one I describe here, were particularly difficult because of the number of people present and the fluidity of the group over time. As such, the transcripts from the group meeting I have included here represent virtually the only taped conversation I was able to record in my 18 months of fieldwork; even during this meeting, I had to turn the recorder off and on to accommodate the wishes of one participant. However, the conclusions I draw from this material were confirmed frequently through my ethnographic research, as I discuss elsewhere (Valentine, 2000).

[d] Given my argument, one might imagine that Nora would have said 'gender' rather than 'sexuality' here. At the same time, however, her use of 'sexuality' indicates the slippage between these categories in talk and practice, and points to the gaps produced by needing to talk about desire in discrete categories.

[e] This argument does not intend to draw away from the organizing and advocacy engaged in by transgender-identified people in claiming this category; nor is it intended to contest the political gains achieved under this category. My goal here is to point to a particular cultural logic that underpins contemporary understandings of both gender variance and homosexuality in order to consider the deeper implications of these politics.

REFERENCES

Bawer, B., 1993. A Place at the Table: The Gay Individual in American Society. Poseidon Press, New York.

Blackwood, E., 1995. Falling in love with an-Other lesbian: reflections on identity in fieldwork. In: Kulick, D., Willson, M. (Eds.), Taboo: Sex, Identity, and Erotic Subjectivity in Anthropological Fieldwork. Routledge, New York, pp. 51–75.

Chauncey, G., 1994. Gay New York: Gender, Urban Culture, and the Makings of the Gay Male World. Basic Books, New York.

Donham, Donald L., 1998. Freeing South African: the 'modernization' of male-male sexuality in Soweto. Cultural Anthropology 13 (1), 3–21.

Foucault, M., 1990 [1980]. The History of Sexuality. Volume 1: an Introduction [trans, by Robert Hurley]. Vintage, New York.

be homosexual? We engage in these political fights with a gender identity system that only allows for male/female and heterosexual/homosexual. Valentine's essay gives us a glimpse of the real, lived, variety of human gender and sexual experience.

Johnson, M., 1997. Beauty and Power: Transgendering and Cultural Transformation in the Southern Philippines. Berg, New York.

Jolly, M., Manderson, L., 1997. Introduction: sites of desire/economies of pleasure in Asia and the Pacific. In: Manderson, L., Jolly, M. (Eds.), Sites of Desire, Economies of Pleasure: Sexualities in Asia and the Pacific. University of Chicago Press, Chicago, pp. 1–26.

Katz, J.N., 1995. The Invention of Heterosexuality. Dutton, New York.

Kulick, D., 1998. Travesti: Sex, Gender, and Culture among Brazilian Transgendered Prostitutes. University of Chicago Press, Chicago.

Kulick, D., 2000. Gay and lesbian language. Annual Review of Anthropology 29, 243–285.

Kulick, D., 2003. Language and desire. In: Holmes, J., Meyerhoff, M. (Eds.), The Handbook of Language and Gender. Blackwell, Oxford.

Lewin, E., 1993. Lesbian Mothers: Accounts of Gender in American Culture. Cornell University Press, Ithaca, NY.

Manalansan, M.F., 1997. In the shadows of Stonewall: examining gay transnational politics and the diasporic dilemma. In: Lowe, L., Lloyd, D. (Eds.), The Politics of Culture in the Shadow of Capital. Duke University Press, Durham, pp. 485–505.

Meyerowitz, J., 2002. How Sex Changed: A History of Transsexuality in the United States. Harvard University Press, Cambridge.

Newton, E., 1979 [1972]. Mother Camp: Female Impersonators in America. University of Chicago Press, Chicago.

Plummer, K., 1992. Speaking its name: inventing a lesbian and gay studies. In: Plummer, K. (Ed.), Modern Homosexualities: Fragments of Gay and Lesbian Experiences. Routledge, New York, pp. 3–25.

Rubin, G., 1984. Thinking sex: notes for a radical theory of the politics of sexuality. In: Vance, C. (Ed.), Pleasure and Danger: Exploring Female Sexuality. Harper Collins, New York, pp. 267–319.

Shokeid, M., 1995. A Gay Synagogue in New York. Columbia University Press, New York.

Sullivan, A., 1995. Virtually Normal: an Argument About Homosexuality. Alfred A. Knopf, New York.

Vaid, U., 1995. Virtual Equality: the Mainstreaming of Gay and Lesbian Liberation. Doubleday, New York.

Valentine, D. 'The calculus of pain': violence, anthropological ethics, and the category transgender. Ethnos 66(2) (in press).

Valentine, D., 2000. 'I Know What I Am': the Category 'Transgender' in the Construction of Contemporary US American Conceptions of Gender and Sexuality. PhD dissertation, Department of Anthropology, New York University.

Warner, M., 1999. The Trouble with Normal: Sex, Politics, and the Ethics of Queer Life. The Free Press, New York.

Weeks, J., 1981. Sex, Politics, and Society: the Regulation of Sexuality since 1800. Longman, London.

Weston, K., 1991. Families We Choose: Lesbians, Gays, Kinship. Columbia University Press, New York.

Wieringa, S., Blackwood, E., 1999. Introduction. In: Blackwood, E., Wieringa, S. (Eds.), Female Desires: Same-sex Relations and Transgender Practices Across Cultures. Columbia University Press, New York, pp. 1–38.

Symbolic and Interpretive Anthropology

Beginning in the 1960s and reaching its fullest expression in the 1970s, symbolic or interpretive anthropology was part of a general reevaluation of cultural anthropology as a scientific enterprise. Materialists insisted that the analysis of culture focus on empirical material phenomena. Ethnoscientists and cognitive anthropologists argued that culture was a mental phenomenon that could be modeled following principles similar to mathematics or formal logic. Symbolic anthropologists agreed with the ethnoscientists and cognitive anthropologists that culture was a mental phenomenon but rejected the notion that culture could be modeled like mathematics or logic. Instead they used a variety of analytical tools drawn from psychology, history, and literature to study symbolic action within culture. Their fundamental interest was in examining how people formulated their reality. Dolgin, Kemnitzer, and Schneider (1977), for example, wrote: "Our concern is not with whether or not the views a people hold are accurate in any 'scientific' sense of the term. . . . In social action, that which is thought to be real is treated as real" (quoted in Lett 1987:111).

The development of symbolic analysis was influenced by the work of Benjamin L. Whorf and Edward Sapir in linguistics and ethnoscientific studies, which gained popularity in the 1950s. Symbolic anthropologists argue that, like language, symbols are a shared system of meaning that can only be understood within a particular historical and social context. Culture, they believe, is embedded in people's interpretations of

the events and the things around them. In other words, symbolic anthropologists believe we construct our cultural reality. Consequently, they take a semiotic approach focusing on the analysis of meaning. As Geertz writes:

> Believing, with Max Weber, that man is an animal suspended in webs of significance he himself has spun, I take cultures to be those webs, and the analysis of it to be therefore not an experimental science in search of law but an interpretive one in search of meaning. (1973:5)

The term *symbolic anthropology* covers a variety of forms of analysis, but two dominant trends in the field are represented by the work of Clifford Geertz (1926–2006) and Victor Turner (1920–1983). Although both are concerned with the interpretation of symbolic action, their approaches are very different. Geertz's emphasis on culture as an organized collection of symbolic systems is typically American in flavor. Turner's work, on the other hand, is in the British structural-functionalist style and is concerned with the operation of symbols in the maintenance of society.

To Geertz, symbols were means of transmitting meaning. His focus was on how symbols affected the way people think about their world, how "symbols operate as vehicles of culture" (Ortner 1984:129). For example, in "Deep Play: Notes on the Balinese Cockfight" (see essay 33), Geertz described and analyzed the various symbolic meanings of the cockfight for the Balinese who engaged in the sport and discussed how these various levels of meaning influenced their lives. Ultimately, he argued that the cockfight does not have any function in the sense of maintaining social solidarity, reinforcing societal norms or filling Malinowskian biopsychological needs. Instead, the cockfight enables the Balinese to share experiences and create meaning from their lives, much in the same way that sports or religious rituals may be organizing experiences for those in the West.

Geertz's type of analysis was focused at the level of the individual participant in society. Although he acknowledged that it was impossible to get inside the head of native informants, he wanted to provide his readers with a sense of what it might feel like to be a member of the culture he was describing. He did this using a technique he called "thick description." Geertz assumed that important symbols and actions had many layers of meaning and that their power derived from this fact. In thick description, the anthropologist attempts to analyze each layer of meaning. Geertz compared doing thick description to peeling an onion. There is layer after layer after layer, but no reward at the center. The onion is its layers; similarly, culture is its meanings (see Geertz 1973:6–10). As the article reprinted here shows, this actor-centered perspective was fundamental to Geertz's form of analysis.

Victor Turner approached symbolic analysis from a different angle. Trained in British structural functionalism, he examined symbols as mechanisms for the maintenance of society. Turner viewed symbols as "operators in the social process, things that, when put together in certain arrangements in certain contexts (especially rituals), produce essentially social transformations" (Ortner 1984:131). Turner argued that social solidarity had to be continually maintained. Ritual symbols, in his view, were the primary tools through which social order was renewed. Turner also made a major contribution to the conceptual vocabulary of symbolic analysis by outlining various properties of symbols such as multivocality, condensation, the unification of disparate significata, and polarization of meaning (Turner 1967b:28). These terms are discussed in essay 32.

Unlike Geertz's "thick description," Turner followed a more formal program of symbolic analysis. He believed that the interpretation of ritual symbols could be derived from three classes of data: (1) external form and observable characteristics, (2) the interpretations of specialists and laypeople within the society, and (3) deduction from specific contexts by the anthropologist.

Turner viewed his work as a contrast to Levi-Strauss' structuralism and to the psychoanalytic analysis of cultural symbols and rituals. In particular, he emphasized study of the social context in which rituals occurred. He understood ritual as part of an ongoing social drama through which underlying social conflicts are worked out. In this, his approach was similar to that of his mentor, Max Gluckman (see essay 13). Through rituals and symbols people evoked, channeled, and domesticated powerful emotions (Turner 1969: 42–43; Deflem 1991). Understanding symbols was critical because they were the smallest analytic unit of ritual. However, it is important to note that for Turner, studying context meant understanding the social-structural positions (and to some extent the personalities) of the individuals and groups involved in ritual. Turner makes almost no mention of the broader contexts of history and colonialism in which those he studied were enmeshed (Kwenda 1993).

One of the great shortcomings of symbolic analysis is that it is primarily descriptive and does not lend itself to general theoretical or methodological formulations. Symbolic anthropologists claim to search for universals of human understanding through the collection of locally particular data. However, much of what symbolic anthropologists know is derived through imaginative insight into particular cultures or events within those cultures. As a result, their knowledge does not provide a theoretical basis for understanding culture as a universal phenomenon.

Mary Douglas (1921–2007) was one symbolic anthropologist whose work defied this generalization. She attempted to analyze universal patterns of symbolism, focusing on beliefs about pollution and hygiene as they were expressed in religions. In her two most famous works—*Purity and Danger* (1966) and *Natural*

Symbols (1970)—Douglas contended that universal patterns of purity-pollution symbolism existed and were based on reference to the human body. She argued her case from a Durkheimian perspective, suggesting that shared symbols "create a unity in experience" (1966:2) and that religious ideas about purity and pollution symbolized beliefs about social order. In the introduction to *Purity and Danger* she wrote:

> I believe that some pollutions are used as analogies for expressing a general view of the social order. For example, there are beliefs that each sex is a danger to the other through contact with sexual fluids. . . . Such patterns of sexual danger can be seen to express symmetry or hierarchy. It is implausible to interpret them as suggesting something about the actual relation of the sexes. I suggest that many ideas about sexual dangers are better interpreted as symbols of the relation between parts of society, as mirroring designs of hierarchy or symmetry which apply in the larger social system. . . . Sometimes bodily orifices seem to represent points of entry or exit to social units, or bodily perfection can symbolise an ideal theocracy. (1966:3–4)

Symbolic anthropology is concerned with studying the process by which people give meaning to their world and how this world is expressed in cultural symbols. Geertz wrote that "Cultural analysis is (or should be) guessing at meanings, assessing the guesses, and drawing explanatory conclusions from the better guesses" (1973:20). However, symbolic anthropologists have never specifically explained a methodology for "guessing at meaning." Anthropologists who do not share Geertz's views often believe that this is a fundamental flaw. Critics claim that the credibility of symbolic interpretation is based on the explanatory skills of the anthropologist and argue that such anthropology often seems closer to literary criticism than social science. In fact, much of the work that characterized the symbolic analyses of the 1970s and 1980s was incorporated into the postmodern movement of the 1990s. Today it is rare to see analytical work such as that conducted by Turner and Geertz. Rather than being concerned with what a symbol "means," contemporary symbolic analyses are much more likely to be concerned with the postmodern issues of agency, power, and positioning.

31. *External Boundaries*

Mary Douglas (1921–2007)

The idea of society is a powerful image. It is potent in its own right to control or to stir men to action. This image has form; it has external boundaries, margins, internal structure. Its outlines contain power to reward conformity and repulse attack. There is energy in its margins and unstructured areas. For symbols of society any human experience of structures, margins or boundaries is ready to hand.[1]

Van Gennep shows how thresholds symbolise beginnings of new statuses. Why does the bridegroom carry his bride over the lintel? Because the

From *Purity and Danger* (1966)

---

[1] Trained in structural functionalism by Evans-Pritchard at Oxford, Mary Douglas was influenced by Durkheim's notions of society and social cohesion. Durkheim argued that religion was essentially a model of society that served to promote social cohesion (see essay 5); Douglas believes that shared symbols promote social solidarity and provide mechanisms for social control. She opens this article with a powerful image of society as a coherently organized whole. Her comment that human experiences of structures or boundaries can serve as symbols of society hints at one of her fundamental ideas—that the human body is a symbol of society.

step, the beam and the door posts make a frame which is the necessary everyday condition of entering a house. The homely experience of going through a door is able to express so many kinds of entrance. So also are cross roads and arches, new seasons, new clothes and the rest. No experience is too lowly to be taken up in ritual and given a lofty meaning. The more personal and intimate the source of ritual symbolism, the more telling its message. The more the symbol is drawn from the common fund of human experience, the more wide and certain its reception.[2]

The structure of living organisms is better able to reflect complex social forms than door posts and lintels. So we find that the rituals of sacrifice specify what kind of animal shall be used, young or old, male, female or neutered, and that these rules signify various aspects of the situation which calls for sacrifice. The way the animal is to be slaughtered is also laid down. The Dinka cut the beast longitudinally through the sexual organs if the sacrifice is intended to undo an incest; in half across the middle for celebrating a truce; they suffocate it for some occasions and trample it to death for others. Even more direct is the symbolism worked upon the human body. The body is a model which can stand for any bounded system. Its boundaries can represent any boundaries which are threatened or precarious. The body is a complex structure. The functions of its different parts and their relation afford a source of symbols for other complex structures. We cannot possibly interpret rituals concerning excreta, breast milk, saliva and the rest unless we are prepared to see in the body a symbol of society, and to see the powers and dangers credited to social structure reproduced in small on the human body.[3]

It is easy to see that the body of a sacrificial ox is being used as a diagram of a social situation. But when we try to interpret rituals of the human body in the same way the psychological tradition turns its face away from society, back towards the individual. Public rituals may express public concerns when they use inanimate door posts or animal sacrifices: but public rituals enacted on the human body are taken to express personal and private concerns. There is no possible justification for this shift of interpretation just because the rituals work upon human flesh. As far as I know the case has never been methodically stated. Its protagonists merely proceed from unchallenged assumptions, which arise from the strong similarity between certain ritual forms and the behavior of psychopathic individuals. The assumption is that in some sense primitive cultures correspond to infantile stages in the development of the human psyche. Consequently such rites are interpreted as if they express the same preoccupations which fill the mind of psychopaths or infants.[4]

Let me take two modern attempts to use primitive cultures to buttress psychological insights. Both stem from a long line of similar discussions, and both are misleading because the relation between culture and individual psyche are not made clear.

Bettelheim's *Symbolic Wounds* is mainly an interpretation of circumcision and initiation rites. The author tries to use the set rituals of Australians and Africans to throw light on psychological

---

[2] Douglas, interested in discovering universals of symbolism, suggests that the most potent symbols are found in the realm of the mundane. Because the form of the human body may be the most common human experience, her analysis centers on the body and its products.

[3] Douglas treats the symbolism of blood, breast milk, and other products of the human body as symbols of society. Ultimately, this argument is based on the organic analogy, a nineteenth-century model of society generally associated with Spencer. But whereas Spencer argued by direct analogy—telegraph wires are the nerves of society, for instance—Douglas' argument is symbolic—society is not a body, but it can be symbolically represented by a body. In the next essay, on Ndembu symbolism, Victor Turner makes a similar point.

[4] Douglas here criticizes psychological interpretations of symbolism, particularly psychoanalytic interpretations, which have tended to treat non-Western peoples as childlike or mentally ill. One line of psychoanalytic thought equates the trancing of shamans or other religious specialists in primitive societies with the acts of psychiatric patients in Western hospitals. See, for example, Kroeber's "Psychotic Factors in Shamanism" (1940) or Devereux's "Shamans as Neurotics" (1961).

phenomena. He is particularly concerned to show that psychoanalysts have overemphasized girls' envy of the male sex and overlooked the importance of boys' envy of the female sex. The idea came to him originally in studying groups of schizophrenic children approaching adolescence. It seems very likely that the idea is sound and important. I am not at all claiming to criticize his insight into schizophrenia. But when he argues that rituals which are explicitly designed to produce genital bleeding in males are intended to express male envy of female reproductive processes, the anthropologist should protest that this is an inadequate interpretation of a public rite. It is inadequate because it is merely descriptive. What is being carved in human flesh is an image of society. And in the moiety- and section-divided tribes he cites, the Murngin and Arunta, it seems more likely that the public rites are concerned to create a symbol of the symmetry of the two halves of society.[5]

The other book is *Life Against Death,* in which Brown outlines an explicit comparison between the culture of "archaic man" and our own culture, in terms of the infantile and neurotic fantasies which they seem to express. Their common assumptions about primitive culture derive from Roheim (1925): primitive culture is autoplastic, ours is alloplastic.[6] The primitive seeks to achieve his desires by self-manipulation, performing surgical rites upon his own body to produce fertility in nature, subordination in women or hunting success. In modern culture we seek to achieve our desires by operating directly on the external environment, with the impressive technical results that are the most obvious distinction between the two types of cultures. Bettelheim adopts this summing up of the differences between the ritual and the technical bias in civilization. But he supposes that the primitive culture is produced by inadequate, immature personalities, and even that the psychological shortcomings of the savage accounts for his feeble technical achievements:

> If preliterate peoples had personality structures as complex as those of modern man, if their defenses were as elaborate and their consciences as refined and demanding; if the dynamic interplay between ego, superego and id were as intricate and if their egos were as well adapted to meet and change external reality—they would have developed societies equally complex, though probably different. Their societies have, however, remained small and relatively ineffective in coping with the external environment. It may be that one of the reasons for this is their tendency to try to solve problems by autoplastic rather than alloplastic manipulation. (p. 87)

Let us assert again, as many anthropologists have before, that there are no grounds for supposing that primitive culture as such is the product of a primitive type of individual whose personality resembles that of infants or neurotics. And let us challenge the psychologists to express the syllogisms on which such a hypothesis might rest. Underlying the whole argument is the assumption that the problems which rituals are intended to solve are personal psychological problems. Bettelheim actually goes on to compare the

[5] Bruno Bettelheim (1903–1990) was an Austrian student of Sigmund Freud who emigrated to the United States in 1939 and spent virtually his whole career at the University of Chicago. Bettelheim was best known for his work with emotionally disturbed children. He was also recognized for his psychoanalytic analysis of ethnographic material, particularly his 1955 work *Symbolic Wounds.*

[6] Geza Roheim (1892–1953) was a Hungarian anthropologist. Early in his career he became a follower of Freud. Roheim spent several years conducting fieldwork in Australia, Africa, and Melanesia and was one of the leading proponents of the psychoanalytic analysis of ethnographic material. When Malinowski attacked Freud's excursions into anthropology, Roheim was one of Freud's staunchest defenders. In his 1925 book *Australian Totemism,* he characterized primitive cultures as autoplastic and Western society as alloplastic. These are medical terms. *Autoplastic* refers to the surgical repair of defects with tissue from another part of the patient's body. *Alloplasty* is replacing a diseased or damaged body part with synthetic material. Using Bettelheim's example from *Symbolic Wounds* that Douglas cites in the paragraph above, Australian Aborigines are autoplastic because a man performs a ritual subincision of his penis in order to simulate the flow of a woman's menstrual blood. Ritual use of a blood substitute, say a red vegetable dye, would be considered alloplastic.

primitive ritualist with the child who hits his own head when frustrated. This assumption underlies his whole book.

Brown makes the same assumption, but his reasoning is more subtle.[7] He does not suppose that the culture's primitive condition is caused by individual personal traits: he allows very properly for the effect of cultural conditioning on the individual personality. But he proceeds to consider the total culture as if it, in its totality, could be compared to an infant or a retarded adult. The primitive culture resorts to bodily magic to achieve its desires. It is in a stage of cultural evolution comparable to that of infantile anal eroticism. Starting from the maxim: "Infantile sexuality is autoplastic compensation for the loss of the Other; sublimation is alloplastic compensation for loss of Self" (p. 170) he goes on to argue that "archaic" culture is directed to the same ends as infantile sexuality, that is, escape from the hard realities of loss, separation and death. Epigrams are, by their nature, obscure. This is another approach to primitive culture which I would like to see fully spelt out. Brown develops the theme only briefly, as follows:

> Archaic man is preoccupied with the castration complex, the incest taboo and the desexualisation of the penis, that is, the transference of the genital impulses into that aim-inhibited libido which sustains the kinship systems in which archaic life is embedded. The low degree of sublimation, corresponding to the low level of technology, means by our previous definitions, a weaker ego, an ego which has not yet come to terms (by negation) with its own pregenital impulses. The result is that all the fantastic wishes of infantile narcissism express themselves in unsublimated form so that archaic man retains the magic body of infancy. (p. 298–9)

These fantasies suppose that the body itself could fulfill the infant's wish for unending, self-replenishing enjoyment. They are a flight from reality, a refusal to face loss, separation and death. The ego develops by sublimating these fantasies. It mortifies the body, denies the magic of excrement and to that extent faces reality. But sublimation substitutes another set of unreal aims and ends by providing the self with another kind of false escape from loss, separation and death. This is how I understand the argument to run. The more material that an elaborate technology imposes between ourselves and the satisfaction of our infantile desires, the more busily has sublimation been at work. But the converse seems questionable. Can we argue that the less the material basis of civilization is developed, the less sublimation has been at work? What precise analogy with infantile fantasy can be valid for a primitive culture based on a primitive technology? How does a low level of technology imply "an ego which has not yet come to terms (by negation) with its own pregenital impulses"? In what sense is one culture more sublimated than another?[8]

[*We have omitted a 1,000-word discussion in which Douglas refutes the psychoanalytic interpretation of excremental magic using an example of what she considers to be Brown's bias in his discussion of a Winnebago Indian trickster myth. She also cites an ethnographic example of how body substances such as blood and spittle may be considered as both polluting or sacred substances. Douglas concludes her discussion of what she calls "body dirt" with a reference to the ritual use of royal corpses. We rejoin the text at the beginning of her discussion of why products of the body are symbols of danger and power.*]

---

[7] The Brown discussed here is the Oxford-educated American scholar Norman O. Brown (1913–2002), best known for his book *Life Against Death* (1959), a psychoanalytic reinterpretation of human history. Today, works such as *Life Against Death* and *Symbolic Wounds* are considered artifacts of a bygone era; even at the time of publication these works were never widely popular among American anthropologists. But Douglas is English, and Freudian theory was taken much more seriously by European anthropologists. When she wrote this book in 1966, she was attacking a view that was still popular among European scholars.

[8] Douglas' central argument is that bodily substances are symbols of danger or power because they symbolize relations within a society. Consequently, she strongly argues against the psychoanalytic notion that the ritualized use of body refuse, such as excrement, is a psychiatric phenomenon based on infantile fantasies.

But now we are ready to broach the central question. Why should bodily refuse be a symbol of danger and of power? Why should sorcerers be thought to qualify for initiation by shedding blood or committing incest or anthropophagy?[9] Why, when initiated, should their art consist largely of manipulating powers thought to inhere in the margins of the human body? Why should bodily margins be thought to be specially invested with power and danger?

First, we can rule out the idea that public rituals express common infantile fantasies. These erotic desires which it is said to be the infant's dream to satisfy within the body's bounds are presumably common to the human race. Consequently body symbolism is part of the common stock of symbols, deeply emotive because of the individual's experience. But rituals draw on this common stock of symbols selectively. Some develop here, others there. Psychological explanations cannot of their nature account for what is culturally distinctive.

Second, all margins are dangerous. If they are pulled this way or that the shape of fundamental experience is altered. Any structure of ideas is vulnerable at its margins. We should expect the orifices of the body to symbolise its specially vulnerable points. Matter issuing from them is marginal stuff of the most obvious kind. Spittle, blood, milk, urine, faeces or tears by simply issuing forth have traversed the boundary of the body. So also have bodily parings, skin, nail, hair clippings and sweat. The mistake is to treat bodily margins in isolation from all other margins. There is no reason to assume any primacy for the individual's attitude to his own bodily and emotional

experience, any more than for his cultural and social experience. This is the clue which explains the unevenness with which different aspects of the body are treated in the rituals of the world. In some, menstrual pollution is feared as a lethal danger; in others not at all. In some, death pollution is a daily preoccupation; in others not at all. In some, excreta is dangerous, in others it is only a joke. In India cooked food and saliva are pollution-prone, but Bushmen collect melon seeds from their mouths for later roasting and eating (Marshall-Thomas, p. 44).[10]

Each culture has its own special risks and problems. To which particular bodily margins its beliefs attribute power depends on what situation the body is mirroring. It seems that our deepest fears and desires take expression with a kind of witty aptness. To understand body pollution we should try to argue back from the known dangers of society to the known selection of bodily themes and try to recognize what appositeness[11] is there.

In pursuing a last-ditch reduction of all behavior to personal preoccupations of individuals with their own bodies the psychologists are merely sticking to their last.

> The derisive remark was once made against psychoanalysis that the unconscious sees a penis in every convex object and a vagina or anus in every concave one. I find that this sentence well characterises the facts. (Ferenczi, *Sex in Psychoanalysis*, p. 227, quoted by Brown)[12]

It is the duty of every craftsman to stick to his last. The sociologists have the duty of meeting one kind of reductionism with their own. Just as

---

[9] *Anthropophagy:* the eating of human flesh.

[10] At the start of this essay, Douglas referred to the work of folklorist Arnold van Gennep (1873–1957), and his influence is evident in this passage. His best known work is *Rites of Passage* (1960 [1909]). Every rite of passage marking a person's change from one status to another, in his view, was outlined by the stages of separation, transition, and incorporation. During the transition phase one is in a liminal state, outside the margins of society, no longer one thing, but not yet another. Thus, separation from the group is necessary because, in the stage of transition, one may be ritually impure or dangerous. Douglas applies this

same principle to the human body. She writes that "all margins are dangerous" and that matter issuing from the body's orifices, because it has traversed the boundary of the body, may be dangerous. One of the classic discussions of liminal states in rites of passage is Victor Turner's "Betwixt and Between: The Liminal Period in Rites of Passage," first published in 1964 and then revised in 1967, in which he referred to this essay by Douglas.

[11] *Appositeness:* suitability or pertinence.

[12] Sandor Ferenczi (1873–1933) was a professor of psychoanalysis and a colleague of Sigmund Freud.

it is true that everything symbolizes the body, so it is equally true (and all the more so for that reason) that the body symbolizes everything else. Out of this symbolism, which in fold upon fold of interior meaning leads back to the experience of the self with its body, the sociologist is justified in trying to work in the other direction to draw out some layers of insight about the self's experience in society.

If anal eroticism is expressed at the cultural level we are not entitled to expect a population of anal erotics. We must look around for whatever it is that has made appropriate any cultural analogy with anal eroticism. The procedure in a modest way is like Freud's analysis of jokes. Trying to find a connection between the verbal form and the amusement derived from it he laboriously reduced joke interpretation to a few general rules. No comedian script-writer could use the rules for inventing jokes, but they help us to see some connections between laughter, the unconscious, and the structure of stories. The analogy is fair for pollution is like an inverted form of humour. It is not a joke for it does not amuse. But the structure of its symbolism uses comparison and double meaning like the structure of a joke.[13]

Four kinds of social pollution seem worth distinguishing. The first is danger pressing on external boundaries; the second, danger from transgressing the internal lines of the system; the third, danger in the margins of the lines. The fourth is danger from internal contradiction, when some of the basic postulates are denied by other basic postulates, so that at certain points the system seems to be at war with itself. In this chapter I show how the symbolism of the body's boundaries is used in this kind of unfunny wit to express danger to community boundaries.[14]

The ritual life of the Coorgs (Srinivas) gives the impression of a people obsessed by the fear of dangerous impurities entering their system. They treat the body as if it were a beleaguered town,

every ingress and exit guarded for spies and traitors. Anything issuing from the body is never to be re-admitted, but strictly avoided. The most dangerous pollution is for anything which has once emerged gaining re-entry. A little myth, trivial by other standards, justifies so much of their behavior and system of thought that the ethnographer has to refer to it three or four times. A Goddess in every trial of strength or cunning defeated her two brothers. Since future precedence depended on the outcome of these contests, they decided to defeat her by a ruse. She was tricked into taking out of her mouth the betel that she was chewing to see if it was redder than theirs and into popping it back again. Once she had realized she had eaten something which had once been in her own mouth and was therefore defiled by saliva, though she wept and bewailed she accepted the full justice of her downfall. The mistake canceled all her previous victories, and her brothers' eternal precedence over her was established as of right.

The Coorgs have a place within the system of Hindoo castes. There is good reason to regard them as not exceptional or aberrant in Hindoo India (Dumont and Peacock). Therefore they conceive status in terms of purity and impurity as these ideas are applied throughout the regime of castes. The lowest castes are the most impure and it is they whose humble services enable the higher castes to be free of bodily impurities. They wash clothes, cut hair, dress corpses and so on. The whole system represents a body in which by the division of labour the head does the thinking and praying and the most despised parts carry away waste matter. Each sub-caste community in a local region is conscious of its relative standing in the scale of purity. Seen from ego's position the system of caste purity is structured upwards. Those above him are more pure. All the positions below him, be they ever so intricately distinguished in relation to one another, are to him

---

[13] Douglas is referring to Freud's *Jokes and Their Relation to the Unconscious* (1960 [1905]), which explored the relationship between dreams and jokes. In this book he outlined different types of jokes and the literary and psychological mechanisms that he believed made them amusing.

[14] Using the example of an Indian caste called the Coorgs, Douglas shows that the four types of bodily purity-pollution practices she outlines are symbolic models of larger social relationships.

polluting. Thus for any ego within the system the threatening non-structure against which barriers must be erected lies below. The sad wit of pollution as it comments on bodily functions symbolizes descent in the caste structure by contact with faeces, blood and corpses.[15]

The Coorgs shared with other castes this fear of what is outside and below. But living in their mountain fastness they were also an isolated community, having only occasional and controllable contact with the world around. For them the model of the exits and entrances of the human body is a doubly apt symbolic focus of fears for their minority standing in the larger society. Here I am suggesting that when rituals express anxiety about the body's orifices the sociological counterpart of this anxiety is a care to protect the political and cultural unity of a minority group. The Israelites were always in their history a hard-pressed minority. In their beliefs all the bodily issues were polluting, blood, pus, excreta, semen, etc. The threatened boundaries of their body politic would be well mirrored in their care for the integrity, unity and purity of the physical body.

The Hindoo caste system, while embracing all minorities, embraces them each as a distinctive, cultural sub-unit. In any given locality, any sub-caste is likely to be a minority. The purer and higher its caste status, the more of a minority it must be. Therefore the revulsion from touching corpses and excreta does not merely express the order of caste in the system as a whole. The anxi-

ety about bodily margins expresses danger to group survival.[16]

That the sociological approach to caste pollution is much more convincing than a psychoanalytic approach is clear when we consider what the Indian's private attitudes to defecation are. In the ritual we know that to touch excrement is to be defiled and that the latrine cleaners stand in the lowest grade of the caste hierarchy. If this pollution rule expressed individual anxieties we would expect Hindoos to be controlled and secretive about the act of defecation. It comes as a considerable shock to read that slack disregard is their normal attitude, to such an extent that pavements, verandahs and public places are littered with faeces until the sweeper comes along.[17]

> Indians defecate everywhere. They defecate, mostly, beside the railway tracks. But they also defecate on the beaches—they defecate on the streets; they never look for cover. . . . These squatting figures—to the visitor, after a time, as eternal and emblematic as Rodin's Thinker— are never spoken of; they are never written about; they are not mentioned in novels or stories; they do not appear in feature films or documentaries. This might be regarded as part of a permissible prettifying intention. But the truth is that Indians do not see these squatters and might even with complete sincerity, deny that they exist. (Naipaul, chapter 3)

Rather than oral or anal eroticism it is more convincing to argue that caste pollution represents

---

[15] In the caste system of India, the purest individuals are leaders and priests; those who are most polluted have tasks dealing with the disposal of human waste and refuse. This association of pollution with human refuse is an extension of body symbolism, a key metaphor in Hindu belief. In the Vedas (sacred Hindu texts), the creation of the world is described as the result of the gods sacrificing a divine being named Purusha. From Purusha's mouth came the priests, from his arms the warriors, from his thighs the merchants, and from his feet the laborers. In other words, the caste divisions were created by the division of Purusha's body. This Hindu myth is a poetic example of the body-society symbolism with which Douglas began the essay.

[16] Douglas suggests that anxiety about one's minority status in a society is typically reflected in rituals concerning the body's orifices. Just as Hindus must be careful about

what goes into their bodies and the disposal of what comes out, the Coorgs, living isolated in the mountains, controlled who came into their communities and who left. The care taken to avoid pollution to their physical bodies is a symbolic manifestation of their desire to protect their political and social integrity as well. Note here that Douglas is outlining a principle she believes is universal; the Coorgs are simply an example.

[17] Douglas' comment that she was shocked to read that Indians defecate in public serves as a reminder that she is conducting cross-cultural comparative research in the tradition of Lévi-Strauss or Radcliffe-Brown. Though she does not make an issue of it as Harris does in essay 19 on the uses of cattle in India, her interpretations are based on her reading of ethnographic material rather than personal field research.

only what it claims to be. It is a symbolic system, based on the image of the body, whose primary concern is the ordering of a social hierarchy.

It is worth using the Indian example to ask why saliva and genital excretions are more pollution-worthy than tears. If I can reverently drink his tears, wrote Jean Genet, why not the so limpid drop on the end of his nose?[18] To this we can reply: first that nasal secretions are not so limpid as tears. They are more like treacle than water. When a thick rheum oozes from the eye it is no more apt for poetry than nasal rheum.[19] But admittedly clear, fast-running tears are the stuff of romantic poetry: they do not defile. This is partly because tears are naturally preempted by the symbolism of washing. Tears are like rivers of moving water. They purify, cleanse, bathe the eyes, so how can they pollute? But more significantly tears are not related to the bodily functions of digestion or pro-creation. Therefore their scope for symbolizing social relations and social processes is narrower. This is evident when we reflect on caste structure. Since place in the hierarchy of purity is biologically transmitted, sexual behavior is important for preserving the purity of caste. For this reason, in higher castes, boundary pollution focuses particularly on sexuality. The caste membership of an individual is determined by his mother, for though she may have married into a higher caste, her children take their caste from her. Therefore women are the gates of entry to the caste. Female purity is carefully guarded and a woman who is known to have had sexual intercourse with a man of lower caste is brutally punished. Male sexual purity does not carry this responsibility. Hence male promiscuity is a lighter matter. A mere ritual bath is enough to cleanse a man from sexual contact with a low caste woman. But his sexuality does not entirely escape the burden of worry which boundary pollution attaches to the body. According to Hindoo belief a sacred quality inheres in semen, which should not be wasted. In a penetrating essay on female purity in India (1963) Yalman says:

> While caste purity must be protected in women and men may be allowed much greater freedom, it is, of course, better for the men not to waste the sacred quality contained in their semen. It is well-known that they are exhorted not merely to avoid low-caste women, but all women (Carstairs 1956, 1957; Gough 1956). For the loss of semen is the loss of this potent stuff . . . it is best never to sleep with women at all.

Both male and female physiology lend themselves to the analogy with the vessel which must not pour away or dilute its vital fluids. Females are correctly seen as, literally, the entry by which the pure content may be adulterated. Males are treated as pores through which the precious stuff may ooze out and be lost, the whole system being thereby enfeebled.

A double moral standard is often applied to sexual offenses. In a patrilineal system of descent wives are the door of entry to the group. In this they hold a place analogous to that of sisters in the Hindoo caste. Through the adultery of a wife impure blood is introduced to the lineage. So the symbolism of the imperfect vessel appropriately weighs more heavily on the women than on the men.[20]

If we treat ritual protection of bodily orifices as a symbol of social preoccupations about exits and entrances, the purity of cooked food becomes important. I quote a passage on the capacity of cooked food to be polluted and to carry pollution (in an unsigned review article on *Pure and Impure, Contributions to Indian Sociology*, III, July 1959, p. 37).

> When a man uses an object it becomes part of him, participates in him. Then, no doubt, this

---

[18] Jean Genet (1910–1986) was a French novelist, playwright, and protégé of the existentialist philosopher Jean-Paul Sartre. Genet was best known for his plays. His works are contributions to the theater of the absurd, a form of drama in which the impossible routinely happens in order to make philosophical points.

[19] *Limpid:* clear or transparent; *treacle:* molasses or syrup; *rheum:* a watery mucous discharge from the eyes or nose.

[20] Douglas says that rules of body purity and pollution are symbolic of a group's place in society as well as the preservation of that group. It follows that because caste membership is transmitted through women, the rules of sexual purity and pollution are more strict for women than for men. Just as sexual restrictions can be symbolic of anxiety about caste membership, the polluting qualities of menstrual blood, semen, or other body products can be symbolic of lineage membership. Yalman's discussion of sexuality and

appropriation is much closer in the case of food, and the point is that appropriation precedes absorption, as it accompanies the cooking. Cooking may be taken to imply a complete appropriation of the food by the household. It is almost as if, before being "internally absorbed" by the individual, food was, by cooking, collectively predigested. One cannot share the food prepared by people without sharing in their nature. This is one aspect of the situation. Another is that cooked food is extremely permeable to pollution.

This reads like a correct transliteration of Indian pollution symbolism regarding cooked food. But what is gained by proffering a descriptive account as if it were explanatory? In India the cooking process is seen as the beginning of ingestion, and therefore cooking is susceptible to pollution, in the same way as eating. But why is this complex found in India and in parts of Polynesia and in Judaism and other places, but not wherever humans sit down to eat? I suggest that food is not likely to be polluting at all unless the external boundaries of the social system are under pressure.[21] We can go further to explain why the actual cooking of the food in India must be ritually pure. The purity of the castes is correlated with an elaborate hereditary division of labour between castes. The work performed by each caste carries a symbolic load: it says something about the relatively pure status of the caste in question. Some kinds of labour correspond with the excretory functions of the body, for example that of washermen, barbers, sweepers, as we have seen. Some professions are involved with bloodshed or alcoholic liquor, such as tanners, warriors, toddy tappers. So they are low in the scale of purity in so far as their occupations are at variance with Brahminic ideals. But the point at which food is

prepared for the table is the point at which the interrelation of the purity structure and the occupational structure needs to be set straight. For food is produced by the combined efforts of several castes of varying degrees of purity: the blacksmith, carpenter, ropemaker, the peasant. Before being admitted to the body some clear symbolic break is needed to express food's separation from necessary but impure contacts. The cooking process, entrusted to pure hands, provides this ritual break. Some such break we would expect to find whenever the production of food is in the hands of the relatively impure.

These are the general lines on which primitive rituals must be related to the social order and the culture in which they are found. The examples I have given are crude, intended to exemplify a broad objection to a certain current treatment of ritual themes. I add one more, even cruder, to underline my point. Much literature has been expended by psychologists on Yurok pollution ideas (Erikson, Posinsky). These North Californian Indians who lived by fishing for salmon in the Klamath River, would seem to have been obsessed by the behavior of liquids, if their pollution rules can be said to express an obsession. They are careful not to mix good water with bad, not to urinate into rivers, not to mix sea and fresh water, and so on. I insist that these rules cannot imply obsessional neuroses, and they cannot be interpreted unless the fluid formlessness of their highly competitive social life be taken into account (Dubois).

To sum up. There is unquestionably a relation between individual preoccupations and primitive ritual. But the relation is not the simple one which some psychoanalysts have assumed. Primitive ritual draws upon individual experience, of course. This is a truism. But it draws upon it so selectively that it cannot be said to be primarily

---

male and female purity is actually a second issue—not the preservation of a social group such as a caste, but the maintenance of gender boundaries.

[21] Douglas refers to the prohibition of eating beef in India, the principles of mana and taboo in traditional Polynesian societies, and the dietary rules about kosher food in Judaism. She suggests that if a society or class feels the need to protect itself from outsiders or foreign influences,

this will be symbolized through rules of behavior and eating. For example, in Polynesia, commoners were forbidden to touch anything associated with the noble classes because these objects contained mana, a power that could harm them. According to Douglas, protecting the body from pollution by guarding the orifices, in this case restricting the diet, symbolizes the protection of traditional beliefs.

inspired by the need to solve individual problems common to the human race, still less explained by clinical research. Primitives are not trying to cure or prevent personal neuroses by their public rituals. Psychologists can tell us whether the public expression of individual anxieties is likely to solve personal problems or not. Certainly we must suppose that some interaction of the kind is probable. But that is not at issue. The analysis of ritual symbolism cannot begin until we recognize ritual as an attempt to create and maintain a particular culture, a particular set of assumptions by which experience is controlled.

Any culture is a series of related structures which comprise social forms, values, cosmology, the whole of knowledge and through which all experience is mediated. Certain cultural themes are expressed by rites of bodily manipulation. In this very general sense primitive culture can be said to be autoplastic. But the objective of these rituals is not negative withdrawal from reality. The assertions they make are not usefully to be compared to the withdrawal of the infant into thumb-sucking and masturbation. The rituals enact the form of social relations and in giving these relations visible expression they enable people to know their own society. The rituals work upon the body politic through the symbolic medium of the physical body.[22]

REFERENCES

Bettelheim, B. 1955. *Symbolic Wounds*. Glencoe, IL.

Brown, Norman O. 1959. *Life Against Death*. London.

Dubois, Cora. 1936. "The Wealth Concept as an Integrative Factor in Tolowa-Tututni Culture." Chapter in *Essays in Anthropology, Presented to A. L. Kroeber*.

Dumont, L. and Peacock, D. 1959. *Contributions to Indian Sociology*. Vol. III.

Marshall-Thomas, E. 1959. *The Harmless People*. New York.

Naipaul, V. S. 1964. *An Area of Darkness*. London.

Posinky. 1956. *Psychiatric Quarterly* XXX, p. 598.

Roheim, G. 1925. *Australian Totemism*.

Yalman, N. 1963. "The Purity of Women in Ceylon and Southern India." *Journal of the Royal Anthropological Institute*

---

[22] Douglas' conclusion reflects the strong influence of Durkheim on her work. Durkheim was concerned with demonstrating that society was a separate phenomenon from individual psychology and that social actions could not be reduced to the sum total of individual actions. In other words, he tried very hard to separate sociology from psychology. Douglas attempts to do the same thing. She insists that the rules of ritual and pollution are what Durkheim called *social facts*. They are not reducible to manifestations of individual psychology. Whatever effects they may have on the individual, they reflect the ways society maintains its structure and solidarity. The essay is profoundly symbolic—a materialist's analysis of the caste system, for example, would have focused on the political and economic inequalities inherent in it, which Douglas ignores. With some modification we could imagine this essay appearing as a chapter in Durkheim's *Elementary Forms of the Religious Life* (1965 [1912]). For example, in the last sentence of the paragraph above, she characterizes ritual as the attempt to create and maintain a particular culture.

---

32. *Symbols in Ndembu Ritual*

Victor Turner (1920–1983)

Among the Ndembu of Zambia (formerly Northern Rhodesia), the importance of ritual in the lives of the villagers in 1952 was striking. Hardly a week passed in a small neighborhood without a ritual drum being heard in one or another of its villages.

By "ritual" I mean prescribed formal behavior for occasions not given over to technological

---

From *The Forest of Symbols* (1967)

routine having reference to beliefs in mystical beings or powers. The symbol is the smallest unit of ritual which still retains the specific properties of ritual behavior; it is the ultimate unit of specific structure in a ritual context. Since this essay is in the main a description and analysis of the structure and properties of symbols, it will be enough to state here, following the *Concise Oxford Dictionary,* that a "symbol" is a thing regarded by general consent as naturally typifying or representing or recalling something by possession of analogous qualities or by association in fact or thought. The symbols I observed in the field were, empirically, objects, activities, relationships, events, gestures, and spatial units in a ritual situation.[1]

Following the advice and example of Professor Monica Wilson, I asked Ndembu specialists as well as laymen to interpret the symbols of their ritual. As a result, I obtained much exegetic[2] material. I felt that it was methodologically important to keep observational and interpretative materials distinct from one another. The reason for this will soon become apparent.[3]

I found that I could not analyze ritual symbols without studying them in a time series in relation to other "events," for symbols are essentially involved in social process. I came to see performances of ritual as distinct phases in the social processes whereby groups became adjusted to internal changes and adapted to their external environment. From this standpoint the ritual symbol becomes a factor in social action, a positive force in an activity field. The symbol becomes associated with human interests, purposes, ends, and means, whether these are explicitly formulated or have to be inferred from the observed behavior. The structure and properties of a symbol become those of a dynamic entity, at least within its appropriate context of action.[4]

STRUCTURE AND PROPERTIES OF RITUAL SYMBOLS

The structure and properties of ritual symbols may be inferred from three classes of data: (1) external form and observable characteristics;

---

[1] This essay, first presented as a paper at a professional meeting in 1958, is one of Turner's most famous works. In it he outlines some basic properties of symbols and contrasts his method of symbolic analysis with psychoanalytic thought using examples from his fieldwork with the Ndembu.

[2] *Exegetic:* the adjectival form of *exegesis,* an interpretation or explanation.

[3] Turner was a student of Monica H. Wilson (1908–1982), a Cambridge-educated South African social anthropologist. In the 1930s, most anthropologists in the structural-functionalist tradition were writing about African societies as static traditions. Wilson, however, focused on economic, political, and social change in African societies, particularly among the Nyakyusa. She is best known for her detailed fieldwork and ethnographies.

Turner speaks of keeping observational and interpretive materials separate from one another because he wrote this article at a time when symbolic interpretation was controversial and because of the training he received from Wilson. The care with which he outlines his argument is in part a reaction to the controversy caused by Freudian interpretations of ethnographic material. Psychoanalytic

analysis relies heavily on the interpreter's explication of the unconscious meaning of a ritual or other symbols. In the British structural-functionalist tradition, Turner considers symbols to be empirically verifiable units and is interested in the laws by which they are used.

[4] Contrary to the psychoanalytic approach, Turner maintains that because ritual symbols are a part of social action they must be analyzed within the social and temporal contexts in which they are expressed. However, Turner thought of these contexts as consisting of elements of the natural world and other social groups and did not consider the effects British colonialism might have had on the societies he studied. The British administration is mentioned briefly and in passing in *The Forest of Symbols* (the book from which this essay is taken) but only to dismiss the importance of its effects. For example, in the introduction, Turner points out that the British have changed the nature of Ndembu hierarchy but then says "The Ndembu . . . still live in the strenuous and heroic past" (1967:3). Turner's structural-functionalist roots are also apparent in this paragraph in that he sees rituals as the mechanism by which groups adjust to changes in their social and external environment.

(2) interpretations offered by specialists and by laymen; (3) significant contexts largely worked out by the anthropologist.[5]

Here is an example. At *Nkang'a*, the girl's puberty ritual, a novice is wrapped in a blanket and laid at the foot of a *mudyi* sapling. The *mudyi* tree *Diplorrhyncus condylocarpon* is conspicuous for its white latex, which exudes in milky beads if the thin bark is scratched. For Ndembu this is its most important observable characteristic, and therefore I propose to call it "the milk tree" henceforward.[6] Most Ndembu women can attribute several meanings to this tree. In the first place, they say that the milk tree is the "senior" (*mukulumpi*) tree of the ritual. Each kind of ritual has this "senior" or, as I will call it, "dominant" symbol. Such symbols fall into a special class which I will discuss more fully later. Here it is enough to state that dominant symbols are regarded not merely as means to the fulfillment of the avowed purposes of a given ritual, but also and more importantly refer to values that are regarded as ends in themselves, that is, to axiomatic values. Secondly, the women say with reference to its observable characteristics that the milk tree stands for human breast milk and also for the breasts that supply it. They relate this meaning to the fact that *Nkang'a* is performed when a girl's breasts begin to ripen, not after her first menstruation, which is the subject of another and less elaborate ritual. The main theme of *Nkang'a* is indeed the tie of nurturing between mother and child, not the bond of birth. This theme of nurturing is expressed at *Nkang'a* in a number of supplementary symbols indicative of the act of feeding and of foodstuff. In the third place, the women describe the milk tree as "the tree of a mother and her child." Here the refer-

ence has shifted from description of a biological act, breast feeding, to a social tie of profound significance both in domestic relations and in the structure of the widest Ndembu community. This latter meaning is brought out most clearly in a text I recorded from a male ritual specialist. I translate literally.

> The milk tree is the place of all mothers of the lineage (*ivumu*, literally "womb" or "stomach"). It represents the ancestress of women and men. The milk tree is where our ancestress slept when she was initiated. To initiate here means the dancing of women round and round the milk tree where the novice sleeps. One ancestress after another slept there down to our grandmother and our mother and ourselves the children. That is the place of our tribal custom (*muchidi*)[a] where we began, even men just the same, for men are circumcised under a milk tree.

This text brings out clearly those meanings of the milk tree which refer to principles and values of social organization. At one level of abstraction the milk tree stands for matriliny, the principle on which the continuity of Ndembu society depends. Matriliny governs succession to office and inheritance of property, and it vests dominant rights of residence in local units. More than any other principle of social organization it confers order and structure on Ndembu social life. Beyond this, however, "*mudyi*" means more than matriliny, both according to this text and according to many other statements I have collected. It stands for tribal custom (*muchidi wetu*) itself. The principle of matriliny, the backbone of Ndembu social organization, as an element in the semantic structure of the milk tree, itself symbolizes the total system of interrelations between groups and persons that makes up Ndembu society. Some of the meanings of

---

[5] Reacting to the ethnoscientists' critique of ethnography, Turner refuses to get drawn into a conflict over the validity of different forms of interpretation. Here he says that observed data, informants' interpretations, and the anthropologist's analysis are all legitimate. In the following paragraph he demonstrates how the symbolism of the *mudyi* tree can be viewed from all three perspectives.

[6] Turner says Ndembu women attribute several symbolic meanings to the *mudyi* tree. The fact that a single symbol can represent many things is called *multivocality*, and it is one of Turner's key ideas. He first defined the term in his article "Ritual Symbolism, Morality, and Social Structure among the Ndembu" (1965b). Note that Turner proposes to call the tree the milk tree, thus imposing a symbolic image of his own. What do the Ndembu call the *mudyi* tree? Is milk tree the English translation of *mudyi*?

important symbols may themselves be symbols, each with its own system of meanings. At its highest level of abstraction, therefore, the milk tree stands for the unity and continuity of Ndembu society. Both men and women are components of that spatiotemporal continuum. Perhaps that is why one educated Ndembu, trying to cross the gap between our cultures, explained to me that the milk tree was like the British flag above the administrative headquarters. *"Mudyi* is our flag," he said.[7]

When discussing the milk tree symbolism in the context of the girls' puberty ritual, informants tend to stress the harmonizing, cohesive aspects of the milk tree symbolism. They also stress the aspect of dependence. The child depends on its mother for nutriment; similarly, say the Ndembu, the tribesman drinks from the breasts of tribal custom. Thus nourishment and learning are equated in the meaning content of the milk tree. I have often heard the milk tree compared to "going to school"; the child is said to swallow instruction as a baby swallows milk and *kapudyi*, the thin cassava gruel Ndembu liken to milk. Do we not ourselves speak of "a thirst for knowledge"? Here the milk tree is a shorthand for the process of instruction in tribal matters that follows the critical episode in both boys' and girls' initiation—circumcision in the case of the boys and the long trial of lying motionless in that of the girls. The mother's role is the archetype, of protector, nourisher, and teacher. For example, a chief is often referred to as the "mother of his people," while the hunter-doctor who initiates a novice into a hunting cult is called "the mother of huntsmanship *(mama dawuyang'a)."* An apprentice circumciser is referred to as "child of the circumcision medicine" and his instructor as "mother of the circumcision medicine." In all the senses hitherto described, the milk tree represents harmonious, benevolent aspects of domestic and tribal life.

However, when the third mode of interpretation, contextual analysis, is applied, the interpretations of informants are contradicted by the way people actually behave with reference to the milk tree. It becomes clear that the milk tree represents aspects of social differentiation and even opposition between the components of a society which ideally it is supposed to symbolize as a harmonious whole. The first relevant context we shall examine is the role of the milk tree in a series of action situations within the framework of the girls' puberty ritual. Symbols, as I have said, produce action, and dominant symbols tend to become focuses in interaction. Groups mobilize around them, worship before them, perform other symbolic activities near them, and add other symbolic objects to them, often to make composite shrines. Usually these groups of participants themselves stand for important components of the secular social system, whether these components consist of corporate groups, such as families and lineages, or of mere categories of persons possessing similar characteristics, such as old men, women, children, hunters, or widows. In each kind of Ndembu ritual a different group or category becomes the focal social element. In *Nkang'a* this focal element is the unity of Ndembu women. It is the women who dance around the milk tree and initiate the recumbent novice by making her the hub of their whirling circle. Not only is the milk tree the "flag of the Ndembu"; more specifically, in the early phases of *Nkang'a*, it is the "flag" of Ndembu women. In this situation it does more than focus the exclusiveness of women; it mobilizes them in opposition to the men. For the women sing songs taunting the men and for a time will not let men dance in their circle. Therefore, if we are to take account of the operational aspect of the milk tree symbol, including not only what Ndembu say about it but also what they do with it in its "meaning," we

---

[7] Like Douglas, Turner inherited the Durkheimian perspective implicit in British structural functionalism. Here you see this perspective expressed in his statement that the *mudyi* tree represents not only breast milk, but at its most abstract level of meaning, Ndembu society. Turner was also influenced by Raymond Firth (1901–2002). A student of Malinowski, Firth was interested in linking the interpretation of symbolism to social structures and social events (Firth 1973:25). Note the symbolic tie between the *mudyi* tree and matrilineality. Here Turner makes the link between kinship and symbolism. In classic functionalist style, Turner focuses on the harmonious, integrative functions of symbols.

must allow that it distinguishes women as a social category and indicates their solidarity.[8]

The milk tree makes further discriminations. For example, in certain action contexts it stands for the novice herself. One such context is the initial sacralization of a specific milk tree sapling. Here the natural property of the tree's immaturity is significant. Informants say that a young tree is chosen because the novice is young. A girl's particular tree symbolizes her new social personality as a mature woman. In the past and occasionally today, the girl's puberty ritual was part of her marriage ritual, and marriage marked her transition from girlhood to womanhood. Much of the training and most of the symbolism of *Nkang'a* are concerned with making the girl a sexually accomplished spouse, a fruitful woman, and a mother able to produce a generous supply of milk. For each girl this is a unique process. She is initiated alone and is the center of public attention and care. From her point of view it is *her Nkang'a*, the most thrilling and self-gratifying phase of her life. Society recognizes and encourages these sentiments, even though it also prescribes certain trials and hardships for the novice, who must suffer before she is glorified on the last day of the ritual. The milk tree, then, celebrates the coming-of-age of a new social personality, and distinguishes her from all other women at this one moment in her life. In terms of its action context, the milk tree here also expresses the conflict between the girl and the moral community of adult women she is entering. Not without

reason is the milk tree site known as "the place of death" or "the place of suffering," terms also applied to the site where boys are circumcised, for the girl novice must not move a muscle throughout a whole hot and clamant[9] day.

In other contexts, the milk tree site is the scene of opposition between the novice's own mother and the group of adult women. The mother is debarred from attending the ring of dancers. She is losing her child, although later she recovers her as an adult co-member of her lineage. Here we see the conflict between the matricentric family and the wider society which, as I have said, is dominantly articulated by the principle of matriliny. The relationship between mother and daughter persists throughout the ritual, but its content is changed. It is worth pointing out that, at one phase in *Nkang'a*, mother and daughter interchange portions of clothing. This may perhaps be related to the Ndembu custom whereby mourners wear small portions of a dead relative's clothing. Whatever the interchange of clothing may mean to a psychoanalyst—and here we arrive at one of the limits of our present anthropological competence—it seems not unlikely that Ndembu intend to symbolize the termination for both mother and daughter of an important aspect of their relationship. This is one of the symbolic actions—one of very few—about which I found it impossible to elicit any interpretation in the puberty ritual. Hence it is legitimate to infer, in my opinion, that powerful unconscious wishes, of a kind considered illicit by Ndembu, are expressed in it.[10]

---

[8] Anthropologist Max Gluckman (1911–1975) was a major influence on Turner. Gluckman, a structural-functionalist, focused on the socially integrative effects of ritual expressions of conflict (see essay 13). Famous for his formulation of the concept of "rituals of rebellion," Gluckman proposed that the ritual enactment of conflict (such as that between women and men in the *Nkang'a* rite) is a form of social catharsis that allows the expression of hostility without endangering the established social order. Having discussed the role that *mudyi* tree symbolism plays in tribal life, Turner tells us that the milk tree also represents differentiation and opposition in a situation that should be harmonious. In the *Nkang'a* ritual the *mudyi* is the "flag" of Ndembu women as they highlight their opposition to men, taunting them and denying them access to their

dance circle. This contradiction is explained in Gluckman's terms. Marxist analysts also placed emphasis on conflict, but used the concept very differently. For structural-functionalists, ritualized forms of conflict prevent social disruption and maintain a society's stability. For Marxists, conflict is the key force propelling revolution and, thus, social evolution.

[9] *Clamant:* noisy.

[10] Elements of both Gluckman and Freud appear in this paragraph. First, Turner explains that the ritual allows the symbolic expression of hostility between the initiate's mother and the larger group of adult women in this matrilineal society. Then, because Turner was unable to elicit any explanation for a mother and daughter's exchange of

Opposition between the tribeswomen and the novice's mother is mimetically represented at the milk tree towards the end of the first day of the puberty ritual. The girl's mother cooks a huge meal of cassava and beans—both kinds of food are symbols in *Nkang'a*, with many meanings—for the women visitors, who eat in village groups and not at random. Before eating, the women return to the milk tree from their eating place a few yards away and circle the tree in procession. The mother brings up the rear holding up a large spoon full of cassava and beans. Suddenly she shouts: "Who wants the cassava of *chipwamp-wilu?*" All the women rush to be first to seize the spoon and eat from it. "*Chipwampwilu*" appears to be an archaic word and no one knows its meaning. Informants say that the spoon represents the novice herself in her role of married woman, while the food stands both for her reproductive power (*lusemu*) and her role as cultivator and cook. One woman told my wife: "It is lucky if the person snatching the spoon comes from the novice's own village.[11] Otherwise, the mother believes that her child will go far away from her to a distant village and die there. The mother wants her child to stay near her." Implicit in this statement is a deeper conflict than that between the matricentric family and mature female society. It refers to another dominant articulating principle of Ndembu society, namely virilocal marriage according to which women live at their husbands' villages after marriage. Its effect is sometimes to separate mothers from daughters by considerable distances. In the episode described, the women symbolize the matrilineal cores of villages. Each village wishes to gain control through marriage over the novice's capacity to work. Its members also hope that her children will be raised in it, thus adding to its size and prestige. Later in *Nkang'a* there is a symbolic struggle between the novice's matrilineal kin and those of her bridegroom, which makes explicit the conflict between virilocality and matriliny.

Lastly, in the context of action situation, the milk tree is sometimes described by informants as representing the novice's own matrilineage. Indeed, it has this significance in the competition for the spoon just discussed, for women of her own village try to snatch the spoon before members of other villages. Even if such women do not belong to her matrilineage but are married to its male members, they are thought to be acting on its behalf. Thus, the milk tree in one of its action aspects represents the unity and exclusiveness of a single matrilineage with a local focus in a village against other such corporate groups. The conflict between yet another subsystem and the total system is given dramatic and symbolic form.[12]

By this time, it will have become clear that considerable discrepancy exists between the interpretations of the milk tree offered by informants and the behavior exhibited by Ndembu in situations dominated by the milk tree symbolism. Thus, we are told that the milk tree represents the close tie between mother and daughter. Yet the milk tree separates a daughter from her mother. We are also told that the milk tree stands for the unity of Ndembu society. Yet we find that in practice it separates women from men, and some categories and groups of women from others. How are these contradictions between principle and practice to be explained?

SOME PROBLEMS OF INTERPRETATION

I am convinced that my informants genuinely believed that the milk tree represented only the linking and unifying aspects of Ndembu social

---

apparel during the *Nkang'a* rite, he assumes the symbolism of the exchange indicates unconscious feelings that the Ndembu censor from conscious expression.

[11] Turner mentions the presence of his wife in this paragraph. Although she accompanied him into the field and helped him conduct research, Edith Turner (b. 1921) is rarely mentioned in his works. She is an accomplished anthropologist in her own right, with several books to her credit including *The Spirit and the Drum: A Memoir of Africa* (1987) and *Experiencing Ritual: A New Interpretation of African Healing* (1992).

[12] Turner's analysis is clearly similar to the work on kinship conducted by Radcliffe-Brown a generation earlier (see essay 12). He states that the ritual actions refer to socio-structural elements of the society as well as express the conflict between matrilineality and virilocality.

organization. I am equally convinced that the role of the milk tree in action situations where it represents a focus of specified groups in opposition to other groups, forms an equally important component of its total meaning. Here the important question must be asked, "meaning for whom?" For if Ndembu do not recognize the discrepancy between their interpretation of the milk tree symbolism and other behavior in connection with it, does this mean that the discrepancy has no relevance for the social anthropologist? Indeed some anthropologists claim, with Nadel (1954, 108), that "uncomprehended symbols have no part in social enquiry, their social effectiveness lies in their capacity to indicate, and if they indicate nothing to the actors, they are, from our point of view, irrelevant, and indeed no longer symbols (whatever their significance for the psychologist or psychoanalyst)."[13] Professor Monica Wilson (1957, 6) holds a similar point of view. She writes that she stresses "Nyakyusa interpretations of their own rituals, for anthropological literature is bespattered with symbolic guessing, the ethnographer's interpretations of the rituals of other people." Indeed, she goes so far as to base her whole analysis of Nyakyusa ritual on "the Nyakyusa translation or interpretation of the symbolism." In my view, these investigators go beyond the limits of salutary caution and impose serious, and even arbitrary, limitations on themselves. To some extent, their difficulties derive from their failure to distinguish the concept of symbol from that of a mere sign. Although I am in complete disagreement with his fundamental postulate that the collective unconscious is the main formative principle in ritual symbolism, I consider that Carl Jung (1949, 601) has cleared the way for further investigation by making just this distinction. "A sign," he says, "is an analogous or abbreviated expression of a *known* thing. But a symbol is always the best possible expression of a relatively *unknown* fact, a fact, however, which is none the less recognized

or postulated as existing." Nadel and Wilson, in treating most ritual symbols as signs, must ignore or regard as irrelevant some of the crucial properties of such symbols.[14]

FIELD SETTING AND STRUCTURAL PERSPECTIVE

How, then, can a social anthropologist justify his claim to be able to interpret a society's ritual symbols more deeply and comprehensively than the actors themselves? In the first place, the anthropologist, by the use of his special techniques and concepts, is able to view the performance of a given kind of ritual as "occurring in, and being interpenetrated by, a totality of coexisting social entities such as various kinds of groups, subgroups, categories, or personalities, and also barriers between them, and modes of interconnexion" (Lewin 1949, 200). In other words, he can place this ritual in its significant field setting and describe the structure and properties of that field. On the other hand, each participant in the ritual views it from his own particular corner of observation. He has what Lupton has called his own "structural perspective." His vision is circumscribed by his occupancy of a particular position, or even of a set of situationally conflicting positions, both in the persisting structure of his society, and also in the role structure of the given ritual. Moreover, the participant is likely to be governed in his actions by a number of interests, purposes, and sentiments, dependent upon his specific position, which impair his understanding of the total situation. An even more serious obstacle against his achieving objectivity is the fact that he tends to regard as axiomatic and primary the ideals, values, and norms that are overtly expressed or symbolized in the ritual. Thus, in the *Nkang'a* ritual, each person or group in successive contexts of action, sees the milk tree only as representing her or their own specific interests and

---

[13] S. F. Nadel (1903–1956) received a doctoral degree in psychology and philosophy from the University of Vienna and studied anthropology at the London School of Economics with Malinowski and Seligman. He is best known for his work with the Nupe in northern Nigeria and the Nuba in Sudan.

[14] Here Turner attempts to deal with the argument that symbolic meaning not recognized by native informants is invalid. Although Turner does not use the terms, this is the same emic-etic debate that was conducted in the United States between ethnoscientists and materialists.

values at those times. However, the anthropologist who has previously made a structural analysis of Ndembu society, isolating its organizational principles, and distinguishing its groups and relationships, has no particular bias and can observe the real interconnections and conflicts between groups and persons, in so far as these receive ritual representation. What is meaningless for an actor playing a specific role may well be highly significant for an observer and analyst of the total system.[15]

On these grounds, therefore, I consider it legitimate to include within the total meaning of a dominant ritual symbol, aspects of behavior associated with it which the actors themselves are unable to interpret, and indeed of which they may be unaware, if they are asked to interpret the symbol outside its activity context. Nevertheless, there still remains for us the problem of the contradiction between the expressed meanings of the milk tree symbol and the meaning of the stereotyped forms of behavior closely associated with it. Indigenous interpretations of the milk tree symbolism in the abstract appear to indicate that there is no incompatibility or conflict between the persons and groups to which it refers. Yet, as we have seen, it is between just such groups that conflict is mimed at the milk tree site.

THREE PROPERTIES OF RITUAL SYMBOLS

Before we can interpret, we must further classify our descriptive data, collected by the methods described above. Such a classification will enable us to state some of the properties of ritual symbols.[16] The simplest property is that of *condensation*. Many things and actions are represented in a single formation. Secondly, a dominant symbol is a *unification of disparate significata*. The disparate *significata* are interconnected by virtue of their common possession of analogous qualities or by association in fact or thought. Such qualities or links of association may in themselves be quite trivial or random or widely distributed over a range of phenomena. Their very generality enables them to bracket together the most diverse ideas and phenomena. Thus, as we have seen, the milk tree stands for, *inter alia,* women's breasts, motherhood, a novice at *Nkang'a,* the principle of matriliny, a specific matrilineage, learning, and the unity and persistence of Ndembu society. The themes of nourishment and dependence run through all these diverse *significata.*[17]

The third important property of dominant ritual symbols is *polarization of meaning*. Not only the milk tree but all other dominant Ndembu

---

[15] Turner says that anthropologists are privileged observers without bias who can view symbolic actions in a wider social context than a ritual participant. Do you agree? Are anthropologists really impartial observers with no particular bias, or do they have their "own particular corner of observation" too? This is a central question for the postmodernists, who claim that an observer cannot be impartial. But even if that is true, an important question remains: Can anthropologists accurately see some things invisible to a culture's participants?

[16] Earlier, Turner defined "dominant symbols" as those referring to "axiomatic," or self-evident, values. In this section, he further explains dominant symbols and describes three of their most important properties: condensation, unification of disparate significata, and polarization of meaning. These principles help explain how symbols can have various and conflicting meanings.

[17] The distinction between condensation and the unification of disparate significata in particular can be difficult to

grasp. The best description we have found is that given by Matheiu Deflem. He points out that in *The Forest of Symbols,* Turner made a distinction between dominant and instrumental symbols, and claimed that dominant symbols had three main properties, condensation, the unification of disparate significata, and the polarization of meaning. Condensation is when one dominant symbol represents many things and actions. The unification of disparate significata refers to the underlying meanings of the symbol being interconnected by common or analogous qualities or by association (Deflem 1991:6). Turner's discussion of the mudyi or "milk" tree is a good illustration of both these properties of symbols. The mudyi tree is called the milk tree because it has a thick white sap and this sap can take on a variety of meanings depending on the ritual context (condensation). Because the sap is milky white it is associated with breast milk, women who produce the milk, and Ndembu matrilineages in general (association of disparate significata).

symbols possess two clearly distinguishable poles of meaning. At one pole is found a cluster of *significata* that refer to components of the moral and social orders of Ndembu society, to principles of social organization, to kinds of corporate grouping, and to the norms and values inherent in structural relationships. At the other pole, the *significata* are usually natural and physiological phenomena and processes. Let us call the first of these the "ideological pole," and the second the "sensory pole." At the sensory pole, the meaning content is closely related to the outward form of the symbol. Thus one meaning of the milk tree—breast milk—is closely related to the exudation of milky latex from the tree. One sensory meaning of another dominant symbol, the *mukula* tree, is blood; this tree secretes a dusky red gum.[18]

At the sensory pole are concentrated those *significata* that may be expected to arouse desires and feelings; at the ideological pole one finds an arrangement of norms and values that guide and control persons as members of social groups and categories. The sensory, emotional *significata* tend to be "gross" in a double sense. In the first place, they are gross in a general way, taking no account of detail or the precise qualities of emotion. It cannot be sufficiently stressed that such symbols are social facts, "collective representations," even though their appeal is to the lowest common denominator of human feeling. The second sense of "gross" is "frankly, even flagrantly, physiological." Thus, the milk tree has the gross meanings of breast milk, breasts, and the process of breast feeding. These are also gross in the sense that they represent items of universal Ndembu experience. Other Ndembu symbols, at their sensory poles of meaning, represent such themes as blood, male and female genitalia, semen, urine, and feces. The same symbols, at their ideological poles of meaning, represent the unity and continuity of social groups, primary and associational, domestic, and political.[19]

[A 569-word section of Turner's article called "Reference and Condensation" has been omitted. In this section, Turner discusses Edward Sapir's discussion of the means by which ritual symbols stimulate emotional responses.]

DOMINANT AND INSTRUMENTAL SYMBOLS

Certain ritual symbols, as I have said, are regarded by Ndembu as dominant. In rituals performed to propitiate ancestor spirits who are believed to have afflicted their living kin with reproductive disorders, illness, or bad luck at hunting, there are two main classes of dominant symbols. The first class is represented by the first tree or plant in a series of trees or plants from which portions of leaves, bark, or roots are collected by practitioners or adepts in the curative cult. The subjects of ritual are marked with these portions mixed with water, or given them, mixed in a potion, to drink. The first tree so treated is called the "place of greeting" (*ishikenu*), or the "elder" (*mukulumpi*). The adepts encircle it several times to sacralize it. Then the senior practitioner prays at its base, which he sprinkles with

---

[18] Turner here imposes a scheme of classification that strongly resembles Lévi-Strauss' nature-culture binary opposition. The poles of meaning that Turner labels ideological and sensory could almost as easily be labeled culture and nature. Why, given that he considers these poles of meaning universal, did Turner not turn to structuralism? In the 1960s and 1970s a structural-functionalist interested in symbolic analysis could turn to Lévi-Strauss or Freud. Like Douglas, who studied the symbolism of body wastes and social boundaries, Turner chose to derive his symbolic meanings from Freud.

[19] Turner is concerned not only with interpreting symbols but also with explaining why they affect people the way they do. He states that blood, genitals, semen, urine, and feces are all represented by basic Ndembu symbols at their sensory and ideological poles of meaning, thus relying on both Durkheim and Freud. He sees symbols as social facts and notes that at the ideological pole these symbols represent "unity and continuity of social groups," which draws on Durkheim. His identification of the sensory pole of meaning as being "flagrantly physiological" shows the influence of Freud, who believed that such physiological symbolism was universal because the experience of these elements in infancy was universal.

powdered white clay. Prayer is made either to the named spirit, believed to be afflicting the principal subject of ritual, or to the tree itself, which is in some way identified with the afflicting spirit. Each *ishikenu* can be allotted several meanings by adepts. The second class of dominant symbols in curative rituals consists of shrines where the subjects of such rituals sit while the practitioners wash them with vegetable substances mixed with water and perform actions on their behalf of a symbolic or ritualistic nature. Such shrines are often composite, consisting of several objects in configuration. Both classes of dominant symbols are closely associated with nonempirical beings. Some are regarded as their repositories; others, as being identified with them; others again, as representing them. In life-crisis rituals, on the other hand, dominant symbols seem to represent not beings but nonempirical powers or kinds of efficacy. For example, in the boys' circumcision ritual, the dominant symbol for the whole ritual is a "medicine" (*yitumbu*), called "*nfunda*," which is compounded from many ingredients, e.g., the ash of the burnt lodge which means "death," and the urine of an apprentice circumciser which means "virility." Each of these and other ingredients have many other meanings. The dominant symbol at the camp where the novices' parents assemble and prepare food for the boys is the *chikoli* tree, which represents, among other things, an erect phallus, adult masculinity, strength, hunting prowess, and health continuing into old age. The dominant symbol during the process of circumcision is the milk tree, beneath which novices are circumcised. The dominant symbol in the immediate postcircumcision phase is the red *mukula* tree, on which the novices sit until their wounds stop bleeding. Other symbols are dominant at various phases of seclusion. Each of these symbols is described as "*mukulumpi*" (elder, senior). Dominant symbols appear in many different ritual contexts, sometimes presiding over the whole procedure, sometimes over particular phases. The meaning-content of certain dominant symbols possesses a high degree of constancy and consistency throughout the total symbolic system, exemplifying Radcliffe-Brown's proposition that a symbol recurring in a cycle of rituals is likely to have the same significance in each. Such symbols also possess considerable autonomy with regard to the aims of the rituals in which they appear. Precisely because of these properties, dominant symbols are readily analyzable in a cultural framework of reference. They may be regarded for this purpose as what Whitehead would have called "eternal objects."[b] They are the relatively fixed points in both the social and cultural structures, and indeed constitute points of junction between these two kinds of structure. They may be regarded irrespective of their order of appearance in a given ritual as ends in themselves, as representative of the axiomatic values of the widest Ndembu society. This does not mean that they cannot also be studied, as we have indeed studied them, as factors of social action, in an action frame of reference, but their social properties make them more appropriate objects of morphological study than the class of symbols we will now consider.

These symbols may be termed "instrumental symbols." An instrumental symbol must be seen in terms of its wider context, i.e., in terms of the total system of symbols which makes up a given kind of ritual. Each kind of ritual has its specific mode of interrelating symbols. This mode is often dependent upon the ostensible purposes of that kind of ritual. In other words, each ritual has its own teleology.[20] It has its explicitly expressed goals, and instrumental symbols may be regarded as means of attaining those goals. For example, in rituals performed for the overt purpose of making women fruitful, among the instrumental symbols used are portions of fruit-bearing trees or of trees that possess innumerable rootlets. These fruits and rootlets are said by Ndembu to represent children. They are also thought of as having efficacy

---

[20] What Turner means is that each ritual has its own design and purpose. An instrumental symbol must be analyzed in terms of the specific ritual context in which it occurs. Dominant symbols are "axiomatic," that is, self-evidently true. The implication here is that, within a culture, dominant symbols are constant in meaning, whereas the meaning of instrumental symbols is dependent on their context.

to make the woman fruitful. They are means to the main end of the ritual. Perhaps such symbols could be regarded as mere signs or referential symbols, were it not for the fact that the meanings of each are associated with powerful conscious and unconscious emotions and wishes. At the psychological level of analysis, I suspect that these symbols too would approximate to the condition of condensation symbols, but here we touch upon the present limits of competence of anthropological explanation, a problem we will now discuss more fully.

THE LIMITS OF ANTHROPOLOGICAL INTERPRETATION

We now come to the most difficult aspect of the scientific study of ritual symbolism: analysis. How far can we interpret these enigmatic formations by the use of anthropological concepts? At what points do we reach the frontiers of our explanatory competence? Let us first consider the case of dominant symbols. I have suggested that these have two poles of meaning, a sensory and an ideological pole. I have also suggested that dominant symbols have the property of unifying disparate *significata*. I would go so far as to say that at both poles of meaning are clustered disparate and even contradictory *significata*. In the course of its historical development, anthropology has acquired techniques and concepts that enable it to handle fairly adequately the kind of data we have classified as falling around the ideological pole. Such data, as we have seen, include components of social structure and cultural phenomena, both ideological and technological. I believe that study of these data in terms of the concepts of three major subdivisions of anthropology—cultural anthropology, structuralist theory, and social dynamics—would be extremely rewarding. I shall shortly outline how I think such analyses might be done and how the three frameworks might be interrelated, but first we must ask how far and in what respects is it relevant to submit the sensory pole of meaning to intensive analysis, and, more importantly, how far are we, as anthropologists, qualified to do so? It is evident, as Sapir has stated, that ritual symbols, like all condensation symbols, "strike deeper and deeper roots in the unconscious." Even a brief acquaintance with depth psychology is enough to show the investigator that ritual symbols, with regard to their outward form, to their behavioral context, and to several of the indigenous interpretations set upon them, are partially shaped under the influence of unconscious motivations and ideas. The interchange of clothes between mother and daughter at the *Nkang'a* ritual; the belief that a novice would go mad if she saw the milk tree on the day of her separation ritual; the belief that if a novice lifts up the blanket with which she is covered during seclusion and sees her village her mother would die; all these are items of symbolic behavior for which the Ndembu themselves can give no satisfactory interpretation. For these beliefs suggest an element of mutual hostility in the mother-daughter relationship which runs counter to orthodox interpretations of the milk tree symbolism, in so far as it refers to the mother-daughter relationship. One of the main characteristics of ideological interpretations is that they tend to stress the harmonious and cohesive aspect of social relationships. The exegetic idiom feigns that persons and groups always act in accordance with the ideal norms of Ndembu society.

[*We have omitted a 700-word section of Turner's article called "Depth Psychology and Ritual Symbolism," in which he discusses the psychoanalytic interpretation of ritual symbols such as the work of Bruno Bettelheim, which was discussed in the previous essay, by Mary Douglas. In this section, Turner claims that psychoanalysts generally reject the ideological pole of meaning and focus on the sensory meanings. He writes that psychoanalysts regard indigenous explanations of symbols as identical to the justifications that neurotics provide for their behavior. Further, Turner says that psychoanalysts look on ritual symbols as being identical to symptoms of neurosis or psychosis or dream symbols of Western Europeans. Turner, of course, disagrees with this point of view. He states that symbols are partly influenced by unconscious motivations and ideas, but his is not a psychoanalytic interpretation. He ends the section in an almost comic manner, referring to "hapless anthropologists" having to choose between competing psychoanalytic interpretations.*]

PROVINCES OF EXPLANATION

I consider that if we conceptualize a dominant symbol as having two poles of meaning, we can more exactly demarcate the limits within which anthropological analysis may be fruitfully applied. Psychoanalysts, in treating most indigenous interpretations of symbols as irrelevant, are guilty of a naive and one-sided approach. For those interpretations that show how a dominant symbol expresses important components of the social and moral orders are by no means equivalent to the "rationalizations," and the "secondary elaborations" of material deriving from endopsychic conflicts. They refer to social facts that have an empirical reality exterior to the psyches of individuals. On the other hand, those anthropologists who regard only indigenous interpretations as relevant, are being equally one-sided. This is because they tend to examine symbols within two analytical frameworks only, the cultural and the structural. This approach is essentially a static one, and it does not deal with processes involving temporal changes in social relations.

Nevertheless, the crucial properties of a ritual symbol involve these dynamic developments. Symbols instigate social action. In a field context they may even be described as "forces," in that they are determinable influences inclining persons and groups to action.[21] It is in a field context, moreover, that the properties we have described, namely, polarization of meanings, transference of affectual quality, discrepancy between meanings, and condensations of meanings, become most significant. The symbol as a unit of action, possessing these properties, becomes an object of study both for anthropology

and for psychology. Both disciplines, in so far as they are concerned with human actions must conceptualize the ritual symbol in the same way.

The techniques and concepts of the anthropologist enable him to analyze competently the interrelations between the data associated with the ideological pole of meaning. They also enable him to analyze the social behavior directed upon the total dominant symbol. He cannot, however, with his present skills, discriminate between the precise sources of unconscious feeling and wishing, which shape much of the outward form of the symbol; select some natural objects rather than others to serve as symbols; and account for certain aspects of the behavior associated with symbols. For him, it is enough that the symbol should evoke emotion. He is interested in the fact that emotion is evoked and not in the specific qualities of its constituents. He may indeed find it situationally relevant for his analysis to distinguish whether the emotion evoked by a specific symbol possesses the gross character, say, of aggression, fear, friendliness, anxiety, or sexual pleasure, but he need go no further than this. For him the ritual symbol is primarily a factor in group dynamics, and, as such, its references to the groups, relationships, values, norms, and beliefs of a society are his principal items of study. In other words, the anthropologist treats the sensory pole of meaning as a constant, and the social and ideological aspects as variables whose interdependencies he seeks to explain.

The psychoanalyst, on the other hand, must, I think, attach greater significance than he now does to social factors in the analysis of ritual symbolism. He must cease to regard interpretations, beliefs, and dogmas as mere rationalizations when, often enough, these refer to social and natural realities. For, as Durkheim wrote (1954, 2–3), "primitive religions hold to reality and express it. One must learn to go underneath the symbol to the reality which it represents and which gives it its meaning. No religions are false,

---

[21] The influence of Durkheim on Turner's analysis is strongly manifested in this section. Turner's description of symbols as forces that incline people to action is quite similar to Durkheim's description of social facts

(see essay 5). In this section, Turner also refers to *The Elementary Forms of the Religious Life* (1965 [1912]), Durkheim's last major work.

all answer, though in different ways, to the given conditions of human existence." Among those given conditions, the arrangement of society into structured groupings, discrepancies between the principles that organize these groupings, economic collaboration and competition, schism within groups and opposition between groups— in short, all those things with which the social aspect of ritual symbolism is concerned—are surely of at least equal importance with biopsychical drives and early conditioning in the elementary family. After all, the ritual symbol has, in common with the dream symbol, the characteristic, discovered by Freud, of being a compromise formation between two main opposing tendencies. It is a compromise between the need for social control, and certain innate and universal human drives whose complete gratification would result in a breakdown of that control. Ritual symbols refer to what is normative, general, and characteristic of unique individuals. Thus, Ndembu symbols refer among other things, to the basic needs of social existence (hunting, agriculture, female fertility, favourable climatic conditions, and so forth), and to shared values on which communal life depends (generosity, comradeship, respect for elders, the importance of kinship, hospitality, and the like). In distinguishing between ritual symbols and individual psychic symbols, we may perhaps say that while ritual symbols are gross means of handling social and natural reality, psychic symbols are dominantly fashioned under the influence of inner drives. In analyzing the former, attention must mainly be paid to relations between data external to the psyche; in analyzing the latter, to endopsychic data.[22]

For this reason, the study of ritual symbolism falls more within the province of the social anthropologist than that of the psychologist or psychoanalyst, although the latter can assist the anthropologist by examining the nature and interconnections of the data clustered at the sensory pole of ritual symbolism. He can also, I believe, illuminate certain aspects of the stereotyped behavior associated with symbols in field contexts, which the actors themselves are unable to explain. For as we have seen, much of this behavior is suggestive of attitudes that differ radically from those deemed appropriate in terms of traditional exegesis. Indeed, certain conflicts would appear to be so basic that they totally block exegesis.

THE INTERPRETATION OF OBSERVED EMOTIONS

Can we really say that behavior portraying conflict between persons and groups, who are represented by the symbols themselves as being in harmony, is in the full Freudian sense unconscious behavior? The Ndembu themselves in many situations outside *Nkang'a*, both secular and ritual, are perfectly aware of and ready to speak about hostility in the relationships between particular mothers and daughters, between particular sublineages, and between particular young girls and the adult women in their villages. It is rather as though there existed in certain precisely defined public situations, usually of a ritual or ceremonial type, a norm obstructing the verbal statement of conflicts in any way connected with the principle and rules celebrated or dramatized in those situations. Evidences of human passion and frailty are just not spoken about when the occasion is given up to the public commemoration and reanimation of norms and values in their abstract purity.

Yet, as we have seen, recurrent kinds of conflict may be acted out in the ritual or ceremonial form. On great ritual occasions, common practice, as well as highest principle, receives its symbolic or stereotyped expression, but practice, which is dominantly under the sway of what all

---

[22] Here Turner distinguishes between cultural symbols and individual psychological symbols. He argues that the former are the province of anthropology, the latter that of psychology. This concern with distinguishing anthropology and sociology from psychology is similar to that expressed by Durkheim at the turn of the century. Both Turner and Durkheim argued that collective phenomena are the subjects of anthropology and that individual consciousness belongs in psychology.

societies consider man's "lower nature," is rife with expressions of conflict. Selfish and factional interests, oath breaking, disloyalty, sins of omission as well as sins of commission, pollute and disfigure those ideal prototypes of behavior which in precept, prayer, formula, and symbol are held up before the ritual assembly for its exclusive attention. In the orthodox interpretation of ritual it is pretended that common practice has no efficacy and that men and women really are as they ideally should be. Yet, as I have argued above, the "energy" required to reanimate the values and norms enshrined in dominant symbols and expressed in various kinds of verbal behavior is "borrowed," to speak metaphorically in lieu at the moment of a more rigorous language, from the miming of well-known and normally mentionable conflicts. The raw energies of conflict are domesticated into the service of social order.[23]

I should say here that I believe it possible, and indeed necessary, to analyze symbols in a context of observed emotions. If the investigator is well acquainted with the common idiom in which a society expresses such emotions as friendship, love, hate, joy, sorrow, contentment, and fear, he cannot fail to observe that these are experienced in ritual situations. Thus, in *Nkang'a* when the women laugh and jeer at the men, tease the novice and her mother, fight one another for the "porridge of *chipwampwilu*," and so on, the observer can hardly doubt that emotions are really aroused in the actors as well as formally represented by ritual custom. ("What's Hecuba to him or he to Hecuba, that he should weep for her?")[24]

These emotions are portrayed and evoked in close relation to the dominant symbols of tribal cohesion and continuity, often by the performance of instrumentally symbolic behavior.

However, since they are often associated with the mimesis[25] of interpersonal and intergroup conflict, such emotions and acts of behavior obtain no place among the official, verbal meanings attributed to such dominant symbols.[26]

THE SITUATIONAL SUPPRESSION OF CONFLICT FROM INTERPRETATION

Emotion and praxis,[27] indeed, give life and coloring to the values and norms, but the connection between the behavioral expression of conflict and the normative components of each kind of ritual, and of its dominant symbols, is seldom explicitly formulated by believing actors. Only if one were to personify a society, regarding it as some kind of supra-individual entity, could one speak of "unconsciousness" here. Each individual participant in the *Nkang'a* ritual is well aware that kin quarrel most bitterly over rights and obligations conferred by the principle of matriliny, but that awareness is situationally held back from verbal expression: the participants must behave as if conflicts generated by matriliny were irrelevant.

[*Several paragraphs totaling about 560 words were omitted from the text. These contained a discussion of the situational suppression of conflict in the ritual expression of dominant symbols.*]

For example, in the frequently performed *Nkula* ritual, the dominant symbols are a cluster of red objects, notably red clay (*mukundu*) and the *mukula* tree mentioned previously. In the context of *Nkula*, both of these are said to represent menstrual blood and the "blood of birth," which is the blood that accompanies the birth of

---

[23] For Turner, apparent conflict reinforces social order, once again illustrating Gluckman's perspective. Although he does not specifically call the *Nkang'a* a ritual of rebellion, it is clear that he has this in mind.

[24] Turner says that it is important for one to analyze symbols in the context of observed emotions. The quotation is from Hamlet, Act II, scene 2, where Hamlet, writing a play in which his father's murder will be re-created, comments on the power of emotion that can be expressed by an actor.

[25] *Mimesis:* imitation.

[26] Turner's emphasis on interpreting behavior rather than thought appears repeatedly in this essay, highlighting the difference between him and the American ethnoscientists of this period. His focus on behavior largely collapsed the emic-etic distinctions so important in American anthropology.

[27] *Praxis:* practice guided by the application of a specific theory.

a child. The ostensible goal of the ritual is to co-agulate the patient's menstrual blood, which has been flowing away in menorrhagia, around the fetus in order to nourish it. A series of symbolic acts are performed to attain this end. For exam-ple, a young *mukula* tree is cut down by male doctors and part of it is carved into the shape of a baby, which is then inserted into a round cala-bash medicated with the blood of a sacrificed cock, with red clay, and with a number of other red ingredients. The red medicines here, say the Ndembu, represent desired coagulation of the patient's menstrual blood, and the calabash is a symbolic womb. At the ideological pole of mean-ing, the *mukula* tree and the medicated calabash both represent (as the milk tree does) the pa-tient's matrilineage and, at a higher level of ab-straction, the principle of matriliny itself. This is also consistent with the fact that *ivumu*, the term for "womb," also means "matrilineage."[28] In this symbolism the procreative, rather than the nutri-tive, aspect of motherhood is stressed. However, Ndembu red symbolism, unlike the white sym-bolism of which the milk tree symbolism is a spe-cies, nearly always has explicit reference to violence, to killing, and, at its most general level of meaning, to breach, both in the social and natural orders. Although informants, when dis-cussing this *Nkula* ritual specifically, tend to stress the positive, feminine aspects of parturi-tion and reproduction, other meanings of the red

symbols, stated explicitly in other ritual contexts, can be shown to make their influence felt in *Nkula*. For example, both red clay and the *mu-kula* tree are dominant symbols in the hunter's cult, where they mean the blood of animals, the red meat of game, the inheritance through either parent of hunting prowess, and the unity of all initiated hunters. It also stands for the hunter's power to kill.[29] The same red symbols, in the con-text of the *Wubanji* ritual performed to purify a man who has killed a kinsman or a lion or leopard (animals believed to be reincarnated hunter kin of the living), represent the blood of homicide. Again, in the boys' circumcision ritual, these symbols stand for the blood of circumcised boys. More seriously still, in divination and in anti-witchcraft rituals, they stand for the blood of witches' victims, which is exposed in necropha-gous feasts.[30]

Most of these meanings are implicit in *Nkula*. For example, the female patient, dressed in skins like a male hunter and carrying a bow and arrow, at one phase of the ritual performs a special hunter's dance. Moreover, while she does this, she wears in her hair, just above the brow, the red feather of a lourie bird. Only shedders of blood, such as hunters, man-slayers, and circumcisers, are customarily entitled to wear this feather.[31] Again, after the patient has been given the baby figurine in its symbolic womb, she dances with it in a style of dancing peculiar to circumcisers

---

[28] Earlier in the article, Turner stated that psychoanalytic interpretations typically focus on the sensory pole of meaning. Here, in his description of the *Nkula* ritual, the symbolism of the calabash as womb and red clay as men-strual blood is very Freudian. At the ideological pole of meaning, the same symbols refer to the patient's matrilin-eage. This is a structural interpretation in the tradition of Radcliffe-Brown. The characteristics of symbols that Turner described earlier in this article—condensation, polarization of meaning, and the unification of disparate significata—allow him to reconcile these seemingly con-tradictory interpretations.

[29] Earlier, Turner characterized instrumental symbols as those that have a ritually specific meaning; here he gives an example. The *mukula* tree represents menstrual blood and the matrilineage in the women's *Nkula* rite, but it also

represents the blood of animals and the hunter's power to kill, among other meanings, in men's hunting rites.

[30] *Necrophagy* is the eating of the dead.

[31] The role reversals in the *Nkula* ceremony—women dressing in hunter's garb and dancing a hunter's dance—are other aspects of the rituals of rebellion that Gluckman described in his research. See for example, his *Custom and Conflict in Africa* (1956). Gluckman's central idea was that while the ritualized reversing of established roles (the poor mock the wealthy, women dress as men) seemed to chal-lenge the established order, in fact, these symbolic rever-sals reinforced it (see essay 13). Similarly, Turner identifies Ndembu women's ceremonial cross-dressing as a demon-stration of male and female roles. He sees the ritual as a symbolic means of forcing women to accept their place as childbearers and not challenge male gender roles.

when they brandish aloft the great *nfunda* medicine of the circumcision lodge. Why then is the woman patient identified with male bloodspillers? The field context of these symbolic objects and items of behavior suggests that the Ndembu feel that the woman, in wasting her menstrual blood and in failing to bear children, is actively renouncing her expected role as a mature married female. She is behaving like a male killer, not like a female nourisher. The situation is analogous, though modified by matriliny, to the following pronouncement in the ancient Jewish Code of Qaro: "Every man is bound to marry a wife in order to beget children, and he who fails of this duty is as one who sheds blood."

One does not need to be a psychoanalyst, one only needs sound sociological training, acquaintance with the total Ndembu symbolic system, plus ordinary common sense, to see that one of the aims of the ritual is to make the woman accept her lot in life as a childbearer and rearer of children for her lineage. The symbolism suggests that the patient is unconsciously rejecting her female role, that indeed she is guilty; indeed, "*mbayi,*" one term for menstrual blood, is etymologically connected with "*ku-baya*" (to be guilty). I have not time here to present further evidence of symbols and interpretations, both in *Nkula* and in cognate rituals, which reinforce this explanation. In the situation of *Nkula,* the dominant principles celebrated and reanimated are those of matriliny, the mother-child bond, and tribal continuity through matriliny. The norms in which these are expressed are those governing the behavior of mature women, which ascribe to them the role appropriate to their sex. The suppressed or submerged principles and norms, in this situation, concern and control the personal and corporate behavior deemed appropriate for man.

The analysis of *Nkula* symbolism throws into relief another major function of ritual. Ritual adapts and periodically readapts the biopsychical individual to the basic conditions and axiomatic values of human social life. In redressive rituals, the category to which *Nkula* belongs, the eternally rebellious individual is converted for a while into a loyal citizen. In the case of *Nkula,* a female individual whose behavior is felt to demonstrate her rebellion against, or at least her reluctance to comply with, the biological and social life patterns of her sex, is both induced and coerced by means of precept and symbol to accept her culturally prescribed destiny.[32]

MODES OF INFERENCE IN INTERPRETATION

Each kind of Ndembu ritual, like *Nkula,* has several meanings and goals that are not made explicit by informants, but must be inferred by the investigator from the symbolic pattern and from behavior. He is able to make these inferences only if he has previously examined the symbolic configurations and the meanings attributed to their component symbols by skilled informants, of many other kinds of ritual in the same total system. In other words, he must examine symbols not only in the context of each specific kind of ritual, but in the context of the total system. He may even find it profitable, where the same symbol is found throughout a wide culture area, to study its changes of meaning in different societies in that area.[33]

There are two main types of contexts, irrespective of size. There is the action-field context, which we have discussed at some length. There is also the cultural context in which symbols are regarded as clusters of abstract meanings. By comparing the different kinds and sizes of contexts in which a dominant symbol occurs, we can often see that the meanings "officially" attributed to it in a particular kind of ritual may be mutually consistent. However,

---

[32] The paragraph concluding Turner's description of the *Nkula* rite highlights the structural-functionalist background that he brings to his analysis. Ritual compels a woman who rebels against her assigned role to "accept her culturally prescribed destiny," thus preserving the stability of Ndembu society.

[33] Note again Turner's view of the anthropologist as neutral omniscient observer—anthropologists can interpret, he says, because they see the total system. The individual immersed in the system does not possess this clarity of vision. Compare this point of view with that of the postmodernists in essays 36–38.

there may be much discrepancy and even contradiction between many of the meanings given by informants, when this dominant symbol is regarded as a unit of the total symbolic system. I do not believe that this discrepancy is the result of mere carelessness and ignorance or variously distributed pieces of insight. I believe that discrepancy between *significata* is a quintessential property of the great symbolic dominants in all religions. Such symbols come in the process of time to absorb into their meaning-content most of the major aspects of human social life, so that, in a sense, they come to represent "human society" itself.[34] In each ritual they assert the situational primacy of a single aspect or of a few aspects only, but by their mere presence they suffuse those aspects with the awe that can only be inspired by the human total. All the contradictions of human social life, between norms, and drives, between different drives and between different norms, between society and the individual, and between groups, are condensed and unified in a single representation, the dominant symbols. It is the task of analysis to break down this amalgam into its primary constituents.

[*The 350-word section called "The Relativity of Depth" was omitted from this text. In it, Turner criticizes the notion that psychoanalytic interpretations of symbolism are "deeper" than anthropological analyses and characterizes symbols as a "force in a field of social action."*]

CONCLUSION: THE ANALYSIS OF SYMBOLS IN SOCIAL PROCESSES

Let me outline briefly the way in which I think ritual symbols may fruitfully be analyzed. Performances of ritual are phases in broad social processes, the span and complexity of which are roughly proportional to the size and degree of differentiation of the groups in which they occur. One class of ritual is situated near the apex of a whole hierarchy of redressive and regulative institutions that correct deflections and deviations from customarily prescribed behavior. Another class anticipates deviations and conflicts. This class includes periodic rituals and life-crisis rituals. Each kind of ritual is a patterned process in time, the units of which are symbolic objects and serialized items of symbolic behavior.

The symbolic constituents may themselves be classed into structural elements, or "dominant symbols," which tend to be ends in themselves, and variable elements, or "instrumental symbols," which serve as means to the explicit or implicit goals of the given ritual. In order to give an adequate explanation of the meaning of a particular symbol, it is necessary first to examine the widest action-field context, that, namely, in which the ritual itself is simply a phase. Here one must consider what kinds of circumstances give rise to a performance of ritual, whether these are concerned with natural phenomena, economic and technological processes, human life-crises, or with the breach of crucial social relationships. The circumstances will probably determine what sort of ritual is performed. The goals of the ritual will have overt and implicit reference to the antecedent circumstances and will in turn help to determine the meaning of the symbols. Symbols must now be examined within the context of the specific ritual. It is here that we enlist the aid of indigenous informants. It is here also that we may be able to speak legitimately of "levels" of interpretation, for laymen will give the investigator simple and esoteric meanings, while specialists will give him esoteric explanations and more elaborate texts. Next, behavior directed towards each symbol should be noted, for such behavior is an important component of its total meaning.[35]

We are now in a position to exhibit the ritual as a system of meanings, but this system acquires

---

[34] In *The Elementary Forms of the Religious Life*, Durkheim argued that Australian Aboriginal religious beliefs were a model of their own society. Here Turner makes a similar claim, not just for Ndembu symbolism, but for the dominant symbols of any society.

[35] Note Turner's comment that different people will interpret symbols differently. A decade later, postmodern writers emphasized this point. They used the term *positioning* and claimed that one's point of view was influenced by social, economic, and political factors. One important

additional richness and depth if it is regarded as itself constituting a sector of the Ndembu ritual system, as interpreted by informants and as observed in action. It is in comparison with other sectors of the total system, and by reference to the dominant articulating principles of the total system, that we often become aware that the overt and ostensible aims and purposes of a given ritual conceal unavowed, and even "unconscious," wishes and goals. We also become aware that a complex relationship exists between the overt and the submerged, and the manifest and latent patterns of meaning. As social anthropologists we are potentially capable of analyzing the social aspect of this relationship. We can examine, for example, the relations of dependence and independence between the total society and its parts, and the relations between different kinds of parts, and between different parts of the same kind. We can see how the same dominant symbol, which in one kind of ritual stands for one kind of social group or for one principle of organization, in another kind of ritual stands for another kind of group or principle, and in its aggregate of meanings stands for unity and continuity of the widest Ndembu society, embracing its contradictions.[36]

THE LIMITS OF CONTEMPORARY ANTHROPOLOGICAL COMPETENCE

Our analysis must needs be incomplete when we consider the relationship between the normative elements in social life and the individual. For this relationship, too, finds its way into the meaning of ritual symbols. Here we come to the confines of our present anthropological competence, for we are now dealing with the structure and properties of psyches, a scientific field traditionally studied by other disciplines than ours. At one end of the symbol's spectrum of meanings we encounter the individual psychologist and the social psychologist, and even beyond them (if one may make a friendly tilt at an envied friend), brandishing his Medusa's head, the psychoanalyst, ready to turn to stone the foolhardy interloper into his caverns of terminology.

We shudder back thankfully into the light of social day. Here the significant elements of a symbol's meaning are related to what it does and what is done to it by and for whom. These aspects can only be understood if one takes into account from the beginning, and represents by appropriate theoretical constructs, the total field situation in which the symbol occurs. This situation would include the structure of the group that performs the ritual we observe, its basic organizing principles and perdurable relationships, and, in addition, its extant division into transient alliances and factions on the basis of immediate interest and ambitions, for both abiding structure and recurrent forms of conflict and selfish interest are stereotyped in ritual symbolism. Once we have collected informants' interpretations of a given symbol, our work of analysis has indeed just begun. We must gradually approximate to the action-meaning of our symbol by way of what Lewin calls (1949, 149) "a stepwise increasing specificity" from widest to narrowest significant action context. Informants' "meanings" only become meaningful as objects of scientific study in the course of this analytical process.[37]

---

difference between Turner's view and that of the postmodernists was that these latter were more influenced by Marxism: They tended to see positioning in terms of conflict and domination of one group over another. Turner notes that positioning exists, but he does not question its effect. He insists that anthropologists occupy a privileged position and are impartial observers.

[36] In the two paragraphs above, Turner provides an outline of his methods of analysis. The sophistication that he brought to symbolic analysis becomes apparent when you compare his work with studies of ritual or religion from the first part of the century, such as Sir James Frazer's *Golden Bough* (1911–1915 [1890]) and Freud's *Moses and Monotheism* (1939). Turner's analysis of the different types of symbols and their properties stands today as one of the seminal works in symbolic anthropology.

[37] The role of symbols in culture and individual psychology is a complex question that has defied definitive explication since it first arose at the turn of the century. In the final paragraphs, Turner, like Durkheim and Douglas, focuses on the intellectual division between anthropology-sociology and psychology.

ACKNOWLEDGEMENT

Victor Turner, from "Symbols in Ndembu Ritual" from *Closed Systems and Open Minds: The Limits of Naïvety in Social Anthropology*, ed. Max Gluckman, pp. 20–51. Copyright © 1964 by Aldine Publishers. Reprinted by permission of AldineTransaction, a division of Transaction Publishers.

NOTES

Read at a meeting of the Association of Social Anthropologists of the Commonwealth in London, March 1958. First published in *Closed Systems and Open Minds: The Limits of Naivety in Social Science*, M. Gluckman, ed. (Edinburgh: Oliver and Boyd, 1964).

[a] *Muchidi* also means "category," "kind," "species," and "tribe" itself.

[b] I.e., objects not of indefinite duration but to which the category of time is not applicable.

REFERENCES

Bettelheim, Bruno. 1954. *Symbolic Wounds: Puberty Rites and the Envious Male*. Glencoe, Ill: Free Press.

Durkheim, E. 1954. *Elementary Forms of the Religious Life*. London: Allen and Unwin.

Fenichel, Otto. 1946. *The Psychoanalytic Theory of Neuroses*. London: Routledge and Kegan Paul.

Jung, Carl G. 1949. *Psychological Types*. London: Routledge and Kegan Paul.

Lewin, K. 1949. *Field Theory in Social Science*. London: Tavistock Publications.

Nadel, S. F. 1954. *Nupe Religion*. London: Routledge and Kegan Paul.

Sapir, E. "Symbols," *Encyclopedia of the Social Sciences*, XIV. New York: Macmillan.

Wilson, M. 1957. *Rituals of Kinship Among the Nyakyusa*. London: Oxford University Press, for the International African Institute.

---

33. *Deep Play: Notes on the Balinese Cockfight*

CLIFFORD GEERTZ (1926–2006)

THE RAID

Early in April of 1958, my wife and I arrived, malarial and diffident, in a Balinese village we intended, as anthropologists, to study.[1] A small place, about five hundred people, and relatively remote, it was its own world. We were intruders, professional ones, and the villagers dealt with us as Balinese seem always to deal with people not part of their life who yet press themselves upon them: as though we were not there. For them, and to a degree for ourselves, we were nonpersons, specters, invisible men.

From *The Interpretation of Cultures* (1973)

---

[1] The work of symbolic anthropologists like Victor Turner and Mary Douglas was concerned with demonstrating what Devons and Gluckman (1964) called the "logic of the irrational." One motive underlying their work was to demonstrate how institutions that seemed irrational to the observer are actually rational, even if the natives themselves are unaware of the cultural logic behind their behavior. Turner and Douglas accounted for this hidden rationality by penetrating the surface behavior and explanations to look for concealed layers of meaning. This form of inquiry ultimately led analysts to resort to psychological explanations of behavior, or semimetaphysical concepts such as social facts or the collective conscience. Geertz, although he too is concerned with the interpretation of cultural symbolism, follows a very different approach: He wishes to provide the reader with an empathic understanding of another society. Geertz believes that culture is acted out in public symbols such as the cockfight and is the mechanism by which members of a society communicate their worldview. He is not trying to uncover the hidden symbolic meaning of the Balinese cockfight, for he believes the Balinese understand the symbolism of the contest as well as anyone. Instead, in this analysis Geertz attempts to situate readers of the essay within the Balinese system in order to facilitate their understanding of the meaning of the cockfight. This is not, in any sense, a scientific goal. His observations are not replicable. Someone else trying to do the same work might well have a very different set of insights.

Geertz's original article is accompanied by 43 voluminous footnotes, which space limitations do not allow us to reprint. Asterisks have been used to show readers the placement of his footnotes in the text.

We moved into an extended family compound (that had been arranged before through the provincial government) belonging to one of the four major factions in village life. But except for our landlord and the village chief, whose cousin and brother-in-law he was, everyone ignored us in a way only a Balinese can do. As we wandered around, uncertain, wistful, eager to please, people seemed to look right through us with a gaze focused several yards behind us on some more actual stone or tree. Almost nobody greeted us; but nobody scowled or said anything unpleasant to us either, which would have been almost as satisfactory. If we ventured to approach someone (something one is powerfully inhibited from doing in such an atmosphere), he moved, negligently but definitely, away. If, seated or leaning against a wall, we had him trapped, he said nothing at all, or mumbled what for the Balinese is the ultimate nonword—"yes." The indifference, of course, was studied; the villagers were watching every move we made, and they had an enormous amount of quite accurate information about who we were and what we were going to be doing. But they acted as if we simply did not exist, which, in fact, as this behavior was designed to inform us, we did not, or anyway not yet.

This is, as I say, general in Bali. Everywhere else I have been in Indonesia, and more latterly in Morocco, when I have gone into a new village, people have poured out from all sides to take a very close look at me, and, often an all-too-probing feel as well. In Balinese villages, at least those away from the tourist circuit, nothing happens at all. People go on pounding, chatting, making offerings, staring into space, carrying baskets about while one drifts around feeling vaguely disembodied. And the same thing is true on the individual level. When you first meet a Balinese, he seems virtually not to relate to you at all; he is, in the term Gregory Bateson and Margaret Mead made famous, "away."* Then—in a day, a week, a month (with some people the magic moment never comes)—he decides, for reasons I have never quite been able to fathom, that you *are* real, and then he becomes a warm, gay, sensitive, sympathetic, though, being Balinese, always precisely controlled, person. You have crossed, somehow, some moral or metaphysi-

cal shadow line. Though you are not exactly taken as a Balinese (one has to be born to that), you are at least regarded as a human being rather than a cloud or a gust of wind. The whole complexion of your relationship dramatically changes to, in the majority of cases, a gentle, almost affectionate one—a low-keyed, rather playful, rather mannered, rather bemused geniality.

My wife and I were still very much in the gust-of-wind stage, a most frustrating, and even, as you soon begin to doubt whether you are really real after all, unnerving one, when, ten days or so after our arrival, a large cockfight was held in the public square to raise money for a new school.

Now, a few special occasions aside, cockfights are illegal in Bali under the Republic (as, for not altogether unrelated reasons, they were under the Dutch), largely as a result of the pretensions to puritanism radical nationalism tends to bring with it. The elite, which is not itself so very puritan, worries about the poor, ignorant peasant gambling all his money away, about what foreigners will think, about the waste of time better devoted to building up the country. It sees cockfighting as "primitive," "backward," "unprogressive," and generally unbecoming an ambitious nation. And, as with those other embarrassments—opium smoking, begging, or uncovered breasts—it seeks, rather unsystematically, to put a stop to it.

Of course, like drinking during Prohibition or, today, smoking marihuana, cockfights, being a part of "The Balinese Way of Life," nonetheless go on happening, and with extraordinary frequency. And, as with Prohibition or marihuana, from time to time the police (who, in 1958 at least, were almost all not Balinese but Javanese) feel called upon to make a raid, confiscate the cocks and spurs, fine a few people, and even now and then expose some of them in the tropical sun for a day as object lessons which never, somehow, get learned, even though occasionally, quite occasionally, the object dies.

As a result, the fights are usually held in a secluded corner of a village in semisecrecy, a fact which tends to slow the action a little—not very much, but the Balinese do not care to have it slowed at all. In this case, however, perhaps because they were raising money for a school that the government was unable to give them, perhaps because raids had been few recently, perhaps, as I gathered from subsequent discussion, there was a notion that the necessary bribes had been paid, they thought they could take a chance on the central square and draw a larger and more enthusiastic crowd without attracting the attention of the law.

They were wrong. In the midst of the third match, with hundreds of people, including, still transparent, myself and my wife, fused into a single body around the ring, a superorganism in the literal sense, a truck full of policemen armed with machine guns roared up. Amid great screeching cries of "pulisi! pulisi!" from the crowd, the policemen jumped out, and, springing into the center of the ring, began to swing their guns around like gangsters in a motion picture, though not going so far as actually to fire them. The superorganism came instantly apart as its components scattered in all directions. People raced down the road, disappeared headfirst over walls, scrambled under platforms, folded themselves behind wicker screens, scuttled up coconut trees. Cocks armed with steel spurs sharp enough to cut off a finger or run a hole through a foot were running wildly around. Everything was dust and panic.

On the established anthropological principle, "When in Rome," my wife and I decided, only slightly less instantaneously than everyone else, that the thing to do was run too. We ran down the main village street, northward, away from where we were living, for we were on that side of the ring. About halfway down another fugitive ducked suddenly into a compound—his own, it turned out—and we, seeing nothing ahead of us but rice fields, open country, and a very high volcano, followed him. As the three of us came tumbling into the courtyard, his wife, who had apparently been through this sort of thing before, whipped out a table, a tablecloth, three chairs, and three cups of tea, and we all, without any explicit communication whatsoever, sat down, commenced to sip tea, and sought to compose ourselves.

A few moments later, one of the policemen marched importantly into the yard, looking for the village chief. (The chief had not only been at the fight, he had arranged it. When the truck drove up he ran to the river, stripped off his sarong, and plunged in so he could say, when at length they found him sitting there pouring water over his head, that he had been away bathing when the whole affair had occurred and was ignorant of it. They did not believe him and fined him three hundred rupiah, which the village raised collectively.) Seeing me and my wife, "White Men," there in the yard, the policeman performed a classic double take. When he found his voice again he asked, approximately, what in the devil did we think we were doing there. Our host of five minutes leaped instantly to our defense, producing an impassioned description of who and what we were, so detailed and so accurate that it was my turn, having barely communicated with a living human being save my landlord and the village chief for more than a week, to be astonished. We had a perfect right to be there, he said, looking the Javanese upstart in the eye. We were American professors; the government had cleared us; we were there to study culture; we were going to write a book to tell Americans about Bali. And we had all been there drinking tea and talking about cultural matters all afternoon and did not know anything about any cockfight. Moreover, we had not seen the village chief all day; he must have gone to town. The policeman retreated in rather total disarray. And, after a decent interval, bewildered but relieved to have survived and stayed out of jail, so did we.

The next morning the village was a completely different world for us. Not only were we no longer invisible, we were suddenly the center of all attention, the object of a great outpouring of warmth, interest, and most especially, amusement. Everyone in the village knew we had fled like everyone else. They asked us about it again and again (I must have told the story, small detail by small detail, fifty times by the end of the day), gently, affectionately, but quite insistently teasing us: "Why didn't you just stand there and tell the police who you were?" "Why didn't you just say you were only watching and not betting?" "Were you really afraid of those little guns?" As always, kinesthetically minded and, even when fleeing for their lives (or, as happened eight years later, surrendering them), the world's most poised people, they gleefully mimicked, also over and over again, our graceless style of running and what they claimed were our panic-stricken facial expressions. But above all, everyone was extremely pleased and even more surprised that we had not simply "pulled out our papers" (they knew about those too) and asserted our Distinguished Visitor status, but had instead demonstrated our solidarity with what were now our covillagers. (What we had actually demonstrated was our cowardice, but there is fellowship in that too.) Even the Brahmana priest, an old, grave, halfway-to-heaven type who because of its associations with the underworld would never be involved, even distantly, in a cockfight, and was difficult to approach even to other Balinese, had us called into his courtyard to ask us about what had happened, chuckling happily at the sheer extraordinariness of it all.

In Bali, to be teased is to be accepted. It was the turning point so far as our relationship to the community was concerned, and we were quite literally "in." The whole village opened up to us, probably more than it ever would have otherwise (I might actually never have gotten to that priest, and our accidental host became one of my best informants), and certainly very much faster. Getting caught, or almost caught, in a vice raid is perhaps not a very generalizable recipe for achieving that mysterious necessity of anthropological field work, rapport, but for me it worked very well. It led to a sudden and unusually complete acceptance into a society extremely difficult for outsiders to penetrate. It gave me the kind of immediate, inside-view grasp of an aspect of "peasant mentality" that anthropologists not fortunate enough to flee headlong with their subjects from armed authorities normally do not get. And, perhaps most important of all, for the other things might have come in other ways, it put me very quickly on to a combination emotional explosion, status war, and philosophical drama of central significance to the society whose inner nature I desired to understand. By the time I left I had spent about as much time looking into cockfights as into witchcraft, irrigation, caste, or marriage.[2]

OF COCKS AND MEN

Bali, mainly because it is Bali, is a well-studied place. Its mythology, art, ritual, social organization, patterns of child rearing, forms of law, even styles of trance, have all been microscopically examined for traces of that elusive substance Jane Belo called "The Balinese Temper."* But, aside from a few passing remarks, the cockfight has barely been noticed, although as a popular obsession of consuming power it is at least as important a revelation of what being a Balinese "is really like" as these more celebrated phenomena.* As much of America surfaces in a ball park, on a golf links, at a race track, or around a poker table, much of Bali surfaces in a cock ring. For it

---

[2] This is one of the most famous stories in anthropology and almost any anthropologist in the United States could tell it to you. Why? First, it is an adventure and a fieldworker's fantasy: Confused anthropologists find empathy and acceptance. Second, it highlights the strength of Geertz's writing style. Not only is it interesting because it is self-revealing, but Geertz was one of the finest writers in anthropology. The essay is full of action and humor. Interestingly, the essay was first published in *Daedalus,* a literary journal; it is aimed at a highly educated audience but not one composed exclusively of anthropologists.

Geertz's self-relevatory style was unusual for ethnographic writing at this time. (See the introduction to Evans-Pritchard's *The Nuer* [1940] for an early example of self-relevatory ethnographic writing.) Although the style is common now, compare his descriptions of the police raid with earlier ethnographic work. Can you imagine Kroeber or Radcliffe-Brown writing an account of their escape from the police? This story is not only fun to read, but Geertz's writing helps a reader visualize the events. He addresses the reader directly: "You have crossed, somehow, some oral or metaphysical shadow line. Though you are not exactly taken as Balinese . . . you are at least regarded as a human being" (1973:413).

The story with which Geertz begins this essay is crucial to his analysis as well. Thanks to a more or less chance occurrence, Geertz gained a particular position in Balinese society that enabled him to make certain kinds of observations. A decade before postmodernism became a serious endeavor within anthropology, Geertz, in this article, discussed his position within Balinese society and the insights it afforded him.

is only apparently cocks that are fighting there. Actually, it is men.

To anyone who has been in Bali any length of time, the deep psychological identification of Balinese men with their cocks is unmistakable. The double entendre here is deliberate. It works in exactly the same way in Balinese as it does in English, even to producing the same tired jokes, strained puns, and uninventive obscenities. Bateson and Mead have even suggested that, in line with the Balinese conception of the body as a set of separately animated parts, cocks are viewed as detachable, self-operating penises, ambulant genitals with a life of their own.* And while I do not have the kind of unconscious material either to confirm or disconfirm this intriguing notion, the fact that they are masculine symbols par excellence is about as indubitable, and to the Balinese about as evident, as the fact that water runs downhill.

The language of everyday moralism is shot through, on the male side of it, with roosterish imagery. *Sabung*, the word for cock (and one which appears in inscriptions as early as A.D. 922), is used metaphorically to mean "hero," "warrior," "champion," "man of parts," "political candidate," "bachelor," "dandy," "lady-killer," or "tough guy." A pompous man whose behavior presumes above his station is compared to a tailless cock who struts about as though he had a large, spectacular one. A desperate man who makes a last, irrational effort to extricate himself from an impossible situation is likened to a dying cock who makes one final lunge at his tormentor to drag him along to a common destruction. A stingy man, who promises much, gives little, and begrudges that, is compared to a cock which, held by the tail, leaps at another without in fact engaging him. A marriageable young man still shy with the opposite sex or someone in a new job anxious to make a good impression is called "a fighting cock caged for the first time."* Court trials, wars, political contests, inheritance disputes, and street arguments are all compared to cockfights.* Even the very island itself is perceived from its shape as a small, proud cock, poised, neck extended, back taut, tail raised, in eternal challenge to large, feckless, shapeless Java.*

But the intimacy of men with their cocks is more than metaphorical. Balinese men, or anyway a large majority of Balinese men, spend an enormous amount of time with their favorites, grooming them, feeding them, discussing them, trying them out against one another, or just gazing at them with a mixture of rapt admiration and dreamy self-absorption. Whenever you see a group of Balinese men squatting idly in the council shed or along the road in their hips down, shoulders forward, knees up fashion, half or more of them will have a rooster in his hands, holding it between his thighs, bouncing it gently up and down to strengthen its legs, ruffling its feathers with abstract sensuality, pushing it out against a neighbor's rooster to rouse its spirit, withdrawing it toward his loins to calm it again. Now and then, to get a feel for another bird, a man will fiddle this way with someone else's cock for a while, but usually by moving around to squat in place behind it, rather than just having it passed across to him as though it were merely an animal.

In the houseyard, the high-walled enclosures where the people live, fighting cocks are kept in wicker cages, moved frequently about so as to maintain the optimum balance of sun and shade. They are fed a special diet, which varies somewhat according to individual theories but which is mostly maize, sifted for impurities with far more care than it is when mere humans are going to eat it, and offered to the animal kernel by kernel. Red pepper is stuffed down their beaks and up their anuses to give them spirit. They are bathed in the same ceremonial preparation of tepid water, medicinal herbs, flowers, and onions in which infants are bathed, and for a prize cock just about as often. Their combs are cropped, their plumage dressed, their spurs trimmed, and their legs massaged, and they are inspected for flaws with the squinted concentration of a diamond merchant. A man who has a passion for cocks, an enthusiast in the literal sense of the term, can spend most of his life with them, and even those, the overwhelming majority, whose passion though intense has not entirely run away with them, can and do spend what seems not only to an outsider, but also to themselves, an inordinate amount of time with them. "I am cock crazy," my landlord, a quite ordinary *afficionado* by Balinese standards, used to moan as he went to move another cage, give another bath, or conduct another feeding. "We're all cock crazy."

The madness has some less visible dimensions, however, because although it is true that cocks are symbolic expressions or magnifications of their owner's self, the narcissistic male ego writ out in Aesopian terms, they are also expressions—and rather more immediate ones—of what the Balinese regard as the direct inversion, aesthetically, morally, and metaphysically, of human status: animality.

The Balinese revulsion against any behavior regarded as animal-like can hardly be over-stressed. Babies are not allowed to crawl for that reason. Incest, though hardly approved, is a much less horrifying crime than bestiality. (The appropriate punishment for the second is death by drowning, for the first being forced to live like an animal.)* Most demons are represented—in sculpture, dance, ritual, myth—in some real or fantastic animal form. The main puberty rite consists in filing the child's teeth so they will not look like animal fangs. Not only defecation but eating is regarded as a disgusting, almost obscene activity, to be conducted hurriedly and privately, because of its association with animality. Even falling down or any form of clumsiness is considered to be bad for these reasons. Aside from cocks and a few domestic animals—oxen, ducks—of no emotional significance, the Balinese are aversive to animals and treat their large number of dogs not merely callously but with a phobic cruelty. In identifying with his cock, the Balinese man is identifying not just with his ideal self, or even his penis, but also, and at the same time, with what he most fears, hates, and ambivalence being what it is, is fascinated by—"The Powers of Darkness."

The connection of cocks and cockfighting with such Powers, with the animalistic demons that threaten constantly to invade the small, cleared-off space in which the Balinese have so carefully built their lives and devour its inhabitants, is quite explicit. A cockfight, any cockfight, is in the first instance a blood sacrifice offered, with the appropriate chants and oblations, to the demons in order to pacify their ravenous, cannibal hunger. No temple festival should be conducted until one is made. (If it is omitted, someone will inevitably fall into a trance and command with the voice of an angered spirit that the oversight be immediately corrected.) Collective responses to natural evils—illness, crop failure, volcanic eruptions—almost always involve them. And that famous holiday in Bali, "The Day of Silence" (*Njepi*), when everyone sits silent and immobile all day long in order to avoid contact with a sudden influx of demons chased momentarily out of hell, is preceded the previous day by large-scale cockfights (in this case legal) in almost every village on the island.

In the cockfight, man and beast, good and evil, ego and id, the creative power of aroused masculinity and the destructive power of loosened animality fuse in a bloody drama of hatred, cruelty, violence, and death. It is little wonder that when, as is the invariable rule, the owner of the winning cock takes the carcass of the loser—often torn limb from limb by its enraged owner—home to eat, he does so with a mixture of social embarrassment, moral satisfaction, aesthetic disgust, and cannibal joy. Or that a man who has lost an important fight is sometimes driven to wreck his family shrines and curse the gods, an act of metaphysical (and social) suicide. Or that in seeking earthly analogues for heaven and hell the Balinese compare the former to the mood of a man whose cock has just won, the latter to that of a man whose cock has just lost.[3]

---

[3] Although Geertz is attempting a very different kind of symbolic analysis than Freud or Lévi-Strauss, the influence of their work is apparent here. The symbolic link between the fighting birds, genitals, and male status is obviously Freudian. Although Geertz is not a structuralist, the binary constructions—man-beast, good-evil, creation-destruction—are based on Lévi-Strauss' nature-culture dichotomy. The human cultural world is repulsed by the animal-natural world, but the two spheres of existence meet in cocks and the cockfight.

THE FIGHT

Cockfights (*tetadjen; sabungan*) are held in a ring about fifty feet square. Usually they begin toward late afternoon and run three or four hours until sunset. About nine or ten separate matches (*sehet*) comprise a program. Each match is precisely like the others in general pattern: there is no main match, no connection between individual matches, no variation in their format, and each is arranged on a completely ad hoc basis. After a fight has ended and the emotional debris is cleaned away—the bets have been paid, the curses cursed, the carcasses possessed—seven, eight, perhaps even a dozen men slip negligently into the ring with a cock and seek to find there a logical opponent for it. This process, which rarely takes less than ten minutes, and often a good deal longer, is conducted in a very subdued, oblique, even dissembling manner. Those not immediately involved give it at best but disguised, sidelong attention; those who, embarrassedly, are, attempt to pretend somehow that the whole thing is not really happening.[4]

A match made, the other hopefuls retire with the same deliberate indifference, and the selected cocks have their spurs (*tadji*) affixed—razor-sharp, pointed steel swords, four or five inches long. This is a delicate job which only a small proportion of men, a half-dozen or so in most villages, know how to do properly. The man who attaches the spurs also provides them, and if the rooster he assists wins, its owner awards him the spur-leg of the victim. The spurs are affixed by winding a long length of string around the foot of the spur and the leg of the cock. For reasons I shall come to presently, it is done somewhat differently from case to case, and is an obsessively deliberate affair. The lore about spurs is extensive—they are sharpened only at eclipses and the dark of the moon, should be kept out of the sight of women, and so forth. And they are handled, both in use and out, with the same curious combination of fussiness and sensuality the Balinese direct toward ritual objects generally.

The spurs affixed, the two cocks are placed by their handlers (who may or may not be their owners) facing one another in the center of the ring.* A coconut pierced with a small hole is placed in a pail of water, in which it takes about twenty-one seconds to sink, a period known as a *tjeng* and marked at beginning and end by the beating of a slit gong. During these twenty-one seconds the handlers (*pengangkeb*) are not permitted to touch their roosters. If, as sometimes happens, the animals have not fought during this time, they are picked up, fluffed, pulled, prodded, and otherwise insulted, and put back in the center of the ring and the process begins again. Sometimes they refuse to fight at all, or one keeps running away, in which case they are imprisoned together under a wicker cage, which usually gets them engaged.

Most of the time, in any case, the cocks fly almost immediately at one another in a wing-beating, head-thrusting, leg-kicking explosion of animal fury so pure, so absolute, and in its own way so beautiful, as to be almost abstract, a Platonic concept of hate. Within moments one or the other drives home a solid blow with his spur. The handler whose cock has delivered the blow immediately picks it up so that it will not get a return blow, for if he does not the match is likely to end in a mutually mortal tie as the two birds wildly hack each other to pieces. This is particularly true if, as often happens, the spur sticks in its victim's body, for then the aggressor is at the mercy of his wounded foe.

With the birds again in the hands of their handlers, the coconut is now sunk three times after which the cock which has landed the blow must be set down to show that he is firm, a fact he demonstrates by wandering idly around the ring for a coconut sink. The coconut is then sunk twice more and the fight must recommence.

During this interval, slightly over two minutes, the handler of the wounded cock has been

---

[4] Geertz describes the cockfight and patterns of betting that take place in great detail. He attempts to re-create the context in which the action takes place in order that the reader may share, as much as possible, in the context in which Balinese cultural meaning is created. Geertz describes this form of analysis as "thick description" (1973:6), which he identifies as uncovering the layers of meaning surrounding an event.

working frantically over it, like a trainer patching a mauled boxer between rounds, to get it in shape for a last, desperate try for victory. He blows in its mouth, putting the whole chicken head in his own mouth and sucking and blowing, fluffs it, stuffs its wounds with various sorts of medicines, and generally tries anything he can think of to arouse the last ounce of spirit which may be hidden somewhere within it. By the time he is forced to put it back down he is usually drenched in chicken blood, but, as in prize fighting, a good handler is worth his weight in gold. Some of them can virtually make the dead walk, at least long enough for the second and final round.

In the climactic battle (if there is one; sometimes the wounded cock simply expires in the handler's hands or immediately as it is placed down again), the cock who landed the first blow usually proceeds to finish off his weakened opponent. But this is far from an inevitable outcome, for if a cock can walk, he can fight, and if he can fight, he can kill, and what counts is which cock expires first. If the wounded one can get a stab in and stagger on until the other drops, he is the official winner, even if he himself topples over an instant later.

Surrounding all this melodrama—which the crowd packed tight around the ring follows in near silence, moving their bodies in kinesthetic sympathy with the movement of the animals, cheering their champions on with wordless hand motions, shiftings of the shoulders, turnings of the head, falling back en masse as the cock with the murderous spurs careens toward one side of the ring (it is said that spectators sometimes lose eyes and fingers from being too attentive), surging forward again as they glance off toward another—is a vast body of extraordinarily elaborate and precisely detailed rules.[5]

These rules, together with the developed lore of cocks and cockfighting which accompanies them, are written down in palm-leaf manuscripts (*lontar; rontal*) passed on from generation to gen-

eration as part of the general legal and cultural tradition of the villages. At a fight, the umpire (*saja komong; djuru kembar*)—the man who manages the coconut—is in charge of their application and his authority is absolute. I have never seen an umpire's judgment questioned on any subject, even by the more despondent losers, nor have I ever heard, even in private, a charge of unfairness directed against one, or, for that matter, complaints about umpires in general. Only exceptionally well trusted, solid, and, given the complexity of the code, knowledgeable citizens perform this job, and in fact men will bring their cocks only to fights presided over by such men. It is also the umpire to whom accusations of cheating, which, though rare in the extreme, occasionally arise, are referred; and it is he who in the not infrequent cases where the cocks expire virtually together decides which (if either, for, though the Balinese do not care for such an outcome, there can be ties) went first. Likened to a judge, a king, a priest, and a policeman, he is all of these, and under his assured direction the animal passion of the fight proceeds within the civic certainty of the law. In the dozens of cockfights I saw in Bali, I never once saw an altercation about rules. Indeed, I never saw an open altercation, other than those between cocks, at all.

This crosswise doubleness of an event which, taken as a fact of nature, is rage untrammeled and, taken as a fact of culture, is form perfected, defines the cockfight as a sociological entity. A cockfight is what, searching for a name for something not vertebrate enough to be called a group and not structureless enough to be called a crowd, Erving Goffman has called a "focused gathering"— a set of persons engrossed in a common flow of activity and relating to one another in terms of that flow.* Such gatherings meet and disperse; the participants in them fluctuate; the activity that focuses them is discrete—a particulate process that reoccurs rather than a continuous one that endures. They take their form from the situation

---

[5] One criticism of Geertz's work is that his interpretation is intuitive, making it difficult for others to replicate. Indeed, one could say that the power of Geertz's analysis is based on his compelling writing style. For example, you may not have noticed that Geertz is not presenting us with a description of one cockfight but rather with a literary construct based on his experience of at least fifty-seven matches.

that evokes them, the floor on which they are placed, as Goffman puts it; but it is a form, and an articulate one, nonetheless. For the situation, the floor is itself created, in jury deliberations, surgical operations, block meetings, sit-ins, cockfights, by the cultural preoccupations—here, as we shall see, the celebration of status rivalry—which not only specify the focus but, assembling actors and arranging scenery, bring it actually into being.[6]

In classical times (that is to say, prior to the Dutch invasion of 1908), when there were no bureaucrats around to improve popular morality, the staging of a cockfight was an explicitly societal matter. Bringing a cock to an important fight was, for an adult male, a compulsory duty of citizenship; taxation of fights, which were usually held on market day, was a major source of public revenue; patronage of the art was [the] stated responsibility of princes; and the cock ring, or *wantilan*, stood in the center of the village near those other monuments of Balinese civility—the council house, the origin temple, the marketplace, the signal tower, and the banyan tree. Today, a few special occasions aside, the newer rectitude makes so open a statement of the connection between the excitements of collective life and those of blood sport impossible, but, less directly expressed, the connection itself remains intimate and intact. To expose it, however, it is necessary to turn to the aspect of cockfighting around which all the others pivot, and through which they exercise their force, an aspect I have thus far studiously ignored. I mean, of course, the gambling.

[We have omitted a 2,200-word section with seven footnotes called "Odds and Even Money," in which

Geertz gives a detailed explanation of cockfight betting patterns. He identifies two types of bets in a cockfight, the main bet between the principals who own the fighting cocks and peripheral bets between members of the audience. The principal bets are large collective wagers involving coalitions of bettors; they are quietly arranged with the umpire in the center of the ring. The second type of bet is typically small and is arranged impulsively by individuals shouting back and forth across the ring.

Because center bets are always for even money, participants typically arrange fair matches. The more evenly matched the cocks, the higher the center bets. The side bets vary wildly according to the odds individual bettors are willing to give. The larger the center bet, the more frenzied the side betting. These fights are considered more interesting because more is at stake in them. In a high-stakes fight, men are risking money and social prestige, as well as valuable fighting cocks. When a match ends, all bets are immediately paid.

We return to Geertz's narrative at the last paragraph in the section, where he introduces the notion of "depth" in the analysis of culture.]

The Balinese attempt to create an interesting, if you will, "deep," match by making the center bet as large as possible so that the cocks matched will be as equal and as fine as possible, and the outcome, thus, as unpredictable as possible.[7] They do not always succeed. Nearly half the matches are relatively trivial, relatively uninteresting—in my borrowed terminology, "shallow"—affairs. But that fact no more argues against my interpretation than the fact that most painters, poets, and playwrights are mediocre argues against the view that artistic effort is directed toward profundity

---

[6] In this paragraph, you get a sense of Geertz's definition of culture: a shared code of meaning that is acted out publicly. Unlike the ethnoscientists, Geertz believes that culture is not a mental model, but exists between people, created by their social actions. In addition, Geertz was interested in the sociology of religion. His reference to Erving Goffman (1922–1982), an important sociologist of the 1960s, gives a clue to the sociological influence on his work. Goffman viewed individual actions as performances and was concerned with delineating the rules governing nonverbal in-

teraction. You can see Goffman's influence in these paragraphs, as Geertz describes people's actions at cockfights.

[7] For Geertz, the secret of decoding the cockfight lies in viewing it as a representation of Balinese society. The long discussion of cockfight betting in the next section leads to a discussion of how betting patterns recapitulate the divisions of the larger society. This insight hearkens back to Durkheim and the structural functionalists, but Geertz does not use his analysis for their purposes.

and, with a certain frequency, approximates it. The image of artistic technique is indeed exact: the center bet is a means, a device, for creating "interesting," "deep" matches, *not* the reason, or at least not the main reason, *why* they are interesting, the source of their fascination, the substance of their depth. The question of why such matches are interesting—indeed, for the Balinese, exquisitely absorbing—takes us out of the realm of formal concerns into more broadly sociological and social-psychological ones, and to a less purely economic idea of what "depth" in gaming amounts to.*

PLAYING WITH FIRE

Bentham's concept of "deep play" is found in his *The Theory of Legislation.** By it he means play in which the stakes are so high that it is, from his utilitarian standpoint, irrational for men to engage in it at all. If a man whose fortune is a thousand pounds (or ringgits) wages five hundred of it on an even bet, the marginal utility of the pound he stands to win is clearly less than the marginal disutility of the one he stands to lose. In genuine deep play, this is the case for both parties. They are both in over their heads. Having come together in search of pleasure they have entered into a relationship which will bring the participants, considered collectively, net pain rather than net pleasure. Bentham's conclusion was, therefore, that deep play was immoral from first principles and, a typical step for him, should be prevented legally.[8]

But more interesting than the ethical problem, at least for our concerns here, is that despite the logical force of Bentham's analysis men do engage in such play, both passionately and often, and even in the face of law's revenge. For Bentham and those who think as he does (nowadays mainly lawyers, economists, and a few psychiatrists), the explanation is, as I have said, that such men are irrational—addicts, fetishists, children, fools, savages, who need only to be protected against themselves. But for the Balinese, though naturally they do not formulate it in so many words, the explanation lies in the fact that in such play, money is less a measure of utility, had or expected, than it is a symbol of moral import, perceived or imposed.

It is, in fact, in shallow games, ones in which smaller amounts of money are involved, that increments and decrements of cash are more nearly synonyms for utility and disutility, in the ordinary, unexpanded sense—for pleasure and pain, happiness and unhappiness. In deep ones, where the amounts of money are great, much more is at stake than material gain: namely, esteem, honor, dignity, respect—in a word, though in Bali a profoundly freighted word, status.* It is at stake symbolically, for (a few cases of ruined addict gamblers aside) no one's status is actually altered by the outcome of a cockfight; it is only, and that momentarily, affirmed or insulted. But for the Balinese, for whom nothing is more pleasurable than an affront obliquely delivered or more painful than one obliquely received—particularly when mutual acquaintances, undeceived by surfaces, are watching—such appraisive drama is deep indeed.

This, I must stress immediately, is *not* to say that the money does not matter, or that the Balinese is no more concerned about losing five hundred ringgits than fifteen. Such a conclusion would be absurd. It is because money *does*,

---

[8] Jeremy Bentham (1748–1832) was an English philosopher and social theorist best known for his doctrine of Utilitarianism, the principles of which are outlined in his 1789 book *An Introduction to the Principles of Morals and Legislation*. Utilitarianism is the belief that the aim of society should be to create the greatest level of happiness for the greatest number of people. Bentham believed that correct conduct was determined by the balance of pleasure over pain that a given act would produce, and that pain and pleasure could be quantitatively measured. Thus legislative decision making could be reduced to a quasimathematical science. Among Bentham's best known intellectual followers were John Stuart Mill (1806–1873) and Herbert Spencer.

When Bentham died, his body was embalmed and his head removed and replaced with a wax replica. His corpse was then dressed and placed on display at University College, London, where it remains to this day.

in this hardly unmaterialistic society, matter and matter very much that the more of it one risks, the more of a lot of other things, such as one's pride, one's poise, one's dispassion, one's masculinity, one also risks, again only momentarily but again very publicly as well. In deep cockfights an owner and his collaborators, and, as we shall see, to a lesser but still quite real extent also their backers on the outside, put their money where their status is.

It is in large part *because* the marginal disutility of loss is so great at the higher levels of betting that to engage in such betting is to lay one's public self, allusively and metaphorically, through the medium of one's cock, on the line. And though to a Benthamite this might seem merely to increase the irrationality of the enterprise that much further, to the Balinese what it mainly increases is the meaningfulness of it all. And as (to follow Weber[9] rather than Bentham) the imposition of meaning on life is the major end and primary condition of human existence, that access of significance more than compensates for the economic costs involved.* Actually, given the even-money quality of the larger matches, important changes in material fortune among those who regularly participate in them seem virtually nonexistent, because matters more or less even out over the long run. It is, actually, in the smaller, shallow fights, where one finds the handful of more pure, addict-type gamblers involved—those who *are* in it mainly for the money—that "real" changes in social position, largely downward, are affected. Men of this sort, plungers, are highly dispraised by "true cockfighters" as fools who do not understand what the sport is all about, vulgarians who simply miss the point of it all. They are, these addicts, regarded as fair game for the genuine enthusiasts, those who do understand, to take a little money away from—something that is easy enough to do by luring them, through the force of their greed, into irrational bets on mismatched cocks. Most of them do indeed manage to ruin themselves in a remarkably short time,

but there always seems to be one or two of them around, pawning their land and selling their clothes in order to bet, at any particular time.*

This graduated correlation of "status gambling" with deeper fights and, inversely, "money gambling" with shallower ones is in fact quite general. Bettors themselves form a sociomoral hierarchy in these terms. As noted earlier, at most cockfights there are, around the very edges of the cockfight area, a large number of mindless, sheer-chance-type gambling games (roulette, dice throw, coin-spin, pea-under-the-shell) operated by concessionaires. Only women, children, adolescents, and various other sorts of people who do not (or not yet) fight cocks—the extremely poor, the socially despised, the personally idiosyncratic—play at these games, at, of course, penny ante levels. Cockfighting men would be ashamed to go anywhere near them. Slightly above these people in standing are those who though they do not themselves fight cocks, bet on the smaller matches around the edges. Next, there are those who fight cocks in small, or occasionally medium matches, but have not the status to join in the large ones, though they may bet from time to time on the side in those. And finally, there are those, the really substantial members of the community, the solid citizenry around whom local life revolves, who fight in the larger fights and bet on them around the side. The focusing element in these focused gatherings, these men generally dominate and define the sport as they dominate and define the society. When a Balinese male talks, in that almost venerative way, about "the true cockfighter," the *bebatoh* ("bettor") or *djuru kurung* ("cage keeper"), it is this sort of person, not those who bring the mentality of the pea-and-shell game into the quite different, inappropriate context of the cockfight, the driven gambler (*potét*, a word which has the secondary meaning of thief or reprobate), and the wistful hanger-on, that they mean. For such a man, what is really going on in a match is something rather closer to an

[9] Geertz claims Max Weber as one of the major influences in his intellectual development. He was first exposed to Weber by one of his professors, Talcott Parsons (1902–1979), while a graduate student at Harvard University. For more information on Geertz's career and academic life, see Handler's 1991 interview with Geertz in *Current Anthropology*.

affaire d'honneur (though, with the Balinese talent for practical fantasy, the blood that is spilled is only figuratively human) than to the stupid, mechanical crank of a slot machine.[10]

What makes Balinese cockfighting deep is thus not money in itself, but what, the more of it that is involved the more so, money causes to happen: the migration of the Balinese status hierarchy into the body of the cockfight.[11] Psychologically an Aesopian representation of the ideal/demonic, rather narcissistic, male self, sociologically it is an equally Aesopian representation of the complex fields of tension set up by the controlled, muted, ceremonial, but for all that deeply felt, interaction of those selves in the context of everyday life. The cocks may be surrogates for their owners' personalities, animal mirrors of psychic form, but the cockfight is—or more exactly, deliberately is made to be—a simulation of the social matrix, the involved system of cross-cutting, overlapping, highly corporate groups—villages, kingroups, irrigation societies, temple congregations, "castes"—in which its devotees live.* And as prestige, the necessity to affirm it, defend it, celebrate it, justify it, and just plain bask in it (but not, given the strongly ascriptive character of Balinese stratification, to seek it), is perhaps the central driving force in the society, so also—ambulant penises, blood sacrifices, and monetary exchanges aside—is it of the cockfight. This apparent amusement and seeming sport is, to take another phrase from Erving Goffman, "a status bloodbath."*

The easiest way to make this clear, and at least to some degree to demonstrate it, is to invoke the village whose cockfighting activities I observed the closest—the one in which the raid occurred and from which my statistical data are taken.

Like all Balinese villages, this one—Tihingan, in the Klungkung region of southeast Bali—is intricately organized, a labyrinth of alliances and oppositions. But, unlike many, two sorts of corporate groups, which are also status groups, particularly stand out, and we may concentrate on them, in a part-for-whole way, without undue distortion.

First, the village is dominated by four large, patrilineal, partly endogamous descent groups which are constantly vying with one another and form the major factions in the village. Sometimes they group two and two, or rather the two larger ones versus the two smaller ones plus all the unaffiliated people; sometimes they operate independently. There are also subfactions within them, subfactions within the subfactions, and so on to rather fine levels of distinction. And second, there is the village itself, almost entirely endogamous, which is opposed to all the other villages round about in its cockfight circuit (which, as explained, is the market region), but which also forms alliances with certain of these neighbors against certain others in various supravillage political and social contexts. The exact situation is thus, as everywhere in Bali, quite distinctive; but the general pattern of a tiered hierarchy of status rivalries between highly corporate but various based groupings (and, thus, between the members of them) is entirely general.

Consider, then, as support of the general thesis that the cockfight, and especially the deep cockfight, is fundamentally a dramatization of status concerns, the following facts, which to avoid extended ethnographic description I shall simply pronounce to be facts though the concrete evidence, examples, statements, and numbers that could be brought to bear in support of them, is both extensive and unmistakable:[12]

1. A man virtually never bets against a cock owned by a member of his own kingroup. Usually he will feel obliged to bet for it, the more so the closer the kin tie and the deeper the fight. If he is

---

[10] The cockfight is not about winning or losing money; it is a simulation of the social interactions between various groups in the community. Geertz contends that this is why the matches are so "deep" to the Balinese.

[11] For Geertz, the cockfight is a symbolic key to Balinese personality because it is the ritual through which the Balinese express their values. Geertz uses the phrase the "migration of the Balinese status hierarchy into the body of the cockfight" to characterize his idea that one can observe the stratification of Balinese society in the organization of people within and around the cockfight area.

[12] Geertz's discussion is reminiscent of Mauss' analysis of the potlatch (see essay 6). The potlatch was a competition for status between individuals representing their kin groups and communities. In the same way, the Balinese cockfight is a competition for status, with men always

certain in his mind that it will not win, he may just not bet at all, particularly if it is only a second cousin's bird or if the fight is a shallow one. But as a rule he will feel he must support it and, in deep games, nearly always does. Thus the great majority of the people calling "five" or "speckled" so demonstratively are expressing their allegiance to their kinsman, not their evaluation of his bird, their understanding of probability theory, or even their hopes of unearned income.

2. This principle is extended logically. If your kingroup is not involved, you will support an allied kingroup against an unallied one in the same way, and so on through the very involved networks of alliances which, as I say, make up this, as any other, Balinese village.

3. So, too, for the village as a whole. If an outsider cock is fighting any cock from your village, you will tend to support the local one. If, what is a rarer circumstance but occurs every now and then, a cock from outside your cockfight circuit is fighting one inside it, you will also tend to support the "home bird."

4. Cocks which come from any distance are almost always favorites, for the theory is the man would not have dared to bring it if it was not a good cock, the more so the further he has come. His followers are, of course, obliged to support him, and when the more grand-scale legal cockfights are held (on holidays, and so on) the people of the village take what they regard to be the best cocks in the village, regardless of ownership, and go off to support them, although they will almost certainly have to give odds on them and to

make large bets to show that they are not a cheapskate village. Actually, such "away games," though infrequent, tend to mend the ruptures between village members that the constantly occurring "home games," where village factions are opposed rather than united, exacerbate.

5. Almost all matches are sociologically relevant. You seldom get two outsider cocks fighting, or two cocks with no particular group backing, or with group backing which is mutually unrelated in any clear way. When you do get them, the game is very shallow, betting very slow, and the whole thing very dull, with no one save the immediate principals and an addict gambler or two at all interested.

6. By the same token, you rarely get two cocks from the same group, even more rarely from the same subfaction, and virtually never from the same sub-subfaction (which would be in most cases one extended family) fighting. Similarly, in outside village fights two members of the village will rarely fight against one another, even though, as bitter rivals, they would do so with enthusiasm on their home grounds.

7. On the individual level, people involved in an institutionalized hostility relationship, called *puik,* in which they do not speak or otherwise have anything to do with each other (the causes of this formal breaking of relations are many: wife-capture, inheritance arguments, political differences) will bet very heavily, sometimes almost maniacally, against one another in what is a frank and direct attack on the very masculinity, the ultimate ground of his status, of the opponent.[13]

---

betting on the birds owned by kinsmen or men of their communities who are competing with people from other communities. A major difference between Geertz and Mauss, however, is that Mauss thought the potlatch was a real competition for status—a defeat in a potlatch meant the loss of a position of leadership. Geertz's point is that the cockfight does not really change anything. In fact, status in Bali is ascribed and cannot change. Although Geertz's analysis is interpretive, the discussion of betting and kin are structural-functionalist in tone. Durkheim or Radcliffe-Brown would have said that the function of the cockfight is to create and reinforce solidarity between these competing kin groups.

[13] The discussion of *puik* is a good place to make another point about Geertz's analysis. Because his work is interpretive, Geertz is often criticized by anthropologists who work in materialist traditions. However, some of Geertz's earlier work was concerned with economics, religion, and ecology. See, for example, his books *Agricultural Involution: The Processes of Ecological Change in Indonesia* (1963a) and *Peddlers and Princes: Social Development and Economic Change in Two Indonesian Towns* (1963b). Here, in one of his most famous works, Geertz does not rule out materialist interpretations; he just is not interested in them. Geertz repeatedly insists that nothing really happens at a cockfight—the conflicts, alliances, wins, and

8. The center bet coalition is, in all but the shallowest games, *always* made up by structural allies—no "outside money" is involved. What is "outside" depends upon the context, of course, but given it, no outside money is mixed in with the main bet; if the principals cannot raise it, it is not made. The center bet, again especially in deeper games, is thus the most direct and open expression of social opposition, which is one of the reasons why both it and matchmaking are surrounded by such an air of unease, furtiveness, embarrassment, and so on.

9. The rule about borrowing money—that you may borrow *for* a bet but not *in* one—stems (and the Balinese are quite conscious of this) from similar considerations: you are never at the *economic* mercy of your enemy that way. Gambling debts, which can get quite large on a rather short-term basis, are always to friends, never to enemies, structurally speaking.

10. When two cocks are structurally irrelevant or neutral so far as *you* are concerned (though, as mentioned, they almost never are to each other) you do not even ask a relative or a friend whom he is betting on, because if you know how he is betting and he knows you know, and you go the other way, it will lead to strain. This rule is explicit and rigid; fairly elaborate, even rather artificial precautions are taken to avoid breaking it. At the very least you must pretend not to notice what he is doing, and he what you are doing.

11. There is a special word for betting against the grain, which is also the word for "pardon me" (*mpura*). It is considered a bad thing to do, though if the center bet is small it is sometimes all right as long as you do not do it too often. But the larger the bet and the more frequently you do it, the more the "pardon me" tack will lead to social disruption.

12. In fact, the institutionalized hostility relation, *puik*, is often formally initiated (though its causes always lie elsewhere) by such a "pardon me" bet in a deep fight, putting the symbolic fat in the fire. Similarly, the end of such a relationship and resumption of normal social intercourse is often signalized (but, again, not actually brought about) by one or the other of the enemies supporting the other's bird.

13. In sticky, cross-loyalty situations, of which in this extraordinarily complex social system there are of course many, where a man is caught between two more or less equally balanced loyalties, he tends to wander off for a cup of coffee or something to avoid having to bet, a form of behavior reminiscent of that of American voters in similar situations.*

14. The people involved in the center bet are, especially in deep fights, virtually always leading members of their group—kinship, village, or whatever. Further, those who bet on the side (including these people) are, as I have already remarked, the more established members of the village—the solid citizens. Cockfighting is for those who are involved in the everyday politics of prestige as well, not for youth, women, subordinates, and so forth.

15. So far as money is concerned, the explicitly expressed attitude toward it is that it is a secondary matter. It is not, as I have said, of no importance; Balinese are no happier to lose several weeks' income than anyone else. But they mainly look on the monetary aspects of the cockfight as self-balancing, a matter of just moving money around, circulating it among a fairly well-defined group of serious cockfighters. The really important wins and losses are seen mostly in other terms, and the general attitude toward wagering is not any hope of cleaning up, of making a killing (addict gamblers again excepted), but that of the horse-player's prayer: "Oh, God, please let me break even." In prestige terms, however, you do not want to break even, but, in a momentary, punctuate sort of way, win utterly. The talk (which goes on all the time) is about

---

losses are all symbolic of things that happen elsewhere. *Puik,* for example, are not caused by cockfight bets; rather, they signal deeper-level conflicts. In the cockfight, all action is symbolic. The real causes lie elsewhere, presumably in material circumstances.

fights against such-and-such a cock of So-and-So which your cock demolished, not on how much you won, a fact people, even for large bets, rarely remember for any length of time, though they will remember the day they did in Pan Loh's finest cock for years.

16. You must bet on cocks of your own group aside from mere loyalty considerations, for if you do not people generally will say, "What! Is he too proud for the likes of us? Does he have to go to Java or Den Pasar [the capital town] to bet, he is such an important man?" Thus there is a general pressure to bet not only to show that you are important locally, but that you are not so important that you look down on everyone else as unfit even to be rivals. Similarly, home team people must bet against outside cocks or the outsiders will accuse them—a serious charge—of just collecting entry fees and not really being interested in cockfighting, as well as again being arrogant and insulting.

17. Finally, the Balinese peasants themselves are quite aware of all this and can and, at least to an ethnographer, do state most of it in approximately the same terms as I have. Fighting cocks, almost every Balinese I have ever discussed the subject with has said, is like playing with fire only not getting burned. You activate village and kingroup rivalries and hostilities, but in "play" form, coming dangerously and entrancingly close to the expression of open and direct interpersonal and intergroup aggression (something which, again, almost never happens in the normal course of ordinary life), but not quite, because, after all, it is "only a cockfight."

More observations of this sort could be advanced, but perhaps the general point is, if not made, at least well-delineated, and the whole argument thus far can be usefully summarized in a formal paradigm:

The more a match is . . .

1. Between near status equals (and/or personal enemies)
2. Between high status individuals

. . . the deeper the match.

The deeper the match . . .

1. The closer the identification of cock and man (or, more properly, the deeper the match the more the man will advance his best, most closely-identified-with cock).
2. The finer the cocks involved and the more exactly they will be matched.
3. The greater the emotion that will be involved and the more the general absorption in the match.
4. The higher the individual bets center and outside, the shorter the outside bet odds will tend to be, and the more betting there will be overall.
5. The less an "economic" and the more a "status" view of gaming will be involved, and the "solider" the citizens who will be gaming.*

Inverse arguments hold for the shallower the fight, culminating, in a reversed-signs sense, in the coin-spinning and dice-throwing amusements. For deep fights there are no absolute upper limits, though there are of course practical ones, and there are a great many legend like tales of great Duel-in-the-Sun combats between lords and princes in classical times (for cockfighting has always been as much an elite concern as a popular one), far deeper than anything anyone, even aristocrats, could produce today anywhere in Bali.

Indeed, one of the great culture heroes of Bali is a prince, called after his passion for the sport, "The Cockfighter," who happened to be away at a very deep cockfight with a neighboring prince when the whole of his family—father, brothers, wives, sisters—were assassinated by commoner usurpers. Thus spared, he returned to dispatch the upstart, regain the throne, reconstitute the Balinese high tradition, and build its most powerful, glorious, and prosperous state. Along with everything else that the Balinese see in fighting cocks—themselves, their social order, abstract hatred, masculinity, demonic power—they also see the archetype of status virtue, the arrogant, resolute, honor-mad player with real fire, the *ksatria* prince.*

FEATHERS, BLOOD, CROWDS, AND MONEY

"Poetry makes nothing happen," Auden says in his elegy of Yeats, "it survives in the valley of its saying . . . a way of happening, a mouth."[14] The cockfight too, in this colloquial sense, makes nothing happen. Men go on allegorically humiliating one another and being allegorically humiliated by one another, day after day, glorying quietly in the experience if they have triumphed, crushed only slightly more openly by it if they have not. *But no one's status really changes.* You cannot ascend the status ladder by winning cockfights; you cannot, as an individual, really ascend it at all. Nor can you descend it that way.* All you can do is enjoy and savor, or suffer and withstand, the concocted sensation of drastic and momentary movement along an aesthetic semblance of that ladder, a kind of behind-the-mirror status jump which has the look of mobility without its actuality.[15]

Like any art form—for that, finally, is what we are dealing with—the cockfight renders ordinary, everyday experience comprehensible by presenting it in terms of acts and objects which have had their practical consequences removed and been reduced (or, if you prefer, raised) to the level of sheer appearances, where their meaning can be more powerfully articulated and more exactly perceived. The cockfight is "really real" only to the cocks—it does not kill anyone, castrate anyone, reduce anyone to animal status, alter the hierarchical relations among people, or refashion the hierarchy; it does not even redistribute income in any significant way. What it does is what, for other peoples with other temperaments and other conventions, *Lear* and *Crime and Punishment* do; it catches up these themes—death, masculinity, rage, pride, loss, beneficence, chance—and, or-

dering them into an encompassing structure, presents them in such a way as to throw into relief a particular view of their essential nature. It puts a construction on them, makes them, to those historically positioned to appreciate the construction, meaningful—visible, tangible, graspable—"real," in an ideational sense. An image, fiction, a model, a metaphor, the cockfight is a means of expression; its function is neither to assuage social passions nor to heighten them (though, in its playing-with-fire way it does a bit of both), but, in a medium of feathers, blood, crowds, and money, to display them.

The question of how it is that we perceive qualities in things—paintings, books, melodies, plays—that we do not feel we can assert literally to be there has come, in recent years, into the very center of aesthetic theory.* Neither the sentiments of the artist, which remain his, nor those of the audience, which remain theirs, can account for the agitation of one painting or the serenity of another. We attribute grandeur, wit, despair, exuberance to strings of sounds; lightness, energy, violence, fluidity to blocks of stone. Novels are said to have strength, buildings eloquence, plays momentum, ballets repose. In this realm of eccentric predicates, to say that the cockfight, in its perfected cases at least, is "disquietful" does not seem at all unnatural, merely, as I have just denied it practical consequence, somewhat puzzling.

The disquietfulness arises, "somehow," out of a conjunction of three attributes of the fight: its immediate dramatic shape; its metaphoric content; and its social context. A cultural figure against a social ground, the fight is at once a convulsive surge of animal hatred, a mock war of symbolical selves, and a formal simulation of status tensions, and its aesthetic power derives from its capacity to force together these diverse realities.

---

[14] W. H. Auden (1907–1973) was a British-born American poet. William Butler Yeats (1865–1939) was an Irish poet and nationalist.

[15] In a 1991 interview (Handler 1991), Geertz stated that a weakness of anthropology before the 1960s was that anthropologists read only other anthropologists. His point was that intellectual development in anthropology is

based on knowledge in a wide range of fields. As you read, look at the diversity of literature that Geertz ties into his work: Balinese sources, poetry, sociology, psychology, mythology, art, and philosophy, to name just a few, all have a place in his thought. Conversely, Geertz is one of the few anthropological theorists widely read by scholars of literature and history.

The reason it is disquietful is not that it has material effects (it has some, but they are minor); the reason that it is disquietful is that, joining pride to selfhood, selfhood to cocks, and cocks to destruction, it brings to imaginative realization a dimension of Balinese experience normally well-obscured from view. The transfer of a sense of gravity into what is in itself a rather blank and unvarious spectacle, a commotion of beating wings and throbbing legs, is effected by interpreting it as expressive of something unsettling in the way its authors and audience live, or, even more ominously, what they are.[16]

As a dramatic shape, the fight displays a characteristic that does not seem so remarkable until one realizes that it does not have to be there: a radically atomistical structure.* Each match is a world unto itself, a particulate burst of form. There is the matchmaking, there is the betting, there is the fight, there is the result—utter triumph and utter defeat—and there is the hurried, embarrassed passing of money. The loser is not consoled. People drift away from him, look around him, leave him to assimilate his momentary descent into nonbeing, reset his face, and return, scarless and intact, to the fray. Nor are winners congratulated, or events rehashed; once a match is ended the crowd's attention turns totally to the next, with no looking back. A shadow of the experience no doubt remains with the principals, perhaps even with some of the witnesses of a deep fight, as it remains with us when we leave the theater after seeing a powerful play well performed; but it quite soon fades to become at most a schematic memory—a diffuse glow or an abstract shudder—and usually not even that. Any

expressive form lives only in its own present—the one it itself creates. But, here, that present is severed into a string of flashes, some more bright than others, but all of them disconnected, aesthetic quanta. Whatever the cockfight says, it says in spurts.

But, as I have argued lengthily elsewhere, the Balinese live in spurts.* Their life, as they arrange it and perceive it, is less a flow, a directional movement out of the past, through the present, toward the future than an on-off pulsation of meaning and vacuity, an arrhythmic alternation of short periods when "something" (that is, something significant) is happening, and equally short ones where "nothing" (that is, nothing much) is—between what they themselves call "full" and "empty" times, or, in another idiom, "junctures" and "holes." In focusing activity down to a burning-glass dot, the cockfight is merely being Balinese in the same way in which everything from the monadic encounters of everyday life, through the clanging pointillism of *gamelan*[17] music, to the visiting-day-of-the-gods temple celebrations are. It is not an imitation of the punctuateness of Balinese social life, nor a depiction of it, nor even an expression of it; it is an example of it, carefully prepared.*[18]

If one dimension of the cockfight's structure, its lack of temporal directionality, makes it seem a typical segment of the general social life, however, the other, its flat-out, head-to-head (or spur-to-spur) aggressiveness, makes it seem a contradiction, a reversal, even a subversion of it. In the normal course of things, the Balinese are shy to the point of obsessiveness of open conflict. Oblique, cautious, subdued, controlled, masters

---

[16] Geertz views culture as shared codes of meaning that are publicly acted out, which makes his analysis a method of dramatic interpretation. The cockfight is like a play the Balinese perform for themselves, and its importance is artistic. Geertz says it has "aesthetic power" because it forces layers of significance, what he calls "diverse realities," together. It expresses what the Balinese are in a way that is "normally well obscured from view."

[17] *Gamelan* is a type of Southeast Asian music using chimes and gongs.

[18] Geertz has led us back from the details of the cockfight to his definition of culture. He stresses that culture does not exist apart from individuals; instead, it is created in people's interpretations of events around them and bound up in public symbols and communication (Applebaum 1987:485). Here he says the cockfight is not a depiction, expression, or example of Balinese life; rather, it *is* Balinese life.

of indirection and dissimulation—what they call *alus,* "polished," "smooth"—they rarely face what they can turn away from, rarely resist what they can evade. But here they portray themselves as wild and murderous, with manic explosions of instinctual cruelty. A powerful rendering of life as the Balinese most deeply do not want it (to adapt a phrase Frye has used of Gloucester's blinding)[19] is set in the context of a sample of it as they do in fact have it.* And, because the context suggests that the rendering, if less than a straightforward description, is nonetheless more than an idle fancy; it is here that the disquietfulness—the disquietfulness of the *fight,* not (or, anyway, not necessarily) its patrons, who seem in fact rather thoroughly to enjoy it—emerges. The slaughter in the cock ring is not a depiction of how things literally are among men, but, what is almost worse, of how, from a particular angle, they imaginatively are.*

The angle, of course, is stratificatory. What, as we have already seen, the cockfight talks most forcibly about is status relationships, and what it says about them is that they are matters of life and death. That prestige is a profoundly serious business is apparent everywhere one looks in Bali—in the village, the family, the economy, the state. A peculiar fusion of Polynesian title ranks and Hindu castes, the hierarchy of pride is the moral backbone of the society. But only in the cockfight are the sentiments upon which that hierarchy rests revealed in their natural colors. Enveloped elsewhere in a haze of etiquette, a thick cloud of euphemism and ceremony, gesture and allusion, they are here expressed in only the thinnest disguise of an animal mask, a mask which in fact demonstrates them far more effectively than it conceals them. Jealousy is as much a part of Bali as poise, envy as grace, brutality as charm;

but without the cockfight the Balinese would have a much less certain understanding of them, which is, presumably, why they value it so highly.

Any expressive form works (when it works) by disarranging semantic contexts in such a way that properties conventionally ascribed to certain things are unconventionally ascribed to others, which are then seen actually to possess them. To call the wind a cripple, as Stevens does, to fix tone and manipulate timbre, as Schoenberg does, or, closer to our case, to picture an art critic as a dissolute bear, as Hogarth does, is to cross conceptual wires;[20] the established conjunctions between objects and their qualities are altered, and phenomena—fall weather, melodic shape, or cultural journalism—are clothed in signifiers which normally point to other referents.* Similarly, to connect—and connect, and connect—the collision of roosters with the divisiveness of status is to invite a transfer of perceptions from the former to the latter, a transfer which is at once a description and a judgment. (Logically, the transfer could, of course, as well go the other way; but, like most of the rest of us, the Balinese are a great deal more interested in understanding men than they are in understanding cocks.)

What sets the cockfight apart from the ordinary course of life, lifts it from the realm of everyday practical affairs, and surrounds it with an aura of enlarged importance is not, as functionalist sociology would have it, that it reinforces status discriminations (such reinforcement is hardly necessary in a society where every act proclaims them), but that it provides a metasocial commentary upon the whole matter of assorting human beings into fixed hierarchical ranks and then organizing the major part of collective existence around that assortment. Its function, if you want to call it that, is interpretive: it is a Balinese

---

[19] Northrop Frye (1912–1991) was an influential literary critic who was particularly concerned with the relationship of literature to myth and society. Gloucester's blinding occurs in Shakespeare's *King Lear,* where the Earl of Gloucester is punished for aiding Lear by having his eyes gouged out. Frye says that the audience does not want to see a real experience (a man's eyes put out); they want a vicarious

experience from the point of view of the imagination. The fact that the blinding does not really happen is crucial to the psychological experience (Frye 1964:98–99).

[20] Wallace Stevens (1879–1955) was an American poet, Arnold Schoenberg (1874–1951) an Austrian composer, and William Hogarth (1697–1764) an English painter and lithographer.

reading of Balinese experience, a story they tell themselves about themselves.[21]

SAYING SOMETHING OF SOMETHING

To put the matter this way is to engage in a bit of metaphorical refocusing of one's own, for it shifts the analysis of cultural forms from an endeavor in general parallel to dissecting an organism, diagnosing a symptom, deciphering a code, or ordering a system—the dominant analogies in contemporary anthropology—to one in general parallel with penetrating a literary text. If one takes the cockfight, or any other collectively sustained symbolic structure, as a means of "saying something of something" (to invoke a famous Aristotelian tag), then one is faced with a problem not in social mechanics but social semantics.* For the anthropologist, whose concern is with formulating sociological principles, not with promoting or appreciating cockfights, the question is, what does one learn about such principles from examining culture as an assemblage of texts?[22]

Such an extension of the notion of a text beyond written material, and even beyond verbal, is, though metaphorical, not, of course, all that novel. The *interpretatio naturae* tradition of the middle ages, which, culminating in Spinoza, at-

tempted to read nature as Scripture, the Nietzschean effort to treat value systems as glosses on the will to power[23] (or the Marxian one to treat them as glosses on property relations), and the Freudian replacement of the enigmatic text of the manifest dream with the plain one of the latent, all offer precedents, if not equally recommendable ones.* But the idea remains theoretically undeveloped; and the more profound corollary, so far as anthropology is concerned, that cultural forms can be treated as texts, as imaginative works built out of social materials, has yet to be systematically exploited.*

In the case at hand, to treat the cockfight as a text is to bring out a feature of it (in my opinion, the central feature of it) that treating it as a rite or a pastime, the two most obvious alternatives, would tend to obscure: its use of emotion for cognitive ends. What the cockfight says it says in a vocabulary of sentiment—the thrill of risk, the despair of loss, the pleasure of triumph. Yet what it says is not merely that risk is exciting, loss depressing, or triumph gratifying, banal tautologies of affect, but that it is of these emotions, thus exampled, that society is built and individuals are put together. Attending cockfights and participating in them is, for the Balinese, a kind of sentimental education. What he learns there is what his culture's ethos and his private sensibility (or,

---

[21] Although rarely discussed in this light, Geertz's article is an attack on structural functionalism. A young generation of American anthropologists, including Geertz, David Schneider, and Eric Wolf, butted heads with a group of British anthropologists, including Max Gluckman and Meyer Fortes, at a conference in Cambridge, England, in 1963. Up to this point in this essay, Geertz has performed an analysis that could have come straight from the pen of a British structural-functionalist ethnographer. In the last few sections, however, he turns the structural-functionalist position upside down, saying that functionalist conclusions are meaningless for the Balinese. Instead he points to an existentialist conclusion. That is, the cockfight is not about social divisions, it is about understanding what it means to be human in Bali and the being and nothingness that are its temporary results.

[22] In this final section, Geertz summarizes his argument and explains how the cockfight attains personal signifi-

cance for Balinese participants. Up to now the analysis has been very particular, but his conclusions try to say something universal about the nature of culture: that cultures are a form of text.

[23] Baruch Spinoza (1632–1677) was an influential philosopher in the rationalist tradition. In one of his best known works, *Ethics*, he set out a geometrical program of definitions, axioms, postulates, and theorems that he proposed was a systematic procedure for the perfection of human nature. His work influenced many later scholars, including Georg Wilhelm Friedrich Hegel.

Geertz's comment concerning the "will to power" refers to a concept Friedrich Nietzsche developed in *Thus Spake Zarathustra* (1954 [1883–1885]). Many of Nietzsche's ideas were deeply influential for anthropologists and other social thinkers. In this book references to Nietzsche also occur in essays by Weber (essay 7), Benedict (essay 14), Bourdieu (essay 34) and Hanson (essay 38).

anyway, certain aspects of them) look like when spelled out externally in a collective text; that the two are near enough alike to be articulated in the symbolics of a single such text; and—the disquieting part—that the text in which this revelation is accomplished consists of a chicken hacking another mindlessly to bits.

Every people, the proverb has it, loves its own form of violence. The cockfight is the Balinese reflection on theirs: on its look, its uses, its force, its fascination. Drawing on almost every level of Balinese experience, it brings together themes—animal savagery, male narcissism, opponent gambling, status rivalry, mass excitement, blood sacrifice—whose main connection is their involvement with rage and the fear of rage, and, binding them into a set of rules which at once contains them and allows them play, builds a symbolic structure in which, over and over again, the reality of their inner affiliation can be intelligibly felt. If, to quote Northrop Frye again, we go to see *Macbeth* to learn what a man feels like after he has gained a kingdom and lost his soul, Balinese go to cockfights to find out what a man, usually composed, aloof, almost obsessively self-absorbed, a kind of moral autocosm, feels like when, attacked, tormented, challenged, insulted, and driven in result to the extremes of fury, he has totally triumphed or been brought totally low. The whole passage, as it takes us back to Aristotle (though to the *Poetics* rather than the *Hermeneutics*), is worth quotation:

> But the poet [as opposed to the historian], Aristotle says, never makes any real statements at all, certainly no particular or specific ones. The poet's job is not to tell you what happened, but what happens: not what did take place, but the kind of thing that always does take place. He gives you the typical, recurring, or what Aristotle calls universal event. You wouldn't go to *Macbeth* to learn about the history of Scotland—you go to it to learn what a man feels like after he's gained a kingdom and lost his soul. When you meet such a character as Micawber in Dickens, you don't feel that there must have been a man Dickens knew who was exactly like this: you feel that there's a bit of Micawber in almost everybody you know, including yourself. Our impressions of human life are

picked up one by one, and remain for most of us loose and disorganized. But we constantly find things in literature that suddenly coordinate and bring into focus a great many such impressions, and this is part of what Aristotle means by the typical or universal human event.*

It is this kind of bringing of assorted experiences of everyday life to focus that the cockfight, set aside from that life as "only a game" and reconnected to it as "more than a game," accomplishes, and so creates what, better than typical or universal, could be called a paradigmatic human event—that is, one that tells us less what happens than the kind of thing that would happen if, as is not the case, life were art and could be as freely shaped by styles of feeling as *Macbeth* and *David Copperfield* are.

Enacted and re-enacted, so far without end, the cockfight enables the Balinese, as, read and reread, *Macbeth* enables us, to see a dimension of his own subjectivity. As he watches fight after fight, with the active watching of an owner and a bettor (for cockfighting has no more interest as a pure spectator sport than does croquet or dog racing), he grows familiar with it and what it has to say to him, much as the attentive listener to string quartets or the absorbed viewer of still life grows slowly more familiar with them in a way which opens his subjectivity to himself.*

Yet, because—in another of those paradoxes, along with painted feelings and unconsequenced acts, which haunt aesthetics—that subjectivity does not properly exist until it is thus organized, art forms generate and regenerate the very subjectivity they pretend only to display. Quartets, still lifes, and cockfights are not merely reflections of a pre-existing sensibility analogically represented; they are positive agents in the creation and maintenance of such a sensibility. If we see ourselves as a pack of Micawbers, it is from reading too much Dickens (if we see ourselves as unillusioned realists, it is from reading too little); and similarly for Balinese, cocks, and cockfights. It is in such a way, coloring experience with the light they cast it in, rather than through whatever material effects they may have, that the arts play their role, as arts, in social life.*

In the cockfight, then, the Balinese forms and discovers his temperament and his society's temper at the same time. Or, more exactly, he forms and discovers a particular facet of them. Not only are there a great many other cultural texts providing commentaries on status hierarchy and self-regard in Bali, but there are a great many other critical sectors of Balinese life besides the stratificatory and the agonistic that receive such commentary. The ceremony consecrating a Brahmana priest, a matter of breath control, postural immobility, and vacant concentration upon the depths of being, displays a radically different, but to the Balinese equally real, property of social hierarchy—its reach toward the numinous[24] transcendent. Set not in the matrix of the kinetic emotionality of animals, but in that of the static passionlessness of divine mentality, it expresses tranquillity not disquiet. The mass festivals at the village temples, which mobilize the whole local population in elaborate hostings of visiting gods—songs, dances, compliments, gifts—assert the spiritual unity of village mates against their status inequality and project a mood of amity and trust.* The cockfight is not the master key to Balinese life, any more than bullfighting is to Spanish. What it says about that life is not unqualified nor even unchallenged by what other equally eloquent cultural statements say about it. But there is nothing more surprising in this than in the fact that Racine and Moliere were contemporaries, or that the same people who arrange chrysanthemums cast swords.*[25]

The culture of a people is an ensemble of texts, themselves ensembles, which the anthropologist strains to read over the shoulders of those to whom they properly belong. There are enormous difficulties in such an enterprise, methodological pitfalls to make a Freudian quake, and some moral perplexities as well. Nor is it the only way that symbolic forms can be sociologically handled. Functionalism lives, and so does psychologism. But to regard such forms as "saying something of something," and saying it to somebody, is at least to open up the possibility of an analysis which attends to their substance rather than to reductive formulas professing to account for them.

As in more familiar exercises in close reading, one can start anywhere in a culture's repertoire of forms and end up anywhere else. One can stay, as I have here, within a single, more or less bounded form, and circle steadily within it. One can move between forms in search of broader unities or informing contrasts. One can even compare forms from different cultures to define their character in reciprocal relief. But whatever the level at which one operates, and however intricately, the guiding principle is the same: societies, like lives, contain their own interpretations. One has only to learn how to gain access to them.[26]

---

[24] *Numinous:* mysterious, surpassing comprehension.

[25] This paragraph is important because it shows that Geertz was moving away from the popular image of culture as an organic whole toward the postmodern vision of culture as the intersection of competing views and interests. Geertz emphasizes that rather than presenting a consistent, integrated message, culture is full of competing voices and messages that are at odds with one another. Jean Racine (1639–1699) and Jean-Baptiste Molière (1622–1673) were French playwrights: the first a great writer of tragedies, the latter famous for his comedies. The last line of the paragraph refers to Ruth Benedict's study of Japanese national character, *The Chrysanthemum and the Sword* (1946).

[26] The notion that a culture is a collection of texts that anthropologists read over the shoulders of those who live them had a powerful impact on the next generation of anthropological theorists. In particular, this idea led anthropologists to borrow some of the tools of textual analysis from literary criticism. Geertz's work provided part of the foundation for postmodernism, which is dealt with in the next section.

This essay was published at a time when the works of modern French critical thinkers such as Roland Barthes (1915–1980) and Jacques Derrida (1930–2004) were becoming available in English. Among their critical insights is the notion that texts are systems of symbols that reveal the assumptions of particular cultures at particular times. As Geertz was writing this essay, the whole idea of deconstructing texts, or culture, was transforming the field of literary criticism. This essay is a critical bridge between literature and anthropological theory.

Background to Postmodernism

In 1917, Marcel Duchamp submitted his work "The Fountain" to a show organized by the Society of Independent Artists, but his work was summarily rejected. In 2004, the BBC reported that 500 art experts had voted Duchamp's piece the most influential work of modern art. In case you're not familiar with it, "The Fountain" is a urinal that Duchamp signed with the name "R. Mutt." The original of "The Fountain" was lost but Duchamp made as many as 11 replicas in the mid-1960s. One of these was purchased for $1.76 million at a Sotheby's auction in New York in 1999. In its origin, "The Fountain" cannot be considered a postmodern work. Duchamp is generally associated with a school of art called *dada*. However, the current day appreciation of works like "The Fountain" definitely portrays a postmodern sensibility. "The Fountain" is postmodern because, for viewers and critics in the late 20th and early 21st centuries, it raises all the right questions. It disorients the viewer and makes the viewer ask what makes something art. It raises questions about the nature of authorship and the control of the author or artist over the works and objects he or she creates. It plays with signs and symbols. It raises questions about authority and power (it is art because the powerful . . . in this case the curators of major museums and the "experts" use their authority to declare it art). For the postmodernist, questions of Duchamp's intentions or the life history that led to the work are irrelevant. We have only the object and we have only our reactions now.

Postmodernism is a movement that began sometime after World War II, affecting art, music, and literature as well as all of the social sciences. To some degree who counts as postmodern is in the eye of the beholder, but some postmodern visual artists include Jenny Holzer and Barbara Kruger. Laurie Anderson might be considered a postmodern musician. Postmodern novelists include David Foster Wallace and Ray Federman. The kinds of questions raised and the play of signs and significance found in "The Fountain" are also found in the works of these artists.

In this book, we are most concerned with postmodernism as it affects the social sciences and humanities, particularly philosophy, literature, history, sociology, and anthropology. Although the postmodern influence in these subjects has many sources, much of it can be traced to developments in France in the 1950s and early 1960s. There a group of mostly young scholars challenged existing orthodoxies and created new understandings of history, literature, and society.

In postwar France, leading intellectuals were drawn both to existentialism and to communism. The French communism of that era was heavily influenced both by its desire to play an active role in the French Government and its ties to the Soviet Union. In the 1950s, this left French communist intellectuals vulnerable on two fronts: Since it generally backed the government, the French Communist Party found itself in support of French colonial wars in both Indochina and Algeria. Since it was tied to the Soviets, it also supported Soviet actions such as the suppression of the Hungarian Revolution of 1956. The issues of colonialism and Soviet domination of Eastern Europe left many intellectuals disillusioned with the communist party. Although most remained staunch leftists, they broke with the party. At the same time, leading French thinkers were also becoming disillusioned with existentialism. The existentialist doctrine that existence precedes essence seemed to suggest that humans were created by the choices they made. However, Marx, as well as the anthropology of Durkheim and Lévi-Strauss, drew scholars' attention to the social structures and systems of classification that determined the range of choices that were available to people.

Disillusioned with both Soviet-style communism and existentialism, French scholars of the 1950s looked for new ways to understand the world. They created these by reinterpreting both Marx and the writings of key 20th century philosophers such as Heidegger, Husserl, and Wittgenstein. They combined these with the linguistics of Saussure and the anthropology of Durkheim and Lévi-Strauss.

In the 1960s, a relatively close-knit group of scholars formed in Paris. Most were about the same age and there were many connections among them. Pierre Bourdieu (1930–2002), Michel Foucault (1926–1984), and Jacques Derrida (1930–2004) were all students of Louis Althusser (1918–1990). Gilles Deleuze (1925–1995) was a friend of Foucault. Paul de Man (1919–1983) was a close friend of Derrida (and Derrida published a book in memory of de Man). Other critical postmodern thinkers working in France at this time included Jean-Francois Lyotard (1924–1998), Jacques Lacan (1901–1981), and Jean Baudrillard (1929–2007). With the exception of de Man, who taught at Yale, all of these thinkers held university positions in and around Paris. The University of Paris has 13 numbered branches as well as several elite institutions designated as "Ecoles." Althusser taught at the Ecole Normale Superieur. Foucault, Lyotard, and Deleuze taught at University of Paris VIII, Baudrillard taught at University of Paris X, Derrida, Bourdieu, and Lacan (along with Lévi-Strauss) taught at the Ecole Practique des Hautes Etudes (later the Ecole Practique des Hautes Etudes en Sciences Sociale). Although many of them moved from institution to institution (for example, Foucault was at the University of Tunis from 1965–1968), they developed their ideas in contact with one another and their work bears the imprint of this.

Many elements tie the work of the postmodernist scholars together. However, among the most important of these are an emphasis on the relationships between language and power. Some have referred to this as the "linguistic turn" in the social sciences and philosophy (Rorty 1967 and many others). Building on the work of Wittgenstein and Saussure, the postmodernists held that languages were systems of signs and symbols that took their meanings from relationships with one another rather than relationships with the empirical world. The empirical world itself remained ineffable, beyond our direct understanding. These ideas articulated nicely with developments in hermeneutic philosophy in the first half of the twentieth century. Hermeneutics is the study of theories of interpretation. Hermaneuticists, particularly Martin Heidegger (1889–1976) and Hans-Goerg Gadamer (1900–2002) argued that it is impossible for people to separate ways of knowing from language and culture.

Paul Ricoeur (1913–2005) a philosopher deeply influenced by Heidegger had a more direct influence on the development of postmodernism. Ricoeur taught at the Sorbonne and was an administrator at Nanterre (University of Paris X) in the 1950s and 60s. Derrida was sometimes his assistant and frequently debated with him. Ricoeur focused on the "double nature" of human beings: at once metaphysical entities and material beings with physical bodies. He held that our self-understandings and our understandings of history are created through imagination and interpretations. However, these understandings are anchored in our physical bodies and in the material world.

In the work of the French postmodernists, the elements we have been describing come together in several prominent themes. The first is an emphasis on understanding society as created and held together through discourse: Society is, somehow, a series of narratives through which we understand how to interpret the world and behave in it. However, because of the nature of language and interpretation, these narratives can never accurately represent the world. Instead, they are made up of signs and symbols that reference one another and can be substituted for one another.

A second element is that such discourses are set within power relationships and are reflective of them. Language is never neutral, never a clear window through which we can perceive the world. Discourses promote ways of understanding and interpreting the world to the favor or disfavor of particular individuals or groups. Postmodernists have been particularly skeptical of grand narratives; totalizing stories that argue for the progress of all humanity or the ultimate triumph of science. For example, in *The Postmodern Condition,* Lyotard argues that "The grand narrative has lost its credibility, regardless of what mode of unification it uses, regardless of whether it is a speculative narrative or a narrative of emancipation" (1984:37). He declares that postmodernism is most simply defined as "incredulity toward metanarratives" (1984:xxiv). Lyotard's attack on science is particularly telling. Rather than a way to understand the world or create a better life for people, Lyotard understands science as simply a discourse, and one that, backed by the power of states, corporations, and the wealthy, is particularly effective at extending the domination of these forces over others. However, if science, (which claims to be an objective way of determining material truth), is simply a discourse, then there can be no agreed on method of determining material truth. Since no appeal to an external reality can ever determine truth, all that is left is competing discourses. In such a competition, the truths of the wealthy, the powerful, the social elites will in most cases triumph over those of the poor, oppressed, or non-elite. Thus, postmodernists claim, power decides what is true. Louis Althusser's ideas were particularly influential in this regard. You will recall that many key postmodern thinkers were among his students. Althusser was a Marxist thinker particularly concerned with social reproduction. He argued that societies had at their disposal both repressive state apparatus (RSA) and ideological state apparatus (ISA). RSAs were institutions of violence through which the state enforced its dominion. ISAs however were institutions such as religion, education, family, law, politics, trade unions, communication, and culture though which the state promulgates its understandings of truth and the nature of the world.

One response of postmodernists to these issues is the idea of deconstruction. Deconstructionism is most closely connected with the work of Jacques Derrida. Derrida argued that narratives, both literary texts and cultural understandings, are incapable of accurately representing reality. Instead, they create particularistic understandings of reality by allowing readers or cultural participants to hear some voices and interpretations while at the same time suppressing (or "delicensing") others. However, Derrida argued that this practice created ruptures: zones of conflict or logical inconsistency. Deconstruction is the practice of finding and interpreting such ruptures in order to reveal underlying cultural assumptions or repressed voices. In *Of Grammatology* for example, Derrida argues that the work of Lévi-Strauss as well as several other writers shows a valuing of speech over written communication. First Derrida explores a variety of reasons why speech might be so valued (writing is only a substitute for speech, speech communicates intention more immediately than writing, etc.). However, he then goes on to show that none of these really make any sense. All of writing's problems can logically be applied to speech, too. He concludes that the privileging of speech cannot be supported by logic but actually reflects the biases and assumptions of Western thought.

In this section, we explore the work of two critical thinkers associated with postmodernism: Pierre Bourdieu and Michel Foucault. Bourdieu was born in Southwestern France in 1930. He studied at prestigious Parisian schools including the École Normale Supérieure, and beginning in the early 1960s, he held increasingly prestigious academic positions at major institutions in and around Paris. In 1968 Bourdieu was named director of the Centre de Sociologie Européenne, a position he held for the rest of his life. Like Foucault, Bourdieu was always a "Man of the Left" (Wacquant 2004). Unlike Foucault, Bourdieu distrusted party politics and, throughout the first half of his career, was not engaged in public politics. However, in the 1980s and 1990s, he became increasingly visible and increasingly outspoken until, by the time of his death, he was one of the most easily recognized public intellectuals in France. In his public political pronouncements, he was harshly critical of left-leaning French governments (first of the government of Francois Mitterrand and later of the government of Lionel Jospin) and argued that the socialist party was both corrupt and co-opted by the right. He also spoke frequently and powerfully against neo-liberalism, free trade, and globalization, considering that these were merely cover for the expansion of wealthy capitalist powers. He railed against the fatalism with which he believed the left accepted these developments.

Bourdieu was very heavily influenced by the linguistic turn in philosophy and anthropological theory. However, more than other postmodern thinkers, he continued to both focus on material aspects of the world and believe in the possibility of a scientific anthropology. Bourdieu created critical new frameworks for exploring social phenomena and much of the vocabulary that he pioneered has become standard in social science. Among his critical concepts are structural violence; cultural, social, and symbolic capital; field; *habitus;* and doxa.

The Bourdieu selection we have reprinted here is a chapter from his 1980 *The Logic of Practice.* In this book, Bourdieu lays out key aspects of his theory including ideas about *habitus,* symbolic capital, and modes of domination. He then applies these to matrimonial strategies and kinship among the Kabyle, a North African group among whom he did ethnographic fieldwork in the late 1950s. In our selection Bourdieu explains the idea of habitus. Thapan (2002:826) has written that Bourdieu "attempted to solve the eternal problem created by the opposing forces of essentialism and determinism primarily through the concept of 'habitus' which mediates between the subject and the object and is therefore crucial to theory."

Foucault was born in 1926 in Poiters, in France. Educated at the prestigious École Normale Supérieure in Paris, he held a series of university positions. In the early 1950s he was a member of the French Communist Party but, like many of his generation, became rapidly disillusioned with it although he remained a political radical throughout his life. In 1960, Foucault met Daniel Defert (b. 1937), then a philosophy student with a deep political engagement with the left. Foucault and Defert lived together openly from 1963 until Foucault's death. In a 1981 interview, Foucault described his relationship with Defert as a state of passion beyond love and reason (Miller 2000:186). When Defert went to Tunisia in 1966 to fulfill his French national service obligations, Foucault followed him, taking a position at the University of Tunis. Foucault and Defert returned to France in 1968. They were important figures in the students' movements of 1968–1969 and were associated with Maoist political parties in the early 1970s. By the end of that decade, Foucault's direct political involvement diminished. In the 1970s, Foucault began to spend increasing time in the United States and became a visiting professor at Berkeley in 1980. He was also increasingly involved with the Gay Liberation Movement. Foucault died of AIDS in 1984. Defert remains a prominent sociology professor and AIDS activist as well as the executor of Foucault's literary estate.

Foucault published a series of books, lectures and interviews beginning with *Madness and Civilization* in 1961. Other well-known works include *The Order of Things* (1966), *Discipline and Punish* (1977), and the multi-volume *History of Sexuality* (first volume published 1976). In these works, Foucault explored the development of certain kinds of knowledge and institutions. He was particularly concerned with the period starting in the mid-seventeenth century and continuing to the twentieth century and he focused on the development of the discourses and institutions of medicine, prisons, and understandings of sexuality in this period. He wished to understand the relationships between these ways of speaking and thinking and power of the government and institutions to intervene in the lives of people and mobilize their labor. Foucault was interested in the ways in which certain kinds of knowledge become dominant, are institutionalized and put to work as well as the way these forms of knowledge are used to dominate and delicense alternative knowledges. The Foucault selection reprinted here comes from the first chapter of volume one of *The History of Sexuality*. Foucault had planned the history of sexuality as a six-volume set and the first three volumes were published in his lifetime. The manuscript of a fourth volume is held in Foucault's estate and cannot be published. The last two volumes were never completed. In volume one, Foucault attempted to analyze the emergence of a new discourse about sexuality starting in the late 17th century. He hoped to show the relationships between power and such a discourse and how this discourse and the institutions that promulgated it became key ways of controlling individuals and populations (Pollis 1987). Foucault's original plan called for additional volumes on specific groups of people and historical periods.

Volume two was intended to cover sexuality in early Christian thinking. Volume three was to discuss the sexuality of children. Additional volumes were planned on the female body, "perverts," and race. However, Foucault's ideas changed after the publication of the first volume. He altered the subjects to focus on his understanding of ethics as it developed in ancient Roman and Greek thought (Davidson 2005).

The work of Bourdieu, Foucault, Derrida, and other scholars associated with postmodernism has been deeply controversial in anthropology. In the introduction to the next section, we describe some of this controversy and the effect that it had on the academic organization of anthropology in the United States. Despite this, there is no doubt that the work of the postmodernists forms a touchstone for many, if not most, anthropologists working today.

34. *Structures,* Habitus, *Practices*

Pierre Bourdieu

OBJECTIVISM CONSTITUTES THE social world as a spectacle offered to an observer who takes up a 'point of view' on the action and who, putting into the object the principles of his relation to the object, proceeds as if it were intended solely for knowledge and as if all the interactions within it were purely symbolic exchanges. This viewpoint is the one taken from high positions in the social structure, from which the social world is seen as a representation (as the word is used in idealist philosophy, but also as in painting) or a performance (in the theatrical or musical sense), and practices are seen as no more than the acting-out

of roles, the playing of scores or the implementation of plans. The theory of practice as practice insists, contrary to positivist materialism, that the objects of knowledge are constructed, not passively recorded, and, contrary to intellectualist idealism, that the principle of this construction is the system of structured, structuring dispositions, the *habitus,* which is constituted in practice and is always oriented towards practical functions. It is possible to step down from the sovereign viewpoint from which objectivist idealism orders the world, as Marx demands in the *Theses on Feuerbach,*[1] but without having to

From *The Logic of Practice* (1980, Eng. trans 1990)

[1] *Theses on Feuerbach* is a short document written by Marx in 1845 summarizing essential points of his thinking at that time. Marx and Feuerbach are more fully discussed in essay 4 in this volume. Bourdieu is probably referring to Marx's First Thesis on Feuerbach, which reads: "The chief defect of all hitherto existing materialism—that of Feuerbach

included—is that the thing, reality, sensuousness, is conceived only in the form of the object or of contemplation, but not as sensuous human activity, practice, not subjectively. Hence, in contradistinction to materialism, the active side was developed abstractly by idealism—which, of course, does not know real, sensuous activity as such."

abandon to it the 'active aspect' of apprehension of the world by reducing knowledge to a mere recording. To do this, one has to situate oneself *within* 'real activity as such', that is, in the practical relation to the world, the preoccupied, active presence in the world through which the world imposes its presence, with its urgencies, its things to be done and said, things made to be said, which directly govern words and deeds without ever unfolding as a spectacle. One has to escape from the realism of the structure, to which objectivism, a necessary stage in breaking with primary experience and constructing the objective relationships, necessarily leads when it hypostatizes these relations by treating them as realities already constituted outside of the history of the group—without falling back into subjectivism, which is quite incapable of giving an account of the necessity of the social world. To do this, one has to return to practice, the site of the dialectic of the *opus operatum*[2] and the *modus operandi*[3]; of the objectified products and the incorporated products of historical practice; of structures and *habitus*.[4]

The bringing to light of the presuppositions inherent in objectivist construction has paradoxically been delayed by the efforts of all those who, in linguistics as in anthropology, have sought to 'correct' the structuralist model by appealing to 'context' or 'situation' to account for variations, exceptions and accidents (instead of making them simple variants, absorbed into the structure, as the structuralists do). They have thus avoided a radical questioning of the objectivist mode of thought, when, that is, they have not simply fallen back on to the free choice of a rootless, unattached, pure subject. Thus, the method known as 'situational analysis', which consists of 'observing people in a variety of social situations' in order to determine 'the way in which individuals are able to exercise choices within the limits of a specified social structure' (Gluckman 1961; cf. also Van Velsen 1964), remains locked within the framework of the rule and the exception, which Edmund Leach (often invoked by the exponents of this method) spells out explicitly: 'I postulate that structural systems in which all avenues of social action are narrowly institutionalized are impossible. In all viable systems, there must be an area where the individual is free to make choices so as to manipulate the system to his advantage' (Leach 1962: 133).[5]

The conditionings associated with a particular class of conditions of existence produce *habitus*, systems of durable, transposable dispositions, structured structures predisposed to function as structuring structures, that is, as principles which generate and organize practices and representations that can be objectively adapted to their outcomes without presupposing a conscious aiming at ends or an express mastery of the operations necessary in order to attain them. Objectively 'regulated' and 'regular' without being in any way the product of obedience to rules, they can be

---

[2] *Opus operatum,* a Latin phrase meaning "the work wrought," often refers to effect inherent in a religious ritual, regardless of those who do the ritual or for whom the ritual is done. In other words, the idea that the performance of ritual is of value and has an effect of its own regardless of who performs the ritual, the reason for its performance, or its intended beneficiary.

[3] *Modus operandi is* a Latin phrase meaning "mode of operation" and generally refers to the manner of working or habits of an individual or group.

[4] In this opening passage, Bourdieu explores the relationship between objectivism: the idea that the actions of individuals and groups can be understood as the direct result of the external relations and forces that impinge on them and subjectivism, the notion that the actions of individuals are the result of their interpretations and understandings of the world around them. Bourdieu finds both of these positions inadequate and proposes the idea of *habitus* as, in part, a way to resolve the conflict between objectivism and subjectivism.

[5] Here Bourdieu critiques the structural functionalist approaches of anthropologists such as Max Gluckman (see essay 13), and to a lesser extent the approach of Lévi-Strauss (see essay 22). He quotes Edmund Leach (1910–1989) a student of Malinowski who was critical of the rigidity of functionalist thinking and became an avid proponent of Lévi-Strauss's structuralism.

collectively orchestrated without being the product of the organizing action of a conductor.[a,6]

It is, of course, never ruled out that the responses of the *habitus* may be accompanied by a strategic calculation tending to perform in a conscious mode the operation that the *habitus* performs quite differently, namely an estimation of chances presupposing transformation of the past effect into an expected objective. But these responses are first defined, without any calculation, in relation to objective potentialities, immediately inscribed in the present, things to do or not to do, things to say or not to say, in relation to a probable, 'upcoming' future (*un a venir*)[7], which—in contrast to the future seen as 'absolute possibility' (*absolute Moglichkeit*) in Hegel's (or Sartre's) sense[8], projected by the pure project of a 'negative freedom'[9]—puts itself forward with an urgency and a claim to existence that excludes all deliberation. Stimuli do not exist for practice in their objective truth, as conditional, conventional triggers, acting only on condition that they encounter agents conditioned to recognize them.[b] The practical world that is constituted in the relationship with the *habitus*, acting as a system of cognitive and motivating structures, is a world of already realized ends—procedures to follow, paths to take—and of objects endowed with a 'permanent teleological character', in Husserl's phrase, tools or institutions[10]. This is because the regularities inherent in an arbitrary condition ('arbitrary' in Saussure's and Mauss' sense)[11] tend to appear as necessary, even natural, since they are the basis of the schemes of perception and appreciation through which they are apprehended.[12]

If a very close correlation is regularly observed between the scientifically constructed objective probabilities (for example, the chances of access to a particular good) and agents' subjective aspirations ('motivations' and 'needs'), this is not because agents consciously adjust their aspirations to an exact evaluation of their chances of success,

---

[6] This paragraph defining *habitus* is notoriously difficult to understand. Bourdieu's student Loic Wacquant defines *habitus* as the system of durable and transposable *dispositions* through which we perceive, judge, and act in the world and notes that the word was not original with Bourdieu but used by Aristotle, Aquinas, Hegel, and others. *Habitus* clearly overlaps with both Durkheim's notion of collective conscience and the American anthropological notion of culture. However habitus is also clearly different from both. For Bourdieu, *habitus* is encoded into the physical body and the mental structures of individuals. *Habitus* interacts with the physical and social structures of the world external to the individual. On the one hand, *habitus* organizes how individuals perceive and act in the world. However, it changes as the result of its encounter with this world. Thus *habitus* both structures and is structured by the encounter of the individual with external reality.

[7] The translator has preserved word play from the French here. Bourdieu draws the reader's attention to the contrast between the word "*l'avenir*" literally "the future" and "*avenir*" literally "to come" (with the word "come" in the infinitive).

[8] Bourdieu was deeply influenced by both Hegel and the French Existentialist philosopher Jean Paul Sartre (1905–1980). In *The Science of Logic* (orig. between 1812 and 1816) Hegel wrote: "There is as good reason for taking everything to be impossible as to be possible: for every content (a content is always concrete) includes not only diverse but even opposite characteristics." By contrast Bourdieu notes that individuals do not perceive everything as possible.

[9] "Negative freedom" frequently refers to freedom from interference from other people and is often associated with the political and philosophical traditions of Hobbes, Locke, and Smith.

[10] Edmund Husserl (1859–1938) considered one of the founders of the philosophical school of phenomenology which focused on experience as the source of knowledge. Teleology refers to the study of design and purpose.

[11] Ferdinand de Saussure (1857–1913) was a Swiss linguist and a critical thinker both in linguistics and the social sciences. Saussure noted that the relationship between a signifier (such as a word) and the signified (such as an object) although conventional was arbitrary. Thus, communication depends on the notion shared by members of a linguistic community that the word "table" refers to the object, but there is no necessary logical relationship at all between a word such as "table" and the object table.

[12] In this passage, Bourdieu notes that although actions influenced by *habitus* may become the focus of rational and conscious calculation, the *habitus* itself is more like a system of automatic actions rather than of cost benefit analysis.

like a gambler organizing his stakes on the basis of perfect information about his chances of winning. In reality, the dispositions durably inculcated by the possibilities and impossibilities, freedoms and necessities, opportunities and prohibitions inscribed in the objective conditions (which science apprehends through statistical regularities such as the probabilities objectively attached to a group or class) generate dispositions objectively compatible with these conditions and in a sense pre-adapted to their demands. The most improbable practices are therefore excluded, as unthinkable, by a kind of immediate submission to order that inclines agents to make a virtue of necessity, that is, to refuse what is anyway denied and to will the inevitable. The very conditions of production of the *habitus*, a virtue made of necessity, mean that the anticipations it generates tend to ignore the restriction to which the validity of calculation of probabilities is subordinated, namely that the experimental conditions should not have been modified. Unlike scientific estimations, which are corrected after each experiment according to rigorous rules of calculation, the anticipations of the *habitus*, practical hypotheses based on past experience, give disproportionate weight to early experiences. Through the economic and social necessity that they bring to bear on the relatively autonomous world of the domestic economy and family relations, or more precisely, through the specifically familial manifestations of this external necessity (forms of the division of labour between the sexes, household objects, modes of consumption, parent-child relations, etc.), the structures characterizing a determinate class of conditions of existence produce the structures of the *habitus*, which in their turn are the basis of the perception and appreciation of all subsequent experiences.[13]

The *habitus*, a product of history, produces individual and collective practices—more history—in accordance with the schemes generated by history. It ensures the active presence of past experiences, which, deposited in each organism in the form of schemes of perception, thought and action, tend to guarantee the 'correctness' of practices and their constancy over time, more reliably than all formal rules and explicit norms.[c] This system of dispositions—a present past that tends to perpetuate itself into the future by reactivation in similarly structured practices, an internal law through which the law of external necessities, irreducible to immediate constraints, is constantly exerted—is the principle of the continuity and regularity which objectivism sees in social practices without being able to account for it; and also of the regulated transformations that cannot be explained either by the extrinsic, instantaneous determinisms of mechanistic sociologism or by the purely internal but equally instantaneous determination of spontaneist subjectivism. Overriding the spurious opposition between the forces inscribed earlier state of the system, outside the body, and the internal forces arising instantaneously as motivations springing from free will, the internal dispositions—the internalization of externality—enable the external forces to exert themselves, but in accordance with the specific logic of the organisms in which they are incorporated, i.e. in a durable, systematic and non-mechanical way. As an acquired system of generative schemes, the *habitus* makes possible the free production of all the thoughts, perceptions and actions inherent in the particular conditions of its production—and only those. Through the *habitus*, the structure of which it is the product governs practice, not along the paths of a mechanical determinism, but within the constraints and limits initially set on its inventions.

---

[13] Note two aspects of Bourdieu's thinking expressed here. First, the *habitus* predisposes individuals to think only about certain possibilities and ignore others. He is probably influenced in this by the work of the Italian Marxist Antonio Gramsci's notion of hegemony. See note 10, page 591 for more information on Gramsci. Second, notice the important role of psychology in Bourdieu's work.

Although Bourdieu is "relentless in his attempts to get rid of psychoanalysis and psychology" (Frere 2004), the idea of *habitus* shows a Freudian influence both in the fact that it is unconscious and in the fact that, like Freud, Bourdieu believes in the particular importance of childhood experience in molding adult response.

This infinite yet strictly limited generative capacity is difficult to understand only so long as one remains locked in the usual antinomies—which the concept of the *habitus* aims to transcend—of determinism and freedom, conditioning and creativity, consciousness and the unconscious, or the individual and society. Because the *habitus* is an infinite capacity for generating products—thoughts, perceptions, expressions and actions—whose limits are set by the historically and socially situated conditions of its production, the conditioned and conditional freedom it provides is as remote from creation of unpredictable novelty as it is from simple mechanical reproduction of the original conditioning.[14]

Nothing is more misleading than the illusion created by hindsight in which all the traces of a life, such as the works of an artist or the events at a biography, appear as the realization of an essence that seems to preexist them. Just as a mature artistic style is not contained, like a seed, in an original inspiration but is continuously defined and redefined in the dialectic between the objectifying intention and the already objectified intention, so too the unity of meaning which, after the event, may seem to have preceded the acts and works announcing the final significance, retrospectively transforming the various stages of the temporal series into mere preparatory sketches, is constituted through the confrontation between questions that only exist in and for a mind armed with a particular type of schemes and the solutions obtained through application of these same schemes. The genesis of a system of works or practices generated by the same *habitus* (or homologous *habitus*, such as those that underlie the unity of the life-style of a group or a class) cannot be described either as the autonomous development of a unique and always self-identical essence, or as a continuous creation of novelty, because it arises from the necessary yet unpredictable confrontation between the *habitus* and an event that can exercise a pertinent incitement on the *habitus* only if the latter snatches it from the contingency of the accidental and constitutes it as a problem by applying to it the very principles of its solution; and also because the *habitus*, like every 'art of inventing', is what makes it possible to produce an infinite number of practices that are relatively unpredictable (like the corresponding situations) but also limited in their diversity. In short, being the product of a particular class of objective regularities, the *habitus* tends to generate all the 'reasonable', 'common-sense',[d] behaviours (and only these) which are possible within the limits of these regularities, and which are likely to be positively sanctioned because they are objectively adjusted to the logic characteristic of a particular field, whose objective future they anticipate. At the same time, 'without violence, art or argument', it tends to exclude all 'extravagances' ('not for the likes of us'), that is, all the behaviours that would be negatively sanctioned because they are incompatible with the objective conditions.[15]

---

[14] Thus Bourdieu argues that the *habitus* obviates the conflict between objectivism and subjectivism by creating a set of dispositions that is both created by action within a social and physical world and generates action in that world. He notes that the *habitus* is not a cookbook-like series of rules that are simply applied to the world in a highly predictive fashion. Bourdieu here may be critiquing ethnoscience and the cognitive anthropology of scholars such as Steven Tyler. In *Outline of a Theory of Practice,* he writes a chapter called Generative Schemes and Practical Logic: Invention Within Limits in which he analyzes the ideas of classification at length (Bourdieu 2002). Bourdieu characterizes this approach as sociologism: the inappropriate application of sociological technique.

[15] In this paragraph, Bourdieu argues that the *habitus* consists of flexible, generative principles that produce more or less consistent effects as they interact with the world. He attacks the notion that individuals or groups have any transcendent essence that can be determined from their lives or works. He points to the critical notion of field. For Bourdieu, social space is composed of fields. Fields are distinct microcosms with their own rules, regularities, and forms of authority (Wacquant 2006). For Bourdieu, fields are spaces structured by differing positions and sites of struggle and contestation.

Notice Bourdieu's use of quotation marks throughout this essay. These serve different purposes in different locations. For example, in this paragraph Bourdieu puts the words 'reasonable' and 'common sense' in quotation marks to suggest that these are not self-evident and transcendent characteristics. There is no universal 'common sense' only the 'common sense' of a particular field. On the other hand, the use of quotation marks around 'art of inventing'

Because they tend to reproduce the regularities immanent in the conditions in which their generative principle was produced while adjusting to the demands inscribed as objective potentialities in the situation as defined by the cognitive and motivating structures that constitute the *habitus,* practices cannot be deduced either from the present conditions which may seem to have provoked them or from the past conditions which have produced the *habitus,* the durable principle of their production. They can therefore only be accounted for by relating the social conditions in which the *habitus* that generated them was constituted, to the social conditions in which it is implemented, that is, through the scientific work of performing the interrelationship of these two states of the social world that the *habitus* performs, while concealing it, in and through practice. The 'unconscious', which enables one to dispense with this interrelating, is never anything other than the forgetting of history which history itself produces by realizing the objective structures that it generates in the quasi-natures of *habitus.* As Durkheim (1977: 11) puts it:[16]

'In each one of us, in differing degrees, is contained the person we were yesterday, and indeed, in the nature of things it is even true that our past personae predominate in us, since the present is necessarily insignificant when compared with the long period of the past because

of which we have emerged in the form we have today. It is just that we don't directly feel the influence of these past selves precisely because they are so deeply rooted within us. They constitute the unconscious part of ourselves. Consequently we have a strong tendency not to recognize their existence and to ignore their legitimate demands. By contrast, with the most recent acquisitions of civilization we are vividly aware of them just because they are recent and consequently have not had time to be assimilated into our collective unconscious.'

The *habitus*—embodied history, internalized as a second nature and so forgotten as history—is the active presence of the whole past of which it is the product. As such, it is what gives practices their relative autonomy with respect to external determinations of the immediate present. This autonomy is that of the past, enacted and acting, which, functioning as accumulated capital, produces history on the basis of history and so ensures the permanence in change that makes the individual agent a world within the world. The *habitus* is a spontaneity without consciousness or will, opposed as much to the mechanical necessity of things without history in mechanistic theories as it is to the reflexive freedom of subjects 'without inertia' in rationalist theories.[17]

Thus the dualistic vision that recognizes only the self-transparent act of consciousness or the

---

or 'without violence, art, or argument' indicates quotes from particular sources. Frequently these quotes are too general for most people to identify. However, in these two cases, the first probably refers to the philosopher Leibnitz whom Bourdieu discusses extensively in the pages to come. The second certainly refers to a passage in Blaise Pascal's *Pensées,* first published in 1662. Pascal (1623–1662) was a French philosopher and mathematician. In Pensées he wrote: "We have to acquire an easier credence—that of habit—which without violence, art, or argument, makes us believe things and inclines all our powers to this belief, so that our mind falls into it naturally."

[16] Note the use of the word "scientific" as well as the first of two long quotations from Durkheim in this paragraph. You will recall that most of Durkheim's students perished during World War I and that apart from Marcel Mauss and Georges Davy (1883–1976) few in France pursued Durkheimian thought. Instead social thinking was domi-

nated by the Marxist analysis of the Soviet Communist Party and, particularly after World War II, existentialism. In the early 1960s, Bourdieu as well as others broke with these political and philosophical schools and moved to rehabilitate Durkheim, reinterpret Marx, and reestablish "the scientific and civic legitimacy of sociology" (Wacquant 2006).

[17] In this paragraph, Bourdieu continues to examine the *habitus* as a way of resolving conflicts between different theoretical positions. He also mentions one of his most influential ideas: capital. For Bourdieu, a capital is any resource that allows one access to position and the ability to benefit within any field (recall that for Bourdieu, fields are microcosms with their own rules, regularities, and forms of authority). Capital comes in three varieties: financial (money), cultural (access to scarce symbolic goods or particular forms of knowledge), and social (status resulting from membership in particular groups).

externally determined thing has to give way to the real logic of action, which brings together two objectifications of history, objectification in bodies and objectification in institutions or, which amounts to the same thing, two states of capital, objectified and incorporated, through which a distance is set up from necessity and its urgencies. This logic is seen in paradigmatic form in the dialectic of expressive dispositions and instituted means of expression (morphological, syntactic and lexical instruments, literary genres, etc.) which is observed in the intentionless invention of regulated improvisation. Endlessly overtaken by his own words, with which he maintains a relation of 'carry and be carried,' as Nicolai Hartmann put it, the virtuoso finds in his discourse the triggers for his discourse, which goes along like a train laying its own rails (Ruyer 1966: 136). In other words, being produced by a *modus operandi* which is not consciously mastered, the discourse contains an 'objective intention', as the Scholastics put it, which outruns the conscious intentions of its apparent author and constantly offers new pertinent stimuli to the *modus operandi* of which it is the product and which functions as a kind of 'spiritual automaton'. If witticisms strike as much by their unpredictability as by their retrospective necessity, the reason is that the *trouvaille* that brings to light long buried resources presupposes a *habitus* that so perfectly possesses the objectively available means of expression that it is possessed by them, so much so that it asserts its freedom from them by realizing the rarest of the possibilities that they necessarily imply. The dialectic of the meaning of the language and the 'sayings of the tribe' is a particular and particu-

larly significant case of the dialectic between *habitus* and institutions, that is, between two modes of objectification of past history, in which there is constantly created a history that inevitably appears, like witticisms, as both original and inevitable.[18]

This durably installed generative principle of regulated improvisations is a practical sense which reactivates the sense objectified in institutions. Produced by the work of inculcation and appropriation that is needed in order for objective structures, the products of collective history, to be reproduced in the form of the durable, adjusted dispositions that are the condition of their functioning, the *habitus*, which is constituted in the course of an individual history, imposing its particular logic on incorporation, and through which agents partake of the history objectified in institutions, is what makes it possible to inhabit institutions, to appropriate them practically, and so to keep them in activity, continuously pulling them from the state of dead letters, reviving the sense deposited in them, but at the same time imposing the revisions and transformations that reactivation entails. Or rather, the *habitus* is what enables the institution to attain full realization: it is through the capacity for incorporation, which exploits the body's readiness to take seriously the performative magic of the social, that the king, the banker or the priest are hereditary monarchy, financial capitalism or the Church made flesh. Property appropriates its owner, embodying itself in the form of a structure generating practices perfectly conforming with its logic and its demands. If one is justified in saying, with Marx that 'the lord of an entailed estate, the first-born

---

18 Nicolai Hartmann (1882–1950) was a German philosopher, probably best known for the idea of *emergence,* the notion that highly complex systems can be produced by many relatively simple, separate interactions. The work of Hartman's student, Hans-Goreg Gadamer (1900–2002), was a key source of postmodern thought. Scholasticism (the Scholastics) was the strongest intellectual tradition in the European Middle Ages based around reconciling seemingly contradictory texts. "Objective intention" is the notion that one can infer people's intentions from their actions. A "trouvaille" is a lucky

find or a sudden insight (but also something of a pun since "trou" is a hole).

In this paragraph, Bourdieu focuses on the interaction between the *habitus,* which is somehow encoded in the physical body and consciousness of the individual, and the institutional setting in which the individual exists. The emphasis is on the actual actions of individuals constrained by the workings of both institutions and *habitus*. Bourdieu referred to his work as a "theory of practice" because he hoped to focus on the physical actions of people in light of *habitus* and the fields in which *habitus* operates.

son, belongs to the land', that 'it inherits him', or that the 'persons' of capitalists are the 'personification' of capital, this is because the purely social and quasi-magical process of socialization, which is inaugurated by the act of marking that institutes an individual as an eldest son, an heir, a successor, a Christian, or simply as a man (as opposed to a woman), with all the corresponding privileges and obligations, and which is prolonged, strengthened and confirmed by social treatments that tend to transform instituted difference into natural distinction, produces quite real effects, durably inscribed in the body and in belief. An institution, even an economy, is complete and fully viable only if it is durably objectified not only in things, that is, in the logic, transcending individual agents, of a particular field, but also in bodies, in durable dispositions to recognize and comply with the demands immanent in the field.[19]

In so far—and only in so far—as *habitus* are the incorporation of the same history, or more concretely, of the same history objectified in *habitus* and structures, the practices they generate are mutually intelligible and immediately adjusted to the structures, and also objectively concerted and endowed with an objective meaning that is at once unitary and systematic, transcending subjective intentions and conscious projects, whether individual or collective. One of the fundamental effects of the harmony between practical sense and objectified meaning (*sens*) is the production of a common-sense world, whose im-

mediate self-evidence is accompanied by the objectivity provided by consensus on the meaning of practices and the world, in other words the harmonization of the agents' experiences and the constant reinforcement each of them receives from expression—individual or collective (in festivals, for example), improvised or programmed (commonplaces, sayings)—of similar or identical experiences.[20]

The homogeneity of *habitus* that is observed within the limits of a class of conditions of existence and social conditionings is what causes practices and works to be immediately intelligible and foreseeable, and hence taken for granted. The *habitus* makes questions of intention superfluous, not only in the production but also in the deciphering of practices and works.[e] Automatic and impersonal, significant without a signifying intention, ordinary practices lend themselves to an understanding that is no less automatic and impersonal. The picking up of the objective intention they express requires neither 'reactivation' of the 'lived' intention of their originator, nor the 'intentional transfer into the Other' cherished by the phenomenologists and all advocates of a "participationist' conception of history or sociology, nor tacit or explicit inquiry ('What do you *mean?*') as to other people's intentions. 'Communciation of consciousnesses' presupposes community of 'unconsciouses' (that is, of linguistic and cultural competences). Deciphering the objective intention of practices and works has nothing to do with 'reproduction' (*Nachbildung*,

---

[19] Bourdieu here quotes from Marx's *Economic and Philosophic Manuscripts of 1844*. One understanding of this paragraph is: The *habitus* in the form of durable adjustable dispositions is created through individual history. It is created by the institutional setting in which a person develops but it also enables individuals to function in these institutions, inhabiting them and thus changing them. It is through this process that institutions become fully realized. On the one hand, individuals are compelled by the roles they occupy: There is no king, for example, without an individual performing the role of hereditary monarch. These roles inscribe themselves in the bodies (consciousnesses) of the members of the society. Any analysis of society must include not only the institutions and formal rules of such a society but also the

dispositions these create in the minds and bodies of the members of society.

[20] To the degree that the *habitus* of different individuals is the product of similar personal histories, the practices they generate are mutually intelligible. Because such practices are set within shared dispositions and assumptions, they transcend individual intention and consciousness. The result of this is an idea of 'common sense' shared by members of a culture and reinforced in institutions and rituals.

The word *sens* is of interest. Richard Nice (the translator) has rendered it as "objectified meaning" (but left us the French original). The simplest translation is "sense." But note that the French title of the book from which this essay is taken (*The Logic of Practice* in English) is *Le sens pratique*.

as the early Dilthey puts it) of lived experiences and the unnecessary and uncertain reconstitution of an 'intention' which is not their real origin.[21]

The objective homogenizing of group or class *habitus* that results from homogeneity of conditions of existence is what enables practices to be objectively harmonized without any calculation or conscious reference to a norm and mutually adjusted in the absence of any direct interaction or, *a fortiori*,[22] explicit co-ordination. The interaction itself owes its form to the objective structures that have produced the dispositions of the interacting agents, which continue to assign them their relative positions in the interaction and elsewhere.[f] 'Imagine', Leibniz suggests (1866c: 548), 'two clocks or watches in perfect agreement as to the time. This may occur in one of three ways. The first consists in mutual influence; the second is to appoint a skilful workman to correct them and synchronize constantly; the third is to construct these two clocks with such art and precision that one can be assured of their subsequent agreement.' So long as one ignores the true principle of the conductorless orchestration which gives regularity, unity and systematicity to practices even in the absence of any spontaneous or imposed organization of individual projects, one is condemned to the naive artificialism that recognizes no other unifying principle

than conscious coordination.[g] The practices of the members of the same group or, in a differentiated society, the same class, are always more and better harmonized than the agents know or wish, because, as Leibniz again says, 'following only (his) own laws', each 'nonetheless agrees with the other'. The habitus is precisely this immanent law, *lex insita*,[23] inscribed in bodies by identical histories, which is the precondition not only for the coordination of practices but also for practices of coordination.[h] The corrections and adjustments the agents themselves consciously carry out presuppose mastery of a common code; and undertakings of collective mobilization cannot succeed without a minimum of concordance between the habitus of the mobilizing agents (prophet, leader, etc.) and the dispositions of those who recognize themselves in their practices or words, and, above all, without the inclination towards grouping that springs from the spontaneous orchestration of dispositions.[24]

It is certain that every effort at mobilization aimed at organizing collective action has to reckon with the dialectic of dispositions and occasions that takes place in every agent, whether he mobilizes or is mobilized (the hysteresis[25] of *habitus* is doubtless one explanation of the structural lag between opportunities and the dispositions to grasp them which is the cause of missed opportunities

---

[21] This passage, set off from the rest of the text, is a critique of other philosophical approaches, particularly "participationism," the notion that participation in collective activities is prior the development of individual consciousness and individual capacity to complete an activity by one's self. Bourdieu also emphasizes the automatic and unconscious nature of much of the action of the *habitus*.

Wilhelm Dilthey (1833–1911) was a German sociologist and philosopher. For Dilthey, *Nachbildung* (literally analog, emulation, or replica) is a conscious process by which an individual experiences someone else's mental process thus making it possible for one person to understand another's reality (Jha 1995).

[22] *a fortiori*: with greater reason.

[23] *lex insita*: underlying principle.

[24] Gotfried Wilhelm Leibniz (1646–1716), German philosopher and mathematician. Like Bourdieu, Leibniz was interested in transcending the dualistic philosophical

approaches of his day, particularly the mind/body dualism of Descartes. His solution was to understand the universe, humans, and god as "monads," indivisible entities that contain within themselves all the properties they currently exhibit and will exhibit in any conceivable future. Leibniz uses the example of the two clocks several times starting in 1696. For Leibniz, the example points to the superiority of pre-established harmony (the third explanation) over other explanations (Scott 1997) and provides evidence of God and of the wholeness and uniformity of the universe. Bourdieu also argues that the third explanation is the best but for him, this is evidence of the workings of the *habitus* which is not universal but must rather be a characteristic of a specific group of people acting in a specific place at a specific time.

[25] hysteresis: the lagging of an event behind its cause (most frequently used in chemistry and in the physics of magnetism). Bourdieu's use of the term here emphasizes the importance of early experiences in the formation of the *habitus*.

and, in particular, of the frequently observed incapacity to think historical crises in categories of perception and thought other than those of the past, however revolutionary). It is also certain that it must take account of the objective orchestration established among dispositions that are objectively co-ordinated because they are ordered by more or less identical objective necessities. It is, however, extremely dangerous to conceive collective action by analogy with individual action, ignoring all that the former owes to the relatively autonomous logic of the institutions of mobilization (with their own history, their specific organization, etc.) and to the situations, institutionalized or not, in which it occurs.

Sociology treats as identical all biological individuals who, being the products of the same objective conditions, have the same *habitus*. A social class (in-itself)—a class of identical or similar conditions of existence and conditionings—is at the same time a class of biological individuals having the same *habitus*, understood as a system of dispositions common to all products of the same conditionings. Though it is impossible for all (or even two) members of the same class to have had the same experiences, in the same order, it is certain that each member of the same class is more likely than any member of another class to have been confronted with the situations most frequent for members of that class. Through the always convergent experiences that give a social environment its physiognomy, with its 'closed doors', 'dead ends' and 'limited prospects', the objective structures that sociology apprehends in the form of probabilities of access to goods, services and powers, inculcate the 'art of assessing likelihoods', as Leibniz put it, of anticipating the objective future, in short, the 'sense of reality', or realities, which is perhaps the best-concealed principle of their efficacy.[26]

To define the relationship between class *habitus* and individual *habitus* (which is inseparable from the organic individuality that is immediately given to immediate perception—*intuitus personae*[27] and socially designated and recognized—name, legal identity, etc.), class (or group) *habitus*, that is, the individual *habitus* in so far as it expresses or reflects the class (or group), could be regarded as a subjective but non-individual system of internalized structures, common schemes of perception, conception and action, which are the precondition of all objectification and apperception; and the objective co-ordination of practices and the sharing of a world-view could be founded on the perfect impersonality and interchangeability of singular practices and views. But this would amount to regarding all the practices or representations produced in accordance with identical schemes as impersonal and interchangeable, like individual intuitions of space which, according to Kant, reflect none of the particularities of the empirical ego. In fact, the singular *habitus* of members of the same class are united in a relationship of homology, that is, of diversity within homogeneity reflecting the diversity within homogeneity characteristic of their social conditions of production. Each individual system of dispositions is a structural variant of the others, expressing the singularity of its position within the class and its trajectory. 'Personal' style, the particular stamp marking all the products of the same *habitus*, whether practices or works, is never more than a deviation in relation to the style of a period or class, so that it relates back to the common style not only by its conformity—like Phidias,[28] who, for Hegel, had

---

[26] In this passage, Bourdieu moves from presenting *habitus* as a characteristic of the individual to presenting it as a characteristic of a class. Note that although he acknowledges the differences among individuals, he argues that the similarity of the experiences of individuals of the same class means these can be safely ignored. Note also the critical role that Bourdieu assigns the *habitus* in creating the reality of experience for members of a class.

[27] *intuitus personae:* taking the personality and personal qualities of the individual into account.

[28] Phidias (circa 480-430 BCE) is commonly regarded as the greatest sculptor of Ancient Greece. Although none of his original works remain, his work is known through Roman copies produced long after his lifetime. In the introduction to *Elements of the Philosophy of the Right* (orig. 1820). Hegel writes: "When a great artist finishes a work we say: 'It must be so.' The particularity of the artist has wholly disappeared and the work shows no mannerism. Phidias has no mannerism: the statue itself lives and moves."

no 'manner'—but also by the difference that makes the 'manner.'[29]

The principle of the differences between individual *habitus* lies in the singularity of their social trajectories, to which there correspond series of chronologically ordered determinations that are mutually irreducible to one another. The *habitus* which, at every moment, structures new experiences in accordance with the structures produced by past experiences, which are modified by the new experiences within the limits defined by their power of selection, brings about a unique integration, dominated by the earliest experiences, of the experiences statistically common to members of the same class.[i] Early experiences have particular weight because the *habitus* tends to ensure its own constancy and its defence against change through the selection it makes within new information by rejecting information capable of calling into question its accumulated information, if exposed to it accidentally or by force, and especially by avoiding exposure to such information. One only has to think, for example, of homogamy,[30] the paradigm of all the 'choices' through which the *habitus* tends to favour experiences likely to reinforce it (or the empirically confirmed fact that people tend to talk about politics with those who have the same opinions). Through the systematic 'choices' it makes among the places, events and people that might be frequented, the *habitus* tends to protect itself from crises and critical challenges by providing itself with a milieu to which it is as pre-adapted as possible, that is, a relatively constant universe of situations tending to reinforce its dispositions by offering the market most favourable to its prod-

ucts. And once again it is the most paradoxical property of the *habitus*, the unchosen principle of all 'choices', that yields the solution to the paradox of the information needed in order to avoid information. The schemes of perception and appreciation of the *habitus* which are the basis of all the avoidance strategies are largely the product of a non-conscious, unwilled avoidance, whether it results automatically from the conditions of existence (for example, spatial segregation) or has been produced by a strategic intention (such as avoidance of 'bad company' or 'unsuitable books') originating from adults themselves formed in the same conditions.[31]

Even when they look like the realization of explicit ends, the strategies produced by the *habitus* and enabling agents to cope with unforeseen and constantly changing situations are only apparently determined by the future. If they seem to be oriented by anticipation of their own consequences, thereby encouraging the finalist illusion,[32] this is because, always tending to reproduce the objective structures that produced them, they are determined by the past conditions of production of their principle of production, that is, by the already realized outcome of identical or interchangeable past practices, which coincides with their own outcome only to the extent that the structures within which they function are identical to or homologous with the objective structures of which they are the product. Thus, for example, in the interaction between two agents or groups of agents endowed with the same *habitus* (say A and B), everything takes place as if the actions of each of them (say a_1 for A) were organized by reference to the reactions which they call forth

---

[29] Bourdieu understands *habitus* as something particular to the individual . . . each individual has his or her own *habitus*. However, he also believes that there is class habitus, the high degree of consistency among individuals who are members of a social class or other social group. In such a group, individuals are variations on a common theme.

[30] homogeny: marriage of individuals who have similar characteristics such as race, ethnicity, religious background, education, socioeconomic status.

[31] In other words, people tend to associate with and listen to those people and institutions that support their under-

standings. This results either from social structure (such as laws or traditions forbidding certain classes of individuals from associating with one another) or from enculturation (our kind of people don't read those kinds of books, watch that sort of TV, go to those sorts of sporting events, eat that kind of food). The Internet and cable TV have made Bourdieu's observation second nature to us.

[32] finalist: finalism is the philosophical position that the world (life, society, etc.) is moving toward a specific goal. It is similar to teleology.

from any agent possessing the same *habitus* (say b_1 for B). They therefore objectively imply anticipation of the reaction which these reactions in turn call forth (a_2, A's reaction to b_1). But the ideological description, the only one appropriate to a 'rational actor' possessing perfect information as to the preferences and competences of the other actors, in which each action has the purpose of making possible the reaction to the reaction it induces (individual A performs an action a_1, a gift for example, in order to make individual B produce action b_1, so that he can then perform action a_1, a stepped-up gift), is quite as naive as the mechanistic description that presents the action and the riposte as so many steps in a sequence of programmed actions produced by a mechanical apparatus.[33]

To have an idea of the difficulties that would be encountered by a mechanistic theory of practice as mechanical reaction, directly determined by the antecedent conditions and entirely reducible to the mechanical functioning of pre-established devices—which would have to be assumed to exist in infinite number, like the chance configurations of stimuli capable of triggering them from outside—one only has to mention the grandiose, desperate undertaking of the anthropologist, fired with positivist ardour, who recorded 480 elementary units of behaviour in 20 minutes' observation of his wife in the kitchen: 'Here we confront the distressing fact that the sample episode chain under analysis is a fragment of a larger segment of behavior which in the complete record contains some 480 separate episodes. Moreover, it took only twenty minutes for these 480 behavior stream events to occur. If my wife's rate of behavior is roughly representative of that of other actors, we must be prepared to deal with an inventory of episodes produced at the rate of some 20,000 per sixteen-hour day per actor. In a population consisting of several hundred actor-types, the number of different episodes in the total repertory must amount to many millions in the course of an annual cycle' (Harris 1964: 74-5).[34]

The habitus contains the solution to the paradoxes of objective meaning without subjective intention. It is the source of these strings of 'moves' which are objectively organized as strategies without being the product of a genuine strategic intention—which would presuppose at least that they be apprehended as one among other possible strategies.[j] If each stage in the sequence of ordered and oriented actions that constitute objective strategies can appear to be determined by anticipation of the future, and in particular, of its own consequences (which is what justifies the use of the concept of strategy), it is because the practices that are generated by the *habitus* and are governed by the past conditions of production of their generative principle are adapted in advance to the objective conditions whenever the conditions in which the *habitus* functions have remained identical, or similar, to the conditions in which it was constituted. Perfectly and immediately successful adjustment to the objective conditions provides the most complete illusion of

---

[33] Thus, Bourdieu argues that actions that seem to be based on rational calculation of future events are, in fact, based on past understandings, particularly those developed early in life, and that such understandings are not explicitly matters of conscious thought. However, since current conditions are never exactly the same as past conditions, practice plays out in ways that are not predictable. The conditions of life as lived feed back into the continuing change and development of the *habitus*.

[34] Bourdieu refers here to Marvin Harris' 1964 *The Nature of Cultural Things*. In that book, Harris proposes an anthropology that "precludes the need to know the actors goals, meanings, and motives" and is "operationally equivalent to the physical sciences" (Metzger 1965).

Harris's system is based on units he called actones. An actone is a specific motion of a body part and the effect of that motion on the environment. Actones were to be grouped into classes called actonemes. These in turn were grouped into higher level patterns of organization called episodes, nodes, scenes and serials. Note that Harris' scheme is similar to the schemes of the ethnoscientists and cognitive anthropologists (see essays 24 and 25). Harris became one of the best known anthropologists of his era but rapidly abandoned this scheme. It gained no support and is largely forgotten. Harris serves as a foil for Bourdieu. Although Bourdieu also wishes to create a scientific anthropology, he believes that the subjective experiences and dispositions of social actors are keys to understanding society.

504 *The Late Twentieth Century and Beyond*

finality, or—which amounts to the same thing—of self-regulating mechanism.[35]

The presence of the past in this kind of false anticipation of the future performed by the *habitus* is, paradoxically, most clearly seen when the sense of the probable future is belied and when dispositions ill-adjusted to the objective chances because of a hysteresis effect (Marx's favourite example of this was Don Quixote[36]) are negatively sanctioned because the environment they actually encounter is too different from the one to which they are objectively adjusted.[k] In fact the persistence of the effects of primary conditioning, in the form of the *habitus*, accounts equally well for cases in which dispositions function out of phase and practices are objectively ill-adapted to the present conditions because they are objectively adjusted to conditions that no longer obtain. The tendency of groups to persist in their ways, due *inter alia*[37] to the fact that they are composed of individuals with durable dispositions that can outlive the economic and social conditions in which they were produced, can be the source of misadaptation as well as adaptation, revolt as well as resignation.[38]

One only has to consider other possible forms of the relationship between dispositions and conditions to see that the pre-adjustment of the *habitus* to the objective conditions is a 'particular case of the possible'[39] and so avoid unconsciously universalizing the model of the near-circular relationship of near-perfect reproduction, which is completely valid only when the conditions of production of the *habitus* and the conditions of its functioning are identical or homothetic. In this particular case, the dispositions durably inculcated by the objective conditions and by a pedagogic action that is tendentially adjusted to these conditions, tend to generate practices objectively compatible with these conditions and expectations pre-adapted to their objective demands (*amor fati*[40]) (for some psychologists' attempts at direct verification of this relationship, see Brunswik 1949; Preston and Barrata 1948; Attneave 1953). As a consequence, they tend, without any rational calculation or conscious estimation of the chances of success, to ensure immediate correspondence between the *a priori* or *ex ante* probability conferred on an event (whether or not accompanied by subjective experiences such as hopes, expectation, fears, etc.) and the *a posteriori* or *ex post* probability that can be established on the basis of past experience.[41] They thus make it possible to understand why economic

---

[35] Here Bourdieu continues to criticize neo-functionalist models such as Harris and Rappaport's (see essays 19 and 20). Bourdieu suggests that the self-regulating, homeostatic mechanism of culture that these theorists perceive is an illusion, an artifact of the operation of the *habitus*.

[36] Marx makes extensive use of Cervantes' work, particularly in Chapter 3 of *The German Ideology* (the selection "Feuerbach" in this book is Chapter 1 of that work) where, among other things, he imagines a duet sung by Bruno Bauer (whom he calls Saint Bruno) and Sancho Panza (whom he calls Saint Sancho).

[37] *inter alia:* among other things.

[38] A strength of Bourdieu's analysis, compared with functionalist and neo-functionalist analyses is that it can account for maladaptation and conflict. Functionalists of all varieties tended to interpret all forms of social action as promoting social solidarity. Bourdieu clearly shows that the *habitus* at the individual level can also be a source of conflict and maladaptation.

[39] The reference here is to Gaston Bachelard (1884–1962) a French philosopher of science who had a strong influence on French scholars of Bourdieu's generation. Bachelard is best known for the idea that the progress of science is not continuous but rather is blocked by certain patterns of thinking. Such patterns must be transcended in an epistemological break for progress to occur.

[40] *amor fati:* literally, love of fate, or love of one's fate; a Latin expression coined by the German philosopher Friedrich Nietzsche (1844–1900).

[41] *a priori:* Latin for "from the former" reasoning from a general law to a particular instance, a conclusion not based on prior study.

ex ante: Latin for "from the latter," a conclusion arrived at by reasoning from observed facts.

a posteriori: reasoning from particular instances to a general principle.

ex post: Latin for "after the fact."

models based on the (tacit) premise of a 'relationship of intelligible causality', as Max Weber[42] (1922) calls it, between generic ('typical') chances 'objectively existing as an average' and 'subjective expectations', or, for example, between investment or the propensity to invest and the rate of return expected or really obtained in the past, fairly exactly account for practices which do not arise from knowledge of the objective chances.

By pointing out that rational action, 'judiciously' oriented according to what is 'objectively valid' (1922), is what 'would have happened if the actors had had knowledge of all the circumstances and all the participants' intentions' (1968: 6), that is, of what is 'valid in the eyes of the scientist', who alone is able to calculate the system of objective chances to which perfectly informed action would have to be adjusted, Weber shows clearly that the pure model of rational action cannot be regarded as an anthropological description of practice. This is not only because real agents only very exceptionally possess the complete information, and the skill to appreciate it, that rational action would presuppose. Apart from rare cases which bring together the economic and cultural conditions for rational action oriented by knowledge of the profits that can be obtained in the different markets, practices depend not on the average chances of profit, an abstract and unreal notion, but on the specific chances that a singular agent or class of agents possesses by virtue of its capital, this being understood, in this respect, as a means of appropriation of the chances theoretically available to all.

Economic theory which acknowledges only the rational 'responses' of an indeterminate, interchangeable agent to 'potential opportunities', or more precisely to average chances (like the 'average rates of profit' offered by the different markets), converts the immanent law of the economy into a universal norm of proper economic behavior. In so doing, it conceals the fact that the 'rational' *habitus* which is the precondition for appropriate economic behaviour is the product of particular economic condition, the one defined by possession of the economic and cultural capital required in order to seize the 'potential opportunities' theoretically available to all; and also that the same dispositions, by adapting the economically most deprived to the specific condition of which they are the product and thereby helping to make their adaptation to the generic demands of the economic cosmos (as regards calculation, forecasting, etc.) lead them to accept the negative sanctions resulting from this lack of adaptation, that is, their deprivation. In short, the art of estimating and seizing chances, the capacity to anticipate the future by a kind of practical induction or even to take a calculated gamble on the possible against the probable, are dispositions that can only be acquired in certain social conditions, that is, certain social conditions. Like the entrepreneurial spirit or the propensity to invest, economic information is a function of one's power over the economy. This is, on the one hand, because the propensity to acquire it depends on the chances of using it successfully, and the chances of acquiring it depend on the chances of successfully using it; and also because economic competence, like all competence (linguistic, political, etc.), far from being a simple technical capacity acquired in certain conditions, is a power tacitly conferred on those who have power over the economy or (as the very ambiguity of the word 'competence' indicates) an attribute of status.[43]

Only in imaginary experience (in the folk tale, for example), which neutralizes the sense of social realities, does the social world take the form of a universe of possibles equally possible for any

---

[42] For background information on Max Weber, see essay 7.

[43] In this passage, Bourdieu critiques economic theory which, he argues, presupposes the existence of a universal economic logic and is based on analyzing and predicting the actions of individuals assumed to be identical. However, for Bourdieu, the logic of the market is not universal but tied to the assumptions and dispositions of individuals in particular times and places. Individuals do not come to the market as random and identical but, because they exist within history and within cultural and social systems, are endowed with different sorts and quantities of capital (see note 17) and therefore face different potential outcomes in the market. These outcomes are strongly tied to social class.

possible subject. Agents shape their aspirations according to concrete indices of the accessible and the inaccessible, of what is and is not 'for us', a division as fundamental and as fundamentally recognized as that between the sacred and the profane. The pre-emptive rights on the future that are defined by law and by the monopolistic right to certain possibles that it confers are merely the explicitly guaranteed form of the whole set of appropriated chances through which the power relations of the present project themselves into the future, from where they govern present dispositions, especially those towards the future. In fact, a given agent's practical relation to the future, which governs his present practice, is defined in the relationship between, on the one hand, his *habitus* with its temporal structures and dispositions towards the future, constituted in the course of a particular relationship to a particular universe of probabilities, and on the other hand a certain state of the chances objectively offered to him by the social world. The relation to what is possible is a relation to power; and the sense of the probable future is constituted in the prolonged relationship with a world structured according to the categories of the possible (for us) and the impossible (for us), of what is appropriated in advance by and for others and what one can reasonably expect for oneself. The *habitus* is the principle of a selective perception of the indices tending to confirm and reinforce it rather than transform it, a matrix generating responses adapted in advance to all objective conditions identical to or homologous with the (past) conditions of its production; it adjusts itself to a prob-

able future which it anticipates and helps to bring about because it reads it directly in the present of the presumed world, the only one it can ever know.[1] It is thus the basis of what Marx (1975: 378) calls 'effective demand' (as opposed to 'demand without effect', based on need and desire), a realistic relation to what is possible, founded on and therefore limited by power. This disposition, always marked by its (social) conditions of acquisition and realization, tends to adjust to the objective chances of satisfying need or desire, inclining agents to 'cut their coats according to their cloth,' and so to become the accomplices of the processes that tend to make the probable a reality.[44]

NOTES

[a] Ideally, one would like to be able completely to avoid talking about concepts for their own sake and so running the risk of being both schematic and formal. Like all dispositional concepts, the concept of the *habitus*, which is predisposed by its range of historical uses to designate a system of acquired, permanent, generative dispositions, is justified above all by the false problems and false solutions that it eliminates, the questions it enables one to formulate better or to resolve, and the specifically scientific difficulties to which it gives rise.

[b] The notion of the *structural relief* of the attributes of an object, i.e. the character that causes an attribute (e.g. colour or shape) 'to be more easily taken into account in any semantic treatment of the signified which contains it' (Le Ny 1979: 190ff.), like the Weberian notion of 'average chances' which is its equivalent in another context, is an abstraction, since relief varies according to dispositions. However, it enables one to escape from pure subjectivism by taking note of the existence of objective determinations of perceptions.

---

[44] In this final paragraph, Bourdieu refers directly to two of the most powerful influences on him: Durkheim and Marx. He begins with Durkheim's notion of the sacred and profane. Durkheim believed that the tendency of people to divide their world into sacred and profane was a universal social fact. Bourdieu juxtaposes this with the idea that one of the most basic elements of the *habitus* is to think in terms of things that are appropriate to us or not appropriate to us. Although he does not use the term here, Bourdieu generally characterizes such shared sets of opinions and unquestioned beliefs that bind members of a community to one another as *doxa* (Wacquant 2006). Bourdieu also

refers to Marx's discussion of the power of money in *The Economic and Philosophic Manuscripts of 1844*. There, Marx says: "The difference between effective demand based on money and ineffective demand based on my need, my passion, my wish, etc., is the difference between *being* and *thinking*, between that which *exists* within me merely as an idea and the idea which exists as a *real object* outside of me." Bourdieu thus combines elements of Durkheim's ideas of collective conscious with the understandings of history, political and economic structures, and power relationships that characterize Marx's work.

The illusion of the free creation of the properties of a situation and, therefore, of the ends of action, no doubt finds an apparent justification in the circle, characteristic of all conditional stimulation, whereby the *habitus* can produce the response objectively inscribed in its 'formula' only to the extent that it confers a triggering efficacy on the situation by constituting it according to its own principles, i.e. making it exist as a pertinent question in terms of a particular way of questioning reality.

[c] In social formations in which the reproduction of relations of domination (and economic or cultural capital) is not performed by objective mechanisms, the endless work required to maintain relations of personal dependence would be condemned to failure if it could not count on the permanence of *habitus,* socially constituted and constantly reinforced by individual or collective sanctions. In this case, the social order rests mainly on the order that reigns in people's minds, and the *habitus,* i.e. the organism as appropriated by the group and attuned to the demands of the group, functions as the materialization of the collective memory, reproducing the acquisitions of the predecessors in the successors. The group's resulting tendency to persist in its being works at a much deeper level than that of 'family traditions', the permanence of which presupposes a consciously maintained loyalty and also guardians. These traditions therefore have a rigidity alien to the strategies of the *habitus,* which, in new situations, can invent new ways of fulfilling the old functions. It is also deeper than the conscious strategies through which agents seek expressly to act on their future and shape it in the image of the past, such as testaments, or even explicit norms, which are simple calls to order, i.e. to the probable, which they make doubly potent.

[d] 'We call this subjective, variable probability—which sometimes excludes doubt and engenders a certainty *sui generis* and which at other times appears as no more than a vague glimmer—*philosophical probability,* because it refers to the exercise of the higher faculty whereby we comprehend the order and the rationality of things. All reasonable men have a confused notion of similar probabilities: this then determines, or at least justifies, those unshakeable beliefs we call *common sense*' (Cournot 1922: 70).

[e] One of the virtues of subjectivism and of the 'moralism of consciousness' (or the examination of conscience) which it often disguises is that, in the analyses that condemn actions subject to the pressures of the world as 'inauthentic' (cf. Heidegger on everyday existence and 'das Man' or Sartre on 'serious-mindedness'), it shows, *per absurdum,* the impossibility of the 'authentic' existence that would absorb all pre-given meanings and objective determinations in a project of freedom. The purely ethical pursuit of 'authenticity' is the privilege of those who have the leisure to think and can afford to dispense with the economy of thought that 'inauthentic' conduct allows.

[f] Contrary to all forms of the occasionalist illusion which inclines one to relate practices directly to properties inscribed in the situation, it has to be pointed out that 'interpersonal' relations are only apparently person-to-person relations and that the truth of the interaction never lies entirely in the interaction. This is forgotten when the objective structure of the relationship between the assembled individuals or the groups they belong to—that is, distances and hierarchies—is reduced to the momentary structure of their interaction in a particular situation and group, and when everything that occurs in an experimental situation is explained in terms of the experimentally controlled characteristics of the situation, such as relative positions in space or the nature of the channels used.

[g] Thus ignorance of the surest but best-hidden basis of the integration of groups or classes can lead some people to deny the unity of the dominant class with no other proof than the impossibility of empirically establishing that the members of the dominant class have an explicit policy, expressly imposed by concertation or even conspiracy; while it can lead others to see the only possible basis for the unity of the dominated class in the awakening of consciousness, a kind of revolutionary cogito that is supposed to bring the working class into existence by constituting it as a 'class in itself.'

[h] It can be understood why dancing, a particular and spectacular case of synchronization of the homogeneous and orchestration of the heterogeneous, is everywhere predisposed to symbolize and reinforce group integration.

[i] It is easy to see that the infinite possible combinations of the variables associated with the trajectories of each individual and of the lineages from which he comes can account for the infinity of individual differences.

[j] The most profitable strategies are usually those produced, without any calculation, and in the illusion of the most absolute 'sincerity', by a *habitus* objectively fitted to the objective structures. These strategies without strategic calculation procure an important secondary advantage for those who can scarcely be called their authors: the social approval accruing to apparent disinterestedness.

[k] Generation conflicts oppose not age-classes separated by natural properties, but *habitus* which have been produced by different modes of generation, that is, by conditions of existence which, by imposing different definitions of the impossible, the possible and the probable, cause one group to experience practices

or aspirations that another group finds unthinkable or scandalous as natural or reasonable, and vice versa.

[1] Emotion, the extreme case of such anticipation, is a hallucinatory 'presenting' of the impending future, which, as bodily reactions identical to those of the real situation bear witness, leads a person to live a still suspended future as already present, or even already past, and therefore necessary and inevitable—'I'm a dead man', 'I'm done for.'

REFERENCES

Attneave, F. 1953: Psychological probability as a function of experienced frequency. *Journal of Experimental Psychology*, 46, 81–6.

Brunswik, E. 1949: Systematic and representative design of psychological experiments. In J. Neymen (ed.), *Proceedings of the Berkeley Symposium on Mathematical Statistics and Probability*. Berkeley, Calif.: University of California Press, 143–202.

Cournot A. 1922: *Essai sure les fondements de la connaissance et sure les caractères de la critique philosophique*. Paris: Hachette (1st edn 1851).

Durkheim, E. 1977: *The Evolution of Educational Thought*. London: Routledge & Kegan Paul. (*L'Évolution pédagogique en France*. 1938).

Gluckman, M. 1961: Ethnographic data in British social anthropology. *Sociological Review*. 9, 5–17.

Harris, M. 1964: *The Nature of Cultural Things*. New York: Random House.

Leach, E. 1962: On certain unconsidered aspects of double descent systems. *Man*, 62.

Le Ny, J. F. 1979: *La Sémantique psychologique*. Paris: PUF.

Leibniz, G. W. 1866: *Second éclaircissement du système de la communication des substances*. (first pub. 1696). In Leibniz *Oeuvres philosophiques*. Ed. P. Janet. Paris: Ladrange.

Marx, K. 1975: *Econonomic and Philosophic Manuscripts of 1844*. In K. Marx, *Early Writings*, Harmondsworth: Penguin.

Preston, M. G. and Barrata, P. 1948: An experimental study of the action-value of an uncertain income. *American Journal of Psychology*, 61, 183–93.

Ruyer, R. 1966: *Paradoxes de la conscience et limites de l'automatisme*. Paris: Albin Michel.

Van Velsen, J. 1964: *The Politics of Kinship: A Study in Social Manipulation Among the Lakeside Tonga*. Manchester: Manchester University Press.

Weber, M. 1922: *Gesammelte Aufsätze zur Wissenschaftslehre*. Tübingen: J. C. Mohr.

——1968: *Economy and Society*, vol I. New York: Bedminster.

---

35. *The Incitement to Discourse*

Michel Foucault (1926–1984)

The seventeenth century, then, was the beginning of an age of repression emblematic of what we call the bourgeois societies, an age which perhaps we still have not completely left behind. Calling sex by its name thereafter became more difficult and more costly. As if in order to gain mastery over it in reality, it had first been necessary to subjugate it at the level of language, control its free circulation in speech, expunge it from the things that were said, and extinguish the words that rendered it too visibly present. And even these prohibitions, it seems, were afraid to name it. Without even having to pronounce the word, modern prudishness was able to ensure that one did not speak of sex, merely through the interplay of prohibitions that referred back to one another: instances of muteness which, by dint of saying nothing, imposed silence. Censorship.[1]

From *The History of Sexuality, Volume 1* (1976, Eng Trans 1978).

---

[1] In this opening paragraph, Foucault makes it clear that his intent is to discuss the historical development of the discourse concerning sexuality in Western Europe. His central thesis is that, beginning sometime in the seventeenth century, the discourse about sexuality began to change from being general and open to being increasingly

Yet when one looks back over these last three centuries with their continual transformations, things appear in a very different light: around and apropos of sex, one sees a veritable discursive explosion. We must be clear on this point, however. It is quite possible that there was an expurgation—and a very rigorous one—of the authorized vocabulary. It may indeed be true that a whole rhetoric of allusion and metaphor was codified. Without question, new rules of propriety screened out some words: there was a policing of statements. A control over enunciations as well: where and when it was not possible to talk about such things became much more strictly defined; in which circumstances, among which speakers, and within which social relationships. Areas were thus established, if not of utter silence, at least of tact and discretion: between parents and children, for instance, or teachers and pupils, or masters and domestic servants. This almost certainly constituted a whole restrictive economy, one that was incorporated into that politics of language and speech—spontaneous on the one hand, concerted on the other—which accompanied the social redistributions of the classical period.[2]

At the level of discourses and their domains, however, practically the opposite phenomenon occurred. There was a steady proliferation of discourses concerned with sex—specific discourses, different from one another both by their form and by their object: a discursive ferment that gathered momentum from the eighteenth century onward. Here I am thinking not so much of the probable increase in "illicit" discourses, that

is, discourses of infraction that crudely named sex by way of insult or mockery of the new code of decency; the tightening up of the rules of decorum likely did produce, as a countereffect, a valorization and intensification of indecent speech. But more important was the multiplication of discourses concerning sex in the field of exercise of power itself: an institutional incitement to speak about it, and to do so more and more; a determination on the part of the agencies of power to hear it spoken about, and to cause it to speak through explicit articulation and endlessly accumulated detail.[3]

Consider the evolution of the Catholic pastoral and the sacrament of penance after the Council of Trent. Little by little, the nakedness of the questions formulated by the confession manuals of the Middle Ages, and a good number of those still in use in the seventeenth century, was veiled. One avoided entering into that degree of detail which some authors, such as Sanchez or Tamburini, had for a long time believed indispensable for the confession to be complete: description of the respective positions of the partners, the postures assumed, gestures, places touched, caresses, the precise moment of pleasure—an entire painstaking review of the sexual act in its very unfolding. Discretion was advised, with increasing emphasis. The greatest reserve was counseled when dealing with sins against purity: "This matter is similar to pitch, for, however one might handle it, even to cast it far from oneself, it sticks nonetheless, and always soils."[a] And later, Alfonso de'Liguori prescribed starting—and possibly going no further, especially when dealing with

---

specific and confined. This was coincident with other changes including the development of capitalism, increases in social control, and increases in specialization of all kinds. Discourse, as Foucault understands it, includes both the words we use to describe sexuality and the ways in which we think about it. Critically, discourse concerns not only what is said, but what one is forbidden to say. Sometimes speech is prohibited as a matter of law. More frequently, censorship is the result of social pressure.

[2] By "the social redistributions of the classical period" Foucault refers to "the class divisions and other social relationships developed and defined during the Eighteenth

Century" (Roughley 2003). Foucault sees the control and regulation of sexual discourse as fundamental to the project of class division and specialization that he believes forms the basis of capitalism.

[3] For Foucault, discourses and their control are fundamentally linked to power. It is not only that the ways of speaking about sex changed, but that this change was fundamentally linked to new expressions of power. To name sex in certain ways, to prohibit speaking of it in certain ways, and valorize speaking in others was to legitimate new divisions of power in the state.

children—with questions that were "roundabout and vague."[b,4]

But while the language may have been refined, the scope of the confession—the confession of the flesh—continually increased. This was partly because the Counter-Reformation busied itself with stepping up the rhythm of the yearly confession in the Catholic countries, and because it tried to impose meticulous rules of self-examination; but above all, because it attributed more and more importance in penance—and perhaps at the expense of some other sins—to all the insinuations of the flesh: thoughts, desires, voluptuous imaginings, delectations, combined movements of the body and the soul; henceforth all this had to enter, in detail, into the process of confession and guidance. According to the new pastoral, sex must not be named imprudently, but its aspects, its correlations, and its effects must be pursued down to their slenderest ramifications: a shadow in a daydream, an image too slowly dispelled, a badly exorcised complicity between the body's mechanics and the mind's complacency: everything had to be told. A twofold evolution tended to make the flesh into the root of all evil, shifting the most important moment of transgression from the act itself to the stirrings—so difficult to perceive and formulate—of desire. For this was an evil that afflicted the whole man, and in the most secret of forms: "Examine diligently, therefore, all the faculties of your soul: memory, understanding, and will. Examine with precision all your senses as well . . . Examine,

moreover, all your thoughts, every word you speak, and all your actions. Examine even unto your dreams, to know if, once awakened, you did not give them your consent. And finally, do not think that in so sensitive and perilous a matter as this, there is anything trivial or insignificant."[c] Discourse, therefore, had to trace the meeting line of the body and the soul, following all its meanderings: beneath the surface of the sins, it would lay bare the unbroken nervure of the flesh. Under the authority of a language that had been carefully expurgated so that it was no longer directly named, sex was taken charge of, tracked down as it were, by a discourse that aimed to allow it no obscurity, no respite.[5]

It was here, perhaps, that the injunction, so peculiar to the West, was laid down for the first time, in the form of a general constraint. I am not talking about the obligation to admit to violations of the laws of sex, as required by traditional penance; but of the nearly infinite task of telling—telling oneself and another, as often as possible, everything that might concern the interplay of innumerable pleasures, sensations, and thoughts which, through the body and the soul, had some affinity with sex. This scheme for transforming sex into discourse had been devised long before in an ascetic and monastic setting. The seventeenth century made it into a rule for everyone. It would seem in actual fact that it could scarcely have applied to any but a tiny elite; the great majority of the faithful who only went to confession on rare occasions in the course of the year escaped

---

[4] In this passage, Foucault uses the phrase "Catholic Pastoral" to refer to the ritual of confession. The Council of Trent (1545–1563) was a series of meetings of Catholic Church officials held in response to the emergence of Protestantism. The Council reaffirmed the centrality and efficacy of the sacrament of Confession and specified that "all the mortal crimes into which the faithful may have fallen should be revealed" (Sess. XIV, c. v). Tamburini refers to Thomas Tamburini (1591–1675) who wrote a five-volume manual on the proper ways for priests to receive confessions (*Methodus expeditæ confessionis* (1647). Tomás Sanchez (1550–1610) wrote in great detail about practices such as fondling, unusual mating positions, coitus interruptus, and female masturbation (Hurteau 1993). Alphonsus

Maria de Liguori (1696–1787), later canonized, was the founder of the Redemptorists, a society of missionary priests. De Ligouri preached exhaustive confession for adults but a much more moderate form for children. Foucault discusses de Ligouri in greater detail in *Abnormal: Lectures at the Collège de France, 1974–1975.*

[5] The Counter Reformation was a move toward increased piety and rigor of practice within the Catholic Church that occurred in the 100 years following the Council of Trent. Thus, Foucault is arguing that the Protestant Reformation and the Catholic response to it were among the key early sources of the increasingly detailed verbal accounting of different types and practices of sexuality.

such complex prescriptions. But the important point, no doubt, is that this obligation was decreed, as an ideal at least, for every good Christian. An imperative was established: Not only will you confess to acts contravening the law, but you will seek to transform your desire, your every desire, into discourse. Insofar as possible, nothing was meant to elude this dictum, even if the words it employed had to be carefully neutralized. The Christian pastoral prescribed as a fundamental duty the task of passing everything having to do with sex through the endless mill of speech.[d] The forbidding of certain words, the decency of expressions, all the censorings of vocabulary, might well have been only secondary devices compared to that great subjugation: ways of rendering it morally acceptable and technically useful. One could plot a line going straight from the seventeenth-century pastoral to what became its projection in literature, "scandalous" literature at that. "Tell everything," the directors would say time and again: "not only consummated acts, but sensual touchings, all impure gazes, all obscene remarks . . . all consenting thoughts."[e] Sade takes up the injunction in words that seem to have been retranscribed from the treatises of spiritual direction: "Your narrations must be decorated with the most numerous and searching details; the precise way and extent to which we may judge how the passion you describe relates to human manners and man's character is determined by your willingness to disguise no circumstance; and what is more, the least circumstance is apt to have an immense influence upon the procuring of that kind of sensory irritation we expect from your stories."[f] And again at the end of the nineteenth century, the anonymous author of *My Secret Life* submitted to the same prescription; outwardly, at least, this man was doubtless a kind of traditional libertine; but he conceived the idea of complementing his life—which he had almost totally dedicated to sexual activity—with a scrupulous account of every one of its episodes. He sometimes excuses himself by stressing his concern to educate young people, this man who had eleven volumes published, in a printing of only a few copies, which were devoted to the least adventures, pleasures, and sensations of his sex. It is best to take him at his word when he lets into his text the voice of a pure imperative: "I recount the facts, just as they happened, insofar as I am able to recollect them; this is all that I can do"; "a secret life must not leave out anything; there is nothing to be ashamed of . . . one can never know too much concerning human nature."[g] The solitary author of *My Secret Life* often says, in order to justify his describing them, that his strangest practices undoubtedly were shared by thousands of men on the surface of the earth. But the guiding principle for the strangest of these practices, which was the fact of recounting them all, and in detail, from day to day, had been lodged in the heart of modern man for over two centuries. Rather than seeing in this singular man a courageous fugitive from a "Victorianism" that would have compelled him to silence, I am inclined to think that, in an epoch dominated by (highly prolix) directives enjoining discretion and modesty, he was the most direct and in a way the most naïve representative of a plurisecular injunction to talk about sex. The historical accident would consist, rather, of the reticences of "Victorian Puritanism"; at any rate, they were a digression, a refinement, a tactical diversion in the great process of transforming sex into discourse.[6]

This nameless Englishman will serve better than his queen as the central figure for a sexuality whose main features were already taking shape with the Christian pastoral. Doubtless, in contrast to the latter, for him it was a matter of augmenting the sensations he experienced with the details of what he said about them; like Sade,

---

[6] In this spectacular passage, Foucault draws a rhetorical line connecting the practices of confession begun in the mid-16th century that demanded the minutely detailed description of sexual acts and thoughts with the work of the Marquis de Sade (1740–1814), and the author of *My Secret Life*. *My Secret Life* is a series of books authored by "Walter" chronicling the details of his extremely active sex life. Controversy remains over the identity of the actual author but the best candidate seems to be Henry Spencer Ashbee (1834–1900), also known for writing bibliographies of pornographic works.

he wrote "for his pleasure alone," in the strongest sense of the expression; he carefully mixed the editing and rereading of his text with erotic scenes which that writer's activities repeated, prolonged, and stimulated. But, after all, the Christian pastoral also sought to produce specific effects on desire, by the mere fact of transforming it—fully and deliberately—into discourse: effects of mastery and detachment, to be sure, but also an effect of spiritual reconversion, of turning back to God, a physical effect of blissful suffering from feeling in one's body the pangs of temptation and the love that resists it. This is the essential thing: that Western man has been drawn for three centuries to the task of telling everything concerning his sex; that since the classical age there has been a constant optimization and an increasing valorization of the discourse on sex; and that this carefully analytical discourse was meant to yield multiple effects of displacement, intensification, reorientation, and modification of desire itself. Not only were the boundaries of what one could say about sex enlarged, and men compelled to hear it said; but more important, discourse was connected to sex by a complex organization with varying effects, by a deployment that cannot be adequately explained merely by referring it to a law of prohibition. A censorship of sex? There was installed, rather, an apparatus for producing an ever greater quantity of discourse about sex, capable of functioning and taking effect in its very economy.[7]

This technique might have remained tied to the destiny of Christian spirituality if it had not been supported and relayed by other mechanisms. In the first place, by a "public interest." Not a collective curiosity or sensibility; not a new mentality; but power mechanisms that functioned in such a way that discourse on sex—for reasons that will have to be examined—became essential. Toward the beginning of the eighteenth century, there emerged a political, economic, and technical incitement to talk about sex. And not so

much in the form of a general theory of sexuality as in the form of analysis, stocktaking, classification, and specification, of quantitative or causal studies. This need to take sex "into account," to pronounce a discourse on sex that would not derive from morality alone but from rationality as well, was sufficiently new that at first it wondered at itself and sought apologies for its own existence. How could a discourse based on reason speak of that? "Rarely have philosophers directed a steady gaze to these objects situated between disgust and ridicule, where one must avoid both hypocrisy and scandal."[h] And nearly a century later, the medical establishment, which one might have expected to be less surprised by what it was about to formulate, still stumbled at the moment of speaking: "The darkness that envelops these facts, the shame and disgust they inspire, have always repelled the observer's gaze. . . For a long time I hesitated to introduce the loathsome picture into this study."[i] What is essential is not in all these scruples, in the "moralism" they betray, or in the hypocrisy one can suspect them of, but in the recognized necessity of overcoming this hesitation. One had to speak of sex; one had to speak publicly and in a manner that was not determined by the division between licit and illicit, even if the speaker maintained the distinction for himself (which is what these solemn and preliminary declarations were intended to show): one had to speak of it as of a thing to be not simply condemned or tolerated but managed, inserted into systems of utility, regulated for the greater good of all, made to function according to an optimum. Sex was not something one simply judged; it was a thing one administered. It was in the nature of a public potential; it called for management procedures; it had to be taken charge of by analytical discourses. In the eighteenth century, sex became a "police" matter—in the full and strict sense given the term at the time: not the repression of disorder, but an ordered maximization of collective and individual forces: "We

---

[7] Note the emphasis in this passage on the relationship between discourse (the act of recounting as well as the words and phrases we use) and effects on the body and society. For Foucault, it is axiomatic that the way we talk about things matters. Note too that for Foucault, this is ultimately related to the development of institutions that promote, control, and regulate both discourse and actions.

must consolidate and augment, through the wisdom of its regulations, the internal power of the state; and since this power consists not only in the Republic in general, and in each of the members who constitute it, but also in the faculties and talents of those belonging to it, it follows that the police must concern themselves with these means and make them serve the public welfare. And they can only obtain this result through the knowledge they have of those different assets."[j] A policing of sex: that is, not the rigor of a taboo, but the necessity of regulating sex through useful and public discourses.[8]

A few examples will suffice. One of the great innovations in the techniques of power in the eighteenth century was the emergence of "population" as an economic and political problem: population as wealth, population as manpower or labor capacity, population balanced between its own growth and the resources it commanded. Governments perceived that they were not dealing simply with subjects, or even with a "people," but with a "population," with its specific phenomena and its peculiar variables: birth and death rates, life expectancy, fertility, state of health, frequency of illnesses, patterns of diet and habitation. All these variables were situated at the point where the characteristic movements of life and the specific effects of institutions intersected: "States are not populated in accordance with the natural progression of propagation, but by virtue

of their industry, their products, and their different institutions . . . Men multiply like the yields from the ground and in proportion to the advantages and resources they find in their labors."[k] At the heart of this economic and political problem of population was sex: it was necessary to analyze the birth rate, the age of marriage, the legitimate and illegitimate births, the precocity and frequency of sexual relations, the ways of making them fertile and sterile, the effects of unmarried life or of the prohibitions, the impact of contraceptive practices—of those notorious "deadly secrets" which demographers on the eve of the Revolution knew were already familiar to the inhabitants of the countryside.[9]

Of course, it had long been asserted that a country had to be populated if it hoped to be rich and powerful; but this was the first time that a society had affirmed, in a constant way, that its future and its fortune were tied not only to the number and the uprightness of its citizens, to their marriage rules and family organization, but to the manner in which each individual made use of his sex. Things went from ritual lamenting over the unfruitful debauchery of the rich, bachelors, and libertines to a discourse in which the sexual conduct of the population was taken both as an object of analysis and as a target of intervention; there was a progression from the crudely populationist arguments of the mercantilist epoch to the much more subtle and calculated attempts at

---

[8] Here Foucault moves the discussion of sex from the domain of the Church and of the perverse to the domain of the state. Control of sexuality with the intention of rationalizing it and putting it to service becomes a goal of the state. The scholars he quotes are models of rationalist, enlightenment thinking. In order, they are the eighteenth century rational progressivist Condorcet (see intro to nineteenth century evolutionism), Auguste Ambroise Tardieu (1818–1879), a pioneer in forensic medicine and author of the first medical text on child sexual abuse (the symptoms characteristic of battered children are often called Tardieu's syndrome in his honor), and Johann Heinrich Gottlob von Justi (1717–1771), another key enlightenment figure who, writing on a wide variety of subjects argued for the rationalization of the economic and social systems of Prussia and other states of the Holy Roman Empire.

Thus, Foucault understands the changes in discourses concerning sexuality to be part of larger changes attempting to rationalize and reform European societies.

[9] "Deadly secrets" is how the eighteenth century demographer Jean-Baptiste Moheau (1745–1794) refers to contraceptives and possibly abortion. Moheau was concerned with depopulation and wrote an essay on the French Population (1778). In an oft-cited phrase, Moheau wrote: "Rich women . . . are not the only ones who regard the propagation of the species as an old-fashioned foolishness. . . . already the deadly secrets unknown to every other animal except man have penetrated the countryside: even in the villages nature is deceived" (cited in McLaren 1974:611). The revolution refers to the French Revolution of 1789.

regulation that tended to favor or discourage—according to the objectives and exigencies of the moment—an increasing birth rate. Through the political economy of population there was formed a whole grid of observations regarding sex. There emerged the analysis of the modes of sexual conduct, their determinations and their effects, at the boundary line of the biological and the economic domains. There also appeared those systematic campaigns which, going beyond the traditional means—moral and religious exhortations, fiscal measures—tried to transform the sexual conduct of couples into a concerted economic and political behavior. In time these new measures would become anchorage points for the different varieties of racism of the nineteenth and twentieth centuries. It was essential that the state know what was happening with its citizens' sex, and the use they made of it, but also that each individual be capable of controlling the use he made of it. Between the state and the individual, sex became an issue, and a public issue no less; a whole web of discourses, special knowledges, analyses, and injunctions settled upon it.

The situation was similar in the case of children's sex. It is often said that the classical period consigned it to an obscurity from which it scarcely emerged before the *Three Essays* or the beneficent anxieties of Little Hans. It is true that a longstanding "freedom" of language between children and adults, or pupils and teachers, may have disappeared. No seventeenth-century pedagogue would have publicly advised his disciple, as did Erasmus in his *Dialogues*, on the choice of a good prostitute. And the boisterous laughter that had accompanied the precocious sexuality of

children for so long—and in all social classes, it seems—was gradually stifled. But this was not a plain and simple imposition of silence. Rather, it was a new regime of discourses. Not any less was said about it; on the contrary. But things were said in a different way; it was different people who said them, from different points of view, and in order to obtain different results. Silence itself—the things one declines to say, or is forbidden to name; the discretion that is required between different speakers—is less the absolute limit of discourse, the other side from which it is separated by a strict boundary, than an element that functions alongside the things said, with them and in relation to them within overall strategies. There is no binary division to be made between what one says and what one does not say; we must try to determine the different ways of not saying such things, how those who can and those who cannot speak of them are distributed, which type of discourse is authorized, or which form of discretion is required in either case. There is not one but many silences, and they are an integral part of the strategies that underlie and permeate discourses.[10]

Take the secondary schools of the eighteenth century, for example. On the whole, one can have the impression that sex was hardly spoken of at all in these institutions. But one only has to glance over the architectural layout, the rules of discipline, and their whole internal organization: the question of sex was a constant preoccupation. The builders considered it explicitly. The organizers took it permanently into account. All who held a measure of authority were placed in a state of perpetual alert, which the fixtures, the

---

[10] In this passage, Foucault develops the idea that a discourse consists not only of what is said but also of strategic silences: what is not said, or not said in certain places. He also considers authorization: the idea that institutions of power authorize or de-authorize certain types of discourses. Ultimately, what concerns Foucault is not specific ideas about sexuality, but the ways in which the discourse about sexuality is used by institutions of power in societies (and the ways in which such usage is resisted and subverted).

Three Essays and Little Hans both refer to Freud's work. Freud published *Three Essays on the theory of sexu-*

ality in 1905. The second of the three essays focused on the sexuality of infants and children. In particular, Freud advanced the theory that infantile sucking was the prototype of future sexual gratification. Little Hans refers to Freud's 1909 paper "Analysis of a Phobia in a Five Year Old Boy," about a young boy's fear of horses. This paper is considered an important step in the development of Freud's theory of the Oedipus complex. Desiderius Erasmus of Rotterdam was a key Renaissance figure and lived from 1466 to 1526.

precautions taken, the interplay of punishments and responsibilities, never ceased to reiterate. The space for classes, the shape of the tables, the planning of the recreation lessons, the distribution of the dormitories (with or without partitions, with or without curtains), the rules for monitoring bedtime and sleep periods—all this referred, in the most prolix manner, to the sexuality of children.[1] What one might call the internal discourse of the institution—the one it employed to address itself, and which circulated among those who made it function—was largely based on the assumption that this sexuality existed, that it was precocious, active, and ever-present. But this was not all: the sex of the schoolboy became in the course of the eighteenth century—and quite apart from that of adolescents in general—a public problem. Doctors counseled the directors and professors of educational establishments, but they also gave their opinions to families; educators designed projects which they submitted to the authorities; schoolmasters turned to students, made recommendations to them, and drafted for their benefit books of exhortation, full of moral and medical examples. Around the schoolboy and his sex there proliferated a whole literature of precepts, opinions, observations, medical advice, clinical cases, outlines for reform, and plans for ideal institutions. With Basedow and the German "philanthropic" movement, this transformation of adolescent sex into discourse grew to considerable dimensions. Salzmann even organized an experimental school which owed its exceptional character to a supervision and education of sex so well thought out that youth's universal sin would never need to be practiced there. And with all these measures taken, the

child was not to be simply the mute and unconscious object of attentions prearranged between adults only; a certain reasonable, limited, canonical, and truthful discourse on sex was prescribed for him—a kind of discursive orthopedics. The great festival organized at the Philanthropinum in May of 1776 can serve as a vignette in this regard. Taking the form of an examination, mixed with floral games, the awarding of prizes, and a board of review, this was the first solemn communion of adolescent sex and reasonable discourse. In order to show the success of the sex education given students, Basedow had invited all the dignitaries that Germany could muster (Goethe was one of the few to decline the invitation). Before the assembled public, one of the professors, a certain Wolke, asked the students selected questions concerning the mysteries of sex, birth, and procreation. He had them comment on engravings that depicted a pregnant woman, a couple, and a cradle. The replies were enlightened, offered without shame or embarrassment. No unseemly laughter intervened to disturb them—except from the very ranks of an adult audience more childish than the children themselves, and whom Wolke severely reprimanded. At the end, they all applauded these cherub-faced boys who, in front of adults, had skillfully woven the garlands of discourse and sex.[m,11]

It would be less than exact to say that the pedagogical institution has imposed a ponderous silence on the sex of children and adolescents. On the contrary, since the eighteenth century it has multiplied the forms of discourse on the subject; it has established various points of implantation for sex; it has coded contents and qualified speakers. Speaking about children's sex, inducing

---

[11] Johann Bernhard Basedow (1724–1790) was the founder of Philanthropinism, a movement in German education. The Philanthropinists hoped to create a rational and scientific form of education. Strongly influenced by Rousseau's key work on education, *Emile* (see Durkheim, What is a Social Fact?, note 5) they conceived education to be less a direct imparting of information and more of a setting of rules and structures in which a child's personality and potential could develop. The Philanthropinists had idiosyncratic views concerning the impor-

tance of semen, which they linked to manliness, strength, and courage. They were extremely concerned with preventing masturbation, which they considered dangerous and had a wide repertoire of tactics designed to eliminate it, including the architectural elements Foucault discusses here (Sumser 1992). Philanthropist ideas about masturbation have not survived and Basedow's Philanthropin in Dessau closed in 1793. However, other elements of their educational program continue to exert a strong influence over education today.

educators, physicians, administrators, and parents to speak of it, or speaking to them about it, causing children themselves to talk about it, and enclosing them in a web of discourses which sometimes address them, sometimes speak about them, or impose canonical bits of knowledge on them, or use them as a basis for constructing a science that is beyond their grasp—all this together enables us to link an intensification of the interventions of power to a multiplication of discourse. The sex of children and adolescents has become, since the eighteenth century, an important area of contention around which innumerable institutional devices and discursive strategies have been deployed. It may well be true that adults and children themselves were deprived of a certain way of speaking about sex, a mode that was disallowed as being too direct, crude, or coarse. But this was only the counterpart of other discourses, and perhaps the condition necessary in order for them to function; discourses that were interlocking, heirarchized, and all highly articulated around a cluster of power relations.[12]

One could mention many other centers which in the eighteenth or nineteenth century began to produce discourses on sex. First, there was medicine, via the "nervous disorders"; next psychiatry, when it set out to discover the etiology of mental illnesses, focusing its gaze first on "excess," then onanism, then frustration, then "frauds against procreation," but especially when it annexed the whole of the sexual perversions as its own province; criminal justice, too, which had long been concerned with sexuality, particularly in the form of "heinous" crimes and crimes against nature, but which, toward the middle of the nineteenth century, broadened its jurisdiction to include petty offenses, minor indecencies, insignificant perversions; and lastly, all

those social controls, cropping up at the end of the last century, which screened the sexuality of couples, parents and children, dangerous and endangered adolescents—undertaking to protect, separate, and forewarn; signaling perils everywhere; awakening people's attention; calling for diagnoses; piling up reports; organizing therapies. These sites radiated discourses aimed at sex, intensifying people's awareness of it as a constant danger, and this in turn created a further incentive to talk about it.[13]

One day in 1867, a farmhand from the village of Lapcourt, who was somewhat simple-minded, employed here then there, depending on the season, living hand-to-mouth from a little charity or in exchange for the worst sort of labor, sleeping in barns and stables, was turned in to the authorities. At the border of a field, he had obtained a few caresses from a little girl, just as he had done before and seen done by the village urchins round about him; for, at the edge of the wood, or in the ditch by the road leading to Saint-Nicolas, they would play the familiar game called "curdled milk." So he was pointed out by the girl's parents to the mayor of the village, reported by the mayor to the gendarmes, led by the gendarmes to the judge, who indicted him and turned him over first to a doctor, then to two other experts who not only wrote their report but also had it published." What is the significant thing about this story? The pettiness of it all; the fact that this everyday occurrence in the life of village sexuality, these inconsequential bucolic pleasures, could become, from a certain time, the object not only of a collective intolerance but of a judicial action, a medical intervention, a careful clinical examination, and an entire theoretical elaboration. The thing to note is that they went so far as to measure the brainspan, study the facial bone

---

[12] Foucault addresses the irony that, far from prohibiting discussions about sex, the subjugation of sexuality to scrutiny by the institutions of state greatly increased the detailed discussion of sex. However, this discussion was embedded in specific power relationships. The ordering and cataloging of sexuality became a method for an increasingly powerful state and a growing world of professionals such as educators and doctors to impose

their control on children as well as other members of society.

[13] The alert reader might consider Mead's discussion of attitudes toward adolescents in the introduction to *Coming of Age in Samoa* (essay 15) as well as the publication of that book, as part of the discourse that Foucault describes in this passage.

structure, and inspect for possible signs of dege-nerescence the anatomy of this personage who up to that moment had been an integral part of village life; that they made him talk; that they questioned him concerning his thoughts, inclina-tions, habits, sensations, and opinions. And then, acquitting him of any crime, they decided finally to make him into a pure object of medicine and knowledge—an object to be shut away till the end of his life in the hospital at Mareville, but also one to be made known to the world of learn-ing through a detailed analysis. One can be fairly certain that during this same period the Lapcourt schoolmaster was instructing the little villagers to mind their language and not talk about all these things aloud. But this was undoubtedly one of the conditions enabling the institutions of knowledge and power to overlay this everyday bit of theater with their solemn discourse. So it was that our society—and it was doubtless the first in history to take such measures—assembled around these timeless gestures, these barely fur-tive pleasures between simple-minded adults and alert children, a whole machinery for speechify-ing, analyzing, and investigating.[14]

Between the licentious Englishman, who ear-nestly recorded for his own purposes the singular episodes of his secret life, and his contemporary, this village halfwit who would give a few pennies to the little girls for favors the older ones refused him, there was without doubt a profound con-nection: in any case, from one extreme to the other, sex became something to say, and to say exhaustively in accordance with deployments that were varied, but all, in their own way, compel-ling. Whether in the form of a subtle confession in confidence or an authoritarian interrogation, sex—be it refined or rustic—had to be put into words. A great polymorphous injunction bound the Englishman and the poor Lorrainese peasant alike. As history would have it, the latter was named Jouy.[o,15]

Since the eighteenth century, sex has not ceased to provoke a kind of generalized discursive erethism.[16] And these discourses on sex did not multiply apart from or against power, but in the very space and as the means of its exercise. Incite-ments to speak were orchestrated from all quar-ters, apparatuses everywhere for listening and recording, procedures for observing, questioning, and formulating. Sex was driven out of hiding and constrained to lead a discursive existence. From the singular imperialism that compels everyone to transform his sexuality into a perpetual discourse, to the manifold mechanisms which, in the areas of economy, pedagogy, medicine, and justice, incite,

---

[14] The important part of this passage is clearly Foucault's claim that in the 19th century, the "inconsequential bu-colic pleasures" of an earlier time were systematized, cat-egorized, and regulated. Control and intervention by power (represented by the government and the profes-sions), mediated by a complex language of sexuality, ex-tended to the exchanges between children and a village simpleton. Many current readers may object to the notion that the game of "curdled milk," presumably involving se-men, could be described as an "inconsequential bucolic pleasure." On the one hand, this may be the result of our acceptance of the dominant discourse of control and reg-ulation of sexuality. On the other, Foucault's own sexual-ity, and his beliefs about sexuality, may have had a strong influence both on his decision to write about sex and on the attitudes he presents in his work. Foucault lived much of his adult life as a more-or-less openly gay man. He was involved in the gay sadomasochist scene in San Francisco in the late 1970s and early 1980s and he died of an-AIDS related illness in 1984. His own position on the borders of the sexual landscape may have given him a particular concern with the relations between power and sexual ac-tions and led him to positions that some may consider both radical and disturbing. For example, he argued that "the criminality of rape is overrated because sexuality is, and that it should be, juridically restricted to the element of bodily harm, any genital transactions being neither here nor there and any denial of this being itself phallocentric" (Rawson 1994:473, see Foucault 1988 *Politics, Philoso-phy, Culture.*)

[15] As the translator notes, Foucault here puns on the French word *jouir*, to play. In addition to the puns noted by the translator, Foucault may also be referring to Derrida's no-tion of free play: the idea that, without a fixed center (a stable, knowable reality), human beings are trapped in a world of endless sign-substitutions (see Hanson, essay 38 in this volume, Derrida 1970).

[16] erethism: abnormal sensitivity of a body part or organ to stimulation.

extract, distribute, and institutionalize the sexual discourse, an immense verbosity is what our civilization has required and organized. Surely no other type of society has ever accumulated—and in such a relatively short span of time—a similar quantity of discourses concerned with sex. It may well be that we talk about sex more than anything else; we set our minds to the task; we convince ourselves that we have never said enough on the subject, that, through inertia or submissiveness, we conceal from ourselves the blinding evidence, and that what is essential always eludes us, so that we must always start out once again in search of it. It is possible that where sex is concerned, the most long-winded, the most impatient of societies is our own.

But as this first overview shows, we are dealing less with a discourse on sex than with a multiplicity of discourses produced by a whole series of mechanisms operating in different institutions. The Middle Ages had organized around the theme of the flesh and the practice of penance a discourse that was markedly unitary. In the course of recent centuries, this relative uniformity was broken apart, scattered, and multiplied in an explosion of distinct discursivities which took form in demography, biology, medicine, psychiatry, psychology, ethics, pedagogy, and political criticism. More precisely, the secure bond that held together the moral theology of concupiscence[17] and the obligation of confession (equivalent to the theoretical discourse on sex and its first-person formulation) was, if not broken, at least loosened and diversified: between the objectification of sex in rational discourses, and the movement by which each individual was set to the task of recounting his own sex, there has occurred, since the eighteenth century, a whole series of tensions, conflicts, efforts at adjustment, and attempts at retranscription. So it is not simply in terms of a continual extension that we must speak of this discursive growth; it should be seen, rather, as a

dispersion of centers from which discourses emanated, a diversification of their forms, and the complex deployment of the network connecting them. Rather than the uniform concern to hide sex, rather than a general prudishness of language, what distinguishes these last three centuries is the variety, the wide dispersion of devices that were invented for speaking about it, for having it be spoken about, for inducing it to speak of itself, for listening, recording, transcribing, and redistributing what is said about it: around sex, a whole network of varying, specific, and coercive transpositions into discourse. Rather than a massive censorship, beginning with the verbal proprieties imposed by the Age of Reason, what was involved was a regulated and polymorphous incitement to discourse.[18]

The objection will doubtless be raised that if so many stimulations and constraining mechanisms were necessary in order to speak of sex, this was because there reigned over everyone a certain fundamental prohibition; only definite necessities—economic pressures, political requirements—were able to lift this prohibition and open a few approaches to the discourse on sex, but these were limited and carefully coded; so much talk about sex, so many insistent devices contrived for causing it to be talked about—but under strict conditions: Does this not prove that it was an object of secrecy, and more important, that there is still an attempt to keep it that way? But this oft-stated theme, that sex is outside of discourse and that only the removing of an obstacle, the breaking of a secret, can clear the way leading to it, is precisely what needs to be examined. Does it not partake of the injunction by which discourse is provoked? Is it not with the aim of inciting people to speak of sex that it is made to mirror, at the outer limit of every actual discourse, something akin to a secret whose discovery is imperative, a thing abusively reduced to silence, and at the same time difficult and necessary, dangerous and

---

[17] concupiscence: a strong desire, particularly sexual desire. Also, in Catholic theology, a desire of the lower appetite (organic needs) contrary to reason (*The Catholic Encyclopedia*).

[18] Note the emphasis on conflict in this paragraph. The expansion of sexual discourses has not been a uniform process but rather different groups have contested for control of different areas of discourse.

precious to divulge? We must not forget that by making sex into that which, above all else, had to be confessed, the Christian pastoral always presented it as the disquieting enigma: not a thing which stubbornly shows itself, but one which always hides, the insidious presence that speaks in a voice so muted and often disguised that one risks remaining deaf to it. Doubtless the secret does not reside in that basic reality in relation to which all the incitements to speak of sex are situated—whether they try to force the secret, or whether in some obscure way they reinforce it by the manner in which they speak of it. It is a question, rather, of a theme that forms part of the very mechanics of these incitements: a way of giving shape to the requirement to speak about the matter, a fable that is indispensable to the endlessly proliferating economy of the discourse on sex. What is peculiar to modern societies, in fact, is not that they consigned sex to a shadow existence, but that they dedicated themselves to speaking of it ad infinitum, while exploiting it as the secret.[19]

NOTES

[a] Paolo Segneri, *L'Instruction du penitent* (French trans. 1695), p. 301.

[b] Alfonso de' Liguori, *Practique des confesseurs* (French trans. 1854), p. 140.

[c] Segneri, *L'Instruction du penitent*, pp 301–2.

[d] The reformed pastoral also laid down rules, alpeit in a more discreet way, for putting sex into discourse. This notion will be developed in the next volume, *The Body and the Flesh*.

[e] Alfonso de' Liguori, *Préceptes sur le sixième commandement* (French trans. 1835), p. 5.

[f] Donatien-Alphonse de Sade, *The 120 Days of Sodom*, trans. Austryn Wainhouse and Richard Seaver (New York: Grove Press, 1966), p. 271.

[g] Anonymous, *My Secret Life*, (New York: Grove Press, 1966).

[h] Condorcet, cited by Jean-Louis Flandrcin, *Familles: parenté, maison, sexualité dand l'ancienne société*, (Paris: Hachette, 1976).

[i] Auguste Tardieu, Étude medico-légale sur les attentats aux moeurs (1857), p. 114.

[j] Johann von Justi, *Éléments généraux de police* (French trans. 1769), p. 20.

[k] Claude-Jacques Herbert, *Essai sur la police general des grains* (1753), pp 320–1.

[l] *Réglement des police pour les lycées*(1809), art. 67: "There shall always be, during class and study hours, an instructor watching the exterior, so as to prevent students who have gone out to relieve themselves from stopping and congregating.

art. 68: "After the evening prayer, the students will be conducted back to the dormitory, where the schoolmasters will put them to bed at once.

art. 69: "The masters will not retire except after having made certain that every student is in bed.

art. 70: "The beds shall be separated by partitions two meters in height. The dormitories shall be illuminated during the night."

[m] Johann Gottlieb Schummel, *Fritzens Reise nach Dessau* (1776) cited by August Pinloche, *La Réform de l'éducation in Allemagn au XVIIIe siècle* (1889), pp. 125–9.

[n] Bonnet and J. Bulard, *Rapport medico-légal sur l'état mental de Ch. J. Jouy*, Janury 4, 1968.

[o] Jouy sounds like the past participle of *jouir* the French verb meaning to enjoy, to delight in (something), but also to have an orgasm, to come. (Translator's note)

---

[19] This final paragraph expresses one of Foucault's central themes but also presents the reader with a dilemma. It expresses Foucault's concern with the fundamental conditions of discourse. He is less concerned with whether various syndromes diagnosed by psychiatrists and government officials are "real" than with the ways in which power and control are exerted and people are classified through the both the silences and the specifications of a discourse. The dilemma is that Foucault here sets a logical model that is impossible to prove or disprove. If we discuss sex in detail, that shows the elaboration of an increasingly complex system of sexual identification and control. However, if we urge people to be silent on the subject of sex, Foucault tells us that our principal aim is to cause people to speak of sex.

Postmodernism

McGee: "I'm having trouble getting started on this introduction to postmodernism." Warms: "Why don't you write about the process of writing the introduction?"

Rich Warms responded to Jon McGee's difficulty starting this introduction in a classic postmodernist fashion, trying to convince him to write it in a postmodern style. We hope that what makes Warms' (unsuccessful) response postmodern will become clear as you read.

Modernism is a term drawn from the study of literature and art as well as the history of science. In general, it reflects the epistemological notion that the world is knowable. People can use the techniques of science, philosophy, and rational inquiry to analyze and understand their world. Proper use of these tools can lead us to a thorough understanding of any subject material to which they are applied. In anthropology, modernism broadly refers to the time period stretching from the early twentieth century until the mid-1970s (Manganaro 1990). Common attributes of modernist writing in anthropology include detachment, the assumption of a position of scientific neutrality, and rationalism.

Postmodernists challenge the assertion that science and rationalism can lead to full and accurate knowledge of the world. They argue that these are specific historically constituted ways of knowing. Therefore, they can create only specific historically constituted sorts of. Since the ideas and practices that we usually refer to when we talk about science and rationality had their historical origin at a certain time and among a cer-

tain class within Western European and North American society, the truths they generate are appropriate to (or empowering of) that group. Although science makes transcendent claims, postmodernists argue that the truths generated by science, or any other system of knowledge are limited. Further, the methods of science and rationality, when applied to other cultures (or other groups within Western culture) are more likely to produce gross distortions than anything else. Postmodernists assert that other peoples have their own ways of knowing, and, since all knowledge is historically constituted, these are just as valid (or just as invalid) as any other.

The postmodernist challenge has led anthropologists to examine the basis of their discipline. For example, historically anthropologists have positioned themselves as authorities on other cultures. They fortify this claim by providing convincing written descriptions of other cultures and emphasizing the importance of their individual experiences of fieldwork. However, postmodern approaches encouraged anthropologists to examine the ways in which their authority, and that of the discipline of anthropology, is established and maintained. Such analysis focused on several areas including the conduct of fieldwork, the literary techniques used in the writing of ethnographies, and the validity of the author's interpretations over competing alternatives.

The conduct of fieldwork is a critical issue to postmodernists because traditionally most ethnography has contained very little information on the actual process of research. Postmodernists argue that it is precisely this process that is crucial in the creation of ethnographic texts. Fieldworkers must, of necessity, be in specific places at specific times. As a result, they see some things and not others. The particular circumstances of fieldwork—the political context in which it occurs, the investigator's preferences and predilections, and the people met by chance or design—all critically condition the understanding of society that results. Consequently, postmodern theorists believe that anthropology can never be purely objective.

Modernist ethnographies were written as if the anthropologist was a neutral, omniscient observer. Postmodernists claim, however, that because the collection of anthropological data is subjective, it is not possible to analyze the data objectively. The Rosaldo essay in this section dramatically illustrates this point. In "Grief and a Headhunter's Rage," Renato Rosaldo (b. 1941) describes his failed attempts to find a logical explanation for Ilongot head-hunting. However, Rosaldo tells us that it was the almost unbearable sorrow he felt after the accidental death of his wife in the field that led him to a visceral understanding of why Ilongot men go head-hunting after the death of loved ones. He argues that it was only this visceral personal experience, not the study of Ilongot custom or society, that allowed him insight into Ilongot society.

Writing ethnography is the primary means by which anthropologists convey their interpretations of other cultures, and ethnographies have usually followed some basic literary conventions, which Marcus and Cushman (1982) have described in detail. Even if you are not a student of ethnographic writing, you will immediately recognize several of these forms. One of the most obvious characteristics of ethnographic writing is that authors claim to represent the native point of view. Of course, an anthropologist cannot possibly present the point of view of everyone in a society; he or she works with selected informants. So the anthropologist chooses who speaks for the society and in his or her translation of the native language decides what words are presented to the audience.

Another common rhetorical device of Anglo-American ethnography is that writers claim to completely describe other cultures or societies even though anthropologists actually know only the part of a culture that they personally experience. One of the techniques through which this is commonly accomplished is the use of the omniscient narrator; the authoritative third-person observer who replaces the fallible first person. Instead of writing, "I saw my informant pour ketchup on his ice cream," a direct statement of what an anthropologist might actually observe, many ethnographies contain statements like "Texas State students pour ketchup on their ice cream." Postmodern critics argue that the use of the omniscient narrator heightens the sense of scientific objectivity projected by the text and improperly severs the relationship between what the ethnographer knows and how he or she came to know it (Marcus and Cushman 1982:32).

One result of the postmodern critique of ethnography was the more revealing style in which some anthropologists began to write. There has always been some self-revelation in ethnography, but in the late 1960s and early 1970s, anthropologists such as Briggs (1970), Geertz (1973), and Rabinow (1977) began to write ethnographies in which the recounting of their own experiences and feelings took a prominent role. For postmodern writers in the 1980s and 1990s, this self-reflexiveness was not simply a more straightforward form of reportage. The recounting of field experiences became a narrative device by which personal goals as well as anthropological understanding were conveyed. Rosaldo, for example, says that the writing of his article was an act of catharsis that helped him deal with his grief as well as giving him new insight into the Ilongot custom of head-hunting.

A second issue that underlies almost all postmodern writing lies in the area of interpretation. Postmodernists maintain that a text is necessarily an author's interpretation. If that author's work is taken as an authoritative account, then other voices and differing interpretations are dismissed. In the postmodern view, writing ethnography is an assertion of power because the only way authors can generate an interpretation that is accepted as true is to "delicense" all others. But can one person's interpretation be more valid than another's? Postmodernists maintain that it cannot. They insist that the acceptance of an interpretation is ultimately an issue of power and wealth. Historically, they say, the interpretations voiced by white males in Western industrialized nations have delicensed all others and silenced them. They ask why this view of events is the only acceptable interpretation and claim that deconstructing the work of this mainstream allows other opinions to be expressed. Postmodernists assert that in history, literature, and politics, the voices of women, minorities, and the poor have long been suppressed. It is only through recognizing and combating "epistemic violence"; the subtle forms of oppression that legitimate and enforce the discourses of the wealthy and powerful, that the voices of the oppressed can be heard.

A final form of postmodern scholarship deals with textual analysis (and this, in fact, informs most other sorts of postmodern thinking). Postmodernists argue that data are, of themselves, mute. Data are just data. Anthropologists participate in the flow of events around them, interpret what they observe, and construct meaning from those observations through the process of writing. Because one must write according to certain literary conventions (tense, voice, and so on), the finished text is of necessity a literary construction of its author. Readers in turn, impose their own interpretation on the author's text. In other words, the written word can never be adequate to represent reality. Instead, writing involves the piling up of layer upon layer of convention and interpretation. Similarly, reading involves its own conventions and each reader brings their own histories and understandings to the act of reading. Thus, a finished text is a thing unto itself. It cannot be an accurate representation of the reality it claims to portray, for this is impossible. Neither can it be understood as accurately reflecting the mind and understandings of its author (since these must be filtered through the conventions of reading and the reader's experience). So, what's a postmodernist to do when a text can tell us very little of the "reality" of its purported subject? Well, the answer is that a postmodernist may deconstruct the ways in which the devices and conventions of writing and reading are exploited in

the text, explores the sorts of meanings that are promoted by the text as well as those that are delegitimized, and examine what this may tell us about the current or historical nature of the society in which the text is written and read. Further, since any form of deconstruction and analysis is itself a literary process, all deconstruction is subject to further deconstruction. Derrida, the father of deconstruction, did not argue that his analysis of texts was authoritative. It was implicit in the process he outlined that deconstruction was a process that changed with the subject of the analysis and who conducted it. There was no authoritative reading to be made.

The issues of reflexivity, desconstruction, voice, power, and interpretation are all important elements that inform the work of authors featured in this section. Lila Abu-Lughod, for example, issued a call for new forms of ethnographic writing in her 1991 essay "Writing Against Culture." There, she argued that the writing of ethnography is inherently an expression of Western power because the concept of culture necessarily contains an element of hierarchy, and ethnographic writing is based on the textual construction of the "other." In other words, the subject of the text is not real people in the context of their lives but a fictional composite people constructed by the author and removed from the reality of the particulars of individually lived lives. Thus she advocates for "writing against culture" and proposes strategies for dealing with these textual forms of oppression. In particular, Abu-Lughod proposes that anthropologists write "ethnographies of the particular" (1991:149). By this she means that, instead of writing broad generalizations of a whole group, anthropologists should write ethnographies of particular people in specific times and places. Abu-Lughod's essay in this volume, "A Tale of Two Pregnancies," is this type of experimental form of ethnography. It contrasts Abu-Lughod's experiences when pregnant with those of Kareema, an Egyptian Bedouin woman who had been pregnant during Abu-Lughod's fieldwork. This essay is an excellent example of Abu-Lughod's notion of an ethnography of the particular because she is the principal subject of her essay. There is very little Bedouin "other" in the essay, most of which consists of specific descriptions of specific events during Abu-Lughod's fieldwork and the period in which she was trying to and eventually succeeded in becoming pregnant. On the one hand, the essay is a good read. Abu-Lughod comments on the nature of fertility medicine in the United States, her experiences in both at home and in Egypt, and various other aspects of modernity. On the other hand, the thoughtful reader might ask what separates this sort of anthropology from the literary essay?

The Hanson essay deals with a different aspect of postmodern thought. Hanson addresses the role colonists, anthropologists, nationalists, and other actors have played in the creation of Maori traditions in New Zealand. He argues that elements of Maori "traditional" culture are actually late nineteenth century European narratives that have been incorporated into current day Maori understandings of "traditional" Maori culture for contemporary purposes. Following Hanson's argument, it is critical for anthropologists to examine how information becomes cultural knowledge and how this knowledge is transmitted through time. More importantly, Hanson argues that the processes he has identified in the 19th and 20th centuries are always going on. People always reinvent, reinterpret, and repurpose their histories. Anthropologists "dip" samples from this process and participate in cultural invention just like everyone else. There is no such thing as a "traditional" culture. The past is unknowable. All we have is interpretations of interpretations. And all such interpretations are goal oriented: set in the context of power and politics.

Postmodernism has been extensively critiqued within anthropology. Many scholars vigorously defend the idea that anthropology is or should be an empirical science. They argue that although some aspects of ethnographic data collection are subjective, anthropologists can accurately observe and record what happens in the field and build useful theories based on this information. They point out that an anthropology that can only make very specific claims about the actions of particular individuals would have little of value to say. To take our example from earlier in this essay: If the only thing an anthropologist

can say is "I saw one of Jon McGee's students pour ketchup on his ice cream" why should anyone care about anthropology? What is the importance of one of McGee's students if his actions can never be generalized? In addition, some have claimed that there are critical logical flaws in postmodern arguments (for example, see O'Meara 1989).

Opponents of postmodernism sometimes argue that, pursued to its logical extreme, postmodernism must result in nihilism. If all voices should be heard, they say, are fascist voices, the voices of white supremacists or neo-Nazis, less worthy of respect than others? Postmodernists argue that power constructs truth. They use this argument, they claim, to recover the voices and agendas of the powerless. In recent years, this has generally been true. Many works by postmodern thinkers attempt to find the voices and represent the interests of those who have historically been oppressed. Throughout the 1990s, postmodernists generally positioned themselves as those who "speak truth to power." However, this notion sits very uneasily with the postmodern idea that truth is determined by power and not all postmodernists have opted to side with the powerless. In the past some whose work was basic to postmodernism chose to side with the powerful. Indeed, during World War II, hermeneuticist Martin Heidegger was an apologist for the Nazis and Paul de Man, who later became a prominent deconstructionist, was a Nazi journalist (Lehman 1992). Today, people representing all shades of the political spectrum seem to struggle to control the discourse and determine how individuals, groups, and history will be represented.

No doubt, taken to its logical extreme, postmodernism can seem nihilistic. Further, if all anthropologists took radical postmodern positions, there would be little difference between anthropology and literature. However, the postmodern critique has been of enduring value. It is rare to find an ethnography of the past twenty years that uses an omniscient narrator. Describing something of the personal history of the author and the conditions of fieldwork is now virtually a requirement for publication. Beyond this, Postmodernism encouraged anthropologists to be aware of issues of rhetoric, power, voice, and perspective. And this awareness continues to enrich our fieldwork and our writing. It helps us to evaluate both our own and other's claims to objectivity. And, since it encouraged anthropologists to be explicit about the specific sources of knowledge for the claims they make, postmodernism may have had the ironic effect of making anthropology more objective. Postmodernists remind us that cultures are never static and that power, conflict, and politics are always present. The postmodern critique of anthropology requires us to remember that these issues are expressed in the cultural structures within which people live, and that they influence peoples' actions, language, and ultimately the stories they tell.

36. *Grief and a Headhunter's Rage*

Renato Rosaldo (b. 1941)

If you ask an older Ilongot man of northern Luzon, Philippines, why he cuts off human heads, his answer is brief, and one on which no anthropologist can readily elaborate: He says that rage, born of grief, impels him to kill his fellow human beings. He claims that he needs a place "to carry his anger." The act of severing and tossing away the victim's head enables him, he says, to vent and, he hopes, throw away the anger of his bereavement. Although the anthropologist's job is to make other cultures intelligible, more questions fail to reveal any further explanation of this man's pithy statement. To him, grief, rage, and headhunting go together in a self-evident manner. Either you understand it or you don't. And, in fact, for the longest time I simply did not.

In what follows, I want to talk about how to talk about the cultural force of emotions.[a] The *emotional force* of a death, for example, derives less from an abstract brute fact than from a particular intimate relation's permanent rupture. It refers to the kinds of feelings one experiences on learning, for example, that the child just run over by a car is one's own and not a stranger's. Rather than speaking of death in general, one must consider the subject's position within a field of social relations in order to grasp one's emotional experience.[b,1]

My effort to show the force of a simple statement taken literally goes against anthropology's classic norms, which prefer to explicate culture through the gradual thickening of symbolic webs

From *Culture and Truth* (1989)

---

[1] From the opening, it is evident that Rosaldo is writing a different sort of anthropology than most of the authors in this book. Most anthropological writing has been built on a scientific model. Essays are written as reports, almost always in the third person. This essay, on the other hand, is conversational in tone, and much of it is in the first and second person. Beyond this, Rosaldo seems, in his opening, to deny the possibility of meaningful anthropological explanation of Ilongot head-hunting. The idea of emotional force which he elaborates below, is not so much explanation as a statement that no further description or explanation is possible.

Rosaldo also introduces the idea of positionality in this paragraph. He argues throughout this essay that an observer's position, that is their personal history and experiences, and their location in the class, racial, and ethnic hierarchy of their own society and the society that they are studying, plays a critical role in what is observed and how it is interpreted. The idea of positionality has some historical depth in anthropology (see Rosaldo's footnote j) it became increasingly popular after the publication of this essay. Indeed, the importance of positionality is a critical insight of postmodern anthropology. However, it also raises fundamental questions: If what you observe and the conclusions you draw from it depend on your positionality, is objective knowledge possible?

of meaning. By and large, cultural analysts use not *force* but such terms as *thick description, multivocality, polysemy, richness,* and *texture.* The notion of force, among other things, opens to question the common anthropological assumption that the greatest human import resides in the densest forest of symbols and that analytical detail, or "cultural depth," equals enhanced explanation of a culture, or "cultural elaboration." Do people always in fact describe most thickly what matters most to them?[2]

THE RAGE IN ILONGOT GRIEF

Let me pause a moment to introduce the Ilongots, among whom my wife, Michelle Rosaldo, and I lived and conducted field research for thirty months (1967–69, 1974). They number about 3,500 and reside in an upland area some 90 miles northeast of Manila, Philippines.[c] They subsist by hunting deer and wild pig and by cultivating rain-fed gardens (swiddens) with rice, sweet potatoes, manioc, and vegetables. Their (bilateral) kin relations are reckoned through men and women. After marriage, parents and their married daughters live in the same or adjacent households. The largest unit within the society, a largely territorial descent group called the *bertan,* becomes manifest primarily in the context of feuding. For themselves, their neighbors, and their ethnographers, headhunting stands out as the Ilongots' most salient cultural practice.

When Ilongots told me, as they often did, how the rage in bereavement could impel men to headhunt, I brushed aside their one-line ac-

counts as too simple, thin, opaque, implausible, stereotypical, or otherwise unsatisfying. Probably I naively equated grief with sadness. Certainly no personal experience allowed me to imagine the powerful rage Ilongots claimed to find in bereavement. My own inability to conceive the force of anger in grief led me to seek out another level of analysis that could provide a deeper explanation for older men's desire to headhunt.

Not until some fourteen years after first recording the terse Ilongot statement about grief and a headhunter's rage did I begin to grasp its overwhelming force. For years I thought that more verbal elaboration (which was not forthcoming) or another analytical level (which remained elusive) could better explain older men's motives for headhunting. Only after being repositioned through a devastating loss of my own could I better grasp that Ilongot older men mean precisely what they say when they describe the anger in bereavement as the source of their desire to cut off human heads. Taken at face value and granted its full weight, their statement reveals much about what compels these older men to headhunt.

In my efforts to find a "deeper" explanation for headhunting, I explored exchange theory, perhaps because it had informed so many classic ethnographies. One day in 1974, I explained the anthropologist's exchange model to an older Ilongot man named Insan. What did he think, I asked, of the idea that headhunting resulted from the way that one death (the beheaded victim's) canceled another (the next of kin). He looked puzzled, so I went on to say that the victim of a beheading was exchanged for the death of one's own kin, thereby balancing the books, so to

---

[2] By invoking the concepts of thick description and multivocality, Rosaldo is referring especially to Clifford Geertz and Victor Turner. The term "thick description" is associated with Geertz and the phrase "forest of symbols" refers to the title of Turner's book from which essay 32 is taken. The important difference between Rosaldo and Geertz can be seen in two different possible interpretations of the following story recounted by Geertz: "There is an Indian story—at least I heard it as an Indian story—about an Englishman who, having been told that the world rested on a platform which rested on the back of an elephant which

rested in turn on the back of a turtle, asked (perhaps he was an ethnographer; it is the way they behave), what did the turtle rest on? Another turtle. And that turtle? 'Ah, Sahib, after that it is turtles all the way down.'" (1973:28–29).

Geertz goes on to say that "cultural analysis is intrinsically incomplete"—meaning that there is always another layer of meaning. His parable can also be interpreted to mean that there is no meaning other than that expressed. It is all just turtles and nothing beyond that. This, perhaps, is the meaning that Rosaldo would prefer.

speak. Insan reflected a moment and replied that he imagined somebody could think such a thing (a safe bet, since I just had), but that he and other Ilongots did not think any such thing.[3] Nor was there any indirect evidence for my exchange theory in ritual, boast, song, or casual conversation.[d]

In retrospect, then, these efforts to impose exchange theory on one aspect of Ilongot behavior appear feeble. Suppose I had discovered what I sought? Although the notion of balancing the ledger does have a certain elegant coherence, one wonders how such bookish dogma could inspire any man to take another man's life at the risk of his own.[4]

My life experience had not as yet provided the means to imagine the rage that can come with devastating loss. Nor could I, therefore, fully appreciate the acute problem of meaning that Ilongots faced in 1974. Shortly after Ferdinand Marcos declared martial law in 1972, rumors that firing squads had become the new punishment for headhunting reached the Ilongot hills. The men therefore decided to call a moratorium on taking heads. In past epochs, when headhunting had become impossible, Ilongots had allowed their rage to dissipate, as best it could, in the course of everyday

life. In 1974, they had another option; they began to consider conversion to evangelical Christianity as a means of coping with their grief. Accepting the new religion, people said, implied abandoning their old ways, including headhunting. It also made coping with bereavement less agonizing because they could believe that the deceased had departed for a better world. No longer did they have to confront the awful finality of death.[5]

The force of the dilemma faced by the Ilongots eluded me at the time. Even when I correctly recorded their statements about grieving and the need to throw away their anger, I simply did not grasp the weight of their words. In 1974, for example, while Michelle Rosaldo and I were living among the Ilongots, a six-month-old baby died, probably of pneumonia. That afternoon we visited the father and found him terribly stricken. "He was sobbing and staring through glazed and bloodshot eyes at the cotton blanket covering his baby."[e] The man suffered intensely, for this was the seventh child he had lost. Just a few years before, three of his children had died, one after the other, in a matter of days. At the time, the situation was murky as people present talked both about evangelical Christianity (the possible

---

[3] The "deeper" explanation of head-hunting for which Rosaldo searched was some sort of accounting modeled on a natural law (here, a mathematical formula, one death cancels another). However, in describing this theory to the Ilongot, Rosaldo faces a problem: Even if the theory explains observed behavior, how can Rosaldo grant it any explanatory power when the idea is utterly unintelligible to the Ilongot themselves? Note that in this passage, Rosaldo implies that for a model to be satisfying, it must be recognized as accurate by the people whose behavior it purports to describe. Consider how different this position is from that of Marvin Harris who, in essay 19, argues that what Hindus think of his explanation of the cattle taboo is irrelevant to its accuracy.

[4] Rosaldo and other postmodern authors share a great deal of concern with the idea of the privileged position. In social science, to privilege a position is to give special credence to certain types of explanation and discount others. Postmodernists argue that Western social science has privileged a particular type of analysis: that which follows the model used in the physical sciences. The closer an explanation is to this model, the more "true" the information it generates, and

the higher the prestige of the field that uses it. The exchange theory Rosaldo has described here sounds like science and therefore it is privileged (but, Rosaldo insists, incorrect)

In some ways, the idea of privileged position is a recasting of the emic-etic dichotomy. A principal source of postmodern thought is ethnoscience and cognitive anthropology, but there is a powerful difference between postmodern thought and ethnoscience. Earlier debate on emics and etics was about the privileging of one or the other of these two positions. Postmodernism confronts the specific interests and positioning of both the anthropologists and their informants. Part of the reason for Rosaldo's misunderstanding of Ilongot head-hunting comes from his attempt to apply a Western scientific model to it.

[5] Although postmodern anthropology draws on ethnoscience, it is critically different in many ways, one of which is shown here. Ethnoscientists viewed culture as a more or less unchanging mental template. For postmodernists, culture is always historically contingent. The actions of individuals and the derivation of meaning within cultures cannot be explained without reference to specific sociohistorical circumstances.

renunciation of taking heads) and their grudges against lowlanders (the contemplation of head-hunting forays into the surrounding valleys).[6]

Through subsequent days and weeks, the man's grief moved him in a way I had not anticipated. Shortly after the baby's death, the father converted to evangelical Christianity. Altogether too quick on the inference, I immediately concluded that the man believed that the new religion could somehow prevent further deaths in his family. When I spoke my mind to an Ilongot friend, he snapped at me, saying that I had missed the point: what the man in fact sought in the new religion was not the denial of our inevitable deaths but a means of coping with his grief. With the advent of martial law, headhunting was out of the question as a means of venting his wrath and thereby lessening his grief. Were he to remain in his Ilongot way of life, the pain of his sorrow would simply be too much to bear.[f] My description from 1980 now seems so apt that I wonder how I could have written the words and nonetheless failed to appreciate the force of the grieving man's desire to vent his rage.

Another representative anecdote makes my failure to imagine the rage possible in Ilongot bereavement all the more remarkable. On this occasion, Michelle Rosaldo and I were urged by Ilongot friends to play the tape of a headhunting celebration we had witnessed some five years before. No sooner had we turned on the tape and heard the boast of a man who had died in the intervening years than did people abruptly tell us to shut off the recorder. Michelle Rosaldo reported on the tense conversation that ensued:[7]

> As Insan braced himself to speak, the room again became almost uncannily electric. Backs straightened and my anger turned to nervousness and something more like fear as I saw that Insan's eyes were red. Tukbaw, Renato's Ilongot "brother," then broke into what was a brittle silence, saying he could make things clear. He told us that it hurt to listen to a headhunting celebration when people knew that there would never be another. As he put it: "The song pulls at us, drags our hearts, it makes us think of our dead uncle." And again: "It would be better if I had accepted God, but I still am an Ilongot at heart; and when I hear the song, my heart aches as it does when I must look upon unfinished bachelors whom I know that I will never lead to take a head." Then Wagat, Tukbaw's wife, said with her eyes that all my questions gave her pain, and told me: "Leave off now, isn't that enough? Even I, a woman, cannot stand the way it feels inside my heart."[8]

From my present position, it is evident that the tape recording of the dead man's boast evoked powerful feelings of bereavement, particularly rage and the impulse to headhunt. At the time I could only feel apprehensive and diffusely sense the force of the emotions experienced by Insan, Tukbaw, Wagat, and the others present.

The dilemma for the Ilongots grew out of a set of cultural practices that, when blocked, were agonizing to live with.[8] The cessation of headhunting

---

[6] A key source of the emphasis on history in postmodernism is Marxism, particularly as filtered by the French Marxist anthropologists and political radicals of the 1960s and 1970s (when many postmodernists were doing their graduate training). Marxists, of course, see culture as part of a historical process that will ultimately result in communism. Postmodernists do not see any end to history, but they do view cultural action as dependent on historical circumstances. It is, for example, critical to the story Rosaldo is telling here that the action takes place in 1974, when head-hunting was made impossible and evangelical Christianity was available as an alternative.

[7] This extended quotation, presumably originally from field notes, is typical of the self-revealing style of postmodernism. Michelle Rosaldo's *Knowledge and Passion* (1980) makes extensive use of such quotations. In traditional ethnography, information from the field is presented in abstract, scientific fashion. Names are rarely mentioned; in fact, pains are sometimes taken to ensure the anonymity of the speakers. Here the opposite is done. Since all knowledge is contingent on the positioning of observers and informants, the fact that specific people are speaking is critical.

[8] Another aspect of Marxist theory absorbed by postmodernists is the emphasis on conflict. Functionalists and ethnoscientists looked for logically consistent systems. Postmodernists believe society to be beset by conflict between social groups (here, the Ilongot versus the government) or

called for painful adjustments to other modes of coping with the rage they found in bereavement. One could compare their dilemma with the notion that the failure to perform rituals can create anxiety.[h] In the Ilongot case, the cultural notion that throwing away a human head also casts away the anger creates a problem of meaning when the headhunting ritual cannot be performed. Indeed, Max Weber's classic problem of meaning in *The Protestant Ethic and the Spirit of Capitalism* is precisely of this kind.[i] On a logical plane, the Calvinist doctrine of predestination seems flawless: God has chosen the elect, but his decision can never be known by mortals. Among those whose ultimate concern is salvation, the doctrine of predestination is as easy to grasp conceptually as it is impossible to endure in everyday life (unless one happens to be a "religious virtuoso"). For Calvinists and Ilongots alike, the problem of meaning resides in practice, not theory. The dilemma for both groups involves the practical matter of how to live with one's beliefs, rather than the logical puzzlement produced by abstruse doctrine.[9]

HOW I FOUND THE RAGE IN GRIEF

One burden of this introduction concerns the claim that it took some fourteen years for me to grasp what Ilongots had told me about grief, rage, and headhunting. During all those years I was not yet in a position to comprehend the force of anger possible in bereavement, and now I am. Introducing myself into this account requires a certain hesitation both because of the discipline's

taboo and because of its increasingly frequent violation by essays laced with trendy amalgams of continental philosophy and autobiographical snippets. If classic ethnography's vice was the slippage from the ideal of detachment to actual indifference, that of present-day reflexivity is the tendency for the self-absorbed Self to lose sight altogether of the culturally different Other. Despite the risks involved, as the ethnographer I must enter the discussion at this point to elucidate certain issues of method.[10]

The key concept in what follows is that of the positioned (and repositioned) subject.[j] In routine interpretive procedure, according to the methodology of hermeneutics, one can say that ethnographers reposition themselves as they go about understanding other cultures. Ethnographers begin research with a set of questions, revise them throughout the course of inquiry, and in the end emerge with different questions than they started with. One's surprise at the answer to a question, in other words, requires one to revise the question until lessening surprises or diminishing returns indicate a stopping point. This interpretive approach has been most influentially articulated within anthropology by Clifford Geertz.[k]

Interpretive method usually rests on the axiom that gifted ethnographers learn their trade by preparing themselves as broadly as possible. To follow the meandering course of ethnographic inquiry, field-workers require wide-ranging theoretical capacities and finely tuned sensibilities. After all, one cannot predict beforehand what one will encounter in the field. One influential anthropologist, Clyde Kluckhohn, even went so

---

between theory and practice (the Calvinist example that follows). The contradictions are not abnormalities that would be eliminated in a smoothly functioning society, but rather a fundamental part of any social system.

[9] The book by Weber to which Rosaldo refers in this paragraph was extremely influential in anthropology and sociology. In it, Weber argued that the beliefs encouraged by Calvinist theology, particularly individualism and the work ethic, contributed directly to the rise of capitalism.

[10] The fundamental implication of Rosaldo's position is that the accounts produced by ethnographers depend on their positioning, that is, the vantage point from which

they view and analyze society. Their positioning is, in turn, contingent on their life experiences rather than being derived from any uniform application of scientific method. The logical extension of this is that postmodern ethnographies are often highly introspective. They become tales about the ethnographer's experiences. The subject of such work is generally the ethnographer's increasing understanding of himself or herself and the people with whom he or she is living. Rather than writing conventional anthropological reports, postmodernists tend to write about the process of doing fieldwork. Although Rosaldo criticizes the worst excesses of this sort of ethnography, he uses this approach himself.

far as to recommend a double initiation: first, the ordeal of psychoanalysis, and then that of field-work. All too often, however, this view is extended until certain prerequisites of field research appear to guarantee an authoritative ethnography. Eclectic book knowledge and a range of life experiences, along with edifying reading and self-awareness, supposedly vanquish the twin vices of ignorance and insensitivity.[11]

Although the doctrine of preparation, knowledge, and sensibility contains much to admire, one should work to undermine the false comfort that it can convey. At what point can people say that they have completed their learning or their life experience? The problem with taking this mode of preparing the ethnographer too much to heart is that it can lend a false air of security, an authoritative claim to certitude and finality that our analyses cannot have. All interpretations are provisional; they are made by positioned subjects who are prepared to know certain things and not others. Even when knowledgeable, sensitive, fluent in the language, and able to move easily in an alien cultural world, good ethnographers still have their limits, and their analyses always are incomplete. Thus, I began to fathom the force of what Ilongots had been telling me about their losses through my own loss, and not through any systematic preparation for field research.[12]

My preparation for understanding serious loss began in 1970 with the death of my brother, shortly after his twenty-seventh birthday. By experiencing this ordeal with my mother and father, I gained a measure of insight into the trauma of a parent's losing a child. This insight informed my account, partially described earlier, of an Ilongot man's reactions to the death of his seventh child. At the same time, my bereavement was so much less than that of my parents that I could not then imagine the overwhelming force of rage possible in such grief. My former position is probably similar to that of many in the discipline. One should recognize that ethnographic knowledge tends to have the strengths and limitations given by the relative youth of field-workers who, for the most part, have not suffered serious losses and could have, for example, no personal knowledge of how devastating the loss of a long-term partner can be for the survivor.

In 1981 Michelle Rosaldo and I began field research among the Ifugaos of northern Luzon, Philippines. On October 11 of that year, she was walking along a trail with two Ifugao companions when she lost her footing and fell to her death some 65 feet down a sheer precipice into a swollen river below. Immediately on finding her body I became enraged. How could she abandon me? How could she have been so stupid as to fall? I

---

[11] Anthropologists in the 1960s were very concerned with the methodology of data gathering. Ethnoscientists and cognitive anthropologists, reacting to the lack of preparation of most fieldworkers, prescribed very specific types of training and interviewing, such as controlled eliciting, to attempt to produce scientifically valid, replicable results. If, on the other hand, anthropology is about the interpretation of culture, then it is dependent on the life experiences of the anthropologist, and training can never be adequate and can never produce scientific, replicable results. Postmodernists insist on good training in language and ethnography, but they do not believe that such skills will result in a scientific anthropology.

Clyde Kluckhohn (1905–1960) was a Harvard based anthropologist with a long-term interest in the Navajo. In 1931 and 1932 Kluckhohn had studied at the University of Vienna and had become interested in psychoanalysis. He used a psychoanalytical approach in *Navajo Witchcraft* (1944) as well as many other papers.

[12] Rosaldo's argument is that interpretation changes with positioning. To understand Ilongot head-hunting, he had to experience grief and loss himself. In this paragraph and later, he describes those personal experiences. Personal revelation is very rare in traditional ethnography but has become commonplace in recent ethnographic accounts. Traditional ethnography does contain occasional glimpses of the fieldworker. For example, Evans-Pritchard, in the introduction to *The Nuer* (1940), tells about his personal experience of Nuerland and his problems living there. However, the reader learns nothing of his background or family life. Here, and later, Rosaldo touches on experiences that are so personal they may make the reader uneasy (because of our own positioning, Michelle Rosaldo is a real person to us in a way that the dead Ilongot uncle described earlier is not). The difference is that Evans-Pritchard did not believe that his background had a critical bearing on his understanding of the Nuer. Rosaldo is convinced that only his personal experiences allow him to understand the Ilongot.

tried to cry. I sobbed, but rage blocked the tears. Less than a month later I described this moment in my journal: "I felt like in a nightmare, the whole world around me expanding and contracting, visually and viscerally heaving. Going down I find a group of men, maybe seven or eight, standing still, silent, and I heave and sob, but no tears." An earlier experience, on the fourth anniversary of my brother's death, had taught me to recognize heaving sobs without tears as a form of anger. This anger, in a number of forms, has swept over me on many occasions since then, lasting hours and even days at a time. Such feelings can be aroused by rituals, but more often they emerge from unexpected reminders (not unlike the Ilongots' unnerving encounter with their dead uncle's voice on the tape recorder).

Lest there be any misunderstanding, bereavement should not be reduced to anger, neither for myself nor for anyone else.[1] Powerful visceral emotional states swept over me, at times separately and at other times together. I experienced the deep cutting pain of sorrow almost beyond endurance, the cadaverous cold of realizing the finality of death, the trembling beginning in my abdomen and spreading through my body, the mournful keening that started without my willing, and frequent tearful sobbing. My present purpose of revising earlier understandings of Ilongot headhunting, and not a general view of bereavement, thus focuses on anger rather than on other emotions in grief.

Writings in English especially need to emphasize the rage in grief. Although grief therapists routinely encourage awareness of anger among the bereaved, upper-middle-class Anglo-American culture tends to ignore the rage devastating losses can bring.[13] Paradoxically, this culture's conventional wisdom usually denies the anger in grief at the same time that therapists encourage members of the invisible community of the bereaved

to talk in detail about how angry their losses make them feel. My brother's death in combination with what I learned about anger from Ilongots (for them, an emotional state more publicly celebrated than denied) allowed me immediately to recognize the experience of rage.[m]

Ilongot anger and my own overlap, rather like two circles, partially overlaid and partially separate. They are not identical. Alongside striking similarities, significant differences in tone, cultural form, and human consequences distinguish the "anger" animating our respective ways of grieving. My vivid fantasies, for example, about a life insurance agent who refused to recognize Michelle's death as job-related did not lead me to kill him, cut off his head, and celebrate afterward. In so speaking, I am illustrating the discipline's methodological caution against the reckless attribution of one's own categories and experiences to members of another culture. Such warnings against facile notions of universal human nature can, however, be carried too far and harden into the equally pernicious doctrine that, my own group aside, everything human is alien to me. One hopes to achieve a balance between recognizing wide-ranging human differences and the modest truism that any two human groups must have certain things in common.

Only a week before completing the initial draft of an earlier version of this introduction, I rediscovered my journal entry, written some six weeks after Michelle's death, in which I made a vow to myself about how I would return to writing anthropology, if I ever did so, "by writing Grief and a Headhunter's Rage. . . ." My journal went on to reflect more broadly on death, rage, and headhunting by speaking of my "wish for the Ilongot solution; they are much more in touch with reality than Christians. So, I need a place to carry my anger—and can we say a solution of the

---

[13] Rosaldo's understanding is conditioned not only by his experiences but by his own culture. Here, he points to the "Anglo-American" understanding of grief. However, note that as a Chicano, Rosaldo is an outsider with respect to this group. One of the principal motivations for postmodern interpretive anthropology is culture critique. For the postmodernist, anthropology allows the opportunity to reflect on and analyze the culture of our own society as much as it allows for the analysis of the other. Here and later, in order for Rosaldo to examine and explain Ilongot practices, he must also examine and explain American practices. Anthropology then becomes a dialogue—a negotiation of interpretation between ethnographers and the cultures they purport to study.

imagination is better than theirs? And can we condemn them when we napalm villages? Is our rationale so much sounder than theirs?" All this was written in despair and rage.[14]

Not until some fifteen months after Michelle's death was I again able to begin writing anthropology. Writing the initial version of "Grief and a Headhunter's Rage" was in fact cathartic, though perhaps not in the way one would imagine.[15] Rather than following after the completed composition, the catharsis occurred beforehand. When the initial version of this introduction was most acutely on my mind, during the month before actually beginning to write, I felt diffusely depressed and ill with a fever. Then one day an almost literal fog lifted and words began to flow. It seemed less as if I were doing the writing than that the words were writing themselves through me.

My use of personal experience serves as a vehicle for making the quality and intensity of the rage in Ilongot grief more readily accessible to readers than certain more detached modes of composition. At the same time, by invoking personal experience as an analytical category one risks easy dismissal. Unsympathetic readers could reduce this introduction to an act of mourning or a mere report on my discovery of the anger possible in bereavement. Frankly, this introduction is both and more. An act of mourning, a personal report, *and* a critical analysis of anthropological method, it simultaneously encompasses a number of distinguishable processes, no one of which cancels out the others. Similarly, I argue in what follows that ritual in general and Ilongot headhunting in particular form the intersection of multiple coexisting social processes.[16] Aside from revising the ethnographic record, the paramount claim made here concerns how my own mourning and consequent reflection on Ilongot bereavement, rage, and headhunting raise methodological issues of general concern in anthropology and the human sciences.

DEATH IN ANTHROPOLOGY

Anthropology favors interpretations that equate analytical "depth" with cultural "elaboration." Many studies focus on visibly bounded arenas where one can observe formal and repetitive events, such as ceremonies, rituals, and games. Similarly, studies of word play are more likely to focus on jokes as programmed monologues than on the less scripted, more free-wheeling improvised interchanges of witty banter. Most ethnographers prefer to study events that have definite locations in space with marked centers and outer edges. Temporally, they have middles and endings. Historically, they appear to repeat identical structures by seemingly doing things today as they were done yesterday. Their qualities of fixed definition liberate such events from the untidiness of everyday life so that they can be "read" like articles, books, or, as we now say, *texts*.[17]

---

[14] Notice the important role that empathy plays in Rosaldo's analysis. He warns against false attribution of our character traits to the other, but his essential insight into Ilongot headhunting occurs only after he has personal experiences that allow him to identify with them in a visceral way. Also consider that although the passages cited by Rosaldo were written in grief and anger, he is suggesting that "a solution of the imagination" is no better than assuaging one's grief by taking the life of a random, innocent person; a radical statement of cultural relativism indeed.

[15] Postmodernists remind us that most of what anthropologists do, we do for our own purposes. Here, Rosaldo's anthropological insights come either as revelation or therapy. As he reports later, writing this essay was a cathartic act and an enormously personal one.

[16] Turner's idea of multivocality runs deeply through Rosaldo's work. Just as symbols do not necessarily have single meanings, cultural action does not have discrete, unique causes. Instead, causation is always multiple. Rosaldo's essay is no exception: It is "an act of mourning, a personal report, and an analysis of anthropological method."

[17] Rosaldo's analysis of anthropological interpretations of mourning is actually a general attack on traditional anthropological method. In some ways, it is an extension of the reasoning of ethnoscience. Ethnoscientists and cognitive anthropologists criticized traditional anthropologists for using their own systems of classification rather than those of the natives. Rosaldo suggests that the problem goes further: The way ethnography is written—the way it delimits events by time, actors, physical location, and so

Guided by their emphasis on self-contained entities, ethnographies written in accord with classic norms consider death under the rubric of ritual rather than bereavement. Indeed, the subtitles of even recent ethnographies on death make the emphasis on ritual explicit. William Douglas's *Death in Murelaga* is subtitled *Funerary Ritual in a Spanish Basque Village;* Richard Huntington and Peter Metcalf's *Celebrations of Death* is subtitled *The Anthropology of Mortuary Ritual;* Peter Metcalf's *A Borneo Journey into Death* is subtitled *Berawan Eschatology from Its Rituals.*[n] Ritual itself is defined by its formality and routine; under such descriptions, it more nearly resembles a recipe, a fixed program, or a book of etiquette than an open-ended human process.

Ethnographies that in this manner eliminate intense emotions not only distort their descriptions but also remove potentially key variables from their explanations. When anthropologist William Douglas, for example, announces his project in *Death in Murelaga,* he explains that his objective is to use death and funerary ritual "as a heuristic device with which to approach the study of rural Basque society."[o] In other words, the primary object of study is social structure, not death, and certainly not bereavement. The author begins his analysis by saying, "Death is not always fortuitous or unpredictable."[p] He goes on to describe how an old woman, ailing with the infirmities of her age, welcomed her death. The description largely ignores the perspective of the most bereaved survivors, and instead vacillates between those of the old woman and a detached observer.

Undeniably, certain people do live a full life and suffer so greatly in their decrepitude that they embrace the relief death can bring. Yet the problem with making an ethnography's major case study focus on "a very easy death"[q] (I use Simone de Beauvoir's title with irony, as she did) is not only its lack of representativeness but also that it makes death in general appear as routine for the survivors as this particular one apparently was for the deceased. Were the old woman's sons and daughters untouched by her death? The case study shows less about how people cope with death than about how death can be made to appear routine, thereby fitting neatly into the author's view of funerary ritual as a mechanical programmed unfolding of prescribed acts.[18] "To the Basque," says Douglas, "ritual is order and order is ritual."[r]

Douglas captures only one extreme in the range of possible deaths. Putting the accent on the routine aspects of ritual conveniently conceals the agony of such unexpected early deaths as parents losing a grown child or a mother dying in childbirth. Concealed in such descriptions are the agonies of the survivors who muddle through shifting, powerful emotional states. Although Douglas acknowledges the distinction between the bereaved members of the deceased's domestic group and the more public ritualistic group, he writes his account primarily from the viewpoint of the latter. He masks the emotional force of bereavement by reducing funerary ritual to orderly routine.[19]

---

on—is, in itself, the imposition of a certain sort of reality on ethnographic material. To postmodernists, such boundaries are artificial, the products of specific observers or specific individuals involved. To report on an event, the ethnographer draws discrete boundaries around it. The type of boundary drawn around the event critically influences its interpretation.

[18] Rosaldo here shows an example of how the preconceptions of the investigator can exert a powerful influence over the ethnography produced. Notice that Rosaldo is not accusing Douglas of misreporting but rather of choosing a point of view within Basque society that confirms his own understanding of that society.

In *A Very Easy Death* (1966) Simone de Beauvoir (see essay 23, note 13) describes the death of her mother from cancer and her reaction to it. De Beauvoir wrote: "For me, my mother had always existed and I had never seriously thought that some day, that soon I should see her go."

[19] One element of Rosaldo's critique of anthropology is a recurring theme first expressed in Boas' attack on the evolutionists. According to Rosaldo, Douglas is not producing ethnography driven by observation but using specific case examples to back his theoretical position. To some degree, this is also true of the symbolic anthropologists, with whom Rosaldo has great sympathy. Symbolic anthropologists tended to concentrate on the analysis of

Surely, human beings mourn both in ritual settings *and* in the informal settings of everyday life. Consider the evidence that willy-nilly spills over the edges in Godfrey Wilson's classic anthropological account of "conventions of burial" among the Nyakyusa of South Africa:[20]

> That some at least of those who attend a Nyakyusa burial are moved by grief it is easy to establish. I have heard people talking regretfully in ordinary conversation of a man's death; I have seen a man whose sister had just died walk over alone towards her grave and weep quietly by himself without any parade of grief; and I have heard of a man killing himself because of his grief for a dead son.[s]

Note that all the instances Wilson witnesses or hears about happen outside the circumscribed sphere of formal ritual. People converse among themselves, walk alone and silently weep, or more impulsively commit suicide. The work of grieving, probably universally, occurs both within obligatory ritual acts and in more everyday settings where people find themselves alone or with close kin.

In Nyakyusa burial ceremonies, powerful emotional states also become present in the ritual itself, which is more than a series of obligatory acts. Men say they dance the passions of their bereavement, which includes a complex mix of anger, fear, and grief:

> "This war dance (*ukukina*)," said an old man, "is mourning, we are mourning the dead man. We dance because there is war in our hearts. A passion of grief and fear exasperates us (*ilyyojo*

likutusila)." . . . *Elyojo* means a passion or grief, anger or fear; *ukusila* means to annoy or exasperate beyond endurance. In explaining *ukusila* one man put it like this: "If a man continually insults me then he exasperates me (*ukusila*) so that I want to fight him." Death is a fearful and grievous event that exasperates those [men] nearly concerned and makes them want to fight.[t]

Descriptions of the dance and subsequent quarrels, even killings, provide ample evidence of the emotional intensity involved. The articulate testimony by Wilson's informants makes it obvious that even the most intense sentiments can be studied by ethnographers.

Despite such exceptions as Wilson, the general rule seems to be that one should tidy things up as much as possible by wiping away the tears and ignoring the tantrums. Most anthropological studies of death eliminate emotions by assuming the position of the most detached observer.[u] Such studies usually conflate the ritual process with the process of mourning, equate ritual with the obligatory, and ignore the relation between ritual and everyday life. The bias that favors formal ritual risks assuming the answers to questions that most need to be asked. Do rituals, for example, always reveal cultural depth?[21]

Most analysts who equate death with funerary ritual assume that rituals store encapsulated wisdom as if it were a microcosm of its encompassing cultural macrocosm. One recent study of death and mourning, for example, confidently begins by affirming that rituals embody "the collective wisdom of many cultures."[v] Yet

---

ceremony and other symbolically complex behavior. They saw these events as the points at which culture displays its greatest richness, therefore making interpretive analysis more productive.

[20] Godfrey Wilson (1908–1944), whom Rosaldo quotes here, was the husband of Monica Wilson. The Wilsons worked together in Tanganyika (now Tanzania) and Northern Rhodesia (now Zambia) in the 1930s and 1940s. Victor Turner was a student of Monica Wilson and refers extensively to her work in essay 32 in this volume.

[21] The notion that great symbolic complexity does not necessarily indicate great meaning to the people involved is

critical to Rosaldo's concept of force. If this is true, exhaustive interpretive treatments of ceremony may not aid much in understanding culture. Great cultural depth may be present in the Nyakyusa ceremonies described in this passage, but as Rosaldo notes later, despite great symbolism there was little depth in the ceremonies he attended for his brother and wife. The notion of force stands in opposition to the symbolic and interpretive anthropology of Geertz and Turner. These anthropologists propose that anthropologists should analyze society by finding complex rituals and exploring their layers of meaning as one might peel an onion. For Rosaldo, complexity is not necessarily a good index of meaning.

this generalization surely requires case-by-case investigation against a broader range of alternative hypotheses.[22]

At the polar extremes, rituals either display cultural depth or brim over with platitudes. In the former case, rituals indeed encapsulate a culture's wisdom; in the latter instance, they act as catalysts that precipitate processes whose unfolding occurs over subsequent months or even years. Many rituals, of course, do both by combining a measure of wisdom with a comparable dose of platitudes.

My own experience of bereavement and rituals fits the platitudes and catalyst model better than that of microcosmic deep culture. Even a careful analysis of the language and symbolic action during the two funerals for which I was a chief mourner would reveal precious little about the experience of bereavement.[w] This statement, of course, should not lead anyone to derive a universal from somebody else's personal knowledge. Instead, it should encourage ethnographers to ask whether a ritual's wisdom is deep or conventional, and whether its process is immediately transformative or but a single step in a lengthy series of ritual and everyday events.

In attempting to grasp the cultural force of rage and other powerful emotional states, both formal ritual and the informal practices of everyday life provide crucial insight. Thus, cultural descriptions should seek out force as well as thickness, and they should extend from well-defined rituals to myriad less circumscribed practices.

GRIEF, RAGE, AND ILONGOT HEADHUNTING

When applied to Ilongot headhunting, the view of ritual as a storehouse of collective wisdom aligns headhunting with expiatory sacrifice.[23] The raiders call the spirits of the potential victims, bid their ritual farewells, and seek favorable omens along the trail. Ilongot men vividly recall the hunger and deprivation they endure over the days and even weeks it takes to move cautiously toward the place where they set up an ambush and await the first person who happens along. Once the raiders kill their victim, they toss away the head rather than keep it as a trophy. In tossing away the head, they claim by analogy to cast away their life burdens, including the rage in their grief.

Before a raid, men describe their state of being by saying that the burdens of life have made them heavy and entangled, like a tree with vines clinging to it. They say that a successfully completed raid makes them feel light of step and ruddy in complexion. The collective energy of the celebration with its song, music, and dance reportedly gives the participants a sense of well-being. The expiatory ritual process involves cleansing and catharsis.

The analysis just sketched regards ritual as a timeless, self-contained process. Without denying the insight in this approach, its limits must also be considered. Imagine, for example, exorcism rituals described as if they were complete in

---

[22] Cultural force, though it may not be present in ritual, frequently appears where powerful emotional states such as rage, anger, fear, or love are expressed. However, traditional ethnography, modeled on scientific writing, deals only very poorly with these. The scientific trope in writing demands that reporting be dispassionate and that writers adopt an emotionally neutral stance toward their subjects. Paul Stoller (b. 1947) contends that "vivid descriptions of the sensoria of ethnographic situations have been largely overshadowed by a dry analytic prose" (1989:8). Although it may be relatively easy to describe a ritual in such prose, Stoller claims that characterizations of others as they lead their social lives are lost in this sort of writing. He argues

for an anthropology that relies more on descriptions of nonvisual sensory information.

[23] In this relatively brief section of the essay, Rosaldo gives an analysis of Ilongot head-hunting that is sensitive to the issues he raises throughout the paper. Rosaldo attempts to break through the boundaries imposed by the act of analysis. For many postmodernists, anthropology is, above all, the acts of observing and writing, which necessarily impose boundaries on events. Because of this, anthropologists tend to write about self-contained events. To escape from this type of analysis, Rosaldo proposes instead that Ilongot head-hunting results from the intersection of three more or less independent processes.

themselves, rather than being linked with larger processes unfolding before and after the ritual period. Through what processes does the afflicted person recover or continue to be afflicted after the ritual? What are the social consequences of recovery or its absence? Failure to consider such questions diminishes the force of such afflictions and therapies for which the formal ritual is but a phase. Still other questions apply to differently positioned subjects, including the person afflicted, the healer, and the audience. In all cases, the problem involves the delineation of processes that occur before and after, as well as during, the ritual moment.

Let us call the notion of a self-contained sphere of deep cultural activity the *microcosmic view,* and an alternative view *ritual as a busy intersection.* In the latter case, ritual appears as a place where a number of distinct social processes intersect. The crossroads simply provides a space for distinct trajectories to traverse, rather than containing them in complete encapsulated form. From this perspective, Ilongot headhunting stands at the confluence of three analytically separable processes.

The first process concerns whether or not it is an opportune time to raid. Historical conditions determine the possibilities of raiding, which range from frequent to likely to unlikely to impossible.[24] These conditions include American colonial efforts at pacification, the Great Depression, World War II, revolutionary movements in the surrounding lowlands, feuding among Ilongot groups, and the declaration of martial law in 1972. Ilongots use the analogy of hunting to speak of such historical vicissitudes. Much as Ilongot huntsmen say they cannot know when game will cross their path or whether their arrows will strike the target, so certain historical forces that condition their existence remain beyond their control. My book *Ilongot Headhunting, 1883–1974* explores the impact of historical factors on Ilongot headhunting.

Second, young men coming of age undergo a protracted period of personal turmoil during which they desire nothing so much as to take a head. During this troubled period, they seek a life partner and contemplate the traumatic dislocation of leaving their families of origin and entering their new wife's household as a stranger. Young men weep, sing, and burst out in anger because of their fierce desire to take a head and wear the coveted red hornbill earrings that adorn the ears of men who already have, as Ilongots say, arrived *(tabi)*. Volatile, envious, passionate (at least according to their own cultural stereotype of the young unmarried man [*buintaw*]), they constantly lust to take a head. Michelle and I began fieldwork among the Ilongots only a year after abandoning our unmarried youths; hence our ready empathy with youthful turbulence. Her book on Ilongot notions of self explores the passionate anger of young men as they come of age.

Third, older men are differently positioned than their younger counterparts. Because they have already beheaded somebody, they can wear the red hornbill earrings so coveted by youths. Their desire to headhunt grows less from chronic adolescent turmoil than from more intermittent acute agonies of loss. After the death of somebody to whom they are closely attached, older men often inflict on themselves vows of abstinence, not to be lifted until the day they participate in a successful headhunting raid. These deaths can cover a range of instances from literal death, whether through natural causes or beheading, to social death where, for example, a man's wife runs off with another man. In all cases, the rage born of devastating loss animates the older men's desire to raid. This anger at abandonment is irreducible in that nothing at a deeper level explains it. Although certain analysts argue against the dreaded last

---

[24] The idea of positioning is again crucial. Rosaldo has spoken earlier of the positioning of the anthropologist; here the positioning of the Ilongot becomes the main object of analysis. Rosaldo does not see Ilongot society as timeless, harmonious, and undifferentiated (as Durkheim, for example, might) but as fixed in historical time and composed of diverse individuals and groups with different interests. Head-hunting happens when historical circumstances make it possible and when the emotional states of young and old men coincide.

analysis, the linkage of grief, rage, and headhunting has no other known explanation.[25]

My earlier understandings of Ilongot headhunting missed the fuller significance of how older men experience loss and rage. Older men prove critical in this context because they, not the youths, set the processes of headhunting in motion. Their rage is intermittent, whereas that of youths is continuous. In the equation of headhunting, older men are the variable and younger men are the constant. Culturally speaking, older men are endowed with knowledge and stamina that their juniors have not yet attained, hence they care for (*saysay*) and lead (*bukur*) the younger men when they raid.

In a preliminary survey of the literature on headhunting, I found that the lifting of mourning prohibitions frequently occurs after taking a head. The notion that youthful anger and older men's rage lead them to take heads is more plausible than such commonly reported "explanations" of headhunting as the need to acquire mystical "soul stuff" or personal names.[x] Because the discipline correctly rejects stereotypes of the "bloodthirsty savage," it must investigate how headhunters create an intense desire to decapitate their fellow humans. The human sciences must explore the cultural force of emotions with a view to delineating the passions that animate certain forms of human conduct.

SUMMARY

The ethnographer, as a positioned subject, grasps certain human phenomena better than others. He or she occupies a position or structural location and observes with a particular angle of vision.

Consider, for example, how age, gender, being an outsider, and association with a neocolonial regime influence what the ethnographer learns.[26] The notion of position also refers to how life experiences both enable and inhibit particular kinds of insight. In the case at hand, nothing in my own experience equipped me even to imagine the anger possible in bereavement until after Michelle Rosaldo's death in 1981. Only then was I in a position to grasp the force of what Ilongots had repeatedly told me about grief, rage, and headhunting. By the same token, so-called natives are also positioned subjects who have a distinctive mix of insight and blindness. Consider the structural positions of older versus younger Ilongot men, or the differing positions of chief mourners versus those less involved during a funeral. My discussion of anthropological writings on death often achieved its effects simply by shifting from the position of those least involved to that of the chief mourners.

Cultural depth does not always equal cultural elaboration. Think simply of the speaker who is filibustering. The language used can sound elaborate as it heaps word on word, but surely it is not deep. Depth should be separated from the presence or absence of elaboration. By the same token, one-line explanations can be vacuous or pithy. The concept of force calls attention to an enduring intensity in human conduct that can occur with or without the dense elaboration conventionally associated with cultural depth. Although relatively without elaboration in speech, song, or ritual, the rage of older Ilongot men who have suffered devastating losses proves enormously consequential in that, foremost among other things, it leads them to behead their fellow humans. Thus, the notion of force involves both

---

[25] In analyzing the head-hunting of the older men, Rosaldo applies his notion of force. He insists that there is no meaningful way to analyze Ilongot rage other than to record it. His insistence that there can be no other explanation of the linkage of grief, rage, and head-hunting is extremely provocative. Many anthropologists find it difficult to accept. Rosaldo has, after all, provided other explanations including the exchange theory that appears earlier in this essay and the "soul stuff" mentioned below. Rosaldo and his Ilongot informants reject these explanations. Others may not.

[26] Postmodern anthropology collapses many of the distinctions upon which more traditional anthropology is based. There is no longer an observer and an observed. Instead there are individuals prepared to know certain things and not others. These are both anthropologists and members of the cultures the anthropologists are analyzing. Accepting Rosaldo's critique renders the distinction between emic and etic meaningless.

affective intensity and significant consequences that unfold over a long period of time.

Similarly, rituals do not always encapsulate deep cultural wisdom. At times they instead contain the wisdom of Polonius.[27] Although certain rituals both reflect and create ultimate values, others simply bring people together and deliver a set of platitudes that enable them to go on with their lives. Rituals serve as vehicles for processes that occur both before and after the period of their performance. Funeral rituals, for example, do not "contain" all the complex processes of bereavement. Ritual and bereavement should not be collapsed into one another because they neither fully encapsulate nor fully explain one another. Instead, rituals are often but points along a number of longer processual trajectories; hence, my image of ritual as a crossroads where distinct life processes intersect.[y]

The notion of ritual as a busy intersection anticipates the critical assessment of the concept of culture developed in the following chapters. In contrast with the classic view, which posits culture as a self-contained whole made up of coherent patterns, culture can arguably be conceived as a more porous array of intersections where distinct processes crisscross from within and beyond its borders. Such heterogeneous processes often derive from differences of age, gender, class, race, and sexual orientation.

This book argues that a sea change in cultural studies has eroded once-dominant conceptions of truth and objectivity. The truth of objectivism—absolute, universal, and timeless—has lost its monopoly status. It now competes, on more nearly equal terms, with the truths of case studies that are embedded in local contexts, shaped by local interests, and colored by local perceptions. The agenda for social analysis has shifted to include not only eternal verities and lawlike generalizations but also political processes, social changes, and human differences. Such terms as *objectivity*, *neutrality*, and *impartiality* refer to subject positions once endowed with great institutional authority, but they are arguably neither more nor less valid than those of more engaged, yet equally perceptive, knowledgeable social actors. Social analysis must now grapple with the realization that its objects of analysis are also analyzing subjects who critically interrogate ethnographers—their writings, their ethics, and their politics.[28]

ACKNOWLEDGEMENT

Renato Rosaldo, "Grief and a Headhunter's Rage" from *Culture & Truth: The Remaking of Social Analysis* by Renato Rosaldo. Copyright © 1989 by Renato Rosaldo. Reproduced with permission of Beacon Press in the format Textbook via Copyright Clearance Center.

NOTES

An earlier version of this chapter appeared as "Grief and a Headhunter's Rage: On the Cultural Force of Emotions," in *Text, Play, and Story: The Construction and Reconstruction of Self and Society*, ed. Edward M. Bruner (Washington, D.C.: American Ethnological Society, 1984), pp. 178–95.

[a] In contrasting Moroccan and Javanese forms of mysticism, Clifford Geertz found it necessary to distinguish the "force" of cultural patterning from its "scope" (Clifford Geertz, *Islam Observed* [New Haven, Conn: Yale University Press, 1968]). He distinguished force from scope in this manner: "By 'force' I mean the thoroughness with which such a pattern is internalized in the personalities of the individuals who adopt it, its

---

[27] Polonius, a character in *Hamlet,* is minister to the king and Ophelia's father. Although he is the king's advisor, he dispenses greeting-card wisdom.

[28] In closing his essay, Rosaldo makes several important points. He refers to the fact that in a world where education in Western languages is increasingly widespread, people who were traditionally the subjects of ethnography are increasingly reading it, and sometimes writing their own. A traditional anthropologist such as Evans-Pritchard did not have to worry about how the Nuer were going to react to his description of them. Current anthropologists write with the knowledge that some of their informants will read and critique their work. This approach has changed the nature of anthropology.

More controversially, Rosaldo asserts that the interpretations of anthropologists must be judged as neither more nor less valid than those of other astute observers. By extension, this implies that anthropological training confers no particular authority. If this is the case, what should be the role of the "human sciences," among which Rosaldo has included anthropology?

centrality or marginality in their lives" (p. 111). "By 'scope,' on the other hand, I mean the range of social contexts within which religious considerations are regarded as having more or less direct relevance" (p. 112). In his later works, Geertz developed the notion of scope more than that of force. Unlike Geertz, who emphasizes processes of internalization within individual personalities, my use of the term force stresses the concept of the positioned subject.

[b] Anthropologists have long studied the vocabulary of the emotions in other cultures (see, e.g., Hildred Geertz, "The Vocabulary of Emotion: A Study of Javanese Socialization Processes," *Psychiatry* 22 [1959]: 225–37). For a recent review essay on anthropological writings on emotions, see Catherine Lutz and Geoffrey M. White, "The Anthropology of Emotions," *Annual Review of Anthropology* 15 (1986):405–36.

[c] The two ethnographies on the Ilongots are Michelle Rosaldo, *Knowledge and Passion: Ilongot Notions of Self and Social Life* (New York: Cambridge University Press, 1980), and Renato Rosaldo, *Ilongot Headhunting, 1883–1974: A Study in Society and History* (Stanford, Calif: Stanford University Press, 1980). Our field research among the Ilongots was financed by a National Science Foundation predoctoral fellowship, National Science Foundation Research Grants GS–1509 and GS–40788, and a Mellon Award for junior faculty from Stanford University. A Fulbright Grant financed a two-month stay in the Philippines during 1981.

[d] Lest the hypothesis Insan rejected appear utterly implausible, one should mention that at least one group does link a version of exchange theory to headhunting. Peter Metcalf reports that, among the Berawan of Borneo, "Death has a chain reaction quality to it. There is a considerable anxiety that, unless something is done to break the chain, death will follow upon death. The logic of this is now plain: The unquiet soul kills, and so creates more unquiet souls" (Peter Metcalf, *A Borneo Journey into Death: Berawan Eschatology from Its Rituals* [Philadelphia: University of Pennsylvania Press, 1982], p. 127).

[e] R. Rosaldo, *Ilongot Headhunting, 1883–1974*, p. 286.

[f] Ibid., p. 288.

[g] M. Rosaldo, *Knowledge and Passion*, p. 33.

[h] See A. R. Radcliffe-Brown, *Structure and Function in Primitive Society* (London: Cohen and West, Ltd., 1952), pp. 133–52. For a broader debate on the "functions" of ritual, see the essays by Bronislaw Malinowski, A. R. Radcliffe-Brown, and George C. Homans, in *Reader in Comparative Religion: An Anthropological Approach* (4th ed.), ed. William A. Lessa and Evon Z. Vogt (New York: Harper and Row, 1979), pp. 37–62.

[i] Max Weber, *The Protestant Ethic and the Spirit of Capitalism* (New York: Charles Scribner's Sons, 1958).

[j] A key antecedent to what I have called the "positioned subject" is Alfred Schutz, *Collected Papers*, vol. 1, *The Problem of Social Reality,* ed. and intro. Maurice Natanson (The Hague: Martinus Nijhoff, 1971). See also, e.g., Aaron Cicourel, *Method and Measurement in Sociology* (Glencoe, Ill.: The Free Press, 1964) and Gerald Berreman, *Behind Many Masks: Ethnography and Impression Management in a Himalayan Village,* Monograph No. 4 (Ithaca, N.Y.: Society for Applied Anthropology, 1962). For an early anthropological article on how differently positioned subjects interpret the "same" culture in different ways, see John W. Bennett, "The Interpretation of Pueblo Culture," *Southwestern Journal of Anthropology* 2 (1946):361–74.

[k] Clifford Geertz, *The Interpretation of Cultures* (New York: Basic Books, 1974) and *Local Knowledge: Further Essays in Interpretive Anthropology* (New York: Basic Books, 1983).

[l] Although anger appears so often in bereavement as to be virtually universal, certain notable exceptions do occur. Clifford Geertz, for example, depicts Javanese funerals as follows: "The mood of a Javanese funeral is not one of hysterical bereavement, unrestrained sobbing, or even of formalized cries of grief for the deceased's departure. Rather, it is a calm, undemonstrative, almost languid letting go, a brief ritualized relinquishment of a relationship no longer possible" (Geertz, *The Interpretation of Cultures,* p. 153). In cross-cultural perspective, the anger in grief presents itself in different degrees (including zero), in different forms, and with different consequences.

[m] The Ilongot notion of anger (*liget*) is regarded as dangerous in its violent excesses, but also as life-enhancing in that, for example, it provides energy for work. See the extensive discussion in M. Rosaldo, *Knowledge and Passion*.

[n] William Douglas, *Death in Murelaga: Funerary Ritual in a Spanish Basque Village* (Seattle: University of Washington Press, 1969); Richard Huntington and Peter Metcalf, *Celebrations of Death: The Anthropology of Mortuary Ritual* (New York: Cambridge University Press, 1979); Metcalf, *A Borneo Journey into Death*.

[o] Douglas, *Death in Murelaga*, p. 209.

[p] Ibid., p. 19.

[q] Simone de Beauvoir, *A Very Easy Death* (Harmondsworth, United Kingdom: Penguin Books, 1969).

[r] Douglas, *Death in Murelaga*, p. 75.

[s] Godfrey Wilson, *Nyakyusa Conventions of Burial* (Johannesburg: The University of Witwatersrand Press, 1939), pp. 22–23. (Reprinted from Bantu Studies.)

[t] Ibid., p. 13.

[u] In his survey of works on death published during the 1960s, for example, Johannes Fabian found that the

four major anthropological journals carried only nine papers on the topic, most of which "dealt only with the purely ceremonial aspects of death" (Johannes Fabian, "How Others Die: Reflections on the Anthropology of Death," in *Death in American Experience,* ed. A. Mack [New York: Schocken, 1973], p. 178).

[v] Huntington and Metcalf, *Celebrations of Death,* p. 1.

[w] Arguably, ritual works differently for those most afflicted by a particular death than for those least so. Funerals may distance the former from overwhelming emotions whereas they may draw the latter closer to strongly felt sentiments (see T. J. Scheff, *Catharsis in Healing, Ritual, and Drama* [Berkeley: University of

California Press, 1979]). Such issues can be investigated through the notion of the positioned subject.

[x] For a discussion of cultural motives for headhunting, see Robert McKinley, "Human and Proud of It! A Structural Treatment of Headhunting Rites and the Social Definition of Enemies," in *Studies in Borneo Societies: Social Process and Anthropological Explanation,* ed. G. Appell (DeKalb, Ill.: Center for Southeast Asian Studies, Northern Illinois University, 1976), pp. 92–126; Rodney Needham, "Skulls and Causality," *Man* 11 (1976): 71–88; Michelle Rosaldo, "Skulls and Causality," *Man* 12 (1977):168–70.

[y] Pierre Bourdieu, *Outline of a Theory of Practice* (New York: Cambridge University Press, 1977), p. 1.

---

37. *A Tale of Two Pregnancies*

LILA ABU-LUGHOD (b. 1952)

ENTERING MY TWENTY-fourth week. Heartburn woke me up this morning, and I turned to my favorite of the three pregnancy guidebooks I keep near my bed—the one organized around anxieties. In the section titled "Heartburn and Indigestion," sandwiched between "Losing Your Figure" and "Food Aversions and Cravings," I read: "It's nearly impossible to have an indigestion-free nine months; it's just one of the less pleasant facts of pregnancy."[1]

I closed my eyes. This was, I thought, what my friend Kareema must have felt.[a] She was the mother of eleven whom I'd seen through two pregnancies in the 1980s. Like all but one of her others, her last pregnancy, at an age closer to my current age than I liked to imagine, had proceeded without the benefit of medical care. She had suffered terrible indigestion, and I remembered those many evenings when, by the light of a kerosene lantern, I had prepared her the fizzy orange drink she swore relieved the pain: effervescent tablets of vitamin C purchased at the local pharmacy, dissolved in a glass of water.[2]

From *Women Writing Culture* (1995)

---

[1] Like the opening to Geertz's analysis of the Balinese cockfight, Abu-Lughod starts this essay with a personal account that immediately draws the reader into her story. Unlike Geertz, who abandons his personal account for a more formal analysis, Abu-Lughod focuses on the personal experience of her pregnancy and writes completely in a personal, reflexive, style. She embraces the postmodern view that ethnography is the creation of the writer, arguing that because ethnographers know things within a personal context, what they write are partial and positioned truths (1991:141). Consequently, in writing about her pregnancy, Abu-Lughod tries to place the reader within her frame of reference as an anthropologist and a woman pregnant with twins.

[2] In her critique of ethnography "Writing Against Culture," Abu-Lughod criticizes the practice of making ethnographic generalizations. She says that generalization is a part of a language of power used by those who stand apart from and outside of those they study (1991:150). She argues that one way to combat generalization is to write "ethnographies of the particular" (1991:149), and indeed her essay is an outstanding example of this approach: She is writing about her pregnancy and her experiences with one specific Egyptian Bedouin woman; she does not try to discuss pregnancy for Bedouin women in general.

In those days I understood little about what Kareema and the other Awlad 'Ali Bedouin women I lived with in Egypt were experiencing. Caught up in my own world and my research, first in my mid-twenties and later in my thirties, I claimed to be, and was, very interested in women's experiences. But I barely noticed anything about their pregnancies except protruding bellies artfully hidden by large red belts. The women worked hard, lifting heavy cooking pots, carrying their other children on their backs, washing clothes, and walking long distances to visit friends and relatives. Pregnancy hardly seemed to interfere. At the end, with the help of a local midwife, their mothers, or their mothers-in-law, these women suddenly produced infants who, by the time I would see them, were lovingly swaddled and lying close to them. Or so it seemed. Except that every older woman who told me her life story mentioned a miscarriage or a stillbirth.

My pregnancy, in contrast, was the ultimate late-capitalist U.S. achievement: assisted by the most recent advances in reproductive technology, monitored from egg production to fetal heartbeats with the help of ultrasound and hormonal analysis, and expensive. I was one of the fortunate women in her late thirties for whom in vitro fertilization had succeeded on the first try. I began the pregnancy with a mix of scientific knowledge, common sense, and holistic medical advice: warned by my books about preeclampsia, prevented from carrying heavy objects by my husband, pampering myself by lying down to allow blood to flow to my placenta, counting my calcium milligrams, balancing my green and yellow vegetables, and studying with some despair the undecipherable diagrams that promise to guide pregnant women through proper exercise regimens.[3]

If I had not known Kareema and the other women in Egypt who had shared their lives with me, I would not have been able to shake my head and laugh at myself for the fuss I was making. I also might not have felt so lucky. My personal experience of the pregnancy was shaped by the double (or hybrid, in Kirin Narayan's view) life I lived as an anthropologist.[b] I moved between the world of "home" in the United States, with my network of friends and family and the resources of feminist scholarship on reproduction to help me think about the facts of life, and "the field" in Egypt, where I was surrounded by women who became pregnant, gave birth, lived with children, and talked to me and to each other about why things sometimes went wrong. I looked to both places for help in understanding what was happening to me, just as I had sought this pregnancy in both places.[4]

---

[3] In "Grief and a Headhunter's Rage" (essay 36), published just two years before this essay, Rosaldo argues that how one understands events depends on one's positioning and that interpretations change as one's positioning changes. Although Abu-Lughod noticed that women were pregnant and had babies, it was not until she became pregnant that these events took on new significance for her. In Rosaldo's terminology, as Abu-Lughod's position changed her Egyptian friends' pregnancies became events with "force." McGee had a similar experience. It was not until McGee's wife, pregnant with their first child, went with him into the field that he thought to ask Lacandon Maya women about pregnancy and childbirth. Like Abu-Lughod he discovered that most women had lost babies or their own daughters in childbirth (McGee 2002:67–70).

Preeclampsia is a condition that occurs in 5 percent to 8 percent of pregnancies. It is characterized by high blood pressure and the presence of protein in the urine. It can be fatal to both mother and child.

[4] In this paragraph Abu-Lughod mentions Narayan's comment on anthropologists leading a "hybrid" life. In other words, Abu-Lughod's viewpoint was created by the intersection of her multiple identities as a woman, anthropologist, wife, mother, her Palestinian background (Abu-Lughod is the daughter of the sociologist Janet L. Abu-Lughod and the political scientist Ibrahim Abu-Lughod), as well as years she spent as a child in Egypt. Through the course of the article she shows us some of these identities in the accounts she gives, as an anthropologist, a patient in an IVF clinic, Kareema's friend and confidant, and a mother.

Kirin Narayan, an anthropologist at the University of Wisconsin, Madison, is the daughter of an American born Indian mother and a Indian-born father. Her recent book *My Family and Other Saints* (2007) describes her childhood and focus on the complex, multicultural life of her older brother.

SEARCHING FOR CHILDREN

Living in what is known as the Western Desert of Egypt, with only a substandard clinic not close enough for easy access, the Bedouin women I knew could not take advantage of the superb doctors and excellent hospital facilities available in Egypt's major cities, Cairo and Alexandria. They gave each other advice, told stories about their pregnancies and those of others, and complained— of headaches, fevers, aches, swelling. That did not stop them from feeling sorry for me, their anthropologist friend, still childless long after their own daughters, who had kept me company on the long winter evenings of my first stay in the late 1970s, had married and given birth to one, two, sometimes three children.[5]

Even though I did not yet want children, they sympathetically told me stories about women who were "searching for children" too. They explained the theory of "blocking"—how conception could be blocked by a sudden fright, by being confronted with someone who has come back from a funeral, or by a donkey who has just given birth. They scared me by offering to take me to healers to have a string sewn through my back or an amulet made. They told me how a second fright could undo a blockage, or how bathing on successive Fridays with water in which a gold necklace had been soaked might counteract a different kind of blockage.

I eagerly scribbled all this in my notebooks; mostly it was material for my book on Bedouin women's stories. I wondered, occasionally, how these notions about flows and blockages fit with our medical narratives about hormones, eggs, sperm, and fallopian tubes. I had long been skeptical of images of how our bodies worked that relied on biological entities whose existence I had to take on faith. Emily Martin's analysis of the mechanical metaphors and bizarre implications of these scientific stories about women's bodies had confirmed my own ambivalence.[c,6]

Later, when I was back in Egypt in 1990 with my husband, I felt it was time to get pregnant. I did not yet know there was a serious problem, but other friends were generous with remedies for infertility. After appointments with the quiet and serious doctor at the Cairo Motherhood Center— where the equipment was sterilized, the sheets clean and white, the ultrasound machine shiny, and the receipts computer generated—I would fly south to the palm-draped village in Upper Egypt where my husband and I were then doing research. My new friend Zaynab, mother of five children conceived on annual visits of her migrant husband, took time from her busy schedule of working her small fields, collecting fodder for her animals, and pressing land claims against her paternal relatives to try to help me.

[5] One of the many insights that postmodern anthropologists have contributed to cultural anthropology is a concern with generalization that Abu-Lughod has already mentioned. In part, avoiding generalizations may help anthropologists to avoid making claims that are beyond their knowledge. Note Abu-Lughod's wording in this paragraph. She is not making a claim to describe the behavior of all Bedouin women, rather she claims to present information from only "the Bedouin women I knew . . ."

[6] Note in this paragraph that Abu-Lughod treats scientific medicine and the folktales of Egyptian infertility equally. She mentions Emily Martin's book *The Woman in the Body: A Cultural Analysis of Reproduction* (1987), in which Martin examines some American women's views of the medical science model of pregnancy and reproduction. As is shown more fully below, postmodernists frequently treat scientific models as the folktales of capitalist and technological society, granting them no more or less credibility than other folktales. The implication of Abu-Lughod's discussion is that rural Egyptian women have one truth, doctors in the IVF clinic another. Some postmodernists claim that because all ethnographic descriptions are the creation of the writer, one truth is as valid as another, and they point out that what is defined as true and who gets to impose that view is an issue of power. However, some issues lend themselves to empirical verification. Although Abu-Lughod may be skeptical of the images and mechanical metaphors by which Western physicians describe how our bodies work, the fact is, in purely practical terms, one form of therapy provided her with amulets and scraps of cloth, the other with twins. Abu-Lughod appears to acknowledge this point later in the essay when she says it is dangerous for feminists to reject science and technology and says, "So what if for two days a petri dish served as my fallopian tubes?"

Zaynab knew of three treatments. First she took me to the ruins of the Pharaonic temple that dominated the small hamlet in which her mud-brick house stood. Calling out to the local guard that we were just going to the well, she saw to it that he waved us on, ignoring the fact that we had no entrance tickets. She took me around the temple and then down some steep steps to a pool of stagnant water. "It is good to bathe with this water," she said. Anticipating my modesty, she had brought with her an empty tin container. "You can do it back at the hotel," she explained as she filled the can with the water.

When we came out of the cool, dark shaft she steered me away from the entrance to the temple. "You have to leave by a different path from the one you used to enter," she said. Later, another old village woman told my husband that Zaynab should have had another woman there, hiding above the shaft, to drop a stone into the water just when I was looking in. This would have frightened me. Although they lived hundreds of miles from the Bedouin and shared little of their way of life, these village women seemed to be working with the same theory of blocking: a second fright undoes the effect of a first, and leaving by a different route literally opens up, or un-blocks, a path to conception and birth.[d]

The next time I came to the village, still not pregnant, Zaynab decided to take me to the Coptic monastery nearby. "It's good," this Muslim woman explained, "to look at those Christian priests with their beards." When we had been admitted by a gentle nun, Zaynab whispered in the hush of the monastery, "Just look at the beautiful things, the velvet curtains, the pictures. The older things are, the better."

Next we went to the monastery's cemetery. Zaynab kept calling out for someone. She seemed agitated and finally hailed a young boy who was riding by on his donkey. "Where is your father?" she asked. "Go get him. Tell them there's a woman here who wants him." Eventually a burly man with a huge grey mustache appeared. He was the undertaker. He led me around the cemetery, explaining so much that I couldn't tell if this was a guided tour meant for a tourist or something special to induce pregnancy.

I realized that he knew why I was there when he took me to a cloth-draped coffin, its cover half on, empty inside. He instructed me to take off my shoes and step back and forth over the casket seven times, using my right foot first each time. Later he took me down to some dusty vaults. Reaching inside, he tore a strip of green cloth off the top of another unused coffin. Zaynab had gone off. "Wrap it under your breasts and bathe three times with it," he said conspiratorially. "But don't tell the woman you're with about this."

Then he told me to climb into the vault. I started in but jumped back in fear as a lizard darted out. Scolding me for being afraid when he was there, he then instructed me to tear another strip of cloth from the cover of the empty coffin in the far corner. He wadded this up and told me to stuff it inside me when I had sex with my husband.

Just then Zaynab returned and reminded him that it was important for me to see the well. So we all walked on. With a key he opened a small structure housing a very old brick well. He told me to look down until I could see my own eye. It was a long way down and there was very little water at the bottom. He explained that the monastery had an electric pump for irrigation and that tanks of water were brought in from the pipeline for drinking. Zaynab and I finally left, she apologetically giving him a small sum (all I had brought with me), he saying he hoped God would grant me what I wanted.

A few weeks later Zaynab decided, with some encouragement from me, that she should take me to visit the local Muslim woman curer. This was an old woman who had married and had five children, spent years in Cairo, and returned to her father's village when her husband died. Her father, himself a religious figure with powers of healing, had appointed her his successor, and she was now famous throughout the area. It was rumored that people came from as far away as Kuwait to seek her help. I had heard about her and was curious.

We waited until the heat of the day had passed and then set off to her hamlet. In her courtyard we saw other women leaving. The healer herself sat in a dark room, a small and wrinkled blind woman with her knees drawn up and her feet tucked neatly under her black dress. Women with children in their laps sat waiting their turn to speak to her. After listening to them, she would talk quickly in a kind of rhyme while deftly winding green thread into small objects they were to take with them. When our turn came, Zaynab first discussed her land dispute. Then she explained my problem and answered questions for me. The old curer prescribed a concoction that my husband was to drink. Zaynab and I pressed some money into her hand and then walked home.

In the end the recipe was too complicated. I didn't know where to get many of the ingredients. I didn't even know what these spices and powders were. Their Arabic names meant nothing to me. And though surely I could have arranged to put the bowl of liquid out on the balcony to catch the starlight, as instructed, where would we get the glowing rod to douse in it, in our Cairo apartment?

The problem, of course, was that my husband and I didn't believe it would work. I had half-heartedly bathed with the water from the Pharaonic temple, wary enough of the dead insects floating in it not to splash sensitive parts of my body—the very parts that were supposed to receive this healing treatment. I had also dutifully stepped over the coffins in the Christian cemetery, feeling silly and hypocritical, but I never wrapped the cloth strips around my chest or stuffed them inside me. Oddly, though, I still have the strips of cloth in my dresser drawer, somehow unable to bring myself to simply throw them away. I also don't quite know what to do with an old amulet I acquired from my Bedouin friends. I had wanted to see what was inside and had even photographed the contents. But then I could not help being awed by people's insistence that amulets were powerful and should never touch the ground or be thrown away. In matters mysterious, like religion and reproduction, one finds oneself uncertain enough about the truth to be half willing to "go native."[7]

INSIDE AND OUTSIDE THE BODY

When I returned home after a year in Egypt, I entered that new world that has become familiar to so many women of my generation and class in the U.S.—the world of laparoscopies, tubal adhesions, endometriosis, amniocentesis, and other such unpronounceables; the world of busy doctors in white coats who inspect and prod and shine lights at parts of you that you cannot see; the world of procedures that, they inform you absentmindedly, might cause slight cramping. I finally was allowed to graduate into the world of IVF, as in vitro fertilization is known. I joined well-dressed women with bags under their eyes who spent the early morning hours waiting their turn to have blood drawn from bruised veins and to lie back in darkened rooms with their legs in stirrups so their ovaries could be scanned on grainy black-and-white screens.

It was a world of sitting by the phone, waiting for your daily instructions. Of injections that quickly cured you of any squeamishness about large hypodermic needles. Sometimes, as you expertly drew from the small vials the correct dosages of Pergonal or Metrodin, or later, progesterone in a viscous base of sesame oil, you wondered if someone watching outside the apartment window might take you for a drug addict. This was, after all, New York.

"Our goal is to make you pregnant," the doctor had explained in our first visit. "Our success rates are the highest in the city. We average about thirty-three percent per three-month cycle." This kind of talk leads to a world of uneasy comparison. You look around the waiting room and wonder who will make the statistics. The woman next to you tells you she has fifteen eggs; yesterday you'd been told that you had five but that one was bigger than the others. "What does that mean?" you ask the busy doctor. "We'll see how they

---

[7] In this essay Abu-Lughod describes herself as a "hybrid," with one foot in the Arab world and another in the West. She writes about how she undergoes the folk remedies of her Egyptian friends to get pregnant and then describes some of her experiences undergoing IVF procedures in New York City. She writes, "In matters mysterious, like religion and reproduction, one finds oneself uncertain enough about the truth to be half willing to 'go native.'" What crosses our minds when we read the last few pages of Abu-Lughod's essay is how Boasian it is. It is a classic telling of folklore much like Paul Radin's articles in the 1920s on Ojibwa folklore, but more personal.

come along. If the others don't catch up, we'll have to cancel the cycle." You beg those little ones to grow.

Another woman tells you that this is her third try; last time she had to be hospitalized for ovarian enlargement. The next day someone tells you about her friend who had so many eggs she froze some. She became pregnant and had twins. Then her husband was killed in a car accident. Now she wants to thaw her other eggs and have another child by him. A tough young woman in blue jeans cheerfully jokes with the nurses as they take her blood. She's been coming for a year. You listen in dismay as another recounts how she got pregnant after four tries and then lost her triplets. She and her husband couldn't stand the strain, so they took a break for two years. You also look around at some of the women and think they're just too old.

All these women are surely bringing down the percentages. You think, with some secret pleasure, that this means your own odds as a first-timer are that much better. You keep talking to your friend and colleague, the one who told you about this clinic and who became pregnant on the first try. She barely seems to remember the anger and frustration you feel, or the uncertainty. She encourages you and tells you what will happen next. You compare notes about the waiting-room experience and tell her what an interesting anthropological study it would make, if only you didn't feel so much hostility to the money-making production line the clinic creates that all you want to do is escape—as soon as you no longer need their services so helplessly.

Retrieval is the clinical term for the procedure of removing your ripe eggs from the ovary to be fertilized outside your body. You go to the hospital for this, feeling perfectly healthy and afraid that when you wake up you won't be anymore. After being kept waiting, as usual, you are walked in your oversized nonskid slippers down corridors, into elevators, and then into an operating room. The room looks familiar from the slide show the nurse gave a few weeks earlier, and you feel less resentful at that two hours wasted in a session of elementary talk about IVF. (The session protects the IVF program by covering in simple language the complex material contained in the pile of consent forms you must sign.) The lights in the room are bright. It's a little cold. An intravenous feeder is put in your wrist, and the nurses talk to you reassuringly. You disappear. You wake up in the recovery room, people groaning all around you, some quite frightening with tubes in their noses. You want to get away but are too groggy to move.

As we were leaving the hospital, my husband and I bumped into one of the doctors. She asked how it had gone. I said no one had told us. Surprised, she went off to telephone the lab. She gave us the first good news: they had retrieved six eggs. She insisted that someone must have come to tell me in the recovery room but I had forgotten. I didn't believe her.

Then we waited for the telephone call our typed instructions said would come as soon as they knew the results. Five eggs had fertilized. One more success. As Sarah Franklin, one of the few feminist anthropologists to study IVF, has noted, the cultural narrative of conception has been rewritten by the infertility specialists so that conception is no longer the natural result of intercourse but a scientific and technological achievement. The road to pregnancy is a complex obstacle course in which hurdles are overcome, one by one.[e,8]

The next step was what they call "the transfer"—from dish to womb. Back at the hospital, I sat on a simple wooden bench with the same

---

[8] Comparing the descriptions of the IVF procedures with the treatments she received from her Egyptian friends it is clear that Abu-Lughod found the IVF procedures unpleasant. In this paragraph she cites Sarah Franklin's work on IVF, in which Franklin concludes that "the cultural narrative of conception has been rewritten by the infertility specialists so that conception is no longer the natural result of intercourse but a scientific and technological achievement." If all truths are positioned truths, then the truths of physicians who are fertility specialists are naturally influenced by their position as doctors, just as the truths of Bedouin women are affected by their positions as women in Egypt. In 2010, the Nobel Prize for medicine was awarded to Robert G. Edwards, the biologist responsible for the development of IVF. Do the traditional medical practitioners Abu-Lughod visited deserve similar awards? Why or why not?

women who had been in the surgical waiting room on the day of the retrieval. Everyone was a little nervous, but cheerful. This part wasn't supposed to hurt. To pass the time we chatted. One of the women asked if I remembered the blonde woman who had been there with us three days earlier. Yes. "Well," she whispered, "her husband was in there for an hour and a half and couldn't do it. So they had to rush me ahead of her in line for the retrieval." We giggled in a mixture of relief that our husbands had performed efficiently and embarrassment at the others' humiliation.

Finally, my turn. I entered the familiar operating room and climbed onto the table. The doctor was joking with the embryologist in the adjoining room. It had been a long day. Suddenly I saw something come into focus on the elevated television screen to my right. My name was typed on the screen, and there were my four fertilized eggs. The fifth, the doctor explained, had disintegrated. An assistant printed out the image on two polaroid snapshots, a general view and a close-up. I had imagined test-tube babies as little fetuses in jars, but these were just cells, clusters of overlapping circles sitting in a petri dish, like illustrations from a biology textbook.

The transfer only took a minute, with some joking about not dropping the catheter as the embryologist rushed from the lab to the table. I was moved onto a trolley and wheeled out, like the women who went before me, clutching my Polaroids.

Abandoned together in a small, otherwise empty ward, we made conversation. One woman's companion helped us exchange our "baby pictures," all we might get for the $8,000 we had had to pay up front (I was counting the days until my insurance company would reimburse me; most of the women had no insurance coverage for IVF). The doctor had told us we could leave after fifteen minutes, but we all insisted on staying for forty-five—superstitious that if we stood up our precious embryos might slide out. One by one, we gingerly climbed out of bed and dressed. I took a taxi home, not wanting to risk the subway.

The month during which I underwent IVF was also the month in which the copyedited manuscript of my book on Bedouin women's stories arrived in the mail.[f] I read over the chapter called "Reproduction," written before I'd entered that strange world of reproductive technology. I could have longed for the more natural character of these women's experiences of becoming pregnant and having babies. I could have viewed pregnancy as an alienation of my body by the medical establishment. But I thought of Donna Haraway, the feminist historian of science, who keeps insisting that it is dangerous for feminists, nostalgic for an organic wholeness, to condemn and reject science and technology. Such associations of the natural with the feminine have been essential to women's confinements to the body and the home; and such rejections of science leave it in the hands of others who may not have women's interests at heart.[g] In the late twentieth century the boundaries between inside and outside our bodies are more fluid. Are glasses to be rejected because they are not our natural eyes? So what if for two days a petri dish served as my fallopian tubes?[9]

Still, I refused to believe the nurse who telephoned twelve days later to say my blood test was positive. I thought the IVF staff would fudge the results so they could publish articles in the medical journals and claim to be the best clinic in the city. Then they'd accuse you, the incompetent female body, of having lost the baby. I didn't believe I was pregnant until two weeks later, when I saw, on that familiar black-and-white television screen, the image of those tiny sacs, each with a

---

[9] Here we reach the passage mentioned in note 6 above. However, consider carefully what Abu-Lughod is saying. Is she saying that it is dangerous for women to reject science because, in so doing, they reject an accurate method of understanding and interacting with the physical empirical world? Or, alternatively, is she saying that it is dangerous for women to reject science because in so doing they confirm their position on the nature side of the nature/culture dichotomy (see Ortner's discussion in essay 23) and leave a powerful discourse "in the hands of others who may not have women's interests at heart." This might be a false dichotomy. Perhaps she is making both points at once.

twinkling star in it. Fetal heartbeats. Multiple gestation, as they call it in the business.[10]

Kareema, on the other hand, knew the other signs of pregnancy. Her period stopped. She began to feel sick. She threw up. She felt fatigued. She couldn't bear to smoke. Some women have cravings; others have aversions to certain foods. Some Bedouin women claim to have aversions to their husbands.

My menstrual cycle had been suppressed by drugs, and it was too early for the other signs. I was dependent on the ultrasound scanner for my knowledge of pregnancy. I recalled Rosalind Petchesky's classic work on fetal imaging and the politics of reproduction. Rather than condemning, along with other feminists, the panoptic gaze the ultrasound technologies afford the male medical establishment or even the disembodiment of the fetus from the mother, demoted to a mere environment for this rights-bearing entity, she drew attention to the possibility that women might experience this technology positively. "How different women," she wrote, "see fetal images depends on the context of the looking and the relationship of the viewer to the image and what it signifies."[h] I couldn't help finding it reassuring to see on the screen to my right what was supposed to be inside me. I was so unsure of my babies that I worried about their having disappeared if I didn't see them every two weeks or so.[11]

COMMUNITIES OF WOMEN

Now, months later, when I have heartburn and the amazement of feeling the babies move in a part of me that had never even existed before, I feel closer to Kareema. The belly I rub with almond oil and look down at is here, not on the screen. It looks the way Kareema's did. My pregnancy book had told me I'd first feel the babies' movements as butterflies or fish swimming around, but the book was wrong. It was a definite thumping—like a heartbeat in the wrong place. I wondered what else the book might be wrong about and instead tried to remember every detail of what the Bedouin women had said and done. How would I cope when the babies came? I tried to remember how these women had managed. How had they breastfed? It had all seemed so natural and easy. How had they coped at night? I don't remember Kareema's babies crying. I realized I hadn't paid much attention to things that now mattered enormously to me. I also understood now that Kareema had probably been feeling that same thumping inside her as she kindly told me folktales to record for my book.

When you are pregnant for the first time, you suddenly see other women you know in a different light. My mother began to tell stories about her pregnancies, and I loved seeing her soften as she reminisced about how exquisite it was to hold an infant. My mother-in-law seemed remarkable for having had seven children. I asked my sister about her experience of giving birth alone in India. She said she had never read a book on the subject and had no idea what was going on. My friends with children began to seem more important. I felt I was crossing a threshold I hadn't noticed before.

This experience of recognizing a commonality among women led me to think back to an article I had begun writing five years earlier about the possibilities for feminist ethnography.[i] I had argued that women ethnographers who studied women unsettled the central divide between Self and Other on which anthropology usually rested. This was not because of any essential, crosscultural sameness of women but because feminist anthropologists had to recognize that womanhood was

---

[10] How is the reader to understand this paragraph? Is it comic relief, or is Abu-Lughod so deeply suspicious of medicine and capitalism that her first response to good news is to assume that she is simply being manipulated for the benefit of the clinic? Although it is certainly conceivable that a clinic could do that, it is a bit surprising that a patient who came to a clinic by choice would react to good news by first assuming it was not only incorrect but guided by immoral purposes as well.

[11] *Panoptic* means "all-encompassing." When Abu-Lughod refers to the "panoptic gaze" the ultrasound technology provided the medical professionals caring for her, she means that her fetuses were completely revealed inside her.

only a partial identity. In the abstract language of academic life I wrote, "By working with the assumption of difference in sameness, of a self that participates in multiple identifications, and another that is also partially the self, we might be moving beyond the impasse of the fixed self/other or subject/object divide."[j] I also noted, however, that there was often a perceived kinship, albeit limited, between women anthropologists and their women subjects that made seeking knowledge of their situations more of a political project that had implications for "home." The kinship Zaynab and other women in Egypt felt for me was apparent in their sisterly concerns about my childless state and their efforts to help me. My feelings for them had led me both to friendships there and to explorations in my anthropological work back home about ways to represent them that might make the complexity of their lives and individual personalities—forms of complexity we recognize in the Self, not the Other—more apparent.[12]

What I did not explore then was another process that could occur: that one's own constructions of personal experience would be shaped by knowledge of these women's lives and even by particular women one had come to know.[k] In being pregnant, I was finding that the cultural resources I had at my disposal to think about what I was experiencing and to fill in gaps in my knowledge of an uncertain terrain included both those from "home" and those from "the field," often juxtaposed. From "home" I had my own family background, the biomedical discourse with which

so many white middle-class women feel comfortable, feminist critiques of this same discourse as well as of the popular cultural representations in media and books, and a patchy familiarity with women who had given birth.[l] From Kareema and the other women I knew in Egypt I had notebooks full of beliefs about reproduction, stories about reproduction, and, most important of all, years' worth of vivid memories of an everyday world rich in pregnancies, births, and children. I now thought and felt with all these resources.[13]

As I begin to gain confidence that the pregnancy really will last, I have started to worry about the birth. I sometimes skip ahead to the later chapters of my pregnancy books and frighten myself with those glossy photographs that seem to have nothing to do with the reassuring text about positions, helpers, and water births. I look at my husband and wonder about my new dependency—will he mop my brow as they show husbands doing in the photographs, will he comfort me, will he find the birth disgusting, will he help me? When I dare look beyond the birth, I am excited. My husband, always more optimistic than I am, reminds me that this is a new adventure for us. When he compliments me for being so brave I swell with pride.

Yet when I think ahead to the days and weeks just after the birth, I envy Kareema. Like most professional women I have good friends, but they don't live nearby. My family too is scattered. My sister, whom I saw every day for more than a month because she gave me my injections, won't be around. I look forward to the new intimacy

---

[12] This essay, published in 1995, is in many ways the companion of an essay Abu-Lughod wrote in 1991, called "Writing Against Culture." In the earlier essay Abu-Lughod writes at length about the divide between self and other, or between writers and their subjects, on which ethnography rests. She says anthropology's avowed goal may be "the study of man [*sic*]," but it is a discipline built on the historically constructed divide between the West and the non-West. It has been and continues to be primarily the study of the non-Western other by the Western self, ". . . And the relationship between the West and the non-West, at least since the birth of anthropology, has been constituted by Western domination." One of the remedies Abu-

Lughod suggests to combat this process of "othering" is to write ethnographies of the particular—exactly what she has done in the essay. However, she implies here that this process of moving beyond the self/other divide will reveal deeply sympathetic characters and universal human passions. Is such an assumption warranted?

[13] Many anthropologists have discovered that lessons they learned in the field can have unexpected applications at home. Although Abu-Lughod makes the point more eloquently, what she describes in this paragraph is what introductory cultural anthropology textbooks call the *process of becoming bicultural*.

with my husband, and I'm counting on him; but I've been warned about the strains. As an academic I think of books as companions, but will they really give me the advice I need? So much is unknown: I don't know how long I'll be in the hospital; whether I'll have a caesarian section; who will deliver me; whether the babies will be in incubators.

When Kareema gave birth, as usual the women in her community dropped everything to come help. She had her baby in the room she likes best for this—a warm room away from the rest of the house. Her cousin and her best friend, women she has known nearly all her life, were there to hold her. Along with some other women and all her children, they stayed with her for a week, busily cooking, doing her laundry for her, and talking. They had all been through this experience. They knew she would be there when it was their turn. They joked and gossiped and told stories late into the night. They made her soothing teas. No men came near, and few demands were made on them. It was a sort of holiday. Kareema's only responsibility was to rest, to nurse and change her new infant, and to receive her women visitors, who came bringing chickens, eggs, bars of soap, and little hand-sewn dresses.

At my wedding four years ago, I missed my Bedouin friends. To bring them in, I recited some songs they would have sung to celebrate my wedding had they been there. It will be harder to find a substitute for the busy companionship they provide to the mother of a newborn. They say a new mother should not be left alone. I expect I will be, from time to time. They say she is vulnerable. We call it postpartum depression. Perhaps I'll wear my Bedouin silver bracelet. They say it is good for a new mother to wear silver; it protects her.[14]

ACKNOWLEDGEMENT

Lila Abu-Lughod, "A Tale of Two Pregnancies." In *Women Writing Culture,* ed. Ruth Behar and Deborah A. Gordon, pp. 339–349. © 1995 The Regents of the University of California. Reprinted by permission of the University of California Press.

NOTES

I am grateful to the women like Kareema and Zaynab in Egypt who taught me about infertility, among other things. A fellowship from the National Endowment for the Humanities through the American Research Center in Egypt enabled me to come to know Zaynab in 1990. Since 1978 I have had generous support for my research among the Awlad 'Ali Bedouin; my most recent extended stay with Kareema and her family was made possible by a Fulbright award. Ruth Behar's insightful suggestions made the essay richer.

[a] All the names used in this essay are pseudonyms.

[b] In a sensitive and sensible rethinking of the misnomer of "native" or "indigenous" anthropologist, Kirin Narayan has drawn attention to the complex and shifting identifications all anthropologists have and has proposed hybridity as a more appropriate characterization of anthropologists' identities. She has also suggested that their texts should embody the enactment of that hybridity. See Kirin Narayan, "How Native Is a 'Native' Anthropologist?" *American Anthropologist* 95 (1993): 671–86.

[c] Emily Martin, *The Woman in the Body: A Cultural Analysis of Reproduction* (Boston: Beacon Press, 1987).

[d] For more on Awlad 'Ali theories of infertility, see Lila Abu-Lughod, *Writing Women's Worlds: Bedouin Stories* (Berkeley: University of California Press, 1993), chap. 3. See also Marcia Inhorn, *Quest for Conception: Gender, Infertility, and Egyptian Medical Traditions* (Philadelphia: University of Pennsylvania Press, 1994), especially its rich descriptions of Egyptian infertility treatments.

[e] Sarah Franklin, "Making Sense of Missed Conceptions: Anthropological Perspectives on Unexplained

---

[14] You have now completed Abu-Lughod's story about pregnancy. Her topic is interesting, her writing style engaging, but stop for a moment and reflect on what you have learned by reading the essay. Do you come away better informed about Egyptian women's ideas on pregnancy and childbirth or in vitro fertilization? The purpose of the essay is for Abu-Lughod to discuss her feelings and experiences, not tell us about Egyptian women (though Abu-Lughod certainly does this in other publications). For

many postmodernists ethnography is not really a descriptive or analytical account of life in another culture, it is a narrative created by the author, little different from a novel. This essay was printed in a volume called *Women Writing Culture,* but Abu-Lughod is telling us much more about herself than about Bedouin culture. One implication of a strong postmodern position is that anthropologists cannot tell us about another culture. They can only tell us about their own experiences.

Infertility," in *Changing Human Reproduction*, ed. Meg Stacey (London: Sage Publications, 1992), 75–91; and "Postmodern Procreation: A Cultural Account of Assisted Reproduction," in *Conceiving the New World Order: The Global Politics of Reproduction*, ed. Faye D. Ginsburg and Rayna Rapp (Berkeley: University of California Press, 1995), 323–45.

[f] Abu-Lughod, *Writing Women's Worlds*.

[g] Among the articles in which Donna Haraway makes this sort of argument, "A Cyborg Manifesto," in her *Simians, Cyborgs, and Women* (New York: Routledge, 1991), 149–81, is probably the most powerful.

[h] Rosalind Pollack Petchesky, "Fetal Images: The Power of Visual Culture in the Politics of Reproduction," *Feminist Studies* 13, no. 2 (Summer 1987): 280.

[i] Lila Abu-Lughod, "Can There Be a Feminist Ethnography?" *Women and Performance* 5, no. 1 (1990): 7–27.

[j] Ibid., 25.

[k] It is difficult for anthropologists to reflect on the ways their sense of self or their experience of life events might have been shaped by the people and ideas encountered in the field. It can be done, however, as exemplified by Dorinne Kondo, "Dissolution and Reconstitution of Self: Implications for Anthropological Epistemology," *Cultural Anthropology* I (1986): 74–88; Renato Rosaldo, "Introduction: Grief and a Headhunter's Rage," in his *Culture and Truth* (Boston: Beacon Press, 1989), 1–21; and Paul Riesman, *Freedom in Fulani Life: An Introspective Ethnography* (Chicago: University of Chicago Press, 1977).

[l] This greater acceptance by middle-class women of the biomedical discourse on reproduction is documented by Martin, *Woman in the Body*, and by Rayna Rapp, "Constructing Amniocentesis: Maternal and Medical Discourses," in *Uncertain Terms: Negotiating Gender in American Culture*, ed. Faye Ginsburg and Anna Lowenhaupt Tsing (Boston: Beacon Press, 1990), 28–42.

---

38. *The Making of the Maori: Culture Invention and Its Logic*

ALLAN HANSON (b. 1939)

ANTHROPOLOGISTS AND HISTORIANS have become acutely aware in recent years that "culture" and "tradition" are anything but stable realities handed down intact from generation to generation. Tradition is now understood quite literally to be an invention designed to serve contemporary purposes, "an attempt," as Lindstrom put it (1982:317), "to read the present in terms of the past by writing the past in terms of the present."[1]

Those contemporary purposes vary according to who does the inventing. When people invent their own traditions it is usually to legitimate or sanctify some current reality or aspiration, be it as momentous as the Greek national identity, Quebec nationalism, or the Hawaiian renaissance (Handler 1984; Handler and Linnekin 1984; Herzfeld 1982; Linnekin 1983), or as uncontroversial as the relatively new form of dual social organization that Borofsky (1987) encountered on the Polynesian island of Pukapuka. People also invent cultures and traditions for others, and then treat them as if their inventions were the actual state of affairs. When the inventors are politically dominant, as has been the case between Western nations and

From *American Anthropologist* (1989)

---

[1] Hanson writes, "Tradition is now understood quite literally to be an invention designed to serve contemporary purposes." This statement is a logical extension of the thinking about culture that was becoming common as a result of postmodern thinking. Postmodernists challenged the positivist notions of culture and ethnography that had been common in most of 20th century anthropology. Boas and his students as well as most other anthropologists of the 20th century believed they were observing, recording, and analyzing culture. However, in the view of postmodernists, there is nothing to preserve except one's own interpretation of what is going on around them. Culture, as you participate in it, is your own construction. The dilemma then, becomes how to talk about beliefs and behaviors which may be common, but are not universal, or which are commonly known, but are the inspiration for only individual or idiosyncratic behavior?

their colonies, the invention of tradition for subordinate peoples is part of a cultural imperialism that tends to maintain the asymmetrical relationship of power (Fabian 1983; Ranger 1983; Said 1978).[2]

It is becoming clear that anthropologists too are inventors of culture. The evolutionary ideas of Sir Henry Maine and Lewis Henry Morgan were major sources for the invention of the Fijian system of land tenure (France 1969; Legge 1958). Although it contains misinterpretations, A. B. Deacon's 1934 book, *Malekula: A Vanishing People in the New Hebrides,* has been adopted by the people of the region as the final arbiter of disputes about traditional culture (Larcom 1982:334).[3] The present intellectual climate has even spawned the notion that the quintessential anthropological activities of ethnographic research and writing inevitably produce cultural inventions (Clifford and Marcus 1986; Geertz 1988; Wagner 1981). This raises fundamental questions about the nature of cultural reality and whether the information that anthropologists produce can possibly qualify as knowledge about that reality.[4]

New Zealand Maori culture forms an excellent context in which to frame these issues. The invention of Maori culture has been going on for more than a century, taking at least two distinct forms in that time, and anthropological interpretations and misinterpretations have joined the contributions of other scholars, government officials, and Maoris themselves (including some Maori anthropologists) in the inventive process. The two historical moments described below are the period around the turn of the 20th century—when the primary aim was to assimilate Maoris into White life and culture—and the present day, when Maoris seek to maintain their cultural distinctiveness and to assume a more powerful position in society. Following that discussion we will be ready to consider more thoroughly the theoretical implications of the invention of culture for the enterprise of anthropology.

THE WHENCE OF THE MAORI

Anthropology's contribution in the early decades of this century to the construction of New Zealand Maori culture stems from that great stream of now-discredited anthropological theory: diffusionism and long-distance migrations. This mode of thinking was largely responsible for the birth and nurturance of two major understandings about traditional Maori culture that, in some quarters, still lead a robust existence. One of these is a set of traditions about the settlement of New Zealand that may conveniently be grouped under the rubric of the "Great Fleet." The other is the idea that pre-European Maori culture featured an esoteric cult dedicated to a supreme being named Io.[5]

---

[2] Many anthropologists today are concerned with issues of power, and western hegemony over the rest of the world, especially though colonialism. One of Hanson's goals in this essay is to show how anthropologists invented Maori traditions that were used to justify Britain's colonial control of New Zealand.

[3] Arthur Bernard Deacon (1903–1927), was a student of A.C. Haddon (see page 150) who died of "black water fever" (a complication of malaria) while doing his first fieldwork. His work was very much in the Torres Straits/Boasian mold, and the idea that an anthropological account could be used to recreate a culture is an enduring notion from Boasian-style anthropology. A final interesting point concerning Deacon: His book was published posthumously by another of Haddon's students, Camilla Wedgewood. She was the great-great-great-granddaughter of Josiah Wedgewood and hence a distant relation by marriage to Charles Darwin.

[4] Hanson published this essay in 1989. The "present intellectual climate" he is writing about is the postmodern critique of ethnography. In this essay Hanson is suggesting that there is no ethnographic reality that can be known in a "scientific" way. He claims the invention of Maori culture has been going on for more than a century and has involved anthropologists, government officials, and Maoris, including Maori anthropologists. Maori cultural "reality" he says, was first created to further the assimilation of Maori into European colonial culture. Today he argues that Maori traditional culture is being recreated to further the rise of Maori political and social power. The essay describes these two distinct periods.

[5] Hanson mentions the "great stream of now-discredited anthropological theory: diffusionism and long-distance migrations." Diffusionism was a popular theory at the turn of the twentieth century with proponets primarily in Germany and England. The German Kulturkreise or Culture

The rudiments of the discovery and settlement theory are these. New Zealand was discovered in A.D. 925 by Kupe, a man from Ra'iatca in the Society Islands. The first settlers, Toi and his grandson Whatonga, arrived from Tahiti in about the middle of the 12th century. Finally, a fleet of seven canoes—Tainui, Te Arawa, Mataatua, Kurahaupo, Tokomaru, Aotea, and Takitumu—set out in about 1350 from a homeland named Hawaiki, which was probably Ra'iatea or Tahiti. After a stop in Rarotonga, the fleet arrived in New Zealand and the migrants dispersed to populate the various parts of the country. Most Maori tribes trace their origin to one or another of the canoes that formed the Great Fleet (Hiroa 1950:5-64; Simmons 1976:3-106; Sorrenson 1979:44-57).

As for the Io cult, it has been claimed that although the Maori pantheon contained many gods, over them all presided Io: an eternal being, itself uncreated, and the creator of the other gods, the universe, and all things (Smith 1913:110-112). The cult of Io was philosophically sophisticated and esoteric, knowledge and worship of the high god being restricted to a few ranking chiefs and high priests. "It is quite probable, indeed, that this superior creed may have been too exalted for ordinary minds" (Best 1973:24).

Before examining how anthropology contributed to their development and promulgation, it is important to know that scholarship in recent decades has thrown both the cult of Io and the Great Fleet story into serious question. The primary source for the Io cult is part 1 of *The Lore of the Whare-wananga*. This is a compendium of religious and mythological lore of the Kahungunu tribe, arranged and translated by S. Percy Smith (1913). After a careful examination of the manuscript material on which the volume is based, David Simmons and Bruce Biggs concluded that chapter 2, which contains the material on the Io cult, is derived from manuscripts whose status as pre-European Maori tradition is questionable (Simmons 1976:382). Te Rangi Hiroa, a half-Maori anthropologist also known as Peter H. Buck, observed that Io's creative activities—bringing forth light from primordial darkness, dividing the waters, suspending the sky, and forming the earth— had rather too much in common with Genesis for their purely Maori provenance to sound convincing (Hiroa 1950:526-536; see also Johansen 1958:36-61).[6]

As far as the Great Fleet is concerned, in 1840 Horatio Hale, a linguist with the United States Exploring Expedition, collected a legend at the Bay of Islands about a fleet of four canoes that were blown off course during a voyage between, he presumed, Samoa and Tonga, and which eventually arrived at New Zealand (Sorrenson 1979:35-36). The army historian A. S. Thomson, writing at mid-century, was also told that migrants to New Zealand set out in a fleet of canoes (Thomson 1859:1:57-68). As with the Io cult, however, Percy Smith was perhaps the key early

---

Circle school of thought was led by Father Wilhelm Schmidt (1868–1964) and Fritz Graebner (1877–1934). Schmidt and Graebner argued that cultural traits spread outward in a circular fashion from a variety of cultural centers. In the 1920s, English diffusionists Grafton Elliot Smith and W. J. Perry proposed that all civilization had originated in Egypt and diffused from that place. This narrative, according to Hanson, played an important part in English thinking about Maori origins in early twentieth century New Zealand. A similar, and better known example of this same type of thinking was Thor Heyerdahl's Kon Tiki expedition in 1947. Heyerdahl hope to demonstrate the possibility that Polynesia was first settled by people from South America who floated across the Pacific on rafts. To support his theory Heyerdahl built the Kon Tiki, a balsa wood raft and launched it from the coast of Peru in April 1947. After a voyage of 101 days, Heyerdahl successfully drifted to the to the island of Raroia where they crashed their raft into a reef. Although one does not have to look far to see examples of diffusion today, modern research has not supported the theories of Schmidt and Smith.

[6] S. Percy Smith (1840–1922) was an English explorer, surveyor, self-trained ethnologist. He was born in England but moved with his family to New Zealand when he was 10. Employed as a surveyor (he was appointed Surveyor General in 1889), Smith used his frequent trips across New Zealand as a way to observe and record information on Maori culture. This material formed the basis of his work as a scholar of Polynesia. He was a founder of the Polynesian society and first co-editor of the Journal of the Polynesian Society.

proponent of migration stories of Kupe, Toi, and the Great Fleet. These are set out particularly in part 2 of *The Lore of the Whare-wananga* (Smith 1915) and *History and Traditions of the Maoris of the West Coast* (Smith 1910).

Simmons and Biggs found the textual material in part 2 of *The Lore* to be a late compilation from a variety of sources (Simmons 1976:386). Simmons conducted an exhaustive study of European writings and Maori traditions from many tribal areas with the aim of ascertaining what Maori traditions actually say about the discovery of and migrations to New Zealand. He concluded that the stories about Kupe, Toi, and Whatonga as summarized above are not authentic Maori tradition (1976:59, 100). In this regard Simmons echoes William Colenso, who, a century before, had written that traditions such as Kupe's discovery of New Zealand and subsequent return to Hawaiki are "mythical rhapsody" that, while entirely believed by some Europeans, were not (at that time) taken as historical fact by the Maoris themselves (Sorrenson 1979:44–45).

While it is undeniable that Maori tribes tell of the arrival of their ancestors in migration canoes, the notion of an organized expedition by a Great Fleet in about 1350 seems to have been constructed by European scholars such as Smith in an effort to amalgamate disparate Maori traditions into a single historical account (Simmons 1976:316). Dating the fleet at 1350 was a particularly blatant work of fiction, since Smith simply took the mean of a large number of tribal genealogies that varied from 14 to 27 generations before 1900. "The date of 1350," Simmons concludes, "has validity only as an exercise in arithmetic" (1976:108; see also Smithyman 1979 for further evaluation of Smith's work).[7]

If the Io cult and the Great Fleet are fabrications about indigenous Maori society, the question arises as to why European scholars so enthusiastically embraced them as fact. The answer pertains to the 19th-century fascination with tracing the various peoples of the world back to a few cradles of civilization. Well before the Great Fleet and Io entered European discourse this penchant of thought produced, as one of the earliest foreign inventions of Maori culture, the idea of the Maoris as Semites. Samuel Marsden, who in 1819 was the first missionary to visit New Zealand, opined that the Maoris had "sprung from some dispersed Jews." He advanced as evidence for this proposition their "great natural turn for traffic; they will buy and sell anything they have got" (Elder 1932:219).

By the late 19th and early 20th centuries scholars were using the Great Fleet and Io theories to suggest kinship between the Maoris and New Zealand's European settlers. The skin color, physical features, and often amorous hospitality of Polynesians had appealed to Europeans since the days of the 18th-century explorers. Now, diffusionist and migration-minded European scholars in New Zealand were pleased to discover in the Maori race the capacity for sophisticated philosophy, as demonstrated by the Io cult, and a history of heroic discoveries and migrations that included the Great Fleet, Kupe, and, in even more remote epochs, intrepid voyages through Indonesia, India, and beyond. This ennobled Maoris in European eyes to the point where it became possible to entertain the possibility of a link with themselves.

Doubtless that possibility became more palatable to British migrants when, as the 19th century drew to a close, the idea emerged that the Maoris were of Aryan stock. Edward Tregear, a high-level civil servant and amateur ethnologist and linguist who participated in the founding of the Polynesian Society, elaborated this thesis in

---

[7] Hanson is setting up a discussion of how the Io cult and Great Fleet stories are actually European narratives that have been incorporated into modern Maori culture for contemporary political and social purposes. However, this is not only an essay about Maori culture, the point is that cultural invention is a common process in all cultures. Just as the Io cult and the Great Fleet stories were created by Europeans in the service of their colonial beliefs, so too these "traditions" have been repurposed by Modern Maori for their own place and times. If you accept Hanson's argument, we must then confront the larger issue of what we know as anthropologists and how we come to know these things. Hanson attempts to address this issue in the last section of his essay.

his 1885 book *The Aryan Maori*. Rejoicing that "Comparative Philology and Comparative Mythology are the two youngest and fairest daughters of Knowledge" (1885:1), Tregear seduced from them a dazzling array of associations between Maori language and lore and that of, among other places, India, ancient Greece, Rome, and Britain. He even demonstrated that although Maori people had long since forgotten the cattle that their ancestors herded in the steppes of Asia and as they migrated through India, the memory remained embalmed in their language. So he found the Sanskrit *gau*, for cow, in several Maori terms containing *kau*. For example, a Maori weapon consisting of "sharp teeth of flint lashed firmly to a piece of wood" was called *mata-kautete* because its shape is reminiscent of a "cow-titty" (1885:30-31). Drunk with the power of comparative philology, Tregear uncovered similar memories in the Maori language of pigs, wolves, tigers, bows and arrows, and frogs (1885:30-37).[8]

Such research was beginning to reveal the dim outlines of perhaps the most splendid chapter in human history: the great Aryan migration. Enthused Tregear of the Maori forerunners,

> No free-booting Huns or Vandals, mad for plunder and the sack of towns were they but colonists seeking new homes beneath strange stars. We of Europe have set out on the same quest. Encircling Africa, the two vast horns of the Great Migration have touched again; and men whose fathers were brothers on the other side of those gulfs of distance and of time meet each other, when the Aryan of the West greets the Aryan of the Eastern Seas. [1885:105]

Building on Renan's (1889:84) remark that Io is one of the many variants of the name Jehovah,

Elsdon Best advanced the same theory (Best 1924:1:90).

The notion of Maoris as Aryans was pertinent to race relations and nation building in fledgling New Zealand. R. Studholme Thompson—who held that the Maoris belonged to the Alpine section of the Caucasian race and came originally from the Atlas mountains of North Africa—explained that his work on Maori origins

> "had a large object in view, viz., the demonstration that the highly-civilized Britain and the Maori, just emerging from barbarism, are one in origin; that in fraternising with the Maori the European undergoes no degradation; in intermarrying with the race he does no violence to the claims of consanguinity. It is thought that when this is thoroughly known there will arise a more cordial feeling between the peoples inhabiting the colony, both equally the subjects of one King." [quoted in Sorrenson 1979:29]

"What better myth could there be for a young country struggling for nationhood and for the amalgamation of its races," asks Sorrenson (1979:30), "than this reunification of the Aryans?"

No one talks seriously anymore about ultimate Maori origins as Aryan or Semitic, but the two most prominent features of the tradition—the cult of Io and the discovery and migration stories concerning Kupe, Toi, and the Great Fleet—remain very much alive. Although they are largely of European construction they have been embraced by Maoris as their authentic heritage. Te Rangi Hiroa accepted the traditions concerning Kupe, Toi, and the Great Fleet (1950:4-64); in his mind the last of these was so significant that it "ranks in historical and social importance with the Norman Conquest" (1950:36). Sir Apirana Ngata, longtime Member of Parliament and

---

[8] In this section Hanson shows how Europeans used diffusionist theories to argue that the Maori were descendent from Aryans. He proposes that such an argument was politically useful to Europeans in the context of nineteenth century New Zealand. The term Aryan here does not refer blonde-haired, blue-eyed people, a twentieth century usage. In the nineteenth century, the term Aryan referred to hypothetical, light-skinned, southern Europeans who were believed to have spread through and conquered the dark-skinned inhabitants of the Middle East and India. The evidence for this theory was largely based on linguistic similarities between Hindi, Greek, Latin, and other European languages. The notion that light-skinned peoples had historically dominated dark-skinned ones nicely fit European colonial efforts and supported the racial thinking of nineteenth century Europeans. Modern archaeological research, however, does not support the conquest theory.

probably the most influential and respected Maori of the 20th century, promoted the idea of a sextennial celebration in 1950 to commemorate the arrival of the Great Fleet (and, not coincidentally, to dwarf the mere centennial of the signing of the Treaty of Waitangi, which the New Zealanders of European descent had celebrated in 1940) (Sorrenson 1979:52). From their discourse, it is clear that Maori authors of today such as Maharaia Winiata (1967:25), Douglas Sinclair (1975:118-119), and Ereura Stirling (Stirling and Salmond 1980:83-84) also accept the tradition of the Great Fleet as historical fact.

Io too lives in Maori minds, as is evident from a recent essay on Maori religion and cosmology by Maori Marsden, chaplain in the Royal New Zealand Navy and Te Aupouri tribal member. Relying solely on sources he has encountered in Maori contexts, such as the transmission of tribal lore and orations at Maori gatherings, Marsden depicts Io as an authentically Maori concept of a creator-god who verbally called the universe into being from a primal void and differentiated light from darkness, the earth and waters from the sky (Marsden 1975:210-211).

Maori reasons for affirming Io and the Great Fleet have not, however, been the same as those of Pakeha (Maori for European or White) New Zealanders. If Maoris have always been willing to accept any qualities of racial greatness that Pakeha scholars might attribute to them, it was not so much to believe themselves worthy of assimilation into the White population and culture as it was to bolster a sense of their own ethnic distinctiveness and value. This sense has grown dramatically in strength and stridency of expression in recent years. That development, indeed, lies at the heart of the second chapter in the invention of Maori culture and tradition that we have to consider.[9]

MAORITANGA

The movement known as Maoritanga (Maoriness) or Mana Maori (Maori Power) is one of the most important developments in New Zealand society today. As with any large social movement, Maoritanga includes diversity, and not all of the tenets discussed below would be endorsed by all of its supporters. What unites them and, interestingly, what they share with turn-of-the-century scholars such as R. Studholme Thompson, is the goal to secure for Maoris a favorable place in the nation being built in New Zealand. Yet the current and earlier images of that place and of the national culture to emerge, are quite different. The earlier vision was to create one culture, European in form, into which Maoris would be successfully assimilated. To promote this goal it was necessary to identify similarities between Maori and European. As we have seen, the invention of Maori culture promulgated by Percy Smith and his contemporaries did just that by using the Io cult as evidence of the Maori capacity for sophisticated thought and the Great Fleet to demonstrate the mettle of Maori ancestors and even to identify them as fellow Aryans.

Maoritanga's vision is different. Its image of the future New Zealand is a bicultural society, in which Maoris are on a par with Pakehas politically and economically and Maori culture is respected as equally valid but distinct from Pakeha culture (see, for example, Sciascia 1984:162). To promote that image, it is necessary to stress the unique contribution that Maori culture has made to national life—different from but no less valuable than the Pakeha contribution. Thus, the Maori tradition that Maoritanga invents is one that contrasts with Pakeha culture, and particularly with those elements of Pakeha culture that are least attractive. In New Zealand as in the

---

[9] We want to review where we are in Hanson's discussion: The Io cult and the Great Fleet stories were invented and promoted by Europeans. Europeans took the tales told them by the Maori and interpreted them for their own end. They put the tales into the frameworks of Christian monotheism and European narratives of discovery. They did this with the goal of establishing the value of the New Zealand colony and its inhabitants and to argue that Maoris were worthy of assimilation into the White population. Modern Maori accept many of the traditions promoted by Europeans and in the following section Hanson discusses Maoritanga, and the ways in which the Maori have used these "traditions" to argue for Maori distinctiveness, independence, and cultural superiority.

United States, human relations among Pakehas are often thought to lack passion and spontaneity; the Pakeha approach to things is detached and coldly rational; Pakehas have lost the appreciation for magic and the capacity for wonder or awe inspired by the unknown; Pakeha culture is out of step with nature—it pollutes the environment and lacks a close tie with the land.[10]

Maori culture is represented as the ideal counterbalance to these Pakeha failings. Maoris cherish the dead, speaking to them and weeping freely over open caskets, while Pakehas mute the mourning process and hide the body from sight (Dansey 1975:177). The Maori has a "close, spiritual relationship with the land"; he "loved his land and identified with it perhaps more closely than any other race" (Sinclair 1975:115). Maori thought appreciates the mystical dimension and transcends reason:

> Abstract rational thought and empirical methods cannot grasp the concrete act of existing which is fragmentary, paradoxical and incomplete. The only way lies through a passionate, inward subjective approach. Only a few foreigners alien to a culture, men like James K. Baxter with the soul of a poet, can enter into the existential dimension of Maori life. This grasp of a culture proceeds not from superficial intellectualism but from an approach best articulated in poetry. Poetic imagery reveals to the Maori a depth of understanding in men which is absent from the empirical approach of the social anthropologist.[11] [Marsden 1975:218-219]

The times have changed a great deal since 1922, when no less respected and proud a Maori than Sir Apirana Ngata could say of a Pakeha scholar, "There is not a member of the Maori race who is fit to wipe the boots of Mr. Elsdon Best in the matter of the knowledge of the lore of the race to which we belong" (quoted in Journal of the Polynesian Society 1932:31). Today Maoris are no longer willing to tolerate being told by Pakehas what is good for them, and even how to be Maori (Rangihau 1975). The notion that the rational Pakeha mind is unsuited to grasp Maori life, together with Maoritanga's major objective of drawing power into Maori hands, have encouraged many Maoris to insist that they, not Pakehas, be the proper custodians and managers of knowledge about the Maori heritage.

This sentiment is strong enough that some advocates of Maoritanga have invited Pakeha scholars out of Maori studies. Michael King, a Pakeha who has written extensively on Maori topics, observed that in 1971 Maori radicals insisted that Pakeha historians write more about Maori subjects, but by 1983 the demand was that they should not write about them at all (1985:161). King's own 1983 book, *Maori—A Photographic and Social History,* has been negatively received by Maori reviewers, who stated the preference that such topics be addressed by Maori writers (King 1985:163). In the university, a Maori student complained that it is ethically wrong to be taught his own heritage by a Pakeha (Mead 1983:343-344).[12]

Pakehas have not been routed from Maori studies. Indeed, because virtually all scholars who deal in Maori topics actively support the goal of Maoris to secure a better position in society and

---

[10] Hanson claims that a part of the invention of Maoritanga is based on being non-Pakeha. The qualities that followers of Maoritanga assign to the Maori are very similar to those attributed to Native Americans in American popular culture (and frequently promoted by Native American peoples).

[11] James K. Baxter (1926–1972) was a major New Zealand poet who struggled with Christian faith as well as alcoholism. In 1968, Baxter had a dream which he believed told him to go to live in "Jerusalem" a small Maori settlement on the Wanganui River. There, he attempted to found a utopian community that would put both Christian and Maori spiritual ideas into practice. He lived at Jerusalem until several months before his death.

[12] The Maori student complaining about being taught Maori culture by a Pakeha might sound radical to most American university students today, but in the 1990s there were similar battles fought in the United States when scholars and popular figures insisted that certain fields should only be taught by particular people. In your university are the majority of faculty in women studies programs women, African American studies, black, Queer studies gay and lesbian?

share the objective of creating a bicultural New Zealand, they have been active participants in the invention of the tradition that Maoritanga presents to the world. Michael King himself, for example, served as editor of the important collection of works by Maori authors that articulated many of the cardinal principles of Maoritanga (King 1975).

A number of writers have fostered the present invention of Maori culture by lending the weight of Pakeha scholarship to the movement. This often takes the form of according special authority to Maoris in matters pertaining to Maori culture. The Pakeha historian Judith Binney acknowledged the premise that Maoris are best equipped to understand and write about Maori topics when, in the preface to her excellent study of the Maori prophet Rua Kenana, she expressed misgivings about her grasp of the material and recorded the hope that one day a Maori scholar would produce a more authoritative account (Binney, Chaplin, and Wallace 1979:11). Anthropologist Anne Salmond has made it one of her professional objectives to promulgate and interpret Maori concepts of knowledge with the aim of incorporating them more fully into a bicultural New Zealand society (Salmond 1982; Stirling and Salmond 1980).[13]

Steps have been taken to avoid offending Maori sensibilities. Preserved and tattooed Maori heads from the early 19th century, only 15 years ago a staple of museum exhibits, are no longer to be found on display in New Zealand institutions. Pakeha scholars have softened critiques of the Io

cult and the Great Fleet, primarily, it seems, because many Maoris accept these traditions as authentic. The first edition of anthropologist Joan Metge's *The Maoris of New Zealand,* published in 1967, contains the following passages about Io: "The existence of a supreme god, Io, was allegedly revealed to those who reached the upper grades of the school of learning" (1967:30), and, from the glossary, "Io: Supreme Being whose existence and cult are claimed to have been revealed to initiates of the pre-European 'school of learning'" (1967:223). The corresponding passages in the second edition of the work, published in 1976, are: "The existence of a supreme god, Io-matua-kore, was revealed to those who reached the upper grades of the school of learning" (1976:23), and "Io: Supreme Being whose existence and worship were revealed to initiates of the pre-European 'school of learning'; identified by many Maoris with the Supreme Being of Christianity and used instead of or in alternation with the name Jehovah" (1976:337). A reference to Io as "the Supreme Being of Classic Maori cosmology" also appears on page 55, in a new chapter written for the second edition. Beyond the generally more positive attitude toward the Io cult, an increased concern about highlighting the views of contemporary Maoris is visible in a change of citation in the glossary entry on Io from Hiroa's skeptical account of the cult in *The Coming of the Maori* (1950) to the 1975 essay by Maori Marsden, discussed above, which accepts Io as authentic tradition.[14]

---

[13] if you agree with the notion that culture is of your own construction and an anthropologist's view of culture is simply their own interpretation of what is going on around them, than should a Maori anthropologist's view of Maori culture be more privileged than a Pakeha scholar's? One postmodern answer to this question might be that Pakeha scholarship has been privileged because ultimately, it is power that controls truth. A Maori anthropologist should be privileged because people have a right to control the content of their own culture. Further, Maori voices have historically been silenced and it is the mission of anthropology to recover these silenced voices. On the other hand, if one follows the postmodern perspective to its logical conclusion than no one view of culture should ever be any more privileged than any other. All are inter-

pretations and there is no objective way to evaluate the relative merits of interpretations.

[14] If one believes that anthropologists have cultural truths to tell, how does one respond to Hanson's statement that Pakeha scholars have softened critiques of the Io cult and the Great Fleet because many Maoris accept these traditions as authentic? An example closer to home: The Navajo (Dine) say that they emerged from the ground at a place in the La Plata Mountains of Southern Colorado. Anthropologists argue that they are Athabascan peoples who entered North America from Siberia and only arrived in the Southwest United States about 750 years ago. Who's right? What forms of evidence are of use in determining the answer? Can these be ranked in terms of reliability? Will

Something similar is happening with the Great Fleet myth. New Zealand archeology has made great strides in recent years, and most discussions of the time and material conditions of early settlement (now established to have occurred by at least the 11th century) rely on archeological evidence. However, in a scholarly presentation of that evidence, Agnes Sullivan carefully states that, while the notion of an organized fleet seems discredited, archeology has produced nothing that disallows the possibility of migrant canoes arriving in New Zealand from East Polynesia up to about the 14th century. This has the effect of muting any archeological challenge to the magic date of 1350 for the arrival of ancestral canoes although, it will be recalled, Smith's settling upon that date is one of the most contrived components of the Great Fleet story. "In traditional terms," Sullivan concludes, "there appear to be no good grounds at present for suggesting that the central themes of most Hawaiki canoe traditions are to be interpreted other than straightforwardly" (1984:62).[15]

One of the most effective projects to publicize Maoritanga's invention of Maori culture was the exhibition "Te Maori: Maori Art from New Zealand Collections" (see Mead 1984b). Anthropology's role in the project is mainly to be found in the person of Sidney Mead, a Maori anthropologist who was one of the central organizers of the exhibition. "Te Maori" was shown in New York, St. Louis, San Francisco, and Chicago in 1984-86, and subsequently toured New Zealand in a triumphant homecoming. Through a stroke of genius in the presentation of the exhibition, Mead and the other Maoris involved in it managed to clothe the ob-

jects with more than simply artistic value. In each city the exhibition opened with a dramatic dawn ceremony in which Maori elders (brought from New Zealand specifically for the purpose) ritually lifted the *tapu* ("taboo") from the objects and entrusted them to the care of the host museum. The ceremony received extensive media coverage in each city, and it conveyed the Maori idea that the objects were infused with a spiritual power that derived from the ancestors and linked them in a mystical union with the Maoris of today. As a result the objects were viewed as more than examples of fine and exotic workmanship, and the notion was inserted into the minds of many Americans who saw or were involved with the exhibition that the Maori people have access to primal sources of power long since lost by more rational cultures (see O'Biso 1987).

The special meanings that became associated with "Te Maori" in the United States also had an impact in New Zealand. Vincent Crapanzano has cogently pointed out (1980:49, 81-87) that it is much easier to believe something about oneself if one succeeds in convincing someone else of it. As the standing of Maori art skyrocketed in international recognition as a result of the exhibition, Maori and Pakeha New Zealanders alike took greater interest and pride in it and became more receptive to the idea of a nonrational, spiritual quality in Maori culture. While the point should not be overemphasized, the exhibition did have some effect in both strengthening Maori identity and increasing Pakeha respect for the Maori people and Maori culture. In this way "Te Maori" advanced the agenda of Maoritanga and the notion of a bicultural New Zealand. Indeed, this was one of

---

different people rank them differently? Is more than one answer to the question possible? Your answers to these questions may indicate the depth to which you accept the postmodern critique of culture.

[15] The careful reader will recognize Sullivan's claim that "archeology has produced nothing that disallows the possibility of migrant canoes arriving in New Zealand from East Polynesia up to about the 14th century" is a logical fallacy (or spurious argument). One cannot prove a negative and the claim would be equally valid no matter what possibilities were placed in the sentence. For example,

"physics has produced nothing that disallows the possibility that flying saucers peopled by extraterrestrials landed at your university yesterday." Unfortunately this kind of non-logic is common. The United States went to War with Iraq in 2002, for example, in part because Saddam Hussein could not show conclusively that he did not have weapons of mass destruction. The lack of evidence for such weapons was not seen as proof that he did not have them, rather it was used to support the characterization of Hussein as cunning and untrustworthy.

the prime purposes and major benefits of the entire project (Mead 1984a:29; 1986:27, 74, 78, 104).

Maoris insisted that art objects produced by their ancestors are tribal treasures (*taonga*), with the result that tribal proprietary rights became an important issue in the mounting of "Te Maori." In the planning stages of the exhibition a distinction was made between the legal ownership of the objects, vested in the museums that hold them, and the cultural ownership, which remained with the tribes. It was decided that no object could leave New Zealand unless the cultural owners agreed. Intense debate raged among elders of the various tribes over this issue, and ultimately the art of the Whanganui region was not included in the exhibition because of tribal disapproval. The concept of cultural ownership of art objects, which had not been enunciated prior to "Te Maori," has enriched the significance of tribal membership for Maori people and represents an important step toward Maoritanga's goal of bringing the Maori heritage under Maori control Mead 1986:99).[16]

Anthropologists and other scholars throughout New Zealand are also attempting to further the cause of Maoritanga by encouraging the growth of Maori Studies programs in the schools and universities, the involvement of program staff in assisting the Maori people with land claims and other projects, and greater Maori university enrollment. The aim is more ambitious than just increasing knowledge of and respect for Maori culture among Pakehas and making the benefits of Pakeha-style education more available to Maoris. As Anne Salmond articulates it, the imperative is to expand social institutions and modes of thinking in New Zealand to the point where they become truly bicultural, so that Maori concerns and Maori epistemology may be included in the national discourse on an equal footing with Pakeha concerns and epistemology. She has registered satisfaction that signs of this are emerging in the university, in the form of a series of master's theses written in Maori by Maori students about the traditional histories of their own tribes, and often presented from the perspective of Maori epistemology. Her main disappointment is that the response from the Pakeha side has been inadequate, for academic anthropology has offered little of relevance to this much-needed injection of Maori ways of thinking and knowing into university-based Maori studies.[17]

> It could be that the anthropology we have inherited from Europe and America is simply not used to epistemological experiments of this sort, because it does not confront the experience of bicultural living, day by day, in the university as well as in the field. The questions of who are "we" and who are the "others" is anything but clear-cut when those who sit in lecture theatres and seminars and those who teach in them, those who write books, theses and articles and those who read them are inextricably both Maori and European; and in such a situation anthropology must change or be discarded. [Salmond 1983:323]

Moving still further along the same road, Sidney Mead has suggested that Maori Studies be elevated from its current program or department

---

[16] The issue of ownership of art objects is not limited to Maori tribes. Greece has been trying to get Britain to return the Elgin Marbles (the frieze from the Parthenon) for decades. In February. 2009, two animal-head sculptures claimed by the Chinese Government but owned by the estate of Yves St. Laurent were auctioned. The winning bidder refused to pay his bid, insisting that the sculptures belonged to China. Pierre Bergé, Laurent's partner who then owned the sculptures, said that he would freely return them to China if China would "observe human rights and give liberty to the Tibetan people and welcome the Dalai Lama" (NYT March 2, 2009). As of this writing (Jan. 2010) the sculptures are still held by the auction house.

Bergé would like to give them to a museum but, so far, no one will accept them.

[17] Here Hanson discusses Maori and Pakeha epistemology. Epistemology is the study of the nature and scope of knowledge. Historically, in Western philosophy, it has generally been assumed that epistemology is universal: The conditions that make something true in one culture make it true in all cultures. Postmodernists argue, however, not only that what is accepted as true in one place is not necessarily true in all places (a mundane claim accepted by all anthropologists) but rather that the conditions for deciding what is true in one culture can be vastly different from the conditions for deciding what is true in other cultures.

status in New Zealand universities to the level of a school; indeed, that a whole University of Aotearoa (the name for New Zealand favored by Maoritanga) be founded. The point is quite radical. It apparently aims to transform Maori Studies from a field of inquiry within the Pakeha-defined university to a general and distinctively Maori epistemological perspective from which not only Maori language and culture but also subjects such as anthropology, sociology, history, education, geography, linguistics, art history, and economics would be investigated (Mead 1983:343–346). Such a school would have a *marae* (in Maori villages, the plaza where visitors are received and community matters are discussed) as its central feature, instruction would be in the Maori language, and most of the staff would be Maori. Although Mead does not specify it, he is certainly not oblivious to the prospect that a University of Aotearoa would command more prestige—and much more substantial government funding—than the various *whare wananga* (traditional Maori schools) sponsored by different tribes. Echoing Maoritanga's cardinal demand for more power in Maori hands, Mead contends that the establishment of a Maori university would make it "possible to repossess our heritage, hold on to it, and to exercise a measure of control over it" (1983:346).[18]

THE LOGIC OF CULTURAL INVENTION

The image of Maori culture that developed around the turn of the 20th century was constructed in the main by scholars who were predisposed to analyze institutions in terms of long-distance migrations, and who cherished the political desire to assimilate Maoris to Pakeha culture. The present image has been invented for the purpose of enhancing the power of Maoris in New Zealand society, and is largely composed of those Maori qualities that can be attractively contrasted with the least desirable aspects of Pakeha culture.

Taken together, these case studies might incline one to the pessimistic view that the reality of traditional culture and history is so irredeemably shrouded behind multiple veils of distortion, some woven from imported fabric and others homespun, that no effort at objectivity could be sufficient to strip them away. But that would miss the distinctive feature of both examples: that the "distortions" have been accepted by Maoris as authentic to their heritage. Io and the Great Fleet have been incorporated into Maori lore and are passed from elders to juniors in storytelling, oratory, and other Maori contexts. Today Maoris, and also those Pakehas who desire to incorporate both sides of bicultural New Zealand into their own experience, make it a conscious point to practice the tenets of Maoritanga. They learn the Maori language and Maori history. They are careful to show respect for elders. They open themselves to the emotional and mystical impact of charisma and the nonrational, and they heighten their appreciation for Maori lore and Maori art. As a result, these and other elements of the current invention of Maori culture become objectively incorporated into that culture by the very fact of people talking about them and practicing them.[19]

---

[18] The notion in the Mead quote that a University of Aotearoa would allow the Maori to repossess their heritage and to exercise a measure of control over it follows from the idea that culture is a more-or-less unified object that is possessed by a group. This notion of culture was popular throughout most of the nineteenth and twentieth centuries. Postmodernists are more likely to hold that culture is not unified but rather more like a process or an arena in which action takes place and different individuals and groups contest for power. If this is the case, then the notion of a Maori university teaching Maori culture seems contradictory: There is no single, unified Maori culture to teach. However, Hansen's point, elaborated in greater detail below, is that such a university makes a great deal of sense as way to represent the interests of at least some Maori people and contest for power within the larger context of New Zealand culture.

[19] Hanson says one can look at his examples here and conclude although there is a cultural reality, that reality is so distorted by history and interpretation that it is impossible to uncover. However, his claim is more radical than that: There is no cultural reality behind the distortions! The distortions, inventions, the ways that culture has been selectively interpreted to favor some interests are all the stuff of Maori culture itself. It has always been thus, and there is no "real" culture other than this.

Therefore, the fact that culture is an invention, and anthropology one of the inventing agents, should not engender suspicion or despair that anthropological accounts do not qualify as knowledge about cultural reality. Inventions are precisely the stuff that cultural reality is made of; as Linnekin (1983) and Handler (1984) have convincingly demonstrated by means of Hawaiian and Quebecois examples, "there is no essential, bounded tradition . . . the ongoing reconstruction of tradition is a facet of all social life" (Handler and Linnekin 1984:276).

To entertain the notion of a historically fixed tradition is to affirm what Jacques Derrida calls the "metaphysics of presence" (1978:281) or "logocentrism" (1974:12). He argues that since Nietzsche, Freud, and Heidegger, among others, it has been necessary to replace the metaphysics of presence with a more fluid, decentered view.[20]

> Henceforth, it was necessary to begin thinking that there was no center, that the center could not be thought in the form of a present-being, that the center had no natural site, that it was not a fixed locus but a function, a sort of non-locus in which an infinite number of sign-substitutions came into play. This was the moment when . . . in the absence of a center or origin, everything became discourse . . . that is to say, a system in which the central signified, the original or transcendental signified, is never absolutely present. . . . The absence of the transcendental signified extends the

domain and the play of signification infinitely. [Derrida 1978:280]

Applied to our examples, a logocentric view would hold that traditional Maori culture existed in determinate form, say, at the moment of effective Western contact by Captain Cook in 1769. That cultural essence was then distorted in one way or another by turn-of-the-century anthropologists as well as by contemporary proponents of Maoritanga—although all of them claim to be holding fast to it. Derrida would maintain, on the contrary, that Maori culture has always been "a sort of nonlocus in which an infinite number of sign-substitutions come into play." From this perspective, discourse about the philosophically sophisticated cult of Io and the arrival in 1350 of a Great Fleet of migrant canoes represents not really a distortion of traditional Maori culture but one set of sign-substitutions in the play of signification that is itself the essence (if we may be allowed to use that word) of Maori culture. Other sign-substitutions include the warmth, passion, and mysticism stressed by Maoritanga. Indeed, they also include whatever lore, conventions, and institutions were in play among Maoris in New Zealand in 1769 on the eve of Cook's visit, for there is no reason to privilege them with some sort of fixed (logocentric) authenticity absent from the other inventions or sign-substitutions that we have considered. Certainly Maoris of the 1760s, no less than contemporary Maori activists,

---

[20] Jacques Derrida (1930–2004) was a French philosopher and a leader of the French postmodern movement. He is particularly known for his attempts to expose and critique fundamental Western modes of thinking by breaking apart philosophical texts, a process he termed *deconstruction*. Through deconstruction, Derrida sought to expose the alternate or repressed meanings in a text beyond that which an author meant to present. Deconstructionists contend that all texts contain elements that betray any stable meaning that an author might seek to impose on them. An analysis of any text will reveal the author's unstated suppositions or unintended contradictions. However, one of Derrida's fundamental points is that depending on who or what one is seeking to deconstruct, these points of contradiction or equivocation change.

Derrida's work was deliberately ambiguous and sometimes contradictory, because he tried to evoke certain ways of thinking rather than telling people what to think. Consequently he did not consider his own reading of text to be authoritative.

Derrida's thought was deeply influential in anthropology. Geertz had declared that culture was a text that members of a culture interpreted, and that anthropologists struggled to read over the shoulders of cultural participants (see essay 33). Derrida's thought gave anthropologists new methods of interpreting those cultural texts. These methods emphasized the variations in understanding, position, and power that condition the ways in which different individuals and groups inhabit, understand, and act within their cultures.

were moved by their own political agendas to appeal selectively and creatively to the tradition of their ancestors; and the same can be said for those ancestors, and so on indefinitely.[21]

It follows from this that the analytic task is not to strip away the invented portions of culture as inauthentic, but to understand the process by which they acquire authenticity. Social reproduction—the process whereby people learn, embody, and transmit the conventional behaviors of their society—is basically a matter of interpersonal communication. Any conventional act, such as greeting someone on the street, is learned by observing how other people do it, modeling one's own behavior on that, and being assured that it is done properly (or alerted that it is not) by the reactions of other people to the behavior. Moreover, each person is teacher as well as learner in the process, because his or her behavior also serves as a model upon which still other people construct their behavior (see Bourdieu 1977; Hanson and Hanson 1981). No one bit of behavior can be said to have ultimate authenticity, to be the absolute and eternal "right way" of which all the others are representations. All of the bits of behavior are models: models of previous bits and models for subsequent ones.[22]

Described like this, the process of ordinary social reproduction is a case of sign-substitution in a play of signification. But, as we have already seen, the invention of culture is also that. This demystifies the process whereby cultural inventions acquire authenticity in the eyes of members of society because the invention of culture is no extraordinary occurrence but an activity of the same sort as the normal, everyday process of social life.

While it is essential to recognize this point, there must nevertheless be something distinctive about culture invention. It is, after all, much too strong a phrase to use for everyday social reproduction. As a first approximation, it might be said that inventions are sign-substitutions that depart some considerable distance from those upon which they are modeled, that are selective, and that systematically manifest the intention to further some political or other agenda. This criterion would authorize us to classify as inventions those sign-substitutions that rework Maori migration canoe legends into a chapter of the great Aryan migration, or that stress Maori respect for the elders and the dead without mentioning that such respect operated within tribes only and was matched by a tendency to revile and cannibalize the elders and dead of other tribes.

Very often, however, the inventive quality of sign-substitutions is recognizable only from outside and when they form clusters. Percy Smith, Edward Tregear, and Elsdon Best worked ingenuously within the tradition of diffusionist anthropology. When compared with the other two, the theories (or sign-substitutions) advanced by any one of them are not radical departures, and certainly they did not consider those theories to be inventions. The same may be said of contemporary advocates of Maoritanga. But when detached observers consider these two movements as wholes, and compare the images of Maori culture

---

[21] Here one can clearly see the postmodern notion of culture as a continuing and fluid process. Derrida talks about "sign-substitution." He derives his understanding of signs from the work of the Swiss Linguist Ferdinand de Saussure (see Bourdieu, note 11). For Saussure, signs (or signifiers) had no meaning apart from their relationship with other signs. The gulf between a thing and the signs that signified it was ultimately unbridgeable. Derrida expanded this notion to argue that since signs endlessly refer to other signs, there can be no "center" of culture, merely endless substitutions. Hansen, invoking Derrida, is arguing that something similar is true of elements of Maori culture. Elements such as the cult of Io can never

BE Maori culture. They are simply signs that refer to other signs that refer to still other signs. It is the relationships among signs that is important and this is a function of political agenda, power, individual personality, and history. Such relationships may be maintained or altered by substitution of one sign for another. The signs do not matter, the relationships among them and the purposes to which they are put do.

[22] Note the influence of Bourdieu who Hansen references here. In this passage, he is describing something very close to Bourdieu's ideas of *habitus* and practice described in essay 34.

they advance and the political agendas they espouse, their status as inventions becomes obvious. Indeed, this highlights one of the main values of the Maori case for the study of culture invention: the fact that there have been two quite distinct inventions of Maori culture makes it much easier to get a clear view of each of them.[23]

We conclude, then, that inventions are common components in the ongoing development of authentic culture, and that producers of inventions are often outsiders (including anthropologists) as well as insiders. This conclusion has a reflexive dimension that pertains to anthropology itself. No less than any other cultural enterprise, anthropology is a discourse consisting of sign-substitutions, of which the present essay is one. To claim otherwise—that anthropology occupies some fixed perspective outside the play of signification of other discourse—would be to sponsor a grotesque mating of logocentrism with professional ethnocentrism.[24]

Granted that this essay is a sign-substitution, but does it qualify as an invention? The comments above distinguishing between the inventive status of individual contributions as opposed to larger aggregates pertain here. Within the rest of the "invention of tradition" literature, which constitutes a kind of paradigm in Kuhn's (1962) sense, this essay is not an invention. But that literature or paradigm, taken as a whole, does make a radical departure from earlier anthropological

thinking about tradition, and thus is an invention. Moreover, this anthropological invention belongs to a larger set of inventive sign-substitutions in contemporary Western social thought, represented by thinkers such as Derrida and described by Clifford (1988:9) as "a pervasive condition of off-centeredness in a world of distinct meaning systems, a state of being in culture while looking at culture, a form of personal and collective self-fashioning."

To acknowledge the presence of inventions in anthropology may appear to jeopardize its capacity to locate truth and contribute to knowledge. But that would be to miss the point of the entire argument. It would assume the existence of some other form of discourse that trades in fixed rules and eternal verities—in short, that logocentrism reigns. To the contrary, the thesis of this essay is that invention is an ordinary event in the development of all discourse, which therefore never rests on a permanent foundation.[1] From this point of view truth and knowledge stem—and always have stemmed—from inventions in the decentered play of sign-substitutions.[25]

NOTES

Acknowledgments. Thanks are due to Rob Borofsky and Alan Howard for the original impetus to write this essay, to John Massad for insights that contributed to the theoretical sections, and to Louise Hanson for contributions to the whole. Oral versions of this paper

---

[23] Here Hanson confronts a critical dilemma: If all of culture is the endless play of sign-substitution, how can you tell if an "important" change has happened? He argues that this is only possible from outside the system. Seen relative to one another, and within their cultural context, the works of Smith, Tregear, and Best seem ordinary and reasonable. It is only when seen from outside that they can be shown as inventions advancing a political position.

[24] Hanson argues that invention is one of the normal, everyday processes of social life, that anthropology is a form of discourse within this process, and that his essay is also part of the process of cultural invention, both within anthropology and within Maori culture. Just as Maori culture is continually invented and reinvented, so too is anthropology continually invented and reinvented.

[25] In these final paragraphs, Hanson turns his gaze on anthropology in general and his own work in particular. He argues that just as the works of Smith, Tregear, and Best are similar to one another but very different from more recent work, his own work is similar to that of others writing about the invention of tradition but that this literature constitutes a radical departure from earlier forms of anthropology. He invokes the historian of science Thomas Kuhn (see essay 25, note 1) arguing that this represents a paradigm shift in anthropology. However, he also argues that to see such a paradigm shift as a threat to the integrity of anthropological science is to miss the point: Anthropology too consists of an endless play of sign-substitutions. Anthropology can't be undermined, since it never existed as a concrete, unified science.

were presented at Columbia University and at the Bob Scholte Memorial Conference on Critical Anthropology, the University of Amsterdam.

[a] Obviously this thesis is closely tied to anthropology's long-standing if ambivalent affair with cultural relativism. The issue of relativism is treated more explicitly in another essay which arrives at a similar conclusion by a different path (Hanson 1979).

REFERENCES CITED

Best, Elsdon. 1924. The Maori. 2 vols. Wellington: Polynesian Society Memoirs, Vol. 5.

——1973[1922] Some Aspects of Maori Myth and Religion. Wellington: Dominion Museum. Monograph No. 1.

Binney, Judith, Gillian Chaplin, and Craig Wallace. 1979. Mihaia: The Prophet Rua Kenana and His Community at Maungapohatu. Wellington: Oxford University Press.

Borofsky, Robert. 1987. Making History: Pukapukan and Anthropological Constructions of Knowledge. Cambridge: Cambridge University Press.

Bourdieu, Pierre. 1977. Outline of a Theory of Practice. Cambridge: Cambridge University Press.

Clifford, James. 1988. The Predicament of Culture. Cambridge, MA: Harvard University Press.

Clifford, James, and George E. Marcus, eds. 1986. Writing Culture: The Poetics and Politics of Ethnography. Berkeley: University of California Press.

Crapanzano, Vincent. 1980. Tuhami: Portrait of a Moroccan. Chicago: University of Chicago Press.

Dansey, Harry. 1975. A View of Death. In Te Ao Hurihuri: The World Moves On—Aspects of Maoritanga. Michael King, ed. Pp. 173–189. Wellington: Hicks Smith and Sons.

Deacon, A. B. 1934. Malekula: A Vanishing People in the New Hebrides. London: George Routledge and Sons.

Derrida, Jacques. 1974. Of Grammatology. Baltimore: Johns Hopkins University Press.

1978. Writing and Difference. Chicago: University of Chicago Press.

Elder, J. R., ed. 1932. The Letters and Journals of Samuel Marsden. Wellington: Reed.

Fabian, Johannes. 1983. Time and the Other: How Anthropology Makes Its Object. New York: Columbia University Press.

France, Peter. 1969. The Charter of the Land: Custom and Colonization in Fiji. Melbourne: Oxford University Press.

Geertz, Clifford. 1988. Works and Lives: The Anthropologist as Author. Palo Alto, CA: Stanford University Press.

Handler, Richard. 1984. On Sociocultural Discontinuity: Nationalism and Cultural Objectification in Quebec. Current Anthropology 25:55–71.

Handler, Richard, and Jocelyn Linnekin. 1984. Tradition, Genuine or Spurious. Journal of American Folklore 97:273–290.

Hanson, F. Allan. 1979. Does God Have a Body? Truth, Reality and Cultural Relativism. Man 14:515–529.

Hanson, F. Allan, and Louise Hanson. 1981. The Cybernetics of Cultural Communication. In Semiotic Themes. Richard DeGeorge, ed. Pp. 251–273. Humanistic Studies, No. 53. Lawrence: University of Kansas Publications.

Herzfeld, Michael. 1982. Ours Once More: Folklore, Ideology and the Making of Modern Greece. Austin: University of Texas Press.

Hiroa, Te Rangi (Peter H. Buck). 1950. The Coming of the Maori. 2nd edition. Wellington: Whitcombe and Tombs.

Johansen, J. Prytz. 1958. Studies in Maori Rites and Myths. Copenhagen: Munksgaard. Journal of the Polynesian Society.

1932. The Late Elsdon Best. Journal of the Polynesian Society 41:1–49.

King, Michael. 1975. [ed.] Te Ao Hurihuri: The World Moves On—Aspects of Maoritanga. Wellington: Hicks Smith and Sons.

1985. Being Pakeha: An Encounter with New Zealand and the Maori Renaissance. Auckland: Hodder and Stoughton.

Kuhn, Thomas. 1962. The Structure of Scientific Revolutions. Chicago: University of Chicago Press.

Larcom, Joan. 1982. The Invention of Convention. Mankind 13:330–337.

Legge. J. D. 1958. Britain in Fiji, 1858–1880. London: Macmillan.

Lindstrom, Lamont. 1982. Leftamap Kastom: The Political History of Tradition on Tanna, Vanuatu. Mankind 13:316–329.

Linnekin, Jocelyn S. 1983. Defining Tradition: Variations on the Hawaiian Identity. American Ethnologist 10:241–252.

Marsden, Maori. 1975. God, Man and Universe: A Maori View. In Te Ao Hurihuri: The World Moves On—Aspects of Maoritanga. Michael King, ed. Pp. 191–219. Wellington: Hicks Smith and Sons.

Mead, Sidney (Hirini) Moko. 1983. Te Toi Matauranga Maori mo nga Ra Kei Mua: Maori Studies Tomorrow. Journal of the Polynesian Society 92:333–351.

1984a. Nga Timunga me nga Paringa o te Mana Maori: The Ebb and Flow of Mana Maori and the Changing Context of Maori Art. In Te Maori: Maori Art from New Zealand Collections. Pp. 20–36. New York: Harry N. Abrams.

1984b [ed.] Te Maori: Maori Art from New Zealand Collections. New York: Harry N. Abrams.

1986. Magnificent Te Maori: Te Maori Whakahirahira. Auckland: Heinemann.

Metge, Joan. 1967. The Maoris of New Zealand. London: Routledge and Kegan Paul.

1976. The Maoris of New Zealand, Rautahi. London: Routledge and Kegan Paul.

O'Biso, Carol. 1987. First Light. Auckland: Pan Books.

Ranger, Terence. 1983. The Invention of Tradition in Central Africa. In The Invention of Tradition. Eric Hobsbawm and Terence Ranger, eds. Pp. 211–262. Cambridge: Cambridge University Press.

Rangihau, John. 1975. Being Maori. In Te Ao Hurihuri: The World Moves On—Aspects of Maoritanga. Michael King, ed. Pp. 221–233. Wellington: Hicks Smith and Sons.

Renan, Ernest. 1889. Histoire du peuple d'Israel, Vol. I. Paris: Calmann Levy.

Said, Edward. 1978. Orientalism. New York: Pantheon.

Salmond, Anne. 1982. Theoretical Landscapes: On Cross-Cultural Conceptions of Knowledge. In Semantic Anthropology. David Parkin, ed. Pp. 65–87. A.S.A. Monograph 22. London: Academic Press.

———1983. The Study of Traditional Maori Society: The State of the Art. Journal of the Polynesian Society 92:309–331.

Sciascia, Piri. 1984. Ka Pu te Ruha, ka Hao te Rangatahi: As the Old Net Piles up on Shore, the New Net Goes Fishing. In Te Maori: Maori Art from New Zealand Collections. Sidney M. Mead, ed. Pp. 156–166. New York: Harry N. Abrams.

Simmons, D. R. 1976. The Great New Zealand Myth: A Study of the Discovery and Origin Traditions of the Maori. Wellington: Reed.

Sinclair, Douglas. 1975. Land: Maori View and European Response. In Te Ao Hurihuri: The World Moves On—Aspects of Maoritanga. Michael King, ed. Pp. 115–139. Wellington: Hicks Smith and Sons.

Smith, S. Percy. 1910. History and Traditions of the Maoris of the West Coast, North Island, New Zealand. New Plymouth, NZ: Polynesian Society Memoirs, Vol. 1.

1913. The Lore of the Whare-wananga, Part 1: Te Kauwae-runga. New Plymouth, NZ: Thomas Avery.

1915. The Lore of the Whare-wananga, Part 2: Te Kauwae-raro. New Plymouth, NZ: Thomas Avery.

Smithyman, Kendrick. 1979. Making History: John White and S. Percy Smith at Work. Journal of the Polynesian Society 88:375–414.

Sorrenson, M. P. K. 1979. Maori Origins and Migrations: The Genesis of Some Pakeha Myths and Legends. Auckland: Auckland University Press.

Stirling, Eruera, and Anne Salmond. 1980. Eruera: The Teachings of a Maori Elder. Wellington: Oxford University Press.

Sullivan, Agnes. 1984. Nga Paiaka o te Maoritanga: The Roots of Maori Culture. In Te Maori: Maori Art from New Zealand Collections. Sidney M. Mead, ed. Pp. 37–62. New York: Harry N. Abrams.

Thomson, Arthur S. 1859. The Story of New Zealand. 2 vols. London: John Murray.

Tregear, Edward. 1885. The Aryan Maori. Wellington: Government Printer.

Wagner, Roy. 1981. The Invention of Culture. Chicago: University of Chicago Press.

Winiata, Maharaia. 1967. The Changing Role of the Leader in Maori Society: A Study in Social Change and Race Relations. Auckland: Blackwood and Janet Paul.

Globalization, Power, and Agency

Samuel Goldwyn, or Yogi Berra, or Casey Stengle once said "never make predictions, especially about the future." In true postmodern fashion, the quote is attributed to all three, and many others besides. We'll never know who really said it first, and there is a website dedicated to tracking claims for its authorship: http://www.larry.denenberg.com/predictions.html. It's impossible to really know the directions anthropological theory will move in the next ten years. However, based on the tendencies of the last decade or so, it seems that work having to do with globalization, power, and agency will probably play an important role in the discipline. In this concluding chapter, we offer three examples of this type of work.

To some degree, interest in globalization is driven by facts on the ground. Today, almost all anthropologists accept the notion that cultures are constantly changing. Authors such as Wolf, Leacock, Stoller, and others have pointed out that most societies studied by anthropologists were deeply affected by the experience of the expansion of Western societies, the emergence of capitalism, colonization, and other external forces. Often, when anthropologists thought they were looking at "primitive" societies and "stone age" peoples, they were, in fact, looking at societies that owed their origin to the policies of European governments.

Despite this, when Napoleon Chagnon went to do research among the Yanomamo in 1964, for example, he could be excused if he believed that they were relatively untouched by the outside world and living in more or less the same way they had for countless generations. This is what they looked like: They had relatively few material goods from outside, had only rarely seen others who did not look like them, and behaved in ways clearly alien to Venezuelan and Brazilian societies. In the past forty years, the Yanomamo have been the subject of endless controversy. Their land has been invaded by gold miners, they have been at the center of disputes about national parks and the rights of native peoples. They have been the subject of both documentary and fiction films. Their leaders have been frequent presences at universities and government hearings. Yanomamo crafts can be purchased on the Internet. We have no wish to take sides in any of the controversies surrounding the Yanomamo. We do wish to point out that, whatever you can say about them, you can't say they have been unaffected by the rest of the world.

The Yanomamo are an extreme (and largely tragic) example. However, what is true of them is also the case just about everywhere else in the world. Almost anywhere you go, at least some people have access to the rest of the world. Television is ubiquitous, and it no longer feels terribly strange to be sitting in a small African village watching American sitcoms. By 2008 there were 376 million cell phone subscriptions in sub-Saharan Africa, enough for about one-third of the population (Acker and Mbiti 2010). No doubt, the distribution of these phones is affected by geography, class, ethnicity, and many other factors, but the numbers are impressive nonetheless. The trappings of consumer society are visible virtually everywhere and this makes globalization one of the most obvious and powerful phenomena in the world. This is particularly clear to anthropologists who (like McGee) have worked in a single location for several decades.

Globalization anthropology has numerous critical theoretical sources. Among the most important of these is surely the work of Eric Wolf. Wolf's contribution is discussed more fully in Part 3, essay 21. Briefly, Wolf, strongly influenced by Marx, argued that the societies anthropologists examined must be seen in their historical contexts. In the past several hundred years, the most critical component of this context was the expansion of power of Europe and the incorporation of societies across the globe in an economic system dominated by capitalism. Globalization theorists do not generally share Wolf's interest in the long-term history of the societies they study. Rather, they tend to focus on the present and the past two or three decades in analyzing the ways in which societies are articulated with the world economy in general and with capitalist enterprises in particular. Critical foci of their studies include the effects of the expansion of multinational corporations, the outsourcing of production and labor, and the ability to move goods and information around the globe.

Although Wolf was concerned largely with large-scale economic and social processes, globalization theorists tend to be interested in specific local effects of economic incorporation. Guided by the work of Antonio Gramsci and Michel Foucault (both of whom have been discussed earlier in this book), they seek to understand the ways in which both the powerful and the powerless perceive and manipulate symbols and comprehend their position in the world; how they choose which objects and activities are desirable; and how they view the goals of society. Gramsci and Foucault were both interested in the relationship between ideas and power. Foucault in particular explored the ways in which knowledge, rather than being abstract and universal, is created and used by powerful people and institutions. For Foucault, there is no truth, in an abstract and absolute sense. Rather there are

"regimes of truth," conditions and processes under which what counts as "truth" in a given society is established and used. Essentially, globalization theorists attempt to describe the truths of capitalist society and elucidate the processes by which these are both established and challenged.

A third influence in globalization theory is the work of the French sociologist Pierre Bourdieu (1930–2002), in particular his ideas regarding habitus (see essay 34) and multiple forms of capital. Bourdieu expands upon the notion of habitus found in the work of Marcel Mauss and Norbert Elias (1897–1990). Habitus is a complex concept, and there is much debate in anthropology over what exactly it means. For Bourdieu, it seems to have the sense of largely unconscious aspects of social life that are inscribed in the body, including dispositions, habits of perception, and action. Habitus is distinct from the notion of a habit. For example, I like to walk my dog at 8:00 in the evening. It's a habit that I've developed over the past several years. It would be habitus if it went without saying that, in my society, if one had a dog, one always walked it at 8 P.M. and if it would not occur to me to walk the dog at any other time. From this description you can see the clear connection between the idea of habitus and Durkheim's notions of social fact and collective conscience. Habitus refers to those aspects of culture of which participants in the culture are not fully conscious.

Economic capital is wealth that can be invested in ownership of the means of production with the goal of increase. Bourdieu points out that in addition to economic capital, individuals in society also manipulate social, cultural, and symbolic capital. Social capital refers to membership in networks of individuals and positions within such networks. An individual with a wide social network can activate it to pursue economic or other goals. Cultural capital refers to the possession of education, special knowledge, and skills. Symbolic capital refers to the possession of prestige and honor (as well as to the actual symbols of those things), which possession determines the degree to which a person's words are likely to be taken seriously. For Bourdieu, these forms of capital inform, along with habitus, what he refers to as a field, a complex interplay of social, physical, economic, and communicatory connections.

The three essays in this section capture much of the flavor of the globalization approach. The first, by Arjun Appadurai, shows a particularly deep debt to French postmodern scholars. In addition to Foucault and Bourdieu, Appadurai also refers to the work of Lacan and Derrida, among others. The world, Appadurai argues, is probably best described as a series of "scapes": ethnoscapes, mediascapes, technoscapes, financescapes, and ideoscapes. He asks us to contemplate the global structure of each of these as well as the relationships between them. Appadurai's notion of a "scape" is clearly similar to Bourdieu's idea of a field.

The second essay, by Philippe Bourgois, is closer to neo-Marxist thinking than the first. Bourgois focuses his attention on the poor of New York and the ways in which they are ensnared in a battle against a system of ideas that justifies the economic order. Bourgois relies heavily on the thinking of Antonio Gramsci, who, within a Marxist framework, emphasized the importance of ideas and symbols in maintaining control of society, and on the work of cultural-production theorists, who stressed the meanings and practices that individuals acquire as a result of their structural position in society as well as the ways they respond to these positions and create new, counter-hegemonic meanings.

Our final essay comes from Theodor Bestor who examines the ways in which the consumption of sushi and the use of convenience stores in Japan are articulated both with technological and organizational changes in international capitalism and Japanese ideas about class structure, gender, as well as the political and legal systems of current day Japan. Bestor's work shows strong influences from Marx and Gramsci as well as from anthropologists such as Sydney Mintz who have been interested in tracing the histories and global impact of the movement of particular commodities.

To some degree, globalization theory represents a synthesis between the materialism and attempted empiricism of the neofunctionalists and neo-Marxists and the more idealist approaches of the cognitive and the symbolic and interpretive anthropologists. Like materialists, they are concerned with people's behaviors and choices. They see these as influenced by economic pressures and economic rationales and set within systems of relations of production. Like symbolic and interpretive anthropologists, they are particularly concerned with the ways in which people create and contest meaning and morality within these structures. Despite this apparent rapprochement, the work of many globalization theorists is more likely to be appreciated by those sympathetic to literary and interpretivist approaches to anthropology than by those who would like to see a natural science of anthropology.

---

39. *Disjuncture and Difference in the Global Cultural Economy*

Arjun Appadurai (b. 1949)

It takes only the merest acquaintance with the facts of the modern world to note it is now an interactive system in a sense that is strikingly new. Historians and sociologists, especially those concerned with translocal processes (Hodgson 1974) and the world systems associated with capitalism (Abu-Lughod 1989; Braudel 1981–4; Curtin 1984; Wallerstein 1974; Wolf 1982), have long been aware that the world has been a congerie of large-scale interactions for many centuries. Yet today's world involves interactions of a new order and intensity. Cultural transactions between

From *Public Culture* (1990)

social groups in the past have generally been restricted, sometimes by the facts of geography and ecology, and at other times by active resistance to interactions with the Other (as in China for much of its history and in Japan before the Meiji Restoration). Where there have been sustained cultural transactions across large parts of the globe, they have usually involved the long-distance journey of commodities (and of the merchants most concerned with them) and of travelers and explorers of every type (Helms 1988; Schafer 1963). The two main forces for sustained cultural interaction before this century have been warfare (and the large-scale political systems sometimes generated by it) and religions of conversion, which have sometimes, as in the case of Islam, taken warfare as one of the legitimate instruments of their expansion. Thus, between travelers and merchants, pilgrims and conquerors, the world has seen much long-distance (and long-term) cultural traffic. This much seems self-evident.[1]

But few will deny that given the problems of time, distance, and limited technologies for the command of resources across vast spaces, cultural dealings between socially and spatially separated groups have, until the past few centuries, bridged at great cost and sustained over time only with great effort. The forces of cultural gravity seemed always to pull away from the formation of large-scale ecumenes, whether religious, commercial, or political, toward smaller-scale accretions of intimacy and interest.

Sometime in the past few centuries, the nature of this gravitational field seems to have changed. Partly because of the spirit of the expansion of western maritime interests after 1500, and partly because of the relatively autonomous developments of large and aggressive social formations in the Americas (such as the Aztecs and the Incas), in Eurasia (such as the Mongols and their descendants, the Mughals and Ottomans), in island Southeast Asia (such as the Buginese), and in the kingdoms of precolonial Africa (such as Dahomey), an overlapping set of ecumenes began to emerge, in which congeries of money, commerce, conquest, and migration began to create durable cross-societal bonds. This process was accelerated by the technology transfers and innovations of the late eighteenth and nineteenth centuries (e.g., Bayly 1989), which created complex colonial orders centered on European capitals and spread throughout the non-European world. This intricate and overlapping set of Euro-colonial worlds (first Spanish and Portuguese, later principally English, French, and Dutch) set the basis for a permanent traffic in ideas of peoplehood and selfhood, which created the imagined communities (Anderson 1983) of recent nationalisms throughout the world.

With what Benedict Anderson[2] has called "print capitalism," a new power was unleashed in

---

[1] In the nineteenth and twentieth centuries, anthropologists tended to understand the object of their study as more or less bounded tribes, ethnic groups, or communities. Though anthropologists sometimes noted connections among communities or between the communities, these were treated as recent and not particularly important. The anthropologists' job was to see beyond them to the original, precontact, pristine community. In the 1970s and 1980s World Systems theorists such as those mentioned in this paragraph argued that this perception was incorrect. The communities anthropologists studied were not bounded and traditional but rather connected to and conditioned by international flows of trade and by wealth. Appadurai follows and extends this argument. In this paragraph and below, he points out that although interaction between cultures has been the rule rather than the exception, the difficulty and expense of communication histori-

cally militated against a world system. Over the past several centuries these factors have steadily diminished in importance until, by the end of the twentieth century (when this piece was written) the transmission of information and transportation of people was both low cost and relatively simple. This has important implications for cultures and the ways in which they are studied.

Two interesting words that Appadurai uses are ecumene and congeries. An ecumene is a civilization or worldwide organization. However, Appadurai uses it to mean some grouping larger than a society that is tied together by any of a number of commonalities. A congerie is an unorganized group of things.

[2] Benedict Anderson (b. 1936) is a scholar of international studies. In his 1983 book *Imagined Communities* he argued that the technology of print and the use of the

the world, the power of mass literacy and its attendant large-scale production of projects of ethnic affinity that were remarkably free of the need for face-to-face communication or even of indirect communication between persons and groups. The act of reading things together set the stage for movements based on a paradox—the paradox of constructed primordialism. There is, of course, a great deal else that is involved in the story of colonialism and its dialectically generated nationalisms (Chatterjee 1986), but the issue of constructed ethnicities is surely a crucial strand in this tale.

But the revolution of print capitalism and the cultural affinities and dialogues unleashed by it were only modest precursors to the world we live in now. For in the past century, there has been a technological explosion, largely in the domain of transportation and information, that makes the interactions of a print-dominated world seem as hard-won and as easily erased as the print revolution made earlier forms of cultural traffic appear. For with the advent of the steamship, the automobile, the airplane, the camera, the computer, and the telephone, we have entered into an altogether new condition of neighborliness, even with those most distant from ourselves. Marshall McLuhan, among others, sought to theorize about this world as a "global village," but theories such as McLuhan's appear to have overestimated the communitarian implications of the new media

order (McLuhan and Powers 1989). We are now aware that with media, each time we are tempted to speak of the global village, we must be reminded that media create communities with "no sense of place" (Meyrowitz 1985). The world we live in now seems rhizomic (Deleuze and Guattari 1987), even schizophrenic, calling for theories of rootlessness, alienation, and psychological distance between individuals and groups on the one hand, and fantasies (or nightmares) of electronic propinquity on the other. Here, we are close to the central problematic of cultural processes in today's world.[3]

Thus, the curiosity that recently drove Pico Iyer[4] to Asia (1988) is in some ways the product of a confusion between some ineffable McDonaldization of the world and the much subtler play of indigenous trajectories of desire and fear with global flows of people and things. Indeed, Iyer's own impressions are testimony to the fact that, if a global cultural system is emerging, it is filled with ironies and resistances, sometimes camouflaged as passivity and a bottomless appetite in the Asian world for things western.

Iyer's own account of the uncanny Philippine affinity for American popular music is rich testimony to the global culture of the hyperreal, for somehow Philippine renditions of American popular songs are both more widespread in the Philippines, and more disturbingly faithful to their originals, than they are in the United States

---

vernacular were essential to the idea of nationhood in Europe. Latin had been universal in Europe. The printing of works in vernacular languages allowed people to conceive of themselves as members of specific language communities. This became one of the building blocks of nationalism. Anderson's notion that nations are the results of very particular—rather than natural and inevitable—historical processes and types of understandings underpins Appadurai's ideas in this essay.

[3] Marshall McLuhan (1911–1980) was a seminal thinker in media studies. In his 1962 book *The Guttenberg Galaxy,* McLuhan argued that advances in communications technology were turning the world into a "global village" in which all people were connected to one another and the transfer of information was instantaneous. McLuhan promoted a theory of technological determinism, arguing that

changes in culture are driven by changes in the technology of communication. Although McLuhan's ideas have been very influential, they are also frequently criticized and deeply controversial. Appadurai clearly appreciates McLuhan's work but argues that the global village is a gross oversimplification.

Propinquity is nearness or affinity and sometimes implies kinship.

[4] Pico Iyer (b. 1957) is a travel writer and journalist. A multicultural individual himself (British born of Indian descent), Iyer's writing focuses on the ironies and paradoxes of globalization. An often-cited quote from him is, "I am a multinational soul on a multinational globe on which more and more countries are as polyglot and restless as airports (in London 1996)."

today. An entire nation seems to have learned to mimic Kenny Rogers and the Lennon sisters, like a vast Asian Motown chorus. But Americanization is certainly a pallid term to apply to such a situation, for not only are there more Filipinos singing perfect renditions of some American songs (often from the American past) than there are Americans doing so, there is also, of course, the fact that the rest of their lives is not in complete synchrony with the referential world that first gave birth to these songs.

In a further globalizing twist on what Fredric Jameson[5] has recently called "nostalgia for the present" (1989), these Filipinos look back to a world they have never lost. This is one of the central ironies of the politics of global cultural flows, especially in the arena of entertainment and leisure. It plays havoc with the hegemony of Eurochronology. American nostalgia feeds on Filipino desire represented as a hypercompetent reproduction. Here, we have nostalgia without memory. The paradox, of course, has its explanations, and they are historical; unpacked, they lay bare the story of the American missionization and

political rape of the Philippines, one result of which has been the creation of a nation of make-believe Americans, who tolerated for so long a leading lady who played the piano while the slums of Manila expanded and decayed.[6] Perhaps the most radical postmodernists would argue that this is hardly surprising because in the peculiar chronicities of late capitalism, pastiche and nostalgia are central modes of image production and reception. Americans themselves are hardly in the present anymore as they stumble into the megatechnologies of the twenty-first century garbed in the film-noir scenarios of sixties' chills, fifties' diners, forties' clothing, thirties' houses, twenties' dances, and so on ad infinitum.

As far as the United States is concerned, one might suggest that the issue is no longer one of nostalgia but of a social *imaginaire*[7] built largely around reruns. Jameson was bold to link the politics of nostalgia to the postmodern commodity sensibility, and surely he was right (1983). The drug wars in Colombia recapitulate the tropical sweat of Vietnam, with Ollie North[8] and his succession of masks—Jimmy Stewart concealing

---

[5] Frederic Jameson (b. 1934) is an American philosopher and literary critic. He is best known for his Marxist critique of postmodernism, which he argues is a feature of corporate capitalism. Jameson's best known work is *Postmodernism: Or the Cultural Logic of Late Capitalism* (1991).

[6] Appadurai refers to Imelda Marcos (b. 1929), wife of former Philippine dictator Ferdinand Marcos (1917–1989). Imelda Marcos was known for her extravagance while in power which included, among other things, her collection of 2,700 pairs of shoes. In a perfectly postmodern twist Appadurai would appreciate, in 2001, Marcos opened a shoe museum in Marikina, a Philippine city with a large shoe industry.

[7] Here Appadurai refers to the work of the French psychoanalytic Marxist Jacques Lacan (1901–1981). Lacan argued that a critical realization for children is their existence as an entity seen by others (he calls this the mirror stage). This gives children a way of understanding and imagining themselves. To create this understanding, children begin to assemble a story of what it is they are like. But, ultimately they cannot truly see themselves. Rather, they compose their self-image out of partial glimpses of themselves, understandings of other children, stories they

are told, pictures they see, and so on. This collection is the *imaginaire*, and, by definition, it is not accurate. Lacan had a genius for and love of puns. *Imaginaire* is an example, connoting both "imaginary" and "made up of images." In another wonderful pun (that doesn't translate as easily), Lacan calls the child with an *imaginaire* an *homme-lette*. In French, this has the connotation of both a "little man" and an omelet—something made out of broken eggs. Appadurai in this passage speaks of America as an *imaginaire*, an idea composed of bits and pieces, of images that are other than reality.

[8] Oliver North (b. 1943) was a US Marine Corps officer who was implicated in the Iran-Contra political scandal of the late 1980s. North was a member of President Ronald Reagan's National Security Council who organized the illegal sale of weapons to Iran in order to secretly finance rebel groups opposed to Nicaragua's leftist government. Although North was convicted of several felonies, immunity agreements he had reached with Congress led to the dismissal of charges against him. North was portrayed as a villain by the left but as a hero by the right. He was featured in *Saturday Night Live* skits and, more recently on *American Dad*. Currently, North is a novelist and a commentator on Fox News.

John Wayne concealing Spiro Agnew and all of them transmogrifying into Sylvester Stallone, who wins in Afghanistan—thus simultaneously fulfilling the secret American envy of Soviet imperialism and the rerun (this time with a happy ending) of the Vietnam War. The Rolling Stones, in their fifties, gyrate before eighteen-year-olds who do not appear to need the machinery of nostalgia to be sold on their parents' heroes. Paul McCartney is selling the Beatles to a new audience by hitching his oblique nostalgia to their desire for the new that smacks of the old. *Dragnet* is back in nineties drag, and so is *Adam-12*, not to speak of *Batman* and *Mission Impossible*, all dressed up technologically but remarkably faithful to the atmospherics of their originals.

The past is now not a land to return to in a simple politics of memory. It has become a synchronic warehouse of cultural scenarios, a kind of temporal central casting, to which recourse can be taken as appropriate, depending on the movie to be made, the scene to be enacted, the hostages to be rescued. All this is par for the course, if you follow Jean Baudrillard or Jean-Francois Lyotard[9] into a world of signs wholly unmoored from their social signifiers (all the world's a Disneyland). But I would like to suggest that the apparent increasing substitutability of whole periods and postures for one another, in the cultural styles of advanced capitalism, is tied to larger global forces, which have done much to show Americans that the past is usually another country. If your present is their future (as in much modernization theory and in many self-satisfied tourist fantasies), and their future is your past (as in the case of the Filipino virtuosos of American popular music), then your own past can be made to appear as simply a normalized modality of your present. Thus, although some anthropologists may continue to relegate their Others to temporal spaces that they do not themselves occupy (Fabian 1983), postindustrial cultural productions have entered a postnostalgic phase.

The crucial point, however, is that the United States is no longer the puppeteer of a world system of images but is only one node of a complex transnational construction of imaginary landscapes. The world we live in today is characterized by a new role for the imagination in social life. To grasp this new role, we need to bring together the old idea of images, especially mechanically produced images (in the Frankfurt School sense);[10] the idea of the imagined community (in Anderson's sense); and the French idea of the imaginary (*imaginaire*) as a constructed landscape of collective aspirations, which is no more and no less real than the collective representations of Émile Durkheim, now mediated through the complex prism of modern media.

The image, the imagined, the imaginary—these are all terms that direct us to something critical and new in global cultural processes: the imagination as a social practice. No longer mere fantasy (opium for the masses whose real work is elsewhere), no longer simple escape (from a world defined principally by more concrete purposes and structures), no longer elite pastime (thus not relevant to the lives of ordinary people), and no longer mere contemplation (irrelevant for new forms of desire and subjectivity), the imagination has become an organized field of social practices, a form of work (in the sense of both labor and culturally organized practice), and a form of negotiation between sites of agency (individuals) and globally defined fields of possibility. This unleashing of the imagination links the play

---

[9] Jean Baudrillard (b. 1929) and Jean-Francois Lyotard (1924–1998) are both well-known postmodern theorists.

[10] The Frankfort School was a group of scholars who examined the Western philosophical tradition and Marxism in light of twentieth-century history. One influential member was Walter Benjamin (1892–1940). In "The Work of Art in the Age of Mechanical Reproduction," Benjamin argued that in traditional societies art had an "aura"; that is, its originality and creativity inspired feelings of awe and respect in those who viewed it. In the modern era, mechanical reproduction has subverted the uniqueness of works of art, and therefore their power was diminished. Benjamin looked upon this as an ambiguous but generally positive development. It meant that people could observe and analyze art free from the mysticism of power. Benjamin believed that media such as radio and film had the potential to liberate, creating alternatives to the high culture of elites. Appadurai refers again to Benjamin later in this essay.

of pastiche (in some settings) to the terror and coercion of states and their competitors. The imagination is now central to all forms of agency, is itself a social fact, and is the key component of the new global order. But to make this claim meaningful, we must address some other issues.

HOMOGENIZATION AND HETEROGENIZATION

The central problem of today's global interactions is the tension between cultural homogenization and cultural heterogenization. A vast array of empirical facts could be brought to bear on the side of the homogenization argument, and much of it has come from the left end of the spectrum of media studies (Hamelink 1983; Mattelart 1983; Schiller 1976), and some from other perspectives (Gans 1985; Iyer 1988). Most often, the homogenization argument subspeciates into either an argument about Americanization or an argument about commoditization, and very often the two arguments are closely linked. What these arguments fail to consider is that at least as rapidly as forces from various metropolises are brought into new societies they tend to become indigenized in one or another way: this is true of music and housing styles as much as it is true of science and terrorism, spectacles and constitutions. The dynamics of such indigenization have just begun to be explored systemically (Barber 1987; Feld 1988; Hannerz 1987, 1989; Ivy 1988; Nicoll 1989; Yoshimoto 1989), and much more needs to be done. But it is worth noticing that for the people of Irian Jaya, Indonesianization may be more worrisome than Americanization, as Japanization may be for Koreans, Indianization for Sri Lankans, Vietnamization for the Cambodians, and

Russianization for the people of Soviet Armenia and the Baltic republics. Such a list of alternative fears to Americanization could be greatly expanded, but it is not a shapeless inventory: for polities of smaller scale, there is always a fear of cultural absorption by polities of larger scale, especially those that are nearby. One man's imagined community is another man's political prison.

This scalar dynamic, which has widespread global manifestations, is also tied to the relationship between nations and states, to which I shall return later. For the moment let us note that the simplification of these many forces (and fears) of homogenization can also be exploited by nation-states in relation to their own minorities, by posing global commoditization (or capitalism, or some other such external enemy) as more real than the threat of its own hegemonic strategies.

The new global cultural economy has to be seen as a complex, overlapping, disjunctive order that cannot any longer be understood in terms of existing center-periphery models (even those that might account for multiple centers and peripheries). Nor is it susceptible to simple models of push and pull (in terms of migration theory), or of surpluses and deficits (as in traditional models of balance of trade), or of consumers and producers (as in most neo-Marxist theories of development). Even the most complex and flexible theories of global development that have come out of the Marxist tradition (Amin 1980; Mandel 1978; Wallerstein 1974; Wolf 1982) are inadequately quirky and have failed to come to terms with what Scott Lash and John Urry have called disorganized capitalism (1987). The complexity of the current global economy has to do with certain fundamental disjunctures between economy, culture, and politics that we have only begun to theorize.[11]

---

[11] Here Appadurai introduces a critical element of his thinking as represented by this essay: that the patterns of economy and culture in the world are far more complex than existing theories suggest. He introduces the term *disjuncture* to characterize this complexity. A disjuncture is a separation, a disconnection, a disunion. Appadurai uses the term to signify ideas that are in some sort of relationship to one another but where that relationship is cannot

be specified because it is characterized by gaps and irregularity. You will recall that much of anthropological theory from the time of Herbert Spencer on envisioned societies and cultures as more or less organic. That is, they understood societies as being composed of a series of elements that stood in certain relations to one another. Together, these elements created the pattern of the culture. This vision of culture received its maximal expression in

I propose that an elementary framework for exploring such disjunctures is to look at the relationship among five dimensions of global cultural flows that can be termed (a) *ethnoscapes*, (b) *mediascapes*, (c) *technoscapes*, (d) *financescapes*, and (e) *ideoscapes*.[a] The suffix scape allows us to point to the fluid, irregular shapes of these landscapes, shapes that characterize international capital as deeply as they do international clothing styles. These terms with the common suffix scape also indicate that these are not objectively given relations that look the same from every angle of vision but, rather, that they are deeply perspectival constructs, inflected by the historical, linguistic, and political situatedness of different sorts of actors: nation-states, multinationals, diasporic communities, as well as subnational groupings and movements (whether religious, political, or economic), and even intimate face-to-face groups, such as villages, neighborhoods, and families. Indeed, the individual actor is the last locus of this perspectival set of landscapes, for these landscapes are eventually navigated by agents who both experience and constitute larger formations, in part from their own sense of what these landscapes offer.[12]

These landscapes thus are the building blocks of what (extending Benedict Anderson) I would like to call imagined worlds, that is, the multiple worlds that are constituted by the historically situated imaginations of persons and groups spread around the globe (see Appadurai 1996: ch. 1). An important fact of the world we live in today is that many persons on the globe live in such imagined worlds (and not just in imagined communities) and thus are able to contest and sometimes even subvert the imagined worlds of the official mind and of the entrepreneurial mentality that surround them.[13]

By *ethnoscape*, I mean the landscape of persons who constitute the shifting world in which we live: tourists, immigrants, refugees, exiles, guest workers, and other moving groups and individuals constitute an essential feature of the world and appear to affect the politics of (and between) nations to a hitherto unprecedented degree. This is not to say that there are no relatively stable communities and networks of kinship, friendship, work, and leisure, as well as of birth, residence, and other filial forms. But it is to say that the warp of these stabilities is everywhere shot through with the woof of human motion, as more persons and groups deal with the realities of having to move or the fantasies of wanting to move. What is more, both these realities and fantasies now function on larger scales, as men and women from villages in India think not just of moving to Poona or Madras but of moving to Dubai and Houston, and refugees from Sri Lanka find themselves in South India as well as in Switzerland, just as the Hmong are driven to London as well as to Philadelphia. And as international capital shifts its needs, as production and technology generate different needs, as nation-states shift their policies on refugee populations, these

---

functionalism but is also present in Boasian anthropology, cultural ecology, and neofunctionalism. It was, to some degree, challenged by Neo-Marxists, who saw cultures as consisting of elements that conflicted and clashed rather than cooperated. Appadurai argues that all existing theories are "inadequately quirky" to explain the global cultural economy and envisions culture as characterized by elements that combine, conflict, cooperate, and separate in ways that seem largely chaotic.

[12] This passage draws the reader to a critical aspect of the essay. Appadurai is describing phenomena that exist at many different levels of scale. We can talk of financescape and ideoscape at the level of the nation, the village, or perhaps the individual. This is an idea he returns to again at the end of the essay. Appadurai's coinage of terms such as ethnoscape has been fairly successful. A Google search for "ethnoscapes" scores over 41,000 hits.

[13] Appadurai owes a critical debt to the Italian Marxist Antonio Gramsci (1897–1931) and notions of hegemony and counter-hegemony. Gramsci focused on understanding ideology within a Marxist framework. He emphasized that power elites set the general rules of understanding and debate within a society. He referred to this as the hegemony of the ruling classes. However, hegemony is negotiated as intellectuals and oppressed classes create counter-hegemonies to challenge elite ideas. In this passage, Appadurai notes that individuals are able to challenge and subvert the "official mind." Additional information on Gramsci can be found in footnote 10 page 591.

moving groups can never afford to let their imaginations rest too long, even if they wish to.

By *technoscape*, I mean the global configuration, also ever fluid, of technology and the fact that technology, both high and low, both mechanical and informational, now moves at high speeds across various kinds of previously impervious boundaries. Many countries now are the roots of multinational enterprise: a huge steel complex in Libya may involve interests from India, China, Russia, and Japan, providing different components of new technological configurations. The odd distribution of technologies, and thus the peculiarities of these technoscapes, are increasingly driven not by any obvious economies of scale, of political control, or of market rationality but by increasingly complex relationships among money flows, political possibilities, and the availability of both un- and highly skilled labor. So, while India exports waiters and chauffeurs to Dubai and Sharjah, it also exports software engineers to the United States—indentured briefly to Tata-Burroughs or the World Bank, then laundered through the State Department to become wealthy resident aliens, who are in turn objects of seductive messages to invest their money and know-how in federal and state projects in India.

The global economy can still be described in terms of traditional indicators (as the World Bank continues to do) and studied in terms of traditional comparisons (as in Project Link at the University of Pennsylvania), but the complicated technoscapes (and the shifting ethnoscapes) that underlie these indicators and comparisons are further out of the reach of the queen of social sciences than ever before.[14] How is one to make a meaningful comparison of wages in Japan and the United States or of real-estate costs in New York and Tokyo, without taking sophisticated account of the very complex fiscal and investment flows that link the two economies through a global grid of currency speculation and capital transfer?

Thus it is useful to speak as well of *financescapes*, as the disposition of global capital is now a more mysterious, rapid, and difficult landscape to follow than ever before, as currency markets, national stock exchanges, and commodity speculations move megamonies through national turnstiles at blinding speed, with vast, absolute implications for small differences in percentage points and time units. But the critical point is that the global relationship among ethnoscapes, technoscapes, and financescapes is deeply disjunctive and profoundly unpredictable because each of these landscapes is subject to its own constraints and incentives (some political, some informational, and some technoenvironmental), at the same time as each acts as a constraint and a parameter for movements in the others. Thus, even an elementary model of global political economy must take into account the deeply disjunctive relationships among human movement, technological flow, and financial transfers.

Further refracting these disjunctures (which hardly form a simple, mechanical global infrastructure in any case) are what I call *mediascapes* and *ideoscapes*, which are closely related landscapes of images. Mediascapes refer both to the distribution of the electronic capabilities to produce and disseminate information (newspapers, magazines, television stations, and film-production studios), which are now available to a growing number of private and public interests throughout the world, and to the images of the world created by these media. These images involve many complicated inflections, depending on their mode (documentary or entertainment), their hardware (electronic or preelectronic), their audiences (local, national, or transnational), and the interests of those who own and control them. What is most important about these mediascapes is that they provide (especially in their television, film, and cassette forms) large and complex repertoires of images, narratives, and ethnoscapes to viewers throughout the world, in which the world of commodities

---

[14] Founded in 1968 by Nobel prize–winning economist Lawrence Klein and supported by the United Nations, Project LINK attempts to create a comprehensive global econometric model. From relatively small beginnings LINK now includes more than 70 different models. It has moved from the University of Pennsylvania to the University of Toronto and the United Nations in New York. The "queen of the social sciences" refers, of course, to economics.

and the world of news and politics are profoundly mixed. What this means is that many audiences around the world experience the media themselves as a complicated and interconnected repertoire of print, celluloid, electronic screens, and billboards. The lines between the realistic and the fictional landscapes they see are blurred, so that the farther away these audiences are from the direct experiences of metropolitan life, the more likely they are to construct imagined worlds that are chimerical, aesthetic, even fantastic objects, particularly if assessed by the criteria of some other perspective, some other imagined world.

Mediascapes, whether produced by private or state interests, tend to be image-centered, narrative-based accounts of strips of reality, and what they offer to those who experience and transform them is a series of elements (such as characters, plots, and textual forms) out of which scripts can be formed of imagined lives, their own as well as those of others living in other places. These scripts can and do get disaggregated into complex sets of metaphors by which people live (Lakoff and Johnson 1980) as they help to constitute narratives of the Other and protonarratives of possible lives, fantasies that could become prolegomena to the desire for acquisition and movement.[15]

Ideoscapes are also concatenations of images, but they are often directly political and frequently have to do with the ideologies of states and the counterideologies of movements explicitly oriented to capturing state power or a piece of it. These ideoscapes are composed of elements of the Enlightenment worldview, which consists of a chain of ideas, terms, and images, including freedom, welfare, rights, sovereignty, representation, and the master term democracy. The master narrative of the Enlightenment (and its many variants in Britain, France, and the United States) was constructed with a certain internal logic and presupposed a certain relationship between reading, representation, and the public sphere. (For the dynamics of this process in the early history of the United States, see Warner 1990.) But the diaspora of these terms and images across the world, especially since the nineteenth century, has loosened the internal coherence that held them together in a Euro-American master narrative and provided instead a loosely structured synopticon of politics, in which different nation-states, as part of their evolution, have organized their political cultures around different keywords (e.g., Williams 1976).

As a result of the differential diaspora of these keywords, the political narratives that govern communication between elites and followers in different parts of the world involve problems of both a semantic and pragmatic nature: semantic to the extent that words (and their lexical equivalents) require careful translation from context to context in their global movements, and pragmatic to the extent that the use of these words by political actors and their audiences may be subject to very different sets of contextual conventions that mediate their translation into public politics. Such conventions are not only matters of the nature of political rhetoric: for example, what does the aging Chinese leadership mean when it refers to the dangers of hooliganism? What does the South Korean leadership mean when it speaks of discipline as the key to democratic industrial growth?

These conventions also involve the far more subtle question of what sets of communicative genres are valued in what way (newspapers versus cinema, for example) and what sorts of pragmatic genre conventions govern the collective readings of different kinds of text. So, while an Indian audience may be attentive to the resonances of a political speech in terms of some keywords and phrases reminiscent of Hindi cinema, a Korean audience may respond to the subtle codings of Buddhist or neo-Confucian rhetoric encoded in a political document. The very relationship of reading to hearing and seeing may vary in important ways that determine the morphology of these different ideoscapes as they shape themselves in different national and transnational contexts. This globally variable

---

[15] *Prolegomena:* an introduction or introductory comments.

synaesthesia[16] has hardly even been noted, but it demands urgent analysis. Thus democracy has clearly become a master term, with powerful echoes from Haiti and Poland to the former Soviet Union and China, but it sits at the center of a variety of ideoscapes, composed of distinctive pragmatic configurations of rough translations of other central terms from the vocabulary of the Enlightenment. This creates ever new terminological kaleidoscopes, as states (and the groups that seek to capture them) seek to pacify populations whose own ethnoscapes are in motion and whose mediascapes may create severe problems for the ideoscapes with which they are presented. The fluidity of ideoscapes is complicated in particular by the growing diasporas (both voluntary and involuntary) of intellectuals who continuously inject new meaning-streams into the discourse of democracy in different parts of the world.[17]

This extended terminological discussion of the five terms I have coined sets the basis for a tentative formulation about the conditions under which current global flows occur: they occur in and through the growing disjunctures among ethnoscapes, technoscapes, financescapes, mediascapes, and ideoscapes. This formulation, the core of my model of global cultural flow, needs some explanation. First, people, machinery, money, images, and ideas now follow increasingly nonisomorphic paths; of course, at all periods in human history, there have been some disjunctures in the flows of these things, but the sheer speed, scale, and volume of each of these flows are now so great that the disjunctures have become central to the politics of global culture. The Japanese are notoriously hospitable to ideas and are stereotyped as inclined to export (all) and import (some) goods, but they are also notoriously closed to immigration, like the Swiss, the Swedes, and the Saudis. Yet the Swiss and the Saudis accept populations of guest workers, thus creating labor diasporas of Turks, Italians, and other circum-Mediterranean groups. Some such guest-worker groups maintain continuous contact with their home nations, like the Turks, but others, like high-level South Asian migrants, tend to desire lives in their new homes, raising anew the problem of reproduction in a deterritorialized context.

Deterritorialization, in general, is one of the central forces of the modern world because it brings laboring populations into the lower-class sectors and spaces of relatively wealthy societies, while sometimes creating exaggerated and intensified senses of criticism or attachment to politics in the home state. Deterritorialization, whether of Hindus, Sikhs, Palestinians, or Ukrainians, is now at the core of a variety of global fundamentalisms, including Islamic and Hindu fundamentalism. In the Hindu case, for example, it is clear that the overseas movement of Indians has been exploited by a variety of interests both within and outside India to create a complicated network of finances and religious identifications, by which the problem of cultural reproduction for Hindus abroad has become tied to the politics of Hindu fundamentalism at home.

At the same time, deterritorialization creates new markets for film companies, art impresarios,

---

[16] *Synesthesia:* an association of sensation, in this case reading, with other sensations. In Appadurai's example, he is discussing the association of reading with hearing and seeing.

[17] Appadurai here employs a fundamental element of postmodern thinking particularly shaped by the work of Jacques Derrida (1930–2004). Derrida argued that authors lose control of their text. Readers understand text based on their own histories and contexts. Thus, meaning can never be fixed. Here Appadurai notes that the lexicon of modern political debate was largely generated by the historical experiences and meanings of Enlightenment Europe. It is now used freely throughout the world and, because of this, takes on meanings its authors could not even imagine

let alone control. So, for example, the authors of the Declaration of Independence did not intend for any of its wording to resonate with either Buddhist or Confucian thinking, which they were not particularly aware of either. Yet, passages of that document may take on special meaning for individuals in those traditions because, by chance, they do so resonate. These meanings may, or may not have anything to do with what the authors intended. From a postmodern perspective, loss of authorial control is an aspect of all text. Appadurai points out that this is much more the case when text (and movies and advertisement and all other forms of communication) move among people of radically different cultures and histories.

and travel agencies, which thrive on the need of the deterritorialized population for contact with its homeland. Naturally, these invented homelands, which constitute the mediascapes of deterritorialized groups, can often become sufficiently fantastic and one-sided that they provide the material for new ideoscapes in which ethnic conflicts can begin to erupt. The creation of Khalistan, an invented homeland of the deterritorialized Sikh population of England, Canada, and the United States, is one example of the bloody potential in such mediascapes as they interact with the internal colonialisms of the nation-state (e.g., Hechter 1975). The West Bank, Namibia, and Eritrea are other theaters for the enactment of the bloody negotiation between existing nation-states and various deterritorialized groupings.[18]

It is in the fertile ground of deterritorialization, in which money, commodities, and persons are involved in ceaselessly chasing each other around the world, that the mediascapes and ideoscapes of the modern world find their fractured and fragmented counterpart. For the ideas and images produced by mass media often are only partial guides to the goods and experiences that deterritorialized populations transfer to one another. In Mira Nair's brilliant film *India Cabaret*,[19] we see the multiple loops of this fractured deterritorialization as young women, barely competent in Bombay's metropolitan glitz, come to seek their fortunes as cabaret dancers and prostitutes in Bombay, entertaining men in clubs with dance formats derived wholly from the prurient dance sequences of Hindi films. These scenes in turn cater to ideas about western and foreign women and their looseness, while they provide tawdry career alibis for these women. Some of these women come from Kerala, where cabaret clubs and the pornographic film industry have blossomed, partly in response to the purses and

tastes of Keralites returned from the Middle East, where their diasporic lives away from women distort their very sense of what the relations between men and women might be. These tragedies of displacement could certainly be replayed in a more detailed analysis of the relations between the Japanese and German sex tours to Thailand and the tragedies of the sex trade in Bangkok, and in other similar loops that tie together fantasies about the Other, the conveniences and seductions of travel, the economics of global trade, and the brutal mobility fantasies that dominate gender politics in many parts of Asia and the world at large.

While far more could be said about the cultural politics of deterritorialization and the larger sociology of displacement that it expresses, it is appropriate at this juncture to bring in the role of the nation-state in the disjunctive global economy of culture today. The relationship between states and nations is everywhere an embattled one. It is possible to say that in many societies the nation and the state have become one another's projects. That is, while nations (or more properly groups with ideas about nationhood) seek to capture or co-opt states and state power, states simultaneously seek to capture and monopolize ideas about nationhood (Baruah 1986; Chatterjee 1986; Nandy 1989). In general, separatist transnational movements, including those that have included terror in their methods, exemplify nations in search of states. Sikhs, Tamil Sri Lankans, Basques, Moros, Quebecois—each of these represents imagined communities that seek to create states of their own or carve pieces out of existing states. States, on the other hand, are everywhere seeking to monopolize the moral resources of community, either by flatly claiming perfect coevality between nation and state, or by systematically museumizing and representing all

---

[18] Khalistan is the name of a proposed Sikh homeland in the Punjab in India. Separatists demanding a Sikh state were most active in the 1970s and 1980s. Between 1980 and 1992 the Punjab was convulsed by a series of rebellions that left almost 25,000 dead, most of them Sikhs (Van Dyke 2009). Numerous famous incidents of terrorism were linked to this movement including the assassina-

tion of Indira Gandhi in 1984 and, most likely, the destruction of Air India Flight 182 off the coast of Ireland in 1985 in which 329 died.

[19] *India Cabaret* (1985) is a made-for-TV documentary that details the lives and expectations of two aging strippers at a rundown Bombay nightclub.

the groups within them in a variety of heritage politics that seems remarkably uniform throughout the world (Handler 1988; Herzfeld 1982; McQueen 1988).

Here, national and international mediascapes are exploited by nation-states to pacify separatists or even the potential fissiparousness[20] of all ideas of difference. Typically, contemporary nation-states do this by exercising taxonomic control over difference, by creating various kinds of international spectacle to domesticate difference, and by seducing small groups with the fantasy of self-display on some sort of global or cosmopolitan stage. One important new feature of global cultural politics, tied to the disjunctive relationships among the various landscapes discussed earlier, is that state and nation are at each other's throats, and the hyphen that links them is now less an icon of conjuncture than an index of disjuncture. This disjunctive relationship between nation and state has two levels: at the level of any given nation-state, it means that there is a battle of the imagination, with state and nation seeking to cannibalize one another. Here is the seedbed of brutal separatisms—majoritarianisms that seem to have appeared from nowhere and microidentities that have become political projects within the nation-state. At another level, this disjunctive relationship is deeply entangled with the global disjunctures discussed throughout this chapter: ideas of nationhood appear to be steadily increasing in scale and regularly crossing existing state boundaries, sometimes, as with the Kurds, because previous identities stretched across vast national spaces or, as with the Tamils in Sri Lanka, the dormant threads of a transnational diaspora have been activated to ignite the micropolitics of a nation-state.

In discussing the cultural politics that have subverted the hyphen that links the nation to the state, it is especially important not to forget the mooring of such politics in the irregularities that now characterize disorganized capital (Kothari 1989; Lash and Urry 1987). Because labor, finance, and technology are now so widely separated, the volatilities that underlie movements for nationhood (as large as transnational Islam on the one hand, or as small as the movement of the Gurkhas for a separate state in Northeast India) grind against the vulnerabilities that characterize the relationships between states. States find themselves pressed to stay open by the forces of media, technology, and travel that have fueled consumerism throughout the world and have increased the craving, even in the non-western world, for new commodities and spectacles. On the other hand, these very cravings can become caught up in new ethnoscapes, mediascapes, and, eventually, ideoscapes, such as democracy in China, that the state cannot tolerate as threats to its own control over ideas of nationhood and peoplehood.[21] States throughout the world are under siege, especially where contests over the ideoscapes of democracy are fierce and fundamental, and where there are radical disjunctures between ideoscapes and technoscapes (as in the case of very small countries that lack contemporary technologies of production and information); or between ideoscapes and financescapes (as in countries such as Mexico or Brazil, where international lending influences national politics to a very large degree); or between ideoscapes and ethnoscapes (as in Beirut, where diasporic, local, and translocal filiations are suicidally at battle); or between ideoscapes and mediascapes (as in many countries in the Middle East and Asia) where the lifestyles represented on both national and international TV and cinema completely overwhelm and undermine the rhetoric of national politics. In the Indian case, the myth of the law-breaking hero has emerged to mediate this naked struggle between the pieties and realities of Indian politics, which has grown increasingly brutalized and corrupt (Vachani 1989).

---

[20] *Fissiparousness:* the tendency of things to break into pieces.

[21] When the first version of this essay was published in 1991, China had recently put down a very widely publicized mass pro-democracy demonstration. In May 1989 hundreds of thousands of students demanded democracy by protesting in Beijing's Tiananmen Square. The movement was crushed by the Chinese Army in late May of that year. The number who died is still unknown, but estimates vary from under 100 to as many as 3,000.

The transnational movement of the martial arts, particularly through Asia, as mediated by the Hollywood and Hong Kong film industries (Zarilli 1995) is a rich illustration of the ways in which long-standing martial arts traditions, reformulated to meet the fantasies of contemporary (sometimes lumpen) youth populations, create new cultures of masculinity and violence, which are in turn the fuel for increased violence in national and international politics.[22] Such violence is in turn the spur to an increasingly rapid and amoral arms trade that penetrates the entire world. The worldwide spread of the AK-47 and the Uzi, in films, in corporate and state security, in terror, and in police and military activity, is a reminder that apparently simple technical uniformities often conceal an increasingly complex set of loops, linking images of violence to aspirations for community in some imagined world.[23]

Returning then to the ethnoscapes with which I began, the central paradox of ethnic politics in today's world is that primordia (whether of language or skin color or neighborhood or kinship) have become globalized. That is, sentiments, whose greatest force is in their ability to ignite intimacy into a political state and turn locality into a staging ground for identity, have become spread over vast and irregular spaces as groups move yet stay linked to one another through sophisticated media capabilities. This is not to deny that such primordia are often the product of invented traditions (Hobsbawm and Ranger 1983) or retrospective affiliations, but to emphasize that because of the disjunctive and unstable interplay of commerce, media, national policies, and consumer fantasies, ethnicity, once a genie contained in the bottle of some sort of locality (however large), has now become a global force, forever slipping in and through the cracks between states and borders.

But the relationship between the cultural and economic levels of this new set of global disjunctures is not a simple one-way street in which the terms of global cultural politics are set wholly by, or confined wholly within, the vicissitudes of international flows of technology, labor, and finance, demanding only a modest modification of existing neo-Marxist models of uneven development and state formation. There is a deeper change, itself driven by the disjunctures among all the landscapes I have discussed and constituted by their continuously fluid and uncertain interplay, that concerns the relationship between production and consumption in today's global economy. Here, I begin with Marx's famous (and often mined) view of the fetishism of the commodity and suggest that this fetishism has been replaced in the world at large (now seeing the world as one large, interactive system, composed of many complex subsystems) by two mutually supportive descendants, the first of which I call production fetishism and the second, the fetishism of the consumer.[24]

---

[22] *Lumpen* is a term from Marxist vocabulary. It generally refers to the underclass, particularly dispossessed and displaced individuals; the very lowest social strata. See also note 9, page 591, where Marx's term *lumpenproletariat* is discussed.

[23] Over the past several paragraphs Appadurai has presented a powerful historical argument. Until perhaps the time of World War II, the various *scapes* that Appadurai characterizes existed in greater or lesser synchrony. Nation-states, capital, media, and so on, overlapped. Firms were tied to national interests and the result was a world characterized by the hegemony of Western wealth, power, and ideas. In the past fifty years or so, these ties have come loose from their moorings, which has radically affected the interests of nations and capitalist firms. The result is a profoundly disjunctive world. On the other hand, Appad-

urai may be extending his argument a bit too far. In the paragraph you just read, he argues that the international popularity of Kung-fu films is a causative factor in the rise in the international arms trade. Appadurai's ideas have been very productive in inspiring research about the ways in which nationalism, capitalism, the media and other aspects of modernity articulate, but it's difficult to imagine exactly what data would show the connection between things such as Kung-fu films and the arms trade.

[24] Commodity fetishism is a critical idea introduced by Marx in *Capital* (1930 [1867]). Marx argues that in capitalism (as distinct from other modes of production) commodities are removed from the conditions of their production through the medium of money. This disjuncture makes it possible to think of a market consisting only of items that are traded against each other and especially

By *production fetishism* I mean an illusion created by contemporary transnational production loci that masks translocal capital, transnational earning flows, global management, and often faraway workers (engaged in various kinds of high-tech putting-out operations) in the idiom and spectacle of local (sometimes even worker) control, national productivity, and territorial sovereignty. To the extent that various kinds of free-trade zones have become the models for production at large, especially of high-tech commodities, production has itself become a fetish, obscuring not social relations as such but the relations of production, which are increasingly transnational. The locality (both in the sense of the local factory or site of production and in the extended sense of the nation-state) becomes a fetish that disguises the globally dispersed forces that actually drive the production process. This generates alienation (in Marx's sense) twice intensified, for its social sense is now compounded by a complicated spatial dynamic that is increasingly global.[25]

As for the *fetishism of the consumer*, I mean to indicate here that the consumer has been transformed through commodity flows (and the mediascapes, especially of advertising, that accompany them) into a sign, both in Baudrillard's sense of a simulacrum that only asymptotically approaches the form of a real social agent, and in the sense of a mask for the real seat of agency, which is not the consumer but the producer and the many forces that constitute production. Global advertising is the key technology for the worldwide dissemination of a plethora of creative and culturally well-chosen ideas of consumer agency. These images of agency are increasingly distortions of a world of merchandising so subtle that the consumer is consistently helped to believe that he or she is an actor, where in fact he or she is at best a chooser.[26]

The globalization of culture is not the same as its homogenization, but globalization involves the use of a variety of instruments of homogenization (armaments, advertising techniques, language hegemonies, and clothing styles) that are absorbed into local political and cultural economies, only to be repatriated as heterogeneous dialogues of national sovereignty, free enterprise, and fundamentalism in which the state plays an increasingly delicate role: too much openness to global flows, and the nation-state is threatened by revolt, as in the China syndrome;[27] too little, and the state exits the international stage, as

---

against money. Economists focus on this market, but in doing so they fetishize commodities, making them magical items that seem to have wills and values of their own, separate from either their uses or their conditions of production. Because of this fetishism, so Marx argues, bourgeois economists misunderstand the true nature of both value (which is tied to the amount of labor in things) and economic relations themselves. Fetishizing the commodity thus acts to disguise or obscure the true nature of the relation of production that created it. In the next paragraphs, Appadurai argues that a similar process has happened for both production and consumption. They have become terms that mask rather than reveal processes and understanding.

[25] Alienation in Marx's sense refers to removal. Recall that Marx believed that workers were alienated to the extent that ownership of the means of production was taken away from them. Here they are doubly alienated because not only are the means of production (the factory) removed from the worker but, despite its physical presence, it is removed from the nation as well. The factory may be physically located nearby, but virtually all aspects of its control, operation, and economic benefits may be managed from afar.

[26] *Baudrillard's sense of simulacrum:* A simulacrum is an image or a representation. Baudrillard (1994) argued that advanced capitalism and, in particular, the media, have detached the image from the real. As we are bombarded with images, we are exposed to models of objects and behaviors that have no counterparts in our actual lives. The notions of masculinity and femininity seen on TV, the homes portrayed on TV and in glossy magazines, and so on, are frequently held up as perfectly desirable. Thus consumerism is fired by an attempt to purchase and create in reality a simulacrum or model that has no origin in reality. Efforts to model reality on such a simulacrum are ultimately doomed and lead to a collapse of meaning. Appadurai, following Baudrillard, argues for a fetishism of the consumer. He claims that analysts focus on consumer behavior, but such a focus misunderstands the true dynamics of the situation. The consumer is buffeted and controlled by elements of capitalism that structure the nature of desire and the possibilities available to satisfy it.

[27] Appadurai here puns on the title of a 1979 American movie *The China Syndrome* about the possible meltdown of the core of a nuclear reactor. The title refers to

Burma, Albania, and North Korea in various ways have done. In general, the state has become the arbitrageur of this *repatriation of difference* (in the form of goods, signs, slogans, and styles). But this repatriation or export of the designs and commodities of difference continuously exacerbates the internal politics of majoritarianism and homogenization, which is most frequently played out in debates over heritage.

Thus the central feature of global culture today is the politics of the mutual effort of sameness and difference to cannibalize one another and thereby proclaim their successful hijacking of the twin Enlightenment ideas of the triumphantly universal and the resiliently particular. This mutual cannibalization shows its ugly face in riots, refugee flows, state-sponsored torture, and ethnocide (with or without state support). Its brighter side is in the expansion of many individual horizons of hope and fantasy, in the global spread of oral rehydration therapy and other low-tech instruments of well-being, in the susceptibility even of South Africa to the force of global opinion, in the inability of the Polish state to repress its own working classes, and in the growth of a wide range of progressive, transnational alliances.[28] Examples of both sorts could be multiplied. The critical point is that both sides of the coin of global cultural process today are products of the infinitely varied mutual contest of sameness and difference on a stage characterized by radical disjunctures between different sorts of global flows and the uncertain landscapes created in and through these disjunctures.

THE WORK OF REPRODUCTION IN AN AGE OF MECHANICAL ART

I have inverted the key terms of the title of Walter Benjamin's famous essay (1969) to return this rather high-flying discussion to a more manageable level. There is a classic human problem that will not disappear however much global cultural processes might change their dynamics, and this is the problem today typically discussed under the rubric of reproduction (and traditionally referred to in terms of the transmission of culture). In either case, the question is, how do small groups, especially families, the classical loci of socialization, deal with these new global realities as they seek to reproduce themselves and, in so doing, by accident reproduce cultural forms themselves? In traditional anthropological terms, this could be phrased as the problem of enculturation in a period of rapid culture change. So the problem is hardly novel. But it does take on some novel dimensions under the global conditions discussed so far in this chapter.[29]

---

the idea that a melting down nuclear core in America would pass through the earth until it reaches China. The notion of meltdown fits nicely with Appadurai's ideas in this paragraph.

[28] Appadurai, referring to South Africa and Poland here, is commenting on the politics of the 1980s. Between the early years of the twentieth century and the early 1990s, South Africa had a legal system of discrimination called *apartheid*. It was eventually brought to an end by a combination of civil disobedience in South Africa and sanctions and diplomatic pressure from the rest of the world. In Poland, a communist nation after World War II, an anticommunist trade union, Solidarity, was founded in 1980. Despite several attempts, the government was unable to suppress the union and by 1989, a Solidarity-led government was in place and union leader Lech Walesa (b. 1943) had been elected president. Note that the collapse of apartheid, the success of Solidarity, and the fall of communism in Eastern Europe and Russia were titanic events that had just happened when Appadurai wrote this essay.

[29] Though he phrases it partially as the anthropological issue of enculturation, Appadurai also locates his argument squarely in neo-Marxist thought. For Marx, every society both produces and reproduces. It produces its livelihood and it reproduces the mode of production. Societies provide their members sufficient resources to reproduce their own living conditions and relations of production as they promulgate ideologies that justify these conditions and relations. Social reproduction is the force that drives society forward in time. Appadurai, punning on the title of Walter Benjamin's most famous essay "The Work of Art in the Age of Mechanical Reproduction," points to the difficulties of social reproduction in an age of global flow. See note 10 in this essay for more information about Walter Benjamin.

First, the sort of transgenerational stability of knowledge that was presupposed in most theories of enculturation (or, in slightly broader terms, of socialization) can no longer be assumed. As families move to new locations, or as children move before older generations, or as grown sons and daughters return from time spent in strange parts of the world, family relationships can become volatile; new commodity patterns are negotiated, debts and obligations are recalibrated, and rumors and fantasies about the new setting are maneuvered into existing repertoires of knowledge and practice. Often, global labor diasporas involve immense strains on marriages in general and on women in particular, as marriages become the meeting points of historical patterns of socialization and new ideas of proper behavior. Generations easily divide, as ideas about property, propriety, and collective obligation wither under the siege of distance and time. Most important, the work of cultural reproduction in new settings is profoundly complicated by the politics of representing a family as normal (particularly for the young) to neighbours and peers in the new locale. All this is, of course, not new to the cultural study of immigration.

What is new is that this is a world in which both points of departure and points of arrival are in cultural flux, and thus the search for steady points of reference, as critical life choices are made, can be very difficult. It is in this atmosphere that the invention of tradition (and of ethnicity, kinship, and other identity markers) can become slippery, as the search for certainties is regularly frustrated by the fluidities of transnational communication. As group pasts become increasingly parts of museums, exhibits, and collections, both in national and transnational spec-

tacles, culture becomes less what Pierre Bourdieu would have called a habitus (a tacit realm of reproducible practices and dispositions) and more an arena for conscious choice, justification, and representation, the latter often to multiple and spatially dislocated audiences.[30]

The task of cultural reproduction, even in its most intimate arenas, such as husband-wife and parent-child relations, becomes both politicized and exposed to the traumas of deterritorialization as family members pool and negotiate their mutual understandings and aspirations in sometimes fractured spatial arrangements. At larger levels, such as community, neighborhood, and territory, this politicization is often the emotional fuel for more explicitly violent politics of identity, just as these larger politics sometimes penetrate and ignite domestic politics. When, for example, two offspring in a household split with their father on a key matter of political identification in a transnational setting, preexisting localized norms carry little force. Thus a son who has joined the Hezbollah group in Lebanon may no longer get along with parents or siblings who are affiliated with Amal or some other branch of Shi'i ethnic political identity in Lebanon. Women in particular bear the brunt of this sort of friction, for they become pawns in the heritage politics of the household and are often subject to the abuse and violence of men who are themselves torn about the relation between heritage and opportunity in shifting spatial and political formations.

The pains of cultural reproduction in a disjunctive global world are, of course, not eased by the effects of mechanical art (or mass media), for these media afford powerful resources for counternodes of identity that youth can project against parental wishes or desires. At larger levels of organization,

---

[30] The idea of habitus is most frequently associated with the work of Pierre Bourdieu (see essay 34). Habitus refers to the common daily practices and beliefs of an individual as a member of a social group that form the basic assumptions about the nature of social life and the world. Two key characteristics of habitus are, first, that its elements are so basic to individuals' understandings that they cannot be thought of directly without difficulty. They are the things that not only go without saying but are extremely difficult

to say. Second, in at least some of its expressions, habitus is a physical thing. It is expressed in people's bodies and the ways in which these are held and used in social interaction. Appadurai here points out that the global economy has the effect of making culture a conscious attribute and a series of choices rather than a habitus, something that is inscribed in our consciousness and our bodies in ways that we can only partially recognize.

there can be many forms of cultural politics within displaced populations (whether of refugees or of voluntary immigrants), all of which are inflected in important ways by media (and the mediascapes and ideoscapes they offer). A central link between the fragilities of cultural reproduction and the role of the mass media in today's world is the politics of gender and violence. As fantasies of gendered violence dominate the B-grade film industries that blanket the world, they both reflect and refine gendered violence at home and in the streets, as young men (in particular) are swayed by the macho politics of self-assertion in contexts where they are frequently denied real agency, and women are forced to enter the labor force in new ways on the one hand, and continue the maintenance of familial heritage on the other. Thus the honor of women becomes not just an armature of stable (if inhuman) systems of cultural reproduction but a new arena for the formation of sexual identity and family politics, as men and women face new pressures at work and new fantasies of leisure.[31]

Because both work and leisure have lost none of their gendered qualities in this new global order but have acquired ever subtler fetishized representations, the honor of women becomes increasingly a surrogate for the identity of embattled communities of males, while their women in reality have to negotiate increasingly harsh conditions of work at home and in the nondomestic workplace. In short, deterritorialized communities and displaced populations, however much they may enjoy the fruits of new kinds of earning and new dispositions of capital and technology, have to play out the desires and fantasies of these new ethnoscapes, while striving to reproduce the family-as-microcosm of culture. As the shapes of cultures grow less bounded and tacit, more fluid and politicized, the work of cultural reproduction becomes a daily hazard. Far more

could, and should, be said about the work of reproduction in an age of mechanical art: the preceding discussion is meant to indicate the contours of the problems that a new, globally informed theory of cultural reproduction will have to face.

SHAPE AND PROCESS IN GLOBAL CULTURAL FORMATIONS

The deliberations of the arguments that I have made so far constitute the bare bones of an approach to a general theory of global cultural processes. Focusing on disjunctures, I have employed a set of terms (*ethnoscape, financescape, technoscape, mediascape,* and *ideoscape*) to stress different streams or flows along which cultural material may be seen to be moving across national boundaries. I have also sought to exemplify the ways in which these various flows (or landscapes, from the stabilizing perspectives of any given imagined world) are in fundamental disjuncture with respect to one another. What further steps can we take toward a general theory of global cultural processes based on these proposals?

The first is to note that our very models of cultural shape will have to alter, as configurations of people, place, and heritage lose all semblance of isomorphism.[32] Recent work in anthropology has done much to free us of the shackles of highly localized, boundary-oriented, holistic, primordialist images of cultural form and substance (Hannerz 1989; Marcus and Fischer 1986; Thornton 1988). But not very much has been put in their place, except somewhat larger if less mechanical versions of these images, as in Eric Wolf's work on the relationship of Europe to the rest of the world (1982). What I would like to propose is that we begin to think of the configuration of cultural forms in today's world as fundamentally

---

[31] In this passage, Appadurai modifies Benjamin's argument. Benjamin was optimistic about mass culture because he saw it as demystifying art and giving it as a tool to the masses. Appadurai, however, sees the media as providing images of violence and sexuality that encourage street and household-level violence by individuals (particularly men) who are denied any meaningful agency in the world at large. Thus, mechanical art becomes not a tool of the people but an avenue to power and profit by the capitalist elite at the expense of the poor.

[32] *Isomorphism:* sharing the same or similar form.

fractal, that is, as possessing no Euclidean boundaries, structures, or regularities. Second, I would suggest that these cultural forms, which we should strive to represent as fully fractal, are also overlapping in ways that have been discussed only in pure mathematics (in set theory, for example) and in biology (in the language of polythetic classifications). Thus we need to combine a fractal metaphor for the shape of cultures (in the plural) with a polythetic account of their overlaps and resemblances. Without this latter step, we shall remain mired in comparative work that relies on the clear separation of the entities to be compared before serious comparison can begin. How are we to compare fractally shaped cultural forms that are also polythetically overlapping in their coverage of terrestrial space?[33]

Finally, in order for the theory of global cultural interactions predicated on disjunctive flows to have any force greater than that of a mechanical metaphor, it will have to move into something like a human version of the theory that some scientists are calling chaos theory. That is, we will need to ask not how these complex, overlapping, fractal shapes constitute a simple, stable (even if large-scale) system, but to ask what its dynamics are: Why do ethnic riots occur when and where they do? Why do states wither at greater rates in some places and times than in others? Why do some countries flout conventions of international debt repayment with so much less apparent worry than others? How are international arms flows driving ethnic battles and genocides? Why are some states exiting the global stage while others are clamoring to get in? Why do key events occur at a certain point in a certain place rather than in others? These are, of course, the great traditional questions of causality, contingency, and prediction in the human sciences, but in a world of disjunctive global flows, it is perhaps important to start asking them in a way that relies on images of flow and uncertainty, hence chaos, rather than on older images of order, stability, and systematicness. Otherwise, we will have gone far toward a theory of global cultural systems but thrown out process in the bargain. And that would make these notes part of a journey toward the kind of illusion of order that we can no longer afford to impose on a world that is so transparently volatile.[34]

---

[33] In this last section of the essay, Appadurai refers to ideas from mathematics and biology. Chaos mathematics was an extremely popular notion of the late 1980s and 1990s. Enthusiasm for it was fired, in part, by James Gleick's popular 1987 account: *Chaos: Making a New Science*. The notion of a fractal is central to chaos theory. A fractal is, technically, a complex figure that can be represented by a mathematical equation. The key characteristic of a fractal is that its pattern repeats itself on both larger and smaller scales. For example, the pattern of a coastline is repeated in the pattern of a smaller section of that coastline, and repeated again in a still smaller section, and so on and so on. Thus, fractals are said to be self-referential. It is not clear that this definition is quite the same as "as possessing no Euclidean boundaries, structures, or regularities," which raises at least two interesting questions: First, is Appadurai simply using *fractal* as a synonym for *chaotic* (and thus mischaracterizing both fractals and the idea of chaos math, which does both seek and find complex patterns)? Second, is the nature of culture properly fractal—that is, are the patterns of global culture reiterated at many different levels: the state, nation, community, individual, and so on?

Appadurai also invokes the idea of *polythetic set*. A group is polythetic if all its members share a number of traits but there is no one identifying trait that is shared by all members. The philosopher Wittgenstein (1889–1951) provides an example. He challenges us to come up with a single trait shared by all games. This is an impossible task, but Wittgenstein (2001) argues that our failure at it is not the result of our lack of understanding the true nature of games but rather indicates that games form a polythetic group and have a family resemblance rather than a single defining characteristic.

[34] In this passage, Appadurai seems to call for a predictive science of anthropology. Invoking chaos mathematics seems to suggest that we could apply some sort of mathematical formula to either predict or explain major geopolitical events with a degree of certainty. It is far from clear that we've made any progress in this direction. A critical problem is that ideas such as ethnoscapes are powerful metaphors and useful tools for thinking about the nature of modernity. However, it is not apparent how such ideas could be quantified in ways that might make rigorous prediction or explanation possible.

Whatever the directions in which we can push these macrometaphors (fractals, polythetic classifications, and chaos), we need to ask one other old-fashioned question out of the Marxist paradigm: is there some pre-given order to the relative determining force of these global flows? Because I have postulated the dynamics of global cultural systems as driven by the relationships among flows of persons, technologies, finance, information, and ideology, can we speak of some structural-causal order linking these flows by analogy to the role of the economic order in one version of the Marxist paradigm? Can we speak of some of these flows as being, for a priori structural or historical reasons, always prior to and formative of other flows? My own hypothesis, which can only be tentative at this point, is that the relationship of these various flows to one another as they constellate into particular events and social forms will be radically context-dependent. Thus, while labor flows and their loops with financial flows between Kerala and the Middle East may account for the shape of media flows and ideoscapes in Kerala, the reverse may be true of Silicon Valley in California, where intense specialization in a single technological sector (computers) and particular flows of capital may well profoundly determine the shape that ethnoscapes, ideoscapes, and mediascapes may take.[35]

This does not mean that the causal-historical relationship among these various flows is random or meaninglessly contingent but that our current theories of cultural chaos are insufficiently developed to be even parsimonious models at this point, much less to be predictive theories, the golden fleeces of one kind of social science. What I have sought to provide in this chapter is a reasonably economical technical vocabulary and a rudimentary model of disjunctive flows, from which something like a decent global analysis might emerge. Without some such analysis, it will be difficult to construct what John Hinkson

calls a "social theory of postmodernity" that is adequately global (1990:84).

NOTES

[a] One major exception is Fredric Jameson, whose work on the relationship between postmodernism and late capitalism has in many ways inspired this essay. The debate between Jameson and Aijaz Ahmad in *Social Text,* however, shows that the creation of a globalizing Marxist narrative in cultural matters is difficult territory indeed (Ahmad 1987; Jameson 1986). My own effort in this context is to begin a restructuring of the Marxist narrative (by stressing lags and disjunctures) that many Marxists might find abhorrent. Such a restructuring has to avoid the dangers of obliterating difference within the Third World, eliding the social referent (as some French postmodernists seem inclined to do), and retaining the narrative authority of the Marxist tradition, in favor of greater attention to global fragmentation, uncertainty, and difference.

REFERENCES

Abu-Lughod, J. L. (1989). *Before European Hegemony: The World System AD 1250–1350.* New York: Oxford University Press.

Ahmad, A. (1987). Jameson's Rhetoric of Otherness and the "National Allegory," *Social Text* 17: 3–25.

Amin, S. (1980). *Class and Nation: Historically and in the Current Crisis.* New York and London: Monthly Review Press.

Anderson, B. (1983). *Imagined Communities: Reflections on the Origin and Spread of Nationalism.* London: Verso.

Appadurai, A. (1996). *Modernity at Large: Cultural Dimensions of Globalization.* Minneapolis: University of Minnesota Press.

Barber, K. (1987). Popular Arts in Africa, *African Studies Review* 30(3) (September): 1–78.

Baruah, S. (1986). Immigration, Ethnic Conflict and Political Turmoil, Assam 1979–1985, *Asian Survey* 26(11) (November): 1184–206.

Bayly, C. A. (1989). *Imperial Meridian: The British Empire and the World, 1780–1830.* London and New York: Longman.

---

[35] In concluding, Appadurai returns again to Marx. In Marxist thought, production and ideology both play important roles, but forces and relations of production are held to be prior to and more important than ideology. Here, Appadurai suggests that no such relationship will hold true for the *scapes* he identifies. Rather, their relationships will need to be determined afresh for each instance of analysis (1995).

Benjamin, W. (1969). The Work of Art in the Age of Mechanical Reproduction [1936]. In H. Arendt (ed.) *Illuminations.* H. Zohn (trans.). New York: Schocken Books.

Braudel, F. (1981–4). *Civilization and Capitalism, 15th–18th Century* (3 vols.) London: Collins.

Chatterjee, P. (1986). *Nationalist Thought and the Colonial World: A Derivative Discourse?* London: Zed Books.

Curtin, P. (1984). *Cross-Cultural Trade in World History.* Cambridge: Cambridge University Press.

Deleuze, G., and F. Guattari (1987). *A Thousand Plateaus: Capitalism and Schizophrenia.* B. Massumi (trans.). Minneapolis: University of Minnesota Press.

Fabian, J. (1983). *Time and the Other. How Anthropology Makes Its Object.* New York: Columbia University Press.

Feld, S. (1988). Notes on World Beat, *Public Culture* 1(1): 31–7.

Gans, E. (1985). *The End of Culture: Toward a Generative Anthropology.* Berkeley: University of California Press.

Hamelink, C. (1983). *Cultural Autonomy in Global Communications.* New York: Longman.

Handler, R. (1988). *Nationalism and the Politics of Culture in Quebec.* Madison: University of Wisconsin Press.

Hannerz, U. (1987). The World in Creolization, *Africa* 57(4): 546–59.

——. (1989). Notes on the Global Ecumene, *Public Culture* 1(2) (Spring): 66–75.

Hechter, M. (1975). *Internal Colonialism: The Celtic Fringe in British National Development, 1536–1966.* Berkeley: University of California Press.

Helms, M. W. (1988). *Ulysses' Sail: An Ethnographic Odyssey of Power, Knowledge, and Geographical Distance.* Princeton, NJ: Princeton University Press.

Herzfeld, M. (1982). *Ours Once More: Folklore, Ideology and the Making of Modern Greece.* Austin: University of Texas Press.

Hinkson, J. (1990). Postmodernism and Structural Change, *Public Culture* 2(2) (Spring): 82–101.

Hobsbawm, E., and T. Ranger (eds.) (1983). *The Invention of Tradition.* New York: Cambridge University Press.

Hodgson, M. (1974). *The Venture of Islam. Conscience and History in a World Civilization* (3 vols). Chicago: University of Chicago Press.

Ivy, M. (1988). Tradition and Difference in the Japanese Mass Media, *Public Culture* 1(1): 21–9.

Iyer, P. (1988). *Video Night in Kathmandu.* New York: Knopf.

Jameson, F. (1983). Postmodernism and Consumer Society. In H. Foster (ed.) *The Anti-Aesthetic: Essays on Postmodern Culture.* Port Townsend, WA: Bay Press.

——. (1986). Third World Literature in the Era of Multi-National Capitalism, *Social Text* 1 (Fall): 65–88.

——. (1989). Nostalgia for the Present, *South Atlantic Quarterly* 88(2) (Spring): 517–37.

Kothari, R. (1989). *State against Democracy: In Search of Humane Governance.* New York: New Horizons.

Lakoff, G., and M. Johnson (1980). *Metaphors We Live By.* Chicago and London: University of Chicago Press.

Lash, S., and J. Urry (1987). *The End of Organized Capitalism.* Madison: University of Wisconsin Press.

Mandel, E. (1978). *Late Capitalism.* London: Verso.

Marcus, G., and M. Fischer (1986). *Anthropology as Cultural Critique: An Experimental Moment in the Human Sciences.* Chicago: University of Chicago Press.

Manttelart, A. (1983). *Transnational and the Third World: The Struggle for Culture.* South Hadley, MA: Bergin and Garvey.

McLuhan, M., and B. R. Powers (1989). *The Global Village: Transformations in World Life and Media in the 21st Century.* New York: Oxford University Press.

McQueen, H. (1988). The Australian Stamp: Image, Design and Ideology, *Arena* 84 (Spring): 78–96.

Meyrowitz, J. (1985). *No Sense of Place: The Impact of Electronic Media on Social Behavior.* New York: Oxford University Press.

Nandy, A. (1989). The Political Culture of the Indian State, *Daedalus* 118(4): 1–26.

Nicoll, F. (1989). My Trip to Alice, *Criticism, Heresy and Interpretation* 3: 21–32.

Schafer, E. (1963). *Golden Peaches of Samarkand: A Study of T'ang Exotics.* Berkeley: University of California Press.

Schiller, H. (1976). *Communication and Cultural Domination.* White Plains, NY: International Arts and Sciences.

Thornton, R. (1988). The Rhetoric of Ethnographic Holism, *Cultural Anthropology* 3(3) (August): 285–303.

Vachani, L. (1989). *Narrative, Pleasure and Ideology in the Hindi Film: An Analysis of the Outsider Formula.* MA thesis, Annenberg School of Communication, University of Pennsylvania.

Wallerstein, L. (1974). *The Modern World System* (2 vols.) New York and London: Academic Press.

Warner, M. (1990). *The Letters of the Republic: Publication and the Public Sphere in Eighteenth-Century America.* Cambridge, MA: Harvard University Press.

Williams, R. (1976). *Keywords.* New York: Oxford University Press.

Wolf, E. (1982). *Europe and the People without History.* Berkeley: University of California Press.

Yoshimoto, M. (1989). The Postmodern and Mass Images in Japan, *Public Culture* 1 (2): 8–25.

Zarilli, P. (1995). Repositioning the Body: An Indian Martial Art and its Pan-Asian Publics. In C. A. Breckenridge (ed.), *Consuming Modernity: Public Culture in a South Asian World.* Minneapolis: University of Minnesota Press.

40. *From Jíbaro to Crack Dealer: Confronting the Restructuring of Capitalism in El Barrio*

Philippe Bourgois (b. 1956)

Following his year and a half of field work in a rural coffee-growing country in the central highlands of Puerto Rico from 1948 through 1949, Eric R. Wolf warned that even the small farmers and coffee pickers in the most isolated and traditional rural barrio that he was studying "in the future will supply many hundreds of hands to the coast, to the towns, and to the United States" (Wolf 1956b, 231). Macroeconomic and political forces proved Wolf's warning to be an understatement. American industrial capital was provided with extraordinary incentives and local agricultural development in Puerto Rico atrophied at the same time that emigration to the factories of New York City was actively promoted. The ensuing exodus over the next three and a half decades of almost a third of Puerto Rico's total population resulted proportionally in one of the larger labor migrations in modern history.[1]

STRUCTURAL CONSTRAINTS OF THE NUYORICAN EXPERIENCE

The majority of the immigrants found employment in New York City's most vulnerable subsector of light manufacturing. They arrived precisely on the eve of the structural decimation of factory production in urban North America. Indeed, the post-World War II Puerto Rican experience provides almost a textbook illustration of what Wolf in his later work refers to as "the growth of ever more diverse proletarian diasporas" that "capitalist accumulation . . . continues to engender" as it

From *Articulating Hidden Histories: Exploring the Influence of Eric R. Wolf* (1995)

[1] This essay first appeared in Articulating Hidden Histories (Schneider and Rapp 1995), a collection of essays dedicated to exploring the legacy of Eric R. Wolf. Wolf (1923–1999) is generally considered one of the most important Marxist-influenced anthropologists of the midcentury (see essay 21). He is particularly interested in the ways in which the expansion of capitalism has affected cultures throughout the world. He explores this theme at length in *Europe and the People Without History* (1982), a book widely considered a classic of the neo-Marxist approach. As you read the essays in this section you will see that they are clearly a synthesis of Marxist and interpretive approaches. Globalization theory provides an intersection between capitalism, power, and meaning. An analysis like Bourgois' illustrates the economic pressures and relations between different elements in an economic system while at the same time illustrating the ways in which people create and contest meaning within these economic structures. In this essay Bourgois discusses how the economic opportunities for young working-class Puerto Rican men have evaporated in the last twenty years as the New York City economy has changed. He shows how these young men attempt to negotiate their way through an unfamiliar cultural landscape in which they are ill-equipped to succeed.

spreads across the globe (1982*a*, 383). Perhaps most interesting and relevant for understanding Nuyorican ethnicity—that is, the experience of New York City-born and raised Puerto Ricans—are the contradictory ways that the "changing needs of capital . . . continuously produce and recreate symbolically marked 'cultural' distinctions" among "the new working classes" who have criss-crossed oceans and continents in their struggle for survival and dignity (Wolf 1982*a*, 379–380).[2]

Depending upon one's formal definition, over the past three or four generations, the Puerto Rican people—especially those living in New York—have passed through almost a half dozen distinct modes of production: (1) from small land-owning semisubsistence peasantry or hacienda peons; (2) to export agricultural laborers on foreign-owned, capital-intensive plantations; (3) to factory workers in urban shantytowns; (4) to sweatshop workers in ghetto tenements; (5) to service sector employees in high-rise inner-city housing projects; (6) to underground economy entrepreneurs homeless on the street.[3]

This marathon sprint through economic history onto New York City's streets has been compounded ideologically by an overtly racist "cultural assault." Literally overnight the new immigrants—many of whom were enveloped in a *jíbaro* (hillbilly)-dominated culture emphasizing interpersonal webs of patriarchal *respeto*—found themselves transformed into "racially" inferior cultural pariahs. Ever since their arrival they have been despised and humiliated with that virulence so characteristic of America's history of polarized race relations in the context of massive labor migrations. Even though the Puerto Rican experience is extreme, it is by no means unique. On the contrary, peoples all through the world and throughout history have been forced to traverse multiple modes of production and have suffered social dislocation.[4]

The historic structural transformations imposed upon the Puerto Rican jíbaro translate statistically into a tragic profile of unemployment, substance abuse, broken families, and devastated health in U.S. inner cities. No other ethnic group except perhaps Native Americans fares more poorly in the official statistics than do mainland U.S. Puerto Ricans. This is most pronounced for the majority cohort living in New York City where Puerto Ricans have the highest welfare dependency and poverty rates, the lowest labor force participation rates, and the fastest growing HIV infection rates of any group (Falcon 1992; Lambert 1990).

---

[2] One of Wolf's key contentions is that the histories of oppressed peoples and minority groups are fundamental to understanding culture and ourselves (Schneider and Rapp 1995:7). Wolf sees such people as fundamental actors driving culture change—a theme he explores in *Peasant Wars of the Twentieth Century* (1969). Bourgois, in dealing with people from the slums of New York, is acting very much in the tradition of Wolf.

[3] The *mode of production* is a fundamental Marxist concept. Unfortunately, Marx never provided a concise definition of it. Briefly, a mode of production is a pattern that combines labor, the machines and raw materials that workers use, and the social and technical relations under which they use them (Suchting 1983:76–77). Marx analyzed the history of Europe as a series of successive modes of production. His modes were Asiatic, ancient, feudal, and modern bourgeois (Lichtheim 1973:151). Traditional Marxist analysis demanded that societies belong to one of these four modes. One of the neo-Marxists' critical innovations

was to expand the mode of production concept to include many societies that did not fit easily into Marx's original modes. This, however, tended to result in a great proliferation of new modes of production. Here Bourgois delineates a number of modes of production, none of which are found in the works of Marx, but each of which describes a pattern of labor, material, equipment, social, and technical relationships that is found in the modern world.

[4] The Boasian tradition in anthropology has often emphasized the unique characteristics of cultures. Ethnoscientists as well as some postmodernists claimed that cultures were essentially incommensurate and no attempt should be made to compare them. Marxism, on the other hand, is a universalizing theory. Marxists claim that fundamental hidden processes underlie all societies. As a result, these societies pass through similar stages and take similar forms. Thus, while much of anthropology emphasizes cultural variation, Marxist anthropologists tend to be more concerned with cultural similarities.

THE ETHNOGRAPHIC SETTING

These contemporary expressions of historical dislocation formed the backdrop for my five years of participant-observation fieldwork on street culture in the "crack economy" during the late 1980s and early 1990s. For a total of approximately three and a half years I lived with my wife and young son in an irregularly heated, rat-filled tenement in East Harlem, better known locally as El Barrio or Spanish Harlem. This two-hundred-square-block neighborhood is visibly impoverished yet it is located in the heart of the richest city in the western hemisphere. Its vacant lots and crumbling abandoned tenements are literally a stone's throw from multimillion-dollar condominiums. Although one in three families survives on public assistance, the majority of El Barrio's 130,000 Puerto Rican and African-American residents comprise the ranks of the "working poor." They eke out an uneasy subsistence in entry-level service and manufacturing jobs in a city with one of the highest costs of living in the world.[5]

In my ethnographic research, I explored the ideologies (i.e., the power-charged belief systems) that organize "common sense" on the street—what I call "street culture." Consequently, over the years, I interacted with and befriended the addicts, thieves, dealers, and con artists who comprise a minority proportion of El Barrio residents but who exercise hegemony over its public space. Specifically, I focused on a network of some twenty-five street-level crack dealers who operated on and around my block.

On the one hand, such an intensive examination of street participants risks exoticizing the neighborhood and may be interpreted as reinforcing violent stereotypes against Puerto Ricans. On the other hand, case studies of the "worthy poor" risk "normalizing" the experience of class and racial segregation and can mask the depths of human suffering that accompanies rapid economic restructuring. Furthermore, the legally employed majority of El Barrio residents has lost control of the streets and has retreated from daily life in the neighborhood. To understand the experience of living in the community, the ideologies of violence, opposition, and material pursuit which have established hegemony over street life—much to the dismay of most residents—have to be addressed systematically. Furthermore, on a subtle theoretical level, the "caricatural" responses to poverty and marginalization that the dealers and addicts represent provide privileged insight into processes that may be experienced in one form or another by major sectors of any vulnerable working-class population experiencing rapid structural change anywhere in the world and at any point in history. Once again, there is nothing structurally exceptional about the Puerto Rican experience except that the human costs involved are more clearly visible given the extent and rapidity with which Puerto Rican society has been absorbed by the United States and the particularly persistent virulence of American ideologies around "race" and culture.[6]

My central concern is the relationship of the street dealers to the worlds of work—that is, the

---

[5] Note that while Bourgois' essay is an analysis of Nuyorican culture, it is also a scathing critique of American capitalism. It is impossible to read this essay without asking yourself, "What kind of system allows this waste of human talent?" Marx, of course, held that capitalism was inherently oppressive and that it would inevitably give way to socialism and communism. In other words, he thought the rise of communism to be a scientific certainty. Most modern Marxists reject this theological notion. However, they generally continue to be harsh critics of capitalism. Bourgois continues to critique American capitalism throughout this essay. He is particularly caustic in its final paragraphs.

[6] This passage expresses several key concerns of current anthropology. The first is the notion of "exoticizing." To exoticize a group of people is to make them appear strange, foreign, and, ultimately, to diminish their humanity. A group that is exotic doesn't have to be taken seriously. A second key concept is "privilege." A privileged insight is one that is to be taken more seriously because of the position of those who offer it. The use of privilege in this manner is often derogatory. Thus, white males of European extraction are held to have privileged positions. That is, for historical reasons, they are the ones whose voices and interpretations are granted the most credibility. Much current anthropology makes an issue of resisting the privileged

legal and illegal labor markets—that employ them and give meaning to their lives. The long-term structural transformation of New York from a manufacturing to a service economy is crucial to understanding this experience. Although economists, sociologists, and political scientists have argued extensively over the details of the statistics, most recognize that the dislocations caused by the erosion of the manufacturing sector are a driving force behind the economic polarization of urban America (Wilson 1987). They also specifically recognize that Puerto Ricans are the most vulnerable group in New York's structural adjustment because of their over-concentration in the least dynamic subsector within light manufacturing and because of their fragile incipient foothold in public sector and service employment (Rodriguez 1989).

Through my ethnographic data I hope to show the local-level implications of the global-level restructuring of capital and, in the process, give voice to some unrepentant victims. In a nutshell, I am arguing that the transformation from manufacturing to service employment—especially in the professional office work setting—is much more culturally disruptive than the already revealing statistics on reductions in income, employment, unionization, and worker's benefits would indicate. Low-level service sector employment engenders a humiliating ideological—or cultural—confrontation between a powerful corps of white office executives and their assistants versus a mass of poorly educated, alienated, "colored" workers.[7]

SHATTERED WORKING-CLASS DREAMS

All the crack dealers and addicts whom I have interviewed worked at one or more legal jobs in their early youth. In fact, most entered the labor market at a younger age than the typical American. Before they were twelve years old they were bagging groceries at the supermarket for tips, stocking beer off-the-books in local *bodegas*, or shining shoes. For example, Julio, the night manager at a video games arcade that sells five-dollar vials of crack on the block where I lived, pursued a traditional working-class dream in his early adolescence. With the support of his extended kin who were all immersed in a working-class "common sense," he dropped out of junior high school to work in a local garment factory:

> I was like fourteen or fifteen playing hooky and pressing dresses and whatever they were making on the steamer. They was cheap, cheap clothes.

---

voices of these people. Here, Bourgois speaks of the privileged voice of the crack dealers, an extremely unprivileged group of people. They are to be taken more seriously because their control of public spaces in the neighborhood and their position in society gives them special insight.

[7] Notice two critical Marxist concerns in the previous two paragraphs. The first is the central importance of work. Marxists take production as the most basic patterning element of society. Marx (in this volume) wrote that "[people] begin to distinguish themselves from animals as soon as they begin to produce their means of subsistence . . ." Marxist analysis thus proceeds outward from labor to meanings and other aspects of life. For Bourgois it is axiomatic that people's lives are given meaning by their work. This might be particularly American understanding. The fact that Marxist analysis starts with production does not necessarily mean that people inevitably experience their jobs as a source of meaning. For example, the work-

ing class youth Paul Willis describes in *Learning to Labor* (1977), understand work as inherently meaningless and do not particularly care about the jobs they take: It's all just work. In that book, Willis shows how working class understandings about labor and manhood, the schools, and governmental structures serve to reproduce the working class. The rebellion of working class youth, rather than threatening the economic system, actually supports it. Bourgois was strongly influenced by Willis' ideas (and references him later in this essay). The second is the notion of conflict. Conflict is central to Marxist analysis. All societies (except the future communist utopia) are riven by conflicts. History and progress are the inexorable working out of these conflicts and the generation of new conflict. You will notice however, that in addition to this focus on production, Bourgois also discusses how young men try to negotiate their worldview within a dominate corporate model, contest that model, and negotiate their own meanings of the world outside the corporate context.

My mother's sister was working there first and then her son, my cousin Hector—the one who's in jail now—was the one they hired first, because his mother agreed: "If you don't want to go to school, you gotta work."

So I started hanging out with him. I wasn't planning on working in the factory. I was supposed to be in school; but it just sort of happened.

Ironically, little Julio actually became the agent who physically moved the factory out of the inner city. In the process, he became merely one more of the 445,900 manufacturing workers in New York City to lose their jobs as factory employment dropped 50 percent from 1963 to 1983 (Romo and Schwartz 1993). Of course, instead of understanding himself as the victim of a structural transformation, Julio remembers with pleasure and even pride the extra income he earned for clearing the machines out of the factory space:

> Them people had money, man. Because we helped them move out of the neighborhood. It took us two days—only me and my cousin, Hector. Wow! It was work. They gave us seventy bucks each.[8]

Almost all the crack dealers had similar tales of former factory jobs. For poor adolescents, the decision to drop out of school and become a marginal factory worker is attractive. It provides the employed youth with access to the childhood "necessities"—sneakers, basketballs, store-bought snacks—that sixteen-year-olds who stay in school cannot afford. In the descriptions of their first forays into legal factory-based employment, one hears clearly the extent to which they and their families subscribed to mainstream working-class ideologies about the dignity of engaging in "hard work" versus education.

Had these enterprising, early-adolescent workers from El Barrio not been confined to the weakest sector of manufacturing in a period of rapid job loss their teenage working-class dream might have stabilized. Instead, upon reaching their mid-twenties they discovered themselves to be unemployable high school dropouts. This painful realization of social marginalization expresses itself generationally as the working-class values of their families conflict violently with the reality of their hard-core lumpenization.[9] They are constantly accused of slothfulness by their mothers and even by friends who have managed to maintain legal jobs. They do not have a regional perspective on the dearth of adequate entry-level jobs available to "functional illiterates" in New York City and they begin to suspect that they might indeed be "vago bons" (lazy bums) who do not *want* to work hard and help themselves. Confused, they take refuge in an alternate search for career, meaning, and ecstasy in substance abuse.[10]

---

[8] In Marxist analysis, the structural factors that drive cultural change are often hidden from cultural participants. In this passage we see Julio actively participating in the change that will lead to poverty for the people around him. Bourgois makes a nice rhetorical point here, but, of course, had Julio refused to take the job moving machinery he simply would have lost the income. Julio could not change the economic structures that led to loss of manufacturing jobs.

[9] The word *lumpenization* comes from Marx's notion of the *lumpenproletariat*. Marx described the lumpenproletariat as comprising "ruined and adventurous off-shoots of the bourgeoisie, vagabonds, discharged soldiers, discharged jail-birds . . . pickpockets, brothel keepers, rag-pickers, beggars," etc. (Bottomore 1991:327). Thus, the lumpenproletariat are the disinherited dregs of society.

Their significance is twofold. First, since workers fear lumpenization, they will accept high levels of exploitation. Second, the lumpenproletariat are politically volatile. Since they are disaffected, they are easily drawn to political radicals and can be mobilized to challenge the power structure.

[10] The work of Antonio Gramsci (1891–1937) has been critical for many modern Marxists, and his effect is felt throughout this essay. Gramsci was a founder of the Italian Communist Party. Imprisoned from 1926 to 1937, he was released because of ill health and died shortly thereafter. Gramsci's key works are his prison notebooks which, since they were written in part to avoid detection by prison censors, are extremely difficult to understand. Gramsci's most important contribution to Marxism is the concept of hegemony, which he does not define with any

Formerly, when most entry-level jobs were found in factories the contradiction between an oppositional street culture and traditional working-class, shop-floor culture was less pronounced—especially when the worksite was protected by a union. Factories are inevitably rife with confrontational hierarchies; nevertheless, on the shop floor, surrounded by older union workers, high school dropouts who are well versed in the latest and toughest street-culture styles function effectively. In the factory, being tough and violently macho has high cultural value; a certain degree of opposition to the foreman and the "bossman" is expected and is considered appropriately masculine.

In contrast, this same oppositional street identity is nonfunctional in the service sector that has burgeoned in New York's finance-driven economy because it does not allow for the humble, obedient, social interaction—often across gender lines—that professional office workers impose on their subordinates. A qualitative change characterizes the tenor of social interaction in office-based service sector employment. Workers in a mailroom or behind a photocopy machine cannot publicly maintain their cultural autonomy. Most concretely, they have no union; more subtly, there are few fellow workers surrounding them to insulate them and to provide them with a culturally based sense of class solidarity.[a] Instead they are besieged by supervisors and bosses from the

alien, hostile, and obviously dominant culture. When these office managers are not intimidated by street culture, they ridicule it. Workers like Willie and Julio appear inarticulate to their professional supervisors when they try to imitate the language of power in the workplace and instead stumble pathetically over the enunciation of unfamiliar words. They cannot decipher the hastily scribbled instructions—rife with mysterious abbreviations—that are left for them by harried office managers. The "common sense" of white-collar work is foreign to them; they do not, for example, understand the logic for filing triplicate copies of memos or for postdating invoices. When they attempt to improvise or show initiative they fail miserably and instead appear inefficient—or even hostile—for failing to follow "clearly specified" instructions.[11]

Their "social skills" are even more inadequate than their limited professional capacities. They do not know how to look at their fellow co-service workers—let alone their supervisors—without intimidating them. They cannot walk down the hallway to the water fountain without unconsciously swaying their shoulders aggressively as if patrolling their home turf. Gender barriers are an even more culturally charged realm. They are repeatedly reprimanded for harassing female co-workers.

The cultural clash between white "yuppie" power and inner-city "scrambling jive" in the service sector is much more than a difference of

---

precision. He most consistently uses *hegemony* to refer to a system of political and moral leadership. It describes the use by the leadership of a society of "intellectual devices to infuse its ideas of morality to gain the support of those who resist or may be neutral, to retain the support of those who consent to its rule . . . " (Kurtz 1996:106). In other words, hegemony is a system of ethical and political ideas propounded by a broad alliance of political and intellectual leaders and believed as "common sense" by the masses. The hegemony of a dominant class is created and reinforced in the institutions, social relations, and dominant ideas of a society (Sassoon 1991:230). In proposing a primary role for hegemony and intellectual leadership, Gramsci provides a counterbalance to the traditional Marxist emphasis on the fundamental importance of economic relations of production. The notion of hegemony has been attractive to Marxist anthropologists because it

gives critical importance to the cultural realm. Gramsci's influence has been particularly felt in Cultural Studies and cultural-production theory (see footnote 24).

The concept of hegemony plays a crucial role in this essay. In this passage, the working-class families of the crack dealers accept the hegemonic ideology of America's power elites: "common sense" about "hard work." The dealers themselves are at least partially accepting of these same ideologies and suspect that they are "vago bons."

[11] These passages reflect and update Willis' work in *Learning to Labor* (1977). Willis argued that the rebellion of working class youth against the school prepared them for life on the shop floor. However, Bourgois asks what happens when the shop floor disappears? The culture of rebellion that worked well for blue collar laborers is completely inappropriate for service workers.

style. Service workers who are incapable of obeying the rules of interpersonal interaction dictated by professional office culture will never be upwardly mobile. In the high-rise office buildings of midtown Manhattan, newly employed inner-city high school dropouts suddenly realize that they look like idiotic buffoons to the men and women they work for. Once again, a gender dynamic exacerbates the confusion and sense of insult experienced by young, male inner-city employees because most supervisors in the lowest reaches of the service sector are women. Street culture does not allow males to be subordinate across gender lines.[12]

"GETTIN' DISSED"

On the street, the trauma of experiencing a threat to one's personal dignity has been frozen linguistically in the commonly used phrase "to diss" which is short for "to disrespect." Significantly, back in the coffee-hacienda highlands of Puerto Rico in 1949, Wolf had noted the importance of the traditional Puerto Rican concept of *respeto*: "The good owner 'respects' [*respeta*] the laborer." Wolf pointed specifically to the role "respect" plays in controlling labor power: "It is probably to the interest of the landowner to make concessions to his best workers, to deal with them on a respect basis, and to enmesh them in a network of mutual obligations" (Wolf 1956*b*, 235; see also Lauria 1964).[13]

Puerto Rican street dealers do not find "respect" in the entry-level service sector jobs that have increased twofold in New York's economy since the 1950s. On the contrary, they "get dissed" in their new jobs. Julio, for example, remembers the humiliation of his former work experiences as an "office boy," and he speaks of them in a race- and gender-charged idiom:

> I had a prejudiced boss. She was a fucking "ho'," Gloria. She was white. Her name was Christian. No, not Christian, Kirschman. I don't know if she was Jewish or not. When she was talking to people she would say, "He's illiterate."
>
> So what I did one day was, I just looked up the word, "illiterate," in the dictionary and I saw that she's saying to her associates that I'm stupid or something!
>
> Well, I am illiterate anyway.

The most profound dimension of Julio's humiliation was being obliged to look up in the dictionary the word used to insult him. In contrast, in the underground economy, he is sheltered from this kind of threat:

> Big Pete [the crack house franchise owner], he would never disrespect me that way. He wouldn't tell me that because he's illiterate too. Plus I've got more education than him. I got a GED.

To succeed at Gloria Kirschman's magazine publishing company, Julio would have had to submit wholeheartedly to her professional cultural style but he was unwilling to compromise his street identity. He refused to accept her insults and he was unable to imitate her culture; hence, he was doomed to a marginal position behind a photocopy machine or at the mail meter. The job requirements in the service sector are largely

---

[12] This passage points up a crucial issue in Marxist analysis, and in much of anthropology. The individuals in Bourgois' study seem to be in "the iron grip of culture." Bourgois' subjects are frightening but somewhat attractive. This comes from the sense that they might be decent individuals trapped by forces beyond their control. In this paragraph, workers are "incapable" of obeying the rules of office culture and forbidden by Puerto Rican street culture from being subordinate to women. Does culture really compel us to this degree?

[13] The theme of this section is the clash of cultures: the "street culture" of the crack dealers versus the office culture in which they seek employment. Although the subjects of his study are Puerto Rican Americans, Bourgois says their experience is not unique and has been reenacted all over the world throughout history. In this, he is focusing his analysis on class and economic conflict rather than race or ethnicity. Notice also that while Bourgois is sympathetic to his crack-dealer subjects, the cultures in question are not equal. The critical dimension of the relationship of crack-dealer culture to office culture is that the members of office-worker culture have power, and despite their demands for respect, crack dealers have none.

cultural—that is, having a "good attitude"—
therefore they conjugate powerfully with racism:

> I wouldn't have mind that she said I was illiter-
> ate. What bothered me was that when she
> called on the telephone, she wouldn't want me
> to answer even if my supervisor who was the
> receptionist was not there. [Note how Julio is
> so low in the office hierarchy that his immedi-
> ate supervisor is a receptionist.]
>
> When she hears my voice it sounds like
> she's going to get a heart attack. She'd go,
> "Why are you answering the phones?"
>
> That bitch just didn't like my Puerto Rican
> accent.

Julio's manner of resisting this insult to his
cultural dignity exacerbated his marginal position
in the labor hierarchy:

> And then, when I did pick up the phone, I used
> to just sound *Porta'rrrican* on purpose.

In contrast to the old factory sweatshop positions, these just-above-minimum-wage office jobs
require intense interpersonal contact with the middle and upper-middle classes. Proximal contact
across class lines and the absence of a working-
class autonomous space for eight hours a day in
the office can be a claustrophobic experience for
an otherwise ambitious, energetic, young inner-
city worker.

Willie interpreted this requirement to obey
white, middle-class norms as an affront to his
dignity that specifically challenged his definition
of masculinity:

> I had a few jobs like that [referring to Julio's
> "telephone diss"] where you gotta take a lot of
> shit from bitches and be a wimp.
>
> I didn't like it but I kept on working, be-
> cause "Fuck it!" you don't want to fuck up the
> relationship. So you just be a punk [shrugging
> his shoulders dejectedly].

One alternative for surviving at a workplace
that does not tolerate a street-based cultural identity is to become bicultural: to play politely by "the
white woman's" rules downtown only to come
home and revert to street culture within the safety
of one's tenement or housing project at night.
Tens of thousands of East Harlem residents man-

age this tightrope, but it often engenders accusations of betrayal and internalized racism on the
part of neighbors and childhood friends who do
not have—or do not want—these bicultural skills.

This is the case, for example, of Ray, a rival
crack dealer whose black skin and tough street
demeanor disqualify him from legal office work.
He quit a "nickel-and-dime messenger job downtown" to sell crack full-time in his project stair-
way shortly after a white woman fled from him
shrieking down the hallway of a high-rise office
building. Ray and the terrified woman had ridden
the elevator together and coincidentally Ray had
stepped off on the same floor as her to make a
delivery. Worse yet, Ray had been trying to act
like a "debonair male" and suspected the contradiction between his inadequate appearance and
his "chivalric" intentions was responsible for the
woman's terror:

> You know how you let a woman go off the ele-
> vator first? Well that's what I did to her but I
> may have looked a little shabby on the ends.
> Sometime my hair not combed. You know. So I
> could look a little sloppy to her maybe when I
> let her off first.

What Ray did not quite admit until I probed
further is that he too had been intimidated by the
lone white woman. He had been so disoriented
by her tabooed, unsupervised proximity that he
had forgotten to press the elevator button when
he originally stepped on after her:

> She went in the elevator first but then she just
> waits there to see what floor I press. She's play-
> ing like she don't know what floor she wants to
> go to because she wants to wait for me to press
> my floor. And I'm standing there and I forgot to
> press the button. I'm thinking about something
> else—I don't know what was the matter with
> me. And she's thinking like, "He's not pressing
> the button; I guess he's following me!"

As a crack dealer, Ray no longer has to confront this kind of confusing humiliation. Instead,
he can righteously condemn his "successful"
neighbors who work downtown for being ashamed
of who they were born to be:

> When you see someone go downtown and get a
> good job, if they be Puerto Rican, you see them

fix up their hair and put some contact lens in their eyes. Then they fit in. And they do it! I seen it.

They turnovers. They people who want to be white. Man, if you call them in Spanish, it wind up a problem.

When they get nice jobs like that, all of a sudden, you know, they start talking proper.

SELF-DESTRUCTIVE RESISTANCE

Third- and second-generation Spanish Harlem residents born into working-class families do not tolerate high levels of "exploitation." In the new jobs available to them, however, there are no class-based institutions to channel their resistance. They are caught in a technological time warp. They have developed contemporary mainstream American definitions of survival needs and emotional notions of job satisfaction. In short, they are "made in New York"; therefore, they are not "exploitable" or "degradable." Both their objective economic needs as well as their personal cultural dignities have to be satisfied by their jobs. They resist inadequate working conditions. Finally, they are acutely aware of their relative depravation vis-à-vis the middle-level managers and wealthy executives whose intimate physical proximity they cannot escape at work.

At the same time that young men like Julio, Willie, and Ray recognize how little power they have in the legal labor market, they do not accept their domination passively. They are resisting exploitation from positions of subordination. They

are living the unequal power struggle that a growing body of anthropological and ethnographic literature is beginning to address (Bourgois in press; Foley 1990; Fordham 1988; Willis 1977; Wolf 1990*b*, 590).

Unfortunately, for people like Julio and Willie, the traditional modes of powerless resistance—footdragging, disgruntlement, petty theft, and so forth—which might be appropriate in traditional peasant or even proletarian settings (see Scott 1985) contradict the fundamental "technological" requirement for enthusiastic "initiative" and "flexibility" that New York's finance-driven service sector demands. In manufacturing, resistance can be channeled through recognized institutions—unions—that often reinforce class consciousness. In fact, oppositionally defined cultural identities are so legitimate on the shop floor that they even serve to ritualize management/worker confrontation.[14]

In the service sector, however, there is no neutral way to express cultural nonconformity. Scowling on the way to brewing coffee for a supervisor results in an unsatisfactory end-of-year performance evaluation. Stealing on the job is just cause for instant job termination. Indeed, petty theft is the avenue for "powerless revenge" most favored by Willie and Julio. They both were skilled at manipulating the Pitney-Bowes postage meter machines and at falsifying stationery inventory to skim "chump change."

More subtle, however, was the damage to Julio's work performance due to his constant concern lest Gloria Kirschman once again catch

---

[14] Here Bourgois focuses on class conflict, a fundamental theme in Marxist analysis. Whereas Durkheim and the functionalist thinkers saw society as fundamentally cooperative, Marx saw it as characterized by conflict. This is illustrated in Bourgois' descriptions of factory workers. The functionalist approach to inequality, often credited to sociologists Kingsley Davis and Wilbert Moore, suggests that people work cooperatively at their level of competence and are rewarded appropriately for their efforts. The center of this model is consensus. We all work together, each doing his or her job, to produce a final product. In Marxist analysis, on the other hand, factory production seems almost secondary to the struggle between workers and over-

seers on the factory floor. Workers are in conflict with managers and owners. Unable, in most circumstances, to openly rebel, they protest their condition by theft and small acts of sabotage. If these are not excessive, such acts are tolerated by owners as a cost of doing business. In fact, tolerating small amounts of theft is one way owners can keep wages low. The critical issue for Bourgois' crack dealers is that in a factory, there is separation of the classes. Management and workers rarely meet face-to-face. This makes small acts of resistance possible. On the other hand, in an office, service workers are in constant contact with management. This means that they must suppress all insubordination or develop subtle ways of showing it.

him off guard and "disrespect" him without his being immediately aware of the gravity of the insult. Consequently, when he was ordered to perform mysteriously specific tasks such as direct mailings of promotional materials that required particular combinations of folding, stuffing, or clipping, he activated his defense mechanisms. Julio had rarely received direct mail advertisements in his project apartment mailbox; consequently, the urgency and the precision with which his supervisor oversaw the logistics of these mailings appeared overbearingly oppressive and insulting. Gloria appeared almost superstitious in the rigor and anxiety with which she supervised each detail and Julio refused to accept the "flexibility" that these delicate mailings required—that is, late-night binges of collating and recollating to make bulk-rate postage deadlines coincide with the magazine's printing and sales deadlines. Furthermore, to Julio, it was offensive to have to bring over the assembled promotional packets to Gloria's home for a last-minute late-night inspection:

> It would be late and I would be at the office to do these rush jobs: collate them, staple them, fold them in the correct way . . . whatever way she said. It was always different. And it had to be just the way she wanted it. I'd stuff them just the right way [making frantic shuffling motions with his hands] and then seal the shit.
>
> I used to hate that. I would box it and take it to the 38th Street Post Office at 10:30 at night.
>
> But then sometimes she would call me from home and I would have to bring papers up to her house on 79th Street and 3rd Avenue [Manhattan's silk stocking district] to double check.
>
> And she would try to offer me something to eat and I would say, "No, thank you," because she would try to pay me with that shit. 'Cause she's a cheap bitch.

> She'd say, "You want pizza, tea, or cookies?" She had those Pepperidge Farm cookies [wrinkling his face with disgust].
>
> But I wouldn't accept anything from her. I wasn't going to donate my time, man.
>
> She thought I was illiterate. She thought I was stupid. Not me boy, charge *every penny*.
>
> From the moment I leave the office that's overtime all the way to her house. That's time and a half.
>
> I used to exaggerate the hours. If I worked sixteen, I would put eighteen or twenty to see if I could get away with it. And I would get away with it. I'm not going to do that kind of shit for free.
>
> And that bitch was crazy. She used to eat baby food. I know cause I saw her eating it with a spoon right out of the jar.

If Julio appeared to be a scowling, ungrateful, dishonest worker to Gloria, then Gloria herself looked almost perverted to Julio. What normal middle-aged woman would invite her twenty-year-old employee into her kitchen late at night and eat baby food in front of him?[15]

Julio's victories over his employer, Gloria, were Pyrrhic.[16] In the cross-cultural confrontation taking place in the corridors of high-rise office buildings there is no ambiguity over who wields power. This unequal hierarchy is constantly reasserted through the mechanisms of cultural capital so foreign to participants in street culture. For example, when someone like Willie, Julio, or Ray is "terminated" for suspicion of theft, the personnel report registers an insulting notation: "lack of initiative," "inarticulate," or "no understanding of the purpose of the company." Julio correctly translates this information into street-English: "She's saying to her associates that I'm stupid!"[17]

---

[15] Like the story above about Ray and the elevator, this story emphasizes the overlap between class and culture. In both stories, attempts to show respect or friendship are misinterpreted. In the first story, Ray's attempt to show respect to a woman on an elevator goes awry when she interprets his actions as those of an assailant. In this story, Gloria almost certainly understands herself as proffering a minimal degree of friendship. Julio interprets this as an insult.

[16] A *Pyrrhic victory* is a victory at a cost so great it harms the victor.

[17] Bourgois invokes Bourdieu's idea of cultural capital (see essay 34 note 17). Lamont and Lareau (1988), interpreting Bourdieu, provide a useful definition of cultural capital: "institutionalized i.e., widely shared, high status cultural signals (attitudes, preferences, formal knowledge, behaviors, goods, and credentials) used for social

Willie and Julio have no frame of reference to guide them through service employment because their social network only has experience with factory work. In their first factory jobs, both Willie and Julio were guided by older family members who were producing the very same products they were making. Still today, for example, Julio's mother is a sweatshop/homework seamstress and Willie's uncle is a factory foreman in the Midwestern town where his metal-chroming company relocated. In contrast, the only socialization available to Willie and Julio in the service sector comes from equally isolated and alienated fellow workers. Willie, for example, who has always been precocious in everything he has done in life—from dropping out of school, to engaging in street violence, to burglarizing, to selling drugs, to abusing women, to becoming a crack addict—immediately understood the impossibility of his supervisor's maintaining an objective quality control in the mailroom where he worked prior to being hired by Julio at the crack house:

> I used to get there late, but the other workers wasn't never doing shit. They was *lazy* motherfuckers—even the supervisor.
>
> They all be sitting, asking each other questions over the phone, and fooling with video games on the computer. And that's all you do at a place like that. My boss, Bill, be drinking on the sneak cue, and eating this bad-ass sausage.

Finally, the precarious tenure of entry-level jobs in the service sector was the immediate precipitating factor in Willie's and Julio's retreat from the legal labor market. When they were not fired for "bad attitude," they were laid off due to economic retrenchment. The companies employing them fluctuated with the unpredictable whims of rapidly changing "yuppie fashions." Julio, for example, lost two different positions in fragile companies that folded: (1) Gloria Kirschman's trendy magazine, and (2) a desktop publishing house.

Surprisingly, in his accounts of being laid off Julio publicly admitted defeat and vulnerability. On repeated occasions I had seen Julio brave violence on the streets and in the crack house. I knew him capable of deliberate cruelty, such as refusing to pay for his fifteen-year-old girlfriend's abortion or of slowly breaking the wrist of an adolescent who had played a prank on him.[18] Downtown, however, behind the computer terminal where he had held his last job "in printing," he had been crushed psychologically by the personnel officers who fired him. Ironically, I registered on my tape recorder his tale of frustration, humiliation, and self-blame for losing his last legal job as a printer only a week after recording with him a bravado-laced account of how he mugged a drunken Mexican immigrant in a nearby housing project:

> I was with Rico and his girl, Daisy. We saw this Mexican. . . . He was just probably drunk. I grabbed him by the back of the neck, and put my 007 [knife] in his back [making the motion of holding someone in a choke hold from behind]. Right here [pointing to his own lower back]. And I was jigging him *HARD* [grinning for emphasis at me and his girlfriend, who was listening, rapt with attention]!
>
> I said: *"No te mueve cabron o te voy a picar como un pernil* [Don't move motherfucker or I'll stick you like a roast pork]." [More loud chuckles from Julio's girlfriend.] Yeah, yeah, like how you stab a pork shoulder when you want to put all the flavoring in the holes.
>
> I wasn't playing, either, I was serious. I would have jigged him. And I'd regret it later, but I was looking at that gold ring he had. [Chuckle.]
>
> The Mexican panicked. So I put him to the floor, poking him hard, and Rico's girl started searching him.

---

and cultural exclusion, the former referring to exclusion from jobs and resources, and the latter, to exclusion from high status groups."

[18] To his credit, Bourgois does not romanticize the central characters in this essay. They are capable of great cruelty and violence. However, in the logic of Marxist analysis, they are victims of economic forces beyond their control.

More specifically, their surroundings have made them who they are. Thus, despite their actions, these young men are depicted in a sympathetic light. Still, many thousands of people are subjected to the same conditions and virtually none of them sell drugs or break the wrists of children. Bourgois' argument is compelling, but is it complete?

I said, "Yo, take that asshole's fucking ring too!"

After she took the ring we broke out. We sold the ring and then we cut-out on Daisy. We left her in the park, she didn't get even a cent. She helped for nothing. [More chuckling.]

As a knife-wielding mugger on the street, Julio could not contrast more dramatically with the panic-stricken employee begging for a second chance that legal employment had reduced him to:

I was more or less expecting it. But still, when I found out, I wanted to cry, man. My throat got dry, I was like . . . [waves his hands, and gasps as if struck by a panic attack].

They called me to the office, I was like, "Oh *shit!*"

I couldn't get through to them. I even told them, "I'll let you put me back to messenger; I will take less pay; just keep me employed. I need the money; I need to work. I got a family."

But they said, "Nope, nope, nope." I left.

I just stood right outside the building; I was fucked, man. All choked up. *Me jodieron* [They jerked me].[19]

THE NEW IMMIGRANT ALTERNATIVE

The flooding of cocaine and then crack onto America's streets during the 1980s infused new energy into the underground economy, making drug dealing the most vibrant equal opportunity employer for Harlem youths. Normally, in order to fill jobs adequately in the expanding service sector, New York's legal economy should have to compete for the hearts and minds of the growing proportion of the inner city's "best and brightest" who are choosing to pursue more remunerative and culturally compatible careers in the underground economy. A wave of cheaper, more docile and disciplined new immigrant workers, however, is altering this labor power balance. These immigrants—largely undocumented—are key agents in New York's latest structural economic adjustment. Their presence allows low-wage employment to expand while social services retrench. This helps explain, for example, how the real value of the minimum wage could have declined by one-third in the 1980s while the federal government was able to decrease the proportion of its contribution to New York City's budget by over 50 percent (Berlin 1991, 10; Rosenbaum 1989, A1). The breakdown of the inner city's public sector is no longer an economic threat to the expansion of New York's economy because the labor force that these public subsidies maintain is increasingly irrelevant.[20]

Like the parents and grandparents of Julio and Willie, many of New York's newest immigrants are from remote rural communities or squalid shantytowns where meat is eaten only once a week, and where there is no running water or electricity. In downtown Manhattan many of these new immigrants are Chinese, but in East Harlem the vast majority are Mexicans from the rural states of Puebla and Guerrero. To them, New York's streets are still "paved in gold" if one works hard enough.

Half a century ago Julio's mother fled precisely the same living conditions these new immigrants

---

[19] These two stories are important because they demonstrate that, at some level, Julio understands the true nature of power. Julio is a violent and abusive individual capable of injuring another person without remorse. He is, however, easily defeated by people such as Gloria Kirschman, who would probably be terrified of him were they to meet on the streets of the barrio. The point is that ultimately power does not stem from the ability of individuals to threaten physical violence, but from the relations of production in which they are enmeshed. Management is able to demolish Julio because he realizes that, despite his bravado, they hold enormous power and he holds almost none. For Marxists, although physical violence may be terrible, the worst sort of violence is structural—that is, the violence done to human beings that stems from exploitative and oppressive relationships of production.

[20] The principle underlying this passage is the notion that in a capitalist society an individual's value is his or her contribution to capitalist production. Individuals who make no contribution have no value. Because they can be easily replaced by new immigrants, Julio and those like him have very little value, and society need not expend much on their support.

are only just struggling to escape. Her reminis-
cences about childhood in her natal village reveal
the trajectory of improved material conditions,
cultural dislocation, and crushed working-class
dreams that is propelling her second-generation
son into a destructive street culture:

> I loved that life in Puerto Rico, because it was
> a healthy, healthy, healthy life.
> We always ate because my father always had
> work, and in those days the custom was to have
> a garden in your patio to grow food and every-
> thing that you ate.
> We only ate meat on Sundays because every-
> thing was cultivated on the same little parcel
> of land. We didn't have a refrigerator, so we ate
> *bacalao* [salted codfish], which can stay out-
> side, and a meat that they call old-meat, *carne
> de vieja,* and sardines from a can. But thanks to
> God, we never felt hunger. My mother made a
> lot of cornflour.
> Some people have done better by coming
> here, but many people haven't. Even people
> from my barrio, who came trying to find a bet-
> ter life [*buen ambiente*] just found disaster.
> Married couples right from my neighborhood
> came only to have the husband run off with
> another woman.
> In those days in Puerto Rico, when we were
> in poverty, life was better. Everyone will tell you
> life was healthier and you could trust people.
> Now you can't trust anybody.
> What I like best was that we kept all our tra-
> ditions . . . our feasts. In my village, everyone
> was either an Uncle or an Aunt. And when you
> walked by someone older, you had to ask for
> their blessing. It was respect. There was a lot of
> respect in those days. [Original in Spanish][21]

Ironically, at sixty, Julio's monolingual Spanish-
speaking mother is the only one of her family who
can still compete effectively with the new immigrants who are increasingly filling Manhattan's
entry-level labor market. She ekes out a living on

welfare in her high-rise housing-project apartment by taking in sewing from undocumented
garment industry subcontractors.

Rather than bemoaning the structural adjustment which is destroying their capacity to survive
on legal wages, street-bound Puerto Rican youths
celebrate their "decision" to bank on the underground economy and to cultivate their street
identities. Willie and Julio repeatedly assert their
pride in their street careers. For example, one
Saturday night after they finished their midnight
shift at the crack house, I accompanied them on
their way to purchase "El Sapo Verde" (The
Green Toad), a twenty-dollar bag of powder cocaine, sold by a reputable outfit three blocks
away. While waiting for Julio and Willie to be
"served" by the coke seller, I engaged three undocumented Mexican men drinking beer on a
neighboring stoop in a conversation about finding work in New York. One of the new immigrants
was already earning five hundred dollars a week
fixing deep-fat-fry machines. He had a straightforward racist explanation for why Willie—who
was standing next to me—was "unemployed":

> OK, OK, I'll explain it to you in one word: Be-
> cause the Puerto Ricans are brutes! [pointing
> at Willie] Brutes! Do you understand?
> Puerto Ricans like to make easy money.
> They like to leech off the other people. But not
> us Mexicans! No way! We like to work for our
> money. We don't steal. We came here to work
> and that's all. [Original in Spanish]

Instead of physically assaulting the employed
immigrant for insulting him, Willie turned the
racist tirade into the basis for a new, genera-
tional-based "American-born," urban cultural
pride. In fact, in his response, he ridiculed what
he interpreted to be the hillbilly naiveté of the
Mexicans who still believe in the "American
Dream." He spoke slowly in street-English as if

---

[21] Marxists hold that capitalism is a system of maximal
exploitation because under capitalism, the individual is
stripped of everything except his or her labor. This has
sometimes led Marxists to romanticize noncapitalist systems of production. In this passage, Julio's mother remi-
nisces about the beauty of life in Puerto Rico, forgetting

for the moment that it was most likely the crushing poverty
and misery of that life that caused her family to emigrate
to New York City. Bourgois uses this rather long quote as a
rhetorical device to emphasize the misery of relations of
production in New York.

to mark sarcastically the contrast between his "savvy" Nuyorican identity versus the limited English proficiency of his detractor:

> That's right, m'a man! We is real vermin lunatics that sell drugs. We don't want no part of society. "Fight the Power!"[b]
>
> What do we wanna be working for? We rather live off the system. Gain weight, lay women.
>
> When we was younger, we used to break our asses too. [Gesturing toward the Mexican men who were straining to understand his English] I had all kinds of stupid jobs too . . . advertising agencies . . . computers.
>
> But not no more! Now we're in a rebellious stage. We rather evade taxes, make quick money and just survive. But we're not satisfied with that either. Ha![22]

CONCLUSION: ETHNOGRAPHY AND OPPRESSION

America was built on racial hierarchy and on blame-the-victim justifications for the existence of poverty and class distinctions. This makes it difficult to present ethnographic data from inner-city streets without falling prey to a "pornography of violence" or a racist voyeurism. The public "common sense" is not persuaded by a structural economic understanding of Willie's and Julio's "self-destruction." Even the victims themselves psychologize their unsatisfactory lives. Most concretely, political will and public policy ignore the fundamental structural economic facts of marginalization in America (see Romo and

Schwartz 1993). Instead the first priority of federal and local social "welfare" agencies is to change the psychological—or at best the "cultural"—orientations of misguided individuals (Katz 1989).[23]

Unfortunately researchers in America have allowed the gap to grow between their hegemonically "liberal" intellectual community and an overwhelmingly conservative popular political culture. From the late 1970s through most of the 1980s, inner-city poverty was simply ignored by all but right-wing academics who filled a popular vacuum with scientifically flawed "best sellers" on the psychological and cultural causes of poverty in order to argue against the "poisonous" effect of public sector intervention (cf. Gilder 1982; Murray 1984). Their analyses coincide with the deep-seated individualistic, blame-the-victim values so cherished in American thought.

There is a theoretical and methodological basis for anthropology's reticence to confront devastating urban poverty in its front yard. Qualitative researchers prefer to avoid tackling taboo subjects such as personal violence, sexual abuse, addiction, alienation, self-destruction, and so forth, for fear of violating the tenets of cultural relativism and of contributing to popular racist stereotypes. Even the "new advocacy ethnography" which is confronting inner-city social crises—homelessness, AIDS, teen pregnancy—in an engaged manner tends to present its "subjects" in an exclusively sympathetic framework (Dehavenon n.d.). The pragmatic realities of a new advocacy anthropology require published data to be politically crafted. A complex critical perspective

---

[22] Gramsci believed that subaltern populations, that is, those who are subordinate or held in positions of oppression and exploitation, produce intellectuals who develop counter-hegemonic ideas. In other words, the oppressed develop new notions of morality and leadership, as well as new alliances that redefine the cultural worlds in which they live. In Gramsci's thought, the organization of a counter-hegemony is critical to developing the revolutionary potential of the masses. In this passage the recent Mexican immigrants echo the hegemonic ideas of bourgeois American society. Willie, in ridiculing these ideas and defying the "hard work makes success" logic of the Mexicans, offers a counter-hegemonic response.

[23] In other words, social institutions serve to reinforce the hegemonic ideas of the power elites. The "cure" for Willie's radicalism, for instance, is to be found in social service organizations that will convince him of the virtues of "common sense" and "hard work." The phrase "pornography of violence" comes from the work of philosopher Abraham Kaplan. According to Kaplan, such violence is "nay saying to life and the human condition, hence immoral and anti-aesthetic . . . [it is] not invariably . . . sexual in content but sex and violence are frequently associated" (Hein 1971: 80).

therefore is often stifled by the necessity of contributing effectively and responsibly to a "policy debate." Defining policy as a political arena for engagement can demobilize both theory and practice.

Regardless of the political, scholarly, or personal motivations, anthropology's cautious and often self-censored approaches to social misery have obfuscated an ethnographic understanding of the multifaceted dynamics of the experience of oppression and ironically sometimes even have served to minimize the depths of human suffering involved. At the same time, there is a growing body of ethnographic literature at the intersection of education and anthropology—sometimes referred to as cultural production theory—which provides insight into how contradictory and complicated forms of resistance often lead to personal self-destruction and community trauma (Foley 1990; Fordham 1988; MacLeod 1987; Willis 1977). Nevertheless, perhaps even these more self-consciously theoretical attempts to grapple with an unpleasant reality tend to glorify—or at least to overidentify with—the resistance theme in order to escape a "blame-the-victim" insinuation (see Bourgois 1989).[24]

Much of the problem is rooted in the nature of the ethnographic endeavor itself. Engulfed in an overwhelming whirlpool of personal suffering it is often difficult for ethnographers to see the larger relationships structuring the jumble of human interaction around them. Structures of power and history cannot be touched or talked to. Empirically this makes it difficult to identify the urgent political economy relationships shaping everyday survival—whether they be public sector breakdown or economic restructuring. For my own part, in the heat of daily life on the street in El Barrio, I often experienced a confusing anger with the victims, the victimizers, and the wealthy industrialized society that generated such a record toll of unnecessary human suffering. For example, when confronted with a pregnant friend frantically smoking crack—and condemning her fetus to a postpartum life of shattered emotions and dulled brain cells—it was impossible for me to remember the history of her people's colonial terror and humiliation or to contextualize her position in New York's changing economy. Living the inferno of what America calls its "underclass," I—like my neighbors around me and like the pregnant crack addicts themselves—often blamed the victim. To overcome such a partial perspective when researching painful human contexts it is especially important to develop a sensitive political economy analysis that "articulates the hidden histories" of the peoples raking themselves over the coals of the latest forms of capitalism.

---

[24] Cultural-production theory is part of the Cultural Studies approach to anthropology and sociology that is closely identified with the work of the Birmingham Centre for Contemporary Cultural Studies and French Marxist Louis Althusser. Cultural Studies scholars focus on studying popular culture expressed in the styles adopted by subcultures as well as in cinema and television aimed at mass audiences. Following Althusser, they believe popular culture expresses the structural relationships between classes and social groups. In addition to expressing this relationship, culture is an ideology that defines the relationship of individuals and groups to the world. This is similar to Gramsci's notion of hegemony and counter-hegemony (see footnotes 11 and 21).

Paul Willis is perhaps the best known cultural-production theorist. He locates his notion of cultural production within the general field of Cultural Studies. However, while Cultural Studies stresses the meanings and practices that individuals acquire as a result of their structural position in society, Willis emphasizes the meanings that individuals create in response to these positions. He claims that individuals are "active appropriators who produce meanings and cultural forms" (1983:114) and sees the production of culture as the active creation, by individuals, of new forms and styles that allow them to occupy (and often challenge) the structural positions capitalist society forces them into. Willis' theory has been widely criticized for political pessimism and romanticization of the oppressed (Walker 1986), hence Bourgois' attempt in the last sentence of this paragraph to distance himself from this theory (1999).

Although Bourgois is critical of some aspects of politically engaged anthropology in these paragraphs he has also said that he thinks that anthropology's "participant observation methods force people to be political or should force people to be political and have a preferential option for the socially vulnerable and also a strategic access to the nitty gritty of how power relations translate into everyday social suffering" (Haanstad 2001).

NOTES

The author would like to thank the following institutions for their support: The Russel Sage Foundation, the Harry Frank Guggenheim Foundation, the Social Science Research Council, the National Institute on Drug Abuse, the Wenner-Gren Foundation for Anthropological Research, the United States Bureau of the Census, and San Francisco State University. Helpful critical comments by Jane Schneider and Rayna Rapp changed the shape of the article. Finally, none of this could have been written without Harold Otto's moral support and typing, as well as final work on the keyboard by Henry Ostendorf and Charles Pearson.

[a] Significantly, there are subsectors of the service industry that are relatively unionized—such as hospital work and even custodial work—where there is a limited autonomous space for street culture and working-class resistance.

[b] "Fight for Power" is a song composed by the rap group Public Enemy.

REFERENCES

Berlin, Gordon. 1991. "The Poverty among Families: A Service Decategorization Response." Photocopied report, Manpower Demonstration Research Corporation, New York.

Bourgois, Philippe. 1989. "Crack in Spanish Harlem: Culture and Economy in the Inner City." *Anthropology Today* 5:6–11.

———. In press. *In Search of Respect: Selling Crack in Spanish Harlem*. New York: Cambridge University Press.

Dehavenon, Anna Lou, ed. n.d. *There Is No Place Like Home: The Anthropology of United States Homelessness and Housing*. Unpublished manuscript.

Falcon, Angelo. 1992. "Puerto Ricans and Other Latinos in New York City Today: A Statistical Profile." Pamphlet, Institute for Puerto Rican Policy, New York.

Foley, Doug. 1990. *Learning Capitalist Culture: Deep in the Heart of Tejas*. Philadelphia: University of Pennsylvania.

Fordham, Signithia. 1988. "Racelessness as a Factor in Black Students' School Success: Pragmatic Strategy or Pyrrhic Victory?" *Harvard Educational Review* 53:257–293.

Gilder, George. 1982. *Wealth and Poverty*. New York: Bantam.

Katz, Michael. 1989. *The Undeserving Poor: From the War on Poverty to the War on Welfare*. New York: Pantheon Press.

Lambert, Bruce. 1990. "AIDS Travels New York-Puerto Rico 'Air Bridge,'" *New York Times* (15 June):B1.

Lauria, Anthony, Jr. 1964. "'Respeto,''Relajo,' and Inter-Personal Relations in Puerto Rico." *Anthropological Quarterly* 37(2):53–67.

MacLeod, Jay. 1987. *Ain't No Makin' It: Leveled Aspirations in Low-Income Neighborhood*. Boulder, Colo.: Westview Press.

Murray, Charles. 1984. *Losing Ground: American Social Policy 1950–1980*. New York: Basic Books.

Rodriguez, Clara E. 1989. *Puerto Ricans: Born in the U.S.A.* Winchester, Mass.: Unwin Hyman.

Romo, Frank, and Michael Schwartz. 1993. "The Coming of Post-Industrial Society Revisited: Manufacturing and the Prospects for a Service Based Economy." In *Explorations in Economic Sociology*, Richard Swedburg, ed., 335–373. New York: Russell Sage Foundation.

Rosenbaum, David E. 1989. "Bush and Congress Reach Accord Raising Minimum Wage to $4.25." *The New York Times* (1 November):A1–A2.

Scott, James C. 1985. *Weapons of the Weak: Everyday Forms of Peasant Resistance*. New Haven: Yale University Press.

Willis, Paul. 1977. *Learning to Labor: How Working Class Kids Get Working Class Jobs*. New York: Columbia University Press.

Wilson, William Julius. 1987. *The Truly Disadvantaged: The Inner City, the Underclass, and Public Policy*. Chicago: University of Chicago Press.

Wolf, Eric R. 1956b. "San Jose: Subcultures of a Traditional Coffee Municipality." In *The People of Puerto Rico: A Study in Social Anthropology*, by Julian Steward et al., pt. 7, 171–264. Urbana: University of Illinois Press.

———. 1982a. *Europe and the People without History*. Berkeley, Los Angeles, London: University of California Press. (Translations: German, Italian, Spanish.)

———. 1990b. "Distinguished Lecture: Facing Power—Old Insights, New Questions." *American Anthropologist* 92:586–596.

41. Kaiten-Zushi *and* Konbini: *Japanese Food Culture in the Age of Mechanical Reproduction*

Theodore C. Bestor (b. 1951)

This chapter examines two different kinds of commercial establishments engaged in the mass distribution of foodstuffs in Japan, both of which have become sine qua non of the contemporary urban commercial landscape. The first of my two types of examples are known as *kaiten-zushi*, sometimes translated as "conveyer belt sushi" or "rotary sushi," restaurants. The second are chain stores known as *konbini*, "convenience stores" (from a Japanese contraction of the English term convenience), which are discussed in much greater detail in Gavin Whitelaw's chapter that follows. At first glance, these two examples perhaps appear to have little in common with one another. One is a kind of restaurant; the other is a kind of retailer. One sells fresh or at least perishable prepared dishes, usually consumed on the spot; the other is a purveyor of packaged, processed foodstuffs, usually to be taken away even if not taken home.[1]

But *kaiten-zushi* and *konbini* are closely linked phenomena in the production, distribution, and consumption of food in contemporary Japan. The connections, parallels, and contrasts that can be drawn between these two genre of businesses provide broader perspectives on food distribution and consumption as an activity deeply embedded in complex domestic as well as global dynamics of Japanese cuisine, consumption, diet, domesticity, labor, leisure, social structure, and the commercial applications of information technology and standardization.

Both types of retailing have become particularly prominent during and after the economic boom (the so-called "Bubble economy") of the 1980s, a period of high inflation, conspicuous consumption, and speculative investment that has been followed (since about 1990) by a prolonged domestic recession during which the Japanese retail environment has adjusted dramatically with increased consolidation of large retail chains (and bankruptcies of small enterprises), steady increases in technological sophistication in production and distribution, greater dependence on foreign imports, and waning consumer spending.

My interest in the relatively new popularity of these retail outlets for industrialized fast food started from the perspective of distribution, based on research at Tokyo's massive Tsukiji wholesale fish market and the supply channels leading to, through, and from it. Tsukiji is the world's largest marketplace for fresh seafood, a hub in both global and national distribution systems, where changing trends of food supply and Japanese consumption directly affect the business of food and the construction of food culture (T. Bestor 1999, 2000, 2001, 2004, in preparation; V Bestor 1998). The growth of *kaiten-zushi* and *konbini* is not just an incremental perturbation in an already complex system of distribution for seafood and related products; rather, these two commercial forms reflect and have helped effect a complex rewiring of the circuitry of food distribution, both domestically and globally.[2]

From *Fast Food/ Slow Food* (2006)

---

[1] This essay originally appeared in *Fast Food/Slow Food* edited by Richard Wilk. The essay that Bestor refers to is "Rice Ball Rivalries: Japanese Convenience Stores and the Appetite of Late Capitalism." The title of Bestor's essay is a reference to Walter Benjamin's famous essay "The Work of Art in the Age of Mechanical Reproduction." Benjamin and this essay are also referenced by Appadurai in "Disjunction and Difference . . ." essay 39 in this book. Benjamin and "The Work of Art . . ." are discussed in notes 10, 29, and 31 in that essay.

[2] Bestor's first act is to situate his essay within a political and economic context. His essay will focus on the ways in which both local and international patterns of finance and

FAST FOOD

In Japan, as is true in many other parts of the world, "fast food" is not a necessarily modern notion. Although sushi has acquired the patina of "high culture"—as something that is simultaneously hip and demanding of connoisseurship both in Japan and in the West—it originated as street food, as pre-industrial fast food, as did many other kinds of Japanese cuisine, such as the *onigiri* (rice balls) that Gavin Whitelaw discusses in chapter 9. These and many other dishes, including *bentō* (box lunches), *yakitori* (grilled chicken skewers), *oden* (vegetable stew), and noodle dishes (*udon* and *ramen*), have been sold by street vendors for generations, in some cases centuries, and are now also the stock-in-trade for the explicitly "Japanese" segments of the Japanese fast food industry (see also Noguchi 1994).

But the identification of dishes as part of a distinctive "traditional" Japanese cuisine also does not necessarily imply historical stasis. Like all other aspects of "tradition," food culture constantly evolves. Many dishes and delicacies now widely regarded as hallmarks of Japanese cuisine are actually of relatively recent introduction or invention. For example, even the basic form of *nigiri-zushi*, a thin slice of fish atop a compact oblong block of vinegared rice—the style characteristic of Tokyo's cuisine and now the world's de facto sushi standard—was an innovation of the mid-nineteenth century, and many of its contemporary features, including exquisitely fresh fish (rather than various kinds of pickled or salted seafood), only became possible in the twentieth century with the advent of mechanical refrigeration and ice manufacturing.[3]

The particular style of Edo-Tokyo sushi, called *nigiri-zushi* ("squeezed" or "hand-molded" sushi) or *Edomae-zushi* (sushi from "in front of Edo"), became the rage of Edo in the 1820s or 1830s (Nishiyama et al. 1984:259-62). One common story of" *nigiri-zushi's* origins puts it in the hands of a famed chef Hanaya Yohei (1799–1858), who invented or perfected the technique in 1824 at his shop in Ryogoku (then one of Edo's major entertainment districts), a shop that survived until the 1930s. A nineteenth-century verse celebrated his popular innovation:

> Crowded together, weary with waiting
>
> Customers wring their hands
>
> As Yohei squeezes sushi[a]

Sushi is just one example, but the point is that the dishes served up by *Kaiten-zushi* and konbini have not brought Japanese consumers a new concept of "fast food."[b] What they have brought is fast food even faster and in enormous but precisely controlled volumes!

INDUSTRIAL FOOD

In this volume Sidney Mintz writes about the creation of a new global food system (see also Mintz 1997), and Japanese contemporary fast food is

---

technology affect both the actual food that appears in Japanese restaurants and the cultural understanding of that food. Bestor's opening is markedly different from earlier anthropological writing. A "traditional" anthropological account might begin by talking about the physical location of the group being studied. For example, compare Bestor's opening lines with the opening of an essay about the Nyakyusa by Monica Wilson "The Nyakyusa are a Bantu-speaking group, numbering some 150,000 who live in a portion of the Great Rift Valley at the north end of Lake Nyasa.

Their country is fertile, the rainfall is heavy and well distributed, and they are skilled and diligent cultivators, growing a great variety of crops" (1950: 111). Bestor also

writes in the first person, telling the reader something of the reasons for his interest in the subject. This reflects a little of the reflexivity encouraged by the Postmodern critics of the 1980s and 1990s.

[3] Note the similarity between Bestor's argument here and the argument that Hanson presents in essay 38. Writing in 1989, Hanson made a strong argument for the effects of politics and power on history. Although Hanson's argument was not new, it still represented a fairly radical approach. By the time Bestor wrote this essay, some 17 years later, Hanson's insight was almost universally accepted. Bestor, passes over a similar statement about the nature of tradition without extensive comment.

certainly deeply embedded in this global system. Part of this system is what Jack Goody refers to as "the industrialization of cuisine" (Goody 1982), a macroscopic and multifaceted set of transformations in which the entire character of a society's sustenance—selections of food resources; methods of production and processing; techniques of distribution, sales, and advertising; daily rhythms of eating; the nutritional content of the daily diet; the re-engineering of familiar foods for mass distribution; and the creation of entirely new foodstuffs as well—is adapted to and shaped by industrial, capital-intensive production.[4]

Typically, industrialization of food changes the repertory of goods available to consumers, increasingly substituting highly standardized, processed, and manufactured foodstuffs for widely varied, locally produced, raw and semi-processed ones. The industrialization of food affects consumers, of course, but the transformations are fundamentally propelled by changes in the economic, political, and social institutions that produce, process, and distribute foodstuffs.

Clearly, twentieth- and twenty-first-century technologies of the food industry—including aquaculture, food additives, freeze-drying, high-speed transportation (on a global scale), and mechanical devices to replace hand-processing—have expanded dramatically the ability to invent and produce "new food." At the same time, new techniques of food processing develop together with new channels of distribution, new kinds of retailers, and new forms of marketing. Proprietary brand names become attached both to newly developed products and to products that previously had been simply generic items from the culinary public domain, and consumers, especially in Japan, come to expect "branded" merchandise, even in culinary domains.[5]

If one looks at the industrialization of cuisine from the perspective of the growth of a "food culture industry," then it is essential to look across an entire food system as an integrated social and cultural phenomenon, including production, content, and reception. Within the scope of this chapter, I cannot touch on all elements of the Japanese food culture industry, ranging across both symbolic and material substance, including: the material realities of harvesting, shipping, and processing, and the social contexts of production, distribution, and consumption; the semi-stable social worlds of producers and the shifting social relations of consumption; the role of the mass media; the symbolism of cuisine and identity; changes in diet and domestic living arrangements; gendered divisions of labor; formal and informal labor markets; issues of food security and insecurity; and the impact of global trade on Japan's retail and service sectors. What I focus on are the elements of mass production—even assembly line production—that are at the core of the *kaiten-zushi* and *konbini* phenomena, which I

---

[4] Bestor here mentions Sidney Mintz (1922–) as informing his work. Mintz studied with both Ruth Benedict and Julian Steward but was deeply influenced by his experiences in the Caribbean and the growing importance of Marxist thought in the 1950s and 1960s. Mintz was also a classmate of Eric Wolf and they sometimes wrote together. In a 1987 interview, Wolf described himself, Mintz, and several others as belonging to "a Marxian stew but not necessarily with any commitment to a particular party line" and wrote "Sid Mintz and I used to march in the May Day parades. Eleanor Leacock would show up wheeling all of her babies" (1987:109). In the early 1980s, Wolf and Mintz each wrote an important book connecting anthropology history with global economic concerns. Wolf's book *Europe and the People Without History* (1985) is discussed on page 262 (Introduction to New-Materialism). Mintz's work *Sweetness and Power* (1985) examined the economics of sugar from the Middle Ages to the 20th century focusing on the deep effects that the production, transportation, and commercialization of sugar had on cultures and populations worldwide.

Jack Goody (1919–) is an important British anthropologist who has written extensively about heredity, the role of writing and literacy, and food.

[5] Note that the perspective here is generally materialist. Bestor is arguing that changes in the food that people consume are driven by technological changes. "New food" happens not because people are bored with "old food" and want to invent new things but because technology and economy make the development of "new food" both possible and profitable.

conceive of as examples of "Fordist food culture."[6]

The elements of Fordism are well-known characteristics of industrial societies, and include: the simultaneous development of both mass production and mass consumption; the substitution of industrial for craft production; the development of process engineering and standardization of both production and products; patterns of vertical integration among economic sectors, in order to control information flows and to manage financial risks; and the invention of the de-skilled assembly line.

Second-stage Fordism—the Japanese version perfected during the high-growth years from the 1960s through the 1980s—made some critical refinements to these basic principles. These include: the creation of flexible systems of industrial production, including "just-in-time production" and "just-in-time distribution" partly based on extensive networks of very well-coordinated subcontractors (dependent not on direct vertical integration but on "relational contracting" among well-established partnerships); philosophies of "total quality management" based on careful collection and statistical analysis of production and distribution information; extremely rapid product cycles; and the micro-segmentation of market niches and product differentiation[7]

This second-stage Fordism, the "Model-J" rather than the "Model-T," enabled the industrial transformation not only of production, but also of the retail and service sectors. Nowhere has that transformation been pushed as relentlessly as in Japan, especially in the 1990s. Time and space have not been annihilated, but have been process-engineered and micro-managed to create ever-finer increments of advantage in distribution, retailing, and the provision of services. *Kaiten-zushi* and *konbini* are exemplars of that acceleration.[8]

KAITEN-ZUSHI

Kaiten-zushi ("conveyor-belt sushi" or "rotary sushi") gained wide popularity among consumers during the late 1990s as an inexpensive but increasingly trendy (and increasingly sophisticated) form of consumption. Restaurants that specialize in *kaiten-zushi* are now ubiquitously part of the urban landscape; some are stand-alone restaurants, others are parts of chains (currently about

---

[6] The word *Fordism* (after the processes used in Henry Ford's factories) was in use in the early 20th century but was popularized by Antonio Gramsci. Background information on Gramsci can be found in note 11 on page 591. In his Prison Notebooks, Gramsci described Fordism as the desire "to develop the workers mechanical side to the maximum, to sever the old psychophysical nexus of skilled professional work in which intelligence, initiative, and imagination were required to play some role and thus to reduce the operations of production to solely the physical aspect" (1992:216, orig. 1930–32). Gramsci believed that this dehumanization along with increasing control of workers lives outside of the factory led to increasing worker dissatisfaction, high worker turnover and industrial sabotage. He argued that under these conditions, force would be inadequate to control workers. Instead, their consent would have to be purchased with increased wages and benefits as well as the promulgation of a new ideology of work. He rejected the notion that increased wages were an indicator of democratization, arguing instead that they were "manipulative responses to meet the demands of the Fordist labor process" (Antonio and Bonanno, 2000:35). Bestor describes some of the characteristics of Fordism in Japanese food production in the paragraphs below.

[7] Think Walmart.

[8] The Ford Model T, the first real mass production car, was manufactured between 1908 and 1927. Ford's second great success, the Model A, was produced between 1927 and 1931. There was no Model J, this is a reference to Japan. His comment about time and space probably refers to a passage in Marx's *Grundrisse* (Outline of the Critique of Political Economy) of 1858. Marx discusses the circulation of commodities as an aspect of the process of production. He writes: "The more production comes to rest on exchange value, hence on exchange, the more important do the physical conditions of exchange—the means of communication and transport—become for the costs of circulation. Capital by its nature drives beyond every spatial barrier. Thus the creation of the physical conditions of exchange—of the means of communication and transport—the annihilation of space by time—becomes an extraordinary necessity for it" (1993:524, orig 1858).

a dozen national chains exist);[d] their decor ranges from nonexistent to high tech; their common characteristic is an emphasis on low-priced sushi.

Kaiten-zushi arrives on a conveyor belt; kitchen workers make small batches of different kinds of sushi and place them on a moving track, and customers take one plate of this or that. Each serving is priced according to the color or shape of the plate itself, and at the end of a meal, an employee simply sorts and then counts the different kinds of plates the customer has stacked up to calculate the total. *Kaiten-zushi* shops make a point of their low prices: 100, 150, or 200 yen per serving for basic offerings (roughly $1.00, $1.50, or $2.00 respectively) with higher prices for servings that go around on fancier plates.

Kaiten-zushi was invented in the 1950s and gained a reputation (deservedly so, in many cases) as quick, cheap, and often tasteless. At wholesale markets like Tsukiji, proprietors of *kaiten-zushi* shops were regarded as bargain hunters, bottom feeders, who bought the cheapest products at the end of the day, items that were overstocked or at the margins of salability. As restaurants, they appealed to a primarily male and often solitary clientele. Such restaurants were places to catch a bite before catching a train; ambience did not come around the belt.

During the 1970s and 1980s, however, a number of factors began to change the character (if not immediately the image) of *kaiten-zushi* shops. One key development, which affected Japanese seafood markets generally, was the decline of the Japanese fishing industry, both in terms of local off-shore production (because of environmental degradation) and the withdrawal of major Japanese fisheries companies from distant water fisheries (because of the shifting geopolitics of fisheries, the expansion of two-hundred-mile fishing zones by many coastal nations, and international criticism of the environmental effects of Japanese fishing fleets). As a result, an increasing proportion of seafood consumed in Japan was imported, often in frozen form and, as food processing technology advanced, often in pre-sliced, portion-controlled packaging. The major Japanese fisheries companies began to shift their focus from direct production to coordination of joint ventures and seafood processing in foreign locations (where labor costs were cheaper than in Japan). Equipment that can skin, de-bone, and custom slice several hundred fish per hour revolutionized the processing of seafood, and super flash freezing (for tuna, to minus 60 degrees Celsius) transformed distribution; in both instances, there was extensive crossfertilization between European and Japanese manufacturers of processing technologies.

In many ways, therefore, seafood from around the globe became widely available, bypassing established wholesale markets, and sushi shops and other retailers are now able to obtain seafood products in portions and styles that exactly match their needs. At least one major (former) fisheries company has a division that is exclusively focused on the processing and distribution of sushi toppings (*sushidane*). *Kaiten-zushi* restaurants are no longer bargain hunters at Tsukiji; they are more likely now to get their fish from channels that run outside the market than from those within it, and this reflects the growing power of large trading companies active in the food import-export business.

Other technological innovations, on the domestic front, included the development of what are known as "sushi robots," an array of mechanical devices that can automatically cook rice, squeeze it into blocks, and plop precut pieces of fish on top, all in the back room where the conveyor belt slips out of sight. Still others depend on pre-made sushi, often frozen, sometimes prepared overseas and shipped to Japan. Aesthetics aside, these enabled high-speed production of highly standardized sushi that could rely on relatively unskilled (and cheaper) labor.

Another unanticipated boost for *kaiten-zushi* came from abroad. In the 1970s *kaiten-zushi* shops began to appear in a few North American cities like San Francisco, Los Angeles, and New York (and later, in the 1980s, in European and Southeast Asian cities (Cwiertka 1999, in preparation; Ng 2001). Non-Japanese clientele were attracted to these restaurants, according to people in the industry, in part by the growing popularity of things Japanese and by the fact that one could see exactly what one was getting without having much if any prior knowledge about sushi; the novelty of Japanese gadgetry—an important aspect of the Western imagery of postwar Japan—was an additional draw. And, as such restaurants acquired a following in foreign cities frequented by Japanese tourists, the idea of *kaiten-zushi* as an aspect of cosmopolitan popular culture was imported back to Japan (Tamamura 2000), a reflection of "Japan's Gross National Cool," a concept now widely embraced within Japan (McGray 2002).

In the Japanese recession of the 1990s, *kaiten-zushi* became widely popular at home and its image (and quality) dramatically improved (Akamoto 2002; Anonymous. 2001; Watanabe 2002; Yagyu 2003). Its newfound popularity (and the idea—oxymoronic to some—of gourmet *kaiten-zushi*) reflects the impact of the recession on consumer spending habits and the wider availability of inexpensive imported seafood (mentioned previously). In addition, the technology of the fast-food industry more generally has been applied to sushi: careful portion control, scanners that can read barcodes or microchips embedded in each plate, and low-paid staff who simply assemble sushi rather than master it.

A major aspect of its appeal is in the demystification of production and consumption. "Traditional" sushi shops—at least during the past generation or two—implicitly valorized the expertise of the *itamae-san*, the sushi chef, as a skilled and discerning *shokunin* (artisan), whose discernment and connoisseurship rendered the customer a passive agent. Many upscale sushi shops were largely male domains where businessmen on expense accounts entertained themselves and developed personal ties with particular chefs. Knowing and trusting a good chef was a sign of a certain kind of consumer connoisseurship, in which price was no object. Young couples, let alone young women on their own, were rarely part of the scene, and for a casual customer, someone who was not an expense-account regular, waiting for the bill—in a system where prices were rarely posted—could be a tense experience.

Kaiten-zushi demystifies the expertise, the discrimination, of the chef, and makes prices transparent. The popularity of *kaiten-zushi* therefore reflects a desire on the part of consumers to know what the meal will cost. The sushi on the conveyor belt provides direct information about what is available (just as, for generations, many Japanese restaurants have displayed extremely accurate plastic models [*mihon*] of their menus in shop windows so that customers can see exactly what their order will look like). Contemporary *kaiten-zushi* shops also have opened consumption up to a much wider spectrum of ages (and genders) and have enabled a feeling of relaxation (or anonymity) that results from uncoupling a meal from one's interactions or relationships with the chef. The chef is no longer an auteur nor an artisan, but simply a service worker in a convivial setting, and a person with whom you do not really need to interact, unless you want to. The automat has been reborn.[9]

---

[9] In this section, Bestor has drawn many different currents together to describe a change in Japanese culinary culture. The role and meaning of *kaiten-zushi* has changed in the last quarter century as a result of global economic factors (the recessions of the 1970s and 1980s), global political factors (the changes in boundary limits and international action against certain forms of Japanese fishing), the development of new technologies in Japan and elsewhere, and the popularity of *kaiten-zushi* in the US and in Europe. Agehananda Bharati (1923–1991) coined the term "pizza effect" to describe a process of re-enculturation similar to what Bestor presents here. Of pizza, Bharati wrote "The original pizza was a simple, hot-baked bread without any trimmings . . . After World War I, a highly elaborated dish, the U.S. pizza of many sizes, flavors, and hues, made its way back to Italy with visiting kinsfolk from America. The term and the object have acquired a new meaning and a new status, as well as many new tastes in the land of its origin . . . " (1970:273). Bestor notes that with the increased popularity of *kaiten-zushi* is, in part a result of the severing of the relationship between chef and customer. He compares this with the automat. The automat was a type of fast food restaurant popular in America in the first half of the 20th century. At an automat, food was dispensed from a machine covering a wall of the restaurant. The machine consisted of hundreds of small doors with a food item behind each one. The customer inserted a coin (or several coins) in a slot beside the door and was then able to open the door and receive the food item. The food was prepared by an unseen staff working behind the wall.

KONBINI

Konbini are franchised chains of "convenience stores" such as 7-Eleven, Lawson, Family Mart, Sunkus, and AM-PM, whose stock-in-trade are ready-to-eat meals, box lunches, and highly processed snack foods. In many Japanese urban areas, konbini have all but replaced traditional small-scale food sellers, especially since the late 1980s.

The first Japanese chain of convenience stores began operation in 1969. Many of the currently dominant chains had their start as joint ventures between American franchise chains and large Japanese trading companies and retail stores; initially, the Japanese side's interest was in acquiring the management expertise for developing highly standardized franchising chains and in training franchisees and workers in highly standardized work routines.[e] Between 1975 and 1995, the number of *konbini* outlets in Japan rose 1600 percent, from about 2,500 to approximately 40,000, a number that has now increased by several fold. As of 1996, one survey estimated that there was one convenience store for every 3,100 residents of Japan; in some urban areas, the density of *konbini* was one per 1,500 residents (Yamashita 1998). In 2005, I personally stood on a street corner in central Tokyo where I could swivel my neck and see six *konbini* (three of them outlets from a single chain).

Konbini are medium-sized, brightly lighted, streamlined shops, usually open twenty-four hours a day and generally located in high-traffic sites. The stores sell ready-to-eat and simple packaged foods, beverages, magazines, toiletries, and basic household goods. Initially, *konbini* were popular primarily with young adults and commuters, but their appeal has spread and their repertoire has expanded enormously. They have become general stores, touted as "lifestyle centers," for young, mobile, free-spending Japanese consumers. They are popular (for many consumers, but not all) because of their hours, the careful branding both of chains and the goods they carry, and the almost total anonymity of the shopping experience; one does not chat or gossip with a *konbini* employee as they scan your purchases.

Current *konbini* services include: selling computer software; providing copying and fax services; offering downloads of music CDs; selling postage stamps and telephone cards; selling tokens for toll expressways; and acting as rail and airline reservation agents. *Konbini* serve as a customer's point for picking up and paying for products ordered over the internet directly from other companies. The advantages for consumers are that they do not have to use a credit card over the internet and that they can arrange for delivery at a time and place convenient for their daily commute (for example, ordering online from their office for a product to be picked up at a branch near their apartment that evening). *Konbini* are also closely linked to the ubiquitous "home delivery services" (*takkyubin*) that can send a purchase (or deliver something to a *konbini* pick-up point) almost any place in Japan within twenty-four hours.

Food remains the mainstay of *konbini*, however. *Konbini* benefit from long-established patterns in Japanese shopping behavior—frequent shopping trips for small quantities—which reflect a combination of consumer preference for daily shopping with practical limitations on domestic storage space in densely populated Japanese cities. Small-scale, family-owned shops have been a major feature of the urban retail, wholesale, and service sectors for generations, and, traditionally, urban neighborhoods were dotted with small-scale shops strung along shopping streets or arcades (known as *shotengai*) that enabled residents to shop quickly, often, and close to home. *Konbini* are heir to this shopping and retailing pattern, but without any of the social relationships that typically existed between shop owner and customer.

During the enduring Japanese economic slump since the late 1980s, *konbini* chains have increased their market share vis-a-vis other categories of large-scale retailers such as supermarket chains and department stores. In 2000, the *konbini* retail sector had an estimated sales volume of six trillion yen, roughly 70 percent of the total sales of department stores and 40 percent of supermarket sales (according to unpublished figures from the Ministry of External Trade and

Industry). For many young and single consumers (and some who are neither), a convenience store is the local food store.[f]

Large trading firms actively developed *konbini* as a strategy to work around restrictions on the size and scale of retail stores (under Japan's Large Retail Store Law) which effectively prevented the expansion of supermarkets and department stores into many commercial districts and most residential neighborhoods: the compact size of *konbini* sets them outside the scope of restrictive law. Building on franchising know-how initially acquired from American retailers, major Japanese trading and retailing corporations engineered ultrasophisticated distribution and inventory systems appropriate to dense networks of small-scale outlets and adapted to the geographic, social, and consumer contexts of contemporary Japan. Food processors have devoted enormous attention to creating products specifically suited to *konbini* product cycles.[g] And, as with *kaiten-zushi* shops, supply channels flow through large trading companies and their domestic and overseas subcontractors; seafood, for example, is obtained by direct imports, processed in central commissaries, and delivered as box lunches, sushi rolls, or stuffed rice balls direct to shops, in several deliveries a day. *Konbini* and supermarkets, along with chain restaurants of all genres, have effectively excluded wholesale markets from their supply chains.

7-Eleven, in particular, is noted for pioneering a retail "just-in-time" distribution and inventory system, which relies on deliveries daily or more often. Their system incorporates sophisticated real-time point-of-sale data collection for inventory control and ordering, as well as consumer analysis and market forecasting. The ag-gressive use of information technology by *konbini* has also enabled the big chains to become major providers of a wide (and increasingly wider) range of electronic services for customers, and they have moved aggressively into e-commerce (examples of which are mentioned previously), through links made with major Japanese manufacturers and merchandisers.

The extensive technological know-how and infrastructure provided by large *konbini* chains has been a critical factor in their successful marketing of franchises to local business people, many of whom have converted old-line specialized retail shops—corner grocers, rice shops, or liquor stores—into *konbini*. Many family-owned businesses occupy valuable commercial locations, but in the past generation this small-scale sector of the economy has faced enormous labor difficulties, between the aging of the population engaged in family enterprises and the reluctance of children to follow in parental footsteps and take over the businesses. *Konbini* therefore offer many small-scale family businesses a good opportunity to capitalize on real estate assets and to retain ownership of a local business, much of the management of which is embedded in the technical know-how and efficiently engineered distribution systems of the large franchise chains. These systems may rely on hands-on management by local proprietors, but that management is framed by chain policies, and the stores themselves can be operated largely with relatively low-cost, low-skilled retail labor. Many stores rely to a great extent on part-time labor (for example, college students and housewives, as well as on the new working class of "freeters" or "free-timers," semipermanent part-time workers).[10]

---

[10] As with Bestor's analysis of *kaiten-zushi,* note the strong role of global and technological factors. The rise of *konbini* is driven by technological change (the advent of information processing and communication technology) as well as the systems of global capital. It is set within a Japanese legal framework that opens some possibilities while foreclosing others. However, Bestor does not portray Japanese entrepreneurs as victims of this system. Rather, they move rapidly to take advantage of the new possibilities that are open to them, jettisoning family businesses in favor to investment in *konbini*.

FORDIST FAST FOOD AND ITS DISCONTENTS[11]

My description and discussion of *kaiten-zushi* shops and *konbini* stores has necessarily been brief and schematic. But some of the commonalities of these two relatively new forms of retailing seem quite clear. In the first instance, they both represent substantial breaks from or transformation of the traditional small-scale sectors of the urban Japanese retail and service economy. Many of their common features reflect aspects of what I call Model-J Fordism, but perhaps an even later model that includes an enormously expanded reliance on global flows of capital, managerial know-how, technological innovation (both in production and information management), and supply networks of foodstuffs, both raw and processed. Both *konbini* and *kaiten-zushi* shops have resulted directly (in the case of *konbini*) and indirectly from huge investments by large corporations, especially Japanese general trading companies, both in Japan and overseas, and from structural realignments within the Japanese fishing and food industries. Both have benefited from sophisticated process-engineering, which in turn relies on intensive use of information technology, including extremely sophisticated POS (point of sales) data collection for inventory control, scheduling of micro-customized deliveries, control of labor costs, and micro-analysis of consumer behavior (known as "data mining"). And both kinds of establishments make use of new managerial models of franchising, which rely on de-skilled labor performing repetitive tasks according to pre-established scripts.

And both kinds of shops are wildly popular. They obviously cater to consumer demand with extreme efficiency, not only in the range of products they provide but also in the social contexts of consumption they establish (or overthrow).

The success of Model-J Fordism as it has been applied to the Japanese retail and service sectors, however, has also spawned controversy, feeding into various of the "moral panics" that regularly sweep through Japan's mass media and the statements of conservative politicians.

Critics of *konbini* and *kaiten-zushi* see them as garishly intrusive shops that purvey a highly impersonal popular culture of consumption that especially targets alienated teenagers and young adults, and indeed encourages that social alienation. The homogenization of foodways and the disappearance of local foodstuffs and specialty dishes is a cause for concern among some, as is the realization that younger Japanese neither know very much about eating Japanese cuisine nor how to prepare it themselves. Equally, these fast-food outlets, of whatever stripe, are seen to destroy local retail competitors and push aside local production and distribution networks in favor of highly centralized major corporations. This economic trend has the side effect of hollowing out the social infrastructure of regional and community life.

Of course, another one of the raps against chain stores is the quality of the food they provide. There is a standard indictment of a nutritional wasteland: preservatives, additives, high sodium, high sugar, high starch, high calories. And in my own informal surveys of the shelves of *konbini*, I have noted that they rarely stock many foodstuffs that would qualify as "ingredients": things out of which one could construct another dish. There is milk, cheese, butter, eggs, *tofu*, *miso* paste, maybe a potato, an onion, a carrot, an

---

[11] The title formula "x and its discontents" has been widely used. It was popularized by Freud's 1930 work *Civilization and its Discontents*. There Freud argues that people long for the control and order that civilization provides. However, the fundamental human drives for sex and violence must also be controlled by civilization. This conflict inevitably creates frustration and discontent. Bestor may also have had Joseph Stiglitz's 2001 *Globalization and its Discontents* in mind. Stiglitz (1943–), a Nobel Award winning economist argues that the free market policies advocated by the International Monetary Fund do not work because they assume economic actors do not have adequate information to make decisions. Discontent results from mismatch between the theoretical workings of the free market and the conditions that actually exist, especially in poor nations.

orange or a banana (each individually wrapped in plastic), salt, pepper, and sugar, but rarely any other vegetables, fruits, let alone fresh fish, meat, or poultry. *Konbini* food is off the rack. (No doubt some future marketing campaign will tout this as "pret-a-porter" cuisine.[12])

Konbini shoppers are themselves pathologized. The pejorative term *konbini* housewife floats around as a scornful comment directed toward young (and some not-so-young) homemakers who rely almost entirely on the pre-packaged and ready-to-eat foodstuffs in which *konbini* specialize; these homemakers hence are assumed to be unable or unwilling to perform the normative role of "good wife and wise mother." A Japanese physiologist recently announced the results of his research on adolescents who hang out at *konbini*, and made a claim that the excessive lighting in such stores (about 2,000 lux compared to 900 lux in typical residential space) creates mood disorders. Concerns about crime and public safety often attach themselves to *konbini*[h] Another nutritionist has calculated the amount of chewing required to eat meals from *konbini* compared with "traditional" meals and claims that today's "soft" cuisine is reshaping the musculature of the jaw and hence the facial shapes of young Japanese (Yamashita 1998). And the anonymity of *kaiten-zushi* and other fast-food restaurants are thought by some to reflect or encourage a form of extreme withdrawal from everyday social contacts that is currently seen as a major problem among young people.[13]

Linguistically, *konbini* and the new service sector have brought criticism as well. Many older Japanese react negatively to the "service voices" that chain store workers affect. Part of it is corporate scrip; some *konbini* chains instruct their employees to greet each customer with the jarring expression: "*Konnichi wa, Irrashaimase!*" Simply translated, this and equivalent phrases simply say,

"Good day! Welcome!" This may be grating because the traditional mercantile greeting is simply "*Irrashaimase!*" (Welcome!) spoken in a variety of registers, none of them requiring a customer's response. "*Konnichi wa,*" however, is a cue to interaction; sociolinguistically it requires a response. "*Howya Doin?*" "*Fine thanks.*" It is a linguistic stealth tactic to get customers to interact with employees, and, according to people in the business, the commercial logic is twofold. First, even minimal interaction is more likely to lead to purchases, but second and more important, interaction dampens the likelihood of shoplifting; pilferage is a major problem in the anonymous world of *konbini*.

Another linguistic annoyance is the affectless, robotic voices that young workers use, seemingly modeled on the speech patterns of video games. For older Japanese, this monotonal, nasal voice is a marker of the "free-timer" phenomenon, the Japanese equivalent of "Generation X," the young part-time workers who are criticized by their elders for a lack of ambition and work ethic, but who—in their defense—are cast into an economy where the only growth sector is in dead-end, de-skilled service jobs.

CONCLUSION

Taken together, these and other critiques point toward the loss of what Sidney Mintz describes elsewhere in this volume as "the thick texture of daily interaction" that underlies the sociability inherent in local and regional food systems. The circumstances of *kaiten-zushi* and *konbini* reflect the ascendance of what Mintz calls "the freedom from intimacy." Although Japanese pundits, politicians, and business people congratulate themselves on Japan's success in revolutionizing mass consumption, seeing this as an exportable commodity, as

---

[12] "prêt-a-porter" Ready to wear, a term used for clothing purchased already finished and in set sizes, clothes "off the rack" (what almost all of us wear). "Prêt a Manger" is a British based sandwich chain that also operates in the U.S. as well as Hong Kong, so perhaps Bestor's future is now.

[13] Bestor here refers to *hikikomori,* Japanese teens and young adults, mostly male, who isolate themselves in their rooms rarely venturing out. *Hikikomori* is often given as an example of a culture bound medical syndrome. *Hikikomori* in Japan are believed to number about one million (see Zielenziger 2006).

part of Japan's new "Gross National Cool" (Mc-Gray 2002), this freedom from intimacy engendered by the automation and process-engineering of mass consumption may raise other significant issues.

The dependence of these highly engineered food systems that rely on the mass and rapid distribution of food from distant and unknowable sources, handled by gigantic and impersonal multinational firms, gives rise to what I call "fast food monoculture," highly susceptible, culturally, to almost instantaneous panics over food security and the contaminations of globalization. And, given the well-documented ability of Japanese mass media to seize on issues of food safety and global risk, recently including *e. coli*, BSE, GMOs, avian flu, and SARS, highly publicized outbreaks or fears of food safety may immediately disrupt Japanese distribution channels on hitherto unimaginable scales and send shock waves throughout the global food system.

And, although the new Japanese food system is inherently dependent on the globalization of food supply, technological innovations, and managerial skills and corporate forms, I would argue that the controversies or moral panics about the domestic changes wrought by (or reflected in) *konbini*, *kaiten-zushi*, and many related genres of business, are much less about domestic change than they are indications of profound ambivalence in contemporary Japan about globalization, perceived as an external rather than an internal or interdependent phenomenon.[14]

NOTES

Acknowledgements. Many institutions have generously supported aspects of the research upon which this chapter is based, including: the National Science Foundation, the New York Sea Grant Program, the Center for Global Partnership of the Japan Foundation, the East Asia Program of Cornell University, and the Reischauer Institute of Japanese Studies of Harvard University. I cannot mention them by name, but I am also extremely grateful to the dozens of individuals throughout the Japanese fishing and food industries who have been willing to answer my many questions and share with me their own expertise. Richard Wilk's extensive comments have dramatically sharpened the focus and improved the style of this chapter. Of course, I am solely responsible for the facts and interpretations expressed in this chapter. Additional information about my research is posted at www.people.fas.harvard.edu/~bestor.

[a] The humor of the original verse is in the word nigiru, used in two senses: wringing one's hands in anticipation, and molding or squeezing rice for sushi, which is known also as *nigiri-zushi* ("hand-molded sushi").

---

[14] Bestor's essay is insightful and well written. Bestor is a professor of anthropology and currently chair of the Department of Anthropology at Harvard. He has done extensive fieldwork in Japan and published books on a Tokyo neighborhood he calls Miyamoto-cho (1989), on the Tsukiji fish market (2004) as well as an edited volume on the experience of doing fieldwork in Japan (2003). However, like many works about globalization, this essay focuses on large scale historical, economic, technological, and political patterns. There is very little in it that reflects Bestor's extensive fieldwork or the depth of his understanding of Japanese culture. If you did not know that Bestor was an anthropologist, would you have been able to guess it from this work? Like many essays in the anthropology of globalization, it feels as if it could have been just as easily written by an economist, a political scientist, a historian, or a journalist.

Bestor speaks of the ambivalence of the Japanese about globalization. In the last page, he swings from paragraphs that seem to ridicule the critics of *konbini* and *kaiten-zushi* (they cause changes in the faces of young people, make *hikikomori*, are patronized by *konbini* housewives, and employ "freetimers," charges that seem unlikely to be true or appear to reflect the prejudices of their authors) to more serious criticism (*konbini* are involved in linguist trickery, they result in "fast food monoculture" that leads to national panics). The essay seems to be generally positive: Mechanical reproduction improves the quality of the product, democratizes it, and creates new possibilities. However these come with a steep price including the severing of old relationships, proliferation of minimally skilled dead-end jobs. Bestor's analysis reflects the ambivalence about globalization about anthropology in general. On the one hand, some aspects of globalization seem to favor the kind of cross cultural exchange and fertilization that has been promoted by anthropologists since the days of Louis Henry Morgan. On the other, this often comes with a flattening of culture and an international economic order that seems to many to be both brutally unfair and deeply oppressive.

[b] Throughout this chapter I restrict my discussion of "fast food" to culinary genres that are identified by contemporary Japanese as distinctively "Japanese" dishes, and exclude discussion of hamburgers, fried chicken, curried rice, donuts, ice cream, pizza, and coffee, all of which are also major segments of the contemporary "fast food" industry in Japan.

[c] Many anthropologists have focused recently on the culture of capitalism and on "multiple capitalisms" as distinct cultural and social forms in different societies (see, for example, Blim 2000; Miller 1997). Japanese economic organization itself has been the object of debates about specific cultural and social characteristics of capitalism (T. Bestor 2004, ch. I). Business and political commentators have at various times either lauded the Japanese economy as a harbinger of future forms of global capitalism based on tight integration and coordination among government, business, and labor (e.g., Johnson 1982), or condemned it as a highly insular, inefficient, and intensely corrupt system that works against consumer interests (van Wolferen 1990).

[d] By Japanese restaurant chain standards, the *kaiten-zushi* chains are quite small; the largest consists of only 250 shops, whereas the largest chains serving "Western" food (e.g., McDonalds, KFC, or Starbucks) each have thousands of outlets (Anon. 2001).

[e] The 7-Eleven chain of convenience stores is owned in both Japan and the United States by the Japanese retailing giant, Ito Yokado. In 1973, Ito Yokado opened its first convenience store in Japan under license from the Southland Corporation, the Texas-based originator of the 7-Eleven franchise, and it began to use the 7-Eleven name in Japan in 1978. In 1991, Ito Yokado acquired 70 percent of the shares of the Southland Corporation. In 1993, the 5,000th Japanese 7-Eleven store was opened, according to the 7-Eleven website.

[f] Occasional surveys on shopping patterns for perishable foodstuffs conducted by the Tokyo Metropolitan Government illustrate larger shifts within which the *konbini* boom has occurred. In 1996, shoppers in their twenties were most likely to patronize small supermarkets and convenience stores (30.4 percent); those in their thirties were most partial to large supermarkets (36.0 percent); and shoppers over the age of sixty favored retail fishmongers (37.1 percent). During the preceding five years, consumers who shopped regularly at retail fishmongers declined by more than 20 percent and those who shopped in supermarkets and convenience stores increased by 16 percent (Tokyo-to 1992:108; 1995:119; 1996:8-13).

[g] I have had several opportunities to visit *konbini* with food chemists from one of Japan's leading food additive manufacturers. My chemist guides are intimately familiar with almost every product on *konbini* shelves and how they have been engineered to specifically meet the needs of *konbini* sales. They tell me that among many other projects, they are actively working on ways to recreate the smell of freshly cooked rice for pre-packaged meals, to duplicate the freshly made "sushi smell" for box lunches, and to mask the subtly different flavor of imported Chinese-raised eels, which are used in the traditional summer delicacy of *kabayaki* (grilled eel).

[h] A national government survey of 3,000 adults, conducted in 2005, found that overall 57 percent of respondents (88 percent of respondents in their 20s, 82 percent in their 30s, and 70 percent in their 40s) considered late-night or 24-hour convenience stores to be a "necessity." However, 41 percent of respondents overall regarded convenience stores as having a negative influence on youth, 28 percent were concerned about noise, and 27 percent worried about crime and safety around such stores (Japan Times, July 17, 2005:2).

REFERENCES

Akamoto, Mariko. 2002. New, Improved Kaiten Shops Herald a Revolution in Dining. *Asahi Shimbun*, September 14–15:36.

Anonymous. 2001. Kaiten-zushi dake! 1200-kan! (Rotary sushi only! 1200 servings!). *Tokyo Isshukan*, December 25.

Apparudai, Arjun. 1990. Disjuncture and Difference in the Global Cultural Economy. *Public Culture* 2(2)1–24.

Bestor, Theodore C. 1999. Wholesale Sushi: Culture and Commodity in Tokyo's Tsukiji Market. In *Theorizing the City: The New Urban Anthropology Reader*. Setha M. Low, ed. Pp. 201–42. New Brunswick, NJ: Rutgers University Press.

2000. How Sushi Went Global. *Foreign Policy*, November/December:54–63.

2001. Supply-Side Sushi: Commodity, Market, and the Global City. *American Anthropologist* 102(1):76–95.

2004. *Tsukiji: The Fish Market at the Center of the World*. Berkeley: University of California Press.

In preparation. Global Sushi. Book manuscript.

Bestor, Victoria Lyon. 1998. Who's Cooking, Whose Kitchen? Paper presented at the New York Asian Studies Conference, New Paint, NY, October.

Blim, Michael. 2000. Capitalisms in Late Modernity. *Annual Review of Anthropology* 29:25–38.

Cwiertka, Katarzyna. 1999. Culinary Globalization and Japan. *Japan Echo*, June.

In preparation. From Ethnic to Hip: Circuits of Japanese Cuisine in Europe. In Japanese Globalizations. H. Befu, T. Bestor, and M. White, eds. Book manuscript.

Goody, Jack. 1982. *Cooking, Cuisine, and Class: A Study in Comparative Sociology*. Cambridge: Cambridge University Press.

Japan Times. 2005. 57% "need" convenience stores. Poll, *Japan Times*, July 17:2.

Johnson, Chalmers. 1982. *MITI and the Japanese Miracle*. Palo Alto: Stanford University Press.

McGray, Douglas. 2002. Japan's Gross National Cool. *Foreign Policy*, May/June 2002:44–54.

Miller, Daniel. 1997. *Capitalism: An Ethnographic Approach*. Oxford: Berg Publishers.

Mintz, Sidney. 1997. Swallowing Modernity. In *Golden Arches East: McDonald's in East Asia*. J. L. Watson, ed. Palo Alto: Stanford University Press.

Ng, Wai-ming. 2001. Popularization and Localization of Sushi in Singapore: An Ethnographic Survey. *New Zealand Journal of Asian Studies* 3(1):7–19.

Nishiyama. Matsunosuke, et al., eds. 1984. *Edogaku jiten* (Encyclopedia of Edo studies). Tokyo: Kobundo.

Noguchi, Paul. 1994. Ekiben: The Fast Food of High-Speed Japan. *Ethnology* 33(4):317–30.

Tamamura, Toyo. 2000. *Kaittn-zushi sekai hitomeguri* (Rotary sushi around the world). Tokyo: Sekaibunkasha.

Tokyo-to. 1992. Shijo Memo (Market memo). Tokyo: Tokyo-to Chuo Oroshiuri Shijo.

Shijo Mtmo (Market memo). Tokyo: Tokyo-to Chuo Oroshiuri Shijo.

———1996. Dai jurokkai seisen shokuryohin oyobi kaki shobi-kambai doko: Chosa Kekka (Results of the sixteenth survey of consumption and sales trends for perishable foodstuffs and flowers). Tokyo: Tokyo-to Chuo Oroshiuri Shijo Tsukiji Shijo.

van Wolferen, Karel. 1990. *The Enigma of Japanese Power*. New York: Vintage.

Watanabe Yonehide. 2002. Kaittn-zushi no ktizaigaku (The economics of kaiten-zushi). Tokyo: Besuto Shinsho.

Yagyu Kyube'e. 2003. Kaittn-zushi no sa-sushi-st-so (The ABCs of kaittn-zushi). Tokyo: Ekusunoreji.

Yamashita Machiko. 1998. From Kitchen: Katei no Shokuji. Osaka: Osaka Gasu Enerugi Bunka Kenkyujo.

BIBLIOGRAPHY

Abu-Lughod, Lila. 1991. Writing Against Culture. In *Recapturing Anthropology: Working in the Present,* Richard G. Fox, ed., pp. 137–162. Santa Fe: SAR Press.

———. 1995. A Tale of Two Pregnancies. In *Women Writing Culture,* Ruth Behar and Deborah A. Gordon, eds., pp. 339–349. Berkeley: University of California Press.

Acker, Jenny C., and Isaac M. Mbiti. 2010. Mobile Phones and Economic Development in Africa. *Journal of Economic Perspectives* 24(3):207–232.

Adams, R. M. 1966. *The Evolution of Urban Society.* Chicago: Aldine.

Agar, Michael H. 1980. *The Professional Stranger: An Informal Introduction to Ethnography.* New York: Academic Press.

Antonio, Robert J. and Alessandro Bonanno. 2000. A New Global Capitalism? From "Americanism and Fordism" to "Americanization-Globalization." *American Studies* 41:2/3: 33–77.

Applebaum, Herbert, ed. 1987. *Perspectives in Cultural Anthropology.* Albany: State University of New York Press.

Ardrey, Robert. 1961. *African Genesis.* New York: Atheneum Publishers.

Asad, Talal. 1973. *Anthropology and the Colonial Encounter.* London: Ithaca Press.

Atkinson, J. J. 1903. *Primal Law.* London, New York, and Bombay: Longman, Green.

Axelrod, Robert. 1984. *The Evolution of Cooperation.* New York: Basic Books.

Bachofen, Johann Jakob. 1992 [1861]. *Das Mutterrecht.* In *Myth, Religion and Mother Right: Selected Writings of J. J. Bachofen,* Ralph Manheim, trans. Princeton, NJ: Princeton University Press.

Barash, D. 1979. *The Whisperings Within.* New York: Harper and Row.

Barnes, Harry E. 1960. Foreword. In *Essays in the Science of Culture in Honor of Leslie A. White,* Gertrude E. Dole and Robert L. Carneiro, eds., pp. xi–xvi. New York: Crowell.

Barnouw, Victor. 1957. The Amiable Side of "Patterns of Culture." *American Anthropologist.* 59(3):532–536.

Barton, Ruth. 1998. "Huxley, Lubbock, and Half a Dozen Others: Professionals and Gentlemen in the Formation of the X Club 1851–1864." *The History of Science Society.* 89(3):410–440.

Bateson, Gregory. 1958 [1936]. *Naven.* Palo Alto, CA: Stanford University Press.

Bateson, Gregory, and Margaret Mead. 1942. *Balinese Character: A Photographic Analysis.* New York: New York Academy of Sciences.

Bateson, M. C. 1984. *With a Daughter's Eye: A Memoir of Margaret Mead and Gregory Bateson.* New York: William Morrow.

Bauer, Bruno. 1974 [1841–42]. *Kritik der Evangelischen Geschichte der Synoptiken.* New York: Hildesheim.

Beardsley, Richard K. 1976. An Appraisal of Leslie A. White's Scholarly Influence. *American Anthropologist* 78(3):617–620.

Behar, Ruth, and Deborah A. Gordon. 1995. *Women Writing Culture.* Berkeley: University of California Press.

Behar, Ruth. 1995. Introduction: Out of Exile. In *Women Writing Culture,* Ruth Behar and Deborah A. Gordon, eds., pp. 1–29. Berkeley: University of California Press.

Bell, V. 1993. *Interrogating Incest: Feminism, Foucault, and the Law.* London: Routledge.

Benedict, Ruth Fulton. 1930. Psychological Types in the Cultures of the Southwest. In *Proceedings of the Twenty-Third International Congress of Americanists* (held at New York, September 17–22, 1928), pp. 572–581. Lancaster, PA: Science Press Printing.

————. 1934a. Anthropology and the Abnormal. *Journal of General Psychology* 10(2):59–82.

————. 1934b. *Patterns of Culture*. Boston, New York: Houghton Mifflin.

————. 1946. *The Chrysanthemum and the Sword: Patterns of Japanese Culture*. Boston: Houghton Mifflin.

————. 1948. Anthropology and the Humanities. *American Anthropologist* 50:585–593.

Benedict, Ruth Fulton, and Gene Weltfish. 1943. *The Races of Mankind*. New York: Public Affairs Committee.

Benjamin, Walter. 1969 [1936]. The Work of Art in the Age of Mechanical Reproduction. In *Illuminations*, H. Arendt, ed., pp. 217–252.

Bennett, John W. and Michio Nagai. 1953. Echoes: Reactions to American Anthropology. *American Anthropologist*. 55(3): 404–411.

Bentham, Jeremy. 1789. *An Introduction to the Principles of Morals and Legislation*. London.

Ben-Zvi, Yael. 2007. Where Did Red Go? Lewis Henry Morgan's Evolutionary Inheritance and the US Racial Imagination. *The New Centennial Review*. 7(2): 201–229.

Berlin, Brent O., Dennis Breedlove, and Peter Raven. 1974. *Principles of Tzeltal Plant Classification*. New York: Academic Press.

Bettelheim, Bruno. 1955. *Symbolic Wounds: Puberty Rites and the Envious Male*. London: Thames and Hudson.

Bharati, Agehananda. 1970. The Hindu Renaissance and its Apologetic Patterns. *The Journal of Asian Studies*. 29(2): 267–287.

Blackburn, J. 1994. *Daisy Bates in the Desert: A Woman's Life among the Aborigines*. London: Secker & Warburg.

Boas, Franz. 1896. The Limitations of the Comparative Method in Anthropology. *Science*, n.s., 4: 901–908.

————. 1901. The Mind of Primitive Man. *The Journal of American Folklore* 14(52):1–11.

————. 1911. *Handbook of American Indian Languages*, Part 1. Smithsonian Institution, Washington DC, Bureau of American Ethnology, Bulletin 40.

————. 1912. Changes in the Bodily Form of Descendants of Immigrants. *American Anthropologist* 14(3): 530–562.

————. 1974. [1938]. *The Background of My Early Thinking: The Shaping of American Anthropology 1883–1911: A Franz Boas Reader*. G. Stocking, ed. New York, Basic Books: 41–42.

Bock, Phillip K. 1988. *Rethinking Psychological Anthropology*. New York: W. H. Freeman.

Borofsky, Robert, ed. 1994. *Assessing Cultural Anthropology*. New York: McGraw-Hill.

Bottomore, T. 1991. Lumpenproletariat. In *A Dictionary of Marxist Thought*, T. Bottomore, ed., p. 327. Oxford: Basil Blackwell.

Bourdieu, Pierre. 1990 (orig. 1980). *The Logic of Practice*. Palo Alto, CA: Stanford Univ. Press.

————. 2002 (1972) *Outline of a Theory of Practice*. Richard Nice, trans. Cambridge: Cambridge University Press.

————. 1990 (orig. 1980). *The Logic of Practice*. Palo Alto, CA: Stanford Univ. Press.

Bourgois, Philippe. 1995. From Jíbaro to Crack Dealer: Confronting the Restructuring of Capitalism in El Barrio. In *Articulating Hidden Histories: Exploring the Influence of Eric R. Wolf*, Jane Schneider and Rayna Rapp, eds., pp. 125–141. Berkeley: University of California Press.

Boyne, Roy. 1966. Structuralism. In *The Blackwell Companion to Social Theory*, Bryan S. Turner, ed., pp. 194–220. Oxford: Blackwell.

Briggs, Jean L. 1970. *Never in Anger: Portrait of an Eskimo Family*. Cambridge, MA: Harvard University Press.

Brillouin, Leon. 1956. *Science and Information Theory*. New York: Academic Press.

Brown, Dee. 1971. *Bury My Heart at Wounded Knee*. New York: Holt, Rinehart, and Winston.

Brown, D. E. 1991. *Human Universals*. New York: McGraw-Hill.

Brown, Jerram L. 1983. Cooperation—A Biologist's Dilemma. *Advances in the Study of Behavior* 13:1–37.

Brown, Norman O. 1959. *Life Against Death: The Psychoanalytical Meaning of History*. Middletown, CT: Wesleyan University Press.

Bucher, Bernadette, and Claude Lévi-Strauss. 1985. An Interview with Claude Lévi-Strauss 30 June 1982. *American Ethnologist* 12(2):360–368.

Bücher, Carl. 1968 [1901]. *Industrial Evolution*. New York: Augustus M. Kelley.

Buffon, Georges Louis Leclerc. 1752–1799. *Histoire naturelle, générale et particulier*. Paris: De l'Imprimerie Royale.

Carneiro, Robert L. 1970. A Theory of the Origin of the State. *Science* 169:733–738.

———. 1981. Leslie White. In *Totems and Teachers: Perspectives on the History of Anthropology*. New York: Columbia University Press.

Carneiro, Robert L., ed. 1967. *The Evolution of Society: Selections from Herbert Spencer's Principles of Sociology*. Chicago: University of Chicago Press.

Caspari, Rachel. 2003. From Types to Populations: A Century of Race, Physical Anthropology, and the American Anthropological Association. *American Anthropologist* 105(1): 65–76.

Casson, Ronald W. 1983. Schemata in Cognitive Anthropology. *Annual Reviews of Anthropology*. 12: 429–462.

Chagnon, Napoleon. 1968. *The Fierce People*. New York: Holt, Rinehart, and Winston.

Chayanov, Aleksandr V. 1966. *The Theory of Peasant Economy*. Daniel Thorner, Basile Kerblay, and R. E. F. Smith, eds. Homewood, IL: R. D. Irwin.

Childe, V. Gordon. 1942. *What Happened in History*. Baltimore: Penguin.

Chodorow, Nancy. 1974. Family Structure and Feminine Personality. In *Woman, Culture, and Society*, Michelle Rosaldo and Louise Lamphere, eds., pp. 43–66. Palo Alto, CA: Stanford University Press.

Clifford, James, and George E. Marcus, eds. 1986. *Writing Culture: The Poetics and Politics of Ethnography*. Berkeley: University of California Press.

Cole, Douglas. 1983. "The Value of a Person Lies in His Herzensbildung, Franz Boas' Baffin Island Letter-Diary, 1883–1884." In *Observers Observed: Essays on Ethnographic Fieldwork*, George Stocking, ed., pp. 13–52. Madison: University of Wisconsin.

Collier, Jane F. 1974. Women in Politics. In *Woman, Culture, and Society*, Michelle Rosaldo and Louise Lamphere, eds., pp. 89–96. Palo Alto, CA: Stanford University Press.

Collier, Jane F., and Sylvia Yanagisako, eds. 1987. *Gender and Kinship*. Palo Alto, CA: Stanford University Press.

Comte, August. 1975 [1922]. Plan of the Scientific Operations Necessary for Reorganizing Society. In *Auguste Comte and Positivism: The Essential Writings*, Gertrud Lenzer, ed., pp. 9–69. New York: Harper Torchbooks.

Condorcet, Jean-Antoine-Nicholas. 1902 [1794]. *Esquisse d'un tableau historique des progrès de l'esprit humain*. Paris: Bibliothèque Nationale.

Conkey, Margaret, and Janet Spector. 1984. Archaeology and the Study of Gender. *Advances in Archaeological Method and Theory* 7:1–38.

Copeland, Lennie. 1985. *Going International: How to Make Friends and Deal Effectively in the Global Marketplace*. New York: Random House.

Coquery-Vidrovitch, Catherine. 1978. Researches on an African Mode of Production. In *Relations of Production: Marxist Approaches to Economic Anthropology*, David Sedden, ed., pp. 261–288. London: Frank Cass.

Corning, Peter A. 1982. Durkheim and Spencer. *The British Journal of Sociology*. 33(3): 359–382.

Cosmides, L., and J. Tooby. 1997. *Evolutionary Psychology: A Primer*. http://www.psych.ucsb.edu/_research/cep/primer.htm, retrieved October 20, 1998.

Crapo, Richley H. 1993. *Cultural Anthropology: Understanding Ourselves and Others*. Guilford, CT: Dushkin Publishing Group.

Crocker, J. Christopher. 1977. My Brother the Parrot. In *The Social Use of Metaphor: Essays on the Anthropology of Rhetoric*, J. David Sapir and J. Christopher Crocker, eds., pp. 164–192. Philadelphia: University of Pennsylvania Press.

Crosby, Alfred W. 1989. *America's Forgotten Pandemic: The Influenza of 1918*. Cambridge: Cambridge University Press.

D'Andrade, Roy. 1995a. *The Development of Cognitive Anthropology*. Cambridge: Cambridge University Press.

———. 1995b. Moral Models in Anthropology. *Current Anthropology* 36(3):399–408.

Darnell, Regna. 2001. *Invisible Genealogies: A History of Americanist Anthropology*. Lincoln: University of Nebraska Press.

Darwin, Charles. 1858. On the Tendency of Species to Form Varieties; and On the Perpetuation of Varieties and Species by Natural Means of Selection. *Journal of the Linnean Society* 3:45–62.

———. 1871. *The Descent of Man and Selection in Relation to Sex*. London: John Murray.

———. 1883 [1868]. *The Variation of Animals and Plants under Domestication*, 2nd ed. New York: D. Appleton.

———. 1952 [1839]. *Journal of Researches* (reprint). New York: Hafner.

———. 1988 [1859]. *On the Origin of Species*. New York: New York University Press.

Davis, K. and Wilbert Moore. 1945. Some Principles of Stratification. *American Sociological Review* 10: 242–249.

———. 1953. Replies to Tumin. *American Sociological Review* 18:394–396.

Davidson, Arnold I. 2005. Ethics as Ascetics: Foucault, the History of Ethics, and Ancient Thought. Pages 123–149 in *The Cambridge Companion to Foucault.* Gary Gutting, Ed. Cambridge: Cambridge University Press.

Dawkins, Richard. 1976. *The Selfish Gene.* New York: Oxford University Press.

Deacon, Desley. 1999. *Elsie Clews Parsons: Inventing Modern Life.* Chicago: University of Chicago Press.

de Beauvoir, Simone. 1952. *The Second Sex*, H. M. Parshley, ed. and trans. New York: Knopf.

Deflem, Mathieu, Ritual, Anti-structure, and Religion: A discussion of Victor Turner's Processual Symbolic Analysis. Journal for the Scientific Study of Religion 1991, 30(1): 1–25.

Delegorgue, Adulphe. 1847 [1990]. *Travels in Southern Africa.* Durbin: Killie Campbell Africana Library; Pietermaritzburg: University of Natal Press.

Deloria, Vine, Jr. 1969. *Custer Died for Your Sins: An Indian Manifesto.* New York: Macmillan.

Derrida, Jacques. 1970. Structure, Sign, and Play in the Discourse of the Human Sciences. Pp. 247–265 in Richard Macksey and Eugenio Donato, eds. The Languages of criticism and the sciences of man: the structuralist controversy. Baltimore: Johns Hopkins.

———. 1998 (orig. 1967) *Of Grammatology.* Baltimore: Johns Hopkins.

Derry, George H. 1902. The Personal Side of Herbert Spencer. *The Sewanee Review.* 10(1):1–11.

Desmond, Adrian. 2001. Redefining the X Axis: "Professionals," "Amateurs" and the Making of Mid-Victorian Biology: A Progress Report. *Journal of the History of Biology.* 34(1):3–50.

Devereux, G. 1961. Shamans as Neurotics. *American Anthropologist* 63:1088–1090.

Devons, Ely, and Max Gluckman. 1964. Conclusion: Modes and Consequences of Limiting a Field of Study. In *Closed Systems and Open Minds*, Max Gluckman, ed., pp. 254–259. Chicago: Aldine.

Diamond, Stanley, ed. 1960. *Culture in History: Essays in Honor of Paul Radin.* New York: Columbia University.

di Leonardo, Micaela. 1991. Introduction to Gender, Culture, and Political Economy: Feminist Anthropology in Historical Perspective. In *Gender at the Crossroads of Knowledge,* Micaela di Leonardo, ed., pp. 1–48. Berkeley: University of California Press.

Dillon, Wilton S. 1980. Margaret Mead and Government. *American Anthropologist.* 82(2): 319–339.

Dolgin, Janet L., David S. Kemnitzer, and David M. Schneider. 1977. *Symbolic Anthropology.* New York: Columbia University Press.

Douglas, Mary. 1966. *Purity and Danger: An Analysis of the Concepts of Pollution and Taboo.* London: Routledge and Kegan Paul.

———. 1970. *Natural Symbols: Explorations in Cosmology.* New York: Pantheon Books.

Dupré, Wilhelm. 1969. Paul Joachim Shebesta (1887–1967). *History of Religions.* 8(3):260–266.

Durkheim, Émile. 1933 [1893]. *The Division of Labor in Society,* George Simpson, trans. New York: Macmillan.

———. 1951 [1897]. *Suicide: A Study in Sociology,* Jon A. Spaulding and George Simpson, trans. New York: Free Press.

———. 1965 [1912]. *The Elementary Forms of the Religious Life,* Joseph Swain, trans. New York: Free Press.

Durkheim, Émile, and Marcel Mauss. 1963 [1903]. *Primitive Classification,* Rodney Needham, trans. Chicago: University of Chicago Press.

Economist. 2005. Race in Malaysia: Failing to Spread the Wealth. *The Economist* April 25, 2005. http://www.economist.com/world/asia/displayStory._cfm?story_id=4323219

Eiseley, Loren. 1961. *Darwin's Century: Evolution and the Men Who Discovered It.* New York: Anchor Books.

Elkin, A. P. 1941. Native Languages and the Field Worker in Australia. *American Anthropologist* 43(1): 89–94.

Engels, Friedrich. 1949 [1888]. *Ludwig Feuerbach and the End of Classical German Philosophy.* Moscow, Foreign Languages Publishing House.

———. 1972 [1884]. *The Origin of the Family, Private Property, and the State.* New York: Pathfinder Press.

Erickson, P. A. W., and L. D. Murphy. 1998. *A History of Anthropological Theory.* Ontario: Broadview Press.

Evans-Pritchard, E. E. 1940. *The Nuer: A Description of the Modes of Livelihood and Political Institutions of a Nilotic People.* Oxford: Oxford University Press.

———. 1951a. *Kinship and Marriage Among the Nuer.* Oxford: Clarendon Press.

———. 1951b. *Social Anthropology.* New York: Free Press.

———. 1956. *Nuer Religion.* Oxford: Clarendon Press.

Fagan, Brian M. 1989. *People of the Earth: An Introduction to World Prehistory.* Glenview, IL: Scott, Foresman.

Fessler, Daniel. 1995. *A Small Field with a Lot of Hornets: An Exploration of Shame, Motivation, and Social Control*. Ph.D. dissertation, University of California, San Diego.

Firth, Raymond. 1964. The Place of Malinowski in the History of Economic Anthropology. In *Man and Culture: An Evaluation of the Work of Bronislaw Malinowski*, Raymond Firth, ed., pp. 209–227. New York: Harper and Row.

———. 1973. *Symbols, Public and Private*. Ithaca, NY: Cornell University Press.

Flannery, Kent V. 1972. The Cultural Evolution of Civilizations. *Annual Review of Ecological Systems* 3:399–426.

Forbes. 2006. Lists, Billionaires, #114 Robert Kuok. http://www.forbes.com/lists/2006/10/ARHN.html.

Fortes, Meyer, and E. E. Evans-Pritchard. 1967 [1940]. *African Political Systems*. London: Oxford University Press.

Foucault, Michel. 1965 [1961]. *Madness and Civilization*. New York: Pantheon.

———. 1972. *The Archaeology of Knowledge*, A. M. Sheridan Smith, trans. New York: Harper Colophon.

———. 1978. *The History of Sexuality*, vol. 1, *An Introduction*. New York: Pantheon.

———. 1980. Truth and Power. In *Power/Knowledge: Selected Interviews and Other Writings, 1972–1977 by Michel Foucault*. Colin Gordon, ed., pp. 109–133. New York: Pantheon.

Fox, Robin. 1972. In the Beginning: Aspects of Hominid Behavioral Evolution. In *Perspectives on Human Evolution*, Sherwood L. Washburn and Phyllis Dolhinow, eds., pp. 358–381. New York: Holt, Rinehart, and Winston.

Frake, Charles. 1962. The Ethnographic Study of Cognitive Systems. In *Anthropology and Human Behavior*, Thomas Gladwin and William D. Sturtevant, eds., pp. 72–85. Washington: Anthropological Society of Washington.

Frank, G. 1997. Jews, Multiculturalism, and Boasian Anthropology. *American Anthropologist* 99(4):731–745.

Frazer, James George. 1911–1915 [1890]. *The Golden Bough: A Study in Magic and Religion*, 3rd ed. London: Macmillan.

Freeman, Derek. 1983. *Margaret Mead and Samoa: The Making and Unmaking of an Anthropological Myth*. Cambridge: Harvard University.

Frère, Bruno. 2004. Genetic Structuralism, psychological sociology and pragmatic social actor theory, Proposals for a Convergence of French Sociologies. *Theory, Culture, Society*. 21(3): 85–99.

Freud, Sigmund. 1939. *Moses and Monotheism,* Katherine Jones, trans. London: Hogarth Press.

———. 1950 [1913]. *Totem and Taboo: Some Points of Agreement between the Mental Lives of Savages and Neurotics,* James Strachey, trans. New York: W. W. Norton.

———. 1960 [1905]. *Jokes and Their Relation to the Unconscious,* James Strachey, trans. New York: W. W. Norton.

———. 1961 [1930]. *Civilization and Its Discontents,* James Strachey, trans. New York: W. W. Norton.

———. 1961 [1928]. *The Future of an Illusion,* James Strachey, trans. New York: W. W. Norton.

———. 1963 [1900]. *On Dreams,* James Strachey, trans. New York: W. W. Norton.

Fried, Morton. 1967. *The Evolution of Political Society.* New York: Random House.

Friedl, Ernestine. 1975. *Women and Men: An Anthropologist's View.* New York: Holt, Rinehart, and Winston.

Friedman, Jonathan. 1974. Marxism, Structuralism, and Vulgar Materialism. *Man* 9(3):444–469.

Frye, Northrop. 1964. *The Educated Imagination.* Bloomington: Indiana University Press.

Gadamer, Hans-Georg. 1975. *Truth and Method,* Garren Burden and John Cumming, trans. New York: Seabury Press.

Galton, F., Sir. 1869. *Hereditary Genius: An Inquiry into its Laws and Consequences.* London: Macmillan.

———. 1883. *Inquiries into Human Faculty and Its Development.* New York: Macmillan.

Garbarino, Merwyn S. 1977. *Sociocultural Theory in Anthropology.* New York: Holt, Rinehart, and Winston.

Gardner, Helen, and Robin J. Wilson. 1993. Thomas Archer Hirst—Mathematician Xtravagant V. London in the 1860s. *The American Mathematical Monthly.* 100(9): 827–834.

Geertz, Clifford. 1963a. *Agricultural Involution: The Processes of Ecological Change in Indonesia.* Berkeley: University of California Press.

———. 1963b. *Peddlers and Princes: Social Development and Economic Change in Two Indonesian Towns.* Chicago: University of Chicago Press.

———. 1973. *The Interpretation of Cultures.* New York: Basic Books.

———. 1975. On the Nature of Anthropological Understanding. *American Scientist* 63:1, 47–53.

———. 1984. Distinguished Lecture: Anti Anti-Relativism. *American Anthropologist.* 86(2): 273–278.

———. 1986. Making Experience Authoring Selves. In *The Anthropology of Experience,* Victor W. Turner and Edward M. Bruner, eds., pp. 373–380. Urbana: University of Illinois Press.

Gennep, Arnold van. 1960 [1909]. *The Rites of Passage,* Monica Vizedom and Gabrielle L. Caffee, trans. Chicago: University of Chicago Press.

Gerth, H. H., and C. Wright Mills. 1946. Introduction: The Man and His Work. In *From Max Weber: Essays in Sociology,* H. H. Gerth and C. Wright Mills, eds., pp. 1–74. New York: Oxford University Press.

Gibbon, Edward. 1942 [1776–1788]. *The Decline and Fall of the Roman Empire.* New York: E. P. Dutton.

Gillis, John R. 2000. *Our Virtual Families: Toward a Cultural Understanding of Modern Family Life.* Working Paper No. 2, The Emory Center for Myth and Ritual in American Life Department of History, Rutgers University, New Brunswick, NJ.

Gleick, James. 1987. *Chaos: Making a New Science.* New York: Viking.

Gluckman, Max. 1947. Malinowski's Contribution to Social Anthropology. *African Studies* 6:57–76.

———. 1949. *Malinowski's Sociological Theories.* Rhodes-Livingstone Paper 16. Livingstone, Northern Rhodesia: Rhodes-Livingstone Institute.

———. 1954. *Rituals of Rebellion in South-East Africa.* The Frazer Lecture 1952. Manchester: Manchester University Press.

———. 1956. *Custom and Conflict in Africa.* Glencoe, IL: Free Press.

———. 1967 [1956]. The Peace in the Feud. In *Custom and Conflict in Africa,* pp. 2–26. New York: Barnes and Noble.

Goldenweiser, Alexander. 1910. Totemism: An Analytical Study. *Journal of American Folklore* 23:179.

———. 1917. The Autonomy of the Social. *American Anthropologist* 19(3):447–449.

Goodenough, Ward. 1956. Componential Analysis and the Study of Meaning. *Language* 32:195–216.

Goody, Jack. 1977. *The Domestication of the Savage Mind.* Cambridge: Cambridge University Press.

———. 1995. *The Expansive Moment: Anthropology in Britain and Africa 1918–1970.* Cambridge: Cambridge University Press.

Gorer, Geoffrey, and John Rickman. 1962 [1949]. *The People of Great Russia: A Psychological Study.* New York: W. W. Norton.

Gould, Stephen Jay. 1981. *The Mismeasure of Man.* New York: W. W. Norton.

———. 1989. *Wonderful Life: The Burgess Shale and the Nature of History.* New York: W. W. Norton.

———. 1994. Cabinet Museums Revisited. *Natural History* 103(1):12–20.

Graebner, F. 1911. *Die Methode der Ethnologie.* Heidelberg: C. Winter.

Gramsci, Antonio. 1994. *Letters from Prison,* Frank Rosengarten, ed.; Raymond Rosenthal, trans. New York: Columbia University Press.

Graves, Robert. 1948. *The White Goddess.* New York: Vintage Books.

Gross, Feliks. 1986. Young Malinowski and His Later Years. *American Ethnologist* 13(3):556–570.

Gunder-Frank, A. 1966. The Development of Underdevelopment. *Monthly Review* 18(4):17–31.

Handler, Richard. 1991. An Interview with Clifford Geertz. *Current Anthropology* 32(5):603–613.

Hardin, Garrett. 1968. The Tragedy of the Commons. *Science* 162(13 December):1243–1248.

Harris, Marvin. 1968. *The Rise of Anthropological Theory.* New York: Thomas Y. Crowell.

———. 1974. *Cows, Pigs, Wars and Witches: The Riddles of Culture.* New York: Random House.

———. 1977. *Cannibals and Kings: The Origins of Culture.* New York: Random House.

———. 1979. *Cultural Materialism: The Struggle for a Science of Culture.* New York: Random House.

———. 1981. *America Now: The Anthropology of a Changing Culture.* New York: Simon and Schuster.

———. 1985. *Good to Eat: Riddles of Food and Culture.* New York: Simon and Schuster.

———. 1994. Cultural Materialism Is Alive and Well and Won't Go Away Until Something Better Comes Along. In *Assessing Cultural Anthropology,* R. Borofsky, ed., pp. 62–76. New York: McGraw-Hill.

Harrison, Faye V., ed. 1991. *Decolonizing Anthropology: Moving Further Toward an Anthropology for Liberation.* Washington, DC: American Anthropological Association, Association of Black Anthropologists.

Harrison, Lawrence E. 1992. *Who Prospers?: How Cultural Values Shape Economic and Political Success.* New York: Basic Books.

Harrison, Lawrence E., and Samuel Huntington, eds. 2001. *Culture Matters: How Values Shape Human Progress.* New York: Basic.

Herdt, Gilbert. 1984. *Ritualized Homosexuality in Melanesia*. Berkeley: University of California.

Herskovits, Melville. 1957. Some Further Notes on Franz Boas' Arctic Expedition. *American Anthropologist* 59:112–116.

Hertz, Robert. 1973 [1909]. The Pre-eminence of the Right Hand: A Study in Religious Polarity. In *Right and Left: Essays on Dual Symbolic Classification*, Rodney Needham, ed., pp. 3–31. Chicago: University of Chicago Press.

Hill, K. 1988. Macronutrient Modifications of Optimal Foraging Theory: An Approach Using Indifference Curves Applied to Some Modern Foragers. *Human Ecology* 16:157–197.

Hill, K., H. Kaplan, K. Hawkes, A. M. Hurtado. 1987. Foraging Decisions Among Ache Hunter-Gatherers: New Data and Implications for Optimal Foraging Models. *Ethnology and Sociobiology*. 8:1–36.

Hobbes, Thomas. 1983 [1651]. *Leviathan*. London: Dent.

Hockett, Charles F. 1973. *Man's Place in Nature*. New York: McGraw-Hill.

Hoebel, E. Adamson. 1949. *Man in the Primitive World: An Introduction to Anthropology*. New York: McGraw-Hill.

Hoernle, Agnes Winnifred. 1925. The Social Organization of the Nama Hottentots of Southwest Africa. *American Anthropologist* 27(1):1–24.

Holland, Dorothy, and Debra Skinner. 1987. Prestige and Intimacy, the Cultural Models Behind Americans' Talk about Gender Types. In *Cultural Models in Language and Thought*, D. Holland and N. Quinn, eds., pp. 78–111. New York: Cambridge University Press.

Holmes, G. 1914. Areas of American Culture Characterization Tentatively Outlined as an Aid in the Study of Antiquities. *American Anthropologist* 16:413–416.

Hsu, Francis L. K. 1980. Margaret Mead and Psychological Anthropology. *American Anthropologist* 82(2): 349–353.

Humboldt, Alexander von. 1874 [1845–1862]. *Kosmos*. Stuttgart: J. G. Cotta.

Humboldt, Wilhelm von. 1963. *Humanist Without a Portfolio: An Anthology of the Writings of Wilhelm von Humboldt*, Marianne Cowen, trans. Detroit: Wayne State University Press.

Hume, Brad D. 2008. Quantifying Characters: Polygenist Anthropologists and the Hardening of Heredity. *Journal of the History of Biology*. 41: 119–158.

Hurteau, Pierre. 1993. Catholic Moral Discourses on Male Sodomy and Masturbation in the Seventeenth and Eighteenth Centuries. *Journal of the History of Sexuality*. 4(1): 1–26.

Hutchins, Edwin. 1994. *Cognition in the Wild*. Cambridge: MIT Press.

Hyatt, Marshall. 1990. *Franz Boas, Social Activist: The Dynamics of Ethnicity*. New York: Greenwood Press.

Hymes, Dell. 1972. *Reinventing Anthropology*. New York: Pantheon.

Jacknis, Ira. 2002. The First Boasian: Alfred Kroeber and Franz Boas, 1896–1905. *American Anthropologist* 104(2):520–529.

Jameson, Fredric. 1991. *Postmodernism, or, The Cultural Logic of Late Capitalism*. Durham, NC: Duke University.

Jha, Stefania Ruzsits. 1995. Michael Polany's Integrative Philosophy. *Polanyiana*. 5(2):36–65.

Jung, Carl Gustave. 1971 [1923]. *Psychological Types*. Princeton, NJ: Princeton University Press.

Kaplan, David, and Robert A. Manners. 1972. *Cultural Theory*. Englewood Cliffs, NJ: Prentice-Hall.

Kaplan, Robert. 1994. The Coming Anarchy. *Atlantic Monthly* 273(2):44–76.

Karp, Ivan, and Kent Maynard. 1983. Reading the Nuer. *Current Anthropology* 24(4):481–503.

Kenyatta, Jomo. 1979 [1938]. *Facing Mount Kenya: The Traditional Life of the Gikuyu*. London: Heinemann.

Keys, Ancel. 1943. Physical Performance in Relation to Diet. *Federation Proceedings* 2:164–187.

———. 1946. Nutrition and Capacity for Work. *Occupational Medicine* 2:536–545.

Kirchhoff, Paul. 1935 [1955]. Principles of Clanship in Human Society. *Davidson Journal of Anthropology* 1:1–10.

Kormondy, E. J., and D. E. Brown. 1998. *Fundamentals of Human Ecology*. Upper Saddle River: Prentice Hall.

Kottak, Conrad Phillip. 1994. *Cultural Anthropology*. New York: McGraw-Hill.

Kroeber, A. L. 1901. Decorative Symbolism of the Arapaho. *American Anthropologist* 3:308–336.

———. 1917. The Superorganic. *American Anthropologist* 19:163–213.

———. 1925. *Handbook of the Indians of California*. Bulletin of the Bureau of American Ethnology, 78.

———. 1939. *Cultural and Natural Areas of Native North America*. Berkeley: University of California Press.

———. 1940. Psychotic Factors in Shamanism. *Character and Personality* 8:204–215.

———. 1959. The History of Personality in Anthropology. *American Anthropologist* 61(3):398–404.

Kuhn, Thomas S. 1962. *The Structure of Scientific Revolutions*. Chicago: University of Chicago Press.

Kuklick, H. 1991. *The Savage Within: The Social History of British Anthropology, 1885–1945*. Cambridge: Cambridge University Press.

Kurtz, Donald V. 1996. Hegemony and Anthropology: Gramsci, Exegesis, Reinterpretations. *Critique of Anthropology* 16(2):103–135.

Kwenda, Chirevo V. 1993. *True Colors: A Critical Assessment of Victor Turner's Study of Ndembu Religion*. Ph.D. dissertation. Department of Religion, Syracuse University.

LaCapra, Dominick. 1972. *Emile Durkheim: Sociologist and Philosopher*. Ithaca: Cornell University.

Lacoste, Yves. 1984. *Ibn Khaldun: The Birth of History and the Past of the Third World*. London: Verso.

Lafitau, Joseph-Francois. 1724. *Mœurs des Sauvages Ameriquains*. Paris: Saugrain.

Lamphere, Louise. 1987. The Struggle to Reshape Our Thinking About Gender. In *The Impact of Feminist Research in the Academy*, Christie Farnham, ed., pp. 11–33. Bloomington: Indiana University Press.

———. 2004. Unofficial Histories: A Vision of Anthropology from the Margins. *American Anthropologist* 106(1):126–139.

Langness, L. L. 1987. *The Study of Culture*. Novato, CA: Chandler and Sharp.

Lavery, David. 2001. The Imagination of Insurance: Wallace Stevens and Benjamin Lee Whorf at The Hartford. *Legal Studies Forum* 24(3–4):481–492.

Layton, Robert. 1997. *An Introduction to Theory in Anthropology*. Cambridge: Cambridge University Press.

Le Bon, Gustave. 1977 [1895]. *The Crowd: A Study of the Popular Mind*. New York: Penguin Books.

Leach, Edmund R. 1954. *Political Systems of Highland Burma: A Study of Kachin Social Structure*. London: London School of Economics and Political Science.

———. 1976. *Claude Lévi-Strauss*. New York: Penguin Books.

———. 1984. Glimpses of the Unmentionable in the History of British Social Anthropology. In *Annual Review of Anthropology*, Bernard Siegel, Alan Beals, and Stephen Tyler, eds., Vol. 13, pp. 1–23. Palo Alto, CA: Annual Reviews.

Leacock, Eleanor. 1983. Interpreting the Origins of Gender Inequality: Conceptual and Historical Problems. *Dialectial Anthropology* 7(4):263–284.

Leacock, Seth. 1954. The Ethnological Theory of Marcel Mauss. *American Anthropologist*. 56:58–71.

Leaf, Murray J. 1979. *Man, Mind, and Science: A History of Anthropology*. New York: Columbia University Press.

Lehman, David. 1992. Paul de Man: The Plot Thickens. *New York Times Book Review*, May 24.

Lesser, Alexander. 1981. Franz Boas. In *Totems and Teachers: Perspectives on the History of Anthropology*, Sydel Silverman, ed., pp. 1–31. New York: Columbia University Press.

Lett, James. 1987. *The Human Enterprise: A Critical Introduction to Anthropological Theory*. Boulder, CO: Westview Press.

———. 1997. *Science, Reason and Anthropology: The Principles of Rational Inquiry*. Lanham, MD: Rowman & Littlefield.

Levine, Norman. 1987. The German Historical School of Law and the Origins of Historical Materialism. *Journal of the History of Ideas*. 48(3): 431–451.

LeVine, Robert A.. 2007. Ethnographic Studies of Childhood: A Historical Overview. *American Anthropologist*. 109(2):247–260.

Lévi-Strauss, Claude 1951 Language and the Analysis of Social Laws. *American Anthropologist*. 53(2): 155–163.

———. 1963a. The Effectiveness of Symbols. In *Structural Anthropology*, pp. 186–205. New York: Basic Books.

———. 1963b. Structural Analysis in Linguistics and in Anthropology. In *Structural Anthropology*, pp. 31–54. New York: Basic Books.

———. 1963c. The Structural Study of Myth. In *Structural Anthropology*, pp. 206–231. New York: Basic Books.

———. 1969 [1949]. *The Elementary Structures of Kinship*, rev. ed. Boston: Beacon Press.

———. 1969. *The Raw and the Cooked*. New York: Harper and Row.

———. 1973. *From Honey to Ashes*. Chicago: University of Chicago Press.

Levy-Bruhl, Lucien. 1966 [1910]. *How Natives Think*, Lillian A. Clare, trans. New York: Washington Square Press.

Lewis, Herbert S. 2001. The Passion of Franz Boas. *American Anthropologist* 103(2):447–467.

Lichtheim, G. 1973. Marx and the Asiatic Mode of Production. In *Karl Marx,* T. Bottomore, ed., pp. 151–171. Englewood Cliffs, Prentice Hall.

Lilla, Mark. 1998. The Politics of Jacques Derrida. *The New York Review of Books* 45(11):36–41.

Locke, John. 1939 [1690]. An Essay Concerning the True Original Extent and End of Civil Government. In *The English Philosophers from Bacon to Mill,* Edwin A. Burtt, ed. New York: Modern Library.

Lorenz, Konrad. 1952. *King Solomon's Ring: New Light on Animal Ways,* Marjorie Kerr Wilson, trans. New York: Crowell.

———. 1966. *On Aggression.* Harcourt, Brace and World.

Lounsbury, Floyd. 1956. A Semantic Analysis of the Pawnee Kinship Usage. *Language* 32:158–194.

Lowe, Donald. 1995. *The Body in Late-Capitalist USA.* Durham, NC: Duke University Press.

Lowie, Robert H. 1913. Military Societies of the Crow Indians. *Anthropological Papers of the American Museum of Natural History* 11:145–217.

———. 1920. *Primitive Society.* New York: Liveright.

———. 1937. *The History of Ethnological Theory.* New York: Holt, Rinehart, and Winston.

———. 1946. Review of a Scientific Theory of Culture and Other Essays by Bronislaw Malinowski. *American Anthropologist* 48(1):118–119.

Lubbock, Sir John. 1865. *Pre-historic Times: As Illustrated by Ancient Remains and the Manners and Customs of Modern Savages.* London: William and Norgate.

———. 1870. *Origin of Civilization and the Primitive Condition of Man: Mental and Social Condition of Savages.* London: Longman, Green.

Lucy, John A. 1997. Linguistic Relativity, *Annual Reviews of Anthropology* 26:291–312.

Lummis, Douglas. 1982. *A New Look at the Chrysanthemum and the Sword.* Tokyo: Shōhaku-sha.

Lutkehaus, N. C. 1995. Margaret Mead and the Rustling-of-the-Wind-in-the-Palm-Trees-School of Ethnographic Writing. In *Women Writing Culture,* R. Behar and D. A. Gordon, eds., pp. 186–201. Berkeley: University of California Press.

Lyell, Sir Charles. 1834. *Principles of Geology.* London: J. Murray.

———. 1863. *The Geological Evidences of the Antiquity of Man.* Philadelphia: G. W. Childs.

Lyotard, Jean-Francois. 1984 (Orig 1979). *The Postmodern Condition: A Report on Knowledge.* Minneapolis: University of Minnesota.

MacCormack, Carol P. 1980. Nature, Culture, and Gender: A Critique. In *Nature, Culture, and Gender,* Carol P. MacCormack and Marilyn Strathern, eds., pp. 1–24. Cambridge: Cambridge University Press.

McDowell, Nancy. 1980. The Oceanic Ethnography of Margaret Mead. *American Anthropologist* 82(2): 278–303.

Macintosh, Sir James. 1828 [1799]. *A Discourse on the Study of the Law of Nature and Nations.* London: H. Goode.

McLennan, John Ferguson. 1865. *Primitive Marriage: An Inquiry into the Origin of the Form of Capture in Marriage Ceremonies.* Edinburgh: A. and C. Black.

Maillet, Benoit de. 1748. *Telliamed, ou, Entretiens d'un philosophe indien avec un missionaire françois sur le diminution de la mer, la formation de la terre, l'origine de l'homme, etc.* Amsterdam: L'honore.

Maine, H. S. 1963. *Ancient Law: Its Connection with the Early History of Society and Its Relation to Modern Ideas.* Boston: Beacon Press.

Malefijt, Annemarie de Waal. 1989. *Religion and Culture: An Introduction to Anthropology of Religion.* Prospect Heights: Waveland Press.

———. 1974. *Images of Man: A History of Anthropological Thought.* New York: Alfred A. Knopf.

Malinowski, Bronislaw. 1922. *Argonauts of the Western Pacific.* New York: E. P. Dutton.

———. 1955 [1927]. *Sex and Repression in Savage Society.* New York: Harcourt, Brace.

———. 1929a. Practical Anthropology, *Africa* 2:22–38.

———. 1929b. *The Sexual Life of Savages in Northwestern Melanesia.* London: Routledge.

———. 1935. *Coral Gardens and Their Magic.* New York: American Book Company.

———. 1939. The Group and the Individual in Functional Analysis. *American Journal of Sociology* 44: 938–964.

———. 1954 [1925]. *Magic, Science and Religion and Other Essays.* New York: Doubleday.

———. 1967. *A Diary in the Strict Sense of the Term.* New York: Harcourt, Brace and World.

Malotki, Ekkehart. 1983. *Hopi Time: A Linguistic Analysis of the Temporal Concepts in the Hopi Language.* (Trends in Linguistics, Studies and Monographs, 20.) Berlin: Mouton.

Malthus, Thomas Robert. 1926 [1798]. *An Essay on the Principle of Population as It Affects the Future Improvement of Society with Remarks on the Speculations* of Mr. Godwin, M. Condorcet, and Other Writers. London: Macmillan.

Manganaro, Marc, ed. 1990. *Modernist Anthropology: From Fieldwork to Text*. Princeton, NJ: Princeton University Press.

Manners, David. 1973. Obituary of Julian Steward. *American Ethnologist,* 75:886–903.

Marcus, George. 1992. Cultural Anthropology at Rice since the 1980s. Provost Lecture, February 17, 1992. http://www.ruf.rice.edu/~anth/research/marcus-provost-lecture.htm

Marcus, George E., and Dick Cushman. 1982. Ethnographies as Texts. *Annual Reviews of Anthropology* 11:25–69.

Marx, Karl. 1930 [1867]. *Capital: A Critique of Political Economy,* 4th ed., Paul Eden and Paul Ceder, trans. New York: E. P. Dutton.

———. 1963 [1844]. On the Jewish Question. In *Karl Marx: Early Writings,* T. B. Bottomore, ed., pp. 3–40. New York: McGraw-Hill.

———. 1993 [1858] *Grundrisse: foundations of the critique of political economy (rough draft)*. New York: Penguin Classics.

Marx, Karl, and Freidrich Engels. 1970 [1846]. *The German Ideology: Part One with Selections From Parts Two and Three, Together with Marx's Introduction* to A Critique of Political Economy, C. J. Arthur, ed. New York: International Publishing.

———. 1972 [1848]. The Communist Manifesto. In *Karl Marx: Essential Writings,* Fredrick L. Bender, ed., pp. 240–263. New York: Harper and Row.

———. 1975 [1845]. *The Holy Family: Or, Critique of Critical Criticism: Against Bruno Bauer and Company*. Moscow: Progress Publishers.

Mason, Otis. 1895. Similarities in Culture. *American Anthropologist* 8:101–117.

Mauss, Marcel. 1967 [1925]. *The Gift: Forms and Functions of Exchange in Archaic Societies,* Ian Cunnison, trans. New York: W. W. Norton.

Mayer, Jean, and Beverly Bullen. 1960. Nutrition and Athletic Performance. *Physiological Reviews* 40(3): 369–397.

McGee, R. Jon. 2002. *Watching Lacandon Maya Lives*. Boston: Allyn and Bacon.

McGee, W. J. et. al. 1900. In Memoriam: Frank Hamilton Cushing. *American Anthropologist*. 2(2):354–380.

McLaren, Angus. 1974. Some Secular Attitudes toward Sexual Behavior in France: 1760–1860. *French Historical Studies*. 8(4): 604–625.

Mead, Margaret. 1928. *Coming of Age in Samoa: A Psychological Study of Primitive Youth for Western Civilization*. New York: William Morrow.

———. 1930. *Growing Up in New Guinea: A Comparative Study of Primitive Education*. New York: William Morrow.

———. 1935. *Sex and Temperament in Three Primitive Societies*. New York: William Morrow.

———. 1939. Native Languages as Field-Work Tools. *American Anthropologist* 41(2):189–205.

———. 1949. *Male and Female: A Study of the Sexes in a Changing World*. New York: William Morrow.

Metzger, Duane. 1965. Review of *The Nature of Cultural Things* by Marvin Harris. *American Anthropologist*. 67 (5):1293–1296.

Metzger, Duane and G. Williams. 1966. Some Procedures and Results in the Study of Native Categories: Tzeltal Firewood. *American Anthropologist* 68: 389–407.

Miller, James and Jim Miller. 2000. *The Passion of Michel Foucault*. Cambridge (MA): Harvard University Press.

Modell, Judith Schachter. 1983. *Ruth Benedict: Patterns of a Life*. Philadelphia: University of Pennsylvania Press.

Montagu, Ashley. 1980. *Sociobiology Examined*. Oxford: Oxford University Press.

Morgan, Elaine. 1972. *The Descent of Woman*. New York: Stein and Day.

———. 1982. *The Aquatic Ape*. New York: Stein and Day.

Morgan, Lewis Henry. 1871. Systems of Consanguinity and Affinity of the Human Family. Smithsonian Contributions to Knowledge no. 218, vol. 17. Washington: Smithsonian.

———. 1966 [1851]. *League of the Ho-dé-no-sau-nee or Iroquois*. New York: B. Franklin.

———. 1985 [1877]. *Ancient Society*. Tucson: University of Arizona Press.

Morgen, Sandra. 1989. Gender and Anthropology: Introductory Essay. In *Gender and Anthropology—Critical Reviews for Research and Teaching,* Sandra Morgen, ed., pp. 1–20. Washington, DC: American Anthropological Association.

Morton, Samuel G. 1839. *Crania Americana*. Philadelphia: J. Dobson.

———. 1844. *Crania Aegyptica*. Philadelphia: J. Penington.

Müller, F. Max. 1977 [1856]. *Comparative Mythology.* New York: Arno Press.

Murdock, George Peter. 1951. British Social Anthropology. *American Anthropologist* 53:465–473.

Murdock, George P. 1959. Evolution in Social Organization. In *Evolution and Anthropology,* B. Meggers, ed., pp. 126–145. Washington: Anthropological Society of Washington.

———. 1960 [1949]. *Social Structure.* New York: Macmillan.

Murphy, R. F. 1994. The Dialectics of Deeds and Words. In *Assessing Cultural Anthropology,* R. Borofsky, ed., pp. 55–61. New York: McGraw Hill.

Murray, Margaret Alice. 1921. *The Witch-Cult in Western Europe: A Study in Anthropology.* Oxford: Clarendon Press.

Nadel, S. F. 1954. *Nupe Religion.* London: Routledge and Kegan Paul.

Nanda, Serena. 1990. *Neither Man nor Woman: The Hijras of India.* Belmont, CA: Wadsworth.

National Cyclopedia of American Biography. 1967. William Graham Sumner, vol. 25, pp. 8–9. Clifton, NJ: J. T. White.

Newman, Fred, and Lois Holzman. 1993. *Lev Vygotsky: Revolutionary Scientist.* New York: Routledge.

Nietzsche, Friedrich. 1954 [1883–1885]. *Thus Spake Zarathustra.* New York: Modern Library.

———. 1956 [1871/1887] *The Birth of Tragedy and the Genealogy of Morals.* Garden City, NY: Doubleday.

Nonacs, P., and L. M. Dill. 1993. Is Satisficing an Alternative to Optimal Foraging Theory? *Oikos* 24: 371–375.

Northrup, F. S. C. 1947. *The Logic of the Sciences and the Humanities.* New York: McMillan.

Obeyesekere, Gananath. 1981. *Medusa's Hair: An Essay on Personal Symbols and Religious Experience.* Chicago: University of Chicago Press.

O'Laughlin, Bridget. 1975. Marxist Approaches in Anthropology. In *Annual Review of Anthropology,* Bernard Siegel, Alan Beals, and Stephen Tyler, eds., vol. 4, pp. 341–370. Palo Alto, CA: Annual Reviews.

O'Meara, J. Tim. 1989. Anthropology as Empirical Science. *American Anthropologist* 91:354–369.

Ong, Aihwa. 1999. *Flexible Citizenship: The Logic of Transnationality.* Durham, NC: Duke.

Ong, Walter J. 1982. *Orality and Literacy: The Technologizing of the Word.* New York: Methuen.

Oppenheimer, Franz. 1914. *The State: Its History and Development Viewed Sociologically,* John M. Gitterman, trans. Indianapolis: Bobbs-Merrill.

Orlove, Benjamin S. 1980. Ecological Anthropology. In *Annual Review of Anthropology,* Bernard Siegel, Alan Beals, and Stephen Tyler, eds., vol. 9, pp. 235–273. Palo Alto, CA: Annual Reviews.

Ortner, Sherry B. 1973. On Key Symbols. *American Anthropologist* 75:1338–1346.

———. 1975. Gods' Bodies, Gods' Food: A Symbolic Analysis of Sherpa Ritual. In *The Interpretation of Symbolism,* Ray Willis, ed., pp. 133–167. New York: John Wiley and Sons.

———. 1984. Theory in Anthropology since the Sixties. *Comparative Studies in Society and History* 26(1): 126–166.

Ortner, Sherry B., and Harriet Whitehead. 1981 [1974]. *Sexual Meanings: The Cultural Construction of Gender and Sexuality.* Cambridge: Cambridge University Press.

Ortner, Sherry B., and Harriet Whitehead. 1981. Introduction: Accounting for Sexual Meanings. In *Sexual Meanings: The Cultural Construction of Gender and Sexuality,* pp. 1–27. Cambridge: Cambridge University Press.

Ospovat, Dov. 1976. The Influence of Karl Ernst von Baer's Embryology. 1828–1859: A Reappraisal in Light of Richard Owen's and William B. Carpenter's "Palaeontological Application of Von Baer's Law." *Journal of the History of Biology,* 9(1): 1–28.

Parezo, Nancy J. 2007. Reassessing Anthropology's Maverick: The Archaeological Fieldwork of Frank Hamilton Cushing. *American Ethnologist.* 34(3): 575–580.

Pathe, R. A. 1988. Gene Weltfish. In *Women Anthropologists: A Biographical Dictionary,* U. Gacs, A. Khan, J. McIntyre, and R. Weinberg, eds., pp. 372–381. New York: Greenwood Press.

Paulme, Denise. 1960. *Femmes d'Afrique Noire.* Paris: Mouton.

Peace, William J. 2004. *Leslie A. White: Evolution and Revolution in Anthropology.* Lincoln: University of Nebraska.

———. 1998. Bernhard Stern, Leslie A. White, and an Anthropological Appraisal of the Russian Revolution. *American Anthropologist* 100(1):84–93.

———. 2004. *Leslie A. White: Evolution and Revolution in Anthropology.* Omaha: University of Nebraska.

———. Leslie A. White and the Socio-Politics of War. *Histories of Anthropology Annual*. 3:1–21.

Peace, William, and David H. Price. 2001. The Cold War Context of the FBI's Investigation of Leslie A. White. *American Anthropologist* 103(1):164–167.

Pike, Kenneth. 1954. *Language in Relation to a Unified Theory of the Structure of Human Behavior*, vol. 1. Glendale, CA: Summer Institute of Linguistics.

Pinker, Steven. 1994. *The Language Instinct: How the Mind Creates Language*. New York: HarperCollins.

Plato. 1993. *Republic*, Robin Waterfield, trans. Oxford: Oxford University Press.

Polanyi, Karl. 1944. *The Great Transformation*. Boston: Beacon.

Polanyi, Karl, Conrad M. Arensberg, and Harry W. Pearson. 1957. *Trade and Market in the Early Empires: Economies in History and Theory*. Glencoe, IL: Free Press.

Pollis, Carol A. 1987. The Apparatus of Sexuality: Reflections on Foucault's Contributions to the Study of Sex in History. *The Journal of Sex Research*. 23(3): 401–408.

Price, David H. 2004 [1960]. *Threatening Anthropology: McCarthyism and the FBI's Harassment of Activist Anthropologists*. Durham, NC: Duke University Press.

Putnam, Robert D. 2000. *Bowling Alone: The Collapse and Revival of American Community*. New York: Simon & Schuster.

Quetelet, Adolphe. 1848. *Du Système Sociale et des Lois qui le Régissent*. Paris: Guillaumin.

———. 1968 [1835]. *A Treatise on Man and the Development of His Faculties*. New York: B. Franklin.

Rabinow, Paul. 1977. *Reflections on Fieldwork in Morocco*. Berkeley: University of California Press.

———. 1986. Representations Are Social Facts: Modernity and Postmodernity in Anthropology. In *Writing Culture: The Poetics and Politics of Ethnography*, James Clifford and George Marcus, eds., pp. 234–261. Berkeley: University of California Press.

Radcliffe-Brown, A. R. 1924. The Mother's Brother in South Africa. *South African Journal of Science* 21: 542–555.

———. 1964 [1922]. *The Andaman Islanders*. New York: Free Press.

———. 1965a. [1940]. On Joking Relationships. In *Structure and Function in Primitive Society*, pp. 90–104. New York: Free Press.

———. 1965b [1935]. On the Concept of Function in Social Science. In *Structure and Function in Primitive Society*, pp. 178–187. New York: Free Press.

Radin, Paul. 1911. Description of a Winnebago Funeral. *American Anthropologist* 13(3):437–444.

———. 1924. Ojibwa Ethnological Chit Chat. *American Anthropologist* 26(4):491–530.

———. ed. 1926. *Crashing Thunder: The Autobiography of an American Indian*. New York: Appleton.

———. 1957 [1927]. *Primitive Man as Philosopher*, 2nd ed. New York: Dover Publications.

Ryang, Sonia. 2004. *Chrysanthemum's Strange Life: Ruth Benedict in Postwar Japan*. Japan Policy Research Institute Occasional Paper 32. University of San Francisco Center for the Pacific Rim.

Rappaport, Roy A. 1967. *Pigs for the Ancestors*. New Haven: Yale University Press.

———. 1984. *Pigs for the Ancestors*, 2nd ed. New Haven: Yale University Press.

———. 1994. Humanity's Evolution and Anthropology's Future. In *Assessing Cultural Anthropology*, R. Borofsky, ed., pp. 153–167. New York, McGraw Hill.

Rawson, Claude. 1994. The Masks of M. Foucault. *The Sewanee Review*. 102(3): 471–476.

Reiter, Reyna, ed. 1975. *Toward an Anthropology of Women*. New York: Monthly Review Press.

Resek, Carl. 1960. *Lewis Henry Morgan: American Scholar*. Chicago: University of Chicago Press.

Ritzer, George. 1992. *Sociological Theory*, 3rd ed. New York: McGraw-Hill.

Rivers, W. H. R. 1900. A Genealogical Method of Collecting Social and Vital Statistics. *Journal of the Anthropological Institute*, n.s., 3:74–82.

———. 1910. The Genealogical Method of Anthropological Inquiry. *Sociological Review* 3:1–12.

Roheim, Geza. 1971 [1925]. *Australian Totemism: A Psychoanalytic Study in Anthropology*. New York: Humanities Press.

Romanucci-Ross, Lola. 2001. Celebrants and the Celebrity: Biography as Trope. *American Anthropologist* 103(4):1174–1178.

Rorty, Richard. 1979. *Philosophy and the Mirror of Knowledge*. Princeton: Princeton University Press.

———. 1980. *Knowledge and Passion: Ilongot Notions of Self and Social Life*. Cambridge: Cambridge University Press.

Roughley, I. R. 2003. Textual Surveillance: The Double Eyes (and I's) of George Bataille's Story of the Eye. *Rhizomes: Cultural Studies in Emerging Knowledge* 6 (2003).

Rousseau, Jean-Jacques. 1974 [1762]. *Émile*, Barbara Foxley, trans. New York: E. P. Dutton.

Rylko-Bauer, Barbara, Merrill Singer, and John van Willigen. 2006. Reclaiming Applied Anthropology: Its Past, Present, and Future. *American Anthropologist* 108(1):178–190.

Sacks, K. 1979. *Sisters and Wives: The Past and Future of Sexual Equality.* Westport, CT: Greenwood Press.

Sahlins, Marshall D. 1964. Culture and Environment: The Study of Cultural Ecology. In *Horizons of Anthropology,* Sol Tax, ed., pp. 132–147. Chicago: Aldine.

———. 1968. *Tribesmen.* Englewood Cliffs, NJ: Prentice Hall.

———. 1972. *Stone Age Economics.* Chicago: Aldine.

———. 1976. *The Use and Abuse of Biology: An Anthropological Critique of Sociobiology.* Ann Arbor: University of Michigan Press.

Sahlins, Marshall D., and Elman R. Service. 1960. *Evolution and Culture.* Ann Arbor: University of Michigan Press.

Said, E. 1978. *Orientalism.* New York: Pantheon.

Sanday, Peggy Reeves. 1980. Margaret Mead's View of Sex Roles in Her Own and Other Societies. *American Anthropologist* 82(2):340–348.

———. 1981. *Female Power and Male Dominance: On the Origins of Sexual Inequality.* New York: Cambridge University Press.

Sanday, Peggy Reeves, and Ruth Gallagher Goodenough, eds. 1990. *Beyond the Second Sex: New Directions in the Anthropology of Gender.* Philadelphia: University of Pennsylvania Press.

Sangren, Steven P. 1988. Rhetoric and the Authority of Ethnography. *Current Anthropology* 29(3):405–435.

Sapir, Edward. 1924. Culture, Genuine and Spurious. *American Journal of Sociology* 29:401–429.

Sassoon, A. S. 1991. Hegemony. In *A Dictionary of Marxist Thought,* T. Bottomore, ed., pp. 229–231. Oxford: Basil Blackwell.

Sawicki, J. 1991. *Disciplining Foucault: Feminism, Power, and the Body.* New York: Routledge.

Scheper-Hughes, Nancy. 1979. *Saints, Scholars, and Schizophrenics: Mental Illness in Rural Ireland.* Berkeley: University of California Press.

———. 1989. Death Without Weeping. *Natural History* 98:8–16.

———. 1992. *Death Without Weeping: The Violence of Everyday Life in Brazil.* Berkeley: University of California Press.

———. 1995. The Primacy of the Ethical: Propositions for a Militant Anthropology. *Current Anthropology* 36 (3):409–420.

Schneider, Jane, and Rayna Rapp, eds. 1995. *Articulating Hidden Histories: Exploring the Influence of Eric R. Wolf.* Berkeley: University of California Press.

Schott, Rudiger. 1976. More on Marx and Morgan. *Current Anthropology.* 17(4): 731–734.

Scott, David. 1997. Leibniz and the Two Clocks. *Journal of the History of Ideas.* 58(3):445–463.

Seligman, Charles G. 1910. *The Melanesians of British New Guinea.* Cambridge: Cambridge University Press.

Service, Elman R. 1962. *Primitive Social Organization: An Evolutionary Perspective.* New York: Random House.

———. 1976. Leslie Alvin White, 1900–1975. *American Anthropologist* 78(3):612–617.

Service, Elman. 1988. Morton Herbert Fried (1923–1986). *American Anthropologist* 90(1):148–152.

Shannon, Claude. 1948. A Mathematical Theory of Communication. *Bell System Technical Journal* 27: 379–423.

Shankman, Paul, and Angela Thieman Dino. 2001. The FBI File of Leslie A. White. *American Anthropologist* 103(1):161–164.

Shapiro, Lawrence. 2004. *The Mind Incarnate.* Cambridge: MIT Press.

Shipler, David K. 2004. *The Working Poor: Invisible in America.* New York: Knopf.

Shipp, E. R. 1980, August 5. Prof. Gene Weltfish Dead at 78; Was a Target of Anti-Red Drives. *New York Times,* p. B101.

Silverman, J. 1967. Shaminism and Acute Schizophrenia. *American Anthropologist* 69:21–31.

Sloan, Richard P. 2006. Trivializing the Transcendant: What Can Science Really Tell Us About Faith? *Christianity Today.*

Smith, Adam. 1976 [1776]. *An Inquiry into the Nature and Causes of the Wealth of Nations.* Oxford: Clarendon Press.

Smith, E. A. 1983. Anthropological Applications of Optimal Foraging Theory: A Critical Review. *Current Anthropology* 24:625–651.

Smith, Grafton Elliot. 1928. *In the Beginning: The Origin of Civilization.* New York: Morrow.

Smith, Watson and John M. Roberts. 1954. Zuni Law, a Field of Values. *Papers of the Peabody Museum, Vol 43.*

Solecki, R., and C. Wagley. 1963. William Duncan Strong (1899–1962). *American Anthropologist* 65(5): 1102–1111.

Spencer, Herbert. 1859. What Knowledge Is of Most Worth? *Westminster Review* 72:1–41.

———. 1860. The Social Organism. *Westminster Review*, n.s., 17:51–68.

———. 1873–1934. *Descriptive Sociology*, 13 vols. New York: Appleton-Century-Crofts.

———. 1898 [1864]. *Principles of Biology*. New York: D. Appleton.

———. 1961 [1873]. *The Study of Sociology*. Ann Arbor: University of Michigan Press.

———. 1967. *The Evolution of Society: Selections from Herbert Spencer's Principles of Sociology*, Robert L. Carneiro, ed. Chicago: University of Chicago Press.

———. 1969 [1851]. *Social Statics: The Conditions Essential to Human Happiness Specified, and the First of them Developed*. New York: A. M. Kelley.

———. 1975 [1885]. *The Principles of Sociology*. Westport, CN: Greenwood Press.

———. 1904. *An Autobiography: Herbert Spencer*. New York: D. Appleton.

Spier, Leslie, A. Irving Hallowell, and Stanley S. Newman, eds. 1941. *Language, Culture, and Personality: Essays in Memory of Edward Sapir*. Menasha, WI: Sapir Memorial Publication Fund.

Spinoza, Baruch. 1930 [1677]. *Ethics*. London: Oxford University Press.

Spradley, James P. 1980. *Participant Observation*. New York: Holt, Rinehart, and Winston.

Spradley, James P., ed. 1987. *Culture and Cognition*. New York: Waveland Press.

Steward, Julian. 1955. *Theory of Culture Change: The Methodology of Multilinear Evolution*. Urbana: University of Illinois Press.

Stirner, Max. 1918 [1844]. *The Ego and Its Own*. Steven T. Byington, trans. New York: Boni and Liveright.

Stocking, G. 1968. The Scientific Reaction Against Cultural Anthropology, 1917–1920. In *Race, Culture, and Evolution: Essays in the History of Anthropology*, _G. Stocking, ed., pp. 270–307. New York: Free Press.

———. 1974. *The Shaping of American Anthropology 1883–1911*. New York: Basic Books.

———. 1987. *Victorian Anthropology*. New York: Free Press.

———. 1992. Ideas and Institutions in American Anthropology: Thoughts Toward a History of the Interwar Years. The Ethnographer's Magic and Other Essays. In *The History of Anthropology*, G. Stocking, ed., pp. 114–177. Madison, University of Wisconsin.

———. 1995. *After Tylor: British Social Anthropology 1888–1951*. Madison: University of Wisconsin Press.

Stoler, Ann Laura. 1989. Making Empire Respectable: The Politics of Race and Sexual Morality in 20th-Century Colonial Cultures. *American Ethnologist* 16(4):634–660.

———. 1995. *Race and the Education of Desire: Foucault's History of Sexuality and the Colonial Order of Things*. Chapel Hill: Duke University Press.

———. 2002. *Carnal Knowledge and Imperial Power: Race and the Intimate in Colonial Rule*. Berkeley: University of California Press.

Stoller, Paul. 1989. *The Taste of Ethnographic Things: The Senses in Anthropology*. Philadelphia: University of Pennsylvania Press.

Strauss, Claudia. 1992. What Makes Tony Run: Schemas as Motives Reconsidered. In *Human Motives and Cultural Models*, Roy D'Andrade and Claudia Strauss, eds., pp. 197–224. Cambridge: Cambridge University Press.

Strauss, Claudia, and Naomi Quinn. 1994. A Cognitive/Cultural Anthropology. In *Assessing Cultural Anthropology*, Robert Borofsky, ed., pp. 284–300. New York: McGraw Hill.

Strauss, David Friedrich. 1892. *The Life of Jesus*, 2nd ed., George Eliot, trans. London: Swan and Sonnenschein.

Strong, W. D. 1994. *Labrador Winter: The Ethnographic Journals of William Duncan Strong, 1927–1928*, Eleanor Leacock, ed. Washington DC: Smithsonian Institution.

Sturtevant, William C. 1964. Studies in Ethnoscience. *American Anthropologist* 66:99–131.

———. 1987. Studies in Ethnoscience. In *Culture and Cognition*, James P. Spradley ed., pp. 129–167. New York: Waveland.

Suchting, W. A. 1983. *Marx: An Introduction*. New York: New York University Press.

Sumner, William Graham. 1963 [1914]. The Concentration of Wealth: Its Economic Justification. In *The Challenge of Facts and Other Essays*, Albert G. Keller, ed., pp. 79–90. New Haven: Yale University Press.

Sumner, William Graham, and Albert G. Keller. 1927. *The Science of Society*. New Haven: Yale University Press.

Sumser, Robert. 1992. "Erziehung." The Family and the Regulation of Sexuality in the Late German Enlightenment. *German Studies Review.* 15(3): 455–474.

Tanner, Nancy, and Adrienne Zihlman. 1976. Women in Evolution, Part I: Innovation and Selection in Human Origins. *Signs* 2(3):585–608.

Taylor, Charles. 1979. Interpretation and the Sciences of Man. In *Interpretive Social Science: A Reader,* Paul Rabinow and W. M. Sullivan, eds., pp. 25–71. Berkeley, University of California Press.

Taylor, William Cooke. 1840. *The Natural History of Society in the Barbarous and Civilized State.* New York: Appleton.

Tax, Sol. 1958. The Fox Project. *Human Organization* 17:17–19.

———. 1960. Action Anthropology. In *Documentary History of the Fox Project, 1948–1959.* Fred Gearing, Robert McC. Netting, and Lisa R. Peattie, eds., pp. 167–171. Chicago: University of Chicago Press.

Thapan, Meenakshi. 2002. Pierre Bourdieu (1930–2002): A Personal Tribute. *Economic and Political Weekly,* 37(9): 826–828.

Thomas, David C., and Kerr Inkson. 2004. *Cultural Intelligence: People Skills for Global Business.* San Francisco: Berrett-Koehler.

Thompson, John B. 1984. *Critical Hermeneutics: A Study in the Thought of Paul Ricoeur and Jurgen Habermas.* Cambridge: Cambridge University Press.

Todorov, Tzvetzn. 1987. *Literature and Its Theorists: A Personal View of Twentieth-Century Criticism,* Catherine Porter, trans. Ithaca, NY: Cornell University Press.

Tönnies, Ferdinand Julius. 1957 [1887]. *Gemeinschaft und Gesellschaft, Community and Society.* East Lansing: Michigan State University Press.

Tooker, Elizabeth. 1992. Lewis H. Morgan and His Contemporaries. *American Anthropologist* 94(2): 357–375.

Trautmann, Thomas, and Karl Sanford Kabelac. 1994 The Library of Lewis Henry Morgan and Mary Elizabeth Morgan. *Transactions of the American Philosophical Society.* 84(6/7):i–336.

Turgot, Anne-Robert-Jacques. 1973 [1750]. *Turgot on progress, sociology and economics: A philosophical review of the successive advances of the human mind, On universal history (and) Reflections on the formation and the distribution of wealth,* Roland L. Meek, trans. Cambridge: Cambridge University Press.

Turnbull, C. 1961. *The Forest People.* New York: Simon and Schuster.

———. 1972. *The Mountain People.* New York: Simon and Schuster.

Turner, Bryan S., ed. 1966. *The Blackwell Companion to Social Theory.* Oxford: Blackwell.

Turner, Edith. 1987. *The Spirit and the Drum: A Memoir of Africa.* Tucson: University of Arizona Press.

———. 1992. *Experiencing Ritual: A New Interpretation of African Healing.* Philadelphia: University of Pennsylvania Press.

Turner, Jonathon H., Leonard Beeghley, and Charles H. Powers. 1989. *The Emergence of Sociological Theory.* Belmont: Wadsworth.

Turner, Victor. 1967a. Betwixt and Between: The Liminal Period in Rites of Passage. In *The Forest of Symbols: Aspects of Ndembu Ritual,* pp. 93–111. Ithaca, NY: Cornell University Press.

———. 1967b. Ritual Symbolism, Morality, and Social Structure among the Ndembu. In *African Systems of Thought,* M. Fortes and G. Dieterlen, eds., pp. 48–58. London: Oxford University Press.

———. 1969. *The Ritual Process: Structure and Anti-structure.* Chicago: Aldine.

Tyler, Stephen. 1969. *Cognitive Anthropology.* New York: Holt, Rinehart, and Winston.

———. 1978. *The Said and the Unsaid: Mind, Meaning, and Culture.* New York: Academic Press.

Tylor, Sir Edward Burnett. 1861. *Anahuac: Or Mexico and the Mexicans, Ancient and Modern.* London: Longman, Green, Longman and Roberts.

———. 1871. *Primitive Culture.* London: John Murray.

———. 1889. On a Method of Investigating the Development of Institutions; Applied to Laws of Marriage and Descent. *Journal of the Royal Anthropological Institute* 18:245–269.

———. 1920. *Primitive Culture,* 2nd ed. London: John Murray.

Vaid, Urvashi. 1993. Speech at the March on Washington. *Gifts of Speech. http://gos.sbc.edu/w/vaid.html* Retrieved September 27, 2010.

Vanoverbergh, Morice. 1925. Negritos of Northern Luzon, *Anthropos,* XX, 148–99, 399–443.

Veblen, Thorstein. 1912 [1899]. *The Theory of the Leisure Class: An Economic Study of Institutions.* New York: Viking Press.

Vico, Giambattista. 1984 [1744]. *The New Science of Giambattista Vico,* Thomas Goddard Bergin and Max Harold Fisch, trans. Ithaca, NY: Cornell University Press.

Wacquant, Loïc. 2006. Pierre Bourdieu. In Rob Stones, ed., *Key Contemporary Thinkers*. 2nd ed. New York: Macmillan.

———. 2004. Pointers on Pierre Bourdieu and Democratic Politics. *Coinstellations* 11 (1): 3–15.

Walker, J. C. 1986. Romanticizing Resistance, Romanticizing Culture: Problems in Willis's Theory of Cultural Production. *British Journal of Sociology of Education* 7(1):59–80.

Wallenchinsky, David, and Irving Wallace, eds. 1975. *The People's Almanac*. Garden City, NY: Doubleday.

Wallerstein, I. 1974. *The Modern World-System; Capitalist Agriculture and the Origins of the European World- Economy in the Sixteenth Century (by) Immanuel Wallerstein*. New York: Academic Press.

Washburn, Sherwood, and C. Lancaster. 1968. The Evolution of Hunting. In *Man the Hunter*, R. B. Lee and Irven DeVore, eds., pp. 293–303. Chicago: Aldine.

Washington Post. 1998. *Campaign Finance Key Players: The Riady Family* http://www.washingtonpost.com/_wp-srv/politics/special/campfin/players/riady.htm

Weber, Max. 1958 [1930]. *The Protestant Ethic and the Spirit of Capitalism*, Talcott Parsons, trans. New York: Charles Scribner's Sons.

———. 1993 [1920]. *The Sociology of Religion*. Boston: Beacon Press.

———. 1978. *Economy and Society: An Outline of Interpretive Sociology*, Guenther Roth and Claus Wittich, eds., Ephraim Fischoff, trans. Berkeley: University of California Press.

White, Leslie A. 1943. Energy and the Evolution of Culture. *American Anthropologist* 43:335–356.

———. 1949. Ikhnaton: The Great Man vs. the Culture Process. In *The Science of Culture: A Study of Man and Civilization*, pp. 233–281. New York: Farrar, Strauss.

———. 1959. *The Evolution of Culture*. New York: McGraw-Hill.

———. 1975. *The Concept of Cultural Systems: A Key to Understanding Tribes and Nations*. New York: Columbia University Press.

Whorf, Benjamin Lee. 1956. *Language Thought and Reality*. Cambridge, MA, M.I.T. Press.

Wierzbicka, Anna. 2005. Empirical Universals of Language as a Basis for the Study of Other Human Universals and as a Tool for Exploring Cross-Cultural Differences. *Ethos* 33(2):256–291.

Willis, P. 1983. Cultural Production and Theories of Reproduction. In *Race, Class and Education*, L. Barton and S. Walker, eds., pp. 107–138. London: Croom Helm.

Wilson, Edward O. 1971. *The Insect Societies*. Cambridge, MA: Harvard University Press.

———. 1975. *Sociobiology: The New Synthesis*. Cambridge, MA: Belknap Press of Harvard University Press.

———. 1984. *Biophilia*. Cambridge, MA: Harvard University Press.

Wissler, Clark. 1917. *The American Indian: An Introduction to the Anthropology of the New World*. New York: D. C. McMurtrie.

———. 1926. *The Relation of Nature to Man in Aboriginal America*. New York: Oxford University Press.

Wittgenstein, Ludwig. 2001. *Philosophical Investigations*. 3rd ed. Oxford: Blackwell.

———. 1981. *Totems and Teachers: Perspectives on the History of Anthropology*, Sydel Silverman, ed. New York: Columbia University Press.

———. 1982. *Europe and the People Without History*. Berkeley: University of California Press.

———. 1959. *Sons of the Shaking Earth*. Chicago: University of Chicago Press.

———. 1966. *Peasants*. Englewood Cliffs, NJ: Prentice-Hall.

———. 1969. *Peasant Wars of the Twentieth Century*. New York: Harper and Row.

Wolf, Eric R., and Joseph G. Jorgensen. 1970, November 19. Anthropology on the Warpath in Thailand. *New York Review of Books*, pp. 26–35.

Woodward, Bob. 1998. Findings Link Clinton Allies to Chinese Intelligence. *Washington Post*. Tuesday, February 10, 1998; Page A01.

Wundt, Wilhelm Max. 1904 [1874]. *Principles of Physiological Psychology*, Edward Bradford Titchener, trans. New York: Macmillan.

———. 1916 [1912]. *Elements of Folk Psychology: Outlines of a Psychological History of the Development of Mankind*. New York: Macmillan.

Yanagisako, Sylvia, and Jane Collier. 1987. Toward a Unified Analysis of Gender and Kinship. In *Gender and Kinship: Essays Toward a Unified Analysis*, pp. 14–50. Palo Alto, CA: Stanford University Press.

Zielengiger, Michael. 2006. *Shutting Out the Sun: How Japan Created Its Own Lost Generation*, New York: Random House.

CREDITS

Arjun Appadurai, "Disjuncture and Difference in the Global Cultural Economy," *Public Culture,* vol. 2, no. 2 (Spring 1990), pp. 1–24. Copyright, 1990, Arjun Appadurai. All rights reserved. Reprinted by permission of the publisher, Duke University Press.

Theodore C. Bestor, "*Kaiten-zushi* and *Konbini*: Japanese Food Culture in the Age of Mechanical Reproduction." In *Fast Food/Slow Food: The Cultural Economy of the Global Food System*, ed. Richard Wilk, pp. 115–130. Copyright © 2006 by Society for Economic Anthropology (SEA). Reprinted by permission of AltaMira Press, a division of Rowman & Littlefield Publishers, Inc.

Rebecca Bliege Bird, Eric Alden Smith, and Douglas W. Bird, "The Hunting Handicap: Costly Signaling in Human Foraging Strategies," *Behavioral Ecology and Sociobiology,* vol. 50 (2001), 9–19. Copyright © 2001 Springer-Verlag. Reprinted by permission of the publisher.

Pierre Bourdieu, "Structures, *Habitus*, Practices." From *The Logic of Practice* by Pierre Bourdieu, translated by Richard Nice, pp. 52–65. Copyright © 1989 by Polity Press. All rights reserved. Used with the permission of Stanford University Press, www.sup.org.

Philippe Bourgois, "From Jíbaro to Crack Dealer: Confronting the Restructuring of Capitalism in El Barrio." In *Articulating Hidden Histories: Exploring the Influence of Eric R. Wolf*, ed. Jane Schneider and Rayna Rapp (Berkeley: University of California Press, 1995), pp. 125–141. Reprinted by permission of Philippe Bourgois.

Harold C. Conklin, "Hanunóo Color Categories," *Southwestern Journal of Anthropology*, vol. 11 (1955), 339–344. Reprinted with permission of the publisher and the author.

Mary Douglas, "External Boundaries" from *Purity and Danger: An Analysis of the Concepts of Pollution and Taboo* (London: Routledge & Kegan Paul, 1966), pp. 114–128. © Mary Douglas 1966. Reproduced by permission of Taylor & Francis Books UK.

Michel Foucault, "The Incitement to Discourse." From *The History of Sexuality, Volume I: An Introduction* by Michel Foucault, trans. Robert Hurley (New York: Random House, 1978), pp. 17–35. Originally published in French as *La Volonté du Savoir*. Copyright © 1976 by Editions Gallimard. Reprinted by permission of Georges Borchardt, Inc., for Editions Gallimard.

Morton H. Fried, "On the Evolution of Social Stratification and the State." In *Culture in History: Essays in Honor of Paul Radin*, ed. Stanley Diamond (New York: Columbia University Press, 1960), pp. 713–731. Reprinted with permission of the publisher.

Clifford Geertz, "Deep Play: Notes on the Balinese Cockfight." Appeared originally in *Daedalus: Journal of the American Academy of Arts and Sciences*, vol. 101, no. 1 (Winter 1972), 1–37. Reprinted with permission.

Max Gluckman, "The License in Ritual" from *Custom and Conflict in Africa* (Oxford: Basil Blackwell, 1956), pp. 109–136. Reproduced with permission of Blackwell Publishing Ltd.

Allan Hanson, "The Making of the Maori: Culture Invention and Its Logic." Reproduced by permission of the American Anthropological Association from *American Anthropologist*, Volume 91, Issue 4, pp. 890–902, 1989. Not for sale or further reproduction.

Eleanor Leacock, excerpts from "Interpreting the Origins of Gender Inequality: Conceptual and Historical Problems," *Dialectical Anthropology*, vol. 7, no. 4 (1983), 263–284. With kind permission from Kluwer Academic Publishers.

Karl Marx and Friedrich Engels, "Feuerbach: Opposition of the Materialist and Idealist Outlook," from *The German Ideology: Part I, with Selections from Parts II and III, Together with Marx's "Introduction to a Critique of Political Economy,"* edited by C. J. Arthur. Translation of Part I, copyright © by International Publishers Co., Inc., 1947; revised translation of Part I © by Lawrence & Wishart, 1970. Reprinted by permission of International Publishers, New York.

Marcel Mauss, excerpts from *The Gift: Forms and Functions of Exchange in Archaic Societies*, trans. Ian Cunnison (New York: W. W. Norton, 1967), pp. 31–45, 76–81. Originally published by Routledge & Kegan

Paul, 1954. Reproduced by permission of Taylor & Francis Books UK and Presses Universitaires France.

Margaret Mead, Introduction (pp. 3–11) from *Coming of Age in Samoa* by Margaret Mead. Copyright © 1928, 1949, 1955, 1961, 1973 by Margaret Mead. Reprinted by permission of HarperCollins Publishers.

Sherry B. Ortner, "Is Female to Male as Nature Is to Culture?" From *Women, Culture, and Society*, edited by Michelle Zimbalist Rosaldo and Louise Lamphere, pp. 67–80, 86–87. Copyright © 1974 by the Board of Trustees of the Leland Stanford Jr. University. All rights reserved. Used with the permission of Stanford University Press, www.sup.org.

A. R. Radcliffe-Brown, "On Joking Relationships," *Africa: Journal of the International African Institute*, vol. XIII, no. 3 (1940), pp. 195–210. Copyright © 1940 International Africa Institute. Reprinted with the permission of Cambridge University Press.

Roy A. Rappaport, "Ritual Regulation of Environmental Relations Among a New Guinea People," *Ethnology*, vol. 6, no. 1 (1967), 17–30. Reprinted by permission of the publisher.

Sally Slocum, "Woman the Gatherer: Male Bias in Anthropology," in *Toward an Anthropology of Women*, ed. Rayna R. Reiter. Copyright © 1975 by Rayna R. Reiter. Reprinted with permission of Monthly Review Foundation.

Julian Steward, "The Patrilineal Band." From *Theory of Culture Change: The Methodology of Multilinear Evolution*, pp. 122–142. Copyright 1955 by the Board of Trustees of the University of Illinois. Renewed 1983 by Jane C. Steward. Used with permission of the author and the University of Illinois Press.

David Valentine, "'I went to bed with my own kind once': the erasure of desire in the name of identity." Reprinted from *Language & Communication*, vol. 23, no. 2, pp. 123–138, Copyright 2003, with permission from Elsevier.

Leslie White, "Energy and the Evolution of Culture," *American Anthropologist* 45, (1943), 335–356. http://www.aaanet.org/publications/anthrosource/

INDEX